THE JEWISH CARAVAN

Other Books by Leo W. Schwarz

A Golden Treasury of Jewish Literature (1937)

Where Hope Lies (1940)

Memoirs of My People (1943; paperback edition, 1963)

The Root and the Bough (1949)

The Redeemers (1953)

Feast of Leviathan (1956)

Great Ages and Ideas of the Jewish People (1956)

Refugees in Germany Today (1957)

Psychiatry and Religious Experience (1958)

The Menorah Treasury (1964)

THE
JEWISH CARAVAN

Great Stories of Twenty-five Centuries

SELECTED AND EDITED BY

Leo W. Schwarz

Revised and Enlarged

SCHOCKEN BOOKS · NEW YORK

First published by SCHOCKEN BOOKS 1976

Published by arrangement with Holt, Rinehart and Winston
Copyright 1935, © 1963, 1965 by Leo W. Schwarz

Library of Congress Cataloging in Publication Data

Schwarz, Leo Walder, 1906-1967 ed.
  The Jewish caravan.

  Reprint of the ed. published by Holt, Rinehart
and Winston, New York.
  Includes bibliographical references and index.
  1. Jewish literature.   I. Title.
[PN6067.S4   1976]   808.83'9'352   75-37043

Manufactured in the United States of America

ACKNOWLEDGMENTS

All copyright materials in this book have been reprinted with the permission of the authors and the following publishers and holders of copyright to whom thanks are due.

The American Scandinavian Foundation, Inc., for "Avrohmche Nightingale" by Meir Aron Goldschmidt from *Denmark's Best Stories,* edited by Hanna Astrup Larsen, copyright 1927, © 1955.

Atheneum House, Inc., for "Never Again" from *The Last of the Just* by André Schwarz-Bart, © 1960 by Atheneum House, Inc., and "The Acid Test of Honesty" from *Look Back, Mrs. Lot!* by Ephraim Kishon, © 1960 by N. Tversky Publishing House, Ltd., Tel Aviv.

Robert O. Ballou, Inc., for "Israel and the Enemy" and "The Rabbi's Son" by Meyer Levin, copyright 1932, © 1960 by Meyer Levin.

Columbia University Press, for "The Clever Judge" from *The Book of Delight* by Joseph ben Meir Zabara, translated by Moses Hadas, and "Rabbi Paltiel" from *The Chronicle of Ahimaaz* by Ahimaaz ben Paltiel, translated by Marcus Salzman, copyright 1924, © 1958 by the Columbia University Press.

E. P. Dutton & Co., Inc., for "The Kiss of God" from *The Life of Moses* by Edmond Fleg, copyright 1931, © 1959 by Edmond Fleg.

The East and West Publishing Co., Inc., for "Another Page to the Song of Songs" by Sholom Aleichem, translated by Maurice Samuel, copyright 1915, 1943 by Sholom Aleichem.

Farrar, Straus & Giroux, Inc., for "The Jewbird" from *Idiots First* by Bernard Malamud, © 1963 by Bernard Malamud, and "The Son" by Isaac Bashevis Singer from *The Menorah Journal,* © 1962 by Isaac Bashevis Singer.

Harcourt, Brace & World, Inc., for "Berman's Joy" from *The Human Season,* © 1960 by Edward Lewis Wallant.

Harper & Row, Publishers, for "The Romantic" from *This People* by Ludwig Lewisohn, copyright 1933, © 1961 by Ludwig Lewisohn.

The Jewish Publication Society of America, for selections from *The Maaseh Book,* translated by Moses Gaster, copyright 1932, © 1960.

Alfred A. Knopf, Inc., Random House, Inc., for "The Death of Sholom Aleichem" from *The World of Sholom Aleichem* by Maurice Samuel, copyright 1943 by Sholom Aleichem, and "Before the Law" from *The Trial* by Franz Kafka, translated from the German by Willa and Edwin Muir, copyright 1937 by Alfred A. Knopf, Inc.

Little, Brown & Company, for "The Lie" by Mary Antin from *Atlantic Narratives, Second Series,* edited by Charles Swain Thomas, copyright 1916, 1944 by Little, Brown & Company.

Liveright Publishing Corporation, Inc., for "Zorakh" from *The Mask* by John Cournos, copyright 1919, 1947 by John Cournos.

The Loeb Classical Library and the Harvard University Press, for "Self-Portrait" from *Josephus,* translated by H. St. John Thackeray, copyright 1925, 1953.

The Macmillan Company and Mrs. Israel Zangwill, for "The Tug of Love" by Israel Zangwill from *Ghetto Comedies,* copyright 1908, 1936 by Mrs. Israel Zangwill.

Scott Meredith Literary Agency, Inc., for "The Golem" by Avram Davidson, © 1955 by Fantasy House, Inc.

Stanley Paul & Company, London, for "A Fair, and Jewish Marriages" from *Fishke the Lame* by Mendele Mocher Seforim, translated by Angelo S. Rappoport.

Paul R. Reynolds, Inc., for "The Testimony of Major Kaufman" from *The Winston Affair* by Howard Fast, © 1959 by Howard Fast.

George Routledge and Sons, London, for "Visit to the Pope" by David Reubeni from *Jewish Travelers,* edited by Elkan Nathan Adler, copyright 1931.

Schocken Books, Inc., for "The Name" by Aharon Megged from *Israeli Stories,* edited by Joel Blocker, translated by Minna Givton, © 1962 by Schocken Books, Inc.

Simon and Schuster, Inc., for "Among Our People" from *"—& Company"* by Jean-Richard Bloch, copyright 1930, © 1958, and "Alfred Engländer" from *The Pure in Heart* by Franz Werfel, copyright 1929, © 1957.

University of Chicago Press, for selections from *The Bible: An American Translation,* edited by J. M. Powis Smith, copyright 1931, © 1959 by the University of Chicago Press.

University of London Press, London, for "A Trip to Heaven" from *Tophet and Eden* by Immanuel ben Solomon Romi, translated by Harmann Gollancz.

The Viking Press, Inc., for "Buchmendel" from *Kaleidoscope* by Stefan Zweig, copyright 1934, © 1962 by The Viking Press, Inc., and "A Ghetto Dog" by Isaiah Spiegel from *A Treasury of Yiddish Stories* by Irving Howe and Eliezer Greenberg, copyright 1953, 1954 by The Viking Press, Inc.

Thomas Yoseloff, Publisher, for "Alte Bobbe" from *When I Was a Boy in Boston* by Charles Angoff, copyright by Charles Angoff.

CONTENTS

CONTENTS

II. UNDER THE CRESCENT AND THE CROSS

MEDIEVAL TIMES

GHETTO LIGHTS AND SHADOWS

CONTENTS

PREFACE

THIS book is more than a compilation of stories; it is a collective portrait of the Jewish people, and reflects, in so far as literature is a reflection of life, the social development of this unique people over a period of almost three thousand years. It is also an effective demonstration of the fact that the Jews, despite a comparatively tragic history and matchless loyalty to religious tradition, have been many-sided human beings, living in a real flesh-and-blood world, a world always tempered by the social and cultural climate of each age and of the people among whom they lived. The incomparable diversity of their living experience is partially indicated by the area of the earth's surface which the Jews have traversed (the catalogue of Jewries reads like an index to an historical atlas) and the wide range of the original languages—Hebrew, Aramaic, Greek, Arabic, Yiddish, French, German, Italian, Spanish, and English—in which these stories were written.

But *The Jewish Caravan* is not an anthology of Jewish literature. Such great collections as the Bible, the Midrash, and the Talmud, the galaxy of poets in the medieval Moslem empires, and the recent revival of Hebrew and Yiddish letters cannot be adequately represented in any one volume. The compilations of Halper, of Fleg, and of Glatzer and Strauss offer no more than hors d'œuvres that whet our appetite precisely because they attempt to include the whole range of Jewish literature. Nor is this an anthology of stories written by authors who happen to be of Jewish birth or extraction. *The Jewish Caravan* is a selection of stories and narratives written by Jewish writers who felt the need of expressing themselves as Jews and of recording and interpreting Jewish life not only for the cultivated few but, perhaps primarily, for the people, and it is arranged to mirror the social and cultural growth of the Jewish people. For example, the wonderful tale of *Jonah,* like the *Letter of Aristeas* in a later period, was an anti-nationalist piece of propaganda written during an age of intense nationalism. The vast sea of Talmudic lore was utilized to comfort, to exhort, and to enlighten the unlettered folk. "The most prominent feature of Rabbinic literature," wrote Professor Louis Ginzberg, "is its popular character." This is equally true of the *Maaseh Book* in the Middle Ages, and of the beautiful, moving Hasidic tales of the eighteenth and nineteenth centuries. Mass movements have been a basic force in Yiddish and Hebrew literatures during the past fifty or more years. But even though, from the point of view of Jewish literature (the monuments of which are chiefly religious classics) this compilation takes us off the main literary highway, yet it does, from the outlook of modern-minded men and women, give us a glimpse into the inner life of the Jewish people, into the social habits and social changes that dominated their everyday existence. In short, it is both a literary feast and a key to the understanding of the Jewish character.

There were several alternatives for the arrangement of the stories. They might have been arranged simply in a chronological order, or according to the countries in which the writers lived, or the languages in which they were written. The present arrangement has been determined by a definite social outlook in the selection of the material. Consequently, we have cut through the accepted chronological and territorial labels, usually circumscribed by the political changes in Jewish history, and arrived at a pattern based upon social forces.

The first division, "The Making of a People," exhibits a minority group struggling for survival in an alien world and finally clinching this struggle by the crystallization of a distinctive culture and Weltanschauung. From the establishment of "normative" or rabbinic Judaism (in the early centuries of the common era) to the nineteenth century, there were two dominating historial forces, Christianity and Mohammedanism, which influenced the intellectual trends in Judaism and even determined the economic and social status of the Jewish people. Hence in our second division, "Under the Cross and the Crescent," is shown how the way of life and the culture developed during the first social epoch acted as a bulwark against persecutions and restrictions, and provided a perennial source of comfort and of strength. Then, with the social and political emancipation of the Jews beginning early in the nineteenth century and their economic restratification as a result of the Industrial Revolution, a new epoch unfolds: "The Modern World." New problems and new forces—assimilation, social and economic antisemitism, the disintegration of traditional religion and culture, nationalism—produced an era of intense conflict and maladjustment, of ceaseless yearning and aspiration. This last division portrays a defenseless minority caught in the maelstrom of titanic social and economic forces which on the one hand press it to the wall, and on the other hand release an enormous vitality and creativeness.

In the selection of the materials substance has been given preference over form and authorship; several stories by lesser known writers have been utilized where the editor felt that they presented the best illustrations of a social trend; and the problem presented by the meagerness of Jewish belles-lettres before the last half-century has been solved by the selection of long excerpts from memoirs, correspondence and chronicles which (as in the autobiographical accounts of Glückel of Hameln, Solomon Maimon and Mordecai Manuel Noah) are unsurpassed for human interest and for sheer drama. Moreover, since the needs of the great body of general readers have been constantly kept in mind, ancient writings, such as the Bible, the Apocrypha and the Agada, have been presented in modern versions; only this consideration can justify the preference of an

intelligible modern translation[1] over the majestic simplicity and moving rhythm
of the King James Version, or the paucity of the Agada selections. Further discussion of the literature and a brief survey of the social and historical background of each period will be found in the Introductions which precede the
three divisions of the book; the literary sources are recorded in footnotes and
in the Biographical Notes.

The editor is aware of omissions, due mainly to the limitations of a single
volume. Anyone acquainted with Jewish literature will miss many stories from
the Bible, the Apocrypha, Hellenistic Jewish literature, the Midrash and Talmud, medieval storytellers, and literally hundreds of modern writers in Hebrew,
Yiddish, and the European languages. That is the inescapable fate of any such
book; for the aim, after all, has been to make the collection representative rather
than comprehensive.

To numerous friends, authors, and publishers who have cooperated in this
undertaking, the editor wishes to express his appreciation. He is particularly
indebted to Mr. Samuel Kreiter, of New York City, and Mr. I. M. Lask, of
Jerusalem, for assistance in the work of translation, and to his former teachers,
Professor Ralph Marcus and Professor Shalom Spiegel, and to Dr. Israel Knox,
for their invaluable suggestions and criticism. To Henry Hurwitz, editor of
The Menorah Journal, he wishes to record his gratitude for generous assistance
and for cooperation which has added much to the quality of the volume.

January 15, 1935   L. W. S.

[1] *The Bible: An American Translation,* edited by J. M. Powis Smith and published by the
University of Chicago Press (1931).

PREFACE TO THE REVISED EDITION

The three decades that have passed since the publication of *The Jewish
Caravan* have been big with events, and the social forces propelling them have
stimulated literary expression everywhere. As a consequence the book has been
revised and enlarged, within the original framework, to mirror the transformation of Jews and Jewish life. My indebtedness to authors, living and dead, is
gratefully acknowledged.

April 15, 1965   Leo W. Schwarz

I. THE MAKING OF A PEOPLE

INTRODUCTION

Jewish history comprises some forty centuries. It is a stream whose tributaries have branched out over five continents. To discover its headwaters we must turn to the Near East, casting an eye on the great cultures that flourished in the valleys of the Nile and the Tigris and Euphrates. From this vantage point, aided by archeology and literature, we can glimpse the early wanderings, struggles, and strivings of the Tribes of Israel and the emergence of their distinctive religion and culture. Even without the remarkable finds of modern archeology, the Hebrew Bible would still portray dramatically the struggle of Israel against the encroachments of the dominant cultures of the ancient Near East as it portrays the development of a people who formed both a kinship community and a national society. Their heirs survived the procession of centuries and still live in most of the centers of modern civilization. The culture of ancient Israel remains a vital part of the lives of twentieth-century Jews, the groundwork of their traditions and institutions, part and parcel of their psychology.

What is that culture? It is derived from the great ancient cultures of the Near East, which the Israelites took over in their conquest of Canaan and reinterpreted in the light of the religious and political philosophy of the Hebrew Prophets. Mentally or temperamentally, King David and the masses which Jeremiah exhorted were not unlike the contemporary non-Israelites. Yet less than a millennium later the Israelite at home in the worship of Yahweh within the borders of Canaan (*King David*)[1] evolved into the cosmopolitan Jew, worshiping the God of the Universe in every part of the far-flung Roman Empire (*Self-Portrait*). The centuries which stand between these two differing culture types witnessed a remarkable social evolution. Let us trace its chief stages.

Under the Judges and early Kings, the Israelites constituted a minority in Canaan. While struggling for a foothold against the Canaanites and the Philistines, they absorbed by conquest and intermarriage many of the local customs and traditions (*The Tragedy of Samson*). The result was a cultural synthesis, but one in which Yahweh maintained the supreme loyalty of the people. The mounting friction between the aristocratic and the agricultural classes came to the surface after the death of Solomon, who had pursued a policy of commercialization and

[1] The titles in parentheses refer to stories or sections of this book.

colonial expansion and, what was resented most by the land- and freedom-loving peasants, of forced labor and military service. An additional irritant was the demonetization of silver (largely in the hands of the masses) caused by the enormous influx of gold which the author of the book of *Kings* describes in words that ring familiar to our own ears: "The king also made silver in Jerusalem as common as stone . . ." The upshot of this policy was the division of the monarchy into the Kingdoms of Israel and Judah and the intensification of internal dissension which ultimately led to the destruction of both kingdoms.

Between the ninth and seventh centuries B.C.E. the conflict between the governing class and the common people expressed itself in the form of religious cleavages. The upper classes were assimilationist: the society dames of Jerusalem imported their gowns from Memphis and Nineveh and their house-furnishings from Tyre and Damascus; their sons intermarried with handsomely dowried daughters of prominent non-Israelitish families. Against them Amos leveled a scathing denunciation:

> Woe unto them that are at ease in Zion,
> And secure in the mountains of Samaria,
> They who lie upon couches of ivory,
> And stretch themselves lazily upon their beds,
> And eat rams from the flock,
> And feed on calves from the stall,
> They who thrum the harp,
> And drink chalices of fine wine,
> And anoint themselves with precious oils.

This whole trend reached its culmination in the attempt of Jezebel, the wife of Ahab (*Ahab and the Prophets*), to superimpose upon Israel the domination of a foreign deity; the outrageous murder of Naboth furnished the springboard for active opposition. Elijah of Tishbeh, an uncompromising patriot of Yahweh and defender of the common people, set himself about the heroic task of re-establishing the supremacy of his god. Unconsciously, he launched a vast social movement—the prophetic movement—which laid the foundations of Judaism and ultimately found its way, through Christianity, into western civilization.

The prophets, from Elijah (ninth century B.C.E.) to Jeremiah (seventh-sixth century B.C.E.), were stern realists. They struggled unyieldingly with the predatory upper classes. They organized public sentiment. They denounced, in the marketplace and at the public festivals: (1) unequal distribution of wealth; (2) social parasites; (3) meaningless religious formalities. They advocated: (1) decent human relations; (2) social equality; (3) religion as an inner experience; (4) leadership based upon moral values rather than political expediency; (5) a complete loyalty to the God of Israel. This platform they identified with the law of God, his demands upon his people, and inevitably associated the practices and beliefs which they denounced with the worship of foreign gods and the cultivation of foreign mores. Thus polytheism and syncretism became symbols of injustice and treachery; and monotheism and social morality became the symbols of justice and loyalty.

The destruction of the northern kingdom by Assyria (721 B.C.E.) gave historical verification to the teaching of the earlier prophets; it increased the prestige of their successors. By the end of the seventh century, the theory of prophetic teaching was elaborated in a practical digest, the book of *Deuteronomy,* which although spurned by the general public, was treasured in prophetic circles. When the unprecedented crisis of 586 B.C.E. (*Jeremiah and the Destruction of Jerusalem*) resulted in the destruction of the state and the national sanctuaries, this book became the constitution of a stateless people. It was the bottle-neck through which the vintage of prophecy flowed into Judaism.

That evil year, 586 B.C.E., marks a new epoch in Israel's long but unfinished drama. Afterwards, with exception of a brief respite under the Hasmoneans, the Jewish people are subject to alien domination. But the major fact of social consequence during the following seven hundred years or more, commonly designated as the Persian, Hellenistic, and Roman periods, was the establishment of the Jews as a diaspora people.

It is true that Israelites left Palestine as soldiers, merchantmen, adventurers and captives, before 586 B.C.E. They are dim but substantial figures in our record; for although some of them, like those carried into captivity by the Assyrians, were absorbed into the surrounding population (they were not "lost"), many, like the small heroic community at Assuan, maintained their identity and probably were later joined by the refugees and captives from Judah. The tolerant policies of Persian rulers, which encouraged cultural autonomy for minorities, helped the growth of Jewish communities throughout their huge empire. By the middle of the first century C.E., when Titus was breaching the walls of Jerusalem, at least two-thirds of the Jews (who as a whole constituted about one-twelfth of the population of the Roman Empire) were living outside Palestine. With Josephus we meet them at Rome; with Paul we find them in the important cities of Asia Minor; Philo gives us a glimpse into their extraordinary community in Alexandria, that Paris of the ancient world; Hillel, an intellectual leader of Palestinian Jewry, hailed from Babylonia; and a Roman geographer, Strabo, who wrote a historical work in the first century of the common era, reported: "They [the Jews] have penetrated into every state so that it is difficult to find a single place in the world in which their tribe has not been received and become dominant" (*Paul Preaches in the Diaspora*). The diaspora had already become the web of the Jewish people, into which the weft of nationality and religion were deftly woven.

The dominance of the prophetic viewpoint after 586 B.C.E. led to the development of a unique concept of nationality. Until the nineteenth century nationality was either identified with or subordinated to the state. But the Jews turned their political losses into spiritual capital. Contrary to the policies of all ancient peoples, they molded and fortified their national life independent of political power, and to the present day they have remained an ethnic, cultural minority.

It should be pointed out that for several centuries the semblance of statehood continued. After Cyrus' decree in 536 B.C.E. (the prototype of the later Napoleonic and British declarations), we know of at least three waves of immigration of Zionists who returned to Judah from Persia. The bare records (*Nehemiah Rebuilds the Temple*) indicate trials and suffering that overshadow those of the modern Palestinian pioneers. Nevertheless a community was reëstablished, the Temple was rebuilt, and, under the sponsorship of Ezra, Nehemiah (fifth century B.C.E.) and their successors, the basic social, religious and legal cast of the community was reconstituted.

But it was not until Alexander had swept through the East and his successors attempted to put into practice a totalitarian state that the Jewish people again embarked upon a brief political career. Antiochus III may have been a tyrant; he was not a "lunatic." This is amply borne out by his understanding of one of the central truths of Jewish history: he knew that this people would oppose him and survive so long as they maintained their ethnic distinctiveness, that to destroy them he must destroy their creative and spiritual essence. But Antiochus failed. The victory over him is still celebrated annually in the colorful festival of Hanukkah (*Courage*). It resulted, among other things, in a brief period of political freedom under the rule of the family of one of the most astute military leaders of ancient times: Judah Maccabee. But the Roman eagle was hovering over the prosperous East. In 139 B.C.E. the Roman senate signed a decree recognizing the independence of the Jewish state. Seventy-six years later Pompey massacred the inhabitants of Jerusalem and made Palestine a province of Syria. The Arch of Titus is eloquent testimony to the disastrous attempt of the Jews to loosen the grip of Rome in the middle of the first century.

The political doom of the Jews had been sealed in 586 B.C.E. However tragic the destruction of the Temple in 70 C.E., its importance has been highly exaggerated. It did not change the political status of the Jewish people. The Patriarch was recognized as the head of all Jewry and given powers equal to those of a Herodian king. It marks, in reality, the beginning of the decline (but not extinction) of Palestinian Jewry, and of the reformulation of Judaism to meet the needs of a changing social order.

Two of the major characteristics of modern World Jewry—the diaspora and the stateless nationality—were fixed in these early times. Another element, closely interwoven with the others, in determining the subsequent fortunes of the Jewish people was their religious tradition (Judaism). This tradition has been misunderstood by many non-Jews who see it through the eyes of Paul's polemics in the New Testament or the theological presuppositions of Church historians. This applies to the Sunday school teacher as well as to Alfred North Whitehead. And by Jews it has been cut to fit their varying intellectual patterns. Compare, for example, the viewpoints of Maimonides, Mendelssohn and Buber; or of the Yiddishist Zhitlovsky, with the nationalist A. D. Gordon.

The theoretical basis of the religious tradition was laid by the prophets. After 586 B.C.E. this theory was slowly translated into life-forms. In Babylonia there appeared a volume by the prophet Ezekiel of Tel Aviv, which may be aptly entitled *The Theory and Practice of the New Judaism*. He envisioned the restoration of Israel in Palestine as a theocracy. He elaborated ideas—the moral value of the individual and the efficacy of individual repentance—which became essential designs in the mosaic of Jewish religious thought. By the waters of Babylon, where the captives "wept, remembering Zion," historical records and the national literature were gathered and revised from the prophetic viewpoint.

In the comparative peace and settled conditions of the Persian empire an extraordinary social and intellectual development proceeded. A world community predicated a world religion; and the majestic writings in the books of *Job, Jonah* and the second *Isaiah* are witnesses to the continuation of the noble thought of the prophets, universally applied. The vision of Isaiah reaches to the skyline of his world, and with matchless poetry and music he sings of the oneness of God and the unity of world history. He portrayed Zion as a vitalizing ethical concept which forever wed the Jewish people, wherever they might dwell, to their homeland. And in *Job* we find an unforgettable word-portrait of what may be considered the high watermark of Jewish ethics:

> . . . I delivered the poor who cried for help,
> And the fatherless, and him that had no helper.
> The blessing of him that was ready to perish came upon me,
> And the heart of the widow I made glad.
> I put on righteousness, and it clothed me;
> Like a robe and a turban was my justice.
> Eyes was I to the blind,
> And feet was I to the lame.
> I was a father to the needy;
> And I investigated the cause which I did not know.
> I broke the talons of the wicked,
> And I drew the prey out of his teeth.

It was this spirit that pervaded the ceremonial and social institutions which were created during these centuries. An apocryphal book, *The Wisdom of Ben Sira*, throws a floodlight upon the institutions and ideas that by 200 B.C.E. were characteristic of the Jewish people. In addition to the elaborate ceremony of the Temple worship and the seasonal feasts and fasts, we discover the synagogue (Bet Hakeneset), the study academy (Yeshivah), the teacher and interpreter of the written and oral law (Sofer) and the Great Assembly. Several hundred years earlier, when Ezra read the law (the equivalent of the Pentateuch) to the Jewish community, it presented a scheme of life which differed considerably. Only through a long struggle, resulting, for example, in the Samaritan schism, was intermarriage finally stopped. But in the third and second century the law was the flesh and bone of the Jewish community. In Alexandria it was translated into Greek for the Greek-speaking Jews of the diaspora.

The failure of Antiochus to bring about the assimilation of Palestinian Jewry is a landmark in Jewish history. It gave the Jews a deep sense of pride; it quickened their religious loyalty (*Judith and Holofernes*); it turned back the rising tide of Hellenism; it resulted, above all, in the growth of a national movement which expressed itself in a neo-Hebrew literature (Aramaic had become the lingua franca of the East) and strengthened the influence of the common people.

And once again a severe social conflict expressed itself in the form of religious cleavages and antagonisms in the struggle between the two major groups, the Pharisees and the Sadducees. How did these groups differ? The Sadducees comprised largely the aristocracy and priesthood who were (1) conservative in religion, resisting the development of the oral law, (2) assimilationist, giving primacy to the western, Hellenistic, cultural tradition, (3) political in national policy, adopting the Greek conception of statehood. The Pharisees constituted the masses and middle classes. They (1) rejected assimilation as a social policy; (2) disavowed political nationalism (it was the Pharisees who sent an embassy to Rome and requested the Romans to remove the priesthood and assume political rule); (3) gave primacy to the development of the oral law. It is this last issue which leads us to the heart of the conflict. The assimilated, educated Sadducees rejected the social and religious tradition (not the ceremonial) which was the breath of the masses who lived it. They rejected certain beliefs (e.g. doctrine of resurrection) and practices not found in the Bible, but which were, in effect, intellectual adjustments to a new age and new conditions.

After the wars with Rome, the Sadducees lost their prestige and their political anchorage. Pharisaism won the day. It was the victory of social democracy over privileged aristocracy. It was the foundation upon which the reformulation of the religious tradition was made in the academies of Palestine and Babylonia.

The need for intellectual reformulation and social reconstruction grew out of a number of historical upheavals and trends during the first to the sixth centuries of the common era. The destruction of the Temple by the Romans has already been noted. These centuries also witnessed the rise and spread of Christianity and its adoption as the state religion of the Roman Empire. As far-reaching in its consequences was the general political and economic decline of the Roman and Persian empires. The effects of these changes upon the Jews were drastic: (1) the diaspora became the basis of the social and political organization of the Jewish people; (2) while the geographic base of the diaspora expanded, the continuous decrease of population reached a danger point; (3) the largest portion of the population, formerly engaged in agriculture, gradually became engaged in commercial pursuits; (4) legal, social, religious and economic restrictions increased in number and severity as these centuries advanced; (5) the crystallization of a new policy, the autonomous international Jewish community, which functioned within the framework of a national state; (6) the crystallization of the religious tradition and its codification in the Talmud.

During the centuries under discussion the stream of Jewish history courses into the "sea of the Talmud." Its religious currents and social cross-currents are incredibly involved, but the opportunity to understand their essential character has been provided for our generation by a group of brilliant interpreters. The admirable writings of Schechter[2] and Ginsberg and the monumental volumes of Moore throw the spotlight of science, learning and understanding upon this much maligned and misunderstood development of Jewish religious thought and expression. ". . . above all its defects of casuistry and trifling and intolerance, the merits of the Talmud soar high. A discipline for the hallowing of life and the attainment of righteousness; a balance of authority and freedom, of law and license; a democratic attitude towards social rank; a syncretism of the material and the spiritual; a refusal to draw too fast a moral line between secular and sacred, or to keep God out of the daily round—to all this the Talmud shows the way more persuasively, more imitably, than do even the Hebrew prophets." (Abrahams)

Out of the pages of the Talmud and the Midrash shines the word "Torah." It is a comprehensive expression for a whole social organization based upon the regimen of the law (Halakah). It implies a society in which institutions and social relations, not verbal ideals or theological dogmas, are the quintessence of religion, in which the pragmatic and the ideal, the desirable and the actual, are completely fused. Every detail of life, every aspect of the workaday world, is the concern of the Torah. The supreme values which it nurtured, as illustrated in the moral myth of the Agada (Torah: Law and Life), are justice, wisdom, independence and goodness; the supreme personality is the Talmid Hakam, the practical scholar; the ultimate goal of human life is a

[2] The reader will find the following volumes highly readable and illuminating: *Some Aspects of Rabbinic Theology* (New York, 1909) and *Studies in Judaism* by Solomon Schechter (New York, 1896); *Students, Scholars and Saints* by Louis Ginsberg (Philadelphia, 1928); and *Judaism in the First Centuries of the Christian Era* by George Foot Moore (Cambridge, 1927-30).

messianic Here and Now. In a noteworthy essay, *Halakah and Agada,* the poet Bialik elaborated the relation between the two branches of the Torah: "Halakah and Agada are two entities that are really one, two sides of the same coin. The relation between them is like that of expression to thought and emotion or of action to speech. Halakah is the condensation, the ultimate quintessence, of Agada; Agada is the substance of Halakah. Agada is the plaintive voice of the heart's longing as it wings its ways to its resting-place; Halakah is the haven where the longing is momentarily satisfied and stilled. As a dream seeks its fulfillment in interpretation, as thought in speech, as flower in fruit, so does Agada seek its fulfillment in Halakah. But the heart of the fruit conceals a seed from which a new flower will sprout. The halakah which is transmuted into a symbol becomes the mother of a new agada which may or may not be like it. A living and wholesome halakah is an agada that has been or will be, and the reverse is also true. Both are one in their beginning and in their end."

So much for the first stages of the development of the Jewish people. By the time the barbarians took their toll of the effete Roman civilization and Mohammed's lieutenants burst upon the East, the Jewish people had been molded in the image of the Torah. How deeply the Torah was engraved upon their soul may be judged when one reflects that, despite the ravages of the intervening centuries, the Jewish people remained, until the modern era, an embodiment of the basic principles established during its early history.

BEGINNINGS

JOSEPH [1]

JOSEPH was thirty years old when he entered the service of Pharaoh, king of Egypt.

After leaving the presence of Pharaoh, Joseph made a tour through the whole land of Egypt. During the seven years of plenty the land produced abundant crops; so he collected all the food of the seven years when there was plenty in the land of Egypt, and thus stored food in the cities, storing in each city the food from the fields around it. Joseph stored up grain like the sands of the sea, in great quantities, until he ceased to keep account of it; for it was past measuring.

Before the years of famine came, two sons were born to Joseph by Asenath, the daughter of Potiphera, priest of On. Joseph called the name of the first-born Manasseh [forgetfulness]; "For," said he, "God has made me forget all about my hardships and my father's home." The name of the second he called Ephraim [fruitfulness]; "For God has made me fruitful in the land of my misfortune."

When the seven years of plenty that had prevailed in the land of Egypt came to an end, the seven years of famine set in, as Joseph had said.

There was famine in all lands, but throughout all the land of Egypt there was food.

When the land of Egypt became quite famished, the people cried to Pharaoh for food; so Pharaoh announced to all Egypt,

"Go to Joseph, and do what he tells you." The famine spread all over the land, so Joseph threw open all that he had locked up, and sold grain to the Egyptians, since the famine was severe in the land of Egypt. People from all lands came to Joseph in Egypt to buy grain; for the famine was severe all over the earth.

When Jacob learned that there was grain to be had in Egypt, he said to his sons,

"Why do you stare at one another? I have just heard," he said, "that there is grain to be had in Egypt; go down there, and buy some for us there, that we may live and not die."

So ten of Joseph's brothers went down to buy grain in Egypt, since Jacob would not let Joseph's brother Benjamin go with his other brothers; "Lest," thought he, "harm should befall him." Thus the Israelites came with the rest to buy grain; for the famine was in the land of Canaan.

Now Joseph was the vizier of the land; it was he who sold the grain to

[1] Selected from *Genesis*, chapters 41:46-46:7. Translated from the Hebrew by Theophile J. Meek.

13

all the people of the land. So Joseph's brothers came and prostrated themselves before him, with their faces to the ground. When Joseph saw his brothers, he recognized them, but he treated them as if he were a stranger, and spoke harshly to them.

"Where have you come from?" he said to them.

"From the land of Canaan to buy food," they said.

Joseph recognized his brothers, but they did not recognize him. Remembering the dreams that he had had about them, Joseph said to them,

"You are spies; you have come to find out the condition of the land!"

"No, my lord," they said to him, "your servants have come to buy food. We are all sons of one man; we are honest men; your servants are not spies."

"Not so," he said to them; "but you have come to find out the condition of the land."

But they said,

"Your servants are brothers, twelve in all; we are sons of a certain man in the land of Canaan; the youngest is at present with our father, while the other is no more."

But Joseph said to them,

"It is as I told you; you are spies. By this you shall be put to the proof: as Pharaoh lives, you shall not leave this place unless your youngest brother comes here. Send one of your number to fetch your brother, while the rest of you remain in custody. Thus shall your statements be put to the proof as to whether you are truthful or not. As Pharaoh lives, you are spies!"

So he bundled them off to prison for three days, but on the third day Joseph said to them,

"Since I am one who fears God, you may save your lives, if you do this: if you are honest men, let one of your brothers remain confined in the prison where you are, and then the rest of you, go and take grain home to your starving households; but you must bring me your youngest brother. Thus shall your words be verified, and you shall not die."

They proceeded to do so, saying to one another,

"Unfortunately, we were to blame about our brother, upon whose distress, when he pleaded with us for mercy, we gazed unmoved; that is why this distress has come to us."

Then Reuben spoke up and said to them,

"Did I not say to you, 'Do not sin against the lad'? But you paid no attention; so now comes a reckoning for his blood!"

They did not know that Joseph heard them; for the intermediary was between them. He turned from them, and wept. On coming back to them, he spoke to them, took Simeon from them, and imprisoned him in their presence. Joseph then ordered their receptacles to be filled with grain, the money of each of them to be replaced in his sack, and provisions to be given them for the journey. This was done for them. Then they loaded their asses with their grain, and departed.

At the camping-place for the night one of them opened his sack to give his ass some fodder, and there he saw his money in the mouth of his sack!

"My money has been put back! It is right here inside my sack!" he said to his brothers.

Thereupon their hearts sank, and they turned to one another in fear, saying,

"What is this that God has done to us?"

On reaching their father Jacob in the land of Canaan, they told him all that had befallen them:

"The man who is lord of the land talked harshly to us, making us out to be spies of the land. But we said to him, 'We are honest men; we are not spies. We are brothers on our father's side, twelve in all; one is no more, and the youngest is at present with our father in the land of Canaan.' Then the man who is lord of the land said to us, 'By this I shall find out whether you are honest men: leave one of your brothers with me, and taking something for your famishing households, be off; and then bring me your youngest brother. Thus shall I know that you are not spies, but honest men. I will restore your brother to you, and you will be free to trade in the land.'"

When they came to empty their sacks, there was the money-packet of each in his sack! On seeing their money-packets, both they and their father were dismayed, and their father Jacob said to them,

"It is I that you bereave. Joseph is no more, Simeon is no more, and now you would take Benjamin! It is on me that all this falls."

Reuben said to his father,

"You may kill my two sons if I do not bring him home to you! Put him in my charge, and I will bring him back to you."

But he said,

"My son shall not go down with you; for his brother is dead, and he alone is left. If any harm were to befall him on the journey that you make, you would bring my gray hairs down to Sheol in sorrow."

The famine continued severe in the land, so when they had finished eating all the grain which they had brought from Egypt, their father said to them,

"Go again, and buy us a little food."

But Judah said to him,

"The man strictly warned us: 'You cannot have audience with me unless your brother is with you.' If you are ready to let our brother go with us, we will go down and buy food for you; but if you are not ready to let him go, we cannot go down; for the man said to us, 'You cannot have audience with me unless your brother is with you.'"

"Why did you bring this trouble on me," said Israel, "by telling the man that you had another brother?"

They said,

"The man persisted in asking about ourselves and our family—'Is your father still living? Have you another brother?' We only gave him the information demanded by these questions of his. How could we possibly know that he would say, 'Bring your brother down'?"

"Let the lad go with me," said Judah to his father Israel; "but we must go at once, if we would save our lives and not die, both we, you, and our dependents. I will be surety for him; you may hold me responsible for him. If I do not bring him back to you and set him before you, you may blame me for it all my life; in fact if we had not wasted so much time, we could have made a second trip by now."

Then their father Israel said to them,

"If it must be so, then do this: take some of the country's best in your receptacles, and take it down to the man as a present—a little balm, a little honey, gum, laudanum, pistachio nuts, and almonds. Also take double the money with you, and so take back with you the money that was replaced in the mouths of your sacks—perhaps there was a mistake. Take your brother too, and go, return to the man. May God Almighty grant you such kindness with the man that he will release your other brother for you, as well as Benjamin. As for me, as I have already suffered bereavement, I may have to do so again."

So the men took this present, and taking double the money with them, as well as Benjamin, they started off, went down to Egypt, and stood in the presence of Joseph. When Joseph saw Benjamin with them, he said to his house-steward,

"Take the men home, kill an animal, and get it ready; for the men are to dine with me at noon."

The man did as Joseph told him, and brought the men to Joseph's house. On being brought to Joseph's house the men became frightened, saying,

"It is because of the money which reappeared in our sacks the first time that we are being brought into the house, in order that he may devise some pretext against us, and falling upon us, take us into slavery, together with our asses."

So they went up to Joseph's house-steward, and spoke to him at the doorway of the house.

"If you please, sir," they said, "we came down the first time specially to buy food, but when we reached the camping-place for the night, and opened our sacks, there was each man's money in the mouth of his sack—our money in full. Accordingly we have brought it back with us, and we have brought other money down with us to buy food. We do not know who put our money in our sacks."

"Be at ease," he said, "do not be afraid! It must have been your God, the

God of your fathers, who put treasure in your sacks for you. I received your money."

Then he brought Simeon out to them.

After bringing the men into Joseph's house, the man gave them water to wash their feet, and he gave them fodder for their asses. Then they set out the present in anticipation of Joseph's arrival at noon; for they had heard that they were to dine there. When Joseph came home, they brought him the present that they had carried into the house, and bowed to the ground before him. He asked after their health.

"Is your father well," he said, "the old man of whom you spoke? Is he still living?"

"Your servant, our father, is well; he is still living," they said, bowing in homage to him.

Raising his eyes, he saw his brother Benjamin, the son of his own mother, and said,

"Is this your youngest brother, of whom you told me?

"May God be gracious to you, my son!" he said.

Thereupon Joseph hastily sought a place to weep; for his heart was deeply stirred at sight of his brother; he retired to his own room, and wept there. Then he bathed his face, and came out, and controlling himself, said,

"Serve the meal."

The meal was served, separately for him, for them, and for the Egyptians that were dining with him; for the Egyptians could not eat with the Hebrews, because that would be abhorrent to the Egyptians. They were seated in his presence in order of age, from the oldest to the youngest, so that the men stared at one another in amazement. He carried portions from his own table to them, but Benjamin's portion was five times as much as any other's. So they feasted, and drank with him.

He then gave orders to his house-steward,

"Fill the men's sacks as full as they will hold with food, and put each man's money in the mouth of his sack; in the mouth of the sack belonging to the youngest put my cup, the silver cup, along with his money for the grain."

He followed the instructions which Joseph gave.

With the dawn of morning the men with their asses were sent on their way. Although they had left the city, they had not gone far, when Joseph said to his house-steward,

"Run at once after the men, and when you overtake them, say to them, 'Why have you returned evil for good? Why have you stolen my silver cup? Is not this the one from which my lord drinks, which in fact he uses for divination? It is a wicked thing that you have done.'"

So he overtook them, and addressed these words to them; but they said to him,

"Why should my lord speak like this? Your servants would never think of doing such a thing! Why, we even brought you back from the land of Canaan the money that we found in the mouths of our sacks. How then could we steal silver or gold from your master's house? That one of your servants in whose possession it is found shall die, and the rest of us will become slaves to my lord."

"Although it may indeed be just as you say," he said, "yet the one in whose possession it is found shall become my slave, but the rest of you shall be held blameless."

Then each of them quickly lowered his sack to the ground, and opened it, and search being made, beginning with the oldest and ending with the youngest, the cup was found in Benjamin's sack. Thereupon they tore their clothes, and each having reloaded his ass, they returned to the city.

Judah and his brothers arrived at the house of Joseph, while he was still there, so they flung themselves on the ground before him.

"What is this that you have done?" Joseph said to them. "Did you not know that a man like me would be sure to use divination?"

Judah said,

"What can we say to my lord? What can we urge? How can we prove our innocence? God has discovered the crime of your servants; here we are, the slaves of my lord, both we and he in whose possession the cup has been found."

"I could not think of doing such a thing," he said; "only the man in whose possession the cup has been found shall be my slave; the rest of you are free to go back to your father."

Then Judah went up to him, and said,

"If you please, my lord, let your servant speak a word in the ear of my lord, and your anger not blaze against your servant; for you are the equal of Pharaoh himself. My lord asked his servants, 'Have you a father or a brother?' And we said to my lord, 'We have an aged father, and a young brother, the child of his old age; his brother is dead, so that he alone is left of his mother's children, and his father loves him.' Then you said to your servants, 'Bring him down to me that I may see him.' But we told my lord, 'The boy cannot leave his father; his father would die if he were to leave him.' Whereupon you said to your servants, 'Unless your youngest brother comes down with you, you cannot have audience with me again.'

"When we went back to your servant, my father, we reported to him the words of my lord. Then our father said, 'Go again and buy a little food for us.' But we said, 'We cannot go down; if our youngest brother accompanies us, we can go down; for we shall not be allowed to have audience with the man unless our youngest brother is with us.' Then your servant, my father, said to us, 'You know that my wife bore me only two children; then one of them left me, and I think he must surely have been torn to pieces; for I have never seen him since. If then you take this one from me too, and harm befall him, you will bring down my gray hairs to Sheol in trouble.'

"And now, when I rejoin your servant, my father, and the boy not with us, his life is so bound up with the boy's that he will die when he sees that there is no boy, and your servants will bring down the gray hairs of your servant, our father, to Sheol in sorrow; for your servant went surety for the boy to my father, saying, 'If I do not bring him back to you, you may blame me for it all my life.' Now then, pray let your servant remain in the boy's place as my lord's slave, but let the boy go back with his brothers; for how can I go back to my father unless the boy is with me, and witness the agony that would come to my father?"

Joseph could no longer control himself before all his attendants, so he cried out,

"Have everyone withdraw from me."

So there was no one with Joseph when he made himself known to his brothers; but he wept so loudly that the Egyptians heard it, and Pharaoh's household heard it. Joseph said to his brothers,

"I am Joseph. Is my father still living?"

But his brothers could not answer him, because they were so dismayed at being in his presence. So Joseph said to his brothers,

"Come nearer to me.

"I am your brother Joseph whom you sold into Egypt. Now do not be distressed nor angry with yourselves that you sold me here; for it was to save life that God sent me ahead of you; for it is two years now that the famine has prevailed in the land, but there are still five years in which there will be no ploughing or reaping. God sent me ahead of you to insure you a remnant in the earth, and to be the means of a remarkable escape for you. So then it was not you, but God who sent me here, and made me a father to Pharaoh, lord of all his house, and ruler over all the land of Egypt. Hurry back to my father and say to him, 'Thus speaks your son Joseph: "Since God has made me lord of all Egypt, come down to me without delay. You shall live in the land of Goshen, and be near me, you, your sons, your grandsons, your flocks, your herds, and all that belong to you; and there I will provide for you, lest you, your household and all that belong to you come to want; for there are still five years of famine to come."' You can see for yourselves and my brother Benjamin for himself that it is I who speak to you. You must tell my father all about my splendor in Egypt, and all that you have seen; hurry and bring my father here."

Then he fell on the neck of his brother Benjamin and wept, while Benjamin wept on his neck. He kissed all his brothers, and wept on their shoulders, after which his brothers talked with him.

When the news was received at Pharaoh's palace that Joseph's brothers had arrived, Pharaoh was delighted, as were also his courtiers. Pharaoh said to Joseph,

"Say to your brothers, 'Do this: load your animals, go back to the land of Canaan, and taking your father and your households, come to me, and I will give you the best of the land of Egypt, so that you shall eat the fat of the land. Also, carry out this order: take wagons from the land of Egypt for your little ones and your wives; convey your father in them, and come back. Never mind your goods; for the best of the whole land of Egypt will be yours.'"

The sons of Israel did so. Joseph gave them wagons in accord with the command of Pharaoh, and he also gave them provisions for the journey. To each of them he gave a festal garment, but to Benjamin he gave three hundred shekels of silver and five festal garments. To his father he sent likewise ten asses loaded with the best products of Egypt, and ten she-asses loaded with grain, bread, and provisions for his father on the journey. Then he sent his brothers away; and as they left, he said to them,

"Do not get too excited on the way."

So they went up from Egypt, and came to the land of Canaan, to their father Jacob.

"Joseph is still living, and he is ruler over all the land of Egypt," they told him.

But he was so stunned that he would not believe them. However, when they told him all that Joseph had said to them, and he saw the wagons that Joseph had sent to convey him, their father Jacob recovered.

"Enough!" said Israel; "my son Joseph is still living; I will go and see him before I die."

So Israel set out with all that belonged to him. On reaching Beersheba, he offered sacrifices to the God of his father Isaac. In a vision by night God spoke to Israel.

"Jacob! Jacob!" he said.

"Here I am," he said.

"I am El, the God of your father," he said; "do not be afraid to go down to Egypt; for there I will make you a great nation. I will myself go down to Egypt with you—yes, and I will bring you up again, when Joseph's hand shall close your eyes."

Then Jacob set out from Beersheba; and the sons of Israel conveyed their father Jacob, with their little ones and their wives, in the wagons which Pharaoh had sent to convey him. Taking their live stock and the property which they had acquired in the land of Canaan, Jacob and all his descendants migrated to Egypt; his sons and his grandsons accompanied him, as well as his daughters and his granddaughters; he brought all his descendants with him into Egypt.

THE RISE OF MOSES [1]

THEN Joseph died, and likewise all his brothers and all that generation; but the Israelites were fruitful and prolific; they increased in numbers, and grew greater and greater, so that the land was filled with them.

Then a new king rose over Egypt, who knew nothing about Joseph; he said to his people,

"See, the Israelite people have become too numerous and too strong for us; come, let us take precautions against them lest they become so numerous that in the case of a war they should join forces with our enemies and fight against us, and so escape from the land."

Accordingly, gang-foremen were put in charge of them, to oppress them with their heavy labor; and they built Pithom and Raamses as store-cities for Pharaoh. But the more they oppressed them, the more they multiplied and expanded, so that they became apprehensive about the Israelites.

The Egyptians reduced the Israelites to rigorous slavery; they made life bitter for them in hard work with mortar and bricks, and in all kinds of work in the fields, all the work that they exacted of them being rigorous.

Then the king of Egypt spoke to the midwives attending the Hebrew women, of whom the name of one was Shiphrah and that of the other Puah.

"When you act as midwives for the Hebrew women," he said, "you are to look at the genitals; if it is a boy, you must kill him, but if it is a girl, she may live."

But the midwives stood in awe of God, and so did not do as the king of Egypt told them, but let the male children live. So the king of Egypt summoned the midwives, and said to them,

"Why have you done this: let the male children live?"

The midwives said to Pharaoh,

"Because the Hebrew women are not like the Egyptian women; but are animals, in that they are delivered before the midwife reaches them!"

So God was good to the midwives; the people multiplied and grew very numerous, and because the midwives stood in awe of God, they established families for them.

So Pharaoh commanded all his people,

"Every boy that is born to the Hebrews, you must throw into the Nile, but you are to let all the girls live."

Now a man belonging to the house of Levi went and married the daughter of Levi. The woman conceived and bore a son, and seeing that he was robust, she hid him for three months. When she could no longer hide him, she pro-

[1] Selected from *Exodus,* chapters 1:6-4:31. Translated from the Hebrew by Theophile J. Meek.

cured an ark of papyrus reeds for him, and daubing it with bitumen and pitch, she put the child in it, and placed it among the reeds beside the bank of the Nile. His sister posted herself some distance away to see what would happen to him.

Presently Pharaoh's daughter came down to bathe at the Nile, while her maids walked on the bank of the Nile. Then she saw the ark among the reeds and sent her maid to get it. On opening it, she saw the child, and it was a boy crying! She took pity on him, and said,

"This is one of the Hebrews' children."

Thereupon his sister said to Pharaoh's daughter,

"Shall I go and summon a nurse for you from the Hebrew women, to nurse the child for you?"

"Go," said Pharaoh's daughter to her.

So the girl went and called the child's mother, to whom Pharaoh's daughter said,

"Take this child away and nurse it for me, and I will pay the wages due you."

So the woman took the child and nursed him; and when the child grew up, she brought him to Pharaoh's daughter, and he became her son. She called his name Moses [drawn out]; "For," said she, "I drew him out of the water."

It was in those days that Moses, now grown up, went out to visit his fellow-countrymen and noted their heavy labor. He saw an Egyptian kill a Hebrew, one of his own countrymen; so, looking this way and that, and seeing that there was no one in sight, he killed the Egyptian, and hid him in the sand. Another day, when he went out, there were two Hebrews fighting! So he said to him that was in the wrong,

"Why do you strike your companion?"

He replied,

"Who made you ruler and judge over us? Are you thinking of murdering me as you did the Egyptian?"

Then was Moses afraid. "The incident must surely be known," he thought.

When Pharaoh heard about the matter, he tried to kill Moses, but Moses fled from Pharaoh and went to the land of Midian, and sat down beside a well.

Now the priest of Midian had seven daughters, who came to draw water, and fill the troughs to water their father's flock, but some shepherds came and drove them off. So Moses went to their rescue and watered their flock. When they came home to their father Reuel, he said,

"How did you come to get home so soon today?"

They said,

"An Egyptian protected us against the shepherds; he even drew water for us, and watered the flock."

"Then where is he?" he said to his daughters. "Why did you leave the man behind? Invite him to have a meal."

When Moses agreed to live with the man, he gave Moses his daughter Zipporah in marriage; and she bore a son, whom he named Gershom [immigrant]; "For," said he, "I am an immigrant in a foreign land."

In the course of this long time the king of Egypt died. The Israelites, groaning under their bondage, cried for help, and their cry because of their bondage came up to God. God heard their moaning, and God remembered his convenant with Abraham, Isaac, and Jacob; God saw the plight of Israel, and took cognizance of it.

While Moses was tending the flock of his father-in-law, Jethro, the priest of Midian, he led the flock to the western side of the desert, and came to the mountain of God, Horeb. Then the angel of the Lord appeared to him in a flame of fire, rising out of a bush. He looked, and there was the bush burning with fire without being consumed! So Moses said,

"I will turn aside and see this great sight, why the bush is not burned up."

When the Lord saw that he had turned aside to look at it, God called to him out of the bush.

"Moses, Moses!" he said.

"Here I am!" said he.

"Do not come near here," he said; "take your sandals off your feet; for the place on which you are standing is holy ground. I am the God of your father," he said, "the God of Abraham, Isaac, and Jacob."

Then Moses hid his face; for he was afraid to look at God.

"I have indeed seen the plight of my people who are in Egypt," the Lord said, "and I have heard their cry under their oppressors; for I know their sorrows, and I have come down to rescue them from the Egyptians and bring them up out of that land to a land, fine and large, to a land abounding in milk and honey, to the country of the Canaanites, Hittites, Amorites, Perizzites, Hivvites, and Jebusites. Now the Egyptians are oppressing them; so come now, let me send you to Pharaoh, that you may bring my people, the Israelites, out of Egypt."

But Moses said to God,

"Who am I, to go to Pharaoh and bring the Israelites out of Egypt?"

"I will be with you," he said; "and this shall be the sign for you that I have sent you. When you bring the people out of Egypt, you shall serve God at this mountain."

"But," said Moses to God, "in case I go to the Israelites and say to them, 'The God of your fathers has sent me to you,' and they say to me, 'What is his name?' what am I to say to them?"

"I am who I am," God said to Moses. Then he said, "This is what you are to say to the Israelites: ' "I am" has sent me to you.' "

God said further to Moses,

"This is what you are to say to the Israelites: 'The Lord, the God of your fathers, the God of Abraham, Isaac, and Jacob, has appeared to me, saying,

"I have given careful heed to you and your treatment in Egypt, and I have resolved to bring you up out of your tribulation in Egypt to the land of the Canaanites, Hittites, Amorites, Perizzites, Hivvites, and Jebusites, to a land abounding in milk and honey." ' They will heed your appeal; and then you and the elders of Israel shall come to the king of Egypt and say to him, 'The Lord, the God of the Hebrews, has paid us a visit; so now, let us make a three days' journey into the desert to offer sacrifices to the Lord our God.' I know, however, that the king of Egypt will not let you go without the use of force; so I will stretch out my hand and smite Egypt with all the marvels that I shall perform in it; after that he will let you go. And I will bring this people into such favor with the Egyptians that you shall not go away empty-handed when you do leave; each woman must ask her neighbor and the guest in her home for articles of silver and gold, and for clothing, which you are to put on your sons and daughters. Thus shall you despoil the Egyptians."

"But suppose they will not believe me," answered Moses, "nor heed my plea, but say, 'The Lord did not appear to you.' "

The Lord said to him,

"What have you in your hand?"

"A staff," he said.

"Throw it on the ground," said he.

He threw it on the ground, and it became a snake. Moses ran away from it, but the Lord said to Moses,

"Stretch out your hand and lay hold of its tail"—stretching out his hand, he seized it, and it became a staff in his hand—"in order that they may be convinced that the Lord, the God of their fathers, did appear to you, the God of Abraham, Isaac, and Jacob."

The Lord said further to him,

"Put your hand into your bosom."

He put his hand into his bosom, and when he took it out, there was his hand leprous, as white as snow!

"Put your hand back into your bosom," he said.

He put his hand back into his bosom, and when he took it out of his bosom, there it was, like the rest of his body again.

"If they will not believe you, nor accept the evidence of the first sign, they may acknowledge the evidence of the second. If they will not be convinced by even these two signs, nor heed your plea, you are to take some water from the Nile and pour it on the dry ground; and the water that you take from the Nile shall become blood on the dry ground."

But Moses said to the Lord,

"Pray, O Lord, I have been no speaker, neither in the past nor recently, nor since thou hast spoken to thy servant; but I am slow of speech and slow of tongue."

The Lord said to him,

"Who gives man a mouth, or makes him dumb, or deaf, or lame, or blind? Is it not I, the Lord? Now go; I will help you to speak, and will instruct you what to say."

But he said,

"Pray, O Lord, commission whom thou wilt."

Then the anger of the Lord blazed against Moses, and he said,

"Is there not your brother Aaron, the Levite? I know that he is a ready speaker, and further, he is just coming out to meet you, and will be overjoyed at seeing you. You must speak to him, and put the words in his mouth; I will help both you and him to speak, and I will instruct you both what to do. He shall speak for you to the people; he shall serve as a mouthpiece for you, and you shall act the part of God to him. You must take this staff in your hand, with which to perform the signs."

Then Moses went off, and returning to his father-in-law Jethro, said to him,

"Pray let me go back to my relatives in Egypt, to see whether they are still living."

"Go in peace," said Jethro to Moses.

The Lord said to Moses in Midian,

"Go, return to Egypt; for all the men who sought your life are dead."

So Moses took his wife and sons, and mounted them on asses, to return to the land of Egypt; Moses also took the staff of God in his hand.

The Lord said to Moses,

"When you return to Egypt, see that you perform before Pharaoh all the portents which I have put in your power; but I will make him obstinate, so that he will not let the people go. You are to say to Pharaoh, 'Thus says the Lord: "Israel is my first-born son; so I said to you, 'Let my son go, that he may serve me'; but you refused to let him go; accordingly I am going to slay your first-born son." ' "

At a camping place in the course of the journey the Lord encountered him, and tried to kill him. So Zipporah took a flint, and cutting off her son's foreskin, she touched his person with it, saying,

"You are my bridegroom in blood."

Then he let him alone.

At that time a person when circumcised was spoken of as a bridegroom in blood.

The Lord said to Aaron,

"Go into the desert to meet Moses."

So he went; and he met him at the mountain of God and kissed him. Then Moses told Aaron all that the Lord had commissioned him to say and all the signs that he had commanded him to perform. So Moses and Aaron went and assembled all the elders of the Israelites, and Aaron spoke all the words that the Lord had spoken to Moses, and performed the signs in the sight of the people, so that the people believed. When they heard that the

Lord had taken note of the Israelites and had marked their plight, they bowed their heads in homage.

THE TRAGEDY OF SAMSON[1]

Now there was a certain man of Zorah, belonging to the Danite clan, whose name was Manoah. His wife was barren and childless; but the angel of the Lord appeared to the woman, and said to her,

"See now, although you have been barren and childless, you are going to conceive, and bear a son. Now then, take care not to drink wine or liquor, nor to eat anything unclean; for you are going to conceive, and bear a son. A razor is not to be used on his head; for the boy is to be a Nazirite to God from conception. He it is who will take the lead in saving Israel from the power of the Philistines."

Then the woman came and told her husband, saying,

"A man of God came to me, whose appearance was like that of an angel of God, very awe-inspiring. I did not ask him where he came from, nor did he tell me his name; but he said to me, 'You are going to conceive, and bear a son; now then, do not drink wine or liquor, nor eat anything unclean; for the boy is to be a Nazirite to God from conception to the day of his death.'"

Then Manoah besought the Lord, and said,

"Pray, O Lord, let the man of God whom thou didst send come back to us, and teach us what to do for the boy that is to be born."

So God acceded to Manoah's request, and the angel of God came back to the woman while she was sitting in the field, her husband Manoah not being with her. Then the woman ran quickly to tell her husband.

"The man who came to me the other day has just appeared to me!" she said to him.

So Manoah rose and followed his wife, and coming to the man, said to him,

"Are you the man who spoke to my wife?"

"I am," he said.

"In case your promise comes true," said Manoah, "what is to be the boy's training and his vocation?"

The angel of the Lord said to Manoah,

"The woman must abstain from everything of which I spoke to her. She must not eat any of the products of the grapevine, nor drink wine or liquor, nor eat anything unclean. All that I commanded her she must observe."

Then Manoah said to the angel of the Lord,

"Pray allow us to detain you, that we may prepare a kid for you."

[1] Selected from *Judges,* chapters 13:2-16:31. Translated from the Hebrew by Theophile J. Meek.

But the angel of the Lord said to Manoah,

"Though you detain me, I will not taste your food; but if you are going to make a burnt-offering, offer it up to the Lord." (For Manoah did not know that he was the angel of the Lord.)

Then Manoah said to the angel of the Lord,

"What is your name, that we may properly honor you when your promise comes true?"

"Why do you ask for my name," the angel of the Lord said to him, "seeing that it is ineffable?"

Then Manoah took the kid, along with the cereal-offering, and offered it up on the rock to the Lord, who performed wonders while Manoah and his wife looked on; when the flame ascended from the altar heavenward, the angel of the Lord ascended in the flame of the altar, while Manoah and his wife looked on, and fell on their faces to the ground. (The angel of the Lord never again appeared to Manoah and his wife.) Then Manoah knew that he was the angel of the Lord; so Manoah said to his wife,

"We shall certainly die; for we have seen God!"

But his wife said to him,

"If the Lord had meant to kill us, he would not have accepted a burnt-offering and a cereal-offering from us, nor would he have showed us all these things, nor would he have told us such a thing as he did just now."

So the woman bore a son, and called his name Samson. The boy grew up, and the Lord blessed him; but the spirit of the Lord first stirred him up at Mahaneh-dan, between Zorah and Eshtaol.

Samson went down to Timnah, and saw a woman at Timnah, one of the Philistine women. When he came back, he told his father and mother.

"I saw a woman at Timnah," he said, "one of the Philistine women; now then, get her for me in marriage."

But his father and mother said to him,

"Is there no woman among the girls of your own kinsmen or among all my people, that you must go and get a wife from the uncircumcised Philistines?"

But Samson said to his father,

"Get her for me; for she is the one that suits me."

His father and mother did not know, however, that it was at the instigation of the Lord that he was picking a quarrel with the Philistines; for at that time the Philistines held sway over Israel.

Then Samson went down with his father and mother to Timnah, and just as they reached the vineyards of Timnah, a young lion came roaring at him. Then the spirit of the Lord came rushing upon him, so that he split it open as one might split a kid, although he had nothing at all in his hands. However, he did not tell his father and mother what he had done. So he went down, and talked to the woman, and she suited Samson. When he returned after a while to marry her, he turned aside to look at the remains of the lion, and there was a swarm of bees in the carcass of the lion, and honey! So he scraped it out into his hands, and ate it as he went along. When he returned to his father and mother, he gave them some to eat, but he did not tell them that it was out of the carcass of the lion that he had scraped the honey.

When his father went down to the woman, Samson made a feast there; for so bridegrooms were accustomed to do. As soon as they saw him, they selected thirty companions to accompany him. To them Samson said,

"Let me propound you a riddle; if you can but solve it for me in the seven days of the feast, and find it out, I will give you thirty linen robes and thirty festal garments; but if you are unable to tell me the solution, then you must give me thirty linen robes and thirty festal garments."

"Propound your riddle," they said to him, "let us hear it!"

So he said to them,

> "Out of the eater came something to eat,
> And out of the strong came something sweet."

When they could not solve the riddle after three days, they said to Samson's wife on the fourth day,

"Coax your husband to solve the riddle for us, lest we burn up you and your father's house. Was it to impoverish us that you invited us here?"

So Samson's wife wept on his shoulder, and said,

"You simply hate me, and do not love me at all. You have propounded a riddle to my countrymen without telling me the solution."

He said to her,

"Why, I haven't told my father or mother; so should I tell you?"

But she wept on his shoulder through the seven days that they kept the feast, until finally on the seventh day he told her, since she pressed him so hard. Then she told the riddle to her countrymen; and on the seventh day, as he was about to enter the bridal chamber, the men of the city said to him,

> "What is sweeter than honey,
> And what is stronger than a lion?"

He said to them,

> "If you had not ploughed with this heifer of mine,
> You would not have found out this riddle of mine."

Then the spirit of the Lord came rushing upon him, so that he went down to Askelon, and killing thirty of them, he despoiled them, and gave the festal garments to those who had solved the riddle. Then, blazing with anger, he went up to his father's house, and Samson's wife went to his rival, who had been a rival to him.

After a while, however, in the time of wheat harvest, Samson paid a visit to his wife with a kid.

"I am going into the bridal chamber to my wife," he said.

But her father would not let him go in.

"I thought of course that you must simply hate her," her father said, "so I gave her to your rival. Is her younger sister not better than she? Take her instead."

Then Samson said of them,

"This time I am going to get even with the Philistines; for I am going to do them harm."

So Samson went and caught three hundred foxes; he then procured torches, and turning tail to tail, he put a torch between each pair of tails. Then, setting the torches on fire, he turned the foxes loose in the standing grain of the Philistines, and burnt up both the shocks and the standing grain, and also the vineyards and olive groves.

"Who has done this?" said the Philistines.

"Samson, the son-in-law of the Timnite," it was said; "because his wife was taken away and given to his rival."

So the Philistines went up, and burned up her and her father's house.

Then Samson said to them,

"You can never do such a thing as this without my taking revenge on you; but after this I will quit."

So he smote them hip and thigh with great slaughter; then he went down, and lived in a cleft of the crag Etam.

Then the Philistines came up, and encamped in Judah, and made a raid on Lehi.

"Why have you come up against us?" said the Judeans.

"We have come up to take Samson prisoner," they said; "that we may do to him as he did to us."

So three thousand of the Judeans went down to the cleft of the crag Etam, and said to Samson,

"Do you not know that the Philistines hold sway over us? What ever have you done to us?"

"As they did to me," he replied, "so have I done to them."

"We have come down to take you prisoner," they said to him, "to turn you over to the Philistines."

"Swear to me that you will not fall upon me yourselves," Samson said to them.

"No," they responded, "we will but take you prisoner, and turn you over to them, but we will not kill you."

So they bound him with two new ropes, and brought him up from the crag. As he reached Lehi, the Philistines came shouting to meet him. Then the spirit of the Lord came rushing upon him, so that the ropes on his arms became like flax that has caught on fire, and his bonds melted off his hands;

and finding a fresh jawbone of an ass, he put out his hand, and seizing it, felled a thousand men with it. Then Samson said,

"With the red ass's jawbone I have dyed them red;
With the red ass's jawbone I have felled a thousand men."

As he finished speaking, he threw the jawbone away; hence that place came to be called Ramath-lehi [the hill of the jawbone]. Then he became very thirsty; so he called to the Lord, saying,

"Thou hast vouchsafed this great victory by thy servant, and am I now to die of thirst, and fall by the hands of the uncircumcised?"

Then God split open the mortar that is at Lehi, and water gushed out of it; and when he drank, his spirits rose, and he revived. That is how its name came to be called En-hakkore [the spring of the caller], which is at Lehi to this day. So he governed Israel in the time of the Philistines for twenty years.

Samson went to Gaza, and seeing a harlot there, had intercourse with her. When the Gazaites were told, "Samson has come here," they came round, and lay in wait for him all night at the gate of the city. They kept quiet all night, saying, "As soon as morning dawns, we will kill him." Samson lay until midnight; but at midnight he rose, and taking hold of the doors of the city gate and the two gateposts, he pulled them up, together with the bar, and putting them on his shoulder, he carried them to the top of the hill that faces Hebron.

Afterwards he fell in love with a woman in the valley of Sorek, whose name was Delilah. Then the Philistine tyrants came to her, and said to her,

"Coax him, and find out why his strength is so great, and how we can overpower him and bind him helpless, and we will each give you eleven hundred shekels of silver."

So Delilah said to Samson,

"Do tell me why your strength is so great, and how you can be bound helpless?"

Samson said to her,

"If I were to be bound with seven fresh bowstrings that have not been dried I should become weak, and be like any other man." Then the Philistine tyrants brought her seven fresh bowstrings that had not been dried, and she bound him with them. Then, having men lie in wait in the inner room, she said to him,

"The Philistines are on you, Samson!"

But he snapped the bowstrings, as a strand of tow is snapped when it comes near fire. So the source of his strength was not discovered.

Then Delilah said to Samson,

"There, you have trifled with me, and told me lies! Do tell me now how you can be bound."

So he said to her,

"If I were but bound with new ropes that have not been used, I should become weak, and be like any other man."

So Delilah took new ropes, and bound him with them. Then she said to him,

"The Philistines are on you, Samson!"

(Meanwhile men were lying in wait in the inner room.)

But he snapped them off his arms like thread.

Then Delilah said to Samson,

"Up to now you have trifled with me, and told me lies. Tell me how you can be bound."

So he said to her,

"If you were to weave the seven locks of my head into the web, and beat them in with the pin, I should become weak, and be like any other man."

So, when he was asleep, Delilah took the seven locks of his head and wove them into the web, and beat them in with the pin. Then she said to him,

"The Philistines are on you, Samson!"

But he awoke from his sleep, and pulled up both the loom and the web.

Then she said to him,

"How can you say, 'I love you,' when you do not confide in me? Three times already you have trifled with me, and have not told me why your strength is so great."

At last, after she had pressed him with her words continually, and urged him, he got tired to death of it, and told her his whole secret.

"A razor has never been used on my head," he said to her; "for I have been a Nazirite to God from conception. If I were to be shaved, my strength would leave me; I should become weak, and be like any other man."

When Delilah saw that he had told her his whole secret, she sent for the Philistine tyrants, saying,

"Come up this once; for he has told me his whole secret."

So the Philistine tyrants came to her, and brought the money in their hands. Then she put him to sleep on her knees, and summoning a man, she had him shave off the seven locks of his head, so that he became quite helpless, and his strength left him. Then she said,

"The Philistines are on you, Samson!"

He awoke from his sleep, and thought, "I shall get off as I have done over and over again, and shake myself free"—not knowing that the Lord had left him. Then the Philistines seized him, and gouged out his eyes, and bringing him down to Gaza, they bound him with bronze shackles, and he spent his time grinding in the prison. But the hair of his head began to grow again as soon as it had been shaved off.

Now the Philistine tyrants gathered to offer a great sacrifice to their god Dagon, and for merry-making, saying, "Our god has delivered our enemy Samson into our power!"

When the people saw him, they praised their god; "For," said they, "our god has delivered our enemy into our hands, the devastator of our lands, and him who slew us in bands."

When they were in high spirits, they said,

"Summon Samson, that he may make sport for us!"

So Samson was summoned from the prison, and made sport before them. When they had stationed him between the pillars, Samson said to the attendant who was holding his hand,

"Put me so that I can feel the pillars on which the building is supported, that I may lean against them."

Now the building was full of men and women, and all the Philistine tyrants were there; and on the roof there were about three thousand men and women, looking on while Samson made sport. Then Samson cried to the Lord, saying,

"O Lord God, pray remember me, and give me strength just this one time, O God, to wreak vengeance but once upon the Philistines for my two eyes!"

Then Samson grasped the two middle pillars on which the building was supported, one with his right hand and the other with his left, and braced himself against them.

"Let me die with the Philistines!" said Samson.

Then he pulled with all his might, so that the building fell in upon the tyrants and all the people that were in it. So those that he killed at his death were more than those that he had killed during his life.

Then his kinsmen and all his father's household came down, and took him up; and bringing him away, they buried him between Zorah and Eshtaol, in the tomb of his father Manoah. He had governed Israel for twenty years.

RUTH AND BOAZ [1]

IN the time when the judges were in power a famine occurred in the land; so a certain man from Bethlehem in Judah emigrated to the country of Moab, along with his wife and two sons. The man's name was Elimelech, his wife's Naomi, and the names of his two sons Mahlon and Chilion— Ephrathites from Bethlehem in Judah. So they came to the country of Moab, and remained there. Then Elimelech, the husband of Naomi, died; and she was left a widow, with her two sons. These married Moabite women, the name of one being Orpah, and the name of the other Ruth. They lived there for about ten years, and then both Mahlon and Chilion died. Then, being bereft of her two children as well as of her husband, the woman, with her daughters-in-law, pre-

[1] The book of *Ruth*. Translated from the Hebrew by Theophile J. Meek.

pared to return from the country of Moab; for she had heard in the country of Moab that the Lord had taken note of his people by giving them food. So she left the place where she was, accompanied by her two daughters-in-law, and they set out on the road to return to the land of Judah. But Naomi said to her two daughters-in-law,

"Go, return each of you to her mother's house. May the Lord deal as kindly with you as you have dealt with the dead and with me! May the Lord enable you to find a home, each of you, in the house of her husband!"

Then she kissed them good-bye; but they lifted up their voices in weeping, and said to her,

"No, we will go back with you to your people."

But Naomi said,

"Turn back, my daughters. Why should you go with me? Have I any more sons in my womb to become husbands for you? Turn back, my daughters; go your way; for I am too old to get married. If I should say that I have hopes both of getting married tonight and of bearing sons, would you wait for them until they were grown up? Would you forego marriage for them? No, my daughters; but I am very sorry for your sakes that the hand of the Lord has been raised against me."

Then they lifted up their voices again in weeping, and Orpah kissed her mother-in-law good-bye, but Ruth clung to her.

"See," she said, "your sister-in-law has turned back to her own people and her own gods; turn back after your sister-in-law."

But Ruth said,

"Do not press me to leave you, to turn back from following you; for wherever you go, I will go; and wherever you lodge, I will lodge; your people shall be my people, and your god my god; wherever you die, I will die, and there will I be buried. May the Lord requite me and worse, if even death separate me from you."

When she saw that she was determined to go with her, she ceased arguing with her. So the two of them went on until they came to Bethlehem. Upon their arrival in Bethlehem the whole city became agitated over them, and the women said,

"Is this Naomi?"

But she said to them,

"Do not call me Naomi [pleasant]; call me Mara [bitter]; for the Almighty has dealt very bitterly with me. I went away full, but the Lord has brought me back destitute. Why should you call me Naomi, seeing that the Lord has afflicted me, and the Almighty has brought evil upon me?"

So Naomi returned from the country of Moab, accompanied by her daughter-in-law, Ruth, the Moabitess. They reached Bethlehem at the beginning of the barley harvest.

Now Naomi had a kinsman of her husband, a man of great wealth, belonging to the family of Elimelech, whose name was Boaz.

One day Ruth, the Moabitess, said to Naomi,

"Let me go to the fields and glean among the ears of grain after him with whom I may find favor."

"Go, my daughter," she said to her.

So off she went, and came and gleaned in the fields after the harvesters; and it was her fortune to come upon the part of the field belonging to Boaz, who belonged to the family of Elimelech. Just then Boaz himself came from Bethlehem.

"The Lord be with you!" he said to the harvesters.

"The Lord bless you!" they replied.

"Whose girl is this?" said Boaz to his overseer in charge of harvesters.

"It is a Moabite girl who came back with Naomi from the country of Moab," the overseer in charge of the harvesters answered. "She said, 'Let me glean, if you please, and gather among the sheaves after harvesters.' So she came, and has remained since morning until now, without resting even a little."

Then Boaz said to Ruth,

"Now listen, my girl. Do not go to glean in another field, nor leave this one, but stay here close by my women. Note the field that they are reaping, and follow them. Have I not charged the servants not to molest you? And when you were thirsty, go to the water jars, and drink some of what the servants draw."

Then she fell on her face, bowing to the ground, and said to him,

"Why have I found such favor with you that you should take notice of me, when I am a foreigner?"

Boaz in reply said to her,

"I have been fully informed of all that you have done for your mother-in-law since the death of your husband, and of how you left your father and mother, and the land of your birth, and came to a people that you did not know before. May the Lord reward your conduct, and may you receive full recompense from the Lord, the God of Israel, under whose wings you have come for shelter!"

"I thank you, sir," she said, "for you have cheered me, and have spoken comfortingly to your maidservant, even though I do not belong to your maidservants."

At mealtime Boaz said to her,

"Come here, and eat some of the bread, and dip your piece in the sour wine."

So she seated herself beside the harvesters, and he handed her roasted grain. She ate until she was satisfied, and had some left over. When she got up to glean, Boaz gave orders to his servants,

"Let her glean right among the sheaves, and do not be rude to her. Indeed pull out some bunches for her, and leave them for her to glean, and do not hinder her."

So she gleaned in the field until evening; then she beat out what she had gleaned, and it amounted to about an ephah of barley. She took it up, and coming into the city, showed her mother-in-law what she had gleaned. Then she brought out and gave her what she had left over after being satisfied.

"Where did you glean today?" her mother-in-law said to her.

So she told her mother-in-law with whom she had worked.

"Boaz is the name of the man with whom I worked today," she said. Then Naomi said to her daughter-in-law,

"May he be blessed by the Lord, whose goodness has failed neither the living nor the dead!"

"The man is a relation of ours," Naomi said to her; "he is one of our close relatives."

"Furthermore," said Ruth, the Moabitess, "he said to me, 'You must stay close by my servants until they have finished all my harvest.' "

"It is best, my daughter," Naomi said to her daughter-in-law, Ruth, "that you should go out with his women, so as not to be molested in another field."

So she stayed close by the women working for Boaz, gleaning until the end of both the barley and wheat harvests; then she returned to her mother-in-law.

Then her mother-in-law Naomi said to her,

"Should I not be seeking a home for you, my daughter, where you may be comfortable? Now then, what about our relative Boaz, with whose women you have been? See, he is going to winnow barley at the threshing-floor to-night. Wash and anoint yourself therefore, put on your best clothes, and go down to the threshing-floor; but do not let your presence be known to the man until he has finished eating and drinking. See to it, however, when he lies down, that you note the place where he lies; then go in, uncover his feet, and lie down yourself; he will let you know what to do."

"I will do just as you say," she responded.

So she went down to the threshing-floor, and did just as her mother-in-law had instructed her. Boaz, having eaten and drunk, had a feeling of contentment and went to lie down at the end of the straw stack. Then she came in stealthily, uncovered his feet, and lay down. At midnight the man started up, and turning over, discovered a woman lying at his feet!

"Who are you?" he said.

"I am Ruth, your maidservant," she said. "Take your maidservant in marriage; for you are a close relative."

"May the Lord bless you, my girl!" he said. "This last kindness of yours is lovelier than the first, in that you have not run after the young men, either poor or rich. And now, my girl, have no fear; I will do for you all you ask; for all the counselors of my people know that you are a woman of worth. Now then, it is indeed true that I am a close relative, but there is another relative closer than I. Stay here tonight, and then, in the morning, if he will do the duty of close relative for you, good; let him do so; but if he does not wish to do the duty of close relative for you, then, as the Lord lives, I will do so for you. Lie down until morning."

So she lay at his feet until morning, but got up before one could recognize another; for he said, "It must not be known that the woman came to the threshing-floor."

"Bring the mantle which you have on," he said, "and hold it out."

So she held it out, and he poured out six omers of barley, and put it on her shoulder; then she went back to the city, and came to her mother-in-law's.

"How did you get along, my daughter?" she said.

Then she told her all that the man had done for her.

"These six omers of barley he gave to me," she said; "'For,' said he, 'you must not go back empty-handed to your mother-in-law.'"

"Wait, my daughter," she said, "until you learn how the matter turns out; for the man will not rest unless he settles the matter today."

Meanwhile Boaz went up to the city gate, and sat down there just as the close relative was passing, of whom Boaz had spoken.

"Come over and sit down here somewhere," he said.

So he came over and sat down. Then Boaz got ten of the elders of the city, and said,

"Sit down here."

When they had seated themselves, he said to the close relative,

"Naomi, who has come back from the country of Moab, is selling the piece of land which belonged to our relative, Elimelech; so I thought that I would tell you about it, suggesting that you buy it in the presence of those who are sitting here, and in the presence of the elders of my people. If you will redeem it, do so; but if you will not redeem it, then tell me, so that I may know; for there is no one but you to redeem it, and I come after you."

"I will redeem it," he said.

Then Boaz said,

"At the time that you buy the field from Naomi, you must also buy Ruth, the Moabitess, the widow of the deceased, in order to restore the name of the deceased to his estate."

Then the close relative said,

"I cannot redeem it for myself, lest I ruin my own estate. Use my right of redemption for yourself; for I cannot do so."

Now this was the ancient custom in Israel: to validate any transaction in the matter of the right of redemption and its conveyance, the one pulled off his sandal, and gave it to the other; this was the manner of attesting in Israel. Accordingly, when the close relative said to Boaz, "Buy it for yourself," he drew off his sandal. Then Boaz said to the elders and all the people,

"You are witnesses today that I am buying from Naomi all that belonged to Elimelech and all that belonged to Chilion and Mahlon. Also Ruth, the Moabitess, the widow of Mahlon, I am buying to be my wife, in order to restore the name of the dead to his estate, so that the name of the dead may not be cut off from among his relatives nor from the counselors of his home; you are witnesses today."

Whereupon all the people at the gate and the elders said,

"We are witnesses. May the Lord make the woman who is comnig into your home like Rachel and Leah, both of whom built up the house of Israel; may you achieve wealth in Ephrath, and gain fame in Bethlehem; and from the offspring that the Lord gives you by this young woman, may you have a house like the house of Perez, whom Tamar bore to Judah!"

So Boaz took Ruth, and she became his wife; he had intercourse with her, and the Lord made her conceive, and she bore a son. Then the women said to Naomi,

"Blessed be the Lord, who has not left you this day without a close relative! May the boy's name become famous in Israel! He shall renew your youth, and be the stay of your old age; for your daughter-in-law, who loves you, has borne him, who herself is more to you than seven sons."

Then Naomi took the child, and laid him in her bosom, and became his nurse; and the women in the neighborhood spread the report of him, "A son has been born to Naomi!" So they called his name Obed. He was the father of Jesse, the father of David.

KING DAVID [1]

Now at the return of spring, at the time when kings go forth, David sent Joab and his servants with him, even all Israel, and they ravaged the Ammonites, and besieged Rabbah. But David remained in Jerusalem. Now one day at sunset, David got up from his couch, and walked to and fro upon the roof of the king's house; and from the roof he saw a woman bathing. And the woman was very beautiful. And David sent and sought for the woman, and said,

"Is not this Bathsheba, the daughter of Eliam, the wife of Uriah the Hittite?"

So David sent messengers and took her; and she came to him, and he lay with her at the time she was cleansing herself from her impurity; then she returned to her house. And the woman conceived; and she sent and informed David, and she said,

[1] Selected from the second book of *Samuel*, chapters 11:1-12:25; 13:1-18:15; 21:1-14; the first book of *Kings*, chapters 1:1-2:11. Translated from the Hebrew by Leroy Waterman.

"I am with child."

Then David sent to Joab,

"Send me Uriah the Hittite."

And Joab sent Uriah the Hittite to David. And when Uriah came to him, David asked concerning the welfare of Joab and the condition of the people and the course of the war. Then David said to Uriah,

"Go down to your house and wash your feet."

So Uriah went out of the king's house, and there followed him a present from the king. But Uriah slept at the entrance of the king's house, along with all the servants of his lord, and did not go down to his house. Now when they told David, Uriah did not go down to his house, David said to Uriah,

"Have you not come from a journey? Why have you not gone down to your house?"

Then Uriah said to David,

"The ark and Israel and Judah dwell in booths, and my master Joab and the servants of my lord are camping in the open field; and should I enter my house to eat and drink and to lie with my wife? As the LORD lives and as you yourself live, I could not do this thing."

So David said to Uriah,

"Remain here today also, and tomorrow I will send you away."

Then Uriah remained in Jerusalem that day. But on the morrow David summoned him and he ate and drank before him, so that he made him drunk; and in the evening he went out to lie on his bed with the servants of his lord, but he did not go down to his house.

So in the morning, David wrote a letter to Joab, and sent it by the hand of Uriah. And he wrote in the letter, saying,

"Put Uriah in the forefront of the hottest fighting, then draw back from him, that he may be stricken and die."

And so as Joab pressed the siege against the city, he put Uriah at a point where he knew the best opposing troops were. And when the men of the city sallied out and fought with Joab, some of the men of David's forces fell, and Uriah the Hittite was also among the slain. Then Joab sent and reported to David the full details of the fighting. And he gave instructions to the messenger, saying,

"When you have finished telling all the details of the fighting to the king, then if the king's anger is aroused, and he say to you, 'Why did you go so near the city to fight? Did you not know that they would shoot from the wall? Who killed Abimelech, the son of Jerubbaal? Did not a woman drop an upper millstone upon him from the wall, so that he died in Thebez? Why did you go near the wall?' Then you shall say, 'Your servant Uriah the Hittite is dead also.'"

So the messenger of Joab set out and came and when he told David all that with which Joab had charged him, even all the details of the fighting, then David was enraged at Joab, and he said to the messenger,

"Why did you go near the city to fight? Did you not realize that you would be attacked from the wall? Who killed Abimelech, the son of Jerubbaal? Did not a woman drop an upper millstone upon him from the wall, so that he died in Thebez? Why did you go near the wall?"

Then the messenger said to David,

"Because the men gained an advantage over us and came out to fight us in the open field, but we fought them back to the very entrance of the gate, and then the archers shot from the wall at your servants; and some of the king's servants are dead, and your servant Uriah the Hittite is dead also."

Thereupon David said to the messenger,

"Thus shall you say to Joab, 'Let not this affair depress you, for the sword devours one as well as another; strengthen your attack upon the city and overthrow it,' and do you encourage him."

And when the wife of Uriah heard that Uriah her husband was dead, she made lamentation for her husband. But when the mourning was over, David sent and removed her to his house, and she became his wife and bore him a son. But the thing that David had done displeased the LORD.

Accordingly the LORD sent the prophet Nathan to David. And he came to him, and said to him,

"There were two men in a certain city, the one rich, and the other poor. The rich man owned very many flocks and herds. But the poor man had nothing but a single little ewe lamb, which he had bought. And he reared it and it grew up with him and with his children. It would eat from his food and drink from his cup, and it lay in his bosom, and it was like a daughter to him. Now there came a traveller to the rich man, and he refused to take from his own flock or his own herd to make ready for the wayfarer who had come to him, but he took the poor man's lamb and prepared it for the man who had come to him."

Then David's anger became furious against the man, and he said to Nathan,

"As the LORD lives, the man that does this is worthy of death, and he shall restore the lamb sevenfold, because he did this and because he showed no pity."

And Nathan said to David,

"You are the man! Thus the LORD GOD of Israel has said, 'I anointed you king over Israel and I delivered you out of the hand of Saul, and I gave you your master's house and your master's wives into your bosom, I also gave you the house of Israel and of Judah, and if that were too little, I would add in this or that way. Why have you despised the LORD by doing that which is evil in my sight? You have slain Uriah the Hittite with the sword, and you have taken his wife to be your wife, having slain him with the sword of the

Ammonites. Now therefore the sword shall never depart from your house, because you have despised me and have taken the wife of Uriah the Hittite to be your wife.' Thus the LORD has spoken, 'Behold, I will raise up evil against you out of your own house, and I will take your wives from before your eyes and give them to your neighbor, and he shall lie with your wives in the sight of this sun, for you did it secretly; but I will do this thing before all Israel in the open light of day.'"

Then David said to Nathan,

"I have sinned against the LORD."

And Nathan said to David,

"The LORD has also taken away your sin; you shall not die. Nevertheless, because you have openly spurned the LORD by this deed, the child also that is born to you shall surely die."

And Nathan went to his house.

And the LORD struck the child that the wife of Uriah bore to David, so that it was taken ill. And David besought the LORD in behalf of the child, and he kept a fast and went in and lay in sackcloth upon the earth. And the older men of his household arose and stood beside him in order to raise him up from the earth, but he would not, neither would he eat food with them.

Now on the seventh day the child died. And the servants of David feared to tell him that the child was dead, for they said,

"Behold while the child was yet alive, we spoke to him, and he heeded not our voice; how can we say to him, the child is dead? How desperate it will make him!"

Now when David saw that his servants were whispering to one another, David perceived that the child was dead, and David said to his servants,

"Is the child dead?"

And they said,

"He is dead."

Then David arose from the earth, and bathed and anointed himself, and changed his garments; and he went into the house of the LORD and worshipped. Then he went to his own house; and he asked for food and they set it before him and he ate. Then his servants said to him,

"What is the meaning of this thing that you have done? You have fasted and wept for the child, while it was alive, but when the child died, you have arisen and eaten food!"

And he said,

"While the child was yet alive, I fasted and wept; for I said, 'Who knows whether the LORD will show himself merciful to me and let the child live?' But now he is dead; why should I fast? Can I bring him back again? I expect to go to him, but he will never come back to me."

Then David comforted Bathsheba his wife, and went in to her and lay with her and she conceived and bore a son, and he called his name Solomon.

And the LORD loved him. And he sent a message through Nathan the prophet; and he called his name Jedidiah, according to the command of the LORD.

Now Absalom, a son of David, had a beautiful sister, whose name was Tamar; and it happened after this that Amnon, a son of David, loved her. And Amnon was so distressed that he made himself sick because of his sister Tamar—for she was a virgin—and it seemed impossible to Amnon to get any approach to her.

But Amnon had a friend whose name was Jonadab, the son of Shimeah, David's brother, and Jonadab was a very shrewd man. And he said to him,

"Why, O prince, are you so depressed morning after morning? Will you not tell me?"

And Amnon said to him,

"I love Tamar, my brother Absalom's sister."

And Jonadab said to him,

"Lie down on your bed, and feign yourself ill. Then when your father comes to see you, say to him, 'Let now my sister Tamar come and serve me some food, and let her prepare the food in my sight, that I may see it and eat from her hand.' "

So Amnon lay down and feigned himself ill. And when the king came to see him, Amnon said to the king,

"Let now my sister Tamar come and make a couple of cakes in my sight, that I may eat from her hand."

So David sent to the house for Tamar, saying,

"Go now to your brother Amnon's house, and prepare food for him."

Then Tamar went to her brother Amnon's house while he was there in bed. And she took dough and kneaded it and made cakes before him, and fried the cakes. And she took the pan and poured them out before him, but he refused to eat. And Amnon said,

"Put out everybody from attending me."

So they all withdrew from him. Then Amnon said to Tamar,

"Bring the food into the chamber, that I may eat from your hand."

So Tamar took the cakes she had made, and brought them into the chamber to Amnon her brother. And when she had brought them near to him to eat, he took hold of her and said to her,

"Come, lie with me, my sister."

And she said to him,

"No, my brother, do not humiliate me, for it is not so done in Israel, do not this disgraceful folly. And as for me, whither could I carry my shame? and as for you, you would become as one of the impious profligates in Israel. Now therefore, I pray you, speak to the king, for he will not withhold me from marrying you."

But he would not listen to her voice, but being stronger than she, he over-powered her and lay with her.

Then Amnon hated her with unutterable hatred, for the hatred with which he hated her was greater than the love with which he had loved her. And Amnon said to her,

"Arise, be gone!"

But she said to him,

"No, my brother; for greater would be this wrong, to send me away, than the first that you have done to me."

Yet he would not listen to her, but called his servant, who ministered to him, and said,

"Put out now this female from my presence, and bolt the door after her."

And she wore a long-sleeved tunic reaching to the ankles, for thus the virgin princesses were formerly wont to clad. So his servant put her out and bolted the door after her. And Tamar put ashes on her head, and rent the long-sleeved tunic which she wore; and putting her hand on her head, she departed, crying aloud as she went along.

Accordingly Absalom her own brother said to her,

"Has Amnon your brother been with you? But now, my sister, be quiet, he is your brother; do not take this matter to heart."

So Tamar remained desolate in the house of Absalom her brother. And when King David heard all these things, he was very angry, but he did not reprove Amnon his son, for he loved him, because he was his first-born. And Absalom spoke to Amnon neither good nor bad; for Absalom hated Amnon, because he had violated his sister Tamar.

Now it happened just two years later, that Absalom had sheep-shearers in Baal-hazor near Ephraim, and Absalom invited all the king's sons. And Absalom went to the king and said,

"See now, your servant has sheep-shearers, let the king and his servants, I pray you, go with your servant."

But the king said to Absalom,

"No, my son, let us not all go now, lest we be a burden to you."

Still he pressed him, however he would not go but he added his blessing. Then Absalom said,

"If not, then I pray you, let my brother Amnon go with us."

And the king said to him,

"Why should he go with you?"

But when Absalom pressed him, he let Amnon and all the king's sons go with him. And Absalom made a feast like a royal feast. Then Absalom commanded his servants, saying,

"See now, when Amnon's heart is merry with wine, and when I say to you, 'Strike down Amnon,' then kill him. Fear not; have I not given you your orders? Be courageous and show yourselves valiant."

And the retainers of Absalom did to Amnon as Absalom commanded. Then all the king's sons arose and each mounted his mule and fled.

And while they were on the way, the report came to David that Absalom had murdered all the king's sons so that there was not one of them left. Then the king arose and tore his garments and lay on the earth, and all his servants who were standing by him tore their garments. But Jonadab, the son of Shimeah, David's brother, answered and said,

"Let not my lord suppose that they have killed all the young men, the king's sons, for Amnon alone is dead, since by the mouth of Absalom this has been determined ever since he violated his sister Tamar. Now therefore let not my lord the king take the report so seriously to heart as to imagine that all the king's sons are dead; but Amnon alone is dead."

And when the youth who kept the watch lifted up his eyes and looked, behold many people were coming in the Horonaim road. And the watchman came and told the king, saying,

"I have seen men coming down from the Horonaim road by the side of the mountain."

And Jonadab said to the king,

"There, the king's sons have come; according to the word of your servant, so it has come about."

And as soon as he had finished speaking, behold, the king's sons arrived, and they lifted up their voice and wept; and the king also and all his servants wept very bitterly.

But Absalom fled and went to Talmai, son of Ammihud, king of Geshur, and David kept on mourning for his son day after day. So Absalom fled and went to Geshur, and he was there three years. And the spirit of King David pined to go out to Absalom, for he was comforted for Amnon, seeing he was dead.

Now when Joab, the son of Zeruiah, perceived that the king's heart was inclined toward Absalom, Joab sent to Tekoa and brought from there a wise woman and said to her,

"Pretend now to be a mourner and put on mourning garments, I pray you, and do not anoint yourself with oil, but become as a woman who has been mourning many days for the dead. And go to the king and speak thus to him."

So Joab put the words into her mouth.

Accordingly when the woman of Tekoa came to the king, she fell on her face to the earth and did obeisance, and said,

"Help, O king!"

And the king said to her,

"What is your trouble?"

And she said,

"Of truth I am a widow, and my husband is dead. And your maidservant had two sons, and the two of them struggled together in the field, and there being no one to part them, the one struck the other and killed him. And now the whole clan has risen up against your maidservant and they say, 'Deliver up the slayer of his brother, that we may kill him for the life of his brother whom he slew,' that they may destroy the heir also. Thus they will quench my remaining coal so as to leave to my husband neither name nor remnant on the face of the ground."

Then the king said to the woman,

"Go to your house and I will give orders concerning you."

And the woman of Tekoa said to the king,

"Upon me, my lord, O king, be the guilt and on my father's house; and the king and his throne be innocent."

And the king said,

"Whoever speaks to you bring him to me and he shall not touch you again."

And she said,

"I pray you, let the king remember the Lord your God, not to allow the avenger of blood to destroy and not to let them murder my son."

And he said,

"As the Lord lives, not one hair of your son shall fall to the earth."

Then the woman said,

"I pray you, let your maidservant speak a word to my lord the king."

And he said,

"Speak."

And the woman said,

"Why then have you devised such a thing against the people of God? For in speaking this word the king is as one that is guilty, in that the king does not bring back his banished one.

"For we must indeed die and are as water poured upon the earth, that cannot be gathered up again; nor can God take it up. Therefore a person should devise plans not to keep in banishment the one who is banished. And now the reason why I have come to speak this word to the king my lord is because the people frightened me, and your maidservant said, 'I will now speak to the king; it may be that the king will perform the request of his handmaid.' For the king will hearken, to deliver his handmaid from the hand of the man who seeks to destroy me and my son from the heritage of the Lord. Then your maidservant said, 'Let the word of my lord the king be a comfort,' for as the Messenger of God, so is my lord the king to hear good and evil. And the Lord your God be with you."

Then the king answered and said to the woman,

"Do not, I pray you, conceal from me anything that I ask of you."

And the woman said,

"Let now my lord the king speak."

And the king said,

"Is the hand of Joab with you in all this?"

And the woman answered and said,

"As sure as you are alive, my lord the king, one cannot turn to the right hand or to the left hand from all that my lord the king has spoken; for your servant Joab, he it was that bade me, and he put all these words in the mouth of your maidservant; in order to change the face of the matter your servant Joab did this thing. But my lord is wise, according to the wisdom of the Messenger of God, so that he knows all things that are in the earth."

Therefore the king said to Joab,

"See now, you have accomplished this thing; go therefore, bring the young man Absalom back."

Then Joab fell on his face to the earth and did obeisance and blessed the king. And Joab said,

"Today your servant knows that I have found favor in your sight, my lord, O king, in that the king has performed the request of his servant."

So Joab arose and went to Geshur, and brought Absalom back to Jerusalem. And the king said,

"Let him live apart in his own house, but he is not to see my face."

So Absalom lived apart in his own house, but he did not see the king's face.

Now in all Israel there was no man so much to be praised for his beauty as Absalom; from the sole of his foot to the crown of his head there was no blemish in him. And when he shaved his head—now at the end of every year he used to cut his hair, because it was heavy on him, therefore he cut it—he used to weigh his hair, two hundred shekels by the royal standard of weight. And there were born to Absalom three sons and one daughter, whose name was Tamar—she was a beautiful woman.

Absalom dwelt two full years in Jerusalem, without seeing the king's face. Then Absalom sent for Joab to send him to the king; but he would not come to him. So he sent again a second time, but he refused to come. Therefore he said to his servants,

"See, Joab's field borders mine, where he has barley; go and set it on fire."

And Joab's servants came to him with torn garments, and said,

"The servants of Absalom have set the field on fire."

Then Joab arose, and went to Absalom at his house and said to him,

"Why have your servants set my field on fire?"

And Absalom said to Joab,

"Behold, I sent to you saying, 'Come here that I may send you to the king, to say, "Why have I come from Geshur? It were better that I were still there." Now therefore let me see the king's face, and if there is guilt in me, let him kill me.'"

And when Joab went to the king and told him, he summoned Absalom.

And he went to the king and did obeisance and fell upon his face to the earth before the king. Then the king kissed Absalom.

Now afterwards Absalom prepared him a chariot and horses and fifty men to run before him. And Absalom used to rise early and stand beside the way of the gate, and whenever any man had a suit to come to the king for judgment, Absalom would take occasion to call to him and say,

"Of what city are you?"

And when he said,

"Your servant is of some one of the tribes of Israel,"

Absalom would say to him,

"It is evident your claims are valid and legitimate; but there is no one deputed by the king to hear you."

Absalom said moreover,

"O that someone would make me a judge in the land, that any man who had a suit or cause might come to me, that I might give him justice!"

And whenever a man came near to do obeisance to him, he would put out his hand and take hold of him and kiss him. And after this manner Absalom dealt with all the Israelites who came to the king for judgment. So Absalom alienated the hearts of the men of Israel.

But at the end of four years, Absalom said to the king,

"Let me go, I pray you, and pay my vow, which I vowed to the LORD, in Hebron. For your servant vowed a vow, while I abode at Geshur in Syria, as follows, 'If the LORD will indeed bring me back to Jerusalem, then I will serve the LORD in Hebron.'"

And the king said to him,

"Go in peace."

So he arose and went to Hebron. But Absalom sent emissaries throughout all the tribes of Israel, saying,

"As soon as you hear the sound of the trumpet, then say, 'Absalom is king in Hebron.'"

And with Absalom went two hundred men from Jerusalem, who went in all innocence as invited guests, and were not aware of any plot.

And Absalom sent and called Ahithophel the Gilonite, David's counsellor, from his city Giloh, where he was offering sacrifices. And the conspiracy was strong, for the people with Absalom kept on increasing.

And when a messenger came to David, saying,

"The heart of the men of Israel has gone after Absalom,"

David said to all his servants who were with him at Jerusalem,

"Up and away; for otherwise there will be for us no escape from Absalom. Make haste to be off, lest he quickly overtake us and set evil in motion against us and put the city to the sword."

Then the king's servants said to the king,

"According to all that my lord the king decides, your servants are ready."

So the king went out and all his household after him. And the king left behind ten concubines to keep the palace. And the king and all his attendants who followed after him went forth and halted at the last house, while all the people marched past him; and all the Cherethites and all the Pelethites and all the men of Ittai the Gittite, six hundred men who had followed him from Gath, passed on before the king.

Then the king said to Ittai the Gittite,

"Why will you also go with us? Return and remain with the king; for you are a foreigner and an exile from your own place. You came but yesterday and shall I today cause you to wander with us, while I go whither I may? Return and lead back your fellow countrymen with you; and the LORD will show you kindness and faithfulness."

But Ittai answered the king and said,

"As the LORD lives and as my lord the king lives, wherever my lord the king shall be—whether for death or for life—there will your servant be."

And David said to Ittai,

"Go and pass on."

So Ittai the Gittite passed on with all his men and all the children that were with him.

Moreover all the countryside was in loud lamentation as all the people were passing by. While the king stood in the Kidron valley, all the people were passing on before him by way of the olive tree which is in the desert. And there too were both Zadok and Abiathar with him, bearing the ark of the covenant of God, and they halted the ark of God until all the people had entirely passed out of the city. Then the king said to Zadok and Abiathar,

"Carry back the ark of God into the city and let it remain in its place. If I shall find favor in the eyes of the LORD, he will bring me back, and show me both it and his abode. But if he say, 'I have no delight in you,' then here I am, let him do to me as seems good in his sight."

The king also said to Zadok and Abiathar the priests,

"Return to the city in peace and your two sons with you, Ahimaaz your son and Jonathan, the son of Abiathar. See, I am going to tarry at the fords of the desert, until word comes from you to inform me."

Therefore Zadok and Abiathar carried the ark of God back to Jerusalem, and they remained there.

But David went up the ascent of Olivet, weeping as he went, with his head covered and walking barefoot, and all the people who were with him covered each his head, and they went up, weeping as they ascended. And when it was told David, saying,

"Ahithophel is among the conspirators with Absalom,"

David said,

"O LORD, I pray, turn the counsel of Ahithophel to foolishness."

And when David came to the top where one worships God, there was

Hushai the Archite to meet him with his tunic torn and earth upon his head.
And David said to him,

"If you accompany me you will be a burden to me. But if you return to the
city, and say to Absalom, 'O king, I will be your servant; and as I have been
your father's servant in time past, so now I will be your servant,' thus you can
defeat for me the counsel of Ahithophel. And are there not there with you
Zadok and Abiathar the priests? Behold, there are with them their two sons,
Ahimaaz, Zadok's son, and Jonathan, Abiathar's son; and you shall send
to me by them everything that you shall hear."

So Hushai, David's friend, came to the city just as Absalom was entering
Jerusalem.

Now when David had passed a little beyond the summit, Ziba, the servant
of Meribaal, met him with a couple of asses saddled, laden with two hundred
loaves of bread, a hundred bunches of raisins, a hundred of summer fruits,
and a skin of wine. And the king said to Ziba,

"Why have you these?"

And Ziba said,

"The asses are for the king's household to ride on, and the bread and the
summer fruit for the young men to eat, and the wine, that those who become
faint in the desert may drink."

And the king said,

"And where is your master's son?"

And Ziba said to the king,

"He remains yonder at Jerusalem, for he has said, 'Today will the house
of Israel give back to me the kingdom of my father.'"

Then the king said to Ziba,

"See, all is now yours that belonged to Meribaal."

And Ziba said,

"I do obeisance. Let me continue to find favor in your sight, my lord,
O king!"

And when King David came to Bahurim, there was a man coming
out from there of the family of the house of Saul, whose name was Shimei,
the son of Gera, uttering a stream of curses as he came along. And he threw
stones at David and all the attendants of King David and at all the people
and all the famous warriors on his right hand and on his left. And thus he
said as he cursed,

"Begone, begone, man of blood and vile scoundrel! The LORD has brought
back upon you all the blood of the house of Saul, in whose stead you have
ruled; and the LORD has delivered the kingdom into the hand of Absalom your
son; and here you are undone; for you are a man of blood!"

Then Abishai, the son of Zeruiah, said to the king,

"Why should this dead dog curse my lord the king? Let me go over now
and take off his head."

But the king said,

"What have I in common with you, O sons of Zeruiah? If he curses when the LORD has said to him, 'Curse David!' then who shall say, 'Why have you done so?'"

And David said to Abishai and to all his attendants,

"See, my own son who came forth from my body seeks my life, how much more now a Benjaminite! Let him alone and let him curse, for the LORD has bidden him. Perchance the LORD will look on my affliction, and the LORD may requite good instead of his cursing today."

And David and his men kept in the road; but Shimei proceeding along the hillside opposite him and cursing as he went along, continued to throw stones and fling dust at him. And the king and all the people who were with him arrived weary at the Jordan, and he refreshed himself there.

Then Absalom and all the men of Israel came to Jerusalem, and Ahithophel with him. Now when Hushai the Archite, David's friend, came to Absalom, Hushai said to Absalom,

"Long live the king, long live the king!"

And Absalom said to Hushai,

"Is this your loyalty for your friend? Why did you not go with your friend?"

Then Hushai said to Absalom,

"No! for whom the LORD and this people and all the men of Israel have chosen, his will I be and with him will I remain. And secondly, whom should I serve? Should it not be his son? As I served your father, so will I serve you."

Absalom also said to Ahithophel,

"Give your counsel. What shall we do?"

And Ahithophel said to Absalom,

"Go in to your father's concubines, whom he has left to keep the house; and all Israel will hear that you are in bad odor with your father and the hands of all who are with you will be strengthened."

So they pitched a tent for Absalom upon the roof; and Absalom went in to the concubines of his father in sight of all Israel. And the counsel of Ahithophel which he gave in those days, was as if one consulted an oracle of God—so was all the counsel of Ahithophel regarded both by David and by Absalom.

Moreover Ahithophel said to Absalom,

"Let me, I pray you, choose out twelve thousand men, and let me arise and pursue after David tonight; thus I will come upon him when he is weary and exhausted and I will throw him into a panic and also all the people who are with him; and I will strike down the king alone. And I will bring back all the people to you as the bride returns to her husband. You seek only the life of one man, and all the people shall be at peace."

And the plan pleased Absalom, and all the elders of Israel.

Then Absalom said,

"Call now Hushai the Archite also, and let us hear likewise what he has to offer."

And when Hushai came to Absalom, Absalom said to him as follows,

"Thus Ahithophel has spoken; shall we carry out his plan? If not, speak out."

Then Hushai said to Absalom,

"This time the counsel that Ahithophel has given is not good."

And Hushai said,

"You know your father and his men, that they are tried warriors and thoroughly aroused, like a bear in the open robbed of her cubs. Furthermore your father is an expert campaigner and will not spend the night with the people. Even now he has hidden himself in one of the caves or in some other place. And in case he falls upon the people at the first, whoever hears the report will say, 'There has been a slaughter among the people who follow Absalom.' Then even the valiant man whose heart is like the heart of a lion, will utterly lose courage; for all Israel knows that your father is a skilled warrior, and those who are with him are valiant men. But I counsel that all Israel be surely gathered together to you, from Dan to Beersheba, as many as the sand that is by the sea, with you yourself marching in their midst. And we will come upon him in some place where he has been located, and we will light upon him as the dew falls upon the ground; and of him and of all the men who are with him there shall not be left even one. But if he withdraws into a city, then all Israel will bring ropes to that city and we will drag it into the valley, until not even a pebble can be found there."

And Absalom and all the men of Israel said,

"The counsel of Hushai the Archite is better than the counsel of Ahithophel."

For the LORD had ordained to frustrate the good counsel of Ahithophel, in order that the LORD might bring evil upon Absalom.

Then Hushai said to Zadok and Abiathar the priests,

"Thus and so did Ahithophel counsel Absalom and the elders of Israel; and then and so have I counselled. Now therefore send quickly and tell David, saying, 'Do not camp tonight at the fords of the desert, but cross over without fail, lest the king and all the people with him be swallowed up.'"

Now Jonathan and Ahimaaz were stationed at Enrogel; and a maidservant used to go and keep them informed, and they would go and tell King David, for they dared not be seen to enter the city. But a lad saw them and told Absalom. Then they both went away in haste and entered into the house of a man in Bahurim, who had a well in his courtyard into which they descended. And a woman took and spread a covering over the well, and strewed dried fruit upon it, so that nothing was known. And when the servants of Absalom came to the woman to the house and said,

"Where are Ahimaaz and Jonathan?"

The woman said to them,

"They are over the source of the watercourses."

And when they had sought and could find no trace, they returned to Jerusalem. Now as soon as they had gone away, the two came up out of the well, and went and told King David and said to David,

"Arise, cross quickly over the water for thus has Ahithophel counselled against you."

Then David and all the people who were with him arose and crossed the Jordan. By daybreak there was not one left behind who had not passed over the Jordan.

Now when Ahithophel saw that his counsel had not been carried out, he saddled his ass and arose, and went home to his own city. And after giving orders concerning his household, he strangled himself, and died and was buried in his father's grave.

Then David came to Mahanaim. And Absalom crossed the Jordan, together with all the men of Israel. And Absalom put Amasa in command of the army in place of Joab. Now Amasa was the son of an Ishmaelite by the name of Jether, who married Abigail the daughter of Jesse, the sister of Zeruiah, Joab's mother. And Israel and Absalom encamped in the land of Gilead. And when David arrived at Mahanaim, Shobi, the son of Nahash of the Ammonite Rabbah, and Machir, the son of Ammiel of Lodebar, and Barzillai, the Gileadite of Rogelim, brought couches and rugs and bowls, and earthen vessels, and wheat, barley, meal, parched grain, beans, lentils, honey, curds, sheep and calves for David, and for the people who were with him, to eat; for they thought;

"The people must have been hungry and weary and thirsty in the desert."

Then David mustered the people who were with him, and appointed over them commanders of thousands and commanders of hundreds. And David divided the people into three divisions, one-third was under the command of Joab, another third under Abishai, the son of Zeruiah, Joab's brother, and another third was under the command of Ittai the Gittite. And the king said to the people,

"I will surely go with you myself."

But the people said,

"You shall not go out; for if we do indeed run away, no one will trouble about us; or if half of us die, no one will trouble about us; but you are equal to ten thousand of us. And now the important thing is for you to be ready to help us from the city."

And the king said to them,

"Whatever seems good in your eyes I will do."

So the king stood at the side of the gate, while all the people marched out by hundreds and by thousands. And the king commanded Joab, and Abishai, and Ittai, saying,

"Deal gently for my sake with the young man, with Absalom!"

And all the people heard when the king gave orders to all the commanders regarding Absalom. Then the people took the field against Israel. And the battle was in the forest of Ephraim. And the people of Israel were defeated there by the servants of David; and the slaughter on that day was great—twenty thousand men. And the battle was there spread out over the whole landscape; and the forest devoured more people that day than the sword.

But Absalom happened to meet the servants of David. And Absalom was riding upon a mule, and the mule went under the thick branches of a great oak and his head caught fast in the oak, and he was left hanging between heaven and earth, while the mule that was under him passed on. And when a certain man saw it, he told Joab and said,

"Behold, I saw Absalom hanging in an oak."

Then Joab said to the man who had told him,

"You mean to say that you saw him! Why then did you not fell him to the ground at once? And it would have been my part to have given you ten pieces of silver and a girdle."

And the man said to Joab,

"Though I were to feel the pressure of a thousand shekels of silver in my hand, I would not put forth my hand against the king's son, for in our hearing the king charged you and Abishai and Ittai, saying, 'Spare for my sake the young man Absalom.' Or if I had treacherously made away with him nothing would have been hidden from the king, and you yourself would have stood aloof."

Then Joab said,

"Not so; I would assuage his wrath."

And he took three weapons in his hand, and thrust them into Absalom's vitals while he was still alive in the midst of the oak. And ten young men who bore Joab's armor gathered around and smote Absalom until he was dead.

Then Joab blew the trumpet, and the people returned from pursuing Israel; for Joab held back the people. And they took Absalom and cast him into a great pit in the forest, and raised over him an enormous heap of stones. And all Israel fled each to his own home. Now Absalom already in his lifetime had taken and set up for himself a pillar which is in the king's dale; for he said,

"I have no son to keep my name in remembrance."

And he named the pillar after his own name. And it is called Absalom's Monument, to this day.

And when Ahimaaz said to Joab,

"Let me run now and bring the news to the king that the LORD has freed him from the power of his enemies,"

Joab said to him,

"You are not the man to carry tidings today. On another day you may carry news, but you shall not do so today, for the king's son is dead."

Then Joab said to the Cushite,

"Go, tell the king what you have seen."

And the Cushite did obeisance to Joab and proceeded to run. But Ahimaaz the son of Zadok said yet again to Joab,

"Whatever happens, I should still very much like to run even after the Cushite."

And Joab said,

"Why is it that you would run, my son, since you will have no reward for news as a result of going?"

And he said,

"However it may be, I would run."

So he said to him,

"Run."

And Ahimaaz ran by way of the plain of the Jordan; and he passed the Cushite.

Now David was sitting between the two gates; and the watchman had gone up to the roof of the gate by the wall. And when he lifted up his eyes and looked, there was a man running alone. Then the watchman called and told the king. And the king said,

"If he be alone, there are good tidings in his mouth."

And he kept on drawing nearer. Whereupon the watchman saw another man running; and the watchman called toward the gate, and said,

"See, another man running alone!"

And the king said,

"He also is bringing good news."

And the watchman said,

"I see that the running of the first is like the running of Ahimaaz, the son of Zadok."

And the king said,

"He is a good man, and comes with good news."

Then Ahimaaz drew near and said to the king,

"All is well."

And he bowed with his face to the earth, and said,

"Blessed be the LORD thy God, who has delivered up the men who lifted up their hand against my lord the king."

And the king said,

"Is it well with the young man Absalom?"

And Ahimaaz said,

"When Joab sent your servant I saw a great tumult, but I did not learn what it was."

And the king said,

"Turn aside and take your stand here."

And he turned aside and stood still. And at that moment the Cushite entered. And the Cushite said,

"Let my lord the king receive the good news that the LORD has freed you this day from all those that rose up against you."

And the king said to the Cushite,

"Is it well with the young man Absalom?"

And the Cushite said,

"Let the enemies of my lord the king and all who rise up against you for evil be as this young man!"

Then the king was deeply moved and went up to the chamber over the gate and wept. And thus he said, as he wept,

"My son Absalom, my son, my son, Absalom! O that I, even I, had died instead of you, Absalom, my son, my son!"

And it was told Joab,

"Behold, the king is weeping and lamenting over Absalom."

And the victory that day for all the people was turned to mourning, since the people heard that day, saying,

"The king is grieved over his son."

Therefore the people stole away furtively into the city, as people who are put to shame when they have fled in battle steal away. But the king covered his face, and cried with a loud voice,

"My son Absalom, Absalom, my son, my son!"

So Joab went to the king in the house and said,

"You have covered with shame today the faces of all your servants, who have preserved your life today, and the lives of your sons and your daughters, and the lives of your wives and your concubines, by loving them who hate you and hating them who love you. For you have shown today that commanders and servants are nothing to you; for now I know that if Absalom were alive and all of us dead today, then you would have been well pleased. Now therefore arise, go forth, and speak reassuringly to your subjects; for I swear by the LORD, if you do not go forth, not a man will be with you tonight, and this will be worse for you than all the misfortune that has befallen you from your youth until now."

Then the king arose and sat in the gate. And when the word passed to all the people, saying, "See, the king is sitting in the gate," all the people came before the king.

Now Israel had fled every man to his home. And all the people murmured throughout all the tribes of Israel, saying,

"The king delivered us from the hand of our enemies, and he has freed us out of the hand of the Philistines, but now he has fled from the land on account of Absalom. And as for Absalom, whom we anointed over us, he has died in battle. Now therefore why do you remain silent about bringing the king back?"

And the word of all Israel came to the king.

Then King David sent to Zadok and Abiathar the priests, saying,

"Speak to the elders of Judah, saying, 'Why are you the last to bring the king back to his house? You are my kinsmen, my bone and my flesh, why then are you the last to bring the king back?' Say to Amasa, 'Are you not my bone and my flesh? God do so to me and more also, if you shall not become commander of the army henceforth instead of Joab.'"

And Amasa swayed the hearts of all the men of Judah as one man, so that they sent word to the king:

"Return, both you and all your followers."

So the king returned and came to the Jordan. And Judah came to Gilgal in order to go and meet the king and bring him across the Jordan.

Now there was a famine in the days of David for three years in succession. And when David sought the face of the Lord, the Lord said,

"It is for Saul and his bloody house, because he put to death the Gibeonites."

And David called the Gibeonites and said to them (now the Gibeonites were not of the Israelites, but of the remnant of the Amorites; however the Israelites had taken oath with them; and Saul had sought to slay them in his zeal for the Israelites and the Judeans),

"What can I do for you? And wherewith can I make expiation, so that you may bless the heritage of the Lord?"

And the Gibeonites said to him,

"It is not a matter of silver or gold between us and Saul or his house; neither is it for us to put to death any man in Israel."

And he repeated,

"What do you say that I shall do for you?"

And they said to the king,

"The man who consumed us, and who planned to destroy us that we should find no place in any of the borders of Israel—let seven men of his sons be given to us, that we may hang them up to the Lord in Gibeon, the mountain of the Lord."

And the king said,

"I will give them."

But the king spared Meribaal, the son of Jonathan, the son of Saul, because of the oath of the Lord which was between them, between David and

Jonathan, the son of Saul. And the king took the two sons of Rizpah, the daughter of Aiah, whom she bore to Saul, Armoni and Meribaal, and the five sons of Merab, the daughter of Saul, whom she bore to Adriel, the son of Barzillai, the Meholathite; and he gave them into the hand of the Gibeonites, and they hanged them in the mountain before the LORD, so that the seven of them fell together; and they were put to death in the first days of harvest, at the beginning of the barley harvest.

Then Rizpah, the daughter of Aiah, took sackcloth and spread it for her on the rock, from the beginning of barley harvest until water was poured upon them from the heavens; and she did not permit the birds of the heavens to light upon them by day nor the beasts of the field by night. And when it was told David what Rizpah, the daughter of Aiah, the consort of Saul, had done, David went and took the bones of Saul and the bones of Jonathan his son from the men of Jabesh in Gilead who had stolen them from the plaza of Beth-shan, where the Philistines had hanged them, on the day that the Philistines overcame Saul at Gilboa. And he brought up from there the bones of Saul and the bones of Jonathan his son and they gathered up the bones of those who were hanged. And they buried the bones of Saul and the bones of Jonathan his son in the land of Benjamin, by the side of the grave of Kish his father, and they did all that the king commanded. And after that God was propitiated toward the land.

Now King David was getting old and well advanced in years, and although they wrapped him in garments he could not keep warm. Therefore his servants said to him,

"Let them seek for my lord the king a young maiden and let her attend the king and act as his nurse; and let her lie in your bosom, that my lord the king may be warm."

So they sought for a beautiful maiden throughout all the territory of Israel, and they found Abishag the Shunammite and they brought her to the king. And the maiden was exquisitely beautiful; and she became the king's nurse, and ministered to him; but the king had no intercourse with her.

Then Adonijah, the son of Haggith, began making his boast, saying,

"I will be king."

And so he prepared for himself a chariot and horsemen and fifty men as runners to go before him. Now his father had never in his life restrained him by saying,

"Why do you do thus and so?"

And he was besides a very handsome man, and he was born next after Absalom. Accordingly he negotiated with Joab, the son of Zeruiah, and with Abiathar the priest, so that they became Adonijah's helpers. But Zadok the priest and Benaiah, the son of Jehoiada, and Nathan the prophet and Shimei and Rei and David's trained warriors were not with Adonijah. Now Adonijah sacrificed sheep and oxen and fat cattle by the Serpent's Stone, which is beside

En-rogel, and he invited all his brothers, the king's sons, together with all the royal officials of Judah; but he did not invite Nathan the prophet, nor Benaiah, nor the trained warriors, nor Solomon his brother.

Then Nathan said to Bathsheba, the mother of Solomon, as follows,

"Have you not heard that Adonijah, the son of Haggith, has been made king and our lord David does not know it? Now therefore let me, I pray you, advise you, that you may save your own life and the life of your son Solomon. Go into King David and say to him, 'Have you not, my lord, O king, sworn to your maidservant, saying, "Solomon your son shall be king after me, and he shall sit on my throne"? Why then has Adonijah been made king?' Now then while you are yet speaking there with the king, I also will come in after you and confirm your words."

So Bathsheba went in to the king to his chamber; (now the king was exceedingly old and Abishag the Shunammite was ministering to the king). Bathsheba then bowed and did obeisance to the king. And the king said,

"What do you want?"

And she said to him,

"My lord, you yourself swore to your maidservant by the LORD your God, 'Solomon your son shall be king after me and he shall sit on my throne.' And now, behold, Adonijah is king and you, my lord, O king, do not know it. He has sacrificed oxen and fat cattle and sheep in abundance, and has invited all the sons of the king, and Abiathar the priest, and Joab, commander of the army; but he has not invited Solomon your servant. Now, my lord, O king, the eyes of all Israel are upon you, that you should tell them who shall sit on the throne of my lord the king after him. As it stands the result will be that when my lord the king shall sleep with his fathers, I and my son Solomon will be regarded as rebels."

But while she was still speaking with the king, Nathan the prophet entered. And they told the king,

"Nathan the prophet is here."

And he came before the king and did obeisance to the king with his face to the earth. And Nathan said,

"My lord, O king, have you said, 'Adonijah shall be king after me, and he shall sit on my throne?' For he has gone down today and sacrificed oxen and fat cattle and sheep in abundance, and invited all the king's sons, and Joab, the commander of the army, and Abiathar the priest, and behold they are eating and drinking before him, and have said, 'Long live King Adonijah!' But as for me, even me your servant, and Zadok the priest, and Benaiah, the son of Jehoiada, and Solomon your servant he has not invited. Has this thing been brought about by my lord the king, and you have not told your servants who should sit upon the throne of my lord the king after him?"

Then King David spoke up and said,

"Call Bathsheba to me."

And she came in before the king and stood before him. And the king swore, saying,

"As the LORD lives, who has ransomed my life out of all adversity, as I swore to you by the LORD, the God of Israel, saying, 'Solomon your son shall be king after me and he shall sit on my throne in my stead,' so will I do this day."

Then Bathsheba bowed with her face to the earth, and did obeisance to the king and said,

"My lord King David live forever!"

And King David said,

"Call for me Zadok the priest, and Nathan the prophet, and Benaiah, the son of Jehoiada."

And when they came before the king, the king said to them,

"Take with you the servants of your lord and cause Solomon my son to ride upon my own mule, and bring him down to Gihon. And let Zadok the priest and Nathan the prophet anoint him there king over Israel; then blow the trumpet and say, 'Long live King Solomon!' You also shall go up behind him and he shall come in and sit upon my throne and he shall be king in my stead; and him have I commanded to be leader over Israel and Judah."

Then Benaiah, the son of Jehoiada, answered the king and said,

"So be it! so my the LORD confirm the words of my lord the king. As the LORD has been with my lord the king, so may he be with Solomon, and make his throne greater than the throne of my lord King David!"

Accordingly Zadok the priest, and Nathan the prophet, and Benaiah, the son of Jehoiada, together with the Cherethites and the Pelethites, caused Solomon to ride on the mule of King David, and brought him to Gihon. Then Zadok the priest took a horn of oil from the tent and anointed Solomon. Whereupon they blew the trumpet and all the people said,

"Long live King Solomon!"

And all the people went up after him playing upon flutes and rejoicing with such great outburst that the earth was rent with their noise.

Now Adonijah and all the guests who were with him heard it just as they finished feasting. And when Joab heard the sound of the trumpet, he said,

"Why this noise of the town in uproar?"

While he was still speaking, there came Jonathan, the son of Abiathar the priest. And Adonijah said,

"Enter, for you are a valiant man and bring good news."

And Jonathan answered and said to Adonijah,

"No, rather our lord King David has made Solomon king. And the king has sent with him Zadok the priest, and Nathan the prophet, and Benaiah, the son of Jehoiada, together with the Cherethites and the Pelethites, and they have caused him to ride on the king's mule. And Zadok the priest and Nathan the prophet have anointed him king in Gihon, and they have gone up from there rejoicing, so that the town is in uproar. That was the noise which you heard. And Solomon also has sat down on the throne of the kingdom. Moreover the servants of the king have already come to congratulate our lord King David, saying, 'May your God make the name of Solomon better than your name and his throne greater than your throne!' and the king bowed himself on his bed. Furthermore thus the king has said, 'Blessed be the LORD, the God of Israel, who has today granted one of my offspring to sit on my throne, my own eyes beholding it.' "

Then all the guests whom Adonijah had were terrified and arose and each went his way. But Adonijah was in such fear of Solomon that he arose and went and caught hold of the horns of the altar. And it was told Solomon, saying,

"See, Adonijah fears King Solomon, and now he has laid hold of the horns of the altar, saying, 'Let King Solomon swear to me first that he will not slay his servant with the sword.' "

And Solomon said,

"If he be a worthy man, not a hair of him shall fall to the earth, but if evil be found in him then he shall die."

So King Solomon sent and they brought him down from the altar, and he came and did obeisance to King Solomon. And Solomon said to him,

"Go to your house."

When David's time to die drew near, he charged Solomon his son, saying,

"I am about to go the way of all the earth. Be strong then and show yourself a man, and keep the charge of the LORD your God, by walking in his ways, by keeping his statutes, his commandments, his judgments and his testimonies, as it is written in the law of Moses, that you may have success in all that you do and in all that you undertake; that the LORD may establish his word that he spoke to me, saying, 'If your sons guard their steps to walk before me in truth with all their mind and with all their zeal, there shall not fail you a man on the throne of Israel.'

"Now furthermore you know what Joab, the son of Zeruiah, did to me, how he dealt with the two commanders of the armies of Israel, Abner, the son of Ner, and Amasa, the son of Jether, how that he slew them and avenged blood shed in war in time of peace, and put innocent blood upon his girdle that was about his loins and upon his sandals that were on his feet. Act therefore according to your wisdom, so that you do not allow his hoary head to go down in peace to Sheol. But show kindness to the sons of Barzillai the Gileadite, and let them be among those who eat at your table; for so they presented themselves to me when I fled from Absalom your brother. There is also with you Shimei, the son of Gera, the Benjaminite of Bahurim, who cursed me with a grievous curse in the day when I went to Mahanaim. But when he came down to meet me at the Jordan, I swore to him by the LORD, saying, 'I will not slay you with the sword.' But do you yourself not hold him guiltless; you are a wise man and know what you should do to him, and you shall bring down his old age with blood to Sheol."

So David slept with his fathers and was buried in the city of David. And the period that David was king over Israel was forty years: seven years he was king in Hebron, and thirty-three years he was king in Jerusalem.

AHAB AND THE PROPHETS [1]

Now Ben-hadad, king of Syria, assembled all his army, and there were thirty-two kings with him, together with horses and chariots. Thereupon he went up and besieged Samaria and fought against it. Moreover he sent messengers to Ahab, king of Israel, into the city, and said to him,

"Thus has Ben-hadad said, 'Your silver and your gold are mine; your wives also and your children are mine.'"

The king of Israel then answered and said,

"According to your statement, my lord, O king, I am yours, together with all that I possess."

Presently the messengers came again and said,

"Thus has Ben-hadad said, 'I sent to you, saying, "You shall deliver to me your silver and your gold, your wives and your children; but about this time tomorrow, I shall send my servants to you and they shall ransack your house and the houses of your servants; and whatever pleases them they shall take in their hand and carry it away."'"

Then the king of Israel called to all the elders of the land, and said,

"Mark, I pray you, and take note how this man is looking for trouble, for he sent to me for my wives and my children, my silver and gold, and I did not deny him."

But all the elders and all the people said to him,

"Obey not, nor consent!"

So he said to the messengers of Ben-hadad,

"Say to my lord the king, 'All that you demanded of your servant at the first I was ready to do, but this thing I cannot do.'"

So the messengers went away and brought him word again. Thus Ben-hadad sent to him and said,

"So may the gods do to me and more also, if the dust of Samaria shall suffice for handfuls for all the people who follow me."

But the king of Israel answered and said,

"Tell him, 'Let not him who is girding on his weapon boast himself as he who is ungirding.'"

[1] Selected from the first book of *Kings*, chapters 20:1-34, 21:1-22:40. Translated from the Hebrew by Leroy Waterman.

Now at the time when he heard this message—he was drinking with the kings in the pavilions—he said to his servants,

"Form in line."

So they formed in line against the city.

At this juncture a certain prophet drew near to Ahab, king of Israel, and said,

"Thus says the LORD, 'Do you see all this great multitude? Behold, I am about to deliver them into your hand today, and you shall know that I am the LORD.'"

But Ahab said,

"By whom?"

So he said,

"Thus says the LORD, 'By the young men under the commanders of the provinces.'"

And he said,

"Who shall begin the battle?"

And he answered,

"You."

Then he mustered the young men under the commanders of the provinces, and they were two hundred and thirty-two. And after them he mustered all the people, even all the Israelites, seven thousand. And at noon they made the attack, while Ben-hadad was drinking himself drunk in the pavilions, together with the thirty-two kings, his allies. Moreover the young men under the commanders of the provinces went out first. And they sent to Ben-hadad and reported, saying,

"Men have come out from Samaria."

And he said,

"Whether they have come out for peace, take them alive; or whether they have come out for war, take them alive."

So these (the young men under the commanders of the provinces) went out of the city, and the force which followed them. Then they slew each his man, so that the Arameans fled. And Israel pursued them, but Ben-hadad, the king of Syria, escaped on a horse with horsemen. Then the king of Israel went out and captured horses and chariots, and made a great slaughter among the Arameans.

Moreover a prophet approached the king of Israel and said to him,

"Go, strengthen yourself, and mark and see what you will do, for a year from now the king of Syria will be coming up against you."

But the servants of the king of Syria said to him,

"Their gods are mountain gods, therefore they were too strong for us; but let us fight against them in the plain, and surely we shall be stronger than they."

So he hearkened to their voice and did so.

Now when the year came round, Ben-hadad mustered the Arameans and went to Aphek to fight against Israel. And the Israelites were mustered and provisioned, and went against them. And the Israelites encamped before them like two prematurely born of she-goats, while the Arameans filled the country. Then a man of God came near and said to the king of Israel,

"Thus says the LORD, 'Because the Arameans say, "The LORD is a god of the mountains and not a god of the valleys," therefore I will deliver all this great multitude into your hand, that you may know that I am the LORD.'"

So they encamped facing each other seven days. But on the seventh day the battle was joined; and the Israelites slew of the Arameans a hundred thousand footmen in one day. And the rest fled to Aphek into the city; and the wall fell upon twenty-seven thousand of the men who were left. Ben-hadad also fled, and came into an innermost chamber. Then the servants said to him,

"Behold now, we have heard that the kings of the house of Israel are merciful kings; let us therefore, I pray you, put sackcloth on our loins, and ropes about our heads, and go out to the king of Israel; perhaps he will spare your life."

So they girded sackcloth on their loins and put ropes about their heads, and went to the king of Israel and said,

"Your servant Ben-hadad says, 'I pray you, let me live.'"

And he said,

"Is he yet alive? He is my brother."

Now the men were trying to divine his meaning, and they quickly caught it from him and said,

"Ben-hadad is your brother."

Then he said,

"Go, bring him!"

And when Ben-hadad came to him, he took him up into his chariot.

So Ben-hadad said to him,

"The cities which my father took from your father I will restore, and you may maintain bazaars of your own in Damascus as my father did in Samaria."

"And I," said Ahab, "will let you go with this understanding."

So he made a covenant with him and he let him go.

Now Naboth the Jezreelite had a vineyard beside the palace of Ahab, king of Samaria. And Ahab spoke to Naboth, saying,

"Give me your vineyard that I may have it for a vegetable garden, because it is close beside my house; and I will give you a better vineyard than it, in its stead, or if you prefer, I will gladly give you its value in money."

But Naboth said to Ahab,

"The LORD forbid, that I should give you the inheritance of my fathers."

Whereupon Ahab came into his house vexed and sullen, because of the word which Naboth the Jezreelite had spoken to him; for he had said,

"I will not give you the inheritance of my fathers."

And he lay on his bed and covered his face and refused food. But Jezebel his wife came to him and spoke to him,

"Why is your spirit so vexed that you eat no food?"

Accordingly he spoke to her,

"Because I spoke to Naboth the Jezreelite and said to him, 'Give me your vineyard for money; or if you prefer, I will gladly give you a vineyard in its stead'; but he said, 'I will not give you my vineyard.'"

Then Jezebel his wife said to him,

"Do you now hold sway in Israel? Arise, eat bread, and let your heart be of good cheer. I will give you the vineyard of Naboth the Jezreelite."

So she wrote letters in Ahab's name and sealed them with his seal, and sent them to the elders and to the nobles who were in his city, who presided with Naboth.

Now she had written in the letters, saying,

"Proclaim a fast and seat Naboth in a conspicuous place among the people. Then seat two unscrupulous men before him and let them bear witness, saying, 'You have cursed God and the king.' Then take him out and stone him to death."

So the men of his city, the elders and the nobles who presided in his city, did as Jezebel had sent to them. As it was written in the letters which she had sent to them they proclaimed a fast, and gave Naboth a seat in a conspicuous place among the people. Also two unscrupulous men came in and sat before him, and the rascals bore witness against Naboth in the presence of the people, saying,

"Naboth cursed God and the king."

So they took him outside of the city and stoned him to death with stones. Then they sent to Jezebel, saying,

"Naboth has been stoned and is dead."

Accordingly, as soon as Jezebel heard that Naboth had been stoned and was dead, Jezebel said to Ahab,

"Arise, take possession of the vineyard of Naboth the Jezreelite, which he refused to give for money; for Naboth is not alive but dead."

Now as soon as Ahab heard that Naboth was dead, Ahab arose to go down to the vineyard of Naboth the Jezreelite to take possession of it.

But the word of the LORD came to Elijah the Tishbite, saying,

"Arise, go down to meet Ahab, king of Israel, who is in Samaria. See, he is in the vineyard of Naboth, whither he has gone down to take possession. Do you speak to him, saying, 'Thus says the LORD, "Have you killed, and also taken possession? Therefore in the place where the dogs licked up the blood of Naboth will the dogs lick up your own blood."'"

And Ahab said to Elijah,

"Have you found me, O my enemy?"

And he said,

"I have. Because you have sold yourself to no purpose, to do that which is evil in the sight of the LORD, behold, I am about to bring evil upon you, and I will utterly sweep you away and will cut off from Ahab every male, both him that is shut up and him that is left at large in Israel. I will also make your house like the house of Jeroboam, the son of Nebat, and like the house of Baasha, the son of Ahijah, because of the indignation which you have aroused and because you have caused Israel to sin. Also to Jezebel the LORD has spoken, saying, 'The dogs shall eat Jezebel in the district of Jezreel.' Whoever belonging to Ahab dies in the city the dogs shall eat; and whoever dies in the field, the birds of the heavens shall eat."

Now as soon as Ahab heard these words he tore his garments and put sackcloth on his flesh and fasted; he also lay in sackcloth, and went about quietly. Then the word of the LORD came to Elijah the Tishbite, saying,

"Have you seen how Ahab has humbled himself before me? Because he has humbled himself before me, I will not bring the evil in his days; in his son's days I will bring the evil upon his house."

Now for three years Syria and Israel continued without war. But in the third year Jehoshaphat, king of Judah, came down to the king of Israel, and the king of Israel said to his servants,

"Do you know that Ramoth-gilead belongs to us, yet we are inactive instead of taking it from the hand of the king of Syria?"

Then he said to Jehoshaphat,

"Will you go with me to fight against Ramoth-gilead?"

And Jehoshaphat said to the king of Israel,

"I am as you, my people as your people, my horses as your horses."

Jehoshaphat also said to the king of Israel,

"Inquire at this time, I pray, for the word of the LORD."

Then the king of Israel gathered the prophets together, about four hundred men, and said to them,

"Shall I go to fight against Ramoth-gilead or shall I forbear?"

And they said,

"Go up; for the LORD will surely deliver it into the hand of the king."

But Jehoshaphat said,

"Is there not here another prophet of the LORD of whom we may inquire?"

And the king of Israel said to Jehoshaphat,

"There is yet a man by whom we may inquire of the LORD, Micaiah, the son of Imlah, but I hate him; for he never prophesies for me good, but only evil."

But Jehoshaphat said,

"Let not the king say so."

So the king of Israel called a certain eunuch and said,

"Bring quickly Micaiah, the son of Imlah."

Now while the king of Israel and Jehoshaphat, the king of Judah, were sitting each on his throne, clad in his purple robes at the entrance of the gate of Samaria, and all the prophets were engaged in ecstatic prophecy before them, Zedekiah, the son of Chenanaiah, made for himself horns of iron and said,

"Thus says the Lord, 'With these you shall gore the Arameans until you have destroyed them.'"

So all the prophets were prophesying, saying,

"Go up to Ramoth-gilead and prosper; for the Lord will deliver it into the hand of the king."

Now the messenger who went to call Micaiah, spoke to him, saying,

"See, now, the prophets with one consent have spoken good to the king; let your words, I pray you, be as the word of one of them and speak good."

But Micaiah said,

"As the Lord lives, I will speak what the Lord speaks to me."

So when he came to the king, the king said to him,

"Micaiah, shall we go to Ramoth-gilead to fight against it or shall we forbear?"

And he said to him,

"Go up and prosper; for the Lord will deliver it into the hand of the king!"

But the king said to him,

"How many times must I adjure you that you speak to me nothing but the truth in the name of the Lord?"

And he said,

"I saw all Israel scattered on the mountains, like sheep without a shepherd. And the Lord said, 'These have no masters; let each of them return to his home in peace.'"

Then the king of Israel said to Jehoshaphat,

"Did I not say to you, that he would not prophesy good concerning me, but evil?"

But Micaiah said,

"Therefore hear the word of the Lord: I saw the Lord sitting on his throne, and all the army of the heavens standing by him on his right hand and on his left. And the Lord said, 'Who will deceive Ahab so that he shall go up and fall at Ramoth-gilead?' And one said one thing and another another, until a spirit came forth and stood before the Lord and said, 'I will deceive him.' And the Lord said to him, 'By what means?' And he said, 'I will go forth and become a lying spirit in the mouth of all his prophets.' Thereupon he said, 'You shall deceive him and also succeed! Go forth and do so.' Now therefore behold, the Lord has put a lying spirit in the mouth of all these your prophets, since the Lord has spoken evil concerning you."

Then Zedekiah, the son of Chenanaiah, came near and struck Micaiah upon the cheek and said,

"Which way did the Spirit of the Lord go from me to speak with you?"

And Micaiah said,

"Indeed, you shall see in that day, when you shall go from one chamber to another to hide yourself."

Then the king of Israel said,

"Take Micaiah and return him to Amon, commander of the city, and to Joash, the king's son, and say, 'Thus says the king, "Put this fellow in the prison house and feed him with scant prison fare of bread and water until I come in peace."'"

But Micaiah said,

"If you do indeed return in peace, the LORD has not spoken by me. Hear, O people, all of you."

So the king of Israel and Jehoshaphat, the king of Judah, went up to Ramoth-gilead. The king of Israel also said to Jehoshaphat,

"I will disguise myself and go into battle, but you can put on your own robes."

So the king of Israel disguised himself and went into the battle.

Now the king of Syria had commanded his thirty-two chariot commanders, saying,

"Fight with neither small nor great, except only with the king of Israel."

Accordingly as soon as the chariot commanders saw Jehoshaphat, they said, "Surely it is the king of Israel."

And they surrounded him to fight against him, but Jehoshaphat cried out. Therefore, as soon as the chariot commanders saw that it was not the king of Israel, they turned back from pursuing him. But a man drew a bow at a venture and shot the king of Israel between the fastenings and the coat of mail. Therefore he said to his chariot driver,

"Turn your hand and take me out of the fight; for I am severely wounded."

Now the battle increased that day, and the king was propped up in his chariot facing the Arameans until evening, and the blood from the wound ran out into the bottom of the chariot. Then at evening he died. And about sunset the cry passed through the army,

"Each to his city and each to his land, for the king is dead!"

So they came to Samaria and buried the king in Samaria. And when they washed off the chariot by the pool of Samaria, the dogs licked up his blood, and the harlots washed in it according to the word which the LORD had spoken. Now the rest of the records of Ahab and all that he did and the ivory house which he built and all the cities that he built, are they not written in the Book of the Chronicles of the Kings of Israel? So Ahab slept with his fathers and Ahaziah, his son, reigned in his stead.

JEREMIAH AND THE FALL OF JERUSALEM [1]

Now when the Chaldean army had raised the siege of Jerusalem, because of the advance of Pharaoh's army, Jeremiah set out from Jerusalem on a journey to the land of Benjamin, to take possession of the property that belonged to him among the people there. But just as he reached the Benjamin Gate, a sentry who was posted there, named Irijah, the son of Shelemiah, the son of Hananiah, arrested Jeremiah the prophet, saying,

"You are deserting to the Chaldeans."

Jeremiah replied,

"It is false; I am not deserting to the Chaldeans."

But he would not listen to him. So Irijah arrested Jeremiah, and brought him to the princes. And the princes were so angry with Jeremiah that they beat him and put him in prison in the house of Jonathan the secretary, which had been turned into a prison. Having thus come to the dungeon-cells, Jeremiah remained there for a number of days.

Then King Zedekiah sent for him, and received him; and the king asked him secretly in his palace, "Is there any word from the LORD?"

And Jeremiah said,

"There is. You shall be given into the hand of the king of Babylon."

Then Jeremiah said to King Zedekiah,

"What wrong have I done to you, or to your servants, or to this people, that you have put me in prison? Where are your prophets who prophesied to you, saying, 'The king of Babylon shall not come against you, nor against this land?' So now, pray, listen to me, O my lord the king; and give a favorable hearing to my supplication, that I may not be sent back to the house of Jonathan the secretary, and left to die there!"

King Zedekiah then gave orders, and Jeremiah was committed to the guard-court, and given a loaf of bread daily from the bakers' street, until all the bread in the city was consumed. So Jeremiah remained in the guard-court.

Now Shephatiah, the son of Mattan, and Gedaliah, the son of Pashhur, and Jucal, the son of Shelemiah, and Pashhur, the son of Malchiah, heard Jeremiah addressing all the people in these terms,

"Thus says the LORD: 'He who remains in this city shall die by sword, famine, and pestilence; but he who surrenders to the Chaldeans shall have his life given to him as a prize of war.' For thus says the LORD: 'This city shall certainly be given into the hand of the king of Babylon's army, and they shall take it.'"

So they said to the king,

[1] Selected from the book of *Jeremiah,* chapters 37:11-39:14; 41:1-3; 42:1-43:7. Translated from the Hebrew by Alex R. Gordon.

"Pray, have this man put to death; for he is disheartening the soldiers that are left in this city, and all the people as well, by addressing such words to them; for this man is seeking not the welfare of this people, but their ruin."

And King Zedekiah said,

"See! he is in your hand; for the king can do nothing against you."

So they took Jeremiah, and cast him into the cistern of Malchiah, the royal prince, which was in the guard-court, letting Jeremiah down with ropes. And as there was no water in the cistern, but only mud, Jeremiah sank in the mud.

But Ebedmelech the Ethiopian, a eunuch in the service of the palace, heard that they had put Jeremiah in the cistern. The king being seated at the Benjamin Gate, Ebedmelech set out from the palace, and addressed the king, saying,

"My lord the king, these men have done wrong in treating Jeremiah as they have done, casting him into the cistern, to die on his feet of famine, because there is no more bread in the city."

The king then gave orders to Ebedmelech the Ethiopian, saying,

"Take with you three men from here, and draw Jeremiah the prophet out of the cistern, before he die."

So Ebedmelech took the men with him and went to the wardrobe of the palace, and took from there same torn and tattered rags, and let them down by ropes to Jeremiah in the cistern. And Ebedmelech the Ethiopian said to Jeremiah,

"Pray, put these torn and tattered rags below your armpits under the ropes."

And Jeremiah did so. And they drew Jeremiah by the ropes, and brought him up from the cistern. And Jeremiah remained in the guard-court.

Then King Zedekiah sent for Jeremiah the prophet, and received him at the third entrance to the house of the LORD; and the king said to Jeremiah,

"I am going to ask you a question, and you must conceal nothing from me."

And Jeremiah said to Zedekiah,

"If I tell you the truth, are you not sure to put me to death? And if I give you advice, you will not listen to me."

So King Zedekiah swore an oath in secret to Jeremiah, saying,

"As the LORD lives, who made this life of ours, I will neither put you to death, nor hand you over to these men who are seeking your life."

Then Jeremiah said to Zedekiah,

"Thus says the LORD, the God of hosts, the God of Israel: 'If you surrender freely to the officers of the king of Babylon, your life shall be spared, and this city shall not be burned with fire; both yourself and your household shall be spared. But if you do not surrender to the officers of the king of Babylon, this city shall be handed over to the Chaldeans, who shall burn it with fire; and you yourself shall not escape from their hand."

Then King Zedekiah said to Jeremiah,

"I am afraid of the Jews who have gone over to the Chaldeans, lest I be handed over to them, and they subject me to indignity."

But Jeremiah said,

"You shall not be handed over. Pray, then, listen to the voice of the LORD, as I declare it to you, that your life may be spared, and all may be well with you. But if you refuse to surrender, this is the word that the LORD has revealed to me. All the women who are left in the palace of the king of Judah shall be led out to the officers of the king of Babylon, saying,

> 'Your bosom friends have deceived you,
>   And have overreached you;
>   They have sunk your feet in the mire,
>   And have turned away from you.'

All your wives and children shall be led out to the Chaldeans, while you yourselves shall not escape from their hand, but shall be captured by the king of Babylon; and this city shall be burned with fire."

Then Zedekiah said to Jeremiah,

"Let no one know of this conversation, on pain of death. And if the princes hear that I have been talking with you, and come and say to you, 'Pray, tell us what you said to the king, and what the king said to you; conceal nothing from us, on pain of death,' you shall say to them, 'I was presenting my petition to the king, that he would not send me back to Jonathan's house, to die there.'"

So when all the princes came to Jeremiah, and questioned him, he answered them in strict accordance with the king's instructions; and they pressed him no further, for the conversation had not been overheard. Jeremiah then remained in the guard-court till the day that Jerusalem was taken.

In the ninth year of Zedekiah, king of Judah, the tenth month, Nebuchadrezzar, king of Babylon, and all his army advanced against Jerusalem and besieged it; and in the eleventh year of Zedekiah, the fourth month, the ninth day of the month, the city was breached. And when Zedekiah, king of Judah, and all the soldiers saw what had happened, they left the city by night, and fled by way of the king's garden, through the gate between the two walls, and made for the Jordan valley. But the Chaldean army pursued them, and overtook Zedekiah in the steppes of Jericho; and they arrested him, and brought him up to Nebuchadrezzar, king of Babylon, at Riblah in the land of Hamath, where he pronounced judgment against him. And the king of Babylon slew the sons of Zedekiah at Riblah before his eyes. The king of Babylon likewise slew all the nobles of Judah. Then he put out the eyes of Zedekiah, and bound him with chains, to carry him to Babylon. The Chaldeans also burned the house of the king and the houses of the people with fire, and demolished the walls of Jerusalem. Then Nebuzaradan, the commander of the guard, carried captive to Babylon the rest of the people that were left in the city, and the deserters who had surrendered to him, together with the artisans that were left. But Nebuzaradan, the commander of the guard, left in the land of Judah a number of the poor people, who had nothing, and at the same time gave them vineyards and fields.

After Jerusalem had been taken, all the officials of the king of Babylon—Nergal-sharezer, the chief councillor, Nebushazban, the chief eunuch, and all the rest of the officials of the king of Babylon—came and took their seats at the middle gate. Now Nebuchadrezzar, king of Babylon, had given orders regarding Jeremiah to Nebuzaradan, the commander of the guard, saying, "Take him, and look after him; do him no harm, but treat him as he tells you." So Nebuzaradan, the commander of the guard, issued orders, and Nebushazban, the chief eunuch, Nergal-sharezer, the chief councillor, and all the chief officials of the king of Babylon sent and took Jeremiah out of the guard-court, and handed him over to Gedaliah, the son of Ahikam, the son of Shaphan, to have him conveyed to his home. So he stayed among the people.

In the seventh month, however, Ishmael, the son of Nethaniah, the son of Elishama, a member of the royal family, accompanied by ten men, came to Gedaliah, the son of Ahikam, at Mizpeh. As they dined together at Mizpeh, Ishmael, the son of Nethaniah, and the ten men who were with him arose, and smote with the sword, and slew Gedaliah, the son of Ahikam, whom the king of Babylon had appointed governor over the land. Ishmael also smote all the Jews who were with him at Mizpeh, as well as the Chaldean soldiers who happened to be there.

Then all the commanders of the forces, including Johanan, the son of Kareah, and Azariah, the son of Hoshaiah, with all the people from the least to the greatest, approached Jeremiah the prophet and said to him,

"Give a favorable hearing to our supplication, and pray to the LORD your God for us, even for all this remnant—for we are left but a few out of many, as you can see with your own eyes—that the LORD your God may show us the way we should go and the thing we should do."

Jeremiah the prophet answered them,

"I have heard your petition. I will pray to the LORD your God, as you request; and whatever answer the LORD may give you, I will tell you—I will hold nothing back from you."

And they said to Jeremiah,

"The LORD be a true and faithful witness against us, if we do not act in perfect accordance with the word which the LORD your God may send you to us! Whether it be pleasant or unpleasant, we will obey the voice of the LORD our God, to whom we are sending you, that we may prosper through obeying the voice of the LORD our God."

At the end of ten days the word of the LORD came to Jeremiah. So he summoned Johanan, the son of Kareah, and all the commanders of the forces that were with him, and all the people from the least to the greatest; and he said to them,

"Thus says the LORD, the God of Israel, to whom you sent me to present your supplication before him: 'If you stay on in this land, I will build you up and not tear you down, and I will plant you and not uproot you; for I regret the harm I have done to you. Do not be afraid of the king of Babylon, of whom you are afraid; do not be afraid of him,' is the oracle of the LORD; 'for I am with you to save you, and to deliver you out of his hand. I will have pity upon you, and will inspire him with pity for you, so that he may allow you to stay in your own land. But if you say, "We will not stay in this land," refusing to obey the voice of the LORD your God, and saying, "No, we will go to the land of Egypt, where we shall see no war, and shall hear no sound of trumpet, and shall have no hunger for bread; and there will we stay," then hear the word of the LORD, O remnant of Judah!' Thus says the LORD of hosts, the God of Israel: 'If you are determined to go to Egypt, and if you go to settle there, the sword which you fear shall overtake you there in the land of Egypt, and the famine which you dread shall cling to your heels there in Egypt; and there shall you die. All the men who are determined to go to Egypt, to settle there, shall die by sword, famine, and pestilence; not one of them shall survive or escape from the doom that I am bringing upon them.' For thus says the LORD of hosts, the God of Israel: 'As my anger and my fury have been poured out upon the citizens of Jerusalem, so shall my fury be poured out upon you when you enter Egypt; and you shall be an execration and a horror, a curse and a scorn; and you shall see this place no more.' So this is the word that the LORD has spoken to you, O remnant of Judah: 'Do not go to Egypt!' And be certain of this—for I forewarn you this day that you will wrong your own selves if, after sending me to the LORD your God, saying, 'Pray to the LORD our God for us; and whatever the LORD our God may say, tell us, and we will do it,' and if, after I have told it to you this day, you do not listen to the voice of the LORD your God in regard to anything that he has sent me to tell you—now be certain of this, that you shall die by sword, famine, and pestilence, in the place where you desire to go and settle."

When Jeremiah had finished speaking to all the people all the words of the LORD their God, even all these words which the LORD their God had sent him to speak to them, Azariah, the son of Hoshaiah, Johanan, the son of Kareah, and all the proud and defiant men said to Jeremiah,

"You are telling a lie. The LORD our God did not send you to say, 'You shall not go to Egypt to settle there'; but Baruch, the son of Neriah, has been egging you on against us, with the object of delivering us into the hand of the Chaldeans, that they may put us to death, or carry us captive to Babylon."

So Johanan, the son of Kareah, and all the commanders of the forces, and all the people, did not listen to the voice of the LORD, bidding them stay in the land of Judah; but Johanan, the son of Kareah, and all the commanders of the forces, took all the remnant of Judah that had returned from all the nations to which they had been driven, to settle in the land of Judah—the men, women, and children, the king's daughters, every person whom Nebuzaradan, the commander of the guard, had left with Gedaliah, the son of Ahikam, the son of Shaphan, including Jeremiah the prophet and Baruch, the son of Neriah—and, not listening to the voice of the LORD, went to the land of Egypt, and arrived at Daphne.

THE ALIEN WORLD

JONAH IS TAUGHT A LESSON[1]

THE word of the Lord came to Jonah, the son of Amittai, as follows:

"Arise, go to Nineveh, that great city, and preach against it; for their wickedness has come up before me."

Then Jonah arose to flee to Tarshish, from the presence of the Lord. So he went down to Joppa, where he found a ship, bound for Tarshish. He paid his fare, and went aboard, to go with them to Tarshish, from the presence of the Lord.

But the Lord hurled a great wind upon the sea, so that there was a great storm on the sea; and it was thought that the ship would be broken up. Then the sailors were frightened, and they cried each one to his god; and they threw overboard the stuff that was in the ship, in order to lighten her.

But Jonah had gone down into the hold of the ship, and was lying fast asleep. So the captain approached him, and said to him,

"Why are you sleeping? Get up; call upon your god. Perhaps that god will bethink himself of us, that we perish not."

Then they said, one to another,

"Come, let us cast lots, that we may know upon whose account this disaster has befallen us."

So they cast lots; and the lot fell upon Jonah. Then they said to him,

"Tell us, now, for what reason this disaster has befallen us. What is your business? Whence do you come? What is your country? And from what people are you?"

So he said to them,

"I am a Hebrew; and I stand in awe of the Lord, the God of the heavens, who made both the sea and the dry land."

"What a wicked thing you have done!"

For the men knew that he was fleeing from the presence of the Lord; because he had told them. Whereupon, they said to him,

"What shall we do with you, that the sea may become calm for us?"

For the sea was running higher and higher. Then he said to them,

"Pick me up, and cast me into the sea, so that the sea may be calm for you; for I know that this great storm is upon you because of me."

But the men rowed hard to bring the ship back to the dry land, yet could not; for the sea was running higher and higher against them. Wherefore, they cried unto the Lord, saying,

"O Lord, we beseech thee, let us not perish for this man's life; and lay

[1] Selected from the book of *Jonah*. Chapter 2:2-9 has been omitted. Translated from the Hebrew by J. M. Powis Smith.

75

not up against us innocent blood; for thou, O Lord, dost do as thou dost please."

Then they picked up Jonah and threw him overboard; and the sea ceased from its raging.

Thereupon the men feared the Lord profoundly; and they sacrificed to the Lord and made vows.

Now, the Lord had assigned a great fish to swallow up Jonah; and Jonah was in the belly of the fish three days and three nights. Then Jonah prayed to the Lord, his God, from the belly of the fish.

Then the Lord commanded the fish, and it vomited Jonah forth upon dry land.

Then the word of the Lord came to Jonah a second time, as follows:

"Arise, go to Nineveh, that great city, and proclaim unto it the proclamation which I shall tell you."

So Jonah arose, and went to Nineveh, as the Lord had said. Now Nineveh was an exceedingly great city, the walk through it requiring three days. And Jonah had gone a day's journey into the city, when he made proclamation, saying,

"Yet forty days, and Nineveh shall be overthrown."

Whereupon the men of Nineveh believed God, and proclaimed a fast, and clothed themselves in sackcloth, from the greatest unto the least of them. When the thing reached the King of Nineveh, he rose from his throne, put off his robe, put on sackcloth, and sat upon the ash heap. He also sent messengers through Nineveh, saying,

"By decree of the king and his nobles, namely, let neither man nor beast, cattle nor sheep, taste a thing; let them not feed, and let them not drink water. But let them put on sackcloth, both man and beast, and let them call aloud unto God; and let each one turn from his wicked way, and from whatsoever violence he has in hand. Who knows but that God will turn and relent, turning from his fierce anger, so that we perish not."

Then God saw their actions, that they had turned from their wicked way. So God relented of the evil which he had said he would do unto them, and he did it not.

But Jonah was greatly displeased and very angry. So he prayed to the Lord, saying,

"O Lord, is not this what I said while I was still upon my own soil? Therefore, I hastened to flee to Tarshish. For I knew that thou wast a gracious God, and merciful, slow to anger, and abounding in grace, and relenting of evil. Now, therefore, O Lord, take my life, I pray thee, from me. For I am better off dead, than alive!"

Then the Lord said,

"Are you so very angry?"

Then Jonah went forth from the city, and sat down to the east of the city; and he made a booth for himself there, and sat under it in the shade, until he should see what would happen in the city. So the Lord, God, gave orders to a gourd, and it grew up above Jonah so as to be a shade over his head, to save him from his discomfort; and Jonah was very glad over the gourd. Then God ordered a worm, when the dawn came up on the morrow, to smite the gourd, so that it wilted. And when the sun arose, God ordered a burning east wind; and the sun smote down upon Jonah's head so that he fainted, and asked that he might die, and said,

"I am better off dead than alive!"

Then God said to Jonah,

"Are you so very angry over the gourd?"

And he replied,

"I am angry enough to die!"

Then the Lord said,

"You have had pity on the gourd, for which you did not toil; nor did you raise it; which grew in a night, and perished in a night! And should not I, indeed, have pity on Nineveh, that great city, wherein are more than a hundred and twenty thousand infants, that cannot distinguish between their right hand and their left, and much cattle?"

NEHEMIAH REBUILDS THE TEMPLE [1]

THE account of Nehemiah, the son of Hacaliah.

Now it happened in the month of Chislev, in the twentieth year, as I was in the citadel of Shushan, that Hanani, one of my kinsmen, came, together with certain men from Judah, and I asked them concerning the Jews who had escaped, who were left from the captivity and concerning Jerusalem. Accordingly they said to me,

"The survivors who are left from the captivity there in the province are in great misery and reproach, and the wall of Jerusalem is broken down and its gates have been destroyed by fire."

Now when I heard these words, I sat down and wept and mourned certain days; and I fasted and prayed before the God of the heavens, and I said,

"I beseech thee, O LORD, the God of the heavens, the great and terrible God, who keeps his gracious covenant with those who love him and keep his commandments. Let thine ears now be attentive and thine eyes open, to hear the prayer of thy servant, which I am making before thee, day and night, for the Israelites thy servants, while I confess, concerning the sins of the Israelites,

[1] Selected from *Nehemiah*, chapters 1:1-2:20; 4:1-6:19; 13:15-31. This memoir, which constitutes (with the book of *Ezra*), a record of Jewish history between 537-433 B.C.E., was written about 430-425 B.C.E. *Nehemiah* and the *Life* of Josephus are the only two autobiographies recorded by Jews until comparatively modern times. Translated from the Hebrew by Leroy Waterman.

which we have sinned against thee, as I myself also and my father's family have sinned. We have acted corruptly against thee, and have not kept the commandments, nor the statutes, nor the ordinances, which thou didst command Moses, thy servant. Remember now the word which thou didst command Moses, thy servant, saying, 'If you trespass, I will scatter you among the peoples; but if you return to me, and keep my commandments and do them, though your outcasts be under the remotest skies, yet will I gather them thence and bring them to the place that I have chosen, there to cause my name to dwell.' Now these are thy servants and thy people, whom thou hast redeemed by thy great power and by thy mighty hand. O LORD, I beseech thee, let thine ear now be attentive to the prayer of thy servant and to the prayer of thy servants, who delight to fear thy name; and prosper, I pray thee, thy servant this day, and grant him mercies in the sight of this man."

Now I was cupbearer to the king. Accordingly it was in the month Nisan in the twentieth year of Artaxerxes, the king, when the wine was served, that I took up the wine and gave it to the king. And I had not formerly been sad. Therefore the king said to me,

"Why is your countenance sad, since you are not ill? This is nothing else but sorrow of heart."

Then I was exceedingly frightened, and I said to the king,

"Let the king live forever: Why should not my countenance be sad, when the city, the place of my fathers' sepulchres is desolate, and its gates have been destroyed by fire?"

Thereupon the king said to me,

"For what then do you make request?"

So I prayed to the God of the heavens. And I said to the king,

"If it please the king, and if your servant is acceptable in your sight, that you would send me to Judah to the city of my fathers' sepulchres, that I may rebuild it."

Then the king said to me, the queen also being seated beside him,

"For how long will your journey be? And when will you return?"

However it pleased the king to let me go; for I proposed to him a time limit. Moreover I said to the king,

"If it please the king, let letters be given me to the governors of the provinces beyond the River, that they may let me pass through until I come to Judah, and a letter to Asaph, the keeper of the king's park, that he may give me timber to furnish the beams for the gates of the citadel, which belongs to the temple, and for the walls of the city, and for the house that I shall enter."

And the king granted my request, according to the good hand of my God that was upon me.

Then I came to the governors of the provinces beyond the River, and gave them the king's letters. Moreover the king had sent with me army officers and horsemen. But when Sanballat the Horonite and Tobiah the Ammonite slave heard of it, it caused them great irritation that a man had come to seek the welfare of the Israelites.

So I came to Jerusalem and was there three days. Then I arose in the night, I and a few men with me, and I told no man what my God had put in my heart to do for Jerusalem, neither was there any beast with me except the beast on which I rode. Accordingly I went out by night through the Valley Gate, even toward the Serpent's Well and to the Refuse Gate, and I examined in detail the walls of Jerusalem, which were broken down, and its gates destroyed by fire. So I passed on to the Fountain Gate and to the King's Pool, but there was no place for the beast that was under me to pass. Then I went on up in the night by the valley carefully examining the wall, whereupon I turned back and entered by the Valley Gate and so returned. And the rulers did not know whither I had gone or what I had been doing, neither had I as yet told it to the Jews nor to the priests nor to the nobles, nor to the rulers nor to the rest who did the work.

Then I said to them,

"You see the serious condition in which we are, how Jerusalem is desolate and its gates are destroyed by fire. Come and let us rebuild the wall of Jerusalem, that we be no longer an object of reproach."

Then I told them of the good hand of my God that was with me, and also of the king's words that he said to me. Thereupon they said,

"Let us arise and build."

So they took courage for the good work. But when Sanballat the Horonite, and Tobiah the Ammonite slave, and Geshem the Arabian heard it they derided and despised us, and said,

"What is this thing that you are doing? Are you about to rebel against the king?"

Then I answered and said to them,

"The God of the heavens, he will prosper us, therefore we his servants will arise and build; but you have no portion nor right nor memorial in Jerusalem."

Now when Sanballat heard that we were rebuilding the wall, he was enraged and very indignant and derided the Jews. Accordingly he spoke before his kinsmen and the army of Samaria and said,

"What are these feeble Jews doing? Will they fortify themselves? Will they sacrifice? Will they finish it in a day? Will they revive the stones out of the rubbish heaps, although they are burned?"

Now Tobiah the Ammonite was with him, and he said,

"Even that which they are building, if a fox should go up he would break down their stone wall."

"Hear, O our God—for we are despised—and turn back their reproach upon their own head, and make them an object of plunder in a land of captivity, and cover not their iniquity and let not their sin be blotted out from thy sight, for they have provoked thee to anger before the builders."

So we built the wall; and all the wall was joined together to half its height, for the people had a mind to work. But when Sanballat, and Tobiah and the Arabians, and the Ammonites, and the Ashdodites heard that the restoration of the walls of Jerusalem was going forward so that the breaches began to be stopped, they were in a great rage. Accordingly all of them conspired together to come and make war on Jerusalem, and make confusion therein. But we made supplication to our God, and set a watch as a protection against them day and night.

Then Judah said,

"The strength of the burden-bearers is overtaxed, for there is much rubbish; so that we are not able to go on with the wall."

Moreover our adversaries said,

"They shall neither know nor see, until we come into their midst, and slay them and cause the work to cease."

And when the Jews came who dwelt beside them, they said to us ten times,

"From all the places where they dwell they will come up against us."

Therefore I assigned some of the lowest parts of the space behind the wall in the exposed places, and appointed the people according to families with their swords, their spears, and their bows. And when I saw, I arose and said to the nobles and to the rulers and to the rest of the people,

"Be not afraid of them. Remember the LORD, who is great and terrible, and fight for your kinsmen, your sons and your daughters, your wives and your houses."

Now when our enemies heard that it was known to us, and that God had frustrated their counsel, we all returned to the wall, each to his own task. Moreover from that day forth while half of my men went on with the work half of them held the spears, the shields, the bows and the coats of mail; and the rulers supported all the house of Judah. The builders on the wall and those who bore burdens were also armed, each with one hand carried on the work and with the other held his weapon; and each of the builders had his sword girded by his side as he built. And the trumpeter was by me. Moreover I said to the nobles and to the rulers and to the rest of the people,

"The work is great and far-extended, and we upon the wall are separated far from each other. In whatever place you hear the sound of the trumpet, rally to us there; our God will fight for us."

Thus we went on with the work, while half of them held the spears from the beginning of dawn until the stars came out. Also at that time I said to the people,

"Let each man with his servant lodge within Jerusalem, that they may be a guard to us by night and ready for the work by day."

So neither I, nor my kinsmen, nor my servants, nor the men of the guard who escorted me, none of us took off our clothes, each kept his weapon in his hand.

Now there arose a great outcry of the people and their wives against their Jewish kinsmen. For there were those who said,

"We are giving our sons and our daughters in pledge in order to secure grain that we may eat and live."

There were also those who were saying,

"We are giving our fields and our vineyards and our houses in pledge that we may secure grain because of the famine."

There were those too who were saying,

"We have borrowed money for the king's tribute. Now our flesh is as the flesh of our kinsmen, our children are as their children; but here we are bringing our sons and daughters into slavery, and some of our daughters are already enslaved; neither is it in our power to help it, for others possess our fields and our vineyards."

Then I was exceedingly angry when I heard their complaint and these assertions. Thereupon after thinking it over, I contended with the nobles and governors and said to them,

"You are taking interest each of his own kinsmen."

So I held a great assembly against them. And I said to them,

"We have, according to our ability, redeemed our Jewish kinsmen who have been sold to the nations; and would you yourselves even sell your kinsmen and should they sell themselves to us?"

Then they were silent and had nothing to say. Therefore I said,

"The thing that you are doing is not good. Ought you not to walk in the fear of our God, because of the reproach of the nations our enemies? For I also, my kinsmen and my servants, lend them money and grain. Let us, I pray you, leave off this interest. Restore now to them at once their fields, their vineyards, their olive yards, and their houses, the hundredth part of the money, the grain, the wine, and the oil that you exact of them."

Then they said,

"We will restore and will require nothing of them; we will do precisely as you say."

Then I called the priests and made them take oath to do according to this promise. Also I shook out the bosom of my garment, and said,

"So may God shake out every man from his house and from the fruit of his labor who does not keep this promise; even thus may he be shaken out and emptied."

And all the assembly said,

"Amen."

And they praised the Lord, and the people did according to this promise.

Moreover from the time that I was appointed to be their governor in the land of Judah, from the twentieth year and even to the thirty-second year of

Artaxerxes, the king, that is for twelve years, neither I nor my kinsmen had eaten the bread due the governor. But the former governors who were before me laid a heavy burden on the people, and took of them bread and wine, besides forty shekels of silver, also their servants domineered over the people. But I did not do so, because of the fear of God. Also I was occupied with the work of this wall, and we bought no land; and all my servants gathered there for the work. Moreover the Jews and the rulers, a hundred and fifty men, besides those who came to us from the surrounding nations, were at my table. Now that which was prepared for each day was one ox and six choice sheep and fowls. They were prepared for me, and once in ten days skins of wine in abundance. But even so I did not exact the bread due the governor, because the service was burdensome upon this people. Remember to my credit, O my God, all that I have done for this people.

Now when it was reported to Sanballat and Tobiah and to Geshem, the Arabian, and to the rest of our enemies, that I had rebuilt the wall and that there was no breach left in it—though even at that time I had not set up the doors in the gates—Sanballat and Geshem sent to me, saying,

"Come and let us meet together in one of the villages in the plain of Ono." But they intended me harm. So I sent messengers to them, saying,

"I am doing a great work, so that I cannot come down; why should the work cease, while I leave it and come down to you?"

But they sent to me four times in this manner, and I replied in the same manner. Then Sanballat sent his servant to me in the same manner a fifth time with an open letter in his hand, in which was written,

"It is reported among the nations, and Geshem affirms it, that you and the Jews are planning to rebel, therefore you are rebuilding the wall, and that you would be their king, and that you have also appointed prophets to preach of you at Jerusalem, saying, 'There is a king in Judah.' And now it will be reported to the king according to these words. Come now, therefore, and let us take counsel together."

Then I sent to him, saying,

"No such things as you say have been done, but you have invented them in your own mind."

For they all would terrify us, saying,

"Their hands shall be weakened from the work, that it may not be done." But do thou strengthen my hands.

Moreover when I went to the house of Shemaiah, the son of Delaiah, the son of Mehetabel, who was confined at home, he said,

"Let us meet together in the house of God, within the temple, and let us shut the doors of the temple for they are coming to slay you, and they are going to slay you by night."

But I said,

"Should a man like me flee? And how should anyone like me enter into the temple to save his life? I will not enter."

Then I perceived clearly that God had not sent him; but he declared his prophecy concerning me because Tobiah and Sanballat had hired him, that I might be afraid and act accordingly and sin; and furnish them an evil report, in order that they might reproach me. Remember, O my God, Tobiah and Sanballat according to these their works, and also the prophets, Noadiah and the rest of the prophets who would have frightened me.

So the wall was finished in the twenty-fifth day of Elul, in fifty-two days. And when all our enemies heard, all the nations round about us feared and fell decidedly in their own esteem, for they perceived that this work had been done with the help of our God.

Moreover in those days the nobles of Judah sent many letters to Tobiah, and those of Tobiah came to them. For many in Judah were under oath to him, because he was the son-in-law of Shechaniah, the son of Arah, and his son Jehohanan had married the daughter of Meshullam, the son of Berachiah. Also they were praising his good deeds before me and reporting my words to him. Then Tobiah sent letters to frighten me.

In these days I saw in Judah men treading wine presses on the sabbath and bringing in heaps of grain loaded on asses, also wine, grapes, figs, and all kinds of burdens which they brought into Jerusalem on the sabbath day; and I protested on the day when they sold provisions. Tyrians also dwelt therein, who brought in fish and all kinds of wares, and sold them on the sabbath to the Judeans and in Jerusalem. Then I contended with the nobles of Judah and said to them,

"What evil thing is this that you are doing, and thereby profaning the sabbath day? Did not your fathers do this and did not our God bring all this misfortune upon us and upon this city? Yet you are bringing more wrath upon Israel by profaning the sabbath."

Accordingly when the gates of Jerusalem began to be in darkness, before the sabbath, I commanded and the gates were shut; and I gave orders that they should not be opened until after the sabbath. And I put some of my servants in charge of the gates, that none should bring in a burden on the sabbath day. So the traders and sellers of all kinds of wares lodged outside Jerusalem once or twice. Then I warned them and said to them,

"Why do you lodge before the wall? If you repeat it, I shall arrest you."

From that time on they came no more on the sabbath. Moreover I gave orders to the Levites that they should purify themselves and that they should come and guard the gates, to keep the sabbath day holy. Remember, O my God, this also to my account and have compassion upon me according to the greatness of thy grace.

In those days also I saw the Jews who had married women of Ashdod, of Ammon, and of Moab, and their children spoke half in the language of

Ashdod, and none of them could speak in the Jews' language, but according to the language of each people. Therefore I contended with them and cursed them and beat some of them and pulled out their hair and made them swear by God, saying,

"You shall not give your daughters to their sons nor take their daughters as wives for your sons or for yourselves. Did not Solomon, king of Israel, sin by these means? Yet among many nations there was no king like him, and he was beloved by his God, and God made him king over all Israel; nevertheless foreign wives were the cause of his sin; and shall it be reported of you that you do all this great evil, and break faith with our God in marrying foreign women?"

Now one of the sons of Joiada, the son of Eliashib, the high priest, was the son-in-law of Sanballat, the Horonite; therefore I chased him from me. Remember them, O my God, because they have defiled the priesthood and the covenant of the priesthood and of the Levites. Thus I cleansed them from all foreigners and established the duties for the priests and the Levites, each for his own task, and for the wood-offering at appointed times, and the first fruits. Remember it, O my God, to my credit.

THE WISDOM OF DANIEL [1]

KING BELSHAZZAR made a great feast for a thousand of his lords, and drank wine before the thousand. Inflamed by the taste of the wine, Belshazzar gave orders to bring in the vessels of gold and silver, which his father Nebuchadnezzar had taken away from the temple at Jerusalem, that the king and his lords, his consorts and his concubines, might drink out of them. So they brought in the vessels of gold and silver, which had been taken away from the temple at Jerusalem; and the king and his lords, his consorts and his concubines, drank out of them. As they drank the wine, they praised the gods of gold and silver, bronze, iron, wood, and stone. Forthwith there appeared the fingers of a man's hand, which wrote on the plaster of the wall of the king's palace, opposite the lampstand; and the king saw the palm of the hand as it wrote. Then the king's face changed color, as his thoughts upset him; the joints of his loins relaxed, and his knees knocked one against another. The king called aloud for the enchanters, the Chaldeans, and the astrologers to be brought in; and the king addressed the wise men of Babylon, saying,

"Whosoever reads this writing, and gives me the interpretation of it, shall

[1] Selected from the book of *Daniel*, chapters 5:1-6:28. The book was written about the year 165 B.C.E. to encourage the Jews not to submit to the attempt of Antiochus Epiphanes (175-164 B.C.E.) to compel them to abandon their worship, but to remain faithful to their God and their Law.

be clothed with purple, and shall have a chain of gold round his neck, and shall be third ruler in the kingdom."

But when all the king's wise men came in, they could not read the writing, nor make known to the king the interpretation of it. Then was King Belshazzar greatly upset, and he changed color; his lords also were thrown into consternation. At the cries of the king and his lords, the queen-mother came into the banqueting-hall; and the queen-mother addressed him, saying,

"O king, live forever! Let not your thoughts upset you, nor your face change color. There is in your kingdom a man in whom is the spirit of the holy gods. In the days of your father there was found in him light, and understanding, and wisdom, like the wisdom of the gods, so that King Nebuchadnezzar, your father, made him chief of the magicians, enchanters, Chaldeans, and astrologers, because there was found in this Daniel, whom the king named Belteshazzar, surpassing ability, knowledge, understanding, and skill in interpreting dreams, solving riddles, and unravelling knots. Let Daniel be called in, then, and he will give the interpretation."

So Daniel was brought in before the king; and the king addressed Daniel, saying,

"You are Daniel, of the exiled of Judah, whom my father the king brought from Judah! I have heard of you, that the spirit of the gods is in you, and that light, and understanding, and surpassing wisdom are found in you. Now the wise men, the enchanters, have been brought in before me, that they might read this writing, and make known to me the interpretation of it; but they could not give the interpretation of the thing. I have heard of you, however, that you can give interpretations, and unravel knots. Now, if you can read the writing, and make known to me the interpretation of it, you shall be clothed with purple, and shall have a chain of gold round your neck, and shall be third ruler in the kingdom."

Then Daniel answered the king, saying,

"Keep your gifts for yourself, and give your rewards to another; but I will read the writings to the king, and make known to him the interpretation of it. O king, the Most High God gave Nebuchadnezzar your father the kingdom, with its greatness, its glory, and its majesty; and because of the greatness that he gave him, all the peoples, nations, and tongues trembled in fear before him— whom he would he slew, and whom he would he kept alive, whom he would he raised up, and whom he would he put down. But when his mind was lifted up, and his spirit became obstinate, so that he bore himself proudly, he was deposed from his kingly throne, and deprived of his glory, he was driven from among men, and his mind was made like that of the beasts, his dwelling was with the wild asses, he was given grass to eat like an ox, and his person was drenched by the dew of the heavens, till he learned that the Most High God rules the kingdom of men, setting over it whom he will. And you his son, O Belshazzar, have not humbled yourself, though you knew all this, but have lifted yourself up against the Lord of the heavens, in that you have had the vessels of his house brought in before you, and have drunk wine out of them— you and your lords, your consorts and your concubines—and have praised the gods of silver and gold, bronze, iron, wood, and stone, which can neither see nor hear nor understand, and have not glorified the God in whose hand our breath is, and to whom belong all your ways. From him, then, has the palm of the hand been sent, and this writing inscribed. This is the writing that has been inscribed: Mene, Tekel, and Peres. And this is the interpretation of the thing: Mene—God has numbered your kingdom, and brought it to an end; Tekel—you have been weighed in the scales, and found wanting; Peres—your kingdom is divided, and given to the Medes and Persians."

Then Belshazzar gave orders, and Daniel was clothed with purple, and had a chain of gold put round his neck, while a proclamation was made concerning him, that he should be third ruler in the kingdom.

That night Belshazzar, the king of Chaldea, was slain; and Dairius, the Mede, received the kingdom, being then about sixty-two years of age.

It pleased Darius to set over the kingdom a hundred and twenty satraps, to administer the whole kingdom, and over them three presidents, of whom Daniel was one, that the satraps might be responsible to them, and the king might suffer no loss. And Daniel distinguished himself above all the presidents and satraps, because surpassing ability was in him; and the king was disposed to set him over the whole kingdom.

Then the presidents and satraps sought to find some ground of complaint against Daniel in connection with his administration of the kingdom; but they could find no ground of complaint or fault, because he was faithful, and no error or fault was to be found in him. So these men said,

"We shall find no ground of complaint against this Daniel, unless we find it in connection with the law of his God."

Then these presidents and satraps thronged to the king, and addressed him as follows:

"O King Darius, live forever! All the presidents of the kingdom, the prefects and the satraps, the ministers and the governors, have agreed in council that the king should lay down a statute, and pass a strict interdict, to the effect that whosoever shall offer a petition to any god or man for thirty days, except to you, O king, shall be cast into the den of lions. Now, O king, lay down the interdict, and sign the document, so that it may not be changed, in accordance with the law of the Medes and Persians, which is unalterable."

Accordingly, King Darius signed the document containing the interdict. Now, when Daniel learned that the document had been signed, he went to his house—which had windows in its upper chamber open toward Jerusalem— and three times a day he continued kneeling upon his knees, praying, and giving thanks before his God, as he used formerly to do. Then these men thronged in, and found Daniel offering petitions and supplications before his God. So they approached the king, and questioned him concerning the king's interdict,

"Did you not sign an interdict, to the effect that whosoever should offer a petition to any god or man for thirty days, except to you, O king, should be cast into the den of lions?"

The king answered, saying,

"The thing stands fast, in accordance with the law of the Medes and Persians, which is unalterable."

Then they answered the king, saying,

"This Daniel, of the exiles of Judah, pays no regard to yourself, O king, nor to the interdict which you have signed, but three times a day he continues offering his own petitions."

When the king heard these words, he was deeply grieved, and applied his mind to saving Daniel; till sunset he exerted himself to rescue him. Then these men thronged to the king, and said to the king,

"You are aware, O king, that it is a law of the Medes and Persians that no interdict or statute which the king lays down can be changed."

So the king gave orders, and Daniel was brought forward, and cast into the den of lions. And the king addressed Daniel, saying,

"May your God, whom you worship consistently, save you!"

Then a stone was brought forward, and laid upon the mouth of the den; and the king sealed it with his own signet, as well as with the signet of his lords, so that no change might be made in respect to Daniel. Then the king went to his palace, and spent the night fasting; no diversions were brought to him, and his sleep fled from him. Then at dawn, as soon as it was light, the king arose, and went in haste to the den of lions. When he came near the den, where Daniel was, the king cried out with a sorrowful voice, and spoke to Daniel, saying,

"O Daniel, servant of the living God, has your God, whom you worship consistently, been able to save you from the lions?"

Then Daniel answered the king, saying,

"O king, live forever! My God has sent his angel, and has shut the mouths of the lions, so that they have not injured me; because I was found innocent before him, and before you also, O king, have I done no injury."

At these words the king was exceedingly glad, and gave orders that Daniel should be taken out of the den. And when Daniel was taken out of the den, no kind of injury was found on him, because he had trusted in his God. Then the king gave orders, and the men who had accused Daniel were brought forward—they, and their children, and their wives—and cast into the den of lions; and before they had reached the bottom of the den, the lions fell upon them, and crushed all their bones to pieces. Then King Darius wrote as follows to all the peoples, nations, and tongues, that live in all the earth:

"Peace be multiplied to you! I hereby make a decree that throughout all the kingdom which I rule men shall tremble in reverence before the God of Daniel;

> For he is the living God,
> Immutable forever;
> His kingdom is one that shall never be overthrown,
> And his dominion is one that shall endure to the end;
> He saves, and he delivers,
> He does signs and wonders
>   In the heavens and in the earth;
> It is he who has saved Daniel
>   From the power of the lions."

So this Daniel prospered during the reign of Darius, and during the reign of Cyrus the Persian.

SUSANNA AND THE ELDERS[1]

THERE lived in Babylon a man called Joakim who married Susanna, the daughter of Chelkias. She was exceedingly beautiful and pious. Her parents also were righteous, and educated their daughter according to the teaching of Moses.

Now Joakim was a very rich man and owned a fair garden adjoining his house. And all the Jews came to him for counsel because he was more respected than all the others.

After the year of Joakim's marriage two of the elders were appointed judges. These men were wicked, such as the Lord spoke of when He said that wickedness came from the elder judges of Babylon. They spent most of their time in Joakim's house, and whoever had a lawsuit went to them.

Now when the people departed at noon, Susanna would stroll in her husband's garden. The two elders saw her enter the garden and stroll every day, and their lust was excited by her beauty. Their minds became distracted so that they disregarded their religion and ceased to render just decisions. Although both of them were aroused by their love for her, one did not disclose his grief

---

[1] The tale of Susanna is one of the most charming stories of the Apocrypha. It has often been called the first detective story, but was probably written (in Hebrew) about the year 90 B.C.E., in the heat of a nationalist revival, to vindicate capital punishment for false witnesses and to impress upon its readers the value of cross-examination of witnesses. The suggestion of immorality among the upper classes precluded the popularity of this skillful tale in the Church and the Synagogue. In 1826 the subscribers of the British and Foreign Bible Society voted a resolution forbidding the distribution of Susanna;—"these unhallowed productions of the wisdom and folly of men that have been so presumptuously associated with the sacred oracles of God." Translated from the Greek by Leo W. Schwarz.

to the other, for they were ashamed to admit their lust and that they desired to have to do with her. Yet they watched attentively from day to day to see her.

Once one elder said to the other,

"Let us go home now, for it is time for the midday meal."

Then as soon as they had left and had separated, they returned to the same place. And after they asked one another the reason and acknowledged their lust, they agreed to meet at a time when they might find her alone.

Now it happened that as they watched at the appointed hour, she entered the garden as usual with only two maidservants. She wanted to bathe because it was hot. There was nobody there except the two elders who had hidden themselves, and watched her. Then she said to her maids, "Bring me oil and soap, and shut the garden doors so that I may bathe." And they did as she asked them, and shut the garden doors and left by a side door to fetch the things that she had ordered. But they did not see the elders because they were hidden.

When the maidservants had left, the two elders got up, ran toward her, and said, "See, the garden doors are closed so that no one can see us. We are in love with you; therefore yield to us and lie with us."

Then Susanna cried aloud and said,

"I am between Death and Satan: for if I do this thing, it will mean my end; if I do not, I cannot escape from you. It is better for me to fall into your power, and not to do it, than to sin in the sight of the Lord." Whereupon Susanna screamed, and the two elders cried out against her. Then one ran and opened the garden door. As soon as the servants of the house heard the cry in the garden, they rushed in at the side door to see what had happened to her. But when the elders told their story, the servants were greatly ashamed; for there had never been such a report made of Susanna.

And it came to pass the next day when the people were assembled before her husband, Joakim, there came also the two elders, bewitched with their evil plotting against Susanna, to put her to death.

In the presence of the people, they said,

"Send for Susanna, the daughter of Chelkias, Joakim's wife."

So they sent for her, and she came with her father and mother, her children, and all her relatives.

Now Susanna was a very delicate woman and beautiful to look upon. And these wicked men commanded that her face be unveiled that they might gratify themselves with her beauty. Therefore her friends and all who saw her wept. Then the two elders stood up in the midst of the people, and laid their hands upon her head. And she, weeping, looked up toward heaven, for she trusted in the Lord.

And the elders said,

"As we walked in the garden alone, this woman came in with two maidservants and shut the garden doors, and dismissed the maids. Then a young man who was hidden there, came to her and lay with her. Then we, standing in a corner of the garden, saw this wickedness and ran toward them. And when we saw them together, we could not hold the man, for being stronger than we, he opened the door, and leaped out. But having taken this woman, we asked who the man was, but she would not tell us. To these facts do we testify."

Then the assembly believed them since they were the elders and judges of the people. So they condemned her to death.

Then Susanna cried out with a loud voice,

"O everlasting God, who knowest the untold things and all things before they happen, Thou knowest that they have borne false witness against me; and, behold, I must die, even though I never did such things as these men have maliciously invented against me."

And the Lord hearkened to her lamentation. Therefore when she was led to be put to death, the Lord incited the holy spirit of a young lad, whose name was Daniel. He cried aloud,

"I am innocent of the blood of this woman!"

Then all the people turned toward him, and asked,

"What is the meaning of what you said?"

So he, standing in the midst of them, said,

"Are you such fools, O children of Israel, that, without examination or knowledge of the truth, you would condemn a daughter of Israel? Return again to the court, for they have borne false witness against her."

Then all the people returned hastily, and the elders said to him,

"Come, sit down among us, and prove your accusation, since God has given you the honor of an elder."

And Daniel said to them,

"Separate these two, and I will cross-examine them."

So when they were separated from each other, he called one of them and said,

"O you who has grown old in wickedness, now all the sins which you have committed in former times have come to light. For you have pronounced false judgment and have condemned the innocent, and have freed the guilty, despite the word of the Lord: 'The innocent and the righteous thou shalt not slay.' Now then, if you saw her, tell me, under what kind of a tree did you see them together?"

He answered,

"Under a mastic tree."

And Daniel said,

"Very well. You have lied against yourself, for even now the divine angel has viewed God's sentence to cut you in two."

So he dismissed him, and commanded them to bring the other. To him he said,

"O you seed of Canaan, and not Judah, beauty has deceived you, and lust has perverted your heart. So have you dealt with the daughters of Israel and for fear they have been your lovers. But the daughter of Judah would not submit to your wickedness. Now, therefore, tell me, under what kind of a tree did you see them together?"

He answered,

"An elm tree."

Then Daniel said to him,

"It is well. You have lied against yourself, for the divine angel is waiting with a sword to destroy you, to cut you in two."

Whereupon the whole assembly cried aloud, and praised God who saves them who trust Him. And they arose against the two elders, for Daniel had convicted them of false witness by their own confession. And according to the law of Moses they treated them as they maliciously intended to do to their neighbor. And they put them to death. Thus on that day an innocent soul was saved.

Therefore Chelkias and his wife praised God for their daughter Susanna, with Joakim her husband, and all the kinsmen because no dishonesty had been found in her.

From that day on Daniel was held in great respect by the people.

THE SECRET ENTRANCE [1]

KING ASTYGES was gathered to his fathers, and Cyrus of Persia received his kingdom. And Daniel was intimate with the king, and was honored above all his friends.

Now the Babylonians had an idol called Bel, and every day they provided it with twelve large measures of fine flour, and forty sheep, and six vessels of wine. And the king worshipped it and went daily to praise it, but Daniel worshipped his own God. And the king said to him,

"Why do you not worship Bel?"

He answered,

"Because I may not worship idols made with hands, but the living God who created the heavens and the earth, and rules over all flesh."

Then the king said to him,

[1] This story, more commonly known as *The Destruction of Bel,* is selected from the Apocrypha. The author is unknown, and although the story is preserved in Greek, it was originally written in Hebrew or Aramaic in the second century B.C.E. The story teaches the speciousness of idolatry and the duty of worshiping the God of the Universe. *The Secret Entrance* proves, as does *Jonah* and the book of *Job,* that post-exilic Judaism was not totally "legalistic" and "exclusive" but, as the late Prof. George F. Moore pointed out, "The influence of the prophets on the religion of the people was in fact the greatest in the age in which it is supposed to have been finally suffocated by the law." Translation by Leo W. Schwarz.

"Do you not think that Bel is a living God? Do you not see how much he eats and drinks every day?"

But Daniel smiled and said,

"O king, be not deceived, for this idol is but clay within and brass without, and did never really eat or drink anything."

So the king was furious, and called for his priests, and said to them,

"If you do not tell me who it is that devours these foods, you shall die. But if you can prove to me that Bel devours them, Daniel shall die, for he has spoken evilly against Bel."

And Daniel said to the king,

"Let it be according to your command."

Now the priests of Bel were threescore and ten, beside their wives and children. And the king went with Daniel into the temple of Bel. Then the priests said,

"Lo, we are going out, but you, O king, may set on the meat, and make ready the wine, and shut the door fast, and seal it with your signet. And to-morrow when you enter, if you find that Bel has not eaten up everything, we shall die; if not, it shall be Daniel who speaks falsely against us."

And they were not very much concerned, for under the table they had made a secret entrance through which they continually entered and ate those things.

So as soon as they had left, the king set the food before Bel.

Now Daniel had commanded his servants to bring ashes which they strew over the floor in the presence of the king alone. Then they went out and shut the door, and sealed it with the king's signet. And so they departed.

In the night the priests with their wives and children came in accordance with their custom, and ate and drank everything.

The king and Daniel arose early in the morning. And the king said,

"Daniel, are the seals whole?"

And he said,

"Yes, O king, they are whole."

And as soon as he opened the door, the king looked upon the table, and cried aloud,

"Great art thou, O Bel, and with thee there is no deceit at all."

Then Daniel laughed, and grasped the king so that he should not enter, and said,

"Now look at the pavement, and notice well whose footsteps there are."

And the king said,

"I see the footsteps of men, women, and children."

And then the king became angry. And he took the priests with their wives and children, who showed him the secret doors where they entered so that they could eat up whatever was upon the table, and he killed them. He delivered Bel into the power of Daniel who destroyed him and his temple.

JUDITH AND HOLOFERNES [1]

Now Holofernes, commander of the armies of Nebuhadnezzar, king of Assyria, and his army marched down toward the seacoast and built garrisons in the high cities, and took out of them picked men for allies. And the people of the cities and the surrounding country received them with garlands and timbrels and dances. But he demolished all their borders and cut down their groves and destroyed all their gods so that all the nations should worship only Nebuhadnezzar, and should regard him as god. And he marched toward Esdrælon near to Judæa, which is over against the mountains of Judæa, and he pitched camp between Geba and Scythopolis, and he remained there a whole month in order to collect all the baggage of his army.

And the children of Israel who lived in Judæa heard all that Holofernes had done to the nations, how he had plundered all their temples and completely ruined them, and they were terrified and distressed for Jerusalem and for the Temple of the Lord inasmuch as they had recently returned from the captivity and all the people of Judæa had been only recently gathered together, and the holy vessels and the altar and the Temple were purified after their profanations. So they sent men to the villages along the coast of Samaria and to Bethoron and Belmaim and Jericho and Koba and Æsora and to the valley of Salem, and they took possession of all the summits of the high mountains and they fortified the villages that were in them, and they stored away food as provisions for war (for their fields had been recently harvested). And Joakim, the High Priest in Jerusalem, wrote to the residents of Betulia and Betomestaim (which is over against Esdrælon toward the plain that is near to Dotaim) commanding them to guard the roads of the hill country because Judæa could be entered through them and, because the approach was narrow with room for no more than two men, it was easy to stop those who came up. And the children of Israel did as Joakim the High Priest and the elders of all the people in Jerusalem had commanded them.

And every man of Israel cried out to God with great fervor and humbled themselves, and they and their wives and their children and their cattle and every stranger and the inhabitants of Jerusalem put on sackcloth and cast ashes on their heads, and they put sackcloth about the altar and prostrated themselves before the Temple. And they cried out to the God of Israel that he should not

---

[1] *Judith* is probably the best known of the apocryphal tales. A stirring plot is enhanced by many details that give a living picture of the social traditions during the second century B.C.E. Prof. A. E. Cowley writes: ". . . the literary excellence of the work is universally recognized even through the uncomely guise of the Greek translation. It was originally written in Hebrew (now lost) for Jewish readers, with the object of encouraging and edifying the people in a time of trial and persecution. In order to carry conviction the more, it aims at the appearance of being historical in its use of well-known names and of precise details, but this historical character is only apparent. . . ." The present translation (abridged) is by Leo W. Schwarz.

give their infants for prey, their wives for spoil, their inherited cities for destruction, and the sanctuary for desecration and opprobrium, a laughing-stock for the nations. And the Lord heard their plea and had mercy upon their affliction, for the people had fasted many days throughout Judæa and in Jerusalem before the sanctuary of Almighty God. And Joakim the High Priest and all the priests and the Levites girded their loins with sackcloth and offered daily burnt-offerings together with the vows and the free gifts of the people; and they put ashes on their mitres and they cried out to God with all their strength so that he would act mercifully toward the House of Israel.

And it was reported to Holofernes, the commander of the Assyrian army, that the children of Israel had prepared for war, had obstructed the roads in the hill country, had fortified the summits of all the high hills and had built blockades in the plains. And he was very angry and summoned all the princes of Moab, the commanders of Ammon, and all the rulers of the sea-coast, and said to them, "O Canaanites, please tell me who is this people which lives in the hill country, which cities they dwell in, how numerous are their forces, wherein is their strength, what king rules over them and leads their army and why are they determined not to respect me as have all the other people of the West?" And Akior, the leader of all the children of Ammon, said to him, "Let my lord listen to an account from the mouth of your servant and I will relate the truth about this people which lives in the hill country near to where you are dwelling, and no lie shall come out of the mouth of your servant. This people is descended from the Chaldeans, and they lived previously in Mesopotamia because they refused to follow the gods of their forefathers who dwelt in Chaldea. Then they diverged from the ways of their forefathers and worshipped the God of heaven whom they knew. So they were driven out of the presence of their gods and fled into Mesopotamia where they sojourned a long time. But their God commanded them to depart from this country and to go to the land of Canaan. And they lived there and grew in riches and their flocks prospered. When a famine raged in the land they went down to Egypt where they sojourned until they waxed strong and their people were innumerable. Then the king of Egypt rose up against them and persecuted them and made them slaves. And they appealed to their God and He smote all of Egypt with incurable plagues so that the Egyptians expelled them; and God dried up the Red Sea and led them by way of Sinai and Kadesh Barnea, and they drove away all the inhabitants of the wilderness. Then they dwelt in the land of the Amorites, and by their power they destroyed all the Heshbonites and, passing over the Jordan, they took possession of all the hill country. And they drove out of the country the Canaanites, the Perizzites, the Jebusites, the Shehemites and all the Girgashites, and they dwelt in that country for a long time. And as long as they sinned not against their God who hates iniquity, He was with them, but when they departed from His laws, they were defeated in many brutal battles and were led away into a foreign land and the Temple of their

God was demolished and their cities were captured by their enemies. But now they have returned to their God and have come back from their dispersion and taken possession of Jerusalem, where their sanctuary is, and dwell in the hill country which was desolate. But now, my lord and master, if they are again sinning against their God, then this is their ruin and punishment, for let us go up and conquer them. But if their people is not lawless, let my lord not interfere lest their Lord defend them and we shall be shamed before the whole world."

Now when Akior had finished his address, all those who surrounded the tent murmured against him, and the captains and nobles of Holofernes and those who dwell by the sea-coast and the Moabites advised their lord to kill him. "We shall not be frightened by the children of Israel," they said, "for lo! they are a people without the power or strength to wage a mighty war. So let us go up, and, lord Holofernes, they will be merely a prey to be devoured by your army."

And when the tumult of the council members ceased, Holofernes, the commander of the army of Assyria, said to Akior, "Who are you, Akior, that you have prophesied among us today, advising that we should not fight against the people of Israel because their God will defend them? Who is God but Nebuhadnezzar? He shall wipe them from the face of the earth, and their God will not save them, but we will utterly destroy them." Then Holofernes commanded his servants, who were waiting in the tent, to take Akior back to Betulia, and deliver him to the Israelites. And they presented him to the rulers of Betulia who assembled all the elders of the city and all the men and the women, and they placed Akior in the midst of the people. And Ozias asked him what had happened, and he answered and related the declaration of the council of Holofernes, and everything that Holofernes had said against the House of Israel. Then the people prostrated themselves and worshipped God, and cried aloud, "O Lord, God of heaven, behold their arrogance, and have mercy upon the helplessness of our people, and assist those who are holy to Thee this day." And they comforted Akior and gave him praise without end. And Ozias took him from the assembly to his house, and made a feast for the elders; and they called upon the God of Israel for help all that night.

Now at that time a report of this reached the ears of Judith, the daughter of Merari. Her husband, Manasses, of her tribe and her family, had died during the barley harvest, for as he stood in the field over the workers who bound the sheaves the heat struck his head and he was forced to his bed, and he died in Betulia; and they buried him with his fathers in the field between Dotaim and Balamon. So Judith was a widow in her house three years and four months: and she built her tent upon the roof of her house and put sackcloth about her loins and wore a widow's garments. And she fasted all the days of her widowhood except the sabbath-eves and the sabbaths and the eves and the days of the new moon and the feasts and days of joy of the House of Israel.

And she had a lovely countenance, most beautiful to look upon; and her husband Manasses left her gold and silver, menservants and maidservants, cattle and property; and she lived on them. And no one spoke an evil word against her for she was pious and God-fearing.

Now when she heard the murmurings of the people against the governor, because they fainted for lack of water, and how Ozias swore that he would deliver the city to the Assyrians after five days, she sent her head maid to summon Ozias and Kabris and Karmis, the elders; and when they came, she said to them,

"Hear me now, O rulers of the residents of Betulia, for the declaration that you have made in the presence of the people today is not just, nor the oath that you have sworn between God and yourselves, promising to abandon the city to our enemies unless within a short time the Lord will come to your aid. Who are you that you should tempt God and take his place among humankind? Now you may probe the Almighty God but you will never know anything. For you will not plumb the depth of the human heart nor can you fathom what man thinks: How, then, can you search out God, the Maker of all these things, and know His mind and comprehend His intention? No, my brethren, do not provoke the Lord our God to anger, for if it is not His intention to aid us within these five days, He has the power to defend us or to destroy us in the presence of our enemies at His will. Do not bind by oaths the counsels of the Lord, for God is not like man that he should be threatened or like the son of man that His intention should falter. Let us wait, then, for His salvation and call upon Him to keep us and if it please Him, He will hear our petition. And now, let us set an example for our brethren because they depend upon us, and the sanctuary and the Temple and the altar rest upon us. Let us also give thanks to the Lord our God who tests us even as He did our fathers. Remember all that He did to Abraham, how He tried Isaac, and all that happened to Jacob in Mesopotamia. He has not tried us in the fire, as He did them, to probe their hearts, nor has He taken vengeance upon us."

And Ozias said to her, "All that you have declared you have spoken with a good heart, and no one shall contradict the truth of it. This is not the first time that you have shown your wisdom but from your early days all the people have known your understanding and the goodness of your heart. But the people were very thirsty and compelled us to speak as we did, and to take an oath which we will not break. Now do you pray for us, for you are a good woman, so that the Lord will send us rain to fill our cisterns and we may no longer be thirsty." And Judith answered, "Listen now; and I shall accomplish something which will be remembered by all the generations of the human race. Tonight you shall stand at the city-gate, and I will leave with my maid, and within the time that you said you would surrender the city to our enemies, the Lord will visit Israel through me. But do not ask about my plan for I will not reveal it until the thing that I will do be accomplished." And Ozias and the rulers said to her, "Go in peace; and the Lord God guide you to take vengeance upon our enemies." And they left the tent and returned to their quarters.

Then Judith prostrated herself and put ashes upon her head and took off the sackcloth that she was wearing. And the evening incense was being offered up in Jerusalem in the House of God, and Judith cried aloud to the Lord and uttered a long prayer, asking Him to help her accomplish her plan and to take vengeance upon the enemies of Israel. And when she had ceased pleading with God, she rose up where she had prostrated herself and called her maid and went into the house wherein she dwelt on the sabbath and feast days; and she took off the garments of her widowhood and washed her whole body with water, and anointed herself with rich ointment and braided her hair and put on a headdress, and clothed herself in bright garments which she was accustomed to wear while her husband Manasses was alive. And she put sandals on her feet and ornaments about her hair, and her rings, her earrings and all her jewels; she adorned herself exquisitely to beguile any man who might see her. And she gave her maid a skin of wine and a cruse of oil, and filled a bag with dried corn and clusters of figs and fine bread; and she packed all these into one bundle and put them upon her back.

Then they went to the city-gate of Betulia where they found Ozias and the elders of the city standing. But when they saw how different she looked, they were amazed at her beauty, and said to her, "May the God of our fathers look kindly upon you and accomplish your purpose to the glory of the children of Israel and to the exaltation of Jerusalem!" And she prayed to God, and said to them, "Command that the city-gate be opened for me and I will proceed to accomplish my plan." So they commanded the young men to open the gate, as she had requested, and they did so.

Then Judith and her handmaid went forth and the men of the city watched her until she had walked down the mountain and had passed the valley and they could no longer see her. And they walked forward in the valley. And the Assyrian watch met her and seized her and asked, "Of what people are you? whence do you come? whither bound?" And she answered, "I am a daughter of the Hebrews, and I fled from them because they are about to fall into your hands; and I am going to Holofernes, your commander, to speak the truth. And I will reveal a road by which he shall be able to march and capture the whole hill country without the loss of a single life." And when the men heard this and saw how exceedingly beautiful she was, they said to her, "Because you have hastened to come down to our lord, you have saved your life; and some of us will conduct you to him. And when you stand before him, fear not but declare all that you have related, and he will treat you well." And they picked a hundred men to accompany her and her maid, and they brought them to the tent of Holofernes.

Now the whole camp assembled and surrounded her (for the report of her appearance had spread abroad among the tents) as she stood outside the tent of Holofernes until they told him of her. And they marvelled at her beauty and at the children of Israel because of her, and each one said to the other, "Who can despise a people that have such women among them? It is not good that even one man of Israel remain alive, for if they are not interfered with, they will be able to deceive the whole earth." And the companions and servants of Holofernes went and brought her into the tent. And Holofernes was resting upon his bed under the canopy which was woven with purple and gold, and emerald and precious stones; and they told him of her so he came out into the space before his tent with lamps of silver lighting the way. And when Judith stood before him and his servants, they all marvelled at her beauty. Then she fell down in obeisance and paid homage to him but his servants raised her up.

And Holofernes said to her, "Woman, be comforted and have no fear for I never harm one who has chosen to serve Nebuhadnezzar, the king of the earth. If your people in the hill country had not set themselves against me, I would not have declared war against them. But they themselves are responsible. And now tell me why you fled from them and came to us, for you have come to save yourself. Be comforted, and you shall live tonight and afterwards; no one shall harm you but all will treat you well as is done to the servants of my lord, king Nebuhadnezzar."

Then Judith said to him, "Accept the declaration of your servant and permit your handmaid to speak before you, and be assured I will tell no lie to my lord this night. And if you will follow the counsel of your handmaid, God will accomplish what I declare and my lord will not fail in his object. Now we have heard that which Akior did declare in your council, for the men of Betulia rescued him and he told them all that he had declared to you. I beg you, O lord and master, do not overlook his counsel but lay it up in your heart, for it is true: our race shall not be punished, neither shall the sword prevail against it unless they sin against their God. But now their sin has overtaken them so that my lord will not be defeated nor will his purpose be frustrated and death will devour them, for they shall provoke the anger of their God. Because their food failed them and their water supply was meagre they decided to take their cattle and consume those things which the laws of God forbid them to eat, and they have resolved to use the first fruits of the corn and the tenth part of the wine and the oil which they had sanctified and set aside for the priests of the Temple in Jerusalem, all foods which the people are not permitted to even touch with their hands. And they have sent messengers to Jerusalem where the inhabitants have also committed this sin, to fetch for them a decree from the Senate. Now when they receive this by the hand of a messenger, on the day that they will commit this sin, they shall be surrendered to you for destruction. That is why I fled from them; and God sent me to perform for you acts such as will make the whole earth marvel. For your servant is religious and serves the God of heaven day and night. And now I will abide with you, and I shall go out into the valley by night to pray to God and He will tell me when they shall have committed their sins. Then I will come and declare it to you and you will march with your whole army and no one will resist you. I will guide you through Judæa until you reach Jerusalem, and I will set you in the midst of the city; and you will drive them like sheep without a shepherd and even a dog will not so much as open his mouth before you, for all this was revealed and declared to me through my foreknowledge, and I was sent to tell you."

And her words pleased Holofernes and his servants. They wondered at her wisdom and said, "There is not another woman from one end of the earth to the other who can compare with you in beauty or wisdom." And Holofernes said, "God did well to send you before the people so that you might possess power and bring destruction to those who despised my lord. Your face is beautiful and your speech is wise, and if you will do as you have declared then your God shall be my God and you will dwell in the palace of Nebuhadnezzar and will be renowned throughout the whole earth."

Then he commanded that she be ushered into the room where his silver vessels were set and ordered his own food to be prepared for her and that she should drink from his own wine. But Judith said, "I will not eat of these things lest it prove a stumbling-block, but provision shall be made for me out of the food that I brought with me." And Holofernes said, "But if the food that you brought be wanting, whence shall we be able to find more? For none of your people is amongst us." And Judith answered, "As you live, my lord, your servant will not consume the food that she possesses until the Lord accomplished by my hand what he has determined." And the servants of Holofernes led her into the tent where she slept until midnight, and toward the morning watch she arose and sent a message to Holofernes, saying, "Let my lord now command that they permit your servant to go forth to pray." And Holofernes ordered his guards not to prevent her; and she dwelt in the camp three days and every night she went out into the valley of Betulia and bathed at the water fountain in the camp. Then she begged the Lord God of Israel to guide her in saving His people. And she returned clean and remained in her tent until she ate in the evening.

Now on the fourth day Holofernes made a banquet for his own servants and invited none of the officers. And he said to Bagoas, the eunuch, who was in charge of all his possessions, "Go now and persuade this Hebrew woman to come here and to eat and drink with us. For if we allow such a woman to depart without having had her company and we draw her close to us, it will be to our discredit and she will laugh us to scorn." So Bagoas left Holofernes and went to her and said, "Let not this beautiful woman fear to come before my lord and to drink wine and be merry with us, and to be made today as one of the daughters of Asshur, who serve in the palace of Nebuhadnezzar." And Judith said, "Who am I that I should be contrary to my lord? Whatever

he desires I will do speedily, and this shall be my joy to the day of my death."
And she arose and clothed herself in all her raiment, and her servant went and
laid the fleeces which she had received from Bagoas for her daily use on the
ground opposite Holofernes so that she might sit and eat on them. And Judith
entered the tent and sat down, and Holofernes said to her, "Now drink and
be merry with us." And Judith answered, "I will drink now, my lord, because
I am exalted today more than all the time since I was born." And she took and
ate and drank before him what her servant had prepared. And Holofernes was
delighted with her and drank much wine, more than he had ever drunk in any
one day.

When evening came on, his servants hastened to depart, and Bagoas shut
the tent from the outside and dismissed all the attendants. And they all went
to sleep for they were all weary because the banquet had lasted a long time.
But Judith remained alone in the tent and Holofernes, glutted with wine, was
stretched out upon his bed. And Judith asked her servant to stand outside her
tent and wait until she went out to pray, as she did daily, and she spoke of this
to Bagoas. Then all left and no one remained, neither great nor small, in the
bedchamber; and Judith, standing beside his bed, said in her heart, "O Lord,
God of all dominion, at this hour watch over the work of my hands for the
glory of Jerusalem, for now is the time to help your people, and carry out my
plan for the destruction of our enemies." And she went to the rail of the bed
where Holofernes' head was resting, and took down his scimitar; and she went
close to the bed and took hold of his hair and said, "O Lord, God of Israel,
strengthen me now." And she smote his neck twice with all her strength and
took away his head from his body and pushed the body off the bed and pulled
down the canopy from the pillars. And after a short time she left and gave
Holofernes' head to her maid who put it in the food-bag. And both of them
went out together to pray in accordance with their custom. And they passed
through the camp and went through the valley and walked up to the mountain
of Betulia until they reached its gates.

Then Judith shouted from a distance to the watchmen, "Open, open the
gate. God is with us to exhibit His power through Israel and His might against
the enemy, even as He has done this day." When the men heard her voice they
hastened down to the city-gate, and they called the elders and they all ran together, both great and small (for it seemed strange to them that she had returned), and they opened the gate. After they had made a fire for light, they
surrounded her, and she said to them, "Praise God, praise God, praise God
who has not deprived the House of Israel of His mercy but has destroyed our
enemies tonight by my hand." And she took the head out of the bag and displayed it and said, "Here is the head of Holofernes, the commander of the
Assyrian army, and here is the canopy in which he was lying in his drunkenness. The Lord smote him by the hand of a woman, and, by the God who
preserved me in the way that I went, I swear that it was my face that deceived

him and led to his destruction; neither did he commit sin with me, nor defile me nor shame me." And all the people marvelled, and bowed down and worshipped God and said in unison, "Blessed art Thou, O our God, who has brought destruction to our enemies this day." And Ozias said to her, "May you be blessed, daughter, in the eyes of the Most High God, above all the women upon the earth, and blessed is the Lord God who created the heavens and the earth, who guided you in cutting off the head of the prince of our enemies. And may God make these things for an eternal memorial to you and visit you only with good, since you did not spare your life because of the affliction of our race, but avenged our lot, walking humbly before our God." And all the people answered, "So be it, so be it."

And Judith said to them, "Listen to me further, my brethren: take this head and hang it upon the battlement of your wall. And when the dawn breaks and the sun comes up, let every valiant one of you take his weapons and go forth from the city. And let a captain be placed in charge of them and act as though you were going down to the plain toward the watch of the Assyrians; but you will not go down. For they will seize their armor and awaken the commanders of their army and run to the tent of Holofernes. But they will not find him and they will become frightened and will flee from you. Then you and all the inhabitants of the coast of Israel will pursue them and destroy them as they attempt to escape. But first summon to me Akior the Ammonite so that he may see and know that when he who despised the House of Israel sent him to us, he was ordering his death."

Then they summoned Akior from the house of Ozias. And when he saw the head of Holofernes in the hand of a man in the assembly of the people, he fainted. And when they revived him, he fell at Judith's feet and paid homage to her, and said, "May you be blessed in every household of Judah, and may your name be a warning to every nation. Pray, tell me everything that you did during these days." And Judith related in the midst of the people all that she had done from the day she had departed. And when she finished they shouted with all their strength and made a joyful uproar throughout the city. And when Akior saw all that God had accomplished he believed in God with all his heart and circumcised the flesh of his foreskin and became a member of the House of Israel to this very day.

Now when it was morning they hung the head of Holofernes upon the wall, and every man took his weapons and they departed in groups to the mountain roads. And when the Assyrians saw them, they sent here and there for their leaders and rulers and rushed to Holofernes' tent and said to his steward, "Waken our lord for the slaves have been bold enough to come down to do battle with us so that they may be utterly destroyed." And Bagoas went in and knocked at the outer door of the tent, for he supposed that he was sleeping with Judith. But when there was no response, he opened it and entered and found his carcass thrown upon the threshold and his head missing. And he cried aloud and, weeping and groaning, he tore his garments. Then he entered Judith's tent but did not find her, and he rushed out to the soldiers and cried, "The slaves have tricked us. One Hebrew woman has brought shame upon the house of King Nebuhadnezzar, for Holofernes' body is upon the ground and his head has been taken." And when the leaders of the Assyrian army heard this, they tore their garments and groaned and raised a great tumult in the camp.

And when the soldiers who were in their tents heard of it they were amazed and dumbstruck, and they were seized with such trembling and fear that no one could face his neighbor, but they rushed out at once and fled by every road of the plain and the hill country. Then every warrior of Israel pounced upon them. And Ozias sent word to Betomastaim and Bebai and Hobai and Hola and to the whole coast of Israel about what had happened, commanding that they should attack their enemies and destroy them. And when the children of Israel received the tidings, they fell upon them and smote them as far as Hobai, and those in Gilead and Galilee fell upon their flank and made a great slaughter until they were past Damascus and its borders. And the Betulians fell upon the Assyrians' camp and despoiled it and enriched themselves with the spoils.

Now Joakim the High Priest and the Senate of the children of Israel in Jerusalem came to see the good things which the Lord showed to Israel, and to see Judith and congratulate her. When they visited her, they blessed her with one accord and said, "You are the exaltation of Jerusalem, the great glory of Israel and the joy of our race. You have accomplished all these things by yourself; you have done well for Israel and God is pleased; may you be blessed with the Almighty God forever." And all the people said, "So be it!"

Then the people despoiled the camp for thirty days, and they gave Judith the tent of Holofernes and all his silver cups, his beds, his vessels and his furniture. And she took them and placed them on her mule and heaped them on wagons. And all the women of Israel ran to see her, and they blessed her and danced for her. And she took branches and gave them to the women who accompanied her; and they made themselves garlands of olive. And she led all the people in the dance and all the men followed in their armor, bearing garlands and singing songs. And Judith sang a song of thanksgiving and all the people joined her in singing it.

And when they came to Jerusalem, they worshipped God; and when the people were purified, they offered their burnt-offerings and their freewill-offerings and their gifts. And Judith dedicated all the spoils of Holofernes, which the people had given her, and gave the canopy, which she had taken for herself out of his bedchamber, for a gift to the Lord. And the people continued feasting in Jerusalem before the Temple for three months, and Judith remained with them. And afterwards everyone departed to his own home, and Judith went away to Betulia, and lived there, and was honored in her time throughout the land. And many desired her, but no man knew her all the days of her life, from the day that her husband Manasses died and was gathered to his fathers. And she increased in greatness and let her maid go free, and she lived in her husband's house until she was a hundred and five years old, and she died in Betulia. And they buried her in the cave of her husband Manasses. And the House of Israel mourned for her seven days. But before she died she distributed her goods to all the nearest of kin to her husband Manasses and to her own relatives. And there was none that frightened the children of Israel in the days of Judith, nor a long time after her death.

COURAGE[1]

Now it happened that a mother and her seven sons were seized and compelled by King Antiochus against the Jewish law to taste swine's flesh, and were tormented with scourges and whips. But one of them, speaking first, said,

"What would you ask or require of us? We are ready to die rather than to transgress the laws of our fathers."

Then the king became furious and commanded pans and cauldrons to be heated. When they were hot, he commanded that the tongue of the lad who spoke first be cut out and that his limbs be cut off while his brothers and mother were looking on. Now when his limbs were mutilated in this way, and while he was yet alive, the king commanded that he be brought to the fire and be fried in the pan. And while the vapors of the pan spread out, they encouraged one another and their mother to die manfully with the following words,

"The Lord God watches us, and in truth has comfort in us, as Moses in his song declared, saying, 'And He shall be comforted in His servants.'"

Now when the first died in this manner, they brought forward the second to make of him a laughingstock. And after they had pulled off the skin of his head with the hair, they asked him,

"Will you eat before every member of your body is mutilated?"

But he answered in his own tongue, and said,

"No."

Then he received the next torment in the same order as his brother. And when he was breathing his last, he gasped,

"In your rage you are depriving us of our present life, but the King of the world shall give us, who have died for His laws, everlasting life."

[1] This tale of superb heroism is a selection from the second book of *Maccabees* (Chap. 7). The whole book is a digest of an earlier history of the Maccabees written by a Greek-speaking Jew, Jason of Cyrene, and has as its object the glorification of the festival of Hanukkah. Translated by Leo W. Schwarz.

After him the third was made a laughingstock. And when it was commanded, he put out his tongue without a murmur; holding out his hands manfully, he said with courage,

"These hands I had from Heaven. For His laws I despise them and from Him I hope to receive them again."

As a result the king and they who were with him marvelled at the young man's courage, for he totally disregarded his pain.

Now when this man was also dead, they tormented and mangled the fourth in a like manner. So when he was on the verge of death, he spoke as follows,

"When one is put to death by men, it is good to trust in God with the hope of resurrection. But *you* shall not be resurrected to life."

Afterwards they brought forward the fifth and also mangled him. Then he stared at the king and said,

"You have power over men but you are perishable. You do what pleases you, yet do not imagine that our nation has been forsaken by God. Wait awhile, and you will behold His power, how He will torment you and your progeny."

After him they brought forward the sixth who, when he was about to die, said,

"Be not deceived without cause. For we suffer this punishment because we have sinned against God. That is why marvellous things happen to us. But you, who take it upon yourself to strive against God, do not imagine that you will escape unpunished."

But, above all, the mother was wonderful, and worthy of honorable memory. For when she saw her seven sons murdered within one day, she bore it all with great courage because of her trust and hope in the Lord. Indeed, she exhorted every one of them in language filled with undaunted courage and unbelievable manliness. She said to them,

"I cannot tell you how you came into my womb; for I neither gave you breath nor life, nor was it I who formed your limbs and body, but the Creator of the world. He who formed the generation of man, and found out the beginning of all things, will also, out of His own mercy, give you breath and life again since you do not consider your own lives for the sake of His laws."

Now Antiochus, thinking himself despised, and regarding the speech as a rebuke, while the youngest was still alive, not only exhorted with words, but also assured him with oaths that he would make him both a rich and happy man, if he would desert the laws of his fathers; and that he would consider him his friend and entrust him with affairs. And when the lad would not hearken to him, the king called his mother and urged her to advise so that the boy's life would be saved. And when he continued to urge her, she promised that she would advise him. But she, bowing herself toward him, laughing scornfully at the cruel tyrant, spoke in her own language as follows,

"O my son, have pity upon your mother who bore you in her womb for nine months, nursed you for three years, nourished you, and raised you to this age, enduring the great trials of education. I beseech you, O my son, not to regard the heaven and the earth and all its creations but to consider that God made all these things and also mankind which had no existence without Him. Fear not this tormentor, but be worthy of your brothers and choose death so that I may receive you again in mercy with your brothers."

Before she had stopped speaking, the youth said,

"Whom are you waiting for? I will not obey the king's commandment, but I will obey the commandment of the law which was given to our fathers by Moses. And you who have been the instigator of all evil against the Hebrews, you shall not escape the hand of God. For we suffer because of our sins. And even though the living God be angry with us for a little while in order to punish and correct us, He shall be reconciled again with His servants. But you, O godless and wicked man, do not be arrogant without cause, or puffed up with uncertain hopes, raising your hands against the servants of God. You have not escaped the judgment of the Almighty God who sees everything. For our brothers who have now suffered but brief pain are dead under God's covenant of everlasting life. But you, through the judgment of God, shall receive just punishment for your pride. But I, like my brothers, offer my body and my life for the laws of our fathers, beseeching God that He may speedily be merciful to our nation; that you, by torments and plagues may confess that He alone is God; and that the wrath of the Almighty, which is justly kindled against our nation, may cease with me and my brothers."

Then the king, greatly enraged, took it to heart that he was mocked and handled him worse than all the rest.

Last of all, after all her sons, the mother died.

THE LETTER OF ARISTEAS [1]

DEMETRIUS of Phalerum, the president of the king's library, received vast sums of money, for the purpose of collecting together, as far as he possibly could, all the books in the world. By means of purchase and transcription, he carried out, to the best of his ability, the purpose of the king. On one occasion when I was present he was asked, 'How many thousand books are there in the library?' and he replied, 'More than two hundred thousand,

[1] This unique story is a selection from *The Letter of Aristeas,* a historical novel of considerable length, which claims to be a contemporary record written by an eye-witness, Aristeas of Alexandria. It was probably written about the first century B.C.E. by an Alexandrian Jew of Pharisaic leanings, as a criticism of such nationalistic writings as III *Maccabees.* In the above selection the author pictures the possibility of racial tolerance and mutual understanding and respect. Translated from the Greek by Herbert T. Andrews.

O king, and I shall make endeavour in the immediate future to gather together the remainder also, so that the total of five hundred thousand may be reached. I am told that the laws of the Jews are worth transcribing and deserve a place in your library.' 'What is to prevent you from doing this?' replied the king. 'Everything that is necessary has been placed at your disposal.' 'They need to be translated,' answered Demetrius, 'for in the country of the Jews they use a peculiar alphabet (just as the Egyptians, too, have a special form of letters) and speak a peculiar dialect. They are supposed to use the Aramaic tongue, but this is not the case; their language is quite different.' And the king when he understood all the facts of the case ordered a letter to be written to the Jewish High Priest that his purpose might be accomplished. The letter of the king ran as follows:

'King Ptolemy sends greeting and salutation to the High Priest Eleazar. Since there are many Jews settled in our realm who were carried off from Jerusalem by the Persians at the time of their power and many more who came with my father into Egypt as captives—large numbers of these he placed in the army and paid them higher wages than usual, and when he had proved the loyalty of their leaders he built fortresses and placed them in their charge that the native Egyptians might be intimidated by them. And I, when I ascended the throne, adopted a kindly attitude towards all my subjects, and more particularly to those who were citizens of yours—I have set at liberty more than a hundred thousand captives, paying their owners the appropriate market price for them, and if ever evil has been done to your people through the passions of the mob, I have made them reparation. The motive which promoted my action has been the desire to act piously and render unto the supreme God a thank offering for maintaining my kingdom in peace and great glory in all the world. Moreover those of your people who were in the prime of life I have drafted into my army, and those who were fit to be attached to my person and worthy of the confidence of the court, I have established in official positions. Now since I am anxious to show my gratitude to these men and to the Jews throughout the world and to the generations yet to come, I have determined that your law shall be translated from the Hebrew tongue which is in use amongst you into the Greek language, that these books may be added to the other royal books in my library. It will be a kindness on your part and a reward for my zeal if you will select six elders from each of your tribes, men of noble life and skilled in your law and able to interpret it, that in questions of dispute we may be able to discover the verdict in which the majority agree, for the investigation is of the highest possible importance. I hope to win great renown by the accomplishment of this work. I have sent Andreas, the chief of my bodyguard, and Aristeas—men whom I hold in high esteem—to lay the matter before you and present you with a hundred talents of silver, the first fruits of my offering for the temple and the sacrifices and other religious rites. If you will write to me concerning your wishes in these matters, you will confer a great favour upon me and afford me a new pledge of friendship, for all your wishes shall be carried out as speedily as possible. Farewell.'

To this letter Eleazar replied appropriately as follows: 'Eleazar the High Priest sends greetings to King Ptolemy his true friend. My highest wishes are for your welfare and the welfare of Queen Arsinoë your sister and your children. I also am well. I have received your letter and am greatly rejoiced by your purpose and your noble counsel. I summoned together the whole people and read it to them that they might know of your devotion to our God. I showed them too the cups which you sent, twenty of gold and thirty of silver, the five bowls and the table of dedication, and the hundred talents of silver for the offering of the sacrifices and providing the things of which the temple stands in need. These gifts were brought to me by Andreas, one of your most honoured servants, and by Aristeas, both good men and true, distinguished by their learning, and worthy in every way to be the representatives of your high principles and righteous purposes. These men imparted to me your message and received from me an answer in agreement with your letter. I will consent to everything which is advantageous to you even though your request is very unusual. For you have bestowed upon our citizens great and never-to-be-forgotten benefits in many ways. Immediately therefore I offered sacrifices on behalf of you, your sister, your children, and your friends, and all the people prayed that your plans might prosper continually, and that Almighty God might preserve your kingdom in peace with honour, and that the translation of the holy law might prove advantageous to you and be carried out successfully. In the presence of all the people I selected six elders from each tribe, good men and true, and I have sent them to you with a copy of our law. It will be a kindness, O righteous king, if you will give instruction that as soon as the translation of the law is completed, the men shall be restored again to us in safety. Farewell.'

The High Priest selected men of the finest character and the highest culture, such as one would expect from their noble parentage. They were men who had not only acquired proficiency in Jewish literature, but had studied most carefully that of the Greeks as well. They were specially qualified therefore for serving on embassies and they undertook this duty whenever it was necessary. They possessed a great facility for conferences and the discussion of problems connected with the law. They espoused the middle course—and this is always the best course to pursue. They abjured the rough and uncouth manner, but they were altogether above pride and never assumed an air of superiority over others, and in conversation they were ready to listen and give an appropriate answer to every question. And all of them carefully observed this rule and were anxious above everything else to excel each other in its observance and they were all of them worthy of their leader and of his virtue. And one could observe how they loved Eleazar by their unwillingness to be torn away from him and how he loved them. For besides the letter which he wrote to the king concerning their safe return, he also earnestly besought Andreas to work for the same end and urged me, too, to assist to the best of my ability. And although we promised to give our best attention to the matter, he said that he was still greatly distressed, for he knew that the king out of the goodness of his nature considered it his highest privilege, whenever he heard of a man who was superior to his fellows in culture and wisdom, to summon him to his court. For I have heard of a fine saying of his to the effect that by securing just and prudent men about his person he would secure the greatest protection for his kingdom, since such friends would unreservedly give him the most beneficial advice. And the men who were now being sent to him by Eleazar undoubtedly possessed these qualities. And he frequently asserted upon oath that he would never let the men go if it were merely some private interest of his own that constituted the impelling motive—but it was for the common advantage of all the citizens that he was sending them.

And, Eleazar, after offering the sacrifice, and selecting the envoys, and preparing many gifts for the king, despatched us on our journey in great security. And when we reached Alexandria, the king was at once informed of our arrival. On our admission to the palace, Andreas and I warmly greeted the king and handed over to him the letter written by Eleazar. The king was very anxious to meet the envoys, and gave orders that all the other officials should be dismissed and the envoys summoned to his presence at once. Now this excited general surprise, for it is customary for those who come to seek an audience with the king on matters of importance to be admitted to his presence on the fifth day, while envoys from kings or very important cities with difficulty secure admission to the court in thirty days—but these men he counted worthy of greater honour, since he held their master in such high esteem, and so he immediately dismissed those whose presence he regarded as superfluous and continued walking about until they came in and he was able to welcome them. When they entered with the gifts which had been sent with them and the valuable parchments, on which the law was inscribed in gold in Jewish characters, for the parchment was wonderfully prepared and the connexion between the pages had been so effected as to be invisible, the king as soon as he saw them began to ask them about the books. And when they had taken the rolls out of their coverings and unfolded the pages, the king stood still for a long time and then making obeisance about seven times, he said: 'I thank you, my friends, and I thank him that sent you still more, and most of all God, whose oracles these are.' And when all, the envoys and the others who were present as well, shouted out at one time and with one voice: 'God save the King!' he burst into tears of joy. For his exaltation of soul and the sense of the overwhelming honour which had been paid him compelled him to weep over his good fortune. He commanded them to put the rolls back in their places and then after saluting the men, said: 'It was right, men of God, that I should first of all pay my reverence to the books for the sake of which I summoned you here and then, when I had done that, to extend the right-hand of friendship to you. It was for this reason that I did this first. I have enacted that this day, on which you arrived, shall be kept as a great day and it will be celebrated annually throughout my lifetime. It happens also that it is the anniversary of my naval victory over Antigonus. Therefore, I shall be glad to feast with you today.' 'Everything that you may have occasion to use,' he said, 'shall be prepared for you in a befitting manner and for me also with you.' After they had expressed their delight, he gave orders that the best quarters near the citadel should be assigned to them, and that preparations should be made for the banquet. And Nicanor summoned the lord high steward, Dorotheus, who was the special officer appointed to look after the Jews, and commanded him to make the necessary preparation for each one. For this arrangement had been made by the king and it is an arrangement which you see maintained today. For as many cities as have special customs in the matter of drinking, eating, and reclining, have special officers appointed to look after their requirements. And whenever they come to visit the kings, preparations are made in accordance with their own customs, in order that there may be no discomfort to disturb the enjoyment of their visit. The same precaution was taken in the case of the Jewish envoys. Now Dorotheus who was the patron appointed to look after the Jewish guests was a very conscientious man. All the stores which were under his control and set apart for the reception of such guests, he brought out for the feast. He arranged the seats in two rows in accordance with the king's instructions. For he had ordered him to make half the men sit at his right hand and the rest behind him, in order that he might not withhold from them the highest possible honour. When they had taken their seats he instructed Dorotheus to carry out everything in accordance with the customs which were in use amongst his Jewish guests. Therefore he dispensed with the services of the sacred heralds and the sacrificing priests and the others who were accustomed to offer the prayers, and called upon one of our number, Eleazar, the oldest of the Jewish priests, to offer prayer instead. And he rose up and made a re-markable prayer. 'May Almighty God enrich you, O king, with all the good things which He has made and may He grant you and your wife and your children and your comrades the continual possession of them as long as you live!' At these words a loud and joyous applause broke out which lasted for a considerable time, and then they turned to the enjoyment of the banquet which had been prepared. All the arrangements for service at table were carried out in accordance with the injunction of Dorotheus. Among the attendants were the royal pages and others who held places of honour at the king's court.

Three days later Demetrius took the men and passing along the sea-wall, seven stadia long, to the island, crossed the bridge and made for the northern districts of Pharos. There he assembled them in a house, which had been built upon the sea-shore, of great beauty and in a secluded situation, and invited them to carry out the work of translation, since everything that they needed for the purpose was placed at their disposal. So they set to work comparing their several results and making them agree, and whatever they agreed upon was suitably copied out under the direction of Demetrius. And the session lasted until the ninth hour; after this they were set free to minister to their physical needs. Everything they wanted was furnished for them on a lavish scale. In addition to this Dorotheus made the same preparations for them daily as were made for the king himself—for thus he had been commanded by the king. In the early morning they appeared daily at the court, and after saluting the king went back to their own place. And as is the custom of all the Jews, they washed their hands in the sea and prayed to God and then devoted themselves to reading and translating the particular passage upon which they were engaged, and I put the question to them, Why it was that they washed their hands before they prayed? And they explained that it was a token that they had done no evil (for every form of activity is wrought by means of the hands) since in their noble and holy way they regard everything as a symbol of righteousness and truth.

As I have already said, they met together daily in the place which was delightful for its quiet and its brightness and applied themselves to their task. And it so chanced that the work of translation was completed in seventy-two days, just as if this had been arranged of set purpose.

When the work was completed, Demetrius collected together the Jewish population in the place where the translation had been made, and read it over to all, in the presence of the translators, who met with a great reception also from the people, because of the great benefits which they had conferred upon them. They bestowed warm praise upon Demetrius, too, and urged him to have the whole law transcribed and present a copy to their leaders.

After the books had been read, the priests and the elders of the translators and the Jewish community and the leaders of the people stood up and said that since so excellent and sacred and accurate a translation had been made, it was only right that it should remain as it was and no alteration should be made in it. And when the whole company expressed their approval, they bade them pronounce a curse in accordance with their custom upon anyone who should make any alteration either by adding anything or changing in any way whatever any of the words which had been written or making any omission. This was a very wise precaution to ensure that the book might be preserved for all the future time unchanged.

When the matter was reported to the king, he rejoiced greatly, for he felt that the design which he had formed had been safely carried out. The whole book was read over to him and he was greatly astonished at the spirit of the lawgiver. And he said to Demetrius, 'How is it that none of the historians or the poets have ever thought it worth their while to allude to such a wonderful achievement?' And he replied, 'Because the law is sacred and of divine origin. And some of those who formed the intention of dealing with it have been smitten by God and therefore desisted from their purpose.' He said that he had heard from Theopompus that he had been driven out of his mind more than thirty days because he intended to insert in his history some of the incidents from the earlier and somewhat unreliable translations of the law. When he had recovered a little, he besought God to make it clear to him why the misfortune had befallen him. And it was revealed to him in a dream, that from idle curiosity he was wishing to communicate sacred truths to common men, and that if he desisted he would recover his health. I have heard, too, from the lips of Theodektes, one of the tragic poets, that when he was about to adapt some of the incidents recorded in the book for one of his plays, he was affected with cataract in both his eyes. And when he perceived the reason why the misfortune had befallen him, he prayed to God for many days and was afterwards restored.

And after the king, as I have already said, had received the explanation of Demetrius on this point, he did homage and ordered that great care should be taken of the books, and that they should be sacredly guarded. And he urged the translators to visit him frequently after their return to Judea, for it was only right, he said, that he should now send them home. But when they came back, he would treat them as friends, as was right, and they would receive rich presents from him. He ordered preparations to be made for them to return home, and treated them most munificently. He presented each one of them with three robes of the finest sort, two talents of gold, a sideboard weighing one talent, all the furniture for three couches.

And with the escort he sent Eleazar ten couches with silver legs and all the necessary equipment, a sideboard worth thirty talents, ten robes, purple, and a magnificent crown, and a hundred pieces of the finest woven linen, also bowls and dishes, and two golden beakers to be dedicated to God. He urged him also in a letter that if any of the men preferred to come back to him, not to hinder them. For he counted it a great privilege to enjoy the society of such learned men, and he would rather lavish his wealth upon them than upon vanities.

SELF-PORTRAIT

by FLAVIUS JOSEPHUS [1]

MY family is no ignoble one, tracing its descent far back to priestly ancestors. Different races base their claim to nobility on various grounds; with us a connexion with the priesthood is the hallmark of an illustrious line. Not only, however, were my ancestors priests, but they belonged to the first of the twenty-four courses—a peculiar distinction—and to the most eminent of its constituent clans. Moreover, on my mothers' side I am of royal blood; for the posterity of Asamonæus, from which she sprang, for a very considerable period were kings, as well as high-priests, of our nation. I will give the pedigree. My great-grandfather's grandfather was Simon surnamed Psellus. He was a contemporary of the high-priest Hyrcanus, the first of the name to hold that office, previously held by his father Simon. Simon "the stammerer" had nine children, of whom Matthias, known as the son of Ephæus, married the daughter of Jonathan the high-priest, who was the first of the line of Asamonæus to attain to the high-priesthood, and brother of Simon who also held that office. Matthias, in the first year of the reign of Hyrcanus, had a son Matthias, surnamed Curtus; who, in the ninth year of the reign of Alexandra, begot Joseph, and he, in the tenth year of the reign of Archelaus, Matthias, to whom I was born in the year in which Gaius Cæsar became Emperor. I have three sons: Hyrcanus, the eldest, born in the fourth, Justus in the seventh, and Agrippa in the ninth year of the reign of Vespasian Cæsar. With such a pedigree, which I cite as I find it recorded in the public registers, I can take leave of the would-be detractors of my family.

Distinguished as he was by his noble birth, my father Matthias was even more esteemed for his upright character, being among the most notable men in Jerusalem, our greatest city. Brought up with Matthias, my own brother by both parents, I made great progress in my education, gaining a reputation for an excellent memory and understanding. While still a mere boy, about fourteen years old, I won universal applause for my love of letters; insomuch that the chief priests and the leading men of the city used constantly to come

---

[1] Josephus (Jewish name, Joseph ben Matthias) was born in 38 C.E. He lived during the turbulent years of the Jewish revolt against Rome; the above selection from the *Life* describes the opening scenes of the Galilean campaign in 66-67 C.E. The immediate occasion for writing this autobiography was the publication of the book of a rival historian, Justus of Tiberias, who placed the responsibility of the war with Rome upon Josephus. It was written not long after 100 C.E., toward the end of his life.

Despite the unfavorable picture that most of his critics have drawn, one cannot help discerning a deep loyalty and patriotism for his people. For his service to the Flavian emperors, we are informed by Eusebius that his statue was erected in Rome and his works placed in the public library. The reader will find a rare appreciation and estimate of Josephus in Lion Feuchtwanger's novel: *Josephus.* Translated from the Greek by H. St. J. Thackeray.

to me for precise information on some particular in our ordinances. At about the age of sixteen I determined to gain personal experience of the several sects into which our nation is divided. These, as I have frequently mentioned, are three in number—the first that of the Pharisees, the second that of the Sadducees, and the third that of the Essenes. I thought that, after a thorough investigation, I should be in a position to select the best. So I submitted myself to hard training and laborious exercises and passed through the three courses. Not content, however, with the experience thus gained, on hearing of one named Bannus, who dwelt in the wilderness, wearing only such clothing as trees provided, feeding on such things as grew of themselves, and using frequent ablutions of cold water, by day and night, for purity's sake, I became his devoted disciple. With him I lived for three years and, having accomplished my purpose, returned to the city. Being now in my nineteenth year I began to govern my life by the rules of the Pharisees, a sect having points of resemblance to that which the Greeks call the Stoic school.

Soon after I had completed my twenty-sixth year it fell to my lot to go up to Rome for the reason which I will proceed to relate. At the time when Felix was procurator of Judæa, certain priests of my acquaintance, very excellent men, were on a slight and trifling charge sent by him in bonds to Rome to render an account to Cæsar. I was anxious to discover some means of delivering these men, more especially as I learnt that, even in affliction they had not forgotten the pious practices of religion, and supported themselves on figs and nuts. I reached Rome after being in great jeopardy at sea. For our ship foundered in the midst of the sea of Adria, and our company of some six hundred souls had to swim all that night. About daybreak, through God's good providence, we sighted a ship of Cyrene, and I and certain others, about eighty in all, outstripped the others and were taken on board. Landing safely at Dicæarchia, which the Italians call Puteoli, I formed a friendship with Aliturus, an actor who was a special favourite of Nero and of Jewish origin. Through him I was introduced to Poppæa, Cæsar's consort, and took the earliest opportunity of soliciting her aid to secure the liberation of the priests. Having besides this favour received large gifts from Poppæa, I returned to my own country.

There I found revolutionary movements already on foot and widespread elation at the prospect of revolt from Rome. I accordingly endeavoured to repress these promoters of sedition and to bring them over to another frame of mind. I urged them to picture to themselves the nation on which they were about to make war, and to remember that they were inferior to the Romans, not only in military skill, but in good fortune; and I warned them not recklessly and with such utter madness to expose their country, their families and themselves to the direst perils. With such words I earnestly and insistently sought to dissuade them from their purpose, foreseeing that the end of the war would be most disastrous for us. But my efforts were unavailing; the madness of these desperate men was far too strong for me.

I now feared that my incessant reiteration of this warning would bring me into odium and the suspicion of siding with the enemy, and that I should run the risk of being arrested by them and put to death. I therefore sought asylum in the inner court of the Temple; the fortress of Antonia being already in their hands. When Menahem and the chieftains of the band of brigades had been put to death I ventured out of the Temple and once more consorted with the chief priests and the leading Pharisees. We were, however, in a state of great alarm; we saw the populace in arms and were at a loss what to do ourselves, being powerless to check the revolutionaries. In such obvious and imminent peril we professed to concur in their views, but suggested that they should make no move and leave the enemy alone if he advanced, in order to gain the credit of resorting to arms only in just self-defence. In so doing we had hopes that ere long Cestius would come up with a large army and quell the revolution.

He came indeed, but in the engagement which ensued was defeated with great loss. This reverse of Cestius proved disastrous to our whole nation; for those who were bent on war were thereby still more elated and, having once defeated the Romans, hoped to continue victorious to the end. To add to this, they had a further ground for hostility. The inhabitants of the surrounding cities of Syria proceeded to lay hands on and kill, with their wives and children, the Jewish residents among them, without the slightest ground of complaint; for they had neither entertained any idea of revolt from Rome nor harboured any enmity or designs against the Syrians. The most outrageous and criminal action of all was that perpetrated by the natives of Scythopolis. Being attacked by hostile Jews from another quarter, they compelled their own Jewish residents to bear arms against their compatriots, which we are forbidden to do, and with their assistance engaged and defeated the invaders; and then, after the victory, with no thought of the allegiance due to fellow-citizens and confederates, put them all, to the number of many thousands, to the sword. The Jewish residents in Damascus met with a similar fate. I have given a more detailed account of these incidents in my volumes on the Jewish War; and I merely allude to them here from a desire to convince my readers that the war with the Romans was due not so much to the deliberate choice of the Jews as to necessity.

After the defeat of Cestius, already mentioned, the leading men in Jerusalem, observing that the brigands and revolutionaries were well provided with arms, feared that, being without weapons themselves, they might be left at the mercy of their adversaries, as in fact eventually happened. Being informed, moreover, that the whole of Galilee had not yet revolted from Rome, and that a portion of it was still tranquil, they dispatched me with two other priests, Joazar and Judas, men of excellent character, to induce the disaffected to lay down their arms and to impress upon them the desirability of reserving these for the picked men of the nation. The latter, such was the policy determined on, were to have their weapons constantly in readiness for future contingencies, but should wait and see what action the Romans would take.

With these instructions I came into Galilee. I found the inhabitants of Sepphoris in great distress concerning their native place, which the Galilæans had decided to pillage because of their leanings towards the Romans and the overtures of loyalty and allegiance which they had made to Cestius Gallus, the governor of Syria. I, however, entirely allayed their fears, by exerting my influence with the populace on their behalf, and by the permission which I gave them to communicate as freely as they chose with their fellow-citizens, who were held as hostages to Cestius at Dora, a city of Phœnicia.

About this time there came to me from the region of Trachonitis two nobles, subjects of the king, bringing their horses, arms, and money which they had smuggled out of their country. The Jews would have compelled them to be circumcised as a condition of residence among them. I, however, would not allow any compulsion to be put upon them, declaring that everyone should worship God in accordance with the dictates of his own conscience and not under constraint, and that these men, having fled to us for refuge, ought not to be made to regret that they had done so. Having brought over the people to my way of thinking, I liberally supplied our guests with all things necessary to their customary manner of life.

Some adventurous young men of Dabaritta lay in wait for the wife of Ptolemy, the king's overseer. She was travelling in great state, protected by an escort of cavalry, from territory subject to the royal jurisdiction into the region of Roman dominion, when, as she was crossing the Great Plain, they suddenly fell upon the cavalcade, compelled the lady to fly, and plundered all her baggage. They then came to me at Tarichææ with four mules laden with apparel and other articles, besides a large pile of silver and five hundred pieces of gold. My own desire was to keep these spoils for Ptolemy, seeing that he was a compatriot and we are forbidden by our laws to rob even an enemy; to the bearers I said that the goods must be reserved for sale and the proceeds devoted to the repair of the walls of Jerusalem. Indignant at not receiving their expected share of the spoils, the young men went to the villages around Tiberias, declaring that I intended to betray their country to the Romans. My assertion about keeping the outcome of their raid for the repair of the walls of the capital was, they said, a mere blind; I had really decided to restore it to its owner. So far, indeed, they correctly interpreted my intention; for, when they left me, I sent for two of the leaders, Dassion and Jannæus, son of Levi, who were special friends of the king, and ordered them to take the stolen goods and dispatch them to him, threatening them with capital punishment if they reported the matter to anyone.

A rumour had now spread throughout Galilee that I was intending to betray the country to the Romans, and the feelings of all were roused to demand my punishment. The young men's statement was credited even by the inhabitants of Tarichææ, who now urged my bodyguards and soldiers to leave me while I was asleep and come at once to the hippodrome, to take part in a general discussion on their commander's conduct. Their persuasion prevailed, and the men joining the assembly found a large crowd already collected, unanimously crying for vengeance on one who had proved so base a traitor. The principal instigator of the mob was Jesus, son of Sapphias, at that time chief magistrate of Tiberias, a knave with an instinct for introducing disorder into grave matters, and unrivalled in fomenting sedition and revolution. With a copy of the laws of Moses in his hands, he now stepped forward and said: "If you cannot, for your own sake, citizens, detest Josephus, fix your eyes on your country's laws, which your commander-in-chief intended to betray, and for their sakes hate the crime and punish the audacious criminal."

After this speech, which was loudly applauded, he hurried, with some soldiers, to the house where I was lodging, intending to kill me. I, quite unaware of what was coming, had, from fatigue, succumbed (to sleep) before the riot. Simon, who was entrusted with the charge of my person and had alone remained with me, seeing the citizens rushing towards me, awoke me and, telling me of my imminent peril, entreated me to die honourably, as a general, by my own hand, before my foes arrived to force me to such action or to kill me themselves. Such were his words; but I, committing my fate to God, hastened to go forth to the people. Changing my raiment for one of black and suspending my sword from my neck, I proceeded by another road, on which I expected that no enemy would encounter me, to the hippodrome; where my sudden appearance, as I flung myself on my face and rained tears upon the ground, aroused universal compassion. Observing the effect produced upon the people, I endeavoured to create dissension among them before the soldiers returned from my house. I admitted that, according to their view of the matter, I was guilty, but craved leave to inform them for what purpose I was reserving the money obtained by the raid, before, if they so ordered, I was put to death. The crowd were just bidding me proceed, when the soldiers appeared and, at sight of me, rushed forward to kill me. At the people's order, however, they stayed their hands; expecting as soon as I had owned to having kept the money for the king, to slay me as an avowed traitor.

Thereupon, amid profound silence, I spoke as follows: "My countrymen, if I deserve to die, I ask no mercy; but, before my death, I desire to tell you the truth. Knowing the lavish hospitality of this city and that it is crowded with vast numbers of persons who have left their homes and gladly come to throw in their lot with ours, I proposed to provide fortifications for it with the money, about which, though it was to be expended on their erection, you are now so indignant." At this a shout was raised by the Tarichæans and their guests, who expressed their gratitude and bade me not be disheartened. The Galilæans and Tiberians, however, still maintained their resentment, and a quarrel arose, one party threatening to have my blood, the other (exhorting me) to disregard (these opponents). But when I further promised to provide fortifications for Tiberias and for any other of their cities which needed them, they, on the strength of this undertaking, retired to their several homes. Having thus, beyond all expectation, escaped from the peril which I have described, I returned to my house, accompanied by my friends and twenty soldiers.

I was not long left in peace. The brigands and the promoters of the disturbance, fearing that they would be called to account by me for their proceedings, again visited my residence, with six hundred armed men, to set it on fire. Apprised of their coming, and considering it undignified to fly, I decided to risk a course requiring some courage. Ordering the house-doors to be closed, I ascended to the upper story and invited them to send some of their number to receive the money, thinking thus to allay their anger. They sent in the most stalwart among them, whereupon I had him soundly scourged, ordered one of his hands to be severed and hung about his neck and in that condition dismissed him to his employers. Panic-stricken and in great alarm, supposing that I had indoors a force outnumbering their own, and fearing, if they remained, to meet the same fate themselves, my opponents made off in haste. Such was the stratagem by which I eluded this second plot.

The feelings of the masses were once again aroused against me by certain persons who asserted that the noble vassals of the king, who had come to me, ought not to live if they refused to conform to the customs of those with whom they had sought refuge; they also falsely accused them of being sorcerers who made it impossible to defeat the Romans. Deluded by specious assertions designed to catch their ear, the people readily believed them to be true. On hearing of this, I again impressed upon the community that such refugees ought to be free from persecution; and ridiculed the absurdity of the charge of sorcery by remarking that the Romans would not maintain so vast an army if they could defeat their enemies by enchantments. My words had a temporary effect; but, after their departure, their passions were again aroused against the nobles by their villainous advisers, and on one occasion they made an armed assault on their house in Tarichææ, intending to kill them. On being informed of this I feared that, if so abominable a crime were committed, the place would be rendered untenable as an asylum for would-be refugees. So I went with some others to the residence of the nobles, locked it up, made a canal leading from the house to the lake, summoned a boat, and embarking with them, crossed over to the frontiers of the district of

Hippos. I paid them the price of their horses, which the conditions of our flight made it impossible for me to bring, and so took my leave, earnestly entreating them to bear their hard fate with fortitude. I was myself deeply distressed at being driven to expose these refugees once more on enemy soil; but I thought it better that they should perish, if such destiny awaited them, under Roman hands than within my own province. After all they escaped, obtaining pardon for their errors from King Agrippa. So ended this episode.

Meanwhile, the hatred borne me by John, son of Levi, who was aggrieved at my success, was growing more intense, and he determined at all costs to have me removed. Accordingly, after fortifying his native town of Gischala, he dispatched his brother Simon and Jonathan, son of Sisenna, with about a hundred armed men, to Jerusalem, to Simon, son of Gamaliel, to entreat him to induce the national assembly of Jerusalem to deprive me of the command of Galilee and to vote for his appointment to the post. This Simon was a native of Jerusalem, of a very illustrious family, and of the sect of the Pharisees, who have the reputation of being unrivalled experts in their country's laws. A man highly gifted with intelligence and judgement, he could by sheer genius retrieve an unfortunate situation in affairs of state. He was John's old and intimate friend, and, at the time, was at variance with me. On receiving this application he exerted himself to persuade the high-priests Ananus and Jesus, son of Gamalas, and some others of their party to clip my sprouting wings and not suffer me to mount to the pinnacle of fame. He observed that my removal from Galilee would be to their advantage, and urged them to act without delay, for fear that I should get wind of their plans and march with a large army upon Jerusalem. Such was Simon's advice. In reply, Ananus, the high-priest, represented the difficulties of the action suggested, in view of the testimonials from many of the chief priests and leaders of the people to my capacity as a general; adding that to accuse a man against whom no just charge could be brought was a dishonourable proceeding.

On hearing this speech of Ananus, Simon implored the embassy to keep to themselves and not divulge what had passed at the conference; asserting that he would see to it that I was speedily superseded in Galilee. Then calling up John's brother he instructed him to send presents to Ananus and his friends, as a likely method of inducing them to change their minds. Indeed Simon eventually achieved his purpose; for, as the result of bribery, Ananus and his party agreed to expel me from Galilee, while everyone else in the city remained ignorant of the plot. The scheme agreed upon was to send a deputation comprising persons of different classes of society but of equal standing in education. Two of them, Jonathan and Ananias, were from the lower ranks and adherents of the Pharisees; the third, Jozar, also a Pharisee, came of a priestly family; the youngest, Simon, was descended from high priests. Their instructions were to approach the Galilæans and ascertain the reason for their devotion to me. If they attributed it to my being a native of Jerusalem, they were to reply that so were all four of them; if to my expert knowledge of their laws, they should retort that neither were they ignorant of the customs of their fathers; if, again, they asserted that their affection was due to my priestly office, they should answer that two of them were likewise priests.

After thus prompting Jonathan and his colleagues, they presented them with forty thousand pieces of silver out of the public funds; and, on hearing that a Galilæan, named Jesus, was staying in Jerusalem, who had with him a company of six hundred men under arms, they sent for him, gave him three months' pay and directed him to accompany the party and obey their orders. They further requisitioned three hundred citizens to follow the deputies, providing money for the maintenance of the whole number. The consent of these recruits being obtained and their preparations for the journey completed, the party of Jonathan set out with them; John's brother and a hundred regulars also accompanied them. They had orders, in the event of my volunteering to lay down my arms, to send me alive to Jerusalem, but if I offered any resistance to kill me regardless of consequences, having the weight of their masters' commands behind them. They had also written to John to be prepared for an attack upon me, and were issuing orders to Sepphoris, Gabara, and Tiberias to send assistance to John.

My information reached me in a letter from my father, to whom the news was confided by Jesus, son of Gamalas, an intimate friend of mine, who had been present at the conference. I was deeply distressed, both by the base ingratitude of my fellow-citizens, whose jealousy, as I could see, had prompted the order to put me to death, and also by the earnest request in my father's letter that I would come to him, as he longed to see his son before his death. I told my friends exactly what had happened and of my intention, in three days' time, to quit the district and go home. All who heard me were overcome with grief and besought me, with tears, not to abandon them to the ruin which awaited them if deprived of my leadership. To these entreaties, out of concern for my own safety, I refused to yield; whereupon the Galilæans, fearing that my withdrawal would leave them an easy prey to the brigands, sent messengers throughout Galilee to announce my intended departure. On hearing of this, large numbers assembled from all quarters, with their wives and children, influenced, I imagine, as much by alarm for themselves as by affection for myself; being convinced that while I remained at my post no harm would befall them. All flocked to the great plain, called the plain of Asochis, in which my quarters lay.

That night I beheld a marvellous vision in my dreams. I had retired to my couch, grieved and distraught by the tidings in the letter, when I thought that there stood by me one who said: "Cease, man, from thy sorrow of heart, let go all fear. That which grieves thee now will promote thee to greatness and felicity in all things. Not in these present trials only, but in many besides, will fortune attend thee. Fret not thyself then. Remember that thou must even battle with the Romans." Cheered by this dream-vision I arose, ready to descend into the plain. On my appearance, the whole crowd of Galilæans, which included women and children, flung themselves on their faces and with tears implored me not to abandon them to their enemies nor, by my departure, leave their country exposed to the insolence of their foes. Finding entreaties unavailing, they sought with adjurations to coerce me to stay with them; bitterly inveighing against the people of Jerusalem for not allowing their country to remain in peace.

With these cries in my ears and the sight of the dejected crowd before my eyes, my resolution broke down and I was moved to compassion; I felt that it was right to face even manifest perils for so vast a multitude. So I consented to remain; and, giving orders that five thousand of them were to join me in arms, bringing their own provisions, I dismissed the rest to their homes. When the five thousand arrived, I set out with them, the three thousand infantry already with me and eighty horse, and marched to Chabolo, a village on the frontiers of Ptolemais, where I kept my forces together, feigning to be making preparations for an engagement with Placidus. The latter had been sent by Cestius Gallus, with two cohorts of infantry and a squadron of horse, to burn the Galilæan villages in the neighbourhood of Ptolemais. While he was entrenching himself in front of that city, I on my side encamped about sixty furlongs from the village of Chabolo. On several occasions we led out our forces, as for battle, but did not proceed beyond skirmishes, because Placidus, in proportion as he saw my eagerness for a combat, became alarmed and declined it. He did not, however, quit his post at Ptolemais.

At this juncture Jonathan arrived with his fellow-envoys, who, as I said, had been sent from Jerusalem by Simon and Ananus the high-priest. Not venturing to attack me openly, he laid a plot to entrap me, writing me the following letter:

"Jonathan and his fellow deputies from Jerusalem to Josephus, greeting. The Jerusalem authorities, having heard that John of Gischala has frequently plotted against you, have commissioned us to reprove him and to admonish him in future to show you proper respect. Wishing to confer with you on a concerted line of action, we request you to come to us with all speed, and with but few attendants, as this village could not accommodate a large military force."

In so writing they expected one of two things to happen: either I would come unprotected and they would have me at their mercy, or, should I bring a large retinue, they would denounce me as a public enemy. The letter was brought to me by a trooper, an insolent young fellow who had formerly served in the king's army. It was the second hour of the night, and I was dining with my friends and the chief men of Galilee. My servant announcing the arrival of a Jewish horseman, this fellow, being called in by my orders, gave me no salute whatever, but reached out the letter and said: "The party who have come from Jerusalem have sent you this. Write your reply immediately, as I am in a hurry to return to them." My guests were astonished at the soldier's audacity; I, for my part, invited him to sit down and join us at supper. He declined. I kept the letter in my hands, as I had received it, and conversed with my friends on other subjects. Not long after I rose and, dismissing the others to their repose, directed four only of my closest friends to stay and ordered my servants to set on wine. Then, when no one was looking, I unfolded the letter, took in at a glance the writers' design and sealed it up again. Holding it in my hands as though I had not yet read it, I ordered twenty drachmas to be presented to the soldier for travelling expenses. He accepted the money and thanked me for it. Noting his cupidity as offering the surest means of gulling him, I said, "If you will consent to drink with us, you shall receive a drachma for every cup." He readily assented and, in order to win more money, indulged so freely in the wine that he became intoxicated and unable to keep his secrets any longer to himself. He told me, without being asked, of the plot that had been hatched and how I had been sentenced to death by his employers. On hearing this I wrote the following reply:

"Josephus to Jonathan and his colleagues, greeting. I am delighted to hear that you have reached Galilee in good health; more especially because I shall now be able to hand over to you the charge of affairs here and return home, as I have long wished to do. I ought certainly to have gone, not merely to Xaloth, but further, to wait upon you, even without your instructions; I must, however, request you to excuse me for my inability to do so, as I am here at Chabolo, keeping watch on Placidus, who is meditating an incursion up country into Galilee. Do you, therefore, on receipt of this letter, come and visit me. Fare you well."

Having written this letter and handed it to the soldier, I sent him off, accompanied by thirty Galilæans of the highest repute, whom I instructed to pay their respects to the deputies, but to say not a word more. To each of them I attached a soldier whom I could trust, to watch them and see that no conversation took place between my emissaries and the other party; and so they set off. Foiled in their first attempt, Jonathan and his friends sent me another letter as follows:

"Jonathan and his colleagues to Josephus, greeting. We charge you in three days' time to join us, without military escort, at the village of Gabaroth, that we may give a hearing to your accusations against John."

Having written this letter and taken leave of the Galilæans whom I had sent, they went on to Japha, the largest village in Galilee, very strongly fortified and containing a dense population. There they were met by a crowd, including women and children, who in abusive language bade them be off and not grudge them their excellent general. Irritated though they were by these outcries, Jonathan and his colleagues did not dare to show their displeasure, and, not deigning to reply, proceeded to the other villages on their route. But on all sides they were met by similar denunciations, the people loudly protesting that none should induce them to alter their determination to have Josephus for their general. Unsuccessful in the villages the delegates withdrew to Sepphoris, the largest city in Galilee. Here the inhabitants, who inclined to the side of the Romans, went to meet them; refraining, however, from either praise or censure of myself. From Sepphoris they descended to Asochis, which gave them a noisy reception similar to that which had greeted them at Japha. Unable longer to restrain their wrath, they ordered their military escort to beat the rioters with cudgels. On their arrival at Gabara they were met by John with three thousand men in arms. Having already understood from their letter that they were determined to attack me, I set out from Chabolo, with a force three thousand strong, leaving my most trusted friend in command of the camp; and, being anxious to be near them, removed to Jotapata, where I was about forty furlongs away. I then wrote to them as follows:

"If you seriously desire me to come to you, there are two hundred and four cities and villages in Galilee. I will come to whichever of these you may select, Gabara and Gischala excepted; the latter being John's native place and the former in league and alliance with him."

On receipt of this letter Jonathan and his colleagues, abandoning further correspondence, summoned a meeting of their friends, John included, and deliberated how they should proceed against me. John was of opinion that they should write to every city and village in Galilee, in each of which there would certainly be found at least one or two adversaries of mine, and call out these persons as against an enemy. He further recommended that a copy of this resolution should be sent to Jerusalem, in order that the citizens, on learning that I had been declared an enemy by the Galilæans, might be induced to pass a similar vote. In that event, he added, even my Galilæan partisans would abandon me in alarm. John's advice was highly approved by the rest of the council. About the third hour of the night news of these proceedings was brought to me by Sacchæus, one of their party who deserted and reported their design to me, adding that there was no time to be lost. So, selecting James, a faithful soldier of my bodyguard, as a fit person, I ordered him to take two hundred men and guard the routes leading from Gabara into Galilee, and to arrest all who passed, especially any caught with letters upon them, and to send them to me. I also dispatched Jeremiah, another of my friends, with six hundred men to the frontier of Galilee, to watch the roads leading from the province to Jerusalem, with similar orders to arrest all found travelling with dispatches; such persons were to be kept in chains on the spot, the letters he was to forward to me.

Having given these orders, I sent directions to the Galilæans to join me on the following day at the village of Gabaroth, with their arms and three days' provisions. I then divided my troops into four companies, formed a body-guard for myself of those whom I most trusted, and appointed officers to take command, charging them to see that no soldier who was unknown to them mixed with their men. Reaching Gabaroth about the fifth hour on the following day, I found the whole plain in front of the village covered with armed men, who, in obedience to my orders, had rallied to my aid from Galilee; while another large crowd was hurrying in from the villages. When I stood up and was beginning to speak, they all greeted me with acclamations, calling me the benefactor and saviour of their country. I thanked them and advised them neither to attack anyone nor to sully their hands with rapine, but to encamp in the plain and be content with their rations, as my desire was to quell these disturbances without bloodshed.

It happened, on that very day, that Jonathan's couriers, carrying dispatches, fell into the hands of my sentries posted to guard the roads. The prisoners were, in accordance with my directions, detained on the spot; the letters I perused and, finding them full of slander and lies, decided, without mentioning a word of them to anyone, to advance to meet my foes.

Jonathan, hearing of my coming, retired, with all his own followers and John, to the mansion of Jesus, which was a great castle, as imposing as a citadel. Here they concealed an armed ambuscade, and, locking all but one of the doors, they waited for me to come, after my journey, and pay my salutations. In fact, they gave orders to the soldiers to admit me only, on my arrival, and to exclude my attendants, hoping thus to have me easily at their mercy. In these expectations they were disappointed; for I, discovering their plot, at the end of my march took up my quarters immediately opposite them and pretended to be asleep. Jonathan and his friends, imagining that I was actually resting and asleep, hastened down to the plain, to create disaffection on the ground of my inefficiency as a general. The result was quite the reverse; for, no sooner had they appeared than the Galilæans raised a shout as hearty as their loyalty for me, their general, and reproached Jonathan's party for coming, unprovoked, upon the scene to throw the province into disorder. They bade them be off, declaring their fixed determination never to receive another governor in my place. Informed of these proceedings I no longer hesitated to show myself, but instantly went down to them to hear what Jonathan was saying. My appearance was the signal for universal applause, and I was hailed with encomiums and expressions of gratitude for my services as commander.

Jonathan and his friends, on hearing these demonstrations, fearing that the Galilæans, out of devotion to me, might make a rush upon them, became alarmed for their lives. They accordingly meditated flight; but on my requiring them to stay, were unable to escape and stood there shamefacedly while I spoke. After bidding the people restrain their applause, I posted the most trusted of my soldiers on the roads to secure us against any surprise attack from John, and advised the Galilæans to pick up their arms, in order to avoid confusion in the event of a sudden assault of the enemy. I then began by reminding Jonathan and his colleagues of their letter, how they had written that they had been commissioned by the general assembly at Jerusalem to settle my quarrels with John and how they had desired me to visit them. While relating these facts I held out the letter for all to see, to prevent any possibility of denial, the document being there to convict them. "Moreover, Jonathan and you, his colleagues," I proceeded, "had my case against John been tried and had I produced some two or three excellent men as witnesses to my behaviour, it is evident that you would have been compelled, after inquiries into their character, to acquit me of the charges brought against me. Now, in order to convince you of the propriety of my conduct in Galilee, I consider three witnesses too few for one who has lived an honourable life, and I present you with all these here present. Ask them what my life has been, and whether in my official capacity here I have acted with perfect dignity, perfect integrity. And you, Galilæans, I adjure to conceal nothing of the truth, but to declare in the presence of these men, as before judges in court, whether I have done anything amiss."

Before I had finished speaking, there was a chorus of voices from all sides calling me benefactor and saviour. They bore testimony to my past conduct and exhorted me upon my course in future; and they all swore that the honour of their womenfolk had been preserved and that they had never received a single injury from me. I then read aloud to the Galilæans two of the letters dispatched by Jonathan, which had been intercepted and forwarded to me by the scouts whom I had picketed on the roads. These were full of abuse and maligned me as acting the part of a tyrant rather than a general, with much else beside, including every variety of shameless falsehood. I told the people that these dispatches had been voluntarily surrendered to me by the bearers, because I did not wish my opponents to know of the scouts' share in the matter, lest they should be deterred from writing again.

The Galilæans, on hearing these calumnies, were so much exasperated that they were starting to kill Jonathan and his companions; and they would have effected their purpose had I not repressed their indignation. To Jonathan and his colleagues I promised pardon for the past on condition that they showed their contrition and returned home and gave a true report of my public life to those who had sent them. With that I let them go, well though I knew that they would fulfil none of their promises. The people, however, burning with rage against them, entreated my permission to punish those who had been guilty of such effrontery. I tried by all means to induce them to spare the men, knowing party quarrels are invariably fatal to the common weal. Popular feeling was, however, too deep-seated to be affected, and they all

rushed towards the house in which Jonathan and his friends had their quarters. Perceiving that their passions were now beyond restraint, I sprang to the
saddle, ordering the crowds to follow me to the village of Sogane, twenty
furlongs distant from Gabara. By this manœuvre I guarded myself against
the imputation of initiating a civil war.

Not long after this Vespasian arrived at Tyre, accompanied by King
Agrippa. The king was met by the invectives of the citizens, who denounced
him as an enemy of their own and of the Romans; because, as they asserted,
Philip, his commander-in-chief, had, under orders from him, betrayed the
royal palace and the Roman forces in Jerusalem. Vespasian, having heard
them, reprimanded the Tyrians for insulting one who was at once a king
and an ally of the Romans; at the same time advising the king to send Philip
to Rome to render an account of his actions to Nero. Thither, accordingly,
Philip was dispatched, but never had an audience of Nero, whom he found in
extremities owing to the prevailing disorders and the civil war, and so returned to the king.

On reaching Ptolemais, Vespasian received indignant remonstrances from
the chief men of the Syrian Decapolis against Justus of Tiberias for setting fire
to their villages. Vespasian handed him over to the king for execution by the
subjects of his realm. The king, however, merely detained him in prison,
concealing this from Vespasian, as previously narrated.

The Sepphorites, who met and saluted Vespasian, were given a garrison
under the command of Placidus. With this force they proceeded into the
interior, being closely followed by me until Vespasian's arrival in Galilee. Of
the manner of his arrival and of his first engagement with me in the neighbourhood of the village of Garis; of my withdrawal from there to Jotapata
and my conduct during the siege of that place; of my capture, imprisonment,
and subsequent liberation; of my conduct throughout the whole campaign
and at the siege of Jerusalem, I have given a detailed description in my books
on the Jewish War. It is, however, I think, incumbent upon me now to
append an account of such particulars of my life as were not recorded in my
earlier work.

After the siege of Jotapata I was in the hands of the Romans and was
kept under guard, while receiving every attention. Vespasian showed in many
ways the honour in which he held me, and it was by his command that I
married one of the women taken captive at Cæsarea, a virgin and a native of
that place. She did not, however, remain long with me, for she left me on
my obtaining my release and accompanying Vespasian to Alexandria. There
I married again. From Alexandria I was sent with Titus to the siege of
Jerusalem where my life was frequently in danger, both from the Jews, who
were eager to get me into their hands, to gratify their revenge, and from the
Romans, who attributed every reverse to some treachery on my part and
were constantly and clamorously demanding of the Emperor that he should

punish me as their betrayer. Titus Cæsar, however, knowing well the varying fortunes of war, repressed by his silence the soldiers' outbursts against me.

Again, when at last Jerusalem was on the point of being carried by assault, Titus Cæsar repeatedly urged me to take whatever I would from the wreck of my country, stating that I had his permission. And I, now that my native place had fallen, having nothing more precious to take and preserve as a solace for my personal misfortunes, made request to Titus for the freedom of some of my countrymen; I also received by his gracious favour a gift of sacred books. Not long after I made petition for my brother and fifty friends, and my request was granted. Again, by permission of Titus, I entered the Temple, where a great multitude of captive women and children had been imprisoned, and liberated all the friends and acquaintances whom I recognized, in number about a hundred and ninety; I took no ransom for their release and restored them to their former fortune. Once more, when I was sent by Titus Cæsar with Cerealius and a thousand horse to a village called Tekoa, to prospect whether it was a suitable place for an entrenched camp, and on my return saw many prisoners who had been crucified, and recognized three of my acquaintances among them, I was cut to the heart and came and told Titus with tears what I had seen. He gave orders immediately that they should be taken down and receive the most careful treatment. Two of them died in the physicians' hands; the third survived.

When Titus had quelled the disturbances in Judæa, conjecturing that the lands which I held at Jerusalem would be unprofitable to me, because a Roman garrison was to be quartered there, he gave me another parcel of ground in the plain. On his departure for Rome, he took me with him on board, treating me with every mark of respect. On our arrival in Rome I met with great consideration from Vespasian. He gave me a lodging in the house which he had occupied before he became Emperor; he honoured me with the privilege of Roman citizenship; and he assigned me a pension. He continued to honour me up to the time of his departure from this life, without any abatement in his kindness towards me.

My privileged position excited envy and thereby exposed me to danger. A certain Jew, named Jonathan, who had promoted an insurrection in Cyrene, occasioning the destruction of two thousand of the natives, whom he had induced to join him, on being sent in chains by the governor of the district to the Emperor, asserted that I had provided him with arms and money. Undeceived by this mendacious statement, Vespasian condemned him to death, and he was delivered over to execution. Subsequently, numerous accusations against me were fabricated by persons who envied me my good fortune; but, by the providence of God, I came safe through all. Vespasian also presented me with a considerable tract of land in Judæa.

At this period I divorced my wife, being displeased at her behaviour. She had borne me three children, of whom two died; one whom I named

Hyrcanus, is still alive. Afterwards I married a woman of Jewish extraction who had settled in Crete. She came of very distinguished parents, indeed the most notable people in that country. In character she surpassed many of her sex, as her subsequent life showed. By her I had two sons, Justus the elder, and then Simonides, surnamed Agrippa. Such is my domestic history.

The treatment which I received from the Emperors continued unaltered. On Vespasian's decease Titus, who succeeded to the empire, showed the same esteem for me as did his father, and never credited the accusations to which I was constantly subjected. Domitian succeeded Titus and added to my honours. He punished my Jewish accusers, and for a similar offence gave orders for the chastisement of a slave, a eunuch and my son's tutor. He also exempted my property in Judæa from taxation—a mark of the highest honour to the privileged individual. Moreover, Domitia, Cæsar's wife, never ceased conferring favours upon me.

Such are the events of my whole life; from them let others judge as they will of my character.

PAUL PREACHES IN THE DIASPORA [1]

THERE were at Antioch in the church there a number of prophets and teachers—Barnabas, Symeon who was called Niger, Lucius the Cyrenian, Manaen, who had been brought up with Herod the governor, and Saul. As they were engaged in worshiping the Lord and in fasting, the holy Spirit said,

"Set Barnabas and Saul apart for me, for the work to which I have called them."

So after fasting and prayer, they laid their hands upon them and let them go.

Being sent out in this way by the holy Spirit, they went down to Seleucia and sailed from there to Cyprus. When they reached Salamis, they proclaimed God's message in the Jewish synagogues. They had John with them as their assistant.

They went through the whole island as far as Paphos, and there they came across a Jewish magician and false prophet named Barjesus. He was attached to the governor, Sergius Paulus, who was an intelligent man. He sent for Barnabas and Saul and asked them to let him hear God's message. But Elymas the magician—for that is the meaning of his name—opposed them,

[1] This selection from *The Acts of the Apostles,* one of the most vivid historical books of ancient times, pictures the missionary activity of Paul of Tarsus among the well-established Jewish communities in the Near East. Because of Paul's animosity toward the Jews, which is generally explained by his temperament and his Hellenistic education, he was called "an Apostate from the Law."

and tried to keep the governor from accepting the faith. But Saul, who was also called Paul, was filled with the holy Spirit, and looked at him and said,

"You monster of underhandedness and cunning! You son of the devil! You enemy of all that is right! Will you never stop trying to make the Lord's straight paths crooked? The Lord's hand is right upon you, and you will be blind and unable even to see the sun for a time."

Instantly a mist of darkness fell upon him, and he groped about for someone to lead him by the hand. Then the governor, seeing what had happened, believed, and was thunderstruck at the Lord's teaching.

Paul and his companions sailed from Paphos and went to Perga in Pamphylia. There John left them and returned to Jerusalem, but they went on from Perga and reached Antioch in Pisidia. On the Sabbath they went to the synagogue there and took seats. After the reading of the Law and the Prophets, the synagogue authorities sent to them, saying,

"Brothers, if you have any appeal to make to the people, proceed."

Then Paul got up, and motioning with his hand, said,

"Men of Israel, and you who reverence God, listen! The God of this people of Israel chose our forefathers, and made the people great during their stay in Egypt, and then with uplifted hand led them out of Egypt. Then after he had taken care of them for forty years in the desert, he destroyed seven nations in Canaan, and settled them upon their land for about four hundred and fifty years. After that he gave them judges, down to the time of the prophet Samuel. Then they demanded a king and for forty years God gave them Saul, the son of Kish, a man of the tribe of Benjamin. Then he removed him and raised David up to be their king, bearing this testimony to him: 'I have found in David the son of Jesse a man after my own heart, who will do all that I desire.' It is from his descendants that God has brought to Israel as he promised to do, a savior in Jesus, in preparation for whose coming John had preached to all the people of Israel baptism in token of repentance. Toward the end of his career, John said, 'What do you suppose that I am? I am not he! No! Someone is coming after me, the shoes on whose feet I am not fit to untie!' Brothers! Descendants of the house of Abraham, and those others among you who reverence God! It is to us that this message of salvation has been sent. For the people of Jerusalem and their leaders refused to recognize him, and condemned him, thus fulfilling the very utterances of the prophets which are read every Sabbath, and though they could find no ground for putting him to death, they demanded of Pilate that he be executed. When they had carried out everything that had been said about him in the Scriptures, they took him down from the cross and laid him in a tomb. But God raised him from the dead, and for many days he appeared to those who had come up to Jerusalem with him from Galilee, and they are now witnesses for him to the people. So we now bring you the good news that God has fulfilled to us, their children, the promise that he made to our forefathers, by raising Jesus to life, just as the Scripture says in the second psalm, 'You are my son! Today I have become your Father!' Now as evidence that he has raised him from the dead, never again to return to decay, he said this: 'I will fulfil to you my sacred promises to David.' For in another psalm he says, 'You will not let your Holy One undergo decay.' Now David, after serving God's purposes in his own generation, fell asleep and was laid among his forefathers and did undergo decay, but he whom God raised to life did not undergo it. You must understand therefore, my brothers, that through him the forgiveness of your sins is announced to you, and that through union with him everyone who believes is cleared of every charge of which the Law of Moses could not clear you. Take care, therefore, that what is said in the prophets does not prove true of you:

> 'Look, you scoffers! Then wonder and begone!
> For I am doing something in your times
> Which you will never believe even when it is related to you!' "

As they were going out, the people begged to have all this said to them again on the following Sabbath, and after the congregation had broken up, many of the Jews and the devout converts to Judaism went away with Paul and Barnabas, and they talked with them, and urged them to rely on the favor of God.

The next Sabbath almost all the town gathered to hear God's message. But when the Jews saw the crowd, they were very jealous, and they contradicted what Paul said and abused him. Then Paul and Barnabas spoke out plainly, and said,

"God's message had to be told to you first, but since you thrust it off and judge yourselves unworthy of eternal life, we now turn to the heathen. For these are the orders the Lord has given us:

> 'I have made you a light for the heathen,
> To be the means of salvation to the very ends of the earth!' "

But Paul and Barnabas stayed on in Antioch and taught, and with many others preached the good news of the Lord's message.

Some time after, Paul said to Barnabas,

"Come, let us go back and revisit the brothers in each of the towns where we made the Lord's message known, to see how they are doing."

Now Barnabas wanted to take John who was called Mark with them. But Paul did not approve of taking with them a man who had deserted them in Pamphylia instead of going on with them to their work. They differed so sharply about it that they separated, and Barnabas took Mark and sailed for Cyprus. But Paul selected Silas and set out, the brothers commending him to the Lord's favor. He traveled through Syria and Cilicia and strengthened the churches.

He went to Derbe and Lystra also. At Lystra there was a disciple named Timothy whose mother was a Jewish Christian while his father was a Greek, and who was highly thought of by the brothers in Lystra and Iconium. Paul wished to take this man on with him, and so on account of the Jews in that district he had him circumcised, for they all knew that his father was a Greek. As they traveled on from one town to another, they passed on to the brothers for their observance the decisions that had been reached by the apostles and elders at Jerusalem. So the churches became stronger and stronger in the faith, and their numbers increased from day to day.

Thus they crossed Phrygia and Galatia. The holy Spirit prevented them from delivering the message in Asia, and when they reached Mysia they tried to get into Bithynia, but the Spirit of Jesus would not permit it, and they passed Mysia and came down to Troas. There Paul had a vision one night; a Macedonian was standing appealing to him and saying,

"Come over to Macedonia and help us."

As soon as he had this vision, we made efforts to get on to Macedonia, concluding that God had called us to tell them the good news.

So we sailed from Troas, and ran a straight course to Samothrace, and next day to Neapolis. From there we went to Philippi, a Roman garrison town, and the principal place in that part of Macedonia.

In this town we stayed for some days. On the Sabbath we went outside the gates, to the bank of the river where we supposed there was a praying place, and we sat down and talked with the women who gathered there. One of our hearers was a woman named Lydia, a dealer in purple goods, from the town of Thyatira. She was a believer in God, and the Lord touched her heart, and led her to accept Paul's teaching. When she and her household were baptized, she appeared to us, and said,

"If you are really convinced that I am a believer in the Lord, come and stay at my house." And she insisted upon our coming.

Once as we were on our way to the praying place a slave girl met us who had the gift of ventriloquism and made her masters a great deal of money by her fortune-telling. This girl would follow Paul and the rest of us, crying out,

"These men are slaves of the Most High God, and they are making known to you a way of salvation."

She did this for a number of days, until Paul, very much annoyed, turned and said to the spirit in her,

"In the name of Jesus Christ I order you to come out of her!" And it came out instantly.

But when her masters saw that their hopes of profits were gone, they seized Paul and Silas, dragged them to the public square, to the authorities, and brought them before the chief magistrates.

"These men," they said, "are Jews, and they are making a great disturbance in our town. They are advocating practices which it is against the law for us as Romans to adopt or observe."

The crowd also joined in the attack on them, and the magistrates had them stripped and beaten. After beating them severely, they put them in jail, and gave the jailer orders to keep close watch of them. He, having had such strict orders, put them into the inner cell, and fastened their feet in the stocks. But about midnight, as Paul and Silas were praying and singing hymns of praise to God, and the prisoners were listening to them, suddenly there was such an earthquake that the jail shook to its foundations; all the doors flew open, and everybody's chains were unfastened. It woke up the jailer, and when he saw that the doors of the jail were open, he drew his sword and was just going to kill himself, supposing that the prisoners had escaped. But Paul shouted out,

"Do not do yourself any harm! We are all here!"

Then he called for lights and rushed in, and fell trembling at the feet of Paul and Silas. He led them out of the jail and said to them,

"Gentlemen, what must I do to be saved?"

"Believe in the Lord Jesus," they said, "and you and your household will be saved!"

Then they told God's message to him and to all the members of his household. And right then in the night, he took them and washed their wounds, and he and all his household were baptized immediately. Then he took them up to his house and offered them food, and he and all his household were very happy over their new faith in God. In the morning the magistrates sent policemen with instructions to let the men go. The jailer reported this message to Paul, saying,

"The magistrates have sent orders that you are to be released. So you can take your leave and go unmolested."

But Paul said to them,

"They had us beaten in public without giving us a trial, and put us in jail, although we are Roman citizens! And now are they going to dismiss us secretly? By no means! Have them come here themselves and take us out!"

The policemen delivered this message to the magistrates, and they were alarmed when they heard that they were Roman citizens, and came and conciliated them, and took them out of the jail, and begged them to leave the town. After leaving the jail they went to Lydia's house, and saw the brothers and encouraged them. Then they left the town.

After passing through Amphipolis and Apollonis, they reached Thessalonica, where the Jews had a synagogue. Paul went to it as he was accustomed to do, and for three Sabbaths he discussed the Scriptures with them, explaining them and showing that the Christ had to suffer and rise from the dead.

"Jesus," he said, "of whom I am telling you, is the Christ!"

He convinced some of them, and they joined Paul and Silas, along with a great many devout Greeks and a number of the principal women. This offended the Jews and they gathered some unprincipled loafers, formed a mob and started a riot in the town. They attacked Jason's house, to find them and bring them out among the people. As they could not find them, they dragged Jason and some of the brothers before the town magistrates, shouting,

"The men who have made trouble all over the world have come here too, and Jason has taken them in. They all disobey the emperor's decrees, and claim that someone else called Jesus is king."

The crowd and the magistrates were very much excited at hearing this, and they put Jason and the others under bonds before they let them go.

The brothers sent Paul and Silas away immediately, in the course of the following night, to Berea. On arriving there they went to the Jewish synagogue. The Jews there were more high-minded than those at Thessalonica, and received the message with great eagerness and studied the Scriptures every day, to find out whether it was true. Many of them became believers and those who worshiped with them, and every day in the public square when the Jews at Thessalonica found out that God's message had been delivered at Berea by Paul, they came there too, to excite and stir up the populace. Then the brothers immediately sent Paul off to the coast, while Silas and Timothy stayed behind. The men who went with Paul took him all the way to Athens, and came back with instructions for Silas and Timothy to rejoin them as soon as possible.

While Paul waited for them at Athens, he was exasperated to see how idolatrous the city was. He had discussions at the synagogue with the Jews and so did no small number of Greek women of position, and men too. But with any whom he happened to find. Some of the Epicurean and Stoic philosophers debated with him. Some of them said,

"What is this rag-picker trying to make out?"

Others said,

"He seems to be preaching some foreign deities."

This was because he was telling the good news of Jesus and the resurrection. So they took him and brought him to the council of the Areopagus and said,

"May we know just what this new teaching of yours is? Some of the things you tell us sound strange to us, and we want to know just what they mean."

For all Athenians and all visitors there from abroad used to spend all their time telling or listening to something new.

Then Paul stood up in the middle of the council and said,

"Men of Athens, from every point of view I see that you are extremely religious. For as I was going about and looking at the things you worship, I even found an altar with this inscription: 'To an Unknown God.' So it is what you already worship in ignorance that I am now telling you of. God who created the world and all that is in it, since he is Lord of heaven and earth, does not live in temples built by human hands, nor is he waited on by human hands as though he were in need of anything, for he himself gives all men life and breath and everything. From one forefather he has created every nation of mankind, and made them live all over the face of the earth, fixing their appointed times and the limits of their lands, so that they might search for God, and perhaps grope for him and find him, though he is never far from any of us. For it is through union with him that we live and move and exist, as some of your poets have said,

'For we are also his offspring.'

So if we are God's children we ought not to imagine that the divine nature is like gold or silver or stone, wrought by human art and thought. While God overlooked those times of ignorance, he now calls upon all men everywhere to repent, since he has fixed a day on which he will justly judge the world through a man whom he has appointed, and whom he has guaranteed to all men by raising him from the dead."

When they heard of resurrection of the dead, some of them sneered, but others said,

"We should like to hear you again on this subject."

So Paul left the council. Some persons joined him, however, and became believers, among them Dionysius, a member of the council, and a woman named Damaris, and some others.

After this he left Athens and went to Corinth. There he found a Jew named Aquila, a native of Pontus, who had recently come from Italy with his wife Priscilla, because Claudius had ordered all Jews to leave Rome. Paul went to see them, and as they practiced the same trade, he stayed with them, and they worked together, for they were tent-makers. Every Sabbath he would preach in the synagogue, and try to convince both Jews and Greeks.

By the time Silas and Timothy arrived from Macedonia, Paul was absorbed in preaching the message, emphatically assuring the Jews that Jesus was the Christ. But as they contradicted and abused him, he shook his clothes in protest, and said to them,

"Your blood be on your own heads! I am not to blame for it! After this I will go to the heathen."

So he moved to the house of a devout proselyte named Titus Justus, which was next door to the synagogue. But Crispus, the leader of the synagogue, believed in the Lord, and so did all his household, and many of the people of Corinth heard Paul and believed and were baptized. One night the Lord said to Paul in a vision,

"Do not be afraid! Go on speaking and do not give up, for I am with you, and no one shall attack you or injure you, for I have many people in this city."

So he settled there for a year and a half, and taught them God's message.

Paul stayed some time longer, and then bade the brothers good-bye and sailed for Syria, with Priscilla and Aquila. At Cenchreæ he had his hair cut, because of a vow he had been under. When they reached Ephesus he left them there. He went to the synagogue there and had a discussion with the Jews. They asked him to stay longer, but he would not consent. He bade them good-bye, saying,

"I will come back to you again if it is God's will."

Then he sailed from Ephesus. When he reached Cæsarea, he went up to Jerusalem and paid his respects to the church, and then went on to Antioch. After spending some time there, he started out again, and traveled systematically through Galatia and Phrygia, reassuring all the disciples.

A Jew named Apollos, a native of Alexandria, came to Ephesus. He was an eloquent man, skilful in the use of the Scriptures. He had had some instruction about the Way of the Lord, and he talked with burning zeal and taught painstakingly about Jesus, though he knew of no baptism but John's. He spoke very confidently in the synagogue at first, but when Priscilla and Aquila heard him, they took him home and explained the Way of God to him more correctly. As he wanted to cross Greece, the brothers wrote to the disciples there, urging them to welcome him. On his arrival there he was of great service to those who through God's favor had become believers, for he vigorously refuted the Jews in public, and showed from the scriptures that Jesus was the Christ.

It was while Apollos was in Corinth that Paul, after passing through the interior, reached Ephesus. Finding some disciples there, he said to them,

"Did you receive the holy Spirit when you became believers?"

"No," they said to him, "we never even heard that there was a holy Spirit."

"How then were you baptized?" he asked.

"With John's baptism," they answered.

"John's baptism was a baptism in token of repentance," said Paul, "and he told the people to believe in him who was to follow him, that is, in Jesus."

When they heard this, they were baptized in the name of the Lord Jesus, and when Paul laid his hands on them, the holy Spirit came on them, and they spoke in foreign tongues and with prophetic inspiration. There were about twelve of them in all.

He went to the synagogue there, and for three months spoke confidently, holding discussions and trying to persuade them about the Kingdom of God. But as some of them were obstinate and refused to believe, finding fault with the Way before the people, he left them, and withdrew the disciples, and held daily discussions in the lecture-room of Tyrannus. This went on for two years, so that everyone who lived in Asia, Greeks as well as Jews, heard the Lord's message.

God did such extraordinary wonders by means of Paul that people took to the sick handkerchiefs or aprons he had used, and they were cured of their diseases, and the evil spirits went out of them. Some Jews who went from place to place casting out demons tried to use the name of the Lord Jesus in the cases of people who had evil spirits in them, saying,

"I command you in the name of Jesus whom Paul preaches!"

A Jewish high priest named Sceba had seven sons who were doing this. But the evil spirit answered,

"I know Jesus, and I know of Paul, but who are you?"

And the man in whom the evil spirit was sprang at them, and over-powered them all with such violence that they ran out of the house tattered and bruised. This came to be known to everyone who lived in Ephesus, Greeks as well as Jews, and great awe came over them all, and the name of the Lord Jesus came to be held in high honor. Many who became believers would come and openly confess their former practices. A number of people who had practiced magic brought out their books and burned them publicly. The value of these was estimated and found to be ten thousand dollars. So the Lord's message went on growing wonderfully in influence and power.

After these events, Paul, under the Spirit's guidance, resolved to go to Jerusalem, and to revisit Macedonia and Greece on the way.

"After I have gone there," he said, "I must see Rome also."

He sent two of his assistants, Timothy and Erastus, to Macedonia, while he stayed on for a while in Asia.

Just at that time a great commotion arose about the Way. A silversmith named Demetrius was making large profits for his workmen by the manu-facture of silver shrines of Artemis. He got the workmen in that and similar trades together, and said to them,

"Men, you know that this business is the source of our prosperity, and you see and hear that not only in Ephesus but almost all over Asia, this man Paul has persuaded and drawn away numbers of people, telling them that gods made by human hands are not gods at all. There is danger, therefore, not only that this business of ours will be discredited, but also that the temple of the great goddess Artemis will be neglected and the magnificence of her whom all Asia and the world worship will be a thing of the past!"

When they heard this, they became very angry, and cried,

"Great Artemis of Ephesus!"

So the commotion spread all over the city, and by a common impulse the people rushed to the theater, dragging with them two Macedonians, Gaius and Aristarchus, Paul's traveling companions. Paul wanted to go before the people himself, but the disciples would not allow it. Some of the religious authorities also, who were friends of his, sent to him and begged him not to venture into the theater. Meanwhile the people were shouting, some one thing and some another, for the meeting was in confusion, and most of them had no idea why they had come together. Some of the crowd called upon Alexander, as the Jews had pushed him to the front, and he made a gesture with his hand and was going to speak in defense of them to the people. But when they saw that he was a Jew, a great shout went up from them all, and they cried for two hours,

"Great Artemis of Ephesus!"

At last the recorder quieted the mob and said,

"Men of Ephesus, who in the world does not know that the city of Ephesus is the guardian of the temple of the great Artemis, and of the image that fell down from the sky? So as these facts are undeniable, you must be calm, and not do anything reckless. For you have brought these men here, though they have not been guilty of disloyalty nor uttered any blasphemy against our goddess. If Demetrius and his fellow-craftsmen have a charge to bring against anyone, there are the courts and the governors; let them take legal action. But if you require anything beyond that, it must be settled before the regular assembly. For we are in danger of being charged with rioting in connection with today's events, though there is really nothing about this commotion that we will not be able to explain."

With these words he dismissed the assembly.

When the confusion was over, Paul sent for the disciples and encouraged them. Then he bade them good-bye and started for Macedonia. After traveling through those districts and giving the people a great deal of encouragement, he went on to Greece where he stayed for three months. Just as he was going to sail for Syria, the Jews made a plot against him, and he made up his mind to return by way of Macedonia. He was accompanied by Sopater of Beres, the son of Pyrrhus, Aristarchus and Secundus, from Thessalonica, Gaius of Derbe, Timothy, and Tychius and Trophimus, from Asia. They went on to Troas and waited for us there, while we sailed from Philippi after the Festival of Unleavened Bread, and joined them at Troas five days later. There we stayed a week.

On the first day of the week, when we had met for the breaking of bread, Paul addressed them, as he was going away the next morning, and he prolonged his address until midnight. There were a great many lamps in the upstairs room where we met and a young man named Eutychus, who was sitting at the window, became very drowsy as Paul's address grew longer and longer, and finally went fast asleep and fell from the third story to the ground, and was picked up for dead. But Paul went downstairs, and threw himself upon him, and put his arms around him.

"Do not be alarmed," he said, "he is still alive."

Then he went upstairs again, and broke the bread, and ate, and after a long talk with them that lasted until daylight, he went away. They took the boy home alive, and were greatly comforted.

We had already gone on board the ship and sailed for Assos, intending to take Paul on board there, for that was the arrangement he had made, as he intended to travel there by land. So when he met us at Assos, we took him on board and went on to Mitylene. Sailing from there, we arrived off Chios on the following day. On the next we crossed to Samos, and on the next we reached Miletus. For Paul had decided to sail past Ephesus, so that he would not have to lose any time in Asia, for he was hurrying to reach Jerusalem, if possible, by the day of the Harvest Festival.

From Miletus he sent to Ephesus for the elders of the church. When they came, he said to them,

"You know well enough how I lived among you all the time from the first day I set foot in Asia, and how I served the Lord most humbly and with tears, through all the trials that I encountered because of the plots of the Jews. I never shrank from telling you anything that was for your good, nor from teaching you in public or at your houses, but earnestly urged Greeks as well as Jews to turn to God in repentance and to believe in our Lord Jesus. I am here now on my way to Jerusalem, for the Spirit compels me to go there, though I do not know what will happen to me there, except that in every town I visit, the holy Spirit warns me that imprisonment and persecution are awaiting me. But my life does not matter, if I can only finish my race and do the service intrusted to me by the Lord Jesus, of declaring the good news of God's favor. Now I know perfectly well that none of you among whom I went about preaching the kingdom of God will ever see my face again. Therefore I declare to you today that I am not responsible for the blood of any of you, for I have not shrunk from letting you know God's purpose without reserve. Take care of yourselves and of the whole flock, of which the holy Spirit has made you guardians, and be shepherds of the church of God, which he got at the cost of his own life. I know that after I am gone savage wolves will get in among you and will not spare the flock, and from your own number men will appear and teach perversions of the truth in order to draw the disciples away from them. So you must be on your guard and remember that for three years, night and day, I never stopped warning any one of you, even with tears. Now I commit you to the Lord, and to the message of his favor, which will build you up and give you a place among those whom God has consecrated. I have never coveted anyone's gold or silver or clothes. You know well enough that these hands of mine provided for my needs and my companions. I showed you in every way that by hard work like that we must help those who are weak and remember the words of the Lord Jesus, for he said, 'It makes one happier to give than to be given to.'"

With these words, he knelt down with them all and prayed. They all wept aloud, and throwing their arms about Paul's neck they kissed him affectionately, for they were especially saddened at his saying that they would never see his face again. Then they accompanied him to the ship.

TORAH: LAW AND LEGEND

From the beginning of the common era until the early middle ages literary expression among the Jews was confined chiefly to formal rabbinical literature. It is out of the interpretative branch of this literature—the Agada—that the following tales have been culled. "The poetical sense of the Rabbis," wrote Israel Abrahams, "expressed itself in a vast and beautiful array of legendary additions to the Bible, but the additions are always devised with a moral purpose, to give point to a preacher's homily or to inspire the imagination of the audience with nobler fancies." But the Agada is something more than "additions" to the Bible. Although it originated in the interpretation and elaboration of Biblical texts, it constitutes a unique, distinctive literature which reflects the social life and the spiritual yearnings of the talmudic Jew. The literary form of the Agada approximates our "short short story"; the substance is as varied and prodigious as life itself. In many cases the names of individual authors have been preserved, but the influence of the Agada came through enormous anthologies—The Midrashim—which in scope and poetic insight have no parallel in world literature.

Moreover, the Agada has had an unbroken history to the present. New anthologies became popular in Hebrew and Yiddish soon after the invention of the printing press; itinerant preachers, orators (Maggidim) and Hasidic saints added abundantly to the rich harvest of the past; and in modern times poets have again turned to the golden treasuries of the Agada for exploration. Hence some examples of the creations of these interpreters—Berdyczevski, Bialik, Buber, Fleg—are incorporated in this section.

Over a hundred years ago Samuel Taylor Coleridge, the English poet, who translated about a half dozen of these tales (see *The Lord Helpeth Man and Beast* and *A Good Wife*), wrote of the value of the Agada in his magazine *The Friend* (1807), and deplored the complete neglect of them in English. Since then numerous collections have been published, but his criticism still holds true. The recently published volume of Bialik, *And It Came to Pass,* a complete saga on the legend and lives of David and Solomon written in Biblical style, and the two volumes of Fleg, *The Life of Moses* and *The Life of Solomon,* serve to illustrate the vast possibilities for an adventurous poet. *Boaz Makes Up His Mind* by Irving Fineman, may be considered an American Agada.

The remainder of the tales are chosen and revised from *The Exempla of the Rabbis* by Moses Gaster, *Hebrew Tales* by Hyman Hurwitz, and the *Sefer Agada* by Bialik and Ravnitsky.

THE LORD HELPETH MAN AND BEAST

During his march to conquer the world, Alexander, the Macedonian, came to a people in Africa who dwelt in a remote and secluded corner in peaceful huts, and knew neither war nor conqueror. They led him to the hut of their chief, who received him hospitably, and placed before him golden dates, golden figs, and bread of gold.

"Do you eat gold in this country?" said Alexander.

"I take it for granted," replied the chief, "that thou wert able to find eatable food in thine own country. For what reason, then, art thou come amongst us?"

"Your gold has not tempted me hither," said Alexander, "but I would become acquainted with your manners and customs."

"So be it," rejoined the other, "sojourn among us as long as it pleaseth thee."

At the close of this conversation, two citizens entered, as into their court of justice. The plaintiff said,

"I bought of this man a piece of land, and as I was making a deep drain through it, I found a treasure. This is not mine, for I only bargained for the land, and not for any treasure that might be concealed beneath it; and yet the former owner of the land will not receive it."

The defendant answered,

"I hope I have a conscience, as well as my fellow-citizen. I sold him the land with all its contingent, as well as existing advantages, and consequently, the treasure inclusively."

The chief, who was at the same time their supreme judge, recapitulated their words, in order that the parties might see whether or not he understood them aright. Then, after some reflection, said,

"Thou hast a son, friend, I believe?"

"Yes."

"And thou," addressing the other, "a daughter?"

"Yes."

"Well, then, let thy son marry *thy* daughter, and bestow the treasure on the young couple for a marriage portion."

Alexander seemed surprised and perplexed.

"Think you my sentence unjust?" the chief asked him.

"Oh, no!" replied Alexander, "but it astonishes me."

"And how, then, would the case have been decided in your country?"

"To confess the truth," said Alexander, "we should have taken both parties into custody, and have seized the treasure for the king's use."

"For the king's use!" exclaimed the chief; "does the sun shine on that country?"

"Oh, yes!"

"Does it rain there?"

"Assuredly."

"Wonderful! But are there tame animals in the country, that live on the grass and green herbs?"

"Very many, and of many kinds."

"Ay, that must, then, be the cause," said the chief, "for the sake of those innocent animals the All-gracious Being continues to let the sun shine, and the rain drop down on your country, since its inhabitants are unworthy of such blessings."

A GOOD WIFE

"HE that hath found a virtuous wife, hath a greater treasure than costly pearls."

Such a treasure had the celebrated teacher, Rabbi Meir, found. He sat during the whole of one Sabbath day in the public school, and instructed the people. During his absence from his house, his two sons, both of them of uncommon beauty, and enlightened in the law, died. His wife bore them to his bed-chamber, laid them upon the marriage-bed, and spread a white covering over their bodies.

Towards evening, Rabbi Meir came home.

"Where are my beloved sons," he asked, "that I may give them my blessing?"

"They are gone to the school," was the answer.

"I repeatedly looked round the school," he replied, "and I did not see them there."

She reached him a goblet; he praised the Lord at the going out of the Sabbath, drank, and again asked,

"Where are my sons, that they may drink of the cup of blessing?"

"They will not be far off," she said, and placed food before him, that he might eat.

He was in a gladsome and genial mood, and when he had said grace after the meal, she thus addressed him: "Rabbi, with thy permission, I would fain propose to thee one question."

"Ask it, then, my love!" he replied.

"A few days ago, a person entrusted some jewels to my custody, and now he demands them again: should I give them back again?"

"This is a question," said Rabbi Meir, "which my wife should not have thought it necessary to ask. What! wouldst thou hesitate or be reluctant to restore to everyone his own?"

"No," she replied, "but yet I thought it best not to restore them without acquainting thee therewith."

She then led him to their chamber, and, stepping to the bed, took the white covering from their bodies.

"Ah, my sons! my sons!" thus loudly lamented the father: "My sons! the light of mine eyes, and the light of my understanding; I was your father, but ye were my teachers in the law!"

The mother turned away, and wept bitterly. At length, she took her husband by the hand, and said,

"Rabbi, didst thou not teach me that we must not be reluctant to restore that which was entrusted to our keeping? See, the Lord gave, and the Lord has taken away, and blessed be the name of the Lord!"

"Blessed be the name of the Lord," echoed Rabbi Meir, "and blessed be His name for thy sake, too! For well is it written, 'He that hath found a virtuous woman, hath a greater treasure than costly pearls. She openeth her mouth with wisdom, and on her tongue is the instruction of kindness.'"

OF LOVE AND FAITH

I

THERE once lived in Jerusalem a plantation owner named Kalba Shebua. He was fabulously rich and exercised his power over numerous workers and his own family like a proud tyrant.

He had one daughter whose loveliness was like the sunset over the hills of the city, and whose wisdom made her precious among the daughters of Israel. But, to her father's dismay, she spurned proffered matches with some of the richest tradesmen of Jerusalem and the wealthiest merchants of Babylonia; for she had fallen in love with Akiba ben Joseph, one of her father's shepherds. He was a poor but noble man, the best of the shepherds in the country. One day, after singing and piping melodies to the girl near his beloved flocks, he revealed to her his love in the golden words of Solomon's rival:

> "Ah, you are beautiful, my love;
> Ah, you are beautiful;
> Your eyes are doves.
> Like a rose among thorns,
> So is my beloved among the maidens."

And after she acknowledged her love for him, saying that his fruit was sweet to her taste, she betrothed herself to him on his promise to leave the fields and devote his life to study and teaching. Then, enfolded in his strong arms, she sang to him:

"Set me like a seal upon your heart,
 Like a seal upon your arm;
 For love is as mighty as death,
 As strong as the grave;
 Many waters cannot quench love, nor rivers overcome it;
 If one were to offer all the substance of his house for love, it would be utterly
    contemned."

When Kalba Shebua heard of the betrothal, he became violent and drove her out of his house. The girl lived with Akiba's mother, and because she belonged to a family of high standing, the neighbors would bring her work secretly while she sent part of her earnings to Akiba, who was studying at the Academy. Despite the drudgery of her position and the sarcasm of the townspeople, she was not discouraged. Did she not smile goodheartedly at a cripple who said to her, "Your hair will turn grey before that shepherd will become a scholar."

Akiba, however, was not certain of attaining his goal, for he was about forty years old when he began his career as a student: he did not believe that he would succeed in swimming safely through the rough seas of Jewish Law. But his wife showed him by practical example how people laughed only once or twice, and then respected a person's conviction. Once he was sitting before a fountain in Lud and saw a large stone with a cavity in the center. When he asked who bored the hole and was told that it had been caused by the rope, with which the bucket was lowered, pressing along the stone, he said to himself: "If such a soft material can dissolve stone, why should not the the words of the Law, which are as hard as iron, make an impression on my heart, which is flesh?" So he devoted himself heart and soul to the study of the Law.

After twelve years Akiba returned to Jerusalem. He was now a renowned scholar and two thousand pupils and disciples followed in his train. All the people crowded the streets to get a glimpse of Rabbi Akiba. Among those who appeared was Kalba Shebua who was presented to the sage. He asked him what he should do with his daughter whom he had driven away from his home. He had made a vow not to support her, but now she was starving and he wanted the great Rabbi to release him from his vow. Akiba asked him the reason for this vow. He said,

"She betrothed herself to an ignorant shepherd who could not even say the blessing over the meals."

"But if he has since become a scholar?"

"If he only knew the blessings," Kalba Shebua replied, "I would give him half my fortune."

"I am the man," said Akiba.

His father-in-law immediately arose, kissed him and thanked the Lord for His generosity and mercy.

As Akiba drew near to his house, his wife came to meet him, fell at his feet and wanted to kiss the hem of his garment. The pupils, not knowing who the woman was, were about to push her aside when Akiba said,

"Leave her alone, for all that you and I know is due to her, for it is the wisdom of the women that builds up the house."

And he had a large tiara, set with many precious stones, made for his wife. When the children asked why he always gave her such valuable presents, he replied that he could never repay her adequately for her love and devotion.

II

Now Rabbi Akiba lived in the most calamitous times. The land of Israel groaned under the iron yoke of the Romans who, attributing the heroic resistance which the people had made against them to the spirit of the Jewish religion, attempted to abolish it by forbidding the observance of the festivals and the study of the Law. Akiba, however, continued to instruct the people in their religious duties, and to teach the Law publicly.

One day, while he was teaching his disciples, Papus ben Judah, a man well known for his learning, took him to task for endangering his life by disobeying the Roman decrees.

"Akiba, are you not afraid of the Romans?" he asked. "Are there not times that require us to yield to circumstances?"

"Papus, are you the man whom people address as a sage? Surely, your questions indicate that you are a fool. When the Law says, 'Thou shalt love the Lord, thy God, with all thy heart, and with all thy soul,' does it not teach us that, when our religion is threatened, we must not, under any circumstances, yield to expediency? Now listen to this fable.

"A fox once took a walk by the side of a river, and observed the fish hurrying to and fro, in the greatest agitation and alarm. Anxious to know the cause of this confusion, he addressed himself to them as follows,

" 'Friends, may I be so bold as to ask why you are so agitated?'

" 'We are attempting to flee from our enemies, and avoid the many nets and snares which they have prepared for us.'

" 'Oh! oh!' said the cunning fox, 'if that is all, I can tell you of an easy way to secure your safety. Come along with me on dry land, where we may dwell together in peace, in the same manner as our ancestors did before us.'

"The fish, perceiving the treachery of their advisor, said to him,

" 'Fox! fox! So you are considered the most sagacious of animals! Surely, your advice proves you are a fool. If, even in our natural element, we are beset with so many dangers, what security can we expect to find in an element so antagonistic to our nature, and so contrary to our habits?'

"It is even so with us," continued Akiba. "If even by partially observing the Law, which is our very life, we experience so much distress and oppression, what do you imagine our lot would be if we entirely abandoned it?"

Akiba was thrown into prison by the Romans. Not long afterwards, Papus was placed in the same dungeon with him. When Akiba saw him, he asked,

"Well, Papus, what brought you here?"

"Blest are you, Akiba," replied Papus, "for you suffer for the Law. Woe to me, who suffers for vain things."

Akiba finally suffered martyrdom. By the order of the emperor Hadrian, he was publicly flayed alive with blazing iron tongs. Before he breathed his last, he cried aloud,

"All my life I have repeated and fulfilled the commandment, 'Thou shalt love the Lord with all thy heart, and with all thy might.' Now I know what it is to love him with 'all my soul.'"

ELISHA BEN ABUYA, SCEPTIC

THE world, declared one of our sages, is like a large cake. It contains many different ingredients which, when kneaded and baked, produce a harmonious delicacy. Life, too, has its diverse elements, good and evil, joy and sadness, pain and pleasure, religion and paganism, saints and sceptics—all of them necessary to make life real, varied, colorful. That is why, said the sage, we should consider ourselves blessed to have had the sage and arch-sceptic, Elisha ben Abuya, in our midst.

When Elisha was born, a group of scholars were present, discussing the Law. At the moment of his birth, a celestial flame leapt from the heavens and encircled the house, and the infant appeared as a luminous precious stone, inundating the inside of the house with an incandescent glow. This so impressed his father that he dedicated his son to the study of the Law. But because he had done so, not that his son should become a scholar, but merely for the sake of honor, Elisha in his late life turned away from Judaism, and became a heretic.

The charges that his fellow-Jews brought against Elisha were manifold: he worked and rode on the Sabbath. In the time of persecution, he assisted the Romans in forcing the Jews to break their Law.

Once Rabbi Meir, his pupil, saw him riding on the Sabbath. He did not reproach him but discussed the Law with him, and found that he showed great erudition. Rabbi Meir tried to induce him to return to the study of the Law but Elisha refused, saying that he once heard a voice behind the Western Wall of the Temple, declaring, "That all who repented should be saved except Elisha ben Abuya who knew My power and rebelled against it."

"Why have you become so rebellious?" asked Rabbi Meir.

Elisha related this tale. Once when he was sitting in the Valley of Genessareth he saw a man climb up a tree on the Sabbath and snatch a nest with a bird and its young. He came down unharmed. Another man, going up the tree, sent the bird away and, in accordance with the Law, kept only the little ones. Coming down he was bitten by a snake, and died. Where was the divine promise that by obeying the Law a man's life would be prolonged? Elisha continued. Once he saw the tongue of Rabbi Nahum, the martyr, eaten by dogs. "Is this the reward of study?" asked Elisha, for he did not believe in the reward after death or in the resurrection of the dead.

Rabbi Meir, however, persisted in his attempt. When he heard that Elisha was dangerously ill, he went to visit him. He again asked him to repent. And Elisha asked,

"Will He receive me now?"

"Yes," replied Rabbi Meir.

Elisha wept and died.

And after a few days Rabbi Meir was told that a fire was issuing out of the grave of his master. He went there, covered it with a mantle, and said,

"Slumber tonight, for perchance the Lord will save you; and if not, *I* will save you. Sleep until morning."

THE ANATOMY OF LEADERSHIP

IN whom shall the leadership and guidance of society be vested? Who is best qualified to administer laws and govern a nation? These questions were being discussed in the Academy when Rabbi Joshua ben Levi told the following fable to illustrate what he considered the inescapable truth.

A serpent's tail had long followed the direction of the head, and all went well. One day the tail became dissatisfied with this natural arrangement and addressed the head as follows:

"I have long, with great indignation, observed your unjust procedure. In all our travels and journeys, it is you who take the lead whereas I, like a menial servant, am obliged to follow behind. You appear everywhere, in the forest and before our fellow-creatures at the head of the parade, but I, like a miserable slave, must remain in the background. Is this fair? Am I not a member of the same body? Why shouldn't I take part in the membership as well as you?"

"You!" exclaimed the head. "You! You, silly tail, want to manage the body! Have you eyes to discern danger, have you ears to be apprized of it, have you brains to prevent or cope with it? Do you not see that it is for your own advantage that I should direct and lead?"

"For my advantage, indeed!" rejoined the tail. "This is the language of all demagogues and oppressors and usurpers. They all pretend to rule for the benefit of their slaves. But I will no longer submit to this state of affairs. I insist, indeed, I demand that I take the lead in my turn."

"Very well, lead on!"

The tail, overjoyed and puffed up with pride, took the lead. Its first exploit was to drag the body into a miry ditch. The situation became quite unpleasant. The tail struggled hard, groped, pulled, turned, and by tremendous effort managed to get out again. But the body was so thickly covered with dirt and filth that it hardly appeared to be the same creature. Its next exploit was to get entangled amongst some briars and thorns. The pain was intense; the whole body was agitated; the more it struggled to free itself, the deeper were the wounds. Here it would have ended its unfortunate career, had not the head hastened to its assistance, and extricated the body from its hazardous situation. The tail, however, was not yet discouraged. It persisted in keeping the lead. It marched on, and as chance decreed, crept into a fiery furnace. It soon began to feel the torture of the hot iron. The whole body was convulsed—all was darkness, terror, confusion, dismay. The head again hastened to offer its friendly aid. Alas! it was too late. The tail was already consumed; and the fire soon reached the vital parts of the body. So the body was destroyed, and the head was involved in the disaster.

What caused the destruction of the head? Was it not because it suffered itself to be guided by the blind tail? It is best, added Rabbi ben Levi, to hearken to the advice of the Torah, "to select from amongst you, wise men, men of understanding, well-known to your tribes."

SEEK PEACE!

THE famous sage Rabbi Meir was accustomed to preach publicly for the edification of the people on the eve of the Sabbath. The public halls were always packed, for the learned man was blessed not only with great erudition but also with remarkable eloquence. His lectures were always illustrated by his extraordinary experiences all over the world, and he clinched his point with anecdotes and fables for which he became celebrated.

Amongst his large audience there was a woman who was so delighted with his discourse that she remained after he concluded, to listen to his answers to the questions of a small group of scholars who had gathered around him. Instructed and pleased, she went home to enjoy the repast which was generally prepared for the honor of the Holy Day. But she was surprised and disappointed when, on arriving near her house, she found the lights extinguished, and her husband standing at the door, apparently in great anger.

"Where have you been?" he inquired in a tone that indicated that he was far from pleased with her absence.

"I have been," she replied mildly, "to hear our learned Rabbi preach, and a delightful discourse it was."

"Was it?" he replied. "Well then, since the Rabbi has pleased you so much, I vow that you shall not enter this house again until you have spit in his face, as a reward for the entertainment he has afforded you!"

The woman, astonished at so unreasonable a demand, thought at first that her husband was joking, and began to congratulate herself on his returning good humor. But she was soon convinced that it was no jest. He insisted that she spit in the preacher's face, as the sole condition of being readmitted into his house. Since she was too pious to offer such an insult to any person, much less to so learned and famous a man, she was compelled to remain in the street. Then a charitable and sympathetic neighbor offered her a refuge, which she gladly accepted.

There she remained for a while, endeavoring in vain to mollify her husband, who still insisted upon keeping his vow. The affair was bruited about in the town, and a report of it reached the ears of Rabbi Meir, who immediately sent for the woman. She came. The good Rabbi asked her to be seated. Pretending to have a pain in his eyes, he, without mentioning what had happened, asked her whether she knew any remedy for it.

"Master," she said, "I am but a poor, ignorant creature. How should I know how to cure your eyes?"

"Well, well," rejoined the sage, "do as I bid you. Spit into my eyes seven times. Some say that it helps."

The woman, who believed that there might be some good in such an act, after some hesitation, complied with his request. As soon as it was done, he said to her,

"Good woman, now go home and say this to your husband: 'It was your desire that I should spit in the Rabbi's face once. I have done so; I have done more, I have spit in it seven times. Now let us be reconciled.'"

The Master's disciples, who had watched this whole performance, ventured to argue with him for permitting an ordinary housewife to offer him such an indignity, observing that this was the way to make the people defy the Law and its interpreters. He smiled gently, and said,

"My sons, do you think that your Master ought to be more punctilious about his honor than our Creator? Even He permitted His holy name to be obliterated (*Numbers* 5:23) in order to promote peace between man and wife. Shall I, then, consider anything as an indignity that can bring this about? Learn this, my sons: no act is disgraceful that tends to promote the happiness and peace of mankind. It is only vice and wickedness that can degrade us."

HADRIAN AND THE AGED PLANTER

WHILE passing near Tiberias in Galilee, the emperor Hadrian observed an old man digging a large trench in order to plant some fig trees. "If you had properly employed the morning of your life," remarked Hadrian, "you would not have to work so hard in the evening of your days."

"I have well employed the morning of my early days, nor will I neglect the evening of my life; and let God do what he thinks best," replied the man.

"How old are you, good man?"

"A hundred years."

"What!" exclaimed Hadrian, "a hundred years old, and you are still planting trees? Do you hope to enjoy the fruits of your labor?"

"Great king," rejoined the hoary-headed elder, "yes, I do hope so; if God permit, I may even eat the fruit of these very trees; if not, my children will. Did not my forefathers plant trees for me, and shall I not do the same for my children?"

Hadrian, pleased with the old man's reply, said,

"Well, old man, if you ever live to see the fruit of these trees, let me know. Yes, let me know. Do you hear, old fellow?" and with these words he left him.

The old man did live long enough to see the fruits of his labor. The tree flourished, and bore excellent fruit. As soon as they were sufficiently ripe, he gathered the choicest figs, put them in a basket, and marched off toward the emperor's residence. Hadrian happened to be looking out of one of the windows of his palace, and noticed the old man, bent with age, with a basket on his shoulders, standing near the gate. He ordered him to be admitted to his court.

"What is your pleasure, old man?"

"May it please your majesty to recollect seeing some years ago a very old man planting some trees; you commanded him, if he ever should gather the fruit, to let you know. I am that old man, and this is the fruit of those very trees. May it please you graciously to accept them as a humble tribute of gratitude for your great condescension."

Hadrian, surprised and gratified to see so extraordinary an example of old age crowned with the full use of all faculties and honest effort, asked the old man to be seated, and ordering the basket to be emptied of fruit, and to be filled with gold, gave it to him as a present. Some courtiers who witnessed this remarkable scene, exclaimed,

"Is it possible that our great emperor should show so much honor to a miserable Jew?"

"Why should I not honor him whom God has honored?" replied Hadrian. "Look at his age, and imitate his example!"

The emperor then very graciously dismissed the old man, who returned home highly pleased and delighted. When he reached his village and exhibited the present he had received, the people were all astonished. Amongst the neighbors whom curiosity had brought to his house, there was a silly covetous woman, who, seeing so much treasure obtained for a few figs, imagined that the emperor must be very fond of this fruit. She therefore hastily ran home, and shouted at her husband,

"You wretch, why are you tarrying here? Have you not heard that Cæsar is very fond of figs? Go, take some to him, and you may become as rich as your neighbor."

The foolish fellow, unable to bear the reproaches of his wife, took a large sack, filled with figs, on his shoulders, and after a strenuous journey, arrived, much fatigued, at the palace-gate, and demanded admittance to the emperor. Being asked what he wanted, he answered that, understanding that his majesty was very fond of figs, he had brought a whole sack full, for which he expected a great reward. The officer on duty reported this to the emperor. Hadrian smiled at the man's folly and impertinence.

"Yes," he said to the officer, "the fellow shall have his reward. Let him remain where he is, and let everyone who enters the gate take one of his figs and throw it at his face until they are all gone: then let him depart."

The order was immediately executed. The wretched man, abused, pelted, derided, instead of wishing for gold, prayed only to see the bottom of his bag. After much patience, and still more pain, his prayer was answered. The bag being empty, the poor fellow was dismissed. Dejected and sorrowful, he hastened home. His wife, who was all the while considering how to spend the unexpected treasure, how many fine gowns and cloaks and jewels she would purchase and relishing the thought of how attractive she would look, how the neighbors would stare to see her dressed in silk and gold—most impatiently awaited her husband's return. He came finally, and though she saw the bag was empty, she imagined that his pockets at least were full. Without even greeting him, or permitting him to take breath, she hastily asked him what good luck he had.

"Have patience," replied the enraged husband, "have patience, and I will tell you. I have both great and good luck. My great luck was that I took to the emperor figs and not peaches, else I should have been stoned to death. And my good luck was that the figs were ripe, else I should have left my brains behind me."

THE NOBLE PHYSICIAN

ABBA UMNA, a Jewish physician, was as celebrated for his piety and humanity as for his medical skill. He made no distinction between rich and poor, and was particularly attentive to students and scholars from whom he could never accept the least reward for his professional services. He considered learned men as fellow-workers whose functions were even more important than his own, since they had the power to cure the diseases of the mind. Unwilling to deter people from profiting by his medical knowledge, yet not wishing to embarrass anyone for the smallness of the fee that they might be able to give, he had a box fixed in his antechamber, into which the patients placed such sums as they could afford.

His fame spread far and wide. Abaye, who was the head of the Academy, heard of it. Anxious to determine whether everything reported of that noble physician was true, he sent to him two of his disciples, who were slightly ill. The physician received them kindly, gave them some medicine, and requested them to stay in his house overnight. The offer was readily accepted. They remained till the next morning, when they departed, taking with them a piece of tapestry which had served as a covering to the couch on which they had slept. This they carried to the market-place, and waiting until their kind host arrived, pretended to offer it for sale, and asked him how much he thought it was worth. Abba Umna mentioned a sum.

"Do you not think it is worth more?"

"No," answered the physician, "this is the very sum I gave for one much like it."

"Why, good man," exclaimed the students, "this belongs to you. We took it from your house. Now tell us, we beg you, after missing it, were you not angry with us?"

"Certainly not. You know that a Jew must not impute evil intentions to anyone, nor judge ill of a neighbor for a single act. Since I was satisfied that no ill use would be made of it, let it ever be so. Sell it and distribute the money amongst the poor."

The students complied with his wishes, departed from him with admiration and thanks, and, by the report of their experience, increased his well-earned fame.

But the most noble trait in Abba Umna's character was that he never accepted any remuneration from the poor, and even provided them with everything, during their illness, that could contribute to their comfort; and when, by his skill and care, he had restored them to health, he would give them money and say,

"Now, my friends, go and purchase bread and meat; these are the best and only medicines you require."

CHARITY

THERE lived in the land of Israel a rich farmer named Aben Judan. His plantations extended to the terraced hills and the fertile valleys; each year at harvest time his threshing floors were overflowing and his vineyards were bursting with luxuriant grapes. His great flocks and herds were sung of in the wayside inns, and brought great prices at the annual fair. His wealth was exceeded only by his goodness and generosity.

Now when the apostles, Rabbi Eliezar, Rabbi Joshua and Rabbi Akiba, used to make their annual tour of the country in order to collect contributions for the poor, they always tarried at the house of Aben Judan. Amongst their many and varied contributors, none gave more liberally nor with more cheerfulness than he. Aben Judan wore the crown of charity with dignity.

Once, however, his fortune took a turn. A severe storm destroyed the fruits of his fields; a raging pestilence swept away the greater part of his flocks and herds; and his extensive fields and vineyards became the prey of his greedy and inexorable creditors. Of all his vast possessions, nothing remained but one small plot of ground. But Aben Judan accepted these reverses with the same cheerfulness and dignity that he had received wealth and prosperity. The teaching of the Torah was engraved upon his mind and heart, and like the unfortunate Job, he said,

"The Lord gave, and the Lord has taken away. Blessed be the name of the Lord."

Then he zealously applied himself to the cultivation of the only field that remained. The land yielded generously to his loving care, and by dint of great labor, and still greater frugality, he managed to support his family; and notwithstanding his comparative poverty, he was cheerful and contented.

A year passed. One evening as he was sitting at the door of his shack to rest from the labors of the day, he observed the Rabbis coming at a distance. Suddenly the memory of his former wealth and his present state at once rushed upon his mind; for the first time he suffered the pangs of poverty.

"What Aben Judan once was!" he exclaimed, "and what is he now?"

Pensive and melancholy, he seated himself in a corner of his shack. His wife, noticing the sudden change, asked tenderly:

"What ails my beloved? Are you ill?"

"Would to God it were in your power, but the Lord alone can heal the wounds he inflicts," replied the distressed man. "Do you remember the days of our prosperity when our corn fed the hungry, our fleece clothed the naked, and our oil and wine refreshed the spirit of the afflicted? The orphans surrounded us and blessed us, and the widow's heart sang for joy. Then we tasted the heavenly pleasures which are the lot of the good and the charitable. But now, alas! we are unable to relieve the faithless and the helpless, since we ourselves are poor. Do you not see yonder the good men coming to make the collection for the poor? What can we give them?"

"Do not grieve, dear husband," answered his good wife, "we still own one field. Suppose we sell half of it, and donate the money for the use of the poor."

The idea delighted Aben Judan. His countenance beamed with joy. He followed his wife's advice, sold half of the field, and when the Rabbis called, gave them the money. They accepted it, and as they departed said,

"May the Lord restore your former prosperity."

Aben Judan resumed his work with good cheer and his customary diligence. He went to plough his small plot. As he labored, the foot of the ox that drew the ploughshare sunk into the ground, and the beast was maimed. While attempting to help the ox, he saw something glittering in the hollow which the foot had made. This attracted his attention; he dug deeper and, to his great astonishment and no less joy, found an immense treasure concealed there. He took it home, moved from the wretched shack in which he lived into a very fine house, and repurchased the lands and possessions which his ancestors had left him but which his former distress had obliged him to sell. Nor did he neglect the poor. He again became a father to the fatherless, and a blessing to the unfortunate.

Now the time arrived when the Rabbis again appeared to make their collection. Not finding their generous contributor in the place where he had lived the year before, they inquired of some of the inhabitants of the village, and asked them what had become of Aben Judan, and how he was.

"Aben Judan!" they exclaimed, "the good and glorious Aben Judan! Who can compare with him in riches, charity, goodness? See yonder flocks and herds? They belong to Aben Judan. Those vast fields, flourishing vineyards and beautiful gardens? They belong to Aben Judan. Those fine buildings? They belong to Aben Judan."

And while they were speaking, the good man happened to pass that way. The wise men greeted him and asked him how he was doing.

"Masters," said he, "your prayers have produced plenty of fruit—come to my house and partake of it. I will make up the deficiency of last year's subscription."

They followed him to his house, where after entertaining them nobly, he gave them a very large contribution. They accepted it, and taking out the subscription list of the preceding year, they said to him,

"See, although many gave greater contributions than you, we placed you at the very top of the list, convinced that the smallness of your gift at that time was due to your lack of means, not want of inclination. It is to men like you that King Solomon alluded when he said,

"'A man's gift extendeth his possessions, and placeth him before the great.'"

PHILOSOPHER AND RABBI

"Your God in his Book calls himself a jealous God, who can endure no other God beside himself, and on all occasions makes manifest his abhorrence of idolatry. How comes it, then, that he threatens and seems to hate the worshippers of false gods more than the false gods themselves?"

"A certain king," replied the Rabbi, "had a disobedient son. Among the worthless tricks of various kinds, he had the baseness to give to his dogs his father's name and titles. Should the king shower his anger on the prince or the dogs?"

"Well turned," replied the philosopher, "but if your God destroyed the objects of idolatry, he should take away the temptation to it."

"Yes," retorted the Rabbi, "if the fools worshipped such things only as were of no further use than that to which their folly applied them—if the idols were always as worthless as the idolatry is contemptible. But they worship the sun, the moon, the host of heaven, the rivers, the sea, the fire, air, and what not. Would you that the Creator, for the sake of these fools, should ruin his own works, and disturb the laws appointed to nature by his own wisdom? If a man steals grain and sows it, should the seed not shoot up out of the earth, because it was stolen? Oh, no! the wise Creator lets nature run her own course; for her course is his own appointment. And what if the children of folly abuse it to evil? The day of reckoning is not far off, and men will then learn that human actions likewise reappear in their consequences, by as certain a law as the green blade rises up out of the buried corn-seed."

THE FALL OF JERUSALEM

One of the leading Jews of Jerusalem once gave a banquet and, through an error of a scribe, his arch-enemy, Bar Kamsa, was invited. When the host discovered him at the banquet table, he ordered him out of his house, despite Bar Kamsa's offer to pay all the expenses of the feast rather than be put to shame. Humiliated and incensed, he decided to wreak his vengeance upon the whole community. He denounced the Jews to the Roman emperor, declaring that they had revolted against his decrees. The emperor could find sufficient proof for his accusation: the Jews would refuse to accept an offering sent to the Temple.

The Romans sent a lamb, which Bar Kamsa intercepted on the way and mutilated in a manner not offensive to the Roman laws but contrary to those of the Jews. Many of the Jews were inclined, for the sake of peace, to offer it up, but Zachariah ben Akilos prevented the sacrifice since it would be contrary to Jewish law. Roman legions marched on Jerusalem, and the commander ordered the soldiers to invest the city. While the commander watched the assault, a Jewish lad passed by, reciting the Scriptures. He asked the lad to repeat the last verse, and he recited,

"Because Edom [Rome] acted revengefully against the household of Judah, and incurred grievous guilt by taking revenge upon them, therefore thus says the Lord God: I will stretch my hand over Edom, and will cut off from it man and beast, I will make it a waste from Teman, and to Dedan shall they fall by the sword. I will execute my vengeance upon Edom by the hand of my people Israel, and they shall deal with Edom in accordance with my anger and fury; and they shall know my vengeance."

This made a deep impression upon him. The commander became frightened, resigned his command, turned Jew, and became the progenitor of Rabbi Meir.

Then Vespasian took command. The siege lasted for several years; the famine increased; people died in the streets; the lovers of peace were compelled by the zealots to fight against their will. But Johanan ben Zakkai was smuggled out of the city in a coffin. He immediately went to Vespasian who received him unhospitably; but Johanan greeted him as befits an emperor. Soon afterwards the report of his election as emperor reached his camp. At the moment he was putting on his sandals but he could not get one on the second foot. Perplexed, he asked Johanan, who was still standing in his presence, to explain why this had happened. The sage said that the good tidings had so elated him that his body had swollen up; let an enemy come before him and his foot would again shrink to its normal size. Vespasian was pleased, and asked why he had not come earlier. Johanan explained that the rebels would not permit him to leave the city. Just then a few of the legion commanders entered and presented a riddle which puzzled them: if a snake is wrapped around a cask of honey, how can the snake be removed without breaking the cask? Johanan solved it for them: one takes pincers and lifts the snake away and so frees the cask without breaking it. Vespasian was delighted, and asked him what favor he could show him. Johanan requested that he be permitted to settle in the city of Jabneh, and that Rabbi Sadok, who had fasted forty years to avert the destruction of Jerusalem and had become a skeleton, be cured. This was granted him.

Then the wicked Titus took command. He went blasphemously into the Temple and committed an immoral act on the scroll of the Law. Then he took a sword and pierced the curtain in the middle of the Temple and when by a miracle, drops of blood oozed out, he cried, "Now I have killed their God."

While he was returning to Rome, a storm arose on the high seas and he said, "The power of their God is only in the waters. He has drowned Pharaoh and Sisera, and now he wants to drown me. Let him come and fight me on dry land!" A Heavenly Voice answered, "O you wicked one! Why, any one of My small creatures has the power to conquer you." When he disembarked an insect found its way into his nostrils and from there it slowly gnawed its way to his brain. He found no other way to ease the pain but to have a smith create a shrill noise with his hammer. They were continuously at work: when the smith happened to be a heathen he paid him four hundred zuzim but when he was a Jew, he said, "It is enough for you to see your God's vengeance on your enemy," and paid him nothing. After a while the insect became accustomed to the noise of the hammers and there was no longer any relief. As he lay dying he ordered his body to be burned and the ashes to be strewn over the seven seas so that the God of the Jews should not be able to find him.

RABBI JOSHUA AND THE PRINCESS

RABBI JOSHUA, the son of Hananyah, was one of those men whose minds are far more beautiful than their bodies. He was so dark that people often took him for a blacksmith, and so plain as almost to frighten children. Yet his great learning, wit, and wisdom, had procured him not only the love and respect of the people, but even the favor of the Emperor Trajan.

Being often at court, one of the princesses rallied him on his want of beauty.

"How comes it," said she, "that such glorious wisdom is enclosed in so mean a vessel?"

The Rabbi, no ways dismayed, requested her to tell him in what sort of vessels her father kept his wine.

"Why, in earthen vessels, to be sure," replied the princess.

"Oh!" exclaimed the worthy Rabbi, "this is the custom of ordinary people: an emperor's wine ought to be kept in more precious vessels."

The princess, thinking him in earnest, ordered a quantity of wine to be emptied out of the earthen jars into gold and silver vessels, but to her great surprise, found it, in a very short time, sour, and unfit to drink.

"Very fine advice, indeed, Joshua, have you given me!" said the princess the next time she saw him. "Do you know the wine is sour and spoiled?"

"You are then convinced," said the Rabbi, "that wine keeps best in plain and mean vessels. It is even so with wisdom."

"But," continued the princess, "I know many persons who are both wise and handsome."

"True," replied the sage, "but they would, most probably, be still wise, were they less handsome."

THE REWARD OF WISDOM

I

ONCE a business man of Jerusalem took a trip to a small town, when he suddenly was taken ill. Learning that he was on the point of death, he summoned the master of the house, begged him to take care of his property until the arrival of his son, and, for fear of imposture, not to deliver it to him unless he first performed three clever acts as a proof of his wisdom.

After the lapse of considerable time the son arrived in the town. Knowing the name of the person with whom his father usually resided, he sought in vain to discover it, since the residents refused to give him any information. While he hesitated, somewhat perplexed and chagrined, he noticed a porter carrying a heavy load of wood on his shoulders.

"How much for that wood?" he asked. They quickly agreed upon an acceptable sum. "Now," said the young man, "go and carry it to so and so's house (mentioning the name of the person for whom he was searching), and I shall follow you."

The porter obeyed his instruction. Arriving at the home, he put down his load.

"What is the meaning of this?" inquired the master of the house. "I have not ordered any wood."

"True, but the person behind me has."

In the meantime the stranger arrived, informed the master who he was, explaining that since no one would disclose his address, he had contrived this stratagem in order to discover it. "You are a clever fellow," said the master. He bade him enter his home and remain as his guest.

Lunch was prepared, the table set. The company, consisting of the master, his wife, two daughters, two sons and the stranger, were seated; and the servant brought a dish containing five chickens, which was placed upon the table.

"Now," said the host to his guest, "will you be good enough to carve?" At first he begged to be excused but at length consented; and executed the office in the following manner: One of the chickens he divided between the master and his wife; another between the two daughters; the third between the two sons, and the remaining two he took for his own share. "A very strange way of carving, this! My guest must be a glutton," thought the master, but he said nothing.

The afternoon and evening were passed in various amusements, and when supper time arrived, a very fine capon was placed upon the table. "You have performed the honors of the table so well today," said the kind host to his guest, "that I must ask you to carve again." The young man undertook the task willingly. He placed the capon before him, cut off its head, and placed it before the master; the inward part he gave to the mistress of the house; to the two daughters he gave each a wing; to the two sons a leg each; the remainder he kept for himself. "Upon my word," said the master, "this is queer; I regarded your method of carving at dinner very strange, but this is still more extraordinary. Is this the way they carve at Jerusalem?"

"Have patience until I explain, and my conduct may, perhaps, not appear quite so strange," replied the guest. "At lunch, five chickens were placed before me; they were to be divided amongst seven persons. Since I could not carve with mathematical precision, I thought it best to do it arithmetically. Now, you, your wife and one chicken, made up the number *three;* your two daughters and a chicken made another *three;* your two sons and a chicken made another *three.* To make up the last number, I was compelled to take the remaining chickens; for two chickens and your humble guest totalled *three.* This is the manner in which I solved that difficult problem."

"You are an excellent mathematician, but a bad carver," commented the master, "but proceed." The stranger continued: "In my carving at supper, I proceeded according to the nature of things. Since the head is the principal part of the body, I gave it to you. Are you not the head of the family? To your wife I gave the inward part as a sign of her fruitfulness. Your two sons are the two pillars of your house; the legs which are the supporters of the animal's body were therefore their proper portion. Your daughters are marriageable and I know that you wish to see them happily settled; I therefore gave them the wings that they may the sooner fly away. As for myself, I came in a boat, and I intend to return in a boat. I therefore took the part which most resembles it."

"Well done!" said the kind host. "I am satisfied that you are the son of my departed friend. Here is your property. Now go and prosper."

II

A rich Israelite who dwelt at a considerable distance from Jerusalem had an only son whom he sent to the Holy City for education. During his absence, the father was suddenly taken ill. Seeing his end approaching, he made his will in which he left all his property to a slave whom he named, on condition that he should permit his son to select out of that property any single thing he might want.

No sooner was the master dead than the slave, elated with the prospect of so much wealth, hastened to Jerusalem, informed the son of what had taken place, and showed him the will. The young man was plunged into the deepest sorrow by this unexpected news. He rent his clothes, threw ashes on his head, and lamented the loss of a parent whom he tenderly loved and whose memory he revered. As soon as the first transports of grief were over, and the days allotted for mourning had passed, the young man began seriously to consider the situation in which he was left. Born in affluence, and growing up with the expectation of receiving, after his father's death, those possessions to which he was entitled, he suddenly saw, or imagined he saw, his expectations disappointed, and his material prospects ruined.

In this state of mind he went to his teacher, a man eminent for his wisdom and piety, acquainted him with his difficult situation, made him read the will, and in the bitterness of distress, ventured to speak his mind: his father, by making such a strange disposition of his property, neither showed good sense nor affection for his only child.

"Say nothing against your father, young man," said the sage; "your father was both a wise man, and an affectionate father. Why, the most convincing proof of what I say is this very will!"

"This will!" exclaimed the pupil. "This will! Surely, honored teacher, you are not in earnest. I can see neither wisdom in bestowing his property upon a slave, nor affection in depriving his only son of his legal rights."

"Your father has done neither," rejoined the sage, "but like a just, loving parent has by this very will secured the property for you, if you have the wisdom to avail yourself of it."

"How! how!" exclaimed the young man in astonishment. "How is it possible? Truly, I do not understand you!"

"Listen, then," began the kindly elder, "listen carefully, and you will have good reason to admire your father's prudence. When he saw his end approaching, and that he must go the way of all flesh, he thought to himself: 'I must die, and my son is too far off to take immediate possession of my estate. My slaves will no sooner be certain of my death than they will plunder my property, and to avoid detection, will conceal my death from my beloved child and thereby deprive him even of the melancholy consolation of mourning for me.' To prevent the first, he bequested his property to a slave whose obvious interest in it would be to take good care of it. To insure the second, he made it a condition that you should be permitted to select something out of that property. The slave, he felt, in order to receive his apparent legal claim, would not fail to notify you immediately, as indeed he has done."

"Well," exclaimed the youth impatiently, "what benefit is all this to me? Will this return to me the property of which I have been so unjustly deprived?"

"Ah!" replied the good man, "I see that wisdom resides with the aged. Do you not know, then, that whatever a slave possesses belongs to his lawful master? And has not your father left you the power of selecting out of his property any one thing that you might choose? What prevents you from choosing that very slave as your portion; and by possessing him, you will of course be entitled to the whole property. This, no doubt, was your father's intention."

The young man, admiring his father's wisdom, no less than his teacher's sagacity, took the hint, chose the slave as his portion, and took possession of his father's estates. Then he gave the slave his freedom, together with a handsome gift, being convinced that "wisdom resides with the aged, and understanding in length of days."

THE KISS OF GOD

by EDMUND FLEG

I T was the sixth day of the month of Adar. In the middle of the day a voice sounded from the sky: "Moses, Moses! There remaineth to thee but one day more to live in this world." "Wherefore is my death so near?" groaned the Prophet. "Hast thou not twice asked to die?" "Lord, Lord, Thou didst show me Thy might on Sinai, and Thy strength in the ten plagues of Egypt; Thou didst show me Thy Mercy in the days of the Golden Calf, and Thy love by the manna in the wilderness. Let me still live to tell Thy glory!"

And in the night the Prophet said fifteen hundred prayers, and in the night he recopied the Torah thirteen times upon scrolls of parchment, thinking: "'The Torah is thy life, and the prolonging thereof.' Perhaps it will prolong mine."

But on the morning of the seventh day of Adar the Voice sounded in the sky: "Moses, Moses! there remain to thee but six more hours to live." And Moses answered: "First let me bless Israel, then I will go to be gathered to my fathers."

Then he assembled the multitude and pronounced over them the blessing.

He spake over Reuben: "Let him be rewarded for saving Joseph, and not punished for defiling Bilhah; let there come forth from him heroes, heroes of might and of the Torah."

He spake over Judah: "Let him be rewarded that he spake for Benjamin, and not be punished that he polluted Tamar. From him let there come forth kings of war, and from him let there come forth kings of peace."

He spake over Levi: "He massacred the Shechemites, but he adored not the Golden Calf; he was overeager to avenge Dinah, but at Shittim his eagerness avenged the Lord. Let priests without blemish come forth from him, and from him the forgiveness of the Eternal."

He called down upon Joseph abundance of dews, upon Zebulon abundance of purple and of gold; to Dan and to Gad and to Issachar he promised increase of flocks, to Naphtali fish, to Asher olives, and to all, the joy of the worship of the Lord. But to Simeon he promised naught, for Simeon had sinned with the daughters of Moab.

Our Rabbis tell us that, although Moses was not the first to bless on earth, his blessing was the most fruitful, for Noah blessed Shem, his son, but cursed Ham; Isaac blessed his two sons Esau and Jacob, but his blessing divided them; Jacob blessed his twelve sons, but in his blessing he chided Reuben; while Moses, since he was unable to bless Simeon, did not name him—in order not to curse him. Wherefore his blessing was perfect.

When he had ended, the Voice from heaven sounded: "Moses, Moses!

there remain to thee but four hours to live in this world." And the Prophet entreated: "Lord, Lord, let me take leave of Israel, then I will go to be gathered to my fathers." And he read to the tribes the whole Torah, and he gave a copy to each of the tribes, saying: "Keep ye the Torah, and may it keep you! And let no word, no sign be changed until the end of the ages, that ye may live unto the end of the ages." All cried: "We will keep it until the end of the ages, so may it keep us!" And then the thirteenth Torah that Moses had copied was taken by the angel Gabriel to bear it back to heaven.

Then the Prophet said: "Often I chided you because of the Torah: forgive me." All answered: "Often we angered thee for thy Torah; forgive us." And they forgave him, and he forgave them. Then he said again: "When ye shall have entered into the land of Israel, remember my bones that shall think of you. And say: 'Alas, alas! the son of Amram who ran before us like a steed, he hath fallen, he hath fallen in the wilderness!'" And all groaned: "Moses, Moses our master, what shall we do without thee?" He answered: "God remaineth with you. It was not for me, but for you, that through me He wrought His wonders. Put not your trust in man of flesh and blood. Ye perceive that he is naught, for death taketh him. The Lord shall send you other prophets: listen to them, follow them; but if ever one of them say to you that he is God, believe him not, for God alone is God." And all cried: "Hear, O Israel, the Lord is our God, the Lord is One." Then the Prophet turned to Joshua and asked him: "Desireth thou some further light upon the Torah? For I go; thou shalt not see me more." "Moses, our master," answered Joshua, "have I ever left thee for a single moment since I have been thy disciple? Hast thou not, night and day, explained to me the Torah? I asked thee everything: thou didst tell me all." "Since thou hast no request more to make to me, let me make one to thee. Embrace me." And Moses embraced Joshua twice, and twice he blessed him, saying: "Let peace be upon thee and upon Israel!"

And as he blessed him, the Voice sounded from the sky: "Moses, Moses! there remain to thee but two hours to live in this world. Go up alone into Nebo, and die in light."

Why, ask our Rabbis, did God wish that Moses should die alone? Because Moses' grave was to remain unknown; for if mankind had known the place, they would have worshipped his tomb as an idol, and Moses as a god. And why, ask our Rabbis, did God wish that Moses should die in light? It was because, if he had died in darkness, mankind would have said: "God was able to take him from us because it was night. In the full light of day we would have taken him back."

But the Prophet still delayed, held in the arms of his mother and his sons and his wife. Again the Voice sounded: "Moses, Moses! go up into the mountain! there remaineth to thee but one more hour to live!" Then he rent his mantle, he covered his head with dust, and said: "Happy the people of

Israel that is not ever to die! Farewell, my brethren, my sons; we shall meet again in another world." And as all rent their garments, and fell groaning with their faces in the dust, he went up alone into the mountain, wailing aloud.

No man, say our Sages, dieth before his day. But however late he die, he dieth always too soon for his desire. For the Prophet, having twice asked for death, and knowing from the mouth of God Himself that he had but one more hour to live, would not yet accept death.

Abandoned by men, he now entreated the mountain and the wilderness, heaven and earth. Climbing up Nebo he said to them amidst his sobs: "Entreat for me the pity of the Lord; may He save me from death!" But the mountain answered: "May He first have pity upon me, hath He not written: *The mountains shall depart and the hills be removed"?* And heaven and earth replied: "May He first have pity upon us, hath He not written: *The earth weareth old like a garment; the heavens dissolve like smoke"?* And the wilderness answered: *"Each thing returneth unto its place; all was dust, to dust shall all return."*

And the Prophet groaned: "Whither go? Whom now entreat? Once a Pharaoh was my slave; I delivered a whole people of slaves; I ordained the Sabbath and the Fast; I decreed life and death; the Torah took my name; I commanded the whole world; I changed the order of things. To the heaven that raineth down water I said: 'Send bread,' and manna fell. To the earth that maketh the bread to come up I said: 'Let water come up,' and water came. God Himself obeyed me. I said to Him: 'Rise up,' and He rose; 'Stop,' and He stopped. I said to Him: 'Punish,' and He punished; 'Forgive,' and He forgave. What am I now? An old man that beseecheth, and to whom none hearken any more." "It is the law of all flesh, My son," God answered him. "Thou hast had thy day, now let another have his. Whose son art thou? Amram's. And whose son was Amram? Kohath's. And Kohath was the son of Levi, and all were the sons of Adam; and all died like Adam. Wherefore shouldst thou not die?"

"Lord, Lord," Moses implored Him, "since Thou canst do all things, canst Thou not also spare me death?" "If thou didst not die in this world, my son, how wouldst thou live again in the other? I have made ready for thee all the joys of Paradise; on earth thou commandedst the sixty myriads of Israel; in heaven thou shalt command the fifty-five myriads of the Righteous, who shall walk in the ways of my Torah. O Moses, thy days will pass, but thy life shall not pass; thou shalt have no need of roof, or mantle, or bread for thine hunger, or oil for thine head, or sandals for thy feet, or sun or moon for thy seeing; for I will shelter thee with My splendor, I will clothe thee in My splendor, I will feed thee upon My delights, I will bear thee upon the wings of My glory. And upon thy face shall shine a light, whose shadow only shone upon thy face on earth."

But Moses did not yet submit. Again he groaned: "King of the World, King of the World, if Thou permit not that I cross the Jordan, If Thou permit not that I behold the Promised Land, permit that I live, Lord, that I live and behold the world! And if Thou wilt not permit that I remain a man, let me live like a beast of the field, let me live like a fowl of the air, but let me live, let me live, O let me not die!"

Thus did the Prophet implore; and the mountains and the seas trembled; the firmament and the abyss howled out in anguish: "Is God, then, about to destroy the universe?" For the prayer of Moses was like a sword to hew and rend the worlds, containing in its plaint the Ineffable Name that created the worlds. Then the Lord ordered all the angels to shut the gates of all prayers, so that the prayer of the prophet should not be received; and the angels sang: "Glory to the Holy One, blessed be He; who knoweth nor favor nor injustice, and maketh death equal for all mortal men."

Moses had now come to the top of the mountain. God said to him: "Wherefore tremblest thou, My son?" "I am afraid." "Of what?" "I am afraid of Samael; I am afraid of death." "Look before thee."

Moses looked. And God said again: "Behold this land, beyond this river; it is the land that I promised to Abraham, to Isaac, and to Jacob, when I sware: 'I will give it to your sons and the sons of your sons.' Thou shalt not enter into it, but thou mayest see it."

And as the Prophet looked, the lord put into his eyes such power that he beheld the whole land from the Jordan to the sea, from Hermon to the wilderness. And every place in the land, from the portion of Naphtali to that of Simeon, from that of Reuben to that of Dan, from the vines of Carmel to the stones of Sodom, from the roses of Sharon to the pastures of Gilead. And as he looked, the Lord put into his eyes such force that he saw, not only every place, but every age in every place: Jericho falling at the blast of the trumpet; Samson bearing the gates of Gaza to the hills of Hebron; Deborah on Mount Tabor raining down stars upon the armies of Sisera; Samuel at Ramoth anointing with oil the head of Saul; David gathering in the brook Elah flint-stones to slay a giant; Solomon leading the Ark of Sinai into the Temple of Moriah amidst the singing of songs. And the Prophet murmured in the joy of his heart: "Lord, Lord, Thou keepest Thy promise and Thy children keep theirs. Thou hast led them into the Land of Thy choice: and thither have they led Thee there to dwell."

But after the victories he saw the defeats; after the sins, the chastisements: Ahab and Jezebel prostituting themselves to the idols in the high places of Samaria; Manasseh commanding a prophet's body to be sewn through on the trunk of a terebinth; Ahaz laying down his bed of stupration in the Holy of Holies beneath the wings of the Cherubim; Jehoiakim in the Valley of Topheth feeding the flesh of his son into the flaming belly of Baal. Then there came upon them, in the noise of their hosts, Nebuchadnezzar with his mitred horsemen and his hairy lancers and his sinewy archers; and Titus with his Romans, his Syrians, his Arabians, his Getæ, bearing the sling and the spear and the pike, and the onager and the catapult, extinguishing in blood the seven stars of the Candlestick, and dragging into exile the groaning remnant of the twelve tribes.

And Moses, in the anguish of his heart, groaned: "Alas, my sons; What do ye? whither go ye? Ye are driven on the roads like cattle, with rings of brass through your nostrils! Ye are dragged in chains, and behind you the son of Edom lifteth up his head in blithe rejoicing! Ye are tracked down barefoot and with bleeding hands through the valleys and through the mountains, beneath the sun and beneath the storm, without a home, without a land, without rest! O Judah, O Gad, O Benjamin, O Ephraim, ye hunger and have no more manna, ye thirst and have no wells! And ye wander, and no more have to lead you a pillar of cloud by day nor a pillar of fire by night! Lord, Lord, canst Thou suffer the shame wherein Thou hast put them? Why deliver them from bondage, and open for them twelve pathways through the sea, and change the sand into gardens, and the rock into fountains, and light up Thy mountain, and from it proclaim Thy Law to Thy people, but to blot out Thyself by blotting them from the world?"

But, lo, beneath the eyes of the Prophet, filling space, a gigantic Temple! Its courts were of onyx and of beryl, its gateways of jasper and of sardonyx, its beams of emerald, its roofs of topaz, its columns of agate, of chrysolite and of amethyst, its altar of ruby, of carbuncle, and of sapphire. And before the Temple waited the Messiah.

And Moses whispered: "Is that the Temple of heaven, or is it the Temple of earth?" "Moses, My father," the Messiah answered him, "this Temple that thou seest is neither of earth nor of heaven; it is the Temple of heaven that the earth shall build." As He spoke, all the seas opened, and by all the pathways of all the seas all the peoples redeemed from sin went up toward the Temple, waving palms and singing songs; and after all the peoples, all the dead of all the ages and of all lands, returned from the Garden of Eden or from Gehenna, waving palms and singing psalms. And before the peoples walked Israel, singing psalms and waving palms. And the Messiah said to the Prophet: "Moses, My father, how couldst thou have entered into the Land of Promise? It is not only beyond Jordan, the country that thou didst seek, it is beyond love, beyond hope. Behold: it is the whole Earth of whole Man." And as He spoke in the vast Temple, a vast table rose up over all the mountains and all the plains, over all the continents and all the seas. Round the table all the peoples were seated, and for the last Passover Adam poured them out wine pressed from the grapes of all vineyards, and portioned to them bread harvested from the corn of all fields. And all celebrated the last Passover, and sang with Adam and with Israel and with the Messiah: "Hosanna! Hosanna! The

Days have come full circle. God is One! Man is One! Peace to man in heaven, peace on earth to God!"

And when like the mists of a dream engulfed by night the visions of the future were devoured by the midday sun, the Lord said to Moses: "I have ordained death for all mortals. For Israel alone have I ordained life, in order that man shall live, and that there shall live the Messiah. If thou desire it, I can change My decree: thou shalt not die, but Israel shall perish. Thy day shall be stayed, thou shalt be eternal, but the Messiah shall not be born." And Moses answered the Lord: "Thou art a God of mercy, King of the World; let the Messiah come and let man live; let Israel live and let me perish."

When the Holy One, blessed be He, saw that the Prophet accepted death, He said to Gabriel: "Go gather up his soul." But the archangel answered: "He hath led Thy people with Thy power in his hand, and Thy word in his mouth. He hath dried up the sea, shattered the Golden Calf; I will not give death to this Righteous One." Then God said to Michael: "Go gather up his soul." But the archangel answered: "He alone uttereth Thine Ineffable Name; Thou hast made him more than an angel and almost a god. I will not give death to this Righteous One."

Now for a hundred and twenty years Samael had waited for Moses to be delivered up to him. He said to the Eternal: "I will go take his soul." The Eternal answered him: "Wouldst thou dare even to approach him? What part of his sacred body could thy myriad eyes even look upon? His countenance? It hath beheld My countenance. His hand? It hath received the Torah from My hand. His feet? They have trod the threshold of My splendor." "Nevertheless, I will go," Samael answered. He grasped his sword, girdled himself with cruelty, clothed himself in anger, and came before Moses. When he saw him, the Prophet, standing upon the summit of the mountain, traced in the air with his radiant fingers the four signs of the Unutterable Name; and, like a motionless lightning in translucent space, the Name remained suspended. Samael was hurled to earth and sought to flee like a wounded serpent. But Moses' knee was upon his throat, and already the angel of death was about to die when a Voice cried from the heaven: "Moses, My son, slay not death; the world hath need of him!" Samael fled, and the Eternal appeared.

He said to the Prophet: "Thinkest thou, My son, that I would have suffered to see thee die like other mortals? Lay thee down. Cross thy feet one above the other. Cross one above the other thine hands." He obeyed.

Then God, calling to himself the Prophet's soul, murmured: "O My daughter, I ordained that thou shouldst dwell for an hundred and twenty years in the body of this man. Leave it now; the hour is come." But the soul replied: "King of the World, I know that Thou art God of all spirits, that

Thou holdest in Thy hands the souls of the quick and the dead. Thou hast created me and Thou hast put me in the body of this Righteous One. Is there in the world a body as pure as his? I love it, I desire not to leave it." "My daughter," God answered, "falter not, obey Me, I will place thee in the highest heaven, beneath the Throne of My Glory, with My Cherubim and My Seraphim." "King of the World," said the soul, "Thine angels themselves have become corrupted; when Azza and Azael came down from the heights to couple with the daughters of men, Thou didst have to chain them betwixt earth and heaven for their chastisement. But Moses, from the moment that Thou gavest him to look upon Thee, face to face, his flesh hath no more known flesh. Wherefore I desire to remain with him."

"Dost thou, then, fear Samael?" the Prophet asked his soul. "In no way: God will not deliver me to Samael." "Dost thou fear that thou wouldst have to weep my death as Israel will weep it?" "In no way: the Lord hath delivered mine eyes from tears." "Fearest thou to be sent into the gulf of hell?" "In no way: God hath promised me the joys of heaven." "Then go, my soul, whither the Lord summoneth thee, and bless with me His love."

The Eternal gathered up the soul from Moses' mouth, and the Prophet died in the kiss of God.

As soon as he was dead, a cry resounded in the camp of the children of Israel wailing, "Woe, woe, he is dead!" And on the next day the manna did not fall. Israel, that had wept Moses thirty days before losing him, made over him ninety days of lamentation. The earth also wept, wailing: "The Righteous One hath left mankind." Heaven also wept, wailing: "Heaven hath left earth." The Eternal cried: "Moses, My son, thou hast said of Me, 'There is no other God in heaven or earth.' I say of thee: 'There shall be no other Moses in Israel!'" And God wept.

Now while all wept the son of Amram, his mother Jochebed could not believe in his death. She went to ask Sinai: "Sinai, Sinai, hast thou seen my son?" "I have not seen him since he made the Torah come down upon me." She went to ask the Wilderness: "Wilderness, Wilderness, hast thou seen my son?" "I have not seen him since he made the manna come down upon me." The sea answered her: "I have not seen him since he changed my waves into dry land." The Nile answered her: "I have not seen him since he turned my waters into blood." And Jochebed journeyed through all the world crying out: "Where is my son? where is my son?"

And now the Prophet went up towards the Eternal. When Adam saw him, he said to him: "Wherefore goest thou higher than I? Was I not created in the image of God?" But a Voice sounded: "He is greater than thou; thou didst lose the glory that thou receivedst of God; what he received, he preserved." Noah said to him: "Wherefore goest thou higher than I? Did I not escape from the Flood?" The Voice sounded: "He is greater than thou, thou savedst thyself alone, he hath saved his people." Abraham said to him: "Wherefore goest thou higher than I? Did I not feed them that passed by?" The Voice sounded: "Thou didst feed them in the inhabited places, he fed them in the wilderness." Isaac said to him: "Wherefore goest thou higher than I? Did I not see upon the rock Moriah the Splendor of God?" The Voice sounded: "Thou didst see it and thine eyes failed; he saw it and his eyes behold it still." Jacob said to him: "Wherefore goest thou higher than I? Did I not wrestle with the angel, and did I not vanquish him?" and the Voice sounded: "He is greater than thou; thou didst vanquish the angel upon earth; he hath vanquished the angels in heaven."

Then Moses went up and seated himself beneath the Throne of Glory. And seated beneath the Throne of Glory, the Prophet, with God, awaits the hour of the Messiah.

OF STUDY AND PRAYER

by MICHA JOSEPH BERDYCZEVSKI

I

THERE once lived a good pious scholar who was exceedingly poor: in his little hut there was neither a morsel of food nor a bit of firewood nor a drop of oil. He sat and worshipped God and contemplated His Law day and night. When it became dark he would recite the liturgy and passages from the Talmud by heart, and pray to God in soft whispering words.

One midnight, while wrapped in study and prayer, he suddenly noticed a ray of light issuing from a hole in the wall. As he observed it, the light brightened. He arose from his little cot, went close to the wall, and behold! he found a large precious stone, glowing with light which flooded the room. The good man did not understand whence it had come or to whom it belonged, and he was greatly astonished.

That night he dreamed a dream. In this dream Elijah the Prophet appeared and said: "There are two ways before you: Either the stone which you found may remain in your possession, and you and your family will thereby become exceedingly rich; or you may leave it where it is, and God will grant you children and grandchildren who will be devoted to the Torah, and whose wisdom will enlighten all mankind." Said the Zaddik: "Neither gold nor silver nor precious stones shall be my portion, but the Law of my God, which I dearly love."

And he awakened from his sleep and beheld streams of light issuing from the hole, and when he came near to it, the precious stone was no longer there. . . .

II

Three men were traveling together in a distant country. Suddenly a terrific storm arose; thunder howled furiously, the lightning flashed, and the downpour of rain filled the men with terror. They observed a cave at the foot of a near-by mountain, and, dashing forward as fast as their legs could carry them, entered it. All night they remained there. And in the morning, when the rain had ceased and the storm subsided, the men gathered together their belongings and were about to leave. But lo and behold! a huge heavy rock, which had fallen from the mountain during the night, had sealed the mouth of the cave, and however they pushed and shoved the three men were unable to move it.

Now the travelers were in great distress, for their provisions had given out and they did not know where they could appeal for help. After a while darkness and hunger, like two evil demons, plagued their souls, and they began to pray to God with great fervor, each in succession, that He might aid them lest they perish.

The first one recalled all the good and just deeds that he had performed during his life. And behold! the rock moved about the length of a finger.

Then the second one began to pray and, like his companion, poured out his heart and recounted even greater deeds of charity and of righteousness. And behold! the rock moved about the length of a hand.

Finally the third one said: "O Lord, I do not know what I have done, but do deliver us from this fearful situation lest we perish." Then he began to pray, and as his words, like organ notes, resounded in the cave, the rock moved entirely from the mouth of the cave, and the three travelers went forth in peace.

THE LEGEND OF THREE AND OF FOUR

by HAYYIM NAHMAN BIALIK

I

KING SOLOMON had a sweet and lovely daughter whose like was nowhere to be found. He loved her as his own soul and guarded her as the apple of his eye. But she was passing strange, differing from all other maidens of her years, disdaining the clamor of pleasure-houses and rather desiring to walk alone and silent through the gardens of the king; or to rise betimes and wander far and wide along the tracks that twined among the vineyards, her spirit absorbed and her eyes gazing far ahead; always did she seem to be dreaming while awake, and there was none that knew her heart. When her time came to be wed, princes from far and near arrived to entreat her from her father; but the king's daughter turned her face away from them and never paid heed to their words; so that they returned one and all, shamed with hanging heads, to their own countries.

Time passed; and when they saw that the maiden persisted in hardening her heart, the princes despaired of her and ceased entreating for her. By reason of this, the king was troubled in spirit on her account and went up to his roof by night to gaze at the stars and perceive who the prince might be that was designed of God for his daughter; and when he would come. He studied the signs of the heavens and discovered that neither king nor prince was matched by God with his daughter, but a poor and needy youth of honest stock would come to her at the appointed season, and take her to wife.

Now this vexed the king exceedingly, and he sought for a stratagem to foil the purpose of heaven. And he decided to hide the maiden away for a while, until the time foretold in the stars should be past and the decree of fate could no longer come about. So he sought him a lonely isle in the sea, far from the ways followed by the ships in their traffic; there he had a lofty castle built, with many a hall and many a chamber; and he ranged a buttressed wall around it on every side, and set his daughter in the castle with seventy Elders of Israel to keep watch and ward over her and serve her every desire; plentiful provision for them did he make, storing them all manner of food and drink and the delights of the world, nothing lacking. Then he closed all the main gates and postern gates and portals and doors of the castle from without with bars of iron and locks and seals so that none might enter or leave; and he said, "Now shall I see the feats of God and His deeds, and whether the intent foretold by the stars shall be brought about or no."

So the king's daughter dwelt within this castle, with the seventy elders mounting guard over her, keeping watch and ward day and night and hastening to satisfy the least as the greatest of her desires. She was permitted whatsoever pastime she might wish, for the king had ordered that she be amused that her loneliness might not oppress her. One thing alone was beyond their power; out of the gates of the castle she could not go since the castle was enclosed from every quarter, none entering and none leaving. If she felt strait and confined within the building she would ascend to the roof and take a turn to and fro in the open air; or would lean against the coping of the battlements, gazing at the width of waters round about and hearkening to the medley of the waves; and she would be eased.

On the wall stood a watchman night and day, his eyes wide on the sea round about, observing the isle lest any ship approach or any strange foot be set on its strand. Twice a day, morning and evening, a speedy skiff would come within bowshot of the isle, one sitting therein who was sent by the king to ask the weal of the maiden. The one in the skiff would wave the white cloth in his hand and ask whether all was well with the king's daughter. And in reply the watchman would wave a white cloth back, signifying that all was well. Then the skiff would straightway turn about and vanish on the horizon.

And the closer came the season which the king did fear, the more did the elders pay heed to their watch and their ward; they stayed awake at their posts by the sealed posterns and gates and portals, their eyes wide, their nostrils sniffing, their ears twitching, starting at the buzzing of a fly as it knocked against a pane of glass or at the scratching claws of a lynx striving to scale the wall; for they were good men and true, such as would not think to deceive while about the king's business.

II

Now a poor lad of good stock who belonged to a family of scribes forsook Acre his city, for he suddenly found that the home of his needy parents was too small for him; and he turned his face afar. He left his home with empty hands, carrying nothing with him save his staff and his body; nonetheless he had no concern and his spirits never fell, since his bones were springing with youth, and his heart bounded with visions and high hopes, and his locks curled and happiness thudded within him all the way, so that he sang as he went. Crossing the fields he watched the grasshopper hopping and the joyous birds at song and the cony of the rocks and the clambering, darting lizard. Every green tree attracted him, and every forgotten booth in a forsaken vineyard. He sustained himself as might a bird from his gleanings in the generous fields, and slept on the ground with a stone for pillow. And wandering wide, passing through villages and cities, he would lend his ears to the converse of the wayfarers, gathering traditions and parables from the people and the elders of the people and storing all such away in his memory; this comforted him in his poverty and restored his soul in his wanderings.

But one day the sun set upon him while he was alone in a desolate, forsaken spot; the evening was rainy and cold, the lad was hungry and thirsty and naked and barefoot, so that frost consumed him and his strength all but vanished. In this plight he saw the carcass of an ox near by and rejoiced, saying: "Blest be God Who hath revealed me a couch in this place; lying therein, I shall grow warmer maybe." So he crept between the ribs of the skeleton, curled himself up and fell asleep.

During his sleep a huge eagle descended, picked up the skeleton in its beak together with him sleeping within it, flew off and set them down on the roof of the princess' castle, where it began to pick the little that was left of the carrion from the bones. Then the youth came out and drove it away, afterwards sitting on the roof all night long, weary and trembling by reason of the cold and the rains.

Morning came and the heavens cleared. The king's daughter mounted to the roof as was her daily custom, saw the strange youth, stood at a distance and asked:

"Who are you and who has brought you hither?"

And he replied very simply:

"Prithee fear not, O maiden, and be not angered with me. An Hebrew am I, a son of poor folk who dwell at Acre; last night the rain caught me in the fields in my hunger and my thirst, with never a garment to cover my flesh; so I lay me down in that skeleton yonder, and the eagle flew away with it and set it down here. Now I do not know the fashion after which I can depart hence, for there is nothing but the sea round about and never a ship in sight."

The king's daughter pitying him, brought him in secret to her bower, where she bathed him and garbed him and gave him to eat and to drink; and thereupon the brightness of his countenance returned to him with his high spirits. She gazed at him, found him handsome and pleasant, rejoiced in him exceedingly and was fain that he should be her companion. So she concealed him in her chambers and the elders knew nothing, since she had not revealed his coming to them and they would not venture to enter her chambers saving if they were summoned. Thenceforward she went forth twice a day to them to report her weal; and the elders paid no attention, thinking it but a whim. And they remained diligent and wakeful about their charges, each remaining in his position as he had been ordered, his eyes darting hither and thither, his ears wide to catch a stirring, his nostrils quivering to sniff; for the men were exceeding, exceeding faithful, doing the king's behest with faith and an entire heart.

III

The king's daughter perceived the wisdom of the poor youth, his good understanding and his pureness of heart, and loved him with all her heart and all her soul. And there came a day when she said to him:

"Am I fitting in thine eyes to be taken for thy wife?"

And the youth rejoined:

"Wherefore dost thou ask? I am thy slave to wash thy feet."

Then the maiden told how great her love was for him; how he was more desirable and precious to her than all the princes in the world; how God Himself had brought him thither on the wings of the eagle; how from the moment she saw him her soul did cleave to him; how in his lack her life would not be a life. Many such words did she utter from her ardent heart, and he answered her with the like, seventy and seven fold; and they made them a covenant of eternal love. The youth arose, let blood from his arm, and wrote with his blood the matter of the covenant on a scroll, signed and sealed, betrothing her according to law, saying: "Witness be the Lord, and witnesses His angels, Michael and Gabriel."

And meanwhile the elders knew of all these matters neither much nor little, though there were none such as they, honest and upright men who turned night into day and remained awake and exceedingly watchful at their posts.

IV

When the season revealed to Solomon by the stars had gone by, he bethought him of his daughter shut into the castle; and he resolved to bring her home again. So he went down to the sea in a ship and came to the isle with its castle; he examined the bars of iron and the locks and the seals on the gates and the posterns and the portals, and found that none had tampered with them and they were whole; so he ordered them to be hacked through and the gates and the portals swung open. Thereupon he entered the castle and the elders sprang up before him, then made obeisance and greeted him with peace.

And the king asked: "Is all well with my daughter? And where is she?"

And the elders replied: "All is well with her, O lord king, and she is within her bower."

Then the king proceeded to the maiden's bower, the elders following. They opened the door; and there was a handsome youth there facing them. And the elders quivered and quaked, and their hearts perished within them. And the king turned his eyes on them and asked:

"Who is this?"

But the elders could not make any answer, for they were so astonished that they might have turned to stone. They stood silent and pale, their heads drooping.

Then the king stamped his foot and cried in fury:

"Answer, or you shall be cut down one and all and hewn in pieces!"

The elders fell on their faces before him and answered in fear and trembling:

"Alas, our lord king. What is there to say and how shall we speak? As God lives we have kept watch and ward over the king's daughter with all our might; we do not know the fashion in which this lad is come hither."

The king turned to the maiden, breathing hard with anger as he asked:

"Wanton, say what this lad is doing here? Who brought him hither?"

The maiden fell at his feet, replying:

"Not in thy wrath, my lord and father! For this thing is come about only from God. He sent His messenger the eagle to bring me this youth my beloved, whose wife I am become. Take him and bless him, O my father!"

Then the king asked the youth:

"Who art thou? And after what fashion art thou come hither?"

And the young man stood erect before the king and answered without fear, relating all that had befallen him. The king observed how fine a youth he was and treated him in friendly fashion, conversing with him and finding him versed in all wisdom and parables more than all the scribes in his entire kingdom. So he enquired his name, his city and the house of his parents; and the young man answered directly and truthfully to all his questions telling him of his poverty and his wanderings, and the wonderful manner in which the eagle had brought him to the roof of the castle, and how the maiden had pitied him and taken him to her, entreating him graciously. And he produced the scroll which he had written and signed with his blood and showed it to the king, in token of the eternal love existing between him and the king's daughter. And Solomon hearkened to all these wonders and understood that he must be the poor youth of whom he had been forewarned in his star-gazing; and he said:

"Now indeed do I know that there is no wisdom nor understanding nor counsel that shall withstand the Lord."

When the elders perceived that the king was no longer in a fury their spirits returned; and they rose from the ground and raised their hands aloft to heaven, saying, "Blest be the Lord Who giveth a man a wife."

v

Then Solomon brought his daughter and her husband to Jerusalem, where he made them a seven-day feast and rejoiced with them greatly. When the feast had come to an end Solomon said to his son-in-law:

"See, thou art the son-in-law of the king, and my domains spread far and wide. Choose thou whatsoever high office thy heart may desire and it shall be thine."

But the youth replied:

"My lord king! Since my childhood I have been but a poor man of letters; my forefathers were scribes and learned of the Lord one and all, never aspiring to greatness nor acquainting themselves with pleasure-houses. Therefore if I find favor in thine eyes, let thy servant be given a secluded home on the seashore, where I may dwell with my spouse, conning the works of God and studying His ways like my fathers before me."

The king granted his request, setting him in charge of the royal scribes. So he dwelt in his home and gathered together all the words of wisdom, proverbs and parables, which Solomon uttered from time to time, and recorded them in a book. Further, the king's son-in-law wrote down some little of his own wisdom, which he had learnt or had fashioned in his meditations; adding them after the proverbs of Solomon the king; these being the words of Agur son of Yakeh.

And among his sayings is to be found:

> There are three too wonderful for me,
>   Four and I know them not.
> The way of an eagle in the heavens,
>   The way of a serpent along the rock,
> The way of a ship in the heart of the sea
>   And the way of a man with a maid.

THE THIRD LEG

by MARTIN BUBER

WHEN Rabbi Ezekiel came to Prague, he addressed his congregation on every Sabbath upon the same subject: the severe distress of the city's needy. Everyone expected to hear profound interpretation and sharp-witted discussion; but he continued, Sabbath after Sabbath, to remind them of the plight of the poverty-stricken. Unchecked and unmitigated, it was spreading rapidly throughout the city, even in their own neighborhood; on this very street where they were attending services. "Help them!" he cried again and again. "Help! This very night go forth and help!" But the people regarded his appeal as a sermon; they were annoyed at its lack of punch and flavor.

Then, on a very busy market day, something odd took place. In the midst of the turmoil the Rabbi appeared. He stood motionless in the center of the thickest crowds as if he had merchandise for sale and was waiting for an opportune moment to dispose of it. To those who knew him his conduct became more and more incomprehensible, while from everywhere tradesfolk and shoppers thronged about him and stared at him. Nobody, however, ventured to question him. At length an onlooker, who fancied that he was his intimate, broke the silence:

"What is our Rabbi doing here?"

Forthwith Rabbi Ezekiel began: "When a table has three legs and a piece of one of them is broken off, what does one do? One props up the leg as well as one can and the table stands again. When, however, a second leg breaks, another support will not make the table stand. What does one do in that case? One shortens the third leg and the table stands again.

"Our sages say, 'The world stands on three things: Learning, Religious Service and Deeds of Loving Kindness.' When a sanctuary is destroyed, then the leg of Religious Service is broken. Our sages provide a support for it in the dictum: 'By prayer is meant service of the heart.' When, however, Deeds of Loving Kindness vanish and the second leg is impaired, how shall the world continue? That is why I left the study and came to the market. We must shorten the leg of Learning so that the table of the world will stand firmly."

BOAZ MAKES UP HIS MIND

by IRVING FINEMAN

W HEN Ruth left him there was just one thin, pale streak, low on the eastern horizon, to show the dawn was coming. The darkness of the autumn night still lay like a tired sleeper in the fields; and within on the threshing floor, among disordered sheaves of grain, the sprawling, shapeless forms of sleeping men were barely discernible.

How like a dream it had been! As if in a dream she had come to him in the night. In the soft, bewitching, autumn night they had stood together, whispering. Whispering lest the sleepers be roused. What ineffable joy and pride in her love and faith had come to him—uncalled—as if out of the opulent night. And then, just before the dawn, he had sent her away, with his promise to see the kinsman.

Silent he stood, as if enchanted, watching Ruth as she descended the low hill through the pasture to the road; her white feet glimmering among the dark grasses, her shapely hips swinging gracefully, her sturdy shoulders bowed under the burden of his generous gift; he watched until her dark form merged with the shadows of the trees by the roadside. There was no sound from the shadowy fields. Behind him Boaz heard only the measured breathing of his sleeping men. How like a dream!

The sun came up; and with it the host of familiar sounds of a workaday world: the incessant twitter of birds from field and wood, the crowing of cocks from the barnyard, the lowing of cattle, the bark of dogs, the stir of waking men from the threshing floor. The sun came up like a clamorous brazen shield, dispelling the enchanting darkness from the land, and the seductive visions from the mind of Boaz. He watched its rays glittering on the waters of a stream that ran gaily down the valleys to the west—ran heedlessly down and away to the Dead Sea. And into the mind of Boaz crept a faint perturbation, seeped in and eddied about and rose—until it swept away all the joy of the night in a flood of anxiety. Doubts assailed him like a multitude of darting arrows—the immortal doubts of a man in the face of marriage.

Before him the sun, shining on his wide fields, drew up to his nostrils the smell of the rich warm soil. From behind him drifted the acrid smoke of a crackling fire and the noise of his young men preparing their food—with their hearty laughter and their free talk, boasting of their prowess in the harvest, in combat, in amorous conquest.

The devil! thought Boaz. Whatever had possessed him in the night? Bewitched, he must have been. . . . After a hard day's work with the harvest— as fine a harvest as any in Judah—he had bathed, eaten with gusto and drunk heartily; he had made merry with his men and lain down to rest, satisfied, without a care—as carefree as the youngest of them. And here he was—overnight—in a fair way to lose this precious freedom. . . .

Bewitched!—overnight. Well, there was no denying she had been a good deal in his thoughts since she first appeared gleaning in his fields. He had been impressed, immensely, at first sight of Ruth. So different, this woman of Moab, from the women he knew—the women of Bethlehem. A magnificent creature, handsome and strong and self-possessed. And when he learned who she was, and heard the tale of her loyalty to old Naomi, he was indeed very much taken with her; he had shown a kindly interest in her welfare, in protecting her from the crude men in his fields. Courageous creature. Other women, to be sure, gleaned in his fields, poor wretches. But Ruth was the widow of Mahlon, the son of Elimelech, of good family. The women of Bethlehem of her class, who considered all labor beneath them, would have died rather than stoop. . . . Boaz grimaced at the thought, and looked up over his olive trees at the walls of the town, glittering in the morning sunlight.

Those gossipy matrons of Bethlehem with their marriageable daughters: senseless girls with not a thought in their giddy heads but to make a good match, their one ambition. Old and young, always angling. Boaz knew that in the town he had long been marked as the great catch: a well-made, valiant fellow, rich, with many broad acres in wheat and barley. And the stratagems, the wiles they had tried upon him. Mothers of the first families of Bethlehem waylaid him in the foyer of the Temple after services: "You poor lonesome man! How you must want a good home-cooked dinner. You must come over and let me and my Sara give you a delicious meal. Sara is a perfect housewife, and would just love it. You haven't met my Sara. Sara, dear, this is . . ." And their fathers, grasping merchants, meeting him in the market place, treating him with unwonted generosity, plying him with patronage and with invitations, dropping hints of dowries that smelt, to Boaz, of barter in cattle. And when he had once been inveigled into calling, how carefully the younger Hannah was hidden from his view while the tiresome Sara was blatantly paraded before him. And finally, when he had failed to respond to the lure of Sara, how desperately the younger Hannah was thrown at his head. . . . He despised them all, did Boaz, the crafty, unscrupulous parents, and their dumb daughters, with their made-up prettiness, their avaricious eyes, and their dull virtues.

And for years he had escaped them; had eluded their wiles; had continued to live his free, robust life, in his broad fields among his men. And now, in the harvest, this miracle; overnight—captured. That was it, taken by surprise. How startled he had been, aroused in the night, to find Ruth at his feet. Strange, courageous woman. With her sturdy bearing, the fine undaunted eyes in her brown face, the roundness of her warm, sunburnt arms. How those cats in the town would talk if they knew she had come to him in the night, alone. . . . She had followed the honest prompting of her heart; in her straightforward manner, she had come to him, without evasion. "I am Ruth . . ." she had whispered in the night, and swept him off his feet. Carried away like a callow youth, he thought . . . and the flood of doubts came back to plague him. What would they not say in the town? Had he resisted the women of Bethlehem only to fall a victim to the bold proposal of this strange penniless woman of Moab? . . .

The devil! he muttered, and turned to his ablutions. The cool water seemed, for a moment, to clear his vision. After all, nothing had been settled finally. He had still to see the kinsman. This kinsman Boaz knew well—a thin beady-eyed, stiff-necked merchant whom he disliked and distrusted: a man, like many in the town, who made nothing with his own hands; who bought and sold, traded with the produce of others; who gilded his fingers, as it were, handling the treasures of others. This kinsman Boaz knew for a shrewd bargainer. Let Boaz but show an interest in the worthless, neglected property of Elimelech, and the kinsman would surely hold out for a profit on his right to redeem it. That, thought Boaz, would let him out. But instead of relief in this thought, he found himself still recalling and debating, over and over, in his disordered mind. . . . Her upturned face, the graceful swing of her hips as she walked, her glimmering feet in the dark. . . . And again the pricking doubts—this woman, an alien, what did he know of her strange ways and desires—upsetting his life, his freedom. . . . Only yesterday his mind had been at peace, and now . . . The devil! He had given his word; he would see it through; anyway he would see the kinsman. And Boaz turned his face to the threshing floor where the beat of the threshers had begun and the chaff rose up in a turbulent cloud.

"It appears that love," said the kinsman maliciously, "is not only blind but deaf."

Boaz, holding the shoe the other had given him as a token of the exchange, had a sudden impulse to fling it at the kinsman's head. But curiosity overcame his irritation, and Boaz kept his peace. His meeting with the kinsman before the elders at the city gate had begun just as Boaz expected. No sooner did he mention his interest in Elimelech's property than the avaricious kinsman said he would redeem the land. But then, unaccountably, Boaz found his heart heavy in his breast. Perversely, in that moment when it appeared that release was in sight, it seemed that, freedom or no freedom, he wanted Ruth. He perceived in a flash that he had not really come to escape the enchantment she had put upon him, but ready to pay dearly for the privilege to this hateful kinsman of hers. How great then was his astonishment and his relief to see the kinsman suddenly lose all interest in the matter, as soon as Boaz announced that the hand of Ruth was involved in the redemption of Elimelech's property. Yet as he watched the kinsman quickly unlace his shoe, the sign of his renunciation, surprise and relief turned to wonder. Boaz became curious; there was something about this too sudden victory; there was something in the mean eye of the kinsman. . . . It was curiosity that prompted Boaz to suggest they seal the bargain with a drink at the inn by the city gate.

Over his wine the kinsman proved only too ready to be drawn out—to air his views; and the more he talked the more he disturbed Boaz, irritated him with his self-righteousness, his mean innuendo.

"Blind and deaf," he repeated, staring malevolently at Boaz over the edge of his goblet. "Every man to his taste, of course," he went on after a pause, "but not for me . . ." He shook his head and pursed his thin lips. Boaz could have wrung his stiff skinny neck. "Too independent," he added crisply. "Woman's place, my dear Boaz, is in the home; and if I had my way," he leaned forward, licking his lips, "it would be in the harem."

Boaz stared at him in amazement.

"They do things differently, it seems, in Moab. But this young woman has got herself talked about in Bethlehem with her independence, boldly running about doing a man's work. Immodesty some people call it, and I may as well tell you that people have been saying things; only this afternoon I heard that late last night she had been seen . . . Well really, my dear Boaz, I mean no offence; only telling you what is being said." He hastily moistened his dry lips and Boaz subsided. "That may all be women's gossip. Anyway I don't mind saying she is not my type. Too sturdy. Personally I prefer them like our Bethlehem girls, soft—you know. That, I admit, my dear Boaz, is a matter of taste. But aside from that, I must say," he continued, "I do not see how you can look with joy on the prospect of old Naomi as your mother-in-law. I am not saying she is not a noble old woman, has had a hard time and all that; but much too crafty. Of course, she cannot be blamed for wanting a good home; and when a man is in love he doesn't mind so much being taken in; but really, my dear Boaz, the way she set out to get a good match for her outlandish daughter-in-law . . . egging her on. . . . Everyone has been talking about it. It may be a romantic accident, my dear Boaz, that the Moabitess came to glean in your fields, but there are people in town, I must tell you, who think differently. Of course, I would not go so far as to say, as some do, that Naomi induced her to come to Bethlehem for the sole . . . Why! my dear Boaz!" For Boaz had flung the shoe, narrowly missing the kinsman's head, and stood up before him in a towering rage.

"You may keep the rest of your slanders for your mean-minded friends—weak, despicable creatures, afraid of strong women. . . ." Yet even as he spoke, conviction failed him, and, in his wrath, words too. He turned and went out. Out of the inn and out of the city gate he strode, and down the road, kicking the dry dust into clouds that rose in the dusk behind him.

Hooked! Boaz muttered. That's what he had been—hooked. It seemed now that he had suspected it all along; that it was this had troubled him. They were no better than the rest—scheming women. All the same. Setting their traps first to catch a man's eye and then his heart. Scheming all the time. What of the night before? The dream of felicity and faith turned to a nightmare of suspicion. The plaguing doubts became horrid certitudes. . . . Naomi preparing Ruth for the visit—instructing her—"Wait, my daughter, until he has eaten and drunk and his heart is merry, and then . . ." That damnable kinsman was right; he had been blind and deaf. But he would not let himself be taken in. He would go to these women now and charge them openly; they would not dare deny. . . . He could have wept for the peace of mind of yesterday that had been changed to this gnawing rancor.

Nor could Boaz have said, even then, whether his spirit was harassed by the knowledge that he had been enslaved by the charms of Ruth, or by the fear that this suspicion of intrigue was taking her from him.

Thus distracted, Boaz suddenly found himself standing at sunset before the rude house that sheltered Ruth and Naomi. He hesitated; the door was open in his hand. The calm of the autumn evening seemed to fall like a balm on his fevered spirit. From within came the voice of Naomi: "Be assured, my daughter," she was saying, "he will not rest until he has settled the matter . . ." Crafty old woman, thought Boaz, it was indeed true; he had not rested. And it seemed to Boaz he had never wanted anything so much as he now wanted rest, and peace from the tormenting business of this day. He entered and Naomi was silent.

She sat by a lamp whose dim light deepened the lines in her face, furrows worn like tracks in an ancient road, as if ridden by recurring sorrows. Boaz, looking down into her patient old eyes, saw there little of craft, but much of wisdom—of the needs of man, and of the perversity of his proud nature. To Ruth, who was bent over the glowing oven, she said, "Boaz is here; come and talk with him"; and went to draw him a cup of wine. He could hear it gurgling from the cask in a dark corner.

About the room hung the pungent, the satisfying aroma of fresh-baked bread; and to his nostrils rose the sharp fragrance of the new-drawn wine Naomi set quietly before him. "Drink, Boaz, and rest," she said; and as he sipped, the plaguing doubts of the day seemed to slip like evil spirits from the heart of Boaz, to lose themselves in the shadows of the quiet room. The devil! he thought, and chided himself. This patient woman, who had been a good mother to her sons and a faithful wife to Elimelech, who had gone bravely with her men to a strange land in their adversity, and suffered there, did she not deserve to find a resting place in her old age? . . . And there before him stood Ruth, silent, expectant, wiping her brown hands on the coarse apron she wore. Ruth with her brave, undaunted eyes, her deep breast, her firm body—sturdy and straight as a cypress. Where was her like in all of Judah? The spell of her eyes, deep, dark and soft as the autumn night, was again upon him. The devil! he wondered; why had he resisted? A mate for a prince! He took her hands; joy and a great peace enfolded him like a cloak; for Boaz had made up his mind.

"She is better to me than seven sons," Naomi murmured; and Boaz answered: "She is worthy to be the mother of kings."

II. UNDER THE CRESCENT AND THE CROSS

INTRODUCTION

THE current of Jewish life,[1] alternately quickened, arrested and diverted at many turns, was determined, from the early Middle Ages until the dawn of the Modern Era, chiefly by two potent cross-currents: Christianity and Mohammedanism. No aspect of Jewish life, economic, social or religious—the Karaite schism, the religious ordinances of Rabbenu Gershom of Mayence, the development of the Kabala, the fortunes of the Maranos in Spain and America, the decline of Polish Jewry, and the career of Moses Mendelssohn—remained untouched by the impact of one of these historical forces.

This long, eventful period is marked by three cardinal changes in the career of the Jewish people: (1) the population and cultural centers shifted from the Eastern cradle to the West; (2) the homogeneity of classical, talmudic Judaism was modified by the development of localized Jewries in western states and of new religious and intellectual trends; (3) a growing differentiation between Jew and Christian was buttressed and exacerbated by the legalization of the Ghetto and Pale with their concomitant economic and social restrictions.

As for the first, the impetus for mass migration was provided by the sensational Moslem conquests in the West. By the middle of the tenth century the time-honored communities of Sura, Pumbedita and Nehardea were supplanted by those of Cairo, Kairawan, Bari, Cordova, Barcelona, Troyes, Worms, Mayence and Oxford (*The Four Captives*). Jews had lived in western Europe from the time that Cæsar's legions penetrated Gaul, and large Jewish settlements appear in the records as early as the fourth century when Christian ecclesiastical councils began to deal with the Jewish question. But it was only in the Middle Ages that the center of gravity of Jewish life shifted to the West. Thus the Christianization of Europe was accompanied by the Europeanization of the Jew.

But the course of Jewish migration and settlement was a zigzag one. By 1500 C.E., as a result of an unbroken series of expulsions and persecutions, the pendulum of Jewish history swings to northern and central Europe and back again to the East (Turkish Empire) where hundreds of thousands of refugees from Spain and Portugal found a haven. The tragic experiences of these leaden-footed wanderers are recorded in the chronicles of contemporaries

---

[1] There are a number of fascinating volumes dealing with various aspects of Jewish life during this period: *Jewish Life in the Middle Ages* by Israel Abrahams (London, 1932); *A World Passed By* by Marvin Lowenthal (New York, 1933); *Jewish Self-Government in the Middle Ages* by Louis Finklestein (New York, 1924); *Venice* by Cecil Roth (Philadelphia, 1930); *The History of the Marranos* by Cecil Roth (Philadelphia, 1932); *The Jews of Angevin England* by Joseph Jacobs (New York, 1893).

and eye-witnesses, such as the *Vale of Tears* by Joseph Hacohen and the *Rod of Judah* by the Vergas. A new group of centers arise in Hamburg, Amsterdam, Posen, Lublin, Wilna, Venice, Solonika, Constantinople, and Safed (*My Journey, from Beginning to End*); and as we approach the nineteenth century we discover the masses of Jewry concentrated in eastern and central Europe, Asia Minor and northern Africa.

Secondly, a new cultural syncretism followed in the wake of the migrations to Moslem centers. Arabic became the language of the Jewish masses and vied with Hebrew as a medium of literary expression. The vast array of Jewish poets, philosophers, commentators, chroniclers and physicians, whose names are associated with Italy, northern Africa and Spain, have justly earned the conventional label by which this era is known, "The Golden Age of Jewish Culture." Saadyah not only grappled with the theological issues that beset his people; he also brought out a new Arabic version of the Bible with a commentary (still read by Yemenite Jews) which served as a cultural link with the contemporary Moslem world, just as the Septuagint had done in a Greek-speaking world a thousand years before. Hasdai ibn Shaprut (*A Jewish Kingdom*), distinguished diplomat and scholar, was Mæcenas to a circle of Hebraists in Moslem lands, notably Menahem ibn Saruk and Dunash ibn Labrat. The exquisite poetry of Solomon ibn Gabirol and Judah Halevi, as well as their unique contributions to philosophy, place them, together with Moses Maimonides, whose octocentennial was recently celebrated throughout the world, among the great creative spirits of medieval times.

The comprehensive culture of the Jews in Moslem countries and Christian Spain differed considerably from that of Anglo-Franco-German Jewries. In the latter communities culture and education were not on a lower level; they embodied more completely the talmudic tradition, and their intellectual life was saturated with the Bible, the Talmud, legal dialectics and liturgy, Rashi (*Rashi and the Duke of Lorraine*) is representative of the leadership on the northern side of the Pyrenees. His life-long exposition of the Bible and Talmud resulted in two commentaries on these collections, which remain to the present indispensable tools of the student and scholar; it has been said that "without Rashi's Commentary the Talmud would today be a sealed book." Like his distinguished predecessor, Rabbenu Gershom of Mayence, Rashi was not concerned with science or philosophy but with the preservation of the religious and literary tradition and their application to social and economic problems. Rashi was succeeded by a school of talmudic dialecticians (Tosaphot) who completed his work. In Poland, where Jews had been driven as a result of brutal massacres of the Crusaders and the devastations of the Black Plague, talmudic exegesis reached the peak of its development in the sixteenth and seventeenth centuries.

The year 1492 C.E. is another landmark in Jewish history. On the one hand it marks the expulsion of the Jews from Spain and the resultant growth of new centers, and on the other hand the spread and the influence of the Maranos in almost every Jewish settlement. Of the importance of this tragic and picturesque body of Jews (*The Testament of a Martyr*), it has been brilliantly written: ". . . in the lands which bordered on both shores of the Northern Atlantic, there sprang up Jewish settlements of a new sort, in which the Jew was able to attain the stature of a man as never before, perhaps since the heyday of the Roman Empire. Persecution was unknown, segregation with its attendant humiliation was no longer the main object of the governmental policy, and there was now possible a healthy individualism in Jewish life instead of the previous differentiatory collectivism. Political disabilities continued till comparatively late, but they were not persecutory. From the very beginning, however, social disabilities were spontaneously removed. Holland, at the close of the sixteenth century, was the first country to open its doors to a colony of Jews of the new type. It was followed by neighboring lands, but especially by England and its colonies. Soon German and Polish refugees, though they lacked the graces and the financial recommendations of their precursors, were able to take advantage of the new atmosphere which the latter had created. It was they who may properly be called in the deepest sense of the term the first modern Jews" (Roth).

In the general upheaval of the fifteenth and sixteenth centuries, in many ways parallel to the present forces of destruction and reconstruction in world Jewry, it is not surprising that the imagination of the Jew should have been captured by the mysticism of the Kabala. Although evidence of cosmological speculation can be traced back to the early centuries of the common era, it was not until the thirteenth and fourteenth centuries that Jewish mysticism was elaborated in semi-philosophic form. The early classics of the Kabala, the *Bahir* and the *Zohar,* were written in northern Spain and Provence as a revolt against the rationalism of the philosophers. But with the tragic expulsions and persecutions that culminated in the destruction of Spanish Jewry, with the fires of the Inquisition taking an incredible toll of human lives, and with the invention of the printing press which permitted a wider circulation of literature, the Kabala spread like wildfire throughout the Jewish world; it was transformed from theosophic speculation to a theurgic method of hastening the coming of the Messiah (*The Awesome Story of Rabbi Joseph de la Reina*) and the restoration of the Jewish state in Palestine. A startling array of adventurers and mystics—David Reubeni (*Visit to the Pope*), Solomon Molko, Joseph Nasi, Manasseh ben Israel, and the leaders of the Safed school, Karo, Luria and Vital—spread out before us like heroic figures of a historical romance. The career of the messianic pretender of the seventeenth century, Sabbatai Zevi, has been the subject of an ever-growing literature: how he influenced his people may be seen from a few sentences out of the record of his contemporary, Glückel of Hameln: "Many sold their houses and lands and all their possessions, for any day they hoped to be redeemed. My good father-in-law left his home in Hameln, abandoned his house and lands and all his goodly furniture, and moved to Hildesheim. He sent on to us in Hamburg two enormous casks packed with linens and with peas, beans, dried meats, shredded prunes and like stuff, every manner of food that would keep. For the old man expected to sail any moment from Hamburg to the Holy Land."

Jewish mysticism reached its culmination in the abortive Frankist movement and the rise and spread of Hasidism in the eighteenth century. On its intellectual side Hasidism leaned upon the ideology of Kabala, but its social origins may be traced to the economic impoverishment of eastern and central European Jewries, and the revolt of the masses against the tyranny of the rabbis and the rich. It was, as Martin Buber has stated, the last great religious movement, and it produced a legendry[2] and folk spirit unparalleled in Jewish history for their incomparable richness (The World of Hasidism).

Thirdly, the Ghettoization of the Jew had, from the social viewpoint, the most serious consequences. By compelling the Jews to isolate themselves within walled quarters, it made them the object of social contempt and mob hostility, and resulted in the eventual impoverishment of the masses. The Ghetto removed them from the influence of modern science, invention and education, thereby giving sanction to the notion that their differences in culture, in religion, and in character made them "alien" and "inferior." How lasting were the effects of the social and economic suppression that the Ghetto concretely symbolized may be judged by the social disabilities and psychological idiosyncrasies characteristic of contemporary Jews. How effective an instrument it was in fostering race prejudice and persecution can be estimated by a study of the former *de jure* ghettos of Morocco and Yemen and the one created in the Third Reich.

It must not be imagined, however, that separate Jewish quarters were the creation of medieval Europe. They were, as a matter of fact, a natural product of the diaspora which required a close communal organization for the preservation of racial purity and social solidarity as well as for protection against mob violence. So long as these autonomous communities were protected by the state in the Roman, Persian and Moslem empires, they functioned as a voluntary social and religious corporation within the framework of the state. A compact social unit in a closed area of residence perpetuated group solidarity and cultural distinctiveness.

It was in medieval Europe, however, that the segregation of the Jew became a form of discrimination. To the Church the Jews were the Antichrist incarnate and by the multiplication of anti-Jewish enactments they were de-

---

[2] The American public was made aware of the beauty of Hasidic folklore by the production of Ansky's *Dybbuk* (1927) about which John Cowper Powys wrote: "Never since the old Greek drama has anything appeared so autochthonous, so woven—like that Jewish garment once diced for by Roman soldiers—'without a seam.'" Translations of Hasidic folklore may be read in *The Golden Mountain* by Meyer Levin (New York, 1932) and *The Hasidic Anthology* by Louis I. Newman (New York, 1935).

prived of public office, of the right to own land or slaves and, by exclusion
from the guilds, of engaging in trade. They became the serfs of the kings
and thus subject to his petty whims and arbitrary decisions. They were forced
into two unsavory economic pursuits, moneylending³ and petty commerce,
which even after hundreds of years have left their mark on their economic
make-up. The legalization of the Ghetto was the last step in their social and
economic degradation. Enforced quarters with gates under lock and key were
established in the bishopric of Mayence in 1349, in Cracow in 1494, and in
Venice in 1516. The complete theory and practice of the Ghetto was crystal-
lized in the bull *Cum nimis absurdum* promulgated by Pope Paul IV in 1555
which commanded the establishment of Ghettos in the cities of the Papal States.
The Ghettoization of all urban Jewish communities followed rapidly, for it
was utilized by the organized merchant and craft guilds of the rising bourgeoisie in the sixteenth century to throttle their severest competitors. Nevertheless a small minority, the "Protected" and the "Court-Jews," managed to purchase certain privileges so that by the beginning of the nineteenth century the
banking families of the Rothschilds, the Oppenheimers, the Gomperzes and the
Speyers had emerged from the ghettos of Frankfort and Vienna.

What has primarily impressed itself upon the mind of our generation is
the squalor and discrimination that the word "Ghetto" suggests. But one need
not search long to discover a unique communal organization and real social
values that were characteristic of ghetto life. One need only mention, as an
example of an admirable group of self-governing institutions, the Council of
Four Lands which regulated Jewish life in Poland from the sixteenth to the
eighteenth centuries. Nor can we fail to be moved by the essential humanity,
the strong moral fiber, the profound sentiment, the feverish imaginativeness and
the quaint but self-critical humor of men and women who accepted their
inferior position in life as God-imposed and found compensation in sweetening
the crumbs of life with the honey of learning and religion (Ghetto Lights and
Shadows).

With the dawn of the nineteenth century appeared titanic forces that within
a century rocked the social, economic and cultural structure of Jewish life.
The blessings and curses that these forces brought to the Jewish people constitute the drama of the Jew in the modern world.

³ The Church outlawed capitalism through a misinterpretation of *Luke* 6:35 which in the
Vulgate reads, "Mutuum date, nihil inde sperantes." The real meaning ("Lend, never despairing") was obscured by the interpretation of the words to mean that no surplus should be expected on merchandise bought or sold and no interest should be asked on the repayment of a loan.

MEDIEVAL TIMES

THE LOST TRIBES OF ISRAEL [1]

by ELDAD THE DANITE

MY departure from the other side of the rivers of Ethiopia was in the following manner.

I and a Jew of the tribe of Asher boarded a small ship to trade with the seamen and alas! at midnight, the Lord caused a strong gale to blow up and the ship was wrecked. Now the Lord had prepared a piece of the wreckage and I seized upon it and my companion, seeing this, also took hold of it, and we went up and down with it, until the sea cast us forth among a people called the Romaranus. And they dwelt in one of the seven kingdoms of Ethiopia and they are black Ethiopians, very tall, without raiment upon their bodies; cannibals, like the beasts of the field.

Now when we came to their country, they seized us, and seeing that my companion was fat and delectable, they slaughtered and ate him, and he cried aloud: "Alas for me, that I should have known this people and the Ethiopians should eat my flesh," but me they put aside, for I was sick on the ship, and they put me in chains until I should grow healthy and fat. And they brought me delicious and fattening food, but forbidden according to our Law, but I ate nothing and hid the food, but when they asked me whether I had eaten, I answered and said, "Yes, I have eaten."

And I was among them a long time until God, blessed be He, performed a miracle for me, for a great army came upon them from another place, who plundered and slaughtered more of them, and took me away with the captives. And those wicked men were fire-worshippers and every morning built a great fire and bowed down and lay prostrate before it. And I dwelt among them four years until on a certain day they brought me to a place called Azania.

And a Jewish merchant of the tribe of Issachar found me and bought me for thirty-two pieces of gold, and brought me back to his country. They live in the mountains of the sea-coast and are ruled by the Medes and the Persians, and they fulfil the command, "the book of this law shall not depart from thy mouth." The yoke of power is not upon them but they live under the yoke of the Law. There are among them military leaders but they fight with no

[1] The author of this account, Eldad the Danite, lived in the ninth century. He has been called an imposter, fabricator and sectarian propagandist, but modern scholars, like Hasdai in the eleventh century and Maimonides in the twelfth, regard his story as substantially historical. He appeared in Kairawan and other cities on the Mediterranean littoral, and some of the correspondence about him between the eastern and western Jewish communities has been preserved. *The Lost Tribes of Israel* is selected from Eldad's letter to the Jews of Spain in 883. The Hebrew employed, as in the diary of another oriental traveler of the sixteenth century, David Reubeni (v. n. page 265), is a Biblical diction. The translation is by Leo W. Scharz.

man, except to protect the Law. They dwell in prosperity and peace and among them are no troublemakers and no evil happenings. They live in a land ten days' journey by ten days, and they have much cattle and camels and asses and slaves, but they do not rear horses. They have no weapons, except the knife for the slaughter of animals, and among them extortion and robbery do not exist, and even if they should find garments or money on a public road, they would not stretch forth their hands to take them. But near them dwell wicked men, fire-worshippers, who take their own mothers and sisters to wife, but our tribes they do not hurt nor help. And they have a Judge, and I inquired about him and they said his name was Nahshon, and they practice the four death penalties—burning, beheading, stoning, and strangling—in the execution of criminals. They speak the Hebrew and Persian tongues.

And the tribe of Zebulun live in the mountains of Paran and extend to the border of Issahar, and they pitch tents of hairy skins which are brought to them from Armenia. And they extend to the Euphrates River and engage in business, and they also practice the four death penalties.

And the tribe of Reuben live on the other side of Mt. Paran, and they dwell in peace, love and unity, and they go together to fight and attack wayfarers and they divide the booty among them; but they observe the laws of the kings of Media and Persia. And they speak the Hebrew and Persian tongues, and possess the Scriptures and Mishnah and Talmud and Haggadah, and every Sabbath they interpret the meaning of the Law and the translation thereof is made in Persian.

And the tribe of Ephraim and the half-tribe of Manasseh live there on the other side of the city of Mecca, the seat of idolatry of the Ishmaelites. They are of tough spirit and of bold heart. They are ready horsemen and attack travelers and are pitiless with their enemies. They live only by booty. They are mighty warriors; one of them can vanquish a thousand enemies.

And the tribe of Simeon and the other half-tribe of Manasseh live in the land of the Kuzars, six months' journey away, and they are the most numerous of all the tribes, and they collect tribute from five and twenty kingdoms and some Ishmaelites pay them tribute.

And in our country we have a tradition among us that we are the children of the captivity, the tribes of Judah and the tribe of Benjamin, living under the dominion of idolators in an unclean land, that we were scattered under the Romans who destroyed our Holy Temple, and under the Greeks and the Mohammedans, may their sword pierce their own heart and may their bones be broken!

We also have an ancient tradition, handed down from father to son, that we are descendants of the tribe of Dan and in those early days we were tent-dwellers in the land of Israel and among all the tribes of Israel there were none like unto us in strength and valor. And when Jeroboam, the son of Nebat, who caused Israel to sin and made two golden calves, caused a revolt, and brought about the division of the Kingdom of David, the tribes gathered together and said, "Let us arise and fight against Rehoboam and against Jerusalem." But the Danites answered, "Why should we fight with our brothers and with the son of our lord David, king of Israel and Judah? God forbid that we should do such a thing!" Then answered the elders of Israel, "In all the tribes of Israel there are no mighty ones like the tribe of Dan. Arise, therefore, and fight with the tribe of Judah." But the Danites refused, saying, "By the life of our father Dan, we will not fight with our brothers, and we will not shed their blood." Whereupon the tribe of Dan took their swords and lances and bows and made ready to depart from the land of Israel, for we saw that we could not remain any longer, and said, "Let us depart now and find a resting-place, for if we wait until the end, we, too, may perish." And then we took counsel and decided to go down to Egypt to lay waste the land and destroy its inhabitants but after deliberation among our princes and nobles we took counsel to go down but not by the way our fathers went and not to lay waste the land but only to pass over the land to cross the river Pishon to Ethiopia. And behold, when we came near to Egypt, all the people trembled and their hearts melted, and sent messengers to us asking, "War or peace?" And we answered, "Peace; we will pass over your country to the river Pishon and there we will find a resting-place for ourselves." But they did not believe us and all the Egyptians were on guard until we passed through their land and arrived in Ethiopia; and we found it a good and fertile land and in it there were fields and vineyards and gardens. The Ethiopians could not prevent our tribe from dwelling with them for we seized the land by force and, because we wished to slay all of them, they had to pay us tribute, and we dwelt with them many years and became fruitful and multiplied and had great riches.

Then arose Sennacherib, King of Assyria, and took captive the tribe of Reuben and the tribe of Gad and the half-tribe of Manasseh and took them to Halah and Habor and the cities of Media. And Sennacherib arose again and took captive the tribe of Asher and the tribe of Naphtali and took them away to Assyria; and after his death the tribes of Naphtali, Gad and Asher left and journeyed to Ethiopia and encamped in the wilderness until they arrived at the border of the country where they still dwell, a twenty days' journey, and they slew the Ethiopians, and to this day they fight with the warriors of the kingdoms of Ethiopia. . . .

And the tribe of Moses, our teacher, peace on him! is surrounded by the sea, three months' journey by three months. They live in fine buildings and castles, and train elephants for themselves. And among them can be found no unclean fowl, cattle, fleas, lice, scorpions, serpents, dogs. They possess only oxen, fowl and sheep which give birth twice a year. They sow and reap twice a year and they have gardens of olives and pomegranates and figs and all manner of beans and melons and plants of strong flavors and barley and wheat, and all of these increase and multiply.

And they are wholly devoted to our religion and their Talmud is all in Hebrew, and this is the manner of their teaching, "Thus did we learn from our Rabbis, from the mouth of Joshua, the son of Nun, from the mouth of our Patriarch, Moses, from the mouth of the almighty." But the later Rabbis they did not know, for these were of the age of the Second Temple and their teaching did not reach them. And they speak only Hebrew and they take ritual baths and never curse. And they raise their voice against him who takes the name of God in vain and they say that cursing is a sin that brings an early death to one's children. . . . And they are all Levites and they abide in the holiness of Moses our teacher, the servant of God. And they see no one except the four tribes which dwell on the other side of the rivers of Ethiopia. There is a certain place they can all see each other and can speak to each other if they shout but the Sambatyon River divides them. And whenever they require anything not in their own land, they take a bird like unto a pigeon and they write their letters and fasten them to the wings or to the feet of the bird, and these fly across the Sambatyon River and reach their kings and nobles. And they possess many precious stones and silver and gold, and they sow flax and grow silk-berries and make myriads of fine garments, more than those that came out of Egypt. Now the breadth of the Sambatyon River is two hundred cubits and the river is glut with large and small stones and the noise they make sounds like a great storm, and during the night the sound of it is heard a day's journey away. And they have six wells which unite into one lake from which they irrigate their land, and which contains clean fresh fish. And the river runs and the stones and sand rumble during the six weekdays but it rests on the seventh day and is quiet until the close of the Sabbath. And on the other side where the other four tribes live there is a fire which flames and glows on the Sabbath and no man can come near within a mile.

And this is my name and genealogy, Eldad Ben Mahali Ben Ezekiel Ben Hezikiah Ben Aluk Ben Abner Ben Shemayah Ben Hater Ben Hur Ben Elkanah Ben Hillel Ben Tobias Ben Pedath Ben Ainon Ben Naaman Ben Taam Ben Taami Ben Onani Ben Gaul Ben Shalom Ben Caleb Ben Omram Ben Dumain Ben Obadiah Ben Abraham Ben Joseph Ben Moses Ben Jacob Ben Kappus Ben Ariel Ben Asher Ben Job Ben Shallum Ben Clihu Ben Ahaliab Ben Ahisamah Ben Hushim Ben Dan Ben Jacob our Patriarch, peace upon him and all Israel.

And these letters prince Eldad sent to Spain in the year 883.

A JEWISH KINGDOM[1]

by HASDAI IBN SHAPRUT

I, HASDAI, son of Isaac, son of Ezra, belonging to the exiled Jews of Jerusalem, in Spain, a servant of my Lord the King, bow to the earth before him and prostrate myself towards the abode of your Majesty, from a distant land. I rejoice in your tranquillity and magnificence, and stretch forth my hands to God in Heaven that He may prolong your reign in Israel. But who am I? and what is my life that I should dare to indict a letter to my Lord the King and to address your Majesty? I rely, however, on the integrity and uprightness of my object. How, indeed, can an idea be expressed in fair words by those who have wandered, after the honor of the kingdom has departed; who have long suffered afflictions and calamities, and see their flags in the land no more? We, indeed, who are of the remnant of the captive Jews, servants of my Lord the King, are dwelling peacefully in the land of our sojourning (for our God has not forsaken us, nor has His shadow departed from us). When we had transgressed He brought us into judgment, cast affliction upon our loins, and stirred up the minds of those who had been set over the Jews to appoint collectors of tribute over them, who aggravated the yoke of the Jews, oppressed them cruelly, humbled them grievously and inflicted great calamities upon them. But when God saw their misery and labor, and that they were helpless, He led me to present myself before the King, and has graciously turned His heart to me, not because of mine own righteousness, but for His mercy and His covenant's sake. And by this covenant the poor of the flock were exalted to safety, the hands of the oppressors themselves were relaxed, they refrained from further oppression, and through the mercy of our God the yoke was lightened. Let it be known, then, to the King my Lord, that the name of our land in which we dwell is called in Hebrew "Sefarad," but in the language of the Arabs, the inhabitants of Andalusia, the name of the capital of the kingdom, Cordova. The length of it is 25,000 cubits, the breadth 10,000. It is situated at the left of the Mediterranean Sea which flows between your country and the Atlantic Ocean, and compasses the whole of your land. Be-

---

[1] The Kingdom of the Kuzars actually existed in the southern part of Russia from the seventh to the tenth centuries. Somewhat before 800 the king, his court, and part of the population embraced Judaism, and adhered to their adopted religion until the kingdom was destroyed by the Russians. The correspondence between Joseph and Hasdai, long believed legendary, are now considered authentic.

Hasdai ibn Shaprut (915-990) played an important rôle in state administration and diplomacy as physician and counselor to the caliph Abd al Rahman III. His prominent position made it possible for him to communicate with the king of Kuzars, and thus help to rescue from oblivion an exciting chapter of medieval history. Hasdai was also the Mæcenas of Spanish-Jewish culture during the tenth century. The above translation is substantially that published in the *Miscellany of Hebrew Literature* (London, 1872).

tween this city and the great sea beyond which there is no farther habitable territory, are nine astronomical degrees; the sun advances one degree on each day,
according to the opinion of the astronomers; each degree contains sixty-six
miles and two parts of a mile, each mile consists of 3,000 cubits; so that those
nine degrees make 600 miles. From the Atlantic the whole distance as far as
Constantinople is 3,100 miles; but Cordova is eighty miles distant from the
shore of the sea which flows into your country (Mediterranean). I have found
in the books of the wise men that the land of Kuzar is sixty degrees longitude,
making 270 miles (from Constantinople). Such is the journey from Cordova
to Constantinople. Before I set forth an account of it I will premise the
measure of the length of its limits. Your servant is not ignorant that the least
of the servants of my Lord the King is greater than the wise men of our
country; but I am not teaching, only recording.

According to the mathematical principles we have found that the distance
of our city from the Equator is thirty-eight degrees, that of Constantinople
eighty-four, of your boundaries forty-seven. I have been induced to state these
facts because of my surprise that we have no account of your kingdom, and
I think this is only due to the great distance of our kingdom from the realm
of my Lord the King. But I recently heard that two men, inhabitants of our
land, had arrived at the dwelling-place of my Lord the King, one of them
called Rabbi Judah, son of Meir, son of Nathan, a prudent and learned man,
the other R. Joseph Haggaris, also a wise man (happy they, and blessed their
lot, whose fortune it was to see the glorious majesty and splendor of my Lord
the King, as well as the state and condition of his servants and ministers), I
thought that it was easy in the sight of God in his great mercy to do a wonder
to me also, and to make me, too, worthy of seeing the majesty and royal throne
of my Lord, and to enjoy his gracious presence. I shall inform my Lord the
King of the name of the King who reigns over us. His name is Abd er-Rahman,
son of Mohammed, son of Abd er-Rahman, son of Hakem, son of Hisham,
son of Abd er-Rahman, who all reigned in succession except Mohammed alone,
the father of our king, who did not ascend the throne, but died in the lifetime
of his father. Abd er-Rahman, eighth of the Ommayads, came into Spain while
the sons of al-Abbasi ruled over it, neighbours of those who are sovereigns in
the land of Shinar at the present time. Abd er-Rahman liberated Spain when
there was an insurrection against it by the sons of al-Abbasi, son of Mu'awiya,
son of Hisham, son of Abdel-Malik, who is called Amir al-Muminim (Ruler
of the Faithful), whose name is universally known. Nor can any of the kings
who went before he compared with him. The extent of Spain which is under
the sovereignty of Abd er-Rahman, the Amir al-Muminim (to whom God be
propitious) is 16 degrees, making 1,100 miles. The land is rich, abounding in
rivers, springs and aqueducts; a land of corn, oil and wine, of fruits and all
manner of delicacies; it has pleasure gardens and orchards, fruitful trees of
every kind, including the leaves of the tree upon which the silkworm feeds,

of which we have great abundance. In the mountains and woods of our country cochineal is gathered in great quantity. There are also found among us mountains covered by crocus and with veins of silver, gold, copper, iron, tin, lead, sulphur, porphyry, marble and crystal. It produces besides what is called in the Arabic language "lulu." Merchants congregate in it, and traffickers from the ends of the earth, from Egypt and adjacent countries, bringing spices, precious stones, splendid wares for kings and princes, and all the desirable things of Egypt. Our king has collected very large treasures of silver, gold, precious things, and valuable such as no king has ever collected. His yearly revenue, I have heard, is about 100,000 gold pieces, the greater part of which is derived from the merchants who come hither from various countries and islands; and all their business transactions are placed under my control.

Praise be to the beneficent God for his mercy towards me! Kings of the earth, to whom His magnificence and power are known, bring gifts to him, conciliating his favor by costly presents, such as the King of the Germans, the King of the Gebalim, the King of Constantinople, and others. All their gifts pass through my hands, and I am charged with making gifts in return. (Let my lips express praise to the God in Heaven who so far extends his loving-kindness towards me without any merit of my own, but in the fullness of his mercies.) I always ask the ambassadors of these monarchs about our brethren the Jews, the remnant of the captivity, whether they have heard anything concerning the deliverance of those who have pined in bondage and had found no rest. At length mercantile emissaries of Khorasan told me that there is a kingdom of Jews who are called Kuzars (and between Constantinople and that country is a sea voyage of 15 days, by land many nations dwell between us and them). But I did not believe these words, for I thought that they told me such things to procure my goodwill and favor. I was therefore hesitating and doubtful till the ambassadors of Constantinople came with presents and a letter from their king to our king, whom I interrogated concerning this matter. They answered me, "It is quite true; there is in that place a kingdom Alkusari, distant from Constantinople a fifteen days' journey by sea, but many peoples are scattered through the land; the name of the king now reigning is Joseph; ships sometimes come from their country to ours bringing fish, skins, and wares of every kind; the men are our brethren and are honored by us; there is frequent communication between us by embassies and mutual gifts; they are very powerful; they maintain numerous armies, which they occasionally engage in expeditions." This account inspired me with hope, wherefore I bowed down and adored the God of Heaven.

I now looked about for a faithful messenger whom I might send into your country in order that I might know the truth of this matter and ascertain the welfare of my Lord and his servants our brethren. The thing seemed impossible to me, owing to the very great distance of the locality, but at length by the will and favor of God, a man presented himself to me named Mar Isaac, son of Nathan. He put his life into his hand and willingly offered to take my letter to my Lord the King. I gave him a large reward, supplying him with gold and silver for his own expenses and those of his servants, and with everything necessary. Moreover, I sent out of my own resources a magnificent present to the King of Constantinople, requesting him to aid this my messenger in every possible way, till he should arrive at that place where my Lord resides. Accordingly this messenger set out, went to the King and showed him my letter and presents. The King, on his part, treated him honorably, and detained him there for six months, with the ambassadors of my Lord the King of Cordova. One day he told them and my messenger to return, giving the latter a letter in which he wrote that the way was dangerous, that the peoples through whom he must pass were engaged in warfare, that the sea was stormy and could not be navigated except at a certain time. When I heard this I was grieved even to death, and took it very ill that he had not acted according to my orders and fulfilled my wishes.

Afterwards I wished to send my letter by way of Jerusalem, because persons there guaranteed that my letter should be dispatched from thence to Nisibis, thence to Armenia, from Armenia to Berdaa, and thence to your country. While in this state of suspense, behold! ambassadors of the King of Gebalim arrived, and with them two Jews; the name of one was Mar Saul, of the other Mar Joseph. These persons understood my perplexity and comforted me, saying, "Give us your letter, and we will take care that it be carried to the King of the Gebalim, who for your sake will send it to the Israelites dwelling in the land of the Hungarians, they will send it to Russ, thence to Bulgar, till at last it will arrive, according to your wish, at its destination."

He who tries the heart and searches the reins knows that I did none of these things for the sake of mine own honor, but only to know the truth, whether the Jewish exiles anywhere form one independent kingdom and are not subject to any foreign ruler. If, indeed, I could learn that this was the case, then despising all my glory, abandoning my high estate, leaving my family, I would go over mountains and hills, through seas and lands, till I should arrive at the place where my Lord the King resides, that I might see not only his glory and magnificence, and that of his servants and ministers, but also the tranquillity of the Jews. On beholding this my eyes would brighten, my reins would exult, my lips would pour forth praises to God, who has not withdrawn his favor from his afflicted ones.

Now, therefore, let it please your Majesty, I beseech you to have regard to the desires of your servant, and to command your scribes who are at hand to send back a reply from your distant land to your servant and to inform me fully concerning the condition of the Jews, and how they came to dwell there. Our fathers told us that the place in which they originally settled was called Mount Seir, but my Lord knows that Mount Seir is far from the place where you dwell; our ancestors say that it was, indeed, persecution, and by one calamity after another, till at length they became fixed in the place where they now dwell. The ancients, moreover, inform us that when a decree of fierce persecution was issued against the Jews on account of their transgressions, and the army of the Chaldeans rose up furiously against them, they hid the Book of the Law and the Holy Scriptures in a cave. For this reason they prayed in a cave and taught their sons to pray there morning and evening. At length, however, through distance of time and days, they forgot and lapsed into ignorance as to the meaning of the cave and why they prayed in it; while they still continued to observe the customs of their fathers, though ignorant of the reason for it. After a long time there came a certain Jew who was desirous of knowing the true meaning of this custom, and when he entered the cave he found it full of books, which he brought out. From that time they resolved to study the Law. That is what our fathers have related to us as it was handed down from ancient times. The two men who came from the land of Gebalim, Mar Saul and Mar Joseph, after pledging themselves to forward my letter to my Lord the King, told me: "About six years ago there came to us a wise and intelligent Jew afflicted with blindness, his name was Mar Amram, and he said that he was from the land of Kuz, that he dwelt in the King's house, ate at his table, and was held in honor by him." On hearing this I sent messengers to bring him to me, but they did not find him, yet this very circumstance confirmed my hope.

Wherefore I have written this epistle to your Majesty, in which I submissively entreat you not to refuse my request, but to command your servant to write to me about all these things; viz., what is your state? what is the nature of your land? what tribes inhabit it? what is the manner of the government, how kings succeed one another—whether they are chosen from a certain tribe or family or whether sons succeed their fathers as was customary among our ancestors when they dwelt in their own land? Would my Lord the King also inform me as to the extent of his country, its length and breadth? what walled cities and what open towns it has; whether it be watered by artificial or natural means and how far his dominion extends, also the number of his armies and their leaders? Let not my Lord take it ill, I pray that I enquire about the number of his forces ("May the Lord add unto them," etc.). My Lord sees that I enquire about this with no other object than that I may rejoice when I hear of the increase of the holy people. I wish, too, that he would tell me of the number of the provinces over which he rules, the amount of tribute paid to him, if they give him tithes, whether he dwells continually in the royal city or goes about through the whole extent of his dominions, if there are any islands in the neighborhood, and if any of their inhabitants conform to Judaism? if he judges his own people himself or appoints judges over them? how he goes up to the house of God? with what peoples he wages war? whether he allows war to set aside the observance of the Sabbath? what kingdoms or nations are on his borders? what are their names and those of territories?

what are the cities near to his kingdom called Khorasan, Berdaa, and Bab al Abwab? in what way their caravans proceed to his territory? how many kings ruled before him? what were their names, how many years each of them ruled and what is the current language of the land? In the time of our fathers there was among us a certain Jew, an intelligent man, who belonged to the tribe of Dan, who traced his descent back to Dan, the son of Jacob. He spoke elegantly and gave everything its name in the holy language. Nor was he at loss for any expression. When he expounded the Law he was accustomed to say, "Thus has Othniel, son of Kenaz, handed down by tradition from the mouth of Joshua, and he from the mouth of Moses who was inspired by the Almighty." One thing more I ask of my Lord, that he would tell me whether there is among you any computation concerning the final redemption which we have been awaiting so many years, whilst we went from one captivity to another, from one exile to another. How strong is the hope of him who awaits the realization of these events. And oh! how can I hold my peace and be restful in the face of the desolation of the House of our glory and remembering those who, escaping the sword, have passed through fire and water, so that the remnant is but small. We have been cast down from our glory, so, that we have nothing to reply when they say daily unto us, "Every other people has its kingdom, but of yours there is no memorial on the earth." Hearing, therefore, of his dominions, and the multitude of his forces, we were amazed, we lifted up our head, our spirit revived, and our hands were strengthened, and the kingdom of my Lord furnished us with an argument in answer to this taunt. May this report be substantiated; for that would add to our greatness. Blessed be the Lord of Israel who has not left us without a kinsman as defender nor suffered the tribes of Israel to be without an independent kingdom. May my Lord the King prosper for ever. . . .

THE REPLY OF JOSEPH, KING OF THE TOGAMI, TO HASDAI, THE HEAD OF THE CAP-TIVITY, SON OF ISAAC, SON OF EZRA, THE SPANIARD, BELOVED AND HONORED BY US.

Behold, I inform you that your honored epistle was given me by Rabbi Jacob, son of Eleazar, of the land of Nemez (Germany). We were rejoiced by it, and pleased with your discretion and wisdom, which we observed therein. I found in it a description of your land, its length and breadth, the descent of its sovereign, Abd er-Rahman, his magnificence, and majesty; and how, with the help of God, he subdued to himself the whole of the East, so that the fame of his kingdom spread over the whole world, and the fear of him seized upon all kings. You also told us had it not been for the arrival of those ambassadors from Constantinople, who gave an account of the people of our kingdom, and of our institutions, you would have regarded all as false and would not have believed it. You also inquired concerning our kingdom and descent, how our fathers embraced the laws and religion of the Jews, how God enlightened our eyes and scattered our enemies; you also desired to know the length and breadth of our land, the nations that are our neighbors, such as are friendly and hostile; whether our ambassadors can go to your land to salute your eminent and gracious king, who draws the hearts of all men to love him and contract friendship with him by the excellence of his character and the uprightness of his actions, because the nations tell you that the Jews have no dominion and no kingdom. If this were done, you say, the Jews would derive great benefit from it, their courage would be reawakened, and they would have an answer and occasion for priding themselves in reply to such as say to them, "There are no Jews remaining who have a kingdom or dominion." We shall, therefore, delighting in your wisdom, answer you with respect to each of these particulars, concerning which you have asked us in your letter.

We had already heard what you have written concerning your land, and the family of the king. Among our fathers there had been mutual intercourse by letters, a thing which is written in our books and is known to the elders of our country. We shall now inform you of what happened to our fathers before us, and what we shall leave as an inheritance to our children.

You ask, also, in your epistle of what people, of what family, and of what tribe we are? Know that we are descended from Japhet, through his son Togarma. We have found in the genealogical books of our fathers that Togarma had ten sons, whose names are these:—Agijoe, Tirus, Ouvar, Ugin, Bisal, Zarna, Kuzar, Sanar, Balgad and Savir. We are of Kuzar, of whom they write that in his days our fathers were few in number. But God gave them fortitude and power when they were carrying on wars with many and powerful nations, so that they expelled them from their country and pursued them in flight as far as the great River Duna (Danube?), where the conquerors live to this day, near Constantinople, and thus the Kuzars took possession of their territory. . . .

As to your question concerning the extent of our land, its length and breadth, know that it is situated by the banks of a river near the sea of Gargal, towards the region of the East, a journey of four months. Near that river dwell very many populous tribes; there are hamlets, towns, and fortified cities, all of which pay tribute to me. On the south side are fifteen very populous tribes, as far as Bab al Abwab, who live in the mountains. Likewise the inhabitants of the land of Bassa, and Tagat, as far as the sea of Constantinople, a journey of two months; all these give me tribute. On the western side are thirteen tribes, also very numerous, dwelling on the shores of the sea of Constantinople, and thence the boundary turns to the north as far as the great river called Jaig. These live in open unwalled towns and occupy the whole wilderness (steppe) as far as the boundary of the Jugrians; they are as numerous as the sand of the sea, and all are tributary to me. Their land has an extent of four months' journey. I dwell at the mouth of the river and do not permit the Russians who come in ships to enter into their country, nor do I allow their enemies who come by land to penetrate into their territory. I have to wage grievous wars with them, for if I would permit them they would lay waste the whole land of the Mohammedans as far as Bagdad.

Moreover, I notify you that I dwell by the banks of the river, by the grace of God, and have in my kingdom three royal cities. In the first the queen dwells with her maids and attendants. The length and breadth of it is fifty square parasangs together with its suburbs and adjacent hamlets. Jews, Mohammedans, Christians and other peoples of various tongues dwell therein. The second, together with the suburbs, comprehends in length and breadth, eight square parasangs. In the third I reside with the princes and my servants and all my officers. This is a small city, in length and breadth three square parasangs; this river flows within its walls. The whole winter we remain within the city, and in the month of Nisan (March) we leave this city and each one goes forth to his fields and gardens to cultivate them. Each family has its own hereditary estate. They enter and dwell in it with joy and song. The voice of an oppressor is not heard among us; there are no enmities or quarrels. I, with the princes and my ministers, then journey a distance of twenty parasangs to the great River Arsan, thence we make a circuit till we arrive at the extremity of the province. This is the extent of our land and the place of our rest. Our country is not frequently watered by rain; it abounds in rivers and streams, having great abundance of fish; we have many springs; the land is fertile and rich; fields, vineyards, gardens and orchards are watered by rivers; we have fruit-bearing trees of every kind and in great abundance.

This, too, I add, that the limit of our lands towards the Eastern region is twenty parasangs' journey as far as the sea of Gargal, thirty towards the South, forty towards the west. I dwell in a fertile land and, by the grace of God, I dwell in tranquillity.

With reference to your question concerning the marvellous end, our eyes are turned to the Lord our God and to the wise men of Israel who dwell in Jerusalem and Babylon. Though we are far from Zion, we have heard that because of our iniquities the computations are erroneous; nor do we know aught concerning this. But if it please the Lord, He will do it for the sake of His great name; nor will the desolation of His house, the abolition of His service, and all the troubles which have come upon us be lightly esteemed in His sight. He will fulfil His promise, and "the Lord whom ye seek shall suddenly come to His temple, the messenger of the Covenant whom ye delight in: behold, he shall come, saith the Lord of Hosts." Besides this we know only the prophecy of Daniel. May God hasten the redemption of Israel, gather together the captives and dispersed, you and I and all Israel that love His name, in the lifetime of us all.

Finally, you mention that you desire to see my face. I also long and desire to see your honored face, to behold your wisdom and magnificence. Would that it were according to your word and that it were granted to me to be united with you, so that you might be my father and I your son. All my people would pay homage to you. According to your word and righteous counsel we should go out and come in. Farewell.

RABBI PALTIEL

by AHIMAAZ BEN PALTIEL [1]

IN those days the Arabians with their armies, with Al Muizz as their commander, overran Italy; they devastated the entire province of Calabria, and reached Oria, on the border of Apulia; they besieged it, defeated all its forces; so that the city was in dire distress; its defenders had no power to resist; it was taken by storm; the storm smote it to the very soul. They killed most of its inhabitants, and led the survivors into captivity. And the commander inquired about the family of R. Shephatiah. He sent for them and had them appear before him. And God let them find grace in his eyes. He bestowed His kindness upon R. Paltiel, His servant, and let him have favor before him. And Al Muizz brought him to his tent, and kept him at his side, to retain him in his service.

One night R. Paltiel and the commander went out to observe the stars. As they were gazing at them, they saw the commander's star consume three stars, not all at one time, but in succession. And Al Muizz said to him, "What meaning dost thou find in that?" R. Paltiel answered, "Give thy interpretation first." The commander replied, "The stars represent the three cities, Tarentum, Otranto and Bari, that I am to conquer." R. Paltiel then said, "Not that, my Lord; I see something greater; the first star means that thou wilt rule over Sicily; the second, that thou wilt rule over Africa, and the third, that thou wilt rule over Babylonia." Al Muizz at once embraced him and kissed him, took off his ring and gave it to him, and took an oath, saying, "If thy words come true, thou shalt be master of my house and have authority over all my kingdom."

Before seven days had passed, a message was brought to Al Muizz. The princes of Sicily sent messengers to him, saying, "Know that the Emir is dead.

---

[1] Of all the discoveries out of university and ecclesiastical archives during the nineteenth century, none was more welcome than the *Chronicle of Ahimaaz* which was found in the Cathedral Library of Toledo by Adolph Neubauer. The author (1017-1054), an elegiac Hebrew poet of considerable importance, was the scion of an Italian Jewish family. "I will relate the story," he says in the beginning of the chronicle, "investigate diligently, and arrange a garner of the traditions of my forefathers; I will set in order their genealogies and add explanatory notes." This family memoir, devoted to the lives and times of the author's distinguished ancestors for a period of two hundred years, has thrown new light on both Byzantine and Italian Jewish history during this period. It is written in rhymed prose. The above selection, taken from the complete translation by Marcus Salzman (*The Chronicle of Ahimaaz*, Columbia University Press), is a superb example of the medieval "âme neuve et naïve."

Come thou in haste and assume authority and dominion over us." He there-upon gathered his troops; with all the captains of his army he embarked on his ships and crossed over into their country, and became their ruler. Then he had faith in the words of R. Paltiel, and did not depart from his advice, either to the left or to the right; he appointed him master over his house and domain. R. Paltiel entered his service as his vizier.

Some time after, Al Muizz went to Ifrikiya, leaving his brother as ruler over Sicily; and R. Paltiel went with him. There he grew in eminence, and added to his fame; he was second in power to the Caliph; his renown spread through all the cities.

At that time, the emperor of Greece sent an embassy with a gift to seek audience with the Caliph of Ifrikiya. The ambassador came in state as was the custom of the Greeks. He asked who was warden of the palace and master of the royal ceremonies. An Arabian said to him, "It is a Jew that gives permis-sion to enter and leave; he is in authority over all the Caliph's dominion; and the Caliph always follows his advice. No one can see him or enter the palace to appear before him without the order and consent of the Jew." But the Greek in his insolence and pride, in his folly and stupidity, replied, "I would rather leave this city and return to Constantinople, to my master who has sent me hither, than deal with the Jew for permission to let me speak to the Caliph." These words reached the ear of R. Paltiel; he was informed of all that had occurred. He then commanded throughout the royal court that no one ap-proach the envoy with a sign of greeting or respect, and that no one take notice of him where he had set up his tent. For about ten days he kept aloof, in anger and raging fury. Then he meekly came up to ask mercy and pardon, begging that he forget his senseless conduct, and forgive the offense he had committed in his stupidity, and the words he had spoken in his folly. R. Paltiel granted that he might come, but not on that day. On the third day, he admitted him into his presence; he received him with honor and splendor, and overwhelmed him with lavish gifts, entertained him with music, and dances, and an abundance of perfumes, with precious stones, onyx and opal, and with the costly and beautiful treasures of the realm. He received him in state, from the gate of his palace to his dining-hall; he adorned the entire hall with hangings of silk and wool; the floor of the court and the walls of the palace were beautified with tapestry of scarlet and fine linen and costly ornaments; he walked in upon rugs of silk. The Greek saw R. Paltiel sitting upon a couch, and, for himself he found a chair of gold. He took his seat and entered into conversation with him, questioned him about the law of the Hebrews, about his kin, and family and native land; R. Paltiel answered him properly and intelligently. And he gave order that water be brought to wash his hands and mouth, in a dish and bowl of onyx and jasper. Secretly he com-manded the servant to break them, after he had washed. The servant carried out the command of his master; he brought the bowl, and its dish; he poured the water over his master's hands, and then fell at his feet, and broke the dishes. Thereupon the Greek arose in amazement and grew pale. But R. Paltiel laughingly turned to him and said before all gathered about him, "Why art thou disturbed; why dost thou rise from thy seat in amazement?" The Greek replied, "Because I have seen great damage done. There is no way of replacing the priceless bowl and dish that have been broken." R. Paltiel then questioned him about the king of the Greeks, as to whether dishes of gold or of precious stone were used in his palace, and the Macedonian ambassador said, "Dishes of gold are used in my master's house." To which R. Paltiel replied, "Thy master is a man of limited means. Dishes of precious stones and gems are more costly than dishes of gold; for those that are made of precious stone cannot be restored when broken, but those of gold, when damaged, can be mended without loss; many dishes of rare stone and gem such as thou hast just seen broken in my house, are broken in the palace of my master the Caliph." Thereupon he dismissed him with honor, to the king of Greece who had sent him.

R. Hananeel, the son of Paltiel, asked permission of the Caliph of Ifrikiya to cross the sea and go to Italy, for at the time of the captivity of Oria, those that were spared sought refuge in Bari and Otranto, bringing their household goods with them, and saving the money of others with their own. So R. Hananeel went to Constantinople, and, sorely depressed and afflicted, entreated the King to receive him with favor, to grant him the authority, under royal seal, to travel through all cities of his kingdom and, with his will and consent, enter any place in which he might find property belonging to him. He took the sealed letter of authority and went to the city of Bari. There he found an old copy of the Scriptures that had been his, and ornaments of the clothes of women, and sewed garments that they wore. The teachers and sages of Bari disputed their possessions with him, in accordance with the principle that he who saves anything from an invading army, from the water or the fire, may claim it as his own; for this was the teaching of Rab, in the interpretation of the Mishna. He replied, "It is as you say, but our sages have also taught that 'the law of the land is the binding law'; here is the written edict with the seal, which the Emperor issued for me." So they divided with him. They gave him the robes and the copy of the Scriptures, and he left them the remainder as a compromise. He went down to Beneventum and the entire community respectfully welcomed him. He remained there an entire year. Then he made his home there, and married one of its women, Esther, daughter of R. Shabbethai, of the family of R. Amittai. In His mercy He turned in kindness, and bestowed His compassion and visited His favor and truth upon the house of R. Shephatiah and R. Hananeel, men of His choice, who serving Him as long as they lived, did not stray from His law. For it is His promise to do good to those who look to His salvation and wait for His help. He favored him in his old age with worthy sons, R. Samuel, his first born, the beginning of his strength, and R. Shabbethai, and Papoleon, and Hasadiah went to Ifrikiya with R. Paltiel, the son of his sister Cassia. R. Samuel came to the city of Capua and there married a woman named Albavera. Some time after, R. Shabbetthai and Papoleon set out with the gift which was sent by the prince of Amalfi to R. Paltiel. After the manner of young men, they entered into conversation with the pilot of the ship, and said, "Let us write the Name, so that we may move at great speed, and reach the coast of Ifrikiya tonight." So they wrote and pronounced the Name of Him that dwelleth on High, and cast the writing into the waters, and they said to the sailors, "Keep very close watch on us, that we do not fall asleep." But their sin brought calamity upon them and deep sleep fell upon them; a storm wind tossed them about on the water; the ship capsized and the men sank in deep waters. The power of the Name took the ship to Spain and Narbonne and the sea of Constantinople; and then brought it back to the sea of Ancona, and finally wrecked it before the city of Amalfi.

Upon the death of the ruler of Egypt, the leaders of Egypt, through reliable couriers, wise and chosen messengers, sent a letter authorized by the princes and nobles and the people of the cities and villages to Al Muizz, Caliph of the Arabians, in which they said, "We have heard of thy mighty deeds, the violence of thy wars, which thou hast waged in thy wisdom, of thy sagacity in which thou excellest the princes that formerly ruled over the kingdom of Syene (Egypt). Now, come to us, be king over us, with the consent of our princes and all the eminent men of our country; we will be thy subjects; thou shalt be our king."

He considered the proposal; R. Paltiel was summoned; and they took counsel together as to what they should do, for it was a long journey, through a barren and desolate land; all the way there was no water; no supplies of food; no tents or places of shelter. R. Paltiel set out in advance and established camps; he erected bazaars and places for lodging, appointed merchants for them, and supplied them with bread, water, fish, meat, garden produce, and everything necessary for soldiers coming from the distant cities. Then the Caliph and princes and courtiers set out; they pitched the tents of their encampments three miles from Egypt (Cairo). All the nobles of Egypt joyfully came forth to greet them, their chiefs and governors, their officials and princes and the masses of people as well. They came up to him and prostrated themselves. He made them take an oath of allegiance, by their law, and accepted their hostages, princes of the people. Then R. Paltiel entered Egypt with a division of forces, detailed them on the walls and towers, that they might guard the city, the palace and the public buildings, and appointed sentinels to be on guard, day and night, on the outskirts and the borders. And then the Caliph with all his army marched in. The nobles and all the people gathered about him, and again swore allegiance to him. He walked into the court and took his seat in his palace, on the throne of his dominion and majesty. They put his sceptre into his hand, and the royal crown upon his head, and he reigned over the kingdom of the South after his heart's desire.

Once, on the Day of Atonement, when R. Paltiel was called to read from the Torah, the whole assemblage arose and remained standing in his presence, the sages, the scholars that were in the school, the young students and the elders, the lads and the children; the entire community was standing. He called to them, saying, "Let the old be seated, and the young stand. If you refuse, I will sit down and refuse to read, for this does not seem right to me." When he finished reading, he vowed to the God of his praise 5000 dinars of genuine and full value; 1000 for the head of the academy and the sages, 1000 for the mourners of the sanctuary, 1000 for the Academy of Geonim at Babylon, 1000 for the poor and needy of the various communities, and 1000 for the exaltation of the Torah, for the purchase of the necessary oil. In the morning he arose early and hurried, for he was always zealous in observing the law, that his evil inclination might not prevail over him to prevent his carrying out his good intention; he engaged men and horses and mules, and provided guards, and sent them forth with the caravans that travelled through the deserts. And they delivered the gold pieces, as R. Paltiel their master had ordered, and distributed them among the schools and synagogues, and the mourners of Zion and the poor of the communities of Israel.

The growth of his authority which the king, through his bounty, had bestowed upon him over his royal domain, having appointed him ruler over the kingdom of Egypt and Syria as far as Mesopotamia, and over all (that had once been) the land of Israel as far as Jerusalem, his eminence and power and wealth with which the king had honored and distinguished him, are recorded in the chronicles of the kingdom of the Nof and Anamin (Egypt).

When Al Muizz was stricken with the sickness of which he was to die, he placed his son on the throne and entrusted him to R. Paltiel, his beloved minister, that he might be his adviser and helper and guardian, that he might govern the kingdom with vigor and success. The Caliph died and slept with his fathers and his son reigned in his stead. All his days had been passed in happiness and security, in peace and content.

When the young caliph sat upon the throne of his kingdom, the officials appointed to conduct the affairs of Egypt told him lying stories about R. Paltiel, continually striking at him with the sharp sword of their tongues, and covertly slandering him. The Caliph's fury raged against them; he repeatedly rebuked them. He told R. Paltiel, the prince, all they said. So together they devised a plan of dealing with them. R. Paltiel and his wife, and friends and all his family went out to his estate, the royal garden that the Caliph had presented to him.

In words of affection the Caliph asked, "Whither has our beloved R. Paltiel, the interpreter of mysteries, gone?" The attendants assembled in the court answered, "He has gone out for recreation, with his friends and all his kin, to the estate which the king has given him." Thereupon the king summoned his magistrates, princes and courtiers, and said to them, "We will go and pay our respects to the venerable scholar in my service, R. Paltiel, so highly esteemed and worthy of honor at my hands." He set out in his chariot and took with him all his lords and princes. The king did this with set purpose; all of this being done as a ruse, ordered by the word of the king, that he might find opportunity to show R. Paltiel his intense love for him, in the presence of the courtiers and princes of the people, to confound his accusers, and cover them with shame and confusion. And as the king drew near the tent of R. Paltiel, he commanded that no one should inform him until he reached the tent. The king descended from the chariot and R. Paltiel approached him. The king, out of his love for him, embraced, caressed and kissed him, and took hold of his hands. They walked away together and took their seats apart from the company. The others remained where they were. Then the jesters and players appeared; they took up the harps and timbrels and made merry before them with pipes, with stringed instruments and songs, playing upon timbrels, cymbals and harps from morning until the decline of the day in the afternoon, until evening when the shadows began to move backward. The king then rode off and returned to Egypt (i.e., to the city). So the face of the accusers was covered with confusion, the enemies and slanderers of R. Paltiel were put to shame. On that day their tongues were silenced, and they did not again speak ill of him. Praised be He that protecteth His saints, that redeemeth and saveth the soul of His servants. Praised be He and praised be His name; praised be the glory of God from His place.

One night R. Paltiel and the king were walking in the open and they saw three bright stars disappear; in an instant their light had vanished. And R. Paltiel said, "The stars that have been eclipsed represent three kings who will die this year; and they will soon be taken off. The first king is John the Greek, the second, the king of Bagdad, in the north"; then the king hastening to interrupt him said, "Thou art the third, the King of Teman," but he replied to the king, "No, my Lord, for I am a Jew; the third is the king of Spain." But the king said, "Thou art in truth the third, as I say."

And in that year R. Paltiel died, the leader of the community of the people of God, settled in Egypt and Palestine, in Palermo and in Africa, and in all the territory of the Arabians (Ishmael), for he ruled over the ancient kingdom of the Hebrews, over that of the Syrians and Egyptians, over the domain of the Arabians and the Land of Israel. May his soul be bound in the bundle of life, secure in Eden, enclosed in the Garden of God, reposing by the side of the Fathers.

THE CLEVER JUDGE

by JOSEPH BEN MEIR ZABARA [1]

S o we continued upon our journey, and our asses bowed down and knelt as if forsooth they meant to pray. When we approached a certain city my companion fell into great confusion and trembling. When I perceived that he was weeping and that his cheeks were moist with tears, I inquired of him, saying, "Wherefore weepest thou, and why do thy tears course down thy cheeks?" He replied, "In this city did my beloved friend and comrade perish; 'tis for him that my tears flow." "What manner of man was he," I asked, "that thou shouldst weep over him?" "A man of wisdom and discernment," he replied, "a man of justice and kindness and faith. He wrought justice ever, in all its forms; nowhere in the world doth any like unto him remain. I will declare to thee a little of his wisdom, and tell thee a moiety of his discernment.

"There came before him once a man, weeping and wailing, and fell upon his face and besought him, 'Give me aid, give me counsel, for overwhelming destruction hath found me.' 'What ails thee that thou criest out,' said he to the man, 'and wherefore do the tears course down thy cheeks?' He replied, 'My lord, I have but one daughter, and for her did I arrange a marriage, giving her to one of the sons of my people. But yesterday I brought unto my house the betrothed lad and his father, and I invited with them my neighbors who are nigh unto me. I showed them her dower of garments and coverings, her mantles and habits, her nose rings and bracelets, her neck chains and pendants: all her ornaments which had been prepared against the day of their wedding, for their gladness and their joy. We arose early in the morning, I and my wife, to cleanse the house and to arrange it, to adorn it and to order it. But we found naught of the garments or ornaments, of the jewels or adornments; there was naught of all her clothing save only her tunic and her slippers. As thine own soul liveth, my lord, that was all my substance and all my wealth, my goods and my possessions, and now I know not what I may do and wherewithal I may dower my clothesless daughter.'

[1] Little more is known about Zabara than that he was a physician and lived and wrote in Spain during the second half of the twelfth century. *The Clever Judge* is a selection from his most important work *The Book of Delight* (Hebrew). The form of this book is similar to that of Chaucer's *Canterbury Tales* and *The Thousand and One Nights,* but its object is "to set forth, frequently by the common medieval device of questions and answers, the sum of his knowledge and of his beliefs, literary, moral and scientific." In the above selection, which really contains three separate tales, we meet the two story-telling protagonists, Enan Hanatas, the evil genius of the book, and Joseph (the author). The selection is from the complete translation by Moses Hadas, *The Book of Delight* (Columbia University Press, 1932).

"But the wise judge spake to him, 'Lead me to thine house that I may see it; mayhap thou wilt yet discover thy goods.' So he brought him unto his house, and he looked upon the walls of the house, and, lo, they were all high, that no thief might ascend the one side and descend to the other, except for one place where there was a breach in the wall, where grew a certain tree of the citrous fruit called naranja. The tree is one filled with prickly thorns and the light doth not penetrate it. 'Who is thy neighbor?' inquired the judge. 'My lord,' he answered, 'my neighbor is a precentor, a man just and upright, righteous in all his deeds and words.' The judge turned hither and thither and then went upon his way. 'Return to me at a like hour on the morrow,' said he, 'I shall do for thee that which thou desirest.'

"And it came to pass on the morrow that he sent for the precentor, whose name was Paltiel, the son of Azan. He came and stood before him, and the judge gazed into his countenance and observed therein indication that the man was not of good faith. The judge then brought him into the chamber and drew off his garments and said to him, 'Do thou draw thy garments off also, and wrestle with me, for last night I saw in my dream that we two were wrangling together being naked, and were wrestling each with the other; and now do I desire to find the interpretation of the dream, wherein may the Lord of peace be our aid.' So the precentor drew off his garments and the judge perceived that his body was filled with sores and bruises and wounds. Just as he had surmised in his heart, so indeed it was; for through that very place had he descended to commit the theft, being naked and without garments, in order that they might not be caught by the thorns which were on the tree.

"Then spake the judge, 'Return that which thou hast stolen, and the dower of thy neighbor's daughter which thou hast taken. If thou refuse, as thy soul liveth, I will scourge thee with rods and with scorpions as a thief and a robber.' Then was the precentor dismayed and affrighted and fell upon his face, nor could he make answer, for that he was confused from before him. And the base evil-doer returned that which he had taken, from a thread even to a shoe latchet. The father returned to the judge as he had been bidden, who then restored to him his daughter's dower. The man fell to the ground full length and kissed his hands and feet for his kindness and his truth, and said, 'Blessed art thou before God most high, for that thy name is a fortress to the poor and a refuge to the humble.' He took all the goods and returned to his house joyful and glad at heart, and ordered his daughter's marriage as pleased herself and as her heart desired."

Said I, "Lo, I marvel greatly at the decision of the judge and at his wisdom, yea, at the greatness of his knowledge and discernment; yet more do I marvel at the deceitfulness of the precentor and at his devious cunning."

"My son," said my companion, "take thou heed of precentors, for they are mostly robbers; trust not in their words, for they are liars."

I asked of my companion, "Good sir, why do men say that a precentor is ever a fool? Wherefore is he a fool?" He made answer: "When he performeth his office he doth stand higher than all men who are with him, and when he beholdeth himself uplifted and exalted in his office, he doth account it as a mark of his own worth and honor, and doth thereby fall into his folly."

"I marvel at thine understanding and thy wisdom," said I, "for no secret is withholden from thee."

Said Enan, "I will tell thee also how that judge by his discernment and clever devices restored to a certain Jew that whereof he had been robbed. There was a certain Jew in Cordova who was called Jacob, the Factor, and he was good and faithful, ready and obedient to the bidding of the judge. One day there was intrusted to him a chain of choice stones and precious pearls to be sold for five hundred pieces of gold. He was walking by the way, carrying the chain in his hand, when he was met by a certain noble of the king's favorites, who thus addressed him: 'Jacob, what manner of chain is that?' He replied to him, 'My lord, it is intrusted to my hand to be sold.' 'And for how much wilt sell it?' 'The price is five hundred pieces of gold,' he replied. Said the noble, 'Wilt sell it for four?' Jacob replied, 'I cannot, for its owner hath laid it upon me not to accept less than five hundred pieces of gold.' The noble said, 'Take it then to my house, and if it please my lady I will buy it.' So he went with him until they reached the gate of his house, where the noble said, 'Stand thou here until I bring out to thee either the money or the chain.' Thereupon he entered into his house but shut the door behind him; the Jew waited until even, but no man came forth from the door of the house.

"And it came to pass when the sun set that Jacob went to his house full of wrath; death had been pleasant to him. Sorrow oppressed his heart and wounded it. He came then and laid him upon the ground, nor partook of bread, neither he, nor his sons, nor his wife, nor did his tunic from off him, nor did he close his weary eyes, but tossed all the night, like clay turned to the seal. In the morning he arose and went to the house of the noble, but lo, he had gone forth from his house. He saw him, and ran to meet him, and said to him, 'My lord, buy the chain if thou wilt, or else return it, and I will sell it to another.' The noble replied, 'Of what chain dost thou speak? Hast thou perchance dreamt of a chain?' But he said, 'The chain of pearls which thou didst take from mine hand but yesterday.' 'Thou art lunatic, afflicted with some evil spirit,' said the noble. 'By my life and the life of the king, did I not respect the position I bear, I would take thy head from upon thee, and thyself would I trample in thy heart's blood.' When Jacob perceived his wrath and the hardness of his words, dread of death fell upon him, and he turned his back and fled from before him, for he saw that the noble glared upon him sore.

"He went to the house of his master, the judge, and when the judge looked upon him he perceived that sorrow had bitten into him with its fangs, until that his appearance and the cast of his countenance were altered. The judge addressed him, 'What ails thee that thou hast altered; hast thou then been sorely afflicted?' He replied, 'My lord, I am in sore straits, nor may I tell thee of it, lest thou shouldst discredit my words and distrust my speech.' But the judge said, 'Do thou but relate the matter, for all thy words are faithful in my sight and thou art righteous in all thy speech.'

"So he related all that had befallen in the matter of the chain and petitioned that his life be spared. Said the judge, 'Remove anger from thy heart and put away sorrow from thine inward parts; tremble not nor groan in thy pain, for I will restore the chain to thee.'

"And it came to pass on the morrow that he summoned all the great men of the city, its elders, and wise men, and sages, to come to the place of judgment, for so was it his wont upon occasion, to send and fetch the wise men and to speak with them of justice. So they all came to his hosue, to hearken to the words of his understanding and his wisdom. But ere they came the judge said to his servant: 'When that certain noble doth come, take thou his shoe and go to his house and say to his wife, "My lord, thy husband, hath sent me to thee, that thou shouldst give him the chain which he bought yesterday or the day before, for he would display its worth and its beauty, and as a sign and testimony, lo, he hath given me his shoe." '

"When the woman saw her husband's shoe she delivered over the chain, and the servant of the judge brought it to his master and hid it in his bosom until that the men should depart from the seat of judgment. When they had so departed, his master spake to him, 'Hast brought the chain?' 'I have brought it,' he replied, and drew it forth from his bosom, and gave it to him. Then the judge sent and summoned Jacob, the Factor, and said to him, 'Be silent, nor sigh longer, for I have returned thee the chain; I have abstracted from the noble's house that which he hath stolen.' When the Jew saw the chain he kissed the judge's hand and blessed him and carried it to his house joyful and glad at heart.

"I shall tell thee also how he returned an inheritance to the lawful heir, when a slave of the deceased, the son of his maidservant, had seized it. There was once a merchant, goodly and honored among the merchants and great among the wealthy, and he had but one son. When the lad grew up he said to his father, 'Send me forth and I will go to the countries across the sea, and I will trade, and see diverse lands and regions, and men of instruction, and men of wisdom and discernment, and I will learn of their instruction and discernment, and I will take of their knowledge and wisdom.' The father hearkened to the voice of his son, for this was his only one, and he had abundance of gold and silver. He purchased for him a ship, and gave him great wealth, and sent him forth in peace with certain friends and acquaintances.

"The man was then left alone in his house with his slave, the son of his maidservant, with whom he did deal as he were the apple of his eye, and did hold him in the place of his son, for the servant prospered in all his ways and was diligent in all his needs.

"And after a certain time this man, the master of the house, was seized with a pain in the heart, and his spirit departed from within him, and he died suddenly, nor did he avail to show his thoughts nor to leave his will regarding any matter. So the servant took hold of all that was his, and lorded it over that which his master's labor had acquired, nor was there any man in the city who knew whether he was son or slave, for during his life had the master caused him to have dominion over all his goods and his wealth.

"About ten years, then, after that man's death, his youthful son returned, his vessel being filled with merchandise, all choice goods of every description. But as he was approaching nigh unto his native city, his ship was like to be destroyed. So they cast overboard all their gear and their merchandise which they had acquired, striving to land; but they could not. The youth did reach land, being faint in body and spirit, and he hied him to the house of his parents, that he might cover his nakedness.

"But when the slave found him there he reproached him and reviled him, saying, 'What business hast thou here and whom seekest thou?' And he smote him and cast him forth out of the house and drove him from his heritage.

"The young man went to the judge's house, weeping as he went, and said to him, 'Thus and so hath my slave used me.' He related all that had befallen him, how that he had smitten him and driven him forth from the house, this slave whom his father had made great and exalted. The judge sent to summon the slave, but the youth wept bitter and sore.

"So the slave came before him, and the judge gazed into his eyes, and him seemed the fellow was base, and he spake to him, and said, 'Is it then true that the man whose portion thou hast taken and whose heritage thou hast seized was indeed thy father? For lo, this one declareth that thou art a slave of the household and that no right of inheritance is thine; that thou seekest the right of possession only by willfulness and deceit.' But the slave answered and said, 'My lord, in good truth he was my father and from his loins did I spring; therefore hath he left me all his heritage and his substance, and treasures, and my heart is sore grieved for his sake, for from my youth he nurtured me as a father.'

"But the judge said, 'Produce thy witnesses that thy speech is upright and that thou hast what thou hast in righteousness.' But the slave remonstrated, 'Prithee, let him produce his witnesses, false one that he is, in that he seeks to work deceit with his tears, for upon him who would deprive another who is in possession rests the burden of proof.' So both of them sought witnesses, but could not find them.

"Thereupon they returned to the judge and said to him, 'Our lord, do thou bring our decision forth to the light, for we have not witnesses and to thee do we look for judgment.' Then said the judge, 'Is there a man of you who knoweth the grave of the deceased?' The slave answered, 'I know it, for I myself buried him, as is meet for a son to bury his father.' Thereupon the judge said to his servants, 'Go with him to the grave of this loathly merchant and cast him forth from his sepulcher and bring me his bones, that I may burn them with fire, for that he hath left no will for his household nor declared whose his heritage should be, but did leave behind him quarrels and strife and great and mighty dissension.'

"Then spake the slave, 'I will go according to my lord's bidding and show them the grave, for thou hast uttered true judgment and hast spoken as a very angel of the Lord.'

"But when the son heard the matter of the burning, he cried out with a soul sore troubled, saying, 'My lord, let the slave take all the heritage of my father, yea, all his glory and all his wealth, but let not my father be cast from his grave.'

"Then said the judge, 'Lo, to thee do I give thy father's heritage and all his wealth and substance, for in truth this fellow is the slave and thou art the son. But as to this slave who hath emboldened his countenance and hath shown no shame, take thou him to be thy slave, and let him serve thee forever.' So the young man went to the house of his parents, taking his bond-slave with him, from whom he received wealth and substance and honor."

Then said I to Enan, "In truth thou dost well to weep for him, for he is of the wise men of the age and of its sages."

THE FOUR CAPTIVES

by ABRAHAM IBN DAUD [1]

AFTER Hezekiah, the last President of the Academy and the last Exilarch, the (Babylonian) academies ceased to exist. But before this happened the Holy One, blessed be He, effected the discontinuance of the income of the academies, which annually came from Spain, Maghrib, Africa, Egypt and Palestine. This state of affairs was brought about in the following manner.

[1] Abraham ibn Daud was born in Toledo about 1110 and died as a martyr in 1180. He was one of the luminaries of the golden era of Spanish Jewish culture; his writings cover a wide range of subjects, chiefly philosophy, astronomy and history. *The Four Captives* is a selection from his historical work, *The Book of Tradition,* which was written in 1161. It gives the medieval explanation of how the centers of Jewish culture and authority shifted from the East to Northern Africa and Europe. The translation, based on the text of Abraham Kahana, *Sifrut Hahistoria Hayisraelit,* is by Leo W. Schwarz.

Out of the city of Cordova sailed a fleet captained by Ibn Damahin, who was sent by Abd Al-Rahman, the Moslem king of Spain. The object of this commander's voyage was the capture of Christian ships and the raiding of towns that were situated near the coasts. They sailed as far as Palestine and maneuvered about the Greek Archipelago and its islands. It was here that they sighted a ship which carried as passengers four great sages who were sailing from Bari to Safsatin. These sages were collecting subscriptions for the Academy. Ibn Damahin captured the vessel and held the sages as slaves. One of them was Rabbi Hushiel, the father of Rabbenu Hananel; the second was Rabbi Moses, the father of Rabbi Enoch (who was then a lad); the third was Rabbi Shemaryah, the son of Rabbi Elhanan; the name of the fourth, I do not know.

The wife of Rabbi Moses was an exceedingly beautiful woman. Bent upon humbling her, the captain attempted to force himself upon this noble woman. At that moment she cried aloud to her husband, asking him in Hebrew whether or not persons devoured in the sea would return to life at the time of the resurrection of the dead. He quickly replied with a verse from the Scriptures: The Lord said: "I will bring them back from Bashan, I will bring them back from the depths of the sea." (Psalm 68:23.) Immediately she threw herself into the sea and was drowned.

The sages were silent about themselves and their importance so the captain sold them as common slaves. He sold Rabbi Shemaryah in Alexandria. Later he went to Cairo where he became the head of a school. Rabbi Hushiel was sold on the coast of Africa. He went to the city of Kairawan which was, in those days, the most powerful of all the Moslem cities in Maghrib. There he became head of a school and there was blessed with his son, Rabbi Hananel. Finally the captain returned to Cordova where he sold Rabbi Moses and his son. They were redeemed by the Jewish community in Cordova but no one knew of their great learning.

Now in Cordova there was a synagogue, and over the school presided Rabbi Nathan, a very pious man. At this time the Jews in Spain were not learned in the writings of our Teachers, may their memory be blessed, but with the modest knowledge at their disposal they carried on their discussions and interpretations of the Law. Once Rabbi Nathan attempted to interpret a law in the tractate [of the Talmud] Yoma, which states that an ablution is required for each sprinkling. Neither he nor his associates could explain the law satisfactorily. Whereupon Rabbi Moses, who happened to be sitting in the corner in the manner of a beadle, stood up before Rabbi Nathan and said to him,

"My master, if the interpretation you have proposed were accepted, too many ablutions would be required."

Hearing this criticism, Rabbi Nathan and his students marvelled and asked him to explain the law, whereupon he gave the accurate interpretation in the manner of the Babylonian academies. Then they asked him to explain all their difficulties, and they posed questions and problems which he answered out of the abundance of his learning and wisdom.

Outside the study hall were waiting litigants who were not permitted to enter until the students had completed their study session. On that day Rabbi Nathan, the judge, came out and said to them,

"I am no longer your judge or teacher. From today this stranger who is clad in sackcloth is my teacher and master. Now appoint him judge of the congregation of Cordova."

This they did. And the congregation provided him with a good allowance and presented him with expensive clothes and a private carriage. And when the captain of the vessel, who had sold Rabbi Moses as a common slave, learned who he really was, he wanted to cancel the sale. But the king would not permit him to do so, for he rejoiced exceedingly in knowing that the Jews of his kingdom no longer needed the guidance of the Jews of Babylonia.

As the report of this event spread throughout Spain and northern Africa, students flocked to Cordova to study under Rabbi Moses. Among his pupils was Rabbi Joseph Ibn Abitur who explained the entire Talmud in Arabic to the Moslem King, Al Hakim. And all the questions which were formerly addressed to the academies in Babylonia were now directed to Rabbi Moses.

This happened in the days of Sherira Gaon, about the year 4750 (989 C.E.).

A MEDIEVAL JEZEBEL [1]

Once upon a time, in the land of Uz, there lived a distinguished rabbi, who was very wealthy and knew the seventy languages. He supported a great yeshibah (college) and had many able students and also educated many young children. He always had at least one hundred pupils in his yeshibah. He also supported an organization for the poor, and many poor people had free access to his house. In short, the rabbi was a pious man and had all the virtues that a good Jew should have. But, as against this, he had a very bad-tempered wife, who could not bear with any of his actions and looked askance at all his deeds. She did not like to see a poor man enter her house.

The proverb, which says: "When the rope is too tight it snaps," was

[1] This folktale and the following one, *Rashi and the Duke of Larraine,* are typical of thousands of stories which circulated among the Franco-German Jewish communities during the Middle Ages. They were popular among the masses, and their social and literary history parallels the more widely known *Gesta Romanorum.* A collection called the *Maaseh Buch* was first published in Basle in 1602. *A Medieval Jezebel* is selected from a recent translation of the book by Moses Gaster (*Maaseh Book,* Jewish Publication Society, 1934).

verified in the case of this pious man. He became so poor that he could no longer give any charity, nor could he do as much good for the young students as he had done formerly. Then the poor rabbi thought to himself: "What shall I do now? All the days of my life I have given freely for God's sake and have done much good to many, and now I am very poor. What shall I do? I will accept my fate willingly from the Lord, blessed be He, who does no injustice. I wonder what sin I have committed." Then he continued: "What is the good of my lamenting my poverty? There always are people who gloat over another's misfortune. There is one thing I can do. I will leave town secretly, so that no one should know what has become of me." So he called his best pupils and said to them: "My dear young men, you know well how faithful I was toward you up to now, how I supplied you with food and clothing and taught you besides. Now I will confide to you a secret, hoping that you will act towards me as I have acted towards you." The pupils replied: "Dear Rabbi, tell us your secret, for we will stand by you as long as God grants us life." So the rabbi told his pupils that he must depart, for he did not understand why he had become so poor. And he asked them to go with him. "For," he said, "I have still a few florins, which I should like to spend with you. Who knows but that God may give me wealth again, and then you will enjoy it again with me as long as you live." The pupils replied: "Dear Rabbi, whatever you desire us to do we will do willingly, and whatever we possess in money and clothes, we will share with you." So the rabbi went away with fifty of his pupils, and not a man in the community knew of his departure. When the poor people learned that their rabbi had gone, they feared greatly, and so did the little children, whom he had brought up by his bounty, as well as the other pupils who remained behind with his wife. Thus he departed together with his pupils, and wherever he came, he was received with the honor he deserved. And no one was surprised to see him traveling about, for they thought he was going to a yeshibah to study.

After traveling about for a year or two, their garments were torn and the money in their purses was spent, as can be easily imagined, and they became dependent upon charity. But wherever they went, people locked the doors in their faces, for nobody knew their circumstances, whether they were vagrants or students. At last the students grew tired of wandering about, and said to the rabbi: "What will be the end of our wandering? We have neither clothes nor money, and cannot help ourselves. And wherever we go, people lock the doors in our faces and look upon us as vagrants. We will therefore return to our parents. Moreover, we are getting older and wish to marry. But we will not tell anyone how you are faring or where you are." When the good rabbi heard this from his pupils, he thought for a while and then said to them: "My dear pupils, I have nothing but praise for the loyalty which you have shown to me. Therefore I beg of you to remain with me four or five days more until after the Sabbath. After that I will let you go in the name of

God. Perhaps God will send us something good and we shall return home together." And the pupils replied: "Very well, dear Rabbi. We have stayed so long with you that we might as well remain a few days longer."

So they continued their travels and came to a clump of small trees. Then the rabbi said to the pupils: "Go ahead and I will be with you soon." The pupils went along, talking among themselves and discussing various points of law. And the rabbi, seeing a small spring, washed his hands and was about to leave, when he saw a small weasel running along with a pretty gold ring in its mouth. He ran after the weasel until it dropped the ring. He picked it up and saw that the ring was of little value, but on examining it more closely, he found an old inscription on the inside, which he easily read. It ran as follows: "Although I look unattractive, my value is inestimable."

Now the rabbi was a very clever man and he suspected that the ring must have a special virtue. He thought as hard as he knew how to find out what kind of charm the ring could have, to be so valuable. Then he thought perhaps it was a magic ring, by means of which one could obtain one's desires, and decided to try it. So he said: "I wish I had a girdle with money." And before he had finished the sentence, he saw a girdle filled with gold lying in front of him. He became cheerful again and, going to his pupils, he said: "My dear boys, be of good cheer, we are going to a place where I have a very rich friend, who will lend me money, for he does not know that I am so poor. I will then buy clothes for you and send you home." But he did not tell his pupils that he had found a magic ring, fearing that they might take it away from him or report him and he would lose it. The pupils rejoiced at the thought of getting new clothes and asked no further questions, having no doubt that their teacher had told them the truth. So they came to the town and after spending a day there, the rabbi dressed them in clothes of pure silk and velvet and dressed himself in clothes similar to those he had worn before. He stayed there a week or ten days, studying very earnestly with his pupils, and the people paid him all the honor which was due to him as a great scholar. One day he went into the town and bought a coach worthy of a prince and said: "My dear pupils, come here and I will pay you back all the money which you laid out for me on the journey, and then we will go home." The pupils had no doubt that his relative who lived in the town and who was a rich man, had lent him a few thousand florins, as the rabbi had told them, so that he might return to his home with honor. They started for home together and where the people had previously shut the door in their faces, they now received them with great honor.

Now as long as the rabbi had been away from his home the people were unhappy, but now a shout went up in the community that the rabbi had come back together with his pupils. And who rejoiced more than the poor? As soon as he had reached home he received everyone with a friendly air, for no one knew that he had gone away because of poverty; they all believed that he had gone to study. The rabbi resumed his old habits of almsgiving, opened his yeshibah and brought up the young children to study. On the Sabbath he was in the habit of taking a nap and then studying tosafot with his pupils. One Sabbath he lay down to take a nap as usual, and his wife said to him: "My dear husband, where did you get so much money? We were so poor before that you had to leave." The rabbi replied: "I had a godsend on my journey." But the wife would not believe this and she worried him so long, as women will do, until the rabbi let himself be persuaded and told her his secret. This was a mistake. For King Solomon said: "Do not confide thy secret to thy wife," for women cannot keep a secret, as happened to the good rabbi, as you will soon hear. If he had not confided his secret to his wife he would have been spared much trouble, and because he told her the secret of the ring, viz., that all one's wishes are fulfilled, he had to suffer great misfortunes.

When the evil-tempered wife heard the story, she thought: "If I had the ring, he would never get it back again," and she would have readily taken it away from him, but it could not be taken off his finger against his will. So she said: "My dear husband, let me see the ring for a while." The rabbi knew what an evil-tempered woman she was and would not give it to her, whereupon she pretended to weep and said to him: "I see you do not love me, for you will not trust me with the ring." And she plagued him until at last he gave it to her. As soon as she slipped the ring on her finger, she put her head under the sheet and said: "I wish my husband were turned into a werewolf and ran about in the woods among the wild beasts." She had scarcely uttered these words when the good rabbi jumped out of the window and ran into the forest, called the Pemerwald (Bohmerwald), and began to devour the people and do damage, so that no one ventured to go through the forest alone for fear of the wolf which struck terror into the heart of the people. The werewolf made himself a dwelling in the forest and took in the charcoal to keep his lair dry. Accordingly all the charcoal burners in the forest ran away also for fear of the werewolf.

Now let us leave the wolf for a while and see what happened in his house. When the time arrived for the rabbi to read tosafot to his pupils, the rabbi's wife (may her name be blotted out!) told them: "The rabbi cannot read tosafot today, as he is not well." The pupils believed her and went away. The next morning they came again, and she said: "The rabbi has gone away and has not told me where, but I believe he will be back in four years." She appeared to be very grieved, but it was only a piece of infamous acting on her part, may her name be blotted out! The poor people came to the door, but she refused to let anyone in. The poor people grieved very much at the loss of the rabbi. The infamous woman was very rich, as one can well imagine. For she was able to obtain everything she desired, hence there was no limit to her wealth. But nobody knew what had happened to the rabbi, or why he had so suddenly disappeared. Moreover, there was no one who could find out, but everyone believed he would return again, as he had done before.

We will leave the wicked woman alone and will return to the poor rabbi, running about in the forest as a werewolf, doing great damage and killing man and beast, for there is no stronger animal than the werewolf. The charcoal burners were asked if they could capture the wolf, but they replied: "No, he is much stronger than a lion and has intelligence besides." When the king heard of this, he arranged a hunt through the forest but he could not catch the wolf. They dug pits in many places but of no avail.

Now among these charcoal burners there was one whom the wolf did not hurt, but on the contrary made friends with him and spent most of its time near his hut. All other people had to avoid the forest for fear of the wolf. Now the king issued a proclamation that he who succeeded in capturing the wolf, alive or dead, would receive the king's daughter as a wife and on the death of the king would succeed to the throne. At the king's court there was an unmarried knight, who was very strong and had taken part in many tournaments. This knight arose and said: "My lord king, if you will keep your word, I will undertake to kill the wolf, for I have fought many battles and luck has always been with me. Therefore, I will try once more." The king repeated his promise on his honor. Accordingly, the knight put on his armor, feeling certain that he would succeed in killing the wolf. He went to the charcoal burner who lived in the forest and was friendly with the wolf and said to him: "Friend, show me the wolf's lair or its whereabouts." When the man saw that the knight intended to attack the wolf, he was very much frightened, fearing the knight would be killed in the encounter, as had almost happened to himself. The charcoal burner said to the knight: "What are you doing in this forest? If the wolf becomes aware of your presence, you will lose your life, great as you are." The knight replied: "Nevertheless, show me his lair, for I have come here to kill him." But the charcoal burner continued: "Sir, I pray you, do not atttempt this. You are playing with your life." The knight replied: "Be quick about it, for it must be." Then the charcoal burner said: "May God have mercy on you," and went with him and showed him where the wolf roamed. The knight took his gun and his spear in his hand and went into the wood, thinking that as soon as he saw the wolf, he would shoot him. When the wolf saw that his life was in danger, he jumped aside, caught the knight by his throat, cast him to the ground, and was about to kill him. When the charcoal burner saw this, he drove the wolf away. The knight was not satisfied and wanted to attack the wolf again, but the coal-burner prevented him. Nevertheless, he rushed at the wolf a third time. Thereupon the wolf became enraged and wanted to tear him to pieces. Then the knight prayed to God to save him from the wolf, promising that he would not attack him. The wolf released his hold and began wagging his tail in fawning fashion. He would not leave him and ran before the knight as a dog runs in front of its master. The knight was very anxious to get rid of him, for he was afraid of him, but the wolf continued to run at his side. So he took off his girdle and, tying it round the wolf, held him by it, the wolf acting as his guide in the forest. And whenever a wild beast desired to do the knight harm, the wolf tore it to pieces. And when he saw a hare or a fox, he caught it and brought it to the knight. Finally the knight brought the wolf to the king. The king and the counselors were seized with fright, for they had heard so many stories about the wolf killing people. So the king told the knight to take the wolf away. The knight replied: "You need not fear, he will do no harm to anyone who will not molest him, I pledge my life on it. On the contrary, he has caught animals for me." So the knight kept the wolf with him and took good care of him, remembering the mercy the wolf had shown to him in sparing him although he had deserved death for having made three attempts upon the wolf's life. He therefore looked after him well and gave him of the best food and drink. Whenever he went hunting, he took the wolf with him and whenever he saw a beast, the wolf caught it and brought it to him.

The king had promised that any man who brought him the wolf alive or dead would obtain his daughter to wife, and as the knight had properly earned this reward, the king kept his promise and gave him his daughter and half of his wealth besides. When at last the old king died, the young knight became king in his stead and obtained the whole land. But all the time he kept the wolf with him and did not want to abandon him as long as he lived, for the wolf had saved his life and was instrumental in his obtaining the kingdom.

One day in the winter after a heavy snowfall, the young king went out hunting and took the wolf with him. As soon as the wolf came out, he began wagging his tail and ran as if he had scented something. The king followed the wolf and saw him in the distance, digging in the snow with his feet. When the king came up, he saw that there was something written in the snow. The king was greatly astonished and said: "There is something strange about the wolf being able to write, perhaps he is a human being who has been turned into a beast by a curse, as has often happened before." But no one was able to read the writing. He sent for all the doctors, but none could read it. Among his counselors there was one who knew Hebrew, and he told the king that it was a writing of the Jews and began to read it as follows: "My dear king, remember the kindness which I showed you when you came into my lair in the forest. I could have torn you to pieces, for I had you under me three times, and in truth would have been justified in taking your life. Nevertheless, I spared you and even helped you to become a king. I have a wife who lives in a town called so-and-so (and he mentioned the name), who put a curse upon me, and unless I recover my ring, I must remain a wolf to the end of my life. But as soon as I get the ring I shall be a human being again. Remember the loyalty I have shown you, go into the town, get the ring from my wife and bring it to me for the sake of our friendship, else I will take away your life." And he gave him a sign by which he might know the ring. All this was written in the snow.

When the king heard this, he said: "I will help him again even if I lose my life in the attempt." Accordingly he took three servants with him and rode into the town which the rabbi named and in which his wife lived. He announced that he had come to buy beautiful rings and Frankish antiques and that he would pay any price to obtain them. He sent for the Jews and asked them if they had any old Frankish gold or rings or precious stones. The Jews replied: "We are poor people, but there is a woman in this old town who has very beautiful rings of all kinds and precious stones." He asked the Jews to take him to the woman, and they did so, not knowing he was a king, but thinking he was a merchant. When he came to the woman, he said: "My good woman, I have been told that you have some old curious gold rings with and without precious stones and old Frankish work. If I like them I will pay you a good price." And he pulled out of his pocket many beautiful rings and said that he had bought them on his travels. The woman said: "I will show you what old gold I have." And she went into her chamber and brought out many beautiful ornaments, such as the king had never seen. And the king was greatly astonished to find such beautiful things in the house of a Jewess. Among other things he saw a string of rings, among which was the gold ring which the wolf had described. Thinking how he might obtain the ring, the king took the rings in his hand and said to himself: "I wish my wolf had the ring in his hand already." And, without pointing to the particular ring, he said to the woman: "What would be the price of these rings?" She replied: "So many hundred florins." The clever king concluded the bargain and bought two rings, at the same time slipping the other ring into his hand without the woman noticing it. Then he paid her the amount, took leave of her, and returned home. When he had reached home, the woman missed the ring but dared not avow it, for she did not know who the merchant was. She grieved very much and mourned like a widow, but no one knew anything about it.

When the king reached home, he ordered a great banquet and invited all the nobles of the kingdom. And as he was sitting at the table and making merry, he called for the wolf, who came in wagging his tail with great joy, for he knew that the king had gone for the ring, but did not know whether he had brought it. The wolf kissed the king and stroked him, and when the king saw the wolf fawning so eagerly, he drew the ring out of the bag and showed it to the wolf. Had the king known the virtue of the ring, he might perhaps not have given it to him. But as it was, he took the ring and put it on one of the wolf's toes, and suddenly there stood a naked man before them. When the king saw it, he threw his mantle over him. All the nobles who were present were frightened, but the king said: "Fear not, the man who stands here before you is none else but the wolf." The man rejoiced greatly and said to the king: "My dear king, I beg of you to grant me leave to return to my home, for I have not been home in three or four years." The king replied: "If it your wish, you may go home, but if you desire to remain here you may stay with me and eat at my table as long as you live, for I cannot repay you for the kindness which you have shown me." But the rabbi preferred to return home. The king wanted to give him many gifts, but the rabbi said: "My lord king, you have seen that I have enough wealth at home, therefore I have no need of your money. You have done me enough good in obtaining the ring for me; for if I did not have my ring, I would have to be a werewolf all my life." Had the king, however, known the secret of the ring, he would not have given it to him so easily, for although the king possessed many valuable things, nothing would have served him as well as the ring. The rabbi took provisions for the journey and departed. On the way he gathered again fifty pupils, dressed them in black velvet and came back to his town. When he had come near the town, he said: "I wish that my wife (may her name be blotted out!) be turned into a she-ass, standing in the stable and eating out of the trough with the other animals."

In the meantime the shout went up that the rabbi had come home, bringing with him fifty pupils dressed in black velvet. The community went out to meet him and received him with great honor. They would have liked to ask him where he had been all that time, but the rabbi said: "If you wish to be kind to me, do not ask me where I have been or what I have done." The rabbi pretended not to know anything about his wife, although he knew very well that she was in the stable. Accordingly, he asked his household: "Where is my wife? I do not see her; perhaps she does not like to see me bringing again fifty pupils." The people of the household replied: "If it will not frighten you, we will tell you." The rabbi said: "I shall not be frightened." The people of the house replied: "When we heard that you were coming home, we hastened to your wife to tell her the good news, but she disappeared and we do not know what has happened to her." The rabbi did not show any fear and pretended not to know. Then he said: "I believe that when she has been away so long as I she will come back."

The rabbi resumed his former mode of life, giving alms to the poor, maintaining a yeshibah and doing works of benevolence generally, so that everybody was happy again. After some time, he prepared a great banquet and invited all the people of the town. Being in good spirits, he said: "Now that God has helped me to come home in safety, I have taken a vow that I would build a beautiful synagogue and the she-ass will carry all the stones required for the building." The she-ass was his wife, but the people did not know that he had put such a curse upon her. Then the people replied: "May God give you strength to carry it out quickly in peace and in good health."

The she-ass meanwhile had been feeding and had grown very fat. Like an animal she showed no shame and mated in the open. But when the rabbi began to use her for carrying stones, she became lean again. When the rabbi saw that she refused to move, he kicked her in the side and said: "Oh, you miserable beast, remember the evil you have done to me, may the lightning strike you!" So he kept on using the she-ass very hard until she grew very thin. This went on for a long time and nobody knew what had become of his wife. When he had completed the building of the synagogue, he made again a great banquet and invited all his wife's friends. And when they were draining their cups, the rabbi told them the whole story of how his wife had made him suffer for so long and how the Lord had helped them to recover. "And now," he added, "I have cursed her that she should become a she-ass and remain such all her life."

When her relatives heard this, they became very much frightened, for they felt pity for her, and begged the rabbi to forgive her this time, saying that she would never do it again. But the rabbi would not trust her. Shortly afterwards the rabbi died and left great wealth to his children. The ring disappeared again and the woman remained all her life a she-ass. This is why king Solomon said that one should not confide his secret to his wife, for had he not revealed the secret of the ring to his wife, the rabbi would not have had the misfortune of running around wild in the forest. But he repaid her fully, for many a one digs a pit for others and falls into it himself.

RASHI AND THE DUKE OF LORRAINE

ONE day the duke of Lorraine, whose name was Godfrey of Bouillon, came with a large army on his way to Jerusalem to fight the Turks. He had heard a great deal of the wisdom of Rashi and was told that he was regarded as a wise man by Jew and Gentile. Nay, he was looked upon as a prophet, which, indeed, he was. So the duke sent for Rashi, to ask his advice. But Rashi refused to go. When the duke heard that Rashi refused to come, he felt very angry that a Jew should disobey his command, and with his army he went to Worms to the house of Rashi. He found all the doors open, the books lying open on the table, but he saw no one in the house. The duke called out in a loud voice, "Solomon, Solomon, where are you?" Rashi replied: "What does your Lordship want?" The duke asked again: "Solomon, where are you?" and Rashi replied: "Here I am, my lord." And as often as the duke called him, Rashi gave answer, but the duke saw no one. The duke was very greatly astonished and went out of the house. Then one of Rashi's students passed and the duke asked him: "Does Rashi live here?" and the pupil replied: "Yes, he is my master." Then the duke said: "Tell your master to come to me. I swear by my head that no harm will come to him." When

Rashi heard it, he came to the duke and fell at his feet. But the duke raised him up and said: "I have seen your cleverness. Now I will tell you why I have come to see you. I wish to ask your opinion with regard to a very great undertaking upon which I have decided. I have collected a large army of infantry and cavalry and I intend to capture Jerusalem, for I am sure that with the help of God I shall defeat the Turks so thoroughly that they will not be able to fight any longer. Now I wish to hear your advice. Speak freely, do not be afraid whether you foretell success or failure. Whatever your advice may be I will follow it, for I know that you are half a prophet and can foretell truly how one will fare in war. Therefore I beg of you to tell me truthfully whether I shall be victorious or not." Rashi replied in a few words: "My lord, I will tell you truth. At first you will be very successful and will capture Jerusalem and reign therein for three days. On the fourth day, the Saracens will gather again and drive you out and you will have to flee. Most of your army will be killed and those who survive will die on the way, and you will come back to the city with three men and one horse's head. Now you may do as you please, but you have heard my opinion."

When the duke heard the words of Rashi, he felt very sad and said to Rashi: "It may be that you are speaking the truth and that I will have the experience you describe, but I promise you that if I return with four men, I will give your flesh to the dogs and will kill all the Jews in my country." And the duke departed with his army. All that Rashi had foretold came to pass, and he returned to Worms with three men and three horses, the duke himself and his horse making four. Meanwhile four years had passed, for the war had lasted all that time.

When he approached Worms he remembered that Rashi had foretold that he would return with three horses, whereas he was coming back with four. His mind was full of evil thoughts and he planned to put Rashi to death. For he had promised that if he came back with four horses, he would give Rashi's flesh to the dogs. But the Lord, blessed be He, frustrates the thoughts of the wicked. For as the duke was about to enter the gate of Worms, a beam with iron spikes (such as are commonly used at the gates and are lowered in front in time of war) fell by itself and knocked off the head of the fourth horse, and the rider had to remain outside. So the duke came to Worms with three men only and not four. The duke became very much frightened and admitted that Rashi had prophesied correctly that he would not enter the town with four horses.

Before going to his own house the duke wanted to go to the house of Rashi to bow down and kneel before him and to thank him for his prophecy. But when he came to the house of Rashi, he found him lying dead in the coffin and about to be buried. When the duke heard of Rashi's death, he mourned him deeply, as such a man should be mourned. May the Lord grant us and the whole of Israel to enjoy the benefits of his merits. Amen.

A TRIP TO HEAVEN

by IMMANUEL BEN SOLOMON ROMI [1]

AND as we ascended Eden's heights, we were destined to see tremendous sights, for there were placed thrones exalted and high, the marvel of miracles it seemed to my eye, to feast upon which the mind could itself not satisfy. Among these there was a shining throne, and the earth was filled with its brightness; it was "like the work of bright sapphire, and as the very heaven for clearness." And as for the footstool under its feet, its entire length was made up of electron, and it was my longing desire to sit thereon. Whereupon I spake, O my lord, for whom is this glorious throne of delight? and for whom is the footstool, work of the sculptor's might? And he replied: By thy life, the throne is reserved for the noblest of the pastors' scion, for Judah spoken of as "the whelp of the lion," he who above his brethren did tower; whilst the splendour which its ornamental blossoms doth shower is "for the law-giver that from between his feet shall not lose power"; to be seated on this seat shall be thy dower, and thou shalt be near him from that hour.

Now hearing this, the excellence of Daniel, my kinsman, I called to mind; he who had led me in the way of truth and caused me the straight path to find; who had befriended me when the fugitive's track around me did wind; he, indeed, the diadem of the holy crown that my forehead did bind, the life of my flesh, and the soul for whom my spirit pined. I bethought me of his distinct greatness and generous dealing of every variety; of his knowledge and wisdom, of his meekness and piety, and how his praise had resounded to the ends of the earth in society. Then said I to the man who took hold of my right: My lord, may I find favour in thy sight, show me the place where Daniel will encamp, my brother-friend, show me the house which they for him to build intend, the spot in which his last rest he shall spend. And he answered me, saying: Know of a surety that exceeding great is the height to which he doth ascend, and the earth is full of praise for him to its very end. And although thy merit, falling short of his, will have before him to retreat, since he the sin of many did bear, and would for the transgressors entreat,

---

[1] Scholars are agreed that there was a definite link, perhaps a warm friendship, between Immanuel and his contemporary, Dante. Immanuel was born in Rome about 1270 and died in Fermo during the first half of the fourteenth century. *A Trip to Heaven* is selected from the twenty-eighth chapter of his major Hebrew work, *Collectanea* (Mehaberoth) which is entitled *Tophet and Eden* (Heaven and Hell), and which in many respects resembles Dante's *Inferno* and *Paradiso*. The work is written in rhymed prose in which Biblical phrases are remarkably interwoven, a style admirably suited to his rich wit and satire for which he has been called "the Heine of the Middle Ages." A complete translation of *Tophet and Eden* by Hermann Gollancz, from which the above selection was chosen, was published for the sexcentenary celebration of Dante's death in 1921.

yet realising by the higher sense that, without thee, his rest he could not with calmness greet, he has suffered his tabernacle near thine to be placed, tho' thy poorer worth cannot at his value be graced. He knoweth, however, that in thy companionship delight he shall see, he being as Moses, and thou his Joshua shalt be. And since all shall say, as (my guide) observes, your souls once united and held fast together, not to be freed, "Shall two walk together, unless they be agreed?", 'tis no marvel that joy upon me has beamed, knowing "my lot in pleasant places to fall has seemed," inasmuch as on his account I shall be redeemed.

Then I said unto the man: As thou livest, my lord, show me the grandeur of his throne whereon he shall rest, for I know that its height will reach unto heaven, the top thereof in the clouds will find its nest. And the man replied, Come with me, and I will show thee; his blissful joy I will trace, and the glory of his resting-place. So I went after him, drawn along by him and receiving his support, until he into the tent of Aholiab ben Ahisamech me brought. And there was Bezalel ben Uri ben Hur, and all the princes of the congregation, and the stalwarts bringing increasingly the vestments for the service of the nation, weaving garments beauteous and fine, full of ornament, which shone forth with splendour as the brightness of the firmament; edged with every stone precious in price, with the sapphire cut in curious device. Tables and candlesticks, thrones and crowns, were there to be seen; they were for the souls that were pure and clean; and there was a throne of ivory, great in size, overlaid with gold in wealth, giving life unto those who reached it, and unto their flesh giving health; and the stones of a crown shone forth upon it on high; whilst garments of blue and purple and scarlet were spread, and about it did lie like polished copper gleaming, unto all lands their beauty beaming. There was a crown above the throne, its weight a golden talent, set with precious stone; fine gold cannot be given in place thereof, nor can silver be weighed for its exchange to stone, and a voice crieth, "Speak and say that its merchandise is but to those who sit before the Lord alone."

And the man who spake to me said, Hast thou seen the crown and the throne exalted on high, upon which thy brother Daniel shall rise up as a lioness, and e'en with the lion shall vie? This is his resting-place for ever, here he shall stay; for unto the Word of the Lord he did hearken, and Him he did obey, and there is none like unto him as the wise worker, to whom the whole earth can allegiance pay.

Thereupon to my God I gave praise and thanksgiving with zest, for having caused me to attain this inheritance of rest, and I spake, Blessed be the One God! No second to be His equal can claim. He hath not forsaken my Master; His kindness and truth are ever the same.

Then we three went straggling along Eden's ways, and all who stood about sent after us their gaze, and a voice was heard unto the distance far, saying, "Immanuel hath come, to merriment there is no bar!"

And when David heard that hither I had come, he ran to meet me, and greeted me with his welcome, the harp and lyre of ten strings in his hand, whilst his glory illumined the whole land. With him were Asaph, Heman, and Juduthun, with the harp and the lyre, and the sons of Korah, sounding the trumpets with fire. Then spake David unto me, "Blessed be he who cometh in the Name of the Lord! Art thou he who the rust from off my pearly utterances did ward?" He then embraced me, and heaped upon me kisses thick, even as close as a girdle to the loins of a man doth stick. And he said unto me, Thou hast done me honour in so far as thou hast explained my Book of Psalms, and hast disclosed in thy comments those excellencies for which it has been awarded the palm, and explained its conceits which hitherto unexplored had enjoyed virgin calm, no man to know them upon them did seize; as I live, since knowledge doth thy soul so please, I will honour thee exceedingly by word and deed, and what thou sayest to me to do I will pay heed. Thereupon David, by the hand of one of those who stood there, sent and summoned all those who explained the Book of Psalms, telling them to bring their comment, and they all came at King David's command, David Kimchi, too, who at their head went. And when they came, they bent low before King David, and with greetings of welfare the air did resound, and they prostrated themselves seven times to the ground; and King David addressed the expounders who before him did stand, Let each of you take the passage, "May God arise, and may there be scattered His enemies' band; may His foes flee away at the waving of His Hand!" Let each reveal the hidden truths therein contained, as his sense doth understand.

They then rose, and took hold each one of his way—one thus and the other thus did say; whereupon David remarked, This one sayeth, This is my comment, this my lore, yet there is none to satisfy me, none my soul to restore. Then David arose, and kissing me said furthermore, This one is the bundle of myrrh: to disclose this psalm's secret, he did himself bestir; no mystery or hint remains for explanation, from the rafters of the ceiling unto the very foundation, which he hath not revealed; he began, and finishing, left nothing concealed. He then bade me rehearse before all the meaning of the psalm, and this I did. Nothing did I withhold, nothing by me was hid. As they listened to my comment and its virtue heard, they directed unto Heaven their prayerful word. Then did David command them to honour me, and they paid me respect, and rendered me service, such as an anointed king might expect.

While yet they with me converse held, lo, Ezekiel, the prophet, we beheld; it seemed as if with his roaring lion's voice we were felled. He speaks: Ten portions are mine in the matter of comment and explanation, and where is he, and who is he, who will dare to drive me from this my station? Then he turned to me saying, Blessed be the Lord, who thee hither has brought! And now is it peace with thee? And I answered, Peace it is which I have sought.

Praise be to God, and thanksgiving I have paid, who has suffered me to reach this exalted grade, to witness while in the life that which no eye hath yet essayed. And he replied, Greatly hast thou honoured me in supplying the passages of my book with a clear interpretation, so that thy comment on the beginning and end of it has afforded balm for others' sickly explanation, for when to the pattern of "The Chariot" thou didst apply thy line of thought, I considered that all doubts relating thereto were set at nought; that all the founts of the great deep were opened and to the surface brought; that the children of Israel of the holy congregation may pass over, uncaught in the midst of the waters of wisdom, to the dry land which they sought.

Whilst he was speaking, behold there came Jeremias, having Elisha at his left, and on his right Elias, and behind them Baruch ben Nerias; and Jeremias stretched forth unto me his hand and said: Blessed be He, who apportioneth unto thee at His command of His glory, and suffereth thee in the region of His majesty to stand. As I live, I shall bind thee as a crown to my head, and place thee as a seal on my heart and my arm, I once said, by reason of the way in which thou didst explain, "Before I formed thee in the womb, by me thou wast known, and before thou camest forth from the womb, the seeds of holiness by me within thee had been sown." The labours of the commentators of the age to elucidate this passage bore no fruit, but thou didst make it clear, aye e'en from branch to root, and thou didst feed those who hungered for the truth with the honey which their palate did suit.

And whilst he spake, see the prophet Isaiah his presence proclaimed, and said unto me: Peace be to thee, thou Expounder among the prophets acclaimed, who, by virtue of thy explanations, hast the life of the world to come obtained. How my heart did rejoice when thou my text didst expound! It was like eating honey from the comb, and fattening myrrh which with balsam did abound. My words in the sight of others were as nought but to be passed by, until thou didst arise, and thy comment was the one agreeable to every eye; 'tis, therefore, no wonder if we, more than for wine, for thy love in remembrance do sigh. By my life, to be thy patron and helper I shall do my best, and every tongue that shall rise against thee shall in judgment be condemned at thy behest, and in the courts of my house with the souls that are pure thou shalt rest; nay, thy praise shall reach unto heaven, and into the clouds shall be thy crest, for thou hast borne the sin of the many, and interceded for those who have transgressed. How precious in my sight was thy skill in explaining the words, "Why be smitten, and continue to be rebellious still?" It was the very thought that was in my mind, and no expounder but thee, sage or prophet, could the true meaning find.

Now, while speaking, King Solomon (may his name be remembered for good!) appeared on the scene, and a company of prophets, authors of the Text, with him was seen, and as they saw me from afar, they knew it was an old friend they would meet, and so, their mouths were filled with merriment, and in the name of the Lord they me did greet, saying: Let him come, with joy our heart heaves, bearing as he does of wisdom the sheaves; the man who, in the task of explaining our works, has revealed the store of golden apples which in the settings on silver lurks.

I then prostrated myself before them as it beseemed, humbly and mute, and in the name of the Lord of Hosts, I gave them the salute; and so they took me and brought me up by the steps of Eden which high up did rise, bringing me to the part in which the tent of Moses, the man of God, lies. And when I saw that the skin of his countenance shone, a dullness came over my eyes, and I said, This is none other than the Man of God in such guise. Then did Moses put upon his face a veil, and I became in his sight as a watered garden, my soul wanting no desire that might avail, and he said unto me, "Happy art thou whose transgression is forgiven, whose sin is covered!" Who has heard such a thing, of whom hath it been discovered, that a man like thyself with a soul polluted, whom fear hath overpowered, should write a comment on books with the prophetic spirit endowered? Not by thy merit nor integrity of heart shalt thou come to inherit everlasting life; but through the merit of thy comments, which make all secrets with meaning rife, shalt thou come not weakened by age to the grave, and redeem thy soul from the pit, the onrush of waters with thy being shalt thou brave.

Now in explaining my Book, the Book of Job, thou didst indeed break through with an attack of great worth, and thou didst make unto thyself a name as that of the great ones in the earth. As a bridegroom didst thou adorn thyself with the priestly dress of beauty, when to unravel the secret of Behemoth and Leviathan thou didst feel it thy duty. Happy thou to have had the merit to enter into their mystery, in which no man preceded thee in history!

Then spake Solomon: By my life, amazement takes hold of my mind, when I think how thou wast able the verses of "Proverbs" to have combined, writing on the portion of the "Valiant Woman," and rising to such marvellous heights, expounding the "Song of Songs" in such wondrous flights, so that the eye cannot feast sufficiently on these lights, even that one verse, "Go forth and see, O ye daughters of Jerusalem, King Solomon in the crown with which his mother him did crown"—not all the wise men of the time were able to grasp its import, in defiance its mystery upon them did frown, until thou didst arise increasing wisdom and honour forsooth, and superadding the splendour of its secret to the inherent truth. And as for the Book of Ecclesiastes, the expounders of the age saw in it no use, and the fools thought some of its expressions folly and abuse, until thou didst enter and fathom the uttermost depths of its recesses, a very forest that as a garden seemed; and so after having been abandoned and sold, it found itself once again redeemed.

While yet they were speaking, lo, Joseph, the righteous (may he in glory rest!), stepped forth from his canopy, as a bridegroom dressed, on his head a great crown of gold; and as he came to the company with joy and gladness he was extolled; his eleven brothers as comrades all filed past according to age, the firstborn first and the youngest last. Now as he beheld in the tent of Moses the beautiful assembly, he prostrated himself with demeanour and humbly, and said, Peace be to thee, Moses, O man of God, planted in the House of the Lord as a green olive-branch that will not fade! Peace to thee who dwellest in the secret place of the Most High, and shelterest in that All-sufficient Shade! Peace, too, to all the Company, whose foundation is on righteousness laid! Then Moses addressed him, saying, Let him come in joy, this ornament of the holy crown of law and propriety, first in wisdom, in meekness and in piety. Peace be to thee! to thee all success and happiness, peace to thy brethren, drawn after thee in loveliness! Now, as Joseph turned about hither and thither, I drew his attention, and he began, By my life, this is the man who in his commentaries of me made mention, and on to my head the royal crown did raise, when by his words he judged me worthy of merit for my ways, and he wrote at length of me and my works in praise. He then took hold of me, so that I could not depart, and said, Peace unto thee, thou man according to my heart! and I answered, saying, May the hosts of peace accompany thee, of the saintly ones the pride, thou who dost speak noble things, and explainest that which its meaning doth hide!

Then Joseph said: As I live, 'tis but to see thee I have come, and I have come forth to bid thee welcome, since honourable mention is made of thee all along, and as a lion thou shalt rise, as a lion shalt thou be strong. Not a day passes but what there is talk of thy might, or that thy conceits do not afford the keenest delight, from the hour when thy friend R. Elias came under the shade of our roof, and made us acquainted with thy songs and thy verses of reproof. And all acknowledge that in song and satire thy intellect gains the upper hand, and they alone are the glory of every land, whereas the songs of others are as scattered chalk-sand, they in public no recognition command. Vanity are they, misleading their trend, and now, Courage! thou pleasant friend, for with us thou shalt abide as a delight to the very end.

And it came to pass when he had finished speaking these words, that he was hid from my sight, and him I could no longer see. I sought him eagerly indeed, but he was not to be found by me. And as I was in the thick of the storm, roaming after him, thinking peradventure I might find him, I was roused from my sleep, and as I called to mind the things which I had seen in a vision, I muttered aught, and then my terror was deep; I feared for my life, and from my phantasy's dream I awoke, and I roused my hand to write down that which my hearing and sight bespoke; all my strength I employed, I omitted nought; and my God, my highest joy, the rock of my strength, my refuge, whose trust I sought, who inspired me with confidence on my mother's breast from the hour when out of her womb I was brought, deign to accept my speech; and may my teaching, dropping upon the hearts of the noble among His people, with the blessing of rain be fraught, my words impressing themselves upon the tablet of their heart, so that I become not as those singing unto the dead, or crying unto idols to take their part! And now, as for me, my hands are unto heaven spread, that whilst His breath is yet within me, I may merit to learn and teach, to observe, and in His precepts tread; and that at the latter end, God's mercy may grant me support, taking hold of my right, and give me my rest in honour in the place where it shall be my delight to meet with those who have brought righteousness unto the many, as the stars for ever and ever shining bright.

MY JOURNEY, FROM BEGINNING TO END

by OBADIAH YAREH DA BERTINORO [1]

M y departure has caused you sorrow and trouble, and I am inconsolable because I have left you at a time when your strength is failing; when I remember, dear father, I cannot refrain from tears. But since I am denied the happiness of being able to serve you as I ought, for God has decreed our separation, I will at least give you an account of my journey from beginning to end in the way which you desired me to do in your letters, which I received in Naples about this time last year, by describing the manners and customs of the Jews in all the places I have visited and the nature of their intercourse with the other inhabitants of these cities.

On the first day of the ninth month (Kislev, 1486), after having arranged all matters in my place of residence, Citta di Castello, I repaired to Rome, and thence to Naples, where I arrived on the twelfth of that month and where I tarried for a long time, not finding any vessel such as I wished. I went to Salerno, where I gave gratuitous instruction for at least four months and then returned to Naples.

In the fourth month, on the fast day (the 17th of Tammuz), 1487, I set out from Naples, in the large and swift ship of Mossen Blanchi, together with nine other Jews; it was five days, however, before we reached Palermo, owing to a calm.

Palermo is the chief town of Sicily, and contains about 850 Jewish families, all living in one street, which is situated in the best part of the town. They are artisans, such as coppersmiths and ironsmiths, porters and peasants, and are despised by the Christians because they wear tattered garments. As a mark of distinction they are obliged to wear a piece of red cloth, about the size of a gold

---

[1] The author of these letters was a distinguished Italian rabbi of the fifteenth century. He was an eloquent preacher, and his commentary on the Mishnah, known as "The Bertinoro," is one of the classics of talmudic literature. The letter, here included, was written between 1487 and 1490. A decade later, he died in Jerusalem. The letter is reprinted from *The Miscellany of Hebrew Literature,* London, 1872.

coin, fastened on the breast. The royal tax falls heavily on them, for they are obliged to work for the king at any employment that is given them; they have to draw ships to the shore, to construct dykes, and so on. They are also employed in administering corporal punishment and in carrying out the sentence of death.

The synagogue at Palermo has not its equal in the whole world; the stone pillars in the outer courtyard are encircled by vines such as I have never before seen. I measured one of them and it was of the thickness of five spans. From this court you descend by stone steps into another which belongs to the vestibule of the synagogue. This vestibule has three sides and a porch in which there are large chairs for anyone who may not wish to enter the synagogue, and a splendid fountain. The entrance is placed at the fourth side of the synagogue which is built in the form of a square, forty cubits long and forty cubits wide. On the eastern side there is a stone building, shaped like a dome, the Ark. It contains the rolls of the law which are ornamented with crowns and pomegranates of silver and precious stones to the value of 4,000 gold pieces (according to the statement of the Jews who live there) and are laid on a wooden shelf, and not put into a chest as with us. The Ark has two doors, one towards the south, and one towards the north, and the office of opening and shutting the doors is entrusted to two of the congregation. In the center of the synagogue is a wooden platform, the Theba, where the readers recite their prayers. There are at present five readers in the community; and on the Sabbath and on the Festivals they chant the prayers more sweetly than I have ever heard it done in any other congregation. On weekdays the number of visitors to the synagogue is very small, so that a little child might count them.

The synagogue is surrounded by numerous buildings, such as the hospital, where beds are provided for sick people, and for strangers who came there and do not know where to pass the night; and again a large and magnificent mansion, where those who are elected sit in judgment and regulate the affairs of the community. There are twelve of these, and they are chosen every year; they are empowered by the king to fix the taxes, to levy fines, and to punish with imprisonment. There is nothing to be said in favor of this arrangement, for men of no name and of bad character frequently prevail upon the governor, by means of gifts, to appoint them members of this body. They then indemnify themselves for their presents by taxing the synagogue and congregation, so that the poor people are overwhelmed with imposts; for this elected body is supported by the governor and has absolute power, and the cry of misery from the oppressed is exceedingly great.

In Palermo I noticed the following customs: When anybody dies, his coffin is brought into the vestibule of the synagogue and the ministers hold the funeral service and recite lamentations over him. If the departed is a distinguished man especially learned in the law the coffin is brought into the synagogue itself, a roll of the law is taken out and placed in the corner of the Ark, while the coffin is placed opposite to this corner, and then the funeral service commences and lamentations are recited; the same thing is done with all the four corners of the Ark. The coffin is then carried to the place of burial outside the town and on arriving at the gate of the town the reader begins to repeat aloud the forty-ninth and other psalms till they reach the burial ground.

I have also noticed the following customs: On the evening of the Day of Atonement and of the Seventh Day of Tabernacles (Hoshana Rabba), after the prayers are finished, the two officials open the doors of the Ark and remain there the whole night; women come there in family groups to kiss the roll of the Law and to prostrate themselves before it; they enter at one door and go out by the other, and this continues the whole night, some coming and others going. . . .

I remained in Palermo from Tammuz 22nd, 5247, till Shabbath Bereshith, 5248 (i.e. from about July to October). On my arrival there the chief Jews invited me to deliver lectures on the Sabbath before the Afternoon Service. I consented, and began on the Sabbath of the New Moon of Ab (5247). My discourses were favorably received, so that I was obliged to continue them every Sabbath; but this was no advantage to me, for I had come to Palermo with the object of going on to Syracuse, which is at the extreme end of Sicily, for I had heard this was the time when Venetian ships going to Beyrut, near Jerusalem, would touch there. The Jews of Palermo then got many persons to circulate false rumors to dissuade me from my intention, and succeeded in taking me in their net, so that I missed the good crossing for the ships to Syracuse; I therefore remained in Palermo to give lectures to the people, about three hours before the Afternoon Service. In my discourses I inveighed against informers and transgressors, so that the elders of the city told me that many refrained from sin, and the number of informers also decreased while I was there; I do not know if they will go back to their old ways. But yet I cannot spend all my life among them, although they honor and deify me, for indeed they treated me as the Gentiles treat their saints.

The common people said that God had sent me to them, while many wanted a piece of my garments for a remembrance; and a woman who washed my linen was counted happy by the rest. They calculated that I would remain there at least a year, and wanted to assign me an extraordinary salary, which, however, I declined, for my heart longed to reach the Promised Land.

On the eve of Tabernacles, 5248 (1487), a French galley came to Palermo, on its way to Alexandria. The worthy Meshullam of Volterra was in it, with his servant, and I rejoiced to travel in his company. The night after the Sabbath we embarked, and on Sunday at midday we left Palermo. All day and night we had a favorable wind, so that in the morning we were close to the Pharos of Messina; we got safely past this and were in Messina on Monday at noon. This town is a trading place for all nations; ships come here from all parts. Messina lies in the middle of the Pharos, so that ships from the east and west pass it by, and its harbor is the only one of its kind in the world; the largest vessels may here come close to the shore. Messina is not so large as Palermo, neither has it such good springs; but the town is very beautiful and has a strong fortress. There are about four hundred Jewish families in it, living quietly in a street of their own; they are richer than those in Palermo, and are almost all artisans; there are only a few merchants among them. They have a synagogue with a porch, open above but enclosed on the four sides, and in the middle of it is a well with spring water. There is an administration consisting of persons who are chosen every year; and this as well as other arrangements resembles that of the Jews of Palermo. At a wedding which took place near my residence I witnessed the following ceremony. After the seven blessings had been repeated, the bride was placed on a horse and rode through the town. The whole community went before her on foot, the bridegroom in the midst of the elders and before the bride, who was the only one on horseback; youths and children carried burning torches and made loud exclamations, so that the whole place resounded; they made the circuit of the streets and all the Jewish courts; the Christian inhabitants looked on with pleasure and no one disturbed the festivity.

On the eleventh of Marheshvan (October) we left Messina to go to Rhodes. We were joined in the ship by a Jewish merchant from Sucari, with his servant, three Jewish leatherworkers from Syracuse, and a Sephardic Jew with his wife, two sons and two daughters, so that together we were fourteen Jewish souls on board. We passed the Pharos in safety, sailed through the Gulf of Venice, and thus reached the Archipelago. The Archipelago is full of small islands—Corfu, Candia, Negropont, Rhodes and Cyprus—and altogether it is said to contain about three hundred inhabited and uninhabited islands. For four days we had a favorable wind; on the fourth day towards evening, we were thrown back by a storm and could only escape the fury of the waves by remaining in a little natural harbor in the mountains, into which we were thrown; these mountains are full of St. John's bread and myrtle trees, and here we remained for three days.

After three days, on Sunday, the 18th of Marheshvan, we left this place and came within sixty miles of Rhodes. All the way we saw islands on both sides, and the Turkish mountains were also visible. But we were driven back eighty miles; and the ship had to cast anchor on the shores of the island Longo, which is under the dominion of Rhodes, and there we had to remain ten days, for the wind was unfavorable. During our stay here, one of the sailors used insolent language to the worthy Meshullam, who complained of it to the master. The master himself went in search of the sailor; the others tried to hide him, but in vain. He commanded him to be tied to the mast and severely flogged, and when the beater seemed to spare him he took the rope himself and continued to punish the insolence of the sailor. He also desired him to make a public apology to the worthy Meshullam. The whole ship's crew were very much annoyed that all this should have happened on account of a few abusive words spoken against a Jew, and from this they began to hate us and no longer treated us as they had done before.

The worthy merchant, Meshullam, took advantage of a small ship that was coming from Rhodes and going to Chios to leave our vessel, intending to go to Chios and thence to Constantinople, for he had given up his intention of accompanying us to Alexandria. On the second day after Meshullam had left us we met a small ship by which we were made aware that a well-armed Genoese man-of-war was coming toward us. This news alarmed the master, for we had no wind; otherwise, if the wind be favorable, the galley does not fear a multitude of other ships, for there is no safer vessel than this. The master therefore made for a little town, Castel San Giovani, on the Turkish mountains, which is under the supremacy of Rhodes, and is the only place in Turkey that has remained in the possession of the Christians. It is small but very strongly fortified, and its extreme environs already belong to the Turks. We arrived there on Friday, the day of the New Moon, Kislev (November) 5248, and were in safety. On Saturday, towards noon, God caused a favorable wind to blow so that we were able to leave the place and to sail all day and night; and on Sunday, Kislev 3rd, 5248, we arrived joyfully at Rhodes, after a twenty-two days' sail.

The inhabitants of Rhodes welcomed us gladly, for the master of our ship was a friend and relative of the governor. The chief men of the Jewish community soon came to our ship, and received us with kindness; for the merchant Meshullam, who had been with us in the ship, was the brother of the physician Rabbi Nathan, the most distinguished man among the Jews of Rhodes. A fine room, provided with all necessities, was assigned to me, while the other Jews who accompanied me were accommodated as well as it was possible, for the Jewish houses in Rhodes had been almost entirely destroyed by the siege of the Turks, under their first emperor, undertaken by him in the year of his death. No one who has not seen Rhodes, with its high and strong walls, its firm gates and battlements, has ever seen a fortress. The Turkish Emperor in the year of his death sent a besieging army against it, bombarded the town with a multitude of stones, which are still to be seen there, and in this way threw down the walls surrounding the Jewish street and destroyed the houses. The Jews here have told me that when the Turks got into the town they killed all before them until they came to the door of the synagogue, when God brought confusion among them, so that they began at once to flee and slay one another. On account of this miracle the governor built a church on the spot and gave the Jews another building instead of it. While I was in Rhodes, he granted them a hundred ducats from the revenues of the town to build a new synagogue.

Not many Jews have remained in Rhodes; altogether there are twenty-two families, all poor, who subsist with difficulty on vegetables, not eating bread or meat, for they never slaughter nor do they buy any wine, for fear of getting into disputes with the Greeks who dwell there. When they buy in the market, they touch nothing that belongs to the Greeks; and they observe the law against wine just as strictly as against pork. The Jews here are all very intelligent and well educated; they speak a pure dialect and are very moral and polite; even the tanners are neatly dressed and speak with propriety. They all allow their hair to grow long and are beautiful in person. Nowhere are there more beautiful Jewesses than in Rhodes; they occupy themselves doing all kinds of handiwork for the Acomodors (the nobles of the land), and in this way support their husbands. The Acomodors hold the Jews in high esteem, often coming into their houses to chat awhile with the women who work there.

When anybody dies there is no coffin made for him; he is buried only in his shroud; an impression of a human form is made in the ground where he is to be buried, for the earth there has never been cultivated so that it receives any impression. The dead body is laid in this cavity, a board is placed over it, and then it is covered with earth. The air in Rhodes is purer and more agreeable than I have yet felt it in any other place; the water is sweet, the soil is clean but poor, and most of the inhabitants are Greeks who are subject to the Acomodors.

In Rhodes we remained from the 3rd of Kislev to the 15th of Tebet (December), because the governor would not allow the ship to sail to Alexandria, fearing lest the king of Egypt would keep it there. For the governor had accepted 120,000 gold pieces from the Egyptian King, promising to deliver up to him the brother of the Turkish Emperor, Dschem by name, who was detained a prisoner in France; but he had not been able to keep his promise from fear of the Turkish Emperor; for this reason he was afraid that the Egyptian King might seize the ship, which contained a vast amount of treasures, together with all the men in it. When, however, time wore on, the master having consulted with the merchants of the ship, thought better to sail in spite of all the danger. On the 15th of Tebet, therefore, we left Rhodes, and after six days we were before Alexandria; the master would not sail into it until he had learnt how matters stood. We therefore remained at Bukari, a place between Alexandria and Rosetta, on the way to Cairo; the water was not deep here but the place was large, and we cast anchor about four miles from the shore. We had a vessel of two hundred tons with us, as tender, which the master had bought and loaded with grain to sell in Alexandria.

The Emir (the representative of the King of Egypt) who had his seat in Alexandria, sent an assurance to the master that the ship and all that was in it might come there in safety, but the latter placed no faith in this promise, and himself sent ambassadors to the king. He was willing, however, to send the smaller ship with wheat and a small crew to Alexandria on the word of the Emir. The Jews therefore resorted to this ship on Friday, expecting to reach Alexandria on the Sabbath. But the Emir would not allow this because the master had refused to place confidence in him, and so we Jews remained in this ship, about a bowshot removed from the galley.

A considerable time had elapsed and the messengers had not yet returned from Cairo; our victuals began to be exhausted, we had no water, and would already have preferred death to life.

On the 18th of Shebat (January), about midnight, a dreadful storm arose; two anchors of our ship suddenly broke, only the weakest remaining. The sailors were terrified and threw many things overboard to lighten the ship; they signalled to the other ship, by firing guns, to send off the boat with men; but nobody heard and nobody answered, for those in the galley were concerned with their own safety and, indeed, it would scarcely have been possible for a bark to have approached us, for the sea was too stormy. It drove us, with the damaged anchor which still remained, on to a whirlpool; the waves went over us, we were tossed hither and thither, and the ship threatened to be wrecked every moment, for it was old and damaged, so that the water penetrated on all sides, and the sea in that part was full of rocks. For about twenty-four hours we were in such danger that we expected death every moment. We each had a pail in our hands to empty out the water which flowed abundantly into the ship; and we tearfully filled our pails and emptied them, till God took mercy on us, and we happily escaped the storm almost miraculously. When the storm was over, the master sent for the people from the damaged vessel and on the morning of the second day we entered into the large ship and remained there until the ambassadors returned bringing a guarantee from the king. There was now again a calm, and the ship could not leave Bukari. The merchants and the Jews in the large ship preferred to go ashore in a bark that their lives might be in safety. We then traveled on foot (not being able to get asses) for eighteen miles of the way, and we reached Alexandria on the 14th of Shebat, tired and weary. Here God gave us favor in the eyes of a generous man who was very much beloved even by the Arabs, by name Rabbi Moses Grasso, dragoman to the Venetians. He came to meet us and released us from the hands of the Arabs who sit in the gate and plunder foreign Jews at their pleasure. He took me in his house, and there I had to remain while I stayed in Alexandria. I read with him a book on the Kabala, which he had in his possession, for he dearly loved this science. By thus reading with him I found favor in his sight and we became friends. On the Sabbath he gave a dinner, to which he invited the Sephardi who had come with me; his two sons were also there when he brought me into the dining-room.

The following is the arrangement of the Sabbath meal customary to Jews in all Arabian countries. They sit in a circle on a carpet, the cupbearer standing near them near a small cloth which is spread on this carpet; all kinds of fruit which are in season are brought and laid on the cloth. The host now takes a glass of wine, pronounces the blessing of sanctification (Kiddush), and empties the cup completely. The cupbearer then takes it from the host, and hands it successively to the whole company, always refilled, and each one empties it, then the host takes two or three pieces of fruit, eats some, and drinks a second glass, while the company say "Health and life." Whoever sits next also takes some fruit, and the cupbearer fills a second glass for him, saying, "To your pleasure," the company join in with the words "Health and life," and so it goes round. Then a second kind of fruit is partaken of, another glass is filled, and this is continued until each one has emptied at least six or seven glasses. Sometimes they even drink when they smell flowers which are provided for the occasion; these flowers are the "dudaim," which Rashi translates into Arabic by "jasmine"; it is a plant bearing only blossoms which have a delightful and invigorating fragrance. The wine is unusually strong, and this is especially the case in Jerusalem, where it is drunk unmixed. After all have drunk to their heart's content, a large dish of meat is brought, each one stretches forth his hand, takes what he wants, and eats quickly, for they are not very big eaters. Rabbi Moses brought us confectionery, fresh ginger, dates, raisins, almonds, and confectionery of coriander seeds; a glass of wine is drunk with each kind. Then followed raisin wine, which was very good, then malmsey wine from Candia, and again native wine. I drank with them and was exhilarated.

There is another custom in the country of the Arabs: On Friday all go to bathe, and on their return the women bring them wine, of which they drink copiously; word is then brought that the supper is ready, and it is eaten in the daytime, before evening. Then they all come to the synagogue, cleanly and neatly dressed. They begin with psalms and thanksgiving and evening prayer is read until two hours after dusk. On their return home they repeat the Kiddush, eat only a piece of bread of the size of an olive, and recite the grace after meals. In this whole district the Afternoon Prayer is read on Friday in private, except in Jerusalem, where the Ashkenazim (Germans) have done away with the custom, and the afternoon and evening prayer are said with minyan as with us, and they eat at night; the evening prayer is not begun, however, until the stars are visible. In these parts the Sabbath is more strictly kept than in any other; nobody leaves his house on the Sabbath, except to go to the synagogue or to the Bet Hamidrash (house of study). I need scarcely mention that nobody kindles a fire on the Sabbath, or has a light that has been extinguished rekindled, even by a Gentile. All who are able to read the Holy Scriptures read the whole day, after having slept off the effect of their wine.

In Alexandria there are about twenty-five families and two old synagogues. One is very large and somewhat damaged, the other is smaller. Most pray in the smaller, because it bears the name of the prophet Elijah; and it is said that he once appeared to somebody in the south-east corner, where a light is now kept constantly burning. I have been told that twenty years ago he again appeared to an old man. God alone knows the truth! In all Arabian countries no man enters the synagogue with shoes on his feet; even in paying a visit the shoes are left outside, at the door, and everybody sits on the ground on mats or carpets.

Alexandria is a very large town surrounded with a wall and encircled by the sea, though two-thirds of it are now destroyed and many houses uninhabited. The inhabited courts are paved with mosaic; peach and date trees are in the middle of them. All the houses are large and beautiful, but the inhabitants are few on account of the unhealthy atmosphere which has prevailed here for many years. It is said that those who are not accustomed to the air, and remain long here, die or at least fall sick. Most of the inhabitants are subject to the diseases of the eye. Merchants come from all parts, and at present there are four consuls here: for Venice, Genoa, Catalonia and Ancona, and the merchants of all nations have to treat with them. The Christians are obliged to shut themselves in their houses every evening; the Arabs close up the streets from without, and open them again every morning. It is the same on Friday from noon till the evening; while the Arabs tarry in the house of prayer, the Christians have to stay in their houses, and whoever is seen in the street has himself to blame if he is ill-treated. The King of Egypt receives an immense sum of money by the export and import duties paid on wares which come to Alexandria, for the tax is very high; even current money that is brought in has to pay two per cent. As for me, by the help of God, I was not obliged to pay entrance duty for my money. Smugglers are not subjected to any special punishment by the Egyptian tax-collectors.

I spent seven days in Alexandria, leaving my effects, which were very few, in the large ship, which was still detained in Bukari by the calm. It happened just at this time that there was a man in Alexandria who had made a vow to celebrate the Passover feast in Jerusalem with his wife and two sons. I joined myself to him, and traveled with him on camels. I commissioned Rabbi Moses Grasso to bring my things from the large ship and send them to Cairo. At Rosetta, on the Nile, we got into a ship. On both sides of the Nile there are towns and villages which are beautiful, large and populous, but all unfortified. We remained two days in Fuah, because the wind was not favorable; it is a large and beautiful place, and fish and vegetables can be got for almost nothing. We came next to Bulak, which already forms the beginning of Cairo. On the Nile I saw the large species of frog which the natives call El Timsah (the crocodile); it is larger than a bear and spots are visible on its skin. The ship's crew say that there are some twice as big. These are the frogs which have remained from the time of Moses, as Nahmanides mentions in his commentary. The Nile is wide and its waters are very sweet but turbid. The part on which we sailed forms merely a branch, for the other goes to Damietta, where it flows into the sea.

Before coming to Bulak we observed two very old dome-shaped buildings which lay on the same side of the stream; it is said that they are the magazines which Joseph built. The door is above in the roof. Although they are now only ruins, yet it is easy to see that they have once been magnificent buildings; the district is uninhabited. Twelve days before Purim, towards evening, we came to Cairo; it was the time of the great harvest and the severe famine which had prevailed in the whole district of Cairo was on the decrease. The barley ripens sooner here than elsewhere by the influence of the waters of the Nile, and the harvest appeared to be very good. In the following month there was great plenty, so that there was no more thought of famine. The inhabitants and their fields are to this day subject to the king, who takes a fifth part of the produce, and sometimes more. Egypt is the only place in the world where the fields are thus subject to the king to the present day.

I shall not speak of the grandeur of Cairo and of the multitude of men to be seen streaming there, for many before me have described them, and all that has been said of the town is true. It is not completely surrounded by a wall, though there are several places here and there protected in that way. The town is very animated, and one hears the different languages of the foreigners who inhabit it. It is situated between the Red Sea and the Mediterranean, and all merchants come from India, Ethiopia, and the countries of Prester John through the Red Sea to Cairo both to sell their wares, which consist of spices, pearls, and precious stones, and to purchase commodities which come from France, Germany, Italy and Turkey, across the Mediterranean Sea through Alexandria to Cairo. In the Red Sea there are magnets; hence the ships which come through them have no iron in them, not so much as a nail. The place where the sea was divided for our forefathers is said to have been identified, and many priests go to visit it, but I have heard of no Jew who has been there. The harbor where the ships coming from the Red Sea unload their cargoes, and from whence the wares are brought to Cairo by means of camels, is said to be not far distant from Mt. Sinai, which is only five days' journey from Cairo. The Christian ecclesiastics live here in a convent and come daily to Cairo, making the journey there and back more frequently than any other people, even than the Arabs, for it is known that they carry no gold with them; the whole way is infested by Bedouin, who rob and plunder at their will in the wilderness; they do no injury, however, to these ecclesiastics who have made an agreement both with the king and with the Bedouin. It is said, indeed, that the Bedouin keep their word to strangers who dwell among them.

In Cairo there are now about seven hundred Jewish families; of these fifty are Samaritans, called also Cutheans, one hundred and fifty are Karaites, and the rest Rabbanites. The Samaritans have only the five books of Moses, and their mode of writing differs from ours—the sacred writing. Maimonides remarks that this writing was customary among the Israelites before the time of the Assyrian exile, as already related in tractate Sanhedrin; but their Hebrew is like ours. Wherever the tetragrammaton occurs in scripture they write Ashima; they are an abomination to the Jews because they offer up sacrifices and frankincense on Mt. Gerizim. Many of them left Cairo with us to bring the passover-offering to Mt. Gerizim, for they have a temple there; they celebrate the Sabbath from the midday of Friday till the midday of

Saturday. There are very few of them in existence now: it is said scarcely five hundred families in all the world.

The Karaites, as you know, do not believe in the words of our sages, but they are familiar with all the Bible. They fix the day of the new moon according to the appearance of the moon; consequently the Karaites in Cairo keep different days for Rosh Hashana (New Year) and the Day of Atonement, from those in Jerusalem, maintaining that there is nothing wrong in this. Every year they send to Jerusalem to observe the month of spring; and when they see that it is necessary to have a leap-year (Ibbur) they add an intercalary month. They do not think it any harm if the Karaites in Cairo add a month and those in Constantinople do not, for every place fixes its calendar according to its own judgment: they fast on the 7th and 10th of Ab. It is well known that they always celebrate Shabuot (Pentecost) on Sunday; they hang the lulab (palm branch) and the other plants in the midst of the Synagogue; they all look upon them, and this they consider sufficient; they have no fire in their houses on the Sabbath, either by day or night; the five rules respecting shehita (slaughtering animals for food) are the same with them as with us, although not expressly mentioned in the Torah; they also observe the regulations to kill with a very sharp knife, free from all notches, and the law respecting wine they keep even more strictly than the Rabbanites. In all the districts through which I passed, I have noticed that the law respecting wine is most strictly kept; there is even a doubt as to whether the honey may be used which the Arabs prepare from the grapes; it is very good, and in preparing it the grapes are not trodden in the same way as in making wine. I was asked to allow the use of it, for there are so many arguments in its favor, but my predecessors had not done it, and I did not wish to make innovations. There is not a single man who would drink wine that had been touched by an Arab, much less by an idolator. The Karaites observe all the laws of purification; if anybody dies they all leave the house and hire poor Rabbanites to carry away their dead, for they will not touch a corpse. I have seen some of their commentaries, such as that of Japhet, which is quoted by Ibn Ezra, and those of Rabbi Aaron, the Karaite. Every day they make new explanations of the Torah, and maintain that even a fundamental law which has been established by the ancients may be altered if it does not appear to one of their wise men now living to agree with the text of the Bible, and they decide everything by the letter of the Torah. In all this they do not consider that either old or living scholars do any wrong. They have a synagogue in Cairo; most of their prayers consist of psalms and other biblical verses; in recent times they have made a rule to read from the Torah on Mondays and Thursdays, which was not done formerly; they have priests and Levites, and it is said of a very rich and honorable Karaite in Cairo, Zadakah by name, that he is really descended from the family of David; he wanted to lay before me his genealogy, attested by witnesses of every generation, but I had not time to meet him.

The Samaritans are the richest of all the Jews in Cairo, and fill most of the higher offices of state; they are cashiers and administrators; one of them is said to have a property worth 200,000 pieces of gold. The Karaites are richer than the Rabbanites, but there are opulent men even among the latter. The custom of the Jews is always to represent themselves as poor in the country of the Arabs; they go about as beggars, humbling themselves before the Arabs; they are not charitable towards one another; the Karaites mix among the Rabbanites and try to become friendly with them.

In Cairo there are about fifty families of forced apostates (Maranos) from Spain, who have all done penance; they are mostly poor, having left their possessions, their parents, their relatives, and come here to seek shelter under the wings of the Lord God of Israel. Among the Jews in Cairo there are moneychangers and merchants, for the country is large, and some branch of industry is open to everyone. For trade there is no better place in the world than Cairo; it is easy to grow rich. Hence one meets there with innumerable foreigners of all nations and languages. You may go out by night as well as by day, for all the streets are lighted with torches; the people sleep on the ground before the shop. The Jew can buy everything that is necessary, such as meat, cheese, fish, vegetables, and in general all that he requires, for everything is sold in the Jews' street; this is also the case in Palermo, but there it is not the same as in Cairo, for in the latter place the Jews cook at home only for the Sabbath, since men as well as women are occupied during the whole week and can therefore buy everything in the market. Wood is very expensive; a load of wood, not so large as the load of a pair of mules, costs upwards of two-thirds of a ducat, and even more; meat and fruit are also expensive; the former is very good, however, especially the tail of the sheep. The Karaites do not eat this, for according to them it belongs to that kind of fat which the Torah has forbidden. I have seen nothing cheap in Cairo except onions of the Nile, leek, melons, cucumbers, and vegetables. Bread is cheap in years of plenty: it is made in the form of a cake and kneaded very soft.

The Jewish Nagid (Prince) who has his residence in Cairo is appointed over all the Jews who are under the dominion of the King of Egypt. He has all the power of a king and can punish and imprison those who act in opposition to his decrees; he appoints the dayyanim (judges) in every community. The present prince lived formerly for a long time in Jerusalem but was obliged to leave it on account of the Elders, the calumniators and informers who were there. He is called Rabbi Nathan HaCohen; he is rich, wise, pious, old and is a native of Barbary. When I came to Cairo he showed me much honor, loved me as a father loves his son, and tried to dissuade me altogether from going to Jerusalem on account of the informers there; all scholars and rabbis formerly in Jerusalem left the city in haste in order to preserve their lives from the oppression of the Elders. The Jews who were in Jerusalem, about three hundred families, disappeared by degrees on account of the great taxes and burdens laid upon them by the elders, so that the poor only remained, and women; and there was scarcely one to whom the name of man could justly be given. These grey-haired criminals went so far as to sell the scrolls of the law with their covers, the curtains, the pomegranates, and all the sacred appurtenances which were in Jerusalem, to Gentiles, who were to carry them away into foreign lands; they sold the numerous books, such as the Talmud and Codes, which were deposited by the Ashkenazim in Jerusalem, so that nothing of value was left there. The Nagid told me he could not well put a stop to this because he feared that the Elders would speak evil against all the Jews to the King, and "the throat of the King is an open sepulchre, and his eyes are not satisfied." About the same time disturbances took place in Egypt; for the King wanted to raise money to give to his generals who were to fight against the Turkish Emperor in Aleppo; and he imposed the heavy tax of seventy-five thousand pieces of gold on the Jews in Cairo, viz. the Samaritans, Karaites, and Rabbanites, and the same on Christians and Arabs, for he wanted to raise an immense sum of money. In Purim of that year there was, therefore, sorrow, fasting and weeping among the Jews; yet I did not lose my courage, my heart was fixed on God.

On the 20th of Adar, I left Cairo in company with the Jew who came from Alexandria, and we came to Chanak which is about two miles distant from Cairo. Before I left New Cairo I went to Old Cairo, called Mizraim Atika, which is also inhabited, though not so closely as New Cairo, and both are quite close together. On the way thither we saw the place where the King sends people every year to prepare a dam against the rising of the Nile, which takes place in the month of Ab (August). I have heard many things about the rising of the Nile, which, however, would be too wearisome to write down, especially as I have not seen it with my own eyes. I saw rain in Cairo, but not much; and while there I felt severe cold at the time of Purim. The people, indeed, wondered and said it had not been so cold for many years, for according to all accounts Egypt is very warm.

In Old Cairo there is a very beautiful synagogue built on large and splendid pillars; it also is dedicated to the prophet Elijah, who is said to have appeared there to the pious in the south-east corner, where a light is kept continually burning. In the north-east corner is a platform where the scroll of Ezra used to be placed. It is related that many years ago a Jew came from the West, and bought it from the temple servant; he set sail from Alexandria, carrying with him the roll of the law, but the ship was not far from Alexandria when it sank, and he was lost, together with the roll of the law. The temple servant, who had sold it to him for a hundred gold pieces, became an apostate, and died shortly afterwards. The case of this roll is still in the synagogue and a light is always kept burning before it. Last year the King wanted to take the pillars on which the synagogue is built for his palace because they are large and very beautiful, but the Jews redeemed them for a thousand gold pieces. According to the date on the wall of the synagogue, it was built thirty-eight years before the destruction of the second temple. Near to it there is another fine large synagogue, but not equal to the former; prayers are offered up here every Sabbath, and the Jews hire a person to watch over it.

I was not so fortunate as to get to Dimo, a place outside Cairo, where Moses is said to have prayed; here there are two synagogues, one belonging to the Rabbanites and one to the Karaites; Divine Service is often held here on Sabbaths and feast days. I was told that the mamelukes of the King feed their horses on the way to it, and that it would therefore be dangerous for a Jew to go there, for the mamelukes were at this time in the habit of beating and plundering Jews as well as Arabs.

In Chanak we remained two days, and there hired five camels, for two men and two women had joined us in Cairo. It is said that this is Goshen, where the Jews sojourned in Egypt. We then came to Salahia where we remained over the Sabbath, waiting for a passing caravan, since the way through the wilderness begins here and it is not safe to make the journey with only five camels. Not a Jew lives on the way from here to Gaza.

We were three days in Salahia when an Arab caravan of eight camels arrived, with which we travelled as far as Katiah, a town in the middle of the wilderness, where no vegetation is to be seen except date-trees. The wilderness between Egypt and Palestine is not large, for from one day's journey to another there are places of encampment for the camels, erected principally for travellers; yet it is all sand, and no vegetation whatever is to be seen except date-trees in well-known places. Water is found after two days' journey, sometimes even after one day's journey, but it is rather brackish.

In the wilderness we came to Arish, said to be the former Succot. The caravans going through the wilderness either encamp at midday and journey in the evening till midnight, or travel from midnight into the first third of the day; this depends on the will of those who have charge of the caravans. Generally speaking, they travel by night rather than by day. Thus we journeyed from place to place in the wilderness, till we came to Gaza without misadventure. Gaza is the first town on coming out of the wilderness leading to the land of the Philistines. It is a large and beautiful city, of the same size as Jerusalem, but without walls, for among all the places under Egyptian dominion, which now extends over Palestine, the country of the Philistines and Syria, Alexandria and Aleppo alone are surrounded by walls. If the account of the Jews living there be correct, I saw in Gaza the ruins of the building that Samson pulled down on the Philistines. We remained four days in Gaza; there is now a Rabbi from Germany there, by name, Rabbi Moses, of Prague, who fled thither from Jerusalem; he insisted on my going to his house, and I was obliged to stay with him all the time that I was in Gaza. On the Sabbath all the wardens were invited to dine with us. Cakes of grapes and fruit were brought; we partook of several glasses before eating, and were joyful.

On Sunday, the 11th of Nisan (April), we journeyed from Gaza on asses; we came within two miles of Hebron, and there spent the night. On Monday we reached Hebron, a small town on the slope of the mountain, called by the Turks Khalil. It is divided into two parts, one beside the Cave of the Patriarchs; the other opposite, a bowshot farther away. I was in the Cave of Machpelah, over which the mosque has been built; and the Arabs hold the place in high honor. All the kings of the Arabs come here to repeat their prayers, but neither a Jew nor an Arab may enter the cave itself, where the real graves of the Patriarchs are. The Arabs remain above, and let down burning torches into it through a window, for they keep a light always burning there. All who come to pray leave money, which they throw into the cave through the window; when they wish to take the money out they let down a young man who is unmarried by a rope, to bring it up—so I have been told by the Jews who live there. All Hebron, with its field and neighborhood, belongs to the cave; bread and lentil, or some other kind of pulse, is distributed to the poor every day without distinction of faith, and this is done in honor of Abraham. Without, in the wall of the cave, there is a small opening, said to have been made just after the burial of Abraham, and there the Jews are allowed to pray, but none may come within the walls of the cave. At this little window I offered up my prayers. On the summit of the opposite mountain is a large cave, said to be the grave of Jesse, the father of David. We went there also to pray on the same day. Between the grave of Jesse and the Cave of the Patriarchs is a well, which the Arabs call the well of Isaac, said to have belonged to the patriarch Isaac. Near to Hebron, between rocks, there is a spring of fresh water, distinguished as the well of Sarah. Hebron has many vineyards and olive-trees, and contains at the present time twenty families, all Rabbanites, half of whom are the descendants of the forced apostates who have recently returned to their faith.

On Tuesday morning, the 13th of Nisan, we left Hebron, which is a day's journey distant from Jerusalem, and came on as far as Rachel's tomb, where there is a round, vaulted building in the open road. We got down from our asses and prayed at each grave, each one according to his ability. On the right hand of the traveller to Jerusalem lies the hill on which Bethlehem stands; this is a small village, about half a mile from Rachel's grave, and the Catholic priests have a church there.

From Bethlehem to Jerusalem is a journey of about three miles. The whole way is full of vineyards and orchards. The vineyards are like those in Romagna, the vines being low but thick. About three-quarters of a mile from Jerusalem, at a place where the mountain is ascended by steps, we beheld the famous city of our delight, and here we rent our garments, as was our duty. A little farther on, the sanctuary, the desolate house of our splendor, became visible, and at the sight of it we again made rents in our garments. We came as far as the gates of Jerusalem, and on the 14th of Nisan, 5248, at noon, our feet stood within the gates of the city. Here we were met by an Ashkenazi who had been educated in Italy, Rabbi Jacob Calmann; he took me into his house, the most part desolate and in ruins. I need not repeat that it is not surrounded by walls, and I remained his guest during the whole time of Passover. The inhabitants of Jerusalem, I am told, number about four thousand families. As for Jews, about seventy families of the poorest class have remained; there is scarcely a family that is not in want of the commonest necessities; one who has bread for a year is called rich. Among the Jewish population there are many aged, forsaken widows from Germany, Spain, Portugal and other countries, so that there are seven women to one man. The land is now quieter and happier than before; for the Elders have repented the evil they have done, when they saw that only the poorer portion of the inhabitants remained; they are therefore very friendly to every newcomer. They excuse themselves for what has happened, and assert that they never injured anyone who did not try to obtain the mastery over them. As for me, so far I have no complaint to make against them; on the contrary, they have shown me great kindness and have dealt honorably with me, for which I give daily thanks to God.

The Jews are not persecuted by the Arabs in these parts. I have traveled through the country in its length and breadth, and none of them has put an obstacle in my way. They are very kind to strangers, particularly to anyone who does not know the language; and if they see many Jews together they are not annoyed by it. In my opinion, an intelligent man versed in political science might easily raise himself to be chief of the Jews as well as of the Arabs; for among all the inhabitants there is not a wise and sensible man who knows how to deal affably with his fellow-men; all are ignorant misanthropes intent only on gain. . . .

The synagogue here is built on columns; it is long, narrow, and dark, the light entering only by the door. There is a fountain in the middle of it. In the court of the synagogue, quite close to it, stands a mosque. The court of the synagogue is very large, and contains many houses, all of them buildings devoted by the Ashkenazim to charitable purposes, and inhabited by Ashkenazi widows. There were formerly many courts in the Jewish streets belonging to these buildings, but the Elders sold them, so that not a single one remained. They could not, however, sell the buildings of the Ashkenazim, for they were exclusively for Ashkenazim, and no other poor had a right to them. The Jews' street and the houses are very large; some of them dwell also on Zion. At one time they had more houses, but these are now heaps of rubbish and cannot be rebuilt, for the law of the land is that a Jew may not rebuild his ruined house without permission, and the permission often costs more than the whole house is worth. The houses in Jerusalem are of stone, none of wood or plaster.

There are some excellent regulations here. I have nowhere seen the daily service conducted in a better manner. The Jews rise an hour or two before day-break, even on the Sabbath, and recite psalms and other songs of praise till the day dawns. Then they repeat the Kaddish; after which the two of the Readers appointed for the purpose chant the Blessing of the Law, the chapter on Sacrifices, and all the songs of praise which follow with a suitable melody, the "Hear, O Israel" being read on the appearance of the sun's first rays. The Kohanim (descendants of the Priests) repeat the priestly benediction daily, on weekdays as well as on the Sabbaths; in every service this blessing occurs. At the morning and afternoon service supplications are said with great devotion, together with the Thirteen Attributes of God; and there is no difference between Mondays and Thursdays, and the other days of the week except that the Law is read on the former.

Jerusalem, notwithstanding its destruction, still contains four very beautiful, long bazaars, such as I have never before seen, at the foot of Zion. They have all dome-shaped roofs, and contain wares of every kind. They are divided into different departments, the merchant bazaar, the spice bazaar, the vegetable market, and one in which cooked food and bread are sold. When I came to Jerusalem there was a dreadful famine in the land. A man of moderate means could have eaten bread the weight of a drachma at every meal, which in our money makes a bolognino of old silver, and he would not have been satisfied. I was told that the famine was less severe than it was at the beginning of the year. Many Jews died of hunger; they had been seen a day or two before asking for bread, which nobody could give them, and the next day they were found dead in their houses. Many lived on grass, going out like stags to look for pasture. At present there is only one German Rabbi here who was educated in Jerusalem. I have never seen his equal for humility and the fear of God; he weaves night and day when he is not occupied with his studies, and for six months tasted no bread between Sabbath and Sabbath, his food consisting of raw turnips and the remains of St. John's bread, which is very plentiful here, after the sugar has been taken out of it. According to the account of a trustworthy man, Jericho, the "city of palms," is only half a day's journey from Jerusalem, and there are at the present day scarcely three palm trees in the town.

Now, the wheat harvest being over, the famine is at an end, and there is once more plenty, praise be to God. Here, in Jerusalem, I have seen several kinds of fruits which are not to be found in our country. There is one tree with long leaves, which grows higher than a man's stature and bears fruit only once; it then withers, and from its roots there rises another similar one, which again bears fruit the next year; and the same thing is continually repeated. The grapes are larger than in our country, but neither cherries, hazelnuts, nor chestnuts are to be found. All the necessities of life, such as meat, wine, olives, and sesame oil can be had very cheap. The soil is excellent, but it is not possible to gain a living by any branch of industry, unless it be that of a shoemaker, weaver, or goldsmith; even such artisans as these gain their livelihood with great difficulty. Persons of various nationalities are always to be found in Jerusalem from Christian countries, and from Babylonia and Abyssinia. The Arabs come frequently to offer up prayers at the temple, for they hold it in great veneration.

I made enquiries concerning the Sambatyon, and I hear from one who has been informed that a man has come from the kingdom of Prester John and has related that there are high mountains and valleys there which can be traversed in a ten days' journey, and which are certainly inhabited by descendants of Israel. They have princes or kings, and have carried on great wars against the Johannites (Abyssinians) for more than a century, but, unfortunately, the Johannites prevailed and Ephraim was beaten. The Johannites penetrated into their country and laid it waste, and the remembrance of Israel had almost died away in those places, for an edict was issued against those who remained prohibiting the exercise of their religious duties as severe as that which Antiochus issued in the time of the Hasmoneans. But God had mercy. Other kings succeeded in India who were not so cruel as their predecessors; and it is said that the former glory of the Jews is now in a measure restored; they have again become numerous, and though they still pay tribute to the Johannites they are not entirely subject to them. Four years ago, it is said, they again made war with their neighbors, when they plundered their enemies and made many prisoners. The enemy, on the other hand, took some of them prisoners, and sold them as slaves; a few of these were brought to Cairo and redeemed by the Jews there. I saw two of them in Cairo; they were black but not so black as the negroes. It was impossible to learn from them whether they belonged to the Karaites or the Rabbanites. In some respects they seem to hold the doctrine of the Karaites, for they say that there is no fire in their houses on the Sabbath; in other respects they seem to observe Rabbanism. It is said that the pepper and other spices which the negroes sell come principally from their country.

It is universally known here that the Arabs who make pilgrimages from Egypt to Mecca journey through a large and fearful desert, forming caravans of at least ten thousand camels. Sometimes they are overtaken in the wilderness by a people of gigantic stature, one of whom can chase a thousand Arabs. They call this people El-Arabes, that is, children of the Almighty, because in their battles they always invoke the name of Almighty God. The Arabs assert that one of these people is able to bear the burden of a camel in one hand, while in the other he holds the sword with which he fights; it is known that they observe the Jewish religious customs, and it is affirmed that they are descendants of Rechab.

No Jew may enter the enclosure of the Temple. Although sometimes the Arabs are anxious to admit carpenters and goldsmiths to perform work there, nobody will go in, for we have all been defiled (by touching bodies of the dead). I do not know whether the Arabs enter the Holy of Holies or not. I also made enquiries relative to the Eben Shethiah where the Ark of the Covenant was placed, and am told that it is under a high and beautiful dome built by the Arabs in the court of the Temple. It is enclosed in this building, and no one may enter. There is great wealth in the enclosure of the Temple. We hear that the monarchs build chambers there inlaid with gold, and the king now reigning is said to have erected a building, more splendid than any other ever built, adorned with gold and precious stones.

The Temple enclosure still has twelve gates. Those which are called the "Gates of Mercy" are of iron, and are two in number; they look towards the east of the Temple and are always closed. They only reach half-way above the ground, the other half is sunk in the earth. It is said that the Arabs often tried to raise them up but were not able to do so.

The western wall, part of which is still standing, is composed of large, thick stones, such as I have never before seen in an old building, either in Rome or in any other country. At the north-east corner is a tower of very large stones. I entered it and found a vast edifice supported by massive and lofty pillars; there are so many pillars that it wearied me to go to the end of the building. Everything is filled with earth which has been thrown there from the ruins of the Temple. The temple-building stands on these columns, and in each of them is a hole through which a cord may be drawn. It is said that the bulls and rams for sacrifice were bound here. Throughout the whole region of Jerusalem, in fields as well as vineyards, there are large caves connected with one another.

In all these districts, in the valleys and mountains, there are toll-collectors, who represent themselves as overseers for the security of the way, and are called "Naphar" in Arabic. These men take as many taxes as they like from the Jews with perfect impunity. From Cairo there are twenty toll-bars; and I for my part paid them altogether about a ducat. The Jews who come from Cairo to Jerusalem have only to pay ten silver denarii at the city gate, while, on the other hand, those who come by way of Jaffa have to pay a ducat. The Jews in Jerusalem have to pay down every year thirty-two silver pieces per head. The poor man, as well as the rich, has to pay this tribute as soon as he comes to the age of manhood.

Everyone is obliged to pay fifty ducats annually to the Niepo (the Governor of Jerusalem) for permission to make wine, a beverage which is an abomination to the Arabs. This is the whole amount of annual taxation to which the Jews are liable. But the Elders go so far in their iniquity that, in consequence of alleged deficits, they every week impose new taxes, making each one pay what they like; and whoever refuses is beaten by order of a non-Jewish tribunal until he submits.

As for me, so far God has helped me, they have demanded nothing from me as yet; how it may fare with me in the future I cannot tell.

The Christians in Jerusalem are divided into five sects—Catholics, Greeks, Jacobites, Armenians and Johannites (Abyssinians); each one declares the faith of the others to be false, just as the Karaites do with respect to the Rabbanites. Each sect has a separate division in the Church of the Sepulchre, which is very large and has a tower surmounted by a cupola, but without a bell. In this church there are always two persons of each sect who are not allowed to leave it.

On Mount Zion, near the Sepulchre of the Kings, the Franciscans have a large Church. The Sepulchre of the Kings also belonged to them a long time ago, but a rich Ashkenazi, who came to Jerusalem, wished to purchase the graves from the King, and so involved himself in strife with the ecclesiastics, and the Arabs then took the graves away from them and have ever since retained them in their own keeping. When it became known in Venice that the graves had been taken from the Catholics through Jews who had come from Christian lands, an edict was published that no Jew might travel to Jerusalem through Venice; but this edict is now repealed, and every year Jews come in the Venetian galleys and even in the pilgrim ships, for there is really no safer and shorter way than by these ships. I wish I had known all this while I was still in those parts, I would not then have remained so long on the journey. The galleys perform the voyage from Venice here in forty days at the most.

I have taken a house here close to the synagogue. The upper chamber of my dwelling is even in the wall of the synagogue. In the court where my house is there are five inhabitants, all of them women. There is only one blind man living here, and his wife attends on me. I must thank God, who has hitherto vouchsafed me His blessing, that I have not been sick, like the others who came at the same time with me. Most of those who come to Jerusalem from foreign countries fall ill, owing to climatic changes and the sudden variations of the wind, now cold, now warm. All possible winds blow in Jerusalem. It is said that every wind before going where it listeth comes to Jerusalem to prostrate itself before the Lord. Blessed be He that knoweth the truth.

I earnestly entreat that you will not despond nor suffer anxiety on account of my having travelled so far away, and that you will not shed tears for my sake. For God in His mercy has brought me to his holy dwelling, which rejoices my heart and should also delight you. God is my witness that I have forgotten all my former distresses, and all remembrance of my native country has passed away from me. All the memories which I still retain of it centre in your image, revered father, which is constantly before my eyes. Mine eyes are dimmed when I remember that I have left you in your old age, and I fear that lest your tears will recall the sins of my youth.

Now, I beseech you, bestow your blessing upon your servant. Let this letter atone for my absence, for it will show you the disposition of your son and you will no longer be displeased with him. If God will preserve me, I shall send you a letter every year with the galley, which will comfort you. Banish all sorrow from your heart. Rejoice with your dear children and grandchildren who sit around your table. They will nourish and sustain your old age. I have prayed for their welfare and continue to do so, in the sacred places of Jerusalem, the restoration of which, by means of the Messiah, God grant us to witness, so that you may come joyfully to Zion. Amen.

Finished in haste in Jerusalem, the Holy City. May it soon be rebuilt in our days.

From your son, OBADIAH YAREH.

On the 8th Ellul, 5248 (1488).

THE TESTAMENT OF A MARTYR

by K. ARTHUR ABRAHAM

Foreword of Leon Gumiel

Lisbon: The third day of Sivan in the year of Creation 5260 (1500). This document, which I, Leon Gumiel, present now to the world, is the statement of Simon Morata, one time a merchant in the town of Seville.

I am the gaoler mentioned in the record who tended him when in his old age he was confined in the cells of the Spanish Inquisition. Now that I have escaped from the toils of my obnoxious office, I have come to Lisbon, and in accordance with the wishes of Simon Morata, have sought out his brother, the Rabbi Joseph, from whom I have obtained permission to make this publication.

There is little I can say or add to this statement; it is the work of a man who, in the days of his darkness, who with the terrible knowledge of the end he was to come to, wrote yet with vision and strength and a brave heart. Of Simon Morata I must record that he was the soul of integrity, conducted his affairs strictly and faithfully, and was held in high esteem by all who knew him.

Now it suffices for me to state the deep appreciation I feel with the knowledge of the faith he placed in me, and the honor he conferred on me in the keeping of this document, and I must thank God that I have been granted the opportunity to fulfil the mission that Simon Morata entrusted to me.

I

TIME is no more to me than pin points of moments that stab the continuity of my life. The future is never, the present always and yet not, and the past a succession of fleeting images that rise and fall in my mind. But these visions that float and intermingle, vanish and return so that I see in flickering intervals the hot sun, the shimmering earth, the tree blossoms waving in the light lustrous day. Now I see the river, sometimes a stream of gold, sometimes a stream of lead, and now the hazy hills climb high in my mind, where last I heard the ram's horn sound strong and triumphant, its echoes reaching to the heavens, rebounding and falling away. Now I see the solemn moon, the silvered night and the myriads of shining stars, and always, always I see faces; faces young and old, pallid and frightened, feeble and strong, austere and meek, wandering in an awesome procession. Sometimes I hear hoarse cries, cold shrieks and tired moans, and when they are gone I live in long silences.

Often I question myself that all these happenings could have occurred; is it because I have lived with them and I am unable to view them distinctly, objectively? I cannot answer this, but, nevertheless, I know they are true, as true as I am in this dark evil cell. For though they have tortured my body, they cannot torture or kill the memory, so that as I grope in the endlessness of my thoughts a strength seems to come to me from some unknown source, and I remember with crystalline clarity and depth, and I place a finger, as it were, on certain pictured episodes that leap up boldly and say: Of this I shall write, and of that.

But now I must stop these random speculations and put down what is already written, and what by God's will shall be written is done by the hand of Simon Morata, now imprisoned in the Castel de Triana, the Palace of the Inquisition of Seville, for the offence of being a Jew.

On the tenth day of Tammuz in this year of Creation 5255 (1495), I reached, by the grace of God, the age of sixty-three.

I was born in Seville, and most of my life have lived here, as did my father and grandfather, may their souls rest in peace!

My grandfather worshipped in the beautiful synagogue of this town until it was taken from our hands. It is some years since it was converted into a church. Ah, but this year I observed the Fast of Ab alone and silently in this cold cell and sadly remembered Rabbi Meir's poem of sorrow. The lamentable cry of this grief-stricken man arises now in my mind, and as I think the words:

> Dismay hath seized upon my soul; how then
> Can food be sweet to me,
> When, O thou Law, I have beheld base men
> Destroying thee?

I feel how much they typify these times. But what beautiful, sad words! What would I not give to be able to write like this.

I am an old man and, though my palsied fingers tremble, I feel stronger as I commence to write. I have not long to live now, for soon they will cast my dismembered and aching body to the flames, and I pray that before my eyes are dimmed I may complete at least a part of the task I have set myself. But let me add that if much of what I write is disconnected or disjointed, it is because I can only work in snatches and by the light of one feeble candle. It splutters and winks, and I must hold one hand round it in such a way that I may shield its gleams from straying beyond this cell; the friars and gaolers here move softly and cunningly, forever watching, waiting, listening.

This will not be in any sense an historical summary of my time, for I am not one to marshal facts and figures; there are better men that I who will present the account faithfully for the future generations.

Rather will I attempt to portray the things that have transpired more intimately with myself; yet I do not wish it to be thought that I am concerned only with myself. But if it will be remembered that I am no isolated case, that I am as one grain in the sack, one of the thousands who unflinchingly in the face of all things obeyed and loved our Law, then shall I feel that I have not labored in vain.

And now, in case it should be wondered how it is that I am able to write at all, let me explain that I am indebted to one certain gaoler by the name of Gumiel who, at the gravest risk to himself, has furnished me with the material for the making of this record. He is Jew, and it is arranged between us that as I complete these sheets he quietly removes them to his home, so that one day, when I am gone from here and he is freed from his cruel duties, he will endeavor to reach my brother who resides in Lisbon, and place them in his hands.

I believe Gumiel, for though he cloaks himself as a Catholic and is bound to perform his horrible work, he is nevertheless a Jew. A thousand ways has he proved this to me, but he is caught up in the meshes of this gigantic tyrannic machine which grinds the life out of this beautiful country, and he must go round with it or be crushed by it. Yet he has done much good work and secretly helped many Jews, just as he assists me.

But he has to exercise great care, for should this manuscript be discovered, then the truth about him would instantly be known and his life would be snuffed out, much as I snuff out the candle before me; nay, but I am mistaken, the candle light dies quickly, unknowingly, but the light of his life would be extinguished slowly, and, with infinite care, painfully.

II

They arrested me one night quite unexpectedly; but this is their procedure, to descend suddenly on the unsuspecting one. It happened in this wise. I had eaten a little food that eve and after sat till late into the night deeply engrossed reading extracts from the *Light of the Lord,* that profound work of Abraham Crescas, who I think was known to my grandfather. Although I am no scholar and struggle hard in discerning the weightiness of his propositions, I have moments of extreme delight when the subtlety of his arguments reach me, but, at the same time, I feel namelessly perturbed and dwarfed in the presence of such mighty thought.

I do not know exactly what made me drop the book and start up with a fearful expectancy, yet I do know that I felt at once oppressed by an immediate danger; and I did not hear their approach at all for the carriage in which they came had leathered wheels and the hoofs of the mules were covered with some kind of noiseless material.

I say that their arrival was unexpected, but still I had perceived that the immunity that I had enjoyed for three years must some day come to an end. And whilst I ponder I discover that no mystery attaches to my sudden incarceration here. For I remember one day early in the year, when my secretary, Philip, entered my study unannounced and saw therein upon my desk the phylacteries I had forgotten to lock away. These, after a lapse of many years, I had taken to wearing again at the morning prayer, and, of surety, it is a mark of a Jew. Perchance he foolishly let slip a word of this to an acquaintance, and then the ferrets of the Holy Office were set busy upon the trail. So all those years I had lived in my daily outward life as a Catholic were counted as against me, and I was at once condemned.

Now, I often ask myself for what reason do they torture me; what do they wish me to say and what not to say? I am a Jew. I have avowed it firmly and in the beginning, for I have the bitter knowledge that once one is entrapped in the webs of the Inquisition there is no escaping. Therefore, rather than give them the satisfaction of breaking a confession from me by torture, I have told them emphatically that I am a Jew, and have always been so, having observed the rites of my faith as far as I was able to in the quietness and secret loneliness of my home. This does not satisfy them; they ask me why I did not leave the country three years ago when the Expulsion Order was made, and then I am silent.

They take me to the torture chamber, where the flickering candles cast lurid shadows upon the grim walls. They tie my hands and hoist and drop and jerk me until my arms seem no more than channels of torment, through which a convulsing agony darts up and down. After a while all feeling is gone and these arms do not belong to me, but are stanchions from which my body dangles. I close my eyes and before them a world of red color reels round and round, and then deep darkness descends. I see no more, I hear no more, but feel the froth bubbling from my lips.

Sense slowly returns and with it a question rushes into my mind. Is it possible, I ask myself, that these devils were children once? This seems absurd, yet how much does it mean!

But I have not spoken. They must not know that it was to be near the grave of my wife that I have remained. Sweet Rachel, reverently I breathe her name, so dear was she in life to me that I, who am alone now—our union was not blessed with children—had resolved never to desert her last resting-place. She lies buried in the little cemetery above the hills, and her burial place I watched and guarded until the moment I was shut in here.

Now should they rack me with all their fourteen tortures, I shall keep silent. They will never know this, for to them to desecrate the grave of a child of Israel is considered a worthy deed. Many a time had I heard my grandfather speak of Vincent Ferrer the Dominican Friar who had said that all things were legitimate in converting mankind to Christianity. Whether he countenanced such vile things as the breaking open of graves I do not know, but it sufficed to have the knowledge that he believed in his mission and led on the people to perpetrate atrocities of unspeakable cruelty.

Methinks it was he who, with an armed band, entered and seized our synagogue and pronounced it a church. If they are to be reviled, perhaps they are to be pitied as well.

This country has been for long in a state of bloodthirsty turmoil and, though the tears blind my eyes as I say it, I thank God that Rachel died before the Inquisition was established in this town. They would have broken her tender body and violated her pure spirit, for she was a true daughter of Israel and the glory of her faith was a beacon that shone always in her heart.

Rabbi Asher ben Yechiel (Asheri) wrote: "Do not obey the Law for reward, nor avoid sin for fear of punishment, but serve God for love," and she lived and died in the spirit of these words.

Could I but say that I have followed this inspiring maxim! I have sinned grievously, but of this later.

III

Restraint and solitude within this gloomy vault sometimes bring despondency which merges into despair, and in my affliction I cup my face in my hands, droop on my low stool and rock myself over far-away dreams.

Youth and my home return to me and I think of my happy boyhood days when, with my brother, I would rove through the long narrow streets and by the river, seeking the nodding reflections of the overhanging trees.

I lived at the time in my grandfather's home, and though he was a stern old man we had a measure of freedom. Holy Days came and were celebrated in the time-honored fashion and now, with a stirring emotion, I feel the poetry and color of that life. Ay, even the Day of Atonement, that grim, long day of abnegation, was surrounded with a halo of its own; the blast of the ram's horn blended in me a feeling of mystery, fear and joy.

Many things spurt up in my mind, but I will tell of one particular episode of my home life that stands out boldly and clear.

Although my grandfather was constantly occupied with his daily affairs, he did not let them entirely distract him from exact observances, and in this he would keep a keen and wise eye upon me, often quelling the waywardness of my turbulent spirit.

I remember one day when I removed my hat soon after a meal and at the moment my grandfather had commenced to say grace. He could not speak immediately to me for the prayer was on his lips, but he signed quickly to me to cover my head. I rather think it was ignorant day-dreaming than boyish obstinacy that made me ignore his unmistakable gestures, for I remained there immovably staring at him, my hat still in my hands.

The prayer ended and then a storm of such severity burst over me that, stricken and dazed, I was unable to utter one word in defence of myself.

"Infidel!" he shouted at me. "Heathen!" he thundered. "Thinkest thou that one can sit during a prayer with the head uncovered? Have they not taught thee better at thy lessons, Never must that happen again, else I shall exact a strict penance from thee, young as thou art."

Such a man was my grandfather. The word, the meaning of tolerance was unknown to him, and, methinks, there was justification in this unrelenting discipline.

To tolerate was to imply countenance of misdeeds, and such relaxation would have been a sign of weakness which would give strength inversely. But I do not think that my grandfather acted from the motive of this thought; he was too truly sincere.

My younger brother was destined to become a rabbi, and, as a boy, was already versed in various studies that showed his bent in that direction. By the goodness of Providence he moved to Lisbon years ago, where he still dwells. My grandfather and my father being engaged in business, it was meet that I should follow in their footsteps.

Hence, as I grew older, I found myself harassed and pressed to attend and to listen to conferences and discussions from which I might gradually learn and fit myself for the things of commerce. Yet youth does not care to be enchained, for the sunlit days call and the scented breezes murmur strange things to the heart.

And so in one year, when feeling all over the country was highly strained, I, who should have been present at a meeting in my grandfather's house to watch the exchanging of certain deeds and the signing of an important contract, escaped, and because of the intricate business in hand, meseems was not missed.

And now I come to the most bitter thing of my young life, the more bitter because of its effect upon me in later years.

But to continue. It was with something akin to delight at my sudden freedom that I went wandering about the streets gazing dreamily on the slow-moving panorama of its life. The Feast of St. Dominic had been celebrated but a few days ago, when a fever and an excitement had rent the air. But the signs of the recent festivity did not appear much in evidence now.

Soon had the market square resumed its lazy hum beneath the warm golden sun, and the white-fronted houses flashed back the light and remained drowsily inert. Voices murmured vaguely and the tinkle of distant swinging bells was but imaginary music to my ears.

Now I came upon sturdy dames, sauntering and chattering volubly, a pomaded cavalier strutted by haughty and alone, and young señors there were who walked slowly and returned quick smiles and glances to the dark-eyed languorous señoritas. And here a singing pedlar came, trotting his fat mule over the rugged stones and passed me by; now a jolly friar with a rotund shining face and mild twinkling eyes would amble along, exchanging sallies with a brother of his order, in whose sly, swarthy face the eyes burnt deeply and cruelly.

How could I see tragedy hovering invisibly in the air, stalking and preparing to violate the poise of this serene atmosphere? How could I, so blissfully unconscious, be aware of the evil, fostered by ignorance, that continually lurked behind those faces and within those heads?

I do not know what made me turn my footsteps towards the Illescas Road, unless it was because I saw many hurrying in that direction, and boyish eagerness for adventure led me on.

How often I now regret and curse that time, for in a moment that was swifter than the movement of an eyelash I found myself caught up in the center of a seething crowd.

With what rapidity events transpired I will not attempt to outline, but the impression of gleaming eyes, distorted faces, brandishing fists, loud cries and shrieks, burning shops and the acrid smell of smoke still remains with me.

"Death to the Jews!" they shouted. "Who killed the child of Gomez?" The cry was uttered by one and was immediately taken up, and like a straw taken up by a mighty wind and tossed in the air it was tossed from mouth to mouth.

The uproar increased, and terror-stricken I fought and tried to push my way out of the mob, but after some vain attempts I realized that my antics would soon give rise to suspicion; to endeavor to escape was to court danger.

Breathless and cowed, I swayed with the crowd and was forced to witness the demoniacal act which will persist in my mind's eye until the end of my days.

I saw the rotund figure of Benjamin Venal, a druggist, appear at the door of his shop; his face was lividly furious, his arms gesticulating wildly. He shouted, cursed, and fought madly with those nearest him, and then suddenly I saw a long knife rise up above him. It curved in its swing, shone like an evil shuddering rainbow in the sunny smoky air, and then swept swiftly down.

One moment I saw Benjamin Venal quivering with life and in the next moment I saw him rock, spin forward and disappear.

Then, still entangled in the crowd, I was carried along with it and watched the headless corpse of Venal dragged through the streets and finally deposited on a great bonfire in the Plaza de San Francisco, where it was consumed.

In later years I gathered that in that riot Miriam, the daughter of Benjamin Venal, had been suddenly seized and violated; her naked body was found afterwards, wounded and torn.

Ah, if there were means whereby one could eradicate from the memory abhorred things such as these, then should I shamelessly possess myself of such means and forever cast from my mind that day's evil picture.

But the scene remains engraved on my memory, hammered in my mind hard as an iron bar embedded immovably in an iron wall, and such was the impression on me that years after, when the passage of time should have stilled the recollection, it reacted on me vividly.

IV

Some three or four years before the edict of Isabella and Ferdinand was issued—that is perhaps seven or eight years ago—this town witnessed another riot of a serious nature, in which I was destined to suffer.

It was the direct result of the fierce preaching of John Sebastion, a Dominican Friar, whom I saw that day haranguing a great concourse of people in the Plaza de San Francisco.

I had business to attend to, but stopped to listen to him for a while, and in that short moment I heard how eloquently and with what force he spoke. His face streaming with perspiration, and with his arms wide flung, he denounced the Jews and cursed them for their unbending obstinacy.

"We are the servants of God," he acclaimed, "and to them who reject and follow not the true church and the true faith we ask them, how can ye hope to enter the Kingdom of Heaven, how can ye have salvation if ye remain self-willed and blind?" Thus he spoke, and the crowd rocked and murmured under the fire of his words, and then afterwards, together with other friars, he led a vast procession through the streets.

Preceded by the Inquisitors, who carried the white silk flag of the Holy Office, with its Christ upon the Cross emblazoned in the centre, the great cortege solemnly wound its way towards the cathedral where, before the grand sculptured portals, Sebastion fell on his knees and in an ecstasy of emotion shook with prayer. And I, in the same moment, in a secret niche, stared and suddenly remembered and thrilled with the words: "Hear, O Israel, the Lord our God, the Lord is One."

I hurried home, however, apprehensive as to the outcome of this unexpected happening, and yet still feeling the inward surge of a triumphant emotion with the memory of those long-remembered words.

The riot broke out later in the day and spread down the Calle de Lugo, burst before my doors, and then, as though I had been guilty of some violent deed, I was dragged from my house, spat upon and shamefully dishonored.

But I will not write of my sufferings for some might say that in them I seek excuse for my sin. Yet this I must tell, that I was at the last extremity and might have never bowed to their insistent demands to become baptized, when the horror of my youth suddenly rose up before my eyes. I saw, in a red fleeting vision, the headless body of Benjamin Venal trailing through the streets. I saw myself, I saw smoke and blood. . . .

In a frenzy of immediate fear I succumbed to their fierce exhortations and consented.

Thence did I become baptized and afterwards in the eyes of all appeared as a good member of Catholicism. Yet my heart muttered unendingly against this apostasy.

This, it murmured, I should not have done, and I lived in shadowed darkness with the thought.

Yet, whilst I whispered, a new thought would insistently arise, and with it a triumphant song would ring within me; because I told myself that I was still a Jew, and this deed and time were but a dark passage of life through which I must go, even if it was unwillingly. It was as though I could see my body being forced through a sunless hole of minute circumference, a hole which it detested, but through which it must go, whilst I myself remained without, wondering and staring at its insensate writhings.

I saw myself aloof, beyond, as this other being crouched beneath me, confusing the eyes of the onlookers. Sometimes a bitter laugh would surge within me, because they could not see me, the invisible, inviolable me, but only this other self of mine, and whilst I saw it tortured and crawling, they saw it upright and true.

I saw myself like this, and thought that I am like this, not because I had willed it, but because circumstance had forced it on me. But I had failed to uphold Asheri's good precepts, and now, when I look back and consider these two selves of mine that I had constructed in my imagination, I do so with a feeling of sorrow and amused pity.

I relaxed through weakness and for fear, but I offer no excuses, for to endeavor to justify myself would be to condone the wrong of the action and to pretend that my conscience remained untroubled, and that would be to lie.

Although I might try to seek out some justification for my conversion, deep in my innermost self it seemed to me that the gift of life was but a sad reward for the harsh rumblings of conscience and the loss of my own self-esteem.

And if I have endeavored to console myself, it was by deep prayer and in the remembrance that Judaism was still the light of my heart and burnt the more brightly for being oppressed. Secretly I turned to it with more readiness than if I had had freedom and plenty of time.

v

Now, I must make record of a singularly beautiful incident, which took place but quite recently within these vaults.

Though the days seem long and slow and fused with an unending weariness, yet time speeds onwards and, with Gumiel's aid, I have counted the months and remembered the Holy Days of the year. The Fast of Ab has gone, New Year and the Day of Atonement have followed. Succot has been and passed, and now Hanukkah has come and gone; Hanukkah, the Feast of Dedication, wherein, fifty years back, I, as a boy, would stand and muse before the dancing candle flames and see fantastic pictures glimmering and hovering about the golden gleams.

And now this Hanukkah within this Palace of Inquisition was suddenly imbued with a significant touching beauty.

It happened on the second day towards eve that I fell into a quiet sleep and was visited with a swift dream of exquisite freedom. I was free once more, wandering beneath a brilliant sky in a day-lighted world again. I saw dear faces, faces of children, of men and women happy and serene. I heard voices, light and gay, and the sound of sweet singing startled my ears, whereupon I awoke and, to my astonishment, found that the singing of my dream was an enchanting reality.

With a beating heart I listened, and the voice I heard was surely that of a boy, boldly singing the hymn, *O Fortress, Rock of My Salvation.*

I was unable to discern from which part of the vault the voice arose, but, with straining ears, I crouched mute and awed by the utter strangeness of this event. Soon I wondered how it was that the gaolers had not interfered and suppressed the singer, yet perhaps they were swayed as much by the magic of the hymn and the appealing softness of the boyish voice, and, affected thus, they were compelled to pretend their ignorance of its meaning.

There was a note of sadness transfusing the hymn, yet it swelled clearly and rang through the iron-barred cells fearlessly, and when it concluded, the hollow silence that followed seemed fraught with a thousand memories. Suddenly I drooped my head and with my heart full the tears rushed into my eyes.

Who was the singer? Gumiel has informed me that he is but a child, a boy not long made a "Son of the Commandment," whose father was one Mendes, a citizen of Valencia. Yet another young life to be stolen away in its early splendor, a boy whose pale moving face flits like a vision before me, and to whom I owe such a debt of gratitude that he can never know, for that moment of unaffected joy he brought me in all these clouded hours.

VI

I feel I cannot write much more now, yet I have still to recount my visit to Granada and the occurrences there, when the illustrious Don Isaac Abrabanel petitioned the King and Queen to revoke the Edict of Expulsion.

I had journeyed to Granada in company with Pedro Gonzolez, a Spaniard, a kindly old man who considered with foreboding the course of events that were transpiring in Castile. Again and again he would quote to me the teaching of St. Bernard, who had written: "Take heed what you do to the Jews, for whosoever touches them is like one who touches the apple of the eye of Jesus, for they are His flesh and blood." This he truly believed, and would utter with a determined shake of his hoary head.

The journey to Granada was long and tedious, and the country across which we travelled was stony, pale and yellow, desolate and treeless, and ranged on the horizon continually with the shadow of distant hills. We fell in with other wayfarers towards the termination of our journey, and finally arrived in Granada some few days before Don Isaac was to appear at the Hall of Ambassadors in the Alhambra.

Granada, with its great open squares, its whitewashed streets, its dark and narrow alleyways, teemed with excited movement and the breathlessness of suspense. Jews from all parts seemed to have foregathered there.

But I had still to maintain my appearance as a Catholic, and hence rested at the home of Pedro Gonzolez. His house was a grand building with marble courts, shaded balconies, bright-hued tiles and urns of blossoming trees set in the patios; most ironically enough each room was blessed with statues or images of the saints.

I, however, really had no eye for these beautiful surroundings, being impatient with the desire to learn of any news that might bring relief to the anxious waiting people.

On the day that Don Isaac had audience with King Ferdinand and Queen Isabella I went out into the streets and joined the palpitating throng.

The road to the Alhambra was lined with Jews; merchants and bankers mingled with hawkers; haughty, scented nobleman rubbed shoulders with bearded Jews; scholars there were, rabbis and artisans and pedlars, all moving forward, watching with eager expectation for the outcome of the negotiations.

I stood amongst them on the edge of the crowd and finally saw Don Isaac return; there was no need for him to speak or to tell of the result of his audience with the ruling sovereigns. His noble face saddened and distraught passed me by and told its tale, and soon it was murmured from ear to ear and spread from lip to lip: the Edict was to remain and all Jews were to leave the country within four months.

Of the great flight, I witnessed more than I can ever hope to write. Harrowing pictures float continually before my eyes, pictures of vast sorrowful movement of humanity who, with the God of Israel quickening their hearts, struck onwards and away from the saddened beauty of the country which had sheltered them for hundreds of years. Would that I could have joined them and sought a new freedom in other countries, but the joy of my life was here, and here I was compelled to remain.

VII

Now I have said most that I wish to say, and though there still arise in my thoughts many untold things, I seek rest now, and will sit in silence to await the end.

But this I must add, that when I die *Adonai, Adonai!* (O God, O God!) will be on my lips, and should they restrain me and muffle my mouth, may my heart take up the cry and shout *Adonai Elohanu, Adonai Ehad!* (The Lord, our God, is One!)

VISIT TO THE POPE

by DAVID REUBENI [1]

I, DAVID, the son of King Solomon, of righteous memory, from the wilderness of Habor, entered the gate of the City of Rome on the 15th day of Adar, 1524, and a Gentile from Venice came to me and spoke with me in Arabic, and I was angry with him. I went to the Pope's palace, riding on horseback, and my servant before me, and the Jews also came with me, and I entered the presence of Cardinal Egidio; and all the Cardinals and Princes came to see me, and with the said Cardinal was Rabbi Joseph Ashkenazi, who was his teacher, and the physician, Rabbi Joseph Sarphati; and I spoke to the Cardinal, and my interpreter was the learned man who came with me, and the Jews heard all that I spoke to the Cardinal, and I said to him that to the Pope I would complete my message. I stayed with the Cardinal all day till the eve of Sabbath, and he promised to bring the matter before the Pope tomorrow. I went away with Rabbi Joseph Ashkenazi and with Rabbi Raphael, the old man who lived in the same house, and we took our Sabbath meal and slept till the morning; and I went with them to the Synagogue in order to pronounce the blessing of deliverance from peril before the scroll of the Law. Men, women, and children came to meet us all the way until we entered the house of the said Rabbi Raphael, and I fasted on that Sabbath day. All day long men and women, Jews and Gentiles came to visit me until evening. Cardinal Egidio sent for Rabbi Joseph Ashkenazi to tell me that the Pope was very pleased, and wished to see me on Sunday before 11. And so in the morning, before prayers, they gave me a horse and I went to Borghetto Santo Gile to the house of an old man, the brother-in-law of Rabbi Joseph Sarphati, before morning

[1] David Reubeni was one of the most romantic figures in the sixteenth century. He claimed to be the ambassador of his brother, supposedly the king of the tribe of Reuben, and that he had been directed to secure munitions from the Pope in order to recover Palestine from the Moslems. His audience with Pope Clement is described in this selection from his diary, the whole of which covers the years 1522-1525 (the complete translation may be found in *Jewish Travelers* by Elkan Adler). According to Abraham Farissol, a contemporary, he was "short, stocky, of a swarthy complexion and an expert horseman." His actual origin remains an historical enigma.

prayer; and I prayed there, and many Jews came to me, may God keep them and multiply them a thousand fold! At eight o'clock I went to the house of the Pope and entered Cardinal Egidio's room, and with me were about twelve old and honoured Jews. As soon as the Cardinal saw me, he rose from his chair and we went, I and he, to the apartment of the Pope, and I spoke with him, and he received me graciously and said, "The matter is from the Lord"; and I said to him, "King Joseph and his elders ordered me to speak to thee that thou shouldst make peace between the Emperor and the French King, by all means, for it will be well with thee and them if thou makest this peace, and write for me a letter to these two Kings, and they will help us and we will help them; and write also for me to King Prester John (i.e. the King of Abyssinia). The Pope answered me, "As to the two Kings between whom thou askest me to make peace, I cannot do it, but if thou needest help the King of Portugal will assist thee, and I will write to him and he will do all, and his land is near to thy country and they are accustomed to travel on the great sea every year, more than those in the lands of those other Kings"; and I replied to the Pope, "Whatever thou wishest I will do, and I will not turn to the right or left from what thou biddest me, for I have come for God's service, and not for anything else, and I will pray for thy welfare and good all the days of my life." And the Pope asked the Cardinal, "Where does the Ambassador lodge?" and he answered, "The Jews asked him to go with them," and the honourable Jews who were with the Pope told him, "Let the Ambassador stay with us, for we will honour him for the sake of thy honour," and the Pope said to them, "If you will do honour to him I will pay all your expenses"; and I said to the Pope, "I wish to come before thee once every two days, for to see thee is as seeing the face of God"; and the Pope answered me that he ordered Cardinal Egidio to come with me every time I came to see him, and I took leave of the Pope and went from before him, and I went with the Jews and rejoiced and was glad of heart. I returned to the old man's house by way of Santo Gile, but Aaron, the warden, was angry that I went to the old man's house, and told the Cardinal that the wardens and the whole congregation had prepared a house for the Ambassador and provided servants for him, because I could not remain alone; the Cardinal wrote me that I should go with them, and I went with them. They prepared for me a fine dwelling with three, big, good rooms, and the master of the house was called Joseph, and he had three sons, the eldest Moses, the second Benjamin, and the third Judah; and they all waited on me, and I stayed in their house six weeks, and I went to the Cardinal's house five days consecutively, for the other Cardinals went to his house and they consulted me from morning to evening, and I fasted in that house six days consecutively; and on Friday they boiled some water for me and put in it many herbs. They did all this for the love of me, because they said that it was medicine after the fast, but my soul was weary, and I wished to drink water, and they gave me the boiled water and I drank a stomach full. This water caused me a great and strong pain in the stomach, for I was not accustomed to drink hot water after a fast. I fasted in Jerusalem six times, seven days and nights, and in Venice, six days and nights, and after all these fasts I drank nothing but cold water with much sugar, and that did me no harm; but they only did it for my good, to give me hot water, because they did not know my constitution, may the householders and the warden be blessed! A great sickness came upon me and I said to them, "Find me a bath of hot water for I wish to go there"; and a man came called Yomtob Halevi, and he prepared me a bath and a good couch to sleep upon, and I entered the bath and slept there, and that day I let much blood, cupping all my limbs, and then I sent for the physician, Rabbi Joseph Sarphati, and said to him, "Look how I am; if thou wishest to get a great name, let me stay in thy house and remain with me until my sickness leaves me." He did so, and I stayed in his house three months, and he paid all the expenses and for all I required, may the lord bless him and his household! He gave me to eat and gave me various kinds of remedies, and boiled wine for me to drink and heated herbs and placed them on my feet, and washed my feet and anointed me, and took olive oil and put it in a big vessel; and I entered and washed in that hot olive oil, and I came out from the hot oil and lay on a good bed, and they changed the sheets each time, and I lay on the bed like a dead man; and they saw that there was gravel in my water, which is a bad sign, and I told them that I would not die from this illness until I had brought Israel to Jerusalem, built the altar, and offered sacrifice; but I got no sleep and was in great pain and lay between life and death, and they said to me, "Wilt thou make confession, for that will neither bring death near nor keep it away"; and I was angered with them, and said, "Go in peace; I do not wish to say the confession, for I trust in God, that he will stay with me and save me." They were astonished at my good constitution and pleased, and God sent a great sweat on me on that day and I was healed from the great sickness. My servants were with me, Hayyim, and the Cantor, and Mattathias, and Yomtob, and David Pirani, and Simcha, and Solomon Gabani, and an Arab Jew, Shua, and his brother Moses, and a third called Sabbatai; and they all stayed in the house of Rabbi Joseph Sarphati, day and night and waited on me and slept in the house, and I called Rabbi Joseph Sarphati and said to him, "Find me a hot bath," and he prepared a bath in the Synagogue of the Sephardim, and I got in and out; and Judah Kutunia prepared for us a great feast, an hour after the bath. Then I returned to the house of Rabbi Joseph Sarphati, but did not wish to reside there because of the sick men in the house, and I called the physician, Rabbi Moses Abudarhin, to find me another house; and he replied that he had a good room in his house, and said to me that he had three sons, Joseph, Samuel and Isaac, who would wait upon me. I stayed in his house from Wednesday until after Sabbath; and he had a grown-up daughter, who could read Scripture, and who prayed daily morning and evening prayer, and on the Sabbath she had great rejoicing and danced from joy, and on the Sunday she was stricken with the plague; and a wise woman called Rabith, a teacher of infants, and the teacher of that girl, came to me and said, "Pray for the daughter of Rabbi Moses Abudarhin, for the fever is come upon her last night"; and, as soon as I heard the words of the woman, I called Rabbi Moses and said to him, "Find me a garden, for I wish to go into the garden"; and I sent for me servants and the three sons of Rabbi Moses, and went with them into a garden, and we stayed there all that day until night, and then I sent Joseph with Rabbi Moses to tell his father that I could not go into his house until eight days had passed and his daughter was healed from her sickness. Joseph went and returned, and said that his father had prepared a room in the house of Rabbi Isaac Abudarhin, his uncle, and all that was needful for me, and I went with him to his uncle's house, which was an evil house and had an evil smell in it; but Rabbi Isaac had a worthy wife, whose name was Perna, who spoke Arabic, and was wise, and I stayed with them, and also the three sons of Rabbi Moses stayed there until their sister's sickness had ceased. They all waited on me and all expenses were paid by Rabbi Moses Abudarhin, and his brother, Abraham, visited me weekly with gifts; and the daughter of Moses Abudarhin died that week, and her brothers stayed in my house until forty days had elapsed. Three months I stayed in this house, only because of my affection for them, for the house was very evil, and the Christian lords came to visit me in a house which was not fitting. After that I sent a letter to the Cardinal to tell him that I had left the house of Joseph Sarphati because of the illness that had come upon me in that house, and that I was now staying in a house which was not fitting nor proper; and immediately he sent to the wardens and requested them to prepare a good and proper house for the needs of myself and four servants. The wardens hired or rented for me four rooms and paid six months' rent, and my servants prepared all the rooms nicely with a nice bed, and in the big room they made a synagogue with a scroll of the law and thirty lamps lighted therein. The servants waited on me for the love of God, and asked no wage of me and vowed to come with me anywhere that I should go, and my scribe, Rabbi Elijah, the teacher, the son of Joab, and his brother, Benjamin, the Cantor, remained with me and waited on me all the time that I remained in Rome. To the servant who came with me from Candia, that wicked Joseph, I gave clothes and money and sent him to his father in Naples, because every day he made quarrels and strife with the other servants and wanted to rule over them. He also slandered me to Don Miguel, the Ambassador of the King of Portugal, saying that I had come hither to bring the Marano Jews back to their Judaism, and the Maranos in Rome heard this and sought to slay him, and I begged them to do him no harm and sent him away, and I stayed in this house until the New Year.

Cardinal Egidio went to Viterbo and I wondered who would help me and stand between me and the Pope. I saw a man whose name was Rabbi Daniel, of Pisa, who used to frequent the Pope, and lived in a house near the Pope's, a very rich man and a Kabalist, and I decided to ask him. I spoke and said to him, "I see that you are honoured and considered by the Pope and all the Cardinals. I want you to be interpreter between me and the Pope, and to advise me and show me the good way, for the love of God and the love of the house of Israel and the love of King Joseph, my brother, and his elders of the wilderness of Khabor; and God will show you more honour than you have yet had if you do this in His service. I have come from East to the West, for the sake of God's service and the love of Israel, who are under the dominion of Edom and Ishmael." I then told him all the secrets of my heart and the hints and the secrets told me by my brother King Joseph; there was nothing I did not tell him, because I saw that he was good and upright in the eyes of man and God; and then I said to him, "God's secret is to them that fear him." The said Rabbi Daniel vowed that he would not journey or move from Rome until he had received letters from the Pope for me, and he would be interpreter between us; and he also vowed not to leave me on the road, but to go with me on the ship I was to enter; and he forthwith wrote a letter to the Pope, and I sent him by Hayyim, my servant, to Ratieri, and he said to him, "The Ambassador gives thee a thousand greetings and sends this letter to you to hand to the Pope, and he wishes to know at what hour he can get an answer to the letter." He took the letter and said to Hayyim, "Go in peace, and come back for the answer in eighteen hours." Next day I sent Hayyim to the Ratieri, and as soon as he entered he said, "Go call thy lord, the Ambassador, and let him come speedily before the Pope, because he summons him." Then Hayyim, my servant, returned with the servant of Rabbi Daniel of Pisa, brought me a horse, and I went to the Pope with all my servants; and they opened all the rooms for me; and I entered the room nearest the Pope and I said to the guards of the Pope's rooms that I did not wish to appear before the Pope until Rabbi Daniel of Pisa should come, because he is interpreter between us; and when Rabbi Daniel came I said to him, "Go thou first before the Pope"; and he entered and returned to me and I went with him and I spoke to the Pope as follows, "I have stood before thee for nearly a year and it is my will for God's sake and thy honour that thou shouldst write me the letters which I asked of thy Holiness for Prester John, and also all the Christians whose lands I shall traverse, whether great or small"; and Rabbi Daniel spoke to the Pope, who said, "I will do all that the Ambassador desires." Then I and Rabbi Daniel of Pisa left the Pope, happy and of good courage, and we went in peace to my home; but there were then in Rome four or five slanderers, and God put repentance in their hearts that they should return from their evil way; and there were also strong Jews in Rome and Italy, mighty and lionhearted for all work, and suitable for war, but the Jews who are in Jerusalem and Egypt and Iraq, and all the Moslem countries, are faint hearted and prone to fear and fright and not fitted for war like the Italian Jews. May the Almighty increase them a thousandfold, and bless them!

Within a few days the letters came from the Pope and Rabbi Daniel gave them to me. That night many Jews came to my house in order to rejoice with me that I had received the letters. Four notables, the heads of the Roman congregation, Rabbi Obadiah of Sforno, and Rabbi Judah of Ascoli, the Physician, and two others came to me. But there were in my house slanderers and spies whom I did not recognize, and they wished to read the brief and the letters which the Pope had written, that they might profit by remembering them; and I was very angry with them, for men told me that they were spies and would go before the scribes of the Pope repeating the words, in order to spoil my business; they caused me much worry and thought. Afterwards the Pope sent for Rabbi Daniel of Pisa and spoke with him about me whether I wished to go, for he would give me leave, and ordered that I should come before him at eighteen o'clock on the 24th of the first Adar, and I and Rabbi Daniel went before him, and I stayed with him about two hours. He spoke to me, saying, "I have given you a letter to King Prester John, and I have also written to the King of Portugal, and I have written to the Christians whose country thou wilt pass so that they should help thee, and honour thee for God's sake and my sake"; and he further said, "Be strong and of good courage and fear not, for God is with thee," and I said to him, "There is none before me but the Almighty and thou, and I am prepared to serve thee all the days of my life, and also King Joseph my brother and all my people's sons are inclined to thee"; and the Pope ordered that they should give me a sign and shield to show to King Joseph my brother, and he also gave me one hundred golden ducats. I would not take the money, but only under compulsion when he said, "Take it for thy servants," and I left the Pope and returned home in peace and joy and a good heart. Then I went to Don Miguel, the King of Portugal's Ambassador, in order to get a safe conduct from him for the journey, and he said, "If thou wishest to go to Pisa, I will write and send thee to Pisa the safe conduct." But he did this by way of trick, and I left his house in anger, and the Pope heard the matter and said to Don Miguel, "Write for him a safe conduct, for I too have written to the King of Portugal"; but he did not obey the Pope, and left Rome for hunting and stayed away a week and returned. I asked a second time for a safe conduct, and he said that he would send it after me to Pisa at any rate, and I believed his words and I went home and Rabbi Daniel went with me, and I said to him that it was my desire to leave Rome tomorrow, in the middle of the month of Nisan, as our fathers left Egypt; and I stayed in Rome till mid-day of the 15th of Adar to arrange my matters and see who of all my servants should go with me. Two went, one called Rabbi Raphael HaCohen, who sang in my home from the day I arrived in Rome, a strong man and warlike, and the second, Jacob HaLevi, even stronger than Raphael Cohen, and he was my servant from the day I arrived in Rome;

and I gave each of them in Rome five ducats in order that they should arrange their affairs, and Rabbi Daniel was with me and promised to give me other servants, and he gave me a third servant, Tobias.

THE AWESOME STORY OF RABBI JOSEPH DE LA REINA [1]

I saw this tale in a very old manuscript which had itself been copied from an even older manuscript found where they store the worn-out books at Safed, may it be builded and established speedily in our days, written by the very hand of Rabbi Judah Meir of blessed memory, the disciple of Rabbi Joseph de la Reina. He was with him at the time of the tremendous work which he performed when he was in the land of Galilee which is Safed, may it be builded and established speedily in our days, and set his heart to importune and bring the Redemption. It seems to me it must have been at a very early time, for we do not know the period at which this work was performed; Rabbi Moses Cordovero of blessed memory quotes it in the book Pardes, *and I have also found it recorded in the books in praise and honor of Rabbi Isaac, the great Ari of blessed memory, that Rabbi Joseph took on flesh in the form of a black dog and kept coming to the Ari of blessed memory, weeping and entreating to be brought back from his evil ways and mended, because he had employed the Divine names of Power. And I have seen fit to copy it here, and thus it reads:*

THERE is the tremendous and awesome tale of Joseph de la Reina, who was a great and wise man, well versed in the knowledge of the Practical Kabala and dwelling in the land of Galilee which is Safed, may it be builded and established speedily, in our days. The time came that he set his heart to importune and bring the Redemption and cause Evil to pass away from the earth. Now he had five disciples with him day and night to attend his requests, and they too were versed in that art of Kabala in the measure that they had learnt from him. And he said to them, "My sons, I have devoted my heart to studying and exploring the wisdom which God has given me; for what profiteth the spending of our days without a purpose and a use; an

---

[1] Rabbi Joseph de la Reina appears to have lived in the early decades of the sixteenth century. Dr. Scholem of the Hebrew University in Jerusalem has found references to him in the kabalistic manuscripts of that period. He is spoken of by Rabbi Moses Cordovero, one of the systematizers of the Kabala, and he appears in the legends of Rabbi Isaac Luria, known as the Ari. The tale told here first assumed its present form some time in the seventeenth century, and immediately became one of the gems of Jewish folklore. The story deals with one of the central themes of Jewish mysticism: the coming of the Messiah and the triumphant Return to the land of Israel. The geography and topography do not apply to the land of Israel of fact; but they are true of the land of Israel of Jewish imagination and legend. Translated from the Hebrew by I. M. Lask.

not for nought has God vouchsafed me of this wisdom, save to render satisfaction to our Creator and cause the spirit of Evil and its abominations to pass away from the earth, and to bring our Messiah who shall free us from our troubles."

Then his five disciples answered as with one voice, "Our lord, our teacher and our rabbi, we stand ready for thy commands and all that thou desirest we shall fulfill; for the Lord thy God is with thee, and we are thy servants and thy disciples; therefore do whatever is thy soul's desire." To that he answered, "If so, do this; purify yourselves, change your garments, be prepared and approach not your womenfolk for three days, and make ready provisions; for on the third day we go forth to the fields, to return to our homes no more until the Children of Israel are settled each one on his own portion in the Holy Land with the aid of the Divine Worker of Wonders in Whose hand is power, Who giveth the weary strength in their right hand, the Lord who is mighty with power."

When the disciples heard the words of their master they rose with great speed and devotion to don new garments, and they purified themselves and changed their under-garments, and prepared themselves provision and food, pure bread which they baked for themselves in purity, and were touched of no woman's hand. On the third day they came to their master and found him in his House of Study in great holiness and purity and alone, with his head bowed between his knees. As they entered he raised his head and said to them, "Come, my sons, blest of the Lord; may the sweetness of the Lord our God be upon us; may it be His will that the Divine Presence should rest upon the work of our hands, and may the Holy and Blest One assent and aid us for the glory of His name." And they answered and said, "Amen, so may the Lord say and may the favour of the Divine Names of Power prosper in your hands."

After these words Rabbi Joseph took all manner of spices and set a scribe's inkhorn at his loins and said to them, "Come, let us go forth." And they went forth and came to Meron, to the grave of Rabbi Simeon ben Yohai; and they prostrated themselves on his grave and lodged there all that night, sleeping no more than in fitful snatches.

In the morning shortly before the morning star arose Rabbi Joseph fell into deep slumber; and Rabbi Simeon with his son Rabbi Eleazar came to him in dream and said to him, "Why dost thou set thy head under a burden too heavy for thee to bear. Nevertheless thy purpose is so desirable as to make it possible for thee to succeed; therefore be exceedingly careful and pay great heed to your soul." And he replied, "The great God knoweth my purpose and the Merciful One seeketh the heart, and will aid me for the sake of the glory of His far-praised name." Then they replied, "May the Lord thy God grant thy wish."

When day came they proceeded toward Tiberias, passing through the countryside till they came to the forest in which there are many, many trees. There they stayed all day, never ceasing from study and fasting, and they neither looked upon nor saw any man or any living thing save birds of the air alone; and they were busied with permutations of the letters of the Divine Names and with the awesome devotions which bring Union with the Divine Presence and which were known to them. And every morning they went to dip themselves twenty-six times successively in the sea of Tiberias, corresponding to the numerical value of HAVAYAH, the name of God the Ever Present; and for each dipping they absorbed themselves in the suitable permutation and devotion of Union with the Divine Presence which was known to them. This they did for three days without ceasing, spending the days in fasting and at night eating nothing that had been alive, neither flesh nor fish, and not wine nor strong drink.

On the third day, about the time of the afternoon prayers, Rabbi Joseph and his disciples arose, and he recited the afternoon prayers in a pleasant voice, with great devotion and closed eyes. When he reached the passage, "Hear our voices," he added, "Answer us." And where the Holy Name of the Ever Present is read as though it were *The Lord,* there they pronounced the Great Name as it is written with the known vowels and the proper devotions for Union with the Divine Presence and he urged and entreated greatly with long prayers and mighty conjurations to all the angels on high with whom he was familiar; and at length he pronounced the name of the Ever Present with the permutation of forty-two letters, crying out, "Answer me at this time and this very season," and by the power of this Great Name he conjured Elijah the prophet to come at once to him in waking and converse with him and instruct him in what he should do in order to bring his thought into action. When he ended his prayer they all fell to earth on their faces, and suddenly Elijah the prophet, hastening at great speed, appeared to them, and said to them, "Behold, I am come now; then what can I do in your behalf and what is your wish that you must urge so with your prayers?" Then Rabbi Joseph and his disciples rose to their feet, bowed to the ground, and he said, "Peace to our Lord, Father, Father, chariot of Israel and the horsemen thereof, prophet of truth, holy of the Lord, bringing good tidings, sounding salvation; let it not be evil in the eyes of my lord that I have been importunate to bring thee to me; for it is open and known to our God that not for my own honor or myself have I put thee to trouble, but because I am zealous for the honor of the Holy and Blest One and His Divine Presence. Now for thee it is indeed fitting that thou be zealous for the Lord of Hosts, for such is thy task; therefore hearken I pray thee to my entreaty, and show me the way by which I can subdue the Other Side, and strengthen and add power to the Side of Holiness."

Then Elijah the prophet answered him, "Know that the thing thou dost think to do is too heavy for thee and thou wilt not prosper for because of transgression the power of the demons and Samael and his retainers has waxed mighty and thou wilt not prevail over them; for there is need of even more holiness and solitude and separation from the business of the world and more penances and ritual bathings; for without these thou wilt not prevail against them, and they will smite thee and harm thee. Yet know that thy wish is desirable and if thou canst turn thy thought into a deed blessed art thou and goodly thy portion. Nevertheless I counsel thee to cease, lest Samael and his hosts smite thee who will not prevail over him."

And Rabbi Joseph answered and said: "My lord, I pray thee not to weaken my hands; but strengthen and sustain me, for I have sworn an oath that I return not home till I bring forth the Holy Presence from the dust to the light and raise it on high. And thou, the blest of the Lord, set thy hand with us and instruct me suitably what I have to do and the commandments I must keep. Whatever my lord may command his servant, for it I am prepared to deliver up my soul and my spirit, even unto death, so be it is for the honor of the Holy and Blest One and His Presence. Let but thy mouth declare what it behooves us to do, for upon thee are our eyes."

When Elijah the prophet heard his words that he was prepared to perish for the honor of the Holy and Blest One and His Presence, he said to him, "What further words can I add? But if thou prosper and canst stand against Samael and his retainers and can cleave to that which I command this day, happy art thou and thy portion is good, and sweet thy lot; now this is the thing thou must do, thou and thy disciples; remain dwelling in the field far from any inhabited place as you have done till now. Let neither man nor beast be seen or found with you. Dwell in this spot for twenty-one days. Eat nothing and drink nothing save from night to night. Let your food and your drink be bread and water alone. Never eat to fullness, but be content with the amount which you yourselves know will sustain you. Night by night diminish the quantity of your food till you have accustomed yourselves to eat the smallest quantity possible. And make yourselves accustomed to smell spices and sweet savours in order that the matter that is in you shall be clear and cleansed, and you will be able to bear the sight of the Angels on High whom you will bring down to hold converse with you. And every day perform twenty-one ablutions according to the numerical value of *Eheye,* the Ever-future. At the end of the twenty-one days make an interruption and fast for three days on end, day and night, performing the twenty-one ablutions on each day. And on the third day, after the afternoon prayers, proclaim the Great Name of forty-two letters which you know, together with its permutations and devotions, and utter the mighty Name emanating from the verse, 'Seraphim stand over him,' in the fashion you know, with its vowels and its roots. In doing this, be swathed in tallith and tefillin, and cover your faces and conjure by these Holy Names the angel Sandalphon together with his camp.

"Summon them to you and when they come, strengthen yourselves with the aid of some fine savour to smell of; for fear and trembling and great weakness will overpower you at the sound of the crashing and the mighty flame. But cast yourselves straightway to the ground and cry out in a very loud voice, 'Blest be the name of the Glory of His Kingdom for evermore'; and at once Sandalphon and his retainers will say to you, 'Why have you done this thing?' As soon as he speaks to you your souls will forsake you because of the mighty thunder of his speech; and you will remain without strength and your words will be shut within you so that you cannot answer him by reason of your great fear and weakness. Therefore for that occasion have pure frankincense beside you to smell of; and beg and entreat the angel I have mentioned to take hold of you and give you strength so that you can speak. And he will tell you what you should do; for he is the guardian of the path and track, so that the Accusing Satan Samael may not enter the quarters of sanctity; he is advised of his devices and stratagems and knows the places where he fortifies himself and in what measure he depends upon them; so that you will be able to do battle with him. And may your desire be the will of God, and Peace be with you."

As soon as Elijah the prophet went his way Rabbi Joseph and his disciples girded themselves together and strengthened themselves with a united heart, and added further holiness unto their former holiness; they did everything which Elijah had advised them, letting nothing slip of all his command-ments; neither day nor night did they cease their study. They paid no heed to the affairs of This World, but devoted themselves to abstraction and the Work of the Chariot till their natural substance all but vanished. And the appointed number of twenty-one days were fulfilled according to the com-mands of Elijah. Then, Rabbi Joseph and his disciples arose in great fear and trembling and awe, and as soon as the hour for the afternoon prayers arrived, wrapped themselves in their talliths and tefillin, covered their heads and began reciting the afternoon prayers with great devotion, saying, "Answer us" in the fashion already described; and for the substituted name of the Ever Present they pronounced the Great and Awful Name according to its writing and the vowels they knew. Ending the prayers, they fell on their covered faces to the earth, then rose at once to their feet, confessed their sins and the sins of all Israel, and at once cried with all their strength in a mighty voice, "Answer us, God of the Chariot, answer us"; and they conjured by the Name of forty-two letters and by the Name which Elijah had told them, deriving from the verse, 'Seraphim stood above him'; and they conjured the angel Sandalphon to reveal himself to them with all his holy retainers at once by virtue of the power of the Holy Names. And when they finished speaking the Heavens were opened and the angel Sandalphon came suddenly upon them with all his train; and they were a chariot of fire and horses of fire and a fiery flame filling the whole world, and a great crashing. Rabbi Joseph was most exceedingly frightened and there was no spirit left in his heart nor in those of his disciples. They fell on their faces, their hearts melted away, trembling possessed them; but they strengthened themselves and smelt the pure frankincense in their hands and their spirits returned; yet they remained possessed by awe and trembling and great weakness so they could not speak.

When the angel Sandalphon reached them with his train he cried, "Son of Adam, crawling worm, how hast thy heart led thee to shake the Upper and the Nether Worlds so that thou didst take no care to heed and perceive thy little worth! Do thyself the honour of remaining at home lest my hosts smite thee to ashes with the breath of their mouths!" But Rabbi Joseph replied in a voice very low and broken by reason of the weakness and the great awe which set all his body and limbs quivering, saying, "My lord angel of the Holy God, what can this thy servant say before thee? Behold, I am left without soul or spirit like a dead man for the greatness of the fear and awe of thee, and a mighty trembling has seized me for fear of this mighty fire so that I cannot answer my lord, saving by the loving-kindness if thou shouldst support me and sustain me and give me leave to speak to my lord."

As soon as the angel heard his words he touched him, saying, "Rise and speak. See, I support thee." Once the angel had touched him, Rabbi Joseph arose, strengthened himself and bowed to the ground, and removed his shoes from off his feet; but his disciples were still lying with their faces to the ground unable to rise; and Rabbi Joseph answered and said, "Peace be unto thee and peace to thy coming, angel of the Lord of Hosts, and peace to all thy holy train. I beseech thee to strengthen me and support me and aid me to bring about my desire; for it is known to the King Who is King of Kings, the Holy and Blest One, that not for my own honour nor for the honour of my father's house do I do this, but to the glory of the living God, the King of the Kings of Kings unto Whom alone is dominion. And now thou, O holy one, and thy holy train, I pray you assent to wage war with me against Amalek and its Prince. Teach me the way I must take to cause evil to pass away from the earth, and how and after which fashion I may succeed in bringing Samael the accusing Satan down from his abode, and raise the trains and the hosts of the holy and set them on high as came about in days gone by."

Then the angel answered Rabbi Joseph, saying, "Indeed your words are good and correct and would they might be heard, and may God be with you; for all the holy hosts, of Seraphs and Erelim and all the holy troops, sit waiting for the vengeance of the Lord to come, and the establishment of His Holy Presence, which has been lowered through Sin to Exile in the Nether Deeps. But know thou, son of Man, that all which thou hast done as yet is nought; wert thou to know the place to which the Accusing Satan and his train have ascended you would not enter upon this work; for who can prevail against him saving the Holy and Blest One alone at the time when His word comes to pass. Now I have come to thee by reason of the glory of the Mighty Name which thou didst pronounce; yet what can I do on thy behalf, since I cannot succeed in knowing wherein lies the great power of Samael and his train and on what depends his fall from that height. This is known to none saving the mighty angel Akathriel and his legions and Metatron, Lord of the Presence and his legions; since but for them he would enter and have power to make an end, of the foes of Israel be it said. But as for me, I have no power to do anything save to guard the Holy paths in the world of Formation whereby the prayers of Israel pass, while I guard them until I hand them over to those selfsame angels. They know and can tell upon what depends the great strength of Samael. Yet who can stand before those tremendous angels? Never wilt thou be able to withstand the great spectacle and mighty dread and the fire-consuming fire of those angels in their lower halves. If thou wert startled at me, how wilt thou bear to stand erect and strong before them? And so regarding the matter of the separation which thou dost need to keep, thou shalt need to do as much again of the like. And now these are my words: stand aside and receive thy reward.—Yet indeed wert thou able to bring about this thing as it should be, thy reward would be exceedingly great and none would be able to stand within thy borders."

Then Rabbi Joseph answered, saying, "I am but young and puny, and I know myself that I am not worthy of doing this deed; for who am I to come before the King? Nevertheless I know that God will not despise a broken and dejected heart, for He does not contemn, neither does He abuse, the humility of the poor; and I have set my mind on sacrificing my soul and my spirit for the holiness of the Holy and Blest One and His Presence, uniting Him completely with His Presence; and whatever Work be necessary I shall perform, and pour forth my soul and my blood and my flesh as an offering before the Holy and Blest One and His Presence. Therefore, O administering angel of the Holy Name, instruct me in that which must be done to bring down Akathriel and Metatron, and the measures of solitude which I must add in holiness and purity, and the Name whereby I may conjure them; for I say let me die this time after seeing the faces of the holy and exalted angels, since thereby I shall gain eternal and victorious life."

Then the angel continued, saying, "Hearken to my words and God be with thee. This thing shalt thou do, and if it be God's command thou shalt prevail, so may it be His will to prosper thy way that thou mayst turn thy thought to a deed. This is the thing that thou shalt do, according to all thou hast done hitherto, whether it be bathing or fasting or purification of thought, so shalt thou continue to do for forty days; let not your minds move from the abstractions of thought for a moment, whether by night or by day; every day diminish somewhat in your food until you accustom yourselves to be sustained with very little; continue to be satisfied by the savors, for they are the sustenance of the soul. After the forty days thou shalt call on the Name of the forty-two letters with all its devotions and vowels and roots which thou knowest, and thereby shalt thou conjure those great and resplendent angels. And before the conjuration, pray and entreat and beseech God to aid you and give you strength to withstand the dreadful terror and the mighty fire so that you may not perish. Thereupon entreat those angels to do your wish for the glory of the Pronounced Name and come to you. Then strengthen thyself as thou hast done but now, and ask of them strength and force for thy words, for they are mighty and resplendent angels; and they will inform thee of the ways of Samael and the manner in which thou canst reduce him and bring him down. Be strong and may we be strengthened for our nation and for the cities of our God. And may the Lord preserve thee from all evil. May He preserve thy soul."

The angel of the Lord went up to Heaven in a tempest while the disciples remained cowering on the ground with fear and awe; and when the angel Sandalphon and his retinue departed they rose and Rabbi Joseph said to them, "My sons, blest of the Lord, be strong and valiant, and let us be heedful in doing all that the angel commanded us." They replied, "Behold us ready and prepared. Happy are we to have seen the sights of God and have heard all their words, albeit we were lying on the ground. And now all that our Lord and instructor will do, that shall we likewise do." And he replied, "Blest be ye in the Lord," and they arose and went thence through the desert to a certain mountain close to Meron where they found a cave in which they dwelt for forty days, living in holiness and purity as they had been commanded, letting no detail slip, till they could scarcely sense anything of the material world in themselves; and all that time they saw neither man nor beast.

When the forty days were at an end they went out into the desert to a place where the River Kishon passed as it came from its source, for there they had performed their bathings throughout the forty days. And they prepared themselves for the recital of the afternoon prayers, and they said, "Answer us" as recorded above and prayed to the Divine Name to this end, praying and weeping greatly. Then they made a circle on the ground into which they entered, and each one gave the next his hand so that they were all linked by their hands within the circle. Then they cried to the Lord after falling on their faces, and cried out and pronounced the Holy Name and conjured the angel Akathriel and his retinue and the angel Metatron and his retinue. And when they uttered the Mighty Name the earth smoked and quaked and there were thunders and lightnings and the heavens were opened and the angels descended with all their followers and wished to smite Rabbi Joseph and his disciples, had they not held their hands united and strengthened themselves by the devotions and Names with which they were familiar; but this only in thought and not in word, for they had no strength to speak but all fell to earth together, but their hands remained joined and they did not separate.

As soon as the angels had descended, they began to cry with great fury, "Who and what is this creature whose heart has led him to employ the Sceptre of the King; how was thy heart so high as to bring thee to this thing,

O flesh and blood, O revolting slime, crawling worm! Who art thou to summon us to the King?" When Rabbi Joseph saw this stupendous spectacle, awe and great fear possessed him at the sound of the tremendous crashings and from the great fire, the riders of fire, the steeds of fire, the angels, the seraphs and their troops filling the entire world, the tempest shifting the hills and shattering the slabs of rock, and the raging fury of the angels who sought to injure him; it was as though he were dumb and thrust down to earth, he and his disciples, and they had no spirit left within them with which to answer to the angels, for they were dumbfounded and terror-stricken before them.

So the angel Metatron touched him and said, "Speak, come answer, noisome slime, what is this great excitement with which thou comest troubling us? Woe to thee that hast no fear for the honour of thy Maker." When the angel touched him, Rabbi Joseph opened his mouth and said in a very weak failing voice, with his eyes tight-closed, "What can this incomplete and humble slave utter to the holy and pure angels if you do not support me; now, my lord, sustain me and permit me to speak, for I am dumb and lifeless as a stone, my breath has forsaken me with my soul." Then the angel Akathriel also stretched out his hand and touched him, saying, "See, I have strengthened thee, speak thy words."

Thereupon Rabbi Joseph, being strengthened, opened his mouth and answered, saying, "The very God knows that not in revolt and not in deceit have I performed all these feats but for the glory of the Holy and Blest One and His Presence, the Which I desire to raise from the dust wherein It lies by reason of our sins; and now with you, ye exalted and holy angels, with you rests this commandment, for my grandeur sufficeth not for this work; but it is indeed more fitting that you angels who are zealous for the Lord of Hosts should perform this thing. Therefore I beseech you, ye ministering angels, by the power of this Mighty Pronounced Name upon which depend the Upper and the Nether Worlds. Give glory to His Name and instruct me wherein lies the strength of Samael and the accusing Satan and his retainers and the fashion in which I can bring him low."

The angels answered together, "Thou hast asked a difficult thing; for would that thou didst but know, by reason of the transgressions of Israel, how powerful he is and strong! There are none to discern this saving us for we keep ward over the Upper Ways against the hordes of Samael and his retainers. And he is indeed powerful and who shall succeed in bringing him low? For his nest is among the stars, where his habitation is surrounded by three barriers by reason of the transgression of Israel. Strong is he and thou shalt not prevail over him save by the Holy and Blest Himself until His words shall come to pass."

But Rabbi Joseph persisted and said, "I have already imperilled my soul unto death for the glory of the Holy and Blest One and His Presence; and after I have seen the troops of the holy and my soul has been delivered I put my trust in the loving-kindness of God; let Him but aid me and I shall succeed if your pure words do suitably inform me what is to be done. Whatever you do tell me that I shall be exceedingly heedful to do."

Then the angels replied, "Hearken, O Joseph, to the word of the Lord. Until this hour it has not been hidden from Him Who spoke and the word sprang into Being that thy desire is acceptable. Nevertheless the hour of redemption has not yet come and the decree has long gone forth, and is proclaimed in the Song of Songs, that love must not be awakened and must not be aroused. And now having regard to the wisdom and the measure of hidden secrets which the Rock of the worlds has vouchsafed thee, through them we are compelled for the glory of His Great Pronounced Name to inform thee and instruct thee concerning the way which thou shalt follow; yet know that thou canst not prevail against him. Therefore do not enter into a place for which thou art not fitted, but thus far shalt thou come and no further. Nonetheless, if thou shouldst desire to be importunate in this matter in face of His Great Name, we shall tell thee what thou shouldst do. And truly if thou couldst possibly succeed how good would be thy portion and how pleasant thy lot!"

Then Rabbi Joseph answered, saying, "Ye holy ones on high, your words are good and correct, but the heart within me grows hot when I see the Presence of His power cast low and I am exceeding zealous for Zion; therefore let the Lord do what is good in His eyes, for even though He slay me in Him I set my trust. I shall not remove my thought from Him. And ye, O angels on high, strengthen me with your best knowledge for me to remember, and I shall not turn aside from it either to the right or to the left, but shall I trust in His Great Name that there may be no stumbling block or snare."

After this Akathriel began and said, "Know thou that on the side facing me Samael has two powerful barriers, one a wall of iron from earth to heaven and one the great barrier of the sea Okeanos, that great sea and broad," and the angel Metatron likewise said that facing him on his side the accusing Samael had a barrier of huge mountains of snow the summit of which reaches to the skies. "And now set thine eyes and thy heart to all which we tell thee and be strong and valiant, for thou must bring low and pass through those three barriers in order to ascend Mount Seir which is Edom to judge Mount Esau. And thus shalt thou do. When thou goest forth from this place bend thy steps towards Mount Seir, and all that thou shalt do below as we tell thee, the like shall we do above; and the likeness of thy soul above is with us. In all the work that thou shalt do below thy soul above shall do the like. Therefore be careful and pay heed not to neglect a single thing of all that we shall tell thee.

"When thou dost come to the way to Mount Seir take heed for your holiness, diminish your food and continue your Unions as you have done till now, for your souls have already ascended so far on high that you are almost in the nature of angels and the ways of the world below are forgotten by you. Be constant in this and let not your thoughts depart from the abstract things even for a moment. Now there on the road a great pack of black hounds will fall upon you. They are the retainers of Samael whom he will send to confuse your purpose. Do not fear them but pronounce against them that name of the Ever Present which is numerically equivalent to 'Son' and 'Hound,' being precise in the vowels and the unity thereof; and they will flee before you. From there you will begin to ascend the Mountain and you will find a great Mountain of snow reaching to the heavens, with no way of passing either to its right or to its left. There you shall utter the name deriving from the verse, 'Didst thou come to the stores of snow,' of which thou knowest the combination and the vowels; and the Mountain will shift from its place. Then utter the name of 'Snow upon Tsalmon' according to the combination and vowels which thou dost know; and the Mountain will vanish entirely from its place and thou shalt continue, bearing these devotions in mind without permitting thy thought to shift until thou dost reach the further barrier of the sea Okeanos, the waves of which do mount up to the heavens. There thou shalt utter the Names deriving from the psalm 'Ascribe to the Lord, ye sons of might' with all their references as they are written and vocalized and combined, together with their root; it will dry up and ye shall pass through the dry land. And after this you shall continue and you shall find a great wall of iron reaching from the earth to the sky. Take in thy hand a knife on which is inscribed the Name deriving from the verse 'A sword for the Lord and for Gideon' with its vowels and its root; hew the iron through with the knife, make an aperture and enter; and take care to hold the aperture open until thy and thy disciples have passed; for after you have passed the aperture will close again.

"And after that you shall continue until you come to Mount Seir, and at the same time we shall cast Samael down from his place and he will already be handed over to you; so have prepared with you a collar of lead with the Mighty Uttered Name engraved upon it, and let there be another collar with the Name engraved upon it which is derived from the verse of Zechariah, 'And he said and thou O evil and he cast them down into the measure, and he cast the leaden stone upon it.' Write the Name deriving from this verse with its vowels and its root, and then go where you will in Mount Seir; and there thou shalt find Samael the evil with his mate Lilith. Seek for them, for they shall flee before you and will hide in a certain ruin in the likeness of two black hounds, dog and bitch. Approach them without any fear and on the dog set the collar with the Holy Uttered Name, and on the bitch set the other collar, and set a rope for a chain about their necks at once, joined to the collars; and they will come with all their retainers. And thereby thou shalt have brought about the desire of the Lord, and thou shalt bring him to judgment on Mount Seir where thou didst pass; and there the great trumpet shall be sounded and Messiah shall be revealed and the spirit of pollution shall pass away from the earth, for the Holy and the Blest One shall slaughter him in front of the saints; and there shall be the complete redemption, and the Kingdom shall be the Lord's. If thou canst perform this work as it should be, happy art thou and how good thy portion and how sweet thy lot; but have a care and be heedful in the aforesaid devotions, both thou and thy disciples; do not cease from them for a single instant; also take exceedingly great care that when Samael is fallen into thy hands with all his retinue, and they weep and entreat thee to give them something to eat or drink or any sort of provision for the sustenance of their forms and bodies, thou shouldst not hearken to them nor give them the slightest thing. If he beseech do not believe him; and be exceedingly careful of this, and also of the devotions; for even though he will already be in thy hands thou shalt require to be very watchful indeed; do not omit a single thing of all that we have instructed thee; may the Lord be thy ascendant star and guard thy feet from slipping."

After this the two holy angels went up to heaven in a tempest, and Rabbi Joseph saw and kneeled and prostrated himself; but his disciples still cowered on their faces and could not raise their heads until they had gone. When the angels had vanished they too arose in great joy. So after the angels had gone Rabbi Joseph and his disciples arose with alacrity and prepared all the orderings of the Names of Power and the Invocations and the devotions which they had been commanded and both of the leaden collars; and they turned their faces toward Mount Seir.

While they were on the path, packs of black dogs came toward them and dashed at them, surrounding them from every side. And they at once uttered the Name that they had been commanded, and they scattered the dogs away from them so that they fled and were seen no more. After that they continued, climbing upward about a day's journey; and towards evening they found an exceedingly great mountain of snow from earth to heaven. At once he strengthened himself with the Names and combinations they knew, and it removed from its place; and by the other combination it vanished away entirely.

They lodged there that night. In the morning they rose betimes and went onward for another two days. On the third day as the morning star arose they found before them a great broad sea tossing and rocking, with its waves mounting to the skies. Thereupon they uttered the Names the angels had told them and passed through the sea on dry land. And at noon they reached the great iron wall mounting from the earth to the skies. Rabbi Joseph took the knife upon which he had inscribed the requisite Names, and hacked through the iron wall which was a hand's breadth thick; and they made an opening in it and held the opening back until all five of the disciples had passed. But in passing one of the disciples, the last of them, delayed, the opening slipped from the hands of Rabbi Joseph, and the wall closed upon the foot of the disciple, who cried out, "Master and teacher, deliver me for my foot is caught." At once Rabbi Joseph drew the knife and hacked at the iron round his foot and freed it; and the opening closed again.

Then they ascended to the summit of Mount Seir and proceeded thence until evening fell. And there in the standing corn they found some ruins, and from them came the barking of dogs. And they entered the ruin and within it they found two great black hounds, dog and bitch, which dashed at them as they entered to consume them. And Rabbi Joseph held the collars in his hands, and recognizing at once that these were Samael and Lilith, he stretched out his right hand and clapped the one collar round the neck of the dog, and the other round the neck of the bitch; and his disciples roped them.

So they tied them up with the collars upon them. And as soon as they saw that the evil had come upon them, the demons divested themselves of the forms of dogs and assumed their own form, that of men with wings full of eyes like burning flame; and they entreated and besought Rabbi Joseph to give them bread and water to sustain them. And they said to him, "Our Lord, now we and all our retinue are bound captive in thy hand and we have no more strength; therefore do unto us what is fitting in thy sight, but give us the wherewithal to keep ourselves alive; for we have been flung from our quarters in which we used to benefit from the shining Presence behind the Veil; and now why should we perish? Give us provision to keep us alive until we reach Mount Seir." But Rabbi Joseph refused as he had been commanded, and would give them nothing.

They proceeded along the way, Rabbi Joseph and his disciples rejoicing and glad at heart, their faces like flames, while Samael and Lilith and all their train went weeping. And in his gladness Rabbi Joseph began to vaunt himself, saying, "Who hath believed our report when they said that we would not succeed? But behold, this day let the heavens rejoice and the earth be glad, and let the nations say that the Lord doth reign." And Samael rejoined, "I know that thou canst indeed prevail and nothing can withstand thee." And he wept greatly and said, "My Lord, why dost thou fear me and all my host; we have no strength any longer nor power, and we are all of us in thy hands to do thy will; but give us something to support our spirits, for how else shall we endure until we come thither?" And Rabbi Joseph answered, "I shall not give thee anything as I have been commanded."

When they approached Mount Seir, Rabbi Joseph took a cone of frankincense to smell at it, and Samael said, "If thou wilt not give me food give me a little of the frankincense in thy hand to savour of it." Rabbi Joseph stretched out his hand and gave him a little of the frankincense; and Samael emitted a spark of fire from his mouth, burnt up the incense while it was still in Rabbi Joseph's hand, snuffed up the smoke into his nostrils, burst the bonds and the ropes and cast the collar from him; and he and his hosts withstood them and attacked the disciples, slaying two at once by the blast and shouting of Samael and his hosts, while two others were smitten and went out of their minds, and Rabbi Joseph was left alone with a single disciple, very weary and worn and astounded. For he did not know that at the peril of his soul he had given him frankincense, which the demon had set smoking in his hand so that he performed idolatrous worship to Samael, thereby effacing the powers of holiness in the collars of lead through the frankincense, and thus sinning in not obeying the words of the angels.

And at that hour the whole mountain was smoking; everything was dark and gloomy; and a voice cried from heaven, "Woe to thee, Rabbi Joseph, and woe to thy soul because thou didst not obey the commands that were given thee but didst commit idolatry and offered incense to Samael, and now he shall pursue thee to destroy thee in this world and the next world."

One disciple was left with Rabbi Joseph, weak and weary and worn, and they reached the Gates of Death, and they sat there to rest under a tree for about two hours. Then they buried the two dead disciples and Rabbi Joseph and his one disciple set out to return to their path; their whole faces were transformed, strange and greenish and exceedingly feeble, while as for the other two a demon had entered into them and they went fleeing by paths which no man knows until they came at last to the city of Safed after about a month, where they soon perished by reason of the pains and suffering inflicted upon them by the demons.

And after this Rabbi Joseph reached the city of Sidon where he settled and turned to evil courses, since he saw that his wish had not come about; and especially when he heard the aforementioned voice from heaven, he despaired of a portion in the World to Come, and made a covenant with the fury Lilith and delivered himself into her hand so that she became his wife. And he polluted himself with every sort of impurity until by the Holy Names and other Names and incantations, which he knew how to misuse for evil purposes, he used to conjure and compel spirits and devils to bring him night by night Whomsoever he might desire. This was his custom for a long time until he finally fell in love, out of all humankind, with the wife of the Grand Turk; he used to have her brought nearly every night, and in the morning he would order her to be taken back.

One day she told her husband that "every night in my dream they bring me to a certain place where a certain man enjoys me, and in the morning I find myself in my bed besmirched with manseed, but knowing not how it comes to me." Then the Grand Turk sensed that there was something strange in this matter and summoned the sorcerers, setting them on the watch in his wife's dwelling with other women, and ordering them to be prepared and nimble in invocations and the Names of Evil, so as to arrest those who would come to take his wife. They did so, remaining on their guard; and that night the demons came at the order of Rabbi Joseph, and they became aware at

once and did their Works and conjured the demons to learn who they were
and why they came. And the demon replied, "We are sent by Rabbi Joseph
who dwells in Sidon." The Grand Turk sent a general with gifts to the lord
of Sidon that Rabbi Joseph be sent to him alive so that he should take vengeance upon him and torture him.

When Rabbi Joseph learnt that evil was to befall him, as he was told by
the demons he had sent, he hastened and flung himself into the sea before the
letter reached the lord of Sidon, and perished. And I, the fifth disciple, am
left alone, lying on a bed of pain all my days, with no cure for my sufferings
and all my members seething; and I have no rest from the demons. I have
written this tale for a memorial, and may the Lord have mercy upon me
and say "enough!" to my troubles. Until here are the words of the disciple
Judah Meir who was present at the above great Work performed by Rabbi
Joseph de la Reina.

ENDED AND COMPLETED

*And I the copyist have copied the ancient and much-worn writings which I
found in the repository of discarded books that is in Safed, may it be rebuilt
and established speedily and in our days. I have written this story as a
sign and a memorial in order that no unworthy man may presume to
hasten the Redemption even though his wisdom might suffice to
bring it about, and also that it may serve to point the moral taught
by Solomon in his wisdom, "Trust to the Lord with all they heart,
but lean not on thine understanding," meaning that one should
not trust in his own understanding and his wisdom, but
that his confidence should be in the Holy and Blest One.
From this story a man should also learn how Samael
and his hosts find support in our iniquities, inasmuch
as through so slight a matter was effaced the power
of the sanctity of the Holy Names, and Samael prevailed and returned once more to his station;
nevertheless it manifests how mighty is the
power of the Holy Names. Through this story
may men learn to fear the glorious and aweful
Name, turning in perfect repentance to Him,
blessed be He, and bring thereby the perfect Redemption, through the Holy and
Blest One Himself, May He restore
His Presence to His Holy Habitation
and Judah and Israel, with the rebuilding of Ariel and the coming
of the redeemer. Amen, may it be
His Will, saith the copyist. Solomon Namaro of Jerusalem.*

GHETTO LIGHTS AND SHADOWS

MURDER IN THE GHETTO

by GLÜCKEL OF HAMELN [1]

ABOUT this time a wonderful incident occurred. There lived in Altona a
man, Abraham Metz by name, may God avenge his blood! He was
married to Sarah, daughter of Elijah Cohen. Before he had moved to
Hamburg he had lived in Herford and had been married to the daughter of
Leib Herford. She died two years after the marriage, and then he moved
to Hamburg and married Sarah. He brought with him a fortune of 3,000 reichstaler. But he was a stranger to Hamburg and knew nothing of the manners
and business customs of the Hamburgers and within a few years had lost his
entire fortune. He was a money-changer and lived at that time in Altona.

One morning his wife came into town and asked all her friends whether
her husband had stayed at any of their houses, but, after innumerable inquiries,
found no one with whom he had stayed. She was greatly alarmed. Many said
she had quarreled with him and he had run away from her. It was three
years to the time of the incident of which I am writing, and nothing more
was heard of this Abraham Metz. Everyone had his own opinion and said
just what he liked. Many said evil things of him, which I do not care to repeat, or mention in connection with such a martyr—God avenge his blood!
But, unfortunately, human weakness is such that we speak with our mouths
of what our eyes have not seen. For three years this poor Sarah was a "living
widow" alone with her sad orphans and had to allow people to talk as they
would and say what they liked of her husband.

There was a Hamburg man, an honest man who although he was not
rich supported his wife and four children quite comfortably. He was a money-
changer. Every money-changer rushes about all day for his living, and toward
evening, at the time of the afternoon prayers, goes home and from there
goes to a synagogue. Each one belongs to a *hevra*[2] and studies with the other
members, and after studying returns home. It was very late on this particular
night when the wife waited for her husband's return from the *hevra,* so that
they could have their supper together. Her waiting was in vain. She ran to

---

[1] Glükel (1646-1724) lived in Germany during the seventeenth century. Her autobiography,
written in Judeo-German, is a fascinating record of her unique experiences and of the tempo of
Jewish life during her times. The above selection, a good example of the author's gift for narra-
tion, depicts the predicament and psychology of the *aguna,* a woman whose husband has disappeared or deserted her and thus cannot change her status as a wife. The translation is by
Beth-Zion Lask. A complete translation has been made by Marvin Lowenthal, *The Memoirs of
Glückel of Hameln* (Harper & Brothers, 1932).

[2] A small group. In this case meeting for the purpose of study: each *hevra* studying a different subject, but all dealing with the Bible and Talmud. Each *hevra* is known by the name of
the subject studied.

all their friends' houses, but could not find him. He was, unfortunately, lost.

The next day there were rumors flying about the town. One said he had seen him here, the other that he had seen him somewhere else. Midday they spoke of it on the Börse. Zanvil the son of Meyer Hekscher related there, "Yesterday a woman came up to me and asked whether I had six or seven hundred reichstaler with me; if I had I should go with her: a distinguished stranger was in her house and had much gold and precious stones to sell. But I had no money and did not go with her." As he finished saying this a man named Lipman who stood near asked him what sort of a woman she was and what she wore. Zanvil answered, "She wore this and that." Upon which Lipman said, "I know the woman! and also know whom she serves. I do not trust her master. Good cannot come of it." And with such talk they left the Börse, everyone going to his own house.

When Lipman reached home, he said to his wife, "Do you know what I am going to tell you? The woman who is a servant of the son of the master of the shipping company, called on Zanvil Hekscher and would have taken him with her if he had had six or seven hundred reichstaler on him. I am sore afraid that the man who is missing went with her and has been murdered." Upon this his wife beat her hands on her head, and cried, "Through our sins! I've just remembered: the same person was also here and wanted to take you or me with her. You know very well what an evil man her master is; he is a murderer; it is certain that the upright, pious man was killed in her house." The woman who was very capable continued, "I will not rest or be still until I bring the whole thing to light."

"Mad woman," cried her husband. "If it is true, what are we to do? We are in Hamburg and dare not utter a word." So, things remained as they were for some days. However, with beat of drum the town council had it proclaimed that anyone who knew anything of the missing Jew, dead or alive, should come forward and say what he knew: he would receive a hundred ducats' reward and his name would be kept secret. But no one came forward and the matter was soon forgotten, in the usual way.

It happened that early one Sabbath morning, in summer, Lipman's wife could not sleep, similarly to what once happened to the King of Spain. He once asked a Jewish scholar, "What is the meaning of the verse, *Hineh lo jonum velo jishon shomer yisroel?*" The scholar translated, "The guardian of Israel neither slumbers nor sleeps." The King answered, "That is not what it means. The real meaning is that God, the guardian, does not let others sleep or slumber. Had I slept as usual this night you would all have been lost as a result of a blood-libel. But the Lord who is your guardian made me unable to sleep and I saw how a child was thrown into a Jewish house. Had I not been witness of this, all Jews would have been put to death."

In the same way Lipman's wife was unable to sleep. Early in the morning she stood at her window. She lived in the Ellern Steinway, a passage through which everyone going in or out of Altona had to pass.

It was on Friday night that the woman could not sleep and disturbed everyone by her mood. Her husband reproached her asking her how much longer this condition of hers was going to last; she would get really mad through it. But she answered that nothing would help her as long as the murder was unavenged. She knew quite well, her heart told her that *that* man was the murderer. Meantime day broke and she still stood looking out onto the street. And there she saw the man whom she took to be the murderer, his wife and a servant carrying a large box, go by. When she saw this, she began to cry out, "O God, stand now by me! This is the beginning of my satisfaction!" She rushed and straightaway snatched up her apron and rain-cloak and ran out of the room. Her husband sprang from bed to restrain her but could do nothing. She ran after those people, followed them to Altona, to the river Elbe and saw them place the box near the water. Rebekah, for this was her name, decided that the corpse of the murdered man was in this box.

She ran to the people in Altona and begged them for God's sake to help her; she knew for certain who was the murderer. But they were unwilling and said, "It is easy to begin anything, but one cannot foretell the end." She insisted that they should go to the President with her and at length two men went with her. They appeared before the President and told him everything. He said to them, "You accuse, but if you cannot prove this, I will take all your goods and chattels from you." Rebekah would not allow herself to be turned aside by this, but answered that she not only risked her property but her blood as well. "I beg you, Herr President, send for the murderer and take him with all that he has with him."

Upon this the President sent police and soldiers to the Elbe, to take them. But the force arrived in time to see them go on board ship for Hamburg, an hour's journey from Altona. If they reached Hamburg in time they would be free, for Hamburg was under other jurisdiction. But they reached them just in time and took the murderer together with his wife and box and brought them before the President who ordered the box to be opened. Nothing but the clothes of the murderer and his wife were found!

Fear and anxiety fell on the poor Jews! The man was closely examined and questioned but would confess nothing. On the contrary, he used threats and terror fell on every Jew for he came of a large, well-known family in Hamburg. All fled in fear, but Rebekah kept saying, "I beg you, dear folk, do not despair: you will see how God will help us." In her great anxiety she ran to town. As she came into the field between Altona and Hamburg, she came face to face with the woman who was in the murderer's service. Rebekah recognized her; she was the one who had gone to the Jewish merchants asking which one had six or seven reichstaler, and had taken him to her master's house. Rebekah went up to her and said, "It is lucky for you and your master and his wife that you have met me. They are imprisoned in Altona for the murder they have committed. They have confessed everything; only your confession is missing. When you have confessed there is a ship already waiting that will take you and your master and mistress away. For we Jews are only eager to know that Abraham is dead, so that his wife may marry again. We want nothing else of you."

She spoke more to the woman, for Rebekah was a very clever woman and persuasive. Because of her gossip, the woman too began to talk. She told everything, how she had met Abraham on the Börse after she had called on Rebekah's husband and other Jews. But no one else was so unfortunate as Abraham when, to his undoing, he had a purse with much money on him. She had shown him a small gold chain and told him that an officer in her master's house had much gold and diamonds to sell. "So Abraham came with me and when he entered the house, his slaughter-bench was ready. My master led him down to his room and together we took his life. We buried him under the threshold." Then, added the woman, "Rebekah, I am telling you all this in confidence. Do not betray me." Rebekah answered her, "Are you a fool? Or don't you know my honest heart? Everything I do is for your master and mistress so that they may soon be released and out of Altona. As soon as you tell all this before our people, everything will be all right."

So the servant went to the house of the President with Rebekah. He heard out the former, and though now she stammered and began to repent, denying that she had said anything, still everything was out. Most important of all, she had already revealed the burial place of the murdered man. In the end, she confessed everything to the President as she had to Rebekah. After this he again examined the master and mistress each separately, but they denied everything and said, "All that the maid has told, the hussy herself has invented." Fear again fell on us. The President said to us, "I can help you no further. Shall I torture these two on the bare word of their servant? And if he does not confess on the rack, what then? You must see to your rights in Hamburg and as soon as possible you must get permission from the government there to search the house for the corpse. If you can find it, as the maid says, you may leave the rest to me."

The *parnassim* immediately got busy and tried to get hold of twenty soldiers to dig the place that the servant had mentioned. They obtained permission to bury the corpse, if it was found, in the Jewish cemetery in Altona. At the same time they were told: "Take care: if the corpse is not found, you will be in great danger. You know the Hamburg mob! It will be impossible for us to restrain them."

We were all in great danger. But Rebekah was everywhere in front as well as behind and told us not to despair: she knew for certain that the corpse would be found, for the servant had sworn on her life and had given her all particulars. Ten trusted men and several sailors known for their trustworthiness went, in God's name, into the house which was not far from Altona, Schragen near Berlei. Meanwhile the news had spread throughout the town and all sorts of workmen and canaille in countless numbers collected before the door of the murderer's house. The mob had decided, "If the Jews find the murdered man, it will be well for them. If not, there will not remain a Jewish hide." But the Holy One, blessed be He, did not leave us long in doubt. As soon as our people entered the house and opened the place which had been revealed to them, they found what they sought. Tears dewed their eyes while joy filled their hearts. They wept that such a fine, pious young man, only twenty-four years old, was found in such tragic circumstances. On the other hand there were rejoicings that the community was out of danger and that vengeance was near. The whole town council was summoned and the corpse shown them and also the place where it had been found, all according to the servant's statement. The council registered and attested this. The corpse was then placed on a wagon and taken to Altona. A multitude of sailors and apprentices was present. The sight was indescribable; perhaps there were a hundred thousand people present but not one bad word was uttered. Though they are a rough people and in quiet times we suffered much evil and distress from them, still this time everything passed off quietly and each person went his way, peacefully.

The day after the *parnassim* brought the attestation to the President of Altona who had the murderer within his jurisdiction. The Jews preferred that the judgment should be in Altona. Again he had the murderer brought before him. He informed him of what had occurred. On this he made a full confession. The widow received a part of the money of her murdered husband, which was still there. The murderer, poor thing, was in prison till the time of his trial.

Meanwhile Sarah was still a "living widow." No news of her husband was to be had, and as already related, there were many rumors. After the unfortunate murder, when everyone knew the murderer so well, it was remembered that before he moved into the house near the old Schragen, he lived with his father who owned the "Schiffergesellschaft," the best known inn in the whole of Hamburg. It is quite near the Börse, and Jewish as well as Gentile merchants who had business, or a reckoning with one another, went there. They used to drink there out of silver dishes. The son was therefore well-known to Jews. When it became known that this very son was a murderer, and remembered that Sarah's husband was a money-changer, it was also remembered that the changers used to meet in that inn and do their business there, counting out money, for the place was well-known for its reliability. Sarah knew also that her husband had been quite friendly with this son. She therefore went to her friends and said, "You know that my husband was lost a few years ago. The murder of Abraham has come to light. My husband used to go in and out of that house often: I believe that the same man killed my husband. Help me, perhaps we may find that my husband lost his life by the same hand."

What need have I to dwell long on this? They went to the President and put this before him. He spoke to the murderer with good and bad words, threatened him with torture to confess that he had killed Abraham Metz. For long he would not confess and only agreed that he had known him well. But the President spoke so long to him that he confessed at last that in his father's house, the "Schiffergesellschaft," he had killed Abraham Metz. He had buried him in a deep hole in the room kept only for cheeses, and filled it up with lime before closing it.

As soon as this was known, the *parnassim* went to the Hamburg council and as before asked permission to make a search. Again the Jews were in dire peril, and worse than before, that such a well-esteemed and distinguished house should be turned into a den of murderers. It was dangerous for fear the corpse should not be found. To our luck it was found; he still wore his red under-waistcoat with silver buttons and a ritual scarf. He also was given a Jewish burial.

There was great mourning in our community, as though they had been killed that day. The friends of my relative Sarah, before they allowed the burial, examined the corpse well. Sarah told of certain marks he had had on his body, so that it might be known for certain that he was indeed her dead husband and that she was really widowed. These were found and she had permission to remarry. After this the result of the trial was made known: the murderer was to be broken at the wheel and his body bound round with iron bands, placed on a stake, that he should be an awful example for a long time. His wife and servant were freed, but had to leave the country. On the day of the trial and sentence there was a great tumult in Hamburg; for more than a hundred years no trial had been so sensational. Jews were in peril, for hatred for them was roused. But God in His full mercy did not forget us that day.

MY GRANDFATHER

by SOLOMON MAIMON [1]

MY grandfather, Heimann Joseph, was farmer of some villages in the neighborhood of the town of Mir, in the territory of Prince Radzivil. He selected for his residence one of these villages on the river Niemen, called Sukovborg, where, besides a few peasants' plots, there was a water-mill, a small harbor and a warehouse for the use of the vessels that come from Königsberg, in Prussia. All this, along with a bridge behind the village, and

[1] Among the numerous intriguing personalities of the eighteenth century, none was more remarkable or tragic than Solomon Maimon (1754-1800). He was born in Lithuania, where he

on the other side a drawbridge on the river Niemen, belonged to the farm, which was then worth about a thousand gulden and formed my grandfather's *hazakah* (tenure). This farm was very lucrative because of the warehouse and the great traffic which passed through it. With sufficient industry and economic skill (*si mens non laeva fuisset*) my grandfather should have been able not only to support his family, but even to become wealthy. The bad climate of the country, however, and the lack of all the equipment necessary for utilizing the land, placed extraordinary obstacles in his way.

My grandfather settled his brothers as tenants under him in the village belonging to his farm. These not only lived continually with my grandfather under the pretense of assisting him in his manifold occupations, but in addition to this they would not pay their rents at the end of the year.

The buildings belonging to my grandfather's farm had fallen into decay from age, and therefore required repairs. The harbor and the bridge also had become dilapidated. In accordance with the terms of the lease the landlord was to repair everything and put it in a condition fit for use. But, like all the Polish magnates, he resided permanently in Warsaw, and could give no attention to the improvement of his estates. His stewards had for their chief object the improvement of their own condition rather than of their landlord's property. They oppressed the farmers with all sorts of exactions, neglected the orders given for the improvement of the farms, and the budget intended for this purpose they applied to their own use. My grandfather indeed made representations to the stewards day after day; he assured them that it was impossible to pay his rent, if everything was not put into proper condition according to the terms of the lease. All this was of no avail. He always received promises but they were never fulfilled. The result was the ultimate ruin of the farm and other evil consequences.

As I have already mentioned, there was a large traffic at this place; and since the bridges were in poor condition, it often happened that these broke down just when a Polish nobleman with his rich train was passing; horse and rider were plunged into the swamp. The poor farmer was then dragged to the bridge, where he was laid down and flogged till it was thought that sufficient revenge had been taken.

My grandfather did everything in his power to guard against this evil in the future. He stationed one of his people to keep watch at the bridge so that if

received a talmudic education, and finally worked his way to Berlin. There he associated with Moses Mendelssohn's circle of intellectuals and made real contributions to philosophy; but because of his cynicism and sharp criticism, he was ostracized by his associates. In 1793 he published his autobiography under the title *Salomon Maimon's Lebensgeschichte* from which *My Grandfather* is a selection. Incidentally, this is the book referred to in George Eliot's *Daniel Deronda*, who, she says, chanced upon a "second-hand book-shop, where, on a narrow table outside, the literature of the ages was represented in judicious mixture. . . . That the mixture was judicious was apparent from Deronda's finding in it something that he wanted—namely, that wonderful piece of Autobiography, the life of the Polish Jew, Solomon Maimon."

any noble were passing and an accident of this sort should occur, the sentinel might bring word to the house as quickly as possible, and the whole family might thus have time to take refuge in the neighboring woods. Everyone thereupon ran out of the house in terror, and not infrequently they were all obliged to remain in the open air the whole night until they ventured to approach the house.

This continued for some generations. My father used to tell of a similar incident which happened when he was still a boy about eight years old. The whole family had fled to their usual retreat. But my father, unaware of what had happened, was playing at the back of the stove. He stayed behind alone. When the angry lord came into the house with his retinue and found nobody on whom he could wreak his vengeance, he ordered every corner of the house to be searched. My father was found at the back of the stove. The nobleman asked him if he would drink brandy. When the boy refused, he shouted: "If you will not drink brandy, you shall drink water." Then he ordered a bucketful of water to be brought, and forced my father, by lashes with his whip, to drink all of it. Naturally this treatment brought on a quartan fever which lasted nearly a whole year and completely undermined his health.

A similar incident took place when I was a child of three. Everyone ran out of the house; and the housemaid who was carrying me in her arms, hurried forth. But as the servants of the nobleman pursued her, she quickened her pace and in her extreme haste let me fall from her arms. There I lay whimpering on the skirt of the wood until a peasant, passing by, lifted me up and took me home with him. It was only after everything had become quiet again and the family had returned to the house, that the maid remembered having lost me in the flight. Then she began to lament and wring her hands. They sought me everywhere, but could not find me, till at last the peasant came from the village and restored me to my parents.

To the terror and consternation into which we used to be thrown on the occasion of such a flight was added the plundering of the house. Beer, brandy and mead were drunk at pleasure; at times the spirit of revenge even went so far that the casks were left to run out and corn and fowl were carried off. Had my grandfather borne the injustice and reconstructed the bridge at his own expense, he would have been able to avoid all these evils. He, however, appealed persistently to the terms of his lease, and the steward made sport of his misery.

And now a word about my grandfather's domestic economy. The manner of life in his home was remarkably simple. The annual produce of the arable lands, pasture lands and truck gardens belonging to the farm was sufficient for the needs of his own family as well as for brewing and distilling. Besides, he could even sell a quantity of grain and hay. His beehives were sufficient for the brewing of mead. He had also a large number of cattle. The principal food comprised a poor kind of cornbread mixed with bran, victuals made of meal and milk, of the produce of the garden but seldom of meat. The clothing was made of poor linen and coarse stuff.

Hospitality was carried very far. The Jews in this neighborhood were continually moving about from place to place; and because there was a brisk traffic at our village, they were frequently passing through it and, of course, they always had to stop at my grandfather's inn. Every Jewish traveller was met at the door with a glass of spirits; one hand making the salaam, while the other reached for the glass. He then had to wash his hands, and seat himself at the table which remained constantly covered with food. The support of a large family along with this hospitality would have had no serious effect upon my grandfather's circumstances if he had introduced a better economy in his house. This, however, was the source of his misfortune.

My grandfather was in trifles almost too economical, but neglected matters of the greatest importance. For example, he looked upon it as extravagance to burn wax or tallow candles; instead, he substituted thin strips of resinous pine, one end of which was stuck into the chinks of the wall while the other was lit. Not unfrequently by this means fires and great damage were caused, in comparison with which the cost of the candles was negligible.

The storeroom, in which beer, spirits, mead, herrings, salt and other provisions were kept for the daily use in the inn, had no windows, but merely apertures through which it received light. Naturally this often tempted the sailors and carriers who put up at the inn to climb into the storeroom and make themselves drunk gratuitously with spirits and mead. What was still worse, these carousing heroes, from fear of being caught in the act, often took flight, on hearing the slightest noise, without waiting to replace the spigot, sprang out through the holes by which they had come in, and let the liquor run as long as it might. In this way whole casks of spirits and mead ran out.

The barns had no secure locks but were shut merely with wooden bolts. Since the barns were at some distance from the dwelling house, one could take from them at pleasure, and even carry off whole wagonloads of grain. The sheepfold had immense holes, by which wolves (the forest being quite near) were able to slink in and feast upon the sheep at their convenience. The cows very often came from the pasture with empty udders. According to the superstition which prevailed there, it was said in such cases that the milk had been taken from them by witchcraft—a misfortune against which it was supposed that nothing could be done!

My grandmother, a good simple woman, when fatigued by her household occupations, often lay down to sleep by the stove, in her clothes, with her pockets full of money; she never kept an account. Of this the housemaid took advantage, and emptied the pockets of half their contents. Nevertheless my grandmother noticed the loss only when the girl played too clumsy a trick.

All these evils could easily have been avoided by repairing the buildings, the windows, the window-shutters and locks, by proper supervision of the manifold lucrative occupations connected with the farm, and by keeping an exact account of receipts and disbursements. But this was never even considered. On the other hand, if my father, who was a scholar, and educated partly in town, ordered for himself a rabbinical suit (for which a finer stuff was required than that in common use) my grandfather did not fail to give him a long and severe lecture on the vanity of the world. "Our forefathers," he used to say, "knew nothing of these newfashioned costumes and yet were devout people. You must have a coat of striped woolen cloth, you must have leather hose with buttons, and everything on the same scale. You will bring me to bankruptcy; I shall be thrown into prison on your account. Ah me, poor unfortunate man! What will become of me?" My father then appealed to the rights and privileges of the profession of a scholar, and showed moreover that, in a well-arranged system of economy, it does not so much matter whether you live somewhat better or worse, and that even my grandfather's misfortunes arose, not from extravagant consumption in housekeeping, but rather from the fact that he allowed himself by his remissness to be plundered by others. All this, however, was of no avail with my grandfather. He could not tolerate innovations. Everything had to be left just as it was.

My grandfather was considered a rich man. He could really have been one if he had known how to make use of his opportunities. And because of this he was envied and hated by all, even by his own family; he was abandoned by his landlord; he was oppressed in every possible way by the steward, and cheated and robbed by his own domestics as well as by strangers. In short, he was the poorest rich man in the world.

There were still greater misfortunes, which I cannot here pass over wholly in silence. The pope (the Russian clergyman in this village) was a dull ignorant blockhead, who had scarcely learned to read and write. He spent most of his time at the inn, where he drank spirits with his boorish parishioners, and let his liquor always be put down to his account, without ever a thought of paying his bill. My grandfather finally became tired of this, and made up his mind to give him nothing more upon credit. The fellow naturally took this very ill, and resolved upon revenge.

For this he found at length a means at which indeed humanity shudders, but of which the Catholic Christians in Poland were wont to make use very often at that time. This was to charge my grandfather with the murder of a Christian, and thus bring him to the gallows. This was done in the following way: A beaver-trapper, who constantly lived in this neighborhood to catch beavers on the Niemen, was accustomed at times to trade in these animals with my grandfather. This had to be done secretly, for the beaver is game preserved and all that are taken must be delivered at the manor. Once the trapper came about midnight, knocked and asked for my grandfather. He showed him a bag which was pretty heavy to lift, and said to him with a mysterious air, "I have brought you a fine big fellow here." My grandfather was going to strike a light to examine the beaver and come to terms about it with the peasant. He however said that this was unnecessary, that my grandfather might take the beaver at any price, and that they would be sure to agree about it afterwards. My grandfather, who had no suspicion of evil, took the bag just as it was, laid it aside, and betook himself again to rest. Scarcely had he fallen asleep again, when he was roused a second time by a loud noise of knocking. It was the clergyman with some roughnecks from the village, who immediately began to search all over in the house. They found the bag, and my grandfather already trembled for he instinctively suspected that he had been betrayed at the manor on account of his secret trade in beavers, and he could not deny the fact. But how great was his horror when the bag was opened and, instead of a beaver, there was found a corpse.

My grandfather was bound with his hands behind his back, his feet were put into stocks, he was thrown into a wagon, and brought to the town of Mir, where he was given over to the criminal court. He was made fast in chains, and put into a dark prison.

At the trial my grandfather insisted upon his innocence, related the events exactly as they happened, and, as was reasonable, demanded that the beaver-trapper should be examined. He, however, was nowhere to be found since he was already over the hills and far away. He was sought everywhere. But the blood-thirsty judge of the criminal court, to whom the trial became tedious, ordered my grandfather three times in succession to be brought to torture. He continued steadfast in his assertion of innocence.

At last the hero was found. He was examined; and since he straightway denied the whole affair, he also was put to torture. Thereupon he quickly blabbed the whole story. He declared that, some time before, he had found this dead body in the water, and was going to bring it to the parsonage for the burial. The parson, however, had said to him, "There is plenty of time for the burial. You know that the Jews are a stiff-necked race, and are therefore damned to all eternity. They crucified our Lord Jesus Christ, and even now they seek Christian blood for their Passsover, which is instituted as a sign of their triumph. They use it for their Passover cake. You will therefore do a meritorious work, if you can smuggle this dead body into the house of the damned Jew of a farmer. You must of course clear out, but your trade you can carry on anywhere."

On this confession the fellow was whipped out of the place, and my grandfather set free; but the pope remained pope.

For an everlasting memorial of this deliverance of my grandfather from death, my father composed in Hebrew an epic poem in which the whole event was narrated and the goodness of God was sung. It was also made a law that the day of his deliverance should be celebrated in the family every year and that this poem should be recited in the same way as the book of *Esther* at the Festival of Haman (Purim).

THREE WHO ATE

by DAVID FRISHMAN

THIS is the story of three who ate. Not on an ordinary day did these three eat, but on the Day of Atonement; not hidden where no one could see them, but openly, in the great synagogue, before the entire congregation did they eat. Nor were they strangers whom no one knew and nobody cared about, but the most honored citizens of the community: the *Rav* and his two *dayanim*. And yet they remained, even after having eaten in public on the Day of Atonement, the most honored citizens of the community. That Day of Atonement I shall not forget!

I was but a child then, understanding little of the significance of the thing they did, yet I vaguely realized that a stirring event had taken place in those bitter days.

Yes, those were bitter days! A great calamity had befallen us from Heaven —cholera! From far away, from the depths of Asia, it had come to our little town. It spread pestilence in the streets; and in the houses it heaped up horror hundredfold. Silent through the nights and invisible through the days it reaped its harvest. Who could enumerate the names of all who died during those days? Who could count the fresh mounds of earth of the graves?

And the worst of its grim work the plague did in the Jewish ghetto. Like flies people fell, young and old. There was no house but had its dead.

Above us, on the second floor, nine had died in one day; below us, in the cellar, a mother and her four children. In the house opposite, we heard, one night, the loud lamentations of the sick, but in the morning there was not a sound.

They who buried the dead grew weary. The corpses lay upon the ground, body against body, yet people no longer cared.

Thus the summer passed. And there came the Holy Days. And the holiest of all—the Day of Atonement. That day I shall not forget!

Evening in the synagogue. Before the Ark stood, not the cantor and two honored citizens, as is the custom, but the *Rav* and his two *dayanim*. Around and around immense wax candles burned. The worshippers stood facing the east wall, wrapped in their white prayer-shawls, swaying to and fro in silence. And the shadows on the walls swayed with them. Were they really shadows? Or were they the shadows of the dead swaying to and fro upon the walls? Shadows of the dead, who finding no peace in their graves, had come to hear *Kol Nidre?*

Silence! The *Rav's* voice rose suddenly, accompanied by his two *dayanim*, with a great sigh that penetrated the congregation. And then the words were heard:

"With the grace of God and the forbearance of the assembled, we permit you to pray together with the transgressors."

I listened. . . . What did the *Rav* mean? Who were now the sinners? And did he not fear that Satan might overhear him now, in such a time, such a bitter time?

A looming dark fear swooped down upon me, and it seemed to me that the same fear fell upon the entire congregation, young and old.

Then I saw the *Rav* mounting the almemar. Did he mean to deliver a sermon to console the mourners and strengthen their faith?

But the *Rav* did not begin a sermon. Despite custom and ritual, he intoned a prayer for the recent dead. How long the list of names! The minutes passed one after another, and there seemed to be no end to his enumeration of the victims of the plague.

Those prayers will ever be vivid in my memory. They were not prayers but a painful moan—a long moan that rose from the hearts of the congregation to pierce the heavy skies. And when the prayers were over no one left the synagogue.

I stood there through the night and felt as if a fog rested on my eyes. I heard the men chanting: "And the angels flutter through the air, and fear and trembling embraces all." Fear and trembling! It seemed to me I could see the clouds through the fog, and the angels fluttering up and down, up and down. And amongst them I discerned in the darkness the Black Angel with his multitudinous eyes—from head to foot eyes—everywhere eyes—and what eyes!

No one left the synagogue that night, yet in the morning two were gone. Two who died in their prayer-shawls—ready to be taken from the House of Prayer to the House on the Dead. From the streets reports filtered in. But no one spoke of them or asked questions, so afraid were they to know what might be in their homes. That *Yom Kippur* eve I shall not forget.

And yet even more frightful was the day that followed. Even now, if I close my eyes for a second, I can see that scene!

Noon of the Day of Atonement. On the almemar stood the *Rav* with his head high and proud. The *Rav* was old, eighty or more years old, his beard was white with a silver whiteness, and the hair on his head was as newly-fallen snow. His face, too, was white; but his eyes, unlike the eyes of old men, were black and glowing. I had known the *Rav* from my earliest childhood. I knew him as a holy man whose wisdom was respected afar, and whose word and judgment was as the word of Moses. I stood in my corner looking at him, at the glowing black eyes that shone from his white face with its white hair. The congregation was silent, waiting for their leader to speak.

At first his voice was low and weak, but it gradually gained in strength and volume. He spoke of the holiness of *Yom-Tov,* and what the Giver of the Torah had meant to convey thereby; he spoke of living and of dying, of the living and the dead. He spoke then of the dreadful plague, of the horror of its pains and of the trail of woe it left behind it. And worst of all—he said—no end to its devastations seemed in sight. His voice rose. The pale cheeks flushed, and the blue lips turned red. Then I heard him say: "And when a man sees that great sorrows have befallen him, then it is that he should search his deeds in his relation to his God, but also in his relation to himself, his own body, his very flesh, his daily needs."

I was but a child then, but I remember that I suddenly turned cold.

And then the *Rav* spoke of the cleanliness that keeps us alive, and the uncleanliness that bereaves us of life; of thirst and of hunger; branding thirst and hunger as evil powers that come, in time of a plague, to kill and to destroy mercilessly. Then I heard him say: "In the holy *Gemara* it is said: 'And he shall live by his virtues and not die through them.' And again the Wise Men said: 'There comes a time when it is considered a virtue to trespass a law of the Torah. There is even a time when it is better that a man destroy all of the Torah if thereby he saves a life for the world!'"

What did the *Rav* mean? At what did his words aim? Of what did he want to persuade his congregation on that day of days?

Then I saw that the *Rav* was weeping. And, as I stood there in my corner, I too began to cry, the tears running to the corners of my mouth.

Even now, as I close my eyes, I can see the *Rav* stretch out his hand and beckon to his *dayanim*. They approach and rise on the almemar. Now the three are standing there, the *Rav,* the tallest of them, in the center, with one *dayan* to the right of him and one *dayan* to the left of him. What does he whisper in their ears that they suddenly turn pale? Why do they lower their heads? A sigh passes through the congregation and is hushed by the voices of the three on the almemar chanting in unison:

"With the grace of God and the forbearance of the assembled, that you may not grow faint in this time of plague—we permit—you—to eat—and to drink—today!"

A deadly silence settled on the synagogue. No one stirred. I remained in my corner and heard my heart beating: one, one-two, one . . . And an inexplicable dark fear seized me. Shadows swam about the walls and among them I seemed to recognize the recent dead—passing in endless procession. Like a rushing tide the realization of what the *Rav* asked of us swept over me. He wanted us to eat! He wanted Jews to eat on the Day of Atonement! Because of the plague! The plague!

I began to cry loudly, but I was not heard. For I was not alone. Many wept. And the three on the almemar wept, too. And the tallest of the three wept like a child. And like a small child he pleaded: "Eat! Go and eat! The time is such! There comes a time when it is a virtue to trespass a law of the Torah! We must live by them, our virtues, and not die on account of them! Go! Go and eat!"

But no one in the synagogue stirred. He stood there pleading, assuring them that he would take upon himself their sin of eating and drinking on this fearful day; that they would appear innocent before God.

No one stirred.

Suddenly the *Rav's* voice changed. He no longer pleaded, but commanded: "I order you to eat! I! I! I!" His words darted forth like arrows.

The congregation listened with bent heads.

Again the *Rav* pleads tearfully: "Why have you all united against me? Must you drive me to the last extremity? Have I not suffered enough this day of days?"

And the *dayanim* plead with him. But no one moves.

The *Rav* pauses. His face turns ash white, his head sinks upon his breast, and a heart-rending sigh escapes his throat. "It is the will of God!" he murmurs. And with a dry, submissive voice he adds: "Eighty-two years have I lived and not been brought to such a trial. It seems God's will that I should not die before I have fulfilled this too!"

The silence of a graveyard!

And the *Rav* calls: *"Shammas!"*

The beadle approaches. The *Rav* whispers something in his ear and the beadle leaves the synagogue. Then the *Rav* turns to his *dayanim,* whispers to them, and they nod their heads in assent. In a little while the beadle returns from the *Rav's* home with wine and cake.

That scene will remain with me to my dying day! The scene of the three who ate, of the three heroic holy men who ate in the synagogue on the Day of Atonement before the entire congregation.

For heroes they were. Who can measure the struggle that must have torn their hearts? Who can weigh their pain and suffering?

"You wanted me to do it—and I did it!" The *Rav* now spoke with a firm clear voice, then added: "Blessed be the name of the Lord!"

And the congregation ate—ate and wept. . . .

WAXENED EARS

by MAX BROD

I

DAYBREAK. . . .

The chill, ashen dawn of a wintry day.

Little David has already been coaxed from his sleep by the gentle words of his mother. It is still quite dark. But one mustn't tarry longer in sleep. For before one goes very early in the morning to *heder* to spend all day, one should study at home at least an hour. To be sure, all children don't. For them the hours of *heder* suffice. But you, David, the son of such a scholar, of such a pious man. . . .

And so the ten-year-old boy sits, frail, shivering, pale, and ghostly as the dawn itself; sits and "learns."

He kneels on his stool; otherwise the table is too high for him. His elbows on the table, his two little fists dug into his cheeks, because he is most comfortable that way.

"And thou shalt love the Eternal, thy God, with all thy heart, with all thy soul and with all thy might." To which the commentator says: With thy *whole* heart; that means with both impulses, with the evil impulse as well as the good.

The boy hesitates. The passage puzzles him. He reads it again, aloud, intoning it, accenting certain words as he has heard his elders do when they debate a moot point in the *Mishnah*. "Thou shalt love the Eternal . . . even with thy evil nature." He does not understand.

But fortunately there is guidance at hand for just such difficulties. In the broad pages of the huge folio the text is surrounded by all the famous commentaries, a framework twice as wide as the text itself; the eternal truth of the Tractate *Berakot* completely encircled by the tiny letters of the commentaries of our great teacher Rashi and the Tosafists' School. But with practiced eye the boy seeks the explaining note, the while he intones the passage and sways his small body back and forth over the broad book.

His thoughts glow. He flings out the last words distinctly and boldly: "Even with thy evil nature?"

How the words resound! A sudden terror seizes him. A light echo rustles through the empty room. The boy is suddenly seized by a fear of the evil spirits of the night. He knows, to be sure, that no spirit has power over him while he is busied with the Holy Word. But he is nevertheless stiff with fright, his thoughts frozen within him. Perhaps he has stumbled unwittingly in those last words on an incantation to summon evil spirits. Dim, obscure powers seem to hover, menacing, about him. He looks anxiously toward the doorposts where the small silver cases containing the inscribed scrolls are fastened. Beyond them no evil spirit can pass. But suppose the *mezuzah* has the tiniest flaw, a missing letter (such things may happen) or the misplaced cap of a letter—then the charm is of no avail, a mere plaything for the evil spirits! Drunk with bad dreams, the child motions the evil spirits away.

But suppose the terrible witch should return, the *Bath-Chorin,* the Daughter of Sin. When you sleep she envelops you, wrapping you round and round. And when you wake she still holds you fast by your finger tips. The boy had been careful to wash his hands very clean as soon as he woke, and to carry the water outside and pour it on the ground, as a charm to drive the *Bath-Chorin* away. But he cannot help feeling that the witch had despite that, somehow, slipped through the chinks of the door. He feels her at his finger tips, where demons love best to cling. The *Shedim,* the dreadful evil spirits, that can assume any human form! But their vulture-clawed feet they cannot change; that telltale mark always betrays them. How often has he not powdered the floor beside his bed with flour so he might see the next morning the imprint of their horrible clawed feet.

The little wax candle on the wooden table flickers. David's heart stops beating. He hears very close to him a knocking, quite distinct.

His father sits in the next room, "learning." Father is always learning. At four in the morning he is already at his books, and it is long after midnight before he allows himself to fall asleep. And he sleeps at the table where all day he learns. He puts his arm across his book, his head on his arm. He sleeps there the whole night through. And he is very angry if he is not awakened after three hours' sleep. For aren't even sixty breaths drawn in sleep a foretaste of death which the pious man may not know? On Friday night alone, the eve of the Sabbath, does Father lie down to sleep in his bed. In this, too, he obeys a precept. Father does nothing which does not fulfill a precept.

The fear of Lilith, the queen of the spirits of the night—Lilith, the mate of Samael—is upon the boy. Lilith it is who tempts the souls of great men. Even Adam lived with her a long time when he turned away from Eve after the fall. Later he turned back to Eve. Since then the hate of Lilith has been visited upon the children of Eve, and Eve's noblest sons she hates most. David wouldn't wonder if Lilith, the fire-witch herself, had broken into his father's room and even now was busy there with her enchantments. The noise again. . . .

The boy is by now too afraid to remain alone. He opens the door of his father's study. He stands motionless in the doorway, as he has seen Mother stand. For no one dares break in upon Father with speech. You must wait still as death until Father looks up and notices you.

But Father is not sitting at the table at all! He has sprung up, flinging his chair back to the floor. With one hand he clutches the silver-white beard which falls to his waist. The other hand is raised aloft, trembling. His lips, white as his beard itself, try to utter something, but cannot.

The boy leaps to the window on which the wide, staring eyes of the old man are fixed.

Underneath lies the snow-covered courtyard with its stack of firewood. A dark figure can be seen slinking by the pile, can be seen scaling the wall.

Life suddenly surges back into the fear-stunned body of his father. He tears open the window, leans far out and shouts loudly, as loudly as he can, after the disappearing figure: "Hefker!"

David understands "Hefker"; it means "ownerless." Father has declared the firewood in the courtyard below ownerless so that a soul might be saved from the terrible sin of stealing. He had been terrified not by the thief, but by the great crime that might have been committed.

Father has already returned to his table and his book. The handsome, finely modeled countenance has quickly recovered its habitual serenity. David would have liked to ask him for an explanation of that passage which had been puzzling him. But he knows he mustn't break in on his father.

On tip-toe he steals back to his room. But he cannot forget the blanched lips of his father as they forced out the word "Hefker." Not that the event impressed him as strange; he had witnessed many similar. Nor does he ever question what his father does, for it is beyond doubt that which is just. . . . But the image of his father, that ghastly look—never before had he seen his father lose control of himself—that look remained with him the whole day long. In *heder* it still haunted him, and distracted him so that he was punished —a rare occurrence—for his inattentiveness.

II

David came home from school at an unusual hour. It is still light and the shop is still open.

There is no one in the store but the deaf-mute servant. A sudden anxiety grips the child. Where is his mother, his busy mother, who never leaves the shop for a moment, who works from early day until far into the night, whose body is nearly worn out from endless toil? She is not there. In vain David shouts into the ear of the deaf-mute. Uncanny, this creature in that death-quiet cavernous room, in which every sound echoes against the dark heaps of old iron and broken tools that lie ceiling-high about him. The boy hears voices, raised now as in heated argument, falling now to a whisper, frightened, strange voices. The whole world becomes to him a mysterious place—and this dark storeroom its most mysterious corner.

He scuttles up the narrow, creaking stairs. He bursts into the room. Mother is there, and Father, too—but not at his books.

Father is sitting at the table and Mother is holding her hand to his ear. David notices that his parents are embarrassed by his presence.

"Back so early today?" asks his father.

But David cannot answer. He cannot take his eyes from his mother's hand. He sees wax in her hand.

And the curious, startled faces of his dear ones. "Have I frightened you?" David wants to say. But he cannot. His mother opens her mouth. But David hopes she will not speak; he feels sure that she is about to tell him something far more grewsome than ever anything that has happened this eventful day, something stranger than that odd business of the Talmudic passage, something wilder even than the terrified look on his father's face that morning.

"Father has caught cold," his mother whispers, "and so I'm putting wax in his ears."

Father turns upon her hotly. "Deborah, what are you talking about? You forget the precept, 'The remnant of Israel shall not speak falsehood, nor shall a deceitful tongue be found in its mouth.' . . . No, no, David, my child, the truth is—"

Mother lifts her hand to stop him.

"The truth is, that by command of the King, through his Counts, three of our community must each week attend church services at St. Valentine's—"

David's mother bursts into tears.

"That this trial, too, should be put upon us for our sins. Three of our community must listen to a special sermon, a conversion sermon. This week the lot fell upon me. One does wrong who shirks his share of the burdens of his community. But we"—a crafty smile passes over his face the like of which David had never seen on his fine, honorable father—"but we make it our practice to guard our ears with wax against the evil words. We used to try sleep; but they set a beadle over us to keep us awake. They've never guessed about the wax. But never believe this will go on forever"—he breaks off, seeing David's shocked face—"how we feel, we shall beg. . . ."

With clenched fists the child starts up.

"Why 'beg, beg'? Why do we always beg?"

"David!"

"Let the others do the begging sometimes. Let *us* command *them;* let *us* be gracious to *them.*"

David's father is silent for a long time. He only looks at his mother, who is still crying, "Wherein have I sinned that my son should be so swollen with pride?" And to David, "I will answer you. I will tell you why we must always beg while the others command—but not today."

"Why not today?"

His father smiles. "David, you mustn't be so headstrong, so impatient. You must learn to wait. Our people have waited almost fifteen centuries. And yet you will not wait even a half year. Today the sun rides low. When the days are at their longest again you shall have your answer."

"Father, dear, so long—so awfully long."

"Do not be angry with him," his mother calls out, as she lays her hand in blessing on the child's head. "It is the mark of a pious man that he be eager for the deliverance. Be pious, my son, and patient."

III

Seven months have passed. It is the eve of the burning of the Temple and the fall of Jerusalem, *Erev Tisha b'Ab*.

The boy had long forgotten the curious events of that strange winter's day when, on this stifling hot evening, his father beckoned him to accompany him to synagogue.

All this bright day sorrow had held undisputed sway in the house. The midday meal had not been eaten at the table; but each had taken his food, as a dog does his bone, into the corner of the room, and there, seated on a footstool, had eaten it. Each is ashamed to let the other see him satisfying a desire. The bread was sprinkled with dust. And besides bread there were only eggs, which are a symbol of mourning, since lacking pores they are like the sorrowing soul that has no outlet for his grief.

Shod only in house slippers, their worst clothes on their backs, they creep out in the dusk to synagogue. No one looks up or greets a friend. It is as if no man knows his neighbor, or as though each has some shameful sin to hide from his fellow. They walk in unbroken silence through the darkening streets.

The old synagogue is steeped in darkness. Not, as on other days, streaming with light, bright with the white prayer-shawls of the congregation as with the wings of angels. Instead, fallen wings, black garments, foreboding figures in the unrelieved gloom of the dark hall. The brass candlesticks are unlit. Each worshipper carries in his hand a small, weak, fitful taper. On this evening there shall be no more light than is necessary to read the prayer-book.

The dreary little tapers may be seen burning dimly, singly and in groups, all very close to the floor. The worshippers are not seated on the benches, as always, but on overturned prayer desks on the floor; in the midst of a disordered clutter they sit huddled, swaying to and fro in prayer. Even the curtains of the Holy Ark no longer hang in their place. The gray leaden door in the wall is bare, without a trace of color. Only the old bloodstains of the martyrs stand out from the black wall.

How often has David thought of this oppressed house of God as a fortress withstanding the attacks of the enemy. With its few small windows, heavy thick wall, it so much resembles a citadel. Here one might defend himself when all else was lost; through these narrow loopholes one might shoot with crossbows and small cannon. And should the enemy break in finally, there is a last refuge, the almemar, where the Law is read, a platform raised three steps from the floor and entirely encircled by bars of iron.

But tonight David's fancy finds little encouragement for such warlike dreams. The worshippers sit huddled together on the floor; there is not a man among them.

"They will break in on us; we will let ourselves be slaughtered like so many fowl," David thinks, shuddering. "Or, at most, we shall have the courage to kill ourselves—as the martyrs did, whose blood the passage of the long years has not wiped out; perhaps we will be so brave."

A great banner, riveted to a column, projects gloomily across almost the entire width of the dark hall. David loves flags. Whatever paper he can get his hands on he scribbles all over with drawings of flags. He is lifting his eyes to the flag when the voice of the cantor, wavering, mournful, in broken rhythm, makes him cast down his eyes again.

"How lonely sitteth the city, once rich in people,
    She is like a widow, she who was once great among the peoples;
    The Princess among the nations has become a slave.
    She weepeth in the night, and her tears are on her cheek."

As he hears these words of the ancient lamentation, wailing breaks out all about him. The worshippers are speechless, overcome with grief; they are convulsed with weeping. The tears run down his father's cheeks, and he draws his boy close to him, and folds him in his great mantle, in the warmth and peace of its folds. Then suddenly his father nudges him.

He hears a quiet, distant voice: "On this day the Lord cast the glory of Israel out of the heaven down to the earth, from a high mountain into a dark pit." David understands. His father wants to call his attention to the passage without speaking of it. For on this evening when all joy is forbidden, how much more is forbidden that highest of all joys, the joy of dwelling on words of learning.

Only after midnight as they are leaving the synagogue does David's father speak:

"Now, son, you understand why we must beg and why others may command."

"Is it because of this day?"

"It is, indeed."

"But, Father, it won't be so forever, will it, not forever and ever?"

" 'On that day'—did you not hear—'on that day God cast out from heaven the glory of Israel?' "

"But, Father, not forever." He remembers now suddenly that gray wintry day when he asked the question his father is just answering.

"Be quiet!"

But the boy rears up with doubting, angry eyes. "Maybe we were wrong to cry out 'Hefker.' . . . And to let them rob us of wealth and home, of strength and honor, and to throw them our blessing in the bargain."

But these last words he dares not utter. Speech fails him under his father's threatening look. Never has his father looked at him with such piercing, such hostile, eyes.

Is it possible that his father can read his mind so utterly that he too recalls, at that instant, the gray winter day which began with the theft of the wood and the declaration of its ownerlessness? In that case it will go hard with him, for his father cannot help understanding, too, the rebellious intent of his look. But surely it is not possible for a grown-up person to recall things so perfectly.

And yet—Father is very wise, very keen-witted. David looks anxiously at his eyes and sees the full recollection unfolding there, sees too his rebellious answer returning in all its grim strength. Oh, for some slip, some weakness! But no, everything is unfolding exactly and clearly.

His father is raising his fist. . . . Yes, he knows everything, and with an awful exactness, too. Never has his father, his even-tempered father, struck him. But he is faced now with impiety and he knows the precept, "The impious, the sharpness of their teeth must be broken."

David awaits the blow.

But his father lets his hand sink. On this day of mourning one is forbidden to strike a child. A day of misfortune is the Ninth of Ab; a day on which all things miscarry; his blow might, too, and prove fatal. It is not by accident, or because of love either (that David knows), that the punishing hand was withheld—but to keep an ancient commandment.

Terrified he stares at his father—a strange countenance on which a cloud of anger seems as if enmarbled forever.

All that stifling night no one sleeps. Father prays, wailing the whole night through, and does not look at the boy. Suddenly David, too, breaks down and weeps. He has been seized by a fear that he will never be able to escape the threat of that ungiven blow of his father.

ADVENTURES IN SHIRAZ AND ISPAHAN

by J. J. BENJAMIN II [1]

I

O N my arrival in Shiraz I found the town in a state of ferment and revolt
in consequence of a change of government in Teheran. Fierce combats
took place in the streets, and it was not until the evening that the
tumult was calmed. The vice-consul received me into his house, and gave me a
safe escort to the Nasi, Mullah Israel. This Nasi, a venerable old man, received
me with the greatest kindness, and according to the Eastern custom, gave me a
hospitable shelter; and I lodged with his son Isaac.

My presence had quickly become known among the Jews, and I was soon
visited by the leading members. From morning until night I was in demand,
my advice and help asked in many matters, and my opinions regarded as
oracles. One day my room became gradually filled by women wearing white
veils, who, one after another, introduced themselves to me. As the Jewish
women are allowed only to wear black veils, in order to distinguish them from
others, this visit disquieted me, for I imagined the house might be attacked
by insurgents. I was, however, pacified when they told me that all these women
belonged to the families who had been compelled to embrace the faith of
Islam, but who in secret adhered to the faith of their fathers. My visitors lifted
their veils, and kissed my forehead and hand. I addressed some words to them
on their apostasy, whereupon the women wept bitterly. One of the men present
came forward and said: "Our brethren know under what fearful circumstances
we were compelled to apostatise: we did it to save ourselves from tyranny and
death. We acknowledge, however, that, notwithstanding our apparent apostasy,
we still cling with all our hearts to the faith of our fathers, and this we testify
by our presence here this day; for were it known, we should all certainly be
lost!" These words much affected me; I tried to console them and said: "Have
patience, my brethren; and continue to put your confidence in God. Perhaps
the monarchs of Europe, under whose protection your fellow-Jews live happily,
may be able to alleviate your misfortunes, and may place noble rulers on

---

[1] Benjamin II is one of the most notable of a long line of Jewish adventurers. He was
born in Moldavia in 1818, spent his early years in the lumber business, and in 1844 set out on a
series of journeys to the Orient to discover the ten lost tribes. The record of his travels in Asia
and Africa, *Eight Years in Asia and Africa,* was published in French, German and English; it is a
bouillabaisse concocted of fact, observation, legend and history. The above selection from this book
gives an intriguing picture of Oriental Jewry in the middle of the nineteenth century. It should
be added that Benjamin traveled in America between 1859-1862 and left a record of his impressions in another volume, *Drei Jahre in Amerika* for which he was decorated by the kings of
Sweden and Hanover and publicly approved by men of the caliber of Humboldt and Richter. He
died in London in 1864, a pauper.

the throne of Persia, who will loosen your bonds, and allow you freely and openly to avow your belief."

Afterwards the leader of the rebels came to the Nasi, in order to force a new tax on him. When he perceived me there, he asked who I was, to which the Nasi replied: "He is a Haham [sage] from Bet-el-Mikdas." Hardly had the Persian heard this, when he addressed me in the following words: "I have been told that the Hahamim of the town are very learned, and understand in particular the art of making amulets; make one for me to protect me in war." At first I wished to disclaim this honor, but my scruples vanished at the sight of his bloodstained *yatagan* (scimitar), and I promised to satisfy his wish on the following day. I set to work, but as I would not profane our sacred customs by this superstition, I turned over irresolutely the leaves of my Bible, and at length came upon the history of Esther. I took the names of the ten sons of Haman, by means of letters joined them into sentences, and in the form of kabalistic amulets wrote them on a square piece of parchment. This I gave to the Persian who expressed great joy on receiving it. And I told him at the same time that the amulet would only be of use as long as he was courageous and brave. Two days later this Persian took part in a combat of the insurgents against the troops, in which the latter were worsted: he now firmly believed in the power of my amulet, brought me presents, and proclaimed that I was a man of God, because my amulet had been so effective. This little affair obtained for me no little consideration.

A few days later, the report was spread that the rebels were going to attack the Jews, who came to me, begging for help and protection. I said that I was a poor pilgrim, and therefore could not help them; but they answered: "You are a learned man, and God is with you; you *can* save us." Thus urged, I advised that they should all assemble in a large house, and arrange a festive entertainment, that at the same time they should all be well armed, should barricade all the entrances, and then, trusting in God's help, await the result. Happily the report was without consequences.

A few months before my arrival, the Nasi Mullah Eliahu had drawn upon himself the ill will of the Imam, and was thrown into prison. The Imam demanded such an enormous ransom for his release that the community was unable to pay it. It was then proposed to him that, in order to be free, he should embrace the Islamic faith. The prisoner declared himself ready to do so, and was conducted before the Kadi. However, since many preparations are requisite before the ceremony takes place, the Nasi sought to gain time by having this deferred. The Imam made inquiries as to the reason for this delay, on which the Nasi declared that he withdrew his word, as he could not make up his mind to abjure at his age a religion which he had followed the whole of his life. Without further parley, the Imam ordered him to receive five hundred *filagos* (blows) on the soles of his feet, and then to be thrown into a damp dungeon. Four days successively this was repeated, so that the unhappy

Nasi received two thousand blows. Without movement, with his face to the ground like a dead man, he lay in that dungeon. Bread and water was all his food, and he would certainly have fallen a victim to these tortures and sufferings, if Providence had not rescued him. During this time a tumult broke out, and on this occasion the rebels released all prisoners, among whom was the Nasi. He then repaired to Bagdad, and it was there I made his acquaintance some time afterwards. His fortune the Imam had appropriated for himself.

Another incident which may give an idea of the desolate condition of the Jews is the following. A Persian took fancy to a Jewish girl, and sought her in the house of her parents. Since these visits became dangerous, he tried to persuade the girl to adopt the Moslem faith so that she might become his wife. "My parents would die of grief," said the Jewess, "if I forsook my religion." "You hear it," said the Persian to his companions, "she will embrace the Islam faith." Notwithstanding all her protestations he hurried to the Achund (Priest and Judge), and corroborated by his companions, stated to him that the maiden wished to embrace Islam. The Achund immediately caused the girl, who had meanwhile been concealed, to be sought for at her parents' house; the messengers treated the parents most cruelly, and the daughter was dragged before the Achund. At the end of the two days the prescribed purifications were concluded, and the girl begged for permission to walk on the terrace in order to enjoy the evening air. This was allowed, and she threw herself down from the terrace and fractured her skull. The Persians, who knew the cause of this suicide, heaped the most dreadful insults on the dead body, hacked it to pieces, and left it in the streets. Only during the night did the Jews venture to collect the remains and bury them.

II

About thirty years ago a poor Jewish jeweler, named Aga Babi, lived in Ispahan. He had three sons, of whom one, Jekutiel, distinguished himself as a dancer, and the great people of the city were so delighted with him that in the dancer they forgot the Jew. At a large fête, which was given in the city in honor of the Shah, Jekutiel was engaged as a dancer. Animated by the presence of the ruler to display the most extraordinary powers of his art, the young man had the boldness in one of his daring leaps to kiss the hand of the monarch, who, admiring his talents, kindly excused his temerity, and induced him to follow him to his court, although the father of Jekutiel endeavored by prayers and remonstrances to keep him back.

The youth grew up under the eyes of his patron the monarch, and proved by his fidelity and zeal that he was worthy of the favor which had been shown him. But even at court, surrounded by flattery and temptation, he never forgot his parentage or his low origin, and long remained faithful to the faith of his fathers. The son of the Shah, his friend and companion, whose amusements he shared, obliged him one day at a feast to partake of forbidden meat: from this time the favorite offered little resistance to the wishes of the prince, and soon afterwards embraced the Islamic faith.

In a short time there was an outbreak at Meshed. The Shah went in person with his army to subdue it. In his company was his young friend and servant Jekutiel, who, after going over to Islam, had taken the name of Ismael. The town of Meshed was sieged, but the rebels defended themselves obstinately, and in a sally put the army of the besiegers to flight. During this general flight the Shah was deserted by his troops, and left alone, without shelter: his faithful Ismael alone remained, and both owed their preservation to the speed of their horses.

When the Shah perceived his faithful servant following him, he called out to him: "Save yourself if you can, and leave me to my fate." But Ismael answered: "I will not leave you, Master; I will save myself with you, or I will perish." The fugitives reached a wood, in which they wandered about for six days. The Shah thought they would perish of hunger, but Ismael shared with him the remains of some biscuit and water. When this slender store was exhausted, the noble youth mounted his horse and rode away to seek for food. After a long search, he at length fell in with a Persian from whom he obtained some bread, and with that he rode back. When he arrived at the spot where he had left the Shah, he was no longer there. In despair he prayed to God, and rushed through the wood in all directions calling him by name. At last he found his master, but in a famished state, and refreshed him with bread. Finally on the seventh day, the fugitives were discovered by some horsemen, who had been sent out to the rescue of the Shah.

In consequence of this fidelity and devotion, the Shah, as soon as he had turned to Teheran, raised his favorite Ismael to be the first minister of his kingdom, and this high post he filled with the greatest zeal up to the death of the Shah. Without becoming proud, he remembered with love those belonging to him, and became an unwearied protector of his former brethren in the faith. When the Shah was near his end, he had his son called to him, and solemnly recommended to him the minister Ismael as his friend, his most faithful servant, and most honest adviser; and he begged the heir of his throne to respect the noble servant as such and allow him to retain his high office. After the death of the Shah, envy and jealousy made the minister an object of suspicion to the young ruler, and almost brought him into disgrace. An extraordinary event, however, kept him in his high position. During the change of succession, the town of Ispahan had revolted, and the young Shah determined to punish it by a demand of 100,000 taumans. For the exaction of this sum he chose the minister Ismael, and promised that, if he fulfilled his duty, he would keep him in his place. In the city an Achund had arranged a new revolt against the emissaries of the Shah; but with a numerous army Ismael suppressed the rebellion, destroyed a portion of the city, chastised the rebels, and carried out successfully his difficult commission. But in these events he had to mourn the death of his father and one of his brothers. The instigator of the rebellion escaped punishment by flight.

These events took place towards the end of the year 1850, shortly after the time I had left Ispahan and during the time I was at Teheran.

Ismael still lives at the court of Teheran, but no longer occupies his former high appointment. In the general esteem and respect which are paid him, he finds compensation for his fall, and still endeavors to alleviate the sufferings of his former brethren.

SHUT IN

by ABRAHAM REISEN

LEBELE is a little boy ten years old, with pale cheeks, liquid, dreamy eyes, and black hair that falls in twisted ringlets, but, of course, the ringlets are only seen when his hat falls off, for Lebele is a pious little boy, who never uncovers his head.

There are things that Lebele loves and never has, or else he has them only in part, and that is why his eyes are always dreamy and troubled, and always full of longing.

He loves the summer, and sits the whole day in heder. He loves the sun, and the Rebbe hangs his caftan across the window, and the heder is darkened, so that it oppresses the soul. Lebele loves the moon, the night, but at home they close the shutters, and Lebele, on his little bed, feels as if he were buried alive. And Lebele cannot understand people's behaving so oddly.

It seems to him that when the sun shines in at the window, it is a delight, it is so pleasant and cheerful, and the Rebbe goes and curtains it—no more sun! If Lebele dared, he would ask:

"What ails you, Rebbe, at the sun? What harm can it do you?"

But Lebele will never put that question: the Rebbe is such a great and learned man, he must know best. Ai, how dare he, Lebele, disapprove? He is only a little boy. When he is grown up, he will doubtless curtain the window himself. But as things are now, Lebele is not happy, and feels sadly perplexed at the behavior of his elders.

Late in the evening, he comes home from heder. The sun has already set, the street is cheerful and merry, the cockchafers whizz and, flying, hit him on the nose, the ear, the forehead.

He would like to play about a bit in the street, let them have supper without him, but he is afraid of his father. His father is a kind man when he talks to strangers, he is so gentle, so considerate, so confidential. But to him, to Lebele, he is very unkind, always shouting at him, and if Lebele comes from heder a few minutes late, he will be angry.

"Where have you been, my fine fellow? Have you business anywhere?"

Now go and tell him that it is not at all so bad out in the street, that it's a pleasure to hear how the cockchafers whirr, that even the hits they give you on the wing are friendly, and mean, "Hallo, old fellow!" Of course it's a wild absurdity! It amuses him, because he is only a little boy, while his father is a great man, who trades in wood and corn, and who always knows the current prices—when a thing is dearer and when it is cheaper. His father can speak the Gentile language, and drive bargains; his father understands the Prussian weights. Is that a man to be thought lightly of? Go and tell him, if you dare, that it's delightful now out in the street.

And Lebele hurries straight home. When he has reached it, his father asks him how many chapters he has mastered, and if he answers five, his father hums a tune without looking at him; but if he says only three, his father is angry, and asks:

"How's that? Why so little, ha?"

And Lebele is silent, and feels guilty before his father.

After that his father makes him translate a Hebrew word.

"Translate *Kimlunah!*"

"*Kimlunah* means 'like a passing the night,'" answers Lebele, terrified.

His father is silent—a sign that he is satisfied—and they sit down to supper. Lebele's father keeps an eye on him the whole time, and instructs him how to eat.

"Is that how you hold your spoon?" inquires the father, and Lebele holds the spoon lower, and the food sticks in his throat.

After supper Lebele has to say grace aloud and in correct Hebrew, according to custom. If he mumbles a word, his father calls out:

"What did I hear? what? once more, 'Wherewith Thou dost feed and sustain us.' Well, come, say it! Don't be in a hurry, it won't burn you!"

And Lebele says it over again, although he *is* in a great hurry, although he longs to run out into the street, and the words *do* seem to burn him.

When it is dark, he repeats the Evening Prayer by lamplight; his father is always catching him making a mistake, and Lebele has to keep all his wits about him. The moon, round and shining, is already floating through the sky, and Lebele repeats the prayers, and looks at her, and longs after the street, and he gets confused in his praying.

Prayers over, he escapes out of the house, puzzling over some question in the Talmud against the morrow's lesson. He delays there awhile gazing at the moon, as she pours her pale beams onto the Gass. But he soon hears his father's voice:

"Come indoors, to bed!"

It is warm outside, there is not a breath of air stirring, and yet it seems to

Lebele as though a wind came along with his father's words, and he grows cold, and he goes in like one chilled to the bone, takes his stand by the window, and stares at the moon.

"It is time to close the shutters—there's nothing to sit up for!" Lebele hears his father say, and his heart sinks. His father goes out, and Lebele sees the shutters swing to, resist, as though they were being closed against their will, and presently there is a loud bang. No more moon!—his father has hidden it!

A while after, the lamp has been put out, the room is dark, and all are asleep but Lebele, whose bed is by the window. He cannot sleep, he wants to be in the street, whence sounds come in through the chinks. He tries to sit up in bed, to peer out, also through the chinks, and even to open a bit of the shutter, without making any noise, and to look, look, but without success, for just then his father wakes and calls out:

"What are you after there, eh? Do you want me to come with the strap?"

And Lebele nestles quietly down again into his pillow, pulls the coverlet over his head, and feels as though he were buried alive.

THE WISE MEN OF HELM [1]

retold by LEO W. SCHWARZ

HOW IT ALL BEGAN

IN Heaven's nurseries there is an angel who is entrusted with the care and distribution of all newly-born souls. One day the Holy One sent this angel to scatter two bags filled with souls in all parts of the earth. One bag contained the souls of wise men; the other, the souls of fools. So the angel flew over the face of the earth and scattered the souls in equal measure: first, a handful of the wise souls, then a handful of the others. Throughout the world, therefore, there were an equal number of wise men and fools.

When the angel was passing over that district upon which was later built the renowned city of Helm, he met with a mishap. His large wings were caught in a very high mountain covered with trees and brush. As he attempted to loosen himself, he fell, and the bagful of wise souls was ripped wide open. Down fell all those souls—sages, teachers, and scholars to be.

In the course of time these souls became men. And they said: "Come, let

[1] The Abderitic city of Helm plays a prominent part in Jewish folklore. Although the tales and anecdotes bear some resemblance to those told in German of Schildburg and Till Eulenspiegel, they are distinctive creations of the Jewish imagination, and together with the countless stories about Motke Habad, Joseph Loktsch and Hershele Ostropoler, they "bear excellent witness to that pungent wit for which the Jews are so justly famous."

us build ourselves a city, and let us call it Helm." That is the name of the city today, and those pioneer builders were the ancestors of all the Helmites, famed for their wisdom throughout the world.

HOW THEY OBTAINED WOOD TO BUILD THEIR HOMES

The Helmites began the task of building their city. Off they went to the forest (it was on the very mountain upon which the angel's bag of souls was torn) to cut down trees. They went up the mountain, cut down the required number of trees, and sawed them into beams. Now they had to get the beams to the bottom of the mountain. The beams were thick and long and heavy: ten men were required to carry one beam from the top of the mountain to the plain below. That was no mean task; it lasted many months.

During the third month a Lithuanian Jew passed by the mountain and observed the Helmites carrying the beams on their backs to the bottom of the mountain. He said to them: "Why do you work so hard to get the beams down to the plain? It would be easier simply to roll down the beams and they will of themselves reach the plain below."

The Helmites got into a huddle and held a meeting to discuss the advice of this Lithuanian fellow. They deliberated seven days and seven nights, and made two important decisions; first, that there must be wise men also among the Lithuanian Jews; secondly, that they would follow the advice of this clever fellow. For, why, after all, should they labor so hard to carry the beams on their shoulders when it was possible to get them to the bottom of the mountain with a mere kick of the foot?

What did the Helmites do?

They immediately went to the plain, took all those beams which they had brought down, carried them straightway to the top of the mountain, and then rolled them down with a mere kick of the foot.

HOW LARGE SHOULD A CEMETERY BE?

After the Helmites had completed their houses, they began to consider the problem of a cemetery. There was some suitable land available on the outskirts of the city, but they did not know precisely how large the cemetery should be. They didn't want it to be too large or too small. No, it must be exactly right.

The Helmites were in a session for several days and nights. They discussed and argued and weighed every proposal. Finally they reached this decision: let the whole community—men, women and children—leave the city and gather on the chosen site. Let every person lie down next to his neighbor, row by row, according to one's station and lineage: the most honored in the best part of the site, the common people in the less desirable parts, the women in separate rows, and the children in the corner. Then a fence should be built all around.

This they did. So the cemetery of Helm was neither too large nor too small but exactly the right size.

HOW HELM WAS ENLARGED

The Helmites increased and multiplied. The city became overpopulated so that it became necessary to enlarge it and to build new homes. But this was not an easy task, for that mountain (where the angel's bag of souls was ripped) spread all over the neighboring land. Not an acre was free for building.

The Helmites convened and became absorbed in endless talk. Several remarkable plans were suggested, plans such as only the wisdom of the Helmites could conceive. At length they made this decision: the whole citizenry—men, women, and children—should go out to the mountain and push it in order to clear the ground for the construction of new homes.

Everyone ran to the mountain. They grasped it with their hands and arms, and pressed their bodies against it. They pushed and pushed. Sweat covered their faces. They pushed and pushed until it became very hot. Then they removed their coats and put them alongside the mountain. Somewhat cooled, they renewed their pushing. While they were exerting themselves in this manner, some thieves passed by and noticed the pile of coats. They grabbed them and hurried off.

The Helmites pushed with all their might for a long time, grew weary, and stopped for a rest. They turned around to see how far they had moved the mountain, and shouted joyfully.

"Look how far we are from the place we started. You cannot even see the coats!"

THE COMMUNITY CENTER

Every day Helm began to look more and more like a model city. And now that each citizen had a home and a plot of ground, the Helmites talked of a large school and community center that would be a credit to their wisdom and an adornment to the city. Up to this time they had used their homes for prayer and study.

They went to the same mountain, cut down the required number of trees, chopped them into long beams, and rolled them down. When they had carried the beams to the city, alas! they discovered something they had not reckoned on: the streets which were lined with houses were very narrow, indeed, only half the width of the beams. When they lifted the beams on their shoulders and, like soldiers on the march, tried to pass into the street which led to the site chosen for the community center, both ends of the lines were halted by the houses. The beams were longer than the width of the street, and they could not pass.

The Helmites called a meeting on the spot. They deliberated and debated and reached this decision: the houses on both sides of the street must be burnt down so that the street would be wide enough to pass through with the beams.

This they did. And when all the beams had been carried to the site of the community center, they returned, jubilant with their success, and rebuilt the destroyed houses.

THE HELMITES ELECT A PRESIDENT

A strange situation arose. There had been two candidates for the presidency of the synagogue, and each of them received an equal number of votes. Since neither would withdraw and it was illegal to have two presidents, the Helmites were perplexed.

A special meeting was called at the community center. After much haggling and discussing, the Helmites agreed to permit each of the candidates to tell a personal experience which should prove his wisdom, and the one whose story was most sage would become president.

The first candidate told this story: "One Saturday afternoon I was strolling along a street when I spied a ten dollar bill. I could not possibly pick it up on the Holy Sabbath, and yet I did not want to lose such a fortune. What did I do? In order to conceal it I covered it with my fur coat. I intended to return for them in the evening after the departure of the Sabbath, but when I returned I found neither the bill nor the fur coat."

The Helmites shook their heads and stroked their beards, so impressed were they with his uncommon wisdom. And now they stretched their necks to hear the story of the rival candidate.

"One night," he began, "I was sitting on my rocking chair and chatting with my wife. I noticed it was getting late so I told her to bolt the door. 'You go,' answered my wife who is by nature a strong-headed woman, 'and bolt it yourself!' 'No, you go,' I insisted. Well, we argued for an hour. Then I said, 'Let's be quiet now, and the one who starts talking will bolt the door.' 'Agreed!' answered my wife.

"We sat and sat and sat. Neither gave in; neither uttered a word. Then we became very sleepy and climbed into bed, leaving the door open. Suddenly I awoke and saw thieves moving in the house. They were putting all our jewelry, silverware and valuables into a sheet which was spread on the floor. But I controlled myself. I did not speak. I did not want to be the first to talk. Then they came over to the bed and were about to take the very pillows from under our heads. That was too much for me, so I coughed vigorously to wake up my wife. She jumped up, and upon seeing the thieves shouted, 'Help! Help! Thieves! Help!'"

The second candidate was unanimously elected to the presidency of the synagogue.

LIGHT FROM HEAVEN

The Helmites were convinced that no city was worthy of the name unless its streets were lit up on the dark nights preceding full moon.

"What shall we do," they asked, "to provide light on nights when the heavens are covered by clouds?"

They convened in the community center for seven days and seven nights, and put their heads together. They debated and talked. All the wisdom in all the heads of these wise men was taxed by this problem. Finally they devised a brilliant trick: when it was full moon, they would place a vessel full of water in the midst of the market-place. They would get the moon into the vessel, spread many sheets and mats over it, and tie them with strong ropes. To insure its safekeeping, they would seal the knots with the seal of the chief officials, the Rabbi and the Dayanim.

In this way they captured the moon on one fine, clear, moonlit evening.

When the end of the month came around and the nights became dark, all the citizens gathered in the market-place to take the moon out of the vessel and suspend it above the city so that it would illumine the streets. They broke the seals, untied the cords, took the sheets and mats from the vessel and—it was dark! Terror seized the hearts of all the Helmites: the moon was missing.

"The moon has been stolen, stolen, stolen," they lamented.

Too bad. For if it had not been stolen, the streets of the city would have been illumined even on the very dark nights preceding full moon.

THE BEADLE OF HELM

Now Helm was a model city. Was it not spacious, didn't it have a beautiful community house, and a cemetery which was neither too large nor too small? But the Helmites set their heart on having a beadle to serve the community, especially to knock on the shutters on the nights during the Holy Days and wake up the citizens for early prayer. So they selected a Helmite worthy of this distinction.

Once the beadle was examining the large oven in the community house. "How fine, how beautiful," he thought; "there's not another one like it!" Suddenly he trembled. "What should happen if thieves came and stole it?" No, that must not happen. What did he do? He took some lime, and wrote on the stove in large letters:

THIS STOVE BELONGS
TO THE COMMUNITY HOUSE OF
HELM

When the Helmites saw what the beadle had done, they praised his wisdom, and were convinced that he was worthy of his position. His faithfulness and ingenuity were never forgotten.

When the beadle was old, his legs became weak and he no longer had the strength to make the rounds at night in order to knock on the shutters. What was to be done? The Helmites removed the shutters from their windows and brought them to the community house so that the beadle would be able to knock on them in one place, so that it wouldn't be necessary for him to run off his legs in the muddy streets during the summer.

THE RABBI

Helm was blessed with a learned Rabbi, a sage worthy of that famous city. But to our day, nobody has been able to discover whether or not the Rabbi had a head.

The question arose only after the Rabbi suddenly disappeared from Helm. The whole community went out to find him. They searched and searched and at length found—a corpse without a head. Was it the Rabbi? Nobody could actually say. If the Rabbi had a head, the corpse was certainly not the Rabbi's. But if they could prove that the Rabbi did not have a head, then it was certainly their Rabbi.

The inquiry began. First, they questioned the beadle who used to serve the Rabbi every day. He said, "I don't know. The Rabbi, may his soul rest in peace, was always wrapped in his prayer-shawl and I saw him *only under the prayer-shawl.*"

They inquired of the community bathkeeper who served the Rabbi in the bath on Friday and holiday evenings. He answered: "I don't know. The Rabbi, peace upon his soul, always took a place on the highest bench which was completely hidden by the steam. I saw *only the lower part of his legs.*"

Finally, the Helmites inquired of the Rabbi's wife. No other woman in Helm could match her wisdom. One day, it is told, the Rabbi asked her whether she gave the goldfish fresh water. "No!" she replied, "they haven't as yet finished the water that I gave them yesterday." Well, *she* certainly would know.

She said: "I do know that he had a *nose,* for on Friday and holiday evenings, he used to prepare snuff for himself. But whether or not he had a *head,* I cannot say."

So even today it is not clear to the Helmites whether or not their Rabbi had a head.

THE SCRIBE

There are not words to describe the wisdom of the scribe who kept the archives of Helm. He, like the beadle and the Rav, was a shining light in Helm.

A few incidents will prove this. Once a group of Helmites visited the scribe at his home. They found him at his desk writing a letter. Not an ordinary letter, but one that could be written only in Helm. The paper was as large as a poster, and the letters of each word were at least a foot long.

"Why are you writing such large letters?" the Helmites asked.

The scribe answered: "I am not writing to you. I am writing a letter to my uncle who is deaf and dumb."

On another occasion the scribe was walking to the next town with a heavy pack on his back. A farmer who was riding by pulled up and invited him to share his seat. The scribe gratefully accepted the invitation, but to the farmer's surprise, did not take the pack from his back.

"Why don't you take the pack and put it in the wagon? Then you can ride comfortably," suggested the farmer.

The scribe answered: "You, my friend, were good enough to invite *me* to share your seat. Would it be fair also to add the burden of my pack?"

If by now, dear reader, you are not convinced of the renown of Helm and the wit and wisdom of the Helmites, you may some day have the good fortune of meeting one of them in person. He will convince you.

TWO SAVIORS

by KARL EMIL FRANZOS

ANYONE who was ever in Barnow was sure to make the acquaintance of Frau Hanna, mother of the chief of the Jewish session; and no one could know her without honestly liking and admiring her: she was so good and kind, and so very quick in understanding and entering into the thoughts and feelings of others. But it would be difficult to convey an adequate idea of her loving-kindness and wisdom to those who never knew her. She was called *Babele* (grannie) by everybody who lived in the little town, and not merely by her own grandchildren; and no wonder. She was never too busy or too tired to help those who needed her assistance either in word or deed; and even those who did not require money or advice used to delight in going to see her, and in hearing her stories of old times; for her renown as a story-teller was as great as her reputation for benevolence.

Anyone passing the old synagogue about the third hour on a Sabbath afternoon in summer, might see with his own eyes what a crowd of attentive listeners she had, and might hear with his own ears how well worth listening to her stories always were. She used to sit on a rug spread out in the shade, with her silent eager auditors, who sometimes numbered fifty men and women, grouped closely around her for fear of losing a single word that fell from her lips. Her stories were all about old days in Barnow—about things that had happened within her own memory, or that she had heard from others. Any attempt to reproduce her stories as she used to relate them would be very difficult, and if I try to do so, it is only because the tale I have chosen is the one she related far oftener than any other. I have heard her tell it scores of times, and will now endeavor to translate it from the Jewish-German in which she used to speak as faithfully as I can.

"Who is great," began Frau Hanna, "and who is small? Who is mighty, and who is weak? We poor shortsighted mortals are seldom capable of deciding this question. The rich and strong are mighty and great in our eyes, while the poor and feeble are regarded as weak and small. But in very truth it is not so. Greatness does not lie in riches or in brute strength, but a strong will and a good heart. And, my friends, God sometimes shows us this very clearly; indeed, we Jews of Barnow can tell how our eyes were opened to this truth. On two different occasions our community was plunged in great danger and suffering from the oppression of the Gentiles around us, and on each of these occasions a savior came forward from amongst us, and delivering us from our distresses, turned our mourning into joy. Who were these saviors of the people? Were they the strongest or the richest of the congregation? . . . Listen to me and I will tell you how it all happened.

"When you cross the market-place, you see a great big block of wood sticking out of the ground in front of the Dominican monastery. It is weather-beaten and decayed, and would have been taken away long ago, were it not kept as a memorial of a time of terror and despair.

"You know nothing of those old days, and you may be thankful for it! If I tell you about that time of misery, it is not that I wish to make your hearts heavy with grief for what is past and gone, or to fill them with bitter anger or hate. No; the sorrows of which I speak are over and done with, and those who suffered from them are dead and buried. It is written amongst the sayings of one of our wise and holy men: 'Forgive those who have trespassed against you, and return good for evil.' What I am going to tell you is the history of a great and noble deed that was done by one who lived and suffered during that time of dire distress,—a deed that should make your hearts beat high when you hear of it, for it is as heroic, good, and great as was ever done on the face of the earth.

"Its author was a simple Jewish woman, whose heart had been steeled to heroism by the force of circumstances. Her name was Leah, and she was the wife of a rich and pious man called Samuel. The family was afterwards given the surname of Beermann when the Austrians came into the country, and made it the law that our people should have German names as well as their old ones; for at the time when these events took place we had no such names. It was more than a hundred years ago, and we were still living under the rule of the Polish nobles.

"The single-headed white eagle was indeed a cruel bird of prey! Long ago, when it was full-plumaged, when its eyes were clear and piercing, and its talons firm and relentless in their grip, it was a proud and noble bird that held its own against both West and North, and protected all who took refuge under its wing most generously. For three hundred years we lived a free and happy life under the shadow of its wings; but when the eagle grew old and weak, and the other birds of prey round about had deprived it of many of its feathers, it became cowardly, sly, and cruel; and because it did not dare to attack its enemies, it turned its wrath upon the defenceless Jews. The power of the kings of Poland became a subject for children to jest about, and then the letters of freedom we had been given of old were no longer of any avail. The nobles became our masters. They oppressed us, extorted money from us, and disposed of our lives and property as it seemed good in their eyes. Oh, that was a time of unspeakable tribulation!

"Barnow belonged even then to the noble family of Bortynski, to whom the good Emperor Joseph afterwards gave the title of Graf (count). Young Joseph Bortynski had entered into possession of his estate that very year. He was a quiet, pious, humble-minded man, and had been educated in a cloister. His ways were different from those of the other young men of his position in the neighborhood, for he hated wine, cards, and women, looked after the management of his property, and prayed four hours a day. He was just and kind in his dealings with his serfs; but we experienced very little of his kindness and justice, for he was hard and cruel to us. He once gave Samuel, the leader of the synagogue, his reason for treating us so badly: 'You crucified my God,' he said. Whenever he was inclined to act towards us with less harshness, he was prevented doing so by his private chaplain, a man who had formerly been his tutor, and who had great influence over him. His name has not come down to us, but he was always talked of as the 'black priest.'

"We Jews used to be very careful of our conduct in those days, and even those of our number who were disposed toward evildoing refrained from deeds of wickedness. 'You crucified my God,' the Graf had said to Samuel, and had then added in a threatening tone: 'I give you fair warning that if I find any of your people guilty of a crime, I shall burn your town as your God once did to Sodom and Gomorrah.' Our fears may be better imagined than described.

"So the spring of 1773 began. The Easter festival was about to commence, when it was rumored that the Empress-Queen at Vienna intended to deprive the Poles of their remaining power, and to govern the land henceforward by means of her own officials. But so far as we could see there was no sign of this intention being carried out.

"Samuel, the leader of the synagogue, and his wife Leah lived in the old house in the market-place that is still known as the 'yellow house.' They were both very much respected by the community: the husband, because of his riches, wisdom, and piety; and the beautiful young wife, because of her gentleness and beneficence. They were in great trouble that Easter, for their only child, a little boy of a year and a half old, had died suddenly a few days before.

Late one Sunday evening they were sitting together in silent grief. The Easter festival was to begin on the following evening, and Leah was very tired, for she had been busy all day long cleaning and dusting the whole house from top to bottom. Suddenly they were startled by a loud knocking at the house door. Samuel opened the window and looked out. An old peasant woman was standing at the door with a bundle on her back. On seeing the master of the house, she moaned out a piteous entreaty for admittance. She was too weak, she said, to walk home to her village that evening, and so she begged Samuel to give her shelter for the night.

" 'This isn't an inn,' answered Samuel, curtly, at the same time shutting the window.

" 'Poor thing,' said Leah. 'Ought we to send her away?'

" 'We're living in dangerous times,' replied Samuel; 'I don't like to admit a stranger into my house.'

" 'But this poor creature is ill and weak,' said Leah.

"And as the old woman outside continued to make an appeal to his pity, Samuel gave way and let her in. The maidservants were all in bed and asleep, so Leah took her guest to a garret-room, and after providing her with food and wine, wished her good-night and left her.

"Next morning the stranger took leave of her hostess very early, and with many expressions of gratitude. Leah was so busy all day making the final preparations for the feast that she had not time to visit the room that had been occupied by the old woman until late in the afternoon, when she was making a last round of the house to see that no leavened bread was anywhere to be found. The room was perfectly neat and tidy, but she was astonished to find it pervaded by a most disagreeable smell. She opened the window, but that had no effect. She hunted about for the cause of the horrible odor. At length, on looking under the bed, she saw what made her blood run cold and her hair stand on end with terror. For under the bed there lay the naked corpse of a half-starved little child, with great wounds in its neck and chest. Leah at once understood what had happened, and struggled hard against the faintness that threatened to overpower her. The old woman had brought the corpse to the house, and had concealed it there, in order that the hideous old story might be revived that the Jews were in the habit of killing Christian children before the feast of the Passover, and terrible would be the vengeance taken by the Christians of the neighborhood. Leah recognized the full horrors of her position, and remembered the Graf's warning to her husband. She was nearly overwhelmed with the weight of her misery. For was it not she, and she alone, who, by inducing her husband to admit the woman into the house, had brought all the sorrow, persecution, and death that would surely come upon the whole Jewish community? While she sat there shivering with fever and anguish, she heard wild cries, shrieks, and the sound of weeping in the street, and also the clank of swords. 'They are coming,' she muttered, and at the same moment a thought flashed into her mind, far more strange and horrible than a woman's brain had ever before conceived, and yet so noble and self-sacrificing that a woman alone could have entertained it. 'It was my fault,' she said to herself, 'and I alone must bear the consequences.' She rose to her feet, pressed her lips firmly together, and after a struggle regained her composure. Then taking up the child's corpse, she wrapped it in a linen cloth and laid it on her knee.

"She listened . . . the minutes seemed to drag. Then she heard the young Graf's voice outside speaking passionately to her husband and another member of the session in these words: 'The woman heard the death-rattle distinctly. I will not leave one stone upon another if I find the body.' She heard the men going through all the rooms in the house. As their steps approached the one in which she was seated, she rose and went to the window, below which the roof fell away steeply, and overhung the paved courtyard of the house.

"The door was thrown open violently; the Graf entered, accompanied by the two members of session, and followed by his men-at-arms. Leah sprang forward to meet them with a wild laugh, showed them the child's body, and then flung it out of the window on to the court beneath. . . .

" 'I am a murderess,' she cried out to the Graf; 'yes, I am, I am, I am. Take me, bind me, kill me! I murdered my own child last night; I don't deny it. You've come to fetch me; here I am!'

"The men stared at her in speechless amazement.

"Then came furious cries, shouts, and questions. Samuel, strong man as he was, fainted away. The other Jews, at once perceiving the true state of the case, and seeing no other way of saving the whole community from certain death, supported her in her statement. Leah remained firm. The Graf looked at her piercingly, and she returned his gaze without flinching: 'Listen, woman,' he said: 'if you have really committed the crime of which you have confessed yourself guilty, you shall die a death of torture far more terrible than anyone has ever yet suffered; but if the other Jews killed the child in order to drink its blood at the feast, you and your husband shall go unpunished, and the others shall alone expiate their crime. I swear this by all that is holy! Now—choose!"

"Leah did not hesitate for a moment. 'It was my child,' she said.

"The Graf had Leah taken to prison and confined in a solitary cell. He saw all the improbability of her story, but he did not believe in any greatness of soul in one of our people. 'If it were not true,' he thought, 'why should the woman have given herself up?'

"The trial threw no light upon the subject.

"All the Jewish witnesses bore testimony against Leah. One told how she had hated her child; another how she had threatened to kill it. Fear of death forced these lies from their lips. The only Christian witness was the black priest's housekeeper—the same woman who had gone to Samuel's house on that fatal evening in the disguise of a peasant to bring destruction on the Jewish community. She told how she had heard the death-rattle of the child during the night. She could not say more without betraying herself, and so her story tallied with Leah's confession. The 'black priest' took no apparent interest in the trial. He probably thought that one victim would suffice for the time, or it may be that he feared the discovery of his crime.

"The Graf's judges pronounced Leah guilty, and condemned her to be broken on the wheel in the market-place and there beheaded. The wooden block in front of the Dominican monastery was placed there for this purpose.

"But Leah did not die on the scaffold: she died peacefully in her own house forty years later, surrounded by her children and grandchildren; for Austrian military law was proclaimed in the district before Graf Bortynski's people had had time to execute the sentence pronounced upon Leah, and an Austrian Government official, whose duty it was to try criminal cases, examined the evidence against her. Samuel went to him and told him the whole story, and he, after due inquiry, set Leah free.

"The wooden block is still standing. It reminds us of the old dark days of our oppression. But it also reminds us of the noble and heroic action by which a weak woman saved the community. . . .

"And eighty years after that, my friends—eighty years after that—when we were once more in danger of losing our lives, who was it that saved us? Not a woman this time; but a timid little man whom no one could have imagined capable of a courageous action, and whose name I have only to mention to send you into a fit of laughter. It was little Mendele. . . . Ah, see now how you are chuckling! Well, well, I can't blame you, for he is a very queer little man. He knows many a merry tale, and tells them very amusingly. And then it is certainly a very strange thing to see a grey-haired man no taller than a child, and with the ways and heart of a child. He used to dance and sing all day long. I don't think that anyone ever saw him quiet. Even now he does not walk down a street, but trots instead; he does not talk, but sings, and his hands seem to have been given him for no other use but to beat time. But—what of that? It is better to keep a cheerful heart than to wear a look of hypocritical solemnity. Mendele Abendstern is a great singer and we may well be proud of having him for our *hazzan* (precentor). It is true that he sometimes rattles off a touching prayer as if it were a waltz, and that when reading the Torah he fidgets about from one leg to the other as if he were a dancer at a theater. But these little peculiarities of his never interfere with our devotions, for we have been accustomed to Mendele and his ways for the last forty years, and if anyone happens to get irritated with him now and then, he takes care not to vent it on the manikin. He cannot help remembering, you see, that little Mendele can be grave enough at times, and that the poor *hazzan* once did the town greater service by his gift of song than all the wise and rich could accomplish by their wisdom or their wealth.

"I will tell you how that came to pass.

"You know that a Jew is looked upon nowadays as a man like everyone else; and that if any noble or peasant dares to strike or oppress a Jew, the latter can at once bring his assailant before the Austrian district judge at the court-hall, and Herr von Negrusz punishes the offender for his injustice. But before the great year when the Emperor proclaimed that all men had equal rights, it was not so. In those old days, the Lord of the manor exercised justice within the bounds of his territory by means of his agent; but what was called justice by these men was generally great injustice. Ah, my friends, those were hard times! The land belonged to the Lord of the manor, and so did all the people who lived on it; and the very air and water were his also. It was not only in the villages that this was the case, but in the towns too, especially when they belonged to a noble, and when their inhabitants were Jews. The noble was lord of all, and ruled over his subjects through his *mandatar* (agent).

"At least it was so with us in Barnow. Our master, Graf Bortynski, lived in Paris all the year round, and gave himself no trouble about his estates or their management. His agent was supreme in Barnow, and was to all intents and purposes our master. So we always used to pray that the *mandatar* might be a good man, who would allow us to live in peace and quietness. And at first God answered our prayers, for stout old Herr Stephan Grudza was as easy-tempered a man as we Jews could have desired. It's true that he used to drink from morning till night, but he was always good-natured in his cups, and would not for the world have made anyone miserable when he was merry. But one day, after making a particularly good dinner, he was seized with apoplexy and died. The whole district mourned for him, and so did we Jews of Barnow. For, in the first place, Herr Grudza had been kind to everyone; and in the second—who knew what his successor would be like!

"Our fears were well grounded.

"The new *mandatar,* Friedrich Wollmann, was a German. Now the Germans had hitherto treated us less harshly than the Poles. The new agent, however, was an exception to this rule. He was a tall thin man, with black hair and bright black eyes. His expression was stern and sad—always, always;—no one ever saw him smile. He was a good manager, and soon got the estate into order; he also insisted on the laws being obeyed; taught evil-doers that he was not a man to be trifled with; and I am quite sure that no one with whom he had any dealings defrauded him of a halfpenny. But he hated us Jews with a deadly hatred, and did us all as much harm as he could. He increased our taxes threefold—sent our sons away to be soldiers—disturbed our feasts—and whenever we had a lawsuit with a Christian, the Christian's word was always taken, while ours was disbelieved. He was very hard upon the peasants too—in fact, they said that no other agent at Barnow had ever been known to exact the *robot* due from the *villein* to his lord with so much severity, and yet in that matter he acted within the letter of the law; and so there was a sort of justice in his mode of procedure. But as soon as he had anything to do with a Jew, he forgot both reason and justice.

"Why did he persecute us so vehemently? No one knew for certain, but we all guessed. It was said that he used to be called Troim Wollmann, and that he was a Christianized Jew from Posen; that he had forsworn his religion because of love for a Christian girl, and that the Jews of his native place had persecuted and calumniated him so terribly in consequence of his apostasy, that the girl's parents had broken off their daughter's engagement to him. I do not know who told us this, but no one could deny the probability of the story who ever had looked him in the face, or had watched his mode of treating us.

"So our days were sad and full of foreboding for the future. Wollmann oppressed and squeezed us whether we owed him money or not, and none that displeased him had a chance of escape. Thus matters stood in the autumn before the great year.

"It isn't the pleasantest thing in the world for a Jew to be an Austrian soldier, but if one of our race is sent into the Russian service his fate is worse than death. He is thenceforward lost to God, to his parents, and to himself. Is it, then, a matter for surprise that the Russian Jews should gladly spend their last penny to buy their children's freedom from military service, or that any youth, whose people are too poor to ransom him, should fly over the border to escape his fate? Many such cases are known: some of the fugitives are caught before they have crossed the frontiers of Russia, and it would have been better for them if they had never been born; but some make good their escape into Moldavia, or into our part of Austrian Poland. Well, it happened that about that time a Jewish conscript—born at Berdychev—escaped over the frontier near Hussiatyn, and was sent on to Barnow from thence. The community did what they could for him, and a rich kindhearted man, Hayyim Grünstein, father-in-law of Moses Freudenthal, took him into his service as groom.

"The Russian Government of course wanted to get the fugitive back into their hands, and our officials received orders to look for him.

"Our *mandatar* got the same order as the others. He at once sent for the elders of our congregation and questioned them on the subject. They were inwardly much afraid, but outwardly they made no sign, and denied all knowledge of the stranger. It was on the eve of the Day of Atonement that this took place—and how could they have entered the presence of God that evening if they had betrayed their brother in the faith? So they remained firm in spite of the agent's threats and rage. When he perceived that they either knew nothing or would confess nothing, he let them go with these dark words of warning: 'It will be the worse for you if I find the youth in Barnow. You do not know me yet, but—I swear that you shall know me then.'

"The elders went home, and I need hardly tell you that the hearts of the whole community sank on hearing Wollmann's threat. The young man they were protecting was a hardworking honest fellow, but if he had been different, it wouldn't have mattered—he was a Jew, and none of them would have forsaken him in his adversity. If he remained in Barnow, the danger to him and to all of them was great, for the *mandatar* would find him out sooner or later—nothing could be kept from him for long. But if they sent him away without a passport or naturalization papers, he would of course be arrested very soon. After a long consultation, Hayyim Grünstein had a happy inspiration. One of his relations was a tenant-farmer in Marmaros, in Hungary. The young man should be sent to him on the night following the Day of Atonement, and should be advised to make the whole journey by night for fear of discovery. In this manner he could best escape from his enemies.

"They all agreed that the idea was a good one, and then partook with lightened hearts of the feast which was to strengthen them for their fast on the Day of Atonement. Dusk began to fall. The synagogue was lighted up with numerous wax candles, and the whole community hastened there with a broken and a contrite heart to confess their sins before God; for at that solemn fast we meet to pray to the Judge of all men to be gracious to us, and of His mercy to forgive us our trespasses. The women and the men were all dressed in white. Hayyim Grünstein and his household were there to humble themselves before the Lord, and amongst them was the poor fugitive, who was trembling in every limb with fear lest he should fall into the hands of his enemies.

"All were assembled and the service was about to begin. Little Mendele had placed the flat of his hand upon his throat in order to bring out the first notes of the *Kol Nidre* with fitting tremulousness, when he was interrupted by a disturbance at the door. The entrance of the synagogue was beset by the Graf's men-at-arms, and Herr Wollmann was seen walking up the aisle between the rows of seats. The intruder advanced until he stood beside the Ark of the Covenant and quite close to little Mendele, who drew back in terror, but the elders of the congregation came forward with quiet humility.

" 'I know that the young man is here,' said Wollmann; 'will you give him up now?'

"The men were silent.

" 'Very well,' continued the *mandatar,* 'I see that kindness has no effect upon you. I will arrest him after service when you leave the synagogue. And I warn you that both he and you shall have cause to remember this evening. But now, don't let me disturb you; go on with your prayers. I have time to wait.'

"A silence as of death reigned in the synagogue. It was at length broken by a shrill cry from the women's gallery. The whole congregation was at first stupefied with fear. But after a time everyone began to regain his self-command, and to raise his eyes to God for help. Without a word each went back to his seat.

"Little Mendele trembled in every limb; but all at once he drew himself up and began to sing the *Kol Nidre,* that ancient simple melody, which no one who has ever heard can forget. His voice at first sounded weak and quavering, but it gradually gained strength and volume, filled the edifice, thrilled the hearts of all the worshippers, and rose to the throne of God. Little Mendele never again sang as he did that evening. He seemed as though he were inspired. When he was singing in that marvelous way, he ceased to be the absurd little man he had always hitherto been, and became a priest pleading with God for his people. He reminded us of the former glories of our race, and then of the many, many centuries of ignominy and persecution that had followed. In the sound of his voice we could hear the story of the way in which we had been chased from place to place—never suffered to rest long anywhere; of how we were the poorest of the poor, the most wretched amongst the miserable of the earth; and how the days of our persecution were not yet ended, but ever new oppressors rose against us and ground us down with an iron hand. The tale of our woes might be heard in his voice—of our unspeakable woes and our innumerable tears. But there was something else to be heard in it too. It told us in triumphant tones of our pride in our nation, and of our confidence and *trust in God*. Ah me! I can never describe the way little Mendele sang that evening; he made us weep for our desolation, and yet restored our courage and our trust. . . .

"The women were sobbing aloud when he ceased; even the men were weeping; but little Mendele hid his face in his hands and fainted.

"At the beginning of the service Wollmann had kept his eyes fixed on the Ark of the Covenant, but as it went on he had to turn away. He was very pale, and his knees shook so that, strong man as he was, he could hardly stand. His eyes shone as though through tears. With trembling steps and bowed head he slowly passed Mendele, and walked down the aisle to the entrance door. Then he gave the soldiers a sign to follow him.

"Everyone guessed what had happened, but no one spoke of it.

"He sent for Hayyim Grünstein on the day after the fast, and, giving him a blank passport, said, 'It will perhaps be useful to you.'

"From that time forward he treated us with greater toleration; for his power did not last long. The peasants, whom he had formerly oppressed, rose against him in the spring of the great year, and put him to death. . . .

"Now, my friends, this is the story of the two saviors of the Jews of Barnow. Let it teach you to think twice before saying who is great and who is small, who is weak and who is mighty!"

A FAIR, AND JEWISH MARRIAGES

by MENDELE MOCHER SEFORIM

"WELL, then, so I am at the fair, standing by the side of my cart and looking about. I see a vast crowd of Jews, all in a great hurry, doing business, and all very much alive. Jews at a fair are like fish in water, that is to say, in their own element. In their case the blessing of our Patriarch Jacob is being realized: 'They shall multiply like fishes in the world.' It is true, Reb Mendele, that it is written like this in our Holy Book? Is it also written, as Jews are in the habit of saying, 'A fair in Heaven'? It evidently means that a Jew's idea of the next world is a fair. Well, never mind. I see Jews running hither and thither, doing business, buying and selling. Among them I perceive Berl Teletze; in olden times he was a teacher's assistant, then an employée, and now he is a well-to-do merchant owning a big shop. I see Jews running about singly and in pairs, gesticulating, pointing with the index, chewing the points of their beards, everyone in a hurry, greatly excited, too busy to say a word. I look at them, and envy creeps into my heart. They are all running after fortune and evidently on the point of making money, whilst I am standing here like an automaton, a clumsy fool, by the side of my cart, exhibiting my wares. What wares? Rubbish; old prayer- and hymn-books; hymns composed by the pious Sarah—all her hymns are worth three pence. You can imagine the profit they will yield. And from these earnings I am supposed to marry off my daughter! In my innermost heart I am cursing my cart, cursing my lean mare, wishing that they had never existed. Enough, I say, enough! I, too, must try my luck, do some big business like others. But what? I push back my cap upon my head, my brain and my hand begin to work. A straw from a neighboring wagon finds its way into my mouth; I chew it, whilst brain and hands are busy. 'Got it,' I exclaim; 'a splendid idea: a marriage between two merchants, well-to-do people owning shops at the fair.' You understand, Reb Mendele, I had made up my mind to turn matchmaker and to bring about a marriage between two well-to-do merchants, one of them being Reb Eljakim Sharogroder, and the other Reb Getzel Greidinger. No sooner has the idea entered my head than I send my cart and my mare, together with the printer, to hell, and assiduously devote myself to my new business. There is hope and there are prospects. I am running from Reb Getzel to Reb Eljakim and from Reb Eljakim to Reb Getzel. I am running hither and thither, thank God, like other business men, very busy, not worse than other Jews; I am working hard, for the business *must* succeed, and at once, that is to say here, at the fair. There is no better opportunity for a marriage than a fair. Well then, quickly, in a hurry, the business is arranged. The fathers of the young people have seen each other and both are very willing; well, what more do you want, since both parties are ready and willing? I am swelling with pride and joy, counting my profits which I look upon as if I had them already in my pocket. I am already calculating how much dowry I would be able to give my girl. On the strength of my profits I buy drilling for bedding and am on the point of bargaining for a velvet overcoat with a second-hand clothes dealer. As for shirts, that is, of course, of minor importance, the last worry; it will be as luck will have it. Well, never mind; but listen what happened. I tell you, Reb Mendele, if you have no luck it is better you had never been born. I had no luck, for when we were already on the point of settling the business and breaking plates, and were incidentally thinking of bride and bridegroom—well, guess what happened! It is a shame and a heartache to relate, but it turned out nothing; no, worse than nothing, it turned out topsy-turvy. Listen to my misfortune, to God's punishment; it turned out that both fathers had—what do you think they had?—both had boys!"

"But, Reb Alter," I exclaimed, breaking out into a loud laugh, "forgive me, I beg you, but how could you have been so silly as to try and bring about a match before making sure which of the parents had a boy and which had a girl?"

"Of course," said Alter, rather offended, "of course you may laugh; but believe me, I am not as silly as you imagine. Thank God, I am endowed with intelligence just as many another man. Are you a Jew and not aware how matches are usually arranged among Jews? You, Reb Mendele, know perfectly well how matches are settled among us Jews. Thus I knew that Reb Eljakim *ought* to have a girl—and what a girl! A beauty! Did I not see her with mine own eyes a year ago? Well, what of it? If you have no luck then your wisdom and your intelligence are of no avail. Just to spite me it turns out that the silly girl had been in a hurry and had taken it into her head to get married without waiting for my assistance. Why on earth had she been in such a tremendous hurry? And how was I to know it? I was quite ignorant of the fact; may I be as ignorant of my poverty. Now I am asking you, Reb Mendele, judge yourself, did I not act properly and like a man of business? I came to Reb Eljakim and thus I spoke to him: 'Reb Eljakim,' say I, 'I should like to bring about an alliance between yourself and Reb Getzel.' Thus, I said, quite properly and like a Jew. Whom could I have had in my mind if not Reb Eljakim's girl, and with whom could I wish to marry her if not with Reb Getzel's boy? To say all this explicitly was superfluous and not businesslike, because it is understood that a marriage is brought about between a girl and a boy and not between two boys. Well, I think that I acted as like a businessman as possible, and no one in my place would have acted otherwise. Without wasting words on matters which had to be taken for granted, I immediately came to the essentials, to brass tacks. I spoke about the dowry, the trousseau, board for the married couple, etc. You must also remember that at a fair you cannnot waste idle words when talking to merchants, for their time is money; you must count your words and only talk business. That is as far as I am concerned. As for Reb Eljakim, he was also right. When I told him that I was anxious to bring about an alliance between himself and Reb Getzel, he naturally thought of his boy. What else could he think of? It never entered his mind that I meant his girl, knowing full well that his girl was already married and that he had a boy to lead under the canopy. Well, so you see that we were both right. Now you understand?"

"Bah!" said I, scarcely able to repress my laughter and making superhuman efforts to keep a serious face.

"Thank God," said Alter, "that you do understand," pointing at me with the index of his right hand. "There you are," he added, as if I had hit the nail upon the head.

To tell the truth, Alter's arguments did not seem quite so silly to me. "Why not?" I thought; marriages among us Jews are indeed being arranged only between the families. It is an alliance between wealth, rank, and position; why should not such mistakes happen? Looking quite kindly at Alter, I said once more, almost involuntarily, "Bah!"

"There you are," said Alter, pointing at me with his finger; "I am right, am I not, when I say that you understand now? But we have not yet finished. A faint hope still lingered within me. When I take up a business I do not so easily give it up."

"But, Reb Alter," I exclaimed, "God be with you! What are you talking about?" I was amazed at his words, imagining that the heat had affected him and turned his brain. "What hope could you have entertained when you knew that both parents had boys?"

"Hush, hush," said Alter, "don't get excited; and let me explain. It is all right, Reb Mendele, I am not mad. The pulse of hope was still beating, for, you see, God Almighty creates the remedy before the disease. There was still Mr. Teletze, who had not yet entered the scene. At the very beginning already I had been thinking of Teletze. He has plenty of girls, lots of them. Eljakim, Getzel, Teletze were crowding my brain, but as my ill-luck would have it, I had just chosen Reb Eljakim and put Teletze aside. When the misfortune befell me, I at once hastened to repair my mistake and led Teletze into the arena, Teletze, a well-to-do, highly respected man. In short, I minimized the mistake, *my* mistake, *their* mistake; never mind. I was a little to be blamed, but above all it was a question of luck and destiny. It had not been decreed in Heaven, you understand? And now I began over again, expatiating upon the merits of Reb Berl Teletze. He is—may the devil eye not touch him!— a very wealthy man and a charitable man; president of many charitable societies. Reb Berl Teletze—who has not heard of Reb Berl Teletze? Needless for me to add that he is also a clever and an intelligent man, for that is already implied in the very word *wealthy*. In short, my spark of hope soon developed into a flame.

"'All is for the best,' I said; 'it is lucky that two boys have emerged like oil upon the water. Now I require two girls for them, and Teletze, the father of several girls, will help me out. With the help of the Almighty it will be quite all right.' To cut a long story short, I began to work hard; I was running hither and thither, was very busy. At first it seemed as if things were going on well, when suddenly, and just to annoy me, the fair came to an end. The fair was over, all the merchants quickly packed up and left, and all my labor had been wasted and lost. Now you understand," Alter continued, turning again to me, speaking as in prayer, stretching out both hands as if he were pouring out his bitter heart and supplicating me to help him. "Now you understand. I tell you, when you have no luck all your cleverness is of no avail. Ah, woe unto me, the anger of God has come down upon me; it is a punishment for my sins!—What were you saying? You were talking of business for cash. Have I a spare copper in my pocket? Woe and woe is unto me."

THE SINNER

by SHOLOM ASCH

So that you should not suspect me of taking his part, I will write a short preface to my story.

It is written: "A man never so much as moves his finger, but it has been so decreed from above," and whatsoever a man does, he fulfils God's will —even animals and birds (I beg to distinguish!) carry out God's wishes: whenever a bird flies, it fulfils a precept, because God, blessed is He, formed it to fly, and an ox the same when it lows, and even a dog when it barks—all praise God with their voices, and sing hymns to Him, each after his manner.

And even the wicked who transgresses fulfils God's will in spite of himself. Why? Do you suppose he takes pleasure in transgressing? Isn't he certain to repent? Well, then? He is just carrying out the will of Heaven.

And the Evil Inclination himself! Why, every time he is sent to persuade a Jew to sin, he weeps and sighs: "Woe is me, that I should be sent on such an errand!"

After this little preface, I will tell you the story itself.

Formerly, before the thing happened, he was called Reb Avrohom, but afterwards they ceased calling him by his name, and said simply the Sinner.

Reb Avrohom was looked up to and respected by the whole town, a God-fearing Jew, beloved and honored by all, and mothers wished they might have children like him.

He sat the whole day in the house-of-study and learned. Not that he was a great scholar, but he was a pious, scrupulously observant Jew, who followed the straight and beaten road, a man without any pride. He used to recite the prayers in Shul together with the strangers by the door, and quite quietly, without any shouting or, one might say, any special enthusiasm. His prayer that rose to Heaven, the barred gates opening before it till it entered and was taken up into the Throne of Glory, this prayer of his did not become a diamond there, dazzling the eye, but a softly glistening pearl.

And how, you ask, did he come to be called the Sinner? In this wise: You must know that everyone, even those who were hardest on him after the affair, acknowledged that he was a great lover of Israel, and I will add that his sin and, Heaven defend us, his coming to such a fall, all proceeded from his being such a lover of Israel, such a patriot.

And it was just the simple Jew, the very common folk, that he loved.

He used to say: A Jew who is a driver, for instance, and busy all the week with his horses and cart, and soaked in materialism for six days at a stretch, so that he only just manages to get in his prayers—when he comes home on Sabbath and sits down to table, and the bed is made, and the candles burning, and his wife and children are round him, and they sing hymns together, well, the driver dozing off over his prayer-book and forgetting to say grace, I tell you, said Reb Avrohom, the Divine Presence rests on his house and rejoices and says, "Happy am I that I chose me out this people," for such a Jew keeps Sabbath, rests himself, and his horse rests, keeps Sabbath likewise, stands in the stable, and is also conscious that it is the holy Sabbath, and when the driver rises from his sleep, he leads the animal out to pasture, waters it, and they all go for a walk with it in the meadow.

And this walk of theirs is more acceptable to God, blessed is He, than repeating "Bless the Lord, O my soul!" It may be this was because he himself was of humble origin; he had lived till he was thirteen with his father, a farmer, in an out-of-the-way village, and ignorant even of his letters. True, his father had taken a youth into the house to teach him Hebrew, but Reb Avrohom as a boy was very wild, wouldn't mind his book, and ran all day after the oxen and horses.

He used to lie out in the meadow, hidden in the long grasses, near him the horses with their heads down pulling at the grass, and the view stretched far, far away, into the endless distance, and above him spread the wide sky, through which the clouds made their way, and the green, juicy earth seemed to look up at it and say: "Look, sky, and see how cheerfully I try to obey God's behest, to make the world green with grass!" And the sky made answer: "See, earth, how I try to fulfil God's command by spreading myself far and wide!" And the few trees scattered over the fields were like witnesses to their friendly agreement. And little Avrohom lay and rejoiced in the goodness and all the work of God. Suddenly, as though he had received a revelation from

Heaven, he went home, and asked the youth who was his teacher, "What blessing should one recite on feeling happy at sight of the world?" The youth laughed, and said: "You stupid boy! One says a blessing over bread and water, but as to saying one over *this world*—who ever heard of such a thing?"

Avrohom wondered, "The world is beautiful, the sky so pretty, the earth so sweet and soft, everything is so delightful to look at, and one says no blessing over it all!"

At thirteen he had left the village and come to the town. There, in the house-of-study, he saw the head of the Academy sitting at one end of the table, and around it, the scholars, all reciting in fervent, appealing tones that went to his heart.

The boy began to cry, whereupon the head of the Academy turned and saw a little boy with a torn hat, crying, and his hair coming out through the holes, and his boots slung over his shoulder, like a peasant lad fresh from the road. The scholars laughed, but the Rosh ha-Yeshivah asked him what he wanted.

"To learn," he answered in a low, pleading voice.

The Rosh ha-Yeshivah had compassion on him, and took him as a pupil. Avrohom applied himself earnestly to the Torah, and in a few days could read Hebrew and follow the prayers without help.

And the way he prayed was a treat to watch. You should have seen him! He just stood and talked, as one person talks to another, quietly and affectionately, without any tricks of manner.

Once the Rosh ha-Yeshivah saw him praying, and said before his whole Academy, "I can learn better than he, but when it comes to praying, I don't reach to his ankles." That is what he said.

So Reb Avrohom lived there till he was grown up, and had married the daughter of a simple tailor. Indeed, he learnt tailoring himself, and lived by his ten fingers. By day he sat and sewed with an open prayer-book before him, and recited portions of the Psalms to himself. After dark he went into the house-of-study, so quietly that no one noticed him, and passed half the night over the Talmud.

Once some strangers came to the town, and spent the night in the house-of-study behind the stove. Suddenly they heard a thin, sweet voice that was like a tune in itself. They started up, and saw him at his book. The small lamp hanging by a cord poured a dim light upon him where he sat, while the walls remained in shadow. He studied with ardor, with enthusiasm, only his enthusiasm was not for beholders, it was all within; he swayed slowly to and fro, and his shadow swayed with him, and he softly chanted the Gemara. By degrees his voice rose, his face kindled, and his eyes began to glow, one could see that his very soul was resolving itself into his chanting. The Divine Presence hovered over him, and he drank in its sweetness. And in the middle of his reading, he got up and walked about the room, repeating in a trembling whisper, "Lord of the World! O Lord of the World!"

Then his voice grew as suddenly calm, and he stood still, as though he had dozed off where he stood, for pure delight. The lamp grew dim, and still he stood and stood and never moved.

Awe fell on the travelers behind the stove, and they cried out. He started and approached them, and they had to close their eyes against the brightness of his face, the light that shone out of his eyes! And he stood there quite quietly and simply, and asked in a gentle voice why they had called out. Were they cold?

And he took off his cloak and spread it over them.

Next morning the travelers told all this, and declared that no sooner had the cloak touched them than they had fallen asleep, and they had seen and heard nothing more that night. After this, when the whole town had got wind of it, and they found out who it was that night in the house-of-study, the people began to believe that he was a Zaddik, and they came to him with petitions, as Hasidim to their Rebbes, asking him to pray for their health and other wants. But when they brought him such a petition, he would smile and say: "Believe me, a little boy who says grace over a piece of bread which his mother has given him, he can help you more than twenty such as I."

Of course, his words made no impression, except that they brought more petitions than ever, upon which he said:

"You insist on a man of flesh and blood such as I being your advocate with God, blessed is He. Hear a parable: To what shall we liken the thing? To the light of the sun and the light of a small lamp. You can rejoice in the sunlight as much as you please, and no one can take your joy from you; the poorest and most humble may revive himself with it, so long as his eyes can behold it, even though a man should sit, which God forbid, in a dungeon with closed windows, a reflection will make its way through the chinks, and he shall rejoice in the brightness. But with the poor light of a lamp it is otherwise. A rich man buys a quantity of lamps and illumines his house, while a poor man sits in darkness. God, blessed be He, is the great light that shines for the whole world, reviving and refreshing all His works. The whole world is full of His mercy, and His compassion is over all His creatures. Believe me, you have no need of an advocate with Him; God is your Father, and you are his dear children. How should a child need an advocate with his father?"

The ordinary folk heard and were silent, but our people the Hasidim were displeased. And I'll tell you another thing, I was the first to mention it to the Rebbe, long life to him, and he, as is well known, commanded Reb Avrohom to his presence.

So we set to work to persuade Reb Avrohom and talked to him till he had to go with us.

The journey lasted four days.

I remember one night, the moon was wandering in a blue ocean of sky that spread ever so far, till it mingled with a cloud, and she looked at us, pitifully and appealingly, as though to ask us if we knew which way she ought to go, to the right or to the left, and presently the cloud came upon her, and she began struggling to get out of it, and a minute or two later she was free again and smiling at us.

Then a little breeze came, and stroked our faces, and we looked around to the four sides of the world, and it seemed as if the whole world were wrapped in a prayer-scarf woven of mercy, and we fell into a slight melancholy, a quiet sadness, but so sweet and pleasant, it felt like on a Sabbath at twilight at the Third Meal.

Suddenly Reb Avrohom exclaimed: "Jews, have you said the blessings on the appearance of the new moon?" We turned towards the moon, laid down our bundles, washed our hands in a little stream that ran by the roadside, and repeated the blessings for the new moon.

He stood looking into the sky, his lips scarcely moving, as was his wont. "Sholom Aleihem!" he said, turning to me, and his voice quivered like a violin, and his eyes called to peace and unity. Then an awe of Reb Avrohom came over me for the first time, and when we had finished sanctifying the moon our melancholy left us, and we prepared to continue our way.

But still he stood and gazed heavenward, sighing: "Lord of the Universe! How beautiful is the world which Thou hast made by Thy goodness and great mercy, and these are over all Thy creatures. They all love Thee, and are glad in Thee, and Thou art glad in them, and the whole world is full of Thy glory."

I glanced up at the moon, and it seemed that she was still looking at me, and saying, "I'm lost; which way am I to go?"

We arrived Friday afternoon, and had time enough to go to the bath and to greet the Rebbe.

He, long life to him, was seated in the reception room beside a table, his long lashes over his eyes, leaning on his left hand, while he greeted newcomers with his right. We went up to him, one at a time, shook hands, and said "Sholom Aleihem," and he, long life to him, said nothing to us. Reb Avrohom also went up to him, and he held out his hand.

A change came over the Rebbe, he raised his eyelids with his fingers, and looked at Reb Avrohom for some time in silence.

And Reb Avrohom looked at the Rebbe, and was silent too.

The Hasidim were offended by such impertinence.

That evening we assembled in the Rebbe's house-of-study, to usher in the Sabbath. It was tightly packed with Jews, one pushing the other, or seizing hold of his girdle; only beside the ark was there a free space left, a semi-circle, in the middle of which stood the Rebbe and prayed.

But Reb Avrohom stood by the door among the poor guests, and prayed after his fashion.

"To Kiddush," called the beadle.

The Rebbe's wife, daughters, and daughters-in-law now appeared, and their jewelry, their precious stones, and their pearls sparkled and shone.

The Rebbe stood and repeated the prayer of Sanctification.

He was slightly bent, and his grey beard swept his breast. His eyes were screened by his lashes, and he recited the Sanctification in a loud voice, giving to every word a peculiar inflection, to every sign an expression of its own.

"To table!" was called out next.

At the head of the table sat the Rebbe, sons and sons-in-law to the left, relations to the right of him, then the principal aged Jews, then the rich.

The people stood round about.

The Rebbe ate, and began to serve out the leavings to his sons and sons-in-law first, and to the rest of those sitting at the table after.

Then there was silence, the Rebbe began to expound the Torah. The portion of the week was Numbers, chapter eight, and the Rebbe began:

"When a man's soul is on a low level, enveloped, Heaven defend us, in uncleanness, and the Divine spark within the soul wishes to rise to a higher level, and cannot do so alone, but must needs be helped, it is a *mizvah* to help her, to raise her, and this *mizvah* is specially incumbent on the priest. This is the meaning of 'the seven lamps shall give light over against the candle-stick,' by which is meant the holy Torah. The priest must bring the Jew's heart near to the Torah; in this way he is able to raise it. And who is the priest? The righteous in his generation, because since the Temple was destroyed, the saint must be a priest, for thus is the command from above, that he shall be the priest. . . ."

"Avrohom!" the Rebbe called suddenly, "Avrohom! Come here, I am calling you."

The other went up to him.

"Avrohom, did you understand? Did you make out the meaning of what I said?

"Your silence," the Rebbe went on, "is an acknowledgment. I must raise you, even though it be against my will and against your will."

There was dead stillness in the room, people waiting to hear what would come next.

"You are silent?" asked the Rebbe, now a little sternly.

"You want to be a raiser of souls? Have you, bless and preserve us, bought the Almighty for yourself? Do you think that a Jew can approach nearer to God, blessed is He, through you? That you are the 'handle of the pestle' and the rest of the Jews nowhere? God's grace is everywhere, whichever way we turn; every time we move a limb we feel God! Everyone must seek him in his own heart, because there it is that He has caused the Divine

Presence to rest. Everywhere and always can the Jew draw near to God. . . ."

Thus answered Reb Avrohom, but our people, the Rebbe's followers, shut his mouth before he had made an end, and had the Rebbe not held them back, they would have torn him in pieces on the spot.

"Leave him alone!" he commanded the Hasidim.

And to Reb Avrohom he said:

"Avrohom, you have sinned!"

And from that day forward he was called the Sinner, and was shut out from everywhere. The Hasidim kept their eye on him, and persecuted him, and he was not even allowed to pray in the house-of-study.

And I'll tell you what I think: A wicked man, even when he acts according to his wickedness, fulfils God's command. And who knows? Perhaps they were both right!

BONTCHE SHWEIG

by ISAAC LOEB PERETZ

D OWN here, in this world, Bontche Shweig's death made no impression at all. Ask anyone you like who Bontche was, how he lived, and what he died of; whether of heart failure, or whether his strength gave out, or whether his back broke under a heavy load, and they won't know. Perhaps, after all, he died of hunger.

If a tramcar horse had fallen dead, there would have been more excitement. It would have been mentioned in the papers, and hundreds of people would have crowded round to look at the dead animal—even the spot where the accident took place.

But the tramway horse would receive less attention if there were as many horses as men—a thousand million.

Bontche lived quietly and died quietly. He passed through our world like a shadow.

No wine was drunk at Bontche's circumcision, no healths were proposed, and he made no beautiful speech when he was confirmed. He lived like a little dun-colored grain of sand on the seashore, among millions of his kind; and when the wind lifted him and blew him over to the other side of the sea, nobody noticed it.

When he was alive, the mud in the street preserved no impression of his feet; after his death, the wind overturned the little board on his grave. The grave-digger's wife found it a long way off from the spot, and boiled a potful of potatoes over it. Three days after that, the grave-digger had forgotten where he had laid him.

If Bontche had been given a tombstone, then, in a hundred years or so, an antiquarian might have found it, and the name "Bontche Shweig" would have echoed once again in our air.

A shadow! His likeness remained photographed in nobody's brain, in nobody's heart; not a trace of him remained.

"No kith, no kin!" He lived and died alone!

Had it not been for the human commotion, someone might have heard Bontche's spine snap under its load; had the world been less busy, someone might have remarked that Bontche (also a human being) went about with two extinguished eyes and fearfully hollow cheeks; that even when he had no load on his shoulders, his head drooped earthward as though, while yet alive, he were looking for his grave. Were there as few men as tramway horses, someone might perhaps have asked: What has happened to Bontche?

When they carried Bontche into the hospital, his corner in the underground lodging was soon filled—there were ten of his like waiting for it, and they put it up to auction among themselves. When they carried him from the hospital bed to the morgue, there were twenty poor sick persons waiting for the bed. When he had been taken out of the morgue, they brought in twenty bodies from under a building that had fallen in. Who knows how long he will rest in his grave? Who knows how many are waiting for the little plot of ground?

A quiet birth, a quiet life, a quiet death, and a quieter burial.

But it was not so in the *other* world. *There* Bontche's death made a great impression.

The blast of the great Messianic Shofar sounded through all the seven heavens: Bontche Shweig has left the earth! The largest angels with the broadest wings flew about and told one another: Bontche Shweig is to take his seat in the Heavenly Academy! In Paradise there was a noise and joyful tumult: Bontche Shweig! Just fancy! Bontche Shweig!

Little child-angels with sparkling eyes, gold thread-work wings, and silver slippers, ran delightedly to meet him. The rustle of the wings, the tap-tap of the little slippers, and the merry laughter of the fresh, rosy mouths, filled all the heavens and reached to the Throne of Glory, and God Himself knew that Bontche Shweig was coming.

Abraham, our father, stood in the gate, his right hand stretched out with a hearty greeting, and a sweet smile lit up his old face.

What are they wheeling through heaven?

Two angels are pushing a golden armchair into Paradise for Bontche Shweig.

What flashed so brightly?

They were carrying past a gold crown set with precious stones—all for Bontche Shweig.

"Before the decision of the Heavenly Court has been given?" ask the saints, not quite without jealousy.

"Oh," reply the angels, "that will be a mere formality. Even the prosecutor won't say a word against Bontche Shweig. The case will not last five minutes."

Just consider: Bontche Shweig!

When the little angels had met Bontche in mid-air and played him a tune; when Abraham, our father, had shaken him by the hand like an old comrade; when he hearrd that a chair stood waiting for him in Paradise, that a crown lay ready for his head, and that not a word would be lost over his case before the Heavenly Court—Bontche, just as in the other world, was too frightened to speak. His heart sank with terror. He is sure it is all a dream, or else simply a mistake.

He is used to both. He often dreamt, in the other world, that he was picking up money off the floor—there were whole heaps of it—and then he woke to find himself as poor as ever; and more than once people had smiled at him and given him a friendly word and then turned away and spit out.

"It is my luck," he used to think. And now he dared not raise his eyes, lest the dream should vanish, lest he should wake up in some cave full of snakes and lizards. He was afraid to speak, afraid to move, lest he should be recognized and flung into the pit.

He trembles and does not hear the angels' compliments, does not see how they dance round him, makes no answer to the greeting of Abraham, our father, and—when he is led into the presence of the Heavenly Court, he does not even wish it "good morning!"

He is beside himself with terror, and his fright increases when he happens to notice the floor of the Heavenly Courthouse; it is all alabaster set with diamonds. "And my feet standing on it!" He is paralyzed. "Who knows what rich man, what rabbi, what saint they take me for—he will come—and that will be the end of me!"

His terror is such, he never even hears the president call out: "The case of Bontche Shweig!" adding, as he hands the deeds to the advocate, "Read, but make haste!"

The whole hall goes round and round in Bontche's eyes; there is a rushing in his ears. And through the rushing he hears more and more clearly the voice of the advocate, speaking sweetly as a violin.

"His name," he hears, "fitted him like the dress made for a slender figure by the hand of an artist-tailor."

"What is he talking about?" wondered Bontche, and he heard an impatient voice break in with:

"No similes, please!"

"He never," continued the advocate, "was heard to complain of either

God or man; there was never a flash of hatred in his eye; he never lifted it with a claim on heaven."

Still Bontche does not understand, and once again the hard voice interrupts: "No rhetoric, please!"

"Job gave way—this one was more unfortunate—"

"Facts, dry facts!"

"When he was a week old, he was circumcised . . ."

"We want no realism!"

"The mohel who circumcised him did not know his work—"

"Come, come!"

"And he kept silent," the advocate went on, "even when his mother died, and he was given a stepmother at thirteen years old—a serpent, a vixen."

"Can they mean me after all?" thought Bontche.

"No insinuations against a third party!" said the president, angrily.

"She grudged him every mouthful—stale, mouldy bread, tendons instead of meat—and *she* drank coffee with cream."

"Keep to the subject," ordered the president.

"She grudged him everything but her finger nails, and his black-and-blue body showed through the holes in his torn and fusty clothes. Winter time, in the hardest frost, he had to chop wood for her, barefoot, in the yard, and his hands were too young and too weak, the legs too thick, the hatchet too blunt. More than once he nearly dislocated his wrist; more than once his feet were nearly frost-bitten, but he kept silent, even to his father."

"To that drunkard?" laughs the accuser, and Bontche feels cold in every limb.

"He never even complained to his father," finished up the advocate.

"And always alone," he continued; "no playmates, no school, nor teaching of any kind—never a whole garment—never a free moment."

"Facts, please!" reminded the president.

"He kept silent even later, when his father seized him by the hair in a fit of drunkenness, and flung him out into the street on a snowy winter's night. He quietly picked himself up out of the snow and ran whither his feet carried him.

"He kept silent all the way—however hungry he might be, he begged only with his eyes.

"It was a wild, wet night in springtime, when he reached the great town; he fell like a drop into the ocean, and yet he passed that same night under arrest. He kept silent and never asked why, for what. He was let out, and looked about for the hardest work. And he kept silent. Harder than the work itself was the finding of it—and he kept silent.

"Bathed in a cold sweat, crushed together under heavy loads, his empty stomach convulsed with hunger—he kept silent.

"Bespattered with mud, spat at, driven with his load off the pavement and into the street among the cabs, carts, and tramways, looking death in the eyes every moment—he kept silent.

"He never calculated how many pounds' burden go to a groschen, how many times he fell on an errand worth a dreier; how many times he nearly panted out his soul going after his pay; he never calculated the difference between other people's lot and his—he kept silent.

"And he never insisted loudly on his pay; he stood in the doorway like a beggar, with a dog-like pleading in his eyes— Come again later! and he went like a shadow to come again later, and beg for his wage more humbly than before.

"He kept silent even when they cheated him of part, or threw in a false coin.

"He took everything in silence."

"They mean me, after all," thought Bontche.

"Once," continued the advocate, after a sip of water, "a change came into his life: there came flying along a carriage on rubber tires drawn by two runaway horses. The driver already lay some distance off on the pavement with a cracked skull. The terrified horses foamed at the mouth, sparks shot from their hoofs, their eyes shone like fiery lamps on a winter's night—and in the carriage, more dead than alive, sat a man.

"And Bontche stopped the horses. And the man he had saved was a charitable Jew, who was not ungrateful.

"He put the dead man's whip into Bontche's hands, and Bontche became a coachman. More than that—he was provided with a wife, and more still— with a child.

"And Bontche kept silent!"

"Me, they mean me!" Bontche assured himself again, and yet had not the courage to give a glance at the Heavenly Court.

He listens to the advocate further:

"He kept silent also when his protector became bankrupt and did not pay him his wages.

"He kept silent when his wife ran away from him, leaving him a child at the breast.

"He was silent also fifteen years later, when the child had grown up and was strong enough to throw him out of the house."

"Me, they mean me!" Now he is sure of it.

"He kept silent even," began the angelic advocate once more in a still softer and sadder voice, "when the same philanthropist paid all his creditors their due but him—and even when (riding once again in a carriage with rubber tires and fiery horses) he knocked Bontche down and drove over him.

"He kept silent. He did not even tell the police who had done for him."

"He kept silent even in the hospital, where one may cry out.

"He kept silent when the doctor would not come to his bedside without being paid fifteen kopeks, and when the attendant demanded another five—for changing his linen.

"He kept silent in the death-struggle—silent in death.

"Not a word against God; not a word against men!

"*Dixi!*"

Once more Bontche trembled all over; he knew that after the advocate comes the prosecutor. Who knows what *he* will say?

Bontche himself had remembered nothing of his life.

Even in the other world he forgot every moment what had happened in the one before. The advocate had recalled everything to his mind. Who knows what the prosecutor will not remind him of?

"Gentlemen," begins the prosecutor, in a voice biting and acid as vinegar—but he breaks off.

"Gentlemen," he begins again, but his voice is milder, and a second time he breaks off.

Then, from out the same throat, comes in a voice that is almost gentle:

"Gentlemen! *He* was silent! I will be silent, too!"

There is a hush—and there sounds in front a new, soft, trembling voice:

"Bontche, my child"—it speaks like a harp—"my dear child Bontche!"

And Bontche's heart melts within him. Now he would lift up his eyes, but they are blinded with tears; he never felt such sweet emotion before. "My child! My Bontche!"—no one, since his mother died, had spoken to him with such words in such a voice.

"My child," continued the presiding judge, "you have suffered and kept silent; there is no whole limb, no whole bone in your body, without a scar, without a wound, not a fibre of your soul that has not bled—and you kept silent.

"There they did not understand. Perhaps you yourself did not know that you might have cried out, and that at your cry the walls of Jericho would have shaken and fallen. You yourself knew nothing of your hidden power.

"In the other world your silence was not understood, but *that* is the world of delusion; in the world of truth you will receive your reward.

"The Heavenly Court will not judge you; the Heavenly Court will not pass sentence on you; they will not apportion you a reward. Take what you will! Everything is yours!"

"Bontche looks up for the first time. He is dazzled; everything shines and flashes and streams with light.

"*Taki?*" he asks shyly.

"Yes, really!" answers the presiding judge with decision; "really, I tell you, everything is yours; everything in heaven belongs to you. Because all that shines and sparkles is only the reflection of your hidden goodness a reflection of your soul. You only take of what is yours."

"*Taki?*" asks Bontche again, this time in a firmer voice.

"*Taki! taki! taki!*" they answer him from all sides.

"Well, if it is so," Bontche smiles, "I would like to have every day, for breakfast, a hot roll with fresh butter."

The Court and the angels looked down, a little ashamed; the prosecutor laughed.

ANOTHER PAGE TO THE SONG OF SONGS

by SHOLOM ALEICHEM

I

"BESSIE, Bessie! Quicker, quicker!" And I caught hold of little Bessie's hand, and together we began to run up the hill. This was the day before Pentecost. "Come, Bessie; the day won't wait for us, little goose, and look what a big hill we've got to cross! And on the other side of the hill is a river, and over the river is stretched a wooden bridge. And the water runs and the frogs croak and the planks of the bridge all creak and shake. And when we get to the other side of the bridge we get to the real, real Paradise, Bessie. That's where my estates begin!"

"Your estates?"

"I mean the meadow—a big, big field. It stretches and stretches away without an end. And it's all covered with a green blanket, and on the green blanket are scattered specks of yellow and shoots of red. Oh, and you should smell the air—the most beautiful spices in the whole world! And you should see my trees—trees, I tell you, without number—great high trees, branching outwards. And I've got a hill there, on which I sit down. I mean to say, if I wish to, I sit on it, but if I don't, well, I just sit down on my magic carpet and I fly away, like an eagle, high above the clouds and mists, over field and forest, over ocean and desert—until I come to the other side of the dark river."

" 'And from there' "—Bessie interrupts me—" 'and from there you go on foot seven miles, till you come to a little lake—' "

"No, you don't know anything about it, Bessie. I come to a dense wood. First I go into the wood, and then I go out of the wood, and I come to a little lake—"

"Then you swim across the water, and you count seven times seven—"

"Yes, and an old, old man with a long white beard grows out of the ground and he asks me, 'Sir, what is your desire?' "

"So I say to him: 'Take me across to the Queen's daughter.' "

Just then Bessie tears her hand from mine, and begins to run downhill; and I run after her.

"Bessie, Bessie! Where are you running to?"

No answer. She is vexed. She doesn't like the Queen's daughter. Bessie likes all my tales except the one about the Queen's daughter. . . .

II

But you ought to know who Bessie is. I think I've already told you once, but I suppose you've forgotten, so I'll tell it to you again.

I had a big brother once—Benny was his name—and he was drowned. And he left behind him a water-mill, a young widow, two horses and a baby. We left the mill there; we sold the two horses; the widow married someone who lived far away; and we kept the baby.

That was Bessie.

Sometimes I really have to laugh. Everybody thinks that Bessie and I are sister and brother. She calls my mother "mamma," and she calls my father "papa." And the two of us live together like brother and sister, and we love each other like brother and sister.

Like brother and sister? Then why are you sometimes so shy with me, Bessie?

Once something happened between us. We were left alone in the house, just the two of us in the whole house. Night was falling; it was beginning to get dark. Father had gone to say prayers for the soul of my older brother Benny, and mother had gone out to buy matches. Bessie and I got into a quiet corner and I began to tell her stories. Bessie loves to hear my stories—all kinds of stories—about school, and from the Arabian Nights. And she snuggled up to me, and her hand was in mine.

"Ah, Sammy, tell me another one, do!"

Silently the night descends. Slowly, slowly, the shadows gather on the walls, tremble and slide downwards, till they reach the floor and spread themselves out. We can hardly see each other. Only I can feel her heart beating, and I can see her eyes shining in the dark. Suddenly, she tears her hand from mine. "Bessie, what's the matter?" "We mustn't do it." "Mustn't do what, Bessie?" "Hold each other's hand." "But why, Bessie? Who said so?" "Nobody said so. I know it myself." "But we're not strangers, little goose. Aren't we brother and sister?" "Oh, Sammy! if we really were brother and sister!" And her words sound like the cry in the Song of Songs: "Oh, that thou wert as my brother!"

It's always the same. Whenever I speak of Bessie I remember the Song of Songs.

III

Oh, what was I telling you? Oh, yes, the day before Pentecost. We're just running downhill; first Bessie and I after her. She is vexed with me about the Queen's daughter. But you needn't worry that Bessie is vexed with me. It lasts just as long as it takes me to tell you about it. In another moment she looks at me again, with her big, bright eyes; she tosses her hair back, and cries:

"Sammy, Sammy, Sammy! Just look at the sky, just look. I do believe you can't see what is up there!"

"Why, you little goose, of course I can see. I can see the sky, and I can feel a soft wind, and I can hear the birds twittering and chirping and flying over our heads—our sky. Bessie, our wind, our birds—everything is ours, ours, ours. Now give me your hand, Bessie."

No! She won't give me her hand. She is shy. Now, why is Bessie shy with me? Why won't she let me hold her hand?

"Over there," says Bessie, and she runs ahead. "Over there, on the other side of the bridge! . . ." And I seem to hear in her words the call of the Shulamite: "Come, my Beloved, let us go forth into the field, let us lodge in the villages. Let us go up early to the vineyards; let us see if the vine flourisheth, whether the tender grape appear, and the pomegranate bud forth. . . ."

And now we have reached the bridge.

IV

The water runs and the frogs croak and the planks of the bridge creak and shake and Bessie trembles in fear.

"Oh, Bessie, Bessie, you're a—what are you afraid of, little goose? Hold on to me tightly, or rather let me put my arms round you—so. My arms round you, and your arms round me. See? Now, like this."

And now we have reached the other side of the bridge.

And with arms around one another, as we have crossed the bridge, we walk over the field, we alone in this paradise. Bessie holds me tightly, very tightly. She is silent, but I seem to hear her speak the words of the Song of Songs: "I am my Beloved's, and my Beloved is mine . . ."

The meadow is green. It stretches and stretches far without an end. And it is all covered with a green blanket and on the green blanket there are scattered specks of yellow and shoots of red. And the scents of the meadow are those of the most beautiful spices in the whole world. And we two walk here with our arms around one another. Just we two, we two alone in this Paradise.

"Sammy," says Bessie, looking straight into my eyes and nestling still closer to me: "When shall we begin to gather greens for Pentecost?"

"There is still plenty of time, little goose," I say, and my face burns. I do not know where to look—shall I look into the great blue covering of the sky, or shall I look at the green blanket of the broad field, or shall I look away to the end of the world yonder, where heavens come down to meet the earth? Or shall I look at Bessie's bright face, into her beautiful wide eyes, which seem to me to be deep, deep as the heavens, and sorrowful, sorrowful as the night? A great sorrow lies hidden in them, and a quiet sadness veils them in a mist. I know what the sorrow is that lies hidden in them; I know the reason of her sadness. And I feel a silent anger rising in me against her mother, who married a strange father, and left her for ever, for ever, just as if they had been strangers. In our house the name of her mother is forbidden, as if Bessie never had a mother. My mother is her mother, my father is her father. And they love her as one of their own children; give her whatever her heart desires. Bessie says she wants to go with me to gather greens for Pentecost (that is why we have come to this field together), and father turns to mother, and says, "Well?" and he looks over the silver rims of his glasses and strokes the silver threads in his beard. And a discussion arises between them as to whether Bessie should go with me out of the city and gather greens for Pentecost.

Father: What do you think about it?

Mother: What do you think about it?

Father: Shall we let them go together?

Mother: Why shouldn't we?

Father: I didn't say we shouldn't let them go.

Mother: Well, then, what do you say?

Father: I simply said, shall we let them go?

Mother: Why shouldn't we let them go?

And so on. I know what there is at the back of their minds. About a dozen times father reminds me—and mother repeats it after him, that over there, on the way, there is a bridge, and under the bridge there is a running water . . . a river . . . a river . . .

v

We, Bessie and I, have long since forgotten the bridge and the river. We wander over the broad, free meadow, under the broad, free skies. We run across the green fields, we tumble and roll about in the sweet-smelling grass; we jump up again, and tumble and roll about again, and we have not even begun to gather greens for Pentecost. I escort Bessie across the length and breadth of the field, and I begin to speak boastfully of my estates.

"Do you see these trees? Do you see this sand? Do you see this little hill?"

"And is everything yours?"

So Bessie asks me, and her wide eyes laugh at me. Her laughter vexes me. It is a habit she has, that of laughing at me. I begin to sulk, and I turn away from her. Then Bessie guesses that I am vexed. She runs in front of me, looks straight into my eyes, takes my hand in hers, and says, "Sammy" and my vexation passes in an instant, and I forget everything. And I take her by the hand, and I lead her to my little hill. This is the little hill I sit on every year. When I feel so inclined I sit there and when I don't wish to sit there I seat myself on my magic carpet and I fly away, like an eagle, right above the clouds and mists, over field and forest, over ocean and desert.

VI

There, on the little hill, we sit, Bessie and I, and we have not even begun to gather greens for Pentecost. We tell stories, that is to say, I tell her stories, and she listens to them. And I tell her of that which is to be in the days to come, when I will grow into a man, and she into a woman, and we will marry each other. . . . We will take our places on the magic carpet and rise above the mists and clouds, and then commence to fly over the whole earth. First we will go to all the countries which Alexander the Great visited; then we will go to Palestine. We will visit the hills where spices grow, fill our pockets with figs and dates and almonds and then fly on and on. And wherever we will come we will play different tricks, for of course, *nobody* will be able to see us. . . .

"Will *nobody* be able to see us?" cries Bessie and catches hold of my hand. *"Nobody, nobody* at all. We will see *everybody* and *nobody* will see us."

"Well, Sammy, I want to ask you a favor."

"A favor?"

"One little favor."

But I know well enough what the favor is to be. She wants us to fly to the far-away city where her mother married a second time, and play some kind of a trick on her stepfather.

"Certainly, why not?" I answer her. "With the greatest pleasure. You may depend on me. I will play them such a trick that they will remember me forever."

"Not them; only him; him alone," she begs of me. But I am not so easily persuaded. It is no safe matter to trifle with my temper. Does Bessie think I am going to forgive her mother? That slut of a woman! Fancy having the impudence to marry another father, and go away with him somewhere to the other end of the earth—and leave her child—never even write her the shortest note! Now I ask you, have you ever heard anything like it, in all your born days?

VII

But I lost my temper in vain. I regret it, regret it bitterly; but it is too late. Bessie has put up both her hands to her face. Is she crying? I want to kick myself. What on earth did I want to open her wounds afresh for? I call myself all the names I can think of—"Donkey! idiot! ass! chatterbox!" I move up to her. I take her hand. "Bessie! Bessie!" I want to speak to her in the words of the Song of Songs: "Let me see thy countenance, let me hear thy voice."

And then, suddenly—where did they spring from?—my father and mother.

VIII

My father's silver-rimmed glasses twinkle from afar. The silver threads of his beard float in the gentle wind, and my mother beckons to us with her shawl. Both of us, Bessie and I, remain sitting as though turned to stone. What are they doing here, my father and mother?

They have come to see that we are quite safe, to make sure that nothing has happened to us—God forbid. Heaven knows what might have happened . . . a bridge . . . a river. . . .

Queer folks, my father and mother.

"And where are the greens?"

"What greens?"

"The greens for Pentecost you went to gather?"

The two of us, Bessie and I, look at each other. I read her eyes and I understood her looks. And she seems to speak to me in the words of the Song of Songs:

"Oh, that thou wert unto me as a brother. Why wert thou not a brother unto me?"

"Well, well, I suppose our greens for Pentecost will come in their own good time," says my father, and smiles above the silver threads of his beard that gleam in the golden sunlight. "Thank Heaven nothing has happened to the children."

"Thank Heaven!" repeats my mother, and with her shawl wipes her red perspiring face.

And both of them look at us and their faces begin to beam. . . .

Queer folks, my father and mother.

TUG OF LOVE

by ISRAEL ZANGWILL

WHEN Elias Goldenberg, Belcovitch's head cutter, betrothed himself to Fanny Fersht, the prettiest of the machinists, the Ghetto blessed the match, always excepting Sugarman the Shadchen (whom love-matches shocked), and Goldenberg's relatives (who considered Fanny flighty and fond of finery).

"That Fanny of yours was cut out for nothing but a rich man's wife," insisted Goldenberg's aunt, shaking her pious wig.

"He who marries Fanny is rich," retorted Elias.

" 'Pawn your hide, but get a bride,' " quoted the old lady savagely.

As for the slighted marriage-broker, he remonstrated almost like a relative.

"But I didn't want a negotiated marriage," Elias protested.

"A love-marriage I could also have arranged for you," replied Sugarman indignantly.

But Elias was quite content with his own arrangement, for Fanny's glance was melting and her touch transporting. To deck that soft warm hand with an engagement ring, a month's wages had not seemed disproportionate, and Fanny flashed the diamond bewitchingly. It lit up the gloomy workshop with its signal of felicity. Even Belcovitch, bent over his press-iron, sometimes omitted to rebuke Fanny's badinage.

The course of true love seemed to run straight to the canopy—Fanny had already worked the bridegroom's praying-shawl—when suddenly a terrible storm broke. At first the cloud was no bigger than a man's hand—in fact, it was a man's hand. Elias espied it groping for Fanny's in the dim space between the two machines. As Fanny's fingers fluttered toward it, her other hand still holding the cloth under the throbbing needle, Elias felt the needle stabbing his heart up and down, through and through. The very finger that held his costly ring lay in this alien paw gratis.

The shameless minx! Ah, his relatives were right.

"Fanny, what dost thou?" he gasped in Yiddish.

Fanny's face flamed; her guilty fingers flew back.

"I thought thou wast on my other side," she breathed.

Elias snorted incredulously.

As soon as Sugarman heard of the breaking of the engagement, he flew to Elias, his blue bandanna streaming from his coat-tail.

"If you had come to me," he crowed, "I should have found you a more reliable article. However, Heaven has given you a second helping. A well-built wage-earner like you can look as high as a greengrocer's daughter even."

"I never wish to look upon a woman again," Elias groaned.

"Schtuss!" said the great marriage-broker. "Three days after the Fast of Atonement comes the Feast of Tabernacles. The Almighty, blessed be He, who created both light and darkness, has made obedient females as well as pleasure-seeking jades." And he blew his nose emphatically into his bandanna.

"Yes; but she won't return me my ring," Elias lamented.

"What!" Sugarman gasped. "Then she considers herself still engaged to you."

"Not at all. She laughs in my face."

"And she has given you back your promise?"

"My promise—yes. The ring—no."

"But on what ground?"

"She says I gave it to her."

Sugarman clucked his tongue. "Tututu! Better if we had followed our old custom, and the man had worn the engagement ring, not the woman!"

"In the workshop," Elias went on miserably, "she flashes it in my eyes. Everybody makes mock. Oh, the Jezebel!"

"I should summon her!"

"It would only cost me more. Is it not true I gave her the ring?"

Sugarman mopped his brow. His vast experience was at fault. No maiden had ever refused to return his client's ring; rather had she flung it in the wooer's false teeth.

"This comes of your love matches!" he cried sternly. "Next time there must be a proper contract."

"Next time!" repeated Elias. "Why, how am I to afford a new ring? Fanny was ruinous in cups of chocolate and the pit of the Pavilion Theatre!"

"I should want my fee down!" said Sugarman sharply.

Elias shrugged his shoulders. "If you bring me the ring."

"I do not get old rings, but new maidens," Sugarman reminded him haughtily. "However, as you are a customer—" and crying, "Five percent on the greengrocer's daughter," he hurried away ere Elias had time to dissent from the bargain.

Donning his sealskin vest to overawe the Fershts, Sugarman ploughed his way up the dark staircase to their room. His attire was wasted on the family, for Fanny herself opened the door.

"Peace to you," he cried. "I have come on behalf of Elias Goldenberg."

"It is useless. I will not have him." And she was shutting the door. Her misconception, wilful or not, scattered all Sugarman's prepared diplomacies. "He does not want you, he wants the ring," he cried hastily.

Fanny indecorously put a finger to her nose. The diamond glittered mockingly on it. Then she turned away giggling. "But look at this photograph!" panted Sugarman desperately through the closing door.

Surprise and curiosity brought her eyes back. She stared at the sheepish features of a frock-coated stranger.

"Four pounds a week all the year round, head cutter at S. Cohn's," said Sugarman, pursuing this advantage. "A good old English family; Benjamin Beckenstein is his name, and he is dying to step into Elias' shoes."

"His feet are too large!" And she flicked the photograph floorwards with her bediamonded finger.

"But why waste the engagement ring?" pleaded Sugarman, stooping to pick up the suitor.

"What an idea! A new man, a new ring!" And Fanny slammed the door in his face.

"Impudent-face! Would you become a jewelry shop!" the baffled Shadchan shrieked through the woodwork.

He returned to Elias, brooding darkly.

"Well?" queried Elias.

"Oh, your love matches!" And Sugarman shook them away with shuddersome palms.

"Then she won't—"

"No, she won't. Ah, how blessed you are to escape from that daughter of Satan! The greengrocer's daughter, now—"

"Speak me no more matches. I risk no more rings."

"I will get you one on the hire system."

"A maiden?"

"Guard your tongue! A ring, of course."

Elias shook an obdurate head. "No. I must have the old ring back."

"That is impossible—unless you marry her to get it back. Stay! Why should I not arrange that for you?"

"Leave me in peace! Heaven has opened my eyes."

"Then see how economical she is!" urged Sugarman. "A maiden who sticks to a ring like that is not likely to be wasteful of your substance."

"You have not seen her swallow 'stuffed monkeys,'" said Elias grimly. "Make an end! I have certainly done with her."

"No, you have not! You can still give yourself a counsel." And Sugarman looked a conscious sphinx. "You may yet get back the ring."

"How?"

"Of course, I have the next disposal of it?" said Sugarman.

"Yes, yes. Go on."

"Tomorrow, in the workshop, pretend to steal loving glances all day long when she's not looking. When she catches you—"

"But she won't be looking!"

"Oh, yes, she will. When she catches you, you must blush."

"But I can't blush at will," Elias protested.

"I know it is hard. Well, look foolish. That will be easier for you."

"But why shall I look foolish?"

"To make her think you are in love with her after all."

"I should look foolish if I were."

"Precisely. That is the idea. When she leaves the workshop in the evening follow her, and as she passes the cake shop, sigh and ask her if she will not eat a 'stuffed monkey' for the sake of peace-be-upon-him times."

"But she won't."

"Why not? She is still in love."

"With 'stuffed monkeys,'" said Elias cynically.

"With you, too."

Elias blushed quite easily. "How do you know?"

"I offered her another man, and she slammed the door in my face!"

"You—you offered—" Elias stuttered angrily.

"Only to test her," said Sugarman soothingly. He continued:

"Now, when she has eaten the cake and drunk a cup of chocolate too (for one must play high with such a ring at stake), you must walk on by her side, and when you come to a dark corner, take her hand and say, "My treasure," or "My angel," or whatever nonsense you modern young men babble to your maidens—with the results you see!—and while she is drinking it all in like more chocolate, her fingers in yours, give a sudden tug, and off comes the ring!"

Elias gazed at him in admiration. "You are as crafty as Jacob, our father."

"Heaven has not denied everybody brains," replied Sugarman modestly. "Be careful to seize the left hand."

The admiring Elias followed the scheme to the letter.

Even the blush he had boggled at came to his cheeks punctually whenever his sheep's eyes met Fanny's. He was so surprised to find his face burning that he even looked foolish into the bargain.

They dallied long in the cake shop, Elias trying to summon up courage for the final feint. He would get a good grip on the ring finger. The tug-of-war should be brief.

Meantime the couple clinked chocolate cups, and smiled into each other's eyes.

"The good-for-nothing!" thought Elias hotly. "She will make the same eyes at the next man."

And he went on gorging her, every speculative "stuffed monkey" increasing his nervous tension. Her white teeth, biting recklessly into the cake, made him itch to slap her rosy cheek. Confectionery palled at last, and Fanny led the way out. Elias followed, chattering with feverish gaiety. Gradually he drew up even with her.

They turned down the deserted Fishmonger's Alley, lit by one dull gas-lamp. Elias' limbs began to tremble with the excitement of the critical moment. He felt like a footpad. Hither and thither he peered—nobody was about. But—was he on the right side of her? "The right is the left," he told himself, trying to smile, but his pulses thumped, and in the tumult of heart and brain he was not sure he knew her right hand from her left. Fortunately he caught the glitter of the diamond in the gloom, and instinctively his robber hand closed upon it.

But as he felt the warm responsive clasp of those soft fingers, that ancient delicious thrill pierced every vein. Fool that he had been to doubt that dear hand! And it was wearing his ring still—she could not part with it! O blundering male ingrate!

"My treasure! My angel!" he murmured ecstatically.

IN THE STORM

by DAVID PINSKI

A PIOUS woman told it to me as a warning to sinners, to the young, to the moderns.

Black clouds began to fleck the clear sky. Dense, heavy storm clouds. At first far off, beyond the forest, but very soon they darkened the whole sky over the village. A violent wind lashed and drove them on, and they sped under its whip, angry and sullen, menacing. The wind—a tornado—raged in all the consciousness of its formidable power, raising pillars of dust as high as the driven clouds, tearing off roofs and uprooting trees.

Terror had descended upon the village. Bright day had of a sudden turned to night, such as well befitted the Sabbath of Repentance, the Sabbath before the Day of Atonement. . . . As frightfully dark, as oppressively heavy as a pious Jew's heart.

Folks shut themselves up in their houses, fastening windows and locking doors. The earnest faces of the penitent Jews became still more earnest. The depressing moods of the Sabbath of Repentance waxed still more depressing. God was scolding. The sad voices of the psalm-singers became deeper and more tearful.

The darkness grew blacker and blacker. Then old Cheyne raised her eyes from the psalms, looked through her spectacles into the street, uttered "Au-hu!" with trembling heart and heaved a sigh.

For a while she sat gazing outside. She shook her head. Her whole soul was full of God's omnipotence.

It refused to grow lighter. The clouds passed by in endless procession, and the wind howled, whirling thick pillars of dust in its path.

She could recite psalms no longer. She removed her spectacles and placed them between the pages of her thick woman's prayer-book, rose from her seat and went into her daughter's room.

"What do you say to . . ."

She did not conclude her question. Her daughter was not there.

The old woman surveyed her room, looked into the kitchen, then returned to the room. Her daughter's bonnet was not in its place. With quivering hands she opened the closet. The jacket was missing!

She had gone! And she had warned her daughter, it seemed, not to go out today—that on the Sabbath of Repentance, at least, she might remain at home and not run off to that "apostate," the former student.

Her aged countenance became as dark as the sky without. And her heart grew as furious as the storm. She gazed about the room as if seeking to vent her rage—strike somebody, break something.

"Oh, may she no longer be a daughter of mine!" escaped in angry outburst from her storming bosom, and she raised her hand to heaven.

She was not affrighted by the curse that her lips had uttered on this solemn Sabbath. At this moment she could curse and shriek the bitterest words. She could have seized her now by the hair, and slapped her face ruthlessly.

Suddenly she threw a shawl over her head and dashed out of the house.

She would hunt them both out and would visit an evil end upon both of them.

A flash of lightning rent the clouds, and was followed by reverberating thunder. Then flash upon flash of lightning and crash upon crash of thunder. One more blinding than the other, one louder than the other!

The horror of the population grew greater. That it should thunder on the Sabbath of Repentance, and in such demoniac fashion! All hearts were touched, all souls went out in prayer.

Old Cheyne, however, scarcely noticed this.

The wind blinded her eyes with dust, tore her scarf from her, blew her skirts about, twisted the wig on her old head.

She rushed along oblivious to all.

She neither heard nor saw anything before her. Within her it thundered and raged; it stormed and something drove her on. And before her all was dark, for her eyes were shot with blood.

Her small form grew even smaller. She strode along fairly doubled up, hastening breathlessly. She seemed to go faster than the wind. The wind lagged behind her. And whenever it caught up with her, it only spurred her on, and she quickened her step.

She did not look around, did not remark the inquisitive eyes that peered at her from behind the fastened windows by which she ran. She neither saw nor heard anything. Her entire being was merged with the fury of nature. Her thought was a curse, a horrible curse, a deadly curse. Not in words. But in her whole soul. Within her it cried, it thundered—drowning out the thunder of the black, angry clouds.

She stormed into the "apostate's" house. She opened the door with a loud bang and closed it with one even louder. Those in the room shuddered at the sudden intrusion and jumped to their feet. She cast a wild, hostile glance at them and dashed through the rooms, from one to the other, from the other to a third. She tore the doors open and slammed them behind her, accompanied by the thunder, as if in a wager as to which of them would make the panes and the windows rattle more violently. A little child took fright and began to cry. She ran from room to room, but neither he nor her daughter was there.

Then she flew back. On the threshold, however, she paused for a moment. She rolled her eyes heavenward and raised her arms to God.

"May flames devour this house!"

Then she departed, pulling the street door violently and leaving it open. The household stood agape, as if the storm itself had torn into the home. Out of sheer stupefaction the persons forgot to close their mouths.

Out of the clouds poured a drenching rain mixed with hail. The tempest seethed like a cauldron.

This boiling tempest, however, raged in Cheyne's bosom. Something stormed furiously within her. She no longer felt the ground beneath her. The flood soaked her through and through, but this could not restrain her. It served only to augment her savage mood.

She ran from house to house, wherever she might have expected to come upon her daughter and the "apostate." She stopped nowhere, uttered never a word, but dashed in and then sped out like a flash of lightning, leaving the household open-mouthed with astonishment.

She would find them! Even under the ground. And she did not stop her cursing and her maledictions.

As she rushed from the last house she paused for a moment. Whither now?

She turned homeward. Her heart told her that her daughter was now at home. Her lips muttered the most terrible imprecations, and the inner fury was at its height; the very air, it seemed to her, was laden with her cries, with her curses and oaths.

With a strong gust of wind, a flash of lightning and a crash of thunder, she tore into her home.

Her daughter was not there. She sank upon a chair and burst into wailing.

There was a terrifying crash of thunder. One of those thunder-claps that work the most widespread havoc. Nature seemed to be shaking off the entire residue of energy that had been left to her by the hot summer.

The inhabitants of the village were rooted to the spot in terror. They looked about, then ventured a glance outside. Hadn't some misfortune occurred? The penitents buried their faces deeper than ever in their prayer-books, and more than ever their voices quivered.

Cheyne, however, had apparently not heard the thunder. She continued to wail, to wail bitterly. Then a wild cry issued from her throat, as wild as the thunder:

"May she not live to come home! May they bring her to me dead! O Lord of the universe!"

The clouds replied with a clap of thunder and the wind sped apace, shrieking.

Suddenly she arose and dashed out as before. The wind accompanied her. Now it thrust her forward from behind, now it ran ahead like a faithful dog, smiting all in its path, raising the dirt from the road and mixing it with the thick drops that fell from the clouds, which were still black, and with the seething drops that coursed from her burning eyes.

She was running to the road just beyond the village.

They had surely gone for a walk on the road, where they had been seen several times. She would meet them on the way, or in Jonah's Inn near the big forest.

On the Gentile's lane, the last one of the village, the dogs in the yards heard her hastening steps upon the drenched earth. Some of them began to bark behind the gates, not caring to venture out into the rain; others were not so lazy and crawled out from under the gates with an angry yelping. She neither saw nor heard them, however. She only gazed far out over the road, which began at the lane, and ran along.

One dog seized her skirt, which had become heavy with water. She did not heed this, and dragged the animal along for part of the way, until it tired of keeping pace with her in the pelting downpour. So it released her skirt. For a moment it thought of seizing her in some other spot, but at once, with a sullen growl, it set out for its yard.

On the road the wind became still stronger. And the thunder reached here with thousands of reverberations from the neighboring forest. Cheyne looked only straight before her, into the distance, through the dense, water-laden atmosphere.

The way was strewn with heaps of twigs and branches that had been severed by the lightning, and even a few trees lay before her, torn up from their very roots, and charred.

"Would to God that the thunder would strike them even so!" she muttered.

She was consumed by an inner cry. Now she had found a definite form for all her curses. The thunder up yonder had torn it from her.

And she ran on, on. . . .

But what is this here?

A few paces before her lie two persons. A man and a woman. With contorted visages. In writhing positions. Their faces black as earth, their eyes rolled back. Two corpses, struck by lightning.

There was a brilliant flash, followed by a deafening thunderclap.

She recognized her daughter.

More by her clothes than by her charred countenance; more by her entire figure than by the horribly staring whites of her eyes.

The girl's arm lay beneath that of the young man. The top of the open umbrella in the youth's hand had been burned off.

The old woman was on the point of shrieking a curse, of adding her thunder to the fury of the storm's thunder; her eyes flashed together with the lightning; in her heart there arose a devastating tempest.

She wished to cry out the most evil of words—that the dead maiden had earned her end. She desired to send after her the most wretched and degrading of names.

Suddenly, however, all grew black before her. A flood of molten lead seemed to pour into her head. Weariness and trembling fell upon her. Her garments, saturated with the rain, seemed to drag her to the earth. Her eyes were extinguished.

The thunder and lightning and shrieking of the wind broke out anew.

But within the old woman all was quiet, dark, dead. She sank to her knees before the corpse of her daughter, stretched over the body her trembling arms, and a dull flame flickered up in her eyes.

Her entire being quivered. Her teeth knocked together. And with a hoarse, toneless voice she gasped:

"My darling daughter! Hennye, my darling!"

THE KERCHIEF

by S. J. AGNON

EVERY year my father of blessed memory used to visit the Lashkowitz fair to do business with the merchants. Lashkowitz is a small town of no more consequence than any of the other small towns in the district, except that once a year merchants gather together there from everywhere and offer their wares for sale in the streets of the town; and whoever needs goods comes and buys them. In earlier times, two or three generations ago, more than a hundred thousand people used to gather together there; and even now, when Lashkowitz is in its decline, they come to it from all over the country. You will not find a single merchant in the whole of Galicia who does not keep a shop in Lashkowitz during the fair.

II

For us the week in which my father went to the market was just like the week of the Ninth of Ab. During those days there was not a smile to be seen on mother's lips, and the children also refrained from laughing. Mother, may she rest in peace, used to cook light meals with milk and vegetables, and all sorts of things which children do not dislike. If we caused her trouble she would quiet us, and did not rebuke us even for things which deserved a beating. I often used to find her sitting at the window with moist lashes. And why should my mother sit at the window; did she wish to watch the passersby? Why, she, may her memory be blessed, never concerned herself with other people's affairs, and would only half hear the stories her neighbors might tell her; but it was her custom, ever since the first year in which my father had gone to Lashkowitz, to stand at the window and look out. When my father of blessed memory went to the fair at Lashkowitz for the first time, my mother was once standing at the window when she suddenly cried out, "Oh, they're strangling him!" Folk asked her, "What are you saying?" She answered, "I see a robber taking him by the throat"; and before she had finished her words she had fainted. They sent to the fair and found my father injured, for at the very time that my mother had fainted, somebody had attacked my father for his money and had taken him by the throat; and he had been saved by a miracle. In after years, when I found in the *Book of Lamentations* the words, "She is become as a widow," and I read Rashi's explanation, "As a woman whose husband has gone to a distant land and who intends to return to her," it brought to mind my mother, may she rest in peace, as she used to sit at the window with her tears upon her cheeks.

III

All the time that father was in Lashkowitz I used to sleep in his bed. As soon as I had said the night prayer I used to undress and stretch my limbs in his long bed, cover myself up to my ears and keep them pricked up and ready so that in case I heard the Trumpet of Messiah I might rise at once. It was a particular pleasure for me to meditate on Messiah the King. Sometimes I used to laugh myself when I thought of the consternation which would come about in the whole world when our Righteous Messiah would reveal himself. Only yesterday he was bandaging his wounds and his bruises, and today he's a king! Yesterday he sat among the beggars and they did not recognize him, but sometimes even abused him and treated him with disrespect; and now suddenly the Holy and Blest One has remembered the oath He swore to redeem Israel, and gave him permission to reveal himself to the world. Another in my place might have been angered at the beggars who treated Messiah the King with disrespect; but I honored and revered them, since Messiah the King had desired to dwell in their quarters. In my place another might have treated the beggars without respect, as they eat black bread even on the Sabbaths, and wear dirty clothes. But I honored and revered them, since among them were those who had dwelt together with Messiah.

IV

Those were fine nights in which I used to lie on my bed and think of Messiah the King, who would reveal himself suddenly in the world. He would lead us to the land of Israel where we would dwell, every man under his own vine and his own fig tree. Father would not go to fairs and I would not go to school but would walk about all day in the Courts of the House of our God. And while lying and meditating thus, my eyes would close of their own accord; and before they closed entirely I would take my *zizith* and knot the fringes according to the number of days my father still had to stay in Lashkowitz. Then all sorts of lights, green, white, black, red and blue, used to come toward me, like the lights seen by wayfarers in fields and woods and valleys and streams, and all kinds of precious things would be gleaming and glittering in them; and my heart danced for joy at all the good stored away for us in the future, in the day that our righteous Messiah would reveal himself, may it be speedily and in our days, Amen. While I rejoiced so, a great bird would come and peck at the light. Once I took my fringes and tied myself to his wings and said, "Bird, bird, bring me to father." The bird spread its wings and flew with me to a city called Rome. I looked down and saw a group of poor men sitting at the gates of the city, and one beggar among them bandaging his wounds. I turned my eyes away from him in order not to see his sufferings. When I turned my eyes away there grew a great mountain with all kinds of thorns and thistles upon it and evil beasts grazing there, and impure birds and creeping abominations crawling about it, and a great wind blew all of a sudden and flung me onto the mountain, and the mountain began quaking under me and my limbs felt as though they would fall asunder; but I feared to cry out lest the creeping abominations should enter my mouth and the impure birds should peck at my tongue. Then father came and wrapped me in his tallith and brought me back to my bed. I opened my eyes to gaze at his face and found that it was day. At once I knew that the Holy and Blest One had rolled away another night of the nights of the fair. I took my fringes and made a fresh knot.

V

Whenever father returned from the fair he brought us many gifts. He was very clever, was father, knowing what each of us would want most and bringing it to us. Or maybe the Master of Dreams used to tell father what he showed us in dream, and he would bring it for us.

There were not many gifts that survived long. As is the way of the valuables of this world, they were not lasting. Yesterday we were playing with them, and today they were already thrown away. Even my fine prayer-book was torn, for whatever I might have had to do, I used to open it and ask its counsel; and finally nothing was left of it but a few dog-eared printed scraps.

But one present which father brought mother remained whole for many years. And even after it was lost it did not vanish from my heart, and I still think of it as though it were yet there.

VI

That day, when father returned from the fair, it was Friday after the noon hour, when the children are freed from school. Those Friday afternoon hours were the best time of the week, because all the week round a child is bent over his book and his eyes and heart are not his own; as soon as he raises his head he is beaten. On Friday afternoon he is freed from study, and even if he does whatever he wants to, nobody objects. Were it not for the noon meal the world would be like Paradise. But mother had already summoned me to eat and I had no heart to refuse.

Almost before we had begun eating my little sister put her right hand to her ear and set her ear to the table. "What are you doing?" mother asked her. "I'm trying to listen," she answered. Mother asked, "Daughter, what are you trying to listen to?" Then she began clapping her hands with joy and crying, "Father's coming, father's coming." And in a little while we heard the wheels of a wagon. Very faint at first, then louder and louder. At once we threw our spoons down while they were still half full, left our plates on the table and ran out to meet father coming back from the fair. Mother, may she rest in peace, also let her apron fall and stood erect, her arms folded on her bosom, until father entered the house.

How big father was then! I knew my father was bigger than all the other fathers. All the same I used to think there must be someone taller than he— but now even the chandelier hanging from the ceiling in our house seemed to be lower.

Suddenly father bent down, caught me to him, kissed me and asked me what I had learnt. Is it likely that father did not know which portion of the week was being read? But he only asked to try me out. Before I could answer he had caught my brother and sisters, raised them on high and kissed them.

I look about me now to try and find something to which to compare my father when he stood together with his tender children on his return from afar, and I can think of many comparisons, each one finer than the next; yet I can find nothing pleasant enough. But I hope that the love haloing my father of blessed memory may wrap us round whenever we come to embrace our little children, and that joy which possessed us then will be possessed by our children all their lives.

VII

The wagoner entered bringing two trunks, one large and the other neither large nor small but medium; and that second trunk seemed to have eyes and smile with them.

Father took his bunch of keys from his pocket and said, "We'll open the trunk and take out my tallith and tefillin." Father was just speaking for fun, since who needs tefillin on Friday afternoon, and even if you think of the tallith, my father had a special tallith for Sabbath, but he only said it in order that we should not be too expectant and not be too anxious for presents.

But we went and undid the straps of the trunk and watched his every movement while he took one of the keys and examined it, smiling affectionately. The key also smiled at us; that is, gleams of light sparkled on the key and it seemed to be smiling. Finally he pressed the key into the lock, opened the trunk, put his hand inside and felt among his possessions. Suddenly he looked at us and became silent. Had father forgotten to place the presents there? Or had he been lodging at an inn where the inn people rose and took out the presents? As happened with the sage by whose hands they sent a gift to Cæsar, a chest full of jewels and pearls, and when he lodged one night at the inn, the inn folk opened the chest and took out everything that was in it and filled it with dust. Then I prayed that just as a miracle was done to that sage so that that dust should be the dust of Abraham our father, which turned into swords when it was thrown into the air, so should the Holy and Blest One perform a miracle with us in order that the things with which the inn keepers had filled father's trunk should be better than all presents. Before my prayer was at an end father brought out all kinds of fine things. There was not a single one among his gifts which we had not longed for all the year round. And that is why I said that the Master of Dreams must have revealed to father what he had shown us in dream.

The gifts of my father deserve to be praised at length, but who is going to praise things that have vanished and are lost? All the same, one fine gift which my father brought my mother on the day that he returned from the fair deserves to be mentioned in particular.

VIII

It was a silk brocaded kerchief adorned with flowers and blossoms. On the one side it was brown and they were white, while on the other they were brown and it was white. That was the gift which father of blessed memory brought to mother, may she rest in peace.

Mother opened up the kerchief, stroked it with her fingers and peeped at father; he peeped back at her and both of them remained silent. Finally she folded it again, rose, put it in the cupboard and said to father, "Wash your hands and eat." As soon as father sat down to his meal I went out to my friends in the street and showed them the presents I had received, and was busy outside with them until the Sabbath began and I went to pray with father.

How pleasant that Sabbath was when we returned from the synagogue! The skies were full of stars, the houses full of lamps and candles, people were wearing their Sabbath clothes and walking quietly beside father in order not to disturb the Sabbath angels who accompany one home from the synagogue on Sabbath Eves: candles were alight in the house and the table prepared and the fine smell of white bread, and a white table-cloth spread and two Sabbath loaves on it, covered by a small napkin out of respect; so that they should not feel ashamed when the blessing is said first over the wine.

Father bowed and entered and said, "A peaceful and blessed Sabbath," and mother answered, "Peaceful and blessed." Father looked at the table and began singing, "Peace be unto you, angels of peace," while mother sat at the table, her prayer-book in hand, and the big chandelier with the ten candles, one for each of the Ten Commandments, hanging from the ceiling, gave light. They were answered back by the rest of the candles, one for father, one for mother, one for each of the little ones; and although we were smaller than father and mother, all the same our candles were as big as theirs. Then I looked at mother and saw that her face had changed and her forehead had grown smaller because of the kerchief wound round her head and covering her hair, while her eyes seemed much larger and were shining towards father who went on singing, "A woman of valor who shall find?"; and the ends of her kerchief which hung down below her chin were quivering very gently, because the Sabbath angels were moving their wings and making a wind. It must have been so, for the windows were closed and where could the wind have come from if not from the wings of the angels? As it says in the Psalms, "He maketh his messengers the winds." I held back my breath in order not to confuse the angels and looked at my mother, may she rest in peace, and wondered at the Sabbath Day, which is given us for an honor and a glory. Suddenly I felt how my cheeks were being patted. I do not know whether the wings of the angels or the corners of the kerchief were caressing me. Happy is he who merits to have good angels hovering over his head, and happy is he whose mother has stroked his head on the Sabbath Eve.

IX

When I awakened from sleep it was already day. The whole world was full of the Sabbath morning. Father and mother were about to go out, he to his little synagogue, and she to the House of Study of my grandfather, may he rest in peace. Father was wearing a black satin robe and a round shtreimel of sable on his head, and mother wore a black dress and a hat with feathers. In the House of Study of my grandfather, where mother used to pray, they did not spend too much time singing, and so she could return early. When I came back with father from the small synagogue she was already seated at the table wearing her kerchief, and the table was prepared with wine and brandy and cakes, large and small, round and doubled over. Father entered, said, "A Sabbath of peace and blessing," put his tallith on the bed, sat down at the head of the table, said, "The Lord is my shepherd, I shall not want," blessed the wine, tasted the cake and began, "A Psalm of David; The earth is the Lord's and the fulness thereof." When the Ark is opened on the New Year's Eve and this Psalm is said there is a great stirring among the congregation. There was a similar stirring in my heart then. Had my mother not taught me that you do not stand on chairs and do not clamber on to the table and do not shout, I would have climbed onto the table and shouted out, "The earth is the Lord's and the fulness thereof"; like that child in the Gemara

(Talmud) who used to be seated in the middle of a gold table which was a load for sixteen men, with sixteen silver chains attached, and dishes and glasses and bowls and platters fitted, and with all kinds of food and sweet-meats and spices of all that was created in the Six Days of Creation; and he used to proclaim, "The earth is the Lord's and the fulness thereof."

Mother cut the cake giving each his or her portion; and the ends of her kerchief accompanied her hands. While doing so a cherry fell out of the cake and stained her apron; but it did not touch her kerchief, which remained as clean as it had been when father took it out of his trunk.

X

A woman does not put on a silken kerchief every day or every Sabbath. When a woman stands at the oven, what room is there for ornament? Every day is not Sabbath, but on the other hand there are Festivals. The Holy and Blest One took pity on His creatures and gave them times of gladness, holidays and appointed seasons. On festivals mother used to put on a feather hat and go to the synagogue, and at home she would don her kerchief. But on the New Year and the Day of Atonement she kept the kerchief on all day long; similarly on the morning of Hoshana Rabba, the seventh day of Tabernacles. I used to look at mother on the Day of Atonement, when she wore her ker-chief and her eyes were bright with prayer and fasting. She seemed to me like a presented prayer-book bound in silk.

The rest of the time the kerchief lay folded in the cupboard, and on Sab-baths and festivals mother would take it out. I never saw her washing it, although she was very particular about cleanliness. When Sabbaths and festivals are properly kept the Sabbath and festival clothes are preserved. But for me she would have kept the kerchief all her life long.

What happened was as follows. On the day I became thirteen years old and a member of the congregation, my mother, may she rest in peace, bound her kerchief round my neck. Blessed be He who is everywhere, who has given His word to guardians. There was not a spot of dirt to be found on the ker-chief. But sentence had been passed already on the kerchief, that it was to be lost through me. This kerchief, which I had observed so much and so long, would vanish because of me.

XI

Now I shall pass from one theme to another until I return to my original theme. At that time there came a beggar to our own town who was sick with running sores; his hands were swollen, his clothes were rent and tattered, his shoes were cracked, and when he showed himself in the street the children threw earth and stones at him. And not only the children but even the grown-ups and householders turned angry faces on him. Once when he went to the market to buy bread or onions the stall-women drove him away. Not that the stall-women in our town were cruel; indeed, they were tender-hearted. Some would give the food from their mouths to orphans, others went to the forest, gathered twigs, made charcoal of them and shared them free among the beggars and poor folk. But every beggar has his own luck. When he fled from them and entered the House of Study, the beadle shouted at him and pushed him out. And when on the Sabbath Eve he crept into the House of Study, nobody invited him to come home with them and share the Sabbath meal. God forbid that the sons of our father Abraham do not perform works of charity; but the ministers of Satan used to accompany that beggar and pull a veil over Jewish eyes so that they should not perceive his dire needs. As to where he heard the blessing over wine, and where he ate his three Sabbath meals—if he was not sustained by humankind he must have been sustained by the Grace of God.

Hospitality is a great thing, since buildings are erected and wardens appointed for the sake of it and to support the poor. But I say it in praise of our townsfolk, that although they did not establish any poorhouse or elect any wardens, every man who could do so used to find a place for a poor man in his own house, thus seeing the troubles of his brother and aiding him and supporting him at the hour of his need; and his sons and daughters who saw this would learn from his deeds. When trouble would befall a man he would groan; the walls of his house would groan with him because of the mighty groaning of the poor; and he would know that there are blows even greater than that which had befallen him. And as he comforted the poor, so would the Holy and Blest One in the future comfort him.

XII

Now I leave the beggars and shall tell only of my mother's kerchief, which she tied round my neck when I grew old enough to perform all the commandments and be counted a member of the congregation. On that day, when I returned from the House of Study to eat the midday meal, I was dressed like a bridegroom and was very happy and pleased with myself because I was now donning tefillin. On the way I found that beggar sitting on a heap of stones, changing the bandages of his sores, his clothes rent and tattered, nothing but a bundle of rags which did not even hide his sores. He looked at me as well. The sores on his face seemed like eyes of fire. My heart stopped, my knees began shaking, my eyes grew dim and everything seemed to be in a whirl. But I took my heart in my hand, nodded to the beggar, wished him peace, and he wished me peace back.

Suddenly my heart began thumping, my ears grew hot and a sweetness such as I had never experienced in all my days took possession of all my limbs; my lips and my tongue were sweet with it, my mouth fell agape, my two eyes were opened and I stared before me as a man who sees in waking what has been shown him in dream. And so I stood staring in front of me.

The sun stopped still in the sky, not a creature was to be seen in the street; but the merciful sun looked down upon the earth and its light shone bright on the sores of the beggar. I began loosening my kerchief to breathe more freely, for tears stood in my throat. Before I could loosen it, my heart began racing with wonder, and the sweetness, which I had already felt, doubled and redoubled. I took off the kerchief and gave it to the beggar. He took it and wound it round his sores. The sun came and stroked my neck.

I looked around. There was not a creature in the market, but a pile of stones lay there and reflected the sun's light. For a little while I stood there without thinking. Then I moved my feet and returned home.

XIII

When I reached the house I walked round it on all four sides. Suddenly I stopped at mother's window, the one from which she used to look out. The place was strange; the sun's light upon it did not dazzle but warmed, and there was perfect rest there. Two or three people passing slowed their paces and lowered their voices; one of them wiped his brow and sighed deeply. It seems to me that that sigh must still be hanging there, until the end of all generations.

I stood there awhile, a minute or two minutes or more. Finally I moved from thence and entered the house. When I entered I found mother sitting in the window as was her way. I greeted her and she returned my greeting. Suddenly I felt that I had not treated her properly; she had had a fine kerchief which she used to bind round her head on Sabbaths and festivals, and I had taken it and given it to a beggar to bind up his feet with. Ere I had ended begging her to forgive me she was gazing at me with love and affection. I gazed back at her, and my heart was filled with the same gladness as I had felt on that Sabbath when my mother had set the kerchief about her head for the first time.

The end of the story of the kerchief of my mother, may she rest in peace.

THE WORLD OF HASIDISM

REB YOSELE AND THE BRAZLAV HASIDIM

by ILYA EHRENBURG

OUTSIDE of Poland the Hasidim are considered to be a small Jewish sect. In reality, the majority of Polish Jews are Hasidim. Nor are they a circle of fanatics. They are simply the Jewish population of Poland: merchants, workers, tradesmen and paupers. The Hasidim participate as a group in the general election campaigns. Some of them are very rich. In Western Poland, or Galicia, a Jew who is not a Hasid is considered a foreigner— "Litvak."

The history of Hasidism is as instructive as the history of any idea, which, while progressing—weakens, conquering—perishes. However, perhaps it is only the law of life, like the life of a tiny flower—a botanical process?

At the beginning Hasidism was a mystic, revolutionary outburst. It became transformed into bigotry and decayed. The first Hasidim revolted against the "law of the Word"; they substituted for it happiness, love, humanitarianism. But three centuries passed. Today the Hasidim are the most fanatical and zealous guardians of law. If only this great Baal Shem Tov could see his followers ready to murder for the least offense against the Canon! It is as if a youth could foresee his days of senility.

The birthplace of Hasidism is Poland. It first appeared in the eighteenth century, based on the tradition of the *Kabala* and *Zohar*. It was a desire for a new life—an everlasting urge to throw off the yoke of the constant fasts, ceremonials and prayers. People were dying amidst bookish dust, amidst the complicated quibblings of the Talmud, amidst such vital questions as: Is it permitted to kill a flea on the Sabbath? This emasculated yet despotical law united the Jews of Saloniki and Vilna, Cracow and Amsterdam. The solid walls of the Ghetto separated the Jews from worldly knowledge. And lacking fresh contacts, Judaism was rapidly dying.

Then in a little Polish village, amid the base debaucheries of the provincial nobility, amid the dark sleep of the ignorant peasantry, amid poverty and snow, the illuminating and great philosophy of Baal Shem Tov (Besht) was born. Translated into everyday language, into the language of the village paupers, it proclaimed: "Long live life." And hearing these words, thousands of hearts began to beat excitedly. Against such a rising the anathemas of the righteous Misnagdim (Talmudists) were powerless.

Hasidism resembles in many respects the Franciscan movement among the Catholics, and the "Starchestvo," or pantheism, of Zosima Dostoyevski among the Russians.

It has been said that the Besht could converse in thirty-six languages. But these were not ordinary languages—not Polish or German. No, he understood the language of birds, dogs, stones, etc. For according to Hasidism everything in the world has its own melody, and the better a man is, the more melodies he hears. Even evil, according to Hasidism, has a divine origin. Morally, it does not repudiate sin, and towards enforced "saintliness" it is rather prejudiced. The Misnagdim were for an exact fulfillment of the "Law"—the Hasidim declared it unnecessary. More important than prayers, they claimed, is the purity of the soul. It is not necessary to pray only in a synagogue, one may pray even in the forest. Nor is it essential to mourn and fast. One should be gay and happy, for only in his childlike happiness is man nearest to God. This, in simplified form, is Hasidism.

It is obvious what hatred it encountered among the orthodox Misnagdim. But it immediately caught the imagination of the poor, village dreamers, and poets. It was a revolt—and the revolt was victorious. However, the cause of its victory was also the cause of its rapid decay.

The Misnagdim devoted their life to solving the puzzles of the Babylonian Talmudist: "How to interpret this or that word." The Hasidim substituted experience for books. Let it be interpreted and judged, they said, not by dead letters, but by living men, virtuous men—"Zaddikim." This was simple and humane. It was also a source of inspiration as long as Hasidism was still in its youthful stage, as long as the Zaddiks were still rebels, prophets and poets. But submitting to the tradition of heredity, it established the "hereditary throne," that is, the oldest son of the Zaddik succeeded his father. And this was even a greater madness than the hereditary monarchy. It was against all the laws of nature—enforced genius. For great fathers often begot insane, mediocre or mean children. At first it paralyzed its development, and soon after Hasidism began to degenerate.

Of course, its history is full of exceptions. Thus, in the sixties of the past century there lived in the city of Kotsk a famous Zaddik, the legends about whom bear a striking similarity to the philosophy of Dostoyevski. All his life he sought for justice and on his death-bed he justified sin. One of the greatest thinkers of his time, unknown, he is spirutually buried within the walls of the Polish Ghetto.

Even today, one may still meet Zaddikim who remember the revolutionary essence of the early Hasidism. But they are few and unknown. The respected, influential, rich Zaddikim are either zealous dogmatists or clever fakers. Some of them are engaged in politics and before elections sell the votes of their followers. Others arrange lotteries for themselves, forcing their Hasidim to buy tickets. Or they enter into agreements with doctors, and when a sick Hasid comes trembling to the Zaddik to ask for advice: "Rabbi, what shall I do?" he is given the address of a doctor—fee fifty-fifty. To be a Zaddik is more profitable than to sell herring.

With difficulty I have at last succeeded in finding a real Zaddik. He is, perhaps, one of the last. His name is Reb Yosele from Skvernovic. He lives in Warsaw, in the neighborhood of the Jewish paupers. A tiny unheated room. I am reminded: "Do not forget to cover your head." This is his only request. The Zaddik is a tall, good-looking Jew of about fifty-five years of age, with a long traditional beard and the kind, yet sad eyes of a village dreamer. He is dressed poorly, and everything around him is poor and shabby. The chairs are broken and the tapestry torn. This Zaddik resembles a great poet who is read only by ten or twenty people. His followers are poor workers from the Nalevki. They do not give, but beg.

The Zaddik offers me a cigarette and lights one himself. By the awkward movement of his fingers, and his strenuous puffing, it is obvious that he is not a habitual smoker. Perhaps, he only lit the cigarette so as to soften the tension of our strange meeting. However, he soon feels at ease and answers my questions. I ask him about the essence of Hasidism. He answers readily without stopping to think a moment; sometimes smiling ironically, sometimes inspired, like a real poet.

"The Misnagdim consider the 'Law' above all. But soldiers are trained differently in different countries. The English soldiers are taught differently from the Polish. However, soldiers of all the world are trained to obey the commands of 'one-two'; the good one forgets everything he has been taught."

The Zaddik caresses his long beard and looks at me questioningly. It seems that he is not certain whether I understood. He adds: "All life is war. . . .

"You ask what is 'Heaven' and 'Hell'? After death a man with strong will power lives his life all over again. The joy from the love and kindness he dispensed through his life is 'Heaven.' And 'Hell'? 'Hell' is shame. . . .

"In order for a man to rise he must first fall. One cannot rise without having fallen. This is the law of life and the law of God. . . .

"Poverty is the path to God. In the book *Zohar* it is said that God has many attires, but he is always dressed in the prayers of the poor."

My last question: "What is more important, the relation between man to God or between man to man?"

The Zaddik smiles.

"At first it seems that his relation to God is the more important. For God is everything, and man—dust. But when you think about it, especially if you have lived and experienced, you will realize that man's relation to man is the most significant. If a man insults God, he has insulted God alone. But when a man insults a man, he has wronged both, God and men."

Reb Yosele has a score of followers. They always come to him for advice: "What's to be done, the daughter is sick?" or "Soloveichik will not return the ten Zlotys he borrowed." His wisdom remains within the four walls, hidden under a faded cap, bent over an old book.

The Zaddik reminds one of an old master who remembers a secret of an ancient craft, but does not know where to apply it. Reb Yosele still remembers the words of the Besht, but his words nobody understands any more. He cures hearts not with his inherited wisdom but with his title of "Zaddik," and with a kind and generous smile.

The rich Jews go to the better-known Zaddikim. There, they too may expect some honor or benefits; the right to sit with the Zaddik at one table, or with his influential assistants in some commercial scheme. These Hasidim wear silk *talletim* (prayer-shawls), their beards are neatly trimmed, and on Saturdays, they wear silk caps with borders of yellow fur. They call themselves Hasidim, but if you ask them about the teachings of Besht, they will not be able to answer. For them more important than the joy and ecstasy is—who will sit today next to the Zaddik, Aaron Shmulevich or Hayyim Rosenberg?

There are still other places where Hasidism is yet alive, not its philosophy but spirit—amid the poor of the synagogue of the so-called "Brazlav Hasidim." They have no Zaddik at all. Their Zaddik died long ago—a century and a half ago. His name was "Reb Nachman from Brazlav." He was a great philosopher and poet. His sayings, legends and poetry were recently published in a German translation. This first emergence of historical Hasidism from the borders of the Ghetto was full of a belated glory, to the classical astonishment of the descendants. "Whence such daring thought? Whence such poetry? From Brazlav? . . . Nobody ever knew about it. . . ."

Yes, only his Hasidim knew it. For them Reb Nachman was a great Zaddik. And when he died, they did not take another one in his place. They have chosen for their adviser the memory of this Zaddik-poet. Among the Brazlav Hasidim there are neither rich nor hypocrites. These have nothing to do here, their place is at the table of the living Zaddik. And here? Here are only the paupers of the Nalevki: peddlers, tailors, cobblers.

I enter the synagogue. It is a small room in a worker's house, dimly lit by a tiny electric lamp. It is crowded to capacity, and with difficulty I manage to elbow my way inside. At first it seems as though it were a trade union meeting. But no, here is a different century, a different chronology. Perhaps it is altogether beyond the concepts of our time. Bearded men in dirty caps who toil the whole week selling rags and herrings, pounding out a monotonous dreary existence. But now is Sabbath Eve. They came here to rejoice. And they are happy, not because it has been prescribed to be happy. No, in them is still alive the belief which is already dead outside of this tiny room. They are meeting the "Sabbath-Queen." They clasp their hands and sing. At first, they say words of prayer. But neither the tongue nor the mind can keep up with the gayness of the soul. Soon, the words are heard no more, only a gay, wide, soul-captivating melody. The feet will not stand in one place any longer, and they begin to jump. And they dance and dance in this tiny and dimly-lit room. Happiness! Life! I observe the faces and wonder. Who changed them? Who erased from their minds the memory of insults, hunger and "Zlotys"? One can speak here even about Catholicism, Freud or "Mass Hypnotism." But is it worth while? These things can be read by everyone in solid books. Would it not be better now, to accept the smile of the Brazlav Hasidim as an extraordinary happiness? Even though it is foreign, inaccessible, but human till the end. The joy of losing oneself in a greater joy, the joy of honesty and forgetfulness, the joy of simple and childish souls. Rejoice! ! ! . . .

ISRAEL AND THE ENEMY

retold by MEYER LEVIN

WHEN Israel was five years old, his father Eleazer was dying. On the day of his death Rabbi Eleazer talked to his son. Eleazer was old, and the wandering that he had done over the earth had creased his body with pain. His eyes were weary, for they had stared many days upon thick clouds to see one instant of heaven. And now he was glad that his death was come.

He said to the boy, "My child, know that the Enemy will always be with you, he will be in the shadows of your dreams and in your living flesh, for he is the other part of yourself. There will be times when like a lightning-stroke you will pierce into his farthest hiding-place, and he will fade before you like a fleeing cloud; and there will be times when he will surround you with walls of darkness, and you will stand alone as upon a raft in the midst of a sea of night. But remember always that your soul is secure to you, for your soul is entire, and he cannot come into it; your soul is a part of God.

"Before you were born it was made known to me that God would always be with you, for within you there lives one of the Innocent souls of heaven. Then go fearless through your life on earth, do not be afraid of man, and do not fear the Enemy, for the highest power is in you."

After the death of Rabbi Eleazer, the Jews of the village cared for his child. Israel was sent to the cheder. But soon he found he could not bear to remain within the schoolroom; he would glide through the door and go into the woods; there he would remain all day long, walking under the trees, sitting among the flowers, or by the running river, absorbed with joy.

The schoolmaster would find him and take him back to the cheder. For a few days Israel would attend dutifully, but then again an urge would come into him, and he would run to the woods.

At last the schoolmaster lost patience with the boy, and left him to do as he pleased.

Then Israel lived joyously, he was brisk as a squirrel. He made himself a mossy place within a cave, and there he slept in the branches of the trees; he lived on berries and fruit, he talked with the birds, he played with the untamed beasts, and sometimes he stood very still, and listened. So Israel grew.

When he was ten years old he came out of the woods to the village of Horodenka, and became a helper to the schoolmaster there. It was Israel's duty to go from one house to another early every morning, to wake the children and lead them to the cheder. In the evening he led them home.

Soon the Jews of Horodenka began to feel that the children were changed. They were like no other Jewish children. Often, they sang.

And this is how it happened that the children of Horodenka sang.

At dawn, the boy Israel went from house to house, calling his followers. When he had gathered all his herd, he would lead them toward the fields, quite in the opposite way from the cheder. And then he would begin to sing. And the other children would also begin to sing; so they would go a long way through the fields and through the woods, going in a great circle until they came to the schoolhouse. In the late afternoon he would lead them again singing through the woods and the fields; they would come carrying green branches in their hands, with the flowers woven in their hair.

Often they sang, "Praised be his Holy name, Amen!" For Israel knew no other song.

The voices of the singing children rose like arrows upward and broke against the heavy clouds of evil that the Enemy had spread over the earth. Every day the voices beat against the clouds, until they pierced into them. Soon a crack was made, and the voices reached the blue sky, and flew toward heaven.

Then the exiled and wandering Spirit, called the Shechina, hearing the singing of the children, raised her head in the hope that the time had come when she might flow back into her Creator, and again be One with Him.

But Satan rose in furious hate and strode straight into heaven.

"Someone there below is interfering with my work!" he cried.

Elijah said, "It is only a band of children singing."

"Let me strive against the children!" Satan demanded of God.

And God nodded his head, saying, "Strive."

Then Satan went down to the earth.

He went to the wood where the boy Israel had lived; there the Enemy crept over the ground, peering at every insect and crawling into the bosom of every flower; of insect and blossom he asked, "Will you carry my poison into the heart of the child Israel?"

But no living thing would turn against the child.

In that wood lived an aged charcoal-burner, who had been born without a human soul. His body lived, and ate, and slept. He did not know what was right and what was wrong. He was afraid of humans, and therefore hid himself in the forest; some people thought he was a sorcerer, and they feared him.

It was true that often at night a demoniac power would creep into the flesh of the old charcoal-burner; then he would feel himself becoming an animal. He would crouch, and sink onto his four paws. His limbs would become covered with fur. Then he would be a werewolf, and prowl under the trees.

Those who went late into the woods were often frightened by the werewolf's moan. But none had felt his teeth.

The charcoal-burner's simple heart shrank under the terrible urge that made him into a werewolf; when he had howled his pain and shame, he would creep under a bush and lie there panting, unable to flee his self, until at last he slept.

So the Enemy found him sleeping.

Satan reached his hand into the breast of the sleeping creature, and took his heart out from his body. That heart Satan buried in the earth. And within the breast of the human werewolf he placed his own heart, that was the innermost kernel of darkness.

When Israel came at dawn with his singing children toward the forest, the werewolf broke from the bush and rushed with snorting nostrils and teeth that flashed like knives toward the flock of children. The children screamed in fright, some fell insensible, some ran into the forest, some into the field, some clung to each other and cried, and some were taken with fever.

The werewolf disappeared.

Israel called to the boys who had been with him, but they had run home crying.

Then the whole village was taken with fright. The children told of the terrifying wolf that had come out of the forest upon them; they shivered and whimpered and trembled, and some lay in the houses, sick with fright. The mothers and fathers said, "It is the fault of the boy who led them into the forest. We will not send the children with him any more."

When the other boys had run to their mothers and fathers, Israel went into the forest. He thought of the words his father had spoken to him, and he knew that what the other children feared, he need not fear.

He walked all morning in the forest.

Then he returned to the village, and went from one house to the other, speaking to the parents of the children.

"Let them come out with me again," he said. "No harm will befall them. A wolf ran by in the field, he was himself frightened of the children. Let them come with me again tomorrow, and you will see how they will be no longer frightened."

And the eyes of the boy were so earnest, and his pleading was so strong, that the parents trusted him and said, "Come for the children in the morning."

At dawn the next day Israel once more gathered his band about him.

He spoke to them earnestly of many things, as a man speaks to his fellows. "Come behind me," he said, "and whatever happens, do not be taken with fright, do not run."

Then he began to sing, and the children followed him singing, "Yiskadal . . . !"

He led them across the fields, to the very edge of the wood. There he stopped and said, "Remain here."

He went alone into the forest. At once the Beast emerged from behind the trees, and came toward Israel.

The boy saw the Beast becoming larger, he saw the Beast grow until his back was a scowling cloud arched beneath the heavens, and his paws clutched the whole earth, and the bloody vapour that issued from his mouth covered the rising sun.

But the boy was not afraid. He walked straight forward, going into the very body of the werewolf, and nothing stopped his steps. He came to the dark glowing heart of the Beast. Round and shining like a black mirror it lay before him; all of the knowledge and all of the desire of the world were drawn into its gloomy depths, and all of the evil and all of the untruth in the world were reflected outward from its surface, reflected with such a black and universal brilliance of hatred that only his universal love of God saved the boy from being blinded, and drawn into the mirror, to become a part of its evil.

That black heart was given into his hand.

He closed his fingers tightly over it, he held it fast.

But then he felt it palpitating within his hand, shivering and jerking like a fish out of water; he felt the blood drop from it, and he knew the immeasurable pain that was in that heart: pain that began before time began, and would endure forever.

Then he took pity, and gave freedom to the heart.

He placed it upon the earth; and the earth opened and swallowed the black heart into itself.

Israel looked around, and saw that he was alone. He went and found his band of children and led them on to the cheder.

At the close of the day, townsfolk found the charcoal-burner lying dead under the bushes in the woods. A smile of simple innocence was on his face. His eyes were closed.

Then, they did not understand why they had ever feared him, saying he became a werewolf at night in the woods. For in death he was like a child.

From that day forward the children of Horodenka ceased to sing as they went after Israel through the fields; they began to be like their fathers, and the fathers of their fathers, with their heads bowed between their shoulders.

THE RABBI'S SON

by NAHMAN OF BRAZLAV

Nот long ago there lived a rabbi who in all his life had scarcely lifted his head from the study of the holy books, and who was so strict in his observance of every last dot in the ritual that he would scarcely raise his eyes to heaven without first seeking a law that might tell him whether it was permitted at that moment and hour to raise one's eyes to heaven. And in all the world there was nothing that angered him so much as the practices of those who were called Hasidim, for in their wild prayer, in their miracles of healing, and in their carelessness of the strictures of the law, he saw the hand of the evil one. And when he found men in his own village going over to the ways of the Hasidim, the rabbi became bitter against them, and he fought with all his strength to prevent another soul from being lost to the erring ones, and he thought, "After I am dead, there will be none to prevent them, and they will all go and become followers of the mad, howling Zaddikim, who disgrace the Sabbath with their loud singing and lusty dancing, and who scarcely know how to read in the holy books." The rabbi longed for a son who would continue after him to keep the people to the observance of the holy law.

When a son was born to him in his old age, he took it joyfully as a sign from above that his way was the only path to heaven, and that the way would not be left without a guide. The rabbi thought, "My son will be a great light against the Hasidim; he will destroy them entirely, with their ignorant Zaddikim, their mad chanting in the woods, and their magic tricks of healing." He was watchful over the boy every instant of day and night, that the child might not touch even the shadow of an impurity.

The youth that grew was remarkable in learning. He sat on a high stool near the table, and studied the books that were before him. But as the young boy sat on the stool, he would sometimes lift his eyes from the pages of the holy books, and his gaze would reach through the window out into the fields, into the distance that was yellow and green with leaves; then his soul would glide forth upon the path of his gaze, and his soul would hover like a bird in the free air.

At those moments the boy felt himself drawn as toward a singing voice, and he was very happy. But then he would remember his books, and force his eyes back upon the page, and hold his head down with both his hands, that he might not err.

More often the longing came upon him, and his soul went out to the call of a song, as a bird answering the song of its mate. And in that time the boy was alight with a holiness that made bright the entire room, and joy was all about him. But when he returned to his books he felt himself dragged down to listen to the mouths of the dead, and there was a yearning and a longing in him for he knew not what.

The flame and the yearning consumed him, his body became weak, and he was as a trembling candle-flame that may die with every puff of the wind. Still he did not know what he desired, but his yearning was as that of the unborn souls that await their embodiment on earth.

The rabbi saw that his son was becoming weak, and he spoke with him of all the wonders of the law's myriad commands, and of his life that was needed to combat the Hasidim on earth. But in all the things that the rabbi said, there was no help for the boy; only when his father spoke of the evil of the Hasidim, only then he felt a trembling within him, and a sudden warmth.

Among the young scholars with whom he sometimes studied, there were two who went secretly among the Hasidim; and when they saw the rabbi's son become so pale, and losing his heart for learning, they said, "What is it that is ill with you?"

He told them, "I feel a longing for something, and I cannot tell what it is."

Then they said to him, "Only one man can help you, and he is the great Zaddik who lives one day's journey from here. You must go to him, for he has the power to release your soul to its destiny."

"Is he pure?" asked the rabbi's son.

"We do not know whether he is pure," they told him, "for he does not keep himself from contact with the sinful. But we do know that he never leaves anyone until he has taken his burden from him."

"Is he learned?" asked the rabbi's son.

"We do not know whether he is learned," they answered, "for he lives in a hut in the forest, and works as a wood-cutter. But he knows the song that the sparrow sings to heaven."

Then the boy went to his father the rabbi and said, "Let me go to see a Zaddik who lives in a little town a day's journey away."

The rabbi was deeply pained at his son's words, for he knew that the Zaddik was but a simple man, a leader of the Hasidim. "What help can he be to you, my son," the rabbi asked, "when you yourself have more learning than he?"

The boy returned to his studies, but again he felt the terrible longing come over his soul and his eyes lifted, and he looked into the distance. Then he went to his father and begged him, "Let me go."

The rabbi saw his son become more frail and wan each day, until when the boy asked him a third time, the rabbi said, "You may not go alone to him, for it may be the evil one who is drawing you on this way. But I will go with you to this ignorant man, that you may see him and forget him."

When they had put the horses to the cart, the rabbi said, "Let us see whether there will be a sign from heaven upon this journey. If nothing happens to delay the journey, it is a sign that this is a true pilgrimage; but if we should be stopped on our way, it is a sign that we must turn back, and we will return."

So they rode forth, and all went well until they came to a shallow brook, but as the cart was crossing the brook, one of the horses slipped and fell and overturned the cart, so that the rabbi and his son were thrown into the water.

When they had come out of the water, and righted the cart, the rabbi said: "You see, my son, heaven has sent us a sign to turn back, for this is an evil journey." So they returned home, and the boy sat again over his books. But soon the heaviness returned to his heart, and he felt the call of the distance. He feared to speak to his father, for he remembered the omen on their journey. Days passed, and each day the boy became weaker, until he was as a dying man who no longer fears what may be said on earth. "Father," he cried, "I must go and speak with the Zaddik!"

Once more the rabbi consented, and they rode on their way. But when they had ridden two-thirds of a day, the cart went over a great stone, and both axles of the cart were broken.

"This Zaddik must surely be an impostor," the rabbi declared, "for we have had another omen, and our journey to him is barred." They mended the wagon, and returned home.

But the boy's soul was more than ever unquiet, until he prevailed upon the rabbi to set out for a third time upon the journey. "But, father," he begged, "let us not take what may befall by chance as an omen from heaven. If the horse slips, or the wagon breaks, have we proof that the Zaddik is sinful?"

The rabbi said, "But if there is a sign of sin against him alone, will you obey?"

"I will obey, and return home, and never ask to go to him again."

They set out on their third journey. All went well; at night they came to an inn not far from the village of the Zaddik. As they sat over their evening meal, the boy dreamy and lost in awaited happiness, the rabbi began to speak with a merchant who sat at a near-by table.

"Where does a rabbi travel?" the merchant enquired.

"On his way," said the rabbi, for he was ashamed to say that he was going to consult a man of no learning. "And you?" he asked.

"I am a merchant; I have just been to a village," said the stranger. And he spoke the name of the Zaddik's place.

Then, as one who remembers the sounds of a name, the rabbi said: "I have heard that many people come to consult with a wonder-worker who lives in that same village."

At this, the merchant laughed out loud. "Don't speak of him!" he shouted. "I have just come from that very man's house!"

The boy raised his head, as one who listens in a dream, and his wide eyes pierced the stranger.

"Is it indeed true," the rabbi asked, "that he is a holy man?"

"A holy man!" the stranger laughed. "He is an imposter and an agent of the evil one! I myself saw him defile the Sabbath!"

Then the rabbi turned to his son and said, "You have heard what the stranger has told us, in all innocence, not knowing where we were bound."

"I have heard," the boy replied, and his voice was as the voice of the dead. They returned home.

Soon after, the boy died.

One night, as the grieving rabbi slept, his son appeared to him in a dream; the youth was wrapped in anger, and as the rabbi asked him, "My son, why are you angry?" the boy cried, "Go to that Zaddik to whom I longed to go!" The rabbi awoke, and remembered his dream, and said to himself, "Perhaps it was a chance dream," and did not go.

But again his son appeared to him as he slept, and the boy wore the form of the Angel of Wrath. And he cried, "Go to the Zaddik! Go!" This time the rabbi thought, "The dream is the work of the evil one." But when his son appeared to him a third time, the rabbi knew that he must go.

And as he came to that same inn where he had stopped with his son, he entered, to pass the night. He sat alone in the room, and did not touch the food that was placed before him; his heart was heavy. Then a voice spoke, a voice of laughter, saying, "Ah, the rabbi is here again."

The rabbi looked up and saw the same merchant whom he had met that other night when he had stopped at the inn.

"The rabbi is here again," the merchant said, "and this time he is alone!"

"Are you not that merchant whom I met here once before?" the rabbi asked.

"Indeed I am!" said the stranger, and laughing, he opened wide his mouth and cried, "If you like, I'll swallow you alive."

The rabbi started with fright. "Who are you!" he murmured, trembling.

"Do you remember," the stranger said, "how you and your son once rode to see the Zaddik, and on the way your horse tripped and fell in the brook? Yet your son made you go again on the way to that holy man, but the second time the axles of your wagon were broken? And the third time you met me here, and I told you that the man was not holy but an imposter who sinned on Sabbath? Then you turned back once more, and so your son died of loneliness and grief? Go, rabbi! Now that I have got rid of your son you may go on your way to the Hasid; for know that in your son there lived the power of the lesser flame, and the power of the greater flame was in the Zaddik, and if they two had come together on this earth, Messiah would have descended! But I placed obstacles in your way, until your son was dead; and now, rabbi, you can go to see the Zaddik!"

With these words, the stranger vanished.

And the rabbi continued on his journey, and came to the hut of the Hasid. And there he wept, "Alas, for him who is lost unto us, and cannot be found again!"

THE ZADDIK OF SOSOV

by JUDAH STEINBERG

IT is said of the Zaddik of Sosov that he loved all the children of Israel. Pious or impious, he loved them all. He would plead for sinners, though they were rotten with wrongdoing as a decayed pomegranate, to lighten their punishment. Nay, more, in his eyes there were no wicked sinners; all the children of Israel were good. Of the common people who interrupted prayers in the Holy Tongue to gossip in the vernacular he was wont to say: "Lord of the Universe! Behold Thy Jews! Even amidst their sinful deeds they pray to Thee and proclaim Thee their Lord and Father!" Of thieves from the fold of Israel, who broke into houses on the Sabbath eve, he would say: "See the ways even of the dregs of Israel! They risk their bodies and souls—and would not shed blood! They are satisfied to take what they need for the Holy Sabbath day and for the sustenance of their families."

And when he saw sinners for whom no allowance could be made he would sigh, and say: "Our Lord in Heaven! Thou who hast created the world and its Jews! Their bodies and souls are in Thy hand! . . . Thou hast created paradise and hell, good spirits and evil spirits . . . and who durst stay Thy hand? Is it not manifest to Thee that it is not we who sin but the Evil Spirit whom Thou hast implanted in our souls?"

Near the house of the Zaddik of Sosov there dwelt a woman who was in great sorrow because of her children who died young. One day she poured out the bitterness of her heart to the Zaddik's wife, censuring the ways of God. The Zaddik's wife bristled with anger: "That a woman like her should dare to speak accusingly in the eyes of the Lord! The Lord is righteous, and we are not even deserving of His mercy." But when the Zaddik heard the words of his wife he became angry and chid her: "You say the Lord is righteous? But is it not written, 'Do not say thus and thus of your Lord' and 'do not say, "His judgments are righteous!"' I say that the poor woman is right! The mother afflicted in her offspring is right! What has God against her? Does not she circumcise her children? Does not she light her candles on Sabbath night? Does not she burn the ritual dough?"

And that very year a child was born to the woman. She lived to see him happily married. And at the wedding the Zaddik was the honored guest.

The kinsmen of the Zaddik used to tell that he was wont to moan to himself: "May I die soon and thus put out all the fires of Hell!"

It came to pass once that an impeachment was brought against Israel in the Court on High. That year, the butcher of Sosov lost his wife, and there remained with him and his children his wife's younger sister, a girl of thirteen, who had been brought up in his house. . . . The butcher sinned with her. . . . And Satan arraigned all Israel because of him, and the house of Israel was near condemned to a total destruction. And all the shofars of Sosov were marred, and all the shofar-blowers stricken in their lips and tongues so that they could not blow the shofar.

And the Zaddik of Sosov resented this thing. So, donning his talith, he left his earthly frame for the Celestial Palace. When he learned there of the butcher's deed he stood up and said: "God in Heaven! Are not the wedding ring and the rabbinical benediction all that are needed to turn this sin into a good deed? Why, what is this but assisting in the affairs of creation! . . ." And Satan was hushed, and the crimson thread of the heavenly altar turned white. And all the shofar-blowers were healed, the shofars cleared, and everybody knew that it was a good omen for the coming year.

And that day at that hour Satan swore by his sword to take vengeance on the Zaddik of Sosov.

On the eve of shofar-blowing the Zaddik went to the bath. And Satan came and stood in his way and showed him on both sides of the road heaps of snow, rime, and ice. And the Zaddik forgot where he was going, that it was the eve of a holiday, and thought it was the month of Adar and that he was going to purify the millstones for the Passover flour. Suddenly he saw in front of him a great house. Because of the charm that was on him, he believed it to be the mill and entered.

But when he opened the door and crossed the threshold the door closed after him. Nor could he open it again. And he found himself in a large and magnificent hall, like the throne room of a king, and in the center of the hall, a golden table, and a beautiful woman sitting on an ivory chair. . . . Beyond words beautiful . . . She smiled and beckoned to him.

A fire glowed on the hearth in the corner of the hall, spreading a clear and pleasant warmth all over the room. And the Zaddik was gladdened, for he was frozen to the marrow of his bones . . . And the woman smiled and laughed and spoke to him in his own tongue. And when he heard her speak in his own tongue the Zaddik rejoiced in his heart that the daughters of Israel were so comely. And the Zaddik determined to ask of God to grant all Jewish maidens such halls and palaces that they might all be so fair.

And the fire on the hearth whispered to him: "Do not be a fool. The eye sees, the heart covets, and life is made for enjoyment."

But the Zaddik merely wondered and was silent.

Then the beautiful woman drew near him and tried to touch his hand with her little finger. But the Zaddik looked at her in amazement and said: "Daughter, do not you know that this may not be done!" And she began to weep: "If you will not let me touch your hand I shall die before your eyes."

"A human life is a great thing," the Zaddik said to himself, "but what shall I do? I am afraid to sin!" Then he thought for some time and finally devised a plan. He drew near the fire and put his hand on the glowing coal till his flesh was burned, so burned that he could not touch it for pain. Then he stretched out his burned hand to her and said in a voice full of pity: "Touch it, my daughter, that you may not die."

And when she touched his hand he felt a terrible pain . . . But he mastered himself and bore the pain with great joy; for had he not saved a soul in Israel?

When the woman saw that she could not allure him with secret temptations she opened her mouth and began to sing sweet songs . . . And her voice was so soft, melodious, so penetrating through all his limbs, that it stirred emotions in his heart.

When the Zaddik felt her voice piercing into his very heart, he knew that sin was coming near to him. And he took a needle from the table, heated it on the fire, and pierced his ear drums till he became deaf.

Then the adulteress did a terrible and ugly deed. She stripped and stood before him naked.

The Zaddik felt a strange emotion in his heart, like the blazing of a fire. And he saw that this flame was of a sinful nature, and led to evil desires. And . . . he blinded his eyes.

Then a storm broke, and thunder and lightning raged in the sky. He saw the lightning and heard the thunder, though he had pierced his ears and eyes. And he knew that they were not sent from heaven. And he wondered much and raised his eyes—the palace was gone, he was standing knee deep in a pool of muddy water.

Then he remembered that it was the eve of a holiday and realized that it had all been the devil's snare and temptation . . . And he stood up and said: "Lord of the Universe! Everyone does Thy bidding. Everyone is serving Thee! Even Satan is doing his work faithfully! What more dost Thou want? Shed Thy mercy on us and quench Thy wrath!"

And the sky cleared at once, and the Zaddik stood in front of the bath. He made his ablutions and went to listen to the blowing of the shofar . . .

That year the shofar emitted a "tekiyoth, shevorim vetruyoth," whose equal no one had ever heard before.

And it was proclaimed from the Court on High: "In the future whoever wants to plead the cause of sinners must first undergo the temptation of the Zaddik of Sosov, else is his plea rejected."

And those versed in the mysteries of the celestial domain secretly tell that the Zaddik of Sosov, on the day of his death, asked the angel of God to lead him through all the fires of Hell, and that since then Hell has cooled very, very much. . . .

IF NOT HIGHER

by ISAAC LOEB PERETZ

AND the Rebbe of Nemirov, every Friday morning early at Sliches-time, disappeared, melted into thin air! He was not to be found anywhere, either in the synagogue or in the two houses-of-study, or worshipping in some minyan, and most certainly not at home. His door stood open, people went in and out as they pleased—no one ever stole anything from the Rebbe—but there was not a soul in the house.

Where can the Rebbe be?

Where should he be, if not in heaven?

It is likely a Rebbe should have no affairs on hand with the Solemn Days so near?

Jews (no evil eye!) need a livelihood, peace, health, successful matchmakings; they wish to be good and pious and their sins are great, and Satan with his thousand eyes spies out the world from one end to the other, and he sees, and accuses, and tells tales—and who shall help if not the Rebbe? So thought the people.

Once, however, there came a Lithuanian—and he laughed! You know the Lithuanian Jews—they rather despise books of devotion, but stuff themselves with the Talmud and the codes. Well, the Lithuanian points out a special bit of the Gemara—and hopes it is plain enough: even Moses our Teacher could not ascend into heaven, but remained suspended thirty inches below it—and who, I ask you, is going to argue with a Lithuanian?

What becomes of the Rebbe?

"I don't know, and I don't care," says he, shrugging his shoulders, and all the while (what it is to be a Lithuanian!) determined to find out.

The very same evening, soon after prayers, the Lithuanian steals into the Rebbe's room, lays himself down under the Rebbe's bed and lies low.

He intends to stay there all night to find out where the Rebbe goes, and what he does at Sliches-time.

Another in his place would have dozed and slept the time away. Not so a Lithuanian—he learned a whole treatise of the Talmud by heart!

Day has not broken when he hears the call to prayer.

The Rebbe has been awake some time. The Lithuanian has heard him sighing and groaning for a whole hour. Whoever has heard the groaning of the Nemirover Rebbe knows what sorrow for All-Israel, what distress of mind, found voice in every groan. The soul that heard was dissolved in grief. But the heart of a Lithuanian is of cast-iron. The Lithuanian hears and lies still. The Rebbe lies still, too—the Rebbe, long life to him, *upon* the bed and the Lithuanian *under* the bed!

After that the Lithuanian hears the beds in the house squeak—the people jump out of them—a Jewish word is spoken now and again—water is poured on the fingers—a door is opened here and there. Then the people leave the house; once more it is quiet and dark, only a very little moonlight comes in through the shutter.

He confessed afterwards, did the Lithuanian, that when he found himself alone with the Rebbe terror took hold of him. He grew cold all over, and the roots of his ear-locks pricked his temples like needles. An excellent joke, to be left alone with the Rebbe at Sliches-time before dawn!

But a Lithuanian is dogged. He quivers and quakes like a fish—but he does not budge.

At last the Rebbe, long life to him, rises in his turn.

First he does what beseems a Jew. Then he goes to the wardrobe and takes out a packet—which proves to be the dress of a peasant: linen trousers, high boots, a pelisse, a wide felt hat, and a long and broad leather belt studded with brass nails. The Rebbe put them on.

Out of the pockets of the pelisse dangles the end of a thick cord, a peasant's cord.

On his way out the Rebbe steps aside into the kitchen, stoops, takes a hatchet from under a bed, puts it into his belt, and leaves the house. The Lithuanian trembles but he persists.

A fearful, Solemn-Day hush broods over the dark streets, broken not infrequently by a cry of supplication from some little minyan, or the moan of some sick person behind a window.

The Rebbe keeps to the street side, and walks in the shadow of the houses.

He glides from one to the other, the Lithuanian after him. And the Lithuanian hears the sound of his own heart-beats mingle with the heavy foot-fall of the Rebbe; but he follows on, and together they emerge from the town.

Behind the town stands a little wood. The Rebbe, long life to him, enters it. He walks on thirty or forty paces, and then he stops beside a small tree. And the Lithuanian, with amaze, sees the Rebbe take his hatchet and strike the tree. He sees the Rebbe strike blow after blow, he hears the tree creak and snap. And the little tree falls, and the Rebbe splits it up into logs, and the logs into splinters. Then he makes a bundle, binds it round with the cord, throws it on his shoulder, replaces the hatchet in his belt, leaves the wood, and goes back into the town.

In one of the back streets he stops beside a poor, tumble-down little house, and taps at the window.

"Who is there?" cries a frightened voice within. The Lithuanian knows it to be the voice of a Jewess, a sick Jewess.

"I," answers the Rebbe in the peasant tongue.

"Who is I?" inquires the voice further. And the Rebbe answers again in the Little-Russian speech:

"Vassil."

"Which Vassil? and what do you want, Vassil?"

"I have wood to sell," says the sham peasant, "very cheap, for next to nothing."

And without further ado he goes in. The Lithuanian steals in behind him, and sees, in the gray light of dawn, a poor room with poor, broken furniture.

In the bed lies a sick Jewess huddled up in rags, who says bitterly:

"Wood to sell—and where am I, a poor widow, to get the money from to buy it?"

"I will give you a six-groschen worth on credit."

"And how am I ever to repay you?" groans the poor woman.

"Foolish creature!" the Rebbe upbraids her. "See here: you are a poor sick Jewess, and I am willing to trust you with the little bundle of wood; I believe that in time you will repay me. And you, you have such a great mighty God, and you do not trust Him! not even to the amount of a miserable six-groschen for a little bundle of wood!"

"And who is to light the stove?" groans the widow. "Do I look like getting up to do it? and my son away at work!"

"I will also light the stove for you," said the Rebbe.

And the Rebbe, while he laid the wood in the stove, repeated groaning the first part of Sliches.

Then, when the stove was alight, and the wood crackled cheerily, he repeated, more gaily, the second part of Sliches.

He repeated the third part when the fire had burnt itself out, and he shut the stove doors. . . .

The Lithuanian who saw all this remained with the Rebbe, as one of his followers.

And later, when anyone told how the Rebbe early every morning at Sliches-time raised himself and flew up into heaven, the Lithuanian, instead of laughing, added quietly:

"If not higher."

HOW THE RABBI OF KALEV FREED A SONG

by MANASSEH UNGER

EVERY soul comes to the earth to accomplish a purpose, the Rabbi from Kalev taught his Hasidim. It is the duty of every man to strive to "release the holy spark" from the lower creations and bring that spark back to the Godhead. My soul—continued the Rabbi—is of the *olam ha-nigun,* the world of song. I came into the world to bring back into our domain all the songs that have fallen to the Evil Power.

And then the Rabbi and his Hasidim would go to the mountain where they could hear diverse sounds. The monotonous murmuring of a little brook, the sighing of a hot afternoon breeze, and sometimes the melancholy lament of a mournful shepherd. For the Rabbi said that the true *niguna* (melody) is not the already assembled tones, but those that, coming from the world of song, are still wandering about the spaces of the world.

"Every day at a certain hour, different tones and voices come down. Sometimes an endless sorrowing cry. Then all who listen sorrow without knowing why, and feel their heart yearn to something. At another time, happy joyful tones fall. Then people feel light-hearted and gay. And from all these scattered tones, men make song, but they do not understand how to find the original song.

"I was created in this world to gather melodies and bring them to their true home. . . ."

The Hasidim listened attentively but understood little. They would see the Rabbi lie down on the earth and strain his ears—listen, now the earth sings a song of praise—and sometimes bending his ear to a tree—now the tree is singing. The Hasidim listened after him, wanted to understand, but they heard nothing except the brushing of a breeze in the twigs of the tree. . . .

The Rabbi used also to teach the Hasidim how to pray. The important thing in prayer is to become one with the Infinite, said the Rabbi, and that is possible through the power of song. Why? Because songs lead to yearning, and yearning to oneness. And if you want to understand what it means to yearn then you must get up very early before the sun has gilded the peaks of the mountains, and go alone to a wood in the hills. There you will understand what it means to yearn. There you will know how to pray. . . .

And so one used to see lonely Hasidim scattered on all the paths, orphaned, going about with their hands hidden in their girdles, their eyes lifted to the skies, experiencing their solitude. They would listen to the songs of the birds, to the running of a brooklet and sometimes stand by a shepherd to carefully note his singing. The Rabbi was always among them to teach them to understand the true sense of the song.

The shepherd would begin to feel at home among the Hasidim. He would leave his sheep to God's care, lay himself down on the grass in the fresh dew with his face to the rising sun, and begin to sing his peasant songs. He sang a verse, then played on his pipes. The Rabbi, hidden in a corner, would listen to the shepherd's song. For the Rabbi said that the shepherd sings with feeling, but he knows not what he sings. He is grown one with nature, he listens to the tones that come from the world of song, but he does not understand them.

The Rabbi gathered his Hasidim to listen to the shepherd. The Hasidim came from all sides. They heard soft plaintive words that the shepherd sang now and then:

> kalah kalah how far you are
> mountain mountain how great you are
> mountain mountain go away from here
> then to my kalah I'll be near.

And the Rabbi said to the Hasidim: Do you know where this melody comes from? It is the yearning song that the *Kneseth-Israel* sings to the *Shekina* (Godhead), and the right way to sing it is this:

> Shekina Shekina how far you are
> Exile Exile how great you are
> Exile Exile go away from here
> So to Shekina I may come near.

The Rabbi had freed the melody and brought it back to its true sense and since then this song is chanted by the Hasidim as the *hishtokikut nigun*.

REB JACOB
Herzl's Hasid

by MOSES SMILANSKI

I

To begin with he was known as Reb Yekele Hornstapoler. Why then Hornstapoler?

It was the name of the town in which lived the sainted Wonder-Rabbi on whom his faith was fixed.

He was born in one of the forsaken villages in the broad plains of Volhynia. There he grew to maturity and lived until he reached the fifties. But he was not called by the name of that village, for what did he care about it and what did it care about him? There he sold brandy, there he did well or did badly, did badly or did well; there he married his wife and had his sons and daughters born to him; there he married them off and raised fresh houses in Israel. In his village he dealt in all these accidentals. But the essence of his life was elsewhere, in Hornstapol, in the sanctum, in the courtyard and in the House of Prayer of his sainted Wonder-Rabbi.

There Reb Yekele *lived*. Thither he went three times in the year: For the final days of Passover, for the Autumn festivals of the New Year and the Day of Atonement, and for the kindling of the first light at Hanukka. That he should go there for the final days of Passover and the Autumn festivals everybody could understand, for it is an accepted custom among all the Hasidim who pin their boundless faith in one or another of the sainted Wonder-Rabbis. But what was the point in going up for the first Hanukka light? That was Reb Yekele's secret. Neither the questioning and cross-examinations of Hasidim nor the complaints of his household were of any avail; Reb Yekele must kindle the first Hanukka light in Hornstapol.

He was a good and tender-hearted man, and when he was "there" his heart and hands were open. More than once and more than twice it happened that he departed full to Hornstapol and returned empty from thence.

"He," may his memory be blessed, was always in great need; as were his sons and grandsons and simple friends whose affairs were going down. For were those suffering from the evils of the time few in number at Hornstapol? Sometimes Reb Yekele would be ashamed to look in the faces of his wife and children when he returned home. In what had these pure innocent lambs sinned? But he knew how to fight against such outlandish thoughts and to remain of his opinions and habits. Occasionally he would grow angry and stubborn, and if he said yes or no at such a time all the winds of the world could not make him budge. Sometimes matters would even reach the saintly seat of the Wonder-Rabbi, so that "He" had to speak pretty plainly to his adherent about it. But at the Feast of Weeks and the Rejoicing of the Law he used to stay at home in his village. All the world went to Hornstapol then but he would stay at home. At the Feast of Weeks when milkfoods are eaten he would prepare a milkfeast for the poor. When things were not going well he laid out his last farthing for this feast of merit. If he was in a really bad way he would take care not to look his wife in the face and would observe his custom. During this feast Reb Yekele was as happy as in Hornstapol, and served his guests and drank and told stories and generally made people feel jolly. At the Rejoicing of the Law he used to dance at the conventicle where the Hornstapol Hasidim of his village prayed, dancing with the scroll of the Torah which he had had written and had given to the conventicle. All the rest of the year the village did not know Reb Yekele the Hasid, the fervent believer in the superhuman, almost semi-divine powers and understanding and righteousness of his sainted Wonder-Rabbi. It only knew Reb Yekele the brandy dealer. Hornstapol knew the Hasid. They used to tell how he took off his shoes there and walked on the tables in his socks in order to serve the guests who sat before Him, long might he live. Nobody knew how to serve as he did. While when Reb Jacob danced before the Rabbi he rose to great things, and his soul mounted aloft in ecstasy. The whole world would climb onto the tables and crane their necks and press their noses against the windows to see Reb Yekele dancing a "Kozako."

Reb Yekele dwelt in his village, lived in Hornstapol, and was therefore known to society at large as Reb Yekele Hornstapoler.

In his old age he received a new name and was called the Rehobothite.

The last twenty years of his life were spent in Rehoboth. There in Rehoboth did I meet him for the first time, get to know him, love him and become a "companion" of his.

II

In the castaway village lost between the broad, gloomy and desolate plains of Volhynia, there are doubtless still ancient cronies sitting together in the Hornstapol conventicle between the afternoon and evening prayers, in the hour that is neither day nor night, and whispering their tales and fables and legends; while stripped, naked souls from the cemetery near by flutter and beat silently against the windows and listen to the whispered tales. The ancients will be sure to tell the tale of Reb Yekele Hornstapoler.

". . . He became obsessed with a mad idea . . ." they whisper, nodding their heads ". . . Peered within at the hidden mysteries and was smitten, the Merciful One deliver us . . ."

It had happened like this. During the pogroms of the eighties of the last century Reb Yekele's village was at its wit's end. The old men and women went out to measure the graves, while Reb Yekele hastened to Hornstapol and rose in front of all the congregation assembled in the large conventicle, crying out, "Rabbi, help us!"

And "He" was silent. He turned his face to the ground and was silent.

And when Reb Yekele returned to his agitated and confused village where he was awaited as though he bore salvation in his hands, he too turned his face to the ground and had nothing to say.

Hard times came to the Hornstapol conventicle. Hasidim entered to pray with dejected faces such as should not be seen among Hasidim who are enjoined to be glad at heart. They would enter silently and leave silently. Even between the afternoon and evening prayers no happy voice would be heard; nothing but a melancholy whisper. And even that whisper might break off suddenly as often as not. Every corner of the building seemed to be in deep mourning.

The hard times passed. The Hasidim returned one by one to their affairs and their worries. The taste of the pogroms grew faint in the mouth. But Reb Yekele was no longer as he had formerly been. He no longer lived in Hornstapol. It began to be whispered from mouth to ear that Reb Yekele was writing a book on the End of Days and the coming of Messiah.

Strange rumors began to reach the forsaken village, the like of which had never before been heard, tidings such as nobody could remember their fathers and grandfathers having told of. When they heard them, the Hasidim shrugged their shoulders and made movements of dismissal with their hands, showing they did not approve. But Reb Yekele listened to these rumors with great attention. Folk began to talk about youngsters who had taken to evil courses, students who had risen overnight and established a society to ascend to the Land of Israel. The youngsters called themselves BILU after the initial letters of the Hebrew verse, "House of Jacob, come let us go."

"Trying to hasten the End of Days . . ."

"Rushing ahead before the band . . ."

"May all I dreamt this night and every night come to pass upon the foes of Israel! They'll go and build a country! Have you ever seen such a House of Jacob in your lives? Heretics, apostates!"

Reb Yekele listened and remained silent to everybody's surprise. How was it he had nothing to say?

Then one day he hurried into the conventicle, stood beside the Holy Ark and cried out, "And I tell you they're right!"

"Who are right?"

"The youngsters."

"God be with you, Reb Yekele, what youngsters?"

"The BILU!"

All the Hasidim were startled. If it had been anyone but Reb Yekele speaking to them they would have let their tongues boil over on him. Had the like ever been heard? Here, in this holy spot, someone trying to justify the heretics with their rushing ahead!

"And tomorrow I'm going to 'Him,'" said Reb Yekele and dashed out of the building.

And sure enough, next day, which was neither a festival nor a holiday, Reb Yekele left for Hornstapol. And the whole village waited breathlessly to hear what message he would bring back from "there."

And in Hornstapol something dreadful happened, the like of which had never before occurred. Reb Yekele came to the house of the Wonder-Rabbi, entered the guest room, took no notice of anybody, never greeted the wardens, never wrote a slip stating what he wanted of the Rabbi according to custom, but burst straight into "His" room. Everybody was astounded and startled; what calamity could have befallen Reb Yekele? A fire? A daughter suffering in a difficult childbirth?

They crowded to the door and strained their ears to listen. To begin with, nothing but a kind of whisper could be heard. Then suddenly they began to hear loud cries, almost shouts, and finally clear, echoing words beating into their ears like hammered nails, so that they hear them to this day.

"And so you are no 'Rabbi.' May the blood of thy people Israel be on thy head!"

The dreadful words were shouted out in a tremendous voice, the voice of Reb Yekele. And the door was suddenly flung noisily open and out rushed Reb Yekele with a flaming face, while the face of the Wonder-Rabbi was pale as death. When they had recovered from their shock the Hasidim set off in pursuit of Reb Yekele "to rend him like a fish," but they did not find him; he had returned home.

When Reb Yekele reached his village he sprang down from his waggon, and instead of going home dashed straight off to the conventicle. It was the time of the afternoon prayer. Hasidim stood in small groups preparing their souls for devotion and prayer.

"Listen to what I tell you today, my masters," thundered Reb Yekele in their ears. "The man who goes to the Land of Israel, even though he be shaven and live against the Law, is greater in my eyes than the 'Rabbi' who dwells in the pollution of Exile at this pregnant hour!"

The Hasidim fell upon him. He returned home beaten and bruised with the last of his strength.

It was not very long before Reb Yekele liquidated his business.

"He just let everything go to smash, sold all his property and goods for a half o' nothing." That is the fashion in which the ancients finish their tale of Reb Yekele. For Reb Yekele went up to the Land of Israel.

III

I first met him twenty-two years ago and found him very lovable.

I had a very soft spot in my heart for the meagre, short old man with the deep wrinkles in his lofty forehead, the thin white beard that framed his fallen cheeks and his blue eyes, innocent as those of a child. He always dressed as he had when he went to visit his Rabbi, wearing a long kapote reaching to his feet, linen breeches and a skullcap on his head under his hat. In his little room were a heap of books, Hasidic books, books on Kabala; and in his trunk lay the manuscript of his own work.

He loved the colony with its houses and vineyards. When a new house was built or a new vineyard planted, he found it an occurrence epoch-making enough to be recorded in his book.

"Children," he used to say to us youngsters, "you can't appreciate how great the work is that you are doing. Every tree you plant, every house you build, help to bring the End of Days nearer."

When he heard of a new stretch of land purchased his eyes began to sparkle with joy. His hat would be pushed back onto the back of his head and the two tails of his kapote would spread away to east and west. He would need very little to set him dancing. Reb Yekele Hornstapoler would revive within him at such times.

He loved us youngsters, and watched us with open affection. He would never miss an opportunity of chatting with us. Sometimes he would wish to bring us back to the paths of righteousness, go up to one of the youngsters, stroke his shaven cheek and say in affectionate remonstrance:

"Do me a favor and just tell me, what do you need this for? Is a beard going to do you any harm? Isn't a fine Jewish face seven times as handsome? Are you really set upon losing your portion of the World to Come? Apostate, all your trouble's in vain. Your portion is prepared and awaiting you in spite of yourself. Every tree you plant is a full and utter atonement for your transgressions. 'They,' they'll rot in Hell. In the Day of Judgment their beards and earlocks won't help them nor their praying shawls and fringes, nor the whole of the Six Hundred and Thirteen Commandments. May the devil take their fathers' fathers' fathers! Sitting there like lords in Hornstapol and busying themselves with carrying out Commandments! Let them come here if they want to be busy with Commandments!"

He always stood up for the youngsters. His defence of the youngsters always came to an end with a bitter outburst against his pious companions who remained dwelling with the Wonder-Rabbi in Exile.

"The youngsters, they know and they understand, while those yonder— they don't know anything and they don't understand anything." So would he always finish.

He would say such things in bitter anger. It seemed as if he found it hard to get them out of his mouth and that his very soul was set on edge when he spoke; but he could not restrain himself, for it hurt him deeply.

Reb Alter, like himself a Hasid, would endeavor to silence him:

"Enough, enough, Reb Jacob. They must be hindering from Heaven. I am sure that 'They' must know. 'They' are greater than us."

"Greater! How are they greater?" Reb Yekele would boil over like a kettle. "Their sins are their only greatness. One shaven chin in Rehoboth balances all your great ones, sunk as they are in the pollution of Exile."

Reb Alter used to put his hands over his ears. He could not bear to hear Reb Yekele's outbursts against the Holy Ones. A group would gather round them. The older folk would grow angry enough to leap in the air with annoyance while the youngsters would stand by to protect their Reb Yekele.

Of me he was particularly fond. It was me he honored with the delicate responsibility of correcting his manuscript.

"You only need to touch up the style a little. That's my weak point. But the ideas! If 'They' will read my book they'll repent, They'll all of them repent. My proofs are as undeniable as the sun that we're right, and I've taken them from the Law and the words of our sages of blessed memory. As clear and undeniable as the sun!"

Reb Jacob had a grand-daughter. She spoke Hebrew with a Sephardic accent instead of the North-European one still customary then. And the old man had a tremendous love for her. He would twist and wrench his tongue trying to speak the "Holy Tongue" with her. And she, mischievous child that she was, used to laugh at his mistakes. And the old man would look at her, fill his ears with her laughter, and his innocent eyes would sparkle afresh with happiness. "Quite right," he would say. "Doesn't she outweigh a hundred rabbis dwelling in the pollution of Exile?"

IV

Reb Jacob loved the colony, the youngsters and his grand-daughter. But most of all he loved Herzl.

From the first day he heard his name he loved, honored and all but idolized him. In Palestine everybody still opposed Herzl for fear that his politics might do damage in the "lofty windows," in Stamboul; but Reb Jacob was already telling signs and wonders of him. He began searching through his calculations regarding the End of Days to find signs and supports and portents for Herzl. Evening by evening, when I returned from my vineyard to my home, I would see Reb Jacob in the distance walking up and down before the entrance of his little house, his hands folded behind him, his skullcap tipped back and his face shining.

"The signs and portents of Herzl are working out well," I would think to myself.

And sure enough I was right. One evening he stood waiting for me at the crossroads.

"It's clear as the sun!"

"What is, Reb Jacob?"

"He's destined for greatness, a greatness that can't even be foreseen or estimated in advance!"

"Who is, Reb Jacob?"

He turned stern eyes on me, as if to say, "Who could we be discussing if not Him?" Naturally I knew what he had in mind, but wanted to tease him.

"Herzl!"

"But our men of affairs are afraid he may spoil things in Stamboul?"

"Wiseacres, addle-pates! He *can't* spoil things! He can't! Each letter of his words, every tittle of his deeds, sum up together in a mighty reckoning. . . . He's born to greatness! Haven't I told you: in the fifties [the 1890's] there'll be a great sign. That's the sign. And in the sixties [1900-1910] there'll be the second sign; the Holy and Blest One will avenge our blood. Do you really and truly suppose that our shed blood is water poured out over the earth? God forbid! The northern people, the great people, Gog Magog, will arise and spread its dominion over the whole earth, and will smite and bring low the pride of those who tread in our blood. And in the seventies [1910-1920] will be the third sign. And from the third sign to the End of Days is but a single step. . . . If only we may merit it, if only we may merit it!"

"Who's the northern people, Reb Jacob? There's no great northern people in the world whom we don't know about."

"You don't know? He knows! There is such, and if there isn't—there will be. It's clear as the sun."

And from that day forward, seeing that the matter was "clear and undeniable as the sun," Reb Jacob began taking up the cudgels on behalf of Herzl. He went into battle with tremendous diligence and devotion, whether in the street, in the synagogue, in the house of the Rabbi of Jaffa, among his youngsters or among the old folk. Once he entered a place there was only one topic: Herzl. He spoke of Herzl as though they were old friends, as though he knew his inmost secrets, as though he had been told everything in his heart. And how happy he became when news was received of Herzl's victories, of his visits to royal courts, of his good relations with the German Kaiser! Reb Jacob's eyes used to burn like coals of fire. If you never saw him in those days you never saw a happy man.

"Isn't that what I told you, that he's meant for great things? He'll stand before kings. Has there been a Jew in our times who has stood before kings and walked among them like one of them?"

And the eyes of a joyful victor would be turned upon those present. If anybody dared differ and say that even before Herzl there were Jews who stood before kings and that Herzl did not walk among them like one of them, Reb Jacob would cover his mouth with his hand and silence him:

"Don't sin, you evil one. You risk your soul."

When he heard that the Congress had met and that Jews had come together from all parts of the world to take counsel and seek a common path, while Herzl had sat at their head and all had accepted his words, he wept for excitement.

"What's it like?" he whispered in my ear. "Like the hour of the Redemption. Then the Baal Shem Tov, the father of all the Hasidim, will rise from his grave and Hasidim of every school will make peace among themselves and all stand before him, a great and mighty camp."

One evening I found Reb Jacob awaiting me again at the crossroads. The expression on his face told me that everything was fermenting and seething within him.

"I've been waiting for you—I mean to say—I wanted to ask you . . . It won't be too much for you?"

"Please tell me straight out, Reb Jacob, what it is you want."

"Just to correct—to correct the language a trifle. . . . Not to touch the ideas, God forbid."

As he spoke he very carefully drew from his pocket a large sheet written on from every possible side and every possible corner and space filled in, with the top of the sheet folded over.

"This is a letter . . . a very important letter."

"Who's it to?"

He stood doubtfully a moment.

"You won't tell anybody? It's a great secret. . . . You mustn't let it out."

"I shan't tell anyone, Reb Jacob, God forbid."

"To Herzl."

It took me a great deal of trouble to understand what was written on the big sheet, and the more the author endeavored to explain and clarify his ideas the more foggy did my comprehension become. I corrected where and what I could without succeeding in making out what he was driving at.

"He has to be told that victory is his, that he'll bring all his foes and his opponents to his feet. . . . His victory is clear as the sun. He has to be told. It will strengthen him and put heart in him."

Reb Jacob copied out the big sheet afresh, added fresh mistakes to the old, added notes wherever they could be squeezed in and left not a single quarter-inch unwritten on; then he sent the letter off. And in the evening Reb Jacob came to me consumed with a great worry; he had forgotten to mention the most important thing of all. If only he could get the letter back. . . .

Nobody else knew anything of the letter. The secret was concealed by us until the sign should come. For many a day did Reb Jacob await that sign. To be more precise: it seemed to him that he waited for many a day. Ere a week had gone by Reb Jacob began to visit the post office of the colony to listen to the addresses on the envelopes being read out, as was then the custom; and listened with the greatest possible attention.

"Reb Jacob," I once whispered to him as we returned from the post, "is it physically possible? The letter can't have arrived there yet."

He said nothing, but the look in his sad, innocent eyes told me that at heart he was saying, yes, it's easy enough for you to wait.

And the sign came.

The whole colony hummed like a beehive that evening.

Reb Jacob stood in the street at the door of his house dressed in nothing but his undergarments. He had already removed his kapote, making himself ready for bed. With trembling hands he held a sheet inscribed with round Roman letters, and under the letter the veritable signature, "With Zion's blessings, Herzl." "Herzl" was written in Hebrew characters. . . .

Round Reb Jacob swarmed at least half the colony.

"Do you see? And what did I tell you?" He confounded the assembly with triumphant questions as though there were someone present who had foretold that he would not receive a reply, and now he was revenging himself in public on the false prophet.

Somebody was found who could read German. Herzl expressed his thanks to Reb Jacob for his letter to him. The old man trembled from head to foot. . . . It took him much effort, apparently, to control his turbulent heart and refrain from weeping, and his eyes gleamed and sparkled like sapphires.

Reb Jacob never slept the whole of that night. I am convinced that when he was alone in his little room he took the letter and wept over it; weeping for the Exile of the Divine Presence, the Exile of Israel.

On the morrow Reb Jacob passed through the entire colony, from house to house, with his letter in his hand:

"Do you see? His own actual signature!"

And everybody touched the letter and examined the signature, while Reb Jacob stood by trembling for the sheet of paper in his hand.

But it sometimes happens that great joy, infinite joy, is hidden away for a man and he does not know of it. Such was the joy that was hidden away for Reb Jacob.

v

He was one of the last to learn that Herzl had come to the Land, that he would be in Rehoboth the following morning. The news never made on him the impression which we had expected. He did not rejoice but was taken aback. It seemed to me as though his eyes said, "I knew that he would assuredly come, but so soon?" He hurriedly secluded himself in his room. Apparently he wanted to work out through his calculations a support for the news which had so startled him and taken him aback. I saw light shining from his window till after midnight. When he came out with the dawn I saw his little bowed figure, armed with the bag for praying-shawl and phylacteries, descending from the hill and hastening to the synagogue.

That morning he had a sharp discussion in the synagogue.

"Today is a festival. We do not say the daily prayer of entreaty," stated Reb Jacob in a voice of finality that brooked no discussion.

"What do you mean?" asked the wondering congregation.

"What do I mean?" stormed Reb Jacob. "Have your ears become stopped up so that you can't hear? Herzl's coming today. It's a festival for us today!"

The cold-hearted members of the congregation, few of whom were Hasidim, would not agree. And even Reb Alter the Hasid held with them for a change. Reb Jacob grew angry and complained, and went out to the entrance hall when they began to say the prayer of entreaty.

A new debate began after the prayers. The heads of the colony and elders wished to meet the guest with "bread and salt." Reb Jacob demanded and insisted that the Scrolls of the Law be brought out of the Holy Ark for him.

"Is he a king then, or a great scholar?" asked one of the cold-hearted ones.

"Whom have we greater than he is? He stands in place of a king for us. . . . 'Great scholar,' indeed! All the great scholars were created only and solely in order to serve him."

This time Reb Jacob prevailed; the Scrolls of the Law were brought forth for the greeting of Herzl.

The first sign was given to prepare for the reception. Reb Jacob hastened home and emerged clad in a long satin coat to his feet (a relic of Hornstapol), wearing a new girdle, a new skullcap and his Sabbath hat on his head, and all of him one mass of radiance.

"It's a festival today, a festival, brethren!" he greeted the crowd assembled outside the colony. Then everybody knew, even the cold-hearted non-Hasidim, that it was indeed a festival that day.

Herzl's coach approached the colony. We riders ranged up in two rows and the coach passed between us. I saw Reb Jacob forcing himself a path by main strength through the crowd to the coach, standing on tiptoe and feasting his eyes on "Him," and standing fixed, not moving his good and innocent eyes once they found their quarry. Reb Jacob's face at that hour is unforgettable; it was the face of one who, in the evening of his days, has had the ineffable happiness of seeing the man whom he had awaited and for whom he had prayed throughout his life. So may a man gaze at the face which he has seen in dream all his life and now suddenly sees in the full light of the sun. When the heads of the colony, having greeted Herzl, moved aside, Reb Jacob approached, stretched out his trembling hand to him and in a loud voice, like a man saying the blessing at the Reading of the Law or when Hallowing the Wine and the Bread, said:

"Blessed art Thou O Lord our God, King of the Universe, Who hath kept us alive and sustained us and brought us to reach this hour. . . ."

A wave of awe, the awe that comes at a holy moment, passed through all those assembled. The moment was sacred. It will be sacred forever.

After that Reb Jacob never left Herzl even for a moment. He followed him. He stood by him, his eyes bathing and bathing again in the light of his countenance, and his heart absorbing every word that fell from his lips. What if Herzl spoke German, a language which he could not understand at all? Let him speak whatever language he wished—he, Reb Jacob, would hearken and understand. Is it the words which express what is in the heart? It is the voice that speaks and expresses everything—and Reb Jacob understood Herzl's voice perfectly. He understood Herzl better than all those who knew German. And more than he understood he sensed and felt.

Sephardic peddlers met Herzl on the hill of the colony; they fell at his feet and kissed his footprints in the sand: so should be done to Messiah, son of Joseph, the forerunner of Messiah, son of David. . . . Reb Jacob leapt with open arms to embrace them. For a few moments they stood conversing with tumultuous hearts. He spoke in his "Holy Tongue" and they answered in their "Hebrew." Neither understood the other's words; but all felt the other's emotion.

And in the evening, after Herzl had left the colony and we stood about in little groups uttering all that was in our hearts, Reb Jacob was to be found in every group, now to the right, now to the left. His long satin robe covered his body and his radiance shone from his face; he was silent and never said a word. And when the riders, who had met Herzl on the road, told how, when they reached the borders of the colony, tears had started from his eyes, he suddenly roused to say:

"You hear!"

As though he had known in advance that Herzl would weep.

And large, heavy tears welled from the eyes of the old man in his festival garb and coursed like a stream down his wrinkled cheeks and his silver-white beard.

VI

The heart draws up its happiness, draws and draws—and then calamity comes.

The impression made on all of us through the tidings of the offer of "Uganda" to the Zionists by the British Government was different from that made on Reb Jacob. We were startled and for a while did not know what to think. We found a stern internal war between emotion and intellect. But Reb Jacob received the news like a slap in the face. He cowered and grew still smaller and more bent. Fear and prayer shone through his eyes. It is the way a child looks when his father catches him and forces him to drink a bitter draught in spite of himself. He could not think, he could only feel. He became still and dumb. He was enwrapped in a deep mourning as though he mourned for someone dead.

When the debates, the quarrels and the fissures began, Reb Jacob kept out of it. He never participated in the debates and never joined one or other side. The Ugandist wanted him to join them, trusting to his boundless "Herzlianism," but he rebuffed them.

"His blood is on your heads!"

Nor did he join us, who remained staunch for Zion.

"You are children, you don't understand. . . . You don't understand anything at all. . . . We need mercy, boundless and infinite mercy!"

He wandered about like a shadow.

Once he brought me into his room.

"Please. . . . Only this once. . . ."

And once again he took from his pocket a large sheet written upon from every side, and slipped it into my hand. It was a summons to the Wonder-Rabbis. And the proclamation brimmed over with curses and maledictions. He cursed the rabbis and the Wonder-Rabbis and strove to awaken their mercy, to have mercy on Herzl, to have pity upon him and not bring him to the grave in his best years. He adjured them to rise together as one man and arouse the people to give their support to Herzl, so that he should be able to redeem the land. But if not, then they, the rabbis and the Wonder-Rabbis, were responsible for his soul and the soul of their people. . . . If not now, then who could say after how long?

The air in the little room under the low ceiling was hot and stifling. The old man's words and the broken fragments of his confused thoughts had their effect on me. He paced up and down the room like an animal in a cage.

"You don't understand. You don't understand anything. The danger is great. . . . So great it can't be estimated. . . . He's in danger, we're in danger, everything is in danger. . . . Reached the breach and there is no strength to labour and give birth. . . . Mercy is wanted. . . . The heavens have to be rent open. . . . The cry must reach as high as the Glory Seat. . . . And there's nobody. . . . Not a man. . . . 'They,' who have the power, remain silent. They have ears but do not hear, eyes but do not see. . . . And you, you're children. . . . You can't do anything. . . . He has to be saved. . . . He is caught. . . . The Powers of Evil are stretching out their hands to strangle him and there is none to deliver him. . . . His soul is fluttering, fluttering and beseeching mercy, and they sit dumb and say nothing in Hornstapol. . . ."

It took me much effort till he let me leave him and go out to breathe the fresh air. The old man stood at the entrance to his room. The moon, as pale and melancholy as himself, shed her light over his sunken face.

"You'll correct it?"

"I'll correct it."

"I'll send it to them. . . . Let them know! The knife is at the throat."

It was the voice of a man making his final desperate effort.

VII

The news of Herzl's death had the same effect on us that the news of Uganda had had on Reb Jacob. But while we were all weeping and in bitter despair, Reb Jacob maintained an awful silence. He said nothing. It was as though he were telling us:

"You've only learnt about the calamity today; I've known it a long time. I've been mourning for him many a day."

And sometimes he would suddenly come to life, rage, shout and bang on the table with his fist:

"They slew him, they turned their hands against his innocent soul. . . . They slaughtered him as though they did it with a knife. . . ."

And when the mourners rose to deliver the memorial addresses for Herzl, Reb Jacob stood amid the congregation, silent. His silence was dreadful, more terrible than all the weeping in the world. His eyes asked us all:

"Why do we speak, why do we mourn? Why don't we remain silent?"

VIII

For several years after Herzl's death Reb Jacob wandered about among us in Rehoboth, his ears open to the footsteps of Redemption and his eyes seeking the signs of the End of Days. At any sign of victory his soul assumed holiday garb, while he dismissed every sign of downfall utterly and entirely. The like had already been, and will be again, but the End will assuredly come! He wandered among us, watching and hearkening; and in the evening he wrote and struck out, rewrote and struck out again. He was writing his book on the End of Days. There was no limit and no end to his book. Nor did he require my aid any longer. His grand-daughter had grown up, and she corrected his errors. She corrected and he wrote afresh and added new errors to the old. What did language and style matter to him? What was essential was the ideas.

Reb Jacob returned his pure soul to the Dweller on High in the late Summer of 1909. I did not have the merit of being present when he passed away. But I know that he died as die the righteous, in perfect peace. The whole of his life was one long tempest; his death must assuredly have been short and restful. Reb Jacob had long been writing and preparing himself for that moment. It would permit him to stand and place himself before the Glory Seat, to seize his beard and earlocks as he stood before the Lord of the Universe and to cry in a loud and bitter voice, Thy people Israel must have mercy!

Can the Merciful and Gracious One be other than merciful?

III. THE MODERN WORLD

INTRODUCTION

"I T would have been absurd and petty," remarked Heine in a conversation
with Alfred Meissner, "if, as I am accused, I had been ashamed of being
a Jew; yet it would be equally ludicrous for me to call myself a Jew."
In this sentence the sagacious poet hit upon one of the central paradoxes of the
modern Jew.[1] Thrust with incredible suddenness into the arena of industrialism
and accepting avidly the slogans and promise of liberalism and democracy, he
completely identified himself with Western culture and statehood. He attempted,
in a spirit of noblesse oblige, to merge himself in the new world by means of
assimilation, conversion and intermarriage. Nationalism, however, and its lusty
handmaiden, anti-Semitism, quickly dissipated the "new springtide of humanity": it was made clear to the Jew that he was at the same time part of and
apart from the land in which he dwelt. Even within his own lifetime, Heine
discovered his fate: "I am no longer the freest man since Goethe. I am no
longer a fat Hellenist with a contemptuous smile for the lean Jews. I am only
a poor, sick Jew, a picture of grim misery, an unhappy being."

This tragic cycle of release, exaltation and disillusionment has become an
individual and collective social pattern of the modern, emancipated Jew. In our
own day it is grotesquely exhibited in the catastrophe of German Jewry in the
Third Reich, but its symptoms—inner conflict and moral defeatism—are discernible everywhere. The philosopher, Asher Ginzberg (Ahad Haam), coined
the phrase "slavery in freedom" to describe an external emancipation accompanied by moral and intellectual slavery to Western civilization. So deep did the
conflict strike at the roots of Jewish life that by the end of the nineteenth century thinkers and leaders began to wonder whether the Jewish people could
survive[2] at all in the modern world, whether the ancestral culture had any
relevancy to modern life. And what of Judaism? "As the ways of thinking and
ways of behaving based on science and conditioned by industry enter into the
texture of the daily life of Jews," writes a contemporary social philosopher,
"Judaism and its institutions fall more and more into an innocuous desuetude."
The first gleam of this social conflict is already discernible in the charming
ghetto tales of the writers of the early and middle of the nineteenth century—
Auerbach, Kompert, Bernstein, Franzos, Goldschmidt, Mosenthal and others

[1] The following books will open the main avenues of modern Jewish life to the reader:
The Jews in the Modern World by Arthur Ruppin (New York, 1934); *Hebrew Reborn* by
Shalom Spiegel (New York, 1930); *Yisröel,* edited by Joseph Leftwich (London, 1933); *The Jews
and Other Minorities Under the Soviets* by Avrahm Yarmolinsky (New York, 1928); *Modern
Palestine,* edited by Jessie Sampter (New York, 1933).
[2] It is not a question of physical survival. The Jewish population has increased fivefold since
the French Revolution.

(To Be or Not To Be?); it pervades the enormous literary output of the Jews during the last fifty years.

But it would be misleading to regard this conflict as an isolated phenomenon. One has to consider it as the result of the impact of the changing modern world upon essentially ghettoized Jewish communities. They felt the pull, first, of economic change. At the beginning of the nineteenth century the majority of Jews were engaged in petty commercial pursuits as land-tenants, innkeepers, brokers and tradesmen, and were living in indescribable poverty; less than two percent were engaged in agriculture and a numerically insignificant minority played a prominent rôle as international bankers. Today more than seventy percent of the Jewish people are engaged in trade and industry, almost seven percent in professional and governmental occupations, and about five percent in agriculture. This extraordinary economic restratification brought in its train a greater interdependence of Jews and non-Jews and a closer knitting together of middle class and proletarian Jews with those who had similar economic interests. The effect upon Jewish life was a progressive weakening of Jewish institutions and mores and, in many instances (e.g. education), their replacement by general institutions and habits of living. Moreover, it resulted, as it did in the case of all the European peoples, in a series of migrations toward western Europe and the Americas, and the increasing urbanization of the Jewish population. Since the Jews were a minority with the baggage of medievalism not entirely cast off, both of these factors affected them more drastically than it did the surrounding populations.

The Industrial Revolution paved the way, but it was civil and political emancipation that opened the portals of Western civilization to the Jews. A number of social and intellectual currents, symbolized in the persons of Voltaire, Rousseau and Paine, culminated in the two major political revolutions of the eighteenth century. These brought about complete equality for the Jews in the United States in 1787, in France in 1791, and in Holland in 1796. The struggle for political freedom continued throughout the nineteenth century when we find Jews among the prominent leaders in the struggles of both of the masses (Marx and Lassalle) and the bourgeoisie (Riesser and Cremieux). It was not, however, until the establishment of the Soviet Union and the granting of minority rights to the central European Jews by the Versailles Treaty that Eastern and Central European Jews were emancipated; there are, however, several countries, like Roumania and Morocco, where they still live under medieval conditions. Thus the Jewish people became part and parcel of the economic, social and intellectual life of Western nations. They became identified with the countries (Bergson the "French" philosopher, Einstein the "German" scientist, etc.) of which they were citizens. They became more and more divorced from Jewish life and institutions.

Conceivably the Jewish people might have been assimilated into the Western nations, but they were not. Some historians and controversialists ascribe this to the rise of modern anti-Semitism. For anti-Semitism in its modern garb was the very antithesis of the social and political objectives of liberalism. It represented the pseudo-scientific conviction that the Jews were different in character, in culture, in ethics, that they were "demonstrably" alien and inferior. It penetrated every class and bred intense hostility and contempt. That anti-Semitism quickened the Jewish people's national consciousness, threw the people upon their own resources, and stimulated auto-emancipatory movements within Jewish life is unquestionable. That it demonstrated the illogic of the preachment of liberalism and the technique of democracy is also true. But another factor, the people's will to survive and to express itself, played as direct a rôle in stemming the tide of assimilation. The inner compulsion to express the folk spirit was especially potent in the masses so that it is among them that the severest struggles for adjustment and rehabilitation took root. But Jews of every economic and social grouping were compelled to weather the storms of this period of transition and thus to make some kind of adjustment. Caught between the anvil of the Machine Age and the hammer of anti-Semitism, they inevitably turned to their reservoir of historical experience and tradition as well as to non-discriminatory social movements to escape dissolution and disintegration. Concretely, they turned to two chief types of self-expression: (1) A number of religious movements[3] arose to preserve intact traditional Judaism (Neo-Orthodoxy), to adjust Judaism to modern life by the introduction of Western forms of worship and customs and by denying the validity of Jewish law and Jewish nationality (Reform Judaism), by utilizing the method and spirit of scientific method, to establish Judaism in the modern world as a humanistic culture (The New Learning), and finally to reëvaluate Jewish life in terms of the spirituality and the romanticism of Jewish mysticism (Neo-Hasidism); (2) With the dominance of nationalism during the nineteenth and twentieth centuries it was natural that national movements should have played a prominent rôle in Jewish life. While some Jews, particularly those resident in Western lands, surrendered themselves to the national culture of their country, others advocated the assimilation of Western culture into Jewish life by fostering Jewish nationalism. This set into motion two powerful and productive movements which stimulated both economic and social adjustments and cultural creativeness. One is distinctly secular in character, insisting upon the cultivation of the Yiddish vernacular as the national language and viewing the establishment of autonomous Jewish communities with minority rights as the solution of the Jewish problem. The second, the Zionist movement, is a union of the traditional national idea with the territorial element in modern nationalism: Zionism advocates the establishment of a Jewish state (or "homeland") in Palestine and the use of Hebrew as the vehicle of cultural expression.

Thus a people singularly uniform and unified for almost fifteen centuries

[3] For a detailed exposition and critique of these movements, see *Judaism as a Civilization* by Mordecai M. Kaplan (New York, 1934).

was torn in many directions. "A people," observed Van Wyck Brooks, "is like a ciphered parchment that has to be held up to the fire before its hidden significances come out." With the rise of the modern world the Jewish people lost its social and political autonomy, became sharply divided, but displayed, above all, the strength that centuries of discipline and suffering had stored up.

In the twentieth century, two world wars and a number of political revolutions set the pendulum of Jewish history in motion again. The center of Jewish life shifted westward to America and brought about an English-speaking era which may become comparable to the Arabic-speaking era of the Middle Ages and the Yiddish-speaking era of the past few centuries. With the Nazi destruction of almost six million Jews and the expunging of East European Jewish culture, the European era in Jewish history appears to be in final decline. The number of Jewish inhabitants of Europe, including those in Soviet Russia, is already exceeded in the State of Israel where Jewish life stands on the brink of a new and different existence.

More than one-half of world Jewry lives in North and South America, where Jewish history runs back to 1492. The largest number—almost six million—are concentrated in the United States, but the origins, problems, and character of the Jewish communities of Montreal, New York, Los Angeles, Mexico City, and Buenos Aires are similar. The Jews have participated enormously in building up the American countries; they have made solid contributions to the cultural development of the New World. In doing so, however, they have emasculated the European traditions they brought with them so that Jewish institutions in the United States, for example, since they lack Jewish content, are in search of new wine to pour into old bottles. The social and intellectual conflicts going on in the American Jew of every walk of life are vividly pictured in a huge body of Anglo-Jewish and Yiddish literature which has poured out of America during the twentieth century (America).

To effect a complete social and economic transformation of Jews in the Soviet Union has been the policy of the regime since its inception. The process has been slow and painful, since the bulk of the Jewish population at the time of the October Revolution was of the lower middle class, without experience in industry or agriculture. The attempts to put Jews on the soil in the Crimea and Birobidzhan seemed to thrive in the twenties and thirties, but since then they either were destroyed by the Nazi invaders or petered out. The once thriving Soviet-Yiddish literature was stifled and in the end the talented writers were imprisoned and executed. There appeared to be a slight relaxation of coercion in the post-Khrushchev regime, but for practical purposes it appeared that the Jews of the Soviet Union were for the most part urbanized and Russified (Soviet Union).

Hitler's plan to exterminate the Jews of Europe, given the code name "The Final Solution," almost succeeded. As the details of extermination unfolded at the Nuremberg trials and in the publication of Nazi documents, the horrifying tragedy slowly found its expression in literature. The moral and spiritual implications of this crime against humanity will continue to be probed; for the time being its meaning lies beneath the surface of contemporary writing (The Holocaust).

The emergence of the State of Israel in 1948—unique among the large number of new states in the post-World War II era—was the salvation of European Jewish culture. Although Israel is essentially European in its origin and orientation, and became within a few decades the center of Jewish and Hebrew learning, the native generations, Hebrew-speaking as is proper, are facing the same problems of alienation and identity as native American Jews. These problems are being faced with immense vitality, as is evident in the many-sided literary expression of current Israeli literature (Israel).

Everywhere, the Jew, like all peoples today, is concerned with his future. The theologian declares: "The Jewish people, like its God, is eternal." "No," observes the social philosopher, "the Jews are an ailing people, perhaps beyond recovery." "True," asserts the radical ideologist, "but the Jew has nothing to lose but the chains of tradition and discrimination; he has a world of freedom and health to gain." A Christian sociologist proposes a remedy in the form of a new mission: "The achievement—let me state it boldly—is the salvaging of Western civilization. That is the challenge to Israel." The mystic sings: "I believe that Judaism has truly not yet arrived at its real task, and that the great forces that live in this most tragic and incomprehensible of all peoples have not yet spoken their most significant utterance in world history."

Which of these is the true prophet? Only Clio knows, but she won't reveal her secret to our generation.

TO BE OR NOT TO BE?

"AMONG OUR PEOPLE"

by JEAN-RICHARD BLOCH

"THEY really are the worthiest people alive," thought Joseph in the train that was bringing him back to Vendeuvre, on the following evening. The Sterns had made much of him. He could not help laughing at Elisa's aspirated sibilants. But it was a hearty laugh. It seemed as though the stout girl had all of a sudden abandoned her pert airs.

"Shall we go to Passe-Lourdin?" Joseph asked Justin the following Sunday, when he came downstairs, shaved to the quick, smelling of soap, sparkling with cold water. Justin was making a fair copy of an exercise by lamplight. Day had not yet dawned.

Sarah brought in their coffee and milk which they took in great earthenware bowls patterned with blue flowers. Joseph devoured in addition half a kugelhopf, two eggs, half a pound of cold meat and a few gherkins.

"Why shouldn't you go with them?" said Sarah to Guillaume in a compelling tone. They set off, a party of four, including Laure. Dawn was staining one corner of the frozen surface of the night.

Guillaume opened his eyes wide when they came to Passe-Lourdin.

"Don't you think this a charming spot?"

"Ye-es. For what purpose?"

Joseph smiled a superior smile: "To live in."

Guillaume's brow wrinkled like an accordion, and with a nervous gesture he sucked one end of his moustaches between his teeth.

"I wouldn't say . . . To live in? And do nothing, you mean?"

"Do what is necessary."

The necessary had, to Guillaume, exactly the same boundaries as the possible: "Listen, you would never dream . . ."

"You know . . . plenty of ideas . . . And why not, after all?"

"But the factory, Choseph, our duty . . ."

"All right, all right. Who spoke of leaving the factory? We shall pay our debts, of course. The rest . . ."

"The rest? Where do you see any rest? Joseph, once more I cannot understand these new ideas. You are not serious. Do you really think of settling down here, in this . . . ? But where will you get the money? To live here by yourself? No! With whom, then, Joseph?"

The question was rather too near the mark. It took Joseph by surprise. He believed, however, that it was answered for him. But it was answered only in theory, not in fact. On the other hand, Guillaume had not accustomed him to making such definite statements, apart from questions of flock or carded wool. Somebody or something was guiding him. Joseph was uneasy rather than irritated.

"Go and play with Justin," Guillaume told Laure.

"No, stay here. What else is there to be said? Besides, you have seen everything, for the present. This is the path that takes us back to Vendeuvre."

"Are we going to stop at Monsieur Le Pleynier's?" asked Laure. Joseph pretended not to hear, and quickened his pace.

In the meantime Sarah had received a letter from Mina. It was not handed round, but it provided the subject of conversation at luncheon. Hippolyte, his wife and daughter-in-law were inexhaustible upon the subject of the Sterns. There was no question of finding where the others had gone for their walk that morning. Only, after luncheon, Sarah took care to have a long discussion with her elder son.

There are certain easy actions in the course of life which the least afterthought transforms into innovations of vast effect.

One of these was the visit which Mlle. Le Pleynier paid to the Simlers' that afternoon. Nothing simpler, one would have thought, than to call upon the ladies of the Boulevard du Grand Cerf in return for their courtesy of the week before. As Monsieur Le Pleynier was going to the Club she made Hilaire drive her to the Simlers'.

We must admit however that the affair appeared slightly more complicated, for Helene, when she heard the bell tinkle inside the house, lost her head altogether. And it was a bloodless apparition that made Hermine start to her feet in a panic and sent a purple flush to Joseph's cheeks.

Sarah, when Laure came up to warn her, concluded her conversation with Guillaume with a peremptory nod, and went downstairs. It was time. Hermine, crushed under the burden of her mother-in-law's confidences, regarded Mlle. Le Pleynier as nothing less than a gorgon's head. Joseph, put to the torment by his sister-in-law's silence and Helene's voiceless pallor, called upon the infernal powers to extricate him from the situation.

When Sarah entered the room, with the majesty of a Proconsul's dame who has prepared herself to receive the homage of a native queen, it was a relief. The stock of goodwill which Helene had brought with her was still in close juxtaposition to the most bellicose tendencies, and Hermine's insignificance would have infuriated an angel.

But it did not take Helene long to estimate the effort that was being required of her. Her voice hesitated for an instant only between the shrill note of provocation and the soft pedal of renunciation. And it was Mme. Hippolyte who was given complete freedom to attack.

It would be untrue to say that this lady did not set to work with her whole heart. Finding the field clear, her assault became a charge. Everything that frigidity, scorn and suspicion can bring to bear, outside the strict limits of the offensive, was put into effect with a dignity and a valour which Helene could not help admiring.

But also the Simler ladies were upon their own ground. Women of their sort show their mettle only within their own doors and among their own furniture. They lose everything by transplantation.

Let it not astonish us either that Mme. Hippolyte was not alarmed by the surprising readiness of a girl whose merit she ought to have appreciated. We must never expect of people what they are unable to give. If twenty centuries of seraglio arm a woman for the inexpiable warfare of the home, they do not, on the other hand, predispose her to equity.

Mlle. Le Pleynier was there, the only one of her sex with any conception of disinterestedness. That she was deeply pained is beyond question. Would she have come, had not a gleam of hope remained? And the presence of Joseph, a helpless onlooker, filled her with a revolt the murmur of which, at several points in the conversation, nearly rose to a shriek.

But she bowed her head. Her grave voice gradually assumed that social resonance which covers everything, and denies everything, even death.

"If I love him, what does it matter to him? If he wishes, let him come and take me. A heart that bleeds does not budge . . ."

Once again, but for the last time doubtless, the demon of humility assumed in her the cast-off cloak of pride and deceived her as to the part it had to play. She who valued her happiness at the price of blood, by what right did she claim to spare another's happiness all struggle?

Did the Clandestine understand the indwelling flaw in her strategy when, twenty minutes later, with a smile on her face, and the chill of death in her heart, she bade the ladies farewell and returned to her dogcart, escorted by Guillaume and Joseph?

She cast a glance as she went by at the factory, and another, slightly more covert, at Joseph.

Although they were mere men, Guillaume, who was forewarned, and Joseph, had missed none of the phases of this duel.

But even if Sarah had not acted under the compulsion of instinct alone, she could have had no more effective policy than that of putting her son at once, as she had just done, under the necessity of making a choice.

She knew that there was no precedent, in the clan, that the alternative had never been stated in the form required by the law of the family. If there was one, Sarah pretended to be unaware of it. What was more, she had provided for it. Not for nothing was she the wife of Hippolyte, the *Königin Simler*. And restricted as her world was, her previsions had always contrived to make, in the present, allowance for the future.

Helene would, in similar circumstances, have despised any other man. She pitied Joseph and forgot to pity herself. She had, moreover, retained this right alone.

"Could the poor fellow have foreseen this?"

When the cart drove away, she studied the lining of her glove, and everything became confused and flickered before her eyes.

Joseph left the house immediately afterwards to pay Hector a visit. Guillaume remained between his mother and his wife, who henpecked him until the evening. Sarah announced that the Sterns would arrive upon Christmas eve, which fell upon Thursday, and decided that Guillaume should discourse with Joseph on various matters, beginning next day.

Guillaume was appalled at this mission. But the calamity of which his mother had given him a hint appalled him even more. Besides, the expedition that morning to Passe-Lourdin had caused him an uneasiness which Mlle. Le Pleynier's visit did not allay.

He could no longer sleep at night. He slept only one night in three. He had begun to waste away and was subject to nervous fits which nothing could control. He had become the destroyer of his own body and of other people.

At five o'clock on Monday morning, Joseph, who had not closed an eye either, came downstairs on tiptoe, when his attention was caught, as he was entering his warehouse, by a faint light which glimmered through the windows of the factory.

He went to examine it more closely. He had arrived at the stage of intellectual disorder when nothing can cause surprise. He saw a familiar figure patrolling the spinning-room between the machines.

Guillaume was carrying in one hand a candle the flame of which he was sheltering from draughts with fingers like pink wax. The candle was guttering over his fingers and scalding him. All of a sudden he started violently and almost dropped the light. Joseph saw a dark object dart across the floor, a huge rat.

He could control himself no longer; he went to the little door, pushed it open and entered the room amid the stiff skeletons of the machines. His ear was caught by a humming sound: Guillaume, at the other end of the room, with his back turned to him, was talking to himself.

Joseph at once said to himself that his brother was mad, and remembered that sleepwalkers may die if they are suddenly awakened.

He called his brother softly: "Wilhelm! Hey, Wilhelm!"

But Guillaume did not hear him, and left the room by the door at the foot of the stair. Joseph followed him upstairs and passed in his wake down the long alley of the weaving-room, overtaking him, then allowing him to regain his lead.

On reaching the attic, which was stuffed with rubbish of every sort, Guillaume seemed to be annoyed by the disorder. He set his candle down on the edge of a case, and tried to push out of the way an old, broken, copper oil-barrel. With the vibration, the candle fell and went out, while the flapping of soft wings was audible from the roof.

"Wilhelm, what on earth are you doing?" cried Joseph.

"Is that you, Jos?" asked a toneless, ageless voice. "I have dropped my candle."

"So I see."

"Help me to get out of here."

Joseph could hear him fumbling and muttering.

"This way. Take my hand. What are you doing here?"

"I couldn't sleep."

"Couldn't sleep, couldn't sleep, that's no excuse for . . . Are you often taken that way?"

"What way?"

"With this sort of sleeplessness."

"Sometimes. Have you found my candle?"

"Don't bother about the candle, come downstairs and get warm. Do you often go roaming about the factory?"

"Sometimes, yes."

The memory of a mysterious confusion that he had found one morning in his office occurred to Joseph: "In the factory only?"

"Why do you ask that?"

"You must know. You have never gone into the warehouse?"

"Possibly. I go everywhere."

"Then it was you?"

"What? . . . Possibly. Listen, I spend so many hours unable to sleep, I cannot remain in bed. Even if I don't move, I waken Hermine and the children. And then, being there alone, sitting up in bed, thinking anything in the world is better than that, I get up, and go down to see if everything is in order."

"In my books? I should never have believed it of you. You have been spying upon me."

"You are mad, Joseph! I, spying upon you? Where do you expect me to go, in the middle of the night? When I have altered my price-list, a dozen times, and answered my letters, I have nothing left to do. If I have opened your books . . ."

Joseph stood at the head of the stair, beside himself with rage: "I should not have made any objection. You had only to ask me for them!"

"Why, what are you imagining, Joseph? I opened your books without any definite idea, to kill time, to see what business we were doing and where we stood. Surely we have no secrets from one another, here."

"That is precisely why. Your behavior has not been frank."

"Do you know what it is to go without sleep for three nights a week, sometimes more? I had no intention of insulting you. But I could not let you know. We don't discuss such things, Jos, after all."

Joseph could not see Guillaume's features. But his voice was strained by his emotion.

"Three nights in a week? You go to sleep every evening at nine."

"I go to sleep at nine, yes, but at eleven, it is all over."

A feeling of shame or of pity made Joseph say: "Then, when we tease you about your habit of falling asleep . . ."

"That is of no importance, Joseph, so long as the rest don't know."

"Has it been going on for long?"

"I don't remember. It must have begun during the war."

"And it is getting worse?"

"Yes."

Joseph began to go downstairs: "Have you found the rail? Take care. You know, it's not good for you, this sort of thing."

"I know. What am I to do?"

"Have you taken anything for it? You ought to see somebody."

"Oh, we have it in our blood. It is devouring us all."

"You have worries?"

"One has always worries."

"You're a thorough Simler, you are!"

"And you?" replied Guillaume, his voice, on this occasion, recovering its trenchant tone. Joseph avoided the point: "Oh, I!"

They groped their way down to the landing outside the weaving-room, the door of which had been left open. A livid glimmer floated through the wide bays of the room.

Down below, Pailloux's lantern was advancing through the darkness towards his engine. Guillaume stepped into the glazed office and tried, with a trembling hand, to light his father's oil lamp.

Now, it must be borne in mind that this oil lamp was the very same which had burned ever since their childhood upon M. Hippolyte's desk. The furniture of the glazed office was the same which had served at a different time and place. And we must not lose sight of the fact that the two men who stood face to face, at that hour, were two Simlers, from Buschendorf, transplanted like cuttings to Vendeuvre, to undergo a new destiny. With the result that, when Guillaume raised his narrow profile, like that of a Persian king, and his eyes hesitatingly sought Joseph's, there was already a considerable change in their relative positions.

And so it was with less assurance, in a tone in which physical weariness was already apparent, that Joseph went on: "What is the cause of your worries?"

Guillaume's conviction thereupon achieved the very stroke which a shrewd policy might have suggested to him.

"Is it true?" he cried, seizing his brother's arm. "Is it true, Choseph?"

Joseph was prepared for anything, save for being forced to look into his own heart.

"What? What do you mean?"

"Ah! Then it is true!" Guillaume concluded on a note of despair. "It is true!" And he released his brother's arm.

"But in heaven's name, tell me!"

"Tell you what? What you know already? What everybody knows!"

"Everybody is very clever and discerning. I don't understand a word of what you're saying."

"Oh! Choseph! Why did you do it?"

By dint of certainty, Guillaume listened to nothing that the other said and went on answering himself. Ten minutes later, there was not a dark corner left in Joseph's consciousness. He knew what he would so gladly not have known yet awhile, and his brother's feverish hand parted, with a mystic frenzy, the viscid lips of the wound.

"You cannot, you cannot do a thing like that."

Rage and grief kept Joseph pacing to and fro in the glazed office. His solid throat buried itself between his shoulders, his fists were forced against the bottoms of his pockets.

"Who gave you leave? Why did you do it?"

Neither of them could make use of any but the vaguest expressions: they had "done it." What was the issue at stake? For Guillaume, it was the maintenance of the inflexible laws of the clan. For Joseph, the protection of intimate aspirations, less easily defined.

"I do not deny that the girl has many merits," drawled Guillaume, carried away by a sacrificant's inebriation, and terrified by his brother's anger.

"What do you know about it? Do you know her? Have you any idea of her worth?"

"I do not deny it, although neither Mamma, nor Hermine, nor myself . . . But you cannot have been entirely mistaken."

"Very good of you. But what are you getting at, may one know that at least?"

"At this, Joseph: whatever may happen, whatever you may feel, there is one thing that is impossible, which is to do anything that affects the family and the factory. You cannot leave us, you cannot create a division among us."

Let those who think that Joseph had merely to reply: "I am going to marry Mlle. Le Pleynier and I am not going to divide myself from you," raise their heads, look around them, in the heart of the Republic One and Indivisible, and say whether there are not more things unwritten than written in the text of the Law.

Joseph had no need, at that moment, of any skill in sociology to discover that thirty centuries of commandments weigh far more heavily in the scales than an inclination a month old.

Whether it was the thirty centuries that were in the right or the month was a wholly different matter. Joseph was to have more than a year in which he was free to weigh them in the balance and start his calculations afresh. He did not fail to do so.

At the moment, he did indeed open his mouth, intending to reply: "What is the connection? I shall marry whom I choose, and I shall not divide myself from you."

But it so happened that he remained there gaping open-mouthed, on his feet, before the lamp, realising, as he unravelled each of his knots, that every-thing was connected and entangled with everything else.

Guillaume, in the meantime, knew better than to develop his line of thought. He barked, chokingly, at his brother, without equalling the speed or the precision with which the consequences outlined themselves in Joseph's mind.

"A *goy* girl among us? . . . You know that it is impossible . . . Mamma . . . you may do what you like . . . don't you see? . . . You know her . . . And besides . . . do you suppose that she . . . that she would consent? Would she turn *yid*? No, no . . . it would mean leaving us . . . leaving us, Joseph! . . . And what then? . . . Is it that Mache . . . Mache-Bourbin, that . . . little house which you showed me yesterday? . . . That, for you? . . . Your life spent there, Joseph? . . . And us? You would leave us, the factory, our debts? . . . To live simply, spend nothing, give up work . . . what you have undertaken? Your duty? . . . And I? When Papa and Uncle Myrtil are no longer with us, I am to be left alone, alone . . . alone?"

The thought of this seized him as it passed. And he was all the more alarmed by it in that he had not said all. He had kept to himself the picture of a Helene whose sole preoccupation would be to make good Catholics of Joseph Simler's children. This was not for want of believing it. In the matter of knowledge of women, you must bear in mind that neither Hermine nor Sarah was capable of error. Guillaume saw—as clearly as they had shown him them—the ruses of a cautious sister-in-law, shrouded in a long black religious veil, creeping along at nightfall and leading a procession of his nephews and nieces to the dark trap of the confessional.

But the fact of his having stopped short of this argument, from a secret male modesty, increased the alarm that he felt at the other prospects which he had revealed. Most of all, the sword of his own eventual solitude pierced him to the heart. It made him stammer with terror.

"Alone! I should have to give up everything, all thought of enlarging the works, of taking on fresh business. Or else, go and look, yes, look for a partner, perhaps . . . Joseph! While you . . ."

An idea shot across his mind; he seized it for what it might be worth, and it turned out to be of the highest order: "It is true that Penchamin, yes, has gone away, but that was to do more, to work. He has had a sense of his duty. I do not share it. But a sense of duty, all the same. Whereas, whereas . . . Ach! it is not possible."

At the end of all the tracks that crossed his own thoughts, Joseph, for his part, could see something dawning which resembled his brother's conclusion. Then he emerged abruptly from his state of semi-hallucination, shrugged his shoulders and turned his back.

Behind him extended the weaving-room. The beam of light shed by the lamp was broken, as it entered that vast space, by the body of the nearest loom. The wood of the batten, polished by use, sped away, taking the light with it, towards a darkness bristling with shadowy forms.

If ever an oily tongue of yellow flame was able to speak for anyone, it was for the two men who were in that office. Each of the fibres of that silence, muscular and hard, had its echo in them. The former nonentity of the Poncet factory, that empty, silent corpse, had not by its own unaided effort acquired substance, strength, mass, been transformed into this dark pomegranate. Their toiling shoulders still recalled the effort of uprooting, and the violent struggle to establish a shadow in a spot where the tree had not grown.

But who knew so well as they that the void was still not far off? Who but a Simler ever knew what is meant by a plank that quivers and sways, poised over an abyss?

And so Guillaume was royally wasting his time in developing, rightly or wrongly, points of view which the weaving-room itself was sufficient to express. From the chaos of contradictions, one conclusion rose now in Joseph's mind: "Is it possible to retain the one while saving the other?"

The man of Buschendorf, the man of cloth, was beginning to realize that to abandon the one was a thing not to be dreamed of. Then the problem appeared to him all of a sudden to have become quite simple: Passe-Lourdin— the day spent here, the night there, life framed in that setting of happy activity:

"And why not?" he growled, turning solidly to face Guillaume. "You will drive me out of my wits! How in the world does my private life affect my work in the factory? Is it the factory that is marrying me?"

"Yes," cried Guillaume without giving himself time to hesitate. And he had no sooner said it than the piercing truth of the word took the breath out of his mouth. Awkwardly, he added, in a quieter tone:

"The factory, the family, there is no difference, two aspects of the same thing."

"And what is that thing?" Joseph sneered. He had almost forgotten the third term of the proposition. The equation became insoluble.

His brother gazed at him in surprise. How could anyone not know things that were so simple that there are not even words in which to express them? Their great-grandfather, Mosche Hertz Simler *selig,* had founded the factory, the grandfather and his sons had enlarged it, against wind and tide, the grandsons had transported it, piecemeal. Today, Chustin was at the head of his class in the lycée, and the Simler team, closely united in good as in evil fortune, was dragging, groaning beneath the yoke, the heavy chariot to the conquest of Vendeuvre.

"What is that thing? It is that we have never been anything but one heart and one mind, and that, *among our people,* it has always been the same."

For an hour and a half these two men had been torturing each other, and the magic word had only now been uttered. But it covered everything. Joseph felt that it was one of those things which we try to elude but which we do not deny. And as if this were not enough, Guillaume, faithful to the spirit of a race which does not know what it is to destroy outside in order to build up inside, held out to Joseph a pair of bony hands, carved in browned ivory, and exclaimed: "Chos! My Chos! We all of us have some inward suffering. And why do we not die of it? Because we must sacrifice ourselves to something. Chos! Remain one of us, do not leave us either in heart or in thought. It is not for myself that I ask you, nor even for Mamma. But there is duty, there is our tradition, our obligations, there is—disinterestedness."

Only the day before, not a hundred yards away, in the presence of these two men, Helene Le Pleynier had repeated this word to herself. Did she deserve that, turned like the finger of a glove, it should now be used against her?

Joseph had failed to understand all that had happened the day before. But he guessed enough of it for this word to wound him keenly. He raised towards Guillaume a swollen, mottled face: "That will do. We shall discuss it another time. You have said enough."

The floor creaked beneath a step. M. Hippolyte came in. He had seen the light, and came hastening with such speed as his gouty legs could muster.

He stopped to scrutinise his sons. The only sound to be heard was his asthmatic wheezing.

Are we to suppose that insomnia had sent him in his turn to join them? Or that, duly informed by his wife, he found no difficulty in interpreting the situation? His large features became drawn together, his eyelids slid down over the bloodshot hemispheres of his eyes, and a contemptuous pity wrinkled the ends of his mouth. He made but a single gesture, which was that of laying his hand upon Joseph's shoulder. A thick voice, loud but restrained, gave utterance to these astonishing words: "We have all gone through it, Choseph. Every man must be unhappy once in his life. You have had no great unhappiness so far. It is an unpleasant thing to say, but now your turn has come. Take as much time as you please. Go away, travel, console yourself. You shall come back and work with us when it has passed."

Then he released his son's shoulder after gripping it for a moment in his swollen fingers, turned his back on him and addressed Guillaume in the imperious tone that he normally used:

"You and I. Myrtil will take charge of the warehouse during Choseph's absence. We shall divide the spinning. You can manage it? Not too tired? Heart not troubling you? No? A serious worker? Very good. Have you a reply from Tuchartin about the cylinder for the machine?"

And he accompanied this speech with an expression of nothing less than benevolence towards his elder son.

When Joseph found himself in the courtyard, he took note of two things: first of all, that his father's unprecented gentleness did not alter the fact that he had been quietly shown the door of the factory for an unspecified time; secondly, that he had neither anywhere to go nor anything to do.

Meanwhile M. Hippolyte was opening the floodgates of his wrath in Guillaume's face.

"The imbecile! So he seriously thought of marrying that *goy?* The daughter of a bankrupt manufacturer? That stuck-up minx? If he does anything of the sort, he can die in his ditch, neither his mother nor I will ever look at him again."

A blow of his fist crushed upon the table a horrible oath, and the flow of his curses made the interior of the glass cage echo until the first wail of the siren.

Guillaume was too exhausted, as he went to open the gate, to observe a motionless form, seated upon a corner-stone, notwithstanding the cold, and bearing a resemblance to his brother.

"Uuu-uh!" moaned the gate as it opened its jaws with an effort. For a quarter of an hour the feet of the workers cluttered in the darkness. Rows of oil lamps punctuated the length of the rooms.

Joseph looked on at this spectacle as though he had never seen it before. The second cry of the siren reverberated over Vendeuvre. The sound of trotting clogs coursed along the avenue. The gate shut with the same wail and the same effort. A roar emerged from the interior of the building. The plunger of the cylinders made a long expectoration. The transmission shafts began to move.

Joseph shut his eyes; the workers were connecting the driving-band with the pulleys of their looms; the little fasteners of the weaving-room were speeding on their course along the rows of shuttles. The first heavy sounds of the weaving-room echoed from the floor above. Farther off, the fulling-mills were set in motion, with a sound as of angry wasps; the outflow of soapy water released, with a Vosgian murmur, a hotly, stalely smelling torrent. A sickly vapour began gradually to invade the courtyard. Joseph could hear, through an open ventilator, the cough of a young woman who was suspected of being consumptive, and the metallic scream of a spinning machine in which a broken piece required changing.

Uncle Myrtil's voice ground for an instant a series of steel knives and was then drowned. Two cries echoed in the distance. Zeller's white overall and muffler crossed the farther end of the courtyard. A shout of childish laughter burst from some unknown quarter, and remained without an echo.

The whole of Vendeuvre was athrob. The dark front of the factory shook from top to bottom. A line of rolling-mills seized a corner of the darkness and drew it towards themselves.

Then the cry of a sort of shrill and hoarse siren, more animal still, if possible, burst from beyond the walls, near or far, it was impossible to say. It aroused others, which continued out of ear shot. The cocks were saluting after their fashion the birth of a day which labour had not awaited.

Joseph turned his head. Something livid and wretched was surmounting the eastern wall. The slightest irregularities of tile or moss were already outlined against this light. A gust of wind flung itself down into the courtyard, as though in a panic. The young man rose, looked round him in every direction, and moved with a sharp step towards the warehouse, the key of which was weighing down his right pocket.

Half an hour later, the other three Simlers appeared there. They found Joseph, who greeted them with a cold, almost menacing stare. They said not a word, and returned each to the place from which he had come.

It was in this singular fashion that there were installed, for the second time, on this morning in December, eighteen hundred and seventy-two, the *Nouveaux Etablissements Simler,* at Vendeuvre.

MILITARY SERVICE

by MICHA JOSEPH BERDYCZEVSKI

"THEY look as if they'd enough of me!"

So I think to myself, as I give a glance at my two great topboots, my wide trousers, and my shabby green uniform, in which there is no whole part left.

I take a bit of looking-glass out of my box, and look at my reflection. Yes, the military cap on my head *is* a beauty, and no mistake, as big as Og, king of Bashan, and as bent and crushed as though it had been sat upon for years together.

Under the cap appears a small, washed-out face, yellow and weazened, with two large black eyes that look at me somewhat wildly.

I don't recognize myself; I remember me in a grey jacket, narrow, close-fitting trousers, a round hat, and a healthy complexion.

I can't make out where I got those big eyes, why they shine so, why my face should be yellow, and my nose pointed.

And yet I know that it is I myself, Hayyim Blumin, and no other; that

I have been handed over for a soldier, and have to serve only two years and eight months, and not three years and eight months, because I have a certificate to the effect that I have been through the first four classes in a secondary school.

Though I know quite well that I am to serve only two years and eight months, I feel the same as though it were to be forever; I can't somehow believe that my time will some day expire, and I shall once more be free.

I have tried from the very beginning not to play any tricks, to do my duty and obey orders, so that they should not say, "A Jew won't work—a Jew is too lazy."

Even though I am let off manual labor, because I am on "privileged rights," still, if they tell me to go and clean the windows, or polish the flooring with sand, or clear away the snow from the door, I make no fuss and go. I wash and clean and polish, and try to do the work well, so that they should find no fault with me.

They haven't yet ordered me to carry pails of water.

Why should I not confess it? The idea of having to do that rather frightens me. When I look at the vessel in which the water is carried, my heart begins to flutter; the vessel is almost as big as I am, and I couldn't lift it even if it were empty.

I often think: What shall I do, if tomorrow, or the day after, they wake me at three o'clock in the morning and say coolly:

"Get up, Blumin, and go with Ossadtchok to fetch a pail of water!"

You ought to see my neighbor Ossadtchok! He looks as if he could squash me with one finger. It is as easy for him to carry a pail of water as to drink a glass of brandy. How can I compare myself with him?

I don't care if it makes my shoulder swell, if I could only carry the thing. I shouldn't mind about that. But God in Heaven knows the truth, that I won't be able to lift the pail off the ground, only they won't believe me, they will say:

"Look at the lazy Jew, pretending he is a poor creature that can't lift a pail!"

There—I mind that more than anything.

I don't suppose they *will* send me to fetch water, for, after all, I am on "privileged rights," but I can't sleep in peace: I dream all night that they are waking me at three o'clock, and I start up bathed in a cold sweat.

Drill does not begin before eight in the morning, but they wake us at six, so that we may have time to clean our rifles, polish our boots and leather girdles, brush our coats, and furbish the brass buttons with chalk, so that they should shine like mirrors.

I don't mind the getting up early, I am used to rising long before daylight, but I am always worrying lest something shouldn't be properly cleaned, and they should say that a Jew is so lazy, he doesn't care if his things are clean or not, that he's afraid of touching his rifle, and pay me other compliments of the kind.

I clean and polish and rub everything all I know, but my rifle always seems in worse condition than the other men's. I can't make it look the same as theirs, do what I will, and the head of my division, a corporal, shouts at me, calls me a greasy fellow, and says he'll have me up before the authorities because I don't take care of my arms.

But there is worse than the rifle, and that is the uniform. Mine is *years* old—I am sure it is older than I am. Every day little pieces fall out of it, and the buttons tear themselves out of the cloth, dragging bits of it after them.

I never had a needle in my hand in all my life before, and now I sit whole nights and patch and sew on buttons. And next morning, when the corporal takes hold of a button and gives a pull, to see if it's firmly sewn, a pang goes through my heart: the button is dragged out, and a piece of the uniform follows.

Another whole night's work for me!

After the inspection, they drive us out into the yard and teach us to stand: it must be done so that our stomachs fall in and our chests stick out. I am half as one ought to be, because my stomach is flat enough anyhow, only my chest is weak and narrow and also flat—flat as a board.

The corporal squeezes in my stomach with his knee, pulls me forward by the flaps of the coat, but it's no use. He loses his temper, and calls me greasy fellow, screams again that I am pretending, that I *won't* serve, and this makes my chest fall in more than ever.

I like the gymnastics.

In summer we go out early into the yard, which is very wide and covered with thick grass.

It smells delightfully, the sun warms us through, it feels so pleasant.

The breeze blows from the fields, I open my mouth and swallow the freshness, and however much I swallow, it's not enough, I should like to take in all the air there is. Then, perhaps, I should cough less, and grow a little stronger.

We throw off the old uniforms, and remain in our shirts, we run and leap and go through all sorts of performances with our hands and feet, and it's splendid! At home I never had so much as an idea of such fun.

At first I was very much afraid of jumping across the ditch, but I resolved once and for all—I've *got* to jump it. If the worst comes to the worst, I shall fall and bruise myself. Suppose I do? What then? Why do all the others jump it and don't care? One needn't be so very strong to jump!

And one day, before the gymnastics had begun, I left my comrades, took heart and a long run, and when I came to the ditch, I made a great bound, and, lo and behold, I was over on the other side! I couldn't believe my own eyes that I had done it so easily. Ever since then I have jumped across ditches, and over mounds, and down from mounds, as well as any of them.

Only when it comes to climbing a ladder or swinging myself over a high bar, I know it spells misfortune for me.

I spring forward, and seize the first rung with my right hand, but I cannot reach the second with my left.

I stretch myself, and kick out with my feet, but I cannot reach any higher, not by so much as a vershok, and so there I hang and kick with my feet, till my right arm begins to tremble and hurt me. My head goes round, and I fall onto the grass. The corporal abuses me as usual, and the soldiers laugh.

I would give ten years of my life to be able to get higher, if only three or four rungs, but what can I do, if my arms won't serve me?

Sometimes I go out to the ladder by myself, while the soldiers are still asleep and stand and look at it: perhaps I can think of a way to manage? But in vain. Thinking, you see, doesn't help you in these cases.

Sometimes they tell one of the soldiers to stand in the middle of the yard with his back to us, and we have to hop over him one at a time. One takes a good run, and when one comes to him, one places both hands on his shoulders, raises oneself into the air, and—over!

I know exactly how it ought to be done; I take the run all right, and plant my hands on his shoulders, only I can't raise myself into the air. And if I do lift myself up a little way, I remain sitting on the soldier's neck, and were it not for his seizing me by the feet, I should fall, and perhaps kill myself.

Then the corporal and another soldier take hold of me by the arms and legs, and throw me over the man's head, so that I may see there is nothing dreadful about it, as though I did not jump right over him because I was afraid, while it is that my arms are so weak, I cannot lean upon them and raise myself into the air.

But when I say so, they only laugh, and don't believe me. They say, "It won't help you; you will have to serve anyhow!"

When, on the other hand, it comes to "theory," the corporal is very pleased with me.

He says that, except himself, no one knows "theory" as I do.

He never questions me now, only when one of the others doesn't know something, he turns to me:

"Well, Blumin, *you* tell me!"

I stand up without hurrying, and am about to answer, but he is apparently not pleased with my way of rising from my seat, and orders me to sit down again.

"When your superior speaks to you," says he, "you ought to jump up as though the seat were hot," and he looks at me angrily, as much as to say, "You may know theory, but you'll please to know your manners as well, and treat me with proper respect."

"Stand up again and answer!"

I start up as though I felt a prick from a needle, and answer the question as he likes it done: smartly, all in one breath, and word for word according to the book.

He, meanwhile, looks at the primer, to make sure I am not leaving anything out, but as he reads very slowly, he cannot catch me up, and when I have got to the end, he is still following with his finger and reading. And when he has finished, he gives me a pleased look, and says enthusiastically "Right!" and tells me to sit down again.

"Theory," he says. "That you *do* know!"

Well, begging his pardon, it isn't much to know. And yet there are soldiers who are four years over it, and don't know it then. For instance, take my comrade Ossadtchok; he says that, when it comes to "theory," he would rather go and hang or drown himself. He says he would rather have to carry three pails of water than sit down to "theory."

I tell him, that if he would learn to read, he could study the whole thing by himself in a week; but he won't listen.

"Nobody," he says, "will ever ask *my* advice."

One thing always alarmed me very much: However was I to take part in the manoeuvres?

I cannot lift a single pud (I myself only weight two pud and thirty pounds), and if I walk three versts my feet hurt, and my heart beats so violently that I think it's going to burst my side.

At the manoeuvres I should have to carry as much as fifty pounds' weight, and perhaps more: a rifle, a cloak, a knapsack with linen, boots, a uniform, a tent, bread, and onions, and a few other little things, and should have to walk perhaps thirty to forty versts a day.

But when the day and the hour arrived, and the command was given "Forward, march!" when the band struck up, and two thousand men set their feet in motion, something seemed to draw me forward, and I went. At the beginning I found it hard, I felt weighted to the earth, my left shoulder hurt me so, I nearly fainted. But afterwards I got very hot, I began to breathe rapidly and deeply, my eyes were starting out of my head like two cupping-glasses, and I not only walked, I ran, so as not to fall behind—and so I ended by marching along with the rest, forty versts a day.

Only I did not sing on the march like the others. First, because I did not feel so very cheerful, and second, because I could not breathe properly, let alone sing.

At times I felt burning hot, but immediately afterwards I would grow light, and the marching was easy. I seemed to be carried along rather than to tread the earth, and it appeared to me as though another were marching in my place, only that my left shoulder ached, and I was hot.

I remember that once it rained a whole night long, it came down like a deluge, our tents were soaked through, and grew heavy. The mud was thick.

At three o'clock in the morning an alarm was sounded, we were ordered to fold up our tents and take to the road again. So off we went.

It was dark and slippery. It poured with rain. I was continually stepping into a puddle, and getting my boot full of water. I shivered and shook, and my teeth chattered with cold. That is, I was cold one minute and hot the next. But the marching was no difficulty to me, I scarcely felt that I was on the march, and thought very little about it. Indeed, I don't know what I *was* thinking about, my mind was a blank.

We marched, turned back, and marched again. Then we halted for half an hour, and turned back again.

And this went on a whole night and a whole day.

Then it turned out that there had been a mistake: it was not we who ought to have marched, but another regiment, and we ought not to have moved from the spot. But there was no help for it then.

It was night. We had eaten nothing all day. The rain poured down, the mud was ankle-deep, there was no straw on which to pitch our tents, but we managed somehow. And so the days passed, each like the other. But I got through the manoeuvres, and was none the worse. Now I am already an old soldier; I have hardly another year and a half to serve—about sixteen months. I only hope I shall not be ill. It seems I got a bit of a chill at the manoeuvres, I cough every morning, and sometimes I suffer with my feet. I shiver a little at night till I get warm, and then I am very hot, and I feel very comfortable lying abed. But I shall probably soon be all right again.

They say, one may take a rest in the hospital, but I haven't been there yet, and don't want to go at all, especially now I am feeling better. The soldiers are sorry for me, and sometimes they do my work, but not just for love. I get three pounds of bread a day, and don't eat more than one pound. The rest I give to my comrade Ossadtchok. He eats it all, and his own as well, and then he could do with some more. In return for this he often cleans my rifle, and sometimes does other work for me, when he sees I have no strength left.

I am also teaching him and a few other soldiers to read and write, and they are very pleased.

My corporal also comes to me to be taught, but he never gives me a word of thanks.

The superior of the platoon, when he isn't drunk, and is in good humor, says "you" to me instead of "thou," and sometimes invites me to share his bed —I can breathe easier there, because there is more air, and I don't cough so much, either.

Only it sometimes happens that he comes back from town tipsy, and makes a great to-do: How do I, a common soldier, come to be sitting on his bed?

He orders me to get up and stand before him "at attention," and declares he will "have me up" for it.

When, however, he has sobered down, he turns kind again, and calls me to him; he likes me to tell him "stories" out of books.

Sometimes the orderly calls me into the orderly-room, and gives me a report to draw up, or else a list or a calculation to make. He himself writes badly, and is very poor at figures.

I do everything he wants, and he is very glad of my help, only it wouldn't do for him to confess to it, and when I have finished he always says to me:

"If the commanding officer is not satisfied, he will send you to fetch water."

I know it isn't true, first, because the commanding officer mustn't know that I write in the orderly-room, a Jew can't be an army secretary; secondly, because he is certain to be satisfied: he once gave me a note to write himself, and was very pleased with it.

"If you were not a Jew," he said to me then, "I should make a corporal of you."

Still, my corporal always repeats his threat about the water, so that I may preserve a proper respect for him, although I not only respect him, I tremble before his size. When *he* comes back tipsy from town, and finds me in the orderly-room, he commands me to drag his muddy boots off his feet, and I obey him and drag off his boots.

Sometimes I don't care, and other times it hurts my feelings.

A LIVELIHOOD

by JUDAH STEINBERG

THE two young fellows, Maxim Klopatzel and Israel Friedman, were natives of the same town in New Bessarabia, and there was an old link existing between them; a mutual detestation inherited from their respective parents. Maxim's father was the chief Gentile of the town, for he rented the corn-fields of its richest inhabitant; and as the lawyer of the rich citizen was a Jew, little Maxim imagined, when his father came to lose his tenantry, that it was owing to the Jews. Little Struli was the only Jewish boy he knew (the children were next door neighbors), and so a large share of their responsibility was laid on Struli's shoulders. Later on, when Klopatzel, the father, had abandoned the plough and taken to trade, he and old Friedman frequently came in contact with each other as rivals.

They traded and traded, and competed one against the other, till they both became bankrupt, when each argued to himself that the other was at the bottom of his misfortune—and their children grew on in mutual hatred.

A little later still, Maxim put down to Struli's account part of the nails which were hammered into his Saviour, over at the other end of the town, by the well, where the Government and the Church had laid out money and set up a crucifix with a ladder, a hammer, and all other necessary implements.

And Struli, on his part, had an account to settle with Maxim respecting certain other nails driven in with hammers, and torn scrolls of the Law, and the history of the ten martyrs of the days of Titus, not to mention a few later ones.

Their hatred grew with them, its strength increased with theirs.

When Krushevan began to deal in anti-Semitism, Maxim learned that Christian children were carried off into the Shul, Struli's Shul, for the sake of their blood.

Thenceforth Maxim's hatred of Struli was mingled with fear. He was terrified when he passed the Shul at night, and he used to dream that Struli stood over him in a prayer robe, prepared to slaughter him with a ram's horn trumpet.

This because he had once passed the Shul early one Jewish New Year's Day, had peeped through the window, and seen the ram's horn blower standing in his white shroud, armed with the Shofar, and suddenly a heartrending voice broke out with Min ha-Mezar, and Maxim, taking his feet on his shoulders, had arrived home more dead than alive. There was very nearly a commotion. The priest wanted to persuade him that the Jews had tried to obtain his blood.

So the two children grew into youth as enemies. Their fathers died, and the increased difficulties of their position increased their enmity.

The same year saw them called to military service, from which they had both counted on exemption, as the only sons of widowed mothers; only Israel's mother had lately died, bequeathing to the Czar all she had—a soldier; and Maxim's mother had united herself to a second provider—and there was an end of the two "only sons"!

Neither of them wished to serve; they were too intellectually capable, too far developed mentally, too intelligent, to be turned all at once into Russian soldiers, and too nicely brought up to march from Port Arthur to Mukden with only one change of shirt. They both cleared out, and stowed themselves away till they fell separately into the hands of the military.

They came together again under the fortress walls of Mukden.

They ate and hungered sullenly round the same cooking pot, received punches from the same officer, and had the same longing for the same home.

Israel had a habit of talking in his sleep, and, like a born Bessarabian, in Yiddish mixed with a large portion of Roumanian words.

One night, lying in the barracks among the other soldiers, and sunk in sleep after a hard day, Struli began to talk sixteen to the dozen. He called out names, he quarreled, begged pardon, made a fool of himself—all in his sleep.

It woke Maxim, who overheard the homelike names and phrases, the name of his native town.

He got up, made his way between the rows of sleepers, and sat down by Israel's pallet, and listened.

Next day Maxim managed to have a large helping of porridge, more than he could eat, and he found Israel, and set it before him.

"Maltzimesk!" said the other, thanking him in Roumanian, and a thrill of delight went through Maxim's frame.

The day following, Maxim was hit by a Japanese bullet, and there happened to be no one beside him at the moment.

The shock drove all the soldier-speech out of his head. "Help, I am killed!" he called out, and fell to the ground.

Struli was at his side like one sprung from the earth, he tore off his Four-Corners, and made his comrade a bandage.

The wound turned out to be slight, for the bullet had passed through, only grazing the flesh of the left arm. A few days later Maxim was back in the company.

"I wanted to see you again, Struli," he said, greeting his comrade in Roumanian.

A flash of brotherly affection and gratitude lighted Struli's Semitic eyes, and he took the other into his arms, and pressed him to his heart.

They felt themselves to be "countrymen," of one and the same native town.

Neither of them could have told exactly when their union of spirit had been accomplished, but each one knew that he thanked God for having brought him together with so near a compatriot in a strange land.

And when the battle of Mukden had made Maxim all but totally blind, and deprived Struli of one foot, they started for home together, according to the passage in the Midrash, "Two men with one pair of eyes and one pair of feet between them." Maxim carried on his shoulders a wooden box, which had now become a burden in common for them, and Struli limped a little in front of him, leaning lightly against his companion, so as to keep him in the smooth part of the road and out of other people's way.

Struli had become Maxim's eyes, and Maxim, Struli's feet; they were two men grown into one, and they provided for themselves out of one pocket, now empty of the last ruble.

They dragged themselves home. "A kasa, a kasa!" whispered Struli into Maxim's ear, and the other turned on him his two glazed eyes looking through a red haze, and set in swollen red lids.

A childlike smile played on his lips:

"A kasa, a kasa!" he repeated, also in a whisper.

Home appeared to their fancy as something holy, something consoling, something that could atone and compensate for all they had suffered and lost. They had seen such a home in their dreams.

But the nearer they came to it in reality, the more the dream faded. They remembered that they were returning as conquered soldiers and crippled men, that they had no near relations and but few friends, while the girls who had coquetted with Maxim before he left would never waste so much as a look on him now he was half-blind; and Struli's plans for marrying and emigrating to America were frustrated; a cripple would not be allowed to enter the country.

All their dreams and hopes finally dissipated, and there remained only one black care, one all-obscuring anxiety: how were they to earn a living?

They had been hoping all the while for a pension, but in their service book was written "on sick-leave." The Russo-Japanese war was distinguished by the fact that the greater number of wounded soldiers went home "on sick-leave," and the money assigned by the Government for their pensions would not have been sufficient for even a hundredth part of the number of invalids.

Maxim showed a face with two wide-open eyes, to which all the passers-by looked the same. He distinguished with difficulty between a man and a tele-graph post, and wore a smile of mingled apprehension and confidence. The sound feet stepped hesitatingly, keeping behind Israel, and it was hard to say which steadied himself most against the other. Struli limped forward, and kept open eyes for two. Sometimes he would look round at the box on Maxim's shoulders, as though he felt its weight as much as Maxim.

Meantime the railway carriages had emptied and refilled, and the locomo-tive gave a great blast, received an answer from somewhere a long way off, a whistle for a whistle, and the train set off, slowly at first, and then gradually faster and faster, till all that remained of it were puffs of smoke hanging in the air without rhyme or reason.

The two felt more depressed than ever. "Something to eat? Where are we to get a bite?" was in their minds.

Suddenly Yisröel remembered with a start: this was the anniversary of his mother's death—if he could only say one Kaddish for her in a Klaus!

"Is it far from here to a Klaus?" he inquired of a passer-by.

"There is one a little way down that side-street," was the reply.

"Maxim!" he begged of the other, "come with me!"

"Where to?"

"To the synagogue."

Maxim shuddered from head to foot. His fear of a Jewish Shul had not left him, and a thousand foolish terrors darted through his head.

But his comrade's voice was so gentle, so childishly imploring, that he could not resist it, and he agreed to go with him into the Shul.

It was the time for Afternoon Prayer, the daylight and the dark held equal sway within the Klaus, the lamps before the platform increasing the former to the east and the latter to the west. Maxim and Yisröel stood in the western part, enveloped in shadow. The Cantor had just finished "Incense," and was entering upon Ashre, and the melancholy night chant of Minchah and Maariv gradually entranced Maxim's emotional Roumanian heart.

The low, sad murmur of the Cantor seemed to him like the distant surging of a sea, in which men were drowned by the hundreds and suffocating with the water. Then, the Ashre and the Kaddish ended, there was silence. The congregation stood up for the Eighteen Benedictions. Here and there you heard a half-stifled sigh. And now it seemed to Maxim that he was in the hospital at night, at the hour when the groans grow less frequent, and the sufferers fall one by one into a sweet sleep.

Tears started into his eyes without his knowing why. He was no longer afraid, but a sudden shyness had come over him, and he felt, as he watched Yisröel repeating the Kaddish, that the words, which he, Maxim, could not understand, were being addressed to someone unseen, and yet mysteriously present in the darkening Shul.

When the prayers were ended, one of the chief members of the congregation approached the "Mandchurian," and gave Yisröel a coin into his hand.

Yisröel looked round—he did not understand at first what the donor meant by it.

Then it occurred to him—and the blood rushed to his face. He gave the coin to his companion, and explained in a half-sentence or two how they had come by it.

Once outside the Klaus, they both cried, after which they felt better.

"A livelihood!" The same thought struck them both.

"We can go into partnership!"

FORLORN AND FORSAKEN

by ISAIAH BERSHADSKI

FORLORN and forsaken she was in her last years. Even when she lay on the bed of sickness where she died, not one of her relations or friends came to look after her; they did not even come to mourn for her or accompany her to the grave. There was not even one of her kin to say the first Kaddish over her resting-place. My wife and I were the only friends she had at the close of her life, no one but us cared for her while she was ill, or walked behind her coffin. The only tears shed at the lonely old woman's grave were ours. I spoke the only Kaddish for her soul, but we, after all were complete strangers to her!

Yes, we were strangers to her, and she was a stranger to us! We made her acquaintance only a few years before her death, when she was living in two tiny rooms opposite the first house we settled in after our marriage. Nobody ever came to see her, and she herself visited nowhere, except at the little store where she made her necessary purchases, and at the house-of-study near by, where she prayed twice every day. She was about sixty, rather undersized, and very thin, but more lithesome in her movements than is common at that age. Her face was full of creases and wrinkles, and her light brown eyes were somewhat dulled, but her ready smile and quiet glance told of a good heart and a kindly temper. Her simple old gown was always neat, her wig tastefully arranged, her lodging and its furniture clean and tidy—and all this attracted us to her from the first day onward. We were still more taken with her retiring manner, the quiet way in which she kept herself in the background and the slight melancholy of her expression, telling of a life that had held much sadness.

We made advances. She was very willing to become acquainted with us, and it was not very long before she was like a mother to us, or an old aunt. My wife was then an inexperienced "housemistress" fresh to her duties, and found a great help in the old woman, who smilingly taught her how to proceed with the housekeeping. When our first child was born, she took it to her heart, and busied herself with its upbringing almost more than the young mother. It was evident that dandling the child in her arms was a joy to her beyond words. At such moments her eyes brightened, her wrinkles grew faint, a curiously satisfied smile played round her lips, and a new note of joy came into her voice.

At first sight all this seemed quite simple, because a woman is naturally inclined to care for little children, and it may have been so with her to an exceptional degree, but closer examination convinced me that here lay yet another reason; her attentions to the child, so it seemed, awakened pleasant memories of a long-ago past, when she herself was a young mother caring for children of her own, and looking at this strange child had stirred a longing for those other children, further from her eyes, but nearer to her heart, although perhaps quite unknown to her—who perhaps existed only in her imagination.

And when we were made acquainted with the details of her life, we knew our conjectures to be true. Her history was very simple and commonplace, but very tragic. Perhaps the tragedy of such biographies lies in their being so very ordinary and simple!

She lived quietly and happily with her husband for twenty years after their marriage. They were not rich, but their little house was a kingdom of delight, where no good thing was wanting. Their business was farming land that belonged to a Polish nobleman, a business that knows of good times and of bad, of fat years and lean years, years of high prices and of low. But on the whole it was a good business and profitable, and it afforded them a comfortable living. Besides, they were used to the country, they could not fancy themselves anywhere else. The very thing that had never entered their heads is just what happened. In the beginning of the "eighties" they were obliged to leave the estate they had farmed for ten years, because the lease was up, and the recently promulgated "temporary laws" forbade them to renew it. This was bad for them from a material point of view, because it left them without regular income just when their children were growing up and expenses had increased, but their mental distress was so great, that, for the time, the financial side of the misfortune was thrown into the shade.

When we made her acquaintance, many years had passed since then, many another trouble had come into her life, but one could hear tears in her voice while she told the story of that first misfortune. It was a bitter Tisha-b'Ab for them when they left the house, the gardens, the barns, and the stalls, their whole life, all those things concerning which they had forgotten, and their children had hardly known, that they were not their own possession.

Their town surroundings made them more conscious of their altered circumstances. She herself, the elder children oftener still, had been used to drive into the town now and again, but that was on pleasure trips, which had lasted a day or two at most; they had never tried staying there longer, and it was no wonder if they felt cramped and oppressed in town after their free life in the open.

When they first settled there, they had a capital of about ten thousand rubles, but by reason of inexperience in their new occupation they were worsted in competition with others, and a few turns of bad luck brought them almost to ruin. The capital grew less from year to year; everything they took up was more of a struggle than the last venture; poverty came nearer and nearer, and the father of the family began to show signs of illness, brought on by town life and worry. This, of course, made their material position worse, and the knowledge of it reacted disastrously on his health. Three years after he came to town, he died, and she was left with six children and no means of subsistence. Already during her husband's life they had exchanged their first lodging for a second, a poorer and cheaper one, and after his death they moved into a third, meaner and narrower still, and sold their precious furniture, for which, indeed, there was no place in the new existence. But even so the question of bread and meat was not answered. They still had about six hundred rubles, but, as they were without a trade, it was easy to foresee that the little stock of money would dwindle day by day till there was none of it left—and what then?

The eldest son, Yossef, aged twenty-one, had gone from home a year before his father's death, to seek his fortune elsewhere; but his first letters brought no very good news, and now the second, Avrohom, a lad of eighteen, and the daughter Rochel, who was sixteen, declared their intention to start for America. The mother was against it, begged them with tears not to go, but they did not listen to her. Parting with them, forever most likely, was bad enough in itself, but worst of all was the thought that her children, for whose Jewish education their father had never grudged money even when times were hardest, should go to America, and there, forgetting everything they had learned, become "ganze Goyim." She was quite sure that her husband would never have agreed to his children's being thus scattered abroad, and this encouraged her to oppose their will with more determination. She urged them to wait at least till their elder brother had achieved some measure of success, and could help them. She held out this hope to them, because she believed in her son Yossef and his capacity, and was convinced that in a little time he would become their support.

If only Avrohom and Rochel had not been so impatient (she would lament to us), everything would have turned out differently! They would not have been hustled off to the end of creation, and she would not have been left so lonely in her last years, but—it had apparently been so ordained!

Avrohom and Rochel agreed to defer the journey, but when some months had passed, and Yossef was still wandering from town to town, finding no rest for the sole of his foot, she had to give in to her children and let them go. They took with them two hundred rubles and sailed for America, and with the remaining three hundred rubles she opened a tiny shop. Her expenses were not great now, as only the three younger children were left her, but the shop was not sufficient to support even these. The stock grew smaller month by month, there never being anything over wherewith to replenish it, and there was no escaping the fact that one day soon the shop would remain empty.

And as if this was not enough, there came bad news from the children in America. They did not complain much; on the contrary, they wrote most hopefully about the future, when their position would certainly, so they said, improve; but the mother's heart was not to be deceived, and she felt instinctively that meanwhile they were doing anything but well, while later—who could foresee what would happen later?

One day she got a letter from Yossef, who wrote that, convinced of the impossibilty of earning a livelihood within the Pale, he was about to make use of an opportunity that offered itself, and settle in a distant town outside of it. This made her very sad, and she wept over her fate—to have a son living in a Gentile city, where there were hardly any Jews at all. And the next letter from America added sorrow to sorrow. Avrohom and Rochel had parted company, and were living in different towns. She could not bear the thought of her young daughter fending for herself among strangers—a thought that tortured her all the more as she had a peculiar idea of America. She herself could not account for the terror that would seize her whenever she remembered that strange, distant life.

But the worst was nearly over; the turn for the better came soon. She received word from Yossef that he had found a good position in his new home, and in a few weeks he proved his letter true by sending her money. From America, too, the news that came was more cheerful, even joyous. Avrohom had secured steady work with good pay, and before long he wrote for his younger brother to join him in America, had provided him with all the funds he needed for travelling expenses. Rochel had engaged herself to a young man, whose praises she sounded in her letters. Soon after her wedding, she sent money to bring over another brother, and her husband added a few lines, in which he spoke of "his great love for his new relations," and how he "looked forward with impatience to having one of them, his dear brother-in-law, come to live with him."

This was good and cheering news, and it all came within a year's time, but the mother's heart grieved over it more than it rejoiced. Her delight at her daughter's marriage with a good man she loved was anything but unmixed. Melancholy thoughts blended with it, whether she would or not. The occasion was one which a mother's fancy had painted in rainbow colors, on the preparations for which it had dwelt with untold pleasure—and now she had had no share in it at all, and her heart writhed under the disappointment. To make her still sadder, she was obliged to part with two more children. She tried to prevent their going, but they had long ago set their hearts on following their brother and sister to America, and the recent letters had made them more anxious to be off.

So they started, and there remained only the youngest daughter, Rivkeh, a girl of thirteen. Their position was materially not a bad one, for every now and then the old woman received help from her children in America and from her son, Yossef, so that she was not even obliged to keep up the shop, but the mother in her was not satisfied, because she wanted to see her children's happiness with her own eyes. The good news that continued to arrive at intervals brought pain as well as pleasure, by reminding her how much less fortunate she was than other mothers, who were counted worthy to live together with their children, and not at a distance from them like her.

The idea that she should go out to those of them who were in America never occurred to her, or to them, either! But Yossef, who had taken a wife in his new town, and who, soon after, had set up for himself, and was doing very well, now sent for his mother and little sister to come and live with him. At first the mother was unwilling, fearing that she might be in the way of her daughter-in-law, and thus disturb the household peace; even later, when she had assured herself that the young wife was very kind, and there was nothing to be afraid of, she could not make up her mind to go, even though she longed to be with Yossef, her oldest son, who had always been her favorite, and however much she desired to see his wife and her little grandchildren.

Why she would not fulfil his wish and her own, she herself was not clearly conscious; but she shrank from the strange fashion of the life they led, and she never ceased to hope, deep down in her heart, that some day they would come back to her. And this especially with regard to Yossef, who sometimes complained in his letters that his situation was anything but secure, because the smallest circumstance might bring about an edict of expulsion. She quite understood that her son would consider this a very bad thing, but she herself looked at it with other eyes; round about *here,* too, were people who made a comfortable living, and Yossef was no worse than others, that he should not do the same.

Six or seven years passed in this way; the youngest daughter was twenty, and it was time to think of a match for her. Her mother felt sure that Yossef would provide the dowry, but she thought best Rivkeh and her brother should see each other, and she consented readily to let Rivkeh go to him, when Yossef invited her to spend several months as his guest. No sooner had she gone than the mother realized what it meant, this parting with her youngest child, and, for the last years, her only child. She was filled with regret at not having gone with her, and waited impatiently for her return. Suddenly she heard that Rivkeh had found favor with a friend of Yossef's, the son of a well-to-do merchant, and that Rivkeh and her brother were equally pleased with him. The two were already engaged, and the wedding was only deferred till she, the mother, should come and take up her abode with them for good.

The longing to see her daughter overcame all her doubts. She resolved to go to her son, and began preparations for the start. These were just completed, when there came a letter from Yossef to say that the situation had taken a sudden turn for the worse, and he and his family might have to leave their town.

This sudden news was distressing and welcome at one and the same time. She was anxious lest the edict of expulsion should harm her son's position, and pleased, on the other hand, that he should at last be coming back, for God would not forsake him here, either; what with the fortune he had, and his aptitude for trade, he would make a living right enough. She waited anxiously, and in a few months had gone through all the mental suffering inherent in a state of uncertainty such as hers, when fear and hope are twined in one.

The waiting was the harder to bear that all this time no letter from Yossef or Rivkeh reached her promptly. And the end of it all was this: news came that the danger was over, and Yossef would remain where he was; but as far as she was concerned, it was best she should do likewise, because trailing about at her age was a serious thing, and it was not worth while her running into danger, and so on.

The old woman was full of grief at remaining thus forlorn in her old age, and she longed more than ever for her children after having hoped so surely that she would be with them soon. She could not understand Yossef's reason for suddenly changing his mind with regard to her coming; but it never occurred to her for one minute to doubt her children's affection. And we, when we had read the treasured bundle of letters from Yossef and Rivkeh, we could not doubt it, either. There was love and longing for the distant mother in every line, and several of the letters betrayed a spirit of bitterness, a note of complaining resentment against the hard times that had brought about the separation from her. And yet we could not help thinking, "Out of sight, out of mind," that which is far from the eyes, weighs lighter at the heart.

It was the only explanation we could invent, for why, otherwise, should the mother have to remain alone among strangers?

All these considerations moved me to interfere in the matter without the old woman's knowledge. She could read Yiddish, but could not write it, and before we made friends, her letters to the children were written by a shopkeeper of her acquaintance. But from the time we got to know her, I became her constant secretary, and one day, when writing to Yossef for her, I made use of the opportunity to enclose a letter from myself. I asked his forgiveness for mixing myself up in another's family affairs, and tried to justify the interference by dwelling on our affectionate relations with his mother. I then described, in the most touching words at my command, how hard it was for her to live forlorn, how she pined for the presence of her children and grandchildren, and ended by telling them that it was their duty to free their mother from all this mental suffering.

There was no direct reply to this letter of mine, but the next one from the son to his mother gave her to understand that there are certain things not to be explained, while the impossibility of explaining them may lead to a misunderstanding. This hint made the position no clearer to us, and the fact of Yossef's not answering me confirmed us in our previous suspicions.

Meanwhile our old friend fell ill, and quickly understood that she would soon die. Among the things she begged me to do after her death and having reference to her burial, there was one particular petition several times repeated: to send a packet of Hebrew books, which had been left by her husband, to her son Yossef, and to inform him of her death by telegram. "My American children"—she explained with a sigh—"have certainly forgotten everything they once learned, forgotten all their Jewishness! But my son Yossef is a different sort; I feel sure of him, that he will say Kaddish after me and read a chapter in the Mishnah, and the books will come in useful for his children—grandmother's legacy to them."

When I fulfilled the old woman's last wish, I learned how mistaken she had been. The answer to my letter written during her lifetime came now that she was dead. Her children thanked us warmly for our care of her, and they also explained why she and they had remained apart.

She had never known—and it was far better so—by what means her son had obtained the right to live outside the Pale. It was enough that she should have to live *forlorn;* where would have been the good of her knowing that she was *forsaken* as well—that the one of her children who had gone altogether over to "them" was Yossef?

POGROM

by ARNOLD ZWEIG

THE ringing of shots awoke Eli Seamen. The double wings of his window, thrown wide open, with their curtains dangling in the wind like the bodies of gallows' birds, admitted the clear crack of the Browning pistols which was carried over the roofs to his bedroom. He sat: the sky above the city was touched with the red either of a conflagration or of a multitude of lights; but directly overhead the legions of the stars worked through the infinite darkness. Against the faint, distant glimmer the window cut out a hard cross right in the center of the Great Bear. Seeing the arrangement of the stars, the boy thought it must be toward eleven o'clock; they are shooting. . . . The door to his father's room was flung wide open, and Inspector Seamen strode over the threshold. "Get up, Eli," he cried, his hard voice wild with excitement. "Pogrom?" the son cried back, leaping with both legs onto the carpet; but no answer was needed.

He dressed himself with quick and trembling hands, while his father sealed a letter by the light of candle stump. The chess board still stood in the throes of the struggle, as they had left it the night before. The masterstroke had just been delivered; the figures loomed black in the candlelight, mustered with their stiff shadows on the divided board. Eli, filled with happy pride, threw one glance at it: his father, stronger player that he was, had been compelled to yield in astonishment before that last triumphant move. . . . But in an instant he was pulled back into the present; while he laced his shoes hastily the thought occurred to him—and it gave him a sense of satisfaction—that things were going badly now for his enemies, those Jewish young boys who threw cakes of mud after him and shouted that he was desecrating the Sabbath and eating uncleanliness; and he felt that it served them right, for they were many, and yet never attacked him singly. "Well, are you ready? Not yet." The inspector, his fur cap on his head, raged up and down in the doorway, stamping in his high boots. He blew impatiently into his thick black beard: "Are you afraid?" And suddenly—he had never thought of this before—Eli realized that he too might be assaulted, for the band could not know that he and his father lived in a state of enmity with the others. But he forgot it again on the spot. "No, no," he answered, angrily. "Here I am. Let's go."

The father locked the letter in the writing desk. "We must see. . . . We must help them out there. . . ."

Then he turned his face on his son and examined the sixteen-year-old boy closely, as if he were a piece of merchandise which had just been delivered; no, he was not afraid.

"Listen, Eli. It's possible that something might happen over there . . . to me too . . . you understand: and if I'm no longer here tomorrow—" "Father!" the boy cried, and his eyes became two black holes. "Anything can happen. In that case, listen—you return to Germany, at once . . ." "Father!" "And then study something decent, see? Engineering." "Oh, please, please, stop," the boy cried in a dying voice, and with both hands he seized his father's arm. "In case you might need it—you're big enough—here!" He thrust the flat pistol toward him. Eli seized the pistol in a strong grasp, though his hands shivered. "Will the police help us, father?" But the inspector had already rushed through the door, in one hand his Browning, and in another a formidable stick, leather on the outside but iron within. His steps sounded down the corridor; hastily the boy snatched his mountain-climbing stick from the corner— a yellow oaken staff pointed with metal at the end. Beyond the outer door he found his father, clearly undetermined. "As a matter of fact, I ought to leave you here. What should you be doing over there. . . ?"

"Without you? I won't let you go alone for a single instant." "I want you to obey me," the father said. "I'll break the door open, and follow you," the powerfully built boy cried. The inspector knew his oldest son. "Well, if you must. . . . It's probably for the best." And smiling weakly he turned the key strongly in the lock.

They stumbled down the three flights of steps, and crossed the broad yard of the factory. In Eli blood ran swiftly and joyfully: adventure! And what an adventure! A pogrom, right on the eve of Easter Sabbath! Tomorrow songs of praise in the churches. He was not at all frightened; his finger pressed happily against the trigger of the weapon. Would he have to shoot? And would he hit his man? Surely if only his hands wouldn't tremble too much. He promised himself to get Gabriel Butterman, the red head, the thrower of stones. That man he wouldn't let escape . . . and he felt the advance happiness of envy which the whole class—and his brother Leos—would feel—when he would tell them about it. . . . He tightened his arm as though in exercise, so that the muscles rose quickly. The schoolboy of the fifth grade lifted up his face, with its arched eyebrows, and its crown of black hair, to the night air. The gatekeeper was still awake; yellow light streamed from the windows of his lodge. The inspector gave him the keys of the house and said, in Polish: "Open the door for me." "It isn't good to go out," the old man argued, while his mustaches, yellowed by smoking, wagged with his speech. "It's true, Janek. But I'll be back at one o'clock. And look after the keys for me." The door shrieked on its hinges; in the distance was heard a faint sound of shots. The father was in such a hurry that Eli was nearly left behind. The streets lay black and deserted; only high up there were a few lighted windows. The two of them turned sharply to the right, went at a trot the whole length of the Petersburgerstrasse—blundering into pools of mud and water—straight across the Patjomkinplatz and right into the Schlusselstrasse. The noise became louder, became a wild tumult. They met people, more people, still more people. 'What's the matter?" the father asked in Russian of a figure hurrying by in the dark. "They're beating the infidel Jews up, uncle, hurry up." "And the police?" "You won't find the soldiers lazy," the citizen answered, laughing contentedly, and hurried on. Eli made up his mind to shoot the soldiers even if they had killed Gabriel.

The street grew brighter in the light of the lanterns and the lamps that streamed from the houses; before long they found themselves in the midst of the crowds. They thrust their way through roughly, and when the father could not proceed fast enough he seized his son by the shoulders and thrust him into the shelter of a high house. "Where now?" the boy asked, excitedly. "Come!" They ran lightly, hastily, up two, three, four flights of steps. From the skylight, a small dirty opening, they peered out on the neighboring streets, for none of the neighboring houses were more than two or three stories high. The square frames of houses enclosed a clear picture, small in the distance, but marvelously sharp in outline. They saw flames flickering through the windows, and thickening smoke, streaked with red; they saw people running, limbs flying, men and women in knots and groups; they heard a deep roaring, the scream of high-pitched voices, single shots here and there, and through the fence, whisper and crack of conflagration, dull thudding noises, as of falling beams and doors smashed open. For a single, hellish instant the horror of it beat up into his face; then suddenly the inspector pulled the son backward and thundered with him down the steps; instead of turning toward the door of the house, he went into the dark courtyard, and holding his stick in his teeth, square across his face, he climbed over the low wall into the neighboring house. Eli threw his cudgel over, leapt up, held on with his fingers, drew himself upward, lifted his legs over the obstacle, just as they did in the gymnasium, and landed on the other side almost on all fours. And now they ran noisily through the back quarters across a second courtyard and by means of a low gate again reached the street. They went swiftly along the houses on the left, through two, three small streets, without seeing a single human being, and they stood again on the Katherinestrasse, which further down, was once more filled with noise, light and smoke. They stood still for a moment, their beating hearts breathless; then they went some seventy steps slowly, easily, down to Metchnikoffstrasse, their Brownings in their hands. There they turned the corner—and something happened.

A woman came running toward them, in her underskirt; on the upper part of her body she wore a brown piece of cloth which covered her shoulders. She was out of breath, unable to utter a sound, her fleshy face distorted with the terror of death; she held her young daughter by the hand; the child had not even a cloth to cover her, her hair hung loose around her face, and the bare feet, scarcely able to keep the pace up, seemed only to be falling forwards. The woman's mouth was wide open, showing all the teeth, and her free hand was pressed against her left breast. Three young ones followed her—with just a short stretch of pavement between her and them; and on that short stretch a young boy, perhaps nine years old, stumbled horribly along, unable to catch up with his mother. . . . Eli thought he recognized Gabriel's younger brother; but at once he might be mistaken. The child reeled and fell, picked itself up, fell again, and as he rose to his feet for a second time, the first of the hooligans ran by; the second one, also running by, thrust a knife into the child's back. "Ma-a—" it cried—the sound beginning high and shrill, then sinking downward and breaking. The mother, hearing that piercing cry, turned her head, stiffened, sank on her knee, without loosening her hold on the girl. Then suddenly Eli was aware that his father, who had just been at his side, had leapt ten paces forward —and, a fiery tumult bursting out within him, he sprang after him. For a single, violent moment he was glad that his mother had long been dead, and then he saw how his father's horrible stick had whirled sideways at the skull of the first hooligan, smashing it as if it had been a clay pot, so that the man fell sideways on the stony ground; and at the same instant he saw two others put themselves on the defensive. And then the fury broke loose. He heard one shot, two shots, and he shifted his Browning to his right hand. His father leapt to the attack of the man who was shooting, but the second man was behind him, his knife uplifted. Eli felt something cold at his heart; and then he stood still, shot, shot again, again; and the knife rang on the hard pavement. A terrific excitement cried out of him: "He's hit!" He heard the piercing cry of the women behind him, the sound of heavy footsteps, a shot thundered darkly behind him, another —no Browning this time, he knew—and then he saw the face of his father turned toward him, a vivid white, with far-off eyes blazing in terrific anger: and then nothing more. He fell forward. "Father . . ." he thought, and at the same time something hammering down upon him flung him to the ground as with a lightning stroke.

　　The police lieutenant wiped his sabre and gave command: "Forward!" And as the policemen retreated swiftly the two women, dumb with horror, fixed a blank dead gaze on the figures lying on the ground: on the man, the youths, the boy and the child.

BEFORE THE LAW

by FRANZ KAFKA

IN THE writings which preface the Law that particular delusion is described thus: before the Law stands a doorkeeper. To this doorkeeper there comes a man from the country who begs for admittance to the Law. But the doorkeeper says that he cannot admit the man at the moment. The man, on reflection, asks if he will be allowed, then, to enter later. 'It is possible,' answers the doorkeeper, 'but not at this moment.' Since the door leading into the Law stands open as usual and the doorkeeper steps to one side, the man bends down to peer through the entrance. When the doorkeeper sees that, he laughs and says: 'If you are so strongly tempted, try to get in without my permission. But note that I am powerful. And I am only the lowest doorkeeper. From hall to hall, keepers stand at every door, one more powerful than the other. And the sight of the third man is already more than even I can stand.' These are difficulties which the man from the country has not expected to meet; the Law, he thinks, should be accessible to every man and at all times, but when he looks more closely at the doorkeeper in his furred robe, with his huge pointed nose and long thin Tartar beard, he decides that he had better wait until he gets permission to enter. The doorkeeper gives him a stool and lets him sit down at the side of the door. There he sits waiting for days and years. He makes many attempts to be allowed in and wearies the doorkeeper with his importunity. The doorkeeper often engages him in brief conversation, asking him about his home and about other matters, but the questions are put quite impersonally, as great men put questions, and always conclude with the statement that the man cannot be allowed to enter yet. The man, who has equipped himself with many things for his journey, parts with all he has, however valuable, in the hope of bribing the doorkeeper. The doorkeeper accepts it all, saying, however, as he takes each gift: 'I take this only to keep you from feeling that you have left something undone.' During all these long years the man watches the doorkeeper almost incessantly. He forgets about the other doorkeepers, and this one seems to him the only barrier between himself and the Law. In the first years he curses his evil fate aloud; later, as he grows old, he only mutters to himself. He grows childish, and since in his prolonged study of the doorkeeper he has learned to know even the fleas in his fur collar, he begs the very fleas to help him and to persuade the doorkeeper to change his mind. Finally his eyes grow dim and he does not know whether the world is really darkening around him or whether his eyes are only deceiving him. But in the darkness he can now perceive a radiance that streams inextinguishably from the door of the Law. Now his life is drawing to a close. Before he dies, all that he has experienced during the whole time of his sojourn condenses in his mind into one question, which he has never yet put to the doorkeeper. He beckons the doorkeeper, since he can no longer raise his stiffening body. The doorkeeper has to bend far down to hear him, for the difference in size between them has increased very much to the man's disadvantage. 'What do you want to know now?' asks the doorkeeper, 'you are insatiable.' 'Everyone strives to attain the Law,' answers the man, 'how does it come about, then, that in all these years no one has come seeking admittance but me?' The doorkeeper perceives that the man is nearing his end and his hearing is failing, so he bellows in his ear: 'No one but you could gain admittance through this door, since this door was intended for you. I am now going to shut it.' "

"So the doorkeeper deceived the man," said K. immediately, strongly at-

tracted by the story. "Don't be too hasty," said the priest, "don't take over someone else's opinion without testing it. I have told you the story in the very words
of the scriptures. There's no mention of deception in it." "But it's clear enough,"
said K., "and your first interpretation of it was quite right. The doorkeeper gave
the message of salvation to the man only when it could no longer help him."
"He was not asked the question any earlier," said the priest, "and you must
consider, too, that he was only a doorkeeper, and as such fulfilled his duty."
"What makes you think he fulfilled his duty?" asked K. "He didn't fulfill it.
His duty might have been to keep all strangers away, but this man, for whom
the door was intended, should have been let in." "You have not enough respect
for the written word and you are altering the story," said the priest. "The story
contains two important statements made by the doorkeeper about admission to
the Law, one at the beginning, the other at the end. The first statement is: that
he cannot admit the man at the moment, and the other is: that this door was
intended only for the man. If there were a contradiction between the two, you
would be right and the doorkeeper would have deceived the man. But there is
no contradiction. The first statement, on the contrary, even implies the second.
One could almost say that in suggesting to the man the possibility of future
admittance the doorkeeper is exceeding his duty. At that time his apparent duty
is only to refuse admittance and indeed many commentators are surprised that
the suggestion should be made at all, since the doorkeeper appears to be a preci-
sian with a stern regard for duty. He does not once leave his post during these
many years, and he does not shut the door until the very last minute; he is
conscious of the importance of his office, for he says: 'I am powerful'; he is respectful to his superiors, for he says: 'I am only the lowest doorkeeper'; he is
not garrulous, for during all these years he puts only what are called 'impersonal
questions'; he is not to be bribed, for he says in accepting a gift: 'I take this only
to keep you from feeling that you have left something undone'; where his duty
is concerned he is to be moved neither by pity nor rage, for we are told that the
man 'wearied the doorkeeper with his importunity'; and finally even his external appearance hints at a pedantic character, the large, pointed nose and the
long, thin, black, Tartar beard. Could one imagine a more faithful doorkeeper?
Yet the doorkeeper has other elements in his character which are likely to advantage anyone seeking admittance and which make it comprehensible enough
that he should somewhat exceed his duty in suggesting the possibility of future
admittance. For it cannot be denied that he is a little simple-minded and consequently a little conceited. Take the statements he makes about his power and the
power of the other doorkeepers and their dreadful aspect which even he cannot
bear to see—I hold that these statements may be true enough, but that the way
in which he brings them out shows that his perceptions are confused by simpleness of mind and conceit. The commentators note in this connection: 'The right
perception of any matter and a misunderstanding of the same matter do not
wholly exclude each other.' One must at any rate assume that such simpleness

and conceit, however sparingly manifest, are likely to weaken his defense of the door; they are breaches in the character of the doorkeeper. To this must be added the fact that the doorkeeper seems to be a friendly creature by nature, he is by no means always on his official dignity. In the very first moments he allows himself the jest of inviting the man to enter in spite of the strictly maintained veto against entry; then he does not, for instance, send the man away, but gives him, as we are told, a stool and lets him sit down beside the door. The patience with which he endures the man's appeals during so many years, the brief conversations, the acceptance of the gifts, the politeness with which he allows the man to curse loudly in his presence the fate for which he himself is responsible— all this lets us deduce certain feelings of pity. Not every doorkeeper would have acted thus. And finally, in answer to a gesture of the man's he bends down to give him the chance of putting a last question. Nothing but mild impatience— the doorkeeper knows that this is the end of it all—is discernible in the words: 'You are insatiable.' Some push this mode of interpretation even further and hold that these words express a kind of friendly admiration, though not without a hint of condescension. At any rate the figure of the doorkeeper can be said to come out very differently from what you fancied." "You have studied the story more exactly and for a longer time than I have," said K. They were both silent for a little while. Then K. said: "So you think the man was not deceived?" "Don't misunderstand me," said the priest, "I am only showing you the various opinions concerning that point. You must not pay too much attention to them. The scriptures are unalterable and the comments often enough merely express the commentators' despair. In this case there even exists an interpretation which claims that the deluded person is really the doorkeeper." "That's a far-fetched interpretation," said K. "On what is it based?" "It is based," answered the priest, "on the simple-mindedness of the doorkeeper. The argument is that he does not know the Law from inside, he knows only the way that leads to it, where he patrols up and down. His ideas of the interior are assumed to be childish, and it is supposed that he himself is afraid of the other guardians whom he holds up as bogies before the man. Indeed, he fears them more than the man does, since the man is determined to enter after hearing about the dreadful guardians of the interior, while the doorkeeper has no desire to enter, at least not so far as we are told. Others again say that he must have been in the interior already, since he is after all engaged in the service of the Law and can only have been appointed from inside. This is countered by arguing that he may have been appointed by a voice calling from the interior, and that anyhow he cannot have been far inside, since the aspect of the third doorkeeper is more than he can endure. Moreover, no indication is given that during all these years he ever made any remarks showing a knowledge of the interior, except for the one remark about the doorkeepers. He may have been forbidden to do so, but there is no mention of that either. On these grounds the conclusion is reached that he knows nothing about the aspect and significance of the interior, so that he is in a state of delusion. But he is deceived also about his relation to the man from the country, for he is inferior to the man and does not know it. He treats the man instead as his own subordinate, as can be recognized from many details that must be still fresh in your mind. But, according to this view of the story, it is just as clearly indicated that he is really subordinated to the man. In the first place, a bondman is always subject to a free man. Now the man from the country is really free, he can go where he likes, it is only the Law that is closed to him, and access to the Law is forbidden him only by one individual, the doorkeeper. When he sits down on the stool by the side of the door and stays there for the rest of his life, he does it of his own free will; in the story there is no mention of any compulsion. But the doorkeeper is bound to his post by his very office, he does not dare go out into the country, nor apparently may he go into the interior of the Law, even should he wish to. Besides, although he is in the service of the Law, his service is confined to this one entrance; that is to say, he serves only this man for whom alone the entrance is intended. On that ground too he is inferior to the man. One must assume that for many years, for as long as it takes a man to grow up to the prime of life, his service was in a sense an empty formality, since he had to wait for a man to come, that is to say someone in the prime of life, and so he had to wait a long time before the purpose of his service could be fulfilled, and, moreover, had to wait on the man's pleasure, for the man came of his own free will. But the termination of his service also depends on the man's term of life, so that to the very end he is subject to the man. And it is emphasized throughout that the doorkeeper apparently realizes nothing of all this. That is not in itself remarkable, since according to this interpretation the doorkeeper is deceived in a much more important issue, affecting his very office. At the end, for example, he says regarding the entrance to the Law: 'I am now going to shut it,' but at the beginning of the story we are told that the door leading into the Law always stands open, and if it always stands open, that is to say at all times, without reference to the life or death of the man, then the doorkeeper cannot close it. There is some difference of opinion about the motive behind the doorkeeper's statement, whether he said he was going to close the door merely for the sake of giving an answer, or to emphasize his devotion to duty, or to bring the man into a state of grief and regret in his last moments. But there is no lack of agreement that the doorkeeper will not be able to shut the door. Many indeed profess to find that he is subordinate to the man even in knowledge, toward the end, at least, for the man sees the radiance that issues from the door of the Law while the doorkeeper in his official position must stand with his back to the door, nor does he say anything to show that he has perceived the change." "That is well argued," said K., after repeating to himself in a low voice several passages from the priest's exposition. "It is well argued, and I am inclined to agree that the doorkeeper is deceived. But that has not made me abandon my former opinion, since both conclusions are to some extent compatible. Whether the doorkeeper is clear-sighted or deceived does not dispose of the matter. I said the man is deceived. If the doorkeeper is clear-sighted, one might have doubts about that, but if the doorkeeper himself is deceived, then his deception must of necessity be communicated to the man. That makes the doorkeeper not, indeed, a deceiver, but a creature so simple-minded that he ought to be dismissed at once from his office. You mustn't forget that the doorkeeper's deceptions do himself no harm but do infinite harm to the man." "There are objections to that," said the priest. "Many aver that the story confers no right on anyone to pass judgment on the doorkeeper. Whatever he may seem to us, he is yet a servant of the Law; that is, he belongs to the Law and as such is beyond human judgment. In that case one must not believe that the doorkeeper is subordinate to the man. Bound as he is by his service, even only at the door of the Law, he is incomparably greater than anyone at large in the world. The man is only seeking the Law, the doorkeeper is already attached to it. It is the Law that has placed him at his post; to doubt his dignity is to doubt the Law itself." "I don't agree with that point of view," said K., shaking his head, "for if one accepts it, one must accept as true everything the doorkeeper says. But you yourself have sufficiently proved how impossible it is to do that." "No," said the priest, "it is not necessary to accept everything as true, one must only accept it as necessary." "A melancholy conclusion," said K. "It turns lying into a universal principle."

THE FRIEND OF THE GHETTO

by EDMOND FLEG

THE type is a new one, but I assure you that it exists, in France at least. The individual of this type usually comes of a good Christian family; sometimes he even goes to mass or to church; or, again, he may be an atheist or a Freemason. Only one condition is essential: He may not be a Jew.

He may be tall or short, young or old, fair or dark, patient or irascible, miserly or generous, a merchant or a lawyer, an army officer or a poet. He has only the one constant and invariable characteristic: He cannot live without the Jews.

He plays whist at the Blochs', and poker at the Kahns'; he goes to exhibitions with the Dreyfuses, and attends dress rehearsals with the Wolfs. He must be present when any of the Bernheims are married at the Synagogue of the Rue de la Victoire, or when any of the Levys are buried in the Cimetière Montparnasse.

He does not know exactly how all this came about. He had not known any of them; then, one day, he met some. His amazement was great: "They eat like anyone else! They drink like anyone else! They sleep like anyone else! They do everything like anyone else! Really, it's extraordinary!"

And, finding them like the rest of the world, he becomes filled with great admiration for them: "The most curious thing of all," he says, "is that they differ among themselves, just as we are not all alike. Not all of them are wealthy, not all of them are Boches, and not all of them are Bolsheviks. They have their cowards and their heroes, their traitors and their saints, their robbers as well as those who are robbed. Why, my dear fellow, I know some who are actual anti-Semites!"

And, having begun by admiring them for being like everyone else, he eventually comes to consider them better than anyone else.

Then he goes off into statistics: "Do you know how many Jews were admitted into the Conservatoire this year? Do you know how many Jews have received Nobel Prizes? Do you know that Jews are not susceptible to tuberculosis? Do you know that alcoholism does not exist among the Jews, that they have no criminals or prostitutes?"

Or he glories in celebrities: "Bergson is a Jew! Freud is a Jew! Einstein is a Jew! Spinoza was a Jew! Jesus Christ was a Jew!"

Or, again, he delves into genealogy: "Gambetta—why, of course he was one, on his mother's side! Montaigne—why, of course he was one, on his grandmother's side! Christopher Columbus—why, of course he was one—his great-grandmother was Jewish!"

Or he utters pious wishes: "If only we had their family affection! If only we had their spirit of solidarity! If only we were as philanthropic as they!"

Or he gushes forth regrets: "Do you know what we need? We don't have enough Jews in France! . . . And the franc! How do you expect it to go up? They didn't let the Jews attend to it. . . . As for the peace, that peace—ah! If, instead of Clemenceau, Lloyd George, Orlando and the others, they had put a half-dozen good Jews around the conference table, then I assure you, we would have had real peace, and a good treaty—they would have known what to do!"

Once he has reached this stage, the Friend of the Ghetto becomes an actual menace, for those Jews who are only half-Jewish, or one-fourth Jewish, or three-tenths Jewish; he takes hold of them, refuses to let go, insists on converting them to one-hundred-per-cent Jewishness:

"My dear fellow, do you mean to tell me that you eat ham? You travel on Saturday? You are going to marry a Christian girl? You won't let your babies be circumcized? You don't pay your shekel? You aren't going to Palestine? You have no right to act like this! Noblesse oblige! . . . Do you realize the responsibility you are taking upon yourself? If all the Jews did as you do, the Jews would soon disappear from the face of the earth! And what would become of us then?"

At this point the Friend of the Ghetto assumes an apocalyptic tone: "What? You who were destined to constitute a race unique among the nations —you would let that race perish? You who were chosen to carry abroad an eternal truth—you would let that truth fall into oblivion? You who were selected to sanctify the world by an endless martyrdom—you drink cocktails on the Place de l'Opera? It is your task to rebuild the holy land of your fathers— and you play golf on the greens of Saint-Cloud? No, my friend, as long as I am here I will not permit such things to happen. And if the fulfilment of your mission and the rebirth of your homeland demands that you be driven back into the Ghetto, then I'll vouch for it that you'll be driven back."

A charming fellow, isn't he, this Friend of the Ghetto? Yet there are Jews who think sometimes that he exaggerates.

MAKING THE CROOKED STRAIGHT

by HAYYIM NAHMAN BIALIK

IT was evening, and three of us were standing on the front platform of the street-car; on one end an elderly Jew, tall and gaunt; I, on the other end, facing him, and between us a fledgling lieutenant—about whose person everything cried, "new!"

At first I paid no attention to the old man. He was leaning, cane in hand, against the wire-meshed grill, keeping himself far in the shadow, where the faint light of the outer lamp hardly reached him. The young officer, who stood between us, shut him off from my view, so that I could see little of him beyond his gray hair fluttering with every jolt of the tram. But when, quite casually, I happened to look in his direction, he turned his head slightly aside and nodded—and instantly I recognized him. He was the old gentleman that I was always running into on the street, and who always nodded to me so politely.

Somewhere I must once have been introduced to him, but when and where I could not remember; nor could I recall ever having exchanged words with him; I knew neither his name nor occupation. Occasionally I would come upon him standing, he and his cane, on some street corner, or sauntering along, pausing to look at posters or the show-windows—and seeing me, he would nod.

His clothes would be threadbare, but fairly clean; his shoes patched in places, but polished. Every morning, it was obvious, the brush had worked assiduously over his clothes, seeking to remedy today what yesterday had spoiled. But never, apparently, with complete success; for whenever he became sensitive to some detecting gaze, the palm of his hand would move quickly to cover a patch or a stain. Sometimes I met him carrying a book or bundle, but his walk would be no more hurried than usual. Passing me, he would nod his head in silence, fix me for a moment with his soft, melancholy eyes, and plod quietly on his way. . . .

Yes, I said to myself, this man is one of those unfortunates who, having no permanent employment, wander all day long, from the time they arise in the morning to the time they retire at night, in a dead emptiness—lose themselves in it and wander about lost, like a tiny cloud in infinite sky. Or, more unhappily, they manage to attach themselves somewhere: through someone's pity, say, or through some casual introduction, they succeed—after numerous rebuffs and refusals—in gaining access to the homes of the well-to-do people. From whom, after being sent away repeatedly with a "come back tomorrow," they eventually obtain some sort of pay. They cannot help but see, poor souls! that the work given them—whether it be cataloguing the house library or arranging the family records (already done for the tenth time), or copying manuscripts (copied already eleven times), or tutoring a youthful gymnast through his bar-mizvah exercises—is neither essential nor suited to their abilities: is given to them, in fact, out of charity. They can make no terms, they must accept what is offered. Entering the rich man's house, they steal in through the back door like trespassers. And when they receive their pay, they lower their eyes, their faces flush, and all self-possession leaves them. They mutter an abrupt good-by, and suddenly find themselves out in the street, without knowing how they got there or through which door they came.

Some, as this man here appears to be, are men of breeding, with refined and gentle souls. Some are hypersensitive and sick with hopeless pride. But all of them suffer from the same sense of inferiority, the same self-consciousness, which conquers their spirit during the day, and gnaws at their bowels in the night. It is not so much poverty that humiliates them, but its outward signs: every patch in their clothing conceals a smarting wound, every stain scorches the flesh underneath it. . . .

So, I thought, one who pities men such as these, who does not wish to aggravate their torture, does well not to look at them any longer than formality requires. And that is how I was careful to act towards my elderly gentleman. I returned his nod with a slight nod and fixed my eyes on the front of the car.

The car stopped. Two more passengers, an older army officer and his wife, mounted the platform. The young officer drew to attention smartly and saluted. They diverted my attention, and I forgot all about the old man.

A few minutes later, however, I saw the young officer suddenly turn to the old man with a polite bow and a genteel wave of his gloved hand, at the same time saying softly:

"Sir, I beg your pardon."

This excessive politeness, like the new uniform he wore, betrayed the tyro. Here was a product of the military academy so recently graduated as to be still punctilious about the rules for a gentleman and an officer that he had learned in school, just as a bar-mizvah boy is careful with his tefillin the first few days he puts them on. How glad he must have been for the opportunity to display his academy manners in the presence of a senior officer!

What had made him beg the old man's pardon? Probably he had unwittingly jostled against him, or elbowed him by accident, or stepped on his toe. Whatever it was, the old man had not been aware of it. Taken aback, therefore, by the junker's unexpectedly courteous attention, he inclined his ear forward, and asked timidly and respectfully:

"What did you say, sir?"

"I humbly beg your pardon, sir," the junker repeated with even more exaggerated politeness than before.

"What? What?" the old man asked in amazement, refusing to believe his ears, and he bent forward even further, until his head was quite close to the young officer's.

Even then the junker did not quite lose his patience, and only his raised voice betrayed his irritation. He repeated his request for a pardon a third time, stressing each word by itself:

"I do ask your pardon, sir, very . . . very . . . much."

Now the old man grasped the matter. This handsome, elegant, young officer was begging pardon; not only that, but had been forced twice to repeat himself. And all on account of him. The old man was terribly embarrassed. Meeting, at this moment, the puzzled stare of the young officer, he was like one who is caught in some shameful act of weakness. With his lips he made a strange sound—*pfff*—accompanying it with a threefold gesture: shrugging his shoulders, spreading out his arms, and twisting his mouth in an odd fashion, all at the same time. It was hard to tell what he meant to convey, whether amazement, or apology, or humiliation, or disdain. Maybe the gesture included them all, and each of the four witnesses—the officer, his wife, the junker and myself—was privileged to the interpretation he liked best.

The old man stood there pitiably restless and ill at ease. That he had brought so much attention upon himself, that so many eyes were looking at him, seemed to hurt him beyond measure. He seemed to feel that all eyes were examining him from head to foot, that he was revealed before everyone in all of his shabbiness and inferiority. It was as if all the humiliating poverty of his life, all the wounds on his soul, and all the wounds on his honor, had suddenly opened mouths and cried out in one bitter voice: Why not? Is it so unusual that a young officer should ask pardon of a man like me? Do I not deserve, for once in my life, some measure of courteous attention? Can I never hope, not even for once in my life, to experience the feelings of a complete man, without patch or stain?

The old man's eyes moved about incessantly, in tortured embarrassment. The palm of his hand moved nervously over his threadbare clothes. It was obvious that he suffered excruciating pain. Yes, every patch had under it a deep sore, and each stain burned the brand of shame into his raw flesh.

He made hasty and furtive efforts to tidy himself. He resorted, all at one time, to all the devices he had ever employed. He hurriedly drew himself straight, smoothed his beard with a hasty gesture, straightened his hat on his head. Then he managed with the same quick motions to button his coat, covering thereby a yellow stain on his trousers. He moved his feet close together, concealing, in the one act, two large patches on his shoes. All these actions he performed hastily, almost all at one time, and, as it seemed to him, secretly, so as to attract no attention from his observers.

And at last he suddenly drew out a handkerchief, not overclean, from his pocket, and blew his nose upon it so violently that all the bystanders were shocked, particularly the polite and elegant young officer.

Poor man! In one moment he wanted to straighten out what so many years had made crooked!

AVROHMCHE NIGHTINGALE

by MEIR ARON GOLDSCHMIDT

THIS is a story about a poor old Jew who hanged himself for love, was cut down, and decided to hang on anyway.

Since it is only fair to tell such a story in detail and to start at the beginning, it would be well to say a few words concerning Leizer Suss.

Probably there are not many people who remember Leizer Suss, partly because he was not officially known by the name of Suss. He was called Lazarus, which is the same as Leizer. Either he must have inherited the name of Suss or obtained it by chance; for it means a horse, and he was by no means what one might call stupid. In the congregation he was respected for his piety, or rather his orthodox observance of all ceremonies. In consideration of this as well as of his poverty, he had been given the duties of a Shohet, that is a butcher and dealer in meat which the congregation could eat with all assurance of its orthodox preparation.

Besides this, there is not much to be said about him. He died almost unnoticed, leaving an elderly widow and six children—one daughter and five sons. According to the Jewish law, the latter had been educated until their thirteenth year, after which they supported themselves as apprentices in various business houses, one in Altona, the others in Copenhagen.

Years passed, and the family lived happily, according to the Latin rule: *Bene vixit qui bene latuit*—he lives well who lives unnoticed. The mother was aging, being about sixty years old, but healthy, active, and a trifle domineering. The daughter, Gitte, at this time nearing the forties, was still unmarried, either because she was poor and the daughter of a Shohet (defects which her beautiful brown eyes could not offset) or because she was unable to look after her own interests. There were probably various reasons which, grouped together, were called the will of God. Her brothers tried to make up for her loss through placid kindness, gifts, and occasional jokes. They were hard working and thrifty. Thus their earnings and consequently their contributions to the support of their mother and sister increased yearly. The four sons who lived in Copenhagen met in their mother's house every Friday evening just as regularly and unfailingly as she lighted and blessed the Sabbath candles.

Besides the slowly and modestly increasing prosperity, one more change had come into the family after the father's death; the brothers had slightly altered their last name. Michael, the oldest son who was living in Altona, had introduced this alteration. He was to be made a partner in the "House"—a haberdashery store—and one day the owner, whose name was also Lazarus, said to him, "Your name is Lazarus. Well, that is a good name—it is not for me to deny it. But one can get too much of a good thing. Lazarus and Lazarus—say what you like, that does not look right on a sign."

"But Lazarus and Co.—" said the future partner modestly.

"Lazarus and Co.? And if somebody asks, who is the Co.? Lazarus!—Turn it as you like: Lazarus and Lazarus!"

"Well, but—" said Michael, and stopped here without courage to express his thought, "Then perhaps you do not want me for a partner?"

After a slight pause the owner continued, "Tell me, had not your lamented father another name than Leizer?"

Michael blushed and did not answer.

"Of course it is between us, and that is not going to disturb your lamented father in his grave. But wasn't he sometimes called Leizer Suss?"

"That may well be," answered Michael.

"Well, there you are! Who says you are to keep every letter of your father's name, especially when he never bore it willingly! We shall change the u to an a. Lazarus and Sass—that isn't bad! That sounds nice!"

Thus the matter was decided, and as Michael, the head of the family, called himself Sass, one after the other of his brothers and, finally, his mother adopted the name. At first they did so with some apprehension, but as nobody objected, they made no further ceremony about it. It is possible or even probable that the congregation joked a little about the change; but as said above, no one objected.

The only person who did not like the new name was Avrohmche Nightingale. From his earliest youth he had been a friend of the family. He appeared at the Friday evening meetings as regularly as any of the sons. He had seen all of them grow up—he was eight years older than the oldest son—he had played with them, shared sorrow and joy with them. Once the possibility of his marrying Gitte had been considered, but it had passed away without causing any disturbance. Now, when along with the new name appeared several new pieces of furniture and a certain new atmosphere fraught with greater pretensions, he had a vague, uncertain sense of losing his hold. It was as if he did not "belong" as completely as formerly, as if his humble trade were noticed more than before. But nothing was tangible; it was only an indefinite perception which appeared one moment and vanished the next. Still, this was why he did not like the name of Sass, but he took good care not to say so.

Here the reader will ask, "But what was his humble trade?" Permit me to lead up to this information by describing the circumstances that decided his profession for him.

His father was called in the congregation Reb Schaie, with the surname of Pollok. He was one of the last men here with a long beard, a caftan, and a fur cap. Although his appearance thus reminded one of a "Polish vagabond," he was an intelligent and active member of society, and carried on a rather extensive business in fur and hides. He kept accounts—of which most business people in those days had a very incomplete knowledge—and was altogether a most exact, serious, and severe man. Of course he wanted his son to take up his business. But his Abraham (Avrohom, diminutive Avrohmche) developed a steadily increasing passion for music and singing. Not only did he insist on hearing good music as often as the chance offered itself, but once in a while he would give vent to utterances which indicated his wish, or rather enthusiastic hope, to perform in public some day—to go on the stage. For a time his father treated this as childishness, as a dream that would vanish when once he was working in the business. Contrary to his custom, he would even joke about the matter, and say with obvious sarcasm, "Avrohmche may still become a hazzan" (cantor in the synagogue). But one evening he happened to enter his son's attic room. There he came upon Avrohmche dressed in tights, with a feathered cap on his head, and singing a bravura to which the old music teacher, Leibche Schwein, also called Levin Snus, played the accompaniment on his guitar. Reb Schaie chased Leibche Schwein down the stairs, and said to Avrohmche, "Knitted underwear and a feathered cap! Why not the Grand Cross of Dannebrog? That my eyes have to see such a meschuggas! Do you realize how mad you are? I shall say only one word to you—listen: Those of the audience who will not hiss you for your long nose and your

crooked mouth—do you know why they will hiss you?"—"No, Father."—
"For your crooked legs."

These cruel but not quite unfair words destroyed an ideal, a hope, a goal
in the heart of Avrohmche. He was only nineteen years old, but from this
moment he was no longer young. He did not show his desperation. He complained to nobody. A spring had been broken in his soul, and it was as if
even the memory of this spring had vanished. But at the same time he had lost
a part of life itself. However, one deep and still passion remained—the passion
for music. As his father from now on gave him a still smaller allowance than
formerly, to prevent him from engaging a music teacher, the idea occurred to
him to rent a box in the theater and sell the tickets, thereby being enabled
to get in for nothing himself. For some time this worked very well; but just
as a plant needs a certain degree of warmth in order to blossom and bear fruit,
so any business undertaking, no matter how modest, needs a certain amount of
time and care. Not all theater tickets sell like hot cakes at all times. One must
be enterprising. There are competitors, chances, conjunctures to be met, and
Avrohmche was often cruelly torn between his duties to his father's business
and his own. The result was that he neglected both. Without knowing the true
reason, his father found more and more cause to be displeased with him, but
finally the whole matter came to light. Avrohmche had contracted debts which
amounted to much more than a single theater subscription would have cost,
and his creditors turned to his father. Reb Schaie paid the debts, gave Avrohmche a sum of money, and said in a low voice in which the Judæo-German
with its mysterious, execrating timbre had a power that could not be expressed in Danish, "Leave my house! Your theater madness will some day make
you look for a nail to hang yourself on! You are useless and good for nothing
on this earth! Out with you!"

At this time Leizer Suss and his wife turned out to be Avrohmche's best
and perhaps only friends. The occasion made Leizer Suss do something very
remarkable for him: He went straight to Reb Schaie to remonstrate with him
about his harshness to his son and to bring about a reconciliation; but he returned very crestfallen and never mentioned what had happened. Then he said
to Avrohmche, "You are not going to suffer want so long as I have a piece of
meat." He and his wife both did what they could to help the young man plan
for the future. As there was no hope of his conquering his passion, it was
deemed best for him to devote his life to the theater—not to the stage itself,
but to the renting of several boxes. His experience and some perseverance
would enable him to earn his living—to cut the matter short, he became a ticket
speculator. Now it is out, and after this introduction it does not seem so
very bad, and will not lessen the reader's sympathy for Avrohmche Nightingale.

But you will ask, "Whence came the surname of Nightingale?" That was
given him because of his unfortunate attempt to sing. The Jews have a remarkable talent for a particular kind of ironical surnames, and Mrs. Sass sometimes

used the name with a certain malice which did not indicate any illwill, but only showed that her friendship had not made her blind to her protégé's short-comings.

Leizer Suss died, and was followed shortly after by Reb Schaie, who left a small fortune to his son. The inheritance was smaller than expected, but still sufficient to have enabled Avrohmche with his modest wants to retire from business and live on his income. But art, even in the farthest corner of its court, has a fascination which few that have ever felt it can resist; and besides it is always hard for a man to give up his activity and his habits. Even the game of a ticket speculator has its emotions. There come triumphs which, although small, gladden his heart; on some evenings he rises to a certain importance, takes part in the life which pulsates so strongly on the stage, reflects in his face the fire of the drama. He could not find openings for other work, or perhaps had neither the wish nor the strength to strike a new path. So Avrohmche Nightingale remained a ticket speculator.

Perhaps at one moment he could have given up his profession. Shortly after his father's death, he thought it his duty to show his gratitude toward the Suss family by offering Gitte his hand and his inheritance. But Gitte refused him, and her mother did not try to influence her, perhaps because she still had other hopes for her daughter. Proposal and refusal were exchanged in all friendliness, and Avrohmche's relations with the family remained the same.

He lived in Pilestraede, where he had rented a room on the fourth floor of a house across the yard, close to the workshop of a carpenter. This gave his clothes a faint but persistent smell of shavings which made his competitors call his box the coffin. Occasionally he retorted wittily and maliciously, but preferred to mumble his pertinent remarks quietly to himself with a faint smile, instead of uttering them aloud. He was satisfied with the conscious-ness that he could retaliate if he wished. As an orthodox Jew and a man who had become a ticket speculator from necessity and not from choice, he felt an inner dignity which raised him above all criticism and even above his very profession.

Whoever met him at this point of his life—about his fiftieth year—saw a rather round-shouldered man, pale, with a gentle, fixed smile; with his hands crossed and hidden in his sleeves; with a curious little motion of his head to one side, as if continually and secretly beating time; while a wink or a twisting of his eyelids kept time with his nodding. He wore a long frock coat in summer and an equally long heavy overcoat in winter. People would have thought that the man's destiny was completed, that he was quietly and peacefully covering the longer or shorter distance to his grave.

Not at all! The crisis in Avrohmche's life was yet to come and was brought about by one single thoughtless word, or rather the thoughtless use of one single word: Suss.

One evening when he arrived at the Sass home, the door was opened by a strange servant girl. Seeing her face he understood at once that the family had changed servants, and in the same instant the old grudge against the name of Sass, with which he could never become familiar, gave him the malicious idea to ask, "Is Mrs. Suss at home?" The word slipped out of his mouth almost without his knowledge. He did not really mean to tell the maid that her mistress should rightfully be called Suss. Perhaps he hardly wanted her to hear the word; yet in that moment of deviltry he needed a confidant, just as King Midas's barber had to betray the secret of his donkey-eared master to somebody, even if only to a little tuft of grass in the field. He rejoiced in pronouncing the word, thus giving vent to his feelings. But the next moment, when the girl answered quietly, "Yes, Mrs. Sass is at home," he regretted it, partly because he felt the answer as a well-merited rebuke, and partly because he was afraid that the girl would report his remark to her mistress. But now it was too late. It would make matters worse to ask the maid to keep still, and moreover he had no time. The next moment he was shown into the living-room.

During the whole evening and the following days he was miserable. He said to himself, "Next time I go there I know how I shall be received. Mrs. Sass will pretend not to see me, and should I sneeze she will ask, 'Who is that? Oh, it's Pollok'—for she will not say Avrohmche. And if in the course of the evening she cuts an orange, she will pass the pieces round the other way, so that there will be nothing left when my turn comes. What do I care for the orange? But the expression of her face! The airs she will give herself! My insides shake with fright. That is the way she will treat me for a week or ten days, or perhaps longer, until a good play comes along, and I ask her to go. Then she may say, 'Well, I think Mrs. Suss might just as well go to the theater for once!' And she will give me a look that will prick my heart like two needles! That is what I get for my cursed talk!"

He did not dare to go to his friends, and yet did not dare to stay away. At last he had to go. He was received in the same natural, almost indifferent way as usual, and thought at first that it was the calm before the storm, staged purposely by the family so as to heighten the effect of the sudden and crushing thunderbolt. But it was soon beyond doubt that the barometer indicated fair weather, and he felt immensely relieved and grateful to Heaven as well as to the maid who had evidently kept quiet. One evening he found some pretext for going there, and brought a penny Christmas cake as a present for the maid. In those days maids and Christmas cakes were probably better than they are now, for she accepted the gift with thanks. Later, when she had to light him downstairs and open the street door for him, she thanked him again.

"You are very welcome," said Avrohmche; "you are a good girl. I am not going to tell you why you are a good girl, but you are. What is your name?"

"Emily."

"Emily! That is a nice name. How old are you?"

"Nineteen."

"Nineteen," said Avrohmche, for the first time looking straight into her pretty and fresh young face. He added naïvely, "You look like a good girl, too. Where is your home? Here in Copenhagen?"

"No, Sir, I am from Nakskov."

"From Nakskov? What was your father's business?"

"He is a currier."

"He is still living? Why did you not stay at home?"

"Father married again, and my stepmother wanted me to leave."

"Poor girl! You are a good girl—keep on being good!"

"Yes, Sir," she answered; but it is doubtful whether both meant the same thing. Avrohmche meant that she should keep on being silent about the word Suss.

Without quite being able to account for it, Avrohmche felt that evening and the following days that something unusual had happened. To be sure, he had been relieved of a great worry and danger; but it was not that alone. Although the conversation with the maid had been most insignificant, yet it was a quite new experience in his life. When did he converse with anybody except about tickets or the commonplace trivialities that were discussed in the Sass home? When did he ask an interested question, and when did the answer awaken such a gentle joy in his mind as these simple remarks from a girl who was content and glad by virtue of her youth? There comes a time in the life of every man when youth acquires a power over him of which he had no idea during his own youth. But his power was felt so much more strongly by Avrohmche because ordinarily nobody looked at him or spoke to him in such a friendly way, least of all anyone as pretty as this girl. A ray of joy shone into the soul of the old man, as if in some strange way he had met a sister whom he did not dare acknowledge, and also did not want to acknowledge; for it was far from any thought of his that there might be a more intimate or even cordial relation between him and a Gentile servant girl.

And yet it was a new joy to him every time the girl lighted him downstairs, and they exchanged a few words which always were almost identically the same as on the first evening. As he only wanted to hear her voice and occasionally glance at her fresh face, it hardly mattered to him what he asked her and what she answered, and he did not realize that he was making himself ridiculous by always repeating the same words—"You are from Nakskov?"— "Yes."—"And your father is a currier?"—"Yes."—"And your stepmother does not want you at home?"—"No."—"You are a good girl. Good-night."—And her clear, laughing voice, returning his good-night, kept ringing in his ears and made him very happy.

Something had entered his ordinary prosaic life, something to think of and long for, and this made him appear younger. He carried himself straighter. He met people with greater confidence and no longer displayed the bad temper which had come over him in his later years and which often had made him lose customers. He bought a new coat; and although he had every reason to do so (the old one was very shabby), this created quite a sensation among his business associates as well as in Kompagnistraede, where Mrs. Sass lived. "What has come over Nightingale?" people asked. If anyone else, even a man in his nineties, had changed this way, one would have said, at least jokingly, "He is in love, he is courting somebody." But nobody thought of making such a joke about Avrohmche, although this was actually the case; and Avrohmche himself did not have the faintest suspicion of the truth. For the first time in his life he enjoyed living. For the first time since his early youth he felt a longing which at the same time gave him happiness. The spring which his father had broken had in its own strange way regained its resilience. This had happened so gently and slowly, with such calmness and innocence, that he himself did not notice it except for his general feeling of joy. Perhaps this is the way the forest feels on a spring-like sunny day in November.

That winter "Svend Dyring's House" made its first appearance, and called forth not only great applause but also strong emotion, especially from the fair sex in the audience. It was said that several ladies had fainted from excitement. The following Friday evening the Sass brothers, who had all seen the play, expressed their delight with it or their approval of the public opinion; but all agreed that Mrs. Sass ought not to see it, the emotion would be too much for her. Avrohmche took a decidedly impartial stand. The play filled the boxes to overflowing—so far, so good. But on the other hand it did not appeal to his ear because it was not an opera, and the music in it was not to his taste. His heart was just then filled with admiration for "Massaniello" which was given during the same season, and even more for the "Slumber Aria"; and he considered the general enthusiasm for "Svend Dyring's House" a passing fad. Yet he wished Mrs. Sass to go and see it from his box and share the delight of her sons. Now more than ever he wanted to give pleasure to this family, and for the moment make himself a man of importance by giving tickets to Mrs. Sass and her daughter and escorting them to and from the theater. For these reasons he protested with unusual energy against the brothers' assertion that their mother would not be able to stand an emotional scene.

"Stand it?" he said. "What is there to stand? What reason is there to faint? I do not see it. A woman next to my box fainted, to be sure. But why did she faint? Because she was a fat brewer woman, and Henriksen had packed the box too full. Henriksen is a retseiach [an inconsiderate brute]. But am I going to pack my box too full when I am inviting a good friend, and will Mrs. Sass not get a good seat in the first row and without any crowding from the front or the back or the sides? Stand it?—Nonsense!"

But one of the sons insisted that the plot of the drama justified their fear. He quoted not incorrectly:

"Every mother full well will know
What milk in my breasts to thee can flow."

"How can mother stand that?" he added.

"Why not?" cried Avrohmche. "Does anybody have to be a woman to understand that? Am I a woman, or don't I know that a dead and buried mother who is nothing but a ghost has no milk in her breasts? If I know it, your mother knows it too, and is not going to faint over it."

Another son said gently and gravely, "Mother will think of our lamented father, may he rest in peace. When the dead woman goes away, and Dyring stretches his hands out to her and asks her to stay, Mother will think of our lamented father in his shroud."

"The Lord forbid!" cried Avrohmche. "I would not have that happen to save my soul! But is not your mother an intelligent woman? Will she not be sensible and say to herself: 'One of those women will have to go away, or the man has two wives, and who is to go? Who else than she who is dead and buried?'"

Perhaps Avrohmche's eloquence would have had no effect if the sons had not themselves chosen an argument which resulted in the opposite of what they had expected; for it is a well-known fact that women enjoy emotion, although they do not admit it openly. Mrs. Sass said with dignity, "I shall not think of your lamented father, may he rest in peace. Why should I? A man's wife has died and comes back—what is that to me? I am going."

During this discussion the servant girl had come and gone, and as she had never been inside a theater, her ideas about plays in general and "Svend Dyring's House" in particular were even hazier than those of the ordinary country girl. If possible, the mysterious repulsion and vast fascination of the play were increased when Mrs. Sass came home accompanied by Gitte and Avrohmche, and was received by all the sons as if returning from a journey. As soon as she entered, she cried proudly, "Did I faint? Was I sick? You tell them, Gitte. I did not even weep—what is there to weep about? But for the sake of appearances I wiped my eyes and blew my nose when the others wept. It certainly was fine— But wasn't she madly in love? Well, I suppose those times were different! But I did not understand that about the baked apple—"[1]

"The baked apple?" cried Avrohmche.

"Well, baked or roasted! What is the difference? Doesn't he roast an apple? What becomes of it? That is not explained—"

She realized from the embarrassment on her sons' faces and Avrohmche's twitching mouth that she had made a blunder, but she had no idea what it was, and maternal dignity did not permit her to dwell upon her mistake. She could not in the presence of her children allow her mind to be improved at the cost of her self-esteem. The subject was changed, and the actors, costumes, knights, the wicked Guldborg, and the poor children were discussed.

---

[1] The hero in "Svend Dyring's House" cuts love runes in an apple. The word riste in the combination riste runer means to cut. It also means to roast.

It seemed to the servant girl that it would be worth years of one's life to see something so wonderful. But how could it be done, how would it be possible to go there? Because Avrohmche Nightingale had given her a Christmas cake it did not at all follow that it was his duty to give her a ticket to the theater. It is true that his portentous secret was in her hands; but she did not even know it. She had not heard, or at least not understood, the profound difference between Suss and Sass, and even if she had known the secret she would hardly have thought of using it to obtain a ticket. In Avrohmche's mind, however, the feeling of his indebtedness was not only unimpaired, but had even grown stronger. Unconsciously the silver of gratitude had been interspersed with the gold of love. A few evenings later, when to his great happiness she was again lighting him down stairs, he said, "Do you know what it is to rist runes?"

"Yes, it is to cut them."

"Not to roast them, is it? Well, then you may go and see the play. Will you? Would you like to have a ticket?"

"Oh, Mr. Nightingale!" she exclaimed, and in an unconscious gesture of clasping her hands nearly dropped the candle.

"Well, my name is not really Nightingale. It is Pollok. But never mind. If you want to say Nightingale, do so; but it really is Pollok."

Probably the girl did not notice any improvement by the change, but she said, "I beg your pardon, Mr. Pollok! But oh, how kind you are!"

She said this with such heartiness in her voice and look that, if Avrohmche had been a young man without the fatal resemblance to the description of him given by his father, he would have been justified in believing that also in her case the silver of gratitude was mixed with a more precious metal. Avrohmche did not see himself but only her, and with the words, "We shall see about it," he went away happy.

The matter turned out to be more difficult than he had imagined, but the difficulties gave reason for joyful excitement. There was much to be considered and discussed. Emily could only go out every other Sunday. She hardly knew how to find the theater, still less the box. It was therefore natural that Avrohmche offered to come for her, wait at the door, take her to the theater, and afterwards see her home. If her own mother had lived, she could not have wished a more innocent escort for her daughter, and for Avrohmche it was a late but veritable rendezvous with all its yearning and secrecy—he was at last young and happy!

Emily had dressed as for a dance, in a lowcut jaconet dress, but with a little silk kerchief laid modestly round her neck. She looked so pretty and almost ladylike that Avrohmche was quite proud to take her to the box. To protect her from too much attention he gave her a seat in the second row. He placed himself behind in the third row and kept bending over her, explaining the proceedings on the stage or preparing her for what was coming. Polite and grateful for his attention, however tiresome it was, she turned toward him as often as possible, whereby the little silk kerchief slipped down unnoticed in the heat of the theater. With the feeling that something was being revealed to his eyes which they had not an honest right to see, Avrohmche gently and conscientiously put the kerchief back in its place every time it fell. This manœuver very soon attracted the attention of a young man in the box next to Emily, whose eyes were not so discreet as Avrohmche's. He thought at first that it was a jealous old husband who had brought his wife to the theater. Soon, however, he recognized Nightingale, and the matter became quite incomprehensible and interesting to him. It seemed to be a nice coquettish young girl whom the ticket speculator volunteered to shield. After the fall of the curtain he addressed a remark to Emily, and since she did not think it right to reveal her position as a stranger among all these charming people who seemed like a big assembly of friends, she answered pleasantly and gratefully, which, however, was quite misunderstood by the young man. Avrohmche could not forbid her to answer, neither could he give her any advice or hint. At the same time he felt all the pangs of jealousy, whether the young man spoke to her or merely looked at her. He wished for the strength and courage of ten men so as to choke the intruder or at least throw him out.

The curtain was again raised, and the progress of the play affected Avrohmche in a hitherto entirely undreamt-of way. A deeply hidden poetic instinct stirred suddenly in his soul, revealing to him that the spirit or mood developing on the stage and taking hold of the audience (we call it romance) was something that he had outgrown long ago or in which, rightly or not, his soul was denied a part, whereas Emily and even the odious young man had the sanction of the world to enjoy the emotion to its full extent. He felt this with unspeakable anguish, as if hearing his own death-warrant or being present at his own funeral. Never had any play impressed him as this one did.

"All the little pictures turned to the wall—"

The knights and ladies and young lovers suddenly remembered his father's words, and said to him, "Why will they hiss you? For your crooked legs!" And he saw himself answering to this description, repulsive and a stranger among the others, miserably rejected. But the music, which he had scorned because it was different from that of "Massaniello," came upon him now and took hold of his organism, gave him artificial youth, tossed him around as if he "belonged," although he knew that he was an outcast.

Why should he not be happy? He could marry the girl. Yes, of course, he could offer his hand to the currier's daughter! He would be excommunicated, but within his soul he would remain a Jew!—And what if they did excommunicate him! What had his life been but a cold, clammy fog! After all, whether as a blessing or a curse, this woman was the only ray of light in his existence— it seemed rank insanity to let her be snatched away from him. He did not have to remain in Copenhagen. He could move to the country and live with her in some quiet, hidden, and cheap place. At least he was an honorable man. Could that be said about the cad in the other box? He would be happy, he was bound to be happy! His decision only needed words to be irrevocable—and here the curtain fell.

Where was his real life? In the box with the girl and the tenderness and jealousy called forth by her? Although he was so close to her, he could not find one fitting word to say, but heard with disgust his own voice saying—"Is it all right? Are you having a good time? Do you like it?" Whereas he wanted to say, "Speak to nobody! Look at nobody! Become my wife!"

Or was real life on the stage where the last act was beginning, where he again was suffering on account of his age, again became young, again made his decision? Verily, the tempest had seized Avrohmche Nightingale. Oh, you sympathetic souls, you would have wept to look into him and laughed to look at him.

Stunned by so many emotions, he left the box with Emily after the end of the play, as a ship leaves the stormy sea for the port. But the young man walked close to them, and at the foot of the stairs, when the collision with the audience from the pit caused a confusion in the crowd, he succeeded in pushing Avrohmche aside and offered his arm to Emily. Avrohmche cried out—his words can be explained only by the storm that had just passed over him, or perhaps by a wish to arouse sympathy, securing some rights for himself. He cried, "Stop! Help! He is stealing my wife!" The young man slipped away like an eel. In the same instant several hundred eyes were turned toward the well-known speculator, and in the sudden silence after his words he had in a flash furnished people with a story to be told at the supper-table or elsewhere.

A few moments later they were in the street. Avrohmche crossed the square silently. The moment had come for him to speak, but there were still too many people around them. He wanted to reach Vingaardstraede before he asked her to sign the document to which he had put his seal. But when he was about to speak and turned toward her, he saw that she was crying.

"What is the matter?" he exclaimed in dismay. "Why are you crying?"

"Because you disgraced me by calling me your wife."

He did not understand that every young girl who is publicly and against her will represented as being married may feel this as a disgrace, and that the country girl felt bitterly that she had been the center of a small scandal. He interpreted her words as the declaration that she considered a marriage with him, the Jew, as a disgrace, and in the same moment he had fallen from his own heaven, even though he was still uncured. He said no word, not even good-night when they parted.

Neither did he say good-evening to the carpenter's journeyman who as usual came out on the stairs and handed him a small lantern, for according to tradition no one was allowed to carry an uncovered light in or near the workshop. The journeyman lived there and was the night-watchman.

As soon as Avrohmche was in his room he gave vent to his feelings.

"Ausgefallene Schtrof'! I must have sinned in my mother's womb so as to be made not only meschugge but meschugge metorf! [stark crazy] To call that out to everybody! Where were my senses? Did I ever have any? Am I born blind and deaf and mad? Shema Yisröel! That will be the death of me! How can one live after having been such a cursed fool? How can one? Oi! Oi! Oi! They all heard it, and they heard still more! Tomorrow they will tell that I have children around here, and how can I prove that it is fiction and lies, that I belied myself? Should I ask her to state—no, that way is still worse than the other—if only she had been willing! But I was willing, I scoundrel, I scoffer of Israel! Can I ever forget? I can never forget it!—Avrohmche, Avrohmche, one minute has made you an unhappy man! Oi! Oi und Weh!"

On this occasion a strange thing happened. He realized his misfortune, but could not quite understand it. Something in his head snapped whenever he tried fully to see and comprehend the double curse upon his fate. He had disgraced himself before the public and the congregation for the sake of happiness, but this happiness had changed to misery and humiliation. The disgrace remained and became intensified. His mind circled wildly round his dilemma, trying to get at the center of it, but screamed with pain before reaching its goal, and rushed back to the circumference.

All this did not take place in silence. Through the thin wall the journeyman heard him rush back and forth, speak to himself, curse and moan; and having noticed his haggard face on the stairs, the young man came up to his room.

"Are you sick, Mr. Pollok?" he asked, looking in.

Avrohmche grasped his head and said, "Toothache! Yes, toothache! Terrible!"

"Is it a molar?" asked the journeyman and came nearer.

"A molar? It is worse than that! It is Schikse!" [Gentile girl] answered Avrohmche, finding a certain relief in confiding in another person without betraying himself.

"Then it is a dog-tooth?"

"No, I wouldn't say that. But I feel like a dog myself. I am tormented like a dog, oh! oh!"

"But where does it hurt?" asked the man, holding the lantern up to Avrohmche's face.

"It is rheumatism. I am getting old. I am an old horse and a big ass, I ought to be dragged out to Amager like the other old horses. Well, they are going to drag me out—just wait and see!"

"Well, I suppose you must have it out; but that cannot be done until tomorrow."

"Tomorrow! I wish tomorrow would never come!" answered Avrohmche with a shudder.

"Come, come, Mr. Pollok!—Don't you want to take something for it?"

"Take something?—What is there to take? What do you know about it? A young and good-looking man like you is happy—I mean," he added, getting better hold of himself, "a young man with such good, fine teeth."

"Still I have been through it."

"You have? What did you do? I tell you, you have not been through it."

"Yes, I poured some brandy on the tooth."

"Brandy on the tooth," said Avrohmche slowly. Instinctively he felt the need of warmth and cheer, and the advice seemed good to him. "Where can I get it? Have you a little?"

With the quiet satisfaction felt by laymen whose remedy for some ailment is being accepted, the journeyman went to his room and brought back a blue flask and a thick, broadfooted glass.

Taking the glass, Avrohmche wanted to say a Jewish prayer, but there came over him a ghastly feeling of having forfeited the right to do this, of having in thought and intention forsaken his God and his people. In despair, he emptied the glass without further ceremony. After the first shock of the unaccustomed drink, he felt warmed through and through, and said, "That was good just the same!"

"It did not quite get to the tooth," said the journeyman.

Avrohmche answered with a strange laugh, "It did not get to the tooth, and still it got there."

"Well, it does you good anyway," said the man, pouring out a glass for himself and emptying it.

"How could it get to the right tooth?" continued Avrohmche. "If it could get to the right tooth, I should not be here, and you would not be here, and there would be no need of it."

The journeyman did not understand this dark, talmudistic speech and answered simply, "Take one more little drink."

"Well, a very small one."

Avrohmche took another swallow and admitted gratefully that he felt much better now. The journeyman bade him good-night and went away.

But when he had gone, the human sympathy and temporary distraction had also vanished, and the dreadful reality burst forth anew, combining with the drink to lash Avrohmche's consciousness to the fever point. The facts seemed impossible to him, yet he could not deny them. It was as if there were some creature in the room with him which now hid in a corner, now would jump at him, seize his throat, throw him down. Meanwhile his thoughts and memories chased around as in the wild whirl of madness, and he saw conflicting events in simultaneous action: Emily, gliding away from the square like a shadow; the young man from the box, laughing in his face; the crowd in the vestibule immeasurably far below him. The air was full of buzzing and laughter, of the ringing music of "Svend Dyring's House" and the rebel scene of "Massaniello"; and in the midst of it all soared his father, pale as death and saying to him, "Your theater madness will some day make you look for a nail to hang yourself on! You are useless and good for nothing on this earth!"— When this horror vanished for a moment, the horror of the morrow rushed out of the corner in the shape of another ghost.

It was unbearable; still he could not shake it off. He could not even utter a shriek, but remained groping in the middle of the darkened room as in a nightmare, with only one vague longing—to slip away from life which held no refuge for him.

What awakens the thought of suicide? The doctors call it a disease, a sort of insanity. But when and how is the harmony of our mysterious secret organism transformed into the discord which reveals insanity and gives us the impulse? And how can insanity make a man hang himself, an undertaking which in the eyes of normal people is difficult and requires a good deal of intelligence? We have some kind of experience in all other ways of suicide. Everybody has sometime in his life cut himself, wounded himself with a pointed instrument, or drunk something nauseating. Those that kill themselves by shooting have previously handled guns or pistols, but no one has had experience in hanging himself on a nail or a hook. And still people do this very thing at the critical moment with an assurance which seems a weird stroke of genius piercing insanity.

How did it occur to Avrohmche to hang himself? He was standing on the brink of insanity, but he had not yet tumbled down. His dead father was pointing to the nail that he was to hang himself on, yet Avrohmche had never taken this for more than a figure of speech. He wanted to have done with life, but had not yet lost the instinct of self-preservation, of love for himself as a living being. A seeming trifle decided his fate. During his terrible delirium he saw something on the wall that had a human shape. It was his old coat hanging on a nail. Suddenly it was as if he had a companion, a fellow-being near him, and he was filled by a great desire to approach this fellow-being. After what seemed an infinitely long time, he managed by exerting his whole strength to take a step toward this friend in need and seize him—only to find that it was a mere empty shell of a man, perhaps of his own father. Through his disappointed or frightened fingers a sensation rose to his brain and completed the madness: With incredible haste and clearness he remembered that the maid had lately stretched a new clothesline outside the window. Then he was certain of having seen a big nail under the ceiling. In an instant he had hauled in the clothesline and had hung himself.

But again he had made more noise than he was aware of, and hardly had accomplished his deed before the journeyman was in the room and had cut him down.

Thus Avrohmche did not kill himself, but was nevertheless more dead than living. The journeyman called for help, and the patient was taken to the hospital.

In the city the strange rumor about his marriage was spread almost simultaneously with the news that he had been taken to the hospital delirious or insane. The latter news swallowed up the former. When a man is overtaken by a commonplace misfortune he ceases to be interesting. Only the Sass family did not quite feel this way. To be sure, their sympathy with him on account of his illness had a hard struggle with their indignation over his secrecy and slyness in getting married. Still his very marriage called forth the conception of something grandly preposterous and inconceivable. The most reliable information from all around the city threw no light on the subject. At his lodging it was said that he had been out of his head and had tried to commit suicide, but the journeyman as well as his master and the whole family were greatly surprised when the question about his wife came up. In the vestibule of the theater he had been seen and his exclamation heard, but nobody in the crowd had noticed his wife. Even though somebody had seen Emily among other women near him, she was the last person in the world to be taken for his companion through life. Some people said indifferently that it was probably no one else than Gitte Sass whom he had married. When the Sass family tried to identify his wife around town, they were to their great surprise directed to their own home. It did not occur to them that her home really might be said to be in their kitchen, and that a single question to their servant girl would have put them on the trail of the truth.

Meanwhile he who could have given the best information, if he had been so minded, was in the hospital. For some time it was not known whether or not his mind was clear, and therefore no visitors were allowed. He was lying there protected against the world by his very illness and the inviolability of the hospital. When his convalescence began, accompanied by the usual state of happiness, impotence, and renewed life, the previous events stood before his mind without pain, veiled in a strange haze. He realized with delight that he was not married and had not forsaken the congregation. Let whoever wanted to do so come and investigate. Even if he had said so himself, it was nevertheless not true. But why had he said so? Here his head began to swim again. He hoped that Emily would keep silent about his love, as she had kept silent about the word Suss, but still this point worried him the most. He did not know that he had never betrayed the secret of his love to her or anybody else.

By this time Mrs. Sass had had an opportunity to reflect and overcome her first indignation over his slyness. She began to doubt it and consider many possibilities. Even if he had not married, he might still do so. Worse things had been known to happen; there were plenty of widows or elderly maids who might be suggested to him by the Jewish matrimonial agent. People knew very well that he had money. How could she have forgotten it, over-

looked it with her eyes wide open? His new coat? If not a sign of his marriage
—all things considered, that was not likely—it was a sign that he was not
averse to change. She did not understand herself. She had only herself to blame
if he had married. She would have deserved the annoyance of seeing him and
his money annexed by another family, by people who had never been good to
him and would not have opened their home to him when his own father had
turned against him. But was he really married or not? For the present all de-
pended on this.

At last the moment came to find out. She was sitting at his bedside and
asked him—or rather did not ask him but remarked, "Avrohmche, people say
that you were taken ill because you have nobody to care for you and are
neglecting yourself altogether."

"Who should take care of me?" asked Avrohmche languidly, and purposely
with great innocence. But at once he became frightened. She might answer,
"Perhaps our servant girl, Emily?" His anxiety made him look so deathly pale
and livid that Mrs. Sass, fearing that he was feeling worse, broke off the conversation. But at home she said, "He is no more married than my cat!"

At her next visit she said, "Avrohmche, are you strong enough to discuss
your future with me?"

He had no objection to the future, if one would only leave the past alone.
So he answered, "The future will be that I shall be buried!"

"Stuff and nonsense! There is nothing the matter with you. You never
looked better than now!"

Avrohmche did not trouble himself about the true meaning of the ambigu-
ous compliment; he was listening as quietly as a mouse.

She continued, "We have spoken of your future before—do you remember?
When my lamented husband was living?"

"Gebenscht soll er sein! If anybody is in Gan Eden [Paradise], it is he."

"Please God, yes. Do you know what he would say if he were alive?"

Avrohmche was again overcome by fear. He expected her to say, "My dear
Leizer would say that you ought not to make a fool of yourself with our
servant girl."—He managed to say, "He would speak gently."

She nodded slowly and significantly as she answered, "Yes, he would
speak gently. He would say, Avrohmche, you are too good to go around in the
rain and cold every evening, and be taken ill and die in the hospital. You must
have somebody to live with you and take care of you and be good to you in
your own home. You ought to marry, Avrohmche."

It was coming—now it was only as much as a hair's breadth away from
him, and in a second the scornful, crushing remark would have reached him,
"You ought to marry our servant girl." He groaned, "It is all over with me,"
and closed his eyes to the lightning.

"Nonsense, Avrohmche! It is never all over.—Do you believe that my son
Isaac is an honest and honorable and decent and hard-working man?"

What was that? She was speaking of her son! Her thoughts were not where he had feared! He opened his eyes.

"Do you believe that?" she repeated.

"Do I? Indeed I do!"

"And do you believe that he understands his business?"

"Kol Yisröel ought to have sons like Isaac! Can I say more?"

"Well, Isaac wants to go into business for himself. You put your little capital into his business, and the Lord will provide for the rest!"

Now Avrohmche understood perfectly. He realized that he was saved and felt it as a miracle, and in return for the marvelous concealment of his dissipation he thought it only fair that he should marry Gitte.

He addressed hurriedly a blessing to the Lord, and asked almost without thinking, "But what is Gitte going to say?"

"Gitte," said Mrs. Sass, "is a sensible girl and past her childhood. And am I not here?"

The next day Gitte came alone.

Without any preamble she said, "Pollok, mother says that you and I must marry."

Avrohmche answered, "She said the same to me."

She continued, "We are no longer children, Pollok. You would get a poor old maid. Well, you know that. But I must ask you something."

"If I can answer you, go ahead, Gitte."

"You can answer. You are the only one that can and the only one that must. Is it a sin to be fond of a Gentile—I mean really to love, to be in love with a Gentile?"

Avrohmche had thought himself perfectly safe; now the question overwhelmed him so that he nearly fainted. But he managed to collect himself and raise a small barricade. "Sin?" he said. "There are greater sins."

"But suppose I had been in love with a Gentile, what then?"

"You!" cried Avrohmche, and a new thought was born in him. He was a man, the lord and judge of women. But at once he wavered. Was it a trap? Or what kind of a tale was this? He dared say no more.

She did not heed him, but went on, "Of course it would be a sin against the Lord if I were going to hide something from the husband He is giving me."

She seemed to be in earnest, and the thought took hold of Avrohmche.

"Who is he?" he cried. "What kind of a man is he? Where did you meet him?"

"He was an officer."

"An officer! Soldiers exist because of our sins, and officers because of our great sins! An officer! How did you meet an officer?"

"I don't know, Pollok. I suppose it was g'sardin. I was walking in the street, and all at once his eyes were looking into mine. I had never seen him before. It was something quite new. It was as if both of us had been created that very moment."

"One pays no attention to such a person—an officer! One simply walks past him."

"Did I not walk past him? I almost went into the wall of the house to make way for him. I turned into air, I turned into nothing, and I passed him."

"Well; past is past. That was the end of it—wasn't it?"

"No. One day as I was sitting at the window, suddenly he stood in the street, looking up. I thought I should fall out of the window. I could not help it."

"Ausgefallene Schtrof'!" cried Avrohmche with a bitterly humorous pun. "I understand—then you began to meet him in the street."

"Then I began to meet him in the street."

"What did he say?"

"For God's sake, Pollok! How could he have addressed me?—I should have screamed! I should have died! Speak to an officer in the street! I never looked at him any more!"

"Well," said Avrohmche with a faint smile, "if you neither spoke to him nor looked at him—"

"Pollok, I am going to tell the truth. That is why I came. I did not speak to him, but I thought of him, and when I met him I felt that he knew it."

"And you say you did not look at him?"

"I did not look at him."

"Schkorum [lies]," murmured Avrohmche and turned half against the wall.

"I did not look at him, and I stayed at home and never went out alone."

"That is good. Very good."

"But he wrote to me."

"He did not speak, but he wrote?—What am I to hear, Gitte? Why beat about the bush? You had much better tell me the whole story straight out."

"But I am telling you that he wrote to me."

"What did he write?"

"He wrote—what does one write to a young girl? He wanted to see me and speak to me; he wanted to meet me."

"That is what they always write. One does not pay any attention."

"One does not pay any attention! Pollok, when you took mother and me to the theater to see 'Svend Dyring's House' and they began to speak of runes, I understood what runes were; but you did not understand it, Pollok."

"Much she knows about it," murmured Avrohmche to himself. After a short silence he went on. "Runes. In the play she runs after him."

"I did not run after him. How could I? How could I have escaped from mother and my brothers?"

"That is so. You are a good girl, Gitte. You stayed at home. And then at last it was over, really over?"

"Then one Friday afternoon I received a letter in which he told me that he was going away Sunday morning, and now he had a wish as urgent as that of a dying man; he wished to see me just once, and I was to decide myself what time I could come on Saturday evening.—And I could have gone, for mother was going to the theater, and my brothers were not coming home. And he implored me like a man before his death!"

"Runes," said Avrohmche, "that *verschwarzte* writing! Those cursed runes! The Lord curse him who invented them! Omein!—Well, then you went?"

"No, for when I was going to write and set the time and place, it was Sabbath eve, and mother had lighted the Sabbath candles, and of course then one is not allowed to write."

"And so you really did not write?" asked Avrohmche, although he found it very natural.

"I had the pen in my hand; but when I was going to put it to the paper and for the first time in my life break the Sabbath, my father arose before me in his shroud."

"Well?"

"Well. And Saturday evening when I could write again, it was too late, and it was all over. And I thanked God."

"When did this happen? How long ago?"

"That was when you proposed to me the first time, twenty years ago."

"Twenty years!" cried Avrohmche, and sat up in bed. "Gitte! In the name of the Almighty God! I have been in love with a Schikse, not twenty days ago!"

"You, Pollok?—Poor Avrohmche!"

"Will you pardon me, Gitte?—It was for her sake that I wanted to hang myself—I was mad, raving mad; but that is why I am lying here! But now it is all over, Gitte; will you bear with me and pardon me?"

"Poor Avrohmche, my husband before God! Let us remember the dead and keep together until the Angel of Death comes!"

Some time after, Avrohmche turned up in his old lodgings to move his belongings to another place which had been prepared for him. He looked just as he had before his great adventure, only paler, but this was rather becoming. The journeyman came to say good-bye, and said to himself that Avrohmche looked as if he had been whitewashed inside, but both men were embarrassed. At last Avrohmche cut the matter short and said, "Well, I was mad, raving mad, and wanted to take my life. You saved me and cut me down—still I hung on! But now I am hanging on to myself in the right way!"

BUCHMENDEL

by STEFAN ZWEIG

Having just got back to Vienna, after a visit to an out-of-the-way part of the country, I was walking home from the station when a heavy shower came on, such a deluge that the passers-by hastened to take shelter in doorways, and I myself felt it expedient to get out of the downpour. Luckily there is a café at almost every street-corner in the metropolis, and I made for the nearest, though not before my hat was dripping wet and my shoulders were drenched to the skin. An old-fashioned suburban place, lacking the attractions (copied from Germany) of music and a dancing-floor to be found in the centre of the town; full of small shopkeepers and working folk who consumed more newspapers than coffee and rolls. Since it was already late in the evening, the air, which would have been stuffy anyhow, was thick with tobacco-smoke. Still, the place was clean and brightly decorated, had new satin-covered couches, and a shining cash-register, so that it looked thoroughly attractive. In my haste to get out of the rain, I had not troubled to read its name—but what matter? There I rested, warm and comfortable, though looking rather impatiently through the blue-tinted window panes to see when the shower would be over, and I should be able to get on my way.

Thus I sat unoccupied, and began to succumb to that inertia which results from the narcotic atmosphere of the typical Viennese café. Out of this void, I scanned various individuals whose eyes, in the murky room, had a greyish look in the artificial light; I mechanically contemplated the young woman at the counter as, like an automaton, she dealt out sugar and a teaspoon to the waiter for each cup of coffee; with half an eye and a wandering attention I read the uninteresting advertisements on the walls—and there was something agreeable about these dull occupations. But suddenly, and in a peculiar fashion, I was aroused from what had become almost a doze. A vague internal movement had begun; much as a toothache sometimes begins, without one's being able to say whether it is on the right side or the left, in the upper jaw or the lower. All I became aware of was a numb tension, an obscure sentiment of spiritual unrest. Then, without knowing why, I grew fully conscious. I must have been in this café once before, years ago, and random associations had awakened memories of the walls, the tables, the chairs, the seemingly unfamiliar smoke-laden room.

The more I endeavoured to grasp this lost memory, the more obstinately did it elude me; a sort of jellyfish glistening in the abysses of consciousness, slippery and unseizable. Vainly did I scrutinize every object within the range of vision. Certainly when I had been here before the counter had had neither

marble top nor cash-register; the walls had not been panelled with imitation
rosewood; these must be recent acquisitions. Yet I had indubitably been here,
more than twenty years back. Within these four walls, as firmly fixed as a nail
driven up to the head in a tree, there clung a part of my ego, long since over-
grown. Vainly I explored, not only the room, but my own inner man, to
grapple the lost links. Curse it all, I could not plumb the depths!

It will be seen that I was becoming vexed, as one is always out of humour
when one's grip slips in this way, and reveals the inadequacy, the imperfections,
of one's spiritual powers. Yet I still hoped to recover the clue. A slender thread
would suffice, for my memory is of a peculiar type, both good and bad; on the
one hand stubbornly untrustworthy, and on the other incredibly dependable.
It swallows the most important details, whether in concrete happenings or in
faces, and no voluntary exertion will induce it to regurgitate them from the
gulf. Yet the most trifling indication—a picture postcard, the address on an
envelope, a newspaper cutting—will suffice to hook up what is wanted as an
angler who had made a strike and successfully imbedded his hook reels in a
lively, struggling, and reluctant fish. Then I can recall the features of a man
seen once only, the shape of his mouth and the gap to the left where he had
an upper eye-tooth knocked out, the falsetto tone of his laugh, and the twitching of the moustache when he chooses to be merry, the entire change of expression which hilarity effects in him. Not only do these physical traits rise before my mind's eye, but I remember, years afterwards, every word the man
said to me, and the tenor of my replies. But if I am to see and feel the past
thus vividly, there must be some material link to start the current of associations. My memory will not work satisfactorily on the abstract plane.

I closed my eyes to think more strenuously, in the attempt to forge the hook
which would catch my fish. In vain! In vain! There was no hook, or the fish
would not bite. So fierce waxed my irritation with the inefficient and mulish
thinking apparatus between my temples that I could have struck myself a
violent blow on the forehead, much as an irascible man will shake and kick a
penny-in-the-slot machine which, when he has inserted his coin, refuses to
render him his due.

So exasperated did I become at my failure that I could no longer sit quiet,
but rose to prowl about the room. The instant I moved, the glow of awakening
memory begain. To the right of the cash-register, I recalled, there must be a
doorway leading into a windowless room, where the only light was artificial.
Yes, the place actually existed. The decorative scheme was different, but the
proportions were unchanged. A square box of a place, behind the bar—the card-
room. My nerves thrilled as I contemplated the furniture, for I was on the track,
I had found the clue, and soon I should know all. There were two small billiard-tables, looking like silent ponds covered with green scum. In the corners,
card-tables, at one of which two bearded men of professional type were playing
chess. Beside the iron stove, close to a door labelled "Telephone," was another

small table. In a flash I had it! That was Mendel's place, Jacob Mendel's. That was where Mendel used to hang out, Buchmendel. I was in the Café Gluck! How could I have forgotten Jacob Mendel? Was it possible that I had not thought about him for ages, a man so peculiar as well-nigh to belong to the Land of Fable, the eighth wonder of the world, famous at the university and among a narrow circle of admirers, magician of book-fanciers, who had been wont to sit there from morning till night, an emblem of bookish lore, the glory of the Café Gluck? Why had I had so much difficulty in hooking my fish? How could I have forgotten Buchmendel?

I allowed my imagination to work. The man's face and form pictured themselves vividly before me. I saw him as he had been in the flesh, seated at the table with its grey marble top, on which books and manuscripts were piled. Motionless he sat, his spectacled eyes fixed upon the printed page. Yet not altogether motionless, for he had a habit (acquired at school in the Jewish quarter of the Galician town from which he came) of rocking his shiny bald pate backwards and forwards and humming to himself as he read. There he studied catalogues and tomes, crooning and rocking, as Jewish boys are taught to do when reading the Talmud. The rabbis believe that, just as a child is rocked to sleep in its cradle, so are the pious ideas of the holy text better instilled by this rhythmical and hypnotizing movement of head and body. In fact, as if he had been in a trance, Jacob Mendel saw and heard nothing while thus occupied. He was oblivious to the click of billiard-balls, the coming and going of waiters, the ringing of the telephone bell; he paid no heed when the floor was scrubbed and when the stove was refilled. Once a red-hot coal fell out of the latter, and the flooring began to blaze a few inches from Mendel's feet; the room was full of smoke, and one of the guests ran for a pail of water to extinguish the fire. But neither the smoke, the bustle, nor the stench diverted his attention from the volume before him. He read as others pray, as gamblers follow the spinning of the roulette board, as drunkards stare into vacancy; he read with such profound absorption that ever since I first watched him the reading of ordinary mortals has seemed a pastime. This Galician second-hand book dealer, Jacob Mendel, was the first to reveal to me in my youth the mystery of absolute concentration which characterizes the artist and the scholar, the sage and the imbecile; the first to make me acquainted with the tragical happiness and unhappiness of complete absorption.

A senior student introduced me to him. I was studying the life and doings of a man who is even today too little known, Mesmer the magnetizer. My researches were bearing scant fruit, for the books I could lay my hands on conveyed sparse information, and when I applied to the university librarian for help he told me, uncivilly, that it was not his business to hunt up references for a freshman. Then my college friend suggested taking me to Mendel.

"He knows everything about books, and will tell you where to find the information you want. The ablest man in Vienna, and an original to boot. The man is a saurian of the book-world, an antediluvian survivor of an extinct species."

We went, therefore, to the Café Gluck, and found Buchmendel in his usual place, bespectacled, bearded, wearing a rusty black suit, and rocking as I have described. He did not notice our intrusion, but went on reading, looking like a nodding mandarin. On a hook behind him hung his ragged black overcoat, the pockets of which bulged with manuscripts, catalogues, and books. My friend coughed loudly, to attract his attention, but Mendel ignored the sign. At length Schmidt rapped on the table-top, as if knocking at a door, and at this Mendel glanced up, mechanically pushed his spectacles on to his forehead, and from beneath his thick and untidy ashen-grey brows there glared at us two dark, alert little eyes. My friend introduced me, and I explained my quandary, being careful (as Schmidt had advised) to express great annoyance at the librarian's unwillingness to assist me. Mendel leaned back, laughed scornfully, and answered with a strong Galician accent:

"Unwillingness, you think? Incompetence, that's what's the matter with him. He's a jackass. I've known him (for my sins) twenty years at least, and he's learned nothing in the whole of that time. Pocket their wages—that's all such fellows can do. They should be mending the road, instead of sitting over books."

This outburst served to break the ice, and with a friendly wave of the hand the bookworm invited me to sit down at his table. I reiterated my object in consulting him; to get a list of all the early works on animal magnetism, and of contemporary and subsequent books and phamphlets for and against Mesmer. When I had said my say, Mendel closed his left eye for an instant, as if excluding a grain of dust. This was, with him, a sign of concentrated attention. Then, as though reading from an invisible catalogue, he reeled out the names of two or three dozen titles, giving in each case place and date of publication and approximate price. I was amazed, though Schmidt had warned me what to expect. His vanity was tickled by my surprise, for he went on to strum the keyboard of his marvellous memory, and to produce the most astounding bibliographical marginal notes. Did I want to know about sleep-walkers, Perkins's metallic tractors, early experiments in hypnotism, Braid, Gassner, attempts to conjure up the devil, Christian Science, theosophy, Madame Blavatsky? In connexion with each item there was a hailstorm of book-names, dates, and appropriate details. I was beginning to understand that Jacob Mendel was a living lexicon, something like the general catalogue of the British Museum Reading Room, but able to walk about on two legs. I stared dumbfounded at this bibliographical phenomenon, which masqueraded in the sordid and rather unclean domino of a Galician second-hand book dealer, who, after rattling off some eighty titles (with assumed indifference, but really with the satisfaction of one who plays an unexpected trump), proceeded to wipe his spectacles with a handkerchief which might long before have been white.

Hoping to conceal my astonishment, I inquired:

"Which among these works do you think you could get for me without too much trouble?"

"Oh, I'll have a look round," he answered. "Come here tomorrow and I shall certainly have some of them. As for the others, it's only a question of time, and of knowing where to look."

"I'm greatly obliged to you," I said; and then, wishing to be civil, I put my foot in it, proposing to give him a list of the books I wanted. Schmidt nudged me warningly, but too late. Mendel had already flashed a look at me—such a look, at once trimphant and affronted, scornful and overwhelmingly superior—the royal look with which Macbeth answers Macduff when summoned to yield without a blow. He laughed curtly. His Adam's apple moved exictedly. Obviously he had gulped down a choleric and insulting epithet.

Indeed he had good reason to be angry. Only a stranger, an ignoramus, could have proposed to give him, Jacob Mendel, a memorandum, as if he had been a bookseller's assistant or an underling in a public library. Not until I knew him better did I fully understand how much my would-be politeness must have galled this aberrant genius—for the man had, and knew himself to have, a titanic memory, wherein, behind a dirty and undistinguished-looking forehead, was indelibly recorded a picture of the title-page of every book that had been printed. No matter whether it had issued from the press yesterday, or hundreds of years ago, he knew its place of publication, its author's name, and its price. From his mind, as if from the printed page, he could read off the contents, could reproduce the illustrations; could visualize, not only what he had actually held in his hand, but also what he had glanced at in a bookseller's window; could see it with the same vividness as an artist sees the creations of fancy which he has not yet reproduced upon canvas. When a book was offered for six marks by a Regensburg dealer, he could remember that, two years before, a copy of the same work had changed hands for four crowns at a Viennese auction, and he recalled the name of the purchaser. In a word, Jacob Mendel never forgot a title or a figure; he knew every plant, every infusorian, every star, in the continually revolving and incessantly changing cosmos of the book-universe. In each literary specialty, he knew more than the specialists; he knew the contents of the libraries better than the librarians; he knew the book-lists of most publishers better than the heads of the firms concerned—though he had nothing to guide him except the magical powers of his inexplicable but invariably accurate memory.

True, this memory owed its infallibility to the man's limitations, to his extraordinary power of concentration. Apart from books, he knew nothing of the world. The phenomena of existence did not begin to become real for him until they had been set in type, arranged upon a composing stick, collected and, so to say, sterilized in a book. Nor did he read books for their meaning, to extract their spiritual or narrative substance. What aroused his passionate interest, what fixed his attention, was the name, the price, the format, the title-page. Though in the last analysis unproductive and uncreative, this specifically antiquarian memory of Jacob Mendel, since it was not a printed book-catalogue but was stamped upon the grey matter of a mammalian brain, was, in its unique perfection, no less remarkable a phenomenon than Napoleon's gift for physiognomy, Mezzofanti's talent for languages, Lasker's skill at chess-openings, Busoni's musical genius. Given a public position as teacher, this man with so marvellous a brain might have taught thousands and hundreds of thousands of students, have trained others to become men of great learning and of incalculable value to those communal treasure-houses we call libraries. But to him, a man of no account, a Galician Jew, a book-pedlar whose only training had been received in a Talmudic school, this upper world of culture was a fenced precinct he could never enter; and his amazing faculties could only find application at the marble-topped table in the inner room of the Café Gluck. When, some day, there arises a great psychologist who shall classify the type of that magical power we term memory as effectively as Buffon classified the genera and species of animals, a man competent to give a detailed description of all the varieties, he will have to find a pigeon-hole for Jacob Mendel, forgotten master of the lore of book-prices and book-titles, the ambulatory catalogue alike of incunabula and the modern commonplace.

In the book-trade and among ordinary persons, Jacob Mendel was regarded as nothing more than a second-hand book-dealer in a small way of business. Sunday after Sunday, his stereotyped advertisement appeared in the "Neue Freie Presse" and the "Neues Wiener Tagblatt." It ran as follows: "Best prices paid for old books, Mendel, Obere Alserstrasse." A telephone number followed, really that of the Café Gluck. He rummaged every available corner for his wares, and once a week, with the aid of a bearded porter, conveyed fresh booty to his headquarters and got rid of old stock—for he had no proper bookshop. Thus he remained a petty trader, and his business was not lucrative. Students sold him their textbooks, which year by year passed through his hands from one "generation" to another; and for a small percentage on the price he would procure any additional book that was wanted. He charged little or nothing for advice. Money seemed to have no standing in his world. No one had ever seen him better dressed than in the threadbare black coat. For breakfast and supper he had a glass of milk and a couple of rolls, while at midday a modest meal was brought him from a neighbouring restaurant. He did not smoke; he did not play cards; one might almost say he did not live, were it not that his eyes were alive behind his spectacles, and unceasingly fed his enigmatic brain with words, titles, names. The brain, like a fertile pasture, greedily sucked in this abundant irrigation. Human beings did not interest him, and of all human passions perhaps one only moved him, the most universal—vanity.

When someone, wearied by a futile hunt in countless other places, applied to him for information, and was instantly put on the track, his self-gratification was overwhelming; and it was unquestionably a delight to him that in Vienna and elsewhere there existed a few dozen persons who respected him for his knowledge and valued him for the services he could render. In every one of these monstrous aggregates we call towns, there are here and there facets which reflect one and the same universe in miniature—unseen by most, but highly prized by connoisseurs, by brethren of the same craft, by devotees of the same passion. The fans of the book-market knew Jacob Mendel. Just as anyone encountering a difficulty in deciphering a score would apply to Eusebius Mandyczewski of the Musical Society, who would be found wearing a grey skullcap and seated among multifarious musical MSS, ready, with a friendly smile, to solve the most obstinate crux; and just as, today, anyone in search of information about the Viennese theatrical and cultural life of earlier times will unhesitatingly look up the polyhistor Father Glossy; so, with equal confidence did the bibliophiles of Vienna, when they had a particularly hard nut to crack, make a pilgrimage to the Café Gluck and lay their difficulty before Jacob Mendel.

To me, young and eager for new experiences, it became enthralling to watch such a consultation. Whereas ordinarily, when a would-be seller brought him some ordinary book, he would contemptuously clap the cover to and mutter, "Two crowns"; if shown a rare or unique volume, he would sit up and take notice, lay the treasure upon a clean sheet of paper; and, on one such occasion, he was obviously ashamed of his dirty, ink-stained fingers and mourning finger-nails. Tenderly, cautiously, respectfully, he would turn the pages of the treasure. One would have been as loath to disturb him at such a moment as to break in upon the devotions of a man at prayer; and in very truth there was a flavour of solemn ritual and religious observance about the way in which contemplation, palpation, smelling and weighing in the hand followed one another in orderly succession. His rounded back waggled while he was thus engaged, he muttered to himself, exclaimed "Ah" now and again to express wonder or admiration, or "Oh, dear" when a page was missing or another had been mutilated by the larva of a book-beetle. His weighing of the tome in his hand was as circumspect as if books were sold by the ounce, and his snuffling at it as sentimental as a girl's smelling of a rose. Of course it would have been the height of bad form for the owner to show impatience during this ritual of examination.

When it was over, he willingly, nay, enthusiastically, tendered all the information at his disposal, not forgetting relevant anecdotes, and dramatized accounts of the prices which other specimens of the same work had fetched at auctions or in sales by private treaty. He looked brighter, younger, more lively at such times, and only one thing could put him seriously out of humour. This was when a novice offered him money for his expert opinion. Then he would draw back with an affronted air, looking for all the world like the

skilled custodian of a museum gallery to whom an American traveller has
offered a tip—for to Jacob Mendel contact with a rare book was something
sacred, as is contact with a woman to a young man who has not had the
bloom rubbed off. Such moments were his platonic love-nights. Books exerted
a spell on him, never money. Vainly, therefore, did great collectors (among
them one of the notables of Princeton University) try to recruit Mendel as
buyer or librarian. The offer was declined with thanks. He could not forsake
his familiar headquarters at the Café Gluck. Thirty-three years before, an
awkward youngster with black down sprouting on his chin and black ringlets
hanging over his temples, he had come from Galicia to Vienna, intending to
adopt the calling of rabbi; but ere long he forsook the worship of the harsh
and jealous Jehovah to devote himself to the more lively and polytheistic cult
of books. Then he happened upon the Café Gluck, by degrees making it his
workship, headquarters, post-office—his world. Just as an astronomer, alone
in an observatory, watches night after night through a telescope the myriads
of stars, their mysterious movements, their changeful medley, their extinction
and their flaming-up anew, so did Jacob Mendel, seated at his table in the Café
Gluck, look through his spectacles into the universe of books, a universe that
lies above the world of our everyday life, and, like the stellar universe, is full
of changing cycles.

It need hardly be said that he was highly esteemed in the Café Gluck,
whose fame seemed to us to depend far more upon his unofficial professorship
than upon the godfathership of the famous musician, Christoph Willibald
Gluck, composer of *Alcestis* and *Iphigenia*. He belonged to the outfit quite as
much as did the old cherrywood counter, the two billiard-tables with their
cloth stitched in many places, and the copper coffee-urn. His table was guarded
as a sanctuary. His numerous clients and customers were expected to take a
drink "for the good of the house," so that most of the profit of his far-flung
knowledge flowed into the big leathern pouch slung round the waist of
Deubler, the waiter. In return for being a centre of attraction, Mendel enjoyed
many privileges. The telephone was at his service for nothing. He could have
his letters directed to the café, and his parcels were taken in there. The excellent old woman who looked after the toilet brushed his coat, sewed on buttons,
and carried a small bundle of underlinen every week to the wash. He was the
only guest who could have a meal sent in from the restaurant; and every
morning Herr Standhartner, the proprietor of the café, made a point of coming
to his table and saying, "Good morning!"—though Jacob Mendel, immersed
in his books, seldom noticed the greeting. Punctually at half-past seven he arrived, and did not leave till the lights were extinguished. He never spoke to
the other guests, never read a newspaper, noticed no changes; and once, when
Herr Standhartner civilly asked him whether he did not find the electric light
more agreeable to read by than the malodorous and uncertain kerosene lamps
they had replaced, he stared in astonishment at the new incandescents. Al-

though the installation had necessitated several days' hammering and bustle, the introduction of the glow-lamps had escaped his notice. Only through the two round apertures of the spectacles, only through these two shining and sucking lenses, did the milliards of black infusorians which were the letters filter into his brain. Whatever else happened in his vicinity was disregarded as unmeaning noise. He had spent more than thirty years of his waking life at this table, reading, comparing, calculating, in a continuous waking dream, interrupted only by intervals of sleep.

A sense of horror overcame me when, looking into the inner room behind the bar of the Café Gluck, I saw that the marble-top of the table where Jacob Mendel used to deliver his oracles was now as bare as a tombstone. Grown older since those days, I understood how much disappears when such a man drops out of his place in the world, were it only because amid the daily increase in hopeless monotony, the unique grows continually more precious. Besides, in my callow youth a profound intuition had made me exceedingly fond of Buchmendel. It was through the observation of him that I had first become aware of the enigmatic fact that supreme achievement and outstanding capacity are only rendered possible by mental concentration, by a sublime monomania that verges on lunacy. Through the living example of this obscure genius of a second-hand book dealer, far more than through the flashes of insight in the works of our poets and other imaginative writers, had been made plain to me the persistent possibility of a pure life of the spirit, of complete absorption in an idea, an ecstasy as absolute as that of an Indian yogi or a medieval monk; and I had learned that this was possible in an electric-lighted café and adjoining a telephone box. Yet I had forgotten him, during the war years, and through a kindred immersion in my own work. The sight of the empty table made me ashamed of myself, and at the same time curious about the man who used to sit there.

What had become of him? I called the waiter and inquired.

"No, Sir," he answered. "I'm sorry, but I hever head of Herr Mendel. There is no one of that name among the frequenters of the Café Gluck. Perhaps the head-waiter will know."

"Herr Mendel?" said the head-waiter, dubiously, after a moment's reflection. "No, Sir, never heard of him. Unless you mean Herr Mandl, who has a hardware store in the Florianigasse?"

I had a bitter taste in the mouth, the taste of an irrecoverable past. What is the use of living when the wind obliterates our footsteps in the sand directly we have gone by? Thirty years, perhaps forty, a man had breathed, read, thought, and spoken within this narrow room; three or four years had elapsed, and there had arisen a new king over Egypt, which knew not Joseph. No one in the Café Gluck had ever heard of Jacob Mendel, of Buchmendel. Somewhat pettishly I asked the head-waiter whether I could have a word with Herr Standhartner, or with one of the old staff.

"Herr Standhartner, who used to own the place? He sold it years ago, and has died since. . . . The former head-waiter? He saved up enough to retire, and lives upon a little property at Krems. No, Sir, all of the old lot are scattered. All except one, indeed, Frau Sporschil, who looks after the toilet. She's been here for ages, worked under the late owner, I know. But she's not likely to remember your Herr Mendel. Such as she hardly knows one guest from another."

I dissented in thought.

"One does not forget a Jacob Mendel so easily!"

What I said was:

"Still I should like to have a word with Frau Sporschil, if she has a moment to spare."

The "Toilettenfrau" (known in the Viennese vernacular as the "Schocoladefrau") soon emerged from the basement, white-haired, run to seed, heavy-footed, wiping her chapped hands upon a towel as she came. She had been called away from her task of cleaning up, and was obviously uneasy at being summoned into the strong light of the guest-rooms—for common folk in Vienna, where an authoritative tradition has lingered on after the revolution, always think it must be a police matter when their "superiors" want to question them. She eyed me suspiciously, though humbly. But as soon as I asked her about Jacob Mendel, she braced up, and at the same time her eyes filled with tears.

"Poor Herr Mendel . . . so there's still someone who bears him in mind?"

Old people are commonly much moved by anything which recalls the days of their youth and revives the memory of past companionships. I asked if he was still alive.

"Good Lord, no. Poor Herr Mendel must have died five or six years ago. Indeed, I think it's fully seven since he passed away. Dear, good man that he was; and how long I knew him, more than twenty-five years; he was already sitting every day at his table when I began to work here. It was a shame, it was, the way they let him die."

Growing more and more excited, she asked if I was a relative. No one had ever inquired about him before. Didn't I know what had happened to him?

"No," I replied, "and I want you to be good enough to tell me all about it."

She looked at me timidly, and continued to wipe her damp hands. It was plain to me that she found it embarrassing, with her dirty apron and her tousled white hair, to be standing in the full glare of the café. She kept looking round anxiously, to see if one of the waiters might be listening.

"Let's go into the card-room," I said. "Mendel's old room. You shall tell me your story there."

She nodded appreciatively, thankful that I understood and led the way to the inner room, a little shambling in her gait. As I followed, I noticed that the waiters and guests were staring at us as a strangely assorted pair. We sat down opposite one another at the marble-topped table, and there she told me the story of Jacob Mendel's ruin and death. I will give the tale as nearly as may be in her own words, supplemented here and there by what I learned afterwards from other sources.

"Down to the outbreak of war, and after the war had begun, he continued to come here every morning at half-past seven, to sit at this table and study all day just as before. We had the feeling that the fact of a war going on had never entered his mind. Certainly he didn't read the newspapers, and didn't talk to anyone except about books. He paid no attention when (in the early days of the war, before the authorities put a stop to such things) the newspaper venders ran through the streets shouting, 'Great Battle on the Eastern Front' (or whatever it might be), 'Horrible Slaughter,' and so on; when people gathered in knots to talk things over, he kept himself to himself; he did not know that Fritz, the billiard-marker, who fell in one of the first battles, had vanished from this place; he did not know that Herr Standhartner's son had been taken prisoner by the Russians at Przemysl; never said a word when the bread grew more and more uneatable and when he was given bean-coffee to drink at breakfast and supper instead of hot milk. Once only did he express surprise at the changes, wondering why so few students came to the café. There was nothing in the world that mattered to him except his books.

"Then disaster befell him. At eleven one morning, two policemen came, one in uniform, and the other a plainclothes man. The latter showed the red rosette under the lapel of his coat and asked whether there was a man named Jacob Mendel in the house. They went straight to Herr Mendel's table. The poor man, in his innocence, supposed they had books to sell, or wanted some information; but they told him he was under arrest, and took him away at once. It was a scandal for the café. All the guests flocked round Herr Mendel, as he stood between the two police officers, his spectacles pushed up under his hair, staring from each to the other bewildered. Some ventured a protest, saying there must be a mistake—that Herr Mendel was a man who wouldn't hurt a fly; but the detective was furious and told them to mind their own business. They took him away, and none of us at the Café Gluck saw him again for two years. I never found out what they had against him, but I would take my dying oath that they must have made a mistake. Herr Mendel could never have done anything wrong. It was a crime to treat an innocent man so harshly."

The excellent Frau Sporschil was right. Our friend Jacob Mendel had done nothing wrong. He had merely (as I subsequently learned) done something incredibly stupid, only explicable to those who knew the man's peculiarities. The military censorship board, whose function it was to supervise correspondence passing into and out of neutral lands, one day got its clutches upon a postcard written and signed by a certain Jacob Mendel, properly stamped for transmission abroad. This postcard was addressed to Monsieur

Jean Labourdaire, Libraire, Quai de Grenelle, Paris—to an enemy country, therefore. The writer complained that the last eight issues of the monthly "Bulletin bibliographique de la France" had failed to reach him, although his annual subscription had been duly paid in advance. The jack-in-office who read this missive (a high-school teacher with a bent for the study of the Romance languages, called up for "war-service" and sent to employ his talents at the censorship board instead of wasting them in the trenches) was astonished by its tenor. "Must be a joke," he thought. He had to examine some two thousand letters and postcards every week, always on the alert to detect anything that might savour of espionage, but never yet had he chanced upon anything so absurd as that an Austrian subject would unconcernedly drop into one of the imperial and royal letterboxes a postcard addressed to someone in an enemy land, regardless of the trifling detail that since August 1914 the Central Powers had been cut off from Russia on one side and from France on the other by barbed-wire entanglements and a network of ditches in which men armed with rifles and bayonets, machine-guns and artillery, were doing their utmost to exterminate one another like rats. Our schoolmaster enrolled in the Landsturm did not treat this first postcard seriously, but pigeon-holed it as a curiosity not worth talking about to his chief. But a few weeks after there turned up another card, again from Jacob Mendel, this time to John Aldridge, Bookseller, Golden Square, London, asking whether the addressee could send the last few numbers of the "Antiquarian" to an address in Vienna which was clearly stated on the card.

The censor in the blue uniform began to feel uneasy. Was his "class" trying to trick the schoolmaster? Were the cards written in cipher? Possible, anyhow; so the subordinate went over to the major's desk, clicked his heels together, saluted, and laid the suspicious documents before "properly constituted authority." A strange business, certainly. The police were instructed by telephone to see if there actually was a Jacob Mendel at the specified address, and, if so, to bring the fellow along. Within the hour, Mendel had been arrested, and (still stupefied by the shock) brought before the major, who showed him the postcards and asked him with drill-sergeant roughness whether he acknowledged their authorship. Angered at being spoken to so sharply, and still more annoyed because his perusal of an important catalogue had been interrupted, Mendel answered tartly:

"Of course I wrote the cards. That's my handwriting and signature. Surely one has a right to claim the delivery of a periodical to which one has subscribed?"

The major swung half-round in his swivel-chair and exchanged a meaning glance with the lieutenant seated at the adjoining desk.

"The man must be a double-distilled idiot," was what they mutely conveyed to one another.

Then the chief took counsel within himself whether he should discharge the offender with a caution, or whether he should treat the case more seriously. In all offices, when such doubts arise, the usual practice is, not to spin a coin, but to send in a report. Thus Pilate washes his hands of responsibility. Even if the report does no good, it can do no harm, and is merely one useless manuscript or typescript added to a million others.

In this instance, however, the decision to send in a report did much harm, alas, to an inoffensive man of genius, for it involved asking a series of questions, and the third of them brought suspicious circumstances to light.

"Your full name?"

"Jacob Mendel."

"Occupation?"

"Book-pedlar" (for, as already explained, Mendel had no shop, but only a pedlar's license).

"Place of birth?"

Now came the disaster. Mendel's birthplace was not far from Petrikau. The major raised his eyebrows. Petrikau, or Piotrkov, was across the frontier, in Russian Poland.

"You were born a Russian subject. When did you acquire Austrian nationality? Show me your papers."

"Papers? Identification papers? I have nothing but my hawker's license."

"What's your nationality, then? Was your father Austrian or Russian?"

Undismayed, Mendel answered:

"A Russian, of course."

"What about yourself?"

"Wishing to evade Russian military service, I slipped across the frontier thirty-three years ago, and ever since I have lived in Vienna."

The matter seemed to the major to be growing worse and worse.

"But didn't you take steps to become an Austrian subject?"

"Why should I?" countered Mendel. "I never troubled my head about such things."

"Then you are still a Russian subject?"

Mendel, who was bored by this endless questioning, answered simply:

"Yes, I suppose I am."

The startled and indignant major threw himself back in his chair with such violence that the wood cracked protestingly. So this was what it had come to! In Vienna, the Austrian capital, at the end of 1915, after Tarnow, when the war was in full blast, after the great offensive, a Russian could walk about unmolested, could write letters to France and England, while the police ignored his machinations. And then the fools who wrote in the newspapers wondered why Conrad von Hotzendorf had not advanced in seven-league boots to Warsaw, and the general staff was puzzled because every movement of the troops was immediately blabbed to the Russians.

The lieutenant had sprung to his feet and crossed the room to his chief's table. What had been an almost friendly conversation took a new turn, and degenerated into a trial.

"Why didn't you report as an enemy alien directly the war began?"

Mendel, still failing to realize the gravity of his position, answered in his singing Jewish jargon:

"Why should I report? I don't understand."

The major regarded this inquiry as a challenge, and asked threateningly:

"Didn't you read the notices that were posted up everywhere?"

"No."

"Didn't you read the newspapers?"

"No."

The two officers stared at Jacob Mendel (now sweating with uneasiness) as if the moon had fallen from the sky into their office. Then the telephone buzzed, the typewriters clacked, orderlies ran hither and thither, and Mendel was sent under guard to the nearest barracks, where he was to await transfer to a concentration camp. When he was ordered to follow the two soldiers, he was frankly puzzled, but not seriously perturbed. What could the man with the gold-lace collar and the rough voice have against him? In the upper world of books, where Mendel lived and breathed and had his being, there was no warfare, there were no misunderstandings, only an ever-increasing knowledge of words and figures, of book-titles and authors' names. He walked good-humouredly enough downstairs between the soldiers, whose first charge was to take him to the police station. Not until, there, the books were taken out of his overcoat pockets, and the police impounded the portfolio containing a hundred important memoranda and customers' addresses, did he lose his temper, and begin to resist and strike blows. They had to tie his hands. In the struggle, his spectacles fell off, and these magical telescopes, without which he could not see into the wonderworld of books, were smashed into a thousand pieces. Two days later, insufficiently clad (for his only wrap was a light summer cloak), he was sent to the internment camp for Russian civilians at Komorn.

I have no information as to what Jacob Mendel suffered during these two years of internment, cut off from his beloved books, penniless, among roughly nurtured men, few of whom could read or write, in a huge human dunghill. This must be left to the imagination of those who can grasp the torments of a caged eagle. By degrees, however, our world, grown sober after its fit of drunkenness, has become aware that of all the cruelties and wanton abuses of power during the war, the most needless and therefore the most inexcusable was this herding together behind barbed-wire fences of thousands upon thousands of persons who had outgrown the age of military service, who had made homes for themselves in a foreign land, and who (believing in the good faith of their hosts) had refrained from exercising the sacred right of hospitality granted even by the Tunguses and Araucanians—the right to flee while time permits. This crime against civilization was committed with the same unthinking hardihood in France, Germany and Britain, in every belligerent country of our crazy Europe.

Probably Jacob Mendel would, like thousands as innocent as he, have perished in this cattle-pen, have gone stark mad, have succumbed to dysentery, asthenia, softening of the brain, had it not been that before the worst happened, a chance (typically Austrian) recalled him to the world in which a spiritual life became again possible. Several times after his disappearance, letters from distinguished customers were delivered for him at the Café Gluck. Count Schönberg, sometime lord-lieutenant of Styria, an enthusiastic collector of works on heraldry; Siegenfeld, the former dean of the theological faculty, who was writing a commentary on the works of St. Augustine; Edler von Pisek, an octogenarian admiral on the retired list, engaged in writing his memoirs—these and other persons of note, wanting information from Buchmendel, had repeatedly addressed communications to him at his familiar haunt, and some of these were duly forwarded to the concentration camp at Komorn. There they fell into the hands of the commanding officer, who happened to be a man of humane disposition, and was astonished to find what notables were among the correspondents of this dirty little Russian Jew, who, half-blind now that his spectacles were broken and he had no money to buy new ones, crouched in a corner like a mole, grey, eyeless, and dumb. A man who had such patrons must be a person of importance, whatever he looked like. The C.O. therefore read the letters to the short-sighted Mendel, and penned answers for him to sign—answers which were mainly requests that influence should be exercised on his behalf. The spell worked, for these correspondents had the solidarity of collectors. Joining forces and pulling strings they were able (giving guarantees for the "enemy alien's" good behaviour) to secure leave for Buchmendel's return to Vienna in 1917, after more than two years at Komorn —on the condition that he should report daily to the police. The proviso mattered little. He was a free man once more, free to take up his quarters in his old attic, free to handle books again, free (above all) to return to his table in the Café Gluck. I can describe the return from the underworld of the camp in the good Frau Sporschil's own words:

"One day—Jesus, Mary, Joseph, I could hardly believe my eyes—the door opened (you remember the way he had) little wider than a crack, and through this opening he sidled, poor Herr Mendel. He was wearing a tattered and much-darned military cloak, and his head was covered by what had perhaps once been a hat thrown away by the owner as past use. No collar. His face looked like a death's head, so haggard it was, and his hair was pitifully thin. but he came in as if nothing had happened, went straight to his table, and took off his cloak, not briskly as of old, for he panted with the exertion. Nor had he any books with him. He just sat there without a word, staring straight in front of him with hollow, expressionless eyes. Only by degrees, after we had brought him the big bundle of printed matter which had arrived for him from Germany, did he begin to read again. But he was never the same man."

No, he was never the same man, not now the miraculum mundi, the magical walking book-catalogue. All who saw him in those days told me the same pitiful story. Something had gone irrecoverably wrong; he was broken, the blood-red comet of the war had burst into the remote, calm atmosphere of his bookish world. His eyes, accustomed for decades to look at nothing but print, must have seen terrible sights in the wire-fenced human stockyard, for the eyes that had formerly been so alert and full of ironical gleams were now almost completely veiled by the inert lids, and looked sleepy and red-bordered behind the carefully repaired spectacle-frames. Worse still, a cog must have broken somewhere in the marvellous machinery of his memory, so that the working of the whole was impaired; for so delicate is the structure of the brain (a sort of switchboard made of the most fragile substances, and as easily jarred as are all instruments of precision) that a blocked arteriole, a congested bundle of nerve fibres, a fatigued group of cells, even a displaced molecule, may put the apparatus out of gear and make harmonious working impossible. In Mendel's memory, the keyboard of knowledge, the keys were stiff, or—to use psychological terminology—the associations were impaired. When, now and again, someone came to ask for information, Jacob stared blankly at the inquirer, failing to understand the question, and even forgetting it before he had found the answer. Mendel was no longer Buchmendel, just as the world was no longer the world. He could not now become wholly absorbed in his reading, did not rock as of old when he read, but sat bolt upright, his glasses turned mechanically towards the printed page, but perhaps not reading at all, and only sunk in a reverie. Often, said Frau Sporschil, his head would drop onto his book and he would fall asleep in the daytime, or he would gaze hour after hour at the stinking acetylene lamp which (in the days of the coal famine) had replaced the electric lighting. No, Mendel was no longer Buchmendel, no longer the eighth wonder of the world, but a weary, worn-out, though still breathing, useless bundle of beard and ragged garments, which sat, as futile as a potato-bogle, where of old the Pythian oracle had sat; no longer the glory of the Café Gluck, but a shameful scarecrow, evil-smelling, a parasite.

That was the impression he produced upon the new proprietor, Florian Gurtner from Retz, who (a successful profiteer in flour and butter) had cajoled Standhartner into selling him the Café Gluck for eighty thousand rapidly depreciating paper crowns. He took everything into his hard peasant grip, hastily arranged to have the old place redecorated, bought fine-looking satin-covered seats, installed a marble porch, and was in negotiation with his next-door neighbor to buy a place where he could extend the café into a dancing hall. Naturally while he was making these embellishments, he was not best pleased by the parasitic encumbrance of Jacob Mendel, a filthy old Galician Jew, who had been in trouble with the authorities during the war, was still to be regarded as an "enemy alien," and, while occupying a table from morning till night, consumed no more than two cups of coffee and four or five rolls. Standhartner, indeed, had put in a word for this guest of long standing, had explained that Mendel was a person of note, and, in the stock-taking, had handed him over as having a permanent lien upon the establishment, but as an asset rather than a liability. Florian Gurtner, however, had brought into the café, not only new furniture, and an up-to-date cash register, but also the profit-making and hard temper of the post-war era, and awaited the first pretext for ejecting from his smart coffee-house the last troublesome vestige of suburban shabbiness.

A good excuse was not slow to present itself. Jacob Mendel was impoverished to the last degree. Such banknotes as had been left to him had crumbled away to nothing during the inflation period; his regular clientele had been killed, ruined, or dispersed. When he tried to resume his early trade of book-pedlar, calling from door to door to buy and to sell, he found that he lacked strength to carry books up and down stairs. A hundred little signs showed him to be a pauper. Seldom, now, did he have a midday meal sent in from the restaurant, and he began to run up a score at the Café Gluck for his modest breakfast and supper. Once his payments were as much as three weeks overdue. Were it only for this reason, the head-waiter wanted Gurtner to "give Mendel the sack." But Frau Sporschil intervened, and stood surety for the debtor. What was due could be stopped out of her wages!

This staved off disaster for a while, but worse was to come. For some time the head-waiter had noticed that rolls were disappearing faster than the tally would account for. Naturally suspicion fell upon Mendel, who was known to be six months in debt to the tottering old porter whose services he still needed. The head-waiter, hidden behind the stove, was able, two days later, to catch Mendel red-handed. The unwelcome guest had stolen from his seat in the card-room, crept behind the counter in the front room, taken two rolls from the bread-basket, returned to the card-room, and hungrily devoured them. When settling-up at the end of the day, he said he had only had coffee; no rolls. The source of wastage had been traced, and the waiter reported his discovery to the proprietor. Herr Gurtner, delighted to have so good an excuse for getting rid of Mendel, made a scene, openly accused him of theft, and declared that nothing but the goodness of his own heart prevented his sending for the police.

"But after this," said Florian, "you'll kindly take yourself off for good and all. We don't want to see your face again at the Café Gluck."

Jacob Mendel trembled, but made no reply. Abandoning his poor belongings, he departed without a word.

"It was ghastly," said Frau Sporschil. "Never shall I forget the sight. He stood up, his spectacles pushed on to his forehead, and his face white as a sheet. He did not even stop to put on his cloak, although it was January, and very cold. You'll remember that severe winter, just after the war. In his fright, he left the book he was reading open upon the table. I did not notice it at first, and then, when I wanted to pick it up and take it after him, he had already stumbled out through the doorway. I was afraid to follow him into the street, for Herr Gurtner was standing at the door and shouting at him, so that a crowd had gathered. Yet I felt ashamed to the depths of my soul. Such a thing would never have happened under the old master. Herr Standhartner would not have driven Herr Mendel away for pinching one or two rolls when he was hungry, but would have let him have as many as he wanted for nothing, to the end of his days. Since the war, people seem to have grown heartless. Drive away a man who had been a guest daily for so many, many years. Shameful! I should not like to have to answer before God for such cruelty!"

The good woman had grown excited, and, with the passionate garrulousness of old age, she kept on repeating how shameful it was, and that nothing of the sort would have happened if Herr Standhartner had not sold the business. In the end I tried to stop the flow by asking her what had happened to Mendel, and whether she had ever seen him again. These questions excited her yet more.

"Day after day, when I passed his table, it gave me the creeps, as you will easily understand. Each time I thought to myself: 'Where can he have got to, poor Herr Mendel?' Had I known where he lived, I would have called and taken him something nice and hot to eat—for where could he get the money to cook food and warm his room? As far as I knew, he had no kinsfolk in the wide world. When, after a long time, I had heard nothing about him, I began to believe that it must be all up with him, and that I should never see him again. I had made up my mind to have a mass said for the peace of his soul, knowing him to be a good man, after twenty-five years' acquaintance.

"At length one day in February, at half-past seven in the morning, when I was cleaning the windows, the door opened, and in came Herr Mendel. Generally, as you know, he sidled in, looking confused, and not 'quite all there'; but this time, somehow, it was different. I noticed at once the strange look in his eyes; they were sparkling, and he rolled them this way and that, as if to see everything at once; as for his appearance, he seemed nothing but beard and skin and bone. Instantly it crossed my mind: 'He's forgotten all that happened last time he was here; it's his way to go about like a sleepwalker noticing nothing; he doesn't remember about the rolls, and how shamefully Herr Gurtner ordered him out of the place, half in mind to set the police on him.' Thank goodness, Herr Gurtner hadn't come yet, and the head-waiter was drinking coffee. I ran up to Herr Mendel, meaning to tell him he'd better make himself scarce, for otherwise that ruffian" (she looked round timidly to see if we were overheard, and hastily amended her phrase), "Herr Gurtner, I mean, would only have him thrown into the street once more. 'Herr Mendel,' I began. He started, and looked at me. In that very moment (it was dreadful), he must have remembered the whole thing, for he almost collapsed, and began to tremble, not his fingers only, but to shiver and shake from head to foot. Hastily he stepped back into the street, and fell in a heap on the pavement as soon as he was outside the door. We telephoned for the ambulance and they carried him off to hospital, the nurse who came saying he had high fever directly she touched him. He died that evening. 'Double pneumonia,' the doctor said, and that he never recovered consciousness—could not have been fully conscious when he came to the Café Gluck. As I said, he had entered like a man walking in his sleep. The table where he had sat day after day for thirty-six years drew him back to it like a home."

Frau Sporschil and I went on talking about him for a long time, the two last persons to remember this strange creature, Buchmendel: I to whom in youth the book-pedlar from Galicia had given the first revelation of a life wholly devoted to the things of the spirit; she, the poor old woman who was caretaker of a café-toilet, who had never read a book in her life, and whose only tie with this strangely matched comrade in her subordinate, poverty-stricken world had been that for twenty-five years she had brushed his overcoat and had sewn on buttons for him. We, too, might have been considered strangely assorted, but Frau Sporschil and I got on very well together, linked, as we sat at the forsaken marble-topped table, by our common memories of the shade our talk had conjured up—for joint memories and, above all, loving memories, always establish a tie. Suddenly, while in the full stream of talk, she exclaimed:

"Lord Jesus, how forgetful I am. I still have the book he left on the table the evening Herr Gurtner gave him the key of the street. I didn't know where to take it. Afterwards, when no one appeared to claim it, I ventured to keep it as a souvenir. You don't think it wrong of me, Sir?"

She went to a locker where she stored some of the requisities for her job, and produced the volume for my inspection. I found it hard to repress a smile, for I was face to face with one of life's little ironies. It was the second volume of Hayn's *Bibliotheca Germanorum erotica et curiosa,* a compendium of gallant literature known to every book-collector. "Habent sua fata libelli!" This scabrous publication, as legacy of the vanished magician, had fallen into toil-worn hands which had perhaps never held any other printed work than a prayer-book. Maybe I was not wholly successful in controlling my mirth, for the expression of my face seemed to perplex the worthy soul, and once more she said:

"You don't think it wrong of me to keep it, Sir?"

I shook her cordially by the hand.

"Keep it, and welcome," I said. "I am absolutely sure that our old friend Mendel would be only too delighted to know that someone among the many thousand he has provided with books, cherishes his memory."

Then I took my departure, feeling a trifle ashamed when I compared myself with this excellent old woman, who, so simply and so humanely, had fostered the memory of the dead scholar. For she, uncultured though she was, had at least preserved a book as a memento; whereas I, a man of education and a writer, had completely forgotten Buchmendel for years—I, who at least should have known that one only makes books in order to keep in touch with one's fellows after one has ceased to breathe, and thus to defend oneself against the inexorable fate of all that lives—transitoriness and oblivion.

THE ENEMIES

by PAUL SCHLESINGER

I T so happened that during the World War two mortally wounded Jews were brought into a hospital, both within the same hour. One was a German—the other was a Frenchman. Their beds adjoined each other. For a long time they lay tossing about, wracked by fever and pain. The Jewish chaplain fluttered from one to another, trying desperately to get them to accept each other as Jews. Before he left them he said:

"I cannot possibly spend any more time with you. Therefore I beg of you—talk to each other. Both of you are Jews, even though one is French and the other is German. Surely, as Jews you both share the same whole-hearted devotion to your fatherlands and to your parents, you are tormented by the same longing for your wives and children at home, by the same anxieties, and the same suffering, and soon both of you will stand before the same God. There certainly must be some virtues as well as vices which you both have in common. Therefore, I must plead with you—unburden your hearts to each other."

The Rabbi went away. The two Jews lay silent for a long time. The Frenchman, who began to feel somewhat better, moved his parched lips: "What have we got to say to each other anyway?"

The German did not answer.

"No doubt you are right for not talking to me. But I believe I am justified in wanting to talk to you. Therefore I say: 'A curse on you Germans for attacking us! A curse on your Hun Kaiser who has ravished Belgium, whose soldiers murder little children and rape women! A curse on all of you!'"

The Frenchman sank wearily back on his pillow. Then the German replied:

"You sound like one of your newspapers. Could I expect you to be otherwise? I never had any great love for our Kaiser, nor for what he said and did. I also never really believed very much in what our newspapers wrote. But if I have to believe any of them I certainly choose to believe our German newspapers more than yours. If I have to obey and sacrifice myself for anybody then I certainly prefer to do it for the Kaiser rather than for any one of you. For after all, he is a German. His language is my language, his virtue is my virtue, and his guilt is my guilt and for it alone I am prepared to atone."

So the two wounded men fell silent again. Night fell and when the dawn broke it found them both in a weaker condition. Once again the Frenchman began to speak:

"What do you fat Germans know about our crystal clear ideas? I know that I am dying now but even in this hour they still flash clear in my mind. I experience the forked lightning of the soul. It illuminates the whole world which is thus made endurable, civilized and free!"

"I too am dying," murmured the German. "The twilight envelops me. I am getting lost in the mist. I feel so much alone! But I will return home now. I will be home soon. It is quiet and warm there. I do not want to think anymore—only to continue feeling—to feel like a German."

The Rabbi, who just entered, overheard these last words and he said to them:

"Why do you persist in quarreling in this last hour? Can't you find something kind to say to each other? You are both Jews."

At this the Frenchman said:

"Don't Christians murder one another?"

And the German, his voice already sounded lifeless, added:

"They have drummed into our heads for too long a time already that brotherly love is an achievement of the Gospels. . . ."

Several hours later, one followed the other into the slumber from which they would never awaken.

A young blond medical assistant who had been listening to the discussion of the two dying men approached the Rabbi and said:

"Please explain to me—"

"What?"

"The Jewish riddle."

The Rabbi turned away from the dead, and followed by the doctor, left the barracks and went out into the fresh air.

"To be a Jew means to live another life not your own. To begin in another, to be fulfilled by another until completely possessed. At times it seems to me as if we were not at all ourselves. No sooner does the Gentile smell something than we begin smelling it too. Just look at the landscape about us, at the vegetation, the animals, the people and the city and surely you will become strangely enchanted by it all. Now who do you think experiences this landscape better and more thoroughly—the native who since childhood has lived in it, who perhaps knows no other—or the one who in passing derives pleasure from it in the sudden recognition of a newly experienced charm? To the native is hardly revealed his own charms. Woe to him if they were! He lives according to the genius of his climate. What he experiences and creates takes place in the style and the tradition of this climate. Because the commonplace and the insignificant are at work within him, therefore the unusual and the great must emerge, opening up new sources of self-development. The alien, on the other hand, cannot react the same way. He can only have impressions of this world that is so alien to him, he can only describe it, translate it, write about it, sing of it.

"We Jews are everlasting strangers everywhere. There has never been a people in the world that has produced in ratio to its population so many musicians, actors, artists, writers as have the Jews. And yet there has never been a people in the world, having such a large number of musicians, actors, artists and writers, that has produced so little for itself. When we Jews sing about other peoples and other lands we sing with a painful devotion, a deeper fervor, and a more dusky passion than when we sing about our own. Indeed, it appears as if all things achieve their fullest expression and their greatest charm through our efforts. The entire world concedes this and therefore cannot dispense with us."

"And how do you think it will be when the Jews return to Palestine?"

The Rabbi smiled and said:

"Boring, my dear doctor."

ALFRED ENGLÄNDER

by FRANZ WERFEL

"Even you! You'll soon be let in for it," said the young gentleman in the black suit (he seemed about twenty-five years old) to Ferdinand, who sat without a movement, frostily crouched in the deep window-seat of the little dormitory. The soaring tower of the Vienna Cathedral filled up, in the rich proximity of its detail, the square space of window-glass behind him. The dormitory was part of the famous Charterhouse of St. Stephen, which sheltered, in those pre-war days, the boarders of the Archiepiscopal Seminary. Ferdinand, with two other alumni in no better case than himself, passed in the stuffy little room what was left of his summer holidays. On this particular Sunday his roommates had made an excursion to Baden; he had remained behind in the half-deserted seminary, alone.

Ferdinand's visitor, the young gentleman in the black suit, paced, swaying from the hips, to and fro in the little room. His name was Alfred Engländer. The impression he gave was of a man not quite at one with himself. He was fairly tall, and already confronted the world with a moderate paunch and a face rotund and rosy, which seemed to indicate an untroubled and comfortable view of life. But across this face, which by rights should have been full-lipped, the mouth made a stern sharp line, while under the forehead there mourned (no less surprisingly) a pair of short-sighted, troubled eyes. Nature in shaping this young man seemed to have fused two contradictory designs.

Ferdinand had got to know Engländer in the lecture rooms of the Archiepiscopal Seminary. Nobody seemed to know at whose instance, or for what purpose, this young, unbaptized Jew came to attend lectures in theology. Ferdinand had responded to the friendly advances of Engländer who had taken him, the nineteen-year-old, under a kind of tutorial protection. Now he sat, as usual, motionless, his eyes fixed on the ground. His callow, undeveloped body was clothed in the kind of soutane usually worn by apprentice clerics. The hands, as a rule, he kept hidden in the cuffs of the fairly wide sleeves. He looked very ill. The fact that his brown hair was cut far back from his forehead, that his drooping lashes melted into the shadows round his eyes, intensified his appearance of ill-health. That negative extinction proper to all children of the State, creatures whose only parent is a government, appeared to have engulfed his whole being. Since his tenth year, since the day when he had left Aunt Caroline and lived in separation from Barbara, he had led a barrack-room existence. First the cadet-school; now this seminary in Vienna. How strange it seemed that there should be people allowed to call their lives their own, people who had no need to accept existence in deep gratitude for the meals they ate and drank, as a necessary evil, a dependency. Such people could go out of doors whenever they liked, eat as they chose, drink, sit down, rest and read. It seemed almost fabulous that Engländer should not be obliged to wear a uniform, that he could go to a tailor and order his clothes as he fancied them.

Alfred Engländer, who had never met anyone like Ferdinand, was struck more forcibly every day with the half-conscious suffering of this prisoner. Since the previous term his visits to Ferdinand had been frequent. He had taken him for walks and smuggled in books for him to read. Although Ferdinand as a rule kept his mouth shut and Engländer did nothing but talk, the elder felt himself far more recipient than benefactor. He was excitable, out of love with himself, and the strange quiet of this prisoner increased his own inward dissatisfaction. Again and again this came to the surface.

"Do you know what I like best about you?" he continued. "You're not clever. Good Lord, how did you manage to preserve yourself—"

He broke off.

"See what I mean? I'm not trying to insult you—it's a mark of distinction. Naturally, I don't think you're a fool—not a person without any intellect— quite the contrary. But it's difficult to say just exactly what's going on inside you. It's a pity that you too will soon be let in for being brainy. No one in this age can ever escape it. And I see it already from some of the things you say."

Engländer came to a halt at Ferdinand's back.

"You see, I come of a different world. I've been brought up by brainy people. My childhood, all my surroundings, my brothers, all my friends, they were a very bright lot indeed. As for me, worse luck, I'm bright by nature—to my finger-tips. A couple of days ago, at a Socialist meeting, I had the most charming experience. One of those clever-clever fools was holding forth on the 'Social Concepts of Primitive Christianity.' After he'd finished, I heard one workman say to another—'You know, this Jesus—he must have been quite a brainy chap, for his time!' That lout, with his ferro-concrete and his dynamos and his horsepower mind, felt infinitely superior to Jesus."

Ferdinand did not laugh. He had given up trying to understand these outbursts. Engländer, who had taken up a book, brought it down with a slam. "Isn't one single axiom of dogmatic theology—one single definition in the Lateranense of the Tridentinium worth all that sort of free-thinking slosh? And not only far more profound—infinitely more scientific."

The sentence rolled out grandiloquently:

"Gratia actualis est internum auxilium supernaturale, quod Deus propter Christi merita homine lapso largitur per modum motionis transeuntis ad operandum in ordine ad ejus sanctificationem."

He reveled in these close-packed, sonorous phrases, following their echoes with delight, as though he himself were not excluded from the grace of this hammered benediction, its essence compressed into such stony and magnificent Latin. Ferdinand, on the contrary, found such axioms heartily detestable. It would have been just as hard to convince a schoolboy whose "Greek for the term" was Homer, of the intrinsic beauties of the Iliad, as to persuade Ferdinand of the worth of a dogmatic formula. These studies had not been his choice; they had been forced upon him, like the rest of his life up to now. It was one of the bitterest aspects of his captivity.

"The intellect has emptied itself of all its content of Divinity—" the voice rose to breaking pitch—"Do you really think that Origen and St. Thomas, for instance, had any less brain than a modern experimental psychologist? Cleverness without God—that's your modern intellectual—or rather, it's your modern fool. There's no such thing as absolute intellect; it's a sheerly formal principle. I defined it once for myself as the subjugation of life to measurements. Technical!—that's what it is! Technical! Technique—the monstrous futile gyration of cleverness. Of course, I'm not so reactionary as to simply despise it all—railway viaducts and ferro-concrete, and cars and skyscrapers, hydraulic power, electric signs, Bleriot's aviation experiments, the Wright brothers, and so on. But even suppose I did? Mankind is accustomed to far greater miracles. The sun and the fixed stars aren't such bad electric signs. But all your modern intellectual wants is to drive the sense of wonder out of humanity. 'What's that shining thing?' you ask. Science says: 'An electric globe.'—'Why does it shine?'—'Because filaments shine.'—'Why?'—'Because an electric current of such and such intensity goes through them.'—'What's an electric current?'—'A substance of accumulated potentiality observed under certain conditions.'—Then all the human being can do is to make a little disappointed bow—and Science begins to sound a warning: 'Above all, my dear chap, no mystery! Miraculous is simply a vulgar word for the little spots I haven't managed to light up yet with my newest electric globe. Tomorrow, I shall explain a bit more clearly. But for heaven's sake don't you go looking for mysteries today; only be thankful that your house is better lighted than your grandfather's.' " Engländer, at this point, jumped up, his fat cheeks flushed with real anger. He yelled—

"But what I say is—it is miraculous!"

The noise made Ferdinand jump. Whenever he heard a loud voice, the terrified feeling came over him that someone in authority must be shouting at him. But Engländer did not notice the effect of his outburst; he was now addressing mankind.

"Aristotle, even, our Master, called mystery the source of all philosophy. But, unfortunately, Aristotle, our Master, was rather a dry old stick. If he hadn't been, he might have added—'There's a hierarchy of mysteries, my dear chap. To be lost in wonder at a vacuum-cleaner isn't quite the same thing as being lost in wonder at original sin.' See what I mean? But 'clever' people can only wonder at vacuum-cleaners. God knows where all this stinking rot began."

Engländer, whose bearing as a rule was most correct, for he did his best to hide his corpulence by an assumption of severe dignity, was so carried away by his theme that he thrust out a careless belly.

"Well, anyway, I know where it all started. The English! Naturally! The English were the people who launched all this modern intelligence stuff."

His plump, good-natured face was creased with hate. For Alfred Engländer, the "English" were an *idée fixe*. He detested them so heartily that he whom fate had burdened with the odious name "Engländer," would have been only too willing to change it had he not been terrified lest people interpret his change of name as a flight from his Jewish nationality. Nothing would have made him more ashamed than that any such misunderstanding should arise, more especially since he was in love with the Catholic philosophy. No shadow of any suspicion that it sprang from some troubled source of opportunism or snobbery must be cast upon this pure enthusiasm. And this same complicated timidity explained why Engländer, whose knowledge of dogmatic and patristic theology was the admiration of many theologians, had never allowed himself to be baptized. If anyone asked him his reasons, he would answer that he did not feel sufficiently free to embrace a martyr's crown of misconstructions. So he kept his name and old religion which in many respects he still venerated. But whenever he happened to mention "the English," his eyes would dart forth hate.

"Of course—the English, and their American spawn! Some Wycliffe, some heretic or other. It began with the denial of a Sacrament. And where's it going to end? With the metaphysic of drainage!"

Suddenly, it came over him like a frenzy. He shut his eyes, stood still in the middle of the room and began intoning, like a curate:

"*Holy Capital,*
        Have mercy on us.
Holy dividends, its truly begotten son,
        Have mercy on us.

Holy business acumen of all the intelligent, third person of the Trinity,
                    Have mercy on us—
You blessed choirs of saints and holy spirits, Petrol, Cotton, Oil, Coal, Leather,
    Rubber, Spare Parts,
                    Pray for us.
You Holy Apostles and Evangelists of the Stock Exchange, the gold market,
    and the modern science that goes with them,
                    Pray for us.
All blessed hermits and solitaries of Trusts and Limited Companies for jerry-
    building, with two w.c.'s, hot and cold water on every floor, central heating
    and Rembrandt reproductions,
                    Pray for us!"

Beads of sweat stood out on his forehead; he paced the room, his fists clenched.

Of this disrespectful parody Ferdinand had grasped as little as the white vaulted walls of the Charterhouse dormitory in which, till now, such sentiments had never echoed. Both he and the room were a trifle disturbed by the outbreak.

Ferdinand made the attempt to lead the conversation back to its starting point. He muttered prudently, as one lays a last and dangerous card on the top of an already tottering card-house—

"What about Revelation?"

In every religious discussion between these oddly assorted friends, the young candidate for Holy Orders took the side of Liberal Free-Thought, and the Jew, of convinced Christianity. It would be inexact to suggest that Ferdinand was plagued with religious doubts. He suffered too acutely from the general enslavement of his life for spiritual matters to have gained any special preponderance. The preachments, formulae and doctrines with which they stuffed his head in the Seminary were matters of supreme indifference. They merely went to create a stuffy atmosphere in which he found it hard to breathe and of whose stifling, unbearable quality Engländer's personality had just begun to make him aware. He had no need to fall away from God, since God, as He existed within him, had never been touched by any of them. They were so much "grind" which one had to learn in order to enter a profession. He, the despised orphan of the State, without other means of support, had had no choice. That these slabs of grind bore any relationship to life, was something he had had to learn from Engländer. The results of this were odd enough—a growing disgust with everything clerical. In the middle of a discussion in which Engländer poured his scorn on medical science, a passionate longing had arisen in Ferdinand's mind. He must be a doctor! That was his profession, the thing for which he was really fitted. The thought of the priesthood to which, mechanically, the government trustees had condemned him, had become a torturing oppression. This new idea, born of his longing to be free, robbed him of his sleep for several nights. Vain hope! Who would ever help him? He had grown so timid that he could not even summon up courage to confide his longings to Engländer. The latter, who had not the least idea what was going on in Ferdinand's mind, hurled himself on the word "Revelation" with all the fire of an apostle.

"Revelation! Good!"—his voice dilated with the full knowledge of irrefutable proof—"Revelation! What about Revelation? I'm delighted to examine Revelation from the standpoint of the very latest, most scientific Biblical criticism. The Old Testament, the Bible, the sacred books of the Jews, are a post-Exilian compendium arranged by Ezra and Nehemiah, two learned politicians, and perhaps—who can tell—full of archeologizing misstatements—an ordinary, human work, written with a purpose from end to end, full of near-Eastern quotations, reaching back as far as the Sumerian Empire and forward to the Hellenistic epoch. In a word an eclectic hotch-potch. I'm delighted, as I said before, without the very slightest misgiving, to accept the modern scientific standpoint—though I do get the feeling in my bones that all this modern scientific detachment is charged with a fair amount of anti-Semitic electricity. And besides, it ought to go without saying that I, as an educated man of today, am convinced that tens of thousands of years ago there were primitive tribes of beings, organized in sympathetic hordes, wandering about this planet without having to wait for Adam and Eve. And they weren't given the Garden of Eden to live and eat each other up in, but some habitable zone in Mexico, Atlantis or Lemuria. So far, so good! And I know that the first appearance of organic life was probably less the result of a command in Hebrew than of the action of ultra-violet rays. Some ultra-violet ray, in its gay and giddy youth, tickled some slothful clod of earth so long that it began to give itself a pain. Lots of people nowadays tell you that this very uncomfortable sensation was the beginning of all life and consciousness. I know all that! I know that my belief in Revelation, the child's belief in me, which would like so much to cling to the contradictions and stupidities of an ancient masterpiece of literature, is going to be forced to capitulate. Good! And yet, so help me God, I can stand here and not capitulate."

We should hasten to add, the better to comprehend these floods of eloquence, that in Engländer they were due to physical weakness. This weakness, in its turn, was the result of a bodily mortification which he would inflict on himself to atone for certain little lapses of the flesh. He was a hearty eater who always relished his food. As a rule, therefore, he would punish his sin by missing a meal. Whenever, in the street, he caught himself giving way to any immodest glance or desire, his backsliding would be followed by the sacrifice of the sweet at his next meal. Should his longings betray him into "following," he would sometimes miss lunch or dinner altogether. But if fleshly sin had been of a more flagrant, positive nature, his fasts would be prolonged over a day, a day and a half, or, in very sinful cases, two whole days. The successful comple-

tion of such a penance would find its reward in a proud glow of spiritual elation, an irrepressible quickening of his flow of thought. Such was Engländer's
case at the moment, for now he had come to the end of the twentieth hour
of his fast.

"Now listen," he shouted, "I want you to use a little intelligence. Two
cosmogonies confront one another. On the one side some professor of biology—
Madenstierer, for instance; on the other, our holy teacher Moses, whether he
ever existed or not. Anyway, I'm perfectly ready to prove to the learned professor Madenstierer that neither Charles the Great, nor Joan of Arc, nor Darwin,
nor he himself, has ever existed either. See? Two cosmogonies then.—In formal
logic, Madenstierer's theory is no whit more evident than Moses'. I imagine
that neither he nor Moses was present at the beginning of the world. But
they both ask me to believe in them. See? The only difference lies in their
methods, that is to say, in the God from whom each of them took his revelation. Madenstierer's God is the intelligence, and he calls his revelation an
hypothesis. But it's just as much based on any beliefs I may choose to bring to it.
I could even go a good step further and affirm that the revelation of Moses, on
which the whole Church is founded, could easily include Madenstierer's hypothesis in itself, as a greater proposition includes a less. Proof?—that holy people,
the Jews—in the eternal sense they are a holy people, in spite of all their present-
day cleverness. Well, then, the Jews! They teach that Revelation, the Bible, can
admit of manifold interpretations—the literal one, the historical one, the
mystic, and the one, last, highest meaning, that only God can interpret. See
what I mean? So that revelation is not just a matter of fact eternally accessible
to humanity, but a deeply veiled, eternal incentive to thought and research. And
that explains the wonderful construction of the Talmud, not unlike the doc-
trinal construction of the Church, since they're both the result of interpretation. And now, I get to my jumping-off place. Interpretation doesn't mean restriction, it's an incentive to free research: and, perhaps, who knows—somewhere or other in the Talmud, or somewhere in St. Thomas—Madenstierer's
hypothesis is contained. The Word of God is an inexhaustible depth of wisdom
in which both theories of causation—the biological and the theological—can
easily exist side by side. It's the mathematical plane of reconciled contradictions.
Proof? All the proof I can give you of that is the relative, magnificent proof of
history. Because, after all, there are only two existing bodies today, which
remain, so to speak, unchanged, eternal: the Catholic Church and Judaism.

"Am I clear? And the thought of God is the one unshakeable foundation,
whether it's been set down in Hebrew, or in Latin or in Chinese characters.
And the only science which survives is the science which binds itself to God.
All Godless intelligence is merely so much subordinate stocktaking. It's a lack
of musical rhythm. Idiots! As though a melody were any less itself because
some kind of sharp-eared schoolmaster can count its beats without grasping
their productive continuity. See what I mean?"

Ferdinand's quiet eyes had been fixed through the whole of this lecture on the workings of Engländer's mouth. The piercing words could reach only his ears. Absence of mind, which of late would so often overcome him in the lecture-room, here also wrapped him in a cloud. What difference did all these things, as remote as the planet Sirius, make to him? He sat in a trance, watching the spittle-bubbles as they oozed from the orator's lips. So every roughness, inequality, zig-zag of thought in Engländer's apologia, which an alert opponent might have seized, passed over his head. Only when the lecturer hit upon an especially happy simile—"An oculist who cannot understand the optic nerve, and yet believes he has grasped the whole essence of light"—did he let out an involuntary sigh. It had nothing to do with the subject.

"Oh, if I could only be a doctor!"

Engländer spluttered and stopped. He looked as though he had only just noticed that somebody had been listening to his flights. He changed his tone.

"Oh, I see. You want to be a doctor, do you? Well, I quite understand your feeling. I can quite understand that anyone should want to be a medico. Well, you'll be one. You'll be one. You'll be anything you want to be. A man like you is bound to be let in for all that intelligence stuff. You have to go through that phase, it's impossible just to jump over it. And very soon you'll have swallowed every atom of the tosh. You'll be thinking, for instance, that some kind of economic system is to blame, instead of just ordinary human godlessness, for the fact that most people behave like a lot of swindling apes, and coldly grin and watch each other perish. Oh, yes, you've got to go through with it. I used to believe in the whole silly bag of tricks myself. So you want to repudiate yourself! Well, I can quite understand—perhaps I may even help you to do it! I say! You haven't got anything to eat here, have you? A hunk of bread, perhaps?"

Ferdinand opened a little cupboard set between two beds. It revealed a few shabby belongings: an extra suit, a second pair of boots, some washing. This evangelical poverty touched Engländer's heart: he began to cogitate seriously the vague promise he had given the little seminarist. Ferdinand took out a plate with a loaf of raisin-bread already cut. This dainty, made of almonds and raisins, a present from Barbara, had come by yesterday's post. Engländer, who had suddenly turned green and begun to look really ill, cut a further huge slab of cake, and began devouring it wolfishly.

In Ferdinand, the word "help" aroused such echoes that his heart set up a wild tattoo. To hide his emotion, no matter how, he went to turn on the light.

"Oh, let it alone—we're all right," grunted Engländer, his fat cheeks bulging with cake.

Ferdinand went back to his window-seat where a shred of daylight was still gleaming. From the table came a voice, impeded by mastication:

"It's odd that I know almost nothing about you. Why don't you ever talk about yourself?"

"Well, you've never asked, and never seemed to want me to," replied the astonished Ferdinand.

"You ought to know what a selfish swine I am."

He dragged up his chair and sat quite close to Ferdinand. But Ferdinand shifted a little, for Engländer had breathed in his face, as he added:

"I might, perhaps, be able to help you to the heresies you seem to need."

This second "help" dropped into Ferdinand's being like water into a deep and dried-up well. Engländer's voice took on a different timbre.

"How is it you happen to be here?"

Tension had relaxed. A warmth began to glow within him. Astonished at the strange sound of his voice, Ferdinand for the first time began talking to Engländer of himself.

LUIGI OF CATANZARO

by LOUIS GOLDING

WHEN the news came through from the Vatican last summer that the Blessed Luigi of Catanzaro was not after all going to be canonized, the disappointment was acute not only in Catanzaro, whither the miracles performed in his name had drawn a countless succession of pilgrims for centuries, but generally throughout the province of Calabria and the whole of Southern Italy. "Il nostro mezzogiorno dimenticato!" was the bitter complaint of cleric and layman alike. "Another instance of North Italian contempt for our wretched forgotten South!" But in point of fact the faithful everywhere in the peninsula were chagrined at the news and it was received with displeasure in Catholic communities as remote as Andalusia and Bohemia. In Bavaria they said that the Jews were at the bottom of it. It was, of course, a purely automatic reaction on the part of the Bavarian gentleman who promulgated the idea. Did it rain? The Jews were at the bottom of it. Did it not rain? The Jews were at the bottom of it. And yet monstrously, marvelously, the fellow had divined the truth this time, though he is still ignorant of the amazing felicity of his imputation. The Jews were at the bottom of it, though not strictly in the sense he implied. That is my story—and Cardinal Bambara's.

You see, not only was there no reason in the world why Luigi should not be canonized; there was, on the contrary, every reason in the world why he should. There were no records of his birth and early upbringing in Calabria, an absence which lent considerable color to the fearful local conviction that there was something supernatural about his birth. Suckled by a goat in the fastness of Aspromonte, the tradition continued, he lived a life of complete isolation among those monstrous caves and forests till his thirtieth year, meditating the doctrine of the Trinity. Then, in recognition of his peculiar merit, Christ himself appeared at the opening of the cave and bade him pick up his oaken staff and his pelt of wolf-skins and make his way to the seashore, even to Cantanzaro; for the plague was raging there at that time and the priests for leagues around the city were either dead in the administration of the holy offices or had fled the neighborhood. Luigi made his appearance a decade or two before the end of the Fifteenth Century; the precise date cannot now be ascertained. But whereas all his history before this time is wrapped in darkness, the whole of his subsequent career, or much of it, is illuminated by a body of consistent tradition, a wealth of references in local ecclesiastical history and a number of documents solemnly attested by high religious and civil officials both immediately after his death and on a large number of occasions subsequently. In a word, there cannot often have been a more complete dossier presented to the *Sacra Congregazione dei Riti,* the Council of Cardinals, prelates and secretaries in the Vatican, whose sole and especial duty it is to deliberate upon beatifications and canonizations and to present their judgment, if favorable, to the final ratification of the Holy Father.

Everything was in order. Of the sanctity of his life there was no question. All that part of the business had been decided at the time of his beatification. He had performed numerous miracles succinctly described by eye witnesses who came to quibble and remained to take the vows as speedily as it could be managed. The plague fell back in rout before him. He healed leprosy, scrofula and all maladies of the digestive organs. He raised a little girl from the dead, and at the earnest solicitation of her pious uncle, who could not bear to see her spotless soul exposed to the iniquities of Catanzaro and the temptations of her own wealth (which he himself inherited and had determined to devote to the foundation of a monastery), Luigi consigned her to the grave again. When he died, his body (I need hardly insist) took the elementary precaution of smelling odorous as a rose-garden for so many days after his demise as he was left unburied, to strengthen the faithful and confute the skeptic.

His posthumous miracles were at least noteworthy. The major part of his relics were preserved with the greatest solemnity in the church of San Stefano, pending such a time as his own canonization made it possible to house them in a church devoted to his own sanctity. But several of his toes, one or two of his finger-joints and an eye-ball managed to find their way into other cities, and their potency was everywhere remarkable. Even shreds of his garments were discovered to be more efficacious than many a thigh-bone abstracted from the bodies of holy men more egregiously advertised than Luigi. The introduction of his sternum into the threshold of a burning house had on several well-authenticated occasions imposed a summary check upon the damage. The bountiful fertility of several successive harvests was achieved by a hebdomadal procession that carried Luigi's cranium with pomp and incense round the fields; and although temporary embarrassment was caused when the same relic was introduced into the chamber of a woman in labor (for she incontinently gave birth to three children and never afterwards could be induced to think kindly of the departed saint), no graver crime could be imputed to Luigi's remains than excess of zeal.

But more than this is required, and rightly, to convince the *Sacra Congregazione* that a given saint is worthy of those ultimate honors they have in their keeping. Not only must a saint's carnal residue be potent upon earth; his spiritual essence must be potent in heaven. Succinct and laborious proof must be given that his intercession before the Celestial Seat has almost invariably insured the efficacy of human prayer. (Invariable success is not exacted, for it is obvious that even the most pious cannot upon occasion forbear making demands of an excessive or indiscreet nature.) The *Sacra Congregazione* had bounteously established the exceptional potency of the Blessed Luigi's intercession. He had interceded on behalf of a Benedictine abbot who had prayed in Luigi's name for a winning number in the State Lottery, in order that he might add a new wing to his monastery. A gentleman from Cotrone had prayed for the unostentatious removal of his first wife, a barren and unprepossessing lady, that he might found, with the assistance of his housekeeper, a charming creature from Piacenza, a numerous and legitimate family to the undying honor of the Holy Church. The first wife had slipped on a pomegranate peel and broken her neck. Need I multiply these instances? It remains for me to add one fact, and not the least important. It seems likely that the increase of Luigi's status from Beatific to Saint might have been achieved a century ago, if nothing more than the merits of the case had been consulted. But it must be realized that sacred processes at the Vatican cost money. Cardinals must live. So must sub-sub-secretaries. And on the day of canonization St. Peter's must be decorated with such splendor that several dukes' ransoms would hardly cover the expenses. Calabria is a poor country.

The financial difficulties in the way of Luigi's promotion had at last, by the grace of God, been overcome. The obols of the peasantry had accumulated for centuries, and had made no great show. But a carter's hunchback son from a back street in Catanzaro emigrated to the States and made a colossal fortune out of tinned tomatoes. He attributed the whole of his success to Luigi, who had presided over every stage of his career and had advised him so shrewdly on Wall Street that he soon had the tinned-tomato world at his feet. He left his fortune without reserve to the cause of promoting Luigi's canonization. No stone was left unturned at the Vatican by his executors. The *Sacra Congregazione* felt more acutely than ever before the beauty and sanctity of Luigi's life. There was not a dissident voice in the council; so overwhelming was their enthusiasm that it was impossible to doubt the issue. They presented the Holy Father with as energetic a recommendation of Luigi's claim as ever passed from the lips and pens of that august body. The matter was not in doubt. For it was well remembered that while still a cardinal, the Holy Father had discussed, upon a certain occasion, with certain friends from Calabria, the title of Luigi and expressed himself wholeheartedly in its favor.

Then the bomb burst. At the very last moment, it seemed, some overwhelming impulse had taken possession of the Father of Christendom. Lugubriously among the mountains of Calabria rumbled the papal "No!" There were tears, there were, I grieve to report, maledictions even. The news, as I have said, was received with displeasure in Catholic communities as remote as Andalusia and Bohemia. As for Bavaria, "The Jews," said they, "the Jews were at the bottom of it!"

They were.

I received the information I am about to convey from Cardinal Bambara himself, the young gentleman whose meteoric career at the Vatican brings our minds back at once to the glorious days of the Renaissance, when exalted office in the Church was awarded not so much for intrinsic virtue (though this sometimes was not overlooked) as for good manners, an elegant appearance or high social distinction. Students of the English peerage will at once recognize below the red hat of Cardinal Bambara the coronet of Lord Laxingworthy. Nor will they have forgotten what august partners were suggested for his hand, in the days when he was one of the first Protestant peers of the United Kingdom. Then one morning the polite world was amazed to learn that young Laxingworthy and his millions had converted to the Church of Rome and that he was already on his way to undertake intimate personal service in the household of His Holiness.

If I may be permitted to say so, I foresaw it all along. I mean Laxingworthy's conversion to the Apostolic and Undivided Church. Ten years ago, he had taken a flattering interest in me during my first, and his own last, term at Oxford, an interest which, I am proud to record, he has never remitted, though our paths have led us into such opposed countries of mind and spirit. He wore ink black shirts and collars in those days and burned black candles before an altar dedicated to Beelzebub. He was your complete undergraduate diabolist, and kept a goat in a suburban garden for the eventual purpose of sacrificing it at a great culminant Mass. He took it all with an engaging seriousness which would have touched the heart of any but the most implacable enemy of Beelzebub. I was perhaps his only friend who knew that a vision—for he is subject to visions and visitations—had won him over to Black Magic; and I am certain he told none but me how another vision had turned his wandering spirit in the direction of Scottish Presbyterianism. That was but a short chapter in his soul's pilgrimage, for he disliked whisky, and Glasgow he could not for a moment tolerate. Rome succeeded Glasgow by way of Boston, Mass., and Hyderabad, and a vision in each case had vouchsafed him the region whither he must next turn his heart. There was evidently a quality of climax in the vision which sent him ecstatic into the bosom of Rome, and thereafter it seemed that Providence need no longer visit him with this clairvoyance and clair-

audience. His soul had attained harbor after perilous seas. It was destined that
the Blessed Luigi of Cantanzaro should slip his soul from its moorings and send
it, tiny and attentive, into vaster oceans than Lord Laxingworthy had ever
traversed before.

It was that solemn moment before His Holiness pronounced his decision.
In a dot of time which was spacious as all time, Cardinal Bambara, standing in
Heaven among the saints of God, saw, heard, understood. Whereas a decision
favorable to Luigi was so much a foregone conclusion among his brethren in
the *Sacra Congregazione* that, before His Holiness had actually given utterance to the fateful monosyllable, they were turning towards each other in easy
and affable conversation, Bambara alone heard the austere negation volleying
down from the empyrean; Bambara alone saw it perch like a bird on the
Pope's lips; Bambara alone understood how none was more astonished at his
own utterance in all that assembly than His Holiness himself.

Here is the tale that Cardinal Bambara told me. I cannot but feel that
Andalusia and Bohemia will receive no little pleasure from hearing the true
story of the Blessed Luigi of Cantanzaro, why he was not canonized. As for
Bavaria—Bavaria may do as it pleases.

There has always, I confess it (said the young cardinal to me), been an
element of the melodramtic in my previous visions—noises of instruments,
unrolling of vapors, swoonings, awakenings. But you cannot conceive how
effortlessly upon this occasion I slid from this state of lesser consciousness to
that other awareness, from flesh to spirit. At one moment I was sitting at the
great table in the council-chamber in the Vatican stretching my legs. At the
next . . . perhaps I ought to admit that I may have nodded for a moment.
You see, old Cardinal Pasqualini had just concluded his long and virtuous
dissertation on the nature of Intercession—a little academic, some of us
thought. He had started the discourse the previous forenoon and it was felt
that he had some time ago exhausted the relevance of his theme to the subject in hand, Luigi's canonization. There is no doubt that even Cardinal Cer-
vone, the postulator of the case, had fallen asleep. I may have nodded a moment
or I may not. At all events it was without any sensation of surprise that I
opened my eyes to find myself in a magnificent institution of which I can only
convey an idea to you if I say it resembled the Athenæum in Piccadilly. Infinitely more spacious of course, but much more like any of the better London
clubs than the somewhat crude conception of Dionysus the Arepogite and
Dante or that regrettable heresiarch, John Milton.

What is that? Where was I? My dear fellow, I was in Heaven! Didn't you
gather that? I hoped not to have to underline the points of my story. In
Heaven, precisely! The House of Commons has been stated to be the most comfortable club in the world. It can't compare with Heaven, I assure you—
You never saw such roomy armchairs. Pleasant little inlaid coffee-tables

dotted the thick-pile carpet, and jolly rugs lay about everywhere. There was a litter of the world's periodicals up and down the place. My eye casually fell upon the Pester Lloyd, the Giornale di Palermo, and the *Buffalo Saturday Night;* St. Appollonia—you remember, the poor girl who had all her teeth extracted in Alexandria—St. Appollonia was deeply immersed in the advertisement columns of the *Dental Surgeon's Gazette.* St. Christopher, who can't read, was poring over the pictures in *La Vie Sportive.* He came from Canaan, you know, where they were never strong on popular education. That was the point. Not even at that first moment was I not aware I was in Heaven, surrounded by the company of the saints. God the Father was sitting in a sort of window-seat behind a dais at the other end of the hall. He tends more and more to keep himself to himself, I gathered. Perhaps, to put it more accurately, he's not quite so interested in the planet Earth and the solar system generally as he once was. There were lots of saints I caught sight of and recognized. Christ himself I didn't see till rather late in the proceedings. Beside him most of the others looked rather garish. He was the only martyr who didn't drag about with him the symbol of his martyrdom. The rest simply would not be separated from their racks, pincers, boilers and so on. Take poor old St. Lawrence, for instance. He had the grid over which he was roasted tied to his belt; of course it dragged after him wherever he went and made a frightful mess of the carpet. St. Barbara's tower also was just a little cumbrous, and St. Bartholomew carrying his own flayed skin did not seem in the very best taste.

They were all surprisingly like their painted and sculptured images in the Uffizi and the Prado and elsewhere. I mean, how could a fellow possibly mistake where he was and who these people were? Talk about nature imitating art. Here was St. Sebastian trying so desperately to look like Sodoma's picture of him in the Academia that he had positively succeeded by now. It had meant rather more readjustment in some cases than others, and St. George, for instance, must have found it a distinct strain to adapt his swarthy Cappadocian features to the pretty and gallant rendering of him by Carpaccio in Venice. You know the one I mean, a series rather, in the School of Schiavoni? I got the impression that one or two saints had never quite made up their minds whose rendering, as between two particularly beautiful ones, they were going to adopt. St. Luke, for instance. Was it to be Van Dyck or Raphael? It had resulted in a curious lack of definition in the evangelist's features which made him hard to recognize at first. The Holy Ghost? Yes, the Holy Ghost was busy flying round and about the place. The noise of his cooing was the only noise I heard on my entrance. He was perched on the crozier that belongs to Nicholas, Bishop and Saint.

Something was engaging the mind of St. Appollonia and St. Christopher, despite all their show of being immersed in the *Dental Surgeon's Gazette* and *La Vie Sportive.* And St. Zeno, St. Florian, St. Roch, St. Jerome (whose lion was behaving disgracefully), St. Panteleon, St. Ignatius Loyola, St. Chad, St.

Elizabeth of Hungary, St. James the Less. You know how sensitive I am to atmospheres. I scented it almost at once. All was not well in Heaven. There was friction somewhere and pretty serious friction.

No, you couldn't possibly guess. The Blessed Luigi of Catanzaro! Surprised? A mere beatific and there are so many thousands upon thousands of them? No mere beatific could have caused such a state of tension among the ranks of the saints in Heaven? Ah, my dear fellow, hold on a moment.

Of course I wasn't told so all at once. Nobody came rushing up to me to enlighten me. Everybody was feeling too raw to take any notice of a little snippety cardinal. I mightn't have existed for all they cared. As I say, I just sensed this distressing atmosphere of strain and trouble. Just the Holy Ghost cooing from St. Nicholas's crozier and a few saints here and there turning over the newspaper with just a little more abruptness—it seems in retrospect—than was strictly necessary. In a sort of special ladies' alcove, several female saints were knitting socks, the usual crowd—St. Agnes, St. Ursula, St. Lucy, and those people. Then of a sudden the air snapped. You never heard anything like it. The whole club was in an uproar and I sidled up as unostentatiously as I could. What was it all about? It was difficult to gather anything straight off, because they talked in the Latin of the Vulgate with a rather perplexing local accent. To intensify the confusion they made the most frantic noise with their saintly symbols. Palms whistled, books slapped, swords clattered, St. Cecilia made her organ screech with temper to drown the noise of St. Ursula's eleven thousand virgins. (St. Ursula never moved a step without them.)

And then I disengaged and pieced together the words: Catanzaro, Luigi of Catanzaro, the canonization of the Blessed Luigi of Catanzaro—yes, no, yes, no, yes, no, yes, no!

And gradually the whole business became clear to me. The matter which was so urgently preoccupying the saints of heaven was precisely the matter which the *Sacra Congregazione* had been debating on earth. From several indications I realized that until quite recently everything had all been plain sailing in the particular issue of Luigi. But what was more important, in the general issue of canonization, one thing became increasingly evident to me: that the Council of the Vatican, so far from deciding these questions off its own bat, so to speak, acts in precise and unconscious correspondence with the decisions arrived at by the congress of saints in Heaven. So that, in point of fact, no beatific is despatched into their assembly without having been carefully examined and passed by them in advance. Beatifications are conducted without their saintly interference, as being of less moment.

And, after all, is not some such thing to be expected? Does any decent club in New York or London admit a new member without the closest scrutiny? Is it not quite reasonable that the saints should require to know whether a projected member is quite the sort of person they care to know?

Luigi of Catanzaro, at all events, had seemed unimpeachable. All his miracles had been in the best taste, and none of them was so preposterously successful as to win over a serious number of their adherents from the established favorites. Expelling the plague, the dead, quickening the womb of the barren or the loins of the impotent—they were all miracles after the best models. The whole business was going through as complacently in Heaven as it was down in the Vatican.

Then some nasty anonymous little angel appeared on the scene and upset everything. The archangels, seraphim, princedoms and the winged powers generally have a club all to themselves. They don't like the architecture of the saints' institution and it cramps their freedom of movement. But the rank-and-file angels are not particularly welcome anywhere. Always carrying tales of what the archangels said about the saints and the saints about the archangels and telling tales about both to God the Father. They brought about a dreadful coolness, apparently, between St. Anthony of Padua and the Archangel Michael. It lasted about four hundred years, till Christ got them to shake hands during the festivities that took place on the acceptance of Joan of Arc into the club. Yes, these angels would have been trodden on ages ago if God the Father hadn't a very soft spot in his heart for them.

Everything was going brilliantly, as I've said, for Luigi. When in rushed one of those offensive young creatures.

"News about Luigi," he cried. "News about Luigi of Catanzaro!"

Everybody crowded round. They didn't like to encourage the fellow, but they all liked Luigi genuinely, so much as they knew of him, and they were interested.

"What's it all about, my fine fellow?" rumbled St. Christopher.

"Yes, indeed?" inquired Saints Cosmo and Damain, in their educated medical voices.

"I've found out who he was!" said the angel.

"But we all know who he was!' said St. Paul, stroking his silky beard. "We've known for five centuries!"

"Yes, but does any of you know who his father was, and where he was born?"

"It never occurred to us to ask!" said St. Genurro severely.

"Who was he anyhow?" somebody else interrupted, not very curiously. The sooner the young fellow delivered his tidbit and made off, the better.

"Yes, who was he?" added another voice—a Jesuit saint it was, one gathered from the clipped cultured syllables. After all it would do no harm to find out just who Luigi and his people were. One had to live at close quarters with one's fellow members and it did no harm to know these things in advance. Quite a number of people suddenly recalled the mists of obscurity which shrouded the birth of Luigi.

"Yes, who was he?"

The little fellow paused, his eyes sparkling with malicious triumph. He look round upon the serried masses of saints, breathless one and all. A strange unease had communicated itself to them.

"Who was Luigi of Catanzaro? Who was he? And you were just going to let them canonize him? You were just discussing the details of the festa you were going to organize in his honor when he made his appearance. Weren't you?"

And they had been.

They were really going to let themselves go. St. Luke had volunteered to paint a magnificent fresco on a triumphal arch to be erected outside the entrance-hall by St. Thomas, patron of architects, Luigi was to approach the arch under a gable of crossed palms and St. Ursula's virgins (room had always to be found for St. Ursula's eleven thousand virgins) were to pelt him with special spineless roses provided by St. Francis of Assisi. During the course of the afternoon the principal martyrs had agreed to give their celebrated show, which they performed only on very special occasions. For they enfiladed before the eyes of the assembled, the highly appreciative company, subjecting themselves to those same tortures which had won them undying glory. St. Catherine getting herself decapitated and St. Lawrence being slowly roasted were always exceptionally successful items.

In the evening the Initiation Proper was to take place. Would in fact, take place. Why should it not?

Then clear and shrill the angel piped across Heaven:

"Luigi of Catanzaro? A common Jew, that's what he was. A Jewish refugee from Saragossa. His father was a low-born little rabbi burned at the stake by the Holy Inquisition. Now you know!"

A cry of dismay resounded across the club.

"A Jew!"

"A Jewish refugee!"

"A common Jew!"

"Prove it!" exclaimed St. Thomas Aquinas peremptorily.

"Prove it?" shrilled the angel. "That won't take me long!" He fumbled about under his left wing and produced a sheaf of papers bound up in blue ribbon. He thrust them under the nose of St. Thomas of Aquinas.

"Everything in order?" he inquired offensively.

St. Thomas impassively examined the documents. His father's and mother's marriage lines, his own birth-certificate, a final notice from the Inquisition authorities that unless Rabbi Nahum (that was the name of Luigi's father) recanted by the second Lord's day from this day, such and such tortures should be imposed, and should these not be successful in winning him from the stubborn abomination, he, and his wife, and his son Aryeh (which is the Hebrew equivalent of Luigi) should be burned at the stake ad majorem Dei gloriam in saecula saeculorum. How Aryeh had escaped was in these papers made plain, how he had spent the first thirty years of his life as a carpenter, who had converted him to the Faith . . .

St. Thomas turned round to the assembled saints.

"Everything," said he, thin-lipped, "everything is in order! Luigi of Catanzaro was by birth and race a Jew, by early profession a carpenter. His own father was a Jewish rabbi burned at the stake for his contumacy. His own subsequent history you are yourselves acquainted with!"

"At all events," said St. Anthony of Padua, "they've beatified him. That can't be undone!"

"So long," said St. Francis Xavier, "as this idea of canonization is dropped. A Jew, that is to say, a Jew!"

"A Jew! A Jew!" The whisper rippled like quickening rivulets.

Boomed like a cataract the voice of the giant from Canaan, colossal Christopher:

"And what's that got to do with it? Canonized he was going to be, and canonized he will be! Jew or no Jew, Turk or Brahmin, you all know the life he lived, the miracles he performed, or don't you? Have you forgotten? A better man than three or four I could mention here. Let there be no nonsense about it, say I! Oo-oo!" H brought his club down on the floor with a terrific impact.

"A Jew!" said St. Peter crossly. "Out of the question, completely out of the question!"

All the apostles echoed his words. "A Jew! O completely out of the question!"

Then a voice chimed like a low, sweet bell. It was St. Francis of Assisi.

"Comrades, comrades. Is it indeed you that speak with so little charity? These are not your voices. Shall not a saint in all ways so lovable, so worthy of our own most lovely sisters and brothers, shall he not be accepted among us with singing, with praises unto the Lord? Comrades, let us continue the discussion of our plans, who shall be deputed to meet him, who to conduct him, who to present him to the Eternal One. The hours grow late . . ."

"Our younger brothers," said St. Paul to St. Peter, "must not allow themselves to be misled by sentiment. In an issue of a purely philosophical nature . . ."

"Philosophy or no philosophy," interrupted St. Denis, "he's a common Jew and that settles it."

"Indeed it does!" said St. Ursula primly.

"Indeed it does!" twittered all her eleven thousand virgins.

"Nothing of the sort!" rapped out St. Cecilia.

The dispute became fast and furious. Then it got worse. It became polite and awkward. Then it subsided into a pained silence. That, as you may by now have forgotten, was the moment of my own appearance.

And then it started again. They threshed it out all over from the beginning, twice, three times, four times. That is how I've been able to reconstruct for my own benefit, and yours, the story up to the point. Of what happened subsequently I was myself a direct witness.

The argument might have gone on indefinitely and His Holiness might even at this moment have been racking his wits to decide the matter one way or the other, had not the idea occurred to St. Bernard of Clairvaux that the only thing to do under the circumstances was to vote on it. You see the situation was unprecedented. In the past the general feeling against or for a particular candidate had been promptly recognizable and speedily acted on, for although the assembly themselves took no part in the process of beatification, it gave them the opportunity of learning all they needed regarding a potential member. They had taken only the most languid interest in the two statutory miracles demanded from Luigi between the times of his beatification and canonization, for his earlier performances had been so numerous and so convincing that his two new miracles had been felt to be more or less perfunctory. It was true that in earlier ages, most especially in the time of the martyrs, the net had been so large that any number of questionable fish had slipped through. What was done could not be undone and they'd all shaken down very comfortably together. But ever since Urban the Eighth in the Seventeenth Century had defined the whole business by those two laborious decrees of his, everything had been plain sailing. One thing was certain. This Jew question had never arisen before.

"Vote on it!" said St. Bernard of Clairvaux brilliantly.

"Vote on it!" caught up a hundred voices with delight. How is it nobody had thought of it before? Really they had all hated upsetting the jolly friendly atmosphere of the club. You might have thought it a pack of angels squabbling, the way everybody had been carrying on.

St. Bernard took the count.

It was distressing. It was dreadfully distressing. The voting was absolutely equal. Such consternation on the faces of St. Peter of Castlenau, St. Gregory, St. Clara, St. Zenobio, St. Romualdo, St. Celsus, St. Alban, as you can't possibly conceive. The situation was rather more desperate than before. Everybody looked helplessly towards St. Bernard. St. Bernard set his lips. St. Bernard puckered his brow. Silence.

Then St. Bernard raised his head and flung his arm out with a gesture of exaggerated ease.

"Nothing," said he, "nothing simpler in the world. Christ shall give his casting vote. We, and Luigi of Catanzaro, and His Holiness, and the *Sacra Congregazione,* shall abide by it. And Calabria, and Andalusia, and Bohemia, and Bavaria. The Faith shall abide by it. Or has any lady or gentleman any other idea to suggest?"

"No!" burst from a thousand throats. "NO, no, no! Good for you, St.

Bernard of Clairvaux! Bully for St. Bernard! But Christ? Where is Christ, by the way? Has anybody seen Christ anywhere?"

Nobody has seen him lately.

"I rather think," said St. Mary Magdalene, "there was some talk of an old widow dying somewhere in Basilicata. She kept on calling for San Luigi Gonzaga; and then for any San Luigi who might care to come along. She insisted on the Luigi, because her husband was Luigi, and so was her first born. Then the boy died and she called her second baby Luigi. And the new Luigi died on the same day as the old one, the father. And this morning, she herself lay dying, but of course all the San Luigis have been too busy on this question of a possible addition to their number.

"So Jesus went."

And at that moment a tired voice whispered—it might have been a flower speaking, *Eccomi*. Here is Christ!" And Christ came in rather foot-sore after his long journey to and from Basilicata, and sat down on an armchair and Mary Magdalene soothed his feet with her tresses.

"Won't you let him recover his breath for a few moments?" whispered St. Mary Magdalene. His mother bent over the back of his chair and stroked his brow.

But the matter was too important to wait, for the peace of mind of the whole club was involved. St. Bernard lost no time explaining how the land lay. Christ had gathered something of the situation upon his journey through the middle air. But the latest developments had eluded him, or his mind had been full of the dying widow's last words. St. Bernard clearly explained what was required from him.

"Give me," whispered Christ, "give me half an hour." He sank his head upon his hands. The saints broke into small groups and paced unquietly up and down the hall. Ten and twenty minutes passed and Christ remained motionless as the chair he sat on. The Magdalene placed her cool cheek against his feet. St. Francis of Assisi looked timidly upon him and besought the others to keep away when they ventured too close.

Christ rose. He moved slowly between the tables towards the inner end of the hall to the dais there, where the lectures and entertainments are held. He lifted his head and spoke.

"Sisters and brothers," he said, "I cannot but regret that this duty, which hitherto you have yourselves so well performed, should now fall upon my shoulders, too little worthy to support it. For the Blessed Luigi of Catanzaro, the object of these present discussions, I have much personal esteem. I might call it affection. I might call it reverence. Those among you who desire to elect him to your company would elect no mean minister, no feeble intercessor, out of his intermediate to these final glories.

"But how shall I place myself in opposition to those others, no less my dear councilors and lovers, who would exclude him? What are the grounds upon which he would be excluded? There are none others, I am right in con-cluding, than that he is a Jew? Sisters and brothers, I cannot but confess that the reason embarrasses me a little. It is true I find that my own beloved apostles are among the most vocal of his rejectors. That the greater part of their company are Jews is not perhaps relevant. . . ."

"That it is!" rumbled St. Christopher.

"Jews!" murmured another. "But of course they're Jews! How can we have lost sight of the fact?"

"There's no need," grumbled St. Peter, who looked hot and uncomfortable, "to rake up these old scandals!"

"Isn't there just!" said the Seven Maccabeans in concert. They had maintained a strict silence hitherto. Being the only pre-Christian saints in the club, they had been feeling their position distinctly uncomfortable all along. We don't see what being a Jew has to do with it!" said the elder Maccabean boldly.

"Indeed we don't!" exclaimed his six brothers.

"The whole objection is ridiculous!" blustered St. Moses of Venice, the converted brigand, who still hoped against hope that somebody would take him for his more illustrious namesake in the Old Testament.

"Autres siècles, autres procès!" said St. Paul pointedly.

"Beloved sisters and brothers!" Christ resumed. "But that is not the sole reason why I find my position so particularly invidious. It will not have been forgotten that I too am a Jew!"

"I'm not at all certain," murmured St. Athanasius, "that the theology is quite sound there!"

"What does theology matter?" said the Magdalene, turning towards him. "Didn't He die on the Cross?"

"What about my grid?" said St. Lawrence.

"Children, children! The knot is too tangled for my fingers to unravel it!" exclaimed Christ piteously. "May I be permitted to submit the issue to the Ancient of Days? He is wiser than his son, than any or all of us. Will you permit it?"

There was a movement amongst the four Latin Fathers.

"It tastes of Aryanism," said one. "The inferiority of the Second Person!" expanded another. They were talked down. If people got on that tack the matter would never be settled this side of doomsday. It was getting late and chilly.

"Ask him!" the cry came. "Ask him!"

Christ walked over to his father and talked to him for a few minutes. Everybody waited. Christ looked up to the old man, gently, fearfully.

"Say it again!" said God. "You know I'm rather deaf!"

Christ began to repeat all he had said in a slightly louder voice. God hollowed his hand about his ear, but this time he did not allow his son to finish. There was a sudden impatient movement of both his arms.

"I won't be bothered! I tell you I won't be bothered! Do you think this is the only religion I've got to attend to? I've got my hands full at the present with this new religion they've started at Boston. And I must keep my eye on Fontainebleau. Settle between yourselves, can't you? Tell them I said so!"

Christ resumed his place on the dais. "You have seen, ladies and gentlemen, you have heard. What is to be done?"

Not a sound was heard in the hall. Everyone looked impotently at everyone else. No one could allow himself to be such a ruffian as to drive Christ to a decision. He looked so tired, he always looked so tired these days. The whole business was lamentable in the extreme.

And at that moment the Holy Ghost cooed long and loud from his perch on the crozier of St. Nicholas.

"The Holy Ghost!" said the saints.

"The Holy Ghost!" whispered Christ. "Here is an arbitration you cannot gainsay?"

"Never! Never! Never!"

Christ clapped his hands. There was a flutter of white wings across the air. "Tell me," murmured Christ. "Tell me!"

The saints lowered their eyes or turned awfully away. The pink feet had come to rest upon Christ's shoulder. He inclined his ear toward the ineffable beak. There was no sound. But the Word had passed between them, too august for utterance, the Word which was in the beginning.

"Beloved sisters and brothers," said Christ. The saints turned and lifted their eyes. *"The Jew, Aryeh, the Blessed Luigi of Catanzaro, will not be canonized.* As it was in the beginning . . ."

"Is now," took up the saints humbly.

"And ever shall be," they continued.

"World without end!" proclaimed the assembly.

The Holy Ghost cooed contentedly from his perch on the crozier of St. Nicholas.

"You might make them understand in Calabria," said Cardinal Bambara, "just how it was, won't you? The Holy Father has taken to heart rather seriously these imputations of a bias against Calabria and the mezzogiorno. You see how unfair they are."

"They were rather upset," I added, "even in Bohemia and Andalusia."

"Let them know," said the Cardinal. "Let them know!"

"And Bavaria?"

"Why not Bavaria?" said the Cardinal, mopping his brow wearily. "By all means let them know in Bavaria!"

Which I herewith do.

THE ETERNAL JEW[1]

by LION FEUCHTWANGER

I

ABOUT a year ago I met the Eternal Jew in Munich. He was sitting in the Café Odeon reading the *Frankfurter Zeitung*. He was elegantly although not too fashionably dressed and disported a small black English beard. His face was carefully shaved and he was a bit paunchy. There was something strangely familiar about the man. I must have seen him often at first nights at the theater, in the restaurants or on the boulevards. However there was a remarkable burning intensity in his eyes and a certain characteristic trick of moving his hands which quite gave him away.

"Good morning," said I. "Do you mind if I sit near you?"

He muttered something which I took for a refusal. Thereupon I sat down beside him.

"You seem to be in a bad humor," I remarked.

"Why shouldn't I be?" he countered irritably, answering my question with another question as was his habit. "Do you call this a trade? Have I a useful function to perform—to be a symbol of something that does not exist? I am putting on flesh. I am growing a paunch and fat ghosts are out of date. I protest! I do not wish to remain an anachronism on two legs!"

"I am innocent!" said I politely and offered him a cigarette.

He flared up.

"Innocent! What do you mean innocent? Nobody is innocent of anything. You will find this written in the books of Abraham ibn Samuel Abulafia. Are you acquainted with Abraham Abulafia?" he interrupted himself. "That short, skinny fellow from Saragossa who looks so comical in his suit of armor."

"Did you say 'armor'?" I asked surprised. "Is the gentleman an actor?"

"What!" he growled. "An actor! You are far too ignorant for an intelligent conversation."

He puffed fiercely at his cigarette.

"Yes, what I wanted to say was that at first he too always twaddled about his innocence. He was a great kabalist, was Abraham Abulafia. Possibly the last time I saw him was six or seven hundred years ago. They hailed him then in Sicily as the Messiah. After that he journeyed to Rome in order to convert Pope Nicholas III to Judaism. But the latter was a disagreeable sort of gentle-

---

[1] *The Eternal Jew* was suppressed by the German government during World War I. Incidentally, the butt of the author's satire became, by a malicious irony, the established order in the Third Reich.

man and things therefore went badly with Abulafia who was condemned to burn, without any loss of time, in the Piazza of Suriano. It happened then to be a public festival. A cardinal was present with his two mistresses. Many farmers arrived with their wives and asses and the innkeeper sold a great deal of wine, anise, artichokes and garlic. And because the stake at which Abulafia was to be burned turned out so attractive to the eye that it pleased his concubines, the Cardinal ordered that three more Jews be tied to it then and there. All the anti-Semites rejoiced, and so also did the Cardinal's two mistresses, the peasants and the asses. They raised a terrible din. And poor Abulafia cried aloud his innocence. Had he not written that Jesus was a misunderstood prophet and that after all there must be something to the Holy Trinity? And as far as he himself was concerned he certainly could not have had a hand in the crucifixion of the Saviour. However, at the very last moment a courier arrived with a message from the Pope and he was released. But from this resulted a great disillusionment in the soul of Abulafia. All night long I argued with him until I finally proved my point. After that he wrote in all his books that nobody is innocent in nothing."

Since I did not know Abraham Abulafia I could not discuss him. So I turned to a subject less remote.

"Is it a long time since you were last here in Munich?"

"Long?" he growled. "What do you mean long? The last time I was here you were ruled by a king who wrote bad verses, had an affair with a good-looking woman, stuck his tongue out and turned anti-Semite merely because Heine's verses pleased people more than his. The nation held nothing against him on account of his verses but it never forgave him his affair with the good-looking woman. At that time all were in favor of beer and the clergy and against art and pretty women. It was a good constellation."

"A good constellation! How so?"

"Wherever people are against art they are also against the Jews. Add on top of that the bad verses, and the anti-Semitic movement is in full bloom. That is why I put such great hope in expressionistic poetry."

"Are you an anti-Semite?" I asked in amazement.

"Just listen to that!" he retorted. "What else do you expect me to be? Am I not a product of anti-Semitism? The Wandering Jew who is everywhere a stranger, who never feels at home anywhere, is undoubtedly an anti-Semitic phantasy. The growth of civilization undermines my raison d'être and diminishes hatred for the Jews. Germany, which has been my strongest bulwark for so long, has furnished me with the worst experiences during the last few decades. Since the time that Moses Mendelssohn made an end of the Yiddish jargon the Jews here have been prospering increasingly. I am ready to vouch for that. Surely you notice how fat I am!" he concluded in a worried tone of voice.

"Yes—yes," he continued after a pause, "the prospects look bad. It is questionable whether I'll survive. My last hope is centered in the Polish land-owners, in the Rumanian peasants, in the Highpriest of the Botoku tribe of the Dalli-Dalli, in certain one-hundred-percent German army officers and students and in expressionist poetry."

"Have you any definite plans while here in Munich?"

"Have I plans? Naturally I have plans. I am establishing an anti-Semitic newspaper here."

"You are establishing—?"

"Why shouldn't I, pray? Shall I stand idly by while they are slowly cutting the ground under my feet? Shall I wait until I am altogether suspended in midair before trying to express my views? Ever since they have done away with race theories, ever since it has been established that the superiority of races and differences in blood are all poppycock and that there is no other criterion for the adhesion of a people than language, I find no air to breathe any more. More and more am I losing my ghostly fluid. What new lease of life the publication of Chamberlain's *Foundations of the Nineteenth Century* gave me! I derived from it a good part of the fat that is on me. But unfortunately it has proven only a brainstorm. Therefore I have turned sour as vinegar. I beg of you, just consider: a fat-bellied bourgeois ghost! Shall I reconcile myself to that state of being? I refuse to be reconciled to it! I will fight, I will bare my teeth, I will strike out! Indeed! I am a tragic person, somewhat repulsive perhaps, admitted, but nevertheless tragic. Shall I become a buffoon, a meditative flowery-arbor ghost à la Lorelei or the dwarf Perkeo? No! I wish to remain an honest ghost! I must get rid of my paunch. I am determined to establish an anti-Semitic newspaper."

"Won't there be difficulties?" I asked timidly. "There is hardly a German of any intellectual consequence from Walther von der Vogelweide and Wolfram von Eschenbach to Klopstock, Lessing and Mommsen, who has not said biting things against anti-Semitism."

"You seem to think you are very clever in making this observation. Naturally, there is no intelligent German of the kind you have mentioned, who has not expressed himself in a similar fashion. But I am hardly pleased with that. What I stand in need of most is clamor, thrashing-flails and resounding sheet-metal. What do you think took place at the disputes during the Middle Ages between the Jewish Rabbis and the Christian theologians? Those were jolly performances! The Jews furnished all the arguments and the others the strong fists."

"And do you believe that in Munich of all places—?"

"Do I believe? I *know*. There, for example, is that Doctor of Philosophy, Marbod Timm—"

"Marbod Timm!" I exclaimed. "The founder of the Scythian League, of the Wotan Union?"

"Yes," said the Eternal Jew, "and also of 'The Secret Order of Black-White-Red from Sirius to the Jungfrau.' "

"I am acquainted with this Marbod Timm," I remarked. "Would you like to meet his fiancée? I am taking tea with her today."

He came along.

"Whenever I read the *Frankfurter Zeitung,*" he said to me as we were crossing the Odeonsplatz, "I become melancholy. Good German stifles me. Good German and anti-Semitism cannot endure each other. Ha!—" The Eternal Jew suddenly interrupted himself with a little cry.

"What is wrong?" I asked, frightened.

"Look! It pricked me!" he exulted, pointing to his swastika stickpin. "For no sooner do I meet with someone or something that can give me assistance or pleasure than my stickpin pricks me."

He bought several newspapers at the street corner.

"There we have it!" he cried triumphantly as he looked through the *Bayrischen Boten.* "What did I tell you? There! Read! That is a German for you! His is the sort I like."

He ecstatically murmured Hebrew exorcisms as he read the newspaper.

"And here—just take a look!" He pointed to the feuilleton. "I should say this feuilleton is the right meat for me! No salt, not a grain of salt in it whatsoever! Goethe, Hebbel, Heine, all of them have verified it. Just watch and see me get rid of my paunch now! I am going to establish my newspaper here!"

He now abandoned himself with ardor to the reading of the newspaper.

"There it goes again!" he jubilated. "There it goes again!" And he pointed to his swastika stickpin. We had now reached the Arcades of the Palace park enriched with the verses Ludwig I had written on the Rottmann frescoes. Hereupon the stickpin cavorted like one possessed. "This is the city where milk and honey flow," rejoiced the Eternal Jew. And he commenced to declaim the King's elegiac verses and ambled about in a dance of triumph to the music of its imperfect scansion.

"You must not dance here," I said gently. "It will attract too much attention."

He calmed down a bit and I continued: "And concerning Munich, you must not indulge in generalizations. To be sure, it is no literature-loving city. Schiller's *Horæ* found only three subscribers here although the novel, *King Ludwig II,* or *The Martyr in Purple Ermine,* sold one hundred thousand copies. But all that proves nothing—nor should it concern us. Just see how much progress had already been made here: a stylized stage, the eight-hour day, the renaissance of the industrial arts, eleven official hangmen, pretzels, the New Pathos and light beer. But of all these fruits of progress only the pretzels and the beer have made any impression upon the citizens of Munich. For this reason I believe your anti-Semitic newspaper will meet with no success. The inhabitants of the town will simply ignore its existence."

The Eternal Jew nodded his head reflectively, slowly fondled his copy of the *Bayrischen Boten,* then folded it and stuck it into his pocket. "We will wait and see," he said.

II

I introduced the Eternal Jew as Dr. A. Has. Gertrud Hohenleitner scrutinized him carefully, but not in any unfriendly way as was usual with her whenever she met someone for the first time.

"Marbod has told me about you," she said. "I believe you have corresponded with him." Her large, handsome face, lit up by her big pale eyes under their drooping dark lashes, struck me as being unusually fresh looking that day. And her very blond hair visibly made an impression upon the Wandering Jew.

"I guess there is nothing doing over here," he whispered to me as we sat down. "She is too clever, too composed. Her hair is like a flock of goats that descend from Mount Gilead. Her teeth are like a flock of sheep that are even shorn, which came up from the washing; Whereof everyone beareth twins, and none is barren among them—"

"Pardon, what did you say?" asked Gertrud as she poured the tea.

"Oh, nothing important, my dear young lady," the Eternal Jew replied hastily. "I only remarked that you bear an astounding resemblance to Abital, the Princess of the Kuzars."

"To whom?" asked Gertrud, lifting her eyebrows.

"To Abital, the Princess of the Kuzars. An unusually pleasing individual, clever, courageous, good-looking and blond as you are. She abolished altogether the old custom of selling children into slavery. This happened more than two hundred years after Bulan, King of the Kuzars, and his entire nation, which, although racially stemming from the Finns, lived in the Crimea, were voluntarily converted to Judaism. Unfortunately, the Kuzars were not long after that annihilated by the invading Russians."

"Are you an historian, doctor?" asked Gertrud.

"To a certain extent, yes," answered the Eternal Jew. "I am an anti-Semite from conviction as well as from inclination. My aim is to prove that all the wickedness that has ever been perpetrated in the world, the crucifixion of socialism and capitalism, the World War and pacifism; in short, all the evil in the world has been caused by the Jews."

"The introduction of syphilis?" I asked wonderingly.

"Very simple. If the Jews had not given assistance to Columbus then he would not have discovered America and syphilis would never have been introduced. Indeed, it is apparent that the Jews aided Columbus only in order to introduce this contagious disease and then, as physicians, to make a pile of money out of it."

"I have similar ideas on this matter," said Gertrud, her large, pale eyes flushing dark with anger. "My fiancé too has the infection. But Marbod is a good man, nevertheless. I confidently hope that I will cure him of this disease."

"And what about my paunch!" angrily cried the Eternal Jew. "Must I resign myself to growing stouter and stouter and more ridiculous from year to year?"

"What has your paunch got to do with Marbod's anti-Semitism?" asked Gertrud in astonishment.

"He is only referring to the possibility that 'The Secret Order of Black-White-Red from Sirius to the Jungfrau' might some day be forced to dissolve," I hastened to explain.

"You ought to be ashamed of yourself," said Gertrud to the Eternal Jew. "And at your age too! A scientific man, too! You ought to keep out of this schoolboy mischief. Tell me, why are you an anti-Semite?"

"From conviction," answered the Eternal Jew.

"Conviction!" jeered Gertrud. "When one wishes to justify to oneself the experience of any cheap emotion then one throws the blame for it on the Jews. Why do you think the anti-Semites employ so much abuse in their discussions? It merely resolves itself into the rage of the incompetent against the competition of the more capable ones. On the other hand there are individuals with vested interests who are determined to throw the blame of their mistakes and villainies on the shoulders of others."

"And what about your fiancé?" asked the Eternal Jew.

"My God! He is young. He is but recently arrived from the trenches. He has been crying for such a long time: 'Down with——!' At first it was: 'Down with the English!'; then, 'Down with the Government!' He must always have someone about whom he can cry: 'Down with——!' It seems as if all young men nowadays stand in need of this particular kind of expression. Now they are shouting: 'Down with the Jews!' And my fiancé shouts along with them. That is only natural."

"And right he is too," said the Eternal Jew with approbation.

"Anti-Semitism," said I, "is something without rhyme or reason. It is always a sure sign that people who generalize are mentally lazy. 'The Jews are to blame for everything.' The Jews! Aren't there Jews great and small, brunette and blond, sympathetic and repulsive? One might as well, and with as much justice, say that all football players, or all those who wear spectacles, are to blame for everything. There certainly are many swindlers and usurers that wear spectacles, as also do some capitalists and Communists. In the perpetration of almost any crime, there is to be found some criminal who wears spectacles. Don't many officers wear monocles? It is those fellows with the monocles that are to blame for militarism. Don't many radicals wear eye-glasses? It is those chaps with the eye-glasses that stabbed the army at the Front in the back during the War. In any case, the wearing of spectacles is thoroughly un-Germanic. I am sure that the ancient Teutons did not wear any spectacles, and it is impossible for me to imagine Hermann the Cheruscan with eye-glasses."

"You are right there!" fervently exclaimed the Eternal Jew. "I very well recall Hermann the Cheruscan. He was a man of affairs, and always was compromising and involving himself in intrigues. He was well-paunched and well-jowled, crafty and jovial. But I did not want to have anything to do with him. Now let me see—whom did he resemble? There! I have it! Prince von Bülow. It would have been good for all the combatants if the battle he engaged in—"

But neither the astonished Gertrud nor I discovered what exactly would have proved good for all the combatants. For at that moment the swastika stickpin began to dance lustily, and Marbod Timm entered.

III

A few days later I went looking for the Eternal Jew in the Hotel Marienbad where he lived. He had just breakfasted, sat in his pajamas at the table, looking through a microscope at an object which I did not recognize.

"What are you after?" I asked.

"Look for yourself," he answered.

I looked through the microscope and saw some small whitish-red organisms that were grown together. I did not know what to make of them.

"These are fission-fungi," he explained. "When exposed to the air they produce blood-red drops of coloring-matter which one frequently sees in bread and in other foods."

"And—?" I asked.

"These fission-fungi also appear occasionally in sacramental wafers," he continued. "Then there is raised the cry that the Host has been defiled by the Jews. Many of the latter are killed. The fission-fungus, as you see, has caused the death of about four hundred thousand Jews.

"In our time, however, it is no longer possible for the Jew-baiters to employ this means. It does not work in the city any more except way down in the sticks. To expect that the Jews be prevented from taking any further part in the intellectual and public life of the nation, that they be confined again in a ghetto and be forced to speak a jargon, appears like a ridiculous contradiction. Also, the falsified statistics concerning the number of Jews in the army have not been manipulated with sufficient ingenuity. New means must be found. Unfortunately the anti-Semites have such sterile imaginations!"

"Tut! tut!" said I. "And what about the fairy tale of Jewish world-domination? Also the fairy tale of Jewish materialism? The fairy tale of Jewish Masonic Lodges and the World War? And the fairy tale of the Jewish Revolution?"

"Of course! That is so!" said the Eternal Jew. "But these fairy tales are too poorly composed. On the one hand they are too incredible, on the other they are not silly enough. They sound imbecilic and certainly lack consistency. If it is charged that capitalism is the means by which the Jews are driving

Germany to ruin, then it is impossible to claim in the same breath that socialism is the means by which they plan to destroy the German nation. It is only possible for the nation to believe in either one of these two theories. The masses are not stupid enough to believe in both at one and the same time."

There he sat, stout and troubled, in his handsome violet pajamas. Carefully shaved, disporting a little black English beard, he might well be met with a hundred times in the theater, at restaurants or on the boulevards. But most remarkable of all, the intense light in his eyes and a certain characteristic way of moving his hands quite gave him away.

"These are hard times," he resumed again. "Germany had provided such a good field for my work before. But ever since the day that Moses Mendelssohn got to realize that it was the Yiddish jargon that called forth the very worst in the Jews, and ever since he put a stop to scrambling languages and issued a death sentence on Yiddish, that I have begun to put on weight. But now the Jews have so deeply entrenched themselves in German culture that my existence no longer has any validity. Upon what then do I pin my last hopes? It is upon the wretched survivals of the Ghetto Masquerade. For should it be attempted to dislodge the Jews from their place in German culture then it is certain that the entire structure will collapse."

"You exaggerate."

"Very little. The anti-Semites came to this conclusion long ago. For this reason they have been trampling upon everything that but faintly resembles intellectuality, art and culture. By this means they expect to strike at the greatest vulnerabilities of the Jews. One anti-Semite has even attempted to prove that Goethe is of Jewish descent."

Once more he looked through the microscope upon the wonderful fission-fungi.

"By the way, do you know what gematria means?" he asked me abruptly. "Also zeruph? notarikon?"

"Yes. Some mystic numerological nonsense. You scramble certain Scriptural verses and all the letters in the name of God and then you transpose them into numerical ciphers."

"Numerological nonsense!" he exclaimed indignantly and shoved the ashtray away from him violently. "Know that the profoundest secrets of the Kabala lie hidden in the science of Numerology! My last hope is centered in it. Much is written in Holy Scriptures about the 'goring ox' and what dangers one runs in getting involved with him." The Eternal Jew moved nearer to me and said mysteriously: "If only I could find the numerical equivalent of the 'goring ox' then I am certain to hit upon the numbers for 'The Crown of Hatred for the Jews.'"

"And what if you find these numbers?" I asked.

"Is it possible that you don't notice the mysterious connection between the 'goring ox' and hatred for the Jews? At the head of the persecution of the Jews

in the year 1298 was a man by the name of Rindfleisch (Beef). The name of
the leader of the Frankfurt uprising against the Jews in 1614 was Fettmilch
(Fat Milk). So you see that there is a connection throughout between cattle
and anti-Semitism. If only I found the third 'goring ox'! The achievement of
'The Crown of Hatred for the Jews' would then be a simple matter."

Suddenly he sprang to his feet. "I know who he is now!" he cried triumphantly. "Would you like to see him? Then come tonight to Dietlindenstrasse 13. Tonight too I will establish my newspaper and I will appoint the
'goring ox' as its editor!"

IV

At Dietlindenstrasse 13 I was led into a room which was piled high with
German Nationalist propaganda literature. It was the office of "The Secret
Order of Black-White-Red from Sirius to the Jungfrau." Huge bull-horns
adorned the walls together with photographs of popular army leaders, of an old
Teuton on a bearskin, of the Trumpeter of Säckingen, and of Admiral Tirpitz.
An immense swastika made of sheet-metal dangled from the chandelier. In-
scriptions on the walls informed one that: "To be a German means to do a
thing for its own sake.—Membership dues, mark fifty.—I no longer know of
any party, I know only Germans.—Down with the Jews!—The Germans will
redeem the world!—Do not spit on the floor."

On the massive table stood huge tankards and through the thick smoke
two men became visible.

The Eternal Jew came quickly forward and introduced me as his secretary.
The two men muttered something that sounded like "Heilo," or else like an
old Teutonic greeting.

A discussion then took place as to what the policy of the proposed anti-
Semitic newspaper should be. Marbod Timm spoke. He was a young man and
looked quite as ordinary as a hundred thousand other young men. He had
a sturdy, powerful physique, although he was a little too thick-set. His face
looked boyish, fresh and pleasant. However, he gave the impression of being
neither clever nor stupid. He and his companion appeared to be mentally
vacuous and were only waiting for a stronger will than theirs to bend them
to any desired end. The Eternal Jew proved to possess the stronger will.

"We, the soldiers who returned from the Front," began Marbod Timm,
"surely deserved to find some pleasant corner to rest our weary bones. Instead,
what did we soon discover? All the good places were already occupied by the
Jews. Who was having a grand time with the girls in the night clubs? Who
was earning money? To whom did the government give all the good jobs?
The Jews!"

He looked angry and insulted. "Those parasites eat till they are ready
to burst while the German people is obliged to go hungry. Can one do anything else but curse the Jews?"

"To curse is not enough," interjected a thick, bass voice. It belonged to Herr Franz Xavier Osterbichler, the head of the southern division of the Old Germanic League. He was a stocky red-headed man with a long, beer-soaked mustache. "That is why the German nation has been going to the dogs," he continued, "because it has despised the motto of its great ancestors. And what has been that motto? 'Strike out!' " He sat down heavily, having risen from his chair in his excitement.

"As God is my witness, your words are inspired!" rapturously cried the Eternal Jew.

Herr Bodo von Zeckenfeld, who was lending an ear to the discussion, drank champagne from a large beer-tankard in approbation of the motto of his great ancestors, the Eternal Jew naturally standing treat. He looked thin and lifeless. At first he had been the publisher of a sports magazine but because of a shady business transaction in which a bad check was passed, he had prudently disappeared from sight for several months. Now he was making his livelihood principally from an education film dealing with white slavers. Of course he was perfectly justified in believing that on account of his ancient lineage he would be welcomed into the German Nationalist movement. To be sure, there is still extant a very charming ballad about one of his ancestors, a certain robber-baron, who was apprehended by the authorities and hanged only after a lot of trouble.

A big man, with a haggard face and a fanatical expression, who somehow recalled portraits of Goethe and of Gerhardt Hauptmann, now rose from his seat.

"Just observe him," whispered the Eternal Jew to me in great excitement. "There he is—the 'goring ox.' His name is Rindleder (Cowhide), Dr. Johannes Borromäus Rindleder. Recall, please: Rindfleisch—Fettmilch—Rindleder."

"I think," began Dr. Rindleder, "that the objectives which I have laid down in my book, *The Fundamentals of Culture,* should be adopted by every German nationalistic society. It is already well established that anything good in the world can be created only by Teutons. As I have proven, in extension of Chamberlain's theory, that not only were the great Italians of the Renaissance and the authors of the Bible Teutons, but also the great Chinese Kung-Fu-Tse and Li-Tai-Po must be regarded as sprung from Teutons. If someday in the future the *Travels of Marco Polo* should be substantiated documentarily—"

"Apropos Marco Polo," interrupted Herr von Zeckenfeld to the Eternal Jew, "I still have standing two railroad cars of tea in Düsseldorf. In case you are interested the price of it will be *loco*—"

"What, for instance, prevents us from accepting the theory that during the migrations of the Germanic tribes in earliest times they reached China? Therefore, not only did we have perfectly justified expansion rights in the acquisition of Kiau-Tshau, but it was also at the same time an inner necessity. It was the call of the blood. In a certain measure it was an irredentist act."

"I have always been for a healthy Colonial policy," said Franz Xavier Osterbichler. "Therefore sensible statesmen must take into consideration the individual needs of every part of the country. The Chinese possessions should be a comfort to Bavaria. Bavaria must have her share of the Far Eastern market. I really cannot think of China except as being managed by Bavaria."

"Comrades," said the Eternal Jew, "we are getting off our subject. We've got to find a name for our newspaper!"

The suggested names came thick and fast: "The Iron Rod—The Eye of Odin—The Limping District Messenger—The One-Eyed Chief Announcer of the Niebelungen—The Blaring Ox-Horn—The Goal-Conscious Bear Skinner."

Finally Dr. Rindleder succeeded in having adopted the name he suggested: *The Fist of Truth.*

"I would like to point out to you, comrades," he said, "that not only does this name suggest symbolically the Teuton's thirst for action, but also his fistic urge. Such a play of words, indirectly disclosing the soul of all things more than the analysis of so-called Science, is well liked both by the Rembrandt-Germans and by Chamberlain."

Herr von Zeckenfeld next discussed the agent's commission he was to receive from the purchase of the newspaper. The Eternal Jew was happy over the election of Johannes Borromäus Rindleder to the post of editor. "His telephone number is 60746," he whispered to me. "If these ciphers are transposed into their corresponding Hebrew letters, then they result either in 'The Crown of Hatred for the Jews' or in the 'goring ox'!"

The Bible of the Teutons, Chamberlain's *Foundations,* was freely quoted from. Dr. Rindleder delivered an address which he climaxed with the assurance that the Germans will redeem the world. Marbod Timm was very much inspired. They also sang German bardic lays. Best of all was the bardic song that Herr von Zeckenfeld rendered:

> *Mädel fein,*
> *Mädel klein,*
> *O du Foxtrott—Mädel mein,*
> *Einmal muss es das erste Mal sein*
> *Hipphipphurra!*

Dr. Rindleder attempted the bardic song about *Fenriswolf,* the one that stuck his tongue out, and about the ash-tree Yggdrasil over whose roots he dribbled. Then Franz Xavier Osterbichler sang the bardic song about that Bavarian hero:

> *Wenns wir beis den Mädchens schlafens,*
> *Sans wir unsern König gleich.*

The Eternal Jew accompanied the singing of the bardic songs with an obbligato on the ox-horn.

V

The Eternal Jew had invited me to celebrate the founding of his newspaper. I drank wine with him.

We sat in the editorial rooms of *The Fist of Truth*. It had formerly been the office of "The Secret Order of Black-White-Red from Sirius to the Jungfrau." The "Swastika Calendar for the German Movement," which hung on the wall, indicated that it was the seventh of Eglfing. A heap of anti-Semitic books and pamphlets, written in every imaginable tongue, was piled high on a table. Even the microscope and the fission-fungi were there, together with such curiosities as an ancient pair of big boots that once had belonged to a feudal knight.

We drank wine and we puffed at our cigarettes.

"There have been times," said he, "when that prophecy of God: 'Behold, I give unto you the nations of the earth to be as your inheritance!' came well nigh of fulfillment. There was, for instance, the Tetrarch Herod. A clever man! He had introduced into Jerusalem Greek and Roman customs and institutions, such as the theater and the gladiatorial contests. If he could only have had his way the Jews would have become a cosmopolitan people at an early period in their history. In that event the world might have had another face today. I once had a large order for shoes from Herod, four thousand pairs of sandals at two drachmas a pair. I wanted to design them in the latest Greek style. Princess Salomé was also for it. They would have been beautiful as well as practical. But the Jewish nationalists were against it. They got Marianne to take sides with them. The result was that Herod, who hated conjugal quarrels, cancelled the order."

He grew silent and sipped his wine.

"Nobody is guilty in nothing," said he after a period of silence. "I am referring to the time when Mohammed appeared on the scene. If the Jewish chauvinists had not offered such bitter resistance to him, had they only agreed on the compromise which Mohammed had suggested to them, Judaism most likely would have taken the form of a discreetly Islamic world-religion instead of Christianity. If that had transpired then, everything would have been tranquil now. It would not have been necessary for my fission-fungi to become so active. I would have disappeared from the earth a long time ago and hence I would not have had the pleasure of sitting with you here drinking the choicest of Markobrunner wines."

His words sounded as if they were coming from a great distance. A strange uneasiness had come over me. My limbs felt paralyzed. A feeling of anguish began to possess me. I had the sensation as if the walls in the room were emitting mist and vapor, as if we were in the midst of strange, eerie creatures who belonged to a bygone age. I was almost certain that watchful eyes were fixed upon me.

"Is anybody else here?" I asked, and my voice sounded hoarse and lifeless.

Was it possible that the Eternal Jew had not heard the question I had put to him? "To serve as the spiritual cement for all the world, to fertilize it with their blood, has been the clear and conscious mission of so many Jews." Then he added, smiling: "And these Jews have always made my mission so difficult! The last and the most resolute of them all was Moses Mendelssohn. But there were others a long, long time before him. You must recall to mind the Jew Alexander whom Josephus Flavius mentions, the Minnesinger Süsskind von Trimberg—"

At that moment I was possessed with the certainty that we were not alone in the room. A whole swarm of human faces, nebulous and intangible, such as I had never seen before and yet were so well known to me, flitted to and fro in an incomprehensible fashion about the room. They neither stirred nor did they stand on one spot and yet—they were there! They did not move their lips and still they were speaking in the thought of all time and of all nations. They flitted by in confused order, regarding me from a thousand eyes. They were Jews, as it were, and yet—they were not Jews! There were present the Greek Livius, Josephus Flavius, and Abraham ibn Sahl: the great Arabic singer of love. There were also among them medieval Frenchmen, Spaniards, and Italians. But quite near to me, although I had never known him, yet paradoxically enough, I was very well acquainted with him, stood that poor Minnesinger with the sorrowful eyes and the large Jewish sugar-cone hat, the Jew Süsskind von Timberg. Over his shoulder peered the Jew Samson Pine who had made the first German translation of the Parsifal legend. And behind Pine's shoulder in turn gazed the Jew Johannes Pauli who, with his abuse and earnestness, had put an end to the farcical literature of medieval Germany. I discerned a thousand faces through the vapor. They spoke in every tongue. They sang in every conceivable musical mode. All the dreams which the imagination of all the peoples on earth had spun passed in review through the image-projections of these Jewish Masters. It was the harmonies of their music which sounded now, the colors of their imaginings which vibrated and glowed. The throng finally paled and imperceptibly was swallowed up in the mist and vapor that seemed to fill the room.

The voice of the Eternal Jew again sounded near. "Anti-Semitism is a lifeless thing without a will of its own. If you only say the right kind of abracadabra then it is sure to become animated and active. It stands outside of all ethical evaluation. It is the sworn enemy of the spirit which withers in its presence. It is a thing of necessity, a law of nature. Now just take a look at these boots!" The Eternal Jew pointed to the ancient pair of boots that once had belonged to a feudal knight. "I have always had a special interest in boots," he remarked laughingly. "It might surprise you to know that by calling I am a boot-manufacturer."

"What do you find so extraordinary about this pair of boots?" I asked.

"Well, look carefully at these soles," he ordered. "As you see, they are made of parchment. Note the Hebrew words on the insoles. These boots were made in the year 1130, during the time when the saintly Bernard de Clairvaux preached the Crusades against the heathen. What wonderful times those were for me! The Jews were slain by the thousands. Their sacred books were burnt, and out of their vellum pages were carved soles for boots. These boots have such soles. They had been ordered by the Chevalier Chrétien de Hautecloque. With his own hands he slew twenty-seven Jews, exclusive of their women folk and children. Then he sallied forth to fight in the Crusades in the Holy Land. These boots he had ordered made of Torah parchment-scrolls. Look closely at them. You may still read the Hebrew words on them. They are a quotation from the Fifth Book of Moses! 'Do not oppress the stranger in thy land nor deal harshly with him. For bondsmen were you in the Land of Egypt.'

"Indeed," continued the Eternal Jew, "wearing these boots, the Chevalier sallied forth to fight the Saracens. And he received absolution for all his sins beforehand. I was then of good assistance to the saintly Bernard. I helped all those who preached the Crusades. I also helped Fernando Martinez and Vincent Ferrer. And this year, as well as last year, when the priests of Poland, Russia and Rumania declared a moratorium on the Sermon on the Mount and exhorted their congregations to kill the Jews and to plunder them of their worldly goods, my hand was also in it. To be sure, I took part in all the doings everywhere. I was, so to speak, in everything." Then somewhat irrelevantly he added: "We took hold of the Hindu doctrine of the transmigration of the soul and introduced it into Europe." He smiled at this. "That is the Asiatic in us."

Again his words grew indistinct as if coming from afar. And once more I was aware that there were more than two of us in the room. Feudal knights sat around the table, in threatening attitudes. They had ruddy, coarse and good-natured faces. The Eternal Jew drank with them. What a remarkable crew to guzzle with! Closer and closer pressed the multitude of apparitions consisting of emaciated, bald-headed and fanatic-looking monks and priests. They had bulldog faces and bestial expressions. Some were dressed in Rumanian peasant dress. Others wore Cossack uniforms. It was clear that all were trying to talk at the same time. Their mouths were wide open. They bellowed, shrieked and roared. But not a sound could be heard.

After that the room began to expand as if by enchantment and became transformed into a vast square which reeked with smoke and blood. Towering heaps of Hebrew books were being burned. Stakes had been erected. They were so high they seemed to pierce the clouds. And the innumerable Jews that were tied to them were being toasted to a cinder. A chorus of priests were intoning: *Gloria in excelsis Deo*. The figures of men, women and children could be discerned moving across the square in every direction. They were naked or in tatters and they had no more apparel upon them than corpses of any variety, whether those burnt to a cinder or strangulated or broken on the wheel or hanged. They had no more clothes upon them than corpses or the charred remains of book-scrolls, of torn, bloodstained, and defiled book-scrolls. And following this multitude was an endless and innumerable throng of men in kaftans and women and children in modern dress. And voices were heard singing: "Mighty rivers are the Euphrates and the Tigris and many are their tributaries that flow into the sea: but mightier are the rivers of blood that Israel has shed for the sanctification of the world."

The vast square now contracted. Again we sat in the noisy editorial room, sipping wine and puffing at our cigarettes. The Eternal Jew again commenced to speak: "I have proven to you that I have fulfilled my duty well. I have done everything that was humanly possible. Wheresoever I saw any sign of stupidity I hastened to the spot without delay and stuck to my purpose tenaciously, undermining and boring from within until I had put everything on the right track, until it resulted in the massacre and expulsion of the Jews. I tried every possible means, not letting anything go untried: the fission-fungus and those Christian children who were victims of Jewish ritual murders, the one-hundred-percent German army officers, the abolition of the Yiddish jargon, Russian priests, the syphilitics, alleged poisonings of wells by the Jews, German swastika students, Cossacks, and finally the falsified statistics about the number of Jews in the army. I have agitated, misrepresented and calumniated for fully two thousand years. So that I can say with justice that what could have happened has already happened.

"As you can see, my paunch is growing bigger, nevertheless. Since Mendelssohn, Lessing and Napoleon it has been growing constantly. I am afraid that I will soon be obliged to settle down quietly."

I could no longer follow him. The martyred Jews and the cosmopolites, the boots belonging to the feudal knight and the one-hundred-percent German army officers, the Minnesinger Süsskind von Trimberg and the holy Bernard de Clairvaux, the fission-fungus and Chamberlain and the German swastika students, all got hopelessly confused in my mind. And the man who was sitting before me, so fashionably dressed, with his double-meaning smile, was he really Dr. A. Has, the editor of *The Fist of Truth,* or, was he merely a symbol of all that never took root, of the eternally nomadic, of all those whom anti-Semitism wished to prevent from ever becoming part of the nation?

"If you have no objection, I would like to open the window," he said suddenly.

He disported a little black beard, was carefully shaved and gave some signs of paunchiness. One surely must have met with him in the theater, in the restaurants and on the boulevards. But what really was remarkable about him was the intense light in his eyes and a certain characteristic way of moving his hands which quite gave him away.

VI

Marbod Timm called on me.

"No doubt you are surprised by my visit," said he. His handsome, boyish face became flushed with embarrassment.

"I cannot pretend that I am not," I said.

"In any case it was Gertrud who made me come here. She has advised me to speak to you openly once and for all."

"Please do so!"

"Not everything is as well as should be in the Germanic movement," he began.

"You don't say so!"

"The aim of our movement is good, is indeed upright. Why cannot we employ honest means of achieving it? For instance, we have an editor. His name is Werner Kotz. You must read his article on Lessing when we recently forced the theater management to take 'Nathan the Wise' off the boards."

"No," said I.

"The thesis of this article was that Lessing's real name was Levi. Now what is your opinion?"

"Whose, mine? *'O Schilda, my Fatherland!'* "

"Well, does it not surprise you? It does seem quite improbable."

"Quite so," I answered. "I too do not think it probable."

"It no doubt will interest you to know that this Kotz fellow had previous to that offered to write for the *Frankfurter Zeitung,* and for that matter also for the *Berlinger Tageblatt.* But they turned him down."

"Even they failed to appreciate sufficiently the beauties of his Germanic style."

"At any rate the entire matter remains highly disputable. I will also pass lightly over the fact that Herr von Zeckenfeld is again being charged with embezzlement, and that Dr. Johannes Borromäus Rindleder has been confined in a madhouse."

"How scandalous!" said I.

"Why the devil doesn't the movement find any better champions?"

I shrugged my shoulders.

"Things were different before," he continued. "There were men like Luther to write against the Jews. His powerful polemic 'Concerning the Jews and their Lies' still remains the breviary of the German-conscious man."

"Luther?" I smiled and took from a bookshelf Luther's work: *Proof That Our Lord Jesus Was Born a Jew.*

"Take a look here, please," I said and pointed to the passage: "Our fools until now have so mistreated the Jews that any good Christian should rather have wished to be a Jew. And had I been a Jew and seen how those boobies ruled and taught, I would sooner have become a pig than a Christian."

Marbod looked perplexed: "You don't mean to tell me that Luther actually wrote those words?" he asked.

"So it appears," said I.

"I must make a confession to you," he began after a pause, with an embarrassed, confidential air which became him well. "My reaction to the Jews has been very curious. Sometimes I find one of them so sympathetic that I get the feeling that I could establish an honest and enduring friendship with him. But at other times I meet one who is so tactless, so servile and arrogant at the same time, that I feel like wholeheartedly joining in the cry: 'Out of Germany with the whole caboodle of them!'"

"Dear Herr Timm," asked I, "haven't you had the same experience with Gentiles?"

And as he stood undecided what to answer, I continued: "Observe, that what in the individual Jew appear to be specifically Jewish traits such as a certain servile arrogance, a meek obtrusiveness, have nothing at all to do with Jewish personality. They are only a consequence of the Ghetto-life into which the Jews were forced by the Germans during the Middle Ages—a consequence of hundreds of years of humiliation, isolation and enslavement."

"But surely there must be some real basis to account for the revulsion that the whole race—!"

"Revulsion? The whole race? To every one hundred and ten Germans there is only one Jew. Therefore only a very small percentage of the German nation has had any real personal contact with them. But for every Jew that there is in Germany appear weekly one hundred copies of anti-Semitic newspapers. That is the source from which the German nation derives its knowledge of Jews. Then you have the one-hundred-percent Germans—"

"Why do you speak with such contempt of the one-hundred-percent Germans?" he interrupted me.

"Contempt? Not that I am aware of. You might have said more correctly—compassion. As a schoolboy I had much to do with the sons of leading one-hundred-percent German families. Many of them were upright, good-natured, but endowed with moderate talents. In the study of languages and history, but particularly in German composition, they were hard put to get by. And several had to thank me for getting out of school a year sooner because they were God-fearing and adroit and copied from my notes. But remarkably enough, they all excelled in sports. They showed themselves sturdy and nimble in jumping, as well as performing on the horizontal bars, on the ladder and in calisthenics. That is certainly very necessary and not at all to be despised. But I never could understand, for instance, why one who is able to give an excellent performance in the high-jump or on the horizontal bars also should be expected to possess those qualities that are necessary for political leadership. And these good athletes, but miserable logicians, who for decades have undertaken the guidance of German political life, are today as well the leaders of the German Nationalist movement.

"They who are driving the national wheelbarrow into the mire would indeed find themselves in a very uncomfortable position were the people, with one voice, to cry out: 'Down with the German Nationalists!' But what great

license they exercise now! At last they have found a way out of their dilemma.
For all at once there has emerged out of the theatrical trap-door the ancient
scapegoat: '*Judæus ex machina*'!"

At this point there was a knock on the door. The Eternal Jew entered.

VII

I received an invitation to a baptism from Marbod and Gertrud Timm.
They had become the proud parents of twins. On my way to their home I met
the Eternal Jew, who was going to the same place.

"I see that your anti-Semitic movement is growing everywhere," I said. "The
hate you have been sowing is now in full bloom."

"Bloom? What do you mean 'bloom'?" he muttered. "It's merely that
The Fist of Truth has gone over big. It has blossomed forth. Take a look at
my paunch."

He appeared to have grown even stouter.

"But I have noticed everywhere—"

"These are but the final convulsions. Now what do you think of that? A
German Christian by the name of Johannes Müller has just written that anti-
Semitism is at the very least a German problem as well as a symptom of the
feebleness of the German national soul. Only that nation, he writes, whose
national ambitions are greater than its ability to realize them, can deteriorate
to such an extent as to wish to blame the Jews for something that every healthy
nation accepts as a matter of pride: responsibility for its own deeds.

"You have observed that an anti-Semitic wave is sweeping the country now,"
continued the Eternal Jew. "That is quite true. After the Germans live among
the Jews for five years they begin to deport themselves in a manner more
erratic and ignoble than the Jews after five hundred years of Ghetto life. However, that is quite beside the point. Anti-Semitism is only an acute illness. I
ought not put any great expectations upon it. And inasmuch as the nation has
finally gotten over its fit of nerves it will no doubt be ashamed to think that
one hundred and ten Germans were afraid of being murdered by one solitary
Jew.

"No, no! It is all over. It is the end. I might just as well pack my baggage.
I am a ghost of yesterday. At very best I am only conceivable as a character in
a play. Naturally I will hold out to the bitter end. I still remain as always the
spearhead of all anti-Semitic propaganda. I flood the country with pamphlets and
under cover of night I paste Jew-baiting posters on drain-pipes and on the walls
of public urinals and water-closets. But I am prepared for the worst. I have
bought myself a house in the Isartal and my Wandering Jew's staff I have
presented as a gift to the property man of the National Theater."

He resumed after a short silence: "You of course notice that the Jews
themselves do not take this sudden anti-Semitic explosion seriously. They do not
lament. You cannot be angry with the cudgel because it is used in beating you!"

"What then are the Jews doing?"

"They are laughing."

"They—what?"

"Yes. They are amused by the lack of talent and the grammatical errors of the anti-Semitic propagandists."

We had finally arrived at the home of the newlyweds.

Marbod Timm pressed my hand warmly. "I was an ass," he said to me. Gertrud proudly exhibited the twins.

"What are their names?" I asked.

"The girl's name is Marie—"

"Marie! Pfui!" exclaimed the Eternal Jew. "That's a Hebrew name. It is a derivative of Miriam. You should have named her Frigg."

"In any case you will like the boy's name. He is called Hans."

"Hans! Pfui!" sneered the Eternal Jew. "It is also Hebrew and derived from Johanan. Why didn't you name him Teut?"

Marbod and Gertrud laughed heartily. "If the Jewish and the German are so well tangled together," said Gertrud, "who can possibly unscramble them again?"

The Eternal Jew sat in an easy chair, fat, smoking comfortably and droning to himself in a sing-song: "To wander is the miller's passion." Carefully shaved as he was, with his little black beard, one might very easily fall in with him in the theater at first nights, in the restaurants and on the boulevards.

"Are you satisfied?" I asked.

"Satisfied!" he growled. "What do you mean satisfied?" He threw me a rapid glance and the remarkable intense light in his eyes flamed up again. He rocked himself and was a picture of well-being.

"Satisfied?" he repeated. And at that he made a characteristic motion with his hands that quite gave him away. He smiled: "And why not, please tell me?"

THE ROMANTIC

by LUDWIG LEWISOHN

I

DURING the hour before sunset the Baron walked in his garden. He was as straight and slender as the poplars which stood dark against the pearly sky. Even when he was alone as now he was faintly aware of the elegance of his figure, the imperturbable grace of his demeanour and the resilience of his tread. He walked up and down a path between the well-tended flower beds which were now filled with the red and russet shrubs, the brilliant scentless flowers of autumn. At the end of the path he turned and stopped and his grey eyes from which at this hour the habitual irony had faded, gazed beyond the hazy city that lay at the foot of the eminence on which his villa stood to the sinuous, shallow glittering river that flowed toward the Carpathian east.

It cost him a perceptible act of the will to leave that higher end of the garden-path from which the landscape could be surveyed; he was tempted to stop there and to fall into a reverie in which he could summon so almost sensibly and tangibly and audibly the scents, the forms, the speech and music of his native land. But he forced himself to walk back, to take the little exercise that he needed. He could no longer race on horseback over the desolate magical plain of his youth; he could not clamber the wild and tangled mountains at the far eastern edge of the plain. He could have travelled, as he had done during the earlier years of his exile. But movement had become futile to him. From here he could at least see the river upon the farther banks of which the speech was spoken and the songs were sung that had forever made a captive of his heart.

Once more he stopped and this time turned his eye toward the villa. Thence came the sounds of a waltz of Chopin played on the piano, played dexterously, competently, quite without zest or fire. The Baron smiled a little and his smile made his nose droop a shadowy bit nearer to his chin and brought into his eyes an old, old expression of mingled irony and kingly contempt. He strode rapidly across paths and lawn, leaped up the few steps of the broad, marble terrace and stepped quietly into the music-room. The light fell upon the back of his wife, sitting there at the piano and playing; it fell upon her rosy dress with old-fashioned tufts at the shoulders, upon her slender bare arms, upon the blond hair which she wore in a knot at the top of her head. Everything about her was elongated; her cheeks, her delicate nose, her admirable teeth. The Baron moved so that he could see her profile. How unbelievably English Ida was! This quality in her had once in the great days of Carpathia and of himself been like a plume and a flag. She was, in addition, the daughter of a knight and Carpathia did not know the degrees of nobility in Britain. Now Ida, her representative function gone, wearied him to the soul with her vapid contentedness. She played Chopin because her governess had taught her to do so; she entertained the Baron's polyglot friends in imperturbable English; she submitted to his increasingly rare embraces with the air of a woman who knew precisely where her duty lay.

The Baron shrugged his shoulders. The shrug was curt and he was careful, as he had been all his life, not to raise his hands as an accompaniment to his shrug. The faint impulse to do so still came to him from time to time. But his body was as disciplined in this matter as his soul. For he could faintly remember, though his consciousness forced his memory to remain an image only, how his mother, across the splendour of a festive table, had regarded his grandfather, the first Baron Tamaczvar, with a pained vigilance. Rosy, enormous, with fat authoritative hands the old Baron had sat at the head of the board talking with that loud, self-satisfied sing-song in his voice, shrugging his shoulders in contempt, raising his hands in astonishment, grasping his neighbour's arm for attention, reflectively laying a finger along the side of his intolerable nose. The grandson remembered; he saw the scene with an etched vividness. Why now? He straightened himself up; he made himself aware of his slender height. He turned from the door of the music-room and, erect and nobly sad, walked up the stairs to his study.

A half-written article lay on his desk. With a troubled eye he regarded the pages. None of the other Carpathian magnates condescended to scribble in newspapers. They held their peace and secretly whetted their swords. But the Baron knew that that way lay destruction, and the death of all hope. The hostility of the world toward his country made him sick to the very soul; the unbelievable injustice of it made him want to cry out in all the market-places of Europe. And now the White Terror established within Carpathia, once he had thought and dreamed the very source of freedom, exposed his faithful heart to yet other wounds. He had to parry, as it were, with a rapier in each hand. Yet the silence about him grew ever more frozen. For his Carpathian peers wanted neither him nor his defence nor his criticism. They wanted their will and their way; they preferred destruction at their own hands to salvation at his. And his curse was that he understood that attitude in them. He recognized its dark and sullen nobility. They wanted to prevail on their own terms or go under, leaving only a legend and a name. But his blood could consent to no such alternative. He had to rebel, to speak out, to plead for peace and hope. He turned the pages of what he had written and a cruel flush crept from his cheeks to his forehead at the memory of a whisper that had come to him. The Count of Nagy-Raföld, once his host and his guest, once his fellow-patron of all the arts, had curtly sentenced him over a card-table in the majestic clubroom of their common youth: "Jewish scribbler!"

II

He lit no light. He let the falling dark flood his study. Wearily he sat down and clasped his hands over his breast. The hard music below had ceased. Ida would be sitting there now, reading a Tauchnitz edition of a novel by Mrs. Belloc Lowndes or the authoress of Pam—a story about nursery governesses and donkey-carts and curates and a young Oxford man making love to an English girl at a charity-bazaar held in tents on a green Surrey lawn. Presently Ida would go and dress for dinner and at dinner she would tell him that she was going to play tennis with some friends that morning. If he spoke of his burning preoccupations, she would listen with an air of sympathy and superficial intelligence and bid him remember his good luck in having the major part of his estates beyond the reach of the present tyrant of Carpathia.

He clasped his hands more tightly; he closed his eyes. What had he to do with this woman and this rented house? What did either know of him? He saw the Carpathian plain with the smoky sphere of the setting sun hung over its edge and next he saw the plain moonlit and wanly silvered. There stood four poplars at the edge of a swampy pool and in the pool lay the images of the trees and of the moon and of a few faint stars. He, young and glowing, in Carpathian hunting-costume, was leaning in the shadow of one of the trees and waiting. Presently from a solitary cottage pricked out from the velvet night by one red lantern sped a lithe figure and sped across the plain toward him. Was it twenty years ago? Were those nights forever gone? But he could still smell the fragrance of Marya's yellow braids; he could still hear her crooning, with his head on her lap, the ballads of the countryside in her strange immemorial tongue.

He was nineteen then. He had gone to his father and told him that he wanted to marry Marya and had asked for nothing but one of the farms of the plain owned by the family. His father, always extraordinarily elegant, a little afraid apparently to relax at all in the great manor-house lest he should seem to strike a note at variance with the traditions of Tamaczvar—his father had first laughed and said: "Kindskopf!" The Baron remembered how it had irritated him that his father had always in intimate moments slipped into the German speech so deprecated by the true Carpathians. But his father's merriment had been brief. "Even the sons of the native nobility do not indulge in such mad pranks! Your marriage must fortify the position of our house. You must marry a magnate's daughter. I am sick of paying for friendship, of losing money to these louts at cards, of endowing all their undertakings. Your grandfather was quite right when he hesitated to accept the title. We have wasted millions on snobs and fools. But you are a Catholic and can marry into the inner circle and possess your position without daily buying it over again. Do you understand?" He had understood and his heart had seemed to turn into ice in his breast. For he had truly forgotten that he was not altogether like his friends and companions. Had he not just been accepted by the most exclusive fraternity at the National University of the Carpathians? Did not his father sit in the Nobles' Council of the Diet? Had not even his grandfather sat in that august assembly? He spoke of these things to his father on that day, not refusing obedience in the matter of Marya, but appealing rather for a confirmation of all he was and changelessly wanted to be. His father had arisen. He could still see the smooth elegant shoes on his father's small, aristocratic feet. He had gone to the fireplace and turned his back to it and spoken. "My son, you are perfectly right. We have flourished extraordinarily in this country; we owe everything to it; we have served it and shall continue to serve it with all we have and are. That is why I caused you and your sister to be baptized Catholics. The step cost me something It cost your grandfather more. But I felt that our family had no longer the right to any separateness from the Carpathian people. Nevertheless it takes more than a generation or two to establish oneself in the bosom of an old, proud race. You never knew my grandfather. I did. Many of my contemporaries remember him. He was a hunchbacked little Jew with a long beard and dirty hands who came over the frontier with a pack on his back. But he had silver in his long old-fashioned purse and he went from manor-house to manor-house and cringed at the back-doors and loaned money to the magnates' sons who had lost too heavily at whoring or gaming and were afraid to face their fathers. He asked for no written security. He required his debtors' word of honour. They often broke their given word. But they learned that he neither betrayed them nor broke his own. Before old age was upon him he had become the most powerful banker in the land; he helped the king wage war and put down rebellion. But he remained a pious Jew and separate from all but Jews to his end. It was only your grandfather, the first Baron, who entered Gentile society. You and I are the first Westerners of our house. You must marry a magnate's daughter. Do you understand?"

The Baron put his hands over his face. How many times in the years between had not that speech of his father come back to stab him? For it had destroyed his innocence; it had curbed his spontaneity; it had changed life from free expression to a problem and a snare. It made him watchful. And now that he watched he became aware of the fact that there were ultimate intimacies from which he was excluded. And there rang in his soul and would ring forever the cry of the closest companion of his youth when it was pro-posed to carouse for three days of winter in a desolate manor-house at the foot of the eastern mountains: "Oh, that wouldn't interest Tamaczvar Sander! Leave him to his foreign books." For this same friend had studied with him through the nights and had gratefully received his instruction. Now there was in his tone, to be sure, neither reproach nor jeer. There was the expression of a cleavage, a separation and the recognition of the fact that the young Baron Tamaczvar cared for other things more than for the traditions of the life of the Carpathian gentry. The cry had hurt so immeasurably because it was true. From that day on the Baron knew that he was different, that he was a stranger here in his own land, by his own hearth and the hearths of his friends, on this beloved plain, beside these pools and trees that broke your heart with their melancholy loveliness.

The Baron arose and went to the open window and stared out into the autumnal gloom. Somewhere beyond, in the darkness, lay the land which he had loved not less, not less but more, since those incidents of his youth. Only his love had become a yearning and unhappy love, like the love of a man for a woman who will never say that she loves him in return nor ever give her-self to him and yet is forever there and seems to be forever on the point of being his. He had lived constantly with that supreme and wounded passion and it had driven him into strange courses, into strange sacrifices and betrayals. Once for a period he had taken to devout practices and to consorting with priests. But the practices had become fantastic and the priests had seemed stupid. Worse than all, his friends of ancient Catholic houses had grinned at his clericalism as at an amiable but unreal eccentricity. And again he had known that they were right. They needed not to go through ceremonies nor be bored by priests. Their Catholicism and royalism had not to be cultivated but were in their blood. Next, in his palace in the capital, he had entertained poets and actors and musicians. These people, by whom alone Carpathia was known in the civilized West, were all of doubtful origin and of disguised names. Their grandfathers or great-grandfathers had come like his own with packs on their backs; their hair curled and their noses were, however delicately moulded, like the noses of the men pictured upon Assyrian ruins. With these people and with these alone had he felt wholly at home, wholly at peace. And upon these associates and friends and lovers—this was the sorest stab—his friends among the magnates and the magnates' sons had not remarked. They had quietly taken it for granted that like seeks like in this world. No one had wondered at his abstention from all religious practices nor at his support of a liberal political party to which he had first fled in the hope that his peers would reproach him and recall him to his duties as one of themselves. There had not arisen so much as a whisper. He invited a Communist leader, whose personality and doctrines he abhorred, to speak at his house. There was no scandal. It came upon him one wintry day suddenly like the scribbling of a sorcerer's hand amid the blue shadows of the snow: the magnates had never believed that he could conceivably be one of themselves; they liked him because he was a pleasant fellow and a millionaire. The delusion had been wholly on his side. They had always seen clear.

But had it been a delusion? Was it a delusion even today in this fourth year of exile? Did anyone love Carpathia more than he? None more. But his love was not wanted; his defence was not wanted; his devotion was not wanted. For all these in him were different in moral quality from the love and the devotion of the sons of the ancient soil. Perhaps the quality of his love was better, nobler, than the quality of theirs? It did not matter. He was a stranger. To be a stranger was his doom.

III

He dressed quickly and went down to dinner. He looked at Ida across the table. A strange woman in a strange house. He had not married a magnate's daughter, after all. He could have had the daughter or sister of some impoverished noble. Somehow his gorge had risen at the thought. For he had waited long enough to face the tragic fact that he would not have been drawn closer to the Carpathian bosom, but that in the innermost core of the innermost circle the lady would be considered to have sold herself to the Jew. He had always liked England, where he was received as a genuine Carpathian Baron. He had seemed so romantic and thrilling to Ida. He had sunned himself in her warm, girlish sense of his exotic charm and splendour. He had put on the gorgeous, corded officer's coat of his Carpathian regiment. Ida had adored him in it. He had been so grateful to her for her belief in him, for her faith, whole and instinctive, in his genuine Carpathianism. He knew that she had no way of perceiving his hybrid position. He wanted to be deluded. He wanted to carry his delusion with him. Ida would probably never even learn the difficult and isolated language of his country. There would be always some- one in those eyes he would be all that he wanted most to be. Thus he had married Ida. And now they faced each other in this rented villa in a foreign land.

She raised her face a little and told him that a man had called to see him twice in the last hour. She had taken it for granted that he did not wish to be disturbed. And the man seemed not to be of any importance. The footman had rather resented the fellow's importunity. He would not give him his name either and the footman had described him as a small and shabby and suspicious-looking. The Baron's heart contracted a little. He had always hoped, foolishly, boyishly, romantically, that his country would call him. Not the bloody tyrant who now ruled that wounded and dismembered land. But those friends and companions of his earlier years, who if words had any meaning or character any stability, must be chafing under that rude and ruthless dic- tatorship. And he had nursed the day-dream in an hundred reveries that an emissary, secret and soft-footed, would come from these friends, from these men who had once, in their youth, been lovers of freedom and beauty and thought, to summon him to take his share in the liberation of their common country. So profoundly had this day-dream become implicated with the Baron's soul that he would watch people who lingered near the gates of his villa and caught with a sudden anxiety the glances of people directed toward him in the streets or in the theatre. His vigilant ear at once became aware of the Car- pathian language in restaurant or coffee-house, or even of the accent which that tongue gave to the speaking of others. With an apparent carelessness he asked his wife to give orders that the stranger, if he called again, was to be admitted. Ida raised her eyebrows ever so little and said she thought that he had wanted for some days to be left quite undisturbed to complete his work. The Baron gave a slight shrug of the shoulders. He forced himself to smile. One never knew, he said, what adventures one was missing. Ida agreed that life had been rather dull recently. Luckily, he added, friends were soon coming from England; the tennis-courts were still in good condition; also, there would be a ball next week at the British Embassy. The Baron had a sensation as though chill, foul water were trickling over his body. But he had himself well in hand. He never let Ida expiate the error and the folly that had been wholly his own.

From far away he heard the faint trill of the doorbell. He clenched his hands under the table. He could feel a pulse throb in his temple. He heard steps. The footman announced that the same questionable individual had arrived. Hoarsely the Baron ordered the man to be taken to his study. He forced himself to swallow a few crumbs of dessert, to take a last sip of wine. He begged Ida to excuse him. He leaped up the stairs, two at a time. Before his eyes danced the springtime acacias of the Carpathian plain. He hesitated at the door of his study. He called himself a dreamer, a fool. He went in and remained standing erect with his back to the door.

IV

Out of an armchair in the middle of the room under the soft light of the chandelier of polished prisms arose a short, thin man, a straight-grown man with small hands and feet who gave the Baron at once the impression of subtle deformity. It was strange that the fellow had neither curved spine nor withered arm nor a club foot. For from him emanated an atmosphere of torment and defectiveness. Standing very straight, he seemed to cringe; normal of limb, he seemed to be cruelly twisted. A thought went through the Baron's mind: perhaps he was tortured in prison; perhaps he has fled from the Dictator's underground dungeon. The man lifted his face; he lifted the upper part of his face into the light. The small black eyes were set preternaturally far apart as in a sheep or goat; the cheek-bones were high and pink and prominent; under the flat Kalmuck nose long, thin, black mustachios drooped over the indistinguishable mouth and chin. A strong, rude voice carefully, too carefully subdued, came from under those drooping mustachios.

"Your Excellency will forgive me for intruding?"

The Baron came forward. He waved to the man to sit down again. He took a chair facing his visitor.

The small, black animal eyes moved rapidly to and fro in their sockets. "Can we be overheard, Your Excellency?"

Again the Baron's heart contracted. He shook his head. But what a messenger for Nagy-Raföld to choose! Yet was not the man the most autochthonous Carpathian type? Was it not these small, black-eyed men who had come from some unimaginable East to conquer the mountains and the plain and to knock triumphantly at the very gates of Rome? Did he love only the Westernized Carpathians? Why should not his friends have chosen a son of the soil, of their soil and of his own? The acacias flickered before his inner eye; he heard the ghostly rustling of the linden-trees beside the ruins of the castle of Zbodöd, the rustling of the lindens that had once blended with the sobs of a poet, of a Carpathian poet who chanted in the speech of this messenger.

"We cannot be overheard," the Baron said.

The messenger lowered his black eyes. "A secret Council of State was held at Keczmeket, Your Excellency, at which it was decided that the country needed the help of all of its true sons. The worthy exiles are to be recalled. His Highness has signed this order of the Council." The messenger raised his eyes and fixed them upon the Baron. Now the eyes were exactly like the black eyes of an animal, grave and polished but without definite expression. "His Highness expects all true sons of the country to heed this call; it will not be issued a second time."

The Baron felt his skull under his head beginning to tingle and this tingling spread gradually over his entire body until for a moment he had the impression of being caught in the impalpable net of a fever. Not his friends rebelling against the Dictator had sent this messenger; it was the Dictator himself and the Baron could see first that hard, fat face, that grey rigid face with its wrenched ravenous eyes, and next he saw grey waves, the grey, grimy waves of a polluted shallow wintry river, the waves of the river into which the Dictator had ordered to be cast the bodies of Communists and Jews. There had been so many; they were not wanted in the Carpathian earth; all rivers reach the sea. The Baron arose and he knew that those black beast's eyes were carefully following his movements. But he arose, as was his want when agitated, and went to the farther end of the room. This was, he said to himself, no moment in which to pamper emotions, however natural and just. It was rather a moment for weighing issues, for a decision on grounds of reason and of ultimate good. If the Dictator's offer was made in good faith, it was because the man was beginning to doubt the security of his arbitrary power. He needed the moral support of the known liberal elements. He probably wanted foreign loans. The Baron smiled sardonically and did not know how like his grandfather's that smile was. One could then, being Tamaczvar, help to conciliate the great Jewish banking-houses of the West and in return demand reforms! Suppose, on the other hand, that the Dictator's invitation was a trick? A faint pang of terror shot through the Baron's vitals. His mind countered immediately. Impossible! There was still a world called Europe. The moral opinion of mankind had its weight. The Carpathian State, even in its present form, had to go on existing in a community of states; it could scarcely outlaw itself. The man would not dare. The Baron knew profoundly that these arguments did not wholly convince him, that the terror did not wholly fade from his breast. He countered again by drawing himself up to his full height. A residuum, alas, of ancestral Jewish prudence and fearfulness. His unhappy country called him. It called him by so strange and sullen and unlovely a voice. Yet it was his country, the only one he had, the land of his youth, of his dreams, speech, song, poetry, heart. Here he dangled miserably, uprooted, homeless, idle, scribbling for newspapers, playing tennis with Ida's friends. Day by day the situation was becoming more insupportable. Besides, even though the Dictator was a conscienceless brute, no man could administer a country single-handed. The most absolute tyrant is dependent on others. And those others were the friends of the Baron's youth, his comrades, playmates, fellow-students, fellow-officers, the chivalric, the loyal and the brave. They had seen him spend his substance and himself on Carpathian art and poetry and music; they had seen him lead his men in the bloody and hopeless defence of the fortress of the East. In these last years they had fallen silent, to be sure; it was this silence that had seemed most ominous and dreadful. But was it not even now being broken, though in so ugly and indirect a fashion? For had not these friends of his remained at home and sworn to support the Dictator? That he could not do nor, perhaps, would he have been permitted to do. His conscience had rebelled. But now evidently a light, however dim, was struggling in the hearts of his friends. He saw their faces; he heard their laughter; he could see them, as he had so often seen them, at his board in his palace, breaking his bread, drinking his wine. From what base ancestral fears and suspicions arose that faint terror which would not leave his heart? There was no knightly gentleman in all Carpathia who was not pledged to him, beyond all differences and controversies, by memories, by common plans and hopes, by the piety toward one's own youth that every gentle soul harbours forever in the heart, by ties of hospitality, humanity and honour. Swiftly he strode back to the silent messenger.

"What credentials have you?"

The man pulled out a worn leather despatch-case. From it he drew a paper. It was a safe-conduct into Carpathia for Warczawsky Sander, Baron of Tamaczvar. The Baron examined the paper. It was official and correct. It bore no date of expiration. There was no haste, then, in spite of the messenger's implied menace that the invitation would not be repeated. The Baron laid the document on his desk.

"I shall come. I am obliged to His Highness."

v

He communicated himself to no one. He kept the safe-conduct in a thin sealskin wallet next his heart. At night it lay in the drawer of a small table beside his bed. He would awake and in an access of slight, sudden fear stretch out his hand and touch the paper. Nevertheless he delayed. He went out into the city during this period of delay more than had been his recent wont; he was observed in the foyer of the former Imperial Opera, very erect, very consciously distinguished, a little pale, receiving with a troubled and yet triumphant eye the greetings of friends and fellow-exiles from Carpathia, fixing upon one or another of them a penetrating glance as though he would peer into their minds for some secret that they stubbornly kept from revealing to him.

It was on one of these nights, Ida not being with him, that at the end of the performance, he almost ostentatiously put his arm through that of the aged Professor Breslavy and invited him to supper in the restaurant of the opera house. They found a table in a deep niche. Out of a forest of black-beard that hid all but his nose, the small brown eyes of Breslavy gazed through the monstrously thick lenses of his steel spectacles. The Baron ordered a bottle of

Rüdesheimer. The amber liquid was softly beautiful in the tall glasses between them. The Professor lifted his glass with gentle reverence to his nose. "A bouquet!" he said. Coldly fierce as an eagle the Baron towered above him and the fat, old hairy hand that held the stem of polished glass began to tremble. "When are you going home to Carpathia?" Precariously the glass reached the table. Leaning forward the Professor put his hands on the cloth. "Are you *meshuggeh,* Sander? Tell me, are you?" The Baron was more pale and held himself more erect than ever. The ancestral vocable, the ancestral sing-song of the voice of his old teacher and friend shocked him unendurably. Not thus had Breslavy permitted himself to speak when he was professor of the History of Law at the National University of Carpathia. Never, not at most intimate moments. When, at rather long intervals some newly arrived student had remarked that the famous scholar was a Jew, comrades and colleagues, except a few, a very few in those days, had laughed at the implication. Breslavy was a Carpathian of the Carpathians, one of the chief glories of the country, the only Carpathian who had ever received the Nobel Prize. The Baron clasped his hands. Was this *that* man? He strained his ears. Had he been mistaken? Was he to hear again that sing-song undertone, almost consciously empha- sized as though in relief from years of restraint? He listened; he heard it. "I ask you that, Sander, seriously. I don't like the way you talk; I don't like the way you look. Don't be a *shlemihl!* What would those dirty little barbarians do to me if I went back? Thank God I put that Swedish prize money in a Swiss bank and escaped the inflations. Go back to Carpathia? Who made their stupid, backward little country into something? We did. Jews did. If they produced a poet, we fed him; if they produced a composer, we listened to his works. We gave them a theatre, a press, a business organization, a name in the world of scholarship. We gave them a position in the world of money and banking and financed their peace and their crazy war. And now they want to expel us and denaturalize us when they don't just let us rot in concentration- camps or pitch us into the river. The swine! For God's sake, Sander. Your father and your grandfather and even your great-grandfather helped to make a civilized country out of a little half-Asian state filled with illiterate peasants and barbarous noblemen. They stank and boozed before our time. They're showing their gratitude to us, aren't they? They listened to us, didn't they? I counselled moderation and restraint, you remember, in my lecture hall and the students howled: 'Alien! Traitor!' That was in nineteen-fourteen. I kept quiet after that. They had to have their war. If they had listened to us there would have been no war and no defeat and no dismemberment. Now they try to make us responsible for their swinishness. *Je m'en fiche!* as we used to say in my student days in Paris. Do you know what the charge against me is for which they would try me and probably execute me if I went back? 'Under- mining the will to victory!'" The Professor expelled the air from his mouth with a gesture of infinite contempt. He took a sip of wine. He lifted a short, fat forefinger. "Their whole ideology was and is an anachronism. So was the ideology of their enemies. I never joined those few perverted idealists among them who flirted with the notion that the Western enemy was any better than they. My principle was—I thought it was yours too, Sander—that nothing but murder, broadly speaking, can come of murder. My post-war conclusion is that no *goy* is entirely civilized. The few exceptions have no influence. *Schluss!*"

The Baron leaned his head on his hand. He had heard such words and such arguments before. He had wondered what was the flaw in them, as far as he was concerned, why he rebelled, why he both subtly and passionately dis-associated himself from them. He had perceptions, gained in his youth on the Carpathian plain, drawn in from the shouts of playmates, inhaled from the fragrance of Marya's hair and from the fragrance of the lilacs and the freshly turned furrows of spring and from the folk-songs heard in his boyhood when the peasants on their wains brought the rich harvest home—he had perceptions which had become passion only. Now at least he could turn them into articulate speech. It was the ancestral melody under his friend's Carpathian or German words that acted as a precipitate of these hitherto floating and dissolved perceptions. "You do not understand. Neither did my father. The Carpathians could not listen to us, nor should they have. For your counsel was a counsel from without; it was, if you like, a counsel from above. It may be that Jews have ethical perceptions that are safer and more rational. But the Carpathian people, like every people, want to live and if necessary to die by the call of their own nature, the impulses of their own souls. You and my father and all the men of your generation conferred unnumbered benefits on Carpathia. But the people do not want the benefits of alien hands and of hearts essentially aloof. In peace and quietude they are dazzled by the benefits; in war and stress they rebel against them. For to accept them in tragic crises would be to accept for themselves the nature and the point of view of the alien benefactors. And that they cannot do. Better for them to die by their own semi-barbarous monitions than to live by that which is contrary to all their instincts, character, historical development, for that thing, though it might save their bodies, will finally cause their souls to wither and to disintegrate. And that is why they rise against the Jews in misery and misfortune. You have none of you identified yourselves. I have. I know that, to be the member of a nation, part of the body of a folk, one must share its instincts. If those instincts lead to darkness and death at a given historic moment, one must choose darkness and death. I too, am a pacifist. My mind too, tells me that violence can do no good. But this abstract intellectual cognition has robbed me of my earth, my land, my friends, of all that makes life significant and dear. Hence I repudiate it. I am a Carpathian, a Central European. These people are mine. I shall live with them and die with them."

Even under his thick black beard the Professor's cheeks could be seen burning with horror and indignation. But he mastered himself. "You are identifying yourself with the worst element of the Gentile world and hence helping to pull it down. You are talking reactionary mysticism of the most muddle-headed kind. You are trying to find a refuge for your floating emotions. Very well, if you must have that kind of a refuge, find it in the life of your own people, of the Jews."

The Baron arose. His smile was sardonic. "Logical but impossible, my dear Professor. I am through with logic and the so-called reason, both very Jewish substitutes for life. I am tired of substitutes. I want to live."

At seven o'clock on the next morning his long, grey car was speeding toward the Carpathian frontier.

VI

In the villages autumnal boughs were hung above the doors of the houses in token of the wine that was being harvested. A cool wind blew in from the east and both the Baron and his chauffeur drew their fur coats tight about them. But in that keen wind the Baron seemed to himself to perceive scents which no longer belonged to this land, but to the land to which he was going. His mood was tense and slightly exalted. He had discovered the intimate truth of life; out of the depth of that truth he was acting. He could submit for the present even to the commands of the Dictator; he could ally himself with the more humane among that bloody tyrant's servitors and thus gradually mitigate the harshness of the White Terror from within. Why had he not seen that before? No good ever came of mere aloofness and recalcitrance. The knightly ideal had always been to serve. But to serve an abstract ideal in a homeless world was only to chill the heart and to make it wither. Better a torn land, a bitter tyrant; better the smell of earth and the smoke of fires on the plain; better the wine of home in a wooden cup than the brackish water of exile in a goblet of gold.

At forty minutes after nine o'clock the Baron's car reached the Carpathian frontier. It stopped before the flagged frontier hut. Two morose, heavily-armed men came out. They first examined the chauffeur's passport, stamped it and gave it back. Sullenly one of them stretched out his hand toward the Baron. He examined the safe-conduct, showed it to his colleague with a significant punch of the elbow and handed it back untouched. The frontier officials had evidently been informed, the Baron thought. He ordered his chauffeur to speed up. In three hours he could be in his palace in the capital. At home at last.

At precisely ten kilometres from the frontier two soldiers of the Dictatorship with drawn revolvers blocked the road. The chauffeur stopped short. The men came to the side of the car. "A new precaution," the Baron thought to himself. He drew the safe-conduct forth once more. The soldier in the road beside him who was, as he now observed, an officer, shook his head. He opened the door of the car and sat down beside the Baron. The other soldier pushed himself in next to the chauffeur. "What is the meaning of this?" the Baron asked. "We will shoot upon the least show of resistance," the officer replied. The Baron felt the intolerable pallor spread, like a leprosy, over his face. "Have you a warrant?" he asked. The officer looked straight ahead of him. "My safe-conduct bears the personal signature of His Highness," the Baron said. "I had assumed that the pledged word of a Carpathian gentleman, even of His Highness, could still be relied upon." The officer gnawed at his moustache. "You are being conducted," he said at last, "to the prison of the State under charges of having insulted the Carpathian people in the person of its princes and representatives, of having urged the overthrow of its government from a foreign point of vantage, of having thus given aid and comfort to its enemies. The final charge against you, therefore, is that of high treason. Further communication between us is forbidden."

The Baron felt a terrible tumult arise in his breast. It was not possible; it was not conceivable. For years he had gone up and down Europe pleading for a mitigation of the wrongs done his country in the insane treaties of the so-called peace. Of course, he was a democrat; of course, he had criticized the bestial excesses of the White Terror. But even that he had done with moderation; he did not want to wound his wounded country more. He clenched his fists. He wanted to cry out. He wanted to speak, to explain, to plead—not for himself, no, but for reason, humanity, ultimate self-preservation! How could Carpathia ever recover if it became so wholly a nest of treachery, of brutality, a steady stench in the nostrils of the civilized world? How? He looked at the face beside him: the narrow, low forehead over the blank ridgeless eyes, the insignificant nose, the stupid military severity of aspect and the foolish laughing-wrinkles. He observed the little red and purple veins on that small nose. A toper and a laugher and a carouser with whores, arrogant and brutal to those in his power, obsequious and slavish to those who gave orders. There was no use. In this creature's mind no idea had ever gleamed. It was packed with ready-made unexamined prejudices. The Baron choked. "May I ask in whose custody I am?" He felt beside him the tension of the muscles of the man's body, even as they would grow tense to salute on a parade-ground. The words came out with a false terseness. There was nothing terse about the fellow's character. He had been trained from babyhood on like an animal. Thus one spoke to inferiors, Jews, prisoners, rabble. "Captain Count Pozsony." "Your older brother Michael," said the Baron, "was a schoolmate of mine." He hated himself at once for the obscure impulse that had made him speak. There was nothing human here with which he could communicate. The Captain turned up the deep collar of his military coat. The car sped on.

The Baron felt himself grow numb within. They would probably imprison him for a period; they would probably confiscate his Carpathian estates; they would probably, though they had no right to do so, revoke his family's patent of nobility. It wasn't all this that mattered. The worst, by far the worst that they were doing, was to rob him a second time of all human and humane bases for his life; they were filching from him a second time his country, all earthly sense of home, of solidarity, of belonging somewhere on this grim and confused earth. They were polluting his memories of childhood and of youth; they were desecrating the graves of his fathers who slept in the Carpathian soil; they were casting him out into a void where there was no faith, no home, no allegiance, nothing to serve or love, no object of loyalty, no aim or goal. The numbness crept from his heart down into his intestines; it seemed to sicker down into his very legs and feet. Life—all life, would hereafter be like food cooked without salt, flat and tasteless and abominable, more flat and abominable, month by month, year by year. There was the possibility that they would try him and that trial would echo throughout Europe and it would arouse the indignation of many men in many lands. But these men would be German and English and American liberals and Jews and friends and comrades of Jews. To such he would have to be grateful. And in truth he would be grateful. But what his heart wanted was not the defence of such, but his country, his compatriots, his early friends, his native soil. The Baron's proud head dropped.

VII

He knew the great grey walls of the prison on the low marshy banks of the fatal river. He gave one glance at the distant castle on its eminence above the city—the castle in the sunlight in which the Dictator held his sullen court. Then the huge wooden doors in the wall of the prison-yard opened, the car entered and the world was wiped out. As he got out of the car the Baron's nerves vibrated strangely. Not, truly not, with fear; but from the stones of this yard and from the rubble of these walls and from these steps which now he had to tread and from this corridor which he must now enter there exhaled to meet him the sorrow and the cruelty with which these things, these dead things, were impregnated: the terrors and the cold sweat, the tears and the despair, the bitter hopeless waiting and watching, the blows and lashes, the blood, the ultimate cries! It seemed to him as though he were immediately conscious of all the tormented flesh that had writhed here and left its ghostly imprint, of all the agonies of the spirit which had here been inflicted by man upon man. He almost held his breath. One had but to try to breathe here to know that this place had no kinship with justice and that the vilest malefactor by the very fact of his being brought here became an object of just pity, became himself as of right both accuser and judge of those who had created a hell like this.

They subjected him to no preliminary examination. He was searched for weapons. He was conducted through corridor after corridor to a cell at the end of the last of the corridors—a cell somewhat larger and better lit than those which he had passed, a cell in which one could walk up and down and catch a glimpse of sky through a window set high but slanting in the wall near the ceiling. The warder placed his hand on the iron door. The Captain assumed his most military attitude. "You are at liberty to choose counsel in your defence, whom we will summon." The Baron looked at the stupid soldier. He opened his lips. He spoke. "Dr. Koralnik." The eyes of the two met. The Baron had recovered his usual irony, now edged and sharpened. The Captain, Count Pozsony, tried to look blank. He failed. His eyes said: They hang together— these Jews! The door slammed. The Baron was alone.

They had not taken his cigarettes. He lit one. He walked up and down. His eyes were not ironical now. He knew that his battle was already lost— not perhaps the legal battle of his trial here. But the battle of the yearning of his life. Not because he did not trust or like Koralnik, whose father had been his father's lawyer and friend. But because at the decisive moment his instinct had spoken, straight, unanswerable, final: You can trust none but a Jew; you dare trust none but a Jew; any Carpathian, even the most liberal, even the most knightly will, if only subconsciously, play into the hands of the Dictator. All that he had passionately denied a thousand times, sincerely, with all his heart—that thing in the hour of peril an unerring instinct had tragically affirmed. Koralnik was his only hope. Koralnik, who had sustained himself here against slander, against the knives of norturnal assassins, against the defection of every Carpathian friend and client—this man alone could understand and succour him. And the Carpathians would say at once that the Jews conspired together and tried to load the dice in their own favour. The Baron sat down on the wooden stool and rested his head on his hands. And they were quite right. Only the Jews were forced to do that if they wanted to be living Jews and not dead Jews. They happened to care whether they were alive or dead. The Carpathians did not. The tragic dilemma was complete, ultimate, hopeless.

In less than two hours Koralnik came, a small, compact, black-bearded man. The guard stood in the open door watching them. The Baron took his friend's hand. Koralnik said quietly: "Speak English." He sat down on the cot. "How could you be so foolish as to walk into a trap? How could you?" The Baron lowered his head. "I had a safe-conduct with the personal signature of the Administrator of the Realm." Koralnik shrugged his shoulders. "They are maddened by the injustice that has been done them—the humiliation, the dismemberment of the land. You and I know how great and terrible the injustice has been. They dare not hate those who have inflicted the injustice because those are too powerful. They must externalize their hatred somehow. They hate whom they can—the defenceless. It is a common human process." "But I have felt so deeply at one with them," the Baron said. Koralnik smiled. "You have tried to and wanted to do so. You have been sincere. But you have not been one of them, only a lover and friend to them. Very well. They do not want your love and friendship." "You stay!" the Baron said. Koralnik drew himself up. "This is my place. I can help both Carpathians who protest and Jews who suffer. I can save the country a little from its own errors." There was a silence. Koralnik leaned nearer his friend. "We have no time for generalities. You are entitled to be tried by your peers—the Council of Nobles. I shall protest at once against your confinement here. You are accused of a purely political offence." The Baron nodded. "What is your opinion of the outcome?" Koralnik rose. He frowned. "Confiscation of your Carpathian estates. Against that we can probably do nothing. The government is out at heels. Next they may want to hold you in the country. We must see to it that you are permitted to leave on condition of engaging in no political activity." The Baron clasped his hands. He thought of the void of exile. "I think I'd rather stay. I could have money brought me by messenger." Koralnik frowned. "You are an incorrigible romantic, Sander. But by all means tell your judges that you would rather stay. They are the surer to let you go."

The Baron, left alone, paced up and down again. Although he had just spoken to his friend from the depth of what he believed to be a sincere feeling, he found himself suddenly in the extraordinary grasp, tight, almost throttling, almost nauseating, of an emotional reaction. He disliked Carpathia; he disliked the Carpathian language; he visualized and disliked the Carpathian landscape. He disliked the patriotic ardours of his youth. He had forgotten in the years of exile that in the old days, before the world catastrophes, he had had on more than one occasion to fight against such revulsions of feeling. He stopped in his pacing. He looked up through the slanting window at the sky. He remembered. A slight nausea overcame him. Perhaps it was the result of his immediate experience. Perhaps it was of deeper origin. He put his hands over his chest. He judged himself. No one who had been suckled at a Carpathian mother's breast could ever feel that profound disgust that threatened to choke him now. Carpathia? It was a home, it was a land that he had wanted. The chance of fate had made him identify that home, that land with Carpathia, even as other wanderers had identified other lands with the lands of their yearning. So long as Carpathia satisfied this yearning, so long as Carpathia seemed, at least, to return his romantic love, he was a Carpathian heart and soul. Now, as on three or four other occasions in the course of his life, he felt hostility and cold disgust—not against the tyrant and his tools, as any liberal Carpathian might have done, but against speech and song, earth and sky, harvest and forest, history and character, gesture and blood. He was sick of the whole business, sick to the very marrow. What had he to do with them? What? He sank on the wooden stool; he hid his face in his hands. He hummed. Why that melody? The German master had wrung the final tone from the Suabian poet's verses: *Du bist Orplid mein Land, das ferne leuchtet!* Orplid—that was the land sought by all homeless idealists, dreamers, yearners. Orplid! He was in prison for a political offence against a real country, a shaggy, cruel, picturesque, alien, half-barbaric land. How absurd! He felt like a play-actor in a coarse melodrama. And yet for the first time in many years, he wept.

VIII

They did not delay his trial. Koralnik frowned. By sure messengers he sent protests across the frontier. Not for the press. That would have infuriated the Baron's accusers. He sent messages to distinguished statesmen and writers in the Western countries, Gentiles, of course, who took the hint and addressed courteous protestations to the Administrator of the Carpathian Realm, describing the Baron as a poet rather than a politician, one whose indiscretions proceeded from a patriotism none the less passionate for being untempered by worldly prudence. The Baron was touched. Koralnik admitted that the people were decent people who were nobly doing all they could. But he asked the Baron not to set too high a hope upon these interventions on his behalf. "Had they been great Jews, your colleagues of the Carpathian nobility would have laughed. Now they laugh too: How clever of the Jews to try to cover their retreat with Gentiles! Throw a cat as you like, it will always fall on its feet. Come what may, the Jew is wrong." The Baron looked up. "You used not to be so bitter." Koralnik met his eyes. "I know better now."

Though in the custody of Captain Count Pozsony, the Baron was permitted to use his own car to drive to the royal castle for the trial. No force was used against him. Erect he walked up the broad stairway and through the tall doors of white and gold into the lofty chamber hung with Gobelins that was now used when the Council of Nobles met in special session. The great room was an imitation of another room in the castle of the city that had once been the imperial capital. The chandeliers were huge, gracefully drooping cascades of prisms; the high wainscoting below the precious hangings was, like the doors, white and gold. The Baron walked up an aisle between the lozenge-backed, red-plush armchairs on which sat, somewhat scattered and thinned in ranks, the Magnates of Carpathia. Except for their military uniforms, their golden cords and glittering orders, this was a room in which the young Mozart might have played. A strain from the Minuet out of *Don Giovanni* went perversely through the Baron's mind.

He reached the end of the aisle. A broad dais had been arranged on which, behind a table of equal length, sat the twelve Magnates who were to judge his cause. Over their military coats and stars, above their stiff, penurious, embroidered coat-collars arose the faces, older and younger, which the Baron knew and had known nearly all his life. There were years in which he would have called these men friends, his father's or his own. How those faces had changed! They were now both blank and bitter. A hostility, an immitigable fear and contempt shone dimly through these living masks. Changed—changed? He put his hand upon his heart and had a vision of older, apparently kinder days and saw these faces with expressions of courtesy, agreement, laughter and saw down the vista of the years behind those superficial gestures the fear and the hostility then curbed and hidden, now hideous in the light of day. They had always feared, these men, that the Jews would dupe them; their blood had always nourished the old hate against those whom they had wronged and accused of foul crime and incredible black magic; their blood had half-believed the old, dark superstitious accusations and had remembered the immemorial days when among their war-like, savage, half-naked ancestors had first come, dispersed and sold into the world by Rome, these astute, awe-inspiring, long-robed and bearded Orientals who could communicate at a distance by means of horrifying symbols painted on parchment, who knew the power of herbs and simples and the powers of the mind and who prayed, wrapped in shawls edged with the purple of the Mediterranean, to an invisible God in empty shrines.

Nagy-Raföld tapped lightly with his gavel. A hush fell. Dr. Koralnik laid a light hand for an instant on the Baron's sleeve. The Baron turned. To their left, facing the judges like themselves, sat the Accuser of the State Szögöd, who with his band of soldiers had publicly hunted and shot down Communists and Jews as one hunts and shoots the fierce beasts of the Eastern mountains. The eyes of Nagy-Raföld were fixed upon the Baron. The examination began. The old ironic light came back into the Baron's eyes. How farcical for these men in this assembly to prepare to ask him his name, his origin, his religion. How seriously they took their trumpery, solemnity of procedure. How evil and how childish at once they were. Hence he answered the first question with an ironic blitheness: "Warczawsky Sander, Baron of Tamazsvar." A silence fell through which suddenly from behind came the shout of a young, amused, taunting voice. "Shmuel Warschauer!" The feeble gavel did not seriously try to stop the male laughter in the hall. The ironic light faced from the Baron's eyes. That had in truth been the name of that great-grandfather of his who had come into the land with a pack on his back and silver in his purse. Three generations had tried to live him down—him to whom they owed all they were. But others had remembered him. His ghost was here. In a flat voice he answered another question. He was born in the year so-and-so at such-and-such a place. "Your religious persuasion?" Nagy-Raföld asked next. What dead formalism! "Catholic." This time the gavel was held aloof. The loud male voices roared in inextinguishable laughter. "With that nose!" someone shouted. The Baron sat down. His legs trembled. Small pulses beat in all parts of his body. His temples ached. A film formed in front of his eyes. He knew that he was fiery red; he knew that his self-esteem, that minimum without which a man cannot well live, was wounded deep beyond all healing, wounded for-ever. These strange, loud, cruel, brave, gallant, stupid men, who hunted and made war, who had been children of their Church and vassals of their Kings for a thousand years and had that faith and that vassalage in their bone and marrow—what had they to do with him or he with them? They had talked liberal theories with him in other years. But to them the talk had been a diversion; to him it had been faith and instinct and life. They had told scabrous anecdotes of priests. Why should they not? They needed neither moral nor intellectual evidence; they were Carpathians and Catholics. They were unalterably what they were. It was he who had always needed to be justifying himself, his attitudes, his allegiances. He had had to do that because they were all false and shoddy and even at his deepest moments of devotion merely romantic or rationalized and opportunist. They were right, these *Goyim*—how the old half-forgotten word beat upon his soul!—he was no Catholic, even though he had been baptized in his cradle. It takes more than a few drops of water and a Latin formula to change a man's nature and his millennial heritage. He should have known; he might have known. Even when they and he used the same forms of speech, especially when they used the same forms of speech, they meant things wholly and forever different. He was pale now. The hammering of the pulses in his body had stopped. His proud head was lowered in resignation and shame.

The accuser arose. It had in recent years, he declared, become apparent to all that the desperate condition of the country was to be traced not least to the penetration into its life of alien and essentially hostile elements. He desired to be just. He did not assert that these elements were always hostile in will; they were always alien, provocative and harmful in fact. A false liberalism had feigned to overlook this truth which had now become clear to all whose hearts were filled with care and anxiety over the nation's fate. These elements, for instance, had always, whatever the circumstances, been in favour of peace— even when peace was dishonourable and sameful, even when their partisanship of peace undermined the morale of the sons of the land whose honour and whose rights demanded that they seize the sword of their ancestors lest that sword be, for the first time in history, stained or broken. And why should not these aliens prefer peace at any price? They were interested wholly in trading or in the practice of the practical professions of law or medicine or journalism. They wanted to pursue the kind of success they desired undisturbed. Hence they resented war. Of national honour and glory they had, by their very nature, no conception. Hence, too, if war proved disastrous and confusion ensued, they used their sudden opportunity—as both Carpathia and Bavaria could testify— to seek to impose upon great peoples aware of their destiny insane and blasphemous social experiments which could have been spawned only by brains devoid of the very notions of nationality, of national honour, of all that binds a true man to his country and its King, to his Church and to his Redeemer. Szögöd paused. There was applause as in a theatre. The Baron saw spare sunlight refracted by the high, red cheek-bones of his adversary.

The accuser sipped water and continued. The accused before this bar of judgment, he said, summed up, as it were, in concrete form, all that he had had the honour to explain in more general terms. The protocols in the hands of the judges bore proof of the fact that this Jew, unhappily disguised by a title conferred upon his family by a mistaken and needy government, had always sedulously opposed the national will. He had fought in the war. But not before he had exerted himself to the utmost to render that war disastrous by pacifist propaganda, by evil prophecy, by poisoning the minds of all with whom he had come in contact. His spiritual treason to the realm was inherent in his nature from the beginning. The disaster he had prophesied had come. The Carpathians, aware of its corrupting seeds in their recent past, had established a government that was strong and in harmony with their nature and traditions, no hypocritic republic squinting and currying favour with rabid proletarians on the one hand or international Jewish finance on the other—a government that, thank God, had stamped out the subversive, the ruinous, the alien! When that government was established and the Administrator of the Realm, standing in the place of the exiled King, had sought to heal the wounds of the Carpathian land, where had this so-called Baron of this realm been? Abroad, in the Capitals of the West, inveighing against the Administrator, inveighing therefore against his King and country. He had academically protested against the dismemberment of the land. A cheap gesture. He had tried to bring into disgrace and obloquy the Carpathian people, forever united to their King and to their Church, forever determined to guard their ancient nobility and dignity and splendour. He had opposed actively and always the will of the nation and had sought to break that will even to the point of pleading for interventionist armies. He had stigmatized His Highness' government as a White Terror, a government by murder and stupidity. He was a traitor, deep-dyed in voluntary guilt, by any definition of that term, an enemy of his King, his country and that Christ whom his lying Jewish lips professed to serve.

In spite of an unutterable weariness the Baron found once more, almost to his surprise, the old ironic smile upon his lips. What anachronistic nonsense they talked and evidently believed. You had appendicitis, for instance, and instead of getting a good surgeon you sent an old peasant wife out to gather leeches to suck the poison out of your belly. It was exactly like that. And then you protested that surgery was a wicked Jewish invention and tried to shout down your pain and hang a few surgeons. What confusion of mind. His heart sank. Had he not himself, out of some dark, romantic, homeless yearning for integration with some folk, some land, plead and reasoned with an equal speciousness? Had he not to himself as well as but the other day to Professor Breslavy used analogous arguments in order to deaden his own inner pain at being hated where he had loved so much? Had he not nourished the murderous errors in his own breast in order to justify his dear foes' hostility to himself? Could self-immolation go further? That, that was what should have been shouted out to these judges. Ha, they would laugh. For once the Jew was duped. What could Koralnik say?

Koralnik arose. Despite the shortness of his stature he was dignified. He lifted his eyes, hitherto lowered, to the judges and a perceptible discomfort vibrated for a moment upon those faces that tried to be stern and succeeded in being only stubborn and lightless. In a clear, penetrating tenor voice Koralnik spoke. The accuser of the State, he began, had defined treason according to a definition that had historically existed. He had enunciated the Roman doctrine of proscription of the party not in power. To apply that to Carpathia: Today all democrats and liberals were to be proscribed as traitors. The same things, then, on the same principle, could happen to the royalists, namely, to the entire exalted assembly here present on some historic tomorrow. Briefly: to stigmatize any difference of political opinion from the government of any specific year or even decade as treason was a terrible two-edged sword. He who had used that sword had never failed to perish by it yet. On that point the evidence of history was complete. Fifteen years ago Carpathia had been one of the most liberal States in Europe. Today it was profoundly conservative. Such changes of polity were natural and legitimate; they had happened before and would again. To stigmatize the opposition of a given hour in history as treacherous was to reduce all government to the periodic clashes of two groups of assassins. The moral opinion of mankind would in the twentieth century remain pitilessly hostile to a State governed on the principle of proscription. Patriotism must be defined as love of the patria, the fatherland, operating in harmony with the innermost nature of the individual citizen or subject. Precisely as men was born Aristotelians or Platonists so they were born liberals or conservatives. That the majority of Jews inclined to liberalism was true. It was, in itself, no reproach. None, upon any rational notion of government or patriotism. He accepted this accusation for his client and would proceed to show that, upon his own principles, he had been a passionate and undeviatingly loyal citizen or subject of the Carpathian State. Koralnik turned to the documents on the table before him and gave a complete account of the Baron's life and activities during his years of exile, eliminating rumour and slander, establishing the sober facts. He sat down amid an icy silence. Szögöd arose for just a minute to say that he need hardly recall the fact to their Excellencies that the arguments just heard were the familiar ones of international liberalism guided everywhere by Jewish brains and that their acceptance meant the death of order, stability, reverence, State and Church. They were the beginning whereof the end was promiscuity, Bolshevism and the destruction of Christian civilization.

Again that grinding weariness overcame the Baron. He felt that he had nothing to do with all this. His brain was not wholly convinced by his friend and advocate; he could see a certain barbaric but not illogical coherence about Szögöd's views. He was not at all sure that a more and more industrialized democracy would not lead more or less inevitably to communism, which he loathed. But he loathed bloody and reactionary authoritarianism just as deeply. Why couldn't he go away, far away, away from all this endless, futile turmoil and agitation and lay his head upon some peaceful bit of earth? He looked at

the judges once more. They were about to withdraw. Their faces made him
think of screened fireplaces. The screens were down; the inner draught made
the red flames leap up. But without was the black screen.

He saw the anxious expression in Koralnik's eyes. He could not summon
any emotional connection with it. He could not recapture a contact with all
this empty palavering as reality, as having to do with him or deciding his fate.
He knew that the resilience was gone from his body and from his soul. Let them
confiscate his estates; let them imprison him. He would not even protest any
more. He was completely worn out. He was disgusted with a homeless world;
he was disgusted with Carpathia. He was disgusted with himself and with
mankind. And God did not exist.

IX

They took him back to his cell. He lay down on his couch. He did not sleep
but sunk into a kind of lethargy in which it came to him that this weariness
and disgust of his life had been with him, had been creeping on him for
a long time. He had resisted by all sorts of half-conscious or semi-conscious
mechanisms of defence. But he had probably walked so eagerly and secretively
into the Carpathian trap because he had unconsciously desired a great danger,
a great upheaval in order to sting his wearied and disgusted soul into activity at
any cost. Confused words and confused images floated into his mind: Marya
on the plain, his grandfather surreptitiously pronouncing a Hebrew blessing,
green lawns in England and then again his grandfather's murmuring voice—he
couldn't have been more than ten when he had heard it last—*Baruch atta
adonai elohenu melech haolam.* He could hear the melody of the strange
words. He sat up suddenly. The heavy door was being opened. He had to wipe
his lids. They were wet.

An unbearably brilliant arc-light had been turned on in the corridor. He
was summoned forth from his cell. Three men stood there, one in a gaudy
military uniform, the other was the warder, the third had on—the Baron
peered incredulously—a soutane. A priest? A cold, sick shiver went through
the Baron's body. The man in the brilliant military uniform drew forth a
document and began to read. It was the sentence. He knew that he ought to
fix his attention upon every word. But he had a humming in his ears and the
glare of the light hurt his eyes. He felt sweat, cold sweat stand out on his
forehead. But he heard phrases concerning the especial responsibilities that
rested upon the nobles of the land and the even more special responsibilities of
any noble of foreign blood and alien origin which the aforesaid Warczawsky
Sander, hitherto Baron of Tamaczvar, had betrayed and outraged in peace and
war and in that defeat which he and his kind had served to bring about. Not
satisfied with the dismemberment and disaster of his country he had assaulted
that country and its rulers by both inherited and divine right with slander
and obloquy, so that patriots had barely saved the ruined land of their birth

from a second invasion and utter destruction. Wherefore the peers of the realm declared him guilty of high treason. The sentence was to be executed at dawn. From the warder the officer in the brilliant uniform took a small, white, wooden staff, lifted it high and, standing on tiptoe, broke it over the Baron's head.

Was he literally sinking, melting, horribly deliquescing into the cement floor? Would his milk-weak knees bear him another moment, only another? Would he be able to keep himself from screaming like a stricken animal? A black veil dropped before his eyes; his stomach seemed literally to turn in his belly. He swayed. The warder took his arm. That touch stung. He did not fall. He dug his nails into his palms, deep, deep, a little deeper. He groaned but held himself erect. He could see again, though dimly. His mouth was dry, horribly dry and horribly bitter. Unspeakably, nauseatingly bitter. Death could be no bitterer than that. He wanted to say something. He forgot what it was. Then it came slowly—he had to chew and mouth and finally mumble the words: "An appeal . . ." "The Council of Nobles is the highest existent Court. No appeal is possible." It was the creature in the gaudy uniform who spoke and who added: "You are advised to accept the consolations of our holy religion." The person in the soutane stepped forward and pushed a long, grey face near to the Baron's. "I will stay with you, my son." The Baron leaned against the wall. He felt his blood that had been congealed begin to flow again. Something began first slowly, then more violently to blaze in his brain. To blaze! The unbelievable swine. The priest who had the effrontery to be mealy-mouthed about the foulest kind of judicial murder. Whose vile lips would not wither as he mumbled the name of that other Jew, Jesus of Nazareth, who had also been murdered by a tyrant. He lifted his arm. He struck the priest full in the face. He laughed.

They pushed him into his cell. He was alone. He was alone with his flesh, with his flesh that again began to shrink from the thought of pain and annihilation. He fell on his cot. Blindly he reached for water for his mouth that was still as bitter as the gall of a fish crushed against the palate. He groped. At last he found the pitcher and the cup of tin. He drank; he drank again. He half sat up. His head fell on his breast. He simmered. Then wave after wave of sheer, sickening animal terror rolled over him. He got up. Insanely he hurried and scurried about from wall to wall, from door to wall. Escape, escape and life, just life, only the naked life of the body on any terms. On any—he stopped very suddenly. A gong struck in his brain. He could hear that gong. He could hear the hammer of that gong. *Baruch atta adonai elohenu* . . . Meaningless words. He did not believe in God. But Jews had died with such words on their lips. They had not cringed or let the animal terror of the body master them. They had always defied the murderers in the end. They were killing him because he was a Jew. He had not lived as a Jew. He was forced to die as a Jew. He would die then as the martyrs of his people had always died.

The waves of animal terror did not cease. From time to time they came again. But with tightly clasped hands, with head a little more erect he mastered each as it came. How many generations of Jews did it take to go from martyrdom to martyrdom? Not many, as history goes. He sat down on the cot; he drew the wooden stool in front of him. He beat softly with his fists on the wooden stool. He must not, not cringe and quiver before those murderous barbarians. He must not. Murderous barbarians. He had tried to exert a civilizing influence over them. He had tried to love them out of their barbarous darkness. A few of that savage blood had tried to do the same. But mainly he and his kind. How could he ever have thought that these people were his people or their thoughts like his own or their emotions like his own? They had mouthed the words; he had meant the meanings. There was no gulf in all the oceans of the earth so deep as the gulf that divided them from him. He had agonized in the war over the consciousness that his soldiers were wounding and killing men, their brothers. He had always known that if ever he were drawn into a bayonet attack, he would rather be killed than kill a brother man. And these nobles—nobles—now for the first time he laughed—these nobles who had borrowed his father's money and his and broken bread in his father's house and his own and taken his intellect and substance for their musicians and their poets—they could murder him and go about their business. Poor Ida, he suddenly thought. But she would have money enough, and everybody in liberal circles in the West would be agreeable to her. And they had no child. Better so. He got up. He must keep hold of this determination, of this state of mind that lifted him above his murderers. If only the dawn would come, if only the dawn and the hour of his supreme testing would come.

A first pale light crept over the slanting window. He fought off his last wave of terror. The pain would be brief and hardly conscious. He repeated those words to himself: brief and hardly conscious. And death is a thing we dread foolishly, for it is no part of our experience. It is no more conscious, it is less conscious than birth. These *Goyim* should not see him cringe; they should not see him falter. Not him nor any Jew.

When the door opened his body fled with back against the wall. His spirit drew it forward. He let his hands be tied behind his back. He smiled ironically at the vested priest with a monstrance held under that thin, long, cruel nose. Erect he walked behind the warder with the priest following down the dim corridors, down the dim stairs into the yard of the prison. Over the high walls he could see the sky, the dear sky beginning to flush rosy over the pearl grey. His eyes grew moist for a moment. Then he saw Captain Pozsony and a squad of ten men. The warder took him to the wall and stood him up against it. The priest came forward. The Baron hurled at him a withering word in the Carpathian tongue. Then he turned to Pozsony. He felt a light breeze of dawn lift the hair from his hot forehead. "Will you permit me to give the word of command?" In spite of himself Pozsony saluted. "Whenever you like, Baron." He saw the men of the squad take aim. He ground his teeth together for a moment. He threw back his head. He forced the word magnificently from his fevered throat: "Fire!"

He fell not ungracefully sidewise against the wall with an enormous ruddy gash in his left breast. Pozsony and the priest walked over to the body. They bent above it. He had died instantly. They drew themselves up and exchanged glances. "A brave man," said the priest, with the bitter lines about his mouth deepening. The Captain nodded. "They die game, these Jews. I've seen it before. Do you know what I think sustains them?" The priest shook his head. The Captain frowned. "Their contempt for us and our religion. That's what it is!" As though to ward off a malign influence the priest crossed himself quickly and began to mumble a Latin prayer.

AMERICA

AN AMERICAN IN TUNIS

by MORDECAI MANUEL NOAH [1]

O N the 30th of July, about noon, we observed signals for a fleet from the tower on Cape Carthage, and shortly after, the American squadron, under full sail, came into the bay and anchored. Nothing can be more welcome to a consul in Barbary than the sight of a fleet, bearing the flag of his nation; he feels that, surrounded by assassins and mercenaries, he is still safe and protected, and an involuntary tribute of admiration is paid by Mussulmen to that nation which has the power and the disposition to command respect. The flags of all the Consulates were hoisted, and I lost no time to ride to the Goletta for the purpose of communicating with the squadron. On my way, a Mameluke on horseback presented me a letter from Commodore Decatur, announcing peace with Algiers, and desired to know the nature of our differences with Tunis. I had already prepared the documents, and arranged the plan of procedure, which I intended to suggest to the Commodore. On my arrival at the Goletta, the Minister of Marine ordered the Bey's barge of twelve oars to be prepared for me, and arranged the silk cushions in the stern, and accompanied by Abdallah, the dragoman, I left the canal.

The squadron lay off Cape Carthage, arranged in handsome order. The *Guerriere,* bearing the broad pennant of the Commodore, was in the center, and the whole exhibiting a very agreeable and commanding sight. In less than an hour, I was alongside of the flagship, and ascended on the quarter deck. The marines were under arms, and received the consul of the United States with the usual honors. Commodore Decatur and Capt. Downs, both in uniform, were at the gangway, and most of the officers and the crew pressed forward to view their fellow-citizen. After the customary salutations, and a few inquiries, Commodore Decatur invited me into the cabin, where, after being seated, he went to his escritoire, and from among a package of letters he handed me one, saying that it was a despatch from the Secretary of State, and requested me to use no ceremony, but to read it. It had the seal of the United States, which I broke, and, to my great surprise, read as follows:

---

[1] The events described here occurred between 1815 and 1816, when Noah (1785-1851) was the American consul in Tunis. The selection is from his volume, *Travels in England, France, Spain and the Barbary States* (1819).

Noah was one of the most colorful Jews in early American history. He was imbued with the spirit of freedom and independence (his father had fought in the War of Independence) which pervaded all his activity and writing. He was a distinguished journalist, playwright and philanthropist. His observation of the misfortune of European Jewries and a deep Jewish pride led him to propose the organization of a Jewish state.

"Department of State, April 25, 1815.

"Sir,

"At the time of your appointment, as Consul at Tunis, it was not known that the Religion which you profess would form any obstacle to the exercise of your Consular functions. Recent information, however, on which entire reliance may be placed, proves that it would produce a very unfavorable effect. IN CONSEQUENCE OF WHICH, the President has deemed it expedient to revoke your commission. On the receipt of this letter, therefore, you will consider yourself no longer in the public service. There are some circumstances, too, connected with your accounts, which require a more particular explanation, which with that already given, are not approved by the President.

I am, very respectfully, Sir,
Your obedient servant,
JAMES MONROE.

(Signed)
"Mordecai M. Noah, esquire, &c. &c."

The receipt of this letter shocked me inexpressibly; at this moment, at such a time, and in such a place, to receive a letter, which at once stripped me of office, of rights, of honor, and credit, was sufficient to astonish and dismay a person of stronger nerves. What was to be done? I had not a moment to determine. I cast my eye hastily on Commodore Decatur. I was satisfied at a glance that he knew not the contents of the letter. It was necessary that he should not, for had he been made acquainted with the determination of the government, it would have been his duty, and he would have exercised it promptly, to have sent an officer on shore, taken possession of the seals and archives of the Consulate, and I should have returned to Tunis, stripped of power, an outcast, degraded, and disgraced, a heavy debt against me; and from my Consulate, from the possession of power, respected and feared, I should, in all probability, have gone into a dungeon, where I might have perished, neglected and unpitied. And for what? For carrying into effect the express order of the government! I had no time to curse such perfidy. I folded up the letter with apparent indifference, put it in my pocket, and then proceeded to relate to Commodore Decatur the nature of our dispute with Tunis, which was corroborated by the documents I had prepared and brought with me. I suggested the propriety of his writing a letter to the minister, and demanding payment for the prizes without delay; and the better to give effect to this demand, it would be well for the Commodore to remain on board his ship until it was complied with. This course I urged with a zeal corresponding to the stake which I had at issue, and with my peculiar situation. The Commodore could not account for this great anxiety to recover the money: my object was to pay the protested bills, redeem the credit of the country, and thus enable me to return home with honor. He must have imagined that other motives dictated this extraordinary warmth, and arguments upon arguments, all of which I enforced with vehemence. "You may probably," said he, "imagine that I am under your orders; if you do, it is proper to undeceive you." I saw a storm gathering, which would destroy all my plans, and I tranquilly assured the Commodore that I requested nothing more than his cooperation to maintain our treaty inviolate, and by such measures as his prudence dictated. We were only there to serve our country in the best manner. Thus satisfied, the Commodore, who originally was pleased at the prompt manner pointed out of terminating this difference, consented to write the letter, which was done forthwith.

Night came on, and I betook myself to rest on the cabin floor, and in a state of mind better imagined than described. At daybreak the next morning, the lively drum and fife played the reveille, the officer on duty furnished me with a boat and hands, which landed Abdallah and myself under Cape Carthage. I had ordered horses to be on the spot at an early hour, and we ascended to the rugged summit to look for their approach. I seated myself on the extreme height of the cape. The sun was just rising, and the beautiful amphitheater by which I was surrounded was tinged with gold. Not a soul was stirring. Below me were the diminished masts of our squadron, which was tranquilly at anchor; at a distance the smooth surface of the Mediterranean, without a solitary bark to break the prospect; the birds were singing cheerfully, everything appeared at ease except myself. I once more read the letter of Mr. Monroe. I paused to reflect on its contents. I was at a loss to account for its strange and unprecedented tenor. My religion an object of hostility? I thought I was a citizen of the United States, protected by the Constitution in my religious as well as in my civil rights. My religion was known to the government at the time of my appointment, and it constituted one of the prominent causes why I was sent to Barbary. If then any "unfavorable" events had been created by my religion, they should have been first ascertained, and not acting upon a supposition, upon imaginary consequences, have thus violated one of the most sacred and delicate rights of a citizen. Admitting, then, that my religion had produced an unfavorable effect, no official notice should have been taken of it; I could have been recalled without placing on file a letter, thus hostile to the spirit and character of our institutions. But my religion was not known in Barbary. From the moment of my landing, I had been in the full possession of my Consular functions, respected and feared by the government, and enjoying the esteem and goodwill of every resident. What injury could my religion create? I lived like other Consuls, the flag of the United States was displayed on Sundays and Christian holidays; the Catholic priest, who came into my house to sprinkle holy water and pray, was received with deference, and freely allowed to perform his pious purpose; the barefooted Franciscan, who came to beg, received almost in the name of Jesus Christ; the Greek Bishop, who sent to me a decorated branch of palm on Sunday, received, in return, a customary donation; the poor Christian slaves, when they wanted a favor, came to me; the Jews alone asked nothing from me. Why then am I to be persecuted for my religion? Although no religious principles are known to the Constitution, no peculiar worship connected with the government, yet I did not forget that I was representing a Christian nation. What was the opinion of Joel Barlow, when writing a treaty for one of the Barbary States? Let the following article, confirmed by the Senate of the United States, answer:

"Article 11th—As the government of the United States of America is not, IN ANY SENSE, founded on the Christian religion—as it has, in itself, no character of enmity against the laws, religion, or tranquillity of Musselmen; and as the said United States never have entered into any war, or act of hostility against any Mohametan nation, it is declared by the parties, that no pretext arising from religious opinions shall ever produce an interruption of harmony existing between the two countries."

If President Madison was unacquainted with the article in the treaty, which in effect is equally binding in all the States of Barbary, he should have remembered that the religion of a citizen is not a legitimate object of official notice from the government; and even admitting that my religion was an obstacle, and there is no doubt that it was not, are we prepared to yield up the admirable and just institutions of our country at the shrine of foreign bigotry and superstition? Are we prepared to disenfranchise one of our own citizens to gratify the intolerant view of the Bey of Tunis? Has it come to this,—that the noble character of the most illustrious republic on earth, celebrated for its justice and sacred character of its institutions, is to be sacrificed at the shrine of a Barbary pirate? Have we then fallen so low? What would have been the consequence, had the Bey known and objected to my religion? He would have learnt, in language too plain to be misunderstood, that whoever the United States commissions as their representative, he must receive and respect, if his conduct be proper. On that subject I could not have permitted a word to be said. If such a principle is attempted to be established, it will lay the foundation for the most unhappy and most dangerous disputes; foreign nations will dictate to us the religions which our officers at their courts should profess.

With all the reflection, and the most painful anxiety, I could not account for this most extraordinary and novel procedure. Some base intriguer, probably one who was ambitious of holding this wretched office, had been at some pains to represent to the government that my religion would produce injurious effects, and the President, instead of closing the door on such interdicted subjects, had listened and concurred. And after having braved the perils of the ocean, residing in a barbarous country, without family or relatives, supporting the rights of the nation, and hazarding my life from poison or the stiletto, I find my own government, the only protector I can have, sacrificing my credit, violating my rights, and insulting my feelings, and the religious feelings of a whole nation. O shame! shame! The course which men of refined or delicate feelings should have pursued, had there been grounds for such a suspicion, was an obvious one. The President should have instructed the Secretary of State to have recalled me, and to have said that the causes should be made to me on my return; such a letter as I received should never have been written, and, above all, should never have been put on file. But it is not true that my religion either had or would have produced injurious effects. The Bey of Algiers had appointed Abraham Busnah his minister at the court of France, Nathan Bacri is Algerine Consul at Marseilles, his brother holds the same office at Leghorn. The Treasurer, Interpreter and Commercial Agent of the Grand Signeur at Constantinople are Jews.

In the year 1811, the British government sent Aaron Cordoza, Esq., of Gibraltar, a most intelligent and respectable Jew, with a sloop of war to Algiers, to negotiate some important point connected with commerce. He was received with deference, and succeeded. The first minister to Portugal from Morocco was Abraham Sasportas, a Jew, who formed a treaty, and was received with open arms. Ali Bey of Tunis sent Moses Massias, the father of Major Massias, who was at present serving in the army of the United States, as ambassador to London. Innumerable instances could be adduced, where the Mussulmen have preferred employing the Israelites on foreign missions, and had any important dispute arose, requiring power and influence to adjust, my religion should have been known, and my success would have been certain. But I had sufficient power and respect, more than have ever been enjoyed by any Consul before me, and none who succeeds me will ever possess a greater share. It was not necessary for a citizen of the United States to have his faith stamped on his forehead; the name of freeman is a sufficient passport, and my government should have supported me, had it been necessary, to have defended my rights, and not to have themselves assailed them. There was also something insufferably little, in adding the weight of the American government, in violation of the wishes and institutions of the people, to crush a nation, many of which had fought and bled for American Independence, and many had assisted to elevate those very men who had thus treated their rights with indelicate oppression. Unfortunate people, whose faith and constancy alone have been the cause of so much tyranny and oppression, who have given moral laws to the world, and who receive for reward opprobrium and insult. After this, what nation may not oppress them?

These reflections I could not avoid making; they were inseparable from my situation, and from the unexpected motives of my recall. Abdallah, my honest dragoman, had taken the pipe from his girdle, filled it, and was seated on some ruins, calmly smoking, occasionally casting on me an eye of anxious solicitude. There was something in this letter which I had not yet examined. Mr. Monroe informs me that there were some circumstances, too, connected with my accounts, which require a more particular explanation, and which the President had not approved of. This was an additional cause of complaint. Yet no officer should be recalled for want of mere explanations in his accounts,—probably my bills were received and not my despatches. Yet had I assumed a power not specially delegated, had I gone beyond orders, squandered or embezzled the public money, this would have been a good and sufficient cause to have recalled me, this would have been the proper ground to have placed the dismissal upon, and not my religion. But the government knew better, they were satisfied that I had kept within the purview of my orders, and was able to give a correct account of my disbursements; on this subject I was perfectly easy; they could not venture to predicate the removal on such objections.

The morning by this time had far advanced. I saw no horses, and left the ruins of Carthage and walked to Marsa, where I met my friend the Danish Consul, to whom I recapitulated the measures we were about to pursue with the Bey. He fully concurred in the promptness and expediency of our steps, and we went to Tunis together. In a short time the Minister of Marine sent for me, he had received the letter from Commodore Decatur, and was in no very pleasant humor. This is not, said he, a proper and respectful manner of doing business. Why does not your Admiral make his complaints to the Bey in person? Why does he demand the payment of us for prizes which the British have illegally carried away, and demand an answer forthwith? We are not accustomed to be treated in this manner. There was a time when you waited our pleasure to establish a treaty, and paid us for it, and gave us presents whenever we demanded them, and all within my recollection. I calmly assured the minister that these measures were indispensable to the preservation of our rights; that he must have anticipated them, and should, as I recommended, have terminated the affair before the arrival of the squadron; that it was now too late; Commodore Decatur had determined not to land without a favorable answer. The minister fully assured me that the money would not be paid, and I left him.

There was some bustle and confusion at Bardo. The Bey sent for Mr. Nyssen, the Dutch Consul, and consulted with him. Nyssen advised him to resist the demand, and stated that we had no authority to declare war, and would not dare to commence hostilities. This was told to me by the Christian slaves. I sent a mild and friendly message to Nyssen, urging him not to interfere in our business; that he would lose his head in twenty-four hours after hostilities had commenced for giving improper advice to the Bey. The minister sent for me three or four times. He appeared to be troubled, yet always assumed that grave and imposing demeanor, which they know so well how to put on. "What is the reason, Consul," said he, "that you are so tranquil? Before your fleet was here you were loud and positive, now that you are backed by a force, you have suddenly become very quiet and indifferent." I stated that remonstrance was no longer necessary, and that war was inevitable, except redress was obtained for the infraction of our treaty; that, having made peace with Algiers on our own terms, the squadron was prepared for new contests, and that it was rather desirable than otherwise, for it was better to have no treaty than to have one that was not respected. The minister, finding me so serious, left Tunis for Bardo. A report reached the palace, that Commodore Decatur, disguised as a common sailor, was seen with four hands in a small boat taking soundings of the bay to ascertain how near the ships could be brought to the fortress of Goletta. I knew not if this were true (it may have been so) but it served to create a great alarm.

In the afternoon, several officers came up to Tunis by land; among them were Captain Gordon and Elliott, with a number of midshipmen. They rushed through the gates of the town with perfect indifference, and appeared to be much at home; the Turks regarded them with astonishment, and on their arrival at the Consulate, they expressed a desire to go to a Turkish bath immediately. I sent Kaleel, the young dragoman, to the principal one to have it ready. These baths are considered very wholesome. The person is carried into rooms of considerable heat raised by steam, which in a short time produces a copious perspiration. They are then rubbed down with woolen cloths, their joints cracked, and thus relaxed, they are rinsed with several pails of tepid water and wrapped up in a sheet to cool gradually. After the ceremony of bathing had been concluded, I went to the bath to see the officers. They were lying on mats arranged round the room like the wards of an hospital, and thus infolded with linen and in a languishing lassitude, they were employed in smoking long pipes of sweet tobacco, and some were sipping coffee. They appeared to be delighted with the operation and effect, and some the next day repeated the visit.

Captains Gordon and Elliott were instructed by Commodore Decatur to accompany me to the palace to learn the ultimatum of the Bey. We were at Bardo at an early hour. Anxiety and curiosity had brought a number of persons about the walls. The hall of audience was crowded, and Hassan and Mustapha, the two sons, were present, and were extremely active and insolent. A commanding appearance has great influence with the Turks. Accustomed to measure everything by the eye, they course over the exterior, and make few allowances for mind or character. Captain Gordon, who is now dead, had not an impressive figure, nor did he carry in his face or person any token of that firmness of character and just and generous sentiments for which he was distinguished. The Bey looked at him with the utmost indifference. He was a short man, worn down by illness. "Who are you?" said he. "I am second in command of that squadron, Sir," said Capt. Gordon, "and I am here to know whether you are ready to do us justice." "Why does not your Admiral come on shore then?" said the Bey. "Why am I treated with so much disrespect by him?" "He will not land, Sir, until you decide to pay the value of these vessels, which you have permitted the British to take from us." Mustapha Bey then interfered, and in a tone of uncommon insolence and violence was about to contend the matter, when Capt. Elliott observed: "We did not come here to be insulted. This interview must be cut short. Will you, or will you not, pay for these vessels? Answer nothing but that." "Well then," said Mustapha, thus pressed, and with a furious look, "we will pay for them, but have a care, our turn comes next. Tell your Admiral to come on shore," said the Bey; "I'll send the money to the Consul. I'm a rich prince, and don't value it. Go."

Thus ended the interview, and thus were the rights of the United States, as guaranteed by treaty, faithfully supported and rigidly enforced. Opposition is invariably made by these people to any demand affecting their interest, but when they are compelled to yield, it is like destiny and is met with resignation. They think no more about it. The Bey ordered a letter to be written to Commodore Decatur, and doubtless felt a respect for that nation which would not abandon a point of honor.

In a few days we took our departure with a pleasant and favorable breeze. We had several French passengers, and a Dutch family, who were emigrating to America, and in forty-four days we entered the Capes of Delaware. After an absence of three years, I landed in my native country, more attached to the soil, to the character of the people and national institutions, from the opportunity of contrasting their advantages with those of foreign nations. I had been daily expected by my friends, who knew not the precise motives which produced my recall, nor the manner in which it had been indicated to me, general rumor having reached them that I had been charged with exceeding my orders, and I had lost no time in proceeding to the seat of government in order to check the circulation of an opinion so very erroneous. I presented myself to Mr. Monroe, then Secretary of State, prepared to give and receive explanations, and with a temper and disposition calculated to forget everything, if suitable indications of justice and liberality were manifested; but, on the contrary, determined to resist any attempt to add to the injustice with which I had already been treated. My reception was altogether as ungracious as it was undeserved, and certainly unexpected, from a citizen possessing the character of Mr. Monroe. Instead of a frank disavowal of any authority to predicate my recall on religion, instead of assurances of a liberal construction of authority, instead of regret that any measures had been accidentally adopted, calculated to wound the feelings of a citizen, or a whole nation, on a very delicate point, instead of a promise, which I confidently expected and which was due to me, of a restoration to an office of equal rank, when my affairs were honorably closed, Mr. Monroe, in a very few words, accused me of going beyond orders, employing a most obnoxious character, expending the public money unnecessarily, justified the recall and its manner, and then told me if I could clear up the affair, and satisfy those friends who had recommended me for the office, that he would be satisfied, and thus our first interview terminated.

Presuming that Mr. Monroe had predetermined the manner of my reception, by the advice of the President, I thought it unnecessary to see Mr. Madison on the subject, and therefore lost no time to collect all my documents and to prepare suitable explanations, which, when concluded, I caused to be printed in pamphlet form in order to lay before Congress, and to demand at their hands that justice which my fellow-citizens in the government had denied to me. My principal object, however, was to cause my letter of recall to be struck from the files of the Department of State, as being a document, not only unconstitutional and discreditable, but calculated to impair, very materially, the rights of an increasing portion of the community; and I calculated that resolutions disapproving the course pursued by the government in my case would have shown to the world the close adherence, the strict regard, the sacred attachment, evinced for the institutions of the country, and their superior influence to personal or political considerations. Prior to taking this step, I sent one of the pamphlets, which was written with mildness and respect, to the Department of State, with the latent hope that the clear explanations which it contained would induce the government to do what was strictly right. The Secretary caused it to be thrown on the table, that every person might read it, and with a view of showing with what indifference they regarded my appeal to the people from their measures and decision. I was pained to see this little spirit exhibited by the government, this fictitious display of power, which we all know is transitory. I had ever supported the government, had been the warm political friend and advocate of the administration, but I had never anticipated such a course, and am persuaded, that the people cannot be acquainted with the operations of such feelings and doctrines in the officers of their choice.

My friends in Congress, who had recommended me for the appointment, were unanimous in their opinion, and expressed to me their regret, and to the government their unequivocal disapprobation of the course pursued. They, however, intimated to me, that no good effect would result from an appeal to Congress, that the body had no control over the documents in the Department of State, and as Mr. Monroe had been nominated for President, it might and would be construed into political hostility and reported so accordingly, which certainly had no connexion with my views. They considered the measures of the government as accidental and unfortunate, but united to assure me that I might place every reliance on the justice of Mr. Monroe, who had ever been remarked, except in this instance, for a prudent exercise of official power. A senator of the United States, and one of the most distinguished, gave me the following letter, directed to the Secretary of State:

"*Sir,*
"*It has been intimated to me by Major Noah that you are desirous of conferring with me in relation to his case. From the character of this gentleman, and the knowledge I have of him, I should suppose him to be incapable of conducting himself improperly on any occasion. Under these circumstances, and as my state of health prevents me from waiting upon you, I feel it to be but an act of justice towards him to declare, that, on examining his statements and documents, I have not been able to discover anything reprehensible in his conduct. The employment of Keene, the charge apparently most relied upon, would seem to be excused, if not justified, sanctioned as it was, by the advice of Mr. Hackley, who had been long in the service and confidence of the government.*
I have the honor, &c."

This letter I delivered open to Mr. Graham, then Chief Clerk of the Department of State. Mr. Monroe, declining to see me, instructed Mr. Graham to inquire what I wanted. I had expressed but one desire, from which I never varied,—it was to do me justice, settle my accounts, and if there is a dollar due me, let me know it officially. That was the first step in my situation, and after mortifying, perplexing, and expensive delays, after twelve months had elapsed, after three special journeys to Washington, the Attorney General was instructed to adjust my claims, and at length I received the following letter:

Department of State, January 14, 1817.

"*Sir,*

"*Your account as Consul of the United States at Tunis has been adjusted at this Department, in conformity with the opinion of the Attorney General of the 30th of December last, of which you have a copy; and a balance of Five Thousand Two Hundred and Sixteen Dollars Fifty-seven cents, REPORTED TO BE DUE YOU, WILL BE PAID TO YOUR ORDER, at any time after Congress shall have made the necessary appropriations. A sum of One Thousand Six Hundred and Sixty-four Dollars, besides a charge of thirty-five per cent loss on the disbursement of your Agent at Algiers, is SUSPENDED, for reasons mentioned in the account of which you have been apprised.*

"*I am, Sir, respectfully,*
"*Your obedient servant,*
(Signed)   "*S. PLEASANTON.*
Mordecai M. Noah, Esq."

Thus ended my connexion with the government, and thus fell to the ground the charge "of going beyond orders." Nothing then remained of the official charge but my religion, a subject which I had reason to believe the President would have reconciled in a suitable manner, but which, after three years' delay, has not commanded his attention.

If I have occupied too much space in this work with recapitulating my official concerns, the reader will bear in mind that this is the first attempt since the adoption of the Constitution of the United States to make the religion of a citizen an objection to the possession of office; a principle so foreign to the Constitution, so much at war with the genius and disposition of the people, and so dangerous to the liberties of the country, that citizens cannot be insensible to the new and dreadful features which it exposes. None can hear with indifference this measure of the government, and none will turn a deaf ear to the representations of an individual who has sustained an injury. Governments have a natural propensity to encroach upon the rights of citizens, and if those rights are worthy of being preserved, the utmost caution should be used to guard them with a vigilance that never slumbers. If a letter such as I received in Barbary had been written by order of a sovereign, presuming that a king could do such a wrong, I should have submitted to it without a murmur, knowing the tenure by which I held my office: but, my fellow-citizen, the

President, to disfranchise me from holding the office of consul at Tunis, when I am eligible to the station which he holds, cannot but be viewed as an assumption of power neither known nor tolerated. Nothing is easier than to establish a principle in governments, and nothing is more difficult than to destroy this principle, when it is found to be dangerous. My letter of recall has become a document on file at the Department of State, which hereafter may, without the present explanations, go to disfranchise a whole nation. I felt it to be my duty to clear up this affair, and as I caused my country to be respected abroad, it was not anticipating too much, when I claimed a reciprocal respect and protection from the government. I had heard it rumored that Col. Lear was the prominent cause of that letter having been written to me. He is now dead, and I have only to express my astonishment at the extraordinary and mysterious influence which he exercised over the administration. I, however, subsequently gave Mr. Monroe an opportunity of doing that justice, which I flattered myself he was disposed to do, by requesting that I might be restored to an appointment of equal rank, but no notice was taken of my application. I had no objections to make. The conferring of appointments is a power correctly vested in the Executive. If he thinks proper to exercise that right in accordance with his own feelings, in advancement with his own views, in support of his own attachments or prejudices, it may be lamented for the sake of the public service, but cannot be prevented. The check in the Senate is all that the Constitution provides. Still it is expected that the Executive, chosen for a transitory period by the people, will in all cases consult what is most acceptable to the people and creditable to the country. It is not necessary for me to say that Mr. Monroe is emphatically an honest man. I measure men by the aggregate of their virtues and vices. All are liable to error. Many pertinaciously adhere to their measures, though they may be manifestly erroneous; and such is the imperfection of our natures, that when a wrong is done intentionally or accidentally, a second wrong is frequently added in confirmation of the first, if complaint is made or clamor heard. Still, with these errors, the balance is greatly in favor of the President for past services, sincere attachment to the country, and strict integrity. He has his weak points like other men. When these do not affect the public service or go to establish dangerous doctrines, they are not necessarily objects of inquiry, but, recurring to the first principles of our government, there is nothing which will tend more securely to preserve our liberties than freedom of speech and the press, a scrutiny into public measures, and a firm but respectful tone to men in power. Mr. Monroe regretted the steps which he had pursued towards me. There was an idea floating on his mind that I had not been well treated, but he regretted it only as it affected him. He had no consideration for my feelings, for my rights or character; he would have been pleased to have arranged the affair in a manner mutually agreeable, had I but presented myself with that submissive tone, with that "bondsmen key and bated breath" that he probably expected. He said I threatened to appeal to Congress; he should have been proud to have seen a citizen thus anxious to support his rights and character, and he should have aided, not opposed, me; not bent the power of government to crush an individual.

I have said this much in proof to political opponents: that I am under no obligation to Mr. Monroe, that my support of the administration is grounded on principle, on nobler motives than personal favor; and as long as he is in the administration, and his measures are calculated to promote the honor and prosperity of our country, so long will I support him. I have no favors to ask, or prejudices to indulge. I have considered it my duty not to labor under suspicions or insinuations, and have thus endeavored to explain them.

> "The evil which men do lives after them,
> The good is oft interred with their bones."

THE LIE

by MARY ANTIN

I

THE first thing about his American teachers that struck David Rudinsky was the fact that they were women, and the second was that they did not get angry if somebody asked questions. This phenomenon subverted his previous experience. When he went to heder (Hebrew school), in Russia, his teachers were always men, and they did not like to be interrupted with questions that were not in the lesson. Everything was different in America, and David liked the difference.

The American teachers, on their part, also made comparisons. They said David was not like other children. It was not merely that his mind worked like lightning; those neglected Russian waifs were almost always quick to learn, perhaps because they had to make up for lost time. The quality of his interest, more than the rapidity of his progress, excited comment. Miss Ralston, David's teacher in the sixth grade, which he reached in his second year at school, said of him that he never let go of a lesson till he had got the soul of the matter. 'I don't think grammar is grammar to him,' she said, 'or fractions mere arithmetic. I'm not satisfied with the way I teach these things since I've had David. I feel that if he were on the platform instead of me, geography and grammar would be spliced to the core of the universe.'

One difficulty David's teachers encountered, and that was his extreme reserve. In private conversation it was hard to get anything out of him except 'Yes, ma'am' and 'No, ma'am,' or 'I don't understand, please.' In the classroom he did not seem to be aware of the existence of anybody besides Teacher and himself. He asked questions as fast as he could formulate them, and Teacher had to exercise much tact in order to satisfy him without slighting the rest of her pupils. To advances of a personal sort he did not respond, as if friendship were not among the things he hungered for.

It was Miss Ralston who found the way to David's heart. Perhaps she was interested in such things; they sometimes are, in the public schools. After the Christmas holidays, the children were given as a subject for composition, 'How I Spent the Vacation.' David wrote in a froth of enthusiasm about whole days spent in the public library. He covered twelve pages with an account of the books he had read. The list included many juvenile classics in American history and biography; and from his comments it was plain that the little alien worshiped the heroes of war.

When Miss Ralston had read David's composition, she knew what to do. She was one of those persons who always know what to do, and did it. She asked David to stay after school, and read to him, from a blue book with gilt lettering, 'Paul Revere's Ride' and 'Independence Bell.' That hour neither of them ever forgot. To David it seemed as if all the heroes he had dreamed of crowded around him, so real did his teacher's reading make them. He heard the clash of swords and the flapping of banners in the wind. On the blackboard behind Miss Ralston troops of faces appeared and vanished, like the shadows that run across a hillside when clouds are moving in the sky. As for Miss Ralston, she said afterwards that she was the first person who had ever seen the real David Rudinsky. That was a curious statement to make, considering that his mother and father, and sundry other persons in the two hemispheres had had some acquaintance with David previous to the reading of 'Paul Revere's Ride.' However, Miss Ralston had a way of saying curious things.

There were many readings out of school hours after that memorable beginning. Miss Ralston did not seem to realize that the School Board did not pay her for those extra hours that she spent on David. David did not know that she was paid at all. He thought Teacher was born on purpose to read and tell him things and answer his questions, just as his mother existed to cook his favorite soup and patch his trousers. So he brought his pet book from the library, and when the last pupil was gone, he took it from his desk and laid it on Miss Ralston's, without a word; and Miss Ralston read, and they were both happy. When a little Jewish boy from Russia goes to school in America, all sorts of things are likely to happen that the School Board does not provide for. It might be amusing to figure out the reasons.

David's reserve slowly melted in the glowing intimacy of these happy half-hours; still, he seldom made any comment on the reading at the time; he basked mutely in the warmth of his teacher's sympathy. But what he did not say orally he was very likely to say on paper. That also was one of Miss Ralston's discoveries. When she gave out the theme, 'What I Mean to Do When I Grow Up,' David wrote that he was going to be an American citizen, and always vote for honest candidates, and belong to a society for arresting illegal voters. You see David was only a greenhorn, and an excitable one. He thought it a very great matter to be a citizen, perhaps because such a thing was not allowed in the country he came from. Miss Ralston probably knew how it was with him, or she guessed. She was great at guessing, as all her children knew. At any rate, she did not smile as she read of David's patriotic ambitions. She put his paper aside until their next quiet hour, and then she used it so as to get a great deal out of him that he would not have had the courage to tell if he had not believed that it was an exercise in composition.

This Miss Ralston was a crafty person. She learned from David about a Jewish restaurant where his father sometimes took him; a place where a group of ardent young Russians discussed politics over their inexpensive dinner. She heard about a mass meeting of Russian Jews to celebrate the death of Alexander III, 'because he was a cruel tyrant, and was very bad to Jewish people.' She even tracked some astonishing phrases in David's vocabulary to their origin in the Sunday orations he had heard on the Common, in his father's company.

Impressed by these and other signs of paternal interest in her pupil's education, Miss Ralston was not unprepared for the visit which David's father paid her soon after these revelations. It was a very cold day, and Mr. Rudinsky shivered in his thin, shabby overcoat; but his face glowed with inner warmth as he discovered David's undersized figure in one of the front seats.

'I don't know how to say it what I feel to see my boy sitting and learning like this,' he said, with a vibration in his voice that told more than his words. 'Do you know, ma'am, if I didn't have to make a living, I'd like to stay here all day and see my David get educated. I'm forty years old, and I've had much in my life, but it's worth nothing so much as this. The day I brought my children to school, it was the best day in my life. Perhaps you won't believe me, ma'am, but when I hear that David is a good boy and learns good in school, I wouldn't change places with Vanderbilt the millionaire.'

He looked at Miss Ralston with the eyes of David listening to 'Paul Revere's Ride.'

'What do you think, ma'am,' he asked, as he got up to leave, 'my David will be a good American, no?'

'He ought to be,' said Miss Ralston warmly, 'with such a father.'

Mr. Rudinsky did not try to hide his gratification.

'I am a citizen,' he said, unconsciously straightening. 'I took out citizen papers as soon as I came to America, four years ago.'

So they came to the middle of February, when preparations for Washington's Birthday were well along. One day the class was singing 'America,' when Miss Ralston noticed that David stopped and stared absently at the blackboard in front of him. He did not wake out of his reverie till the singing was over, and then he raised his hand.

'Teacher,' he asked, when he had permission to speak, 'what does it mean, "Land where my fathers died"?'

Miss Ralston explained, wondering how many of her pupils cared to analyze the familiar words as David did.

A few days later, the national hymn was sung again. Miss Ralston watched David. His lips formed the words 'Land where my fathers died,' and then they stopped, set in the pout of childish trouble. His eyes fixed themselves on the teacher's, but her smile of encouragement failed to dispel his evident perplexity.

Anxious to help him over his unaccountable difficulty, Miss Ralston detained him after school.

'David,' she asked him, when they were alone, 'do you understand "America" now?'

'Yes, ma'am.'

'Do you understand "Land where my fathers died"?'

'Yes, ma'am.'

'You didn't sing with the others.'

'No, ma'am.'

Miss Ralston thought of a question that would rouse him.

'Don't you like "America," David?'

The boy almost jumped in his place.

'Oh, yes, ma'am, I do! I like "America." It's—fine.'

He pressed his fist nervously to his mouth, a trick he had when excited.

'Tell me, David, why you don't sing it.'

David's eyes fixed themselves in a look of hopeless longing. He answered in a whisper, his pale face slowly reddening.

'My fathers didn't die here. How can I sing such a lie?'

Miss Ralston's impulse was to hug the child, but she was afraid of startling him. The attention she had lavished on the boy was rewarded at this moment, when her understanding of his nature inspired the answer to his troubled question. She saw how his mind worked. She realized, what a less sympathetic witness might have failed to realize, that behind the moral scruple expressed in his words, there was a sense of irreparable loss derived from the knowledge that he had no share in the national past. The other children could shout the American hymn in all the pride of proprietorship, but to him the words did not apply. It was a flaw in his citizenship, which he was so jealous to establish.

The teacher's words were the very essence of tact and sympathy. In her voice were mingled the yearning of a mother and the faith of a comrade.

'David Rudinsky, you have as much a right to those words as I or anybody else in America. Your ancestors did not die on our battlefields, but they would have if they'd had a chance. You used to spend all your time reading the Hebrew books, in Russia. Don't you know how your people—your ancestors, perhaps!—fought the Roman tyrants? Don't you remember the Maccabean brothers, and Bar Kochba, and—oh, you know about them more than I! I'm ashamed to tell you that I haven't read much Jewish history, but I'm sure if we begin to look it up, we'll find that people of your race—people like your father, David—took part in the fight for freedom, wherever they were allowed. And even in this country—David, I'm going to find out for you how many Jews there were in the armies of the Revolution. We don't think about it here, you see, because we don't ask what a man's religion is, as long as he is brave and good.'

David's eyes slowly lost their look of distress as his teacher talked. His tense little face, upturned to hers, reminded her of a withered blossom that revives in the rain. She went on with increasing earnestness, herself interested in the discoveries she was making, in her need.

'I tell you the truth, David, I never thought of these things before, but I do believe that the Pilgrim Fathers didn't all come here before the Revolution. Isn't your father just like them? Think of it, dear, how he left his home, and came to a strange land, where he couldn't even speak the language. That was a great trouble, you know; something like the fear of the Indians in the old days. And wasn't he looking for the very same things? He wanted freedom for himself and his family, and a chance for his children to grow up wise and brave. You know your father cares more for such things than he does for money or anything. It's the same story over again. Every ship that brings your people from Russia and other countries where they are ill treated is a *May-flower*. If I were a Jewish child like you, I would sing "America" louder than anybody else!'

David's adoring eyes gave her the thanks which his tongue would not venture to utter. Never since that moment, soon after his arrival from Russia, when his father showed him his citizenship papers, saying, 'Look, my son, this makes you an American,' had he felt so secure in his place in the world.

Miss Ralston studied his face in silence while she gathered up some papers on her desk, preparatory to leaving. In the back of her mind she asked herself to how many of the native children in her class the Fourth of July meant anything besides fire-crackers.

'Get your things, David,' she said presently, as she locked her desk. 'It's time we were going. Think if we should get locked up in the building!'

David smiled absently. In his ears ran the familiar line, 'Land where my fathers died—my fathers died—fathers died.'

'It's something like the Psalms!' he said suddenly, himself surprised at the discovery.

'What is like the Psalms, dear?"

He hesitated. Now that he had to explain, he was not sure any more. Miss Ralston helped him out.

'You mean "America," sounds like the Psalms to you?'

David nodded. His teacher beamed her understanding. How did she guess wherein the similarity lay? David had in mind such moments as this when he said of Miss Ralston, 'Teacher talks with her eyes.'

Miss Ralston went to get her coat and hat from the closet.

'Get your things, David,' she repeated. 'The janitor will come to chase us out in a minute.'

He was struggling with the torn lining of a coat-sleeve in the children's dressing-room, when he heard Miss Ralston exclaim:

'Oh, David! I had almost forgotten. You must try this on. This is what you're going to wear when you speak the dialogue with Annie and Raymond. We used it in a play a few years ago. I thought it would do for you.'

She held up a blue-and-buff jacket with tarnished epaulets. David hurried to put it on. He was to take the part of George Washington in the dialogue. At sight of the costume, his heart started off on a gallop.

Alas for his gallant aspirations! Nothing of David was visible outside the jacket except two big eyes above and two blunt boot-toes below. The collar reached to his ears; the cuffs dangled below his knees. He resembled a scarecrow in the cornfield more than the Father of his Country.

Miss Ralston suppressed her desire to laugh.

'It's a little big, isn't it?' she said cheerily, holding up the shoulders of the heroic garment. 'I wonder how we can make it fit. Don't you think your mother would know how to take up the sleeves and do something to the back?'

She turned the boy around, more hopeless than she would let him see. Miss Ralston understood more about little boys' hearts than about their coats.

'How old are you, David?' she asked absently, wondering for the hundredth time at his diminutive stature. 'I thought the boy for whom this was made was about your age.'

David's face showed that he felt reproved. 'I'm twelve,' he said apologetically.

Miss Ralston reproached herself for her tactlessness, and proceeded to make amends.

'Twelve?' she repeated, patting the blue shoulders. 'You speak the lines like a much older boy. I'm sure your mother can make the coat fit, and I'll bring the wig—a powdered wig—and the sword, David! You'll look just like George Washington!'

Her gay voice echoed in the empty room. Her friendly eyes challenged his. She expected to see him kindle, as he did so readily in these days of patriotic excitement. But David failed to respond. He remained motionless in his place, his eyes blank and staring. Miss Ralston had the feeling that behind his dead front his soul was running away from her.

This is just what was happening. David was running away from her, and from himself, and from the image of George Washington, conjured up by the scene with the military coat. Somewhere in the jungle of his consciousness a monster was stirring, and his soul fled in terror of its clutch. What was it—

what was it that came tearing through the wilderness of his memories of two worlds? In vain he tried not to understand. The ghosts of forgotten impressions cackled in the wake of the pursuing monster, the breath of whose nostrils spread an odor of evil sophistries grafted on his boyish thoughts in a chimerical past.

His mind reeled in a whirlwind of recollection. Miss Ralston could not have understood some of the things David reviewed, even if he had tried to tell her. In that other life of his, in Russia, had been monstrous things, things that seemed unbelievable to David himself, after his short experience of America. He had suffered many wrongs,—yes, even as a little boy,—but he was not thinking of past grievances as he stood before Miss Ralston, seeing her as one sees a light through a fog. He was thinking of things harder to forget than injuries received from others. It was a sudden sense of his own sins that frightened David, and of one sin in particular, the origin of which was buried somewhere in the slime of the evil past. David was caught in the meshes of a complex inheritance; contradictory impulses tore at his heart. Fearfully he dived to the bottom of his consciousness, and brought up a bitter conviction: David Rudinsky, who called himself an American, who worshiped the names of the heroes, suddenly knew that he had sinned, sinned against his best friend, sinned even as he was planning to impersonate George Washington, the pattern of honor.

His white forehead glistened with the sweat of anguish. His eyes sickened. Miss Ralston caught him as he wavered and put him in the nearest seat.

'Why, David! what's the matter? Are you ill? Let me take this off—it's so heavy. There, that's better. Just rest your head on me, so.'

This roused him. He wriggled away from her support, and put out a hand to keep her off.

'Why, David! what is the matter? Your hands are so cold—'

David's head felt heavy and wobbly, but he stood up and began to put on his coat again, which he had pulled off in order to try on the uniform. To Miss Ralston's anxious questions he answered not a syllable, neither did he look at her once. His teacher, thoroughly alarmed, hurriedly put on her street things, intending to take him home. They walked in silence through the empty corridors, down the stairs, and across the school yard. The teacher noticed with relief that the boy grew steadier with every step. She smiled at him encouragingly when he opened the gate for her, as she had taught him, but he did not meet her look.

At the corner where they usually parted David paused, steeling himself to take his teacher's hand; but to his surprise she kept right on, taking his crossing.

It was now that he spoke, and Miss Ralston was astonished at the alarm in his voice.

'Miss Ralston, where are you going? You don't go this way.'

'I'm going to see you home, David,' she replied firmly. 'I can't let you go alone—like this.'

'Oh, teacher, don't, please don't! I'm all right—I'm not sick,—it's not far—Don't, Miss Ralston, please!'

In the February dusk, Miss Ralston saw the tears rise to his eyes. Whatever was wrong with him, it was plain that her presence only made him suffer the more. Accordingly she yielded to his entreaty.

'I hope you'll be all right, David,' she said, in a tone she might have used to a full-grown man. 'Good-bye.' And she turned the corner.

II

All the way home Miss Ralston debated the wisdom of allowing him to go alone, but as she recalled his look and his entreating voice, she felt anew the compulsion that had made her yield. She attributed his sudden breakdown entirely to overwrought nerves, and remorsefully resolved not to subject him in the future to the strain of extra hours after school.

Her misgivings were revived the next morning, when David failed to appear with the ringing of the first gong, as was his habit. But before the children had taken their seats, David's younger brother, Bennie, brought her news of the missing boy.

'David's sick in bed,' he announced in accents of extreme importance. 'He didn't come home till awful late last night, and he was so frozen, his teeth knocked together. My mother says he burned like fire all night, and she had to take little Harry in her bed, with her and papa, so's David could sleep all alone. We all went downstairs in our bare feet this morning, and dressed ourselves in the kitchen, so David could sleep.'

'What is the matter with him? Did you have the doctor?'

'No, ma'am, not yet. The dispensary don't open till nine o'clock.'

Miss Ralston begged him to report again in the afternoon, which he did, standing before her, cap in hand, his sense of importance still dominating over brotherly concern.

'He's sick, all right,' Bennie reported. 'He don't eat at all—just drinks and drinks. My mother says he cried the whole morning, when he woke up and found out he'd missed school. My mother says he tried to get up and dress himself, but he couldn't anyhow. Too sick.'

'Did you have the doctor?' interrupted Miss Ralston, suppressing her impatience.

'No, ma'am, not yet. My father went to the dispensary but the doctor said he can't come till noon, but he didn't. Then I went to the dispensary, dinner time, but the doctor didn't yet come when we went back to school. My mother says you can die ten times before the dispensary doctor comes.'

'What does your mother think it is?'

'Oh, she says it's a bad cold; but David isn't strong, you know, so she's scared. I guess if he gets worse I'll have to stay home from school to run for the medicines.'

'I hope not, Bennie. Now you'd better run along, or you'll be late.'

'Yes, ma'am. Good-bye.'

'Will you come again in the morning and tell me about your brother?'

'Yes, ma'am. Good-bye.—Teacher.'

'Yes, Bennie?'

'Do you think you can do something—something—about his record? David feels dreadful because he's broke his record. He never missed school before, you know. It's—it's too bad to see him cry. He's always so quiet, you know, kind of like grown people. He don't fight or tease or anything. Do you think you can, teacher?'

Miss Ralston was touched by this tribute to her pupil, but she could not promise to mend the broken record.

'Tell David not to worry. He has the best record in the school for attendance and everything. Tell him I said he must hurry and get well, as we must rehearse our pieces for Washington's Birthday.'

The next morning Bennie reeled off a longer story than ever. He described the doctor's visit in great detail, and Miss Ralston was relieved to gather that David's ailment was nothing worse than grippe; unless, as the doctor warned, his run-down condition caused complications. He would be in bed a week or more, in any case, 'and he ought to sleep most of the time, the doctor said.'

'I guess the doctor don't know our David!' Bennie scoffed. 'He never wants at all to go to sleep. He reads and reads when everybody goes to bed. One time he was reading all night, and the lamp went out, and he was afraid to go downstairs for oil, because he'd wake somebody, so he lighted matches and read little bits. There was a heap of burned matches in the morning.'

'Dear me!' exclaimed Miss Ralston. 'He ought not to do that. Your father ought not—Does your father allow him to stay up nights?'

'Sure. My father's proud because he's going to be a great man; a doctor, maybe.' He shrugged his shoulders, as if to say, 'What may not a David become?'

'David is funny, don't you think, teacher?' the boy went on. 'He asks such funny questions. What do you think he said to the doctor?'

'I can't imagine.'

'Well, he pulled him by the sleeve when he took out the—the thing he puts in your mouth, and said kind of hoarse, "Doctor, did you ever tell a lie?" Wasn't that funny?'

Miss Ralston did not answer. She was thinking that David must have been turning over some problem in his mind, to say so much to a stranger.

'Did you give him my message?' she asked finally.

'Yes'm! I told him about rehearsing his piece for Washington's Birthday.'
Bennie paused.

'Well?'

'He acted so funny. He turned over to the wall, and cried and cried without any noise.'

'The poor boy! He'll be dreadfully disappointed not to take part in the exercises.'

Bennie shook his head.

'That isn't for what he cries,' he said oracularly.

Miss Ralston's attentive silence invited further revelations.

'He's worrying about something,' Bennie brought out, rolling his head ominously.

'Why? How do you know?'

'The doctor said so. He told my father downstairs. He said, "Make him tell, if you can, it may help to pull him off"—no, "pull him up." That's what the doctor said.'

Miss Ralston's thoughts flew back to her last interview with David, two days before, when he had broken down so suddenly. Was there a mystery there? She was certain the boy was overwrought, and physically run down. Apparently, also, he had been exposed to the weather during the evening when he was taken ill; Bennie's chatter indicated that David had wandered in the streets for hours. These things would account for the grippe, and for the abnormal fever of which Bennie boasted. But what was David worrying about? She resolved to go and see the boy in a day or two, when he was reported to be more comfortable.

On his next visit Bennie brought a message from the patient himself.

'He said to give you this, teacher,' handing Miss Ralston a journal. 'It's yours. It has pieces in it for Washington's Birthday. He said you might need it, and the doctor didn't say when he could go again to school.'

Miss Ralston laid the journal carelessly on a pile of other papers. Bennie balanced himself on one foot, looking as if his mission were not yet ended.

'Well, Bennie?' Miss Ralston encouraged him. She was beginning to understand his mysterious airs.

'David was awful careful about that book,' the messenger said impressively. 'He said over and over not to lose it, and not to give it to nobody only you.'

III

It was not till the end of the day that Miss Ralston took up the journal Bennie had brought. She turned the leaves absently thinking of David. He would be so disappointed to miss the exercises! And to whom should she give the part of George Washington in the dialogue? She found the piece in the journal. A scrap of paper marked the place. A folded paper. Folded several times. Miss Ralston opened out the paper and found some writing.

Dear Teacher Miss Ralston,—

'I can't be George Washington any more because I have lied to you. I must not tell you about what, because you would blame somebody who didn't do wrong.

'Your friend,

'David Rudinsky.'

Again and again Miss Ralston read the note, unable to understand it. David, her David, whose soul was a mirror for every noble idea, had lied to her! What could he mean? What had impelled him? *Somebody who didn't do wrong.* So it was not David alone; there was some complication with another person. She studied the note word for word, and her eyes slowly filled with tears. If the boy had really lied—if the whole thing were not a chimera of his fevered nights—then what must he have suffered of remorse and shame! Her heart went out to him even while her brain was busy with the mystery.

She made a swift resolution. She would go to David at once. She was sure he would tell her more than he had written, and it would relieve his mind. She did not dread the possible disclosures. Her knowledge of the boy made her certain that she would find nothing ignoble at the bottom of his mystery. He was only a child, after all—an overwrought, sensitive child. No doubt he exaggerated his sin, if sin there were. It was her duty to go and put him at rest.

She knew David's father kept a candy shop in the basement of his tenement, and she had no trouble in finding the place. Half the children in the neighborhood escorted her to the door, attracted by the phenomenon of a teacher loose on their streets.

The tinkle of the shop-bell brought Mr. Rudinsky from the little kitchen in the rear.

'Well, well!' he exclaimed, shaking hands heartily. 'This is a great honor —a great honor.' He sounded the initial h. 'I wish I had a palace for you to come in, ma'am. I don't think there was such company in this house since it was built.'

His tone was one of genuine gratification. Ushering her into the kitchen, he set a chair for her, and himself sat down at a respectful distance.

'I'm sorry,' he began, with a wave of his hand around the room. 'Such company ought not to sit in the kitchen, but you see—'

He was interrupted by Bennie, who had clattered in at the visitor's heels, panting for recognition.

'Never mind, teacher,' the youngster spoke up, 'we got a parlor upstairs, with a mantelpiece and everything, but David sleeps up there—the doctor said it's the most air—and you dassn't wake him up till he wakes himself.'

Bennie's father frowned, but the visitor smiled a cordial smile.

'I like a friendly kitchen like this,' she said quietly. 'My mother did not keep any help when I was a little girl and I was a great deal in the kitchen.'

Her host showed his appreciation of her tact by dropping the subject.

'I'm sure you came about David,' he said.

'I did. How is he?'

'Pretty sick, ma'am. The doctor says it's not the sickness so much, but David is so weak and small. He says David studies too much altogether. Maybe he's right. What do you think, ma'am?'

Miss Ralston answered remorsefully.

'I agree with the doctor. I think we are all to blame. We push him too much when we ought to hold him back.'

Here Bennie made another raid on the conversation.

'He's going to be a great man, a doctor maybe. My mother says—'

Mr. Rudinsky did not let him finish. He thought it time to insure the peace of so important an interview.

'Bennie,' said he, 'you will go mind the store, and keep the kitchen door shut.'

Bennie's discomfiture was evident in his face. He obeyed, but not without a murmur.

'Let us make a covenant to take better care of David in the future.'

Miss Ralston was speaking when Mrs. Rudinsky appeared in the doorway. She was flushed from the exertions of a hasty toilet, for which she had fled upstairs at the approach of 'company.' She came forward timidly, holding out a hand on which the scrubbing brush and the paring knife had left their respective marks.

'How do you do, ma'am?' she said cordially but shyly. 'I'm glad to see you. I wish I can speak English better, I'd like to say how proud I am to see David's teacher in my house.'

'Why, you speak wonderfully!' Miss Ralston exclaimed, with genuine enthusiasm. 'I don't understand how you pick up the language in such a short time. I couldn't learn Russian so fast, I'm sure.'

'My husband makes us speak English all the time,' Mrs. Rudinsky replied. 'From the fust day he said to speak English. He scholds the children if he hears they speak Jewish.'

'Sure,' put in her husband. 'I don't want my family to be greenhorns.'

Miss Ralston turned a glowing face to him.

'Mr. Rudinsky, I think you've done wonders for your family. If all immigrants were like you, we wouldn't need any restriction laws.' She threw all possible emphasis into her cordial voice. 'Why, you're a better American than some natives I know!'

Mrs. Rudinsky sent her husband a look of loving pride.

'He wants to be a Yankee,' she said.

Her husband took up the cue in earnest.

'Yes, ma'am,' he said, 'that's my ambition. When I was a young man, in the old country, I wanted to be a scholar. But a Jew has no chance in the old country; perhaps you know how it is. It wasn't the Hebrew books I wanted. I wanted to learn what the rest of the world learned, but a poor Jew had no chance in Russia. When I got to America, it was too late for me to go to school. It took me all my time and strength to make a living—I've never been much good in business, ma'am—and when I got my family over, I saw that it was the children would go to school for me. I'm glad to be a plain citizen, if my children will be educated Americans.'

People with eyes and hands like Mr. Rudinsky's can say a great deal in a few words. Miss Ralston felt as if she had known him all his life, and followed his strivings in two worlds.

'I'm glad to know you, Mr. Rudinsky,' she said in a low voice. 'I wish more of my pupils had fathers like David's.'

Her host changed the subject very neatly.

'And I wish the school children had more teachers like you. David likes you so much.'

'Oh, he liked you!' the wife confirmed. 'Please stay till he veks up. He'll be sorry to missed your visit.'

While his wife moved quietly around the stove, making tea, Mr. Rudinsky entertained their guest with anecdotes of David's Hebrew school days, and of his vain efforts to get at secular books.

'He was just like me,' he said. 'He wanted to learn everything. I couldn't afford a private teacher, and they wouldn't take him in the public school. He learned Russian all alone, and if he got a book from somewhere—a history or anything—he wouldn't eat or drink till he read it all.'

Mrs. Rudinsky often glanced at David's teacher, to see how her husband's stories were impressing her. She was too shy with her English to say more than was required of her as hostess, but her face, aglow with motherly pride, showed how she participated in her husband's enthusiasm.

'You see yourself, ma'am, what he is,' said David's father, 'but what could I make of him in Russia? I was happy when he got here, only it was a little late. I wished he started in school younger.'

'He has time enough.' said Miss Ralston. 'He'll get through grammar school before he's fourteen. He's twelve now, isn't he?'

'Yes, ma'am—no, ma'am! He's really fourteen now, but I made him out younger on purpose.'

Miss Ralston looked puzzled. Mr. Rudinsky explained.

'You see, ma'am, he was twelve years when he came, and I wanted he should go to school as long as possible, so when I made his school certificate, I said he was only ten. I have seven children, and David is the oldest one, and I was afraid he'd have to go to work, if business was bad, or if I was sick. The state is a good father to the children in America, if the real fathers don't mix in. Why should my David lose his chance to get educated and be somebody, because I am a poor business man, and have too many children? So I made out that he had to go to school two years more.'

He narrated this anecdote in the same simple manner in which he had told a dozen others. He seemed pleased to rehearse the little plot whereby he had insured his boy's education. As Miss Ralston did not make any comment immediately, he went on, as if sure of her sympathy.

'I told you I got my citizen papers right away when I came to America. I worked hard before I could bring my family—it took me four years to save the money—and they found a very poor home when they got here, but they were citizens right away. But it wouldn't do them much good, if they didn't get educated. I found out all about the compulsory education, and I said to myself that's the policeman that will keep me from robbing my David if I fail in business.'

He did not overestimate his visitor's sympathy. Miss Ralston followed his story with quick appreciation of his ideals and motives, but in her ingenuous American mind one fact separated itself from the others: namely, that Mr. Rudinsky had falsified his boy's age, and had recorded the falsehood in a public document. Her recognition of the fact carried with it no criticism. She realized that Mr. Rudinsky's conscience was the product of an environment vastly different from hers. It was merely that to her mind the element of deceit was something to be accounted for, be it ever so charitably, whereas in Mr. Rudinsky's mind it evidently had no existence at all.

'So David is really fourteen years old?' she repeated incredulously. 'Why, he seems too little even for twelve! Does he know?—Of course he would know! I wonder that he consented—'

She broke off, struck by a sudden thought. 'Consented to tell a lie,' she had meant to say, but the unspoken words diverted her mind from the conversation. It came upon her in a flash that she had found the key to David's mystery. His note was in her pocketbook, but she knew every word of it, and now everything was plain to her. The lie was this lie about his age, and the person he wanted to shield was his father. And for that he was suffering so!

She began to ask questions eagerly.

'Has David said anything about—about a little trouble he had in school the day he became ill?'

Both parents showed concern.

'Trouble? what trouble?'

'Oh, it was hardly trouble—at least, I couldn't tell myself.'

'David is so hard to understand sometimes,' his father said.

'Oh, I don't think so!' the teacher cried. 'Not when you make friends with him. He doesn't say much, it's true, but his heart is like a crystal.'

'He's too still,' the mother insisted, shaking her head. 'All the time he's sick, he don't say anything, only when we ask him something. The doctor thinks he's worrying about something, but he don't tell.'

The mother sighed, but Miss Ralston cut short her reflections.

'Mrs. Rudinsky—Mr. Rudinsky,' she began eagerly, 'I can tell you what David's troubled about.'

And she told them the story of her last talk with David, and finally read them his note.

'And this lie,' she ended, 'you know what it is, don't you? You've just told me yourself, Mr. Rudinsky.'

She looked pleadingly at him, longing to have him understand David's mind as she understood it. But Mr. Rudinsky was very slow to grasp the point.

'You mean—about the certificate? Because I made out that he was younger?'

Miss Ralston nodded.

'You know David has such a sense of honor,' she explained, speaking slowly, embarrassed by the effort of following Mr. Rudinsky's train of thought and her own at the same time. 'You know how he questions everything— sooner or later he makes everything clear to himself—and something must have started him thinking of this old matter lately—Why, of course! I remember I asked him his age that day, when he tried on the costume, and he answered as usual, and then, I suppose, he suddenly realized what he was saying. I don't believe he ever thought about it since—since you arranged it so, and now, all of a sudden—'

She did not finish, because she saw that her listeners did not follow her. Both their faces expressed pain and perplexity. After a long silence, David's father spoke.

'And what do you think, ma'am?'

Miss Ralston was touched by the undertone of submission in his voice. Her swift sympathy had taken her far into his thoughts. She recognized in his story one of those ethical paradoxes which the helpless Jews of the Pale, in their search for a weapon that their oppressors could not confiscate, have evolved for their self-defense. She knew that to many honest Jewish minds a lie was not a lie when told to an official; and she divined that no ghost of a scruple had disturbed Mr. Rudinsky in his sense of triumph over circumstances, when he invented the lie that was to insure the education of his gifted child. With David, of course, the same philosophy had been valid. His father's plan for the protection of his future, hinging on a too familiar sophistry, had dropped innocuous into his consciousness, until, in a moment of spiritual sensitiveness, it took on the visage of sin.

'And what do you think, ma'am?'

David's father did not have to wait a moment for her answer, so readily did her insight come to his defence. In a few eager sentences she made him feel that she understood perfectly, and understood David perfectly.

'I respect you the more for that lie, Mr. Rudinsky. It was—a noble lie!'

There was the least tremor in her voice. 'And I love David for the way he sees it.'

Mr. Rudinsky got up and paced slowly across the room. Then he stopped before Miss Ralston.

'You are very kind to talk like that, Miss Ralston,' he said, with peculiar dignity. 'You see the whole thing. In the old country we had to do such things so many times that we—got used to them. Here—here we don't have to.' His voice took on a musing quality. 'But we don't see it right away when we get here. I meant nothing, only just to keep my boy in school. It was not to cheat anybody. The state is willing to educate the children. I said to myself "I will tie my own hands, so that I can't pull my child after me if I drown." I did want my David should have the best chance in America.'

Miss Ralston was thrilled by the suppressed passion in his voice. She held out her hand to him, saying again, in the low tones that come from the heart, 'I am glad I know you, Mr. Rudinsky.'

There was unconscious chivalry in Mr. Rudinsky's next words. Stepping to his wife's side, he laid a gentle hand on her shoulder, and said quietly, 'My wife has been my helper in everything.'

Miss Ralston, as we know, was given to seeing things. She saw now, not a poor immigrant couple in the first stage of American respectability, which was all there was in the room to see, but a phantom procession of men with the faces of prophets, muffled in striped praying-shawls, and women radiant in the light of many candles, and youths and maidens with smouldering depths in their eyes, and silent children who pushed away joyous things for—for—

Dreams don't use up much time. Mr. Rudinsky was not aware that there had been a pause before he spoke again.

'You understand so well, Miss Ralston. But David—' he hesitated a moment, then finished quickly—'how can he respect me if he feels like that?'

His wife spoke tremulously from her corner.

'That's what I think.'

'Oh, don't think that!' Miss Ralston cried. 'He does respect you—he understands. Don't you see what he says: *I can't tell you—because you would blame somebody who didn't do wrong*. He doesn't blame you. He only blames himself. He's afraid to tell me because he thinks I can't understand.'

The teacher laughed a happy little laugh. In her eagerness to comfort David's parents, she said just the right things, and every word summed up an instantaneous discovery. One of her useful gifts was the ability to find out truths just when she desperately needed them. There are people like that, and some of them are school-teachers hired by the year. When David's father cried, 'How can he respect me?' Miss Ralston's heart was frightened while it beat one beat. Only one. Then she knew all David's thoughts between the terrible, 'I have lied,' and the generous, 'But my father did no wrong.' She guessed what the struggle had cost to reconcile the contradictions; she imagined his bewilderment as he tried to rule himself by his new-found standards, while seeking excuses for his father in the one he cast away from him as unworthy of an American. Problems like David's are not very common, but then Miss Ralston was good at guessing.

'Don't worry, Mr. Rudinsky,' she said, looking out of her glad eyes. 'And you, Mrs. Rudinsky, don't think for a moment that David doesn't understand. He's had a bad time, the poor boy, but I know— Oh, I must speak to him! Will he wake soon, do you think?'

Mr. Rudinsky left the room without a word.

'It's all right,' said David's mother, in reply to an anxious look from Miss Ralston. 'He sleeps already the whole afternoon.'

It had grown almost dark while they talked. Mrs. Rudinsky now lighted the lamps, apologizing to her guest for not having done so sooner, and then she released Bennie from his prolonged attendance in the store.

Bennie came into the kitchen chewing his reward, some very gummy confection. He was obliged to look the pent-up things he wanted to say, until such time as he could clear his clogged talking-gear.

'Teacher,' he began, before he had finished swallowing, 'what for did you say—'

'Bennie!' his mother reproved him. 'You must shame yourself to listen by the door.'

'Well, there wasn't any trade, ma,' he defended himself, 'only Bessie Katz, and she brought back the peppermints she bought this morning, to change them for taffy, but I didn't because they were all dirty, and one was broken—'

Bennie never had a chance to bring his speeches to a voluntary stop: somebody always interrupted. This time it was his father, who came down the stairs, looking so grave that even Bennie was impressed.

'He's awake,' said Mr. Rudinsky. 'I lighted the lamp. Will you please come up, ma'am?'

He showed her to the room where David lay, and closed the door on them both. It was not he, but Miss Ralston, the American teacher, that his boy needed. He went softly down to the kitchen, where his wife smiled at him through unnecessary tears.

Miss Ralston never forgot the next hour, and David never forgot. The woman always remembered how the boy's eyes burned through the dusk of the shadowed corner where he lay. The boy remembered how his teacher's voice palpitated in his heart, how her cool hands rested on his, how the lamp-light made a halo out of her hair. To each of them the dim room with its scant furnishings became a spiritual rendezvous.

What did the woman say, that drew the sting of remorse from the child's heart without robbing him of the bloom of his idealism? What did she tell him that transmuted the offence of ages into the marrow and blood of persecuted virtue? How did she weld in the boy's consciousness the scraps of his mixed inheritance, so that he saw his whole experience as an unbroken thing at last? There was nobody to report how it was done. The woman did not know nor the child. It was a secret born of the boy's need and the woman's longing to serve him; just as in nature every want creates its satisfaction.

When she was ready to leave him, Miss Ralston knelt for a moment at David's bedside, and once more took his small hot hands in hers.

'And I have made a discovery, David,' she said, smiling in a way of her own. 'Talking with your parents downstairs I saw why it was that the Russian Jews are so soon at home here in our dear country. In the hearts of men like your father, dear, is the true America.'

ZORAKH

by JOHN COURNOS

To live in an inferno day after day is to get used to it. To greet morning with a sigh, and night with a curse, is to lapse into a habit, which would be painless but for new, rare and more terrible diversions. To walk in the fetid darkness for ever and ever, without a gleam of light, is to merge with it, become lost in it, steeped in it: a dark fetid thing in the fetid darkness. Habit walks at your side, holding your hand, habit—which is a demon of the fetid, sordid darkness; the darkness that is both of day and night, continuous, everlasting. Men become like insects in the mire, feeding on darkness, and are the food of darkness. Fortunate the rare few for whom the dark way in which they wander is illuminated at intervals by flashes of lightning, even though these illuminations reveal horrors exceeding the darkness itself. Certain things happen—rare and terrible diversions, and it is these that break the routine of your inferno, make your inferno interesting, make you conscious that you are in an inferno. And these things either kill or save."

In such a manner did John Gombarov dwell many years afterward on his childhood days in Philadelphia, on those terrible days and nights, which were like one long darkness, save for those sudden, those bewildering flashes, which came and went; they were the sharp, forked lightnings, and they clove the darkness and revealed for but an instant an inferno terrible to behold, fantastic and unimaginable; then the darkness closed in upon him, and he wandered on in the darkness, shaken by the flash, the memory of the flash haunting him for days and days.

Sitting many years afterward with his friend Douglass in an A.B.C. shop in London, Gombarov poured out a tale of one of those rare and terrible diversions in his life, and strange it seemed to the sun-loving Englishman to hear his friend thrice-bless so sombre a diversion, and only later, as he sat musing in his own room in silence, did it dawn upon him how narrowly Gombarov's life was saved from being merely sordid by tragic illuminations. This is the tale that Gombarov told:

"You will remember," he began, "the boy, living in our house, who first introduced me to selling papers. He lived with his parents on the floor above us. There were three other children in the family younger than the boy. They had come some years before from Russia, driven by the pogroms. At home Zorakh was a first-class men's tailor, who could make a complete garment and took pride in making it well. There, in the small Russian town, he worked slowly and deliberately. So it was quite natural that his efforts to establish himself as an independent tailor in Philadelphia should prove a failure. He soon found out that only speed and quantity counted here, and, giving up his shop, he began to look for work. Everywhere he heard the same story. They did not employ tailors: they employed only cutters and basters and sewers and button-sewers and button-hole makers and pressers; a man who could make a whole garment was not wanted because it was against the idea of speed; a man who could make a whole garment was likely to get too much interested in his work, like an artist. At last, swallowing his pride, he began to look for a job as a cutter, thinking it would be the least obnoxious part in the making of a machine-made garment. But he failed to reckon on the law of demand and supply: there was in fact a plethora of cutters, but there was a shortage of button-hole makers. And so, swallowing his pride a second time, Zorakh became a button-hole maker. All day he sat making button-holes. Efficiency being a passion with him, he took great pains with these button-holes, but as he was paid so much for so many button-holes—the price depending upon the quality of the cloth—he soon found out that unless he hustled he would not be able to supply his own wants, not to speak of the wants of his family. He soon knew the meaning of the word sweat-shop! His only joy was when he had a better-class garment to do and the button-holes required better care in doing.

"Zorakh, being a sensitive, nervous man, began to see button-holes everywhere; they floated before his eyes in black outlines, but at night they looked at him out of the darkness like green luminous malignant eyes, which followed him in spite of every movement of his head to escape them. But sitting all day in the fetid air of the shop, bent over into a half-arch, even a worse fate overtook him: he began to spit blood. A doctor advised open-air employment. And so Zorakh became a huckster of vegetables and fruits. Bravely, day after day, he pushed his laden cart through the streets, and shouted his wares. He had been at this job hardly more than a week when one of those periodical raids on hucksters was made by 'plain-clothes men.' Sometimes the prostitutes were raided and led through the streets half-naked, shivering in the night; sometimes the poor hucksters were rounded up and driven toward a police station, pushing their own carts under a sweltering sun. It was pitiful to see a huge inhuman paw on the collar of each, as if they could escape! and it was pitiful to hear the jeers of the street boys and now and then even of older men. It was both pitiful and grotesque. And only the Jewish men and women stood on the pavements and in the doorways wildly gesticulating, indignantly chattering, crying their 'Woe to Columbus!' How helpless they were! Their discomfiture gave the hoodlums great joy, it was such fun to see the Jews in such a fuss!

"The commotion in the street brought us all to the window. We saw what was happening, and we nearly cried to see poor Zorakh in that moving confusion; he pushed his cart with great effort, urged on by a big, burly six-foot-four Irishman, who held up his free fist at one moment in the air as though he meant to strike, at the same time giving a wink at the passers-by on the sidewalk. I remember that my blood boiled in me. I didn't know why these men were rounded up—perhaps they had no huckster's license—but whatever the reason I felt it was unjust—these men were trying to make an honest living. The sense of justice was even then most curiously developed in me, and it seems to me that in my indignation I could almost have thrown a stone or a rotten egg at Zorakh's tormentor at that moment, regardless of consequences. I remember I looked up at my stepfather. His face was pale, his features drawn, and his fists were clenched. My mother held his arm, as though she feared he would do something rash. She must have thought of that night in Russia, when in his fury he pulled up a young birch sapling from the ground and belaboured with it some unwelcome visitors, who ran from the demonlike man in sheer terror of their lives. He did not speak until the little procession had passed. Then he said: 'One can understand why Moses killed the Egyptian.'

"Zorakh was taken with the others before a magistrate, unable to pay his fine, his cart with its contents was confiscated, and he got seven days besides to make up the measure. Poor Zorakh served his seven days, then went home, and to bed. He was very ill, beyond hope of saving. He lingered on for some weeks, and between the earnings of the boy and the small charities, his family managed to go on living.

"I remember knocking on the door one afternoon, hoping to find the boy in. Serele, a little girl, opened the door to me. She had a frightened look on her face. 'Father is looking so queer, and there is no one at home. I only wish mother would come in.' With a fluttering heart I went into Zorakh's room. He was lying on the bed with his eyes wide open, and his body rose and fell with his heavy breathing. On seeing me he tried to speak, and though his lips moved the words would not come for some time. One of his hands appeared to seek, to grope, for something. I then understood, he wanted a hand. I put my warm hand on his cold one, and that appeared to revive him for a moment. A smile struggled to his eyes, and words to his lips. 'I w-wish—I w-wish you—a happy—' He did not finish his words. Something suddenly seemed to lift him from his bed, shake him violently, and drop him back on his pillow. Seeing him very, very still, and as it were smiling just a little, I became frightened, and ran out of the room, with Serele at my heels. Zorakh was dead.

"Yet it was not Zorakh's death that was the terrible diversion I spoke of in the beginning, but what happened afterward, on the day of his burial.

"Imagine then to yourself the same sordid room; a pine box containing Zorakh, supported on two chairs, is in the middle of the room, the sun penetrates the drawn green blinds and falls in a ghastly green glare on Zorakh's pale face, softened somewhat by the gentle but flickering light of the candles at the four corners. Three old women, their figures bent, their heads wrapped in pale bandanna shawls, their faces unseen, sit at the head of the coffin like three lamenting fates, and they drone and croon in a low monotone a dirge-like primitive litany, which sounds strangely as though from afar, a faint murmuring from dumb inarticulate throats—sorrowful and endless.

"A terrible curiosity drew me to look at Zorakh. The same smile I had seen before still seemed to hover in some indefinable way, appeared to suggest the harbouring of some happy momentary fancy, the passing of some benevolent thought, which had become arrested at the very instant the spirit had left the body.

"The widow, a tall gaunt woman, with a demented look in her eyes under a bulging forehead, sat in the next room and was being comforted by her neighbours. Death had wrought a truce in her relations with the dead—for poverty is no friend of conjugal happiness—and for the while softened the hardness of her second nature, which, as you may know, is nearly always stronger than the first; she recounted again and again his manifold virtues, which would surely be considered at the Seat of Judgment; she told of his brave uncomplaining days in bed; of course, he had left her ill-provided for— what with her three little ones that three hundred dollars of lodge money wouldn't go very far; still he must have expressed a death-bed wish for her welfare, and the good Lord, the Caretaker of widows and orphans, would surely not disregard it; she believed in the death-bed wish as strongly as she did in the existence of an omnipotent God and of the Evil Eye. She wondered, and again she wondered, as to what his wish might have been: if she only knew! if she only knew!

"I happened to sneeze at the moment.

" 'There!' she said, 'it's as true as he's sneezed!'

"A cold sweat suddenly passed over me as I suddenly realized that Zorakh's death-bed wish was for me! And I thought: if she only knew!

"And what was worse, Serele was there, Serele heard it also! Suppose Serele should tell!

"At that moment three or four of Zorakh's friends were standing in the doorway, discussing the sad happening.

" 'He was a good man—a good man!' one of them was saying.

" 'He was not only a good man—he was also a good Jew,' added an old bent man with beard and locks, whom Rembrandt might have painted. He was attired in a black capote and black velvet skullcap, a Jew unmistakably of the old school.

" 'Oh, yes, rabbi, but he worked on Saturdays!' said derisively the youngest of the group, who was a Socialist and did not believe in God.

" 'That's very true, young man, but we are in exile, and God will forgive us much. If it is to sustain our lives, He will forgive us even the eating of pork. As one of our sages tells us, there are only three things He won't forgive: Idol worship, murder, unchastity.'

"That aroused the ire of the Socialist.

" 'Oh, yes!' he cried, 'the really unforgivable sin you do not mention at all. It's capitalism, and includes all three. You talk of idol worship—but you have men here who worship the dollar; you talk of unchastity, yet these men have driven more girls to the street than the Lord can ever hope of saving; you talk of murder—murder—look then at Zorakh—is it not murder? I tell you it's murder—worse than murder—because they kill you so slowly.'

" 'Perhaps it was eating pork that did it!' went on the Socialist pitilessly. 'And what will be Zorakh's reward in the next world? I suspect he will be put to making button-holes on the garments of the dear little angels.'

"Then while the rabbi went to attend to his duties, a third speaker intervened with the ironical suggestion that Pharaoh had his Moses; the capitalist of today his Marx; that Marx indeed was an up-to-date Moses, who ejected the God of Tablets of the Law, and had put in his place the God of Statistics. The argument waged hot and might have gone on indefinitely, had not something happened just then, something terrible and grotesque, something quite unlooked for.

"It was just after the coffin had been nailed down and was being lifted by four men that a tall gaunt woman with dishevelled hair swept past the disputants like a whirlwind, almost knocking them over, and leaping through the door she hurled herself upon the coffin, and made it fall; it rattled violently as it struck the floor.

"It was Zorakh's wife.

"When I saw what happened a great fear possessed me, for I at once understood that my terrible secret was out, that Serele had told her.

"She fell upon the coffin, clutched at it as if it were a living thing, hammered it hard with her bony hand, and cried all the while:

" 'Have me in mind, my husband! Me—and not the boy! Do you hear, husband? Have me in mind! I am your wife and you have children—and it's me you ought to think of.'

"The pine box resounded hollow under the blows of her hands. There was consternation among the mourners. Two men laid their hands on her shoulders and tried to drag her away, but she embraced the coffin in the deathlike grip of both her arms, and sobbed, and cried through her sobs:

"'Your last wish must be for me—me—me—I say me!'

"When at last they stood her upon her feet, she was assailed with questions:

"'What is the matter?'

"'Why make such a scene?'

"She tried to tear herself out of the hands of those who held her. Suddenly she caught sight of Serele, who stood frightened in front of her. She managed to seize the child by the arm.

"'Tell them, Serele, what he said to the boy before he died. He wished him luck, him—a stranger, and me he forgot. D'you hear, people, he wished me nothing!'

"She stood there like an animal at bay. She wanted to throw herself on the coffin again, to beat it with her head, her hands; she wanted to tear her hair, to shriek so that the dead might hear. They had great trouble in leading her away, and she went on shrieking as she was being led away:

"'Have me in mind—me! me! me!'

"The coffin was borne quickly out of the house, placed in an ordinary cart which waited for it, and was hurriedly driven away."

Some minutes passed by before John Gombarov spoke again.

"Well, that shook me up," he said at last. "I could not sleep for nights, thinking of that tragic flash. What was my own darkness, my own pathos and sadness, to that mad woman's sharp tragic pangs on seeing her world slipping from her forever, a world which had hung on so frail and perilous a thread as a death-bed wish, now irrevocable? Although it was not my fault, I felt full of pity and remorse, as if deliberately I had taken from her all the hope she had; gladly, gladly, I would have given her wish back to her—if only I could! And yet, lying there of nights, sleepless, a great comfort came to me from that terrible event. My troubled darkness receded and receded, became a nothingness before the fierce tragic blaze, and at those moments I ceased to think of myself and my troubles. And only later, much later, I began to understand why this was so. The illumination came to me during my first days in London, where, lonely and troubled, I used to take down from my shelf a play by Sophocles or Euripides, and found that it soothed me, rested me, lifted something from me, absorbed my own petty sorrows as light absorbs darkness, as the great sea of sorrows takes to its welling bosom all the sad rivers and streams. And I began to understand why the Greeks dedicated their theatre-temples to sorrow, why their tragic plays were as much a religious ceremony among them as any other religious ceremony. How fortunate was the Athenian in that he had a way of purging himself of his sorrow, in losing his own sorrow in the tragic doom of Medea, Agamemnon and Œdipus Tyrannus!

"And so it was that the stranger's sorrow helped me on my dark way. If it had been merely sordid it would have added to my sordidness, but being so sharply tragic it absorbed all sordidness. I don't mean to say that the thing was as great as a Greek play. But it was, in its own way, a profound and tragic illumination, which at the time seemed to have served a need in my life."

"All I can say," observed Douglass at the end of Gombarov's narrative and philosophic reflection thereupon, "is that you were not born in the right age. The time is out of joint for you. What makes me think so is a play I saw the other day. It was called 'Barnborough Sits Up' or some name like that. Barnborough, you see, is the usual Yorkshire industrial town, and when the curtain goes up, that is when the fourth wall is removed—for that accursed forth wall is responsible for nearly all modern drama—you are dragged in, as it were, to witness the usual family squabble in the usual Barnborough household. There is the usual bawling by the usual factory girl, who lost her virtue to the usual scapegrace son of the usual factory owner on the usual week-end, which began with the usual joy-ride. The week-end, as you may know, is a great institution. If it were abolished the English lawyer and the English dramatist would lose their occupations. To return to the Barnborough household. There is of course a great fuss made about the girl's lost virtue, and it is unanimously decided by her parents and his parents and the real fiancée of the guilty young man that, having robbed the poor girl of her virtue, he ought to take the girl with it. And so he is coerced into making a proposal to her. Well, you would say that never could a girl have been seduced under more auspicious circumstances. But no! The dramatist gets in his great stroke of work here. She will simply have nothing to do with the young man! She has had a jolly good time while it lasted, and that was all there was to be said about the matter. There is a sensible girl for you. Moral of the play: There is no reason for making such a hulabaloo about a factory girl's lost virtue. Well, Gombarov, I wouldn't advise you to see this play if you have a sorrow that you want lifted from your heart."

"It seems to me, Douglass, that the subject ought to make a fine comedy, and the next best thing to a fine tragedy for lifting one's sorrows is a good comedy. The Greeks had Aristophanes as well as Sophocles."

"That may be true," answered Douglass, "but the trouble with this play is that it is neither a tragedy nor a comedy, it is a sordedy."

The two friends laughed, and Douglass called for liqueurs.

A PICNIC

by S. LIEBIN

Ask Shmuel, the capmaker, just for a joke, if he would like to come for a picnic! He'll fly out at you as if you had invited him to a swing on the gallows. The fact is, he and his Sarah once went for a picnic, and the poor man will remember it all his days.

It was on a Sabbath towards the end of August. Shmuel came home from work, and said to his wife:

"Sarah, dear!"

"Well, husband?" was her reply.

"I want to have a treat," said Shmuel, as though alarmed at the boldness of the idea.

"What sort of a treat? Shall you go to the swimming-bath tomorrow?"

"Ett! What's the fun of that?"

"Then, what have you thought of by way of an exception? A glass of ice water for supper?"

"Not that, either."

"A whole siphon?"

Shmuel denied with a shake of the head.

"Whatever can it be!" wondered Sarah. "Are you going to fetch a pint of beer?"

"What should I want with beer?"

"Are you going to sleep on the roof?"

"Wrong again!"

"To buy some more carbolic acid, and drive out the bugs?"

"Not a bad idea," observed Shmuel, "but that is not it, either."

"Well, then, whatever is it, for goodness' sake! The moon?" asked Sarah, beginning to lose patience. "What have you been and thought of? Tell me once for all, and have done with it!"

And Shmuel said:

"Sarah, you know we belong to a lodge."

"Of course I do!" and Sarah gave him a look of mingled astonishment and alarm. "It's not more than a week since you took a whole dollar there, and I'm not likely to have forgotten what it cost you to make it up. What is the matter now? Do they want another?"

"Try again!"

"Out with it!"

"I—want us, Sarah," stammered Shmuel, "to go for a picnic."

"A picnic!" screamed Sarah. "Is that the only thing you have left to wish for?"

"Look here, Sarah, we toil and moil the whole year through. It's nothing but trouble and worry, trouble and worry. Call that living! When do we ever have a bit of pleasure?"

"Well, what's to be done?" said his wife, in a subdued tone.

"The summer will soon be over, and we haven't set eyes on a green blade of grass. We sit day and night sweating in the dark."

"True enough!" sighed his wife, and Shmuel spoke louder:

"Let us have an outing, Sarah. Let us enjoy ourselves for once, and give the children a breath of fresh air, let us have a change, if it's only for five minutes!"

"What will it cost?" asks Sarah suddenly, and Shmuel has soon made the necessary calculation.

"A family ticket is only thirty cents, for Yossele, Rivele, Hannahle, and Berele; for Resele and Doletzke I haven't to pay any carfare at all. For you and me, it will be ten cents there and ten back—that makes fifty cents. Then I reckon thirty cents for refreshments to take with us: a pineapple (a damaged one isn't more than five cents), a few bananas, a piece of watermelon, a bottle of milk for the children, and a few rolls—the whole thing shouldn't cost us more than eighty cents at the outside."

"Eighty cents!" and Sarah clapped her hands together in dismay. "Why, you can live on that two days, and it takes nearly a whole day's earning. You can buy an old ice-box for eighty cents, you can buy a pair of trousers—eighty cents!"

"Leave off talking nonsense!" said Shmuel, disconcerted. "Eighty cents won't make us rich. We shall get on just the same whether we have them or not. We must live like human beings one day in the year! Come, Sarah, let us go! We shall see lots of other people, and we'll watch them, and see how *they* enjoy themselves. It will do you good to see the world, to go where there's a bit of life! Listen, Sarah, what have you been to worth seeing since we came to America? Have you seen Brooklyn Bridge, or Central Park, or the Baron Hirsch baths?"

"You know I haven't!" Sarah broke in. "I've no time to go about sight-seeing. I only know the way from here to the market."

"And what do you suppose?" cried Shmuel. "I should be as great a greenhorn as you, if I hadn't been obliged to look everywhere for work. Now I know that America is a great big place. Thanks to the slack times, I know where there's an Eighth Street, and a One Hundred and Thirtieth Street with tin works, and an Eighty-fourth Street with a match factory. I know every single lane around the World Building. I know where the cable car line stops. But you, Sarah, know nothing at all, no more than if you had just landed. Let us go, Sarah; I am sure you won't regret it!"

"Well, you know best!" said his wife, and this time she smiled. "Let us go!"

And thus it was that Shmuel and his wife decided to join the lodge picnic on the following day.

Next morning they all rose much earlier than usual on a Sunday, and there was a great noise, for they took the children and scrubbed them without mercy. Sarah prepared a bath for Doletzke, and Doletzke screamed the house down. Shmuel started washing Yossele's feet, but as Yossele habitually went barefoot, he failed to bring about any visible improvement, and had to leave the little pair of feet to soak in a basin of warm water, and Yossele cried, too. It was twelve o'clock before the children were dressed and ready to start, and then Sarah turned her attention to her husband, arranged his trousers, took the spots out of his coat with kerosene, sewed a button onto his vest. After that she dressed herself, in her old-fashioned satin wedding dress. At two o'clock they set forth, and took their places in the car.

"Haven't we forgotten anything?" asked Sarah of her husband.

Shmuel counted his children and the traps. "No, nothing, Sarah!" he said.

Doletzke went to sleep, the other children sat quietly in their places. Sarah, too, fell into a doze, for she was tired out with the preparations for the excursion.

All went smoothly till they got some way uptown, when Sarah gave a start.

"I don't feel very well—my head is so dizzy," she said to Shmuel.

"I don't feel very well, either," answered Shmuel. "I suppose the fresh air has upset us."

"I suppose it has," said his wife. "I'm afraid for the children."

Scarcely had she spoken when Doletzke woke up, whimpering, and was sick. Yossele, who was looking at her, began to cry likewise. The mother scolded him, and this set the other children crying. The conductor cast a wrathful glance at poor Shmuel, who was so frightened that he dropped the hand-bag with the provisions, and then, conscious of the havoc he had certainly brought about inside the bag by so doing, he lost his head altogether, and sat there in a daze. Sarah was hushing the children, but the look in her eyes told Shmuel plainly enough what to expect once they had left the car. And no sooner had they all reached the ground in safety than Sarah shot out:

"So, nothing would content him but a picnic? Much good may it do him! You're a workman, and workmen have no call to go gadding about!"

Shmuel was already weary of the whole thing, and said nothing, but he felt a tightening of the heart.

He took up Yossele on one arm and Resele on the other, and carried the bag with the presumably smashed-up contents besides.

"Hush, my dears! Hush, my babies!" he said; "wait a little and Mother will give you some bread and sugar. Hush, be quiet!" He went on, but still the children cried.

Sarah carried Doletzke, and rocked her as she walked, while Berele and Hannahle trotted alongside.

"He has shortened my days," said Sarah; "may his be shortened likewise."

Soon afterwards they turned into the park.

"Let us find a tree and sit down in the shade," said Shmuel. "Come, Sarah!"

"I haven't the strength to drag myself a step further," declared Sarah, and she sank down like a stone just inside the gate. Shmuel was about to speak, but a glance at Sarah's face told him she was worn out, and he sat down beside his wife without a word. Sarah gave Doletzke the breast. The other children began to roll about in the grass, laughed and played, and Shmuel breathed easier.

Girls in holiday attire walked about the park, and there were groups under the trees. Here was a handsome girl surrounded by admiring boys, and there a handsome young man encircled by a bevy of girls.

Out of the leafy distance of the park came the melancholy song of a workman; near by stood a man playing on a fiddle. Sarah looked about her and listened, and by degrees her vexation vanished. It is true that her heart was still sore, but it was not with the soreness of anger. She was taking her life to pieces and thinking it over, and it seemed a very hard and bitter one, and when she looked at her husband and thought of his life, she was near crying, and she laid her hands upon his knee.

Shmuel also sat lost in thought. He was thinking about the trees and the roses and the grass, and listening to the fiddle. And he also was sad at heart.

"Oh, Sarah!" he sighed, and he would have said more, but just at that moment it began to spot with rain, and before they had time to move, there came a downpour. People started to scurry in all directions, but Shmuel stood like a statue.

"Shlimm-mazel, look after the children!" commanded Sarah. Shmuel caught up two of them, Sarah another two or three, and they ran to a shelter. Doletzke began to cry afresh.

"Mame, hungry!" began Berele.

"Hungry, hungry!" wailed Yossele. "I want to eat!"

Shmuel hastily opened the hand-bag, and then for the first time he saw what had really happened: the bottle had broken, and the milk was flooding the bag; the rolls and bananas were soaked, and the pineapple (a damaged one to begin with) looked too nasty for words. Sarah caught sight of the bag, and was so angry she was at a loss how to wreak vengeance on her husband. She was ashamed to scream and scold in the presence of other people, but she went up to him, and whispered fervently into his ear, "The same to you, my good man!"

The children continued to clamor for food.

"I'll go to the refreshment counter and buy a glass of milk and a few rolls," said Shmuel to his wife.

"Have you actually some money left?" asked Sarah. "I thought it had all been spent on the picnic."

"There are just five cents over."

"Well, then go and be quick about it. The poor things are starving."

Shmuel went to the refreshment stall, and asked the price of a glass of milk and a few rolls.

"Twenty cents, mister," answered the waiter.

Shmuel started as if he had burnt his finger, and returned to his wife more crestfallen than ever.

"Well, Shlimm-mazel, where's the milk?" inquired Sarah.

"He asked twenty cents."

"Twenty cents for a glass of milk and a roll? Are you Montefiore?" Sarah could no longer contain herself. "They'll be the ruin of us! If you want to go for another picnic, we shall have to sell the bedding."

The children never stopped begging for something to eat.

"But what are we to do?" asked the bewildered Shmuel.

"Do?" screamed Sarah. "Go home, this very minute!"

Shmuel promptly caught up a few children, and they left the park. Sarah was quite quiet on the way home, merely remarking to her husband that she would settle her account with him later.

"I'll pay you out," she said, "for my satin dress, for the hand-bag, for the pineapple, for the bananas, for the milk, for the whole blessed picnic, for the whole of my miserable existence."

"Scold away!" answered Shmuel. "It is you who were right. I don't know what possessed me. A picnic, indeed! You may well ask what next? A poor wretched workman like me has no business to think of anything beyond the shop."

Sarah, when they reached home, was as good as her word. Shmuel would have liked some supper, as he always liked it, even in slack times, but there was no supper given him. He went to bed a hungry man, and all through the night he repeated in his sleep:

"A picnic, oi, a picnic!"

SOLOMON

by I. RABOY

THAT day Solomon went to work as usual. He sauntered through the shop with his hands folded behind his back, making his way along the aisle between two long rows of tables at which many girls were at work. They cast sidelong glances at him. The sewing machines whirred tumultuously. They were racing all at one time. During abrupt pauses of split seconds the whirring noise dissolved in tattered shreds of diminishing sound. The girls who operated the machines looked stealthily at him. He took them all in with a stern, comprehensive look, noticing what was at fault with the minutest detail of their work. He paused only long enough to snap out sharp orders to his subordinates to see that things were done right. The latter searched his face anxiously but found nothing unusual or disturbing in it for themselves.

When he had completed his inspection of the shop Solomon entered his office. At a large, low desk sat his daughter. She was just about to begin her typing.

"Good morning, daughter," he said.

The girl looked up startled.

"Hello, papa!" she murmured.

"I was just saying 'good morning' to you."

"Well, I returned your greeting. Haven't I, papa? I believe I said: 'Hello, papa!'"

"So you did," he answered and lit a cigarette. He held it between two fingers in characteristic Jewish-tailor fashion and blew spirals of smoke from the corners of his mouth. "Tell me, daughter," he began suddenly. "How many languages do you know besides English?"

"I cannot express myself freely in any other language except English," she answered.

"Have you ever read anything in any other language?"

"Yes, I have."

"Did you read *that* letter yesterday in the Yiddish newspaper?"

"I read *that* letter even before it was published in the Yiddish newspaper."

"What I demand from you is a frank answer: Did you read *that* letter in the Yiddish newspaper or did you not?"

"Not yet, papa. I have no interest to read it a second time."

"Answer me honestly!"

"What do you mean, papa? I have nothing to hide. I will answer any question you will put to me!"

"Was it your name which was affixed to that letter?"

"If the name is Rosie then it is mine."

"So you do know another language besides English!"

"Papa, believe me, I don't know any other language in which I can express myself freely and—"

He did not allow her to finish. The severe lines on his face grew harsher.

"Don't you try to confuse me and what's more, don't you get tangled up in your explanation. Only tell me: Did you or did you not write that letter, Rosie?"

"Yes, I did!"

"Did you send it to the Yiddish newspaper?"

"Yes."

"Now answer me: Am I your father or am I not? Are you or are you not my daughter?"

At these questions Rosie rose hurriedly from her seat and dashed to the clothes-closet, muttering confusedly:

"What funny questions you ask! Who knows what other—"

Her father rudely intercepted her and planted himself determinedly with his back against the closet. He put his hands out as if to prevent her from getting her wraps.

"What do you wish to do?" he asked.

"Let me go! I want to go home!" clamored Rosie, first in a suppressed, low voice and then louder and more shrill.

"Do you have a home? I have not suspected that at all."

"Pa, I am going to run out into the street without my hat and coat."

"Little fool, the doors are locked."

"In that case I will go into the shop and join the girls. I will go home with them."

"Just try!"

"The girls are my best friends. They will help me."

"Go ahead! But you will have to do the same kind of work they are doing."

"That suits me perfectly! I have been wishing to do that for a long time already. I have so many friends working here! I know I will be happier there. Here in the office I am all alone."

"Poor thing!" answered her father derisively. "Well, since you want it so much, come along! I will give you the chance to try out the friendship of the girls inside. Now come with me!"

He seized Rosie's hand roughly and dragged her, resisting, into the shop.

At first Rosie butted her head against her father's chest. Her hair became unloosened and fell over her shoulders. These efforts brought a deep flush to her cheeks. But when the shop door had closed on her father Rosie pranced about and sang with joy. The girls received her with open arms.

All day long Rosie worked at a sewing machine. She chatted gaily with the girls who taught her to sew. The foremen looked abashed and guiltily at one another. At the work tables and at the sewing machines the girls were impatiently waiting for the end of the day. They longed to escape from the shop and to enter into another world of experience. Finally, when closing time came, all the girls clustered around Rosie, chatted gaily with her and kissed her good-bye.

Rosie returned home flushed with excitement, just as if she had but left the arms of her sweetheart Philip. Her father had come in shortly before her. He already was sitting at the table waiting for dinner to be served. As soon as she entered her mother threw her a significant look. Evidently she already knew what had happened, thought Rosie. Yet she was certain that her mother would not dare take her part in the presence of her father.

Rosie freshened up a bit for dinner. She pretended that nothing had happened. Only she felt that something had happened inside of her which had radically changed her. And she could not put this thought away from her. She looked at her father with amazement. He behaved as if nothing untoward had taken place between them. Rosie ate with relish.

After dinner they sat lounging at the table as was usual with them. Rosie's father lit a cigarette. Her mother picked her teeth. And Rosie, leaning back in her chair, thought about her sweetheart Philip who was expected shortly.

Silence reigned in the room. One could almost hear the shadows of the advancing evening creeping along the walls of the houses.

Then Solomon arose and took himself off into his room. His wife, too, went away to seclude herself. And Rosie remained alone in the dining-room. She surrendered herself in thought to the strong arms of one invisible who embraced her and joined her in the silence.

So neither her father nor her mother thought it necessary to say even one word to her at dinner! Rosie felt offended. But she found some consolation in the observation that affairs of business must not be introduced into the home. A moment later her injured pride began to smart again at the thought that she was being treated like a stranger in her own home.

A sudden ring at the door caused Rosie to jump up with a start. She listened attentively. A sound similar to that of a practised hand beating rhythmically upon a drum floated up the stairway. Rosie was gripped by fear. That was the characteristic way Philip climbed the stairs.

She opened hastily the door of the small foyer and hid herself behind it. Philip entered. In the manner of an actor he took his hat off at the door. He did not notice that Rosie was hiding. She slowly tiptoed behind him and tickled the back of his neck with her finger. Philip stopped short. Instinctively he felt that the tickling finger belonged to Rosie. He staggered back in mock simulation of falling. Rosie put out her arms and he sank reversed into them. She felt his full weight crushing her and was frightened.

"Philip!" she cried protestingly.

He wheeled about laughing hilariously. They embraced, kissed and hand in hand entered the house.

Rosie rang for the maid. Philip switched on the light. The maid hurried in with a guilty air and began to clear the table. When she was through with her work and left them alone together, Philip said:

"I longed for you so much yesterday!"

"I missed you too," answered Rosie, toying with a fold in her dress. "The house seemed bigger and lonelier than it actually is. I could find no peace for myself."

"Why didn't you come to see me?"

"To see you! In the first place, I'll never come to you again. In the second place, I did not do so yesterday because I did not dare leave the house after what I—"

"Did you really write that letter in the Yiddish newspaper?" interrupted Philip.

"I always do what I say I will do."

"How could you—about your own father!"

"I can see no connection between my loyalties at home and my business relations with my father in the factory."

"But it is this very factory which has made your home possible, Rosie."

"Philip!" began Rosie in a reproachful voice.

"Rosie!" pleaded Philip, not allowing her to say any more. "Just think what you are doing! I love you. God, you and I know the truth of it best. You can believe me when I say that I do not look forward to your father's financial assistance when we get married. But I cannot but help feeling outraged at the thought that you have committed such an unpardonable act against your own father."

"I don't need your love and I don't need your preaching," answered Rosie angrily and, rising from her chair, stormed out of the room.

Philip looked very much upset by her sudden flight. He carefully went over in his mind all that she had said to him and all that he had answered her. He lit a cigarette to steady his nerves and then went in search of Rosie.

He found her in another room leaning out of a window that opened upon the street. He too leaned out of the open window. And so they stood side by side, looking mutely out upon the deserted street. After some hesitation he put his arm around her waist and tried to draw her to him. But she repulsed him without a word and looked in the opposite direction.

Thereupon he drew deeply upon his cigarette and blew a mouthful of smoke directly into her face. Rosie averted her gaze still more and stubbornly kept silent. At this Philip made an angry, impatient gesture. Rosie then drew back from the window, pulled Philip away with her and shut the window.

"You can't frighten me, Philip, with whatever you intend to do. You will only succeed in making me hate you the more."

"Hate me then, but that shouldn't keep you from talking to me. I have only given you my opinion. And that is: if I were a father and a daughter of mine were to do what you did to—"

"Philip!" interrupted Rosie. "You're talking like an old grandaddy now. How will you talk when you get older, I'd like to know?"

"Enough of your sarcasm! Well and good—you have done something which you cannot possibly recall. I know how your father feels about it. But what is your mother's reaction?"

"I don't know. She says nothing. I am not even sure if she knows anything about the matter."

"What? She doesn't know anything about it! Why didn't you tell her about it yourself?"

"What difference does it make? She will know about it in the morning anyway."

"Will you tell her, Rosie? You must tell her. She is your mother."

"She will find out about it herself tomorrow morning."

"Will your father inform her?"

"My father is not that kind."

"Shall I talk to her about it?"

"No, no! Not you! Let her find out herself."

"How will she find out?"

"She will see me get up very early in the morning."

"Why so early?"

"All girls who work in my father's factory have to be there early."

"I don't understand what you are talking about."

"I will have to rise early enough to be on time for work. Is that clear to you now?"

"So! Then your father has punished you and you are going to look for another job!"

"I have already found one. My job will be at the sewing-machine in my father's factory among all the other working-girls. And I have chosen it myself."

"Well, what do you say to that!" exclaimed Philip, flabbergasted.

"Just what you hear!"

"Are you going to learn a trade?"

"Yes, Philip. The girls will teach me."

"How exciting! Very exciting!" exclaimed Philip derisively. "And what if the wages your father offers to pay you should be less than you expect—will you break with him and then go looking for another job?"

"Not only will I be on the outs with him in case he will wish to underpay me but should he exploit and mistreat the other girls I will take their part against him."

Rosie was on her guard. Although the room was dark she felt instinctively that Philip was smiling at her, bemused. He had nothing more to say to her. He paced silently to and fro in the darkened room.

Rosie then bethought herself that certain details were missing in the picture of herself in the striking circumstances she was in and that it was her duty to make everything clear to Philip. So she continued:

"And should my father discharge me from my job and even if he should force me to leave home I will come to you for help, Philip. You understand me, don't you, Philip?"

Philip nodded that he understood. And out of politeness he stayed a little longer. He finally took his leave and she heard him tearing down the stairs as if he were pounding rhythmically upon a drum.

Next morning Rosie tumbled out of bed very early, just as she had planned to. It was a sunny morning and she was under the impression that she would be late for work. She hastened with her toilette and moved about as noiselessly as possible so that she might steal out of the house unnoticed by her mother. But no matter how careful and expeditious she tried to be, everything seemed to go wrong. As if by sheer deviltry, she could not help knocking against things and making an awful clatter.

Her mother suddenly came out of her room and noticing that Rosie was fully dressed, she turned pale.

"Good morning, mother!"

"Rosie! What is the matter? Just see how you look!"

"Oh, mother, with you it's always: 'Just see how you look!' said Rosie, smiling. "I don't look any different now than at any other time. Only I am in a hurry today."

"Are you going picnicking with Philip? Why didn't you tell me last night? I would have prepared lunch for you."

"No, mother. I am not going picnicking. And if you don't mind I'll prepare my own breakfast."

"I simply don't understand you. You are not going on a picnic—you get up scandalously early, and now you insist on making your own coffee."

"Just so! I am in a hurry to go to work."

"To work! What work? All so suddenly! Tell mother, Rosie. You seem so upset today."

By this time Rosie had finished dressing and started for the door which led into the kitchen. Thereupon her mother obstructed her way.

"Well, mother, if you will not let me go into the kitchen, I'll go to work without my coffee."

"Have you gone out of your wits?" pleaded her mother. "Or is it all a nightmare?" She began to dab her eyes with her handkerchief. "I will wake your father if you will insist on going. I will ask him not to let you go."

"Mother, I beg you not to create any unpleasant scene. You can trust me to do the right thing."

But her mother ignored Rosie's plea. Sobbing and wringing her hands she went to wake her husband. This gave Rosie the opportunity of grabbing up her hat and coat and running out of the house.

Five hundred girls were suddenly overjoyed. They clipped the letter which their boss's daughter Rosie had published in the Yiddish newspaper. Then they had every word of it transposed and stamped on white linen. This they drew tight upon frames and proceeded to embroider with fine silk-thread. They wished to keep it as a memento, to have it framed and hung upon the wall so that their children and their children's children might remember this phenomenal act everlastingly. And the following are the words of Rosie's letter which they embroidered:

"To the Editors:

"I am the daughter of Solomon. Do not be surprised if I make unexpected revelations about my father. He is greatly honored by the community and well thought of because he gives money lavishly to Jewish charities. But I have had the good fortune of receiving a Jewish education. I have absorbed myself in the writings of our great Jews and I have also read biographies of them. I have learned a great deal from those men. For instance I have learned that the great men of our race in both thought and action were dedicated to the service of society. They issued from the people, lived for it and died for it.

"Allow me therefore to inform you that my father has no rightful place in the Jewish community, among its leaders, among men of enlightenment and social responsibility. My father has climbed to riches on a ladder braided by fragile women's hands. Immured in my father's factory are five hundred girls. They work for a pittance that even slaves would spurn. Day in and day out these five hundred girls are grinding out riches for my father. They dare not even laugh as healthy young girls should. They dare not sing as every normal girl should and wants. They dare not exchange a word with one another because my father's watch-dogs stand guard over them from early morning until late at night.

"And now allow me please to ask you, is it just that such a man as my father should be honored by you, that the Jewish community should rejoice over him, because of the banquets that he makes for them, because of his wine that they drink, because of his food that they eat? All are bought with the money created by the sweat and blood of the five hundred girls who wear themselves away for my father in his factory.

"I wish to sign myself with the name of

"—Rosie."

ALTE BOBBE

by CHARLES ANGOFF

How old she was when she died in 1915 I don't know, and neither does anybody else. Whenever one of her thirteen children, ten grandchildren, and about twenty great-grandchildren asked her for the date of her birth, she would smile and say, "Who knows such things? Only in America they remember birthdays. I was born when the good Czar Alexander II was a little boy, God have mercy on his soul. Don't ask me any more foolish questions."

Her oldest daughter, my grandmother, however, who also didn't know her birthday, once gave her brothers and sisters more detailed information; and on the basis of that, Great-grandmother Jeannette must have been ninety-five at the very least when she died. Very likely she was more than a hundred.

In Yiddish her name was Yente, or Alte Bobbe Yente, Great-grandmother Yente. Her family called her that in Russia and in Boston, until the census man came around in 1910. He asked one of her grandchildren what Yente's name was in English.

She knew hardly any English, but this question she did understand. It made her laugh. "Tell him I'm too old to have an English name," she said.

The census man persisted. He claimed he couldn't put it down just Yente Schneider. Finally an idea struck him. "Why not call her Jeannette?" he asked.

"Jeannette," my great-grandmother repeated and laughed. The census man also laughed because in those days, at least in Boston, Jeannette was a name assumed by girls who thought they were better than they were. For a while the mention of Jeannette would cause guffaws of laughter in the house. Then, for some strange reason, the name lost its potency as a laugh inciter, and great-grandmother became Yente again to her friends, and Alte Bobbe to all her off-spring, near and far. It sounded more respectful, yet more familiar. Anyway, I, her oldest and favorite great-grandchild, always called her Alte Bobbe. The name Jeannette never appealed to me. It was at best a joke for grownups, while it lasted, not for us younger fry.

She was short, about five feet two, and she had remarkable bearing to the very end. She weighed only about 100 pounds, walked erect, never wore glasses, and her face was round and kindly and had fewer lines than many women half her age. In accordance with orthodox Jewish rite, her hair was closely shorn and she wore a kerchief instead of a hat. She used a wide variety of kerchiefs, some of them quite colorful, though on Saturdays, Yom Kippur, Rosh Hashanah, and other holidays, she always wore a pure white woolen kerchief. It gave her a truly angelic appearance. She was meticulously tidy, manicuring her fingernails every Friday afternoon in order to greet the Eve of the Sabbath in a worthy manner.

She lived with her oldest daughter, my grandmother, but she really managed the house as if it were her own. She was not dictatorial, but she took an interest in everything that went on, helping out with the housework wherever possible. As long as she lived, her house was the center of the whole family, including all the relatives. Every one of her children and grandchildren visited her at least once a week, and she visited them at least three times each year: on Rosh Hashanah, Passover, and Hanukkah, three important Jewish holidays and feast days. On the first two holidays she would bring sponge cake and a little wine to each family, take a sip of wine, and continue with her visits. On Hanuk-kah she used to carry a bag of pennies and give each of the youngsters two or three cents as a present.

Of course she would visit a family more often if there was need for her services or advice. She settled domestic difficulties, made sure that the children got proper religious training, and occasionally administered to the physical ailments of young and old. As far as I know, she was never ill herself. She was a great believer in sleep as a healer, and after that she put most stress on chicken soup, boiled beef, black bread, and tea. The only three vegetables that made sense to her were potatoes, carrots, and horse-radish. I often heard her say, "If chicken soup and sleep can't cure you, nothing will. They are God's gift to the poor man." She had little respect for doctors, and there was a slight touch of superstition in her. She cured mild colds and toothaches with a knife and magic words. She would make three circles with the knife around the head or throat if the patient suffered with a cold, and around the jaw if the patient had a toothache, touching the skin in each case lightly, and whispering holy Hebrew words as she did so. However, she never relied completely on this magic. She insisted on chicken soup and sleep in addition, saying that the incantation wouldn't work otherwise.

While she made sure that all the children got religious training, she didn't push her piety upon the oldsters. She would never light a match on Saturday or even carry a dish across the street. Both were work, which was forbidden on the Sabbath. But she didn't object to her children and grandchildren going to their jobs on the Sabbath. "God does not want the poor to starve," she would say. "He understands and will forgive." The children and grandchildren returned this consideration by not smoking cigarettes or sewing or doing any other forbidden thing on Saturday in front of her. This pleased her so much that she at times violated her own convictions. Some of her sons and grandsons, she knew, were heavy smokers, and she was sorry that on Friday night they had to abstain on account of her. So around nine o'clock she would say, "Harry, Fishel, don't you want to take a little walk?" They always did. They knew it meant that if they went into the street and had a cigarette or two, it would be all right with her.

My own only religious disagreement with her took place when I was seven years old; she was then in her late eighties or early nineties. One of my sisters and I had arrived in America with her, in steerage, of course. (My mother and two other children had to remain in Libau, Latvia, for a few months.) As was customary in those days, steerage passengers had to spend a day or more on Ellis Island for medical examination, and some organization sent over baskets of fruit and cookies for the poorer immigrants. Each unit received one or more baskets. I ripped open the basket allotted to us, and was immediately fascinated by a long yellowish object. I examined it from every angle, and the girl who brought the basket peeled it for me. It was a banana, of course, the first I had ever seen. I began to eat it, and offered it to my sister to taste. Whereupon Alte Bobbe seized it from my sister, and turning to me said, "You don't have to be in such a hurry to forget your Judaism." She thought it was pork done up in a special way.

Her advice in the realm of marriage and love helped to smooth out many difficulties. She herself was married at fifteen, and while she thought that was perhaps too early an age, she believed that every girl should have a husband by the time she was eighteen. "A woman must have a man to make up her mind for her," she used to say, "and to give her children." She looked upon childless marriages as a curse. Any family with less than six or seven children was not a real family. She said that in all her life she never knew a woman who was really happy without a flock of her own children.

She had clear and definite ideas about the relationship between husband and wife. I once heard her say to an aunt of mine who complained about her husband, "I don't care what he did or what he said. If there is a quarrel between a wife and her husband, it's always the wife's fault. Look into your heart and change your ways." To the men she spoke with equal plainness, and sometimes with sharpness. To one of them who was a bit of a miser she said, "Yes, they'll erect a golden gravestone in your memory." To another who was mean-tempered and selfish she said, "Consider how small you are. When a fine Jew says, 'Good day,' to another, the other replies, 'A good year to you.' A whole year for one day! You don't even reply, 'Good day.' "

While she lived in this country only six years and knew only a few words of English, she loved America almost from the day she arrived. "A country that has sidewalks," she said, "is God's country. I'm sure there are sidewalks in Heaven," she would add with a smile. The village she came from had no side-walks. The roads were muddy nearly all year round. She admired President Wilson: "He has so much grace and learning. It's a wonderful country where a professor, a man like that, can become the head. When he makes mistakes, it's only like bad weather. It goes away." Her pet, however, was Louis D. Brandeis, upon whom she looked as a neighbor because he lived in Boston. She said that his face was "like evening on a mountain." For a while she regretted that he didn't have a beard. "A Jew should have a beard, as a mountain should have foliage." But she soon overlooked that. I often think what a pity it was that she didn't live long enough to be told of Brandeis' elevation to the Supreme Court. She would have been thrilled as only a woman in her nineties can be thrilled.

A year or two before she died, she began to weaken perceptibly. I used to walk with her almost every Saturday morning to the synagogue—a journey that meant going down a steep hill and crossing a congested streetcar junction—and I began to notice that she held onto my arm more firmly than before. In the synagogue she used to sit in the balcony, where all women sit in an orthodox synagogue, and I noted that she would doze off occasionally, a thing she had not done previously, to the best of my knowledge. When she returned from the synagogue, she took longer rests before dinner. In the evening she would amble over to the hot-water boiler by the coal stove in the kitchen, lean against it for hours, and apparently go to sleep, though she maintained that she heard everything that was said.

Her children pleaded with her to permit Dr. Golden, the family physician, to examine her thoroughly. She would say, "I'll see him. He's a fine man, but I won't let him examine me. There's nothing wrong with me. I'm only a little tired. When my time comes, he won't be able to help. And besides, I've lived long enough. All my children are married happily, and that's all a woman really wants in life. So don't disturb Dr. Golden."

Dr. Golden knew Alte Bobbe very well. He used to talk with her at length when he visited others in the family. Once in a while she'd allow him to put the stethoscope to her heart, but no more. He told the men folk in the family that Alte Bobbe's heart was none too good, that age was beginning to take its toll. A few times he told her to rest more often. She replied, "I'll take a good long rest when I'm dead. You'll die before me with all your medicines. Now tell me how your wife is, and the children. You don't look too good yourself. You should sleep more and have more chicken soup."

The inevitable last day came. She was unable to get up from her bed to wash and go to the front room, where she used to pray by herself before breakfast. She asked her oldest daughter to give her a little tea. She finished the tea and then said, "Call all the children. This is the end. I'm not afraid. Don't you be afraid. It's God's will. I thank God I am dying in my own house, with all my children around, and in a good country, where Jews are treated like human beings. I'm sorry I'm not leaving anything of value. I make only two requests: remember me every year by burning a lamp on this my last day, and put a picture of the whole family in my coffin." The entire family had had a group picture taken two years before, at her suggestion.

Her oldest daughter protested such talk.

Alte Bobbe said, "Do as I tell you."

We all came over as soon as possible, some thirty of us, young and old. Dr. Golden was also called. He examined her. She did not object. After the examination he walked out of Alte Bobbe's bedroom, his eyes red. Three or four hours later Alte Bobbe died, fully conscious to the end and as peacefully as anybody could have wished. Her two oldest sons picked her up from the bed and put her down on the floor, in accordance with orthodox Jewish custom, and placed two candles at her head. All of us then walked by her and asked her to plead for us in the other world. My turn came, and I said the Hebrew words my mother told me. I wasn't afraid. Alte Bobbe looked the same as I had always known her, calm, kindly, and as beautiful as snow on a hill not far away. I saw the family picture by her feet. I was inexpressibly glad I was in it, and I always will be.

MEETINGS AND PARTINGS

by CHARLES REZNIKOFF

GOOD-BYE GRANDPA

I CAME to say good-bye. I was going away to the University of Missouri. My grandfather turned from the window at which he sat, looking across the lots at the parkway. To eyes used to the droshkies and sleighs, sleds, wagons and slow carts of the Ukrainian roads, the parkway was new, I suppose: its smooth surface—with orderly, swift automobiles and trucks, shining in the sun or under the streetlights—in a great sweep between rows of tall houses and brand-new little trees.

My grandfather knew Yiddish and Hebrew and a smattering of Russian, and I—except for the languages I had learned a little of at school—only English and a smattering of Yiddish. A man whose only study was Torah and Talmud, he had found when he came to this country that I had been brought up unable to recite a blessing or to read a word of Hebrew. So we could say little and had little to say to each other. Sick, his skin yellow, his eyes red and bleared, his hair still dark brown—for he had hardly any gray hair in his beard or on his head— I used to see him sitting at the window, reading a Hebrew book, or thinking about a sad, secret matter, or watching the automobiles and trucks along the parkway turn the curve.

As I came in, he rose with difficulty—he had been expecting me, it seems— stretched out his hands and blessed me in a loud voice—in Hebrew, of course, and I did not know what he was saying. Then he turned aside and burst into tears. "It is only for a little while, Grandpa," I said in my broken Yiddish. "I'll be back in June." (By June he had been dead seven months.)

He did not answer me. Perhaps he was in tears for other reasons. Perhaps because, in spite of all the learning I had acquired in school, I knew not a word of the sacred text and was now going out into the world with none of the accumulated wisdom of my people to guide me, with no prayers with which to talk to the God of my people, a soul—for it is not easy to be a Jew, or perhaps a man—doomed by his ignorance to stumble and blunder. Perhaps he wept because he alone of his family was true to the sacred—and so pleasant—ways of his fathers, and now he was about to die. Perhaps he wept because he was about to die. No, Achilles was a heathen; my grandfather would not weep because he was about to die.

WHY MY FRIEND PRACTICED FALLING

I had a friend at school who practiced falling. After school we would go to a playground. There were boys at handball, though the ground was uneven and covered with pebbles—no one could tell how the ball would bounce. But each day, while the others played games, ran after each other, or swung on the bars and rings, my friend persisted at learning how to fall. He would work his way up the inclined ladder, higher and higher each time, and drop to the ground. The small clumsy body would drop heavily upon the hard-packed sand, pick itself up, and then the short arms—the body jerking—would work their way up the ladder again. The trick, he explained, was to land lightly, and not sting the soles of one's feet.

"Why learn how to fall?" I would ask him. "What good is it?"

"I don't know," he would answer and look puzzled. "I want to."

Once, when I was in his house, I stood at the window looking into the yard. My friend's father had a little store in front—a few bolts of cloth, a few dirty and broken paper boxes, a dusty showcase with pins and buttons, needles and thread. The yard was full of old wagons, the shafts in the air like masts. Along the back fence, almost as high as the second story, cats were walking gracefully, and now and then one jumped to the ground, landing lightly on its feet.

WHY I DO NOT FAST ON THE DAY OF ATONEMENT

Until I was twenty-one I had never fasted on the Day of Atonement. I kept only the feasts. But that year—to meet the daughters of the congregation—I joined a synagogue in our neighborhood. And since everybody went to synagogue on the Day of Atonement, I thought it would not be nice for me not to go. That meant, it seemed to me, that I should fast because it would be hateful to sit, sated and belching, among the fasting worshipers. And it seemed to me that it might even be pleasant in that slight exaltation that comes from hunger to listen to the cantor and the choir chanting, to lose myself in the Hebrew of the prayers, to wrap myself in a silk prayer shawl and in meditation upon the Eternal forget myself. So I went to synagogue and fasted.

It was a warm day, as warm as a day in summer. About three o'clock I had gone down and up a depression, I no longer found the chanting and the prayers tiresome, my collar sticky, the air close, and, though my head ached a little, my spirit was nimble and joyous, conversing with the cherubim.

A member of the congregation greeted me. "How are you?" he asked. "You are really fasting?" he added surprised.

"How can you tell?"

"By your lips—they are dry and white. Come, let us go for a walk—a little walk. You will feel better."

"But I feel fine."

"Come, it is lovely outside. We will be back soon."

I was somewhat flattered at his attentions. We walked along the boulevard; the trees had on their holiday leaves of red and yellow. "How is it that a clever young man like you," began my companion, when we were a decent block or so from the synagogue, "carries so little insurance?"

I found my headache worse, excused myself, went home, and ate heartily. Since then I never fast: I am afraid that someone will sell me insurance, or who knows what, when I am weakened.

SUNDAY AFTERNOON

In the street one day Daniel met Rose who had lived on the same block as he seven years before. He recognized her at once, but she did not know him. Of course. He had been fourteen and she had been a woman of twenty-four. In those days she would condescend to talk to him of the books he was reading; and he remembered a tall pale woman with deep blue eyes and a pleasant laugh. Now that he was a man she seemed not tall at all, in fact he was more than a head taller; she was thin, pale, and her eyes were a watery blue. But she spoke cheerfully as ever. He had tickets for a concert—Fritz Kreisler. Would she come? What was she doing? She was still a teacher. And now he was about to become a lawyer.

When he called for her, he was shown into the parlor: a small room with heavy furniture like a herd of pachyderms in a cage. He could hear Rose quarreling with her sister in an undertone. Rose had gone to the closet to get her coat. "Who took my rubbers?" she was saying. "Mine had my initial in them and you had no business to take them. It was not a mistake. You had no business to take them."

When they were in the street, he turned to the subway. "I can't ride in the subway," she said. Of course, he should have signaled a taxicab in the first place, but he did not have the money for it. The tickets had been more than he could afford.

"Shall we go by—?" and he looked at the elevated tracks a block away.

"That will do," she said. Luckily, she had a seat. As he held onto a strap in front of her, "I have no patience," she said, "with those girls—whenever we go out together—who want to sit in cheap seats. If they can't afford to sit in good seats, they ought not to go. I get dizzy when I am far from the stage, and if I don't enjoy myself, I'd rather not go."

"I hope," said Daniel, "that you will not be dizzy in our seats; they are in the balcony."

"As long as they are not in the gallery, they will do. Besides, this is music and not a play. But I do hope that we are not too far away; I should like to see what Fritz Kreisler looks like."

They certainly were not near Fritz Kreisler. They sat quietly and never turned in their seats or rustled a program, but Daniel acknowledged that he had not been more than mildly interested. As for Rose, she too had been somewhat disappointed. "I expected more," she said calmly, as if the disappointment did not matter much.

"Shall we have coffee?" Daniel asked, as they passed a place with many trays of pastry in the large windows.

"I am very particular about coffee," Rose said.

"I know nothing about it; we drink tea at home. But let's try this place; it looks good." His eye had caught the price of coffee on the menu pasted on one of the windows; it was only ten cents, and pastry would be fifteen or twenty.

They had their coffee. "How is the coffee?" Daniel asked.

"Mediocre, perfectly mediocre," she answered, a trace of vexation in her voice.

When he brought her home, her father and sister were about to have supper; there was a platter of smoked salmon, another of sliced meat, and a heap of boiled potatoes, smoking hot.

A large pot of coffee, no doubt excellent coffee such as Rose liked, was on the table. But no one asked Daniel to stay, and Rose was glad to have him go—at least, she said good-bye when he ventured to say it, quickly and cheerfully, without the mild protestation that Daniel expected.

OLD ACQUAINTANCE

Once, when Daniel was in the gallery watching a play, he heard one of the girls behind him whisper, "There's Laura! She used to be Laura Stein. How pretty she still is!"

Daniel had known a Laura Stein years before—had been in love with her—and he looked eagerly at the faces about him. There was a woman, somewhat like the girl he had known, in the second row. He knew that she had married and that she had a child.

How pretty Laura had been, especially when flushed with games or dancing. The girls, then, wore their hair coiled on the back of their heads like the statue of Diana. Some, who did not have hair enough for that, used to wind it about a contraption of wire called a "mousetrap." Laura's would be sticking out of her hair after a game. She was the liveliest and, when she set herself going, ribbons, bands, pins, and hooks-and-eyes had a hard time of it. Once the placket of her skirt was open, and Daniel was furious at a boy for pointing at it, and tried not to see it.

Daniel greeted her, as she came up the aisle with her husband, when the play was ended. Yes, it was Laura, but the lithe body had become broad, and as she set down her quick little heels they sounded on the stairs and sidewalk. They walked to the corner. Would he come to see them any Sunday afternoon? He would. And the very next Sunday he did go.

Laura lived in a suburb where there were many large houses with broad lawns. But her house was one of a row of little wooden ones, unpainted, as alike as clothespins, set close together. Her street was narrow and the others were broad; it was unpaved, without trees or gardens. As Daniel walked up the rickety steps to the little porch, he could see thick black cobwebs in the corners and under the railing. As he looked at them and at a broken baby carriage on the porch, his heart failed him. Of course, their invitation had been merely a formality, and he turned away.

DELICATESSEN

I was in a delicatessen store. A boy of seven or eight came in, neither timid nor noisy like a schoolboy, but sedate. I supposed him to be in business—a newsboy who had sold his papers or an errand boy for one of the stores. He considered the meats on the counter and ordered his sandwich, gave the clerk a dime and was given four cents in change. He counted this at a glance and slipped it carelessly into his pocket. As he chewed his sandwich, he eyed the bowl of pickles.

"How much," he asked, "for a small one?"

"Two cents," and the clerk dug his hand into the bowl.

"Too much. Haven't you any for a penny?"

"Two cents is the cheapest. I'll give you a good one, see!" And the clerk took out a pickle and held it up. I could smell the good smell of dill. The boy eyed it, shook his head, and went on chewing his sandwich.

A CAGE

I was in a factory. There was a boy of three or four on a stool in a corner of the office, who smiled shyly at me and looked away. He had the stub of a pencil and a sheet of paper before him, but most of the time he was looking out of the window. There was only a row of buildings with shops in them to see, and all he could hear was the noise of the machines. "That is your little boy, I suppose," I said to the manufacturer.

"No, he is the child of one of the operators. He is too young to go to school, and she has no one with whom to leave him; so I let her bring him here." Later, I saw a woman dart into the office to steal a glance at the boy.

"When do you come here?" I asked him.

"Eight o'clock in the morning."

"And when do you go away?"

"Six o'clock." He smiled, his black eyes shining.

Next morning I had to go there again. The youngster was on his perch in the office. He had some empty spools before him to play with, but he was not playing.

A PEDDLER

I went to see my uncle, the jobber, and found one of his customers in a passionate discourse on some difficulty in the Talmud. "He is the son of a great rabbi," whispered my uncle to me. The discourse came to an end at last, and the son of the great rabbi turned to look at a heap of sweaters, the merits of which my uncle was proclaiming.

Walking down a street a week or so later, I was somewhat surprised to see, so far from any ghetto, a Jew carrying a bundle—he must have carried it a long way, for he was finding it heavy; with his derby on, he was no more than five feet tall; the sweat trickling from under the brim had soaked through the hatband and was soaking into his beard; his coat was too big for him, and for that matter so was his hat, and both had been well powdered by the dust of the street; his face was thin, the cheeks and lips pale, and his large black eyes were lost in thought. It was the discourser on the Talmud.

THE DEATH OF SHOLOM ALEICHEM

by MAURICE SAMUEL

FOR Sholom Aleichem the pilgrimage was permanently broken off on Saturday, May 13, 1916. The way station where he died was an apartment house at 968 Kelly Street, the Bronx, and the time was the middle of the First World War.

Those were dark, bitter years to die in, for a Jew sensitive to the fate of his people. The Yiddish-speaking world of Europe was the battlefield in the vast war of movement between Russia and Germany. Nicholas I was still on the throne—what hopes could the Jews repose on a Russian victory? But Germany was the cradle of modern anti-Semitism. The greatest Jewish historian of our time has pointed repeatedly to this fact. His *History of the Jews of Poland and Russia,* published thirty years ago, made the dilemma clear even before the First World War began. What hope, then, was there for the Jews in a German victory? No wonder Sholom Aleichem himself said, in his *New Arabian Nights—* the record of the Jewish agony in the First World War: "Of course this is a Jewish war—its purpose is the annihilation of the Jewish people." The spirit of the time, and his own share in the flight from Europe, helped undermine the resistance which he had put up for nearly a decade against tuberculosis and diabetes; and the death of a son came to him as a solemn forewarning of his own impending departure.

He did not foresee that worse was to follow for the Jews; the Polish pogroms and the mass slaughters organized under the Ukrainian hetman Petlura (one cannot speak of them simply as pogroms) were yet to come. And in the not too remote future, after a breathing spell in Poland and a liberation in Russia, there was to follow the total eclipse of Hitler's advance over the remnants of the Yiddish world. But what he lived to witness was bad enough—and he closed his eyes to it, defeated at last.

There he lay, used up and burned out, in the little apartment in the Bronx. Three bearded old Jews of Pereyeslav, the townlet of his birth, had performed the last rites for him, washed his body, wrapped it in cerements, swathed him in his praying shawl. For thirty-six hours—two nights and a day—a permanent guard of Yiddish writers stood over him, while an interminable line of mourners wound through the adjoining streets to take a last look at the tired, clever, puckish face, relaxed in death. They tiptoed in, stood for a few moments staring down at the waxen features under the candlelight, and passed on. Fifteen thousand of them managed to get a last glimpse of Sholom Aleichem in the flesh, and thousands more came too late on the morning of Monday. A hundred and fifty thousand lined the streets at the stopping-places of the cortege, at the Ohav Tzedek synagogue at One Hundred and Sixteenth Street and Fifth Avenue, at the Jewish community center at Second Avenue and Twenty-first Street, at the offices of the Hebrew Immigrant Aid Society, and at the building of the Educational Alliance on East Broadway.

In a sense it might be said that his pilgrimage was not broken off—it had come to its end. Those who believe that the tempo of a man's work is dictated unconsciously by the number of years placed at his disposal may add Sholom Aleichem to the evidence. It was in 1908, the forty-ninth year of his life, that he was first struck down by sickness. But that same year was marked, all over the Jewish world, by an extraordinary celebration of Sholom Aleichem's completion of a quarter of a century of literary activity. It was a demonstration which probably has not its like in the exilic history of Jewry. In hundreds of towns in Russia, Poland, England, the Americas, South Africa—wherever Yiddish was read—in the Kasrielevkys of the Pale, Kasrielevky on the Hudson, Kasrielevky on the Pampas, Kasrielevky in the Transvaal, there were meetings at which his works were read forth, and the *Kasriels* in exile laughed with Sholom Aleichem and at themselves, wept with him and over themselves. He had by then achieved a place in the folk which was final and unchangeable. He wrote much that was great in his last eight years; when he died he was engaged on great work, and had great works in mind. They would have added to the delight of his readers, not to his name.

In another sense, too, he had completed his pilgrimage. He had known all the vicissitudes of a Jew, he had tasted all the experiences which were peculiar to the history of his people. He had been a *cheder* boy in old Kasrielevky, and a Russian Gymnasium student; he had passed from the medieval to the modern; he had been a tutor, a Crown Rabbi, a businesman; he had dealt in sugar, had gambled on the Yehupetz stock exchange, had turned insurance agent; he had been very rich, and very poor. He had been a Maecenas of literature, and he had known what it was to need a Maecenas and not to find one. He had published lavishly the works of lesser writers, and had been unable to find publishers for his own. He had been adored and ignored. He had had his plays turned down by producers, he had been bullied by New York newspaper editors who told him they knew better than he what the public wanted. And always he had written. He wrote in health and sickness; he wrote on trains, in droshkies, on the kitchen table, at his business desk, in the midst of ledgers, balance sheets, and

IOU's. He wrote even on his deathbed. He was driven by an intolerable creative strength. The excessive imagination, the gifts of observation and of memory, and the irresistible impulse to mimicry which had made him a portent in his *cheder* days stayed with him to the end. But never was he the less a man, living with his fellow men, because he was the writer; and as a man he had lived through all that his people had suffered.

It is not a formality to speak of the thousands who poured out into the streets of New York on that day as "mourners." It was not formality that caused hundreds of unions, brotherhoods, societies, Zionist clubs, benevolent orders, and Socialist organizations to call hasty meetings on the Sunday of May 14, and to send their representatives to the cemetery on the morning of the 15th. It was not formality that brought delegations to New York from every town in America within overnight distance. Nor was it Sholom Aleichem himself that they mourned. It was a part of their life which had been torn away from them. They were attending the rehearsal of their own obsequies, saying the *Kaddish* in advance over their way of life, for they knew that none would say it afterward. Brighter days might indeed come for the Jewish people, but the savor of their world would not be tasted by their children, and they would be a mystery to their own posterity.

This "they" felt. And who were "they"? None other than the people he had written of. Tevyeh himself left his milk cart at the corner of Intervale Avenue, and came with Goldie to say farewell to Sholom Aleichem. Menachem Mendel the *schlimihl,* came with them. Not far off was Sholom Ber of Teplik, no longer the *nogid,* but a rag peddler; and behind him limped along Berel the Lame, who had gone to Heissin in his company on a memorable day. Mottel the cantor's son, and Ellie the tailor, and Leizer Wolf the butcher, and old Reb Yozifel, the pietists and the revolutionaries, the skullcaps and the bowler hats—they filed through the living room where he lay in state, they darkened the streets of the lower East Side, they waited for him at the cemetery. They heard the singing of the requiem—"God, full of mercy"—and it was as though a people were being consigned to the grave. Why, then, should they not mourn? Who was to speak for them now that Sholom Aleichem was dead, and who was to remember them if he was forgotten?

Sholom Aleichem lies buried in Mount Nebo Cemetery in Cypress Hills, Brooklyn. He had asked that his body be transferred, after the war, to the cemetery of his beloved Yehupetz; but this could not be done, and it is better so. In other respects the provisions of his testament were carried out. His grave is simple, and only his epitaph distinguishes it from those that surround it. He had said: "Let me be buried among the poor, that their graves may shine on mine, and mine on theirs."

THE SON

by ISAAC BASHEVIS SINGER

THE ship from Israel was due to arrive at twelve o'clock, but it was late. It was evening before it docked in New York, and then I had to wait quite a while before any passengers were let off. Outside it was hot and rainy. A mob of people had come to wait for the ship's arrival. It seemed to me that all the Jews were there: assimilated ones, and rabbis with long beards and side-locks; girls with numbers on their arms from Hitler's camps; officers of Zionis-tic organizations with bulging portfolios, Yeshiva boys in velvet hats, with wildly growing beards; and worldly ladies with rouged faces and red toenails. I realized I was present at a new epoch in Jewish history. When did the Jews have ships? And if so, their ships went to Tyre and Sidon, and not to New York. Even if Nietzsche's crazy theory about the eternal return were true, quadrillions and quintillions of epochs would have to pass before the smallest part of any-thing happening in the present would have happened before. But this waiting was boring and tedious. I measured everybody with my eyes, and each time I asked myself the same question: What makes him my brother? What makes her my sister? The New York women fanned themselves, spoke all at once with hoarse voices, refreshed themselves with chocolate and Coca-Cola. A non-Jewish toughness stared out of their eyes. It was hard to believe that only a few years ago their brothers and sisters in Europe went like sheep to the slaughter. Mod-ern Orthodox young men with tiny skullcaps hidden like plasters in their dense hair spoke loudly in English and cracked jokes with the girls, whose behavior and clothes showed no sign of religion. Even the rabbis here were different, not like my father and grandfather. To me, all these people appeared worldly and clever. Almost all, except myself, had secured permits to board the boat. And they got acquainted unusually fast, shared information, shook their heads know-ingly. The ship's officers began to descend, but they seemed stiff in their uni-forms, which had epaulettes and gilded buttons. They spoke Hebrew, but they had accents like Gentiles.

I stood and waited for a son whom I hadn't seen in twenty years. He was five years old when I parted with his mother. I went to America, she to Soviet Russia. But apparently one revolution was not enough for her. She wanted "the permanent revolution." And they would have liquidated her in Moscow if she hadn't had someone who could reach the ear of a high official. Her old Bol-shevik aunts who had sat in Polish prisons for Communist activity had inter-ceded for her, and she was deported, together with the child, to Turkey. From there, she had managed to reach Palestine, where she had brought up our son in a kibbutz. Now he had come to visit me.

He had sent me one photograph taken when he had served in the army and fought the Arabs. But the picture was blurred, and in addition he was wearing a uniform. Only now, as the first passengers began to come down, did it occur to me that I did not have a clear image of what my son looked like. Was he tall? Was he short? Had his blond hair turned dark with the years? This son's arrival in America pushed me back to an epoch which I had thought of as already belonging to eternity. He was emerging out of the past like a dream or a phantom. He did not belong in my present home, nor would he fit into any of my relationships outside. I had no room for him, no bed, no money, no time. Like that ship flying the white and blue flag with the Star of David, he constituted a strange combination of the past and the present. He had written me that of all the languages he had spoken in his childhood, Yiddish, Polish, Russian, Turkish, he now spoke only Hebrew. So I knew in advance that, with what little Hebrew I possessed from the Pentateuch and the Talmud, I would not be able to converse with him. Instead of talking to my son, I would stammer and have to look up words in dictionaries.

The pushing and noise increased. The dock was in a tumult. Everyone screamed and shoved themselves forward with the exaggerated joy of people who have lost the standard to measure achievement in this world. Women cried hysterically; men wept hoarsely. Photographers took pictures, and reporters rushed from person to person, conducting hurried interviews. Then occurred the same thing that always occurs when I am part of a crowd. Everyone became one family, while I remained an outsider. Nobody spoke to me, and I didn't speak to anybody. The secret power which had joined them kept me apart. Eyes measured me absent-mindedly, as if to ask: What is *he* doing here? After some hesitation, I tried to ask someone a question, but the other didn't hear me, or at least he moved away in the middle of my sentence. I might just as well have been a ghost. After a while I decided what I always do decide in such cases, to make peace with fate. I stood out of the way in a corner and watched everyone as they came off the boat, sorting them out in my mind. My son could not be among the old and middle-aged. He could not have pitch-black hair, broad shoulders, and fiery eyes—one like that could not have stemmed from my loins. But suddenly a young man emerged strangely similar to that soldier in the snapshot, tall, lean, a little bent, with a longish nose and a narrow chin. This is he, something screamed in me. I tore myself from my corner to run to him. He was searching for someone. A fatherly love awoke in me. His cheeks were sunken and a sickly pallor lay on his face. He is sick, he has consumption, I thought anxiously. I had already opened my mouth to call out, "Gigi" (what his mother and I had called him as a small boy), when suddenly a thick woman waddled over to him and locked him in her arms. Her cry turned into a kind of barking; soon a whole bunch of other relatives came up. They had snatched a son from me, who was not mine! There was a kind of spiritual kidnaping in the whole thing. My fatherly feelings became ashamed and stepped back in a hurry into that hiding place where emotions can stay for years without a sound. I felt that I had turned red with humiliation, as if I had been struck in the face. I decided to wait patiently from now on and not to allow my feelings to come out prematurely. Then for a while, no more passengers emerged. I thought: What is a son after all? What makes my semen more to me than somebody else's? What value is there in a flesh and blood connection? We are all foam from the same caldron. Go back a number of generations and all this crowd of strangers probably had a common grandfather. And two or three generations hence, the descendants of those who are relatives now will be strangers. It's all temporary and passing—we're bubbles on the same ocean, moss from the same swamp. If one cannot love everybody, one should not love anybody.

The passengers again began to come out. Three young men appeared together, and I examined them. None was Gigi and, even if one were, no one would snatch him from me anyhow. It was a relief when each of the three went away with someone else. None of them had pleased me. They belonged to the rabble. The last one had even turned around and thrown a bellicose look at me, as if he had in some mysterious way caught my deprecating thoughts about him and those like him.

If he is my son he will come out last, it suddenly occurred to me, and even though this was an assumption, somehow I knew that it would happen that way. I had armed myself with patience and with that resignation which is always there in me ready to immunize my failures and curb any desire I might have to free myself from my limitations. I observed each passenger carefully, guessing from the way he looked and was dressed his character and personality. Perhaps I only imagined it, but each face gave me its secrets and I seemed to know exactly how each of their brains was working. The passengers all had something in common: the fatigue of a long ocean trip, the fretfulness and unsureness of people arriving in a new country. Each one's eyes asked with disappointment: Is this America? The girl with the number on her arm angrily shook her head. The whole world was one Auschwitz. A Lithuanian rabbi with a round gray beard and bulging eyes carried a heavy tome. A bunch of Yeshiva boys were waiting for him, and the moment he met them he began to preach with the angry zeal of one who has learned the truth and is trying to spread it quickly. I heard him say, Torah . . . Torah . . . I wanted to ask him why the Torah hadn't defended those millions of Jews and kept them from Hitler's crematoriums. But why ask him when I knew the answer already?—"My thoughts are not your thoughts." To be martyred in God's name is the highest privilege. One passenger spoke a kind of German dialect, which was neither German nor Yiddish but a gibberish out of old-fashioned novels. And how strange that those who waited for him should chatter in the same tongue.

I reasoned that in the whole chaos there are precise laws. The dead stay dead. Those who live have their memories, calculations, and plans. Somewhere in the ditches of Poland are the ashes of those who were burned. In Germany, the former Nazis lie in their beds, each one with his list of murders, tortures, violent or half-violent rapes. Somewhere there must be a Knower who knows every thought of each human being, who knows the aches of each fly, who knows each comet and meteor, each molecule in the most distant galaxy. I spoke to him. Well, Almighty Knower, for you everything is just. You know the whole and have all the information . . . and that's why you're so clever. But what shall I do with my crumbs of facts? . . . Yes, I have to wait for my son. The passengers had again stopped coming out and it seemed to me that they had all disembarked. I grew tense. Hadn't my son come on that ship? Had I overlooked him? Had he jumped into the ocean? Almost everybody had left the pier, and I felt the attendants were ready to put out the lights. What should I do now? I had had a premonition that something would go wrong with that son who for twenty years had been for me a word, a name, a guilt in my conscience.

Suddenly I saw him. He came out slowly, hesitantly, and with an expression that said he didn't expect anybody would have waited for him. He looked like the snapshot, but older. There were youthful wrinkles in his face and his clothes were mussy. He showed the shabbiness and neglect of a homeless young man who had been years in strange places, who had gone through a lot and become old before his time. His hair was tangled and matted, and it seemed to me there were wisps of straw and hay in it—like the hair of those who sleep in haylofts. His light eyes, squinting behind whitish eyebrows, had the half-blind smile of an albino. He carried a wooden satchel like an army recruit, and a package wrapped in brown paper. Instead of running to him immediately, I stood and gaped. His back was already bent a little, but not like a Yeshiva boy's, rather like that of someone who is used to carrying heavy burdens. He took after me, but I recognized traits of his mother—the other half that could never blend with mine. Even in him, the product, our contrary traits had no harmony. The mother's lips did not pair with the father's chin. The protruding cheekbones did not suit the high forehead. He looked carefully on both sides, and his face said good-naturedly: Of course, he didn't come to meet me.

I approached him and asked unsurely, "*Atah,* Gigi?"

He laughed. "Yes, I'm Gigi."

We kissed and his stubble rubbed my cheeks like a potato grater. He was strange to me yet I knew at the same time I was as devoted to him as any other father to his son. We stood still with that feeling of belonging together that needs no words. In one second I knew how to treat him. He had spent three years in the army, had gone through a bitter war. He must have had God knew how many girls, but he had remained as bashful as only a man can be. I spoke to him in Hebrew, rather amazed at my own knowledge. I immediately acquired the authority of a father and all my inhibitions evaporated. I tried to take his wooden box but he wouldn't let me. We stood outside looking for a taxi but all the taxis had already gone. The rain had stopped. The avenue along the docks stretched out—wet, dark, badly paved, the asphalt full of ditches and with puddles of water reflecting pieces of the glowing sky, which was low and red like a metal cover. The air was choking. There was lightning but no thunder. Single drops of water fell from above but it was hard to know whether these were spray from the former rain or a new gust beginning. It hurt my dignity that New York should show itself to my son so gloomy and dingy. I had a vain ambition to have him see immediately the nicer quarters of the city. But we waited for fifteen minutes without a taxi appearing. Already I had heard the first sounds of thunder. There was nothing else to do but walk.

We both spoke in the same style—short and sharp. Like old friends who know one another's thoughts, we did not need long explanations. He said to me almost without words: I understand that you could not stay with my mother. I have no complaints. I myself am made of the same stuff. . . .

I asked him, "What kind of a girl is she—the one you wrote me about?"

"A fine girl. I was her counselor in the kibbutz. Later we went into the army together."

"What does she do in the kibbutz?"

"She works in the barns."

"Has she at least studied?"

"We went to high school together."

"When are you going to marry?"

"When I go back. Her parents demand an official wedding."

He said this in a way that meant—naturally, we two don't need such ceremonies, but parents of daughters have a different logic.

I signaled a taxi and he half protested. "Why a taxi? We could have walked. I can walk for miles." I told the man to drive us across Forty-second Street, up the lighted part of Broadway, and later to turn into Fifth Avenue. Gigi sat and looked out through the window. I was never so proud of the skyscrapers and of the lights on Broadway as that evening. He looked and was silent. I somehow grasped that he was thinking now about the war with the Arabs, and all the dangers which he had survived on the battlefield. But the powers which determine the world had destined that he should come to New York and see his father. It was as if I heard his thoughts behind his skull. I was sure he too, like myself, was pondering the eternal questions.

As if to try out my telepathic powers, I said to him, "There are no accidents. If you are meant to live, you have to remain alive. It is destined so."

Surprised, he turned his head to me. "Hey, you are a mind reader!"

And he smiled, amazed, curious, and skeptical, as if I had played a fatherly trick on him.

THE TESTIMONY OF MAJOR KAUFMAN

by HOWARD FAST

AFTER Major Kaufman had been sworn in and had given details of rank and position, Adams asked him to describe the events of the morning in question.

There was an electric quality in the courtroom on this afternoon. Outside, the clouds were gathering for rain. The heat was heavy and oppressive, and the ceiling fans, moving so slowly, appeared to be turning in liquid. Major Kaufman sat erect and withdrawn, the object of the whole population of the room, the officers of the court watching him seriously and intently, Major Smith and his two assistants sitting with the impatient frustration of hunters. The observers aslo watched and waited. Even Winston was intermittently held by the quality and mood of the place.

The thought came to Adams that this was a sanctuary—the only sanctuary in a world torn and twisted with every conceivable violence and hurt. But history was full of sanctuaries that crumbled.

Major Kaufman spoke to the court, yet he spoke through them and past them. Before he took the stand, he had offered no word or greeting to Adams. Adams could only wonder what his thoughts were—but such wonder and doubt were not a new experience during the last few days. Adams had come to ponder a great deal on the problems of a great many people.

"Lieutenant Winston," Major Kaufman said, "was brought to the hospital by two military policemen. That was early in the morning. These two policemen had been instructed by Major Kensington to bring their prisoner to the psychiatric section of the hospital. When the prisoner had been brought into our receiving room, Lieutenant Sorenson called for me. I came immediately, and as soon as I saw the prisoner, Lieutenant Winston, I realized that he was in a state of acute depression and, to some degree, shock."

"Mr. President?" Major Clement said to Thompson.

Thompson nodded, and Clement asked Kaufman, "How were you able to see that immediately, Major?"

"There were unmistakable signs. Depression translates into a condition of indifference. But the indifference is profound and pathological. The drive to live, to exist, a very important part of man's emotional structure, is submerged. When you have seen acute depression, you recognize it. Also, his breathing was labored. He sweated excessively. His facial muscles were without tone. And he was only in part aware of his surroundings—and therefore able to respond to those surroundings in a most limited sense. You must understand, sir, that I am attempting to describe a medical phenomenon in lay language."

"I realize that," Clement replied.

Colonel Winovich wanted to know exactly what Major Kaufman meant by depression. "I have heard that term for two days now, like someone might say cholera. I've been depressed. I imagine you have, Major. Why treat it like some hellish disease?"

"Because it can be more hellish than most diseases, sir, and because it is a disease. When a normal person is depressed, he is not experiencing what we call, in a medical sense, depression—and, happily, most people never have that experience. I'll try to explain this as simply as I can. Depression, pathologically, is a combination of fear and hostility turned inward against the organism which is experiencing this fear and hostility. In its extreme form, it is a condition of total repression, total frustration, and total hopelessness. That is why we speak of the very deep depression as being suicidal. Most suicides are the result of this type of pathological depression, although many different mental conditions can bring about depression."

"Is this a physical condition, Major?" Thompson asked him. "Like heart disease or kidney trouble?"

"It has its physical aspects. It affects the entire organism rather than any single organ, and it is accompanied by changes in blood pressure, pulse beat, and so forth. But the profound physical changes, I imagine, are chemical and have to do with various ductless glands and probably with the basic adrenaline-histamine balance."

"You say you imagine? Are you guessing? Don't you know?"

"There is a great deal about all disease that we don't know, sir, a great deal about the body that baffles all physicians. We grope and guess and attempt to learn. As for diseases of the mind, well, until a generation ago they were for the most part treated no better or more wisely than in the Middle Ages."

"Did you examine the patient, Major?" Adams asked now.

"I did."

"How often?"

"I examined him physically when he was admitted, that is, I took blood pressure, pulse, listened to heartbeat and breathing, tested reflexes, examined his eyes and ears—the whole procedure of a thorough physical examination. I ordered a cardiogram, since his pulse was rapid and his blood pressure dangerously high, and a blood test and urine analysis. This was repeated two days later. Each day, he had a superficial physical. In addition to this, I examined him verbally each day for five days."

"What do you mean by verbally, Major?"

"That is a method of conversation or interview by which we attempt to more fully diagnose the nature of a psychosis. Actually, I ask questions. The patient answers them. I attempt to lead the conversation and to elicit salient points of knowledge."

"Now, when the patient was admitted, he was sick, was he not?"

"I should not have admitted him if he was not sick."

"Was his sickness at the time of admittance mental or physical?"

"There is no separating the two, Captain. A man's mind is a part of his body—his brain and nervous system, these are parts of the body. Lieutenant Winston was a very sick man when we admitted him. He has recovered in some part from the fatigue and shock which he was suffering then, and I managed to bring his blood pressure down somewhat, but he is still a very sick man."

Major Smith rose with this and objected that Major Kaufman had no right to a diagnosis of a man he had not examined for weeks.

Mayburt put the objection aside, telling Smith, "We will not get into a dispute over this use of competence. The witness is a physician, and physicians are entitled to their observations as part of diagnosis."

"What is the nature of Lieutenant Winston's disease?" Adams then asked.

"Lieutenant Winston is suffering from paranoia. Paranoia is a generic term for a group of mental diseases which fulfill the terms of a general description. Medically speaking, I would describe paranoia as an organized irrational system of mentation and response—which is characterized by projecting into external society causation by unreal factors. It is persecutory in its direction and usually accompanied by intermittent depression."

"Could you describe it in lay terms, making the description at least in part a direct diagnosis of the defendant?"

Winston's interest had at last been wholly caught, and he watched witness and counsel with intense, trembling concentration.

"I can try, sir. Our habit is not to think these things through in ordinary language, and perhaps that is a fault. Let me begin by saying that the paranoid personality is not uncommon; but we do not consider people who have this personality pattern to be psychotic. We differentiate and ascribe the psychotic factor to the mind which organizes an entire irrational system. I am trying to simplify, but it is not easy.

"In the case of the defendant, the paranoid roots go back to childhood, and even in childhood the irrational system was in process of organization. In other words, Lieutenant Winston began to create in his mind a picture of society in general and human beings in particular that departed more and more from the reality, until at last he was utterly incapable of coming to grips with reality. At this point, he became the prisoner of his own system.

"Why this happened, I cannot say. There are factors in our society that do this to children but, I would speculate, only to children who have an area of specific weakness. These children develop a fear of people, a fear which increases with growth and intensifies itself constantly. And since this fear is unreal, without any foundation in society, it can be handled and controlled only with unreal defenses. Thus we get the persecution complex, which is the common and vulgar explanation of the paranoiac. But the paranoiac is basically afraid, and his fear is a disease, a sickness which so far society has not been able to cure.

"The paranoiac, as he matures, has only two choices—either to cope with his fears or to destroy himself. When he sets out to cope with his fears, he begins to fulfill a pattern which has come to be known as the power compulsion. Again, a misleading vulgarization. It is not power in itself which the paranoiac is driven to command—for power in itself is meaningless—it is power over those whom he fears. And since he fears all mankind, the accomplishment of power can never cure or even balance the paranoiac. It is only an analgesic, a temporary assuagement of his terrors.

"The other alternative is depression—and its ultimate conclusion, suicide. When the paranoiac's defenses of power and authority over others finally crumble beyond hope of repair or reconstruction, then the fear begins to submerge his personality. His personality begins to disintegrate, and this disintegration is progressive. In a manner of speaking, he retreats into himself, cuts his connections with the outer and real world, turns his fear and hatred upon himself—and destroys himself. Even if prevented from suicide, this disintegration will continue and the soul will die. It is usually during this stage that he becomes delusionary. Bereft of real power, he invents power and sometimes comes to believe that he is a tool of God, or more usually, he the master of God and God the tool. Thus, he frequently places God within him, as part of himself."

They were all listening intently, Winston's face staring and fixed, only the tic on his mouth breaking the immobility, the court leaning forward over the table—even Smith caught, attentive and silent.

It was not Adams but Colonel Mayburt who broke the silence after Kaufman had finished, asking, "Did this breakdown—the beginning of this disintegration you speak of—did this come as a result of the murder of Sergeant Quinn?"

It was to the point, the key to the point; and Kaufman considered it before he answered. Then he said, "No. It was the other way around. Lieutenant Winston was the only commissioned officer at Bachree. He had the power and the authority. But Sergeant Quinn broke down this authority. He undermined Lieutenant Winston. He laughed at him and mocked him, and the process of disintegration began. The murder of Sergeant Quinn was the last desperate effort of Lieutenant Winston to defend himself with the exercise of power. But already, at that point, he was insane. Yes, he was insane then and he is insane now," Kaufman finished coldly.

Winston rose, pointed a shaking finger at Kaufman, and screamed, "You're a lousy, mother-friggen Jew bastard liar! I'm sane! Sane! Sane—do you hear me, sane!"

BERMAN'S JOY

by EDWARD LEWIS WALLANT

IT HAD snowed just a little during the night, probably sometime around dawn; the horses' halters and yokes were lightly dusted with it and the streets had just enough of a fine, powdery snow to leave footprints. Everything was gray and the air was cold, with a damp penetration. Looking about at the buildings and stores made darker and dingier by the outlining white of the snow, Berman was surprised at his feeling of exaltation. He smiled at the cap of snow on a barber pole and the myopic stare of the barber peering through his steamed window as though at a blizzard.

What was it, he asked himself, trying to breathe reason into his mood. Just another morning heading for work with nothing to look forward to in the hours of the day except hard, cold work and the steady stream of insults from the anti-Semitic Irishman who bossed the job. He looked around the grimy, unattractive street as though to find some logical excuse for his feeling of happiness, for that peculiar airiness of spirit. In shop windows there were little tokens of Christmas and in some of the narrow front yards he passed, scraggly evergreens were decorated with baubles of bright-colored glass. It wasn't *his* holiday, although Hanukkah was also a week away. He thought briefly of the good, rich smell of his mother's cooking and of the warmth there would be in his house that night when relatives came to call and maybe some of his friends came up to drink glasses of his mother's homemade sweet wine and sit around one corner of the living room cracking walnuts and arguing politics until the older folks began shushing and tossing frowns at them.

But why feel so good, he asked himself, ignorant of the blessing of his youth and strength, for he knew only that. Only, he guessed, as though at a brief peek at mystery, there were times when joy awoke in him with a violence that declared itself invulnerable. This morning was one of those times. He felt he could go through all manner of terrors and pain with his joy showing intact at the end. Perhaps it was nothing more than a subtle physiological cycle, which gave him from time to time a great, instinctive appreciation for the very flow of blood in his veins. There were times like that morning in which the ability to swing his legs and taste the air seemed aspects of a stupendous endowment, which he acknowledged by smiles or little chuckles, so that people he came in contact with returned his good nature condescendingly, as though they thought him simple-minded. His own voice was a marvel to him, an amazing instrument he had to try even when he had nothing special to say. His mother and his older brother turned frowns on his little spurts of words, which showered on them like spray from an invisible source. Their own pleasures and happinesses were better integrated, were mixed more thoroughly with their grievances. They were always pretty much the same people.

"Hanukkah and Christmas—something, hah?" he had said to their sleepy morning faces, his voice throaty as though a laugh were just beneath. "Big doin's, some of the family coming over, all the Christmas trees for the *goyim*. Oh boy, it's something, I'll tell you." And he would know he was raving even before his brother growled that he was. But Berman knew, too, that his brother was powerless before that awesome vitality, and he only chuckled at his mother's disapproval.

He came up to the huge open trench in the street where a few of the men were already gathered, preparing to minister to the dark wound in the snowy roadway. His teeth sucked the cold, wet air from behind his smile. He had to chuckle at the irritated looks on their pinched faces, and that only made their expression deepen into anger.

"What's so funny, Yid?" the foreman demanded. He had thick, big-pored skin, and his shapeless fighter's nose was perforated and huge like an old potato. "You got a stupid face, you know that!"

"I got what God gave me," Berman said good-naturedly, shrugging and looking at the rest of the men, who seemed to relent, one or two even awarding him smiles in return.

"I got what God gave me," the foreman mocked. "Cut out the bullshit and let's get to work, hah! What do you think this is, Yid, a bank or somethin'? It's quarter to eight. Get your dumb Jew self down in that hole and start diggin'."

"Yessir, Mr. Foreman," Berman said, leaping gracefully down into the slushy trench.

One after another the other men followed, making wet, plopping sounds in the mucky trench bottom. The dirt was heavy with wetness and the throw to the top required a long heave. Before long the men stopped their conversation, putting everything into the great grunts of effort. Only Berman worked with a queer little smile. The foreman walked the length of the trench and back, his frown deepening every time his eyes fell on Berman. From down below almost everything on earth was invisible. Only the sky related to them, gray and shifty, impossible to gauge for depth or distance, so that one moment Berman saw it as an infinite realm of rolling, pearly space, only to feel in the next moment that he could reach up and touch it, that indeed it lay on his shoulders with great weight. Along the dark, raw-red edge of the ditch the foreman moved like some strange, menacing indicator, foreshortened and powerful.

Berman tossed him the flat smile as he straightened joyfully against the weight of the heavens, and rage piled up in the bitter, pitted face. Yet silence held, except for the abrasive sound of the shovels, the occasional clinks as they turned aside stones, and the heavy grunting. The dampness encompassed them, coming off the dirt walls of the hole like the wet breath of a great sleeping animal. With each effort, each straining of muscle, Berman's inexplicable joy mounted. Like a silent paean of music the sourceless delight swelled in him. He began singing, in a low monotone, the words of an old Hebrew song.

"*Dy dy, anu, dy, dy, anu, dyanu, dyanu-u . . .*"

The foreman's face came alight with threat. He almost seemed to be smiling in relief as though Berman had given him something he had been looking for.

"Cut out them Jew songs, Yid. And cut out that standing up to rest every five minutes. You're getting me mad, Yid." He squatted down on the lip of the trench to be closer to Berman, and his eyes shone with a gay war light. "Standin' there with that crappy grin on yer crappy Jew face . . . I'm gettin' fed up with you, Yid."

"I'm getting fed up with you, too," Berman said, matching the fierce gaiety of the Irishman. And then, deliberately, with his eyes on the potato nose just a few feet away, he began again to sing, "*Dy, dy, anu, dy, dy, anu . . .*" standing erect so it came out like some ancient war cry while all around him the other men stopped to lean on their shovels under the infinite height of the gray sky. The half-exposed pipe gleamed rustily in its wetness and the puddles in the mud reflected the pale light like flat chips of glass. A little wind blew tiny particles of wet snow off the top of the trench and Berman's face shone and tightened with its cold touch as he sang to the brooding, vital face over him.

"*Dyanu, dyanu-u-u . . .*"

"Your mother's a whore, Yid," the Irishman said, with a grin for the imminence of combat. And oddly Berman knew the foreman had lost his malevolence, that the fantastic insult was a sort of tribute, a ritual gesture toward battle. For the first time the Irishman was acknowledging him an equal, and he knew a perverse affection for the brutal-faced man because he himself was a battler deep inside, under the traditional repugnance for violence that Jews have.

So his own smile widened in abandon for a moment before he lunged for the man's feet and pulled them toward him. The heavy figure crashed into him and they fell into the soft, wet bottom of the trench. For a moment he was shocked at the dangerous strength of the embracing arms, the prodigious weight. They rolled silently in the mud while a low, awed murmur went up among the watching men. Berman found his face in the thick, watery mud. His eyes saw nothing and his mouth opened to the viscous atmosphere of earth and water. The powerful arms forced his ribs in on his lungs and for a moment he thought he would drown there in that viewless pit to the sound of splashing limbs and the low calls of encouragement from an invisible audience; until, with a spasm of desperate strength, he threw his own body into a spin and saw the colorless sky through his dirt-clogged lashes. But the massive arms continued the terrible oppression and blackness began filling the sky, too, as his brain died for air. He brought his head forward until his chin touched his chest, then snapped it back suddenly to crack with dull impact on the face of his opponent. And the arms opened to the snarl of pain so that Berman could spin his body over and over away from the squeezing arms. Then they were on their knees a few feet apart, each staring in amazement at the mud-covered visage of the other.

"C'mon, kike," the foreman said in a thick, hoarse voice as though he, too, had swallowed some of the mud. And Berman, with the gritty edge to his teeth, smiled his slumberous Yiddish curses and rose to his feet.

The foreman rushed him but Berman had time to bring up a punch of half-strength which put the heavier man into a halt just out of reach. Now he saw the size and great advantage in weight of his opponent as though for the first time, and he seized a hand-size rock from the ground near his feet. At that, the foreman, an old shillelagh fighter, gave a chuckle of pleasure and came up with a small Stillson wrench from out of nowhere.

"Oho, Yid," he cried, finding new delights in his opponent at every turn.

"Yes," Berman answered in acknowledgment as he swung his rock-laden hand. He met the thick shoulder of the Irishman, who bellowed his pain yet immediately swung his wrench in an expert counterblow which caught Berman on the lower chest with a crunching sound of breaking ribs. And Berman's gurgle of pain came out like a chuckle for the terrible game they played. He pushed the rock straight out in a spasmodic jab. It met the Irishman's face dead center and left a welter of blood mingled with the mud on the broken features.

The foreman wiped at his ruined mouth, looked at the undecipherable smear on his hand, and then lunged too suddenly for Berman to parry. The first blow caught Berman over the ear and knocked him down beside the half-exposed pipe. Then, as he felt his consciousness fade, the second blow, right after, crushed his hand against the cold pipe.

He smiled at the strangeness of not feeling that blow. Then he lay back to face the gray sky, and passed out.

He opened his eyes three days later. He was in his bedroom and there was a smell of raisins and chicken fat in his nostrils. Three of his friends ranged the wall shyly; a smile passed from one to another of them at the sight of his opened eyes. His mother came into the room, severe with her gray hair back in an iron-hard bun. Steam rose from her hands and as she drew close he saw she carried a bowl of soup for him.

"It's a party?" he queried brightly, his voice hoarse from disuse. "All my friends, dinner in bed . . . How come . . . just for this?" he said, touching the thickness of bandage on his head and glancing up toward it with a ludicrous expression. And then, as he lowered his hand, he saw the peculiar bandaging, in which he was unable to account for all the fingers.

"Misery, torturer, it's not enough, the aggravation you give me?" his mother said. "Oh, don't worry, you'll drive me to my grave soon enough. Go, joke that you only have a small hole in your head, that you only lost one finger. . . ."

Berman looked at his finger, or where his finger had been. Then he looked up at the faces of his friends, who looked away uncomfortably in anticipation of his shock. But he only began a broad grin, which widened and widened until it seemed his cheeks would split. His mother glanced worriedly toward the door, where his elder brother stood behind his thin, old-looking face.

"It's affected his head," his brother said solemnly.

Berman concurred, nodding the heavy weight of bandages and holding the bandaged stump up in the air.

"It's affected my head and my hand, too," he said in a strangled voice. "But you should see the other guy." Then he began to laugh, holding his hand to his head as though to keep it from shattering over the violence of his mirth.

And one by one, a little timidly in fear of the mother's disapproval, his friends began to laugh, too—stifled, mouth-covered laughs at first until, caught by the irrepressible merriment of the patient, they began bellowing with helpless shrugs for the mother and the frowning brother. And the room seemed to pulse and breathe with the sound until there was room for nothing else, so the mother began to smile angrily, then shake furtively for a moment. Then, defeated, she squealed and waved her condemnation at the folly of it. Even the older brother went through an elaborate series of winces and face-making, caught himself, and, horrified at his own weakness, whirled and hurried out of sight.

"Oh, you Berman," the short, wiry boy with the square head howled.

"Eeee-eee-eeeey-Yussel," shouted the husky youth named Riebold. "Such a time to laugh!"

"*Mashuginah,* insane, insane," Berman's mother protested, her apron up over her mouth. "Stop, stop before you hurt . . ." But she was engulfed in the laughter and went out defeated, her apron over her head as though in shame.

The friends writhed, hit each other, dropped into chairs, only to spring up again as though stung. And all the time Berman lay with the bandaged hand up to the bandaged head as though keeping the symbol of his peculiar delight before them, while he shook silently, tears streaming from his eyes, which he kept closed. His head throbbed to his shaking but he could not stop any more than his friends, who had become so susceptible because they had expected sorrow and pain and had been unnerved by relief when they found something altogether different.

One by one they emptied themselves of the hysteria and sank down on chairs, wiping their eyes and shaking out the little residues of mirth. Berman, too, lowered his hand weakly at last and began dabbing at his face with the sheet.

"Such a hero," Riebold said. "What's a finger to Berman!"

"Even the head is nothing to him," the small, wiry boy, whose name was Fox, cackled.

"Even the head," the third youth, a fat boy named Bonoff, echoed as though it were an example of the utmost wit.

"How's the Irisher?" Berman asked.

"Uglier than before," Fox said.

"He sent you a get-well card," Riebold said.

And they laughed at that again, not quite so hard as before, but fondly rather, as though in reminiscence of the uproarious joviality.

And Berman looked at his spirit to find his joy in one piece as he had known it would be, or maybe even greater now that it had been tried. His heart sang with that mysterious exaltation that had no basis in reason, no foundation of motive or history. There in the green-painted room with the cracks painted over like healed scars, among his friends and the cherished bric-a-brac his mother had brought from Russia with all the other worthless heirlooms, with the cold New England air intolerant against the puttied panes, in a world of common pain, present in his body and anticipated in his mind, he held to that odd transcendence, that bodiless flame both fragile and mighty which held him in a solitude he would not relinquish for all its loneliness.

His mother came in with a tray that held a bottle of wine and various-shaped glasses and a plate of her *kiche,* which melted on the tongue with the delicacy of a snowflake. So they sat around the bed, sipping the sweet wine, munching, talking, chuckling, toasting their fallen friend, who sat up now against his pillows like a king. Even his older brother came in to spread cigar smoke over the other warm smells. The lamp shone orange through the colored-glass shade, glinting on the lately displaced gas jets and making the smoke into floating amber yarn. The mother sat beside Bonoff and let herself be consoled, nodding to his murmured cheer, smiling a little as though half-convinced now that pain and worry were vanquished for the while.

But later, alone in the room which was suddenly invaded by moonlight as the clouds parted, Berman felt pain, strong and living in his head and where his finger had been, and he was swollen with the joy of it, burned with recognition, as though it were the overpowering evidence, irrefutable, of some towering presence.

THE JEWBIRD

by BERNARD MALAMUD

THE window was open so the skinny bird flew in. Flappity-flap with its frazzled black wings. That's how it goes. It's open, you're in. Closed, you're out and that's your fate. The bird wearily flapped through the open kitchen window of Harry Cohen's top-floor apartment on First Avenue near the lower East River. On a rod on the wall hung an escaped canary cage, its door wide open, but this black-type long-beaked bird—its ruffled head and small dull eyes, crossed a little, making it look like a dissipated crow—landed if not smack on Cohen's thick lamb chop, at least on the table close by. The frozen foods salesman was sitting at supper with his wife and young son on a hot August evening a year ago. Cohen, a heavy man with hairy chest and beefy shorts; Edie, in skinny yellow shorts and red halter; and their ten-year-old Morris (after her father)—Maurie, they called him, a nice kid though not overly bright—were all in the city after two weeks out, because Cohen's mother was dying. They had been enjoying Kingston, New York, but drove back when Mama got sick in her flat in the Bronx.

"Right on the table," said Cohen, putting down his beer glass and swatting at the bird. "Son of a bitch."

"Harry, take care with your language," Edie said, looking at Maurie, who watched every move.

The bird cawed hoarsely and with a flap of its bedraggled wings—feathers tufted this way and that—rose heavily to the top of the open kitchen door, where it perched staring down.

"Gevalt, a pogrom!"

"It's a talking bird," said Edie in astonishment.

"In Jewish," said Maurie.

"Wise guy," muttered Cohen. He gnawed on his chop, then put down the bone. "So if you can talk, say what's your business. What do you want here?"

"If you can't spare a lamb chop," said the bird, "I'll settle for a piece of herring with a crust of bread. You can't live on your nerve forever."

"This ain't a restaurant," Cohen replied. "All I'm asking is what brings you to this address?"

"The window was open," the bird sighed; adding after a moment, "I'm running. I'm flying but I'm also running."

"From whom?" asked Edie with interest.

"Anti-Semeets."

"Anti-Semites?" they all said.

"That's from who."

"What kind of anti-Semites bother a bird?" Edie asked.

"Any kind," said the bird, "also including eagles, vultures, and hawks. And once in a while some crows will take your eyes out."

"But aren't you a crow?"

"Me? I'm a Jewbird."

Cohen laughed heartily. "What do you mean by that?"

The bird began dovening. He prayed without Book or tallith, but with passion. Edie bowed her head though not Cohen. And Maurie rocked back and forth with the prayer, looking up with one wide-open eye.

When the prayer was done Cohen remarked, "No hat, no phylacteries?"

"I'm an old radical."

"You're sure you're not some kind of a ghost or dybbuk?"

"Not a dybbuk," answered the bird, "though one of my relatives had such an experience once. It's all over now, thanks God. They freed her from a former lover, a crazy jealous man. She's now the mother of two wonderful children."

"Birds?" Cohen asked slyly.

"Why not?"

"What kind of birds?"

"Like me. Jewbirds."

Cohen tipped back in his chair and guffawed. "That's a big laugh. I've heard of a Jewfish but not a Jewbird."

"We're once removed." The bird rested on one skinny leg, then on the other. "Please, could you spare maybe a piece of herring with a small crust of bread?"

Edie got up from the table.

"What are you doing?" Cohen asked her.

"I'll clear the dishes."

Cohen turned to the bird. "So what's your name, if you don't mind saying?"

"Call me Schwartz."

"He might be an old Jew changed into a bird by somebody," said Edie, removing a plate.

"Are you?" asked Harry, lighting a cigar.

"Who knows?" answered Schwartz. "Does God tell us everything?"

Maurie got up on his chair. "What kind of herring?" he asked the bird in excitement.

"Get down, Maurie, or you'll fall," ordered Cohen.

"If you haven't got matjes, I'll take schmaltz," said Schwartz.

"All we have is marinated, with slices of onion—in a jar," said Edie.

"If you'll open for me the jar I'll eat marinated. Do you have also, if you don't mind, a piece of rye bread—the spitz?"

Edie thought she had.

"Feed him out on the balcony," Cohen said. He spoke to the bird. "After that take off."

Schwartz closed both bird eyes. "I'm tired and it's a long way."

"Which direction are you headed, north or south?"

Schwartz, barely lifting his wings, shrugged.

"You don't know where you're going?"

"Where there's charity I'll go."

"Let him stay, papa," said Maurie. "He's only a bird."

"So stay the night," Cohen said, "but no longer."

In the morning Cohen ordered the bird out of the house but Maurie cried, so Schwartz stayed for a while. Maurie was still on vacation from school and his friends were away. He was lonely and Edie enjoyed the fun he had, playing with the bird.

"He's no trouble at all," she told Cohen, "and besides his appetite is very small."

"What'll you do when he makes dirty?"

"He flies across the street in a tree when he makes dirty, and if nobody passes below, who notices?"

"So all right," said Cohen, "but I'm dead set against it. I warn you he ain't gonna stay here long."

"What have you got against the poor bird?"

"Poor bird, my ass. He's a foxy bastard. He thinks he's a Jew."

"What difference does it make what he thinks?"

"A Jewbird, what a chuzpah. One false move and he's out on his drumsticks."

At Cohen's insistence Schwartz lived out on the balcony in a new wooden birdhouse Edie had bought him.

"With many thanks," said Schwartz, "though I would rather have a human roof over my head. You know how it is at my age. I like the warm, the windows, the smell of cooking. I would also be glad to see once in a while the *Jewish Morning Journal* and have now and then a schnapps because it helps my breathing, thanks God. But whatever you give me, you won't hear complaints."

However, when Cohen brought him a bird feeder full of dried corn, Schwartz said, "Impossible."

Cohen was annoyed. "What's the matter, crosseyes, is your life getting too good for you? Are you forgetting what it means to be migratory? I'll bet a helluva lot of crows you happen to be acquainted with, Jews or otherwise, would give their eyeteeth to eat this corn."

Schwartz did not answer. What can you say to a grubber yung?

"Not for my digestion," he later explained to Edie. "Cramps. Herring is better even if it makes you thirsty. At least rainwater don't cost anything." He laughed sadly in breathy caws.

And herring, thanks to Edie, who knew where to shop, was what Schwartz got, with an occasional piece of potato pancake, and even a bit of soupmeat when Cohen wasn't looking.

When school began in September, before Cohen would once again suggest giving the bird the boot, Edie prevailed on him to wait a little while until Maurie adjusted.

"To deprive him right now might hurt his school work, and you know what trouble we had last year."

"So okay, but sooner or later the bird goes. That I promise you."

Schwartz, though nobody had asked him, took on full responsibility for Maurie's performance in school. In return for favors granted, when he was let in for an hour or two at night, he spent most of his time overseeing the boy's lessons. He sat on top of the dresser near Maurie's desk as he laboriously wrote out his homework. Maurie was a restless type and Schwartz gently kept him to his studies. He also listened to him practice his screechy violin, taking a few minutes off now and then to rest his ears in the bathroom. And they afterwards played dominoes. The boy was an indifferent checker player and it was impossible to teach him chess. When he was sick, Schwartz read him comic books though he personally disliked them. But Maurie's work improved in school and even his violin teacher admitted his playing was better. Edie gave Schwartz credit for these improvements though the bird pooh-poohed them.

Yet he was proud there was nothing lower than C minuses on Maurie's report card, and on Edie's insistence celebrated with a little schnapps.

"If he keeps up like this," Cohen said, "I'll get him in an Ivy League college for sure."

"Oh I hope so," sighed Edie.

But Schwartz shook his head. "He's a good boy—you don't have to worry. He won't be a shicker or a wifebeater, God forbid, but a scholar he'll never be, if you know what I mean, although maybe a good mechanic. It's no disgrace in these times."

"If I were you," Cohen said, angered, "I'd keep my big snoot out of other people's private business."

"Harry, please," said Edie.

"My goddamn patience is wearing out. That crosseyes butts into everything."

Though he wasn't exactly a welcome guest in the house, Schwartz gained a few ounces although he did not improve in appearance. He looked bedraggled as ever, his feathers unkempt, as though he had just flown out of a snowstorm. He spent, he admitted, little time taking care of himself. Too much to think about. "Also outside plumbing," he told Edie. Still there was more glow to his eyes so that though Cohen went on calling him crosseyes he said it less emphatically.

Liking his situation, Schwartz tried tactfully to stay out of Cohen's way, but one night when Edie was at the movies and Maurie was taking a hot shower, the frozen foods salesman began a quarrel with the bird.

"For Christ sake, why don't you wash yourself sometimes? Why must you always stink like a dead fish?"

"Mr. Cohen, if you'll pardon me, if somebody eats garlic he will smell from garlic. I eat herring three times a day. Feed me flowers and I will smell like flowers."

"Who's obligated to feed you anything at all? You're lucky to get herring."

"Excuse me, I'm not complaining," said the bird. "You're complaining."

"What's more," said Cohen, "even from out on the balcony I can hear you snoring away like a pig. It keeps me awake at night."

"Snoring," said Schwartz, "isn't a crime, thanks God."

"All in all you are a goddamn pest and free loader. Next thing you'll want to sleep in bed next to my wife."

"Mr. Cohen," said Schwartz, "on this rest assured. A bird is a bird."

"So you say, but how do I know you're a bird and not some kind of a goddamn devil?"

"If I was a devil you would know already. And I don't mean because of your son's good marks."

"Shut up, you bastard bird," shouted Cohen.

"Grubber yung," cawed Schwartz, rising to the tips of his talons, his long wings outstretched.

Cohen was about to lunge for the bird's scrawny neck but Maurie came out of the bathroom, and for the rest of the evening until Schwartz's bedtime on the balcony, there was pretended peace.

But the quarrel had deeply disturbed Schwartz and he slept badly. His snoring woke him, and awake, he was fearful of what would become of him. Wanting to stay out of Cohen's way, he kept to the birdhouse as much as possible. Cramped by it, he paced back and forth on the balcony ledge, or sat on the birdhouse roof, staring into space. In the evenings, while overseeing Maurie's lessons, he often fell asleep. Awakening, he nervously hopped around exploring the four corners of the room. He spent much time in Maurie's closet, and carefully examined his bureau drawers when they were left open. And once when he found a large paper bag on the floor, Schwartz poked his way into it to investigate what possiblities were. The boy was amused to see the bird in the paper bag.

"He wants to build a nest," he said to his mother.

Edie, sensing Schwartz's unhappiness, spoke to him quietly.

"Maybe if you did some of the things my husband wants you, you would get along better with him."

"Give me a for instance," Schwartz said.

"Like take a bath, for instance."

"I'm too old for baths," said the bird. "My feathers fall out without baths."

"He says you have a bad smell."

"Everybody smells. Some people smell because of their thoughts or because who they are. My bad smell comes from the food I eat. What does his come from?"

"I better not ask him or it might make him mad," said Edie.

In late November Schwartz froze on the balcony in the fog and cold, and especially on rainy days he woke with stiff joints and could barely move his wings. Already he felt twinges of rheumatism. He would have liked to spend more time in the warm house, particularly when Maurie was in school and Cohen at work. But though Edie was goodhearted and might have sneaked him in, in the morning, just to thaw out, he was afraid to ask her. In the meantime Cohen, who had been reading articles about the migration of birds, came out on the balcony one night after work when Edie was in the kitchen preparing pot roast, and peeking into the birdhouse, warned Schwartz to be on his way soon if he knew what was good for him. "Time to hit the flyways."

"Mr. Cohen, why do you hate me so much?" asked the bird. "What did I do to you?"

"Because you're an A-number-one trouble maker, that's why. What's more, whoever heard of a Jewbird? Now scat or it's open war."

But Schwartz stubbornly refused to depart so Cohen embarked on a campaign of harassing him, meanwhile hiding it from Edie and Maurie. Maurie hated violence and Cohen didn't want to leave a bad impression. He thought maybe if he played dirty tricks on the bird he would fly off without being physically kicked out. The vacation was over, let him make his easy living off the fat of somebody's else's land. Cohen worried about the effect of the bird's departure on Maurie's schooling but decided to take the chance, first, because the boy now seemed to have the knack of studying—give the black bird-bastard credit—and second, because Schwartz was driving him bats by being there always, even in his dreams.

The frozen foods salesman began his campaign against the bird by mixing watery cat food with the herring slices in Schwartz's dish. He also blew up and popped numerous paper bags outside the birdhouse as the bird slept, and when he had got Schwartz good and nervous, though not enough to leave, he brought a full-grown cat into the house, supposedly a gift for little Maurie, who had always wanted a pussy. The cat never stopped springing up at Schwartz whenever he saw him, one day managing to claw out several of his tailfeathers. And even at lesson time, when the cat was usually excluded from Maurie's room, though somehow or other he quickly found his way in at the end of the lesson, Schwartz was desperately fearful of his life and flew from pinnacle to pinnacle—light fixture to clothes-tree to door-top—in order to elude the beast's wet jaws.

Once when the bird complained to Edie how hazardous his existence was, she said, "Be patient, Mr. Schwartz. When the cat gets to know you better he won't try to catch you any more."

"When he stops trying we will both be in Paradise," Schwartz answered. "Do me a favor and get rid of him. He makes my whole life worry. I'm losing feathers like a tree loses leaves."

"I'm awfully sorry but Maurie likes the pussy and sleeps with it."

What could Schwartz do? He worried but came to no decision, being afraid to leave. So he ate the herring garnished with cat food, tried hard not to hear the paper bags bursting like fire crackers outside the birdhouse at night, and lived terror-stricken closer to the ceiling than the floor, as the cat, his tail flicking, endlessly watched him.

Weeks went by. Then on the day after Cohen's mother had died in her flat in the Bronx, when Maurie came home with a zero on an arithmetic test, Cohen, enraged, waited until Edie had taken the boy to his violin lesson, then openly attacked the bird. He chased him with a broom on the balcony and Schwartz frantically flew back and forth, finally escaping into his birdhouse. Cohen triumphantly reached in, and grabbing both skinny legs, dragged the bird out, cawing loudly, his wings wildly beating. He whirled the bird around and around his head. But Schwartz, as he moved in circles, managed to swoop down and catch Cohen's nose in his beak, and hung on for dear life. Cohen cried out in great pain, punched the bird with his first, and tugging at its legs with all his might, pulled his nose free. Again he swung the yawking Schwartz around until the bird grew dizzy, then with a furious heave, flung him into the night. Schwartz sank like stone into the street. Cohen then tossed the birdhouse and feeder after him, listening at the ledge until they crashed on the sidewalk below. For a full hour, broom in hand, his heart palpitating and nose throbbing with pain, Cohen waited for Schwartz to return but the brokenhearted bird didn't.

That's the end of that dirty bastard, the salesman thought and went in. Edie and Maurie had come home.

"Look," said Cohen, pointing to his bloody nose swollen three times its normal size, "what that sonofabitchy bird did. It's a permanent scar."

"Where is he now?" Edie asked, frightened.

"I threw him out and he flew away. Good riddance."

Nobody said no, though Edie touched a handkerchief to her eyes and Maurie rapidly tried the nine-times-table and found he knew approximately half.

In the spring when the winter's snow had melted, the boy, moved by a memory, wandered in the neighborhood, looking for Schwartz. He found a dead black bird in a small lot near the river, his two wings broken, neck twisted, and both bird-eyes plucked clean.

"Who did it to you, Mr. Schwartz?" Maurie wept.

"Anti-Semeets," Edie said later.

THE GOLEM

by AVRAM DAVIDSON

THE gray-faced person came along the street where old Mr. and Mrs. Gumbeiner lived. It was afternoon, it was autumn, the sun was warm and soothing to their ancient bones. Anyone who attended the movies in the twenties or the early thirties has seen that street a thousand times. Past these bungalows with their half-double roofs Edmund Lowe walked arm-in-arm with Leatrice Joy, and Harold Lloyd was chased by Chinamen waving hatchets. Under these squamous palm trees Laurel kicked Hardy and Woolsey beat Wheeler upon the head with codfish. Across these pocket-handkerchief-sized lawns the juveniles of the Our Gang Comedies pursued one another and were pursued by angry fat men in golf knickers. On this same street—or perhaps on some other one of five hundred streets exactly like it.

Mrs. Gumbeiner indicated the gray-faced person to her husband.

"You think maybe he's got something the matter?" she asked. "He walks kind of funny, to me."

"Walks like a *golem*," Mr. Gumbeiner said indifferently.

The old woman was nettled.

"Oh, I don't know," she said. "*I* think he walks like your cousin Mendel."

The old man pursed his mouth angrily and chewed on his pipe stem. The gray-faced person turned up the concrete path, walked up the steps to the porch, sat down in a chair. Old Mr. Gumbeiner ignored him. His wife stared at the stranger.

"Man comes in without a hello, good-bye, or howareyou, sits himself down and right away he's at home. . . . The chair is comfortable?" she asked. "Would you like maybe a glass tea?"

She turned to her husband.

"Say something, Gumbeiner!" she demanded. "What are you, made of wood?"

The old man smiled a slow, wicked, triumphant smile.

"Why should *I* say anything?" he asked the air. "Who am I? Nothing, that's who."

The stranger spoke. His voice was harsh and monotonous. "When you learn who—or rather what—I am, the flesh will melt from your bones in terror." He bared porcelain teeth.

"Never mind about my bones!" the old woman cried. "You've got a lot of nerve talking about my bones!"

"You will quake with fear," said the stranger. Old Mrs. Gumbeiner said that she hoped he would live so long. She turned to her husband once again.

"Gumbeiner, when are you going to mow the lawn?"

"All mankind—" the stranger began.

"*Shah!* I'm talking to my husband. . . . He talks *eppis* kind of funny, Gumbeiner, no?"

"Probably a foreigner," Mr. Gumbeiner said, complacently.

"You think so?" Mrs. Gumbeiner glanced fleetingly at the stranger. "He's got a very bad color in his face, *nebbich*. I suppose he came to California for his health."

"Disease, pain, sorrow, love, grief—all are nought to . . ."

Mr. Gumbeiner cut in on the stranger's statement.

"Gall bladder," the old man said. "Guinzburg down at the *shule* looked exactly the same before his operation. Two professors they had in for him, and a private nurse day and night."

"I am not a human being!" the stranger said loudly.

"Three thousand seven hundred fifty dollars it cost his son, Guinzburg told me. 'For you, Poppa, nothing is too expensive—only get well,' the son told him."

"*I am not a human being!*"

"Ai, is that a son for you!" the old woman said, rocking her head. "A heart of gold, pure gold." She looked at the stranger. "All right, all right, I heard you the first time. Gumbeiner! I asked you a question. When are you going to cut the lawn?"

"On Wednesday, *odder* maybe Thursday, comes the Japaneser to the neighborhood. To cut lawns is *his* profession. *My* profession is to be a glazier—retired."

"Between me and all mankind is an inevitable hatred," the stranger said. "When I tell you what I am, the flesh will melt—"

"You said, you said already," Mr. Gumbeiner interrupted.

"In Chicago where the winters were as cold and bitter as the Czar of Russia's heart," the old woman intoned, "you had strength to carry the frames with the glass together day in and day out. But in California with the golden sun to mow the lawn when your wife asks, for this you have no strength. Do I call in the Japaneser to cook for you supper?"

"Thirty years Professor Allardyce spent perfecting his theories. Electronics, neuronics—"

"Listen, how educated he talks," Mr. Gumbeiner said, admiringly. "Maybe he goes to the University here?"

"If he goes to the University, maybe he knows Bud?" his wife suggested.

"Probably they're in the same class and he came to see him about the homework, no?"

"Certainly he must be in the same class. How many classes are there? Five *in ganzen*: Bud showed me on his program card." She counted off her fingers. "Television Appreciation and Criticism, Small Boat Building, Social Adjustment, The American Dance . . . The American Dance—nu, Gumbeiner—"

"Contemporary Ceramics," her husband said, relishing the syllables. "A fine boy, Bud. A pleasure to have him for a boardner."

"After thirty years spent in these studies," the stranger, who had continued to speak unnoticed, went on, "he turned from the theoretical to the pragmatic. In ten years' time he had made the most titanic discovery in history: he made mankind, *all* mankind, superfluous: he made *me*."

"What did Tillie write in her last letter?" asked the old man.

The old woman shrugged.

"What should she write? The same thing. Sidney was home from the army, Naomi has a new boy friend—"

"*He made* ME!"

"Listen, Mr. Whatever-your-name-is," the old woman said, "maybe where you came from is different, but in *this* country you don't interrupt people the while they're talking. . . . Hey. Listen—what do you mean, he *made* you? What kind of talk is that?"

The stranger bared all his teeth again, exposing the too-pink gums.

"In his library, to which I had a more complete access after his sudden and as yet undiscovered death from entirely natural causes, I found a complete collection of stories about androids, from Shelley's *Frankenstein* through Capek's *R.U.R.* to Asimov's—"

"Frankenstein?" said the old man, with interest. "There used to be Frankenstein who had the soda-*wasser* place on Halstead Street: a Litvack, *nebbich*."

"What are you talking?" Mrs. Gumbeiner demanded. "His name was Franken*thal,* and it wasn't on Halstead, it was on Roosevelt."

"—clearly showing that all mankind has an instinctive antipathy toward androids and there will be an inevitable struggle between them—"

"Of course, of course!" Old Mr. Gumbeiner clicked his teeth against his pipe. "I am always wrong, you are always right. How could you stand to be married to such a stupid person all this time?"

"I don't know," the old woman said. "Sometimes I wonder, myself. I think it must be his good looks." She began to laugh. Old Mr. Gumbeiner blinked, then began to smile, then took his wife's hand.

"Foolish old woman," the stranger said, "why do you laugh? Do you not know I have come to destroy you?"

"What!" old Mr. Gumbeiner shouted. "Close your mouth, you!" He darted from his chair and struck the stranger with the flat of his hand. The stranger's head struck against the porch pillar and bounced back.

"When you talk to my wife, talk respectable, you hear?"

Old Mrs. Gumbeiner, cheeks very pink, pushed her husband back in his chair. Then she leaned forward and examined the stranger's head. She clicked her tongue as she pulled aside the flap of gray, skinlike material.

"Gumbeiner, look! He's all springs and wires inside!"

"I *told* you he was a *golem,* but no, you wouldn't listen," the old man said.

"You said he *walked* like a *golem.*"

"How could he walk like a *golem* unless he *was* one?"

"All right, all right. . . . You broke him, so now fix him."

"My grandfather, his light shines from Paradise, told me that when Mo-HaRaL—Moreynu Ha-Rav Löw—his memory for a blessing, made the *golem* in Prague, three hundred? four hundred years ago? he wrote on his forehead the Holy Name."

Smiling reminiscently, the old woman continued, "And the *golem* cut the rabbi's wood and brought his water and guarded the ghetto."

"And one time only he disobeyed the Rabbi Löw, and Rabbi Löw erased the *Shem Ha-Mephorash* from the *golem's* forehead and the *golem* fell down like a dead one. And they put him up in the attic of the *shule* and he's still there today if the Communisten haven't sent him to Moscow. . . . This is not just a story," he said.

"*Avadda* not!" said the old woman.

"I myself have seen both the *shule and* the rabbi's grave," her husband said, conclusively.

"But I think this must be a different kind *golem,* Gumbeiner. See, on his forehead: nothing written."

"What's the matter, there's a law I can't write something there? Where is that lump clay Bud brought us from his class?"

The old man washed his hands, adjusted his little black skullcap, and slowly and carefully wrote four Hebrew letters on the gray forehead.

"Ezra the Scribe himself couldn't do better," the old woman said, admiringly. "Nothing happens," she observed, looking at the lifeless figure sprawled in the chair.

"Well, after all, am I Rabbi Löw?" her husband asked, deprecatingly. "No," he answered. He leaned over and examined the exposed mechanism. "This spring goes here . . . this wire comes with this one . . ." The figure moved. "But this one goes where? And this one?"

"Let be," said his wife. The figure sat up slowly and rolled its eyes loosely.

"Listen, Reb *Golem*," the old man said, wagging his finger. "Pay attention to what I say—you understand?"

"Understand . . ."

"If you want to stay here, you got to do like Mr. Gumbeiner says."

"Do-like-Mr.-Gumbeiner-says . . ."

"*That's* the way I like to hear a *golem* talk. Malka, give here the mirror from the pocketbook. Look, you see your face? You see on the forehead, what's written? If you don't do like Mr. Gumbeiner says, he'll wipe out what's written and you'll be no more alive."

"No-more-alive . . ."

"*That's* right. Now, listen. Under the porch you'll find a lawnmower. Take it. And cut the lawn. Then come back. Go."

"Go . . ." The figure shambled down the stairs. Presently the sound of the lawnmower whirred through the quiet air in the street just like the street where Jackie Cooper shed huge tears on Wallace Beery's shirt and Chester Conklin rolled his eyes at Marie Dressler.

"So what will you write to Tillie?" old Mr. Gumbeiner asked.

"What should I write?" old Mrs. Gumbeiner shrugged. "I'll write that the weather is lovely out here and that we are both, Blessed be the Name, in good health."

The old man nodded his head slowly, and they sat together on the front porch in the warm afternoon sun.

SOVIET RUSSIA

THE REVOLUTION AND THE ZUSSMANS

by DAVID BERGELSON

FROM Moscow came a letter from Mottie, the eldest, the disbarred student, and from Aleck, the "neither here nor there," the youngest, the redhead, who had been hanging around with Mottie for several years without coming to anything.

The letter was written in Mottie's cold hand, and opened with cold, formal greetings:

> To Father Hirshl Zussman,
> To Mother Sheindel,
> To Sister Mani,

(That is, to no one in particular.)

Both Mottie and Aleck signed, with stiff signatures one under the other, as to a protocol.

And both begged they be understood (the word "understood" underscored three times) and that the family enter their names for them in one of the new collectives, for a parcel of land located on the main road. The land was close to home—that was first, and secondly, neither of them, neither Mottie nor Aleck, could find anything to do in Moscow, nor anything, for that matter, to do at home. And—the Devil take it all!—there was no other way out.

At the Zussmans the letter was coldly read and considered (as if it were a letter from a sister-in-law asking for contributions toward her daughter's dowry) and afterwards shoved out of sight under the linen of the dining-room table, where were stored letters which were neither urgent nor yet to be entirely ignored: letters one would not want lost, but not always to be staring one in the face either.

The head of the house, tall, gaunt Hirshl Zussman, gray-blond, with deep pouches under his eyes, tapped with his fingers on the table, as if he were playing a piano. His tiny pupils, almost drowned in the whites of his eyes, lifted to the tops of his glasses, and stared over them in astonishment, as if they failed to recognize the world around him.

"What's the use?" he said mildly. "They are jackasses."

Sheindel, his wife, was a much more bitter person. Out of bitterness she had not spoken to her own sister for sixteen years.

The morning the letter arrived she had been returning from market (which the Soviet authorities had ordered, like a leper, outside the city proper). Her bag was heavy, and on her way she stopped a small boy and asked him in her most elegant manner: "Come here, little boy, and help me a little way with this bag."

But just as the boy started to relieve her of the bag, a young drayman called out from a nearby stall in the market: "Hey, boy, wait a minute! Drop that bag! We've been carrying bags for her long enough."

As soon as she arrived home she took herself to bed. The family was used to this. "She has a weak heart, and shouldn't even talk," they would say. Her bosom heaved, and she was obviously distressed, but whether it was because of the letter that had been received from her good-for-nothing sons, or because of what had happened in the market place, it was hard to tell.

The huge, nickel-plated bed on which she lay was in the smaller of the two rooms into which the Zussmans had been crowded, by Soviet order, with all of their cumbersome and ornate furniture. Reclining there, Sheindel had spoken to no one all day long, as if she were indeed seriously ill amid all the sick-bed paraphernalia, the pills and the lemons and the tubes and glasses. Or, as if it were one of those days long ago when she had just returned from some foreign watering place, and had exhausted herself telling all she had seen and done there. "Marvelous! They do things so wonderfully abroad."

Hirshl came into her room several times during the day, seated himself by her bed and sighed: "What's the use? They are jackasses."

Sheindel kept her head turned away from him. When he left the house, however, she raised herself slightly, and began to call out, in the plaintive voice of a sick person, but with the strength of a well one, to her daughter, Mani, a girl God had made taller than the rest of the girls in town for the express purpose of enabling her to wear a longer and hence more expensive fur coat than any of them. Mani answered her mother with reluctance. She would have much preferred to remain where she was at the window, staring out into the world. Until recently she had worn high heels and a tightly laced corset and, although with the changing times she had abandoned them, she still walked with mincing steps and spoke in a stifled tone. A thick sense of oppression hung over her, as if at any moment she expected the arrival of bad news. Well, now the bad news had arrived. And of all the letter that Aleck and Mottie had sent them there remained in her mind but one phrase, which, to say the truth, they might not even have written, but which stood out, nevertheless, clearly between the lines.

"What's the use of fooling ourselves any longer!"

She was afraid if she were to enter her mother's room with these words on her tongue, her mother would pick them up with a squeal.

"Of course! What's the use? We're hopelessly ruined."

And for this reason she dreaded to enter, because more than anything else she hated to hear her mother squeal.

Meanwhile, lanky Hirshl Zussman was dashing about the streets like mad, speaking to this and to that chance acquaintance, regardless of quality, for all the world as if the civil war were still raging and the town under bombardment. In which case, as Zussman had been fond of saying, "Rich and small are equal all."

More than with anyone, however, he consulted with Alter the butcher, of Little-Buczacze, an old sock of seventy, who had not forgotten to this day that he had once served the grandfather of Hirshl Zussman, and that the grandmother of this same Hirshl had lent him the money with which he had set up in business as a butcher.

So to Alter the butcher Zussman now told all of his troubles, just as in the old days on a journey he used to unburden his heart to his coachman.

Of this new confident, Hirshl himself once said, half in earnest: "What's the harm? Once we used to ask advice of the wealthy, today we have to ask it of the poor. Because today the poor are the wise ones. . . . No?"

And Alter advised him thus: "What is there to lose? Suppose you do enter the names of your children, what's the harm?"

Shortly afterwards, the butcher called on Zussman to inform him that he and his five sons were all going to enter their names. And that if he intended to sign for Mottie and Aleck it would be better for all parties concerned if they all went into the same collective. And that he had already spoken to his children about it.

Some evenings later he paid a second call, and sat for a long time silent, yet all the while smiling as if pleading without words for them to listen to him as to a good friend. And when no one encouraged him, he burst suddenly into speech, saying:

"In God's name—if they are actually giving away two to three desyatins land to each member of the family, then why not? Why not all sign? It would be a pity to lose the extra six to nine desyatins, especially since the land seems to be good land, so they say at any rate. First class."

Several weeks passed. And not a single mention was made in the house of the fact that the father, Hirshl, had entered all their names. The mother held her tongue because she did not wish her sons, her burdens, God spare them, to accuse her of failing to do her duty towards them, of placing obstacles in their way. And Mani kept quiet because she feared another call from the Little-Buczacze butcher.

Until one fine day they received a visit from a strange young man, who carried a heavy portfolio under his arm. He seated himself, and spread out a number of strange documents on the table before him. And he inquired whether these were not the same Zussmans who once owned the brandy distillery in Dobra. Whether they had not once owned the house they now lived in, and other houses, since nationalized.

The Zussmans brightened up at once. Some time ago they had written abroad inquiring about payment of insurance due them on a policy they held with the American Insurance Corporation, with whom they had been insured previous to the war. And here!—a proof that writing could do no harm, since the company had for a fact sent its agent.

But the strange young man stared at them in wonder.

"Policy? What policy?"

It turned out he was no agent, but a Jew and a Communist, sent to investigate applicants for land in the new settlements.

He gazed thoughtfully at the tall, gaunt Hirshl; he addressed a few words to Sheindel, who hastily excused herself, saying she had a weak heart and could not talk, and should as a matter of fact be lying in bed. He threw a hasty glance in the direction of the languid figure of Mani, who stood at the window with her back turned as if she were angry with them all. At length he asked: "And who among you will work the land?"

To which Zussman answered hastily that there were two other children, sons, in Moscow. That one of them was a disqualified student, but that the real difficulty was with the second son. "A sort of—I don't know how to describe him—just a plain rascal. A redhead, of all things, with freckles on every part of his face, and even on his ears. When he was born, everyone marveled. How was it possible? For never before in the history of our family has there been a redhead." And he was the real reason for their wanting the land. He was the real trouble. You sent him to school, and he played truant, for what, did you suppose? So that he could help the coachman clean the stables. And in time, he, too, began to smell of the stables. No matter how much you washed him and scrubbed him, the odor of the stables still clung to him.

All this he told the strange young man, in familiar and friendly fashion. Almost with enthusiasm.

But the thoughts of the young man seemed elsewhere. The story of the redhead, the rascal, he seemed scarcely to hear. And as Zussman continued, he showed signs of increasing dissatisfaction. He shifted in his seat, and he began to ask questions that had nothing to do with the subject.

Questions that involved a suspicion that the Zussmans were, perhaps, not so poor as they appeared. That they might have hidden resources, gold, or jewels, say, or other treasures. When the young man left he was still far from satisfied.

But some days later they heard their application had been accepted. And immediately it became clear that the land really must have some value, "since, see, they do not give it to anybody."

And there called on them again, and sat until late in the evening, the sticky-eyed butcher of Little-Buczacze, who rambled on in this fashion: "My advice . . . you should not wait for the boys to arrive, but grab right away, and build yourself an any-sort-of house near the land that is being divided. Because nowadays, if you grab nothing, you have nothing. And once you have grabbed, nobody can take it away from you. That is one thing."

Another thing. How much, in God's name, could such a piece of land cost? And if they did not wish to retain it, if things went badly, they could find a purchaser. Even he, Alter or one of his sons, might buy it. He could talk it over with his sons, who planned to leave for the settlements within a week, to go on the land.

Early summer came to the settlements, and not far from the zemliankes, lean-tos with thatched, slanting roofs, thrown up by the sons of Alter the butcher, stood a newly-built cottage, whitewashed once, and then over again, and left with open windows and doors facing the sun. The Zussmans had had it built. . . . Even if they didn't settle on the land, it wouldn't hurt to have a cottage for the summer. What harm was there in that?

Around the house in all directions wild, green fields.

Winds that were meant to turn the long arms of windmills swept over the fields. And since there were no windmills to turn, they amused themselves by whirling through the open door and windows of the house, into the kitchen and out again. And the rains washed away all signs of whitewash, of newness, and the cleared space around the house grew green again in great haste.

July came, with thirty-one days, much as other years. But this year they were long-drawn, parched and dusty days, driving people from the city to summer places.

So one midday, under the blazing sun, there drove up to the house, first a wagon-load of furniture, and afterwards, in a hired carriage, Hirshl Zussman, his wife and daughter. They surprised the house in its desolateness, and for a while they stood in the middle of the road amazed, and as if they had come for no other purpose than to gaze and to wonder:

"Well now! . . . In the middle of an empty field!"

"Well now! . . . Not one tree!"

From being shaken up and down during the five-hour journey, Sheindel had acquired a hiccough, and they went to the nearby settlement to get her a glass of water. Alter and his sons were away in the fields, so they sought refuge in a strange lean-to, whose sole occupant was a pregnant woman who sat fanning herself in the shade. There they drank milk, without knowing whether or not to pay (the woman might feel offended) and chatted with her about various things, the dust, the heat in town, the hard times. And to live out here in the fields, they observed, was also, it would seem, no great pleasure.

"Hard, these days, what?"

They conversed thus amiably with the woman, chiefly of the heat in the city, from which, they said, they had simply had to run away.

Toward evening they went back to their own hut, reluctantly, and on the face of each was a look that denied responsibility for having come. At the door of their cottage they paused.

"Quite a walk, so to speak."

"Breathe deep, breathe deep. Breathe the air. Like sauerkraut."

As if angry with all the world, they retired early.

The next day, however, they hung curtains on the windows, and placed heavy iron bars on the door. They would remain only as long as the hot weather lasted. And this they were doing only because of Sheindel's health.

But when all was said and done, it was less dusty here than in town. All around were open, fresh fields, and not too far from the house, moreover, there was a small green forest, where one could go during the heat of the day and find refuge in the shade.

Husband and wife became extremely solicitous of each other's health, and began to exhort each other to take long walks, to breathe deeply the fresh air, to take on flesh. And because the place was really empty and bare as compared with a real summer home, Hirshl Żussman found it necessary to repeat several times a day: "I tell you, Sheindel, it's not half bad here."

Every morning Zussman promenaded around the house as punctually as if he were under doctor's orders. As he walked, his mind revolved many things: the white linen bag that contained the family treasures, because of which they had barred doors and windows; figures that had to do with former property and investments; how much would the nationalized houses be worth, or the distillery, if, for example, they were turned back to him this very day? His mind grew lighter adding up the imaginary profits and his heart lifted. He gained in health and in spirits. And finding himself lighter of heart, he began to take notice of things around him, to listen to the twittering of the birds in the woods on the other side of the main road. He would call out to his wife: "Sheindel! Hurry! Come out here! Sheindel, listen! How nice!"

Thus the hot summer months came to an end, and found the Zussmans with healthy full cheeks, tanned faces, bodies that had begun to fill out into natural lines and to take on the odor of things around them, of green fields and green forest.

The days grew shorter. Night fell with unexpected suddenness. Sly, chill wisps of air gave sudden and unexpected tickles to body and spirit. Idle hours began to weigh heavy pounds. The floors in the little hut began to answer one's tread, sorrowfully, and echo one's thoughts: "What now shall we do here?"

And now during the twilights, sounds that had not reached them when the air was thick and heavy drifted with ease across the fields. The weary summer withdrew its weight from the air, and its chirping insects from the fields. The noises from the colony could be heard plainly now in the Zussman home. And every call that came floating over the fields, every sound of laughter, every blow of a hammer seemed to Zussmans to carry a reproach for their idleness and isolation.

The ears of the Zussmans became sharpened. They strained to hear these accusations, and when all was silent it was even worse. Then they felt as if they were being completely ignored, as if the settlers were indifferent to what was being done, or not being done, in the hut of the Zussmans. They felt cut off, alone.

Often on such twilights the yellow buggy of the agricultural expert stood outside the settlement while the expert made his rounds among the settlers.

To the expert would flock the people of the settlement. They would surround him, listen attentively to his talk, explain and argue. They would take him from cottage to cottage, show him their implements, their farms, their possessions, besiege him with requests for advice, with stories of their troubles. Lights would appear in the windows of the huts, one after another, as the expert entered them, and as he went from house to house the crowd would follow him.

During all this buzz of activity, the Zussmans would remain inside their hut, hushed and trembling, in a state of terror lest at any moment the expert enter their house and inquire: "And in what department are you entered in the collective? What work are you doing?"

Yet, when they heard the sound of the buggy's wheels departing, they felt, somehow, not relieved, but slighted and angry. Why did not the expert visit them, after all? True, he was a Communist, but after all an educated man, really one of them, and maybe of a good family.

"Why? Why?"

The first rains began to fall, in a steady downpour. Sheindel remembered her weak heart, and took to her bed. And as she stayed day after day in bed, not only she but every member of the family seemed to be suffering from a weak heart. They spoke in whispers, and the tall daughter, Mani, returned to her post by the window and stood for long hours staring into the rain. She seemed, as always, to be expecting bad news. She waited so long that at last, one day at noon, she heard a familiar noise in the house; she awoke as if from a dream to hear a familiar voice, crying: "Mazeltov!"

The old butcher, Alter, was calling on them again.

Alter the butcher had just returned from the city. He brought with him the distressing news that during their absence their lodgings had been turned over to another family, only two weeks ago. Sheindel, in the next room, caught his words, and let out a shriek that could be heard for miles around. Everyone began talking at once.

"Our rooms . . . taken!"

"Who could have known?"

"But who leaves a house unoccupied in such times?"

"So . . . we're stuck here."

"Do you hear? Just two weeks ago."

"And now it's too late."

They gave Zussman no rest, until one day he left for the city, to be gone several days. He accomplished nothing, but looked almost as pleased when he returned as if he had run into a great stroke of luck.

"Listen," he said. "The man who has taken our lodgings, he's not at all unreasonable. 'Move out?' he said. 'By all means. Only find me another lodging.'"

Therefore, the old man, the Little-Buczacze butcher, began to call on the Zussman family regularly every evening to give advice. From his shrunken body came the smell of the fields and of sour pickles. He sat in a chair, blinked his swollen eyes, took snuff, and with exasperating slowness recited the troubles of the colonists, told what the future held for them, explained just how each member of the settlement stood now that the first summer was over.

"Some tell me this summer is for our credit in the next world, but I tell them, not so. Here are the figures. You will manage through the winter. You will manage."

The air around him is charged with impatience. The women in the house are tense and nervous. They refuse to leave the bedroom as long as Alter the butcher remains; they lie both in one bed, and listen angrily through the wall. Zussman himself paces the floor nervously. He, too, is waiting for his visitor to go, but the old man has plenty of time.

"Che . . . I am no fool. The others are skeptical, but I say, from the earth one can make a living."

When he is gone, and the family has retired, Hirshl pulls his blanket over his ears to escape the sound of his wife's reproaches.

"We must get out of here. We must escape."

"Get done with it, do you hear?"

"Find a house in the city!"

"Well . . . then we will rent a place. Why don't you rent a place?"

Zussman begins to make frequent trips to the city to rent a lodging there. And it reaches the point where they are prepared to move, when a letter comes from their two sons, whom they had almost forgotten. The letter says, wait! They, Mottie and Aleck, are coming. The family reads the letter with dilated nostrils, and with bitter protest on their lips.

"What are they running here for? . . . What's so wonderful here?"

The first to arrive from Moscow was the youngest, Aleck, the good-for-nothing redhead with the freckles.

The first thing he did on arrival was to prepare rough bedding for himself on the hard kitchen floor on which he flung himself face down and slept for a good two hours.

While he slept, his baggage, his clothes, his personal effects were closely examined.

"Look! Look at the holes!"

"Look, how ragged!"

"He has come here without a penny."

"And without an idea in his head."

The ideas, they reasoned, Mottie would have. Mottie would have plans for the future.

"Aleck, when will Mottie be here?"

Aleck awakes, rubs his eyes and yawns. Without answering he goes to the kitchen sink and washes himself. And before they can begin to talk to him he is gone. Away to the settlement, where he holds long conversations with Alter's sons. He inspects their household, hops on their wagon and is off with them to the fields.

From one of them he borrows an axe.

With the axe he disappears for long hours into the woods, returning on a borrowed wagon, loaded with poles and branches. And without further ado, he begins to build a fence around the house.

The Zussmans watch him with heavy hearts.

"What is he up to now? . . . What can be the purpose of that?"

Mani, from her station at the window, has a view of all that he is doing, but she stares beyond him and his work. The line of poles that Aleck is planting has reached the window, and now Aleck notices his sister and calls out to her: "Annie! Annie! Come out and hold this pole a minute."

His sister stares at him with eyes full of hatred and contempt, and without answering leaves the window and retreats into the depths of the bedroom. Aleck calls out to her a second time, but she does not answer. So Aleck leaves, and returns shortly afterwards with the granddaughter of Alter the butcher, a sturdy girl of fifteen, with broad feet, broad nose and mouth, and a plump smiling face. She holds the pole with both hands while Aleck refills the hole around it with the fresh-dug earth, and stamps it with both feet. The butcher's granddaughter grins as she watches him. At intervals, with shameless curiosity, she peers into the window of the cottage.

This is too much for the Zussmans inside. They draw the curtains and retreat to the privacy of the inner room, where they remain until the work outside is finished and the girl gone home.

The next day they give Aleck money to buy a suit and overcoat and a pair of shoes for himself in town.

They say to him: "You look like a tramp!"

Aleck drives to town, and returns with five chickens and a rooster, but with no suit or overcoat or shoes.

With part of the money, they learned later, he entered into an arrangement with a neighbor, whereby part of a field was his to plant. Meanwhile he put the chickens into the enclosure and gathered crumbs and bits of food from the table to feed them. He also raked up a bit of ground for them to scratch around and watched them with great glee when they began to find worms. As soon as he woke in the morning, he went immediately into the yard to tend his poultry. And almost every day the butcher's granddaughter came over, tapped the bellies of the chickens and told him which ones contained eggs.

"He is the only soul in the wide world on whom the years make no impression," said his family. "Neither the years nor the family misfortunes. He has remained with the mind of a child."

The final blow was when he found it necessary to his health and well-being to buy a dog, a hound of dubious ancestry, which he kept chained in the yard, and for which he built a kennel not far from the house.

This dog was a lazy, woebegone creature, with not enough spirit even to bark at the approach of strangers. But no sooner had the dog arrived than the rooster began to perk up, to feel at home, to crow lustily every morning early, under the window, destroying the last luxury that remained to the Zussmans from their former days of prosperity—the luxury of sleeping late, forgetful of the world and its troubles.

Sheindel groaned loudly whenever the rooster crowed; groaned loudly, and called out loudly to Hirshl, so that Aleck might hear.

"Hirshl . . . I have a weak heart. I beg you, Hirshl, go out into the yard, I beg you, Hirshl, and strangle that rooster."

A month later Mottie arrived, a shrunken, haggard figure of a man, stooped, as if he wished to conceal within himself his great height.

Instead of his pince-nez, he now wore small eyeglasses with nickel rims, the sort that peasants buy from pushcarts at a groschen a pair. His black mustache was too large for his peaked, narrow face; his long hands he kept crammed deep in his pockets, as if to hide them from sight. And about him was an air of melancholy that was a silent accusation against his parents who had sought to make him an intellectual, cramming his head since childhood with knowledge, until now in his nine-and-twentieth year he had discovered it all valueless, had found it necessary to take himself in hand, to say to himself, short and sharp: Look here, young man, nobody needs your learning.

Outside of his habit of keeping his hands deep in his trousers pockets, he had brought nothing back from Moscow.

When he had been home a few days his father began to discuss matters with him, as with an older, wiser person. How his property had been taken from him down to the very last house, and how to the very end it had appeared that something would turn up, someone would intervene in his behalf. Well, and after that, they had closed the distillery, which had remained closed for a time, and now was being opened under new management.

"That's what really hurts. The young fellows who now have the distillery in charge, they are brothers-in-law, so they say, who before the war kept a koropke in Charkov. Well, I'll tell you, when they begin to look around, when they begin to consider, they will wonder whether it really pays to change. What do you think?"

And the mother complained to Mottie of Aleck's conduct, how strangely Aleck was acting.

"Crazy! . . . Chickens and dogs and butchers' granddaughters. Working like a peasant. . . . Others in the city haven't knuckled under. . . . They are still doing something. . . . And what will become of us when we eat up the last of our savings?"

Mottie looks at his mother and father, not with his eyes, but with his eyeglasses, and seems to hear them in the same fashion, with his eyeglasses. When they are near him, he seems desperately unhappy. He is silent and reserved, like a stranger.

With Aleck he is a different person. They talk in brotherly fashion. Together they walk out into the yard, and Aleck explains to Mottie how things will look when he is finished, shows him the stable that is being erected, and the barn. The other Zussmans watch them through the window, mystified.

Mottie goes out with Aleck to the plowed fields, and together they cross over to the settlement. The agricultural expert drives up in the yellow buggy, and the brothers join in the circle that forms around him.

That evening Hirshl takes himself again to his son; and the sister, Mani, leaves the house and is gone a long while. She cannot stand Mottie's silence. When she returns both Mottie and Aleck are asleep on pallets they have spread for themselves on the kitchen floor. But the house is not yet quiet. From the second chamber comes the sound of her father's voice, reasoning, pleading with Sheindel.

"But who listens to me? . . . And if nobody listens, what's the use of speaking?"

Long, interminable expostulations.

There is a pause. The conversation shifts to Mani. Papa, Mamma, they never stop worrying about her, about their daughter—her future, her age and prospects. Mani lifts her head from the blanket, knocks on the intervening wall, and calls: "Be still! I want to sleep!"

The next morning, more trouble.

Aleck wants money. He wants to buy a wagon and two horses. It is already the end of August, he points out, and all the other colonists have their fields ready for the winter crops.

The answer comes as if it has been long prepared: "There is no money. . . . Where shall we get it?"

Aleck looks at them sharply, and winks towards the second chamber.

"From in there . . . from the linen sack, under the mattress."

No one answers him.

Then Aleck calls, "What do you say, eh, Mottie?"

Instead of answering, Mottie puts on his hat and coat, and walks out of the house.

Aleck points in the direction of the departing Mottie, strikes an attitude, and shows his teeth.

"Look . . . he hates you all, he does. Because of you he was shut out of the university. Yes, because of you. You gave us an education, you did. . . . Well, what good are we?"

At this the tall girl turns around from her customary post at the window and glares at Aleck.

"Idiot!" she says. "You are acting theater!"

And Aleck gets no money.

Nevertheless, a week later, he rides away in good spirits with a neighbor, and when he returns he is seated in a new wagon, drawn by two horses. Behind the wagon trots a colt.

Quiet for a few days. Then one morning a piercing shriek comes from the second room. Hirshl and Mani rush in to find Sheindel in a dead faint. Before her lies open the linen bag that contains the family treasures. Everything is in good order. Only a small jewel box containing a diamond ring is missing.

Mottie and Aleck were not at home. They left for the fields at dawn, and did not return until the lamps had been lit. When they came back that night, they rode in the new wagon, drawn by two horses, and behind the wagon followed the colt. This could only mean one thing. Mottie was definitely on Aleck's side, Mottie would not care if Aleck had bought the horses and wagon with the stolen ring.

Zussman paced the floor day and night, turning over in his mind this new and alarming development. His wife gave him no rest. She kept pushing him to speak to Mottie.

"Well, aren't you going to do anything about it?"

Zussman had prepared in his mind everything he was going to say: "I understand. . . . The spirit of the times . . . Children know more nowadays than the parents. They have the right to take matters in their own hands, apparently."

And more in the same sarcastic vein. But when he finally gained courage to approach Mottie it was nightfall, and the brothers had just come back from the fields. Mottie cut him short at the first words: "Let me alone! I'm tired."

And turned aside to help Aleck unharness the horses.

These were the last words they got from Mottie. "Let me alone." Now the sons no longer talk to the other members of the family. The family is definitely split into two factions. On one side, Hirshl, his wife and daughter. On the other side, Aleck and Mottie.

The two sons work every day in the fields, from morning until night. They forget to wash their faces, they neglect to shave their beards. And in this fashion, unshorn and unkempt, they go among people, to the meetings in the settlements. They help carry lumber to the houses that are being built for the winter months, and take, like the others, a portion of hay as payment for their labors. And they come home exhausted, fall asleep immediately, without a word to any member of the family. They give no ear to Zussman's daily argument about his nationalized houses and his distillery which is in operation again, under new management. . . .

This last Zussman learns from Alter the butcher, who carries meat every day to Dobra.

Alter fills the cottage with the smell of freshly killed meat, blinks his red eyes, takes snuff, and marvels how everything has turned somersault and back.

"The sugar-factory is operating. . . . The distillery is operating. . . . In a word—just like in the good times."

He has nothing else to tell, but lingers nevertheless.

"They'll be needing oxen now in the distillery, don't you think? . . . And live-stock is cheap these days. Dirt-cheap."

His talk creates a stir in Zussman's bosom.

When the butcher is gone, he paces the floor in his carpet slippers, and cannot fall asleep until late in the night. And in the morning, as soon as he rises, he begins to write furiously on little scraps of paper: how many thousand pounds grain, how much wood, how many horses and oxen; and how much this same grain, wood, and so on, would be worth at the current prices, let us say. He goes over these figures again and again, week after week. And because no one else in the house takes the slightest interest in figures, Zussman little by little forms the third party in his house, with a separate life of his own.

The first snows have fallen in the fields. Sheindel gives her husband no rest: when will they be moving back to town? When will he rent a house in town? And she talks of the bargain he might make with the tenant who now occupies their house in town. But Hirshl scarcely hears her. He is entirely occupied with his figures, and mutters often to himself: "Well, yes . . . the reckoning is correct."

In the fields the winter winds blow and howl in far different fashion than they do in town, far more ferociously. The winds clap hands in joy, clap hands in derision, sweep the snow into mounds which they tumble down again, play a game of cat and mouse with each individual snowflake. From the cottage that stands close to the road one can watch this game being played, day in, day out.

The tall girl, Mani, leans against the window frames and gazes dreamily out into the open fields. The roof above her creaks and groans, and threatens to cave in under its burden of snow.

Mottie and Aleck come on the scene, intrude themselves into her vision. They find it necessary, for some strange reason, to heap up straw against one side of the house, and as fast as they pile the straw up, the wind tears into it, snatches away the straw, and carries it off into the fields. Someone from the settlement comes over to give advice. They borrow ladders, and place weights on top to press the straw down. The wind howls, and snatches mischievously at the heap, but must content itself now with smaller handfuls.

In the fields the winds whirl and blow in far different fashion, much more fiercely than they do in town.

Fiercely they whirl and blow for eight days, and then calm down. The snow stops, and it is possible to dig a path. Cloaked and covered so that only the tip of his nose and his blond-gray mustache can freeze, Hirshl Zussman sits in a sleigh belonging to one of the butcher's sons, and thinks as he drives to town: "We must make an end—once and for all!"

But on the other hand: "What if it is not possible?"

In town he met one Chaim Barim, the same whose son is also a disqualified student. Barim had also been rich before the change, and he had said when Zussman went on the land: "Once he had money. Now he is a fool."

When Zussman met Barim, the former landowner was wearing a patched overcoat, torn shoes, and a ragged beard that was neither clipped nor yet full grown.

Said Zussman to Barim: "Well, what's new?"

And Barim answered: "What should be new? I'm still alive."

"And what else?"

Barim answered: "There are seven words in the Holy Tongue which describe a pauper."

"Well?"

"Well, not one of them fits me. I am looking for an eighth word."

And looking keenly at Zussman he asked: "Maybe you are looking for the same word?"

In town Zussman learned that the Dobra distillery was indeed in operation again, and running as before. And this bit of information was the sole fruit of his visit.

It had begun to snow again in the fields when he returned. And the winds had resumed their play of cat and mouse with the snowflakes. Leaning languidly against the window posts, and with her face close to the window, stood the tall daughter of Hirshl Zussman, and stared absently into the open fields. . . .

The snow is packed high on either side of the road that has been cleared for the passage of sleighs. Down the narrow way that has been formed lumbers the wagon belonging to Mottie and Aleck. The lads are on the way to the railroad station to deliver a load of timber cut from the nearby forest. They make several such trips a day.

When Mottie and Aleck return home late in the evening, as soon as they come in the house is filled with an odor of sweat and manure and of the coarse soap they have used to wash themselves. And the smell drives out all hope the Zussmans may have had of the good old days. They realize now that there are peasants in the family. Sheindel finds consolation in sleep, and Hirshl in figures—so many flasks of oil, so many thousand poods of grain, so many barrels of brandy.

Every morning, after the boys have left for the fields, the daughter, Mani, cleans after them, throws open the windows, sweeps and airs their room with a grimace on her face. But in the evening, when the boys return, the odor returns with them. They keep to themselves in the kitchen, but the smell seeps into the next room, making the evening unbearable for the other Zussmans. Even worse is the loud laughter and loud talk that comes from the kitchen. The breach in the family widens beyond all hope of repair. . . .

The days grow warmer. The days grow beautiful and queenly. The sun beats warmly down, and on both sides of the road murmurs a rush of retreating waters, of melted snow, whose overflow spreads to the road and reflects the shining day.

On such a day the boys are at work in the road, repairing their wagon, which has broken down. They have almost completed the job when an automobile drives up and comes to a halt in front of them. Two young men, strangers, spring out of the car, and one of them asks the way to Dobra, to the brandy distillery.

Mottie and Aleck continue their labors, without looking up, and Mottie answers indifferently through his nose.

"Straight ahead. . .`. Follow the road."

The winter has passed, and the road is filled again with passing wagons, which rattle along, fresh and active, as they do after a good night's rest. Darting, turning, in and out among the wagons, speeds the automobile, bearing the two strangers from the city to the distillery, and from the distillery to the city. Every day it is the same thing. The day is warm, the wagons rattle pleasantly over the road, their drivers dozing, and suddenly the harsh cry of the auto horn fills the air, and the bellicose machine comes into view, crying to all and everything to make way.

Hirshl Zussman sits indoors, lost in thought and fills sheets of paper with figures. The heavy total staggers him, and he goes over his figures again. With these he plans to confront the young men of the distillery. And because no one in the house seems to understand or to be interested in the importance of these figures, he seeks refuge and solace in the company of the little old butcher. He calls him into conference and places before him the figures, just as he intends to place them before the young men, and he puts the proposition up to Alter in the same way. These figures are honest figures, he says. They are not puffed up; they are honest. And no matter how unreasonable the young men may be, something, if only a small portion, the tiniest per cent, they must give him. Because these are true figures. What does the butcher say? Isn't it so? The figures will do the work.

The butcher blinks his red eyes, takes a pinch of snuff, and adopts a respectful air of attention, as he always does when he remembers that he once served in the oxen stalls owned by the grandfather of this same Hirshl Zussman.

He admits that it is even so. That it is logic. No matter how little, no matter how small a sum, something they will give.

Zussman's eyes shine as in a dream. He looks beamingly down upon the little butcher.

"Yes, certainly . . . that is the way it will be. . . ."

It is the last week before Passover. The figures are completed. The young men of the distillery are liable at any time to leave for the Passover holidays. Hirshl Zussman cannot wait for the drayman, who makes occasional trips to town. He makes arrangements to leave on foot. And because Alter the butcher is journeying the same way, they both rise at dawn and set out together. . . .

It is around eleven in the morning, and Alter and Hirshl are well on the way.

Alter is driving a lean milch cow, which he has to take to the slaughter house in Dobra to have it killed there and made kosher so that he can sell it in town.

He is terribly afraid of being late. The shohet at Dobra has informed him that he will not slaughter by lamplight, his eyesight being bad. Also that on the following day he is leaving for a few days. The butcher looks at the sun, with anxiety in his eyes, and he looks at Hirshl Zussman. But the aristocratic Hirshl Zussman is by no means accustomed to planting his feet one after another as needed. After the first few miles he began to tire, to drag his feet, and to take frequent rests by the wayside. He moves his feet as if they are shackled, and every few minutes he asks of Alter, "You don't see the automobile with the two young men, ha? Do you suppose they have left town yet?"

And a little later: "Is it far to Dobra? Hey, Alter. Is it far?"

"Listen to me," says the little butcher. "You had better take off your shoes, and carry them in your hands. Just as I do. The road, Mr. Zussman, is warm, and it is a pleasure, I tell you. Besides the walking is much easier. And besides, nowadays, if you have a good pair of shoes, you have to guard them like an only son. Boots are dear nowadays."

But no sooner has the genteel Mr. Zussman taken his shoes and stockings in his hands, and stepped with bare feet gingerly into the road, than from a distance comes the sharp note of that automobile horn.

The horn cries out with wild joy that the sun is shining, that the air is clear, that everything within hearing distance must take heed of its voice. Down a winding side road the automobile rushes, spattering mud, splashing lustily along the flooded road. It swings into the main highway: the twisted

bowels of its nickel-plated horn catch the rays of the morning sun. The horn
blows threateningly, and dozens of slow-moving wagons swerve to one side
to let it pass. The peasants in the wagons stare after the automobile with fear
and distaste. They catch sight of the sharp faces of the two young men in the
automobile, and they say to themselves: "Jews!"

The automobile continues on its way. It catches up with Alter and
Hirshl, who crawl over the road like two black insects.

"Pitch! Pitch!" cries the horn. "Pitch! Pitch! Pitch!" And Alter and Hirshl
huddle by the side of the road until it passes.

"Eighty black years!" Alter shouts after it. "Eighty black years!"

The lean cow becomes frightened, and runs off into the furrowed fields.
The old butcher pursues it, shouting, and Hirshl is left alone in the road. His
hat has fallen from his head, swept off by the rush of wind when the automobile passed him. His lips tremble.

"Uh wah," he says to himself. "A fiend! a devil!"

He is angry, and he sits down by the side of the road to meditate. But
Alter has returned with the cow, and has not time for reflection.

"Come, Reb Hirshl," he says. "Come, it is getting late. . . ."

It is early evening, and Hirshl and Alter are returning by the same road.
The butcher carries upon his shoulders the freshly skinned pelt of the slaughtered cow. From the pockets of Zussman's old-fashioned overcoat protrude
the corked necks of two brandy bottles. The bottles swing as he walks, and
beat against his thighs, hindering his movements.

On the way they are again overtaken by the automobile carrying the two
young men, traveling this time in the opposite direction.

"T-t-t-t," says the butcher. "Different times. Times are changed."

But Hirshl Zussman is past all powers of speech.

Before his eyes is a picture of the seething cauldrons, the flagged yard of
the distillery, the electric lights recently installed. The employees are the same
as before, most of them. The same that had once worked for him. But there are
several new ones, and one of these stops him to ask his business; wants un-
pleasantly to know who let him in.

Before his eyes is a picture of the two young men of the distillery, very
busy and very stern. They have no time for strangers, they have no time to talk
to him. And when he shows them the figures, one of them motions him away
with a wave of his hand.

"We are not allowed," the young man says, "we are not allowed to deal
with former owners."

And he waves him aside to make way for other petitioners. But Hirshl
remains standing, his hand stretched out, holding the papers. The young man
bites his lip. An employee who worked for Zussman in the old days approaches
the desk and whispers to the young man, and the young man whispers in
return. The old employee approaches Zussman, leads him gently out into the

yard, and tells him to wait a few minutes. When he returns he is carrying two bottles of brandy, which he sticks in Zussman's coat pockets—the same two bottles which are now banging against his thighs, hindering him as he walks. . . .

Alter the butcher says something to Zussman, but Zussman does not hear him. He keeps asking:

"Is it far from home? Is it very far?"

At length, late in the evening, they reach home. The butcher leads him almost to his door, but Zussman is still in a daze.

"Go . . . go," he says to the butcher. "I will find the way myself."

The butcher leaves him, and slowly he begins to realize where he is. He takes the two bottles from his pockets, and looks at them uneasily.

"No," he murmurs, "God forbid! I do not want them."

He goes into the yard, and sticks one of the bottles deep under the manure heap. He waits a minute irresolutely, and sticks away the other bottle.

He feels somehow as if a burden has been lifted from him. He goes with lighter steps towards the house, but hesitates before he knocks, uncertain whether or not the people in the house are awake.

It is late in summer. From the city of Little-Buczacze comes Hayyim Barim's son, a disbarred student also, who knew Mottie in Moscow. He has wandered down to the colony to take a look around, to see whether . . .

"Who knows . . . maybe . . . a plan."

When Mottie and Aleck return from the fields they find Hayyim Barim's son awaiting them.

"Oh," says Mottie, jumping from his wagon. His manner is as if he remembers the student, but cannot think of his name.

Mottie stands before young Barim, peers at him with his nearsighted eyes, and they talk for a long while.

"What do I advise?" says Mottie finally. "Well, I don't know. . . . We have been here a year. . . . And we are still here."

GEDALI

by ISAAC BABEL

On the eve of Sabbath I am oppressed by the dense sadness of memories. Long ago on such evenings my grandfather used to stroke with his yellow beard the tomes of Ibn-Ezra. My granny, with a little lace cap on her head, would weave charms with her knotty fingers over the Sabbath candle, and sob sweetly. On such evenings my child's heart rocked like a little boat on enchanted waves. O withered Talmuds of my childhood! O dense sadness of memories!

I am wandering through Zhitomir, looking for the timid star. Near the ancient snyagogue, by its yellow and indifferent walls, old Jews are selling chalk, blueing wicks—old Jews with beards of the prophets, with passionate rags on their sunken chests.

I behold the market place, and the death of the market place. The fat soul of abundance is slain. Dumb locks hang on the shop doors, the granite of the pavement is clean like the bald head of a corpse. The timid star winks and splutters.

My good fortune came later, my good fortune came just before sunset. The shop of Gedali was hidden amidst the rows of locked stores. Dickens, where was your genial ghost on that day? You would have seen in this curiosity shop gilded slippers and ship cordage, an ancient compass and a stuffed eagle, a huntsman's Winchester with the year 1811 engraved on it and a broken pan.

Old Gedali struts around his treasures in the rosy emptiness of the evening, a tiny proprietor in smoky glasses and in a green frock-coat to the floor. He rubs his white little hands, he plucks at his gray sparse beard, and with a bent head he listens to the invisible voices that have come flocking unto him.

This shop resembles the little box of an inquisitive and solemn boy who may grow up into a professor of botany. There are buttons in this shop, and there is a dead butterfly, and the name of its tiny proprietor is Gedali. Everybody has left the market place, but Gedali is still there. He glides through the labyrinth of globes and skulls and dead flowers, he waves a many-colored duster made of cock feathers, and he flicks the dust off the dead flowers.

There we sit on empty beer barrels. Gedali twists and untwists his narrow beard. His tall silk hat sways above us like a black tower. The warm air is floating by us. The sky changes colors. Up above tender blood flows from an overturned bottle, and I am enveloped by a light odor of decay.

"The Revolution—we shall say yes to her, but are we to say no to Sabbath?" thus begins Gedali, and entwines me with the silken straps of his smoky eyes. "Yes, I shout to the Revolution. Yes, I shout to her; but she hides from Gedali, and sends forth only fusillades."

"The sun does not enter eyes that are shut," I answer the old man, "but we shall rip open the eyes that are shut."

"The Pole has shut my eyes," whispers the old man under his breath, "the Pole, the malicious dog. He takes the Jew and tears his beard out, ach, the dog! And behold, they beat him, the malicious dog. That's fine, that's—Revolution. But then the one who beats the Pole says to me: 'I must confiscate your gramophone, Gedali.' 'I love music, Madame,' I answer the Revolution. 'You don't know what you love, Gedali. I am going to shoot at you, then you will know. I cannot help shooting, because I am—the Revolution.'"

"She cannot help shooting, Gedali," I say to the old man, "because she is—the Revolution."

"But the Pole was shooting my kind, sir, because he is—the Counter-Revolution; you shoot because you are—the Revolution. Now Revolution—that's delight and joy. And joy does not like to make orphans in the family. A good man does good deeds. The Revolution is a good deed done by good men. But good men do not kill. It follows that the Revolution is made by bad men. But then the Poles too are bad men. Who will tell Gedali where is the Revolution and where the Counter-Revolution? I once studied the Talmud, I am fond of the commentaries of Rashi and of the books of Maimonides. And there are other men of understanding in Zhitomir. And behold, all of us, men of learning, fall on our faces and cry out aloud: woe unto us, where is the sweet Revolution?"

The old man became silent. We perceived the first star as it was wending along the milky way.

"Sabbath is coming on," said Gedali solemnly. "Jews must go to the synagogue. Sir comrade," he said rising, and the silk hat began to sway on his head like a black tower, "bring to Zhitomir a little bit of good men. Ai, how we miss them in our town, ai, how we miss them! Bring good men, and we shall let them have all the gramophones. We are not ignoramuses. International—we know what the International means. What I want is an International of good men, I want that every soul be registered and be given a ration of the first category. Here, soul, have nourishment, please, take your delight in living. International, sir comrade, it's you who don't know with what it is eaten."

"It is eaten with powder," I answered the old man, "and it is spiced with the best blood."

And behold, youthful Sabbath ascended her throne out of the blue darkness.

"Gedali," said I, "today is Friday, and it is already evening. Where can one get a Jewish cracknel, a Jewish glass of tea, and a bit of that forbidden joy inside of the glass of tea?"

"Nowhere," answered Gedali, locking up his little box. "There is a tavern next door, and good people used to run it, but they no longer eat there, they weep in there."

He fastened his green frock-coat on three bone buttons. He wafted himself with the cock feathers, splashed some water on his soft palms, and moved away—a tiny, lonely man, in a black silk hat, and with an enormous prayer-book under his arm.

Sabbath is coming on. Gedali, the founder of the Fourth International, is off for the synagogue to pray.

THE DISPUTE

by S. GODINER

THEY sat through the long blue winter night in the spacious old room. The mute shadows of grandparents and great-grandparents, with long silvery beards and the dusty melancholy of eternity, wavered in the dim corners. They disputed with the hearty devotion one had for the other, but with savage divergence.

Neither of them desired it now.

Nor were they of the same age.

Nor were their paths drawn in a straight line, hand in hand. Somewhere the goal gleamed, in the farthest distances and unknown futures, like a glowing star, gleaming and trembling, twinkling and calling to both:

—Come to me, to me! I shall wrap you in my light, melt suns for you to do with them as you please. . . .

The goal was the same for both.

And both sprang from the same stem.

Of the same stem but in two different eras—aged father and young son.

Events, like waves of an angry sea, tossed the son into his father's arms. Old, wisely-shrewd eyes dropped a quiet tear into silver strands and pleaded.

—Tell me, my son, where and how are you living; tell your old father.

A small, golden-curled beard fluttered, eyes kindled behind glasses, illuminating two bright stars, and a smile lit up a bright young face:

—What for, father?

Something like a tremor passed over the face framed in tarnished gold. A small transparent cloud veiled a large white forehead.

—Don't you know yourself?

—Are you still on the same path?

—Yes, father.

—And why have you come here?

—Do you resent it?

—No. . . . But you will accomplish nothing here.

—Don't be my enemy, father. Our ways have parted a long time ago.

—Yes. . . . But you did not travel mine till the end. Has anything convinced you that my path leads to nothing? You left it in the middle . . . uprooted yourself, and started everything anew.

He raised high his gray gold head, and pride rang in his old voice:

—And if a wanderer should change directions every minute, drift into twisted by-paths and back-paths, could he never reach anywhere? And what are we here if not stranded sojourners?—

Then quietly, imploring so:

—Come with me, my son. An old affirmed path is mine. . . . Great-grand-fathers and fathers have traveled upon it. . . . Thanks to them it is without a stumbling block. Every possible pitfall was foreseen by them far unto the end. . . . And to what purpose did they live if you turn aside? Come with me, my son! I have not far to go, but will watch your step with my last look. . . . You will go farther and farther, drawing the thread and extending the road, our road, and you will shorten the distance between yourself and salvation. . . .

And with the sorrow of a millennium:

—We have reached nowhere! We are in the middle of the road. If you should desert me now I would be cut off and lost. Who will carry on? . . .

—I will, father.

—You have deserted me.

—I am younger and can see better. So I take the short cuts.

—On unknown roads.

—What does it matter if one goes towards everything?

—Everything is nothing, son, everything is—look out through the window— the whole blue sky with its milliards of stars. But can they light up the room? Our smoky lamp with its small darkly-red flame amounts to something. . . . Put it out and the room is plunged into darkness. Everything—the stars—gives off a weak light, a faint glimmer. . . . Something—the lamp—illumines your face which is a delight to me. . . . Everything, son, is the world, all nations and creatures. Something—that's you, your body, mine, the memory of my being, of my having been . . .

Quietly, almost forlornly:

—If you lose everything you lose nothing. If you lose something you lose all. We are something, therefore we need something. . . .

—Your thought, father, has clipped wings. It grovels on the floor in search of only something. . . .

—Your thoughts, son, are in the clouds and without substance. . . .

And so on and on far into the blue noiseless night. The old gray head is taxed with hard slices of rigid wisdom sucked from big glass book-cases, from surviving but decadent generations, from unreturning experiences. . . . Youthfully curled, golden head has the breath of sunlight, the vastness of space, the energy of the living world. . . . Old lips pour forth mountains of stones taken from thousand-year-old ruins which were once built by great-grandfather, by grandfather and their successors. . . . Young lips smile, smile to themselves, and speak mincingly. . . . They swim in the bigness of the world, and feel its rhythm. They cut short the dispute and invite old father to the window:

—Look, father, day is breaking . . .

—And—

—Listen!

Old gray father listens intently to the sounds surging in the dawn, soft, gentle, aggressive sounds rising with the waves of fresh dew on a young spring morning:

> "This will be the last
> And decisive battle. . . ."

Old man inquires uneasily:

—What does it all mean? What does that thundering song mean?

—Calling us together, to assemble, father.

—And . . . you are joining them?

—Yes. And taking the shortest distance. . . .

This spoken so evenly, with such an assured smile and tone that they caused old feet to cave in, and lips to stammer:

—Taking the shortest distance to where?

—To salvation, if you will.

—Whose?

—Everybody's. Yours, father. Farewell! And away.

The young man leaves the old house, the aged father, and follows the song which resounds in the break of light. Left alone among the mute shadows of great-grandparents wavering in the corners, near the dim-red flame of the smoky lamp, the old man muses serenely: "I have brought up a son to sow unrest on the Russian highways . . . to search for salvation. . . ."

But a moment later, when his eyes fall upon the flickering flame in the lamp, flickering and yet leaping heavenward in the wild exultation, this occurs to him:

"Perhaps . . . Does anyone really know from where the great tidings will come?"

An old wall-clock is ticking hoarsely, keeping time with the exultation and burdened doubts of the sinking lamp-flame and of the old Jew.

—Tick-tick, tick-tick, tick-tick . . .

—Does anyone really know from where the great tidings will come? . . .

FROM BODANA'S DIARY

by I. KIPNIS

Those who have met me in this big town, particularly my patients, know what a busy man I am. Still, sufficient time is left for me, after office hours and after my visits to the sick at home, to call on a girl I know, a Communist pioneer. Whenever I find her home I am glad to spend an hour or two with her.

My visits to this girl are no secret at my home. Bodana (that's her name) is of my native town. Moreover, she is my sister, to boot. In the town which we left behind lives a dear and lovable woman who longs for us unremittingly. That woman is our mother.

Back home I was the oldest of my brothers and Bodana the youngest of my sisters. Here she visits me rarely. She says she is busy. I therefore put pride aside and visit her, for which I am well rewarded. For there I often find a letter on the table from our mother, and also a tastily baked wheat cake which she sends us from home. In addition Bodana's friends, both male and female, are there when I call. She places a hand on the open book before her, or on her diary which she keeps, and narrates incidents which remind us of home.

I would put the best book aside in order to listen to her stories. It is not so easy to retell them. But recently, while rummaging through her papers, I came upon some notes in her own handwriting. And I am passing on their content to you, word for word:

I. HOW THE BIG CITY FRIGHTENED ME FROM AFAR

. . . Many things are probably sorry that I have left home. But, on the other hand, I miss them as much, if not more. . . . I shall never forget the scene of my leave-taking, and that of my sitting on the wagon. We were eight miles from the town. I sat on the wagon with eyes closed. The few passengers around me were talking quietly among themselves. I heard nothing of their talk. I mused as though I were in a sleep. Only the evening before everything had been just as any other day. Now I had a peculiar feeling. The driver was prodding his nags. The wagon was shaking me up. The dust irritated my face. Under the seat, hard by my feet, was my bundle. Still I didn't know where I was heading for and that made me sad.

It seems to me that I am a good pioneer. Nevertheless, I thought, what am I going to do in a big city where no one knows me? They might even run after me as though I were some queer-looking creature. . . . I know that my brother and sister-in-law live there. I shall go to school and study, which will be a good thing. But last night when our calf came home from the pasture (and

I am beginning to miss our calf), it looked so tiny that I believed I could have lifted it on my back and carried it wherever I pleased. Of reddish skin, with blue fresh horns, and with somewhat dark streaks in the face, particularly around the mouth and eyes. Our calf understands everything.

It was then that I did not feel like leaving home. I was beginning to take notice of things which I had ordinarily ignored. The box upon which I used to sit while milking the cows had a square hole in it. The chimney in the kitchen, where I would strain the milk, was black with smoke and soot. Helping out my mother was apparently little in my mind. . . . Why didn't I rise in the middle of the night and polish the stove, bring in pails of water from the well and tidy up the kitchen until it looked like a palace? . . . Weeping isn't the thing for a pioneer to do. But what can I do when I journey forth far away? I don't know anybody in the big city nor about what to talk with people.

I took farewell from my circle, but they promised to come again in the evening. The children of our aunt and neighbours were all envious of me because I was to ride on the train and live in a big city. A week ago I was envious of myself for it. Now, however, the children appeared to me so foolish that it made me bawl. And in the depth of my thoughts lurked an idea that the whole story was a lie. I was riding nowhere. I should remain a good pioneer at home and study. And in good health. One always is in a small town. And help out my mother in the house.

However, my things were all packed. The calf probably understood that all my things were packed, for she often turned her head and looked at me with the eyes of a saddened human being.

My things were all ready and my little brother went out to reserve a place for me with one of the horse and wagon drivers.

The pioneers of my circle visited me again that evening. They sensed at once that I felt disheartened. What was the use of laughing when in the morning the wagon would come and take me away and I wouldn't know whether I shall ever return! . . .

When the wagon came to a stop before a well in some village in order to water the horses, I opened my eyes.

—Were you dozing?—inquired the driver.

I answered him with a "hm." Just the same I couldn't keep my eyes open. I felt groggy but tried to recall one thing to my mind: that my mother spoke little to me the day before I left. She did not want me to leave home. I also recalled (in the morning the driver was hurrying me so that I had no time to think, but it was clear to me now) that at night, while asleep, I suddenly felt someone standing beside me and stroking my head for a long, long time. When I opened my eyes no one was there. But as soon as I closed them again I felt someone bending over and kissing me. As I stirred someone hastened away. When I lay inert someone was again beside me. Finally when I sat up fully awake I saw my mother retreat to her room with a light trembling in her hand. . . .

The wagon stumbled over a rock and jerked me out of my reverie. . . . The driver turned to me merrily:

—Are you asleep, Bodana? Sleep, sleep! I can already hear the train shrieking in the distance.

And the wheels spun into a lively clatter upon the Iskorosta road.

II. IN THE WOODS

Once I was coming from the Tsotchen district. . . . Tsotchen is a village, three miles from us, where I was delegated to organize the peasant children. Mother refused to tolerate it and father wouldn't hear of "my imparting the Torah to Gentiles."

—They don't want to become Communists—said he—and if they did, God would send them a teacher from elsewhere!

The youngsters of Tsotchen clung to me as though for dear life.

—Remember!—my people would warn me—a bandit will catch you some day and wrench your head off. Bandits have no use for such as you! . . .

It was twilight when I walked home from the village. The peasant lads asked me to bring them more paper on my next visit.

—And matches—added Kalistrat.

—I shall,—I promised and felt elated that nineteen boys had listened to my talk.

I was already beyond the village gate and out on the fields. As the dusk was settling, the idea of taking a dip in the pond near Hrischke's flour-mill occurred to me. At home the cow would be attended to, and I was looked upon askance by the family anyway (they often accused me of shirking housework). . . . I felt that a different path was laid out for me. . . .

I walked and walked. The trees, the hills, appeared familiar and yet strange. . . . I quickened my pace. It grew dark. Suddenly, unexpectedly, I found myself in an unfamiliar forest. Tsotchen, I knew, was fringed with woodland leading to the rear of the town through scattered hamlets. I quickly turned back towards Tsotchen. But not a glimmer of the village was anywhere to be seen. Then, how could there be if I was already an hour and a half from the village? Nevertheless I retraced my steps. I walked and walked—and came to a point where roads crossed. I didn't remember having seen roads cross. And they appeared alike. And that had to happen to me at night! The roads that stretched before me had rugged surfaces. They extended in silence as though conspiring against me.

That was, after all, a small matter. For how far was I really from home? A two-hour walk at most. I could see the bowl of steaming hot potatoes on the table. And I could sniff the grease in the anteroom. I could feel the warmth of the chickens huddling in the coop. . . .

I stood before the crossroads and the darkness made me dizzy. I was beginning to see the things with which my mother would scare me:

Decrepit hags?

No.

And brigands—Yes!

They are tough fellows and my mother is right about the terror they instil. Ah? What is that? Really? No. It's not true! I turn about and take the road leading away from Tsotchen. Maybe I'll see there a guiding gleam of light, or smoke from a chimney. . . . I stray again into the forest. I have nothing on my person—am barefoot and in only a red dress.

—Forest, forest,—I muse—where are your bears? Where are your tigers and leopards? Let me see them at once! And where are your roving cut-throats? Nothing here. Just forest. Only my steps have a strange sound, as though I walked on broken wires.

Well, whatever will happen, will happen. If only it weren't so quiet. There is no trodden path under my feet. The grass is astir with hopping, circling insects. Somewhere an owl is hooting, like the crying of a child. The devil take it! I had better find an elevated dry spot where I can rest till dawn. It is dry under a pine tree, not under an oak tree. I take shelter under a pine tree. Let the owl hoot! Let the moon taunt me—as if to imply:

—Aha, pioneer woman! At home you are brave hiding behind your mother's apron.

—Well, so what? How does it concern you?

The long summer day tired me out, so let the forest be my home, not the whole forest, but the place where I am resting. And, as at home, so here I would not mind something to eat: a hot potato, a slice of bread—anything. We pioneers would do well to pitch tents here for at least a month during the summer. . . . A summer month in the woods would be good for us. But now I want so terribly much to talk to someone. If there were only a dumb animal beside me,—a dog, a cat, or a cow. I am aching to call out to someone. Let it be an old woman, a murderer!!!—

With these thoughts in mind I fell asleep. . . .

I was dreaming that I was cold.

I dreamt I was at home sleeping on a hard couch. The room is like any other room. Maps decorate the walls. Then my cover dropped to the floor. I opened my eyes but felt too lazy to pick it up. Mother, after all, is right when she says of me: "For the sake of her friends she would run the world around, but for herself she wouldn't lift as much as a glass of water." . . . Mother, I believe, is right. For what could be simpler than to reach down and pick up the quilt? . . . I forced my eyes open. I searched and scratched in the grass and wondered how I came to be out here, in the open, instead of at home. . . . Trees, the moon, and an owl somewhere . . . I know that it is perched on a tree even if it stopped hooting. . . .

My younger brother sleeps with our cousin Moische on the hayloft in the barn. He will make believe that I had not yet returned from the lectures.

Good, let him think so. I turn on the other side and draw my feet up under my dress. The boys of Tsotchen probably know the way out here better than I do. . . . Recently I lectured them on why one mustn't kill birds in their nests, mustn't pick unripe cherries, and destroy branches of fruit trees . . .

Old peasants edged closer in order better to catch the substance of my talk, and they seemed to like it.

—That's the very thing—they agreed—they should know.

—This is so fine a lesson—echoed the peasant women—that nothing better is needed. . . .

A horseback rider passed not far from me among the trees and whistled. Chilled to the bone I lay still and thought of nothing. Afterwards I reproved myself: What if someone did pass by on horseback and whistle?

Meanwhile the moon grew dim. Again I opened my eyes and imagined myself in an orchard guarding the fruit. I want so much to sleep but I am in charge of the fruit trees and afraid of thieves. I am a janitress, my husband a janitor. A wedding is in progress at my home which is on the outskirts of the town. . . . I run off with my braids flying, trying to escape someone. . . . The music pursues me. . . . My home is brilliantly lighted and glimmers in the night. . . . The wedding guests dance drunkenly. And someone is trying very badly to embarrass me in their presence, to drag me back by my hair and in my weekday clothes. . . .

Galia Ovsayevna, my oldest school teacher, is attempting to protect me. She says something about a child, someone's child. Anyway, she says, we know everything. The child is a pioneer, four years, six years, twelve years old, and already a Communist.

Galia's words fill my heart with tears. A warm smoke spirals upward from the chimneys. And as I walk and walk and walk a lake spreads out into view. The lake is wide but not deep. In it flocks of gold fish swim about playfully. They are within reach of my hand. In some places the water runs as thin as cigarette paper. It laps against the shore and is iridescent in the sunlight. I'd like to thrust a hand into the water and catch some of the fish, but I don't. Perhaps I am dreaming. As I wake up, a warm sun ray darts at me through the foliage. I close my eyes and hear the gurgle of a warm water stream. Finally, when I open my eyes once more I find myself in the woods. I feel so hungry that my heart goes out. Yet I am in no great hurry to get up. For I still want to sleep, if only for another wink. . . .

At last I rouse myself to my feet with great effort. The breeze braces me up and I feel refreshed all over my body. It is not a field breeze, but one of the woods, secretive, penetrating. And I am already on my way.

I don't care where I am going, so long as it is daytime and I am going.

III. THE MEETING WITH KIRILKA

At this point begins the story of Kirilka. A dog barks forlornly in the distance. I see fenced-off fields, grazing cows, and a barn. When I come closer to the barn I hear someone groaning inside. I look in to see if it is any one of my pioneers. The dog shuffles towards me. I don't know what the dog wants. Maybe he is one of those quiet, sullen creatures who may, at any moment, seize me by my bare feet. So I call inside the barn and out comes, crawling on hands and knees, Kirilka, the younger son of Ivan, our neighbor. He recognizes me at once and begins to whimper:

—Akh, Bodanka, dear girl, save me! . . .

He speaks like an old man but his eyes light strangely at the sight of me.

He is an orphan, without a mother, and his father hired him out to a peasant farmer!

This is his second summer working for the same employer. Well, it's nothing. He is alone in the forest and his job is to mind the cattle. The employer sends him food two or three times a week. Now he complains of a severe pain in the stomach. Yesterday when the boss passed by he found him sick.

—What's the matter?—he inquired.

Instead of answering, he grasped himself by the abdomen and burst into tears.

—And what did the boss say to that?

—Ignore it, Kirilka,—he said,—it's nothing. You must have overeaten a bit. Drink less warm milk and eat more small dried pears.

And he rode off.

I listen to him carefully and conclude that he is suffering from dysentery. His eyes are glittering. His face looks tired. He shivers and squeals for help.

What can I do?—I think to myself—carry him on my back I couldn't. For him to walk is equally impossible. He can hardly stand on his feet, and has no mother to the bargain.

The employer's counsel is not at all unwise.

—Ignore it, it's nothing. You have simply overeaten yourself.

—Do you know what?—I say to Kirilka—I am going over to your house and will bring your father with me.—

—Sure?

—Sure.

—You won't forget, Bodanka?

—No—I promise—I give you my word as a pioneer!

And he cries, poor thing, bathing his face in tears.

Home is about seven miles from here. He tells me exactly how to go. The dog, ostensibly, feels that Kirilka is in need of human contact. He runs after me for a few paces, then turns back. I hasten my steps.

The distance shouldn't take more than two hours to cover. But I want to save Kirilka, to spare him more than ever before.

Three years ago, while they carried his mother out of the chapel to the grave and he followed her coffin in white sandals, I did not feel too sorry for him. Afterwards he hated me for a different reason. When the seven-year school reopened in our district and the blackboards and books were missing, I told the teacher that Philip and Kirilka had stolen them. . . . So they went there with policemen and recovered about two hundred books. . . .

But now I am ready to forgive him everything, only let him be well again.

Wagons come rattling by. Many of them are familiar to me. Most of them are without uprights, heading to the forest for timber. I walk faster. Meet flocks of cattle at the beginning of the forest. It is still early. It is the first time in my life that I meet with so many cattle (our cow is not among them for it grazes near our home). . . .

And . . . as I enter the house they are still in bed. I tell them I'll be back shortly. They think I spent the night at a friend's house. Without taking as much as a piece of bread I rush out of the house and straight to Ivan.

I find Ivan puttering around in the yard near the shed.

—Harness your horses—I command him—and let's go and fetch Kirilka. He is very sick.

Ivan begins to scratch his head. . . .

He thought, he says, of taking manure out to the field. . . .

—To the devil:—All right! . . . We'll go. But I'll have some stew first before I hitch the horses to the wagon. . . . Want to come along, Bodana?

—Certainly!—I answer.

In less than an hour I am on Ivan's wagon and we are making fast for the woods through the outlying hamlets to where the owner of the barn lives. He isn't in, but nearby, and is soon called.

And you should have seen how two peasants talk between themselves. It's really curious. As though they take nothing to heart.

As we approach the barn Kirilka is so overjoyed that he raises himself on his knees, supports himself with his hands on the floor, and gives us one long look.

—Ah—he says—our horses have arrived! . . . and a strange luster creeps into his eyes and he drops to the floor. The dog circles around him, sniffs him in a peculiar way. And when we place Kirilka on the wagon, his head hangs down. The dog rests on his hind legs, with snout upraised, and begins to whine mournfully because Kirilka is no longer living.

The two peasants did not exchange a word. Ivan pulls a cloak over Kirilka and rides off without saying good-by.

Abandoned the flock, abandoned the owner, abandoned the forest, abandoned the dog.

On the way home Ivan does not say a word to me nor I to him.

The team of "our horses" runs along and snorts in the sunlight. I sense that Ivan is angry at the interference with his work. He might have brought out two wagon-loads of garbage on the fields when suddenly—the interruption. . . . Now he will have to drive the horses to the grazing ground, to go in search of boards for a makeshift coffin, run for a priest, and call a few people together —too much work! . . .

I reflect that if Kirilka's mother had been alive she would not just have wept, but screamed and beat her head on the ground. For a mother is not a father. And if she had bawled right then and there on the wagon the pity for Kirilka might have been lessened.

My brother asked me:

—Where did you spend last night? At Eva's home?

I answered him:

—Have patience and I will tell you.

At first my mother was angry with me. But as I cleaned my hands, rolled up my sleeves, and dived straight into the vat of dough to knead the bread, she softened considerably. Then I told them the story of "our horses have arrived." . . .

Mother raked up the fire in the stove, listened attentively, and tears welled up in her eyes.

—What foolish children!—she exclaimed—what tasks they take upon themselves! !—she couldn't finish, smiled, and turned away with brimming eyes.

—It is really tragic—she said—and the way you told the story can grip the heart of anyone. . . .

THE HOLOCAUST

A GHETTO DOG

by ISAIAH SPIEGEL

ANNA NIKOLAIEVNA, widow of Jacob Simon Temkin, the fur dealer, had only time enough to snatch up a small framed photograph of her husband, for the German was already standing in the open doorway shouting "R-*raus-s!*"

There were no more Jews in the house by now, and if she had failed to hear the noise they made as they fled it was because with age she had grown hard of hearing and because that very morning, before the light had seeped through the heavy portieres, a desire had come over her to open her piano—a grand piano, black—and let her old parchmentlike fingers glide over its yellowed keys. One could scarcely call what she was playing music, since her fingers, which were as gnarled as old fallen bark, had been tremulous with age for years. The echoes of several tunes had been sounding in her deaf ears the whole morning, so that she had failed to hear the German when he appeared shouting on the threshold.

All the while Nicky, the widow's dog, had been lying near one of the heavy portieres, dozing and dreaming an old dog's dream, his pointed muzzle resting on his outstretched paws. He was well along in years; his coat was shedding and light patches showed in its sandy hue. His legs were weak, but his big eyes—brownish with a blue glint—reminded one that he too had once been a puppy.

The widow and her dog led a lonely life. Nicky wandered through the rooms on his weak stumpy legs, his head drooping, and swayed mournfully, his whining quieted by weary thoughts. The Temkins had got him from a farm a long time ago. After his master's death the widow used to listen all day to Nicky moving through the stillness of the house. Whenever she sat by the table and Nicky was in the bedroom opposite (he had refused for several days to leave the bed where his master had died), it seemed to her as though her late husband were again walking through the bedroom in his house slippers. She used to listen to the least noise from the bedroom, pricking up her deaf ears, and as a sudden pallor spread over her wrinkled forehead she seemed actually to hear Jacob Simon's soft slow tread. Any moment now he would appear on the threshold of the bedroom, seat himself in the plush *fauteuil,* reach out for a plaid rug, and throw it over his knees, which had been rheumatic for so many years.

Between the widow and her dog there had formed a mesh of otherworldly thoughts and dreams. She saw in his drooping old head, in his worn-out fur and his pupils with their blue glints, a shadow of her husband. Perhaps this was because Nicky had been close to his master for so many years and had been ready to lay down his life for him, or perhaps because with time he had taken on his master's soft tread over the rugs, his master's lax mouth and watery eyes—

whichever it was, the widow had never clasped the dog's head without feeling some inner disquiet. Between them there was that bond which sometimes springs up between two lonely creatures, one human and the other brute.

While the German was still in the open doorway, and before the widow had time to snatch up the photograph, Nicky had already taken his stand at the threshold. He raised his old head against the German, opened his mouth wide to reveal his few remaining teeth, let out three wild howls, and was set to leap straight for the German's throat. One could see Nicky's hackles rise and hear his old paws scrape as he dashed about, ready to leap at the stranger in the outlandish green uniform. Suddenly the dog had shed his years; his legs straightened and hot saliva drooled from his muzzle as if he would say, "I know you're our enemy. I know! But you just wait—wait!"

The German at the door became confused for a moment. Taken aback by the fire glinting in the old dog's eyes, he clutched at his pistol holster.

"Have pity!" the old woman quavered. "It's only a poor animal—"

With her old body she shielded Nicky from the German and at the same time began patting the dog. In a moment he lay quiet and trembling in the old woman's arms. At last the widow tugged at his leash, and the two of them made their way through the dark hallway and into the street. As she hurried through the hallway she seized a small black cane with a silver knob; without this cane, a memento of her husband, she could hardly take a step.

She found herself in the street, leaning on the black cane with the silver knob, the rescued photograph safe in her bosom, and tugging the dog on his leash. Her eyes could scarcely be said to perceive what was going on around her. The day was frosty, blue; a blue silvery web of mist, spun by the early Polish winter, was spreading over the houses, the street, the sidewalks. The faces of the fleeing Jews were yellow, pallid. Nicky was still restless and was drawing back all the time; he did not know where his mistress was leading him. From time to time he fixed his eyes on the widow's face, while she, as she trudged along, felt a sudden icy fear grip her heart. From the dog's eyes raised to hers there peered the watery, lifeless gaze of her late husband. And here were the two of them, linked together in the web of frosty mist that was swirling under a lowering dark sky. The two of them were now plodding close to each other, their heads downcast. Cold, angry thoughts kindled in her drowsy old mind. She actually felt a chill breath swishing about her ears and she caught words—far-off words, cold and dead.

The widow who had for so long lived a life apart from Jews and Jewishness had suddenly come to herself, as if awaking from a state of unconsciousness. She had been driven out of her house, of course, as a Jew like any other, although for many years her house had been like any Christian's. Her only son had become an apostate, had married a Christian girl and gone off to Galicia, long before the war, where he was living on his father-in-law's estate. During the Christian holidays various gifts would arrive from him. She knew beforehand what he would send: a big, well-fattened turkey and half a dozen dyed Easter eggs. The turkey she could use, but when it came to the colored eggs the old woman had a strange oppressive feeling. They would lie around for months, gathering dust on their shells, until some evening she peeled them in the bright light of the girandole and then left them on the window sill for the hungry sparrows.

She herself had been estranged from Jewishness since her very childhood. For years on end no Jewish face appeared at her threshold. The war, which had come so suddenly to the town, had during the first few days failed to reach her comfortable home. The catastrophe that had befallen the Jews had not touched her, and the angry prophecy of the storm that was raging in the streets had not beaten upon her door.

When the German had opened it that morning, he had aroused the little old woman from her torpor and had reminded her that she was a Jew and that heavy days had come for her and all other Jews. And though the old woman had during so many years been cut off from Jewishness and Jews, she had accepted the sudden misfortune with courage and resignation, as if an invisible thread had connected her to her people all through the years.

Now she was trudging through the streets with so many others whose faces were strange and distracted. She recognized these faces from her remote youth, faces framed in black unkempt Jewish beards and surmounted by small round skullcaps, which Jacob Simon used to ridicule so in his lifetime. Jews in gaberdines, Jewish women wearing headkerchiefs and marriage wigs, were dragging their children by the hand. Anna's heart was filled with a friendly feeling as, leaning on her black, silver-knobbed cane, she led Nicky with her left hand. The fleeing Jews cast surly sidelong looks at her and the dog. Nicky plodded on without once lifting up his head; the light had gone out of his eyes. A small spotted dog suddenly emerged from the crowd, ran up to Nicky, and placed a paw on the old dog's neck as if seeking consolation; thereafter both dogs walked side by side.

Nicky sensed the strange atmosphere as they turned into the next street. It was poorly paved, with gaping pits; the press was greater here. He could barely make his way among the thousands of unfriendly feet. They kept stepping on his paws, and once his mistress almost fell. Anna held her head higher and was pulled along by the crowd of Jews. She drew the leash closer to her, every so often saving Nicky from being trampled. By now he kept closer to her, mournful, and with his head still lower.

Fine, wet snowflakes swirled in the air, unwilling to fall to the ground, and settled on Nicky's grizzled, closely curled coat.

The widow found herself in a narrow squalid street in the Balut district of Lodz, where all the hack-drivers, porters, and emaciated Jewish streetwalkers lived. She had come here with a host of strangers who quickly made themselves at home in a huge empty barn. The Jewish streetwalkers brought them all sorts of good things baked of white flour. The widow sat in the barn, her gray disheveled head propped on the silver knob of her cane, while Nicky sprawled at her feet and took in the angry din made by the strange people.

It was late at night before everyone in the barn was assigned quarters in the district. The widow found herself in the room of a tart known as Big Rose—a very much disgruntled tart, who did not want a dog in the house.

"It's enough that I have to take in a female apostate!" she kept yelling. "What do I need a sick old hound for?"

Anna stood on the threshold before the tart, the dog close to her on his unsteady legs; his body emanated a forlornness that was both animal and human.

"Quiet, quiet!" The widow's hand fell shakily on Nicky's drooping head and patted it.

The room where Big Rose lived lay under a gabled roof. It held a small shabby sofa, strewn with yellow and red cushions. A low ceiling made the place dreary and depressing. Outside the window was the hostile night, spattered with the silver of the first frost. This night-silver interlaced with the reflections of light from the room and fell on the windowpanes like dancing stars.

The nook that sheltered the widow and her dog was very dark; the warmth lingered there as if in a closed warm cellar. Throughout the room there hovered a sour odor of sin and lust. The old woman did not realize where she had come to; nothing mattered any longer. She and her dog huddled in their nook and for a long while squatted there like two huge rigid shadows. From time to time Nicky put his head in her lap, and a soft, long-drawn-out whine issued from the dark nook, like the moan of a hopelessly sick man.

Later that night, when the old woman and the dog had stretched out in their nook on some rags, Big Rose closed the red hangings which screened the shabby sofa from the rest of the room. The little red flame of the small night lamp hanging on the wall wavered slowly and angrily, licking at the musty darkness around it.

Only now, when everything had become utterly quiet, did certain huge shadows appear in the darkness of the threshold. The shadows entered one by one; each hovered for a moment on the threshold, looked about, then disappeared within the hangings. In the dark little hallway on the other side of the door other shadows gathered and waited for the door to open. They did not have to wait long: each shadow, after darting out from behind the hangings, rushed through the door and disappeared down the dark stairs.

The widow was dozing by now. From time to time she awoke and put her arms around Nicky's warm neck. The dog continued snoring with a low, canine snore. Each time the door opened and a shadow darted within the hangings, from which there immediately issued Big Rose's witchlike snicker, Nicky would emit a low growl.

This suddenly angered Big Rose. She sprang up naked by the drawn-back hangings and, brandishing her arms, shouted at the widow in the nook, "My grand madam! May a curse light on you! Maybe madam would like to step out for a little while on the balcony with the hound? He's driving everybody away, may the devil overtake him! I'll poison that hound!"

The widow, startled from her sleep, was frightened by Big Rose's stark nakedness and its pungent reek.

"Sh, sh, sh!" she at last managed to whisper to the dog.

She stood up in her nook, took Nicky's head, and started for the door. Through the small dark hallway the two of them, the widow and the dog, reached the deserted balcony. Below them lay a tangle of dark Balut streets. The wind drove nearer and scattered the grayish, tenuous whiteness of the still swirling night snow. From the south side of the city the dusty glow of electric lights was borne through the night. The widow watched these lights blinking on and off, like inflamed eyes.

"See there, Nicky? Over there—there. That's our house, our street—"

The dog lifted his head, stood up on his hind legs, and peered into the darkness. For a while he stood thus, with the widow's arms around him, then suddenly let out a howl. It rent the sky like lightning, beat against the clouds, and then died away in the cold darkness of the earth.

In the morning, when the chilled widow awoke in her nook, the dog was no longer by her side. Nobody had any idea where he had vanished to. Big Rose kept saying that this was no dog but a werewolf and that she hadn't even heard the dog leaving the house.

He was gone the whole day, and only toward evening did they hear him scraping at the door. He fell into the nook in great excitement, with foam on his hanging tongue, and threw himself on the frightened widow's lap.

Nicky lay on her knees, quivering with an ardent, old-dog sob. The widow took his shivering head and for some time gazed into his watery pupils, as if into the small openings of two wells. She could not understand what had happened to the dog. He barked in a subdued way, as if some words were struggling to escape him, as if he were straining to tell everything to the old woman bending over him. His whole body quivered, and his narrow face seemed to wear the twisted grimace of a dog in lament. Yet this was not whining; rather a noisy outburst of joy and consolation. He kept lifting his paws and putting them on the old woman's knees. The widow took the paws and brought them to her aged, withered lips, bent over, and for a long, long time, with her eyes closed, rested her head upon them.

For a long time the widow sat in the darkness embracing the dog, while the night lamp, which had been turned low and had been burning all day near the red hangings, now cast a mysterious reddish reflection on the wall. The sharp silhouette of the dog's pointed head and the widow's arms swayed on the ceiling in a network of dancing shadows.

The next morning Nicky again disappeared and did not come back until nightfall. This was repeated day after day.

These disappearances coincided with the time the Germans built a wall around the ghetto, barbed wires dividing the Balut from the rest of the city. Nobody was allowed to leave or enter the Jewish district. But just the same Nicky used to disappear every day and come back only at night.

Once, when Nicky returned as excited as always, the old woman put her hands on his head and drew them back: they were sticky with blood. His fur was split and torn with open wounds. He was holding his paws on her knees, as always, but this time his pupils were reddish, glowing, and little green fires kept dancing across his watery eyes.

The widow applied rag after rag soaked in cold water to the dog's open wounds. Only now did she realize that Nicky had been crawling through the barbed wire, that each morning he had run off to the city and each evening he had come running home. The widow kept on washing the warm blood and applying the cold wet rags, while Big Rose ran to fetch basins of water. The bitterness she had felt in her heart for the dog had quickly vanished. She took a white blouse from her closet and tore it into narrow bandages; she also procured from somewhere a salve that was good even for human wounds. She smeared torn strips with the salve and then, kneeling by the door, started to bind the dog's wounds.

A sudden fright came over Big Rose; an otherworldly expression appeared on her face, as if she felt a cold breath upon her. She could have sworn by all that was holy that, as she had been binding the dog's wounds, he had given her a mournful human look.

From the day Big Rose had bound the open wounds the dog had got by crawling through the barbed wire strung around the ghetto—from that day her attitude toward the widow had undergone a complete change. She took down the red hangings that had divided the room in two and asked the old woman to leave her dark nook and share the room with her. All three of them, the two women and the dog, now used the sofa. Nicky lay propped up by the colored cushions, lost in an old dog's dream.

This happened just about the time when the Germans issued an order that all animals—horses, cows, goats, and dogs—must be turned over to them. Only two broken-down horses were allowed to remain in the whole ghetto. For generations the old Jewish residents of the Balut had made their meager living as animal breeders. The hack-drivers and cabbies, the milk dealers, small middlemen, organ-grinders, and innkeepers had to give up the horses and cows they had tended in the crowded dark stables and stalls. They unharnessed their horses for the last time and embraced the warm necks of their cows; they led out the mournful Jewish cows and the frightened Jewish goats. The draymen led their beautiful, glossy chestnut draft horses through the streets, the whole family marching in step with them, wringing their hands as if they were following the dead to a yawning grave. The women dragged the cows and goats along—the animals became stubborn and refused to budge. At the tail end of the procession, on ropes and leashes, other Jews were leading watchdogs, Dalmatians, poodles with mournful eyes, and common household pets with bobbed tails. The Jews hoped that their dumb creatures would be better fed than they had been in the ghetto. The horses and cows were taken into the city, but the dogs were immediately shot in a field close to the market place.

At daybreak Big Rose had thrown a torn black shawl with long fringes over her, and the widow, without uttering a word, had taken Nicky on his leash with one hand and her small silver-knobbed cane in the other. Both women were going to take the dog to the market place. Big Rose kept mauling her cheeks and softly weeping. The widow's disheveled hair, gray and lifeless, hung over her ashen face.

The compulsory surrender of her dog had come as such a shock to the widow that at first, when Big Rose had shouted the news into her face, she had clutched her head with her withered fingers and had remained still for several minutes. Big Rose thought the old woman had died, standing with her fingers in her hair, and her eyes not even blinking. She just stood there, stunned and stone-cold.

The dog let them do with him whatever they liked. He dropped at their feet and held his pointed head up to them, then yawned and let his muzzle sink to the cold floor.

The two women started out through the small courtyard, Nicky on his long leash between them. The snow was coming down in flakes as slender and chill as needles, and stabbed their hands, their faces, and the dog's fur. It was bitter cold. Although dawn had broken a comparatively short while ago, the ghetto seemed already to be in twilight—night can fall abruptly in that region.

Big Rose bit her lips as she walked along. She peered out from the black shawl in which she was wrapped and could see nothing but the widow's half-dead face. Nicky still had his back bound in rags.

As they neared the market place they saw Jewish children emerging from the surrounding little streets, leading gaunt, emaciated dogs on ropes and leashes. There was a pound in the market place where the Germans collected the dogs. The horses and cows had already been transferred to German civilians to bring into the city proper. The dogs within the pound were looking out on the ghetto through barbed wire, their eyes watering. A shadowy terror was frozen upon their frightened, pointed muzzles.

A German stationed near the wicket leading into the pound relieved each owner of his or her dog, pushed the wicket open, kicked the dog with the point of his boot—and the animal found itself in the pound. Rarely or ever did any dog snarl at the German. Sudden shock paralyzed the dogs, depriving them of their strength and numbing their rage. Perhaps this was due to the reek that now came to them from the field where the dogs were being killed.

By the time the widow and Big Rose approached the pound with Nicky it was full of Jewish dogs. They were jammed together, huddled in two's and three's, their heads resting on one another's shoulders. Perhaps they did this because of the cold, which beat down upon them from the sky. A few of them were close to the barbed wire, prodding it with their paws in an attempt to get free. But they had to fall back with a childlike whimper when they felt their paws become sticky with blood. The barbs of the wire were sharp and rusty and stuck out like little knife points.

The widow and Big Rose halted before the German. He was waiting for the old woman to let go of the leash. But, instead of letting go, she wound the leash still tighter about her wrist and even her forearm. She did this with her eyes closed, the way a Jew winds the straps of a phylactery on his forearm. The German snatched at the leash. The widow staggered on her old legs, since Nicky was by now pulling her into the pound. She let herself be dragged along. In the meantime the German kicked the wicket shut. His loud, tinny laughter ran along the barbed wire.

Big Rose saw the widow standing inside the enclosure ringed by a pack of dogs and still holding Nicky on the leash. In her left hand she had the small cane with the silver knob and was keeping it high over the heads of the dogs. She stood there with her cane raised, her hair disheveled, the dogs circling at her feet. Some of the dogs lifted up their mournful heads and looked into the old woman's face. Nicky alone remained unperturbed. His back was still bound up in the white rags torn from Big Rose's blouse. From time to time he lifted his head toward the wicket where Big Rose was standing, petrified.

Exhausted, the widow sank to her knees in the snow. By now one could barely make out her body. The snow was falling more heavily, in bright shimmering stars. The widow's head stood out in the whiteness like a dazzling aureole.

Big Rose saw another wicket fly open on the other side and someone begin driving the dogs out into an open field. The widow stood up, leaned on her small silver-knobbed cane, and, with Nicky leading, started toward the field. . . .

Big Rose wrapped the small black shawl more tightly about her head. She did not want to hear the dull, tinny sounds that came from the sharp-edged shovels scooping up the frozen ground of the Balut. It was only the wind, playing upon the shovels that delved the narrow black pits—only the wind, chanting its chill night song.

A DAY IN THE VILNA GHETTO

by MARK DWORZECKI

MIDNIGHT

DARKNESS all around. On wooden bunks, on tables and chairs moved together lie inert figures; eight, twelve, fifteen people in a room. Whole families lie huddled together, some undressed, others half-clad. The windows are hung with black sheets. Strict black-out is enforced.

The door opens softly and a dim shadow glides across the room and bends over another shadow.

"Shlomo, get up, it's time for your watch."

"Coming right away. What news in the ghetto?"

"Everything's quiet. Some policemen were running about a while ago, must have been looking for someone. But on the whole it's quiet. Hope it keeps up."

ONE A.M.

A silvery winter night. There's snow on the ground. The ghetto is steeped in the pale glow. Walls and leaves cast broken shadows. The cold is intense.

A night watchman, wrapped in a number of overcoats, paces the alley at 44 Zawalna Street. His steps crunch softly in the snow.

The steps of the watchmen in neighboring courtyards sound far away. From time to time they stop to hail one another and their voices echo bleakly against the walls.

Gaps in the walls connect the yards. It is easy to pass from one yard to another. It is very quiet.

A sound of movement is heard from the direction of the ghetto gate. Something is going on.

The gate at 44 Zawalna Street opens on a street outside the ghetto. Beyond lies freedom, or death. But the gate is securely locked and bolted.

Some of the watchmen go to the gate and throw a faint beam from a blacked-out pocket flashlight. Nobody there. Must have imagined things.

But no. One of the boards seems to have been moved a little out of place. The flashlight is switched on again. There's a little bag on the ground. Somebody on the other side must have pushed it through, prying one of the boards loose.

There's a soft footfall and a shadow approaches.

"Shlomo, did you find a little packet near the gate?"

"I did."

"Keep quiet about it. Come, I'll tell you what's in it. Someday this packet is going to be very, very useful."

TWO A.M.

A door opens. One dim shadow glides over to another.

"Avram, get up for your watch. I've done my two hours. It's your turn now."

The night watch in the ghetto yards is changed every two hours. The watchmen keep a lookout for drunken Germans or Lithuanians or Poles who might break through the ghetto gates. In case trouble is brewing, at the smallest sound of suspicious movement members of the night watch run at once from house to house to give the alarm:

"Wake up, everybody! Wake up! Something's going on in the ghetto!"

In a few moments every man, woman, and child is up. Those without identification papers run to the nearest hide-out.

Whatever the cause of the alarm, it is always best to play safe.

FOUR A.M.

People stir in their rooms. Kerosene lamps are lit cautiously, after black-out precautions have been checked. Everyone dresses at the same time—men, women, and children—quickly yet without shame. Social conventions have long been cast aside. No one pays any attention to the others.

Women cluster round the single little stove in the kitchen; they quarrel about who should be the first to cook something for her husband before he goes out to his day's forced labor.

The janitress, or "house commandante" as she is called, a large strong-featured woman, reads out the day's chores from a list on the wall:

"Today Malka sweeps all the rooms and the staircase.

"Sara scrubs the floors.

"Golda does the doors and windows.

"Listen all of you, all those buckets have got to be out of the corridors before daylight. Remember, there's going to be a sanitary inspection today, so you'd better get everything in order. This is the last time I'm warning you. I'm not going to prison on account of you."

The women glare at her, furious:

"Just listen to her! Who do you think you are, a princess? You could also give a hand, you know."

"I work just as hard as you do, if not harder, in the forced-labor squad. And you know it. You can have my job!"

The men intervene:

"Quiet, women, easy there. You've got to do what the *commandante* tells you. The place has to be kept in order. Are you looking for trouble?"

FIVE A.M.

Graying dawn in the distance. There is already some movement in the streets. Queues for tea form at the canteens of the *Judenrat*. Shawled women run back and forth with kettles of hot water. Husbands must drink something warm before going to work.

Men walk up and down with little boxes:

"Who wants to buy saccharine, real German saccharine?"

A woman stops.

"I'll take two packs, if it's real. I don't want the local rubbish."

"You don't know what you're talking about, local rubbish! My son stole this saccharine from a German, at the place where he works. It's genuine Czech saccharine. He also lifted three lemons. Maybe you know somebody who's sick and needs a lemon?"

"How much d'you want for one?"

"Five kilos of bread. My boy ran a terrible risk getting them, you must understand."

SIX A.M.

The labor battalions are lined up at the special assembly yard. Rows and rows of tired men and women. Each group is led by a Jewish squad leader.

The laborers are all dressed differently, in whatever garments or rags they could get their hands on. Each has a rope round the waist and carries a soup can and a small box for bread.

The squads file out of the assembly yard toward the gate of the ghetto.

At the gate stand SS troopers and Lithuanian police. They are the "Gate Watch."

The squads rush through the gate on the double. The lines are counted. The same number must return in the evening. The Jewish squad leader is held responsible for this. If one of his men is missing, he will pay for it with his life.

SEVEN A.M.

The streets are quiet. All the labor squads have left. The ghetto is practically deserted except for the women who have stayed behind, children, ghetto officials, and those without papers who officially do not exist.

Sleepy-eyed children get dressed. A thin soup cooks on the stove. Women once again run to the canteens for hot water—the second breakfast shift.

News of the night's events begins to seep through: who was arrested, where searches were made.

Fresh notices have been pasted on the walls. Groups cluster around them. They do not bear good tidings.

EIGHT A.M.

Children scamper off to the ghetto schools, laborers hurry to the ghetto workshops, *Judenrat* employees go to their offices, the hospital, or the cooperative store.

Ghetto policemen sell the only available newspaper, an anti-Semitic Polish daily, one ruble per copy.

Jews snatch up the paper, glance at the headlines, spit in disgust.

"May they die a foul death, these Jew-baiters. How can anybody read such a paper!" Still, one must get hold of some news somehow, and there's always a chance of learning something between the lines.

NINE A.M.

Life proceeds as usual in the ghetto.

Jewish doctors inspect the sanitation in yards, outhouses; they go from room to room, exhorting, pleading with all and sundry:

"Air the bedclothes. Wash the floors. Wipe the windows. Clean out the latrines. Empty the rubbish cans. Anybody with lice can get a free ticket to the public baths. If your hands begin to itch go down to the antiscurvy clinic for some ointment. If you've got a fever you can have your temperature taken. Here! Please don't break that thermometer, it's the only one we have. Folks! guard against disease."

Dejected Jews react to the exhortations of the doctors and nurses in different ways.

Some grumble, indignant:

"Nothing else to worry about but cleanliness. What about making a living? What about an identity card? And what's this news we hear about Ponar? [1]

Others receive them courteously, invite them to be seated on the wooden bunks:

"Poor doctor. There was a time when you had nice consulting rooms, and look at you now—going around from house to house like the *shames* waking people for Selichot." [2]

"Let's hear a good word, doctor, some piece of good news. Surely you know more than we do."

The news is passed from one flight of stairs to the other:

"The Jewish doctor is coming! The Sanitary Nurse is here! Start mopping the floors! Here, sweep those stairs!"

"Why be afraid of the Jewish doctor? He's not a German, he understands what it's like. You can't get everything done all at once. I bet his wife is still scrubbing her own floors."

Caretakers are tidying up the yards and cleaning out the latrines. Carts are drawn up near the rubbish bins—the peasants have come from outside the ghetto to collect the refuse. They are amazed how so much refuse could have

---

[1] Ponar—a notorious extermination camp in the Vilna district, a dread name for all ghetto inmates.

[2] Selichot—prayers recited daily before dawn during the month preceding the High Holidays.

accumulated overnight, so many potato peelings, beet and cabbage leaves.

A Jewish woman saunters past one of the peasants and whispers furtively:
"Michael, remember me? You once used to buy cloth at my store. Maybe you need a nice blouse for your wife?"

"Of course I remember you. My word, how you've changed! Hurry, bring the blouse down before anybody sees.

"You'll get two kilos of bread, three kilos of potatoes, an egg, and a beet for it."

The deal is made. The red blouse, wrapped in thick paper, vanishes among the refuse on the cart.

The bakeries open their doors. People stand in long queues to buy the hot, strictly rationed loaves. One feels safer when there's a bit of bread in the house. One never knows when it may be necessary to run to the cellars again.

The little stores called "Ghetto Cooperatives" begin to open. The rations are chalked up on the doors: "Frozen potatoes—three kilos, half a kilo of carrots, and one kilo of beets, per ration card."

Queues have formed outside the stores. Don't turn up your nose at frozen potatoes. Wash them well then grate them and make a pie. Anything is better than going hungry.

The offices of the *Judenrat* are a hive of activity. Officials write furiously registering names, issuing ration cards, affixing stamps, drawing up lists. Impatient queues besiege the offices.

The ghetto workshops reverberate with the sound of hammer upon metal. The mechanical saw whines in the ghetto sawmill. Out of the mill come little wagons, laden with logs and drawn by children of the ghetto Transport Brigade.

Outside the public baths people queue up to buy tickets or to be deloused.

Shrill voices of school children at a singing lesson:

"This is how the farmer
Sows his corn, sows his corn . . ."

"Teacher, where does he sow it? What does corn look like?"

From another schoolroom the voice of the teacher carries through the paneless windows:

"When the Romans were besieging Massada."

ELEVEN A.M.

A secret alarm bell rings in the *Judenrat*. This bell, connected with the ghetto gate, gives a prearranged signal—Muhrer is coming! [3]

Jewish ghetto police run from one yard to the other giving the alarm.

[3] Muhrer—SS Lieutenant-Colonel, Ghetto Commissioner of Vilna. He was arrested in Austria in 1947, extradited to Russia, and sentenced to death in 1948.

"Muhrer is coming!"

The streets are cleared as if by magic. The hawkers and peddlers, those without identification papers, everyone with a sprinkling of gray in his beard,[4] all vanish into thin air.

Dead silence in the streets, suspense in the hide-outs. Caretakers seize brooms and begin sweeping out the courtyards in frenzied haste. The janitress runs through the rooms:

"Sweep those floors! Clean up! Hurry, tidy everything up, Muhrer is coming!"

Life comes to a standstill.

Sometime later the news is flashed from house to house, from room to room:

"M has been to the *Judenrat* and the ghetto prison. Didn't take anybody away with him."

"M has gone!"

Jews flock into the streets once more. Queues are re-formed. Carts and wagons rattle through the streets. Children's singing voices can be heard above the din.

Life resumes its beat.

NOON

Public kitchens are tightly packed. Today's menu: Cabbage soup and boiled potatoes (frozen).

"How long can such food keep a man on his feet?"

The poor of the ghetto and those without families have their midday meal at the public kitchens. Others take the soup back to their homes, augment it with whatever they have been able to scrape up, smuggle, or buy.

ONE P.M.

Early afternoon lull. Quiet streets. No Germans are to be seen at the gate; it is their *mahlzeit*. A few Lithuanian police are hanging about, but their palms have been well greased. The Jewish policemen are at their posts and look unconcerned. No SS men in sight. Suddenly a cart appears at the gate laden with old rags and scraps of wood. It seems to have sprung up from nowhere. The gate swings open and the cart turns into a nearby yard where it is swiftly unloaded—potatoes, carrots, bags of flour.

The cart leaves, carrying refuse.

All's quiet, no SS in sight.

A second cart rumbles into the ghetto. A few dozen loaves, some bags of flour and peas are pulled out from under the logs.

Bread will cost less in the ghetto this evening.

---

[4] Persons showing signs of age were the first to be exterminated.

FOUR P.M.

There is activity at the gate. The first labor battalions returning from nearby begin to arrive.

The people present a curious appearance. Some have strange humps and protuberances about their persons, others limp, have swollen calves and thighs, distended bellies, grotesquely broad shoulders—caused by the potatoes and flour they try to conceal about their bodies.

They huddle together furtively as the count is taken. The number tallies. The check is perfunctory. They scuttle through.

Children eagerly await them in the doorways:

"Got through all right, Papa? What have you brought?"

"A couple of slices of bread, some potato soup in the tin, and two spools of thread."

"Papa, you're great, you bring home so much. There's some beet soup on the stove, let's mix it with the soup you brought. With the thread you pinched we'll get some more bread. That'll be fine, won't it, Papa?"

"That's fine, son; as long as we're still alive . . ."

SIX P.M.

Endless lines of returning forced laborers wait for admittance. There is a delay at the gate. SS troopers have arrived to make a thorough check.

Policemen run searching hands over shrinking bodies, produce a handful of potatoes, half a loaf of bread.

Levas, the policeman, stands by with his rubber truncheon and lets every smuggler feel the weight of it.

A woman, suspiciously on the stout side, shuffles past, is stopped and searched. A young rooster flies from her ample bosom and runs around cackling and crowing. All the police—Germans and Lithuanians—chase the rooster, who leads them on, flaps his wings in their faces, eludes them, crowing tauntingly.

Scores of Jews take advantage of the confusion to rush through the open gates, clinging to the precious packages. They disappear into the darkness.

The woman tries to slip away. Levas goes after her with his rubber truncheon.

SEVEN P.M.

The ghetto streets are quiet again.

The laborers who have returned from "outside" recount the news of the day to eager families and friends:

"Farmers on the road said the Russians are quite near."

"The bridge beyond Lyda has been blown up."

"The trains were carrying 'frozen apples' [Germans frostbitten on the Russian fronts]."

"A large transport of 'chopped cabbage' [severely wounded soldiers] passed through the railway station today."

"Another train blown up near Villaika. Wonder who could have done it?"

"There was a search at the tailoring workshop today. They found a spool of thread on one woman. Took her away."

"Our German foreman at the factory whispered in my ear: 'Run away while you still have the chance, they're going to do away with the lot of you.'"

"A plague on him! It's just like him to rub it in. Where can we run to, and who's going to take us in? I say that what has to happen will happen, and there's nothing to be done about it."

Spitalna Street is the street of the ghetto hospital.

At the corner, a group of ghetto "strategists" cluster around Dr. Yashpan, the "political commentator," who reviews the news of the day with an air of importance:

"A report has come in that the German Thirteenth Division has been completely destroyed."

"Where did you get that from?"

"What do you care? If I tell you the news came in, I know what I'm saying. . . . The Twenty-third Corps is surrounded. The Twenty-first Division is in a tight spot and can't get out, they're absolutely cut off."

Hope dawns.

"Bless you doctor! May I only live to see the day when they are defeated."

Evening trade is brisk in Shavelska and Strashun, the two main streets of the ghetto. Goods smuggled in during the day are now brought out into the open.

Men, women, and children walk up and down crying their wares.

"Potatoes, three rubles a kilo, potatoes!"

"Real saccharine, genuine saccharine!"

"Beets, nice big beets!"

"Radishes, as big as pumpkins!"

"Needles, pins, shoelaces!"

"Pea flour, good for cooking, good for baking!"

"Cigarettes! German, Polish, Spanish cigarettes!"

Women and small boys peddle local ghetto products.

"Pies! Pancakes! Potato cakes! Meal pancakes!"

"Sweets, candy, three rubles each! Caramels—melt in your mouth—six rubles apiece!"

"Soap! Real, genuine soap! Makes a lather! Stamped with the original trademark!"

Two well-known ghetto merchants stand at the corner:

"Who has a gold watch for a Polish nobleman? Payment in cash."

"I need a white wedding dress for my former porter. I guarantee a kilo of white bread and a quarter kilo of butter."

Business flourishes.

Outside the library on Strashun Street, sixteen-year-old Nachumke has set up his stand. In a half-hiss, half-whisper, he offers his goods for sale:

"Cyanide! D'you want to buy some cyanide? Die in a moment!"

"Is it the real stuff?"

"Test it at the pharmacy if you don't believe me."

"How much for a single dose?"

"Thousand rubles a dose. Cheap for a quick death. Keep you out of Ponar!"

The Jew stands there thinking it over and strokes his beard:

"If I buy one dose for myself, it's not fair to the wife. . . . A couple of doses would cost me two thousand rubles—a lot of money. . . . I can live on it for two months. . . ."

Nachumke urges:

"What's the use of saving your money now. For another two months of this? Afterwards it'll be too late, you won't be able to get this stuff. How will you stop them from sending you to Ponar then?"

"Buy my own death? Take my life? Run away from the sort of death that awaits me? No. I'll die the way I'm destined to die."

(I came across Nachumke sometime later in an Estonian concentration camp, badly beaten up and dying of dysentery. He recognized me and spoke with genuine regret: "Sold everybody cyanide. Left none for myself. Couldn't afford it. Had to support my family. Gave so many people the chance to die whenever they wanted. Didn't leave myself a single dose of cyanide. Had to buy potatoes and bread. Not a single dose . . .")

A small group of women in the yard of the *Judenrat*. One says:

"I heard them say today that some truck driver came across a labor gang of Vilna Jews working on the road near Minsk. They say he brought some woman a letter from her husband who had been taken away during one of the deportations. It looks as if not all of them have been killed. Some of them must still be alive!"

Her neighbor asks:

"Who is this woman? Maybe I can find out if my husband is also alive?"

"Can't find out who she is. She won't let on. Must be afraid the others will be jealous of her."

A wide-eyed, pale child of six clutches the hand of a thin young woman. She says excitedly:

"They're alive . . . somewhere . . . maybe near Vitebsk, or around Minsk . . . but I know they're alive. Last night I dreamt I saw my husband . . . he was taken away last summer . . . he beckoned to me . . . he said we'd all be together soon. . . ."

"What does that mean . . . all be together soon?"

EIGHT P.M.

The young people are taking their evening stroll in two's and three's. The streets are very crowded.

Youngsters laugh and joke, exchange glances, flirt, forgetting for the moment the grim squalor and the ever-present sense of dread that pervades the ghetto.

Thronged main streets. Rudnitzka, Shavelska, Strashun Streets look almost festive. The ghetto café offers black, unsweetened coffee—roasted bran extract.

Romantic couples stroll to the yard of the *Judenrat*. There stands a tree—the only tree in the ghetto—giving the illusion of a park.

The lumber yard at 6 Strashun Street is the tryst for young lovers. Perched on the heaps of timber they hold hands and sing the sad, stirring Russian songs. Refrains are caught up, voices blend:

> "We shall meet again
> At the cannon's breech . . ."

There is a performance at the ghetto theater. In the ghetto café people crowd around the little tables, recounting the hardships and horrors of day. The evening prayers are recited in the synagogue. Committees of the Underground hold their consultations. The ghetto choirs sing Hebrew and Yiddish songs.

News bulletins of the Partisan Organization circulate from hand to hand.

NINE P.M.

Crowds queue for the latrine and the water tap before retiring for the night into the suffocation of the cramped quarters. Some still discuss the latest scraps of news.

"Do you think we'll be able to sleep in peace tonight?"

"Look, Leibel, just nip outside and find out if there's going to be any trouble tonight. We might as well know if we can get undressed, or just go to bed in our clothes."

In the crowded darkness of the rooms the wooden bunks are put up, blankets are spread on tables and floors, on chairs. The occupants lie down to sleep. Someone whispers:

"Well, another day's passed, at any rate."

"Don't say 'passed.' The night has only begun."

TEN P.M.

The ghetto sleeps. The streets, the houses are enveloped in silence, except for faint, indistinguishable sounds that come from the cellars and the attics—Partisans training in the use of arms, or constructing new hide-outs.

The first night watch goes out to its posts.

ELEVEN P.M.

A distant muffled drone is borne across the sleeping skies—Allied airplanes.

"Come in your thousands! Come every day, every hour! Bring the liberation nearer and nearer."

Again the stillness of death. A watchman nudges his comrade:

"Listen!"

"It's nothing."

Another member of the watch, a Biblical student, softly calls out the ancient scriptural phrase:

"Watchman, what of the night?"

A voice answers.

Then again silence.

THE BUNKER

by M. J. FEIGENBAUM

B Y DAY, nine of us hid in a corn patch. However, the farmers were working up to the harvest; soon the fields would be stripped, and with them our hiding place laid bare. We had to find another refuge if we were to survive. So we set out, late at night, on July 20, 1943, to look for a place where no human eye might see us. We found none, and at daybreak we climbed to the attic of the first house in sight, determined to continue our search the following night. That was when I thought of some Christian women my family had known, who owned an orchard and barn at the city limits. I decided to go there, to ask if they would help us hide, or at least supply us with food.

Two of us started out while it was still dark, so as to have our talk with the women the first thing in the morning. We made it safely, in plenty of time; so, after stilling our hunger on fresh fruit, we went to sleep beneath a clump of young fir trees.

The rising sun bathed the orchard in light when we awoke. The women received us doubtfully. They listened to what we had to say, but would not be persuaded. Only a little while ago, they told us, a whole family had been arrested on suspicion of harboring Jews. How could they risk the lives of their folks?

That night we rejoined our friends in the attic. Before long, however, shepherd boys had spied us there, and we had to go back, once more, to the fields. Meanwhile two of our group, Justman and Hofer, had managed to buy some food from peasants in the neighborhood; one of them even agreed to supply us regularly. Having paid him for future orders, Justman and Hofer returned, the night of July 25th, with more food and the news that the man had shown them a cellar in his barn that could be easily transformed into a bunker. He had offered to take in the two of them as well as a third person for a consideration; the price was to be named when they went back again for food the next night.

Anxiously we waited, all the rest of that night and the day after. Finally it was dark again. We had resigned ourselves to breaking up into small groups, as it was impossible to find a hiding place for nine people. Consequently, Samuel Gwiodze and his wife left, to go back to Siedlec, while Justman and Hofer set out to conclude their negotiations with the peasant. Five of us remained, crouching amid the sheaves of corn, impatient for their return.

The sound of approaching footsteps cheered us momentarily. We waited eagerly for the password. But then there was the sound of many footsteps. We could hear Hofer's voice, pleading with someone. . . . Hardly daring to breathe, we sank deeper into the corn. Hours passed, still our comrades did not return. Evidently, the peasant had plans of his own for Jews with money, lurking in the fields. . . .

That night, too, crept away at last. But now we could no longer remain in the corn patch. We moved in among the barley stalks, and lay all day without food or water, beneath the blistering sun. Our plan was made: we would wait until midnight, on the chance that our comrades might yet return; otherwise, we were to head for the orchard and barn. So we lay and waited, but no one came; we listened to empty air.

Another of our number, meanwhile, had decided to go back to his home town. That left four of us—Sara Cahn, her brother, Preter, Isaac Koniar, and myself—as we started out, busy with plans to save ourselves. On the way over, we quenched our thirst at a well; then, coming to the orchard, we picked some of the tart green apples. There we once more parted company. Preter and I stayed behind to seek out the Polish women in the morning, to change some money and renew our pleas for a hiding place. Mrs. Cahn went on toward town to see what she could find; Koniar had remained hidden in the grain.

It was Wednesday, an eventful day, for we learned that Mussolini had fallen; yet we were no better off. Once again I talked to the Polish women about concealing us. They answered with tears: "If it were just a fine, or prison . . . but it's our lives. We also want to get through these few weeks. . . ." But we did not go hungry that day.

Shelter was as remote as ever when we met that night. Now that the grain was no longer safe, we moved into the shrubbery. At night we haunted the orchard, drawing water for the coming day, picking some apples and cucumbers. The days dragged on. Where would we go? Our grandiose plans had collapsed.

The dog days were unbearable. We kept running short of water and could hardly wait for night to replenish our stores. Days passed with a dull sameness. After the heat came the rains, and soon we wished for summer to be back. We froze and rotted in our damp clothes. No one felt like eating; life had become too horrible.

And then I had an idea. A crazy idea, but we grasped at it nevertheless. We would dig a pair of bunkers, like unmarked graves, to hide us, in the orchard. However, we would need lumber, and we had neither material nor tools. We decided to venture out into the woods at night and cut down some trees. It was risky. But what had we to lose?

A deserted barn and field kitchen, once a camp for Jews draining the swamps, stood on the way. There was just a chance we might find something there. . . .

"Today is Tuesday," I said, "a lucky day for Jews."

So we started out, carrying a shovel and a dull ax, at once tools for work and arms for defense. We were in luck, for upon reaching our destination an hour later we found lumber of all shapes and sizes, as though made to order for us. Preter and Koniar, who had climbed in the tiny window, now handed out the boards the same way, and we hauled our precious load over six kilometers back to "our" orchard. At dawn we selected a likely spot for our first bunker in the thick of the fir trees, having first cached our lumber in a field of buckwheat nearby.

All that day was spent in organizing our project. As soon as night fell, we eagerly tackled the job. For the moment our most pressing problem was how to dispose of the dirt we dug up; we solved that eventually by spreading the freshly dug earth along the fence, unaware how it would look by daylight. Carrying our load in a potato sack, we never dreamed that a hole two meters long, one meter wide, and a little less than two meters deep could hold so much earth. It took us three nights to finish the job, and in the end we lay down in the tight little dugout, grateful at finding shelter at last.

In spite of our precautions, we were found out immediately. The farm women were quick to grasp the meaning of the freshly dug earth and broken fir branches. They came to our bunker. But they were compassionate; their discovery proved our blessing, for they undertook to provide for us. And so they did, with unselfish devotion and solicitude. Whenever important news of the war reached them, moreover, they would slip out to hearten us.

We had yet to build the entrance to our bunker, a ticklish assignment, as it would have to be so contrived that even persons standing nearby would see nothing to arouse their suspicions. A bunker is really a grave for the living, but we had forgotten that the living need air. On one occasion, for instance, when Preter had to see the Polish women, the three of us crawled in, while he closed the entrance with boards and covered them with earth. Lying there, in the dark, we fell asleep. Koniar was the first to wake up, choking. He began to tear at his clothes, and woke us too. Vaguely, I understood what had happened. Straining at the boards, I finally managed to move them, and let in some precious air.

A week later, we had completed our first bunker and started on the second, also among fir trees. Working through the night, we lay concealed in our bunkers throughout the day. Then, when darkness fell again, we went back to work, sweat pouring from us. With no possibility of washing regularly, we became filthy and vermin-ridden. Delousing was to be, in fact, an important part of our daily routine. Yet when we had completed our bunkers and lay all day without a lick of work to do, we found we'd have to think of a way to keep busy. To begin with, we decided to make our bunkers more comfortable, to turn them into tiny underground cabins instead of the living graves they were. There was plenty of wood only six kilometers away, and we made several nightly forays. The dark of night protected us, and as we returned, heavily laden with lumber, we would hum the Polish song:

> Ours is the night,
> We have nought else . . .

Stretched out in our de luxe cabins, at length, we only began to realize what risks we had taken in the past month, and the part that luck had played in our venture. There were military encampments, all too close for comfort. Suppose all that digging and hammering had been overheard! . . . Yet we were proud of our handiwork too; architects really ought to familiarize themselves with this new branch of construction.

After we had tidied the bunkers and covered the wooden floor and walls with straw mats, it was our turn to clean up: nor did we skimp on soap or water. Finally we changed our underwear. Clean and comfortable at last—the bunkers were now equipped with clothes hangers and shelves, as well as lamps —we grew hungry and began to wish for some home cooking. We managed to get hold of a primus stove, and Mrs. Cahn, our housekeeper, regaled us with tasty dishes. After all, there were lots of things for our table in the fine orchard where we were living. Working by moonlight, our housekeeper also washed our clothes in water boiled in the primus, and we dried them in the bunkers. At the same time, the two Polish women and their young farmhand attended to all our needs.

On warm, fragrant nights when we had nothing else to do, we would stroll through the orchard and look longingly toward the city. You wanted to laugh because you had hidden under the enemy's very nose; and you wanted to cry at each glimpse of the city, your birthplace, where joy and hope had vanished with wife and child, mother and sisters.

Lying in the cabin of your underground yacht by day, when sleep will not come, you remember the times you hoped for such a hiding place; now that you have it you are apathetic and only long for death. Our Christian friends, who pump courage into us, bring us good news of the war. We lie and wait for peace, momentarily expecting the women to come running, panting with the news.

Time passes. It is August—almost a year since my first loss, the first blow to our family, when my sisters were killed. It seems like yesterday, remembering my mother as she blessed the candles on Yom Kippur eve, and friends came to offer New Year's wishes. And suddenly my mother burst into convulsive sobs and beat her head with her fists. . . . Then comes August 25, another fatal anniversary, when part of my life ended with the loss of my wife and child. I didn't think I could survive it; yet more than a year has passed since. Sometimes it seems as if it all happened only yesterday; then again it seems so far away you begin to doubt you ever had a home.

Lying in your de luxe grave with your grim memories, you hear cheerful sounds above. The orchard resounds with gaiety. It is Sunday, and friends of the Polish women have come for a stroll. There is life up there; the grave is for the dead. In the evening, when the forbidden lights in the cabin grow fainter and shadows lengthen on the walls, there is a soft tapping on the bunker. We open the door, and our friend brings us news. She tells us the Italians have surrendered and leaves some newspapers.

The calendar moves to another grievous day, October 6, when my mother was deported to Treblinka. Her life seemed worthless after she had lost her three daughters. She made not the slightest effort to save herself, but voluntarily joined the death transport.

Autumn has come. Nature is dying and so, I feel, am I. Perhaps I'll go to sleep and wake up in the spring. The orchard looks funereal now. Trees rustle soundlessly. The feeble sunbeams barely reach our bunker. Red and yellow leaves are falling; the ghostly trees are naked. In the evening we sit around a pot of warm food, talk and play dominoes. By day we read—if there is something to read. When there is nothing else to do, we sleep. Generally, we sleep a great deal. Though our dreams are bad, it is better than being awake.

We doubled up in one bunker the night of November 6, discussing our problems. As we emerged at dawn, we found the orchard blanketed with snow, its dazzling white spread over fields and trees. Cautiously we crept back, trying not to leave too many tracks. Then and there, we worked out a plan to restrict our movements, because of the telltale footprints. We would install a telephone over the fifteen meters between the two bunkers. The construction was quite primitive, consisting of a hammer and a small board attached to a wire. Communication was made by tapping. The wire itself was concealed among the fir trees. Writing, now, I hear the telephone tap out the message that dinner is ready.

We crept out of our bunkers at night and looked south toward the Russian war-prisoners' camp. One day, perhaps, the camp would be gone; then we would know that the end is near. But night by night, we kept seeing its lights and heard the melancholy notes of nostalgic Russian melodies.

With the coming of winter, life in our graves became more difficult. We were snowbound. "I used to love the snow," the young farmhand would say, "but now it makes me sad and afraid." We dug a hole in one of the bunkers and filled it with potatoes, so he and the women would not have to come too often. And so we lay in our graves and trembled with the cold. Drawing water became a problem. Though the well in the orchard was about fifteen meters deep, it yielded little water. Moreover the rope broke, leaving us with a piece in hand while the rest, pail and all, lay at the bottom of the well. Christmas came; we sent our friends greetings.

Shrouded in white, the orchard sleeps its winter sleep. Who'd ever believe that buried underneath the fir trees are living human beings, whose only wish is to look for once upon a free world? Who'd think that people live beneath the frozen ground and crawl out on wintry nights to look up at the sky, the stars, and the moon? Yet though the winter nights are long, they pass quickly. After partaking of hot food, we turn to our bookkeeping lesson. I am the teacher. Then we study Russian. We wind up playing chess or dominoes—I carved all the pieces myself, in two nights.

In spite of all, the tedium of our underground existence becomes unendurable at last. So overpowering is my desire to see another face that I decide to tempt fate by visiting my town. I start out across the fields, just as the shadows on our bunker wall begin to lengthen. Underneath my coat, I carry the dull ax. It will serve me as identification papers.

It is Friday, a dull, cloudy evening. I crawl through the deep snowdrifts in my wooden shoes. My path leads through the Jewish cemetery, every trace of which had been destroyed. Only when I approach the Catholic cemetery do I realize that I have been walking over the graves of our ancestors. "Forgive me, my dear ones," I whisper, "for disturbing your eternal rest."

There are more people nearer to town. My heart beats wildly. Death stalks me like a shadowy creature that might pounce at any moment. The snowy streets are dark. People seem to float past and disappear. Now I am in the Jewish quarter. Vacant lots and ruined buildings. Houses untenanted, their doors and windows ajar.

I call on my acquaintance, the Volkdeutsche. Dumfounded, he stares at me as though I had returned from the dead. I ask if he has news of my brother, in Lublin. As to that he knows nothing, but he tells me about the war. The Red Army is near Kowel, the Germans on the Eastern front are surrounded. In two weeks—a month at the latest—he thinks the Russians will be here. He gives me some things and I start back. But I cannot leave without passing our house. As I draw near, I seem to hear my father's voice, bidding me welcome. I want to fall down and kiss the cold stones. But I only stand there, like a Jew at the Wailing Wall.

Though the winter is not severe, its dreary, sunless days weigh heavily upon us. Droves of crows swoop over our graves; their angry cawing grates on our nerves. Once a week, one of us goes to the barn to pick up our provisions from the farmhand and have a talk with him. Face to face with reality, hope melts like snow beneath the sun. The front is still far away.

Finally the calendar ushers in the long-awaited spring. Yet nature in her capriciousness has just begun winter. Snow is piled high, and the frost burns fiercely. The tiny pane of our bunker window is a frozen mosaic. Weeks pass, with no relief. The de luxe cabins are dark and desolate catacombs.

Yet we have lately noticed increased military activity in our area. At dawn, on March 30, we are aroused by sounds of shouting. Peering out of our bunker, we see that the fence around the orchard has been knocked down on two sides, and men with shovels are working in the fields. What can it mean? We listen closely, but all we hear is the howling of yet another snowstorm.

We had thought the orchard safe. But now, with the fence down . . . it came to us that they must be digging trenches. That night we repaired the fence and retired, somewhat reassured. The morning proved our guess correct. Men were, in fact, digging trenches not far from the orchard. We had a new job now. Each night we would slip out to see what direction the trenches were taking, mortally afraid that they might pass through the orchard. The digging kept coming closer. Once more the Germans tore the fence down. We felt certain, now, that they would cut straight into our bunker. Just the same, we repaired the fence as usual, that night, before we lay back in our graves. Yet it was not disturbed again; evidently the trenches would not cross the orchard, after all.

On Easter our Christian friends brought us cakes and meats, welcome delicacies. At long last, the snows had begun to melt. Soon peasants would be in the fields with their plowshares. On May 1, we had some evening entertainment, in the form of a Soviet air raid over Brzesc. Clouds of smoke and flame appeared in the skies, and we heard the echoes of crashing bombs. The orchard grew greener; trees burst into bloom; fresh air sweetened our breath. I lay in the bunker and recorded the murder of our people. In the evening we strolled down the lanes among the trees, talking politics and military strategy. Then, at the first rays of sunshine, we returned reluctantly to the bunker.

On the second day of Shevuoth, the Feast of Weeks, we were met with bad news at the other bunker. During the day, the husband of one of the Polish women and a friend of his had been tending to a young sapling in the orchard. The friend, who had lingered among the fir trees, suddenly called out: "Look, there's a hole here!" Putting his hand down the hole of the concealed opening, he lifted the cover over the entrance, then quickly dropped it. "There's some kind of lid here," our friends heard him say; "you can see people have been walking among the fir trees." The owner stammered something and changed the subject. I might add, he almost never came to our bunker, as if he didn't want to know of our existence.

Our friends were sure they hadn't been seen, as they had covered themselves with something dark. Maybe the visitor hadn't caught on, after all. . . . Our bunkers were well covered with grass and difficult to detect. Unfortunately, a heady wind that day had parted the grass. Would we be forced to leave and go back into the fields, after all these months? No one felt like eating that evening.

We waited to be dispossessed. In the morning, however, when the farm-hand rapped on our bunker as usual, he made no mention of the incident. We were about to breathe a sigh of relief. But then, the second morning, he told us we would have to leave; the women said so. We asked to see them first.

The younger woman came, with downcast eyes, ashamed to face us. We suggested that if worst came to worst, we could double up in one bunker; after all, we hadn't yet been discovered. In any case only one man knew the secret, and he was a good friend—a reliable person. Naturally, if there was real danger, we would get out.

"Where will you go?" she lamented. "You're so helpless. . . ."

It was decided that she would visit their friend and find out what he suspected.

Several days passed. We waited impatiently. Then she came back and related the conversation to us:

"I hear you found something in our orchard," she said. "A lid. My husband looked, but couldn't see anything suspicious."

"I found nothing suspicious either," he answered. "Just a lid over an opening, like a sewer."

So we remained in our graves.

Once I saw a tiny piece of paper flutter through the opening into the bunker. In the reflection of the setting sun, I read: "Today, June 6, in the early hours, the invasion began between Cherbourg and Le Havre. Rome has been occupied by the Allies."

But weeks passed, and our life was as tedious and depressing as ever. We had survived the fall, winter, and spring in our bunkers, but now it seemed as if the summer might drive us out. Rain flooded our catacombs. One bunker became unfit for habitation, and we had to crowd into the other, while repairs were made. The air was stuffy; food spoiled; bread became moldly. The Russian front was steadily advancing. At night the Russian air force furnished grandiose spectacles while bombing German objectives. The lights of the Russian prisoner-of-war camp were gone; we no longer heard the captives' plaintive songs. We began to think that these really were our last days in the bunker. Anticipating our departure, we stared at the walls whose dampness had soaked into our lungs for months.

Lost in thought, I suddenly heard someone tapping outside. It was one of our Polish women. Her face beamed. "This time, I have good news for you." The Germans were packing, she told me; the post office was no longer functioning. Next morning, the farmhand brought us more news. Meanwhile, we observed the changes at night. The huge searchlight that used to comb the skies for Soviet aircraft was to be seen no more. There was no movement on the roads. The sky was red for miles around. Lit by flames, the orchard was light as day.

On July 24, there was dead silence all around. From time to time, the bunker heaved with distant explosions. Then, for two days, no one came near us. We went out early one evening, having observed some movement in the trenches along the orchard. Now we could hear the booming of artillery. We didn't cook that night, but made preparations to prolong our stay in the bunkers, in case we were immobilized by the nearness of the front. From now on, we would sleep at night and wake in the morning, like normal human beings.

The morning silence, occasionally broken by a burst of shrapnel, unnerved us. Then—footsteps near the bunker. Who could it be? But then came the familiar tapping, louder and surer this time. "Out of the grave!" the young farmhand called to us. "You are free!"

Yet I was not overcome with joy. For I remembered my loneliness; my homelessness. Red Army soldiers were swarming over the orchard, their automatics at the ready. In broken Russian, we told them who we were, repeating again and again, "Mi Yevreyi" (We are Jews). They told us we could go into the town; we'd have to leave the orchard, which had now become part of the front lines.

We washed and put on clean clothes. Then we climbed out of our graves for the last time.

UNDERGROUND COURIER

by WLADKA MEED

Fɪʀsᴛ, you had to find arms. You'd risk your life, but you'd get them. Then, you had to smuggle them into the ghetto. Crossing over in itself was no easy matter, let alone transporting packages. As long as you had nothing on you, you could fall in with one of the labor gangs on the way home from the Aryan side. But there was always the danger of being searched and caught at the gate, if you carried something.

One night comrade Michal smuggled in a revolver, under the very noses of the Germans. The job was to have been done by another smuggler, a Gentile, working inside the ghetto. When the man failed to show up at the appointed hour, Michal decided to go ahead on his own. All the time he was crossing the Umschlagplatz, he kept his hand firmly on the gun in his pocket, ready to shoot if he were stopped. Fortunately, he was able to make his delivery and get back without a hitch. But we had to find another way to continue operations.

The ghetto wall extended all along Okpowa and Dzika. In between, there is a narrow street called Parysowski Place. The guards at that point had been bribed, and a brisk business in smuggling was carried on over the wall. Traders of the Kerceli market would crawl over, to buy clothes, shoes, underwear, sewing machines, etc. at ridiculously low prices. Others ventured to break into abandoned Jewish homes, dismantle beds, chests, credenzas and other articles of furniture, and transport them bit by bit over the wall. Eventually the Germans uncovered most of the smuggling points, and shot a number of smugglers. Once more, crossing the wall became difficult.

Michal introduced me to the smuggling point on Parysowski. He and another worker, Yurek, had smuggled our first shipment—about a dozen revolvers that representatives of the Jewish Coordinating Committee had obtained from the Polish underground—by this approach. The revolvers were packed in small boxes, covered with a layer of nails, and loaded on a wheelbarrow, like ordinary supplies. Our Polish landlord, Stefan Mahai, pushed the wheelbarrow, while Michal and Yurek followed at some distance, each with a gun in his pocket. All went well, until a policeman stopped Stefan at Dzika, right near the smuggling point, and asked to see his permit to move goods. Fortunately, a few zlotys helped satisfy his curiosity, and he let them go their way. Michal gave the password, and one of our comrades of the Jewish Fighter Organization on the other side of the wall climbed up, took the boxes Michal, Yurek, and Stefan handed up to him, and lowered them into the ghetto. If any of the fighter group had been intercepted, Michal told me, they would have shot their way out. None would dream of letting the revolvers, for which they had waited so long, fall into unauthorized hands.

I was to use this route frequently myself, later on. The first time, I had gone along with Michal to deliver a box of steel files, destined for the Fighter Organization. I held the package, while Michal slipped into a tumbledown building opposite the ghetto, where the Gentile "operators" had their headquarters. Having paid in advance for the privilege of crossing, we had to wait until a young Pole gave us the all-clear signal. Thereupon Michal swiftly scaled the wall; I handed him the package, watched him disappear on the other side, then went home.

The next time, I went to Parysowski Place alone, in charge of delivering three packages of dynamite. It was deathly still along the wall when I arrived. Suspecting that something had happened, I stopped an elderly woman.

"Why's everything so dead?" I asked.

"Two smugglers were shot this morning," she told me. "Others were arrested. Now they've got special patrols on duty."

The news wasn't exactly sensational. There were always these risks in smuggling. The question was, what to do now. Delay was out, as the dynamite was badly needed in the ghetto. Comrades were almost certainly waiting for me on the other side of the wall at that very moment. Consequently I telephoned the ghetto, reported what had happened, and said that I would try to smuggle in the packages through Feifer's factory.

Feifer's leather factory was situated on Okpowa, near Gliniana, at the border of the ghetto. Jews often used the building to slip out. I rang the bell; the watchman opened the door. The old man was badly frightened. It took me a long time to talk him into letting me smuggle a small package into the ghetto. However, the prospect of money and liquor finally convinced him. Well satisfied, I called my comrades again, and asked them to wait for me at six that evening on the ghetto side of Feifer's factory.

I was on my way to the factory at the appointed hour, with my package of dynamite in tow. It was dusk; there was little movement on the street. Unfortunately, the German sentry on guard at the Jewish cemetery on the opposite side of Okpowa also kept an eye on the factory. I ducked into a nearby doorway, and watched the guard. I'd have to wait, I decided; better try it after dark. Then I saw the guard turn aside to light a cigarette. I bolted to the factory gate, and rang the bell.

We are inside now, my package of dynamite and I. The watchman bids me follow him. We pass several rooms, upstairs and down, and finally come to one filled with boxes and crates. I look around for some opening through which to conduct our smuggling. The watchman understands, and points to a corner. "Get ready," he says, and turns off the light. The room is plunged into darkness. I hear something being moved. Then, as I strain toward the corner, I begin to recognize the outlines of a small, grated window.

"Hurry up and hand out your package," the watchman orders.

I peer out the window into the darkness. Not a sound anywhere. Have my comrades left already? Very softly, I call out the password:

"Yurek! Yurek!"

"At last!" comes the whispered reply.

A shadow appears at the window. I recognize Janek Bilak, a courageous member of the Fighter Organization, always ready for the most dangerous missions. I pick up my dynamite—but, worse luck—the package is too big to pass between the grates.

"Faster! Faster!" the voice outside urges me.

"Wait a minute, I must repack," I answer softly.

I have no choice. The old man is beside me. Nervously our fingers flutter over the boxes. It is taking too long. Why didn't the old man tell me to make small packages? The watchman is quaking all over. Outside, they keep pressing me.

We are finished, at last. I shove the dynamite past the grating. As soon as the last package is out, the watchman locks the window and switches on the light. Flushed and perspiring he stands there, without a word. I gather up the remaining paper and some spilled dynamite dust.

"No reason to be afraid," I say. "You see, it went off fine."

"I won't risk it again," the watchman gasps. "I was frightened to death."

I hand him three hundred zlotys and a bottle of whisky, as I say good-bye. The old man's hand is still trembling.

"Tell me the truth," he asks suddenly, "what was in those packages?".

"Nothing special. Just some boxes of paint."

"That all?" The old man peers into my eyes.

"That's all."

On the lists of the Coordinating Committee were the names of several Jews in the nearby city of Radom. A number of Warsaw Jews as well, among them Abraham Meltzer (now in New York) and Kotlar (now in Israel) were known to be working there, in the German printing plant. But the Committee had no names of Gentiles through whom contact might be established. Eventually, I was sent with money and instructions to contact the surviving Jews of Radom. My immediate assignment was to bring them aid, discuss their problems with them, and urge them to organize an underground relief committee, to cooperate with the Warsaw Coordinating Committee.

Radom was a German military center. There were almost no civilians on the streets, and hardly any open shops. A numbing fear seemed to grip the city. German rules and restrictions were rigidly enforced.

From the railway station, I headed straight for the printing plant, on Nowomieyska Street. Upon arriving there, however, I found the lowslung brick building locked, its windows shuttered, and no sign of activity anywhere. Some Germans sauntered past the office next to the main gate. How was I to learn anything?

Fortunately, I had noticed a Polish woman selling apples at the corner. I bought some of her wares, and fell into a conversation with her.

"Could you tell me where I might buy some old clothes?" I asked. "I understand Jews sell them cheaply. But where are they?"

The old woman looked around cautiously, then whispered:

"You can't do business with Jews any more. They've sold all their good stuff long ago. All they've got now is the rags they pull off their backs, but it wouldn't pay you to buy them. Besides, a lot of smugglers were caught and shot by the Germans."

I interrupted to ask where the Jews were. I'd see for myself if the stuff was worth buying. The old woman pointed to the building I had just passed.

"In there," she said. "You can see them at noon. Try going down the second street, toward the city baths. The Jews bathe today."

I turned down the second street. It was just ten—two more hours to go. I had been lucky about my first information; I hoped it would lead somewhere.

The two hours passed. Suddenly I saw a group of people with white armbands near a solitary gray brick building. Surely, those were Jews!

There were a number of wooden huts not far from the group. Gentile trader-women with baskets crouched behind the huts. I joined them, expecting to learn something. Instead, the women insisted that I leave. It was their territory, their business; they wouldn't stand for competition. I convinced them I wasn't there on business; all I wanted was a few things for myself. Anyway, they'd see. It worked. They quieted down and let me stay.

Under cover, I observed the Jews. Men, women, and a few children were walking about the lot. Some were not too badly dressed, but most presented a pitiful sight. They kept signaling us, but couldn't come near. Finally, the Germans left. The trader-women took off at a run; I followed. All at once, I was besieged by men and women asking: "Have you got bread? Potatoes? Lard?"

"Sorry, no."

Now I regret that I brought nothing. I note their yellow, wizened faces, their sunken eyes and thin, shrunken bodies. They can barely stand up. An elderly woman, holding up two worn sheets for sale, attracts my attention. Her wrinkled face, gray hair, and dark, sad eyes inspire confidence. I tell her I have some Jewish acquaintances in the camp, and mention the names the Committee gave me. Could she help me find them? No, she hasn't been here long; but if I'll wait, she'll call a Radom Jew, who'll be able to give me the information.

Just then, there is a mad scampering and tumult. Someone is coming! The Jews retreat toward the baths, the trader-women run headlong for the huts. I run with them; it is safer to stay close to experienced smugglers. Then I see the cause of the disturbance: two civilians wearing hats—Germans. As soon as they pass from sight, the women run back to the Jews. This scuttling back and forth is repeated several times. Everyone is on edge, and keeps looking about nervously. Business is concluded in this atmosphere of terror.

I look for my emissary. She comes toward me with a short, thin man. He knows the people whose names I mentioned; they were taken away at the first deportation, he tells me. The Jew speaks calmly, without fuss. A trustworthy man. I take him aside, and hastily tell him about my mission: underground relief and distributing money. His face turns deathly pale. Finally, he says dryly:

"Don't tell me any stories about relief. You asked about Jews and I told you." Then he adds ironically, "Don't think Jews don't recognize such tricks."

He leaves me standing there, stunned. The Jew did not believe me, he is afraid of me. I run after him; there is no one near us. I speak to him in

Yiddish, our mother tongue. He stands open-mouthed, speechless. When I have finished, he says unsteadily:

"Perhaps you speak the truth. But I won't take any money."

"Why not? It's for your own good."

"There are lots of spies and informers in our camp," he tells me. Jews have been denounced and put to death because of contact with Gentiles. No, he won't take anything from me. I'd better talk to the Jews in the printing plant. They might be willing to take up relief work; he is afraid.

He says good-bye, with a friendly smile. Alone once more, I am angry at myself and at this Jew. It would have been so easy to give him the money and discuss the work—instead, nothing has been accomplished.

The scurrying begins again. Embittered, I duck behind the huts and decide to try the printing plant again. The entrance is now guarded by a Jewish policeman. Beyond the gate, I can see Jews darting about with bowls and mess kits. It is the noon recess. I ask the guard to call the worker, Mrs. Meltzer; he leaves the gate a moment, then comes back with a young woman. I whisper that I have money and letters for her from Warsaw. The woman doesn't know what to make of me. She says something to the policeman, who opens the gate and lets me in. Would I wait a minute?

Mrs. Meltzer returns with her husband and brother-in-law. Once more, I review the purpose of my mission: money, relief, the Coordinating Committee. Joyous smiles spread over their faces. It is hard for them to believe this is not a dream. Yes, they'll organize the relief program. As long as they have not been forsaken!

The Jewish policeman signals that my time is up. I pass them the money and the letter from the Coordinating Committee. They promise to get a message to me, summing up their needs and listing the addresses of their children, left with kindly Poles. I leave the factory, well pleased. The trader-women are gone, but there are some children still playing at the gate. Suddenly something strikes my back. The children laugh and let go with another stone. Instantly, they start shouting:

"Look! She didn't buy anything from them!"

Others pick it up: "She must be one of them!"

They chant in chorus: "Yid, dirty Yid! Yid, dirty Yid!"

I scream at them, but they only shout louder. It is a bad situation, I must get out of sight. I turn down a street. The children follow, still shouting: "Yid, dirty Yid!" I duck into a courtyard, then another. Passers-by begin to stop. My face is burning. Confused, I hail a droshky, and tell the driver to take me to the station. In the distance, the children's voices are still calling, "Yid, dirty Yid!" Why no one stopped me, I'll never know.

All that night, I squatted in the station. Should I return to Warsaw? Could I break off this link, barely established as yet? Early in the morning, I set out for the factory, to pick up the letter Meltzer promised me; I reasoned that the children wouldn't be out at that hour. Guarded by Jewish policemen, the group were on their way to work when I arrived. For a minute I fell in with the marchers, took the letter from Meltzer, then vanished.

There were about four thousand Jews in Radom at the time, living in specially built wooden barracks outside the city limits. From there work gangs were sent on all sorts of jobs, the two largest employers being the local munition factory and the German printing plant. Conditions were the same as in any camp: hard work, hunger, disease, selections, and death—though starvation, perhaps, was a little worse in Radom. Soon after my visit, Meltzer, Kotlar, Greenberg, and some others set up a relief committee. About one hundred of the neediest Jews thus benefited from the first monies received.

On my next call, I had more money—fifty thousand zlotys—underground literature and letters. I went directly to the printing plant, but saw no one near, even during the noon recess. I circled the building. The entire area had been fenced in with barbed wire. Signs posted at intervals warned: "Do not approach! Pain of death!" Turning down an alley, I could see Jews behind the barbed wire. They no longer wore their own clothes but the regulation blue-and-white striped garb of prisoners. Heavily armed Germans and Ukrainians kept watch.

I turned down another street, and slipped into a doorway opposite the fence. I made tiny rolls of the money and printed matter and hid them beneath the lid of my shopping basket. But what good were these preparations if I couldn't make a move without the guard seeing me? I'd have to go to the soldier himself, and ask his permission to buy something from the Jews.

With a nonchalance I did not feel, I left my cover and in my most innocent tone asked the guard to be good enough to let me buy a pair of shoes from the Jews. A Ukrainian, he was gruff at first, but soon fell in with my bantering tone. We talked for some minutes that seemed like an eternity to me. Beyond the barbed wire, I could see the Jews watching the scene. Finally I persuaded him. I ran up to the barbed wire, but saw none of my former contacts. Nervously I asked if Meltzer and Kotlar were still in the camp.

"Yes, they're here. We'll call them," one of the Jews said. I urged them to hurry. The guard came over to the fence.

"Who has shoes for her?" he asked in German.

"I want to buy a pair of shoes," I repeated in Polish.

The Jews asked if I'd care for a dress or a sweater. They looked upon me as an ordinary smuggler.

"No, just shoes."

Meanwhile, my contacts appeared. They whispered to a third person who called the guard aside, handed him something through the wire, and drew him into conversation. Meltzer stood near me, watching the guard. As soon as the Ukrainian turned away, I handed Meltzer the package. He hid it beneath his pajama top, and promptly disappeared. The Jews around us had seen this, but kept quiet. People brought me shoes. I tried them on and kept chattering to the guard, who was now back with me. One of my contacts reappeared and carefully passed me a letter. Our business was accomplished.

I bought no shoes that day. On leaving, I promised the Ukrainian I'd meet him that evening. Needless to say, I didn't keep the date. . . .

The smuggling was not always successful. There were frequent failures, one of which almost cost the life of my friend, Olye Margolis. It happened in Piotrkow, where I once had to deliver fifty thousand zlotys from the Coordinating Committee. I had done it with the help of a Polish factory guard. Olye succeeded in getting inside the factory, and handed over the money and letters to the Jews directly. Some passing Germans, however, spotted her. She was arrested and found guilty of trespassing in a prohibited area. The Jews she had just helped turned the camp upside down. They beseeched all the German officers and civilian officials to release the "innocent Aryan." They eventually bought her freedom with the very money she had brought them.

Other failures ended in death. Nevertheless, we were able to continue our relief work in various camps until the end of the war.

DIALOGUE WITH THE DEAD [1]

by MORDECAI STRIGLER

PROUD woman, prototype of myself, you are no longer alive. It was the dense, unknown woods leading from the Skarzicko concentration camp into the heart of the ravaged world that swallowed up your body and dragged you away, together with hundreds of others, down the dark roads of question-marked destiny. I do not know why, but it is you who have begun lately to turn my ascetic hallucination into a torture and to awaken me that I may come alive for you minutes, hours, after your certain death.

I see you again as in my fantasy of that Tisha B'Ab day, the last day in the camp, the whole lovely image of you. Red, bloody dots streak through in secret script the history of your ultimate extinction. Your golden curls are loath to vanish into the cold earth along with your body; they nestle in the grass as if seeking there a final refuge. On your face I still see as a last blessing the dew of young womanhood, but silently the colors of life steal away, as if in shame for abandoning you, alone and bullet-ridden, in the middle of the German desert.

[1] This reverie is the Prologue to a work titled *In the Death Factories*, published in Buenos Aires in 1948.

You are still lying on your side. Your firm breast is thrust forward, as if, with your last scrap of courage, you were taking aim at His Mightiness, Death, who is approaching.

Two Polish hoodlums, showing big jagged teeth, make merry over your dead loveliness, and I, the shadowy one, stand to one side. My body still awaits its destined punishment, as do those which the forest was unable to lure. But it is I who, having arrived by wavering paths, stand over you, Jewishly powerless, paralyzed. No one sees me here, no one can drive me away or make me silent as you, you who have escaped and perished. I look at the wooded gloom that called, enticed, and consumed you and looking at you, I see you as exalted lowliness, dying. I myself do not know how it comes about that my lips are whispering something, a mixture of passion and regret over the dead one that should not, dared not, be dead. Do I mutter your name?

Above me emerges the form of him who entangled himself in your days and with whom you made your escape from the camp into the forest. The fire in his eyes lights up his ash-blackened face. He flashes over me with the brilliance that only the extinguished possess. My senses stunned, I hear deviously, through my skin and hair rather than my ears, your quiet, astonished reproof. You, too! You, too, are weeping over me? He falls with one hand outstretched toward you. Guffaws of nauseating laughter, bursting skunklike from the two figures with jagged teeth swirl frenziedly about, seeking a hiding place and roll heavily away among the trees. My forehead burns with his last wrathful glance. I want to retreat, as I did once before, but seeing you motionless, I can no longer find a stronghold. The battle with myself, once fought with reinforcements of tomorrow's days and the dazzling hopes of the future, has now shifted. At this point the waiting has ended. You have crossed that border beyond which all is too late and every breath of consolation is sealed in an abyss. Only an indestructible regret wells up. Now there is nothing left.

Did he run after you in order to retain his right over you even there, on the blue steppes of Death? But I am still here and will never reach either of you. Why does his glance sear me so? And why do you appear, you too, on sleepless nights and entangle yourself in my hallucinations?

Today the agonies of freedom have made me desperate, and I drive your image from me. I sharpen my tools and force myself to conjure up the darkest, most contemptible part of you, and blacken the pallid paper with it. To perpetuate your disgrace, or to still my own yearning, to stifle the longing you did not appease? Have I set myself to pin the insignia of a whore on you, or did you really wear them brazenly, as ornaments? See how stern I am, how I aim my barbs at your awakening image in me? Today you come to me, the lost one, long since swept away by flood tides that can bring back only an unblemished image. Must I penetrate the darkness that surrounds you because your flesh and blood have been kneaded for eternity into naked desire, or shall I go my way in silence, so that you and I may never grieve again?

Your image from behind my eyelids invades the secret cells of my brain, and I, the gray-haired recluse, inwardly plead for help, invoking a stronger inner self, for succor against you. But now you are merciless.

"Once," you say, scarcely moving your lips, "you weakened and called to me in your thoughts, stretching out your arms to emptiness. Don't you know for whom? I was close to your soul and heard you.

"Now you cast me out, as you had once forced yourself to abandon me. But I'll rekindle the very feelings you concealed from yourself and me. I come to stir you with the nudity of a corpse, past all earthly joy or pleasure. Not for my sake, but for those debts of rapture left untapped, that linger in the world in vain."

I wish to say something, to reply, but your image towering above me overwhelms me, drowns out my voice: "Be silent!" Of all my words and protestations, only one brief question forces its way to my lips: "What, then, do you want of me?"

Her brows knit threateningly.

"You once wrote something in which you appointed yourself moral arbiter and lashed everyone with your pen. Remember? You denounced me and all those around me; I sickened when I read it. I was still alive and full of boasting then; now I only want to warn you to stop. You came bemoaning the death of millions and sought to spread the spirit of the dead over the living who were themselves waiting to die. Would you want life to fade away while hot blood is still seething? Don't you sense your own blood condemning you for it?

"You were there with the rest of us. You saw how we had to gulp down a lifetime in days, for the weeks would surely cut short our span. We had envisioned years stretching before us, until a cloud blotted out our future; so we seized each vibrant hour, to balance the expectant years in our limbs. Weren't you caught up in it, too? Didn't you hear life cry out within you: 'Open the flood gates and let the storm rage! Leave nothing but a weary emptiness for the grave!' You couldn't do it, because you were too weak, too cowardly, to break the chains that bound you to yesterday. In your innermost self, perhaps, you waited for someone to sweep you with the force of chaos into the senseless game of complete forgetfulness. No one came, and you remained an outcast from your past, without moorings anywhere. Perhaps you only moralized because chaos, with its grip of steel, failed to loosen your fetters. Possibly you screamed in anger, not in pain, at being passed by. Have you ever taken stock of yourself, sought the truth within, before condemning others?

"You speak of the 'soul.' Remold your own soul first. Hunched up in your isolation you write, with a mummy's hand, lines that have never known the light of day. A determined recluse, you withdraw from the world, from our times, so none may intrude upon you. Your pen is sharp and pointed. You revive us only to impale us, because of our hunger for life, the lustful craving of those days that weren't days at all. So I've come to warn you. Don't point your finger like a prophet of old, shouting imprecations. It ill behooves you from the seclusion of your tiny room. Caress first and be caressed; breathe the fragrant forest air; feel each healing touch of the finger of life. Then, perhaps, you may cry out: 'I understand!' and 'I desire!' Who are you to rail at the living like a bleached skeleton, with a skeleton's envy: 'You, there! Be damned for your will to live! For every moment that you wrest from oblivion, reflect whether you will use or stifle it, reflect until your moment is past and the opportunity gone.'

"For years, you wrote; you leafed through thousands of written pages, in a kind of intoxication. What of all that, now? Wake up, you mystic denier of life! For the very fate that whirled you naked past all dangers and washed you ashore safely at last, robbed you of ten years of your work. You wrote and fate destroyed, a contest between creation and destruction. Has it taught you nothing, you prober of events? Would you start anew by condemning all desire for the warmth of the body, its life-giving sustenance, though achieved in the ungainly fashion that nature forces upon us? Or will you try to understand us and confess that deep down you, too, are no different? No one can force life upon you. 'Not after what I've been through, not after what I've seen,' you amend. What, then, have you seen and been through but an appalling tragedy, to be avoided in the future? Must all survivors be cold as marble, stamped with the seal of death?

"Deep down, you craved the tumult of chaos, but habit made you grit your teeth and suppress your desire. You cast out my image, with all that remained of your youthful instincts; now you are purging your very memories, so you may be the prophet of an indignant justice. Strangle your own youth, if you will, but don't demand the same of others! You prepare an indictment against us, whom reality repeatedly snatched from your grasp. But before passing judgment, yield to life; experience it in your own flesh, feel it to your marrow. Don't try from your mouse hole to judge the actions of those who heard life calling to them over the stockades of the camp, and responded to the voice of the blood. If you'll lift up your face to the sun, our story will be written differently, and though you may be angry, you will not revile us.

"Once more, I try to affirm that I know life and understand it, in spite of my seclusion. I have observed certain restraints, though not with the warped instincts of the kill-joy. I did not create those restraints nor would I impose them on others; rather, I sought to test their validity at moments when the most vital among us were bound by a measure of moral constraint and grief. But I cannot launch my first work on the eve of a new life without a testimonial to what has been, even though much that we sensed may not be understood.

"You'll never prove it!" a voice thunders in reply; hers, or the voice of my inner self? "Life has its own limitations. At the very core of ecstasy, nature has posted its warning sign: 'So far and no further!' The coward alone will not venture near the outer bounds."

Her voice speaks out clear and distinct: "Would you be free of my tormenting presence now? Very well, I'll not force my memory upon you. Dead, I'll vanish into oblivion. Only let me warn you: writing of us is no mere personal obligation. So try not to speak for those who have gone before into the all-engulfing horror. Do not appoint yourself persecutor in their behalf. Who knows what message may have been conveyed to us from their graves? Did they bid us to live out our last few days as pariahs, or did they cry out: 'We have fallen! Save your remaining moments from the holocaust!' Can you be certain you understand their bidding? Write, if you will, but write truthfully, on behalf of all. Beyond that, your intuition will show you the right way. Are you equal to it?"

I want time to think it over, but that other self within me cries out, "Yes!"

So I'll no longer turn a deaf ear to these objections, any more than I shall wholly dismiss the memory of painful things I've seen. This is an account of events as they occurred, omitting both indignation and anger against those who surely do not merit our resentment. Mindful that none is so blameless as to judge, we stand before you in our nakedness; let courage and righteousness interpret and understand, condone or accuse.

NEVER AGAIN

by ANDRÉ SCHWARZ-BART

THE hours that Ernie Levy lived through in the sealed freight car were lived through by a host of his contemporaries. When the fourth night fell on the chaos of tangled bodies—a Polish night squatting on their smashed souls like some fantastic beast against which some of the adults were still struggling, blowing on their hands or rubbing frostbitten limbs—no complaint, no protest, no lament issued from the children's half-open mouths. Even gentleness was powerless to make them speak. They stared expressionlessly. Now and then those who were cramped against an adult's body scratched at random with their insensate talons like little animals, not to remind the world of their existence but rather, in spasms born in the still tepid depths of their entrails, in a kind of attenuated pulsation that prolonged circulation artificially—a vague rush of life perpetuating itself in bodies abandoned by their extinct souls but still without the consolations of God. Inert, his back to the wall, Ernie did not dare to search for a breath of life in Golda's face, resting against his shoulder, to see if she had not been silently drained of what made her—because of, in spite of, the horrors of the flesh—the object of his love. But for some time he had been incapable of the slightest movement, and only the upper part of his body floated over the mass of small bodies clinging to him, bodies that had slowly enveloped him. One clambering over the other, attracted by the memory of his words, they had then frozen in position as they were now, a wave of cold flesh stabilized at the level of his heart, binding him in a network of hands flat upon his skin or clawing deep into his flesh. Occasionally, thinking that one of them might be able to hear him, Ernie created gentle, happy words in the ice palace of his mind, but in spite of all his efforts the words never issued from his sealed lips.

The locomotive whistled, shuddered, ground reluctantly to a halt. A ghostly tremor ran through the car. But when the first barking of dogs was heard, an electrifying, fluid terror struck the outstetched bodies one by one, and a leaden Ernie stirred too, supporting Golda, who had been jolted out of her stupor. The surviving children screamed with all their poisonous breath, surrounding Ernie with a gaseous ring of decomposing entrails. Outside, pincers were already snipping through the seals affixed at the Drancy station, and the doors slid back, admitting the first SS death's-heads in a blinding flow of light. Carrying whips and bludgeons, restraining black mastiffs on taut leashes, they plunged with gleaming boots into the stormy tide of deportees, channeling it out onto the platforms with shouts and blows that roused even the dying, setting them suddenly into motion like a flock of sheep jostling and crushing. At dawn the platforms seemed unreal beneath the floodlights, and the jerry-built station opened out on a strange plaza bounded by a chain of SS men and dogs, and by a barracks dimly visible in the agonizing fog. Ernie never knew how, with Golda and a child clinging to his arms, he succeeded in running the length of the platform amid the mad panic of the survivors, many of whom were absurdly dragging bundles or suitcases. In front of them a woman tripped over her valise, which had burst open; her skirts flew up to her waist. Immediately a German stepped forward with one of those savage animals baying on his leash, and obviously addressing himself to the animal, he shouted before the terrified eyes of the motionless group, *"Man, destroy that dog!"* At the poor woman's outcry, Ernie started running again, aware of nothing but the crackle of his flaming brain and the pressure of Golda's and the child's hands. He wondered suddenly if that tiny, sharp shriek belonged to a girl or a boy. . . .

Beneath the blackish heights of the dawn, the plaza, trampled by hundreds of Jewish feet, also seemed unreal. But Ernie's wary eye soon noted alarming details. Here and there on the hastily swept pavement—just before the train's arrival, it was obvious—there still lay abandoned possessions, bundles of clothing, opened suitcases, shaving brushes, enameled pots. . . . Where had they come from? And why, beyond the platform, did the tracks end suddenly? Why the yellowish grass and the ten-foot barbed wire? Why were the new guards snickering incomprehensibly at the new arrivals? These, catching their breath, were trying to settle into their new life, the men wiping their foreheads with kerchiefs, the girls smoothing their hair and holding their skirts when a breeze sprang up, the old men and women laboriously trying to sit down on their suitcases—silent, all of them, in a terrible silence that had fallen over the entire flock. Aside from the snickering and the knowing laughter, the guards seemed to have exhausted their anger, and while they calmly gave orders, blows, and kicks, Ernie realized that they were no longer driven by hate but were going through the motions with the remote sympathy one feels for a dog, even when beating him. If the beaten animal is a dog, it may be supposed with a fair degree of probability that the beater is a man. But as he examined the barracks building, again a vague gleam shone through the fog, high in the gray sky, capped by a cloud of black smoke. At the same moment he became aware of the nauseating odor that hovered in the plaza, which differed from the stagnant effluvium of dysentery in that it had the pungency of organic matter in combustion.

"You're weeping blood," Golda said suddenly in amazement.

"Don't be silly," Ernie said, "nobody weeps blood." And wiping off the tears of blood that furrowed his cheeks, he turned away from the girl to hide from her the death of the Jewish people, which was written clearly, he knew, in the flesh of his face.

The crowd was thinning out in front of them. One by one the deportees passed before an SS officer bracketed by two machine gunners. With the end of his swagger stick, the officer directed the prisoners distractedly to left or right, gauging them with a quick, practiced glance. Those on the left, men between twenty and forty-five whose outward aspect was relatively sturdy, were lined up behind the chain of SS men along a row of roofless trucks that the lifting fog had just revealed to Ernie's haggard investigations. On one of those open trucks he even noticed a group of men apparently wearing pajamas, each of whom was holding a musical instrument. They composed a kind of peripatetic orchestra waiting farcically on the truck, wind instruments to their lips, drumsticks and cymbals raised, ready to blare forth. The prisoners on the right, all children, women, old men, and invalids, huddled together raggedly near the barracks, shrinking before a wide grating set directly into the wall of that strange building.

"They're going to separate us," Golda said coldly. And as if echoing her fears, the few children who had mysteriously found Ernie's trail through the crowd pressed closer around him, some of them simply offering the mute reproach of their heavy eyes, swollen like abscesses, and others clinging to his sleeve or the tail of his pitiful black jacket. Quite sure now of their imminent destiny, Ernie caressed their little heads, and contemplating Golda's anxious face and widening his eyes fogged by the blood congealing under the lids, he drank deeply one last time of the girl's beloved features, of her soul so well made for the simple marvels that earth dispenses to men, from which the curt movement of the SS doctor's swagger stick would shortly separate him forever.

· "No, no," he said, smiling at Golda while a fresh flow of blood streamed from his eyes, "we'll stay together, I swear it." And to the children, many of whom were now risking feeble groans, "Children, children," he reassured them, "now that we've come to the kingdom, do you think I'd stay out? We shall enter the kingdom together," he went on in the solemn, inspired voice, the one thing that could touch their souls so full of darkness and terror. "In a little while we shall enter it hand in hand, and there a banquet of tasty foods awaits us, a banquet of old wines, of tasty foods full of marrow, and of old wines, clear and good. . . . There, my little lambs . . ."

They listened without understanding, gentle smiles shadowing their tortured lips.

I am so weary that my pen can no longer write. "Man, strip off thy garments, cover thy head with ashes, run into the streets and dance in thy madness. . . ."

Just one incident interrupted the ceremony of selection. Alerted by the smell, a woman suddenly cried, "They kill people here," which gave rise to a brief panic, in the course of which the flock fell back slowly toward the platforms masked by the strange floodlit façade, like a stage set for a railway station. The guards went into action immediately, but when the flock was calm again, officers went through the ranks explaining politely—some of them even in unctuous, ministerial voices—that the able-bodied men had been called up to build houses and roads, and the remainder would rest up from the trip while they awaited assignment to domestic or other work. Ernie realized joyfully that Golda herself seemed to grasp at that fiction and that her features relaxed, suffused with hope. Suddenly the band on the truck struck up an old German melody. Stunned, Ernie recognized one of those heavily melancholy lieder that Ilse had been so fond of. The brasses glittered in the gray air, and a secret harmony came from the band in pajamas and their languidly glossy music. For an instant, a brief instant, Ernie was certain in his heart of hearts that no one could decently play music for the dead, not even that melody, which seemed to be of another world. Then the last brassy note died and, the flock duly soothed, the selection went on.

"But I'm sick, I can't walk," he murmured in German when at his turn the swagger stick had flicked toward the small group of healthy men who had been granted a reprieve.

Dr. Mengele, the physician in charge at the Auschwitz extermination camp, conceded a brief glance to the "Jewish dung" that had just pronounced those words. "All right," he said, "we'll fix you up."

The swagger stick described a half circle. The two young SS men smiled slyly. Staggering with relief, Ernie reached the sad human sea lapping at the edges of the barracks building. With Golda hugging him and the children's little hands tugging at him, he engulfed himself in it, and they waited. Finally they were all gathered together. Then an *Unterscharenführer* invited them, loudly and clearly, to leave their baggage where it was and to proceed to the baths, taking with them only their papers, their valuables, and the minimum they needed for washing. Dozens of questions rose to their lips: Should they take underwear? Could they open their bundles? Would their baggage be returned? Would anything be stolen? But the condemned did not know what strange force obliged them to hold their tongues and proceed quickly—without a word, without even a look behind—toward the entrance, a breach in the wall of ten-foot barbed wire beside the barracks with its grating.

At the far end of the plaza the orchestra suddenly struck up another tune and the first purring of the motors was heard, rising into a sky still heavy with morning fog, then disappearing in the distance. Squads of armed SS men divided the condemned into groups of a hundred. The corridor of barbed wire seemed endless. Every ten steps, a sign: "To the Baths and Inhalations." Then the flock passed along a tank-trap bristling with *chevaux de frise,* then a sharp, narrow, rolled-steel wire, tangled like a briar, and finally down a long open-air corridor between yards and yards of barbed wire. Ernie was carrying a little boy who had passed out. Many managed to walk only by supporting one another. In the ever more crushing silence of the throng, in its ever more pestilential stench, smooth and graceful words sprang to his lips, beating time to the children's steps in reverie and to Golda's with love. It seemed to him that an eternal silence was closing down upon the Jewish breed marching to slaughter —that no heir, no memory, would supervene to prolong the silent parade of victims, no faithful dog would shudder, no bell would toll. Only the stars would remain, gliding through a cold sky. "O God," the Just Man Ernie Levy said to himself as bloody tears of pity streamed from his eyes again, "O Lord, we went forth like this thousands of years ago. We walked across arid deserts and the blood-red Red Sea in a flood of salt, bitter tears. We are very old. We are still walking. Oh, let us arrive, finally!"

The building resembled a huge bathhouse. To left and right large concrete pots cupped the stems of faded flowers. At the foot of the small wooden stairway an SS man, mustached and benevolent, told the condemned, "Nothing painful will happen! You just have to breathe very deeply. It strengthens the lungs. It's a way to prevent contagious diseases. It disinfects." Most of them went in silently, pressed forward by those behind. Inside, numbered coat hooks garnished the walls of a sort of gigantic cloakroom where the flock undressed one way or another, encouraged by their SS cicerones, who advised them to remember the numbers carefully. Cakes of stony soap were distributed. Golda begged Ernie not to look at her, and he went through the sliding door of the second room with his eyes closed, led by the young woman and by the children, whose soft hands clung to his naked thighs. There, under the showerheads embedded in the ceiling, in the blue light of screened bulbs glowing in recesses of the concrete walls, Jewish men and women, children and patriarchs, were huddled together. His eyes still closed, he felt the press of the last parcels of flesh that the SS men were clubbing into the gas chamber now, and his eyes still closed, he knew that the lights had been extinguished on the living, on the hundreds of Jewish women suddenly shrieking in terror, on the old men whose prayers rose immediately and grew stronger, on the martyred children, who were rediscovering in their last agonies the fresh innocence of yesteryear's agonies in a chorus of identical exclamations: *"Mama! But I was a good boy! It's dark! It's dark!"* And when the first waves of Cyclon B gas billowed among the sweating bodies, drifting down toward the squirming carpet of children's heads, Ernie freed himself from the girl's mute embrace and leaned out into the darkness toward the children invisible even at his knees, and he shouted with all the gentleness and all the strength of his soul, "Breathe deeply, my lambs, and quickly!"

When the layers of gas had covered everything, there was silence in the dark sky of the room for perhaps a minute, broken only by shrill, racking coughs and the gasps of those too far gone in their agonies to offer a devotion. And first a stream, then a cascade, an irrepressible, majestic torrent, the poem that through the smoke of fires and above the funeral pyres of history the Jews—who for two thousand years did not bear arms and who never had either missionary empires nor colored slaves—the old love poem that they traced in letters of blood on the earth's hard crust unfurled in the gas chamber, enveloped it, vanquished its somber, abysmal snickering: "SHEMA YISRAEL ADONOI ELOHENU ADONOI EHAD . . . Hear, O Israel, the Lord is our God, the Lord is One. O Lord, by your grace you nourish the living, and by your great pity you resurrect the dead, and you uphold the weak, cure the sick, break the chains of slaves. And faithfully you keep your promises to those who sleep in the dust. Who is like unto you, O merciful Father, and who could be like unto you . . . ?"

The voices died one by one in the course of the unfinished poem. The dying children had already dug their nails into Ernie's thighs, and Golda's embrace was already weaker, her kisses were blurred when, clinging fiercely to her beloved's neck, she exhaled a harsh sigh: "Then I'll never see you again? Never again?"

Ernie managed to spit up the needle of fire jabbing at his throat, and as the woman's body slumped against him, its eyes wide in the opaque night, he shouted against the unconscious Golda's ear, "In a little while, *I swear it!*" And then he knew that he could do nothing more for anyone in the world, and in the flash that preceded his own annihilation he remembered, happily, the legend of Rabbi Chanina ben Teradion, as Mordecai had joyfully recited it: "When the gentle rabbi, wrapped in the scrolls of the Torah, was flung upon the pyre by the Romans for having taught the Law, and when they lit the fagots, the branches still green to make his torture last, his pupils said, 'Master, what do you see?' And Rabbi Chanina answered, 'I see the parchment burning, but the letters are taking wing.'" . . . "*Ah, yes, surely, the letters are taking wing,*" Ernie repeated as the flame blazing in his chest rose suddenly to his head. With dying arms he embraced Golda's body in an already unconscious gesture of loving protection, and they were found that way half an hour later by the team of *Sonderkommando* responsible for burning the Jews in the crematory ovens. And so it was for millions, who turned from *Luftmenschen* into *Luft*. I shall not translate. So this story will not finish with some tomb to be visited in memoriam. For the smoke that rises from crematoriums obeys physical laws like any other: the particles come together and disperse according to the wind that propels them. The only pilgrimage, estimable reader, would be to look with sadness at a stormy sky now and then.

And praised. *Auschwitz.* Be. *Maidanek.* The Lord. *Treblinka.* And praised. *Buchenwald.* Be. *Mauthausen.* The Lord. *Belzec.* And praised. *Sobibor.* Be. *Chelmno.* The Lord. *Ponary.* And praised. *Theresienstadt.* Be. *Warsaw.* The Lord. *Vilna.* And praised. *Skarzysko.* Be. *Bergen-Belsen.* The Lord. *Janow.* And praised. *Dora.* Be. *Neuengamme.* The Lord. *Pustkow.* And praised . . .

Yes, at times one's heart could break in sorrow. But often too, preferably in the evening, I can't help thinking that Ernie Levy, dead six million times, is still alive somewhere, I don't know where. . . . Yesterday, as I stood in the street trembling in despair, rooted to the spot, a drop of pity fell from above upon my face. But there was no breeze in the air, no cloud in the sky. . . . There was only a presence.

"FOR YOSL—FOR EVERYTHING—"

by LOUIS FALSTEIN

ANTEK inserted a coin in the turnstile and pushed it. He walked to the gum-vending machine with the *Out of Order* sign and stopped. He heard the rush of the oncoming Express and felt his body tensing. The train stopped, the doors flew open. He went into the nearest car but he did not find Hornbostel. He ran out onto the platform again and started toward the front end of the train, gazing intently at the faces inside the cars, his panic mounting. What if Hornbostel escaped? Suddenly he caught sight of him in a car up ahead and wedged himself between the middle doors of the car just as they were closing.

Hornbostel was at the front end, his head rising above the crowd. Antek remained standing near the doors, nailed to the spot. He moved only when someone shoved him.

There was a nightmarish quality about his being in the same car with Hornbostel. He could hardly believe he was awake. During the last few days, when he had considered confronting the ex-guard in this way, he had told himself that he must stay calm. This must be done rationally. From his own experiences in the ghetto fighting he knew that rage was a poor substitute for calm and determination. But in spite of himself, the sight of Hornbostel brought on blind rage. He felt his fists flexing at his sides and he was conscious of a pain in his fingers. He needed a few precious moments to plan a method of attack. But his body was propelling him toward the ex-guard and only the tightly massed crowd arrested his movements. He wondered if he could possibly make his way to Hornbostel's side before the train stopped at the next station. Supposing Hornbostel got out at the next stop?

Antek stopped pushing and measured the distance between them. Several determined lunges and he would be able to lay his hands on him. And then? What if the assassin fought back? What if the crowd proved hostile? He had to remember that he was in a world of Gentiles with whom he could not even communicate. The fish mustn't wriggle away this time—or there might never be another opportunity.

He realized with something of a shock that in a brown suit of American cut, a brown felt hat on his head, the ex-guard looked like any well-to-do American businessman. The look of the killer that had been stamped on his face in Tiranka was gone; so was the tight sneer that had always lurked in the corners of his mouth. He was heavier in the body and had jowls; he even carried a briefcase! What was the ex-pimp doing with a briefcase? For that's what he had been before he started Jew-killing, Antek wanted to shout to the crowd, a pimp on the docks of Bremen!

"HORNBOSTEL!"

He hadn't meant to shout. He hadn't even meant to call. He had planned to do it differently. But he heard himself repeating the ex-guard's name, which was like gall in his mouth. "Hornbostel, Emil—criminal from war—Tiranka —kill everybody—"

There was a brief commotion in the car, a ripple of comment that he did not understand, exclamations of shock and surprise. Suddenly he hurled himself at those who were blocking his path. Some passengers tried moving out of his way, others did not give way. He was aware of faces turning toward him questioningly, then looking away. Their glances bewildered him, and he thought he read in them the embarrassment that comes with an unwilling intrusion into some situation of intimacy. He was also conscious of an indifference in them verging on hostility.

Hornbostel moved unobtrusively from his spot and disappeared into the next car. Antek plunged after him. Perhaps they *would* help him if his tongue were not tied. The words he had shouted in English seemed to him clear enough. But evidently they didn't understand him. Or didn't they want to understand? The devil with them! A policeman, that's what was necessary! Antek elbowed his way through the incurious crowd toward where Hornbostel had disappeared.

A rush of air struck Antek as he crossed into the next car. If he lost him now, he would never see him again. It was necessary to lay hands on him and drag him to the police station. There would be time enough then to worry about proof, evidence, affidavits—legalisms.

The train stopped suddenly and Hornbostel sprang out onto the platform. Antek ran after him. "Hornbostel, you're not going to get away this time—" He saw the other stop momentarily, and advanced. He was the shorter of the two but he had massive shoulders and the clublike fists of a bread baker. And in his heart there was a wild and bitter rage.

He made a leaping dive but missed the surprisingly agile ex-guard, who started up a flight of stairs. Once he looked over his shoulder at the pursuing Antek and his face was ashen gray. He mumbled something, but Antek did not hear him. He was heading for a wooden elevated structure.

Antek halted at the top of the stairs and regarded the platform suspiciously. It was less crowded than the subway station below. A four-coach wooden train was filling up rapidly. Hornbostel ran inside the second car just as the conductor swung shut the iron gates and pulled the cord twice. The train started. Antek ran alongside of it for an instant.

Suddenly he grabbed the iron railing with one hand and hoisted his body over it. He heard the conductor shout, "Yal get killed!" Passengers on the little platform were eying him curiously. He felt a sharp twinge of pain in his ankle from his leap, and his breath came in harsh spasms. *A slight exertion,* he thought bitterly, *and I'm on the brink of collapse.*

During the fighting in Warsaw he had gone without sleep for what seemed like weeks, roaming behind the enemy lines in the "Aryan" part of Warsaw. He realized with something of a shock that he was too old for such violent activities.

He entered the car and stared up and down the benches but he did not see Hornbostel. Next car, maybe. He started toward the head of the train, examining the faces of the passengers as he went, as if he believed that Hornbostel's slyness might have enabled him to change his appearance, even his identity, in that short time.

"Son of a bitch—" he muttered in Polish. Hornbostel was nowhere in the cars. Antek was tempted to shout the name aloud, pull the cord, and cry out an alarm. The six-foot ex-Nazi had apparently evaporated into thin air two stories above the city!

The train marking, *Myrtle Avenue,* had no meaning for him, but he repeated it several times, consciously memorizing the words for possible future use. As the train passed through the Bedford-Stuyvesant section of Brooklyn, he caught sight of rooftops crowded with television antennas. They reminded him of metal tank traps. They passed above a Negro neighborhood and he saw people hanging out the windows, resting their elbows on pillows, their faces shiny with perspiration. The piles of rubble on the street, the crumbling, condemned buildings wrenched his mind back to the war and the screeching bombs, and it did not seem at all strange that he should be chasing the killer of his parents and brother in such surroundings. In his mind, rubble and piles of brick would always recall the Nazis, just as smoke from any chimney brought to mind crematoriums.

The train lumbered into a station and he jumped off and stood on the wooden platform and felt it trembling under his feet, his eyes flashing in all directions. Hornbostel did not come out. Vanished.

They started again. *He must be on the train,* Antek thought, and resumed his mad search. If only there were a policeman on the train! He needed someone to help him. On the left, in the distance, the Manhattan sky line came into view, he recognized the Empire State Building, its tower looking like a thermometer stood on its head. The city, wrapped in a bluish haze, seemed many miles away.

Now they were heading toward a prairie, a vast stretch of intense green and patches of copper where the grass had been burned by the summer sun. For an instant he imagined himself back in Warsaw, in the suburb of Prahl, where he'd gone on picnics. An old iron bridge leaped into view and beyond it was a vast field of crosses that bent over the rim of the horizon. A graveyard without end, a city of the dead, bigger than anything he had ever seen.

Near the entrance to the cemetery, under floodlights—though it was still daylight—men were playing baseball. He saw a ball sail up into the air and his eyes followed its flight and descent among the tombs. A player ran after it there and ran back to the playing field.

"Last stop!" the conductor called.

The train began to slow down; the passengers rose, like runners getting ready for a last swift dash. When the train stopped, Antek hurried out onto the platform. Suddenly he caught sight of Hornbostel climbing down from the roof of the first car. The ex-guard lost his footing and fell to the platform but rose quickly and hurled himself at the exit.

"Hold him!" Antek shouted, starting in pursuit. But nobody seemed to be paying any attention. He reached the street and turned sharply to the right, his eyes finding Hornbostel, who looked back, once, without stopping. They were on a broad avenue, lined on both sides with huge flower shops and monument works. Ahead the graveyard took over both sides of the traffic-jammed street.

Hornbostel's speed had not slackened. In fact it seemed to Antek, who was tiring rapidly, that the ex-guard's speed was putting distance between them. Much as he resented the difference in their stamina, it was understandable. Hornbostel, after all, had never been a skeleton.

Antek saw him suddenly swing to the right and disappear into the cemetery through a tear in the high wire fence. He stopped short in surprise. He had not expected him to do that. Could he have had this in mind all along, or was this a sudden decision inspired by the hole in the fence? Did Hornbostel mean to make a stand there, among the graves?

Antek followed through the gap in the fence. He felt the soft earth under his feet. He trampled over flowers, freshly laid and strong-scented, and barked his legs against stone markers and bumped into large stone crosses. But in spite of this, he was beginning to gain on Hornbostel.

"Hornbostel—you had better stop—" He was aware of using the cursed German language again, but what was worse, and almost brought on a feeling of nausea, was the sound of the hated name in his ears. "Hornbostel, you won't get away, not this time!"

Then, surprisingly, the husky man with the briefcase stopped suddenly, turned and spoke: "There must be a mistake—I don't believe I've had the honor—"

"Then why are you running?" Antek retorted, shocked by the lie, the soft voice, and the formality. Even the voice had changed but not the cunning. "I'll refresh your memory. Section Three, Tiranka. The numbers on the forearm. Here!" He made a step forward but, when the other retreated, he stopped. "My nose, you smashed it with your gun butt." He paused. "Do any of these things I mention refresh your memory? My name is Prinz—"

The man with the briefcase cocked his ear as if he were sampling the sound of the voice and the name. He shook his head with slow regret. "It does not strike a familiar chord, I'm sorry to say. . . . Do you mind getting out of my path?" But instead of advancing, he took a few steps backward, knocking over a small white cross.

"I will further refresh your memory, Squad Leader Hornbostel," Antek cried, incensed at the man's brazen denial. "My brother, Yosl—you murdered him *one day before liberation*. You knew as well as I that the war was over, that nothing would be gained by another killing—"

"I don't know what you are talking about," the other said in his native tongue, glancing furtively over his shoulder, as if charting a route of escape.

"I will further refresh your memory—" Suddenly Antek realized that Hornbostel had bounded away.

Antek stepped around a freshly dug grave, his foot sinking into the soft earth almost to the ankle. In Tiranka, he recalled, only dogs and Nazis had graves dug for them. The graves of both his parents were in the sky. The smoke from the chimneys had been a common grave. There were a million others buried with them there. He heard the sound of feet shuffling on gravel and caught sight of Hornbostel darting in and out among the tombs.

The two men were plunging deeper into the city of the dead. Behind them the fence and the avenue were no longer visible, but Antek could still hear the shouts of the baseball players; their voices reached him in incoherent snatches.

He skirted a large, square mausoleum and saw Hornbostel disappearing from sight not more than ten feet away. The spring seemed to have gone from the ex-guard's step. How much longer could they keep up this chase? Both of them were too old for this game, which should have been played out a long, long time ago.

A crushing exhaustion weighed Antek down. He had not eaten since morning. A pine tree near one of the graves gave off a living, pungent fragrance, and Antek looked at it suspiciously as he ran by, wondering what it was doing among the dead.

"Hornbostel," he continued to shout desperately, "you are not going to get away this time!"

The other, as if attracted by the shouts, stopped and showed his tired, sweat-drenched face from behind a large, marble monument.

"I insist there must be a mistake," he said, gasping for breath. "You will please get out of my way. I will be forced to call the—police."

Antek shook the sweat out of his eyes. "Call them," he taunted as Hornbostel might have done to his victims of another time. "Come, I'll help you call the police."

The ex-guard's voice rose to a higher pitch, as if he were already summoning them. "I'm innocent, I tell you—"

"Aren't you Emil Hornbostel?" Antek flung the German words from his mouth, eager to be rid of them. "Will you deny before the police that you are Hornbostel, ex-Squad Leader and SS man?"

"My name is Sleicher, Conrad Sleicher."

"Will you go to the police with me, Conrad Sleicher?"

"I have never seen you before."

"Ay—" Antek muttered, in a frenzy of doubt now. Could he really be mistaken? Was he dealing with a man or a devil? Was this Hornbostel, with all the black cunning of a former pimp from the docks of Bremen, or really an innocent stranger named Conrad Sleicher?

"My God!" Antek cried in bewilderment. He retreated several steps, as if he were getting out of the man's way. Suddenly he noticed again the ring on the man's finger.

"Jew-burner!" he roared. "I saw when you cut that ring off Shenkman's finger. You *are* Hornbostel, you blood of a stinking bitch! I'll tear you—" He started at Hornbostel with a gesture of violence.

"Herr Prinz."

Antek stared at him dumfounded.

"Herr Prinz, let's be reasonable. This is 1950. Why are you bringing up what happened a long time ago and in another country? A man sometimes"— he hesitated—"has to do what is ordered, especially in war. I hated the Nazis no less than you, I—" his voice dropped to a low, intimate whisper, as if he did not want the dead to hear: "I tried to do what I could for you. It was I who spared your life."

"Not you, Hornbostel," Antek retorted. The outright lie did not shock him, but he wanted the record to remain straight. "It was that pig, Hoffman."

"Herr Prinz, I'll make you an offer."

"It's too late for offers," Antek said.

Hornbostel took off again without warning and disappeared behind the monument. Then he started running across a shallow clearing with low mounds and wilted flowers that gave off a smell of decay. He had lost his hat, and Antek could see a bald spot on the back of his head that had not been there before.

It had grown darker, and the monuments had taken on the shapes of ossified trees. He was reminded of the nights he had spent in the forest with a band of Jewish guerrillas under the command of Itzhok Dorfman, whose father had been a rabbi on the Nalivkes. For a moment he imagined himself back in the forest where he had left off almost seven years ago. All the rest, the intervening time, the meeting with Lisa, their marriage, Joe's birth, their trek across Europe to America, all of these were the long pause, the breathing spell, before the return to the forest. In the distance he caught sight of a cross outlined in light bulbs atop a high white church tower; it was that which jolted his mind back to the present.

"If you let me go," Hornbostel's voice reached out of the stillness of the tombs to say, "I will make it worth your while. I will reward you, Herr Prinz, generously."

"With money, eh?" Antek said bitterly. "Or will it be with earrings or gold fillings?" As he spoke, he was probing the darkness with his eyes, trying to determine where the sound came from.

"I will let you name your own price."

"You don't have that much to give. Not all the loot—"

"Let me go, Herr Prinz. I will make you rich." Hornbostel paused, and when there was no response continued: "I will give you five hundred dollars now. And I will sign a note for whatever sum you name. On my word of honor."

"Come out, Hornbostel. My hands are bare, just like yours. But you are not a hero with bare hands, are you? You need a gun butt. 'Word of honor!'" he cried derisively at the darkness. "Don't be a fool. The money you deposited in Switzerland—I know where that came from. It came from gold fillings you dug out of Jewish mouths, and rings you tore off Jewish fingers, and bracelets you hacked off Jewish wrists. It's all blood money, the blood of my people. It's not yours to give away!" He paused.

"Come out, Hornbostel, my hands are bare, like yours," he said again.

"There are laws in this country." The voice seemed to come from within arm's reach. "You must keep in mind," it went on, "that this is not the Third Reich, not Hitler Germany. This is the United States of America. If any harm comes to me, you will be held strictly to account."

"Who will hold me to account?"

"The American law."

"And all your crimes and atrocities? Is that a settled matter? I'll drag you to court and we'll see if it is!"

"I'm ready to settle it now. I'll pay whatever sum you name. . . . Have pity, Herr Prinz."

"Super race!" Antek bellowed at the silent tombs. "Yosl, my brother, here is the super race for you!" As though he and Yosl and the others now dead hadn't known all along that those who strutted among them wearing swastikas on their sleeves were a race of cowards. When you took away their guns, what were they? Cowards! Even when, armed to the teeth, they had besieged the Warsaw ghetto, how long it had taken them to subdue the starved fighters, whose weapons were often no more than a bottle filled with gasoline, and a bitter curse!

He heard the sudden swish of gravel and Hornbostel exploded before his startled eyes, his right arm raised to strike. Antek dodged, but the rock in the ex-guard's fist struck sharply at his skull, drowning his senses in a rush of darkness. But even as he felt the world plunging away, Antek's powerful arms shot out blindly and found their target.

The shutter in his brain fell away and he realized that his hands were gripping Hornbostel's throat. Squeezing with all his might, he felt the springy neck muscles and the slippery Adam's apple. Inside his own skull a furnace was raging. He felt Hornbostel's knee smash into his groin but he held on, despite the agony, pressing with the last of his strength, tasting his own blood that trickled down from his matted hair, moving his lips in a low whisper:

"For Yosl—for everything—"

ISRAEL

THE WAY OUT

by JOSEPH HAYYIM BRENNER

I

EARLY every morning, when the little train from Tulkarem arrived to stack
wood for fuel, the old work-instructor would go out on his terrace, shade
his eyes and gaze away from the hamlet to see if they had not come.
They should have been there. They might come any day.

It was by that little train coming to stack wood that they should arrive—
from over there where the trouble was. From the place where the land had been
made desolate, trees had been hewn down and dwellings destroyed; where the
few colonists had paid the soldiers billeted on them to cut down their last
almond trees and bring them to them, the colonists, as fuel; where unground
Indian corn was regularly eaten to give the belly its fill and escape the curse of
famine: where damp, filthy, stinking, verminous, rat-infested booths had for
months on end provided shelter for women and children freezing in winter's
cold and twisted in sickness; where four or five out of every hundred were removed dead day after day; where there was no place on which to set the dozens
who fell ill every day, where there was no shirt for them or sheet to set under
them; where the inhabitants did nothing all day long but listen to the guns,
argue military tactics and moan, "Oh, the Migration Committee's killing us!
It's murdering us!"; where thieves, robbers and swindlers were growing
wealthy, heaping up napoleons, while dozens of hale and hearty lads came from
the north, ate eggs and jam, played cards day and night and awaited the long-
delayed "redemption."

"Can you hear? They're shooting!"

"Our folk, that must be."

"What are you talking about? Those shots don't come from our folk."

"Ours are lying over there, and that's where the shots are from."

"And if it's from ours, it means *they're* on their way."

"The aeroplanes are hanging about all day long."

"And this morning one flew round for two hours straight off."

"And have you seen the Golem? I've seen it."

(The Golem was the captive balloon.)

"The rains are late."

"Well, one thing's sure; when the rains are over we'll go on to Jaffa."

But the rains had passed, Passover had gone without unleavened or leaven
bread for that matter, and instead of returning to the South, to Jaffa, the home-

less exiles had had to bundle their rags and tats together and move weakly north again.

And what would happen? What would happen? They would all come, spent, broken, starving, naked, sick with infectious diseases, would be dropped from the train and would remain there under the heavens, consumed by the sun's heat in the daytime and by the cold and dew at night; bits of broken earthenware unable to move, incapable of shifting for themselves in anything, in anything. . . . Who would give them food or drink? Who would heal them? What would happen?

II

Another few days passed, yet they did not come. There were rumours that they had been sent direct to Galilee and would not be seen thereabouts. The heart began to beat more easily and thoughts to return to the daily round.

And then, one flaming May morning, the news was passed on:

"Forty-two!"

"Where?"

"There. Can't you see them round the wood-stack? That's where they're creeping about."

"Well, if so"—the old work-instructor was all confused—"something has to be done, hasn't it—water . . ."

"They're already filling a barrel with water to take out to them. . . . They mustn't come here to drink. . . . Children here. . . . The doctor says we mustn't have anything to do with them till they've been disinfected."

"Only the horses aren't back yet. . . . Nothing to take it over on," came the report alongside the news about the water.

"And how about bread?" The old man was not listening. "We must have some bread to go on with, at least. A couple of loaves for a bite."

It was a tiny spot with just a single oven, and not too much bread. He himself had two loaves. One he put in the basket; after a moment's thought he broke off half the other loaf and added it. Then he went to each of the five houses in turn to "borrow" loaves and slices of bread for the migrants. Forty-two souls. . . .

The womenfolk knew their duty. It's hard for a housewife to remain without bread, but those people had been starving all the winter through. . . . Now they had come, thirsty, hungry, unfortunate. One woman borrowed loaves, half-loaves and slices from the other—and the basket filled up.

Then the old man hurried to the new arrivals: the water-barrel had not been prepared yet. There were all kinds of delays.

III

Human shadows. Old men. Old women. They lay beside scattered bundles. Women with uncovered bosoms in torn shifts. Unwashed girl-faces from which the marks of youth had vanished. Seven or eight dried-up orphans.

"Jews! Don't rush! Don't crowd round!" cried a small young man with a yellow beard who came over to the bringer of bread. "It must be divided in order, the same to everyone according to the list. Sh, sh. Here's the list, let's share it out! You can't behave like that! You'll tear the old man to pieces."

"Bread! Bread!" rejoiced an old migrant woman. "Here's England; they hand out bread."

"And wagons?" demanded one ginger man, the only ginger person among them, who stood beside five strong and heavy boxes with iron locks. "Is this all the Committee has sent us? Rogues! They're all rogues and swindlers. May the name and fame of the Migration Committee be blotted out! At Kfar Saba we were promised hills and mountains and here we're allowed to stay out in the open. And nobody thinks of how to move us to Kolonia!"

The old instructor answered him, explaining that he was not from the Migration Committee of the neighboring colony but had come of his own accord from the outlying hamlet nearby. In a little while, he, the instructor, would go himself to the branch of the Migration Committee in the colony to inform them of the arrivals.

"And what would it be possible, for instance, to get at the colony to eat with the bread?" asked one young woman. "I shared out bread myself at Kfar Saba. Honey; they say there's lots and lots of honey here. Butter, honey—and how much is meat a pound?"

"And how about it if I wanted to settle in the colony?" asked the wife of the ginger Jew after receiving her share; on her own statement she was the sister of the young woman who had herself distributed bread at Kfar Saba. "Could I find an apartment here?—A room at least, but with a ceiling and roof. . . . Not for nothing, God forbid—I'm quite prepared to pay—let them ask what they want. Only I'm sick of living without an apartment."

"Woe's me, everybody knows that at Kfar Saba I had a grand apartment," lamented the distriburess.

"A doctor, bring a doctor here!" Another woman caught at the old man. "Come and have a look, Mister Jew—the baby's dying. She can't eat bread, a two-year-old child and looks like two months. The father had to stay in Petah Tikva. She hasn't even tasted a spoonful of water for two whole days. The mother's starved and has no milk. On the way there—come and have a look, Mister Jew."

In the arms of a barefoot woman of about twenty, lean as the board beside her, who sat alone some distance away among the trees, quivered a naked baby, white and consumed by mosquitoes, lice and bugs. Covered with sores, she lay dumb and silent with open, glassy eyes.

"If only—some milk," could be heard the ghost of a breath from the mother.

"It's a doctor you want here, a doctor," urged the woman who had called him over.

"Did you ever see anything like it?" interrupted one of the other women.

"A doctor and milk is what they must have, and my children haven't even any water."

"There's no milk to be got at the hamlet," stammered the old man. "But there's water there. They'll bring it in a little while, and for the present—have you any vessel?" He turned to the complaining woman. "Come with me and I'll give you water. It's only ten minutes away."

"There's water nearer at hand!" said the young man with the list in his hand, "over by the bridge."

"God forbid!" the old man shuddered. "Don't drink it. It's swamp water. There's sweet water over at the hamlet. Who's coming with me for some?"

Nobody went. Who would go that distance? The angry young woman gave her kettle to a volunteer orphan and sent him to the bridge to fetch water from the neighborhood for her children.

IV

The colony Committee Room, where migration affairs were also decided, was closed. Everything went on as usual round about. The old instructor sat on the porch and felt, uneasily, how all the ardour flaming within him while he hurried from "station" to the colony was beginning to die away in front of this closed door. He had imagined that he would bang the table with his shrivelled fist, would shout (and maybe would drive his long fingernails into the beard of the committee chairman): "Murderers! Why are you sitting still doing nothing?" But during the half-hour before the closed door some kind of petrification affected him. The beadle passing by had told him that the chairman would arrive in a little while—he was taking a nap just then; but even when he came, what would he, the teacher, have to say to him? And, after all, what was the chairman able to do, really?

"I've come to tell you," he began in a low voice when the chairman arrived about an hour later, "that there are forty-two souls, migrants, arrived. . . ."

"I know," answered the chairman.

"Well, what's going to happen?" asked the instructor shamefacedly.

"What ought to happen? I've arranged that they shouldn't be allowed in the colony without prior disinfection. . . . And anyhow, these are going straight ahead and have nothing to do here in the colony. . . ."

"Yes, so today yet they'll get wagons?" asked the glad instructor.

"This wagon affair is a bad business just now," said the vice-chairman as he entered. "It's the work season now, and which of the farmers will want to hire out a wagon? A wagon—why, it's gold."

"All the same, we'll impound two wagons till the morning," said the chairman with pride.

"Two wagons for forty-two souls?" commented the instructor.

"Well, anyhow—for the baggage. The people can go afoot."

"They're sick and suffering mostly—and children. . . ."

"We know, we know," the vice cut him off. "If we can get a wagon—that's a hundred and twenty gold francs." The chairman was silent.

"And tonight they're to stay in the open?"

The vice made no answer. After a few moments' silence he began to tell the chairman of the conversation he had had over the phone with the chief of the Central Migration Committee. There had been officers in the room and he had not wanted to state, in front of them, how many napoleons the Central Head had to send for the expenses of the new arrivals, so he'd put it cleverly and said twice as much as had been sent the day before yesterday, which meant a hundred and fifty napoleons. And the money had already arrived by special messenger.

"So we can buy the durra?" asked the chairman.

"They want thirty-nine mejidis a bushel."

"Really!" cried the chairman. "We ought to buy. We can't trouble about prices now."

"I believe you still have some durra left for sale?"

And within a moment the building was overflowing with grain-dealers and agents. The vice stuck his hands in his breeches pockets and shovelled out streams of gold napoleons. One agent could be heard joking:

"It's all right. Migrants aren't swine. They'll eat even durra like this."

"It's half dust!"

"Malesh!" (What's the odds!)

"So it's all decided?" The instructor suddenly broke in again. "They're to stay without shelter? And we'll have the right to say 'Our hands have not shed this blood'?"

And as there was no answer he flung another verse among them.

" 'How are the hearts become stone!' "

"But they're used to it," said one of the farmers who had been summoned for hiring wagons. "They've already spent a whole winter at Kfar Saba!"

"Since they haven't been disinfected we can't have anything to do with them. It's doctor's orders," explained the head of the colony.

"Then you'd better keep clear of me. Because I've been with them, without any disinfection. And I've brought all the microbes with me!" screeched the old instructor.

"Very clever, I must say!" The vice had become very serious and stopped jingling the napoleons. "Really, you shouldn't have come here, you know."

"There's no joking in these matters."

"You can't fly in the face of hygiene."

And negotiations were finished.

v

The instructor stayed overnight in the colony. He could not return to his room, for he doubted whether the wagons would be sent in the morning if there was nobody to urge them on.

At midnight a cold mist descended and covered this entire neighborhood. He stood outside, gazed at the wisps of vapour, shivered silently, but did not enter any house. No, he would not enter any house.

He wandered about the colony through the mist until dawn. When it became light he took up his stand before the closed door of the Council room. When the two wagons left at nine in the morning the mist had not entirely vanished.

He rode to the woodpile in one of the wagons, thinking that if no fresh ones were sent today, those who arrived yesterday could be fixed up somehow. The poorest would be sent on further, while those with baggage, if they insisted on staying there, and particularly if they made it quite clear that they would not "be a burden," could be disinfected and allowed into the colony.

But if an additional transport arrived today, with all this disorder and indifference round about, then he was lost.

He drew close and saw, through the mist clinging to the shivering bodies, that they had not increased.

Everything shrank together within him, and a few tears fell.

Apart from the ginger Jew, who was hidden within a tiny booth made by two Yemenites, since the previous day, out of his trunks, linen curtains, sticks and eucalyptus branches, they were all, grown-ups and children, lying on the ground, shivering and huddled up with damp and thirst.

"Sodom!" The yellow-bearded young man, who seemed to have grown smaller overnight, passed judgment on the colony.

"And what are you going to give us today, Mister Jew?" asked the woman who had spoken gratefully of "England" the day before.

"They're going to bring bread," the old man promised. "Durra bread," he found it his duty to add.

He cast his eyes about him for the mother of the sick child (he had succeeded in getting a pint of milk for her in a tin can), but could not see her. She had gone to the colony. Gone to the doctor. Without prior disinfection. Paid no attention to the order. She had gone with her child.

"And what would you advise, Mister Jew?" came the distraction. "Should I stay here or go on?"

The reasons for and against were numberless. The chief reason for staying was: How was it possible to go ahead when the saviors might arrive there the very next day?

Meanwhile the trunks of the ginger Jew were loaded on the wagons with the aid of the wagoners, and the young man who had set himself in charge. The trunks were full of cloth and it was impossible to shift them. A great quantity of toil, panting and moaning was sacrificed to them. And once they were loaded, the Jewish carter who had been sent by one of the farmers refused to allow as much as a straw to be added. The orphans were lifted up and lifted down half a dozen times. But he wasn't going to kill his mules for migrants! It didn't matter! There were other wagons in the colony and the Migration Committee wasn't so sick and sore that it couldn't hire as many as it needed! It was the second carter, the Arab, who had no clear idea as to what the Migration Committee was, who consented to take, besides the three trunks on the wagon (the Jew carried only two), a few extra bundles as well as two impatient old men, who climbed up—as one might to martyrdom in order to hallow the Name —resolved to go on whatever happened.

"And they're not going to send any more wagons?" asked the other migrants in astonishment, staring at one another.

"And they won't give me and my children a wagon at all?" The woman who had demanded water the day before could not understand it.

After turmoil, shrieks, curses, gnashing of teeth, arguments, demands, good advice, inventions, discoveries and witticisms, the greater part of the caravan remained where they were that day as well.

The remnants of the shelter of the red Jew, who had journeyed further, led to many quarrels. Each one claimed to have taken possession first, till finally they pulled the cover to pieces and scattered it in all directions.

The orphans sat playing on the scattered branches spitting the good water —which had at length been brought—one over the other.

And the instructor returned to the colony to report. There were a few youngsters who had not gone to work and who were willing to spend the day arranging the disinfection and putting up tents, so that those left behind might enter the colony and not sleep out in the open.

But the matter was not arranged. The Colony Council claimed that the authorities did not permit migrants to enter the colony. This colony, the vice explained, was a military camp, and the authorities were afraid that the migrants might spread sicknesses among the soldiers.

The tents were left halfway.

The bath-house owner did not want to let the bath-house be used for disinfection when he was asked. It was impossible to get a big pot at any price. The migrants remained where they were and the old instructor with them, idle and powerless. That night the dew fell on him and he had a bad spell of fever. And in the morning the train brought another hundred and forty-seven souls from Tulkarem. There was no way out.

VI

Fever flaming within him, the old man stormed from the migrants' camp back to the colony, feeling himself lost. But there he found his way out.

Among the trees on the slope, beside some migrants' rubbish which had reached there Lord knows how, stood a group of men, including some ragged and hungry Turkish soldiers, round a thin, barefoot woman who sat on the ground with a dead child beside her.

The dead child, who had been naked as at birth in the migrants' camp two days before, now lay in a little shift.

"The doctor put a spoonful of milk into her mouth; he poured it in but she didn't swallow. . . . It was plain that nothing could be done," said one of the bystanders.

The mother herself was silent. She sat barefoot and lean as she had two days before. She wanted them to take the dead child away for burial, and not to forget to bring her, the living one, the child's rations of durra bread for that day. She was ravening with hunger.

There was no change in the child save for the shift. Her mouth was shut and her eyes were open. The pallor of her cheeks had neither increased nor lessened. The sores were as they had been.

"Why don't they bury her?" complained the bystanders.

"We've been three times to the Council already," came the answer. "There's nobody to speak to. Nobody to go to the *Hevra Kadisha*. Putting it off from hour to hour . . ."

"I'm burying her!" cried the old work-instructor. "Will someone give me a shovel?"

People went in search of a spade, went to every house in the colony, and came back empty-handed.

"There's a little hoe. That soldier's holding it."

The old man took a bishlik from his pocket and turned to the soldier without a word, holding it up.

The man in soldier's uniform nodded. With a queer movement the old man picked up the tiny body and carried it straight to the cemetery, as God-parents carry the eight-days child to the circumcision—on the two hands extended straight before him.

It was a hard way through sand. The feverish man set the body under his armpit whence it dangled. He strode with the last of his strength, the soldier in his tailless tarbush before him.

After a half hour they reached their haven of desire.

The fence round the cemetery had been broken down. The staples were missing, and where they had been there were now deep, narrow holes in the ground.

He was covered with sweat, though he had taken a gramme and a half of quinine some hours back; and his fever was beginning to leave him. It was already too much for him, though this load was not nearly as heavy as the basket of bread he had brought to the camp two days earlier. His eyes dimmed and he could not see. "Child, my child! How lovely you are! What a beautiful woman you could have become! Who knows whose happiness enters the grave with you today! Little girl, my little girl!"

His foot caught in one of the holes. He took it out quickly, not even feeling that he had dislocated the big toe of his left foot.

"Here!" said he to the soldier and stopped.

The soldier put his hoe to the ground and set to work. Simply, without argument or question. He continued for about ten minutes, like a big child playing with sand. When the hole had been dug he raised his childlike eyes to his commander, who was giving him the bishlik; and the old man, who had meanwhile put the child on the sand, ordered him with eyes and gestures to dig deeper. . . .

"We must, so that the dogs shouldn't drag the body out," he thought.

The soldier went on; the grave was prepared; the digger straightened himself; and the old man did all that was necessary. He took off the shift for some reason, lowered the sweet little body, wasted by mosquitoes and hunger, into the grave and covered it with loose earth with his own hands. The soldier put the discarded shift under his tailless tarbush, bent down, moved the shift from under the tarbush into a tear in his coat which resembled a pocket, and immediately began to devote himself to scattering earth in the grave, aiding in the burial of this daughter of a strange God.

They returned to the colony as fellow-workers might.

The old man was limping and could hardly walk. The big toe was paining more and more. But he felt that there was still something left for him to do, that the business was not at an end, that he could not part from his dark-skinned companion in such a fashion. When they reached the colony he entered a shop in order to treat him to a glass of wine, to drink with him and toast "Good health! Good health, brother in adversity! Good health, patient Anatolian peasant!" But there was no wine in the shop; the Mukhtar had taken it all. The Commandant was staying with him. All to the good, thought the old man as he remembered that wine is prohibited to Moslems and that the soldier might have been perplexed if he were treated to something forbidden. Instead he bought his companion a packet of cigarettes and a piece of hard, white cheese, added the bishlik, shook hands with him warmly, and the Turk departed full of heartfelt gratitude, the little child's shift gleaming white from his torn pocket.

But he, the old man, could not go. The hole left by the removal of the staple from the cemetery fence, doubtless for military purposes, had injured him seriously; not until dark was he brought home from the colony on a donkey, with the aid of a worker-pupil.

At his request the pupil brought him a basin of cold water and left him.

It was growing dark in the room. He lay alone. He set his toe in the cold water, and it swelled so that later he could not even move to attend to his physical needs. But, anyway, he was free of all other needs. Entirely free. The load was lifted.

The half-loaf, lying on his table among his books and linen for two days, reminded him that for three days he had not even eaten. But the pain in the toe was great enough to drive away all thought of food. For some reason he stretched out his hand to feel the bread, which had grown too dry to eat. And he felt sorry that he had not taken it with the other loaves. What a pity, what a pity, he thought, every crumb of bread now . . . But the sorrow speedily passed and was replaced by a great relief in his heart. A bare ten minutes' walk away a hard, unpleasant night spread its wings over the third transport of transmigrants as well as sixty-nine souls who had arrived at noon, which was not the time arranged. He knew about it. His pupil had told him on the way. But it did not affect him. He did not venture out or go across to them. He could not walk. He had been relieved.

THE YEAR OF ABUNDANCE

by MOSES STAVSKY

G OD relented. And the whispered prayers of the toiler returned not empty, and the tears of the sower reached to heaven.

With great, with manifold mercy the windows of heaven were flung open, flung wide by a generous hand to abundance and rich blessing.

At the beginning of Heshvan the rains began to fall, beautiful in their order and pleasant in their seasons. Week in and week out, Sabbath to Sabbath, Sabbath to Wednesday, and Wednesday to Sabbath alternately, with slight pauses until the plowing and sowing were done, and again from week to week, Sabbath to Sabbath, Sabbath to Wednesday, and Wednesday to Sabbath, as in the generations of complete purity and God-fearing men.

And when Tebet came, the fields were all plowed, plowed and sown, pregnant with fruit, rich in blessing, and drunken with rain.

To the farthest horizon, as far as the eye encompassed, it fed on verdure, bright green and yellow green. Soft and gentle and pale were the first sprigs of wheat which cracked the crust of the earth and shot forth their heads into air, delicate, languid and tender.

Light green and dark green, sun bright—beans and barley, vetch and barley, vetch and oats—light green and dark green. Sun and rain—deep-rooting, high-stretching, black-spreading—sated and oversated, filled to overflowing. Like a well-favored child who rests on the knees of a mother blessed with abundant milk and sucks his fill, and being replete pushes away the breast without sucking to the end—not half—not a third—and falls with his head thrown back, weary of fullness, and foam dribbles from his mouth and about his neck, foam and saliva, sweet foam, sweet and white.

Joy, satiate joy, rises from the earth, fills the spaces of the air, rises and pours itself over the face of the earth like the savor of good ointments—joy and blessing.

To the village abundance reached, and to the colony, to the large colony and to the small colony, to the moshav and to the kvutzah; it knocked at the doors of the Arab husha, at the doors of mansions and huts, at the tent flap and wooden barracks. It knocked exultingly, with exceeding joy. It shouted, "Here am I. I have come to you with blessing. Once in seventy years. Few are the graybeards that remember me.

"Behold your prayers are answered, the tears of your babes have reached me. I have come to you—and with me grass for the cow and the goat, milk for the suckling and the calf, seeds for the hen and pigeon, grain for the millstone, grain for sowing, grain for the granary."

At once worry fell away, strife ended, and hate was torn up by its roots—complete strangers with careworn faces looked at one another joyfully—delight and gladness were companions—exultation met with rejoicing.

People heavy with age and full of trouble sought out the tenderest words and the pleasantest names to call their happiness. In ringing voices like the clinking of gold against silver—

> The most blessed year, the greenest year—
> Year of milk, year of corn!
> The whitest year, the greenest year,
> Year of the lamb, year of the calf—
> The rainiest year, the most blessed year!

In the oldest of the settlements, the mother of the settlements, abundance overflowed its banks. Mud to the neck. And it was easy and pleasant to wallow in abundance, to leap from stone to bank, and hop from bank to stone, amused and smiling lightly: Did you ever see a wanton like this, such a bully—ever in all your days?

Easy it was and pleasant, for the fields were already sown, sown correctly and in their appointed time, the harvest was growing prettily, and many were eager for it.

Pleasant it was and easy. For the ditches in the vineyard were open already . . . wide open . . . they stretched from tree to tree, ditch touched ditch . . . the price of almonds was higher than last year . . . new vines will be planted this year . . . grapes are paid for in advance . . . there are great preparations in the winepress . . . everyone has his hands full of work.

Pleasant it was and easy. For there was so much water that it was impossible to get to the orange grove. One could only go out and stand far off by the acacia hedge, and from there gaze at the long, entangled, heavy-laden rows of greenage. Laden with abundant blessing, a green, ripening blessing, ripening and yellowing. And while you are standing, as a thief might stand outside the fence, your own fence, you take account, you reckon and set prices, you grow fantastic, exaggerate, and know that you exaggerate, and understand your folly. And you are satisfied and brimming with pleasure at this folly of yours.

Pleasant it was and easy. For this week a donkey sank in the swamp of the hamrah. Bells clanged and people gathered. Noise and tumult. The village folk rushed to the hamrah, some on foot, some horseback, some with rope, some with sticks. But they could not pull the donkey out. At last they harnessed a pair of mules and tied them to the donkey, jerked him out, dragged him through the whole village, pulled him from street to street singing and clamoring. People came out of their houses to whistle and hiss after them. Loafers beat on tins, trilled with their fingers on their lips, shrill feverish shrieks like the wailing lament of Arab women mourners.

Idle days they rode to the city to amuse themselves, one to the tailor or dressmaker, another to the theater or movie. Anyone who owned a horse wore riding trousers. His legs encased in boots, a kafia on his head, and an abya on his shoulders. He and comrades his own age go down to the threshing floor, the one dry spot in the village, to sport with the horses. One remembers his friend in a neighboring village, puts double sacks on his saddle and gifts in the sacks, a branch loaded with oranges, some green and some ripe, branch and leaves and fruit together. In the evening he comes home with a gift to the house, honey, eggs and chickens that peep out of the sacks.

In the evening neighbor visits neighbor, housewife visits housewife, to sip tea, eat sweets and gossip.

The old men pass their time in the synagogue, one pondering over a holy book, another in secular talk.

And the village band, from its room in the council house, from early evening until late at night, booms through all the village with its great brass instruments. Out of satiety and pleasure, with childlike folly and innocent joy —boom boom—till midnight and later—boom boom—we are blessed this year, a wonder like this comes but once in seventy years.

Boom—boom—boom—

Slow moving as the waters of Siloam, abundance poured itself out over the face of the earth. Lovely in its order and pleasant in its season. Week after week, Sabbath after Sabbath, every Sabbath and every Wednesday. When Shevat comes, the wells of Jerusalem are brimful of water, and every throat hoarse with praise and song. Every shoe and every sandal torn with dancing.

And the pasture floods over the face of the earth like a green river. Like the waters of early spring in western lands. Like the Nile at the end of summer. Wherever grass could strike its roots it climbed: sand, stone, mountain, valley, tree and roof.

The dew is still on the ground and the herd returns to the village to be shut up in the stalls a day and a night, until the morning of the morrow. Filled, glutted, every belly a barrel's width. All day and all night, they chew and ruminate, until their jaws are tired and white foam, greenish foam, dribbles from their mouths, weary of chewing, and paints all the ground about them green and white.

The calves suckle and do not empty the tits, not half, not a quarter, and they weary of sucking—they grow weary from too much sucking.

The flock are weary of carrying their fatted skins, and because of the heaviness of their fleshy rumps the lambkins move lumberingly and lazily.

In the middle of Tebet a letter was sent from brother to brother—from Ain Hai, which is in Kfar Saba near Petach Tikva, to Tel Adashim, which is in Emek Israel, saying:

"Cauliflower is plentiful here. We have so many that we could pave the streets with them. I talked it over with my wife Zipporah and she says perhaps it would be well to send you some, for who knows whether cauliflower has grown well with you this year."

And the man in Tel Adashim, which is in the Emek, answered his brother who is in Ain Hai, which is in Sharon:

"We have packed cauliflower in cans. We collected all the cans of Nazareth and Haifa, and it is impossible to get any more. And as for carrots, we have more than we can pull up, more than we can gather. I beg you to come to us. You were fond of tzimmus, and my wife Tobah will cook tzimmus for you as you liked it in the old days, as mother cooked it, may she rest in peace, for the Sabbath meal when we were still in our father's house."

And in the beginning of the month of Shevat a message was sent by word of mouth from Kfar Saba, which is near Petach Tikva, through a worker going to Tel Aviv. By word of mouth, because the sender was not in the habit of writing. Nor had he the time, for he was alone at his work. And there was his vegetable garden and tree nursery of orange trees on which he must keep an eye, and the cowshed where the cows must be fastened, watered and milked.

The message was addressed to the house of the produce agent in Mercaz Mischari, Tel Aviv, who was to give it to a comrade who kept cows in Tel Nordia; and it was phrased in these words:

"The calves which were nearly dead at the end of last summer from lack of pasture in the fields will not die. Their skin is almost bursting with fat. And so I beg you to send your cattle to my pastures. For there is too much grass and the blessing of God is going to waste."

And a comrade of Magdel brought his old mother and young sister up to Erez Israel from Motomashav, which is in the kingdom of Poland. He harnessed his horse and cart and drove to Tel Aviv himself to fetch them from the ship. Himself: first, because pennies are scarce among workers on the land and he hadn't the price of an auto; and, second, because he longed to show off, to boast, to strut before them like a child.

"Just look, what a driver! How handsomely he manages a horse!"

And they, the whole way, could not fill their eyes with looking, nor their hearts with marveling.

"See, see, what a driver. Look at the farmer, no evil eye upon him. . . ."

Look, look how sunburnt and how dirty he is! Look, how cracked his hands are, his dear hands."

And the sister who had been a comrade of the chalutz in Poland laughed through her tears and wept in her laughter. She took the reins in her hands and learned how to drive the horse, and then in the softest, gentlest voice she called to the horse, the big horse who was pulling the cart—my dove, my bird, my cat, my darling, my love. They got home late, tired from the journey, and overwrought with joy. And long they spoke and much they recountered, questioned and answered, until drowsiness fell upon them, and they slept.

And an old peasant, a man of Bertuvia in Shephelah, which is in Judah, returned at sunset from the fields, unyoked his oxen, watered them, put fodder before them, washed himself, prayed minha and maarev peacefully and earnestly. And when he had refreshed himself with food, he sent to a neighbor for pen and ink. He tore an empty page from a notebook that belonged to his grandchild, mounted his glasses on his nose and sat down to write a letter to his son who lived in Nahalal, which is in the Emek, in a fine Yiddish seasoned here and there with bits of Russian. And this is the translation:

"First, I wish you and your wife and children peace and good health.

"Secondly, Mother, long life to her, asks how you are and how your wife and children are, may they be found worthy of long life and good health. Also I must tell you, my son, that the barley has come up beautifully this year, higher than a man's head. Perhaps you would lose nothing if you were to come to me, you and your horse and your wagon together to help us to reap our fields."

And the son, who dwelt in Nahalal, which is in the Emek, returned from the fields to his house, set the yard and cowshed in order, and after he had washed and dressed, eaten and drunk, he turned his step to the council house. (Once there had been pen and ink in his house, but the pen rusted and the ink dried from the heat—and the boy was still in kindergarten, so there was no notebook to tear a piece of paper from.) And from the council house he wrote a letter to his father, who was in Bertuvia, in pure Hebrew—and this was its content:

"To my honored father and teacher and my mother who bore me—may you have long life. The barley and vetch have grown this year beyond all other years. We are tired of too much labor. Perhaps my father would consent to come to his son to help him gather the fruit of his fields."

The letters met at the station, Lydda, and separated, one in one direction and the other in another direction, this one to Bertuvia, which is in the Shephelah, and that one to Nahalal, which is in the Emek.

And a Jew who dwelt in the settlement Hederah, a firmly planted Jew, broad-boned, a solid rich peasant, wrote to his daughter who was a shopkeeper in Jaffa, in Beneve Shalom:

"Lock the store and come, you, your husband and your children. There is plenty of work and plenty of food . . . milk and eggs and vegetables . . . more than we can eat . . . no one buys and no one sells!" . . .

And a farmer, a man of Ekron, met a worker of his in a street of Tel Aviv. And they recognized one another—by the smell of the field and cowshed they knew one another. The smell clung to them and they carried it with them amid the sand and stone of the city. Both strong men, bent in stature, sunburnt faces. One in boots and the other in jacket, vest and tsitsot. They knew each other and rejoiced—they rejoiced wholeheartedly.

The plow had bent both their backs and made them equals.

"Do you know that in Mansorah each dunam gave two full sacks of wheat?"

"Do you know that with us in Ain Tivon the oats have grown higher than a man's head, so that when the watchman gets off his horse among the grain both horse and rider vanish?" . . .

And the comrades of Tel Hai wrote to their comrades in Tel Josef.

"Perhaps you can send us a few scythes. Our scythes broke this year. Each stalk of hay is thicker than a finger, and is almost impossible to cut."

And the comrades of Tel Josef, which is in the Emek, answered their comrades in Tel Hai, who dwell in the mountains of Upper Galilee.

"We have set up a carpenter to make handles for the scythes. Perhaps you are able to send us oak wood. For it is impossible to get any wood here except eucalyptus wood." . . .

And the writer of the story, who was shut up between the sand and stone of Tel Aviv, met a comrade of his one day in Allenby Street, a comrade of many days gone by, a companion of the plow and scythe, broad-shouldered, sturdy and sunburnt. And he remembered his first month of work, that sweet, as it were, honeymoon of his workdays, that bright singing month rose in his heart—horse, cow and cowshed, plow, scythe and field, grass, sun and rain—earth—and sky—and God—

And the comrades rejoiced—rejoiced exceedingly—tears came to their eyes out of excessive joy. They questioned each other, told one another stories. Until the writer grew silent and his friend, the man of the colony, continued to recount, to relate joyously, out of his great joy.

"Beyond belief.

"Beyond conception.

"One year in seventy, one year in eighty, weary is the earth of great blessing, tired are the sowers of overwork, and every hand is heavy with overabundance."

The writer listens and is silent, tears choke in his throat, and his heart murmurs a prayer and a silent blessing.

"Blessed be the hands that have chosen hard labor for their lot.

"Blessed be ye in your houses, blessed in your gardens, blessed your garners and baking troughs, blessed your flocks and your herds, blessed your plows and your scythes—

"Even to the smallest weed of your field that grows by the wayside."

THE THREE HALUZOT

by AVIGDOR HAMEIRI

I. "MURDERESS"

My friend the sculptor took me by the arm and said:

"Come on, you've got to come and see something that has been driving me crazy lately. You must come and see a woman's body."

"I've seen them. More than once. I used to drop in at Franz Stuk's studio. I've seen them."

"You've seen devils, my boy, not women's bodies. That Stuk of yours paints devils and witches. Come along and I'll show you a real angel of the Lord, a real fairy."

Well and good. We went down to the seashore.

It was sunset. A Jaffa sunset with all its futurist magic. The sea was flaming, poured-out molten gold; and the disc of the sun descended to the sea like a woman smiling as she goes down to her scented bath.

The foreshore was filled with bathers, old and young together. They were bathing, splashing and skylarking, like dragonflies round forest pools.

My friend the sculptor paced hither and thither, staring and searching, reassuring me with the hand held behind him: "Right away, right away. She's here every day, she bathes here. I'll find her at once."

I followed him.

But I found her before he did. I noticed a group of women lying on the sand with all their eyes frozen on one spot in the sea. The spot was she.

"There she is," I told my friend.

"Aha. Yes."

"Well?"

"My old teacher, Rodin," said my friend excitedly, "once said to me categorically, 'Never model a woman's body till you find one that robs you of your rest and brings you to the belief that even if you were shown no more than one breast you would be able to say exactly how old she is.'

"Well, there she is. For the last few days I can't eat or drink or sleep like an ordinary human being. You know how I always eat like a brewer's horse

and sleep like a dormouse. Now I eat like a dormouse and sleep like a horse—
I hardly close my eyes."

I gazed at her while he added: "That's her public, that group of curious
women. They talk of her as the young beauty. They know she comes to bathe
here every day at this time and they come to stare at her and feel sorry for
themselves."

"Yes. She's a beauty. Who is she?"

"Who is she? I'll tell you the truth; I want to go round and ask, but I'm
afraid of the answer. Why? Just look at her.—Now tell me, can you estimate
how long it took for that woman's body to evolve out of hairy ape-mother Eve?
How many millions of years have gone by to bring the body to this stage? And
who and what has brought it as far as this?"

"Who? I suppose that quiet, petted, sheltered lives of gentle culture and of
careful, prolonged nurture have been the lot of mother and daughter for ages
and ages. Care of the entire body from her hair to her toenails."

"That's it. And that's what strikes a discord in my creative enthusiasm. A
girl nurtured enough to make the working masses rise! Someone told me that
she's a haluza.[1] I believed him for a moment and then realized how far I was
from acting on my teacher's instructions. How could I imagine even for a second that she was a haluza? When you look at your worn-out haluzot, tired
out and withered up before their time with hard work, you'll go raving mad
at that girl; her beauty flourishes at the cost of all holy and unfortunate
daughters of Israel, who can't even afford to buy a cake of decent toilet soap."

"That's no affair of an artist."

"I know, but what can I do? I know it's the sort of philosophizing you can
expect from a Socialist. But it's gone so far that instead of modeling the body
of a beautiful woman I've decided to introduce an idea of cruelty. I'd hardly
begun to model when the right name struck me for the piece—Cattleia
Necans. Do you know the Cattleia Necans Orchid, the loveliest of them all?
It's a wonderful flower, a destructive flower, climbing over plants and trees and
pouring its tendrils over any number of other plants; it twines round them, embraces them and slays them with a kiss, sucks their sap and flourishes, its
blossom laughing to the sun in all its colors and its scent making you drunk
far away.—And this witch here is a blossom of the same kind. She preens herself at the cost of thousands of her sisters who toil and dry up like wild roses
and who shrivel up under the flaming sun. Cattleia Necans—murderess!"

I wanted to say something to him, something in the style of Samson's
"Out of the strong came forth sweetness." But she had just come out of the
sea alone.

The sun was sinking, a disc of pure gold, and the girl stood stretching herself. She made a step and her head entered the circle of flaming light. The rim
of the sun was a diadem set round her black head.

[1] Pioneer working in the Palestinian communes.

"Just look how Chance is mocking us. A glory of gold round her head. Come along, let's go. That's enough."

As we walked along he repeated:

"Murderess . . . murderess."

II. MOTHER

I met the sculptor again and he was in quite a different mood. He had a new idea. His murderess had been dropped halfway. He was true to his social theories and did not care even for the sanctities of Art, if they did not agree with his theories. He hated that murderess and a hater cannot be a creator. Now he had a holy idea.

"I've an idea for something I've long felt the need of."

"Well?"

"The Jewish Mother. It's like this. Next door to me live a couple with two kiddies, a boy and a girl. The boy's sick lately. The wall's real Tel Aviv manufacture, thick as three sheets of writing paper, and I can hear everything that's going on. And among the rest I've found out something that never struck me. I've found out what a Jewish mother is.—It's something I can't make out. This mother hasn't slept a wink for nearly three months—not a wink. I work at night, as you know, and she's up and busy with the baby all night long. She doesn't close her eyes even for five minutes. She just doesn't sleep. How is it possible?"

"Maybe she sleeps in the daytime?"

"That's the thing! I know that in the daytime she's at work somewhere. I haven't even seen her yet. Once I got up in the morning because I hadn't been working the night before, and I heard her attending to the two children. She was suckling the little boy and singing to him, and teaching the little girl. Pure Hebrew instruction. She speaks a Hebrew we can envy her. Lately there's nobody there all day long; it's only in the morning I hear her while she's suckling the boy. I hear things that are enough to make you melt away. She suckles the baby and speaks to him in her song. I noted down some of it."

He took out his notebook and read:

"Little red flower, tiny blossom, here is a little milk, take my pure white life. Take my white blood. Drink, drink, my weeny ram, drink and become a lion. Judah is a lion's whelp. Judah-lion's-whelp must not be sick. Many are the beasts of prey, my little son. You must grow and roar, not for prey, my son, but for the word of the Lord. A lion roars, who doth not fear; the Lord doth speak, who can but prophesy? Drink, drink, my son, my milk and blood. La-la-la, la-la-la, la-la."

He closed his notebook and raised his eyes to me. His eyes were moist.

"Well, what do you think?"

"A Jewish mother. You're right."

"She's awake at night. Doesn't let her eyelids close. And by day it's Judah, the lion's whelp, and then to work somewhere or other. Sure, she's a haluza. 'Take my white blood'—Lord! We have mothers like that."

"And who's her husband?"

"I have no idea. I'll tell you the truth; I've no great desire as yet to meet her. Come along to my place!"

As we entered his room we heard the voice of a woman singing to herself.

"She's at home," whispered the sculptor.

After listening a moment:

"She's washing herself—she's about to go out. Do you know what? Let's go down to the entrance and wait for her."

We went down and stood in the entrance hall, and did not have long to wait. She appeared and went into the street. We could not see her face well for it was hidden by a blue summer-veil. She passed us quickly, a tastefully-dressed young woman. I looked after her and saw that her hands were not well kept.

"Spoiled hands," I said. "They're hard and bony. A haluza."

"A pity," said my friend. "Those are holy hands."

He looked after her and was silent. Suddenly he roused himself.

"Eh, my lad! What a piece, what a creation that will be! Do you know the name I've found for it?"

"Well?"

" 'Thy mother, the lioness.' "

III. HALUZA

"You're looking for a subject and must have a social theme? Come to my place!" I said to my sculptor friend a few days later. "Come and visit me after noon. I've got something for you to chew over. After you've looked you'll do a piece with a clear, fine, simple name, 'Haluza.' "

"Something in that. You're right. That idea never struck me. 'Haluza,' the sculpture of the age."

He visited me the following afternoon.

In the middle of the sands across the street a house was being built.

"Come here," said I. "Do you see that girl over there? That one, with a red handkerchief round her head?"

"Yes, I see her. Well?"

"Just sit down by the window and watch her for a while. Sit down and watch her working."

He sat down and I left him to himself.

Half an hour later I returned. He sat like an image and stared. When he sensed that I had come in he jumped up.

"Well?" I asked.

"Do you know the conclusion I've come to?" said he as though thinking aloud. "That the first of all revolts is the revolt of the women. You know, it's a real dirty trick; why do women get a smaller wage than men? Why, that girl over there does more alone in a single second than three men in ten minutes! Just look how she's working! She's as strong as a giant, that girl. Look! Just look how she's picking up that iron bar!"

He started forward as though he wished to run and help her.

Meanwhile the singing of a woman reached us. She was singing at her work. A sweet and pleasant voice, light, but agreeable to the ear and appealing to the heart. The men would answer back in snatches and every now and again she would laugh at their gruffness, like a stream murmuring through the soughing of the trees.

My friend was all aflame.

"What am I against such a creature?" said he in despair. "All my attempts are hopeless against such an original. 'Haluza,' of course! Still, I'll try. And she's still young and fresh, you can see. Lovely girl."

We listened again to her happy singing and gazed in astonishment at her strength and diligence, wayward as a flowing fountain.

"Let's cross over!" proposed my friend. "I want to look at her nearby."

"All right. They're finishing right away, anyhow."

We went across and were a moment or two late. They were already leaving. We followed her. She was walking with her husband.

They turned into the street in which my friend the sculptor lived. When we reached the house in which his room was, they entered.

We looked at one another like two clowns.

"That's your mother lioness," said I. "You're a great artist and no mistake. How was it you didn't know?"

We entered his room and heard her speaking through the wall:

"You attend to the children meanwhile. I won't be back for about an hour. It's two days since last I bathed."

We stared at each other as the same idea struck us. Perhaps this was the beautiful girl?

"Some hopes," said my friend. "You jump too fast. You're silly."

"Silly if you like, but come down to the hallway all the same."

We went down and in a moment she came out. It was the same "Jewish mother" we had seen coming out a few days earlier.

Looking at her face, naturally I recognized the beautiful bathing girl.

"A poet's hallucination," said my friend with mocking assurance.

We followed her in silence.

She proceeded straight to the sea.

When we arrived and found her in the sea we stared at one another as though we had gone silly.

The sun was setting. My friend caught my hand and pulled me to the right.

"Over here. Come over here. That's right."

I did not understand for a moment. But when I moved I saw her black head in the gold disc of the sun and the haluza stood on the sands, bright with a glory.

"Well, my lad, what name can you suggest for this piece?"

THE PANGS OF MESSIAH

by MOSES SMILANSKI

I

R EB YOSI, the beadle, scion of the Baal Shem Tov, dwelt at Meron at the entrance to the Cave of Rabbi Simeon Ben Yohai, which is on the slopes of Mount Atzmon, loftiest of the mountains of this side of Jordan, which rears its head over all Galilee. There he tended the holy Eternal Lamp over the sacred grave of the saintly rabbi; for were it to be extinguished, God forbid, the whole world might return to void and emptiness.

All the forty years of his life Reb Yosi had been poor to despair. He had inherited his post from his father of blessed memory. He, his spouse, his only daughter and her husband, a fisherman in partnership with one of the Gentile fishers of Tiberias, sustained themselves from one Sabbath to the next with very little more than a measure of carobs. His face was seamed and withered as that of an old man. But age had come upon him not from the toil of making a living nor from the pursuit of wealth, but—this was revealed only to the humble of spirit, and then just from mouth to ear—because he was among those who calculate the End of Days and the coming of Messiah. Ever since he had known his own mind he had been drawn to calculations of the End, and was thoroughly versed in them.

Since the time of his return from the Yeshiva at Safed to Meron, and his inheritance, after his father had passed away, of the duty of tending the Holy Grave, he had sunk himself heart and soul in these reckonings. Nobody knew the nature of his discoveries save his modest spouse, to whom, on occasion, he might reveal the slightest part of his calculations. She would listen, nod her head in agreement, and moan. Not out of desire for the coming of the End of Days, however. She was too intent on her own calculations of how far her few farthings would go in her preparations for the Sabbath. Her husband received one mejidi a week as wages, and another mejidi a month as his portion from the money collected in the Exile for the upkeep of the Jewish communities in the land of Israel. Her son-in-law, the fisherman, brought home no more than fish for Sabbath. She alone had to worry concerning their living and more still concerning the Sabbath.

Reb Yosi derived no great pleasure from his calculations of the End. He had spent many a year at them, turning night into day with his reckonings.

He computed his correspondence and dived into the sea of numerical equivalents, finding many a false date for the End, may the Merciful deliver us from evil. But the one true End he could not discern. Satan stood accusing. Sometimes he would find the correct way, and radiance would illumine the path from beginning to end. Sometimes he would feel with his entire being that it was very near, and he could all but take hold of it in his hand. Yet another day of balanced understanding and settled thought, maybe two days, and he would possess the time of the End.

Then dreadful news would arrive. Riots had broken out aaginst Israel; destruction had been decreed; Israel had been falsely accused in a fashion to profane the honor of Israel and the Torah. Reb Yosi would rend his garments, put ashes on his head and don sackcloth, and sit fasting at the entrance to the cave, mourning as one does the dead. Every calamity befalling all Israel was his own calamity. What then did he possess in the world save the honor of Israel and the Torah?

At such times he would forget all the long and ordered chain of his computations in his grief, and the solutions which had been clear as the sun to him. The threads that had begun to wind together into a single powerful strand were broken off. The light vanished. Darkness oppressed his brain. When his grief died down, he would begin again at the beginning, toiling and laboring till he found what he sought. Then would come a fresh calamity and the cycle would be repeated. The accusing Satan stood in the way.

Nevertheless the twenty-two years which he had spent tending the Holy Grave had not been spent in vain. He had labored indeed, resting from his calculations only on Sabbaths and Festivals. Then, on Sabbaths and Festivals, he devoted himself to the Supplementary Soul which descends upon the Jew, honoring it and benefiting from its brightness. In addition he did not indulge in his work during the regular fasts nor during the extra forty days' fast which he took upon himself year by year; during those times he was mourning the Exile of the Holy Presence. Excepting such periods, both his days and his nights were devoted to his sacred work. Morning by morning, after he had dipped to cleanse himself and prayed, he would leave the care of the Eternal Light to his granddaughter, who tended it like the pupil of her eye, while he went wandering far and wide through the district, without returning home until the hour of the afternoon prayer.

He would set his midday meal, which consisted of a hunk of black bread, in his wallet, would wash his hands at the springs and would sing the grace after food among the rocks, which always echoed amen. Throughout the entire district there was not a rock he did not know, never an herb he had not studied, not a cave to the end of which he had not penetrated. Then he also knew the dervishes and the hajjis, they, their manner of speech and their ways of thought; for he spoke a pure Arabic. And from them all—from mountain and from rock and from herb and from cave and from dervish and from the men of the countryside—he would derive fine threads which he wove into the fabric of his calculations concerning the End of Days. And who knows? But for the hour of the afternoon prayers which would interrupt him in his thoughts and meditations, simultaneously snapping the magic thread unifying him with his surroundings and with the tracks of those distant saints who had trodden these selfsame hills thousands of years ago—who call tell? Maybe he would already have discovered the secret of the End. . . .

But his duties would interrupt him and he would return to the cave with the grave within, and his house at the foot of the mountain. The magic thread would be snapped and only on the morrow might he begin to spin it anew. At night he would sit alone in the cave, a wax candle in one hand and a copy of the holy "Zohar" in the other, with a creased sheet of paper and the stub of an old pencil before him for his calculations. He would read and reckon and make notes. There would be no end to the numbers and the calculations. . . .

Then the hour of midnight would arrive. Once again his duty would interrupt him. Reb Yosi would devote himself to the solitary Midnight Service of Reparation, weeping bitterly for the Exile of the Divine Presence and for the shame of the Jewish people. He would forget the entire world in which he lived, his calculations as well. After the Midnight Service he would sleep the short sleep of duty, rousing himself speedily to serve the Creator; the dawn breaking would find him in the cave, pale as death, his heart empty, his brain empty, broken as a shattered potsherd and thinking to collapse. Were his modest wife not to bring him a hot drink at that hour he would collapse in earnest. . . .

But after all, Reb Yosi had not toiled and labored in vain all these twenty-two years. Much had been made clear to him. Though all the kings of the West and the East might come to him, with all the saints in the world, they would not be able to make him budge the least little bit in this matter. Three of the figures of the year of Redemption he had already discovered; these were the thousands, the hundreds and the units. It was only the decade that he did not know. There lay the secret which was withheld from him. Yet he felt with all the ardor of his soul that the hour was approaching; that it was impossible for the hour to be greatly delayed. How long are the years of a man's life? Seventy years, and if he be strong—even eighty. The sign should be given in his own days. That was clear to him as the light of the sun.

And it came about that he all but discovered the fourth, the missing, figure. A great light was revealed to him and he all but seized it in his hand. Then again came the operations of Satan. Through the maiden was the light revealed to him, and through her was it concealed again.

II

Early one Friday morning Reb Yosi dipped the three requisite times, prayed, prepared the Eternal Lamp and filled it with pure olive oil, told his granddaughter to watch the flame and tend it with seven eyes, took his stick and wallet and went out awandering among the rocks. A few days earlier he had noticed a certain wild flower which had won his heart. Its strange fragrance, the charm of its petals and its entire remarkable construction told him that there was some secret concealed therein. He recognized that this particular plant was not like all the other wild flowers of the mountains. And so he bent his steps to it.

But before he reached the rock underneath which he had seen the wonderful flower growing, he raised his head and gasped; beside the flower was a woman on her knees. She was examining the flower with her fingers and her eyes. The Holy, Unutterable Name all but left his lips, so startled was he; there was not the slightest doubt in his mind but that Satan in the likeness of a woman stood before him, with the full intent of confusing Reb Yosi so that he should not be able to understand the nature of the plant. But before he could utter a sound the woman stood upright and turned her eyes on him. The eyes were black and simple as those of a little child, but filled with some boundless, endless grief, and a spark of sanctity gleamed within her pupils.

"Peace be with you, grandsire! Surely you are Reb Yosi, who tends the holy grave of Rabbi Simeon Ben Yohai?"

In her voice was the undertone of pure heartfelt prayer, fresh as the dew of dawn and spiritual and ardent as the Midnight Prayers.

"Peace be with you, my daughter. Yes, I am he. What is your desire? Tell me."

Only after he had said these words did Reb Yosi look closely at the woman in front of him, and his soul all but perished within him. Her legs were bare from her knees down. Her arms were uncovered and her hair was in no way concealed but fell in clusters of curls on her neck. Suspicion returned to him and his face turned pale.

"Who are you?" he asked in an angry yet tremulous voice.

"I am a worker from the neighboring colony beyond the mountain."

"And what is your name?"

"Ruhama."

"And what are you doing here?"

"I seek God, the God of Redemption who shall be zealous for his people and give those who abase them according to their merits."

Reb Yosi stood perplexed and wondering at what he saw and heard. He had already heard reports of the "colonies" which had been established in the country, where the settlers tilled the soil and the women worked in the field like the men. But he had not seen them and they in no way attracted him, since their bad reputation was sufficient to keep him away. Why, their avowed intention was to rebel against the Kingdom of Earth and the Kingdom of Heaven—let no man open his mouth to Satan. And here was one of the people of the colonies standing before him. Yet what was this holy grief in her eyes? What was this light burning eternally in her pupils? What was this charm in the sun-tanned face? She spoke in the name of God, and the zeal of His people consumed her. A strange text to expound.

"Why look at me so, grandsire? Because I am black?—The sun has scorched me. Because my heart is twice as black?—The troubles of my people have made it black. Grandsire, why do all cities stand in their places while foxes traverse the streets of Jerusalem?"

"Daughter, the measure of punishment is not yet ended for the Holy People. The End has not yet come."

"Measure of punishment? Our blood is loot for all, our honor is booty for all. Our Torah is spoil for all. We have neither yesterday nor tomorrow. There is no sense in our lives and we perish in shame. How can the measure of punishment contain more?"

Reb Yosi's heart became soft as wax and he had to gulp down his tears. Suddenly he raised his head and said aloud:

"Do not cower so in spirit, daughter, and do not utter complaint. The End is not distant. I see it—and it is near by. I look upon it and it is here and now, in the nearest times. That is a tried and tested matter, as clear as the light of the sun."

He was startled at his own words and stepped back, trembling like a leaf in the wind. It was the first time that his secret had slipped from his lips; and to whom? To this barefoot, bareheaded girl. Shame on him!

Now the situation was changed. The girl stood as though enchanted, listening to the old man with all her attention.

"Is what folk tell about you true, grandsire? That you reckon the time of the End of Days?"

And she suddenly fell to the ground and laughter burst from her lips. The fragments of the laughter scattered throughout the neighborhood, dropped amid the rocks and slabs and down among the shrubs and thickets in the valley, and their echo returned and rattled round the heads of the pale old man and the girl, who had stopped laughing and also stood pale as chalk.

"No, grandsire, that is not the way! You, the simple and upright, calculate the End of Days in the cave yonder; while they, the sinners, pollute the country. They have sold God and the Redemption for profit. And no man takes it to heart, and no man avenges the insult of the Lord. Hatred consumes without and slavery bereaves within. No, grandsire, with prayers the country cannot be rebuilt. With blood and sweat can it be redeemed. Do you see this wild flower? If its seed falls on a place where blood and sweat have sunken into the ground it will take root and flourish for many a decade."

Reb Yosi quivered all over, as though something had struck him in the face. He roused from the enchanted, stone-like stupor into which the shameless words of the maiden had cast him, pulled himself erect and cried out:

"Daughter! How many? How many? Oh, please tell me, how many?"

But the girl did not hear him and paid no attention to him. Her gaze wandered in the distance as though seeking aid from the rocks and the valleys. Bitter words fell from her lips.

"Not on our blood and not on our sweat has this wild flower grown. The people is sold to the golden calf." And still speaking, she vanished amid the rocks. And the old man fell on his face and prayed:

"God, merciful God! Reveal me now but this one thing: How many years shall this wild flower live?"

His prayer died away on the hillside. There was no answer. . . .

He returned to the cave before sunset, his mind made up. At the end of the Sabbath he would gird up his loins and go down to the colony behind the mountain, seek the maiden and find her, and ask her concerning the flower. But at home he heard his son-in-law telling his daughter that the fishers had taken the body of a girl out of the Kinneret with their nets.

"A girl? A Jewess? What did she look like?" cried he, trembling.

Yet at that very moment the terrified voice of his granddaughter startled him:

"Grandfather! Grandfather! The Eternal Lamp is all but going out! Here! Here!"

His soul almost forsook him. He rushed to the cave to prevent the Eternal Lamp going out, God forbid.

III

When the Sabbath had ended, Reb Yosi went down to Tiberias and from thence to the small colony beyond the mountain, entering into speech with the fishers who had withdrawn the body of the girl from the Kinneret, with her fellow-colonists and with the rabbi of the city. On Sunday night he returned to Meron, even more sad and doleful than before. What he had heard had set him thinking.

Her companions, who had all of them rent their clothes and were sitting in mourning for the requisite seven days, had told him that two months earlier she had left them and gone to the mountains; and until that Friday, when her body was drawn out of the Kinneret, they had not known anything of her actions.

The fishermen told how, on the Friday morning about two hours before noon, they had seen a girl in the distance descending from the mountains, her head up and her feet taking her direct into the lake. She reached the water and continued walking. The waters reached her throat, mounted and covered her head and she vanished. They dashed to her aid, spread their nets, and dragged her dead body out of the water.

And the trembling rabbi of the congregation whispered to him that on the Eve of the Sabbath the sun's setting had been delayed until the grave-diggers had returned from the cemetery; while the grave-diggers had sworn before him on oath that the clods of earth flung into the grave had stood like an arch above the boards without touching them, and it was only with the greatest difficulty that they had forced all the earth back into the heap. . . .

Reb Yosi began to be troubled in spirit after a fashion with which he had but rarely been acquainted. He suddenly knew something which he had not known since he had become mature. This girl, who had drowned herself in the Kinneret, had become dearer to him than a daughter, than the wife of his bosom and all which he had. Never in his life had anything attracted him and never had he wrapped his feelings in any person. He had devoted himself entirely to the holy work set upon him. Yet this woman had become like a portion of all that was sacred herself.

He mourned deeply for her.

Had she committed suicide? Why? And what were the signs of honor shown her from the skies? And was there any reparation for her soul? Or was hers as the fate of all other stripped souls, the road of suffering and everlasting incarnation without rest? In his distress he called on the aid of the saint. More than once and more than twice in his difficult tests had the Baal Shem Tov, his revered forefather, been his counsellor.

He left the Eternal Lamp to his granddaughter, giving further instructions concerning it to his spouse. Then he robed himself in sackcloth, put ashes on his head, and began wandering alone through the length and breadth of the mountains. And he mourned, and afflicted his soul by fasting, three days and three nights. He ate no bread, he drank no water, and did not permit his eyelids to close in slumber. And he poured forth his supplication before the Baal Shem Tov to light up his soul and stand for him at the judgment before the Seat of Glory, in order to beg mercy and pardon and salvation for her soul, that she might not suffer the stern punishment that awaited her.

Nor did he neglect to beg for the revelation of the secret of the blossom, the strange wild flower.

During those three days there was a tempest in the mountains. The north winds burst from their hiding-places, wailed and thundered, uprooted bushes and shrubs, heaved the stones out of place and shook the roots of the mountains. The visage of Mount Atzmon, on which Meron stands, was menacing and black. Its jagged rocks jutted out sharper than ever, its summit loomed above, seeming to utter one last warning to the entire world. Jotapta between the Mountains of Zebulon seemed sadder than ever; as though the tempest had rent from it the film formed by length of days, and now exhibited it naked for all to see. The gullets of the deep caves gaped wider than ever, as though the storm had stretched them. And a weeping, a moaning like that of a spirit brought back to earth by conjurations, sounded louder than the tumult of the storm, wrapping round mountains and valleys, rolling and tumbling into every crevice and cranny and dell, and filled all space; to Reb Yosi it seemed as if the voices of those tortured and slain for the Sanctity of the Name of God and the Name of Israel had stolen with the storm out of the caves in which they had been sealed. The light of the sun had vanished. The deep mourning lowering above Gischala seemed deep sevenfold, seeming blacker than black with the encrusted blood of the carcasses fallen in the lost War for Freedom. Yet the summit of Tabor, which could be seen between the boulders and crags, was as round and green as ever; brightness was there, hope and faith; a sense of bravery seemed to hover over it, comforting, sustaining and proclaiming the Redemption.

On the fourth night Reb Yosi fell fast asleep and dreamed. In his dream he found himself standing in a great, light holy chamber, with the holy Baal Shem Tov his own august self sitting before him on a seat of gold and asking him:

"My son, what is this trouble which you bring to me?"

"My instructor and master, forgive thy servant. A soul is in my question, and the soul of a daughter of Israel is my request. If a human soul transgress and knowingly destroys the life in its body, is there any mercy for it in judgment?"

"None."

"Pardon thy servant this once more. Is it nothing but pollution which takes a man beyond his senses, or is it possible that a surplus of holiness, such as the human creature born of woman cannot hold, can lead to the same?"

"Pollution alone, my son."

A deep sigh burst from the very heart of Reb Yosi and troubled the entire hall.

"What ails you, my son, that you should sigh?"

"Holy father, I mourn for the shame of thy people Israel. Its honor has been reduced to the dust and the shame thereof drives the Sons and Daughters of Israel out of their minds. . . ."

"My son, do not your words refer to her who was drawn from the waters of Kinneret on the Sabbath eve?"

A spark of hope lit up the gloom of the old man's heart. He roused and said:

"Aye, holy father. My soul is in my question, and the redemption of her soul is my request. I know her and she is pure and spotless."

The sainted Baal Shem Tov sighed so that the pillars of the universe were shaken.

"My son, I have been told from behind the veil. It is decreed."

"And what is the sentence on this stripped soul?"

There was a dead silence. The old man bowed the knee and dropped his head in his bitter sorrow. The suffering of the saint was plain to see. Then came his still, small voice.

"My son, the hour has come to reveal to thee the beginning of the End of Days."

The old man trembled like a windblown leaf, and lifted up his eyes in a holy prayer.

"My son, turn back the veil over the window of the chamber and see that which comes about beyond the veil."

His knees shaking, Reb Yosi approached the window and raised an edge of the veil. Messiah stood there, bound to a pillar of marble by fetters of iron. And the hand of a maiden was snapping the links at his wrists and his ankles. A loud cry burst from the old man, and he fell on his face. The girl standing prepared to snap the fetters of the Messiah was the one he had seen standing by the wild flower.

He awoke and it was a dream. His spirit tossed within him. And he prayed:

"Lord of the Universe! It was Thy will to reveal to me a span; why didst Thou conceal a double span? When shall that sign be?"

But the Heavens were hard and dumb. Broken and depressed, suffering and afflicted, he returned home, keeping his vision a secret.

IV

Years passed by. Reb Yosi had grown very old indeed. His daughter had become a widow. Her husband's fishing boat had foundered on Kinneret and he had been drowned. His granddaughter, who had formerly tended the Eternal Lamp, had married. And now she was passing through her first pregnancy. The poverty had increased. The demands of the mouths were great, while income remained as it had been. The granddaughter's husband was likewise a fisher, who earned no more than his deceased father-in-law, may he rest in peace.

But it was not the hardship of making a living nor the vexations of bringing up children which had aged Reb Yosi. The dark mist which had clouded over his calculations on the day he had met the girl had not cleared down to that very day. Hard times had come to him, times of doubt and evil thoughts, such as the heart would fear to reveal to the mouth. Sometimes it seemed to him that the iron wall was tottering and he began to cast doubts. And sometimes he felt as though he were going out of his mind. The blood of Israel was still being poured forth like so much water, the honor of Israel was a byword. Yet the tracks of Messiah were not to be seen. Every day in turn brought the pangs preceding Messiah—yet Messiah was not come. Sometimes he would rouse like a lion to console himself for the mourning in his soul:

"If not now—the time cannot be long delayed. . . . Though I may not merit—yet my son shall merit. . . ."

But while thinking this same thought he would start up as though stung by a scorpion, and would return and calculate afresh. Why should it not be in his own time?

Then he had a further trouble at heart, a trouble which he would not admit clearly even to himself, yet which ate like a fester at his bones. God had granted him no son. . . . This and something more; he had received a tradition from his father, and his father from his grandsire, that on the Nineteenth day of Kislev, the anniversary of the day on which the saintly foundation of the world, Reb Shneur Zalman, the wonder-Rabbi of Ladi, had been released from the prison into which he had been cast by false accusations many a year before, there would be born the one who would precede the coming of the Messiah. Now Reb Yosi never desired greatness at all during the entire course of his life. Nevertheless, as though it were Satan's handiwork, every time his wife had been pregnant and after her her daughter, his thought had automatically and illicitly set about making a calculation of the end of the days of carrying, to see whether it would occur on the Nineteenth of Kislev. Whenever he would catch himself reckoning, Reb Yosi would start back, spit out at something, rebuke something, and heavily turn his steps to the grave.

And Reb Yosi had had no luck. His wife's first pregnancy had ended in a miscarriage; the second had brought him his daughter. Then she had stopped bearing, and he had had no son. His daughter's first pregnancy had brought him his granddaughter; then her womb had closed too. Now his granddaughter was big with child. When his wife had whispered him of the first signs of the pregnancy he had vowed to make no calculations and not to think of the matter in any shape or form. If he caught himself at the faintest suggestion of such a thought, he used to beat himself over the heart and dash headlong to the grave as though to seize the corners of it and thereby be delivered from the persecutions of a certain Thing. Yet in some hidden corner at the bottom of his heart, covered over by a heap of ashes, there still glowed on a spark of hope.

v

The Nineteenth of Kislev fell on a Sabbath, and hence the Eve of the Nineteenth was the Sabbath Eve. It was always Reb Yosi's custom on this night to add a candle of his own at the grave of the saint. After the evening prayer he would hallow the evening over wine and would eat some of the fish which his wife had prepared in honor of the Sabbath day.

From the Friday morning Reb Yosi had seemed to be all but tipsy. He hummed a sad and compelling melody of those Braslav melodies for which he cherished a special affection, coming as they did from the great wonder-Rabbi who, like him, had been a descendant of the Baal Shem Tov, and who had seen and loved the Land of Israel and Meron. He had felt this mood upon him when he had gone to the ritual spring to dip, when he had donned his tefillin, when he prepared the lamp and chopped wood for his spouse in honor of the Sabbath, and while he proudly watched the preparations of his spouse as she prepared and salted the great fish which his granddaughter's husband had brought up from Tiberias for them while it was still broad day.

It was a huge fish such as Reb Yosi did not remember having seen before, large and fat and still quivering under the knife as though it wished to protect itself. Who could say whether it might not be the habitat of some transmigrant stripped and naked soul?

At noon, when he rose and washed his hands before eating, his granddaughter passed in front of him, her belly between her teeth, as the Hebrew has it, busy preparing the house for the Sabbath, and smiled at him in the great affection she felt for him. A shadow, whether of satisfaction or pain, it was hard to tell which, crossed Reb Yosi's face. And his spouse, who entered the room just then, whispered to him:

"Another month to go. . . . God guard her from all evil and mischance."

"Mm . . . mm . . . mm . . ." muttered the old man, as though to remind her that he could not talk on lay affairs before having said the blessing over bread and tasting a piece. What he wished to say, if he wished to say anything at all, they never knew. Yet it was clear that the good humor in which he had been all the morning had suddenly deserted him. Some trouble clouded his brow and covered his face. His wife wondered with regret what had happened, and whether she could have spoilt his mood, biting her lips to see him so again. And on this occasion the slice of white bread with prepared radish stood like a bone in her throat.

The sun already began to sink while he was busied at his holy labor. Its rays turned the waters of Kinneret yellow as it lay on the horizon between the mountains. The skies were crystal clear. In the uttermost north above Hermon could be seen a cloud about the size of a man's hand; and the gate-keeper, the black hajji, who came to tend the flame on the Sabbath day ever since the time of Reb Yosi's father of blessed memory, turned his left eye—the right being closed since his childhood—on the Kinneret, calm as the dead, and the tiny cloud about the summit of the grandsire of the mountains, and shook his head doubtfully. Reb Yosi took no notice of the gate-keeper, the Kinneret or the little cloud; he was too busy making his preparations for receiving Queen Sabbath. He returned again and dipped in the spring within the cave, put on the white chalat and the satin kapote which he had inherited from his father of blessed memory, and bound about his loins the girdle of silk. His stockings were white as snow, his pumps had been polished by his granddaughter while it was yet day. And on his head he set his huge round three-tailed "Shtreimel." His face was bright with the shining holiness. He prepared the Eternal Lamp in front of the grave as was meet, poured more than sufficient oil into it to last until and even after the close of the Sabbath, and left the care of it to the hajji, who faithfully observed this trust and in whose hands nothing had ever yet been permitted to go wrong.

He was still busily employed when the old woman appeared on the threshold, with troubled face and hasty steps, and signed him with her hand to come to her. Her lips were moving but no sound could be heard. Reb Yosi paid no attention until the gate-keeper called him. Then he looked at her but could not understand the sign, nor the silent whisper on her lips. He felt annoyed that she should trouble him at such an hour, and going over, he said:

"What is it you must trouble me for?"

"Yosi . . . Yosi . . . Listen, Yosi. . . . Listen. . . . The granddaughter . . . Yosi . . . The granddaughter . . ."

"What ails her? What ails the granddaughter? Tell me!"

"Sh-sh-h . . . Yosi, she's about to give birth. . . . The birth-pangs have begun. . . . Woe's me. . . . Hasten to pray to the Saint. . . ."

Reb Yosi's face suddenly became bright as the dawn. He seized his spouse and looked at her in joy.

"Wife, why are you so upset? Let us raise our hands in thanks to the Lord of the Universe for his great loving-kindness."

"Husband, you are crazy! It is a difficult birth. . . . There's danger. . . . May I not open my mouth to Satan. . . . A full month to run yet. . . ."

"Hush, you silly. Don't presume to rebuke the Powers on High. . . . What's a month, what's a year, what's a generation? Like moisture on a jar, like dust on the scales before the will of Him who can do all things. . . . Wife, wife—the eve of the Nineteenth of Kislev . . . The longed-for day has come . . . bring lights! I order you as your husband! Bring out all the lights! . . . Pour out all the oil! Let's light the candles, let's light the oil, let's make a great illumination, wife! Come, let's sing, let's all rejoice! Come, dance with me. The day of the Redemption is coming, it's on its way! Listen, listen! The very trumpet of Messiah! There it is cleaving its way up through the mountains! The day of vengeance has come, the day of payment, the day of salvation! Wife, the dawn has broken! A great light is shown us!"

"Have you gone mad or started on evil courses? The horn has sounded from Safed, and it's the hour of kindling the lights, and you two old sillies go billing and cooing like a couple of turtle-doves!"

The voice of the old hajji roused Reb Yosi from his vision and he quivered. So did the old woman, who looked at him with entreaty and prayer as though she besought mercy for her own soul, for his soul, for the soul of the woman in her birth-pangs and for the soul of the whole world.

"Wife, the blessing over the lights! The honor of the Sabbath precedes all things. . . . Wife, the lights!"

The old woman hastened back and Reb Yosi lit his special Sabbath candle and then returned to the house to hear his wife say the blessing over the Sabbath candles. Then, just as she had lit the candles and ended the blessing— the old man stood riveted to his place. A weird roar passed right across the world, as it seemed. Savage laughter, a mocking, poisonous hiss. The crack of a tremendous whip in the air. It was answered from every side, from every rock, from every boulder, from every crag, from every cave by eldritch, eery voices such as could never have been heard by human ear since the earth has been heaven's footstool—wild, protesting, angry, furious, inciting, menacing, blood-filled, blood-lusting voices. The sky was covered with heavy black clouds like a barrier of iron between heaven and earth.

And a gale burst out from beyond Hermon, and boomed and bellowed and threatened to swallow heaven and earth. It turned a somersault and swept away and destroyed all it found in its path. It uprooted trees, overturned houses, shifted the very hills from their places. A storm rose on Kinneret. Wave after wave rose high and swallowed whatever might be upon the face of the waters, and charged far beyond the bounds set for the lake. It was as though the end of the world had come, and all living creatures were to perish together. There was none to stand in the breach, none to preserve Man from destruction. The Gates of Mercy were locked, and the deep flung its jaws wide.

There were but three who were not confused and remained at their posts. The one-eyed hajji covered the Eternal Lamp with his body and abaya to keep the wind away.

The old woman lit her five big candlesticks, one light for each soul of the household and an extra sixth one for the soul about to enter the world. The wind seized the four corners of the house as though to turn it over upon the head of the old woman, of the woman in childbed and the lights. But the old woman did not move. She took her silken Sabbath apron, which she had inherited from her mother of blessed memory, and spread it out as a canopy over the lights so that the wind could not reach them.

And the corners of Reb Yosi's kapote, of his earlocks and his beard, streamed in the wind, his black eyes burnt like two flaming torches, and his mouth continued pouring forth its song and praise to Him who dwells on High. He did not stay in one place. Now he ran to the grave to encourage the old hajji. Now he ran to the house to look at his spouse and sustain her spirits. Now he lent an ear to the thin, persistent moaning which forced its way out into the storm. And he encouraged the woman in childbed and prayed on her behalf.

"Elder, elder!" Reb Yosi heard the cry of the hajji, and saw his hand beckoning him. He approached.

"Elder! There is no aid and no help saving that we diminish her wrath!"

"Whose wrath?"

The gate-keeper bent his head low and whispered to Reb Yosi:

"The wrath of Kinneret. . . ."

"Why? What does it mean?"

"She rages. Because of the fish which you take from her every Eve of Sabbath to honor the presence of the Queen Sabbath. She envies her."

"You speak nonsense!"

"Do not grow wroth. You—a tender of the Holy Grave are you and wise. I—am a gate-keeper with much experience. I have heard it from the elders.

During the six Days of Creation she, the Kinneret, was the very body of Allah; but on the Seventh day your Lady Sabbath took her place. Ever since then she restrains her suffering and her jealousy within her own breast without complaint. Satan desired to comfort her and she, the foolish one, thrust him off. Once only in a Jubilee, once in a Jubilee of years, does she burst forth and storm her recriminations against the Heavens. Is her reproach so little that they have to take of her honor, her fishes, to honor her supplanter!—And then, when her wrath bursts forth, nothing can calm her again save the flesh of one of those daughters of Israel who prepares the fishes; nothing else can still her fury."

"Idolatry!" cried Reb Yosi, spitting toward the hajji.

"No idolatry, elder, but your faith. The Sabbath is yours. Kinneret was likewise yours and will return unto you. It will not be redeemed saving with your blood. Do you remember the woman whom the fishers drew from Kinneret with their nets? She wished to offer herself to the lake in order to redeem it and never merited. Another was merited . . ."

"Silence!"

"I shan't be silent. There is no other way, elder, than to assure her the flesh of the one who is about to be born of your granddaughter. . . . Otherwise we are lost. The lamp over the grave will be extinguished in a little while. The candles in front of the old woman will be blown out, her apron is already rent to tatters. The entire world will return to chaos and void. The nether powers have vanquished the upper powers. Promise her to the lake, elder, and we shall all be delivered on her account. . . ."

"Old demon, old Ashmedai, hold your tongue! Now I know you, now I recognize you! All this time you have concealed yourself in the flesh of the gate-keeper. Your day has come, it has come indeed! The one to be born on the Nineteenth of Kislev brings news of the Redemption. Let me but call on the name of the one whose coming is foretold by the unborn child, and all your stories cease, and you turn into a heap of dust, and all the power you have gathered together to overturn us will be as nought! I call on his name—the Messiah!"

Before the word had left Reb Yosi's lips a thin wail, the cry of a newborn child, was heard from the house. . . . Reb Yosi dashed thither. The candles lit by his spouse were burning upright. The wind and the storm, with all the weird pipings and eldritch howlings, were as though they had never been. He returned to the cave. There was no sign of the old gate-keeper, nothing save a little pile of dust settling down after the wind. And the Eternal Lamp burnt steady. Sabbath calm could be felt now, as though Queen Sabbath had blessed the entire world with her presence.

Reb Yosi returned to the house once again, his hands on high and his lips filled with song and praise.

"Yosi, Yosi, a good Sabbath and a happy sign! Our granddaughter has borne a daughter in a happy hour!" cried his wife, hurrying in from the birth chamber.

He fell fainting to the ground.

VI

That night, when deep sleep had fallen upon Reb Yosi, the Baal Shem Tov his own honored self came to him and spoke thus:

"Yosi, my son, do not be aggrieved. This child born in your house at the hallowing of the Sabbath—within her days shall be the commencement of the work which I showed you."

The old man trembled and asked:

"Holy father, what name shall I give her?"

"Raise your eyes and look yonder."

He did so and his heart stopped within him. She stood before him, her legs bare from the knees down, her arms uncovered, no hat on her hair, which fell in curls down to her shoulders; and the hair was interwoven with the weeds and grasses from the deeps of the Kinneret. . . . And her great black eyes sparkled with something holy, seeming to utter some dumb pure prayer. . . .

"She?—After her name?" he asked, quivering.

"Yes, Yosi, my son, after her name. Your granddaughter's child is no other than the transmigration of her soul."

"Grandsire—but she . . . Has her soul received salvation?"

"Do not inquire as to that which is beyond you. Great are the searchings of heart. But do you act as you have heard from me. It has been told me from behind the veil."

On the Sabbath, when ten Jews from Safed and Tiberias were assembled to pray at the grave of Rabi Simeon Ben Yohai, Reb Yosi, while they read the Torah, gave the name in Israel of "Ruhama" to the child born of his granddaughter. And ere the taper separating the Sabbath from the weekday was extinguished, his soul departed in purity; and he was laid to rest in the grave of his fathers.

The following year the old woman his wife died as well. Then the widowed daughter and the granddaughter, with her husband and child, left Meron and settled in the colony beyond the mountain, and the granddaughter's husband became a tiller of the soil, fertilizing the ground with his toil and eating his bread in the sweat of his brow. For so they had found written in clear words, black and white, in the Will which Reb Yosi had left for the conduct of his house.

THE NIGUN

by DAVID SHIMONOVITCH

And when he grew blind, Reb Yosey,
What was Reb Yosey wont to do?
He would say, "Since the chant is so holy,
I shall chant and serve thus the Lord too."

Seeing Reb Yosey was not one
With great grasp and memory choice,
He did not know the Torah by heart.
But God had blessed him with a voice.

Not strong and not big was his voice,
Yet sweet indeed his "Rava says . . ."
And although those who studied might smile
His voice brought their spirit to praise,

While when with deep study and thought
The lads would grow weary and tire,
Or when Samael the beguiler
Would entice with forbidden desire,

Then would the voice of Reb Yosey
Restore them their parching souls;
Then would the voice of Reb Yosey
Cleanse their hearts of things evil, things false,

And now that Reb Yosey was blind
His voice grew more sweet than before.
As of old he stood bowed at the lectern
And without the Gemara would pour

The chant of the Law forth again.
Nothing was heard but the ringing;
He did not know the Torah by heart,
So studied without words by singing.

Some testy old scholar might snort,
"Isn't derision within?
Doesn't his chant run to waste?
Why, by my faith, it's a sin. . . ."

But just like a bone halfway down,
Not to be chewed or be spued,
The grumbling would suddenly stick
In the throat of the scholar, berued.

His face he would hide in his tome,
Not bringing his words to an end,
And louder to hide his confusion
He would lift up his voice, "This is meant . . ."

And days passed, the years sped away,
While the old House of Study stood there.
Students had parted and gone.
Who counted them? How did they fare?

But just as of old Reb Yosey
Would stand at the lectern and sway.
Nothing was heard but the ringing,
The warm wordless tune flowed away.

And as of old, of that school
Wonderful legends men told;
How all those who studied were mighty
In Torah, its warriors bold

Who knew the whole ocean of Talmud
And sailed to its uttermost sea,
Had they wished they were also able
To account for each "let it be."

Saving one, Yosey the blind,
Whose name was not famed through the land.
No Sinai he to move mountains.
And although not a boor, God forfend. . . .

Yet who knows? Maybe he'd forgot
The little he'd known from before?
Apart from the chant, not a sound
Passed his lips in years more than a score!

The days passed, the years sped away,
Time galloping by like the wind,
And unto the Upper Assembly
Was summoned Reb Yosey the blind.

His comrades made no mournful speeches.
They silently bore him to earth,
Since he was no mighty scholar,
But a toiler of simple worth.

For good they remembered his sweetness
In chanting the Talmud tune,
Meanwhile deriding in hints
A scholarship little or none.

Then they forgot him with speed;
For indeed of the work there is store.
Sea shoreless, authorities endless,
No bound to the deeps of our lore!

Each to his lectern! To study!
Daylong and nightlong in turn
The school rings and echoes again
To the chant of the scholars who learn.

But see! A wonder indeed!
From the time the tune became dumb
On the lips of Reb Yosey the blind,
It seemed that a blemish had come

Upon the keen brains of the scholars.
In the texts they would cease to advance.
Not this the old depth and the sharpness,
Not this the grasp at a glance,

While what had been simple before
As out of milk taking a hair
Was hard now as though sealed to them;
Molehills were grown mountains there.

No longer did this school ascend
O'er Houses of Study unknown;
Here too not all were great scholars,
Nor were prodigies found there alone.

The wardens, they saw it with pain,
The community saw it with grief,
How honor was leaving the school
And its praises grew small past belief.

But great as might be the grief,
Great was the wonder as well.
What was the cause of the change?
Who had sealed Torah's well?

Until the day that a saint
Happened to come to those parts.
They told him the story; he asked
To hear it again where it starts,

And when they came to refer
To the blind and the humble one,
Then the holy man listened with care,
And his face shone as though from the sun,

And he suddenly cried in a blaze,
To all of the learned men there:
"If then you saw a great light
'Twas by his flawless merits and rare.

"For the tune of Reb Yosey alone
Like a shepherd tending his flocks
Led you ever safely across
That sea with its shoals and its rocks.

"The fire of his tune scattered sparks
That lit up your darkened mind.
And so you saw light through the gloom
From the shining soul of the blind.

"And while you caressed and adorned
The outward Torah you saw,
He caressed and embraced its soul,
He knew the full light of the Law.

"And while you were chewing the husk
The kernel he swallowed with zest—
Therefore his chanting was pleasant,
Therefore the sweet song was blest.

"For everybody may come
To study; none will gainsay;
Yet to sing the true Torah song
—Of a thousand just one knows the way."

FOALING SEASON

by EDWARD ROBBIN

THE sun hung in the sky just over the hills and men stopped at their work and waited for it to fall. The land was ripe and full. The pomegranates were splitting through their hard skins; the grape clusters pulled the drunken vines down to the earth; almonds lay in yellow heaps among the lacy trees and their green shellings were scattered around them. The air was ahum with the buzzing of contented insects. On the threshing floor rose the tall hills of yellow grain dancing against the quiet hips of gentle Gilboa.

Javniel turned the plough from the furrow, unhitched one side of the shaft so that it dragged freely, and jumped astride one of the mules. Heinrich, among the banana trees, stood watching the water run muddily through the new canals he had just dug. A group of the women unbent from their weeding among the vegetables, and the men who had been digging the ditch for the new cement drainage canal that was to cut across the length and breadth of the fields shouldered their tools and turned toward the kvuzah.

Voices are heard clearly from afar. There are shouts from the men to the women and back again, and a full song of naked desire is in the voices. Laughter breaks out of the rising breasts of the women, leaps from mouth to mouth, bounds against the hills and back to the men. Answering peals of laughter burst from the men. They are not tired today. They are ripe like the grain, splitting with ripeness like the earth, running over with honey, like the hives.

There must be an excuse for laughter, so Greenbaum tells how last night he saw Aaron and that new girl, Rachel, who works in the chicken house, walking together.

"You'd have thought he was leading a horse, the way he walked her about. Never a word, never a word. I was walking about five paces back of them."

Laughter spread, rang to the hills, to the women, like echoing summer thunderclaps.

"Here's the big lummox Aaron, and here's Rachel, and they walk all around the threshing floor, perfectly dumb, never sitting down. Then at last they come back and he goes off without as much as mumbling good night."

"That's all right, Greenbaum," said Heinrich, "you'd better let Aaron alone, even though he is slow. Rachel is his. Let him go about with her in his own way."

"But the helplessness of him! As if she were a horse, I tell you. I wanted to give him directions. 'Now, Aaron, you big golem, put your arm around her, now ask her to sit down. Hey there, Aaron, get busy.' I tell you it was heartbreaking."

Peals of laughter cracking like summer lightning against the sky.

A wagon rumbled down the road, and the men climbed into it and jolted homeward.

Aaron trailed a horse toward the brook that ran swiftly out of the rocks of Gilboa through the wood. He pushed her into midstream and, rolling up his trousers, waded in himself. Then he poured bucketsful of water over her and brushed her down.

"When are you going to give us that young foal, eh, Bruria?" he said, rubbing her down. "Two or three days I guess. Maybe less. You're not telling."

The horse snorted, threw back its head, and its skin quivered under the dash of icy water.

Aaron thought as he rubbed the mare down that he would take a walk with Rachel again tonight. Would they walk about the threshing floor as they had last night and the night before?

Aaron heard some of the men splashing somewhat upstream and the shrill cries of the women as they plunged into the water still further upstream.

Would he at last ask her to sit down on one of the haystacks? Would they lie side by side with their backs on the warm hay?

Aaron slapped Bruria on the flanks and rubbed down her sides and belly gently. The foal lying there curled up in the belly. He felt it moving about under his hand.

Aaron squinted and a frown gathered on his low forehead. What should he say to her? One of his great broad shoulders sagged as though he were lifting sacks of meal and fodder for the beasts. What should he say to her?

When he got back to the stables he started to shovel up the manure. He rehung the harness that the men had tossed carelessly on the nails.

And all the time it was there in his head: What should he say to Rachel when they walked out at night?

He watered the horses. They stamped and neighed, shook the flies from their heads, and blinked them out of their eyes. They rubbed against the posts and against Aaron as he passed among them.

There was plenty of grain, plenty of fodder. The sacks were full. The granaries would soon be overflowing. The foaling season had come and the horses would soon be trailing their young after them in the fields.

Aaron listened contentedly to the noises of his beasts. He heard the milkers in the cow stalls clanking their pails as they moved about the heavy udders.

Aaron felt his great strength rise like a wall within him. What should he say to Rachel, he laughed to himself. Oh, he would find the right words, and he began to hum in a hoarse tuneless voice.

When supper was over, Aaron sidled up to Rachel. He steered her through the crowd of comrades who were standing outside the heder ochel, buzzing kvuzah politics. There would be a meeting tonight. Figures would be submitted: how many sacks the threshing had brought in, what the grapes were valued at, how many men would be needed to build the three new houses. The comrades would chew over these figures, repeat them to one another, discuss them, add them, divide them and multiply them. And the next day they would ruminate over them in the fields.

Aaron too was to be seen at these meetings. Usually he stood outside and only his large low-browed head hung in at an open window. He never said anything unless the talk turned on the stables. But then he glowered at anyone else who spoke, and hampered the discussion at every turn, snapping like a dog.

But tonight Aaron did not wait for the meeting. He went off with Rachel down the wide road that led out to the fields.

Rachel was a large, cow-eyed dark girl. She moved with slow grace like a beast. The lines of her body were full.

They turned down the path towards the vineyards. It was narrow and her white starched dress brushed against him like a leaf. He quivered and his arms moved like the limbs of a tree shaken in the wind.

Aaron felt his mouth dry, his tongue loose in his mouth. They did not speak.

That afternoon Rachel had lain flat on her back in the chicken-house after she had fed the chickens and they had gathered close about her. As she lay with the warm chickens nestled about her, a great tenderness, a desire to fold the shaggy ugly head of Aaron to her breast, had swept all her body. Then after work she had gone down to the stream. On the way she saw Aaron rubbing down the foaling mare and slapping its flanks. Way upstream she stripped off her clothes and dipped into the icy water. The water swept about her hot sweaty limbs in a cold stream. Then she leaped out and dressed in a clean fresh petticoat and a starched white dress. And now as she walked with Aaron she stiffened against him and her ripe body hungered for warmth and completion.

Stiffly and silently they walked through the fields where the full earth sang with contentment; through the vineyards where the ripened fruit hung from the vines. Aaron shook his uneven shoulders as though he were in harness.

Suddenly there was a cry from the kvuzah. "Aaron! Aaron!"

Aaron stopped as though he were being called out of another world.

"Bruria is foaling, Bruria is . . ."

Rachel clutched his arm. Aaron turned suddenly to her. She stood stiff and waiting. Aaron put his hard hand on her thigh and rubbed it. Then he seized her, and they fell through the vine leaves crushing the clusters of grapes into the loose earth.

They hurried back to the kvuzah, hot hand in hand, panting. "Come, Rachel, we may catch the little one yet." He squeezed her hand.

When they got to the kvuzah they found a crowd gathered in a semi-circle, and tensely watching the heaving foaling mare which lay in the center. The mare heaved and groaned and tried to struggle to its feet, and then as the spasm of pain faded away, fell back breathing heavily. Its lids fell over the bloodshot eyes and its tongue hung loosely out of its mouth.

The crowd made way for Aaron. He prepared cord, water and a litter of straw. The mare was easier when it felt his hand upon her. At last a terrible spasm, and someone let out a quivering half-cry of delight.

"The legs . . . it's coming . . ."

In a moment the foal was out, a sleek, beautiful, wide-awake creature, striving to scramble to its long, thin, unmanageable legs. Aaron took it up tenderly and placed it on the litter at the head of the mother. He patted it happily and nosed the mother and foal. The mare lay back wearily and licked her sleek foal, who jerked and twitched under her tongue, poking his long head uncertainly into her neck.

The comrades gathered closer about the foal and the mare, and held a lantern over it to look at it. An ecstatic joy seized upon them. They cried out names for the foal amid laughter and congratulations. Someone started to play a harmonica. The tune surged through the night. The crowd broke and formed a circle. Arm to shoulder, arm to shoulder, swaying, tugging, stamping out the full sensuous rhythm, faster, beating, stamping, tugging, swaying . . . Hey dey de de . . .

Rachel leaned back against the stable weary and content, and passed her hand over her full warm pulsing breasts.

RAHAMIN THE PORTER

by H. HAZAZ

ONE sunny day Menashke Bezprozvani, lean as a pole, wandered through the streets of Jerusalem, his face seamed and sickly-looking, his mouth unusually fleshy and red, his eyes discontented and disparaging.

Bitterness gnawed at his heart, piercing through him like some venom—a bitterness of heart which was unconscious rather than clearly expressed, resulting from the years he had spent without achieving anything, neither contentment for himself, nor property nor a family; the bitter, gloomy quintessence of fever and hunger, of unsettled wandering from kvuzah (commune) to kvuzah, of vexations and suffering and troubles enough to send a man out of his mind and make him lose his strength, and all the other effects of his past experiences, his lack of employment, and his present sickness.

His despair set him in a fury. All sorts of evil thoughts possessed him, recriminations and accusations directed against the Labor Federation and Zionism, against, "the domination of the Zionist Imperialism"; against everything in the world, it seemed. As though one might claim that everything was fine and bright, he would have had a job, his spirit would be refreshed, he might have everything he desired and the whole of life could be brilliant, were it not for the worthless leaders and the Zionist Imperialism that hindered things.

All these were the complaints of a dejected, despairing person who, more than he wished to comfort himself, wished to torture himself, to cry out aloud and rebel and remonstrate against the whole state of affairs. But his complaining was only half-hearted. Like it or not, he possessed a great love for the Land and a great love of the Hebrew language; a strong, deep, irrational, obstinate love that went past all theories and views, and led beyond all personal advantage. And since his complaints were no more than half-hearted, he complained all the more, denying everything and destroying everything in thought without getting anywhere, and just making himself uncomfortable.

Apart from all his bitterness, the excessive heat was tiring him. It was the middle of July. The heat was like that of an oven stoked with glowing coals, and the white light dazzled to blindness and distraction. The roadway quivered uncertainly in the light as though in a dream; it might have been so much barren soil or else a field left fallow because of drought; or it might have been anything you like in the world. The sun quarreled with the stones and the windows. The slopes of the mountains on the horizon shone yellow-brown through the dryness, while the skies in their purity of blue called eternity and worlds without end to mind.

A yell stopped him as he walked. A dozen or so Arabs dashed excitedly among the crowd in the street, yelling at the tops of their voices as though attacked by robbers:

"Barud! Barud!" (Blasting going on!)

Menashke Bezprozvani stood among the group of stationary folk pressed together, until the road echoed to a loud explosion and stones flung aloft scattered around and fell here and there in confusion. When he began to resume his walk he found himself accompanied by a man riding a donkey.

"Noise, eh!" said this stranger, turning his face to him with a smile of satisfaction and wonder.

He was a short individual with thick black eyebrows, a beard like a thicket, his face bright as a copper pot and his chest uncommonly virile and broad. He was dressed in rags and tatters, rent upon rent and patch upon patch, a rope girded round his loins and a basket of reeds in front of him on the donkey's back.

Menashke Bezprozvani glanced at him and made no answer, but the stranger entered into conversation and drew him to reply.

"Got a missus?" he turned on the donkey's back to ask.

"What do you want to know for?"

"Ain't got one, a missus?" wondered the man on the donkey.

"No, I haven't, I haven't!"

"Not good," the owner of the donkey commiserated with him, as though he saw something strange and impossible in front of him. "Take you a missus!"

"I'm poor and I have nothing. How shall I keep my wife?" Menashke Bezprozvani answered, half mocking, half protesting.

"His Name is merciful!"

"How's His Name merciful? I'm an old bachelor already and so far He hasn't shown me any mercy!"

"His Name is merciful!" maintained the owner of the donkey. "Him, everything He knows. Me, got nothing and His Name never forsook me."

"That's you and this is me."

"What's matter, eh! Must be everything all right. I had sense and got missus! Plenty all right."

He lowered his head between his two shoulders and closed his eyes tight with satisfaction and contentment.

"Plenty all right, His name be blessed!" He opened his eyes and went on speaking. "Plenty all right . . . One day was in shop, I brought boxes. I saw there's one missus there . . . First, long, long before men gave me a missus and wasn't luck. His Name never give . . . I heard they told me, it is a missus come from Babylon (Baghdad) wants to marry. Goes to Kiryat Shaul—and that's the missus from the shop . . . From heaven, eh! No money I had—not got money what'll you do! Look, look, took six pound in Bank and did business. At Muharram I made five pound also—and married! His Name be blessed, plenty all right . . . Take you a missus, a worker, a fat one, be all right. His name is merciful . . ."

He rapped his two soft sandals on the belly of the donkey which was plodding slowly under him, while his face expanded and broadened till it beamed like two copper pans.

"Never get on, no man, without a missus!" He moved from where he was sitting toward the donkey's crupper, speaking in a tone of absolute and assured finality. "No mountain without top, no belly without belly-button, no man get on without a missus!"

"And how many wives have you?" asked Menashke Bezprozvani, looking at him from the corner of his eye. "Two? Three?"

"Two, is two." He raised his outstretched palms aloft as though saying, Come and see, I have no more than two . . .

"Do they live at peace?"

"Eh! Mountain looks at mountain and valley between them . . ." He turned a mouthful of strong white teeth toward him. "If a young one in house, old one always brrr, brrr . . ."

"And how much do you earn? Are you a porter or what?"

"Yes, mister."

And having found himself a comfortable part of the donkey's back to sit on and settled himself firmly there, he began telling him all his affairs. To begin with, he said, he had been a plain porter, and now he was porter with a donkey! This donkey under him was already his eighth, and from now nobody swindle him more. He was already a big expert on donkeys, old and well-versed donkey-doctor! Through a bad donkey and a bad wife, said he, old age comes leaping on a man, but a good donkey and a good wife, nothing better than them in the world. Like a fat pilaff to eat, or the hot pot on the Sabbath! And His Name be blest, he earned his daily bread. His Name is merciful! Sometimes one shilling a day, sometimes two shilling a day, and sometimes one mil. . . . There were these and those, all sorts of days!

"Then was all right, long before," he passed his hand over the back of his neck as he spoke, "earned four shilling a day also! Then was all right."

He put his hand into the reed basket before him and took out a few dirty eggs.

"Take the ecks." He held them out to his companion. "Take, mister. Fresh as the cooperative!"

Menashke Bezprozvani did not wish to take them.

"Have you a chicken-run?" he asked, in a better humor.

"His Name be blest! Got seven hens!" replied the other contentedly and with pride. "All make ecks, eck a day, eck a day . . . Take, mister! Please, like the cooperative . . . Chickens all right, His Name be blest!"

Were it not, said he, for the money he needed, he himself would eat the ecks his hens made, so all right were those ecks! But his little daughter lay sick in the Hadassah and not a farthing did he have. Yesterday he had bought her bananas for half a piastre and she ate . . .

"Eating already!" he said as one who announces great tidings, while his face lit up in a smile of good nature and happiness. "Eating already, blest be His Name!"

While he put the eggs back in the basket. Menashke Bezprozvani noticed that he wore two rings on his fingers, two copper rings set with thick projecting colored stones. He asked:

"What are these?"

"This? Rings. And you haven't got?"

"Haven't got."

"That's it," he smiled into his beard. "I'll tell you saying they tell by us in Babylon . . ."

And he began telling him the story of a certain man who loved a beautiful woman. "Once it happened he had to go a long journey. He said to her, to that beauty: Lady! because that I love you much, you give me your ring, and as long as I see it on my finger I remember you and long for you. And that beauty who was sharp never wish to give him her ring but said to him: Not so, only every time you look at your finger and see my ring not there, you remember me because I never give you ring, and you long for me . . ."

Ending his tale, he burst into a peal of laughter.

"Ha, ha, ha!" He threw his head back and filled the whole road with his powerful, noisy laughter. "And so you also, ha, ha, ha!"

His laughter and the yarn he had spun turned Menashke Bezprozvani's mind in a different direction. Despite himself he began to think of his own girl, her merits, her queernesses, and the whole of that chapter.

The donkey, left to its own devices, was proceeding lazily and heavily while the porter sat shaking on its back, his face ruddy as copper and glinting, his beard spread in his satisfied smile and his mood good as though he found everything satisfactory in the whole world. Menashke Bezprozvani turned his eyes to him and observed the way in which he sat on the donkey's back among his wooden vessels and ropes and pieces of metal; short and broad, a sort of doubled-over and redoubled-over man. It looked almost as though his height had been doubled over into breadth, his backbone was double, and the teeth in his mouth were double; his laugh echoed from one end of the road to the other, with childhood in it that scattered itself throughout the universe; and the Holy and Blest One was with him, near to him, at home with him among his children and his wives, his chickens and his donkey. . . .

He walked slowly beside him and pictured the other at home. Here, his thoughts gradually emerged in clear pictures, he sits at the entrance to his home of an evening in the closed courtyard beside the cistern built over with stones. The children, a mixed heap of children, hang round him and tumble over him from every side, squalling and yelling. The womenfolk are busy at the fire. They cook the evening meal and quarrel among themselves on his account with vituperations and curses. Both are heavy and solid as two well-filled feather-beds, and ready for sowing as two well-dug garden plots; and he makes peace between them looking at one with affection and at the other with even more; every glance of his falls like rain upon the thirsty soil. At the side lies his sick father, a heap of rags in a corner; an old man, he and his days draw near to die. The fire crackles cheerfully and brightly, the pot boils, and one of the wives begins singing, rolling her voice toward the stars and drawing out her song. . . .

"How did you come to the land of Israel?" he interrupted his reverie to ask.

"With the help of His Name!"

And ere a moment had elapsed he was telling him all his wanderings. Thus and thus, he was a Kurdi from Zacho. Did he know Zacho? . . . One day he heard there's a legion in the land of Israel, warriors of the Children of Israel. He said: wish to be a Jewish warrior—what is! He rose and went from Zacho to Mosul and from Mosul to Baghdad and from Baghdad to Basra.

And already in Basra he was a servant to a Jew who has a shop to wear clothes, a rich man, plenty blessing he has, His Name be blest. He made bread, he made food, everything, everything . . . Because a man is better fit for work than a missus, fit much more . . . And then from Basra he went to Bombay, as the way to Damascus was then, long, long before, closed because of the war with the Turk. He stayed in Bombay two months, and every day, every day walked in the garden of Señor Sassoon, eating and drinking and walking . . . Until at last he went to the land of Israel. Did he know Haifa? . . . As yet then in Haifa the Commercial Centre wasn't, eh! The lads told him there in Haifa: stay with us, Rahamin! But he didn't want—to Jerusalem, to the Jewish Legion! So he came to Jerusalem and the Legion wasn't. . . .

"None there!" He clapped his hands together, speaking in a downcast, long-drawn-out voice.

For a while he was silent, shifting on his saddle. He turned his eyes and casually glanced at Menashke Bezprozvani, and his face changed. It was as though something astonishing had occurred to him just then.

"What for you're so sad?" he asked in a slow, soft voice.

Since Menashke Bezprozvani did not answer, he scratched the back of his neck two or three times and stirred himself.

"Late already," he said, raising his head aloft.

He kicked his heels into the donkey's belly and tugged at the reins in his hand. The donkey tossed its head, put its feet one here and one there, and began kicking up its heels and galloping.

"Take a missus! His Name is merciful!" he turned his head and shouted back to Menashke. "Peace! Peace to Israel!"

The donkey changed its gait, began to be precise in its steps, and its tiny hoofs tapped in the roadway like castanets.

Menashke Bezprozvani remained alone and walked on, his body heavy and his spirit worn down and weary. Strange feelings were pricking at his heart, chop and change, piecemeal, in turn, then all tossing within him in confusion; half-recollections of his childhood, the affairs and misadventures of his girl and all his suffering and distractions. For some reason he remembered the days at Migdal, the baths at Tiberias, Ras al Ain and Kfar Gileadi; and the rhythm of a tune which was still indistinct to himself began to trouble him, half-remembered, half-forgotten, half-forgotten, half-remembered; he could not bring it fully to mind. . . .

Until he heard the sound of a donkey's hoofs clacking on the roadway like castanets. He raised his eyes and saw that the porter had turned back toward him. He stood in surprise, blinking his eyes in the sun, and stared.

When the porter reached him, he pulled up his donkey and stopped.

"Mister! Mister! . . . Listen!" He lowered his head to him with a wayward smile, his face strangely affectionate and humble. "Mister! . . . Don't be sad! By my life! . . . Be all right! By my life! His Name is merciful!

"His Name's merciful . . ." he explained again, with a modest, almost maternal, smile. "Don't be sad! My life! On my head and eyes! Be all right!"

Menashke Brezprozvani stood astonished with nothing to say. His heart leapt within him, and the beginnings of a confused smile were caught frozen at the corner of his mouth. The other had already left him and vanished along the road, but he still stood where he was as though fixed in the ground, his heart leaping and his spirit in a protracted, dark turmoil, like a distant echo caught and hanging all but still of an evening. And he could not understand it. It was as though something had happened within him, something big, but he did not know what. As though—as though—the guilty and soothing smile of that porter and his face which had been bright with love and humility did not disappear from his thoughts, but soothed him, comforting him and raising his spirits above all the errors and mistakes and recriminations and bitternesses.

After a while he moved and turned and moved to go. He descended into open space covered with dry thorns, with many sunken stones in it, and a few twisted old olive trees. Under one of the trees stood five or six sheep pushing their heads one under the other and standing as though bewitched. A little donkey, desolate and wearied and patient as all its kind, quieter than all the other animals in the world, passed before him with a heavy load.

Menashke Bezprozvani sat himself down on a stone, which burnt like fire in the heat of the sun, and looked casually after the sheep and the donkey. Before his eyes stood the likeness of the porter with his guilty smile tugging at the heart; his spirits rising within him, his thoughts divided, he began to hum to himself the words of the song which the children had been accustomed to sing at Kfar Gileadi in those days of hardship and hunger:

> In Kfar Gileadi, in the upper court,
> Next to the runnel, within the big butt
> There's never a drop of water . . .

IN THESE HEAVY HOT DAYS—

by GERSHON SHOFMAN

THE newspapers are full of news about suicides. Merchants and businessmen fall in their struggle to live, and the item is always the same: "The chambermaid, suspicious because she got no answer to her rings and knocks, called the police, and the police called a locksmith who with much trouble opened the door by force, and then . . ."

The people in the streets look like exhausted soldiers on the battlefield. This storekeeper who cleans the dust off his goods with a feather, the terror of the abyss is in his eyes. Tomorrow, the day after tomorrow, I shall probably read the usual item in the papers about him. My heart is aleap toward my four-year-old son, he who is so gentle in his being and to whom this business of hurry is so strange: what will he do when he grows up in this world? What will he do, what will he do?

There he runs to me with his hammer in his hands. I take him up and press him to my heart, as I have never pressed him before, and meanwhile decide: I shall give you to a locksmith, my son, to a locksmith. In the cloudy future, be you the man whom the police will ask to open the door . . .

THE NAME

by AHARON MEGGED

G RANDFATHER Zisskind lived in a little house in a southern suburb of the town. About once a month, on a Saturday afternoon, his granddaughter Raya and her young husband Yehuda would go and pay him a visit.

Raya would give three cautious knocks on the door (an agreed signal between herself and her grandfather ever since her childhood, when he had lived in their house together with the whole family) and they would wait for the door to be opened. "Now he's getting up," Raya would whisper to Yehuda, her face glowing, when the sound of her grandfather's slippers was heard from within, shuffling across the room. Another moment, and the key would be turned and the door opened.

"Come in," he would say somewhat absently, still buttoning up his trousers, with the rheum of sleep in his eyes. Although it was very hot he wore a yellow winter vest with long sleeves, from which his wrists stuck out—white, thin, delicate as a girl's, as was his bare neck with its taut skin.

After Raya and Yehuda had sat down at the table, which was covered with a white cloth showing signs of the meal he had eaten alone—crumbs from the Sabbath loaf, a plate with meat leavings, a glass containing some grape pips, a number of jars and so on—he would smooth the crumpled pillows, spread a cover over the narrow bed and tidy up. It was a small room, and its obvious disorder aroused pity for the old man's helplessness in running his home. In the corner was a shelf with two sooty kerosene burners, a kettle and two or three saucepans, and next to it a basin containing plates, knives, and forks. In another corner was a stand holding books with thick leather bindings, leaning and lying on each other. Some of his clothes hung over the backs of the chairs.

An ancient walnut cupboard with an empty buffet stood exactly opposite the door. On the wall hung a clock which had long since stopped.

"We ought to make Grandfather a present of a clock," Raya would say to Yehuda as she surveyed the room and her glance lighted on the clock; but every time the matter slipped her memory. She loved her grandfather, with his pointed white silky beard, his tranquil face from which a kind of holy radiance emanated, his quiet, soft voice which seemed to have been made only for uttering words of sublime wisdom. She also respected him for his pride, which had led him to move out of her mother's house and live by himself, accepting the hardship and trouble and the affliction of loneliness in his old age. There had been a bitter quarrel between him and his daughter. After Raya's father had died, the house had lost its grandeur and shed the trappings of wealth. Some of the antique furniture which they had retained—along with some crystalware and jewels, the dim luster of memories from the days of plenty in their native city—had been sold, and Rachel, Raya's mother, had been compelled to support the home by working as a dentist's nurse. Grandfather Zisskind, who had been supported by the family ever since he came to the country, wished to hand over to his daughter his small capital, which was deposited in a bank. She was not willing to accept it. She was stubborn and proud like him. Then, after a prolonged quarrel and several weeks of not speaking to each other, he took some of the things in his room and the broken clock and went to live alone. That had been about four years ago. Now Rachel would come to him once or twice a week, bringing with her a bag full of provisions, to clean the room and cook some meals for him. He was no longer interested in expenses and did not even ask about them, as though they were of no more concern to him.

"And now . . . what can I offer you?" Grandfather Zisskind would ask when he considered the room ready to receive guests. "There's no need to offer us anything, Grandfather; we didn't come for that," Raya would answer crossly.

But protests were of no avail. Her grandfather would take out a jar of fermenting preserves and put it on the table, then grapes and plums, biscuits and two glasses of strong tea, forcing them to eat. Raya would taste a little of this and that just to please the old man, while Yehuda, for whom all these visits were unavoidable torment, the very sight of the dishes arousing his disgust, would secretly indicate to her by pulling a sour face that he just couldn't touch the preserves. She would smile at him placatingly, stroking his knee. But Grandfather insisted, so he would have to taste at least a teaspoonful of the sweet and nauseating stuff.

Afterwards Grandfather would ask about all kinds of things. Raya did her best to make the conversation pleasant, in order to relieve Yehuda's boredom. Finally would come what Yehuda dreaded most of all and on account of which he had resolved more than once to refrain from these visits. Grandfather Zisskind would rise, take his chair and place it next to the wall, get up on it carefully, holding on to the back so as not to fall, open the clock and take out a cloth bag with a black cord tied round it. Then he would shut the clock, get off the chair, put it back in its place, sit down on it, undo the cord, take out of the cloth wrapping a bundle of sheets of paper, lay them in front of Yehuda and say:

"I would like you to read this."

"Grandfather," Raya would rush to Yehuda's rescue, "but he's already read it at least ten times . . ."

But Grandfather Zisskind would pretend not to hear and would not reply, so Yehuda was compelled each time to read there and then that same essay, spread over eight long sheets in a large, somewhat shaky handwriting, which he almost knew by heart. It was a lament for Grandfather's native town in the Ukraine which had been destroyed by the Germans, and all its Jews slaughtered. When he had finished, Grandfather would take the sheets out of his hand, fold them, sigh and say:

"And nothing of all this is left. Dust and ashes. Not even a tombstone to bear witness. Imagine, of a community of twenty thousand Jews not even one survived to tell how it happened. . . . Not a trace."

Then out of the same cloth bag, which contained various letters and envelopes, he would draw a photograph of his grandson Mendele, who had been twelve years old when he was killed; the only son of his son Ossip, chief engineer in a large chemical factory. He would show it to Yehuda and say:

"He was a genius. Just imagine, when he was only eleven he had already finished his studies at the Conservatory, won a scholarship from the Government, and was considered an outstanding violinist. A genius! Look at that forehead. . . ." And after he had put the photograph back he would sigh and repeat, "Not a trace."

A strained silence of commiseration would descend on Raya and Yehuda, who had already heard these same things many times over and no longer felt anything when they were repeated. And as he wound the cord around the bag the old man would muse: "And Ossip was also a prodigy. As a boy he knew Hebrew well, and could recite Bialik's poems by heart. He studied by himself. He read endlessly, Gnessin, Frug, Bershadsky. . . . You didn't know Bershadsky; he was a good writer. . . . He had a warm heart, Ossip had. He didn't mix in politics, he wasn't even a Zionist, but even when they promoted him there, he didn't forget that he was a Jew . . . He called his son Mendele, of all names, after his dead brother, even though it was surely not easy to have a name like that among the Russians. . . . Yes, he had a warm Jewish heart. . . ."

He would turn to Yehuda as he spoke, since in Raya he always saw the child who used to sit on his knee listening to his stories, and for him she had never grown up, while he regarded Yehuda as an educated man who could understand someone else, especially inasmuch as Yehuda held a government job.

Raya remembered how the change had come about in her grandfather. When the war was over he was still sustained by uncertainty and hoped for some news of his son, for it was known that very many had succeeded in escaping eastward. Wearily he would visit all those who had once lived in his town, but none of them had received any sign of life from relatives. Nevertheless he continued to hope, for Ossip's important position might have helped to save him. Then Raya came home one evening and saw him sitting on the floor with a rent in his jacket. In the house they spoke in whispers, and her mother's eyes were red with weeping. She too had wept at Grandfather's sorrow, at the sight of his stricken face, at the oppressive quiet in the rooms. For many weeks afterward it was as if he had imposed silence on himself. He would sit at his table from morning to night, reading and rereading old letters, studying family photographs by the hour as he brought them close to his shortsighted eyes, or leaning backward on his chair, motionless, his hand touching the edge of the table and his eyes staring through the window in front of him, into the distance, as if he had turned to stone. He was no longer the same talkative, wise, and humorous grandfather who interested himself in the house, asked what his granddaughter was doing, instructed her, tested her knowledge, proving boastfully like a child that he knew more than her teachers. Now he seemed to cut himself off from the world and entrench himself in his thoughts and his memories, which none of the household could penetrate. Later, a strange perversity had taken hold of him which it was hard to tolerate. He would insist that his meals be served at his table, apart, that no one should enter his room without knocking at the door, or close the shutters of his window against the sun. When anyone disobeyed these prohibitions he would flare up and quarrel violently with his daughter. At times it seemed that he hated her.

When Raya's father died, Grandfather Zisskind did not show any signs of grief, and did not even console his daughter. But when the days of mourning were past it was as if he had been restored to new life, and he emerged from his silence. Yet he did not speak of his son-in-law, nor of his son Ossip, but only of his grandson Mendele. Often during the day he would mention the boy by name as if he were alive, and speak of him familiarly, although he had seen him only in photographs—as though deliberating aloud and turning the matter over, he would talk of how Mendele ought to be brought up. It was hardest of all when he started criticizing his son and his son's wife for not having foreseen the impending disaster, for not having rushed the boy away to a safe place, not having hidden him with non-Jews, not having tried to get him to the Land of Israel in good time. There was no logic in what he said; this would so infuriate Rachel that she would burst out with, "Oh, do stop! Stop it! I'll go out of my mind with your foolish nonsense!" She would rise from her seat in anger, withdraw to her room, and afterward, when she had calmed down, would say to Raya, "Sclerosis, apparently. Loss of memory. He no longer knows what he's talking about."

One day—Raya would never forget this—she and her mother saw that Grandfather was wearing his best suit, the black one, and under it a gleaming white shirt; his shoes were polished, and he had a hat on. He had not worn these clothes for many months, and the family was dismayed to see him. They thought that he had lost his mind. "What holiday is it today?" her mother asked. "Really, don't you know?" asked her grandfather. "Today is Mendele's birthday!" Her mother burst out crying. She too began to cry and ran out of the house.

After that, Grandfather Zisskind went to live alone. His mind apparently had become settled, except that he would frequently forget things which had occurred a day or two before, though he clearly remembered, down to the smallest detail, things which had happened in his town and to his family more than thirty years ago. Raya would go and visit him, at first with her mother and, after her marriage, with Yehuda. What bothered them was that they were compelled to listen to his talk about Mendele his grandson, and to read that same lament for his native town which had been destroyed.

Whenever Rachel happened to come there during their visit, she would scold Grandfather rudely. "Stop bothering them with your masterpiece," she would say, and herself remove the papers from the table and put them back in their bag. "If you want them to keep on visiting you, don't talk to them about the dead. Talk about the living. They're young people and they have no mind for such things." And as they left his room together she would say, turning to Yehuda in order to placate him, "Don't be surprised at him. Grandfather's already old. Over seventy. Loss of memory."

When Raya was seven months pregnant, Grandfather Zisskind had in his absent-mindedness not yet noticed it. But Rachel could no longer refrain from letting him share her joy and hope, and told him that a great-grandchild would soon be born to him. One evening the door of Raya and Yehuda's flat opened, and Grandfather himself stood on the threshold in his holiday clothes, just as on the day of Mendele's birthday. This was the first time he had visited them at home, and Raya was so surprised that she hugged and kissed him as she had not done since she was a child. His face shone, his eyes sparkled with the same intelligent and mischievous light they had in those far-off days before the calamity. When he entered he walked briskly through the rooms, giving his opinion on the furniture and its arrangement, and joking about everything around him. He was so pleasant that Raya and Yehuda could not stop laughing all the time he was speaking. He gave no indication that he knew what was about to take place, and for the first time in many months he did not mention Mendele.

"Ah, you naughty children," he said, "is this how you treat Grandfather? Why didn't you tell me you had such a nice place?"

"How many times have I invited you here, Grandfather?" asked Raya.

"Invited me? You ought to have *brought* me here, dragged me by force!"

"I wanted to do that too, but you refused."

"Well, I thought that you lived in some dark den, and I have a den of my own. Never mind, I forgive you."

And when he took leave of them he said:

"Don't bother to come to me. Now that I know where you're to be found and what a palace you have, I'll come to you . . . if you don't throw me out, that is."

Some days later, when Rachel came to their home and they told her about Grandfather's amazing visit, she was not surprised:

"Ah, you don't know what he's been contemplating during all these days, ever since I told him that you're about to have a child. . . . He has one wish —that if it's a son, it should be named . . . after his grandson."

"Mendele?" exclaimed Raya, and involuntarily burst into laughter. Yehuda smiled as one smiles at the fond fancies of the old.

"Of course, I told him to put that out of his head," said Rachel, "but you know how obstinate he is. It's some obsession and he won't think of giving it up. Not only that, but he's sure that you'll willingly agree to it, and especially you, Yehuda."

Yehuda shrugged his shoulders. "Crazy. The child would be unhappy all his life."

"But he's not capable of understanding that," said Rachel, and a note of apprehension crept into her voice.

Raya's face grew solemn. "We have already decided on the name," she said. "If it's a girl she'll be called Osnath, and if it's a boy—Ehud."

Rachel did not like either.

The matter of the name became almost the sole topic of conversation between Rachel and the young couple when she visited them, and it infused gloom into the air of expectancy which filled the house.

Rachel, midway between the generations, was of two minds about the matter. When she spoke to her father she would scold and contradict him, flinging at him all the arguments she had heard from Raya and Yehuda as though they were her own, but when she spoke to the children she sought to induce them to meet his wishes, and would bring down their anger on herself. As time went on, the question of a name, to which in the beginning she had attached little importance, became a kind of mystery, concealing something preordained, fearful, and pregnant with life and death. The fate of the child itself seemed in doubt. In her innermost heart she prayed that Raya would give birth to a daughter.

"Actually, what's so bad about the name Mendele?" she asked her daughter. "It's a Jewish name like any other."

"What are you talking about, Mother"—Raya rebelled against the thought

—"a Ghetto name, ugly, horrible! I wouldn't even be capable of letting it cross my lips. Do you want me to hate my child?"

"Oh, you won't hate your child. At any rate, not because of the name . . ."

"I should hate him. It's as if you'd told me that my child would be born with a hump! And anyway—why should I? What for?"

"You have to do it for Grandfather's sake," Rachel said quietly, although she knew that she was not speaking the whole truth.

"You know, Mother, that I am ready to do anything for Grandfather," said Raya. "I love him, but I am not ready to sacrifice my child's happiness on account of some superstition of his. What sense is there in it?"

Rachel could not explain the "sense in it" rationally, but in her heart she rebelled against her daughter's logic which had always been hers too and now seemed very superficial, a symptom of the frivolity afflicting the younger generation. Her old father now appeared to her like an ancient tree whose deep roots suck up the mysterious essence of existence, of which neither her daughter nor she herself knew anything. Had it not been for this argument about the name, she would certainly never have got to meditating on the transmigration of souls and the eternity of life. At night she would wake up covered in cold sweat. Hazily, she recalled frightful scenes of bodies of naked children, beaten and trampled under the jackboots of soldiers, and an awful sense of guilt oppressed her spirit.

Then Rachel came with a proposal for a compromise: that the child should be named Menachem. A Hebrew name, she said; an Israeli one, by all standards. Many children bore it, and it occurred to nobody to make fun of them. Even Grandfather had agreed to it after much urging.

Raya refused to listen.

"We have chosen a name, Mother," she said, "which we both like, and we won't change it for another. Menachem is a name which reeks of old age, a name which for me is connected with sad memories and people I don't like. Menachem you could call only a boy who is short, weak and not good looking. Let's not talk about it any more, Mother."

Rachel was silent. She almost despaired of convincing them. At last she said:

"And are you ready to take the responsibility of going against Grandfather's wishes?"

Raya's eyes opened wide, and fear was reflected in them:

"Why do you make such a fateful thing of it? You frighten me!" she said, and burst into tears. She began to fear for her offspring as one fears the evil eye.

"And perhaps there *is* something fateful in it . . ." whispered Rachel without raising her eyes. She flinched at her own words.

"What is it?" insisted Raya, with a frightened look at her mother.

"I don't know . . ." she said. "Perhaps all the same we are bound to retain

the names of the dead . . . in order to leave a remembrance of them . . ." She
was not sure herself whether there was any truth in what she said or whether it
was merely a stupid belief, but her father's faith was before her, stronger than
her own doubts and her daughter's simple and understandable opposition.

"But I don't always want to remember all those dreadful things, Mother.
It's impossible that this memory should always hang about this house and
that the poor child should bear it!"

Rachel understood. She, too, heard such a cry within her as she listened to
her father talking, sunk in memories of the past. As if to herself, she said in
a whisper:

"I don't know . . . at times it seems to me that it's not Grandfather who's
suffering from loss of memory, but ourselves. All of us."

About two weeks before the birth was due, Grandfather Zisskind appeared
in Raya and Yehuda's home for the second time. His face was yellow, angry,
and the light had faded from his eyes. He greeted them, but did not favor
Raya with so much as a glance, as if he had pronounced a ban upon the
sinner. Turning to Yehuda he said, "I wish to speak to you."

They went into the inner room. Grandfather sat down on the chair and
placed the palm of his hand on the edge of the table, as was his wont, and
Yehuda sat, lower than he, on the bed.

"Rachel has told me that you don't want to call the child by my grandchild's name," he said.

"Yes . . ." said Yehuda diffidently.

"Perhaps you'll explain to me why?" he asked.

"We . . ." stammered Yehuda, who found it difficult to face the piercing
gaze of the old man. "The name simply doesn't appeal to us."

Grandfather was silent. Then he said, "I understand that Mendele doesn't
appeal to you. Not a Hebrew name. Granted! But Menachem—what's wrong
with Menachem?" It was obvious that he was controlling his feelings with
difficulty.

"It's not . . ." Yehuda knew that there was no use explaining; they were
two generations apart in their ideas. "It's not an Israeli name . . . it's from
the *Golah*." [1]

"*Golah*," repeated Grandfather. He shook with rage, but somehow he
maintained his self-control. Quietly he added, "We all come from the *Golah*. I,
and Raya's father and mother. Your father and mother. All of us."

"Yes . . ." said Yehuda. He resented the fact that he was being dragged
into an argument which was distasteful to him, particularly with this old man
whose mind was already not quite clear. Only out of respect did he restrain
himself from shouting: That's that, and it's done with! . . . "Yes, but we were
born in this country," he said aloud; "that's different."

---

[1] Diaspora: the whole body of Jews living dispersed among the Gentiles.

Grandfather Zisskind looked at him contemptuously. Before him he saw a wretched boor, an empty vessel.

"You, that is to say, think that there's something new here," he said, "that everything that was there is past and gone. Dead, without sequel. That you are starting everything anew."

"I didn't say that. I only said that we were born in this country. . . ."

"You were born here. Very nice . . ." said Grandfather Zisskind with rising emotion. "So what of it? What's so remarkable about that? In what way are you superior to those who were born *there*? Are you cleverer than they? More cultured? Are you greater than they in Torah or good deeds? Is your blood redder than theirs?" Grandfather Zisskind looked as if he could wring Yehuda's neck.

"I didn't say that either. I said that *here* it's different. . . ."

Grandfather Zisskind's patience with idle words was exhausted.

"You good-for-nothing!" he burst out in his rage. "What do you know about what was there? What do you know of the *people* that were there? The communities? The cities? What do you know of the *life* they had there?"

"Yes," said Yehuda, his spirit crushed, "but we no longer have any ties with it."

"You have no ties with it?" Grandfather Zisskind bent toward him. His lips quivered in fury. "With what . . . with what *do* you have ties?"

"We have . . . with this country," said Yehuda and gave an involuntary smile.

"Fool!" Grandfather Zisskind shot at him. "Do you think that people come to a desert and make themselves a nation, eh? That you are the first of some new race? That you're not the son of your father? Not the grandson of your grandfather? Do you want to forget them? Are you ashamed of them for having had a hundred times more culture and education than you have? Why . . . why, everything here"—he included everything around him in the sweep of his arm—"is no more than a puddle of tapwater against the big sea that was there! What have you here? A mixed multitude! Seventy languages! Seventy distinct groups! Customs? A way of life? Why, every home here is a nation in itself, with its own customs and its own names! And with this you have ties, you say . . ."

Yehuda lowered his eyes and was silent.

"I'll tell you what ties are," said Grandfather Zisskind calmly. "Ties are remembrance! Do you understand? The Russian is linked to his people because he remembers his ancestors. He is called Ivan, his father was called Ivan, and his grandfather was called Ivan, back to the first generation. And no Russian has said: From today onwards I shall not be called Ivan because my fathers and my fathers' fathers were called that; I am the first of a new Russian nation which has nothing at all to do with the Ivans. Do you understand?"

"But what has that got to do with it?" Yehuda protested impatiently. Grandfather Zisskind shook his head at him.

"And you—you're ashamed to give your son the name Mendele lest it remind you that there were Jews who were called by that name. You believe that his name should be wiped off the face of the earth. That not a trace of it should remain . . ."

He paused, heaved a deep sigh and said:

"O children, children, you don't know what you're doing . . . You're finishing off the work which the enemies of Israel began. They took the bodies away from the world, and you—the name and the memory. . . . No continuation, no evidence, no memorial, and no name. Not a trace . . ."

And with that he rose, took his stick, and with long strides went toward the door and left.

The newborn child was a boy and he was named Ehud, and when he was about a month old, Raya and Yehuda took him in the carriage to Grandfather's house.

Raya gave three cautious knocks on the door, and when she heard a rustle inside she could also hear the beating of her anxious heart. Since the birth of the child Grandfather had not visited them even once. "I'm terribly excited," she whispered to Yehuda with tears in her eyes. Yehuda rocked the carriage and did not reply. He was now indifferent to what the old man might say or do.

The door opened, and on the threshold stood Grandfather Zisskind, his face weary and wrinkled. He seemed to have aged. His eyes were sticky with sleep, and for a moment it seemed as if he did not see the callers.

"Good Sabbath, Grandfather," said Raya with great feeling. It seemed to her now that she loved him more than ever.

Grandfather looked at them as if surprised, and then said absently, "Come in, come in."

"We've brought the baby with us!" said Raya, her face shining, and her glance traveled from Grandfather to the infant sleeping in the carriage.

"Come in, come in," repeated Grandfather Zisskind in a tired voice. "Sit down," he said as he removed his clothes from the chairs and turned to tidy the disordered bedclothes.

Yehuda stood the carriage by the wall and whispered to Raya, "It's stifling for him here." Raya opened the window wide.

"You haven't seen our baby yet, Grandfather!" she said with a sad smile.

"Sit down, sit down," said Grandfather, shuffling over to the shelf, from which he took the jar of preserves and the biscuit tin, putting them on the table.

"There's no need, Grandfather, really there's no need for it. We didn't come for that," said Raya.

"Only a little something. I have nothing to offer you today. . . ." said Grandfather in a dull, broken voice. He took the kettle off the kerosene burner and poured out two glasses of tea which he placed before them. Then he too sat down, said, "Drink, drink," and softly tapped his fingers on the table.

"I haven't seen Mother for several days now," he said at last.

"She's busy . . ." said Raya in a low voice, without raising her eyes to him. "She helps me a lot with the baby. . . ."

Grandfather Zisskind looked at his pale, knotted, and veined hands lying helplessly on the table; then he stretched out one of them and said to Raya, "Why don't you drink? The tea will get cold."

Raya drew up to the table and sipped the tea.

"And you—what are you doing now?" he asked Yehuda.

"Working as usual," said Yehuda, and addded with a laugh, "I play with the baby when there's time."

Grandfather again looked down at his hands, the long thin fingers of which shook with the palsy of old age.

"Take some of the preserves," he said to Yehuda, indicating the jar with a shaking finger. "It's very good." Yehuda dipped the spoon in the jar and put it to his mouth.

There was a deep silence. It seemed to last a very long time. Grandfather Zisskind's fingers gave little quivers on the white tablecloth. It was hot in the room, and the buzzing of a fly could be heard.

Suddenly the baby burst out crying, and Raya started from her seat and hastened to quiet him. She rocked the carriage and crooned, "Quiet, child, quiet, quiet . . ." Even after he had quieted down she went on rocking the carriage back and forth.

Grandfather Zisskind raised his head and said to Yehuda in a whisper: "You think it was impossible to save him . . . it was possible. They had many friends. Ossip himself wrote to me about it. The manager of the factory had a high opinion of him. The whole town knew them and loved them. . . . How is it they didn't think of it . . . ?" he said, touching his forehead with the palm of his hand. "After all, they knew that the Germans were approaching. . . . It was still possible to do something . . ." He stopped a moment and then added, "Imagine that a boy of eleven had already finished his studies at the Conservatory—wild beasts!" He suddenly opened eyes filled with terror. "Wild beasts? To take little children and put them into wagons and deport them . . ."

When Raya returned and sat down at the table, he stopped and became silent, and only a heavy sigh escaped from deep within him.

Again there was a prolonged silence, and as it grew heavier Raya felt the oppressive weight on her bosom increasing till it could no longer be contained. Grandfather sat at the table tapping his thin fingers, and alongside the wall the infant lay in his carriage; it was as if a chasm gaped between a world which was passing and a world that was born. It was no longer a single line to the fourth generation. The aged father did not recognize the great-grandchild whose life would be no memorial.

Grandfather Zisskind got up, took his chair and pulled it up to the clock. He climbed onto it to take out his documents.

Raya could no longer stand the oppressive atmosphere.

"Let's go," she said to Yehuda in a choked voice.

"Yes, we must go," said Yehuda, and rose from his seat. "We have to go," he said loudly as he turned to the old man.

Grandfather Zisskind held the key of the clock for a moment more, then he let his hand fall, grasped the back of the chair and got down.

"You have to go. . . ." he said with a tortured grimace. He spread his arms out helplessly and accompanied them to the doorway.

When the door had closed behind them the tears flowed from Raya's eyes. She bent over the carriage and pressed her lips to the baby's chest. At that moment it seemed to her that he was in need of pity and of great love, as though he were alone, an orphan in the world.

THE ACID TEST OF HONESTY

by EPHRAIM KISHON

SOMETIME ago my wife declared that she could no longer cope with her household duties, which had grown out of all proportion since we acquired the canary. She therefore demanded the immediate hiring of an experienced charwoman.[1]

After a thorough inquiry, we decided on Mazal, a woman with an immaculate reputation in the neighborhood. Mazal is a middle-aged member of the Oriental community with a somewhat scholarly air due to a pair of wire-rimmed glasses precariously perched on the tip of her nose. It was a case of love at first sight: we knew that Mazal was just the person to relieve my overworked spouse.

All was smooth sailing until our neighbor, Mrs. Shavua Tov, planted the seeds of distrust in our all-too-willing ears.

"Simpletons," Mrs. Shavua Tov said, when she called on us one morning and found Mazal briskly pushing a broom. "If a woman like Mazal agrees to work for you, she certainly does not do it for the sake of the measly salary you pay her."

"So what else would she want?"

"To steal!"

We indignantly rejected this baseless slander. Mazal would never do such

---

[1] Israel women hate to take care of their households, because of the heat and the tedium of it all. Mothers take on jobs and do not mind if they spend their whole salaries on maids, if only they do not have to suffer in their own households. A logical solution would be for two friends to manage each other's households for suitable and identical salaries.

a thing. Next Monday, however, my wife noticed that while sweeping the floor, Mazal never looked us in the eyes—just like Raskolnikov in *Crime and Punishment*—also that the woman's dresses had outsize pockets.

In the best Hercule Poirot tradition I furtively watched her while pretending to read the paper, and noticed that she was cleaning our silverware with almost morbid pleasure. The suspicious signs grew in number. Tension mounted and became unbearable. I proposed calling in the police.

But my wife, who is an ardent reader of detective stories, drew my attention to the fact that so far all our evidence against Mazal was of the circumstantial variety. We therefore urgently asked Mrs. Shavua Tov for advice.

"You must trip up the monster," our neighbor urged us. "Hide something, for instance a bank note, somewhere in your flat, and if she finds and does not return it, you can drag her to court."

Next day we set the trap.

After careful deliberation, we decided to hide a five-pound note under the bathroom rug.

I was so tense all day long that I did hardly any work, and when we met in the afternoon, my wife complained of a splitting headache. We worked out a detailed plan of operations, the gist of which was that the wife would delay the criminal by craft and cunning, while I would alert the security forces.

"*Shalom*," [2] Mazal greeted us. "I found ten pounds under the bathroom mat."

We mumbled a few disappointed words, then withdrew to our lair, completely flabbergasted. For a few minutes we could not look each other in the eye.

"In fact I have always trusted our Mazal," my wife finally said. "I knew you were wrong when you stubbornly insisted that such an honest creature could bring it upon herself to steal from her employers."

"So it was I who said that she stole!" I roared. "That's a fine thing to say! For the past two days I have tried to protect this model woman against your slanderous insinuations."

"Hahaha. You are very funny, my dear."

"So I am funny, what?" I lost my temper. "Then perhaps you could tell me why you hid a ten-pound note under the bath mat, when we had agreed on a five-pound one? Had Mazal pinched the money—which naturally was out of the question—we would needlessly have lost five pounds."

We did not speak to each other until the evening.

When Mazal had finished her day's work, she came to say good night. "Good night, Mazal," my wife said cordially. "Don't be late tomorrow."

"All right," the charwoman replied. "Is there anything madam wishes to give me?"

[2] This is the accepted Hebrew greeting. It means "Peace" and is the world's most beautiful and expressive greeting—except, of course, "Hi!"

"Give you something? No, Mazal, I don't think so."

This answer sparked the neighborhood's noisiest brawl in two thousand years.[a]

"So madam does not want to give me anything!" Mazal shrieked, and her eyes spurted fire and brimstone. "And what about my money? Hey? You know only too well that you put a five-pound note under the bathroom mat, so that I should steal it! The smarties wanted to 'test' me!"

My wife changed color and I hoped the ground would open under my feet, but it did not.

"Well, what are you waiting for?" Mazal became impatient. "Perhaps you want to keep my money?"

"Sorry, ma'am." I smiled ingratiatingly. "Here are your five pounds, ma'am."

Mazal grabbed the five pounds out of my hand and put them into one of her outsize pockets.

"It goes without saying," she added, "that I won't work in a house where they steal. Luckily I found out in time. . . . One can't trust anybody nowadays. . . . Terrible."

We never saw her again. And the worst part of the affair is that Mrs. Shavua Tov has spread the rumor all over the neighborhood that we tried to rob a poor woman.

TWO TREES

by MENDEL MANN

A NARROW donkey track links the abandoned Arab villages. On the mosque height near the stone cupola the narrow track bends, and the cool stones of the mosque wall drink the well water like thirsty sheep. A bright path drops swiftly at that point, twining like a new cascade of water and losing itself amid cactuses and dry citrus groves. Here and there the path runs through low coffee-colored grasses where there is a bright naked sandy dust; and it mirrors itself in the sun like a snake which has just crept out of hiding.

The birds in the bush do not fly aloft. Instead they hop about from cactus leaf to tree branch. Their little wings are full of dust. No bird-talk is to be heard in the hot noon hours: only the quiet creaking of last year's thin twigs

[a] With us, everything that happens is a "first in two thousand years," due to the extremely long break that intervened in our State's life. We thus have the first riding school in two thousand years, the first scooter factory in two thousand years, and believe it or not, this is the first English-language collection of Israeli satirical short stories in two thousand years. It therefore deserves a certain amount of reverence.

and branches cracking as they dry, to remind one that somewhere in the thicket there is a swarming bird life.

A row of cactuses rest their weary heads by the flaming donkey track. One side of the path is half in shadow, full of rounded little dapplings of sunshine. The yellow dog wandering from village to village passes with its head down, keeping to the side of the path where the shadows of the green-gray cactuses fall.

At the castor tree the path is cut by a swarming black ribbon that runs into the thick grasses. These are ants flowing over the clear sand—ant after ant.

The weary dog stops at the moving thread of ants, his dry nostrils writhing and quivering. He raises a front paw, looks at the quivering grasses, and goes away.

Two trees rise on either side of the path, one facing the other. It seems as though the skies above them are loftier, the sad distances even more distant. The bushes by the wayside, the coffee-colored grasses, the gray interwoven branches, the prickly leaves and dead twigs nearby are trifling and small.

One tree spreads its rounded branches afar. It seems to comprehend the distant horizons. Its green is the green of cold steel, its leaves are long and thin as knives. The veins in the leaves are hard, with the dead yellow of ivory. The slender trunk is beautiful, with ridges like the necklets around the throats of the women who used to walk along this path. A silvery dust gleams on it after dark, bestrewing the branches and the trunk ridges with moonlight.

It seems as though the tree were supporting the weight of the melancholy distances. Its branches sustain the distant vaulted heavens. On *khamsin* days it raises its proud head to the topmost fiery heights while its foot cools itself in its own shadow, the cool, breeze-filled shadow where the grass-birds gather together.

That is the palm; a rarely beautiful date palm.

On its thin branches the other tree wears a fresh bright green; the kind of green which is found only in countries where broad streams run amid pastures or near half-concealed springs. The leaves of this tree are small, and they quiver. The trunk is not to be seen. From the ground to the treetop it wears a foaming green garb of leaves, fine and delicate, as transparently thin as green gossamer in the field. There is no shade in its branches. Yet the sun shows its mercy to the tree. Its fires slide off the green amber leaves and remain lying at the foot of the slender, leafy trunk.

All through the winter the tree stands naked, dead, its branches stretching out on high, forcing themselves aloft. The treetop is narrow, thin, and sways with the faintest breeze. It begins to blossom late in May, when the fig tree and the mulberry are already spreading their shade. It remains leafless even when the distances around are green and sated with the later rains. Its translucent leaves fall at the very beginning of autumn.

The tree behaves after the style of its distant place of origin, somewhere along Slavic roads. It has inherited the old calendar. It blossoms, withers, and continues to behave according to the old arboreal fashion of the North. When the first cold autumn winds begin blowing in the Slavic countries it flings off its leaves beside the donkey track, although this is high summer here as before, and there is not even a sign of cold. But yonder in the land of its origin the leaves are falling now, so the tree discards them here as well.

For hundreds of tree generations it has been bearing within it this rhythm of withering and blossoming. It opens its buds when the soil in the Vistula basin has long been warmed, after the snowy cover has melted and the waters have run down to the streams and the time of blossoming has begun.

This is the poplar, which has found its way into this country and is to be met with at the wayside, in the windbreaks of the citrus groves.

How the poplar comes to have joined the palm here, along the forgotten donkey track, will remain an everlasting secret. Who planted the two trees? Whose hands tended the little sprouts? And who rested in their shades?

The bird marks on the path are covered over. The traces of the lizards in the sand erase the last track of the sheep flocks. On the left-hand side of the path there are still signs of human feet. Where the two trees face one another they suddenly cease and vanish.

Nobody knows the secret of the two trees, nor will the tracks in the sand reveal it. The dry twittering of the birds, the hoarse croaking of the birds reveal nothing at all about the empty path.

Who brought the two distant alien worlds together and set them face to face? Who planted, at the edges of the donkey track, the hard green dusty-gray date palm next to the light-green delicate poplar tree?

The palm fronds stretch out with their veined leaves, growling the song of the deserts, the song of melancholy distances. The poplar branches quiver with silky whispering of songs that are sung in the green glades.

Somewhere the songs must meet. Somewhere hot and cold springs flow and join together. Somewhere beneath our feet, in the deeps of the earth, are roots being interwoven.

A heavy dark tractor made its way into the dry citrus grove. Branches snapped with a sudden sharp dry crackle. Brown roots leapt up with pieces of raw earth and fell on a lofty heap. A piece of cactus fence shook, shuddered, and fell to earth with its thousand heads as though they all wished to conceal their grief from the bright sunlight. Here was a large area that was being cleared to put up tents for newcomers.

The tractor clattered for a long time between the trunks and the dead roots, taking up more and more of the donkey track, until its front wheels came to a standstill in front of the poplar. The tractor lightly touched the tall green tree. The trunk did not tremble at all.

Then once again.

This time the tip of the poplar shuddered as though an autumn wind had sped by it.

For a while the tractor withdrew with a quiet murmur as though its motor were about to stop. Then it angrily growled and raised its lower wheels. Chunks of earth flew off like startled birds, and with raging impetus the tractor butted at the trunk.

The poplar bowed. A few leaves dropped. It fell quietly and gently. Nothing was heard but a swishing of green leaves. Or rather it was a hovering, the gasping flight of a sick bird.

The poplar lay on the ground, resting not on its trunk but on its branches, with some of its roots still in the ground. Once again the tractor circled and approached the tree. Its excavating iron cut into the roots, the motor growled and rattled. The tree jumped. Naked light roots appeared and shook a cloud of red earth from themselves.

Suddenly a piece of the sandy track rose up. The palm, which had quietly observed the death of the poplar, spread its own rounded fronds, and its trunk fell with a hollow thunder, its ridged breast to the bare earth. . . .

For the roots of the two trees had united and interlaced under the surface. Together they had drunk from hidden springs. And when the tractor cut through the poplar roots, the date palm also fell.

The two trees lay with bare interlaced roots. And like two hands the palm fronds seemed to be embracing the quivering green of the poplar trunk.

THE WORLD IS A ROOM

by YEHUDA AMIHAI

THEY came back a different way. Cutting through a high-lying thicket they came to a valley that was completely empty: empty of stones, and of trees, and of people. In the distance they heard the yelling of children at play. He took out the camera and photographed her. Then she photographed him. Afterward, they were left with a picture of the two of them embracing. Yet his camera was not automatic and there was no one in the valley but them. The valley was empty, like a newly discovered star. Who had photographed them? Who developed their fate? Who held their faint smile against the air, as he examined the negative.

They returned by way of Tibeon. As they climbed the hill, her body divided again. Her head was tired. All the childhood in her was tired, as was the sea in her eyes that had all the sea's fish and longing. But her body grew stronger with every step. He put his arm around her shoulders and her small head rested on his arm as though it was broken. He brought her up from the valley as though he were bearing her dead. They sat in a small coffee house, the only one in the place. Someone was singing a wonderful melody over the radio. A long time later, when he remembered that evening, it seemed to him that right after the melody the war began, that the last bars and the first shots sounded together. Actually, there were several hours between them. That night everything changed in the country. The world's voice was altered, like an adolescent's. It turned scaly and hoarse, but they did not know it, and so they remembered only the world's clear voice.

They got up and paid for the coffee. They never forgot to pay and for this peaceful evening they paid with many nights of war. Lovers pay no attention to prices. Generally speaking, there is no difference between a world without trees and without people like that empty valley in the afternoon and one that is covered with all sorts of camouflage. Then they returned to the city. He went to his bachelor's room. The landlord was not in, and he took a hot bath. When he was finished he rinsed the tub and watched the last of the water drain out. He thought, the water was draining slowly, like those last summer days. That night there was the decision to partition the country. Everybody ran out into the street and the firemen's band played and there was tremendous dancing all night. She came to him that night like a marvelously unexpected find. There as they sat together, the commotion covered them and they hid underneath it. Joy that night was a big ball that rolled above the celebrating crowd, skipping from head to head. In the gap between heads it fell to the ground where it rolled till morning, when it disappeared with the first shots. By then automobiles containing serious, pale men and women with concealed weapons were driving through the street; other automobiles were adorned with the first dead.

Two or three days later for the first time she saw a person who had been killed. It was a woman. The dead woman lay on her side, where she had been shot. Fashions that season emphasized feminine lines. The dead woman's hips protruded as she lay on her side, her long hair in a pool of sticky blood.

She volunteered to go down to the lower city, which was cut off from the rest of the city and surrounded by Arab homes. She worked as a teacher in a small school that was attended by the children of the Salonika longshoremen. One day the Arabs rolled barrels of explosives down the slope of the street. The children and she fell to the floor. When she got up she was covered with plaster and slivers of glass. That day she accompanied the children home. An English policeman guarded them. When they reached the big square, the Arabs began shooting at them from every side and there was no place to take shelter. The English policeman disappeared. She walked on with her children, erect, dividing the bullets like the Red Sea. Snipers raced and fell sprawling on their faces, but she crossed the empty square erect. Behind her, the waves of shooting closed again. There was always a protective cover over her: once it was a *hamsin*, once joy, and now it was war.

Evenings the two of them would meet and their talk would become odd and fateful.

"I knew. I knew this would happen."

"It seems to me it's getting dark."

"Open the shutter."

"I opened it."

"Don't leave me."

"It's good to hear a loaded truck go down the hill."

"You're a fine man."

"It seems to me it's getting dark."

"It's as though they're closing the mouth of our cave."

"With big stones."

"There are a lot of stones in the world."

"Once, on Purim, my mother had an attack of kidney stones. It's hard for me to imagine big stones in my mother, the way there are in a mountain. This was at the Purim feast, and we had guests. My mother's pain was not theirs, it was only ours. So they left."

"It seems to me it's dark already."

"Open the shutter."

Afterward he told her he would have to join one of the companies in three days. He took her home. They heard an explosion and the sound of windows shattering. She told him they should take away all the fragile vessels from people. Showcases may be all right for future generations or for angels to fit into the sky's windows. But the people of our world are not fit to take care of fragile things. The first things that get broken in this world are glass vessels.

They passed by a Red Magen David first-aid station. A bus came along, bullet-scarred and with wounded people inside. Instead of going to the bus station it drove over to the first-aid house. They walked through the public garden. The path led through two beds of flowers. A lantern on either side. As they walked through, they took away some of the light on their hair and their backs. Afterward they sat down and read about what had happened that day. They found a typographical error in the newspaper: Instead of reading "Two of the fighters fell," it read "Two of the blighters fell." They thought it was a wonderful error—one of the errors that gives significance to the world and the deeds of this world. Like the error that attached itself to her body when it grew heavy and wonderful while her head remained narrow and childish, the eyes full of sea-longing.

The third day he went off. He left her a power of attorney. A power of attorney for her heart, that was left without power of its own. She was in the fullness of her beauty their last night together and he was in the fullness of his strength with her. There was joy that suddenly turned into a fearful sadness. Among the things she said to him was: "We have a lot in common—a few books, a season ticket to the orchestra, the ability to adapt to every situation, and a lot of other things." She was wearing a black skirt. All at once he said to her: "The flowers in this flower pot know more about us than you imagine." Afterward he left her his will, saying: "Here is my will, I am leaving against my will." His watch was well trained. Otherwise, it would have burst and gone past the time. Time is fate's courtesy.

As her bus moved away, she waved her hand to him. She could not find a place to sit so she had to stand, holding the straps. Her palms were busy holding on to the straps in the shaky bus, or she would have wiped away the tears. And so she stood, arms raised, the hollows of her armpits shouting like a dark mouth. When she came home she opened the refrigerator and took out something to eat. Afterward she heard two or three explosions and then she heard groans, but the groaning came from her throat.

He joined the company that was breaking the siege of Jerusalem. Once he was standing on the roof of a water station near the road. It was during a rest period between actions. He wrote his name on the railing in black. Whenever his name is mentioned, people say: "Just a minute. I know that name." What they do not realize is that everyone who comes and goes to Jerusalem reads his name several times. Now his name is fading because of the rain and the wind. Afterward they began to write letters to one another. Then he went south. There he came to know still other soils. He said to himself, With my love, so it is with war. I have come to know many different soils. My forehead, my chin, my elbow, my knees have touched stony soil, sandy soil, rich soil. And the thornbushes have guarded my weary head like sentries. There were landscapes he could recognize only at night, as Isaac recognized Jacob: by groping, and by touch, and by smell. And he did not know whether to bless or curse. He was not a hero, and neither was he afraid.

After many battles, he was fatigued. Once he fell asleep during a bombing. Fate grew fatigued, too: an artilleryman was sent to his unit. It was an infantry unit. All over the country they were looking for artillerymen and this one was sent to an infantry company. In a battle he was shot and died, death by error. Afterward they retreated through white and fearful sand. The dead artilleryman remained there lying on the railroad tracks that were no longer in use. Then there was an English Christian whose name was Shelley. All night, marching to the battle that ended in retreat, he kept thinking about the Englishman's name, the same as that of the poet, whose poems he probably didn't know. The English volunteer wore a tropical hat, broad-rimmed, a memento of the Empire days in India. They had known one another before the war when they stayed together in an abandoned military camp. The buildings were turning white and you could see where the slaughterhouse used to be and the officers' club and the bathhouse. Later, in the first morning watch, the English-

man Shelley died of his wounds. His eyes died under the broad-rimmed tropical hat. And the memory of the poet died with him. What was left of the
company retreated to a kibbutz, through the dilapidated military camp. Before
they retreated from the kibbutz, he lay down to rest in a room that had been
cleared of its owners. On the chest of drawers stood a number of ceramic vessels. In the bookstand there were books by Marx, Rosenzweig, Buber's translation of the Bible, and Rilke's poems. Outside the window were trees, and there
were still other trees a little further off, near the enemy positions.

The next day airplanes appeared and everybody shouted, Ours! Ours!—until one of the planes shot at them and dropped bombs. Returning to his dugout
near the hill he wrote her a letter: "After a while I'll return north. When there's
no more siege." Another time he wrote her: "When the clouds are rain, and the
rain fields, and the fields joy, I'll come." And he added she was not to cry. To
which she answered that the death of tears is in the desert, where all things
finish.

An ancient wind blew from Mesopotamia drying her tears and his sweat.
He lost all sense of how hard the days were. Hard things die in soft: stone sinks
in sand. The hard words of Isaiah sink in the soft hearts of men without
affecting them. His hardened spirit sank in his love.

She was called up too and was sent to Galilee to teach Hebrew to immigrant soldiers. One day he left the siege behind, in an airplane for which
many torches were lit in the dust-filled airport. Next day he traveled to Safed
where her unit was camped. He crossed the bridge and came to the monastery
that housed staff headquarters. He went to the office. . . . Where are you
from? He told them where he was from. As he spoke he saw Lake Kinneret
through the window. Sometime back he had gotten into the habit of looking
out windows. He thought that was more important than to look at the person
he was speaking to. They sent him to the women's corps officer. From her he
learned that his girl had been injured in a road accident and was lying in a Haifa
hospital. The women's corps officer proposed that he spend the night in camp.
He asked if there was a bus to Haifa. There was none, so he went to Rosh
Pinnah. He waited for the bus but it did not turn up. He saw that night had
fallen. The world seemed to him to be a big room, and all the cities and villages
its furniture. So he began walking toward Tiberias. The world was a big
room, and at the end of the room his girl lay in her bed. He walked toward her
and his footsteps echoed clearly. He heard voices behind him. Two white
blouses rose from the voices. The voices and the blouses belonged to two girls
from the nearby kibbutz. Their shorts were black like the night in which only
their bare legs and white blouses gleamed. Where was he from? He told them
and they discovered people they knew in common. The whole country consisted of people one knew in common with other people, and they were all in
one company or another, one brigade or another, and some of them were already dead. They reached the kibbutz and he stood between the two voices,

pausing. They told him to come in and spend the night there. The farmhouse stood on the side of a high hill whose top could not be seen at night. He touched one of the girls on the hair and she said, Come along. He went to the kitchen with her. Near the kitchen was a trench in which a cannon lay covered by a net. He ate till he was full in the large kitchen, alone with the two girls who served him. Afterward a truck came along driven by a man whose face could not be made out in the darkness and they all got into it.

In Ayelet Hashahar there was a chamber music concert. Artillerymen and other soldiers sat in the dining hall with the kibbutz members. He sat at a table, a girl at either hand. He thought, This is like a fairy tale! In the night they returned to the small kibbutz. Again, there was nothing to be seen but the girls and himself and a number of covered cannons. They explained where the shower was and the toilet. One of them fetched him some fresh cake. Then he accompanied them to their room. There was a third bed. He took off his wrist watch so the band wouldn't cramp his wrist while he slept. Then he took his papers out of his pocket and put the Palmach army pin on the chair, the way they used to remove their armor in the old days. He lay down on his back, in his clothes. They said, There's hot water. He got up and they gave him a towel. Between the spurts of the jetting shower he heard the girls on the other side of the partition whispering to one another. The night was fragrant with the smell of the butter cake the girls had fetched him and of the abandoned earth. The two of them were still sitting and reading when he came into the room. He asked to be excused from conversation because he was tired. They said, You can take your clothes off, you don't have to be shy. We're all alone here with you and some cannons covered with nets that look like fish just hauled out of the sea. He undressed near the three beds. They undressed too, and there were three piles of clothes near three beds. They were the kind of girls who do not wear much clothing in the summer, particularly when they are alone in the cease-fire between battles near quiet cannons. The three of them lay there, open eyes staring at the ceiling, not going near one another. He tried to match the rhythm of his breathing with the rhythm of theirs but did not succeed. Not falling asleep, he wondered whether to go to them. They were good to him and young and the world was an empty room where they were alone. Finally, he perceived that one of the girls had fallen asleep but the other was still awake. He approached her bed and she let him sit next to her. He put his palm on her thigh. She took his hand and laid it on her stretched belly where the muscles trembled.

The next morning when he woke the girls' beds were empty. He went down to the highway and traveled to Haifa. Bursting into the hospital, he entered a hall where he saw a long line of beds that seemed endless because of the perspective. When he was a child he used to beg his father to draw rooms and houses for him in perspective. It had been a kind of magic trick. Since then he had learned to draw in perspective and was perfectly familiar with the changes that take place because of the distances between objects.

She convalesced and the war resumed. On furloughs they saw one another. At times he smelled the sharp fig smell of his love for her. It would hit him suddenly and he would not know how to escape. Once he surprised her from behind and put his palms over her eyes. He asked her, Guess who? And though she knew who it was, she would not guess. In the same way there were times when fate came along and asked, Guess who? And they did guess: They guessed names of enemies and names of lovers, and names of various other things. But they did not guess who it really was that put his hand over their eyes. So fate's palms remained on their eyes and they were as blind.

Once she visited him in a military camp two days before the conquest of Beersheba or some other place. They went outside and saw a solitary carob tree. They made love under it. He said to her, Now we've contributed toward the settlement of the country: we've crushed some bushes and cleared some ground. The spot where they lay was slightly higher than the surrounding ground to the south, so they threw good-luck casts all over the lowlands. Afterward they returned to camp. They went into the dining room and found that the meal was already over. A sweet and sticky California melon jam was spread out on the tables between leftover pieces of drying bread. He pulled her to him and kissed her. Some people came along and saw that she belonged to him. There began a whispering in the corners of the world. And the moon rose and stood on the gun barrel of the tank that stood in the courtyard.

The war did not touch them at all. They were like ducks oiled against the water. She was involved in the problem of her heavy body and childish head. And he in the problem of his future and the landscape pictures on the other side of the window. Since they did not oppose fate and the war, the war passed over them without doing injury. Like an empty house through whose open windows the wind blows.

And such was their end. She married the soldier with whom she had tumbled out of the automobile when they were injured together. This was a fine and logical conclusion to a shared road accident, to two people rolling together down the slope of a mountain in the Upper Galilee. And he, since he did not fall in the war and was not injured either, he no longer interests us. He was a man who did not live in the shadow of his end. There are people who live in a valley at the foot of a high mountain that casts its shadow over them, affecting their life and their end. But he was not such a man. Nothing compelled him and nothing compelled her and the ties between them were perhaps just an illusion, as in fairy tales.

BIOGRAPHICAL NOTES

SAMUEL JOSEPH AGNON (1888-1970) was born in Buczacz, Galicia. Here he soaked himself in Jewish learning and the rich ghetto life and lore that became the subject matter of much of his subsequent literary production. He resided in Palestine from 1907-1913 when he went to Germany and lived in Berlin, Munich, and other cities. He returned to Palestine in 1924. Agnon undertook to record, in a prose that is as sensitive and epic as its subject, the traditional East European culture which the Nazis expunged. He was awarded the first Bialik Prize for Hebrew Literature (1934) and the Nobel Prize for Literature (1966). During his last three decades the land of Israel, especially the life of Jerusalem, was the focus of his writing. Many of his books have been translated into English including *The Bridal Canopy, In the Heart of the Seas, Days of Awe, A Guest for a Night,* as well as the collections *Twenty-One Stories,* and *Two Tales.* The story in this book, translated by I. M. Lask, was selected for translation by Agnon himself.

YEHUDA AMICHAI was born in Germany in 1924 and was brought to Palestine at the age of twelve. He served in the British Army in World War II and was a member of the Palmach, the commandos of the Israeli Army, during the War of Independence. Educated at the Hebrew University, he spent a year in England and the United States, and afterwards taught at a high school in Jerusalem. He has produced four volumes of verse and short stories, and a novel, *Not of This Time . . .* (1963). Amihai lives in Tel Baruch, a suburb of Tel Aviv. The story in this book was translated from the Hebrew by Jacob Sloan.

CHARLES ANGOFF was born in Minsk, Russia, in 1908, and brought to Boston, Massachusetts, at the age of six. After graduation from Harvard College in 1923, he became a newspaperman and then an editor of the *American Mercury, The Nation,* and the *North American Review.* He has published about thirty books including autobiography, fiction, biography, verse, and contributed stories and criticism to many literary periodicals. *Summer Storm,* the sixth of a projected series of ten novels, appeared in 1963. The story here included is reprinted from *When I Was a Boy in Boston.* Mr. Angoff and his family live in New York City.

MARY ANTIN (1881-1949), a native of Polotsk, Russia, was brought to the United States in her girlhood. She studied at Barnard College and Teachers College, Columbia University, and began her career by writing engrossing stories of immigrant life and problems in literary journals. *The Lie,* included here, is representative. The same theme pervades her subsequent novels: *From Polotsk to Boston, The Promised Land,* and *They Who Knock on Our Gates.* She died in Suffern, New York.

SHOLOM ASCH (1880–1957) was born in Kutno, Poland, where he received a traditional education and was introduced into general culture by his wife. His early stories depicting life in the *stetl,* especially his novel *Dos Stetl,* won him high rank among the Yiddish writers. Subsequently, he lived in Paris and New York, traveled widely, and produced over fifty books, including novels, plays, travelogues, and apologias. Novels like *Three Cities* and *The Nazarene,* the first of three controversial Messianic novels, achieved for him international repute. He spent his last years in Israel and died during a visit to London, England. The story included here, translated by Helena Frank, is reprinted from *Yiddish Tales.*

ISAAC BABEL (1894–1941), the son of a Jewish tradesman, was born and educated in Odessa, Russia, and moved to St. Petersburg at the age of twenty-one. He served with the Cossacks in their campaign against the White Russians and the Poles. His work was first published by Gorky, and his two books *Odessa Tales* and *Red Cavalry* (combined in *Isaac Babel: The Collected Stories,* 1955) won him an international reputation. The mystery of his silence during the thirties and his disappearance was cleared up by his sister in *Isaac Babel: The Lonely Years 1925– 1939* (1964). He disappeared in a concentration camp during one of the Stalinist purges. His story in this book, translated from the Russian by Alexander Kaun, first appeared in the January, 1929, issue of *The Menorah Journal.*

AHIMAAZ BEN PALTIEL (1017–1054) lived in southern Italy. He was a member of a family of distinguished poet-scholars and statesmen whose family traditions reached back a thousand years. He himself was a master of Hebrew rhymed prose. For further details, see the footnote on page 205.

IMMANUEL BEN SOLOMON ROMI (See footnote on page 228)

J. J. BENJAMIN II (1818–1864) (See footnote on page 311)

MICHA JOSEPH BERDYCZEVSKI (1865–1921) was born in Mezibuz, Poland. He lived in a Hasisic environment, attended the famous Yeshibah in Volozshin, and began early to contribute essays and stories to Hebrew periodicals and later also wrote in German and Yiddish. During the latter part of his life he lived in Berlin and Breslau, where he became absorbed in philosophy and aesthetics. Deeply influenced by Nietzsche, his writings introduce a new note of gloom and introspection into Jewish letters. Among his unique contributions are an interpretive rendering of Agadic literature. His collected Hebrew works appeared between 1922 and 1926 in twenty volumes. He died in Berlin.

DAVID BERGELSON (1885–1952) was born in Achrimova, near Uman, Russia, of a middle-class family and left a lucrative practice of dentistry to become a writer. His pre-Revolution fiction won him a reputation as a master storyteller. Following the March Revolution, he became a director of the Cultural League in Kiev, and he supported the Yiddish literary revival in the Ukraine. After a visit to Berlin in 1921, he returned to the Soviet Union and continued writing fiction in which he idealized life in the new proletarian society. During the Stalinist liquidation of Yiddish writers, he was executed by a firing squad on August 12, 1952. The story in this book, translated by Louis Berg, first appeared in the December, 1929, issue of *The Menorah Journal*.

ISAIAH BERSHADSKI (real name Isaiah Domashevitski, 1871–1908) was born in Derechin, Lithuania, and after attending Jewish schools and a trade school decided to devote himself to Hebrew literature. He served as one of the editors of the first Hebrew daily, *Hazman*, and contributed to Hebrew periodicals under various pseudonyms. In his novels and stories he pictured the decline of the Jewish bourgeoisie of the nineties under the impact of modern industrialism. *Forlorn and Forsaken* was translated by Helena Frank. He died in Warsaw.

HAYYIM NAHMAN BIALIK (1873–1934) was born in the village of Radi, Russia, and suffered severe poverty in his boyhood. While he wandered and worked as a printer's apprentice, he mastered Hebrew and secular culture. His poetry was one of the spiritual factors helping to shape the Zionist movement, and his writings, including verse, prose, translation, won him recognition as a commanding figure in contemporary Hebrew literature. The Bialik Prize for Hebrew Literature is a memorial to his pre-eminence. Much of Bialik's poetry has been translated into English as well as his autobiography, *Aftergrowth*. His story in this book, translated by Aaron Frankel, first appeared in the November-December, 1930, issue of *The Menorah Journal*.

JEAN-RICHARD BLOCH (1884–1947) was born in Paris and was regarded as one of the outstanding men of letters in France during his time. In his fiction he succeeded in blending the qualities of both the Judaic and French traditions, and his books of criticism and travel are among the best in those fields. Among his books are *Kurdish Night, Sybilla, The Last Emperor, Levy,* and *"— & Company,"* from which the story in this book is excerpted.

JOSEPH HAYYIM BRENNER (1881–1921) was born in the Ukraine, was educated in a yeshiva, and after a brief period of manual labor, he served as librarian of a Jewish cultural society in Homel, White Russia. He became imbued with both socialism and Tolstoyan idealism. After escaping from the Czarist Army, he fled to London and learned the printing trade. He settled in Palestine in 1908, and as a worker and pioneer he suffered great hardship. Brenner's writings, comprising novels, essays, and stories, in both Hebrew and Yiddish, were of great influence in labor circles. He was killed in Jaffa by Arab rioters. *The Way Out*, translated from the Hebrew by I. M. Lask, gives a graphic picture of the suffering and disillusionment of the early Zionist settlers in Palestine.

MAX BROD (1884–1968) was born in Prague and received his doctorate in philosophy at the University of Prague. He worked as a government official but soon turned to journalism and a literary career. With an intensely Jewish and Zionist background, he was among the brilliant Prague literary circle which fell under the spell of Martin Buber's Neo-Hasidism. A close friend of Franz Kafka, he became his literary executor and was instrumental in helping Kafka achieve posthumous fame. Among his books which have been translated into English are *Tycho Brahe's Way to God* and *Reubeni, Prince of the Jews,* from which the story included here, translated from the German by Hannah Waller, is taken. Brod settled in Israel after World War II.

MARTIN BUBER (1884-1965) was born in Vienna, studied at the universities of Vienna, Berlin, Leipzig, and Zurich, and taught at the University of Frankfurt and the Hebrew University, Jerusalem. He was one of the intellectual leaders of the Zionist movement and an eloquent advocate of Neo-Hasidism. His existentialist-tinged theology is in great vogue in both Christian and Jewish religious circles. Among his important literary works are a German translation of the Hebrew Bible (with Franz Rosenzweig) and many volumes of Hasidic lore. His parable in this book was translated from the German by Leo W. Schwarz. Buber died at his home in Jerusalem in 1965.

JOHN COURNOS was born in a Russian village in 1881 and was brought to Philadelphia at the age of ten. After working at various jobs, he decided upon a literary career and went to England "to learn English on English soil." He has distinguished himself as novelist, editor, critic, and translator. *Zorakh* is from his novel *The Mask,* which together with *The Wall* and *Babel* constitute a trilogy of autobiographical novels. He began writing poetry when he was seventy-nine and his volume of verse, *With Hey, Ho . . . and The Man with the Spats* was praised highly by the critics. He lives in New York City.

AVRAM DAVIDSON was born in Yonkers, New York, in 1924, and attended New York University and Yeshiva University. During 1942–1946 he served with the U. S. Navy, participating in the missions of the 5th Marines in the Pacific. After the war, he engaged in various occupations, spent two years in Israel, and contributed to *Midstream, Commentary,* and other magazines. Turning to science fiction, he served as editor of *Fantasy and Science Fiction* and published several volumes of stories and novels, among them *Or All the Seas With Oysters, Mutiny in Space,* and *The Great Year.* His story in this book, *The Golem,* was included in *The Best From Fantasy and Science Fiction* (1956). He lives in Berkeley, California.

MARK DWORZECKI was born in Vilna, Lithuania, in 1903, and was a practicing physician there and a delegate to the City Council when the Ghetto was set up by the Nazis. He was an inmate of several concentration camps. On the way to Dachau, he escaped into a forest shortly before liberation by American forces in April, 1945. While living in Paris after V-E Day, he was an active member of a Yiddish literary group and wrote a number of monumental volumes about the Vilna Ghetto. He has lived in Tel Aviv, Israel, since 1948. The memoir in this book, translated from the Yiddish by Shlomo Katz, was reprinted from the May, 1952, issue of *The Jewish Frontier.*

ILYA EHRENBURG (1889-1967) was born in Moscow and, except for short periods of residence in Paris, spent his life in the Soviet Union. His numerous works include essays, biography, politics, travel, fiction, and memoirs. Among his novels translated into English are *The Second Day* and *The Extraordinary Adventures of*

Julio Jurenito. In his earlier writings he occasionally depicted Jewish characters, as he does in the Hasidic story included here, translated from the Russian by Leon Dennen. The story first appeared in the February, 1932, issue of *Opinion*.

ELDAD THE DANITE (See footnote on page 193)

LOUIS FALSTEIN was born in the Ukraine in 1914 and was brought up in Chicago. During World War II he served as an aerial gunner with the U. S. 15th Air Force, an experience which he used as background for his novel, *Face of a Hero*. He has taught writing at New York University and contributed stories, articles, translations, and book reviews to national magazines. Among his other works are a novel, *Laughter on a Weekday* (1965), and a biography of Sholom Aleichem. The story in this book is part of his novel, *Sole Survivor*. He lives with his family in Brooklyn, New York.

HOWARD FAST was born in New York City in 1914 and began writing fiction in his early twenties. He has excelled as a short-story writer and his historical novels, including *The Unvanquished, Citizen Tom Paine,* and *My Glorious Brothers,* rank with the best in the field. His collection of science fiction stories, *The Edge of Time,* is an original creation in that genre. The story in this book is an excerpt from his war novel, *The Winston Affair*.

MOSES JOSEPH FEIGENBAUM was born in Biale, Poland, in 1914, where he grew up and worked as a bookkeeper. The story of his escape from the Nazis during their occupation of Poland, as told in the story included here, translated from the Yiddish by Lucy Davidowicz, was published in *Fun Letzten Churbon* (Munich, 1947). After liberation he participated in the work of the Central Historical Commission in Lodz, and following the disturbances there in 1946, he emigrated to Munich where he helped to organize the Historical Commission of the Central Committee of Liberated Jews. He edited and contributed to *Sefer Biale-Podlaska* (Tel Aviv, 1961), a volume recording the history and destruction of the Jewish community of his native town. He emigrated to Israel in 1949 and resides in Tel Aviv.

LION FEUCHTWANGER (1884–1958), the son of a prosperous Jewish manufacturer, was born in Munich, Germany, and studied at the Universities of Berlin and Munich. He instantaneously achieved a literary as well as a popular success with his works. His lampooning of Hitler and the Nazis in the novels *Success* and *The Oppermanns* brought upon him the hatred and vengeance of the Nazi rulers. He fled for his life to southern France, and then came to the United States where he continued a productive literary career. Among his last notable historical novels were *Raquel* and *Jephta and His Daughter*. The story included here was translated from the German by Nathan Ausubel. Feuchtwanger died in California.

IRVING FINEMAN, a native of New York City, was born in 1893. He studied at the Massachusetts Institute of Technology and Harvard, taught engineering at the University of Illinois and lectured on literature at Bennington College. During World War I he served in the U. S. Navy as an engineer officer. His first stories and reviews were published in *The Menorah Journal*. Among his memorable novels of Jewish interest are *Hear, Ye Sons* and *Ruth*. He has also worked in Hollywood, and now lives in Shaftsbury, Vermont. The story included here first appeared in the June-July, 1926, issue of *The Menorah Journal*.

EDMOND FLEG (1874–1964), a native of Geneva, Switzerland, studied at various European universities, saw service at the front in World War I, for which he was awarded the Croix de Guerre, and since then has lived in Paris and devoted himself to literary pursuits. He was one of the creators of a renascence of Jewish letters among the postwar generation in France. During the Nazi Occupation he fled to southern France and Italy; he returned to his home in Paris in 1944, continued his literary work and helped to rebuild Jewish cultural institutions. Fleg was pre-eminent as poet, critic, playwright, and translator. Among his works that have been translated into English are *Why I Am a Jew, The Jewish Anthology, Jesus,* and *The Life of Moses*. He died in Paris.

KARL EMIL FRANZOS (1848–1904) was born in Podolia and studied law and medicine at the Universities of Vienna and Gratz. He traveled throughout Europe and the Near East and finally settled in Berlin. While he held various government positions, he wrote travel memoirs, novels, and short stories. His fame, however, was achieved chiefly by his stories of Jewish life in the Galician ghettos of Poland. *The Jews of Barnow,* from which *Two Saviors* is chosen, was translated into many European tongues. Franzos died in Berlin.

DAVID FRISHMAN (1863–1922) was born of wealthy parents in Lodz, Poland. Educated by tutors and at Breslau University, he began writing Hebrew stories in his youth, and in his twenties collaborated with Smolenskin and Sokolow in the publication of Hebrew journals. For almost forty-five years he exercised a critical, humanistic influence on Hebrew literature; he translated into Hebrew the works of Andersen, Eliot, Tagore, Wilde, Shakespeare, and a score of other European masters. A complete edition of his Hebrew and Yiddish writings was published in 1927. The story here included first appeared in the August-September, 1926, issue of *The Menorah Journal*.

SAMUEL GODINER (1893–1942) was born in Telechan, District of Minsk, Russia, and after the October Revolution became one of the better known of the new vintage of Soviet Yiddish writers. His short stories and novels concern the struggle and conflicts of the old and new order. The story included here, translated from the Yiddish by Samuel Kreiter, is taken from *Af Barikadn*. He was killed in action during World War II.

LOUIS GOLDING (1895–1958) was born in Manchester, England, and educated at the Manchester Grammar School and Oxford University. He served with the British Army in World War I, and throughout his life traveled as widely as any contemporary writer. He distinguished himself as poet and critic and short-story writer; but his travel books and novels such as *Day of Atonement* and *Magnolia Street* gained for him a large audience in the English-speaking world. He was married shortly before his death, in London. *Luigi of Cantanzaro* first appeared in the December, 1925, issue of *The Menorah Journal*.

MEIR ARON GOLDSCHMIDT (1818–1887) was born in Vordingborg, Denmark, and died in Copenhagen. Educated in Danish schools but unable to take a degree because he was a Jew, he launched upon a career of vigorous political journalism for which he was frequently fined and sentenced to prison. After 1862 he devoted himself exclusively to fiction. He produced many notable novels and short stories of Jewish and Danish life, which won for him wide acclaim and were translated into Hebrew, Yiddish, and other European tongues. The story included here is reprinted from *Denmark's Best Stories* (Hannah Astrup Larsen, ed.).

ALBERT HALPER was born in Chicago, Illinois, in 1904 and was educated at Northwestern University. He became a frequent contributor of stories and essays to numerous literary journals, and with the publication of his *Union Square* and *On the Shore*, he quickly took high rank among the younger American novelists. He was a Guggenheim Fellow in 1934, and since then has published a score of volumes of fiction and short stories. He lives in New York City. The story here included appeared in the April, 1929, issue of *The Menorah Journal*.

AVIGDOR HAMEIRI (1886–1970) was born in Bereo, Hungary, and educated at the Rabbinical Seminary of Budapest. He saw action at the front during World War I, was taken prisoner by the Russians, and settled in Palestine in 1922. His poetry and prose are dominated by memories of war experiences and the havoc wrought upon humanity. He wrote a volume of sketches of Odessa during the immediate postwar period, which compare favorably with Babel's *Red Cavalry*. The story here included, *The Three Haluzot*, was translated from the Hebrew by I. M. Lask.

GLÜCKEL OF HAMELN (See footnote on page 289)

HAYYIM HAZAZ was born in the Ukraine in 1898, where he was educated and witnessed the Bolshevik Revolution. He left Russia for Paris and Constantinople where he began to write novelettes on Jewish village life in Russia during the Revolution. Settling in Palestine in 1931, he was soon recognized as one of the most original of the new generation of Hebrew writers. He has written numerous short stories, a four-act play, a tetralogy, and four novels of which one appeared in English under the title *Mori Said*. Especially noteworthy are his short stories on Biblical episodes. The story included here, translated by I. M. Lask, was chosen by Hazaz himself for this volume.

ABRAHAM IBN DAUD (See footnote on page 216)

HASDAI IBN SHAPRUT (See footnote on page 197)

JOSEPH BEN MEIR ZABARA (See footnote on page 211)

FLAVIUS JOSEPHUS (See footnote on page 112)

FRANZ KAFKA (1883–1924) was born in Prague, Czechoslovakia. He studied law at Karls-Ferdinand University in Prague, and, although the son of a wealthy businessman, he supported himself by a job with the insurance division of the government. A member of a literary circle which included Karel Capek and Franz Werfel, he published only a few stories and poems during his lifetime. Max Brod, his literary executor, arranged for the publication of Kafka's novels and diaries, which have now been recognized as twentieth-century classics. The selection in this book, translated from the German by Willa and Edwin Muir, is taken from *The Trial*. Kafka died of tuberculosis and was buried in Prag-Straschnitz.

ISAAC KIPNIS was born in a Russian village in 1896. He began writing in Hebrew, Yiddish, and Russian in his youth and earned his living as a lumberman and tannery worker. In 1920 he moved to Kiev and began publishing stories and articles in Yiddish anthologies circulating in the Soviet Union. He achieved prominence as a Soviet-Yiddish writer with his book *Months and Days,* from which the story in this book, translated from the Yiddish by Samuel Kreiter, is taken. He survived purges and war and is reported to be living in Kiev.

EPHRAIM KISHON was born in Budapest, Hungary, in 1924, where he was educated and became a publicist. He settled in Israel in 1949, mastered the Hebrew language, and since 1952 has written a column in the Hebrew daily *Maariv,* which is translated and published in eight languages. He has published eight books of comedies, plays, and satires and he founded the Green Onion, a satirical theater in Israel. He was awarded the Nordau Prize for Literature in 1955 and the Arlozoroff Prize for Journalism in 1958. Mr. Kishon resides with his family in Tel Aviv. The story in this book, translated from the Hebrew by Yohanan Goldman, is taken from *Look Back, Mrs. Lot!*

MEYER LEVIN was born in Chicago, Illinois, in 1905. He was educated at the University of Chicago and studied art in Paris. He started newspaper work on the Chicago *Daily News,* worked as a pioneer in a Palestinian commune where he wrote his novel *Yehuda,* conducted experimental marionette theaters in Chicago and New York, and served as a war correspondent in World War II. He has written a score or more of books, including short stories, plays, memoirs, and translations. He has achieved recognition for his novels, particularly for *The Old Bunch, Compulsion,* and *The Fanatic.* He now lives with his family in Israel. The Hasidic tale he retells in this book is taken from his rendering of the tales of Israel Baalshem and Nachman Bratzlaver, *The Golden Mountain.*

LUDWIG LEWISOHN (1882–1955) was born in Berlin and was brought to America by his parents in 1890. He was educated at the College of Charleston and Columbia University. He began his academic career in 1910 at the University of Wisconsin as an instructor in the German language and literature, and in 1911 was appointed a professor in that subject at Ohio State University. Later, due to his resentment of campus anti-Semitism, recorded in *Upstream,* he lived in New York and Paris, achieving an imposing position in American letters as critic and novelist. In the last decades of his life his reconversion to Judaism and espousal of Zionism gave his writings a new verve. He was serving as librarian of Brandeis University when he died. *The Romantic* is one of five novelettes in *This People* (1933).

SOLOMON LIEBIN (real name Israel Hurwitz, 1872–1955) was born in Gorki, Russia, and emigrated twenty years later to New York by way of London. He earned his living as a newsboy and factory worker. His first literary efforts were published in Yiddish labor journals; after the split in the ranks of the Socialist Party, he allied himself with the writers on the *Vorwarts,* a New York daily with which he was associated until his death. He is the author of three volumes of touching tales of immigrant life in the New York ghetto, of which *A Picnic,* translated for this volume by Samuel Kreiter, is typical.

SOLOMON MAIMON (See pages 294–295)

BERNARD MALAMUD was born in Brooklyn, New York, in 1914 and educated at City College of New York and Columbia University. His second novel, *The Assistant* (1956), brought him to the fore as a novelist, and his two collections of short stories, *The Magic Barrel* and *Idiots First,* from which the story in this book is taken, have established him as a significant American writer. He has won the National Book Award for fiction and the Daroff Annual Award for the best Jewish novel.

MENDEL MANN was born in Warsaw, Poland, in 1916, and began his career as an artist. Turning to literature in 1938, he published several volumes of verse and fiction. He was in Warsaw when the war broke out, and he escaped to Russia and enlisted in the Red Army. He fought at Moscow when the city was besieged by the Germans, and took part in the eastern campaign up to the fall of Berlin. After the war he returned to Lodz and resumed his writing. His volume of Yiddish ballads was the first Jewish book published in Poland after the holocaust. After the Kielce pogrom in 1946, he fled to Regensburg, Germany, where he edited a weekly, *Der Nayer Moment.* He went to Israel in 1948 and during the following decade wrote novels and stories of life in Israel. He has lived in Paris since 1961. His works have been translated into French, German, Swedish, and a novel, *At the Gates of Moscow,* has been translated into English. The story included here was translated from the Yiddish by I. M. Lask.

WLADKA MEED (née Feige Peltel), a native of Warsaw, Poland, was born in 1922, and soon after her graduation from high school became a member of the Fighter Organization in the Warsaw Ghetto in German Occupied Poland. She helped to smuggle arms into the ghetto and acted as a courier to groups outside the ghetto. The engrossing story is told in her book, *On Both Sides of the Ghetto Wall,* from which the excerpt in this volume, translated from the Yiddish by Lucy Davidowicz, is taken. She came to America with her husband in 1946, studied at Columbia University, has lectured in the United States, Europe, and South America, and has contributed articles to the *Forwartz.* The Meeds have two teenagers and live in New York City.

AHARON MEGGED was born in Poland in 1920 and brought to Palestine by his parents at the age of six. He was one of a group which established Sdot Yam, a fishing kibbutz, and later traveled throughout the country, doing manual work. He served as a cultural representative of the Jewish Agency for Palestine in 1937–48. He has written fiction and plays; his novel *Hedva and I* won the 1954 Ussishkin Prize.

His story "The Name," translated from the Hebrew by Minna Givton, appeared in *Israeli Stories,* edited by Noel Blocker. Megged is the editor of the literary supplement of the newspaper *Lamerhav* and resides in Tel Aviv.

MENDELE MOCHER SEFORIM (real name Sholem Jacob Abramovitch, 1836–1917) was born in Kopyl, Lithuania, and spent his boyhood studying in yeshibot of Slutsk and Vilna. When his widowed mother married the owner of a flour mill, who lived in the village of Melniki, Mendele joined them and there, in the midst of a beautiful countryside, the "Muse came to me." He wrote both in Hebrew and Yiddish, but his Yiddish fiction, attacking religious fanaticism and Hasidism and mass ignorance and social injustice, became popular and controversial. The creator of a new style, he became known as the "grandfather" of modern Yiddish literature. His novel *Fishke the Lame* has been translated into English. The story included here, translated from the Yiddish by Joseph Gaer, is reprinted from the August-September, 1926, issue of *The Menorah Journal.*

NAHMAN OF BRAZLAV (1772–1811), the great-grandson of Israel Baalshem, the founder of Hasidism, was born in Medzibuz, Poland. He was deeply influenced by the family tradition and from early youth was recognized as a Zaddik. His chief disciple and amanuensis, Nathan of Nemerow, in his *Life of Our Master,* has portrayed him as a remarkable personality and a man of profound religious inclinations. Besides works on ethics, mysticism, and liturgy, he left a unique collection of symbolic folk tales which were written down in Yiddish by his disciples, and then, at Nahman's request, translated into Hebrew. Most of these tales, together with the legends of the Baalshem, were freely translated by Meyer Levin in *The Golden Mountain,* from which the story in this book is reprinted.

MORDECAI MANUEL NOAH (1785–1851) was born in Philadelphia, Pennsylvania, to parents who were of aristocratic Sephardic lineage and patriots in the American Revolution. He showed great interest in the Chestnut Street theater and joined a group of amateur actors in his native city. He studied law in Charleston, South Carolina, and entered politics. He also distinguished himself as a journalist and playwright. For further details, see the footnote on page 567.

OBADIAH YAREH DA BERTINORO (See footnote on page 234)

ISAAC LOEB PERETZ (1852–1915), a native of Zamascz, Poland, received a traditional Jewish education and at the same time saturated himself in Polish, French, and German literature. His career as a lawyer in Warsaw was cut short by the government because of his radical political views, and while serving the Kehilla as clerk in charge of cemetery registrations, he advocated the cause of the poor and working classes and devoted himself to Yiddish literature. His genius found expression in poetry, drama, journalism, and, particularly, folk tales, and his Hasidic tales, like *Bontche the Silent* included here, have won general acclaim. Peretz died in Warsaw; the fiftieth anniversary of his death was commemorated throughout the world.

DAVID PINSKI (1872–1959), a native of Mohilev, Russia, had already established his reputation as a writer when he came to America in 1899 at the invitation of a

New York labor newspaper. An ardent apostle of Labor Zionism, his numerous novels, stories, and plays deal with the worker's plight in an industrialized society. His plays were produced on the American stage in both Yiddish and English; *The Treasure* was produced by the Theater Guild. Among his other writings that have been translated into English are *Arnold Levenberg* (novel), *Temptations* (short stories), and *Ten Plays*. He died in Haifa, Israel.

ISAAC RABOY (1882–1944) was born in Zawale, Poland, but he spent his early years in Bessarabia. He was well versed in Hebrew, Yiddish, and Russian literature and began to write in all three tongues. Arriving in America in 1904, he worked by day in garment factories and carried on his literary labors by night. Disgusted finally by his struggle to survive in the city, he attended an agricultural school and worked on a ranch in North Dakota. As a consequence, he turned from idyls of his childhood in Bessarabia to stories of farm folks and ranchers. His story *The Jewish Cowboy* was the first of its kind in American Jewish literature. He died in Los Angeles at sixty-one, leaving behind ten published books. *Solomon* was translated from the Yiddish by Samuel Kreiter.

ABRAHAM REISEN (1876–1953), a major figure in Yiddish literature, was born in Koidanov, Russia, and, encouraged by Sholom Aleichem, his poetry and fiction won a large audience among the Yiddish-reading masses. He was well known when he emigrated to America where he continued to write lyrical verse and fiction and struggled for the acceptance of Yiddish as the national language of the Jewish people. He published several journals of literature and criticism which influenced the younger generation of Yiddish writers. His stories, as illustrated by *Shut In*, translated by Helena Frank, portray the character of his people with lyric simplicity and gentle irony. He died in New York.

DAVID REUBENI (See footnote on page 265)

CHARLES REZNIKOFF was born in Brooklyn, New York, in 1894, and was educated at the University of Missouri and New York University (LL.B.). He contributed verse, drama, and fiction to *The Menorah Journal* for over thirty years and served as a Contributing Editor. Among his numerous published works are *The Lionhearted*, a novel, and *By the Waters of Manhattan*, a volume of selected verse with an Introduction by C. P. Snow. He serves as Editor of the *Jewish Frontier* and lives in New York City. His story in this book first appeared in the Spring, 1932, issue of *The Menorah Journal*.

EDWARD ROBBIN was born in Chicago in 1907 where he attended the public schools. He interrupted his studies at the University of Illinois to bum across the country and travel around Europe on a bicycle. After several years with theater groups in Chicago and New York, he took his wife and child to Greece and then to Palestine. There he spent four years working in the communes and at a variety of random jobs. It was during these years that he contributed to *The Menorah Journal* verse and a number of graphic stories dealing with life in the agricultural colonies. *Foaling Season* movingly and poetically portrays the impact of the new environment upon two sturdy pioneers. He resides in Los Angeles.

MAURICE SAMUEL (1885-1972) was born in Macin, Rumania, and came to America in 1914. He studied at the high school in Manchester, England, and at Manchester University. A lifetime advocate of Zionism and a brilliant lecturer, he excelled also as a novelist, essayist, critic, and translator. His dialogues with Mark Van Doren on television, dealing with Biblical and literary themes, were memorable. Among his noteworthy literary studies are *Prince of the Ghetto* (on Peretz), *Certain People of the Book,* and *The World of Sholom Aleichem,* from which the story in this book is an excerpt.

PAUL SCHLESINGER (1878–1928), whose journalistic pseudonym was von Sling, was born in Berlin and educated at the University of Berlin. In Munich he was a member of the cabaret group *Elf Scharfrichter.* Later he was a court reporter and an editor of the *Vossische Zeitung* in Berlin. His attacks on the courts for their many miscarriages of justice won him wide appreciation. A collection of his most interesting court trial reports was posthumously published (Berlin, 1929) under the title *Richter und Gerichtete.* Among his other books is *Das Slingbuch* (1926), from which the feuilleton in this book, translated by Nathan Ausubel, was taken. He died in Berlin.

LEO WALDER SCHWARZ (1906-1967) was born in New York City and attended Harvard University and New York University. He served in the 3rd U. S. Army in the European Theater, traveled much in Europe, the Near East and Africa, and lectured in the United States and Canada. He edited magazines and books, among them *Memoirs of My People* and *The Menorah Treasury.* Among his other books are *The Redeemers* and *Refugees in Germany Today.* He adapted the folk tales of Helm for this book from old Hebrew and Yiddish chapbooks.

ANDRÉ SCHWARZ-BART was born in Metz, France, in 1928. His parents had emigrated from Poland in 1924, and in 1941 they were caught in a Nazi roundup and died in an extermination camp. During the Nazi occupation of France, he served in the Maquis. After the war he worked as a laborer, mechanic, and librarian, where he was able to satisfy his thirst for books. He studied at the Sorbonne and spent several years writing and rewriting drafts of *The Last of the Just,* from which the story in this book, translated by Stephen Becker, is excerpted. The book won the Prix Goncourt, France's leading literary award, in 1959, and, translated into English and other tongues, quickly won acclaim as a masterpiece of the literature of the Holocaust.

DAVID SHIMONOVITCH (1886–1956) was born in Bobruisk, White Russia, and settled in Palestine in 1909. He worked as a laborer and as a guard (*shomer*) in the colonies until 1914 when he became a teacher in the Herzliah School in Tel Aviv. Deeply influenced by Lermontov, Pushkin, and Tolstoi, whose work he translated into Hebrew, he distinguished himself as a lyric Hebrew poet, ranking close to Bialik, Tchernihovski, and Shneour. His idyls are among the best poetic descriptions of the Yishub and he produced a considerable number of verse fables of a high order from which *The Nigun,* translated by I. M. Lask, was chosen for this book.

SHOLOM ALEICHEM (real name Sholom Rabinowitz, 1859–1916), the son of a Hasidic squire, was born in the Russian village of Voronko. He began writing in

Hebrew and Russian in his youth, but, influenced by the writing of Mendele Mocher Seforim and Alexander Zederbaum, the editor of *Folksblatt,* he turned to writing in Yiddish. He became a great folk figure of the Jews of Eastern Europe and his popularity has grown over the years. On the hundredth anniversary of his birth, celebrations were held throughout the world. His books and adaptations of his works for the theater became popular in the United States in the sixties. Maurice Samuel's *The World of Sholom Aleichem* (1943) is a masterly re-creation of the great humorist. The story included here, translated by Maurice Samuel, first appeared in the *East and West* magazine (1916).

GERSHON SHOFMAN (1880-1972) was born at Orsha, Mohilev, White Russia. He was deeply involved in Socialist activities, served in the Russian Army in World War I, and after living as a refugee in Germany and Austria, emigrated to Palestine in 1938. His subject matter is life during war and people set adrift by the consequences of war, and his writing is confined to the short story and the short short story where he has compressed the juices of life in a semifabular, symbolic style. He edited the Hebrew periodicals *Peret* and *Shalehet.* The short short story included in this book, translated from the Hebrew by A. Aaroni-Botzman, appeared in the October, 1924, issue of *The Menorah Journal.*

ISAAC BASHEVIS SINGER was born in Radzymun, Poland, in 1904, of a family of notable rabbis and writers, and joined his brother, I. J. Singer, in New York City in 1935. A member of the staff of the *Jewish Daily Forward,* he has written numerous novels and short stories, many of which, including *The Family Moskat* and *The Slave,* have appeared in English translation and brought him international acclaim. The recipient of many coveted prizes, in 1964 he was elected a member of the American Academy of Arts and Letters. The story included in this book, translated from the Yiddish by the author and Elizabeth Pollet, first appeared in the Valedictory Issue of *The Menorah Journal* (1962).

MOSES SMILANSKI (1874–1953) was born in Talpino in the Ukraine, and settled in Palestine as a Zionist pioneer in 1890. He worked in the first Jewish colonies and later bought a plot of land in Rehovot where he lived until his death. During World War I, he served in the Jewish Legion. He achieved a reputation as a Hebrew journalist and a short-story writer. In his stories he related the experiences of the struggles of his generation, and tells of Arab life in the villages and tents, always with sympathy and understanding. *The Pangs of the Messiah,* translated by I. M. Lask, gives us a glimpse of what Herzl meant to the early pioneers of the Yishub.

ISAIAH SPIEGEL was born in Lodz, Poland, in 1906, and grew up in Warsaw. He is a survivor of the Warsaw Ghetto, and resides in Israel. He has devoted himself to writing stories on the theme of the Holocaust. *A Ghetto Dog,* translated from the Yiddish by Bernard Guilbert Guerney, is reprinted from *A Treasury of Yiddish Stories,* edited by Irving Howe and Eliezer Greenberg.

MOSES STAVSKY (1891–1964) was born in Grodno, Russia. He emigrated to Palestine in 1911, worked first as a teacher and then as a farmer, and later became the manager of a large dairy farm. Writing in both Yiddish and Hebrew, he was among the first storytellers in those tongues to deal with domestic animals and farm life. The story included in this book, translated from the Hebrew by Edward Robbin, first appeared in the April, 1930, issue of *The Menorah Journal*.

JUDAH STEINBERG (1861–1908), the son of a famous Zaddik, was born in Bessarabia. He earned a livelihood by instructing children in Hebrew and in 1897, with the publication of *In City and Country*, a collection of stories, he won a large Hebrew-reading public. His collected works were published in four volumes in Berlin in 1910. Together with Peretz and Berdychevski, he is a notable interpreter of Hasidism in stories. Two volumes of his stories, *In Those Days* (1915) and *The Breakfast of the Birds* (1917), have been translated into English. *The Zaddik of Sosov*, translated from the Hebrew by Simon Chasen, appeared in the October, 1925, issue of *The Menorah Journal*.

MORDECAI STRIGLER was born in Zamascz, Poland, in 1921, where he received an intensive education in Hebrew and Talmud. He began writing in his youth in local Yiddish journals, and after 1937 he lived and wrote in Warsaw. During the German Occupation he was an inmate of several concentration camps, just escaping death on a number of occasions. During 1945–52 he resided in Paris, France, where he edited *Undzer Wort* and published *In a Fremden Dor*, a volume of verse. At the same time he wrote six volumes about concentration camps and the Holocaust, which established him as one of the distinguished postwar Yiddish writers. He came to New York in 1952 and since then has served as editor of *Yiddisher Kemfer*. *Dialogue With the Dead*, translated from the Yiddish by Adah Fogel, is the Prelude to *In di Fabrikn fun Toit*, one of the cycle of Strigler's autobiographical books on the Holocaust.

MENASSAH UNGER, the scion of an Hasidic dynasty, was born in Zabno, Galicia, in 1900. He lived in Vienna for five years, left to work as a pioneer in a Palestinian commune, and then returned to Poland where he was active as a Yiddish publicist and an official of the Yiddish Scientific Society (YIVO) in Vilna, Lithuania. He has written Hasidic stories and essays for the New York Yiddish newspaper, *The Day*, and published several books on Hasidism, among them studies of the Besht and Nahman of Bratzlav. The story here included, translated from the Yiddish by Edward Robbin, appeared in the March, 1929, issue of *The Menorah Journal*.

EDWARD LEWIS WALLANT (1926–1962) was born in New Haven, Connecticut, and educated at the Pratt Institute, Brooklyn, and the New School for Social Research. After serving with the U. S. Navy as a gunner's mate in World War II, he became art director for a New York advertising agency. In 1962–63 he spent five months abroad on a Simon Guggenheim Memorial Foundation Fellowship. His four novels established him as an important American novelist. *The Pawnbroker* has been made into a film. *The Human Season*, from which the story here included is an excerpt, won the Daroff Memorial Award from the Jewish Book Council for "1960's best Jewish book in the fiction field." Wallant died of a brain hemorrhage on December 5, 1962, in Norwalk, Connecticut, leaving a wife, a son, and two daughters.

FRANZ WERFEL (1890–1945), the son of a wealthy Jewish merchant, was born and educated in Prague where he was an ardent member of Martin Buber's Neo-Hasidic coterie. However, due to the temperamental instability of his genius he abandoned this interest in socialism and then successively became an adherent of anarchism, internationalism, communism, Catholicism, and finally, as a direct result of Fascist persecution of the Jews, he fled to England and became a devout Jew. Werfel was hailed by Romain Rolland as one of the greatest poets and novelists of his time. He spent his last years in California where he died. Among his novels in vogue in the English-reading world are *The Forty Days of Musa Dagh* and *The Pure in Heart,* from which the story in this book is excerpted.

ISRAEL ZANGWILL (1864–1926), the most distinguished of Anglo-Jewish authors, was born in London and received the B.A. degree with highest honors from London University. Besides being an eminent novelist, critic, and playwright, he became best known as an interpreter of Jewish life, and his books about the London Jewish ghetto have become classics. He also played a notable role as a champion of the downtrodden and persecuted. He allied himself with Theodor Herzl in the Zionist movement, and later organized the Jewish Territorial Association (JTO) for the purpose of establishing autonomous Jewish countries for persecuted Jews in various parts of the world. *Tug of Love* is taken from *Ghetto Comedies.*

ARNOLD ZWEIG (1887–1963) was born in Glogau, Silesia. Although the son of a harness maker, he nevertheless acquired extensive academic training at the Universities of Breslau, Munich, Berlin, Göttingen, and Tübingen. He saw active service at the front in World War I, and acquired experience that turned him into a militant pacifist. After the war he devoted himself to writing as a career, and his novels, especially *The Case of Sergeant Grisha,* short stories, and essays gained him international recognition. As an exponent of the Zionist-Socialist viewpoint, he wrote extensively on Palestine Jewish labor, and after his exile from Nazi Germany, he lived in Haifa. He returned to the East German Republic in 1953 and lived there until his death. *Pogrom* is reprinted from the July, 1930, issue of *The New Palestine.*

STEFAN ZWEIG (1881–1942) was born of wealthy parents in Vienna and educated at the University of Vienna. His literary career was interrupted by the outbreak of World War I, when his pacifism took him to Switzerland. There he joined Romain Rolland in a militant international peace movement, and he wrote his antiwar play, *Jeremiah,* later produced by Max Reinhardt. He became a voluntary exile from Fascist Austria, lived for a while in London, and then sought refuge in Brazil where, depressed by exile and war, he committed suicide. The author of thirty-one books, Zweig excelled as a novelist, biographer, poet, short-story writer, dramatist, critic, and psychologist. He won high regard internationally as a brilliant man of letters. *Buchmendel,* included here, is reprinted from his volume of stories, *Kaleidoscope.*

INDEX OF TRANSLATORS